Bill James presents. . .

STATS™
Major League Handbook
1997

STATS, Inc. • Bill James

STATS
PUBLISHING

Published by STATS Publishing
A Division of Sports Team Analysis & Tracking Systems, Inc.
Dr. Richard Cramer, Chairman • John Dewan, President

Cover by Ron Freer and the Big Blue Image

Photo by Tony Inzerillo/Sporting Views

First Edition: November, 1996

Printed in the United States of America

ISBN 1-884064-30-2

Acknowledgments

There's a mad, wild, hectic crazy and (all in all) fun period each year that is known at STATS as "the fall book season." During that period, we put together three books—the *Major League Handbook*, *Minor League Handbook* and *Player Profiles*—in a little less than two weeks. It's a daunting task, and we'd like to thank the folks who help us bring the books in on time.

John Dewan, STATS President and CEO, has brought our company from the "home office" days to its current period of unprecedented success. John is capably assisted by Heather Schwarze.

The Systems Department, headed by Sue Dewan, Mike Canter and Art Ashley, crunches the truly amazing array of numbers you see in this book. The Systems staff consists of Dave Carlson, Marty Couvillon, Mike Hammer, Stefan Kretschmann, Steve Moyer, Brent Osland, Dave Pinto, Pat Quinn and Jeff Schinski. Special thanks go to the indefatigable Stefan, who serves as chief programmer for this book.

The task of collecting the data belongs to our Operations Department, and they verify every figure down to the last "team earned run." Jeff Chernow, Jason Kinsey, Jim Osborne, Allan Spear and Peter Woelflein head up a reporter network which is, quite simply, the best in the business.

The STATS Publications Department takes all those numbers and makes a book (actually, *many* books) out of them. Ethan Cooperson, Jim Henzler, Chuck Miller, Tony Nistler and Mat Olkin make up a team of all-star "prose boys."

Our Marketing Department has the job of making sure the world knows about STATS. Jim Capuano is Director of National Sales, and he is assisted by Kristen Beauregard. Ron Freer is our advertising guru, and Jim Musso and Oscar Palacios make our fantasy games the best in the business.

The Departments responsible for Publications Sales, Finances and Administration, headed by Bob Meyerhoff, handle numerous responsibilities which are vital to our company. The group includes Marc Elman, Drew Faust, Mark Hong, Betty Moy, and Mike Wenz. Stephanie Seburn manages the Administrative group's responsibilities, with assistance from Ken Gilbert, Virginia Hamill, Tiffany Heingarten, Antoinette Kelly and Leena Sheth.

And finally, thanks to Bill James. Without Bill, none of us would be where we are today.

—Don Zminda

**This book is dedicated to
STATS baseball reporter Stan Reynolds,
whose courage is an inspiration to us all.**

Table of Contents

Introduction

What was the most amazing thing about 1996? We certainly have plenty of candidates for the honor. Brady Anderson clubbed 50 homers, Hideo Nomo twirled a no-hitter at Coors, Barry Bonds entered the exclusive 40-40 club, Kevin Brown became just the third pitcher since 1986 to finish with a sub-2.00 ERA *and* qualify for the title, the Rockies boasted three players who broke the 40-homer mark, the magic total of 240 by the 1961 Yankees was topped by the Orioles, Mariners and Athletics, Roger Clemens fanned 20 Detroit Tigers in one game, Mark McGwire made a run at Maris. . . and that's just the short list. All are strong candidates, but all are runners-up. *The* most amazing thing about 1996 was the fact that the word "strike" was actually used more frequently in reference to pitch counts than labor relations. We'd almost forgotten how much fun a full season can be!

So in celebration, we decided to sit down, take out the fine-toothed comb, and go through our best-selling publication page by page. The result? The *STATS 1997 Major League Handbook.* What you *won't* find is a complete overhaul—if you've been with us before, we think you'll agree that we had a pretty good model to begin with—but you *will* find plenty of new stats. . . all from the most complete set of data in the business. A sampling? We've added such things as holds and save opportunities to our Career Stats section, and even took the time to count up the different positions (and games at those positions) every big leaguer played in the 1996 season. We bulked up our Team and Managers sections, and made numerous additions to our Special Pitchers section. We think you'll find our time was well spent.

Speaking of time, we *didn't* want to change how long it took to get the *Handbook* to your doorstep. Our long-standing commitment to be first still drives us every season. And of course, we always welcome your comments and suggestions.

So just how much fun can a whole season be? Open up and take a look for yourself!

—Tony Nistler

What's Official and What's Not

The statistics in this book are technically unofficial. The Official Major League Baseball Averages are not released until December, but we can't wait that long. If you compare these stats with the official ones, you'll find no major differences. We take extraordinary efforts to insure accuracy.

Career Stats

The career data section of this book includes the records of all players who saw major league action in 1996.

You probably know what most of the abbreviations stand for, but just in case:

Age is seasonal age based on July 1, 1997.

For Batters, **B** = Bats; **T** = Throws; **DH** = Designated Hitter; **PH** = Pinch Hitter; **G** = Games; **AB** = At-Bats; **H** = Hits; **2B** = Doubles; **3B** = Triples; **HR** = Home Runs; **Hm** = Home Runs at Home; **Rd** = Home Runs on the Road; **TB** = Total Bases; **R** = Runs; **RBI** = Runs Batted In; **TBB** = Total Bases on Balls; **IBB** = Intentional Bases on Ball; **SO** = Strikeouts; **HBP** = Times Hit by Pitches; **SH** = Sacrifice Hits; **SF** = Sacrifice Flies; **SB** = Stolen Bases; **CS** = Times Caught Stealing; **SB%** = Stolen Base Percentage; **GDP** = Times Grounded into Double Plays; **Avg** = Batting Average; **OBP** = On-Base Percentage; **SLG** = Slugging Percentage.

For Pitchers, **SP** = Starting Pitcher; **RP** = Relief Pitcher; **G** = Games Pitched; **GS** = Games Started; **CG** = Complete Games; **GF** = Games Finished; **IP** = Innings Pitched; **BFP** = Batters Facing Pitcher; **H** = Hits Allowed; **R** = Runs Allowed; **ER** = Earned Runs Allowed; **HR** = Home Runs Allowed; **SH** = Sacrifice Hits Allowed; **SF** = Sacrifice Flies Allowed; **HB** = Hit Batsmen; **TBB** = Total Bases on Balls; **IBB** = Intentional Bases on Ball; **SO** = Strikeouts; **WP** = Wild Pitches; **Bk** = Balks; **W** = Wins; **L** = Losses; **Pct.** = Winning Percentage; **ShO** = Shutouts; **Sv** = Saves; **Op** = Save Opportunites; **Hld** = Holds; **ERA** = Earned Run Average.

An asterisk (*) by a player's minor league stats indicates that these are his 1996 minor league numbers only; previous minor league experience is not included. Figures in **boldface** indicate the player led the league in that category.

For pitchers, thirds of an inning were not kept officially prior to 1982. Therefore, there are no thirds of an inning for 1981 and before for older pitchers.

For players who played for more than one major league team in a season, stats for each team are shown just above the bottom line career totals.

Some Class-A and Rookie Leagues are denoted with a "+" or "-" (like A+) to indicate the caliber of competition within the classification.

Jim Abbott

Pitches: Left **Bats:** Left **Pos:** SP-23; RP-4   **Ht:** 6'3" **Wt:** 210 **Born:** 9/19/67 **Age:** 29

Year Team	Lg	G	GS	CG	GF	IP	BFP	H	R	ER	HR	SH	SF	HB	TBB	IBB	SO	WP	Bk	W	L	Pct.	ShO	Sv-Op	Hld	ERA
1996 Vancouver *	AAA	4	4	1	0	29	118	16	12	11	3	1	0	0	20	0	20	2	0	0	2	.000	0	0--	—	3.41
1989 California	AL	29	29	4	0	181.1	788	190	95	79	13	11	5	4	74	3	115	8	2	12	12	.500	2	0-0	0	3.92
1990 California	AL	33	33	4	0	211.2	925	246	116	106	16	9	6	5	72	6	105	4	3	10	14	.417	1	0-0	0	4.51
1991 California	AL	34	34	5	0	243	1002	222	85	78	14	7	7	5	73	6	158	1	4	18	11	.621	1	0-0	0	2.89
1992 California	AL	29	29	7	0	211	874	208	73	65	12	8	4	4	68	3	130	2	0	7	15	.318	0	0-0	0	2.77
1993 New York	AL	32	32	4	0	214	906	221	115	104	22	12	4	3	73	4	95	9	0	11	14	.440	1	0-0	0	4.37
1994 New York	AL	24	24	2	0	160.1	692	167	88	81	24	9	5	2	64	1	90	8	1	9	8	.529	0	0-0	0	4.55
1995 ChA-Cal	AL	30	30	4	0	197	842	209	93	81	14	8	4	2	64	1	86	1	0	11	8	.579	1	0-0	0	3.70
1996 California	AL	27	23	1	2	142	654	171	128	118	23	4	10	4	78	3	58	13	1	2	18	.100	0	0-0	0	7.48
1995 Chicago	AL	17	17	3	0	112.1	474	116	50	42	10	5	1	1	35	1	45	0	0	6	4	.600	1	0-0	0	3.36
California	AL	13	13	1	0	84.2	368	93	43	39	4	3	3	1	29	0	41	1	0	5	4	.556	1	0-0	0	4.15
8 ML YEARS		238	234	31	2	1560.1	6683	1634	793	712	138	68	45	29	566	27	837	46	11	80	100	.444	6	0-0	0	4.11

Kurt Abbott

Bats: R **Throws:** R **Pos:** SS-44; 3B-33; 2B-20; PH-16   **Ht:** 6'0" **Wt:** 185 **Born:** 6/2/69 **Age:** 28

Year Team	Lg	G	AB	H	2B	3B	HR	(Hm	Rd)	TB	R	RBI	TBB	IBB	SO	HBP	SH	SF	SB	CS	SB%	GDP	Avg	OBP	SLG
1996 Charlotte *	AAA	18	69	26	10	1	5	—	—	53	20	11	7	0	18	1	0	1	2	0	1.00	1	.377	.436	.768
1993 Oakland	AL	20	61	15	1	0	3	(0	3)	25	11	9	3	0	20	0	3	0	2	0	1.00	5	.246	.281	.410
1994 Florida	NL	101	345	86	17	3	9	(4	5)	136	41	33	16	1	98	5	3	2	3	0	1.00	5	.249	.291	.394
1995 Florida	NL	120	420	107	18	7	17	(12	5)	190	60	60	36	4	110	5	2	5	4	3	.57	6	.255	.318	.452
1996 Florida	NL	109	320	81	18	7	8	(6	2)	137	37	33	22	1	99	3	4	0	3	3	.50	7	.253	.307	.428
4 ML YEARS		350	1146	289	54	17	37	(22	15)	488	149	135	77	6	327	13	12	7	12	6	.67	21	.252	.305	.426

Kyle Abbott

Pitches: Left **Bats:** Left **Pos:** RP-3   **Ht:** 6'4" **Wt:** 215 **Born:** 2/18/68 **Age:** 29

Year Team	Lg	G	GS	CG	GF	IP	BFP	H	R	ER	HR	SH	SF	HB	TBB	IBB	SO	WP	Bk	W	L	Pct.	ShO	Sv-Op	Hld	ERA
1996 Midland *	AA	15	15	0	0	88	377	93	54	44	11	6	2	3	34	1	48	5	0	3	5	.375	0	0--	—	4.50
1991 California	AL	5	3	0	0	19.2	90	22	11	10	2	3	0	1	13	0	12	1	1	1	2	.333	0	0-0	0	4.58
1992 Philadelphia	NL	31	19	0	0	133.1	577	147	80	76	20	6	5	1	45	0	88	9	1	1	14	.067	0	0-0	0	5.13
1995 Philadelphia	NL	18	0	0	3	28.1	122	28	12	12	3	0	1	0	16	0	21	2	1	2	0	1.000	0	0-0	0	3.81
1996 California	AL	3	0	0	1	4	26	10	9	9	1	1	0	0	5	0	3	1	0	0	1	.000	0	0-1	0	20.25
4 ML YEARS		57	22	0	4	185.1	815	207	112	107	26	10	6	2	79	0	124	13	3	4	17	.190	0	0-1	0	5.20

Bob Abreu

Bats: Left **Throws:** Right **Pos:** PH-8; LF-6; RF-1   **Ht:** 6'0" **Wt:** 160 **Born:** 3/11/74 **Age:** 23

Year Team	Lg	G	AB	H	2B	3B	HR	(Hm	Rd)	TB	R	RBI	TBB	IBB	SO	HBP	SH	SF	SB	CS	SB%	GDP	Avg	OBP	SLG
1991 Astros	R	56	183	55	7	3	0	—	—	68	21	20	17	0	27	1	2	3	10	6	.63	3	.301	.358	.372
1992 Asheville	A	135	480	140	21	4	8	—	—	193	81	48	63	1	79	3	0	3	15	11	.58	5	.292	.375	.402
1993 Osceola	A+	129	474	134	21	17	5	—	—	204	62	55	51	1	90	1	1	3	10	14	.42	8	.283	.352	.430
1994 Jackson	AA	118	400	121	25	9	16	—	—	212	61	73	42	3	81	3	0	6	12	10	.55	2	.303	.368	.530
1995 Tucson	AAA	114	415	126	24	17	10	—	—	214	72	75	67	9	120	1	0	8	16	14	.53	6	.304	.395	.516
1996 Tucson	AAA	132	484	138	14	16	13	—	—	223	86	68	83	3	111	2	2	2	24	18	.57	5	.285	.391	.461
1996 Houston	NL	15	22	5	1	0	0	(0	0)	6	1	1	2	0	3	0	0	0	0	0	.00	1	.227	.292	.273

Mark Acre

Pitches: Right **Bats:** Right **Pos:** RP-22   **Ht:** 6'8" **Wt:** 240 **Born:** 9/16/68 **Age:** 28

Year Team	Lg	G	GS	CG	GF	IP	BFP	H	R	ER	HR	SH	SF	HB	TBB	IBB	SO	WP	Bk	W	L	Pct.	ShO	Sv-Op	Hld	ERA
1996 Edmonton *	AAA	39	0	0	28	43	175	33	11	10	1	3	1	0	16	5	50	1	0	6	2	.750	0	8--	—	2.09
1994 Oakland	AL	34	0	0	6	34.1	147	24	13	13	4	3	1	1	23	3	21	1	0	5	1	.833	0	0-1	3	3.41
1995 Oakland	AL	43	0	0	10	52	236	52	35	33	7	1	2	2	28	2	47	2	1	1	2	.333	0	0-4	5	5.71
1996 Oakland	AL	22	0	0	11	25	124	38	17	17	4	1	0	2	9	4	18	0	0	1	3	.250	0	2-3	2	6.12
3 ML YEARS		99	0	0	27	111.1	507	114	65	63	15	5	3	5	60	9	86	3	1	7	6	.538	0	2-8	7	5.09

Terry Adams

Pitches: Right **Bats:** Right **Pos:** RP-69   **Ht:** 6'3" **Wt:** 205 **Born:** 3/6/73 **Age:** 24

Year Team	Lg	G	GS	CG	GF	IP	BFP	H	R	ER	HR	SH	SF	HB	TBB	IBB	SO	WP	Bk	W	L	Pct.	ShO	Sv-Op	Hld	ERA
1991 Huntington	R+	14	13	0	0	57.2	300	67	56	37	1	1	2	6	62	0	52	4	4	0	9	.000	0	0--	—	5.77
1992 Peoria	A	25	25	3	0	157	682	144	95	77	7	8	6	9	86	0	96	13	1	7	12	.368	1	0--	—	4.41
1993 Daytona	A+	13	13	0	0	70.2	320	78	47	39	2	2	3	1	43	0	35	9	2	3	5	.375	0	0--	—	4.97

Year Team	Lg	G	GS	CG	GF	IP	BFP	H	R	ER	HR	SH	SF	HB	TBB	IBB	SO	WP	Bk	W	L	Pct.	ShO	Sv-Op	Hld	ERA
1994 Daytona	A+	39	7	0	21	84.1	383	87	47	41	5	4	2	4	46	3	64	8	1	9	10	.474	0	7--	—	4.38
1995 Iowa	AAA	7	0	0	6	6.1	25	3	0	0	0	0	0	0	2	0	10	1	0	0	0	.000	0	5--	—	0.00
Orlando	AA	44	0	0	36	44	174	26	9	6	2	0	1	2	18	1	36	5	1	2	3	.400	0	24--	—	1.23
1995 Chicago	NL	18	0	0	7	18	86	22	15	13	0	0	0	0	10	1	15	1	0	1	1	.500	0	1-1	0	6.50
1996 Chicago	NL	69	0	0	22	101	423	84	36	33	6	7	3	1	49	6	78	5	1	3	6	.333	0	4-8	11	2.94
2 ML YEARS		87	0	0	29	119	509	106	51	46	6	7	3	1	59	7	93	6	1	4	7	.364	0	5-9	11	3.48

Willie Adams

Pitches: Right **Bats:** Right **Pos:** SP-12 **Ht:** 6'7" **Wt:** 215 **Born:** 10/8/72 **Age:** 24

Year Team	Lg	G	GS	CG	GF	IP	BFP	H	R	ER	HR	SH	SF	HB	TBB	IBB	SO	WP	Bk	W	L	Pct.	ShO	Sv-Op	Hld	ERA
1993 Madison	A	5	5	0	0	18.2	84	21	10	7	2	1	1	0	8	0	22	1	1	0	2	.000	0	0--	—	3.38
1994 Modesto	A+	11	5	0	6	45.1	181	41	17	17	7	2	0	0	10	0	42	2	3	7	1	.875	0	2--	—	3.38
Huntsville	AA	10	10	0	0	60.2	256	58	32	29	3	2	3	5	23	2	33	1	1	4	3	.571	0	0--	—	4.30
1995 Edmonton	AAA	11	10	1	1	68	288	73	35	33	2	2	2	6	15	5	40	3	0	2	5	.286	0	0--	—	4.37
1996 Edmonton	AAA	19	19	3	0	112	466	95	49	47	12	1	1	6	39	2	80	4	0	10	4	.714	1	0--	—	3.78
1996 Oakland	AL	12	12	1	0	76.1	329	76	39	34	11	3	2	5	23	3	68	2	0	3	4	.429	1	0-0	0	4.01

Joel Adamson

Pitches: Left **Bats:** Left **Pos:** RP-9 **Ht:** 6'4" **Wt:** 185 **Born:** 7/2/71 **Age:** 25

Year Team	Lg	G	GS	CG	GF	IP	BFP	H	R	ER	HR	SH	SF	HB	TBB	IBB	SO	WP	Bk	W	L	Pct.	ShO	Sv-Op	Hld	ERA
1990 Princeton	R+	12	8	1	3	48	204	55	27	21	2	1	0	3	12	1	39	6	7	2	5	.286	0	1--	—	3.94
1991 Spartanburg	A	14	14	1	0	81	333	72	29	23	5	2	4	3	22	0	84	3	2	4	4	.500	1	0--	—	2.56
Clearwater	A+	5	5	0	0	29.2	125	28	12	10	1	2	1	1	7	0	20	2	1	2	1	.667	0	0--	—	3.03
1992 Clearwater	A+	15	15	1	0	89.2	378	90	35	34	4	2	1	7	19	0	52	0	1	5	6	.455	1	0--	—	3.41
Reading	AA	10	10	2	0	59	255	68	36	28	10	3	1	0	13	1	35	3	0	3	6	.333	0	0--	—	4.27
1993 Edmonton	AAA	5	5	0	0	26	125	39	21	20	5	1	1	0	13	0	7	0	1	1	2	.333	0	0--	—	6.92
High Desert	A+	22	20	6	1	129.2	571	160	83	66	13	3	4	4	30	0	72	5	7	5	5	.500	3	0--	—	4.58
1994 Portland	AA	33	11	2	16	91.1	402	95	51	44	9	5	2	5	32	5	59	0	0	5	6	.455	2	7--	—	4.34
1995 Charlotte	AAA	19	18	2	0	115	471	113	51	42	12	0	3	6	20	0	80	4	2	8	4	.667	0	0--	—	3.29
1996 Charlotte	AAA	44	8	0	14	97.2	424	108	48	41	15	3	3	3	28	2	84	1	0	6	6	.500	0	3--	—	3.78
1996 Florida	NL	9	0	0	1	11	56	18	9	9	1	2	1	1	7	0	7	0	0	0	0	.000	0	0-0	0	7.36

Rick Aguilera

Pitches: Right **Bats:** Right **Pos:** SP-19 **Ht:** 6'5" **Wt:** 203 **Born:** 12/31/61 **Age:** 35

Year Team	Lg	G	GS	CG	GF	IP	BFP	H	R	ER	HR	SH	SF	HB	TBB	IBB	SO	WP	Bk	W	L	Pct.	ShO	Sv-Op	Hld	ERA
1996 Fort Myers *	A+	2	2	0	0	12	50	13	5	5	1	0	1	0	1	0	12	1	0	2	0	1.000	0	0--	—	3.75
1985 New York	NL	21	19	2	1	122.1	507	118	49	44	8	7	4	2	37	2	74	5	2	10	7	.588	0	0--	—	3.24
1986 New York	NL	28	20	2	2	141.2	605	145	70	61	15	6	5	7	36	1	104	5	3	10	7	.588	0	0--	—	3.88
1987 New York	NL	18	17	1	0	115	494	124	53	46	12	7	2	3	33	2	77	9	0	11	3	.786	0	0-0	1	3.60
1988 New York	NL	11	3	0	2	24.2	111	29	20	19	2	2	0	1	10	2	16	1	1	0	4	.000	0	0-0	1	6.93
1989 NYN-Min		47	11	3	19	145	594	130	51	45	8	7	1	3	38	4	137	4	3	9	11	.450	0	7-11	1	2.79
1990 Minnesota	AL	56	0	0	54	65.1	268	55	27	20	5	0	0	4	19	6	61	3	0	5	3	.625	0	32-39	0	2.76
1991 Minnesota	AL	63	0	0	60	69	275	44	20	18	3	1	3	1	30	6	61	3	0	4	5	.444	0	42-51	0	2.35
1992 Minnesota	AL	64	0	0	61	66.2	273	60	28	21	7	1	2	1	17	4	52	5	0	2	6	.250	0	41-48	0	2.84
1993 Minnesota	AL	65	0	0	61	72.1	287	60	25	25	9	2	1	1	14	3	59	1	0	4	3	.571	0	34-40	0	3.11
1994 Minnesota	AL	44	0	0	40	44.2	201	57	23	18	7	4	1	0	10	3	46	2	0	1	4	.200	0	23-29	0	3.63
1995 Min-Bos	AL	52	0	0	51	55.1	223	46	16	16	6	1	4	1	13	1	52	0	0	3	3	.500	0	32-36	0	2.60
1996 Minnesota	AL	19	19	2	0	111.1	484	124	69	67	20	1	3	3	27	1	83	6	0	8	6	.571	0	0-0	—	5.42
1989 New York	NL	36	0	0	19	69.1	284	59	19	18	3	5	1	2	21	3	80	3	3	6	6	.500	0	7-11	1	2.34
Minnesota		11	11	3	0	75.2	310	71	32	27	5	2	0	1	17	1	57	1	0	3	5	.375	0	0-0	0	3.21
1995 Minnesota	AL	22	0	0	21	25	99	20	7	7	2	0	2	1	6	1	29	0	0	1	1	.500	0	12-15	0	2.52
Boston	AL	30	0	0	30	30.1	124	26	9	9	4	1	2	0	7	0	23	0	0	2	2	.500	0	20-21	0	2.67
12 ML YEARS		488	89	10	351	1033.1	4322	992	451	400	102	39	26	27	284	35	822	44	9	67	62	.519	0	211--	—	3.48

Jose Alberro

Pitches: Right **Bats:** Right **Pos:** RP-4; SP-1 **Ht:** 6'2" **Wt:** 190 **Born:** 6/29/69 **Age:** 28

Year Team	Lg	G	GS	CG	GF	IP	BFP	H	R	ER	HR	SH	SF	HB	TBB	IBB	SO	WP	Bk	W	L	Pct.	ShO	Sv-Op	Hld	ERA
1991 Rangers	R	19	0	0	16	30.1	121	17	6	5	1	1	0	4	9	0	40	1	2	2	0	1.000	0	6--	—	1.48
Charlotte	A+	5	0	0	0	5.2	33	8	9	6	0	1	0	2	7	2	3	3	0	0	1	.000	0	0--	—	9.53
1992 Gastonia	A	17	0	0	6	20.2	84	18	8	8	2	0	1	1	4	0	26	1	0	1	0	1.000	0	1--	—	3.48
Charlotte	A+	28	0	0	20	45	175	37	10	6	2	1	1	1	9	0	29	1	1	1	1	.500	0	15--	—	1.20
1993 Tulsa	AA	17	0	0	16	19	78	11	2	2	2	1	0	0	8	1	24	2	1	0	0	.000	0	5--	—	0.95
Okla. City	AAA	12	0	0	7	17	85	25	15	13	2	1	2	0	11	0	14	4	0	0	0	.000	0	0--	—	6.88
1994 Okla. City	AAA	52	0	0	35	69.2	314	79	40	35	6	6	4	5	36	2	50	3	0	4	3	.571	0	11--	—	4.52
1995 Okla. City	AAA	20	10	0	7	77.2	331	73	34	29	4	2	3	4	27	2	55	6	0	4	2	.667	0	0--	—	3.36

4

	HOW MUCH HE PITCHED						WHAT HE GAVE UP										THE RESULTS					
Year Team	Lg	G	GS	CG	GF	IP	BFP	H	R	ER	HR	SH	SF	HB	TBB	IBB	SO	WP	Bk	W	L	Pct.	ShO	Sv-Op	Hld	ERA
1996 Okla. City	AAA	29	27	4	0	171	720	154	73	66	12	6	0	8	57	1	140	9	2	9	9	.500	0	0- -	—	3.47
1995 Texas	AL	12	0	0	7	20.2	101	26	18	17	2	0	1	1	12	1	10	2	0	0	0	.000	0	0-0	0	7.40
1996 Texas	AL	5	1	0	1	9.1	46	14	6	6	1	0	1	0	7	1	2	0	0	0	1	.000	0	0-0	1	5.79
2 ML YEARS		17	1	0	8	30	147	40	24	23	3	0	2	1	19	2	12	2	0	0	1	.000	0	0-0	1	6.90

Scott Aldred

Pitches: Left **Bats:** Left **Pos:** SP-25; RP-11 **Ht:** 6'4" **Wt:** 215 **Born:** 6/12/68 **Age:** 29

	HOW MUCH HE PITCHED						WHAT HE GAVE UP										THE RESULTS					
Year Team	Lg	G	GS	CG	GF	IP	BFP	H	R	ER	HR	SH	SF	HB	TBB	IBB	SO	WP	Bk	W	L	Pct.	ShO	Sv-Op	Hld	ERA
1990 Detroit	AL	4	3	0	0	14.1	63	13	6	6	0	2	1	1	10	1	7	0	0	1	2	.333	0	0-0	0	3.77
1991 Detroit	AL	11	11	1	0	57.1	253	58	37	33	9	3	2	0	30	2	35	3	1	2	4	.333	0	0-0	0	5.18
1992 Detroit	AL	16	13	0	0	65	304	80	51	49	12	4	3	3	33	4	34	1	0	3	8	.273	0	0-0	0	6.78
1993 Col-Mon	NL	8	0	0	2	12	65	19	14	12	2	2	0	1	10	1	9	2	0	1	0	1.000	0	0-1	0	9.00
1996 Det-Min	AL	36	25	0	0	165.1	748	194	125	114	29	7	7	6	68	4	111	10	1	6	9	.400	0	0-0	1	6.21
1993 Colorado	NL	5	0	0	1	6.2	40	10	10	8	1	2	0	1	9	1	5	1	0	0	0	.000	0	0-0	0	10.80
Montreal	NL	3	0	0	1	5.1	25	9	4	4	1	0	0	0	1	0	4	1	0	1	0	1.000	0	0-1	0	6.75
1996 Detroit	AL					43.1	217	60	52	45	9	3	2	3	26	3	36	6	1	0	4	.000	0	0-0	0	9.35
Minnesota															42	1	75	4	0	6	5	.545	0	0-0	1	5.09
5 ML YEARS														1	151	12	196	16	2	13	23	.361	0	0-1	1	6.13

Bats: L **Ht:** 5'11" **Wt:** 185 **Born:** 1/29/61 **Age:** 36

Year Team									IBB	SO	HBP	SH	SF		SB	CS	SB%	GDP	Avg	OBP	SLG
1986 San Fr								3	4	34	2	4	1		1	3	.25	3	.250	.353	.389
1987 San Fr								3	5	50	0	4	2		6	0	1.00	6	.325	.396	.462
1988 San Fr								6	13	65	0	1	3		6	5	.55	10	.267	.357	.329
1989 Montr								9	0	30	1	1	2		1	3	.25	4	.221	.316	.316
1990 Montr								7	2	31	1	0	1		1	2	.33	2	.242	.385	.317
1991 SD-C								9	1	41	0	1	2		1	3	.25	1	.242	.364	.298
1993 Oakl								4	2	45	0	3	0		1	1	.50	7	.267	.353	.443
1994 Oakl								0	1	35	0	0	3		2	0	1.00	2	.242	.313	.337
1995 Oak-C								9	1	31	1	0	3		0	0	.00	4	.268	.349	.403
1996 Cal-N								4	0	19	0	0	1		0	1	.00	1	.213	.301	.435
1991 Clev								3	0	4	0	0	0		0	1	.00	1	.000	.167	.000
Cleve								6	1	37	0	1	2		1	2	.33	0	.262	.380	.322
1995 Oakl								9	1	23	1	0	2		0	0	.00	3	.272	.367	.432
Calif								0	0	8	0	0	1		0	0	.00	1	.250	.240	.250
1996 Calif								5	0	4	0	0	0		0	0	.00	3	.150	.239	.400
New								9	0	15	0	0	0		0	1	.00	1	.250	.338	.456
10								314	29	381	5	14	18		19	18	.51	43	.263	.356	.377

...ander **-1; P-1** **Ht:** 5'10" **Wt:** 160 **Born:** 3/20/71 **Age:** 26

Year Tea								TBB	IBB	SO	HBP	SH	SF		SB	CS	SB%	GDP	Avg	OBP	SLG
1992 Bal								0	0	3	0	0	0		0	0	.00	0	.200	.200	.200
1993 Bal								0	0	0	0	0	0		0	0	.00	0	.000	.000	.000
1995 Bal								20	0	30	2	4	0		11	4	.73	2	.236	.299	.318
1996 Bal								3	0	27	0	2	0		3	3	.50	2	.103	.141	.103
4								23	0	60	2	6	0		14	7	.67	4	.206	.265	.270

...fonzo **Ht:** 5'11" **Wt:** 187 **Born:** 11/8/73 **Age:** 23

	BATTING														BASERUNNING				PERCENTAGES		
Year Team	Lg	G	AB	H	2B	3B	HR	(Hm Rd)	TB	R	RBI	TBB	IBB	SO	HBP	SH	SF	SB	CS	SB%	GDP	Avg	OBP	SLG
1991 Mets	R	54	175	58	8	4	0	— —	74	29	27	34	0	12	2	3	7	6	4	.60	1	.331	.431	.423
1992 St. Lucie	A+	4	5	0	0	0	0	— —	0	0	0	0	0	0	0	0	0	0	0	.00	0	.000	.000	.000
Pittsfield	A-	74	298	106	13	5	1	— —	132	41	44	18	1	31	0	2	4	7	5	.58	6	.356	.388	.443
1993 St. Lucie	A+	128	494	145	18	3	11	— —	202	75	86	57	3	51	5	4	9	26	16	.62	13	.294	.366	.409
1994 Binghamton	AA	127	498	146	34	2	15	— —	229	89	75	64	6	55	0	5	7	14	11	.56	9	.293	.369	.460
1995 New York	NL	101	335	93	13	5	4	(0 4)	128	26	41	12	1	37	1	4	4	1	1	.50	7	.278	.301	.382
1996 New York	NL	123	368	96	15	2	4	(2 2)	127	36	40	25	2	56	0	9	5	2	0	1.00	8	.261	.304	.345
2 ML YEARS		224	703	189	28	7	8	(2 6)	255	62	81	37	3	93	1	13	9	3	1	.75	15	.269	.303	.363

Luis Alicea

Bats: Both **Throws:** Right **Pos:** 2B-125; PH-16 **Ht:** 5'9" **Wt:** 177 **Born:** 7/29/65 **Age:** 31

Year Team	Lg	G	AB	H	2B	3B	HR	(Hm	Rd)	TB	R	RBI	TBB	IBB	SO	HBP	SH	SF	SB	CS	SB%	GDP	Avg	OBP	SLG
1988 St. Louis	NL	93	297	63	10	4	1	(1	0)	84	20	24	25	4	32	2	4	2	1	1	.50	12	.212	.276	.283
1991 St. Louis	NL	56	68	13	3	0	0	(0	0)	16	5	0	8	0	19	0	0	0	0	1	.00	0	.191	.276	.235
1992 St. Louis	NL	85	265	65	9	11	2	(2	0)	102	26	32	27	1	40	4	2	4	2	5	.29	5	.245	.320	.385
1993 St. Louis	NL	115	362	101	19	3	3	(2	1)	135	50	46	47	2	54	4	1	7	11	1	.92	9	.279	.362	.373
1994 St. Louis	NL	88	205	57	12	5	5	(3	2)	94	32	29	30	4	38	3	1	3	4	5	.44	1	.278	.373	.459
1995 Boston	AL	132	419	113	20	3	6	(0	6)	157	64	44	63	0	61	7	13	9	13	10	.57	10	.270	.367	.375
1996 St. Louis	NL	129	380	98	26	3	5	(4	1)	145	54	42	52	10	78	5	4	4	11	3	.79	4	.258	.350	.382
7 ML YEARS		698	1996	510	99	29	22	(12	10)	733	251	217	252	21	322	25	25	31	42	26	.62	41	.256	.342	.367

Jermaine Allensworth

Bats: Right **Throws:** Right **Pos:** CF-61; PH-3 **Ht:** 6'0" **Wt:** 190 **Born:** 1/11/72 **Age:** 25

Year Team	Lg	G	AB	H	2B	3B	HR	(Hm	Rd)	TB	R	RBI	TBB	IBB	SO	HBP	SH	SF	SB	CS	SB%	GDP	Avg	OBP	SLG
1993 Welland	A-	67	263	81	16	4	1	—	—	108	44	32	24	0	38	12	2	1	18	3	.86	2	.308	.390	.411
1994 Carolina	AA	118	452	109	26	8	1	—	—	154	63	34	39	0	79	11	5	3	16	14	.53	2	.241	.315	.341
1995 Carolina	AA	56	219	59	14	2	1	—	—	80	37	14	25	0	34	5	2	0	13	8	.62	4	.269	.357	.365
Calgary	AAA	51	190	60	13	4	3	—	—	90	46	11	13	0	30	5	1	0	13	4	.76	3	.316	.375	.474
1996 Calgary	AAA	95	352	116	23	6	8	—	—	175	77	43	39	6	61	7	1	1	25	5	.83	4	.330	.406	.497
1996 Pittsburgh	NL	61	229	60	9	3	4	(4	0)	87	32	31	23	0	50	4	2	2	11	6	.65	2	.262	.337	.380

Roberto Alomar

Bats: Both **Throws:** Right **Pos:** 2B-142; DH-10; PH-3 **Ht:** 6'0" **Wt:** 185 **Born:** 2/5/68 **Age:** 29

Year Team	Lg	G	AB	H	2B	3B	HR	(Hm	Rd)	TB	R	RBI	TBB	IBB	SO	HBP	SH	SF	SB	CS	SB%	GDP	Avg	OBP	SLG
1988 San Diego	NL	143	545	145	24	6	9	(5	4)	208	84	41	47	5	83	3	16	0	24	6	.80	15	.266	.328	.382
1989 San Diego	NL	158	623	184	27	1	7	(3	4)	234	82	56	53	4	76	1	17	8	42	17	.71	10	.295	.347	.376
1990 San Diego	NL	147	586	168	27	5	6	(4	2)	223	80	60	48	1	72	2	5	8	24	7	.77	16	.287	.340	.381
1991 Toronto	AL	161	637	188	41	11	9	(6	3)	278	88	69	57	3	86	4	16	5	53	11	.83	5	.295	.354	.436
1992 Toronto	AL	152	571	177	27	8	8	(5	3)	244	105	76	87	5	52	5	6	2	49	9	.84	8	.310	.405	.427
1993 Toronto	AL	153	589	192	35	6	17	(8	9)	290	109	93	80	5	67	5	4	5	55	15	.79	13	.326	.408	.492
1994 Toronto	AL	107	392	120	25	4	8	(4	4)	177	78	38	51	2	41	2	7	3	19	8	.70	14	.306	.386	.452
1995 Toronto	AL	130	517	155	24	7	13	(7	6)	232	71	66	47	3	45	0	6	7	30	3	.91	16	.300	.354	.449
1996 Baltimore	AL	153	588	193	43	4	22	(14	8)	310	132	94	90	10	65	1	8	12	17	6	.74	14	.328	.411	.527
9 ML YEARS		1304	5048	1522	273	52	99	(56	43)	2196	829	593	560	38	587	23	85	47	313	82	.79	111	.302	.371	.435

Sandy Alomar

Bats: Right **Throws:** Right **Pos:** C-124; PH-4; 1B-1 **Ht:** 6'5" **Wt:** 215 **Born:** 6/18/66 **Age:** 31

Year Team	Lg	G	AB	H	2B	3B	HR	(Hm	Rd)	TB	R	RBI	TBB	IBB	SO	HBP	SH	SF	SB	CS	SB%	GDP	Avg	OBP	SLG
1988 San Diego	NL	1	1	0	0	0	0	(0	0)	0	0	0	0	0	1	0	0	0	0	0	.00	0	.000	.000	.000
1989 San Diego	NL	7	19	4	1	0	1	(1	0)	8	1	6	3	1	3	0	0	0	0	0	.00	1	.211	.318	.421
1990 Cleveland	AL	132	445	129	26	2	9	(5	4)	186	60	66	25	2	46	2	5	6	4	1	.80	10	.290	.326	.418
1991 Cleveland	AL	51	184	40	9	0	0	(0	0)	49	10	7	8	1	24	4	2	1	0	4	.00	4	.217	.264	.266
1992 Cleveland	AL	89	299	75	16	0	2	(1	1)	97	22	26	13	3	32	5	3	0	3	3	.50	7	.251	.293	.324
1993 Cleveland	AL	64	215	58	7	1	6	(3	3)	85	24	32	11	0	28	6	1	4	3	1	.75	3	.270	.318	.395
1994 Cleveland	AL	80	292	84	15	1	14	(4	10)	143	44	43	25	2	31	2	0	1	8	4	.67	7	.288	.347	.490
1995 Cleveland	AL	66	203	61	6	0	10	(4	6)	97	32	35	7	0	26	3	4	1	3	1	.75	8	.300	.332	.478
1996 Cleveland	AL	127	418	110	23	0	11	(3	8)	166	53	50	19	0	42	3	2	2	1	0	1.00	20	.263	.299	.397
9 ML YEARS		617	2076	561	103	4	53	(21	32)	831	246	265	111	9	233	25	17	15	22	14	.61	60	.270	.313	.400

Moises Alou

Bats: R **Throws:** R **Pos:** RF-123; LF-33; CF-7; PH-1 **Ht:** 6'3" **Wt:** 195 **Born:** 7/3/66 **Age:** 30

Year Team	Lg	G	AB	H	2B	3B	HR	(Hm	Rd)	TB	R	RBI	TBB	IBB	SO	HBP	SH	SF	SB	CS	SB%	GDP	Avg	OBP	SLG
1990 Pit-Mon	NL	16	20	4	0	1	0	(0	0)	6	4	0	0	0	3	0	1	0	0	0	.00	1	.200	.200	.300
1992 Montreal	NL	115	341	96	28	2	9	(6	3)	155	53	56	25	0	46	1	5	5	16	2	.89	5	.282	.328	.455
1993 Montreal	NL	136	482	138	29	6	18	(10	8)	233	70	85	38	9	53	5	3	7	17	6	.74	9	.286	.340	.483
1994 Montreal	NL	107	422	143	31	5	22	(9	13)	250	81	78	42	10	63	2	0	5	7	6	.54	7	.339	.397	.592
1995 Montreal	NL	93	344	94	22	0	14	(4	10)	158	48	58	29	6	56	9	0	4	4	3	.57	9	.273	.342	.459
1996 Montreal	NL	143	540	152	28	2	21	(14	7)	247	87	96	49	7	83	2	0	7	9	4	.69	15	.281	.339	.457
1990 Pittsburgh	NL	2	5	1	0	0	0	(0	0)	1	0	0	0	0	0	0	1	0	0	0	.00	1	.200	.200	.200
Montreal	NL	14	15	3	0	1	0	(0	0)	5	4	0	0	0	3	0	0	0	0	0	.00	0	.200	.200	.333
6 ML YEARS		610	2149	627	138	16	84	(43	41)	1049	343	373	183	32	304	19	9	28	53	21	.72	46	.292	.348	.488

6

Garvin Alston

Pitches: Right **Bats:** Right **Pos:** RP-6　　**Ht:** 6'1" **Wt:** 185 **Born:** 12/8/71 **Age:** 25

Year Team	Lg	G	GS	CG	GF	IP	BFP	H	R	ER	HR	SH	SF	HB	TBB	IBB	SO	WP	Bk	W	L	Pct.	ShO	Sv-Op	Hld	ERA
1992 Bend	A-	14	12	0	0	73	320	71	40	32	1	5	5	9	29	0	73	7	8	5	4	.556	0	0--	—	3.95
1993 Central Val	A+	25	24	1	0	117	538	124	81	71	11	6	6	8	70	0	90	10	2	5	9	.357	0	0--	—	5.46
1994 Central Val	A+	37	13	0	20	87	382	91	51	35	9	5	0	6	42	1	83	5	2	5	9	.357	0	8--	—	3.62
New Haven	AA	4	0	0	1	4.1	22	5	6	6	1	0	0	0	3	0	5	0	0	0	0	.000	0	1--	—	12.46
1995 New Haven	AA	47	0	0	20	66.2	271	47	24	21	1	4	2	3	26	3	73	4	0	4	4	.500	0	6--	—	2.84
1996 Colo. Sprng	AAA	35	0	0	26	34.1	171	47	23	22	3	1	0	1	27	0	36	2	0	1	4	.200	0	14--	—	5.77
1996 Colorado	NL	6	0	0	4	6	30	9	6	6	1	0	2	1	3	0	5	1	0	1	0	1.000	0	0-0	0	9.00

Tavo Alvarez

Pitches: Right **Bats:** Right **Pos:** RP-6; SP-5　　**Ht:** 6'3" **Wt:** 235 **Born:** 11/25/71 **Age:** 25

Year Team	Lg	G	GS	CG	GF	IP	BFP	H	R	ER	HR	SH	SF	HB	TBB	IBB	SO	WP	Bk	W	L	Pct.	ShO	Sv-Op	Hld	ERA
1990 Expos	R	11	10	0	0	52	214	42	17	15	0	1	3	1	16	0	47	1	0	5	2	.714	0	0--	—	2.60
1991 Sumter	A	25	25	3	0	152.2	663	152	68	55	6	4	3	3	58	0	158	3	6	12	10	.545	1	0--	—	3.24
1992 W. Palm Bch	A+	19	19	7	0	139	542	124	30	23	0	2	1	3	24	0	83	2	0	13	4	.765	4	0--	—	1.49
Harrisburg	AA	7	7	2	0	47.1	191	48	15	15	3	1	1	2	9	0	42	0	0	4	1	.800	1	0--	—	2.85
1993 Ottawa	AAA	25	25	1	0	140.2	636	163	80	66	10	5	7	4	55	2	77	6	0	7	10	.412	0	0--	—	4.22
1995 Harrisburg	AA	3	3	0	0	16	70	17	8	4	0	0	0	1	5	0	14	0	0	2	1	.667	0	0--	—	2.25
Ottawa	AAA	6	6	0	0	37.2	153	34	14	10	1	0	0	1	10	0	25	1	0	4	2	.667	0	0--	—	2.39
1996 Ottawa	AAA	20	20	2	0	113	485	128	66	59	12	3	0	2	25	1	86	5	0	4	9	.308	1	0--	—	4.70
1995 Montreal	NL	8	8	0	0	37.1	173	46	30	28	2	1	0	3	14	0	17	1	0	1	5	.167	0	0-0	0	6.75
1996 Montreal	NL	11	5	0	3	21	96	19	10	7	0	2	0	1	12	1	9	0	0	2	1	.667	0	0-0	0	3.00
2 ML YEARS		19	13	0	3	58.1	269	65	40	35	2	3	0	4	26	1	26	1	0	3	6	.333	0	0-0	0	5.40

Wilson Alvarez

Pitches: Left **Bats:** Left **Pos:** SP-35　　**Ht:** 6'1" **Wt:** 235 **Born:** 3/24/70 **Age:** 27

Year Team	Lg	G	GS	CG	GF	IP	BFP	H	R	ER	HR	SH	SF	HB	TBB	IBB	SO	WP	Bk	W	L	Pct.	ShO	Sv-Op	Hld	ERA
1989 Texas	AL	1	1	0	0	0	5	3	3	3	2	0	0	0	2	0	0	0	0	0	1	.000	0	0-0	0	0.00
1991 Chicago	AL	10	9	2	0	56.1	237	47	26	22	9	3	1	0	29	0	32	2	0	3	2	.600	1	0-0	0	3.51
1992 Chicago	AL	34	9	0	4	100.1	455	103	64	58	12	3	4	4	65	2	66	2	0	5	3	.625	0	1-1	3	5.20
1993 Chicago	AL	31	31	1	0	207.2	877	168	78	68	14	13	6	7	122	8	155	2	1	15	8	.652	1	0-0	0	2.95
1994 Chicago	AL	24	24	2	0	161.2	682	147	72	62	16	6	3	0	62	1	108	3	0	12	8	.600	1	0-0	0	3.45
1995 Chicago	AL	29	29	3	0	175	769	171	96	84	21	5	5	2	93	4	118	1	2	8	11	.421	0	0-0	0	4.32
1996 Chicago	AL	35	35	0	0	217.1	946	216	106	102	21	5	2	4	97	3	181	2	0	15	10	.600	0	0-0	0	4.22
7 ML YEARS		164	138	8	4	918.1	3971	855	445	399	95	36	21	17	470	18	660	12	3	58	43	.574	3	1-1	3	3.91

Rich Amaral

B: R **T:** R **Pos:** LF-63; CF-26; PH-26; 2B-15; 1B-10; RF-5; DH-4; 3B-1　　**Ht:** 6'0" **Wt:** 175 **Born:** 4/1/62 **Age:** 35

Year Team	Lg	G	AB	H	2B	3B	HR	(Hm	Rd)	TB	R	RBI	TBB	IBB	SO	HBP	SH	SF	SB	CS	SB%	GDP	Avg	OBP	SLG
1991 Seattle	AL	14	16	1	0	0	0	(0	0)	1	2	0	1	0	5	1	0	0	0	0	.00	1	.063	.167	.063
1992 Seattle	AL	35	100	24	3	0	1	(0	1)	30	9	7	5	0	16	0	4	0	2	2	.67	4	.240	.276	.300
1993 Seattle	AL	110	373	108	24	1	1	(0	1)	137	53	44	33	0	54	3	7	5	19	11	.63	5	.290	.348	.367
1994 Seattle	AL	77	228	60	10	2	4	(2	2)	86	37	18	24	1	28	1	7	2	5	1	.83	3	.263	.333	.377
1995 Seattle	AL	90	238	67	14	2	2	(1	1)	91	45	19	21	0	33	1	1	0	21	2	.91	3	.282	.342	.382
1996 Seattle	AL	118	312	91	11	3	1	(1	0)	111	69	29	47	0	55	5	4	1	25	6	.81	6	.292	.392	.356
6 ML YEARS		444	1267	351	62	8	9	(4	5)	456	215	117	131	1	191	11	23	8	74	22	.77	22	.277	.348	.360

Ruben Amaro

Bats: B **Throws:** R **Pos:** PH-35; RF-28; CF-7; 1B-1　　**Ht:** 5'10" **Wt:** 175 **Born:** 2/12/65 **Age:** 32

Year Team	Lg	G	AB	H	2B	3B	HR	(Hm	Rd)	TB	R	RBI	TBB	IBB	SO	HBP	SH	SF	SB	CS	SB%	GDP	Avg	OBP	SLG
1996 Syracuse *	AAA	16	50	12	1	0	0	(—	—)	13	8	2	10	0	11	4	1	0	6	2	.75	0	.240	.406	.260
Scrnton-WB *	AAA	52	180	50	10	3	2	(—	—)	72	28	22	14	0	29	3	1	0	7	1	.88	4	.278	.340	.400
1991 California	AL	10	23	5	1	0	0	(0	0)	6	0	2	3	1	3	0	0	0	0	0	.00	1	.217	.308	.261
1992 Philadelphia	NL	126	374	82	15	6	7	(5	2)	130	43	34	37	1	54	9	4	2	11	5	.69	11	.219	.303	.348
1993 Philadelphia	NL	25	48	16	2	2	1	(0	1)	25	7	6	6	0	5	0	3	1	0	0	.00	1	.333	.400	.521
1994 Cleveland	AL	26	23	5	1	0	2	(0	2)	12	5	5	2	0	3	0	0	0	2	1	.67	0	.217	.280	.522
1995 Cleveland	AL	28	60	12	3	0	1	(1	0)	18	5	7	4	0	6	2	2	0	1	3	.25	1	.200	.273	.300
1996 Philadelphia	NL	61	117	37	10	0	2	(1	1)	53	14	15	9	0	18	3	1	0	0	0	.00	3	.316	.380	.453
6 ML YEARS		276	645	157	32	8	13	(7	6)	244	74	69	61	2	89	14	10	3	14	9	.61	17	.243	.321	.378

Brady Anderson

Bats: Left **Throws:** Left **Pos:** CF-143; PH-4; DH-2 **Ht:** 6'1" **Wt:** 195 **Born:** 1/18/64 **Age:** 33

Year Team	Lg	G	AB	H	2B	3B	HR	(Hm	Rd)	TB	R	RBI	TBB	IBB	SO	HBP	SH	SF	SB	CS	SB%	GDP	Avg	OBP	SLG
1988 Bos-Bal	AL	94	325	69	13	4	1	(1	0)	93	31	21	23	0	75	4	11	1	10	6	.63	3	.212	.272	.286
1989 Baltimore	AL	94	266	55	12	2	4	(2	2)	83	44	16	43	6	45	3	5	0	16	4	.80	4	.207	.324	.312
1990 Baltimore	AL	89	234	54	5	2	3	(1	2)	72	24	24	31	2	46	5	4	5	15	2	.88	4	.231	.327	.308
1991 Baltimore	AL	113	256	59	12	3	2	(1	1)	83	40	27	38	0	44	5	11	3	12	5	.71	1	.230	.338	.324
1992 Baltimore	AL	159	623	169	28	10	21	(15	6)	280	100	80	98	14	98	9	10	9	53	16	.77	2	.271	.373	.449
1993 Baltimore	AL	142	560	147	36	8	13	(2	11)	238	87	66	82	4	99	10	6	6	24	12	.67	4	.263	.363	.425
1994 Baltimore	AL	111	453	119	25	5	12	(7	5)	190	78	48	57	3	75	10	3	2	31	1	.97	7	.263	.356	.419
1995 Baltimore	AL	143	554	145	33	10	16	(10	6)	246	108	64	87	4	111	10	4	2	26	7	.79	3	.262	.371	.444
1996 Baltimore	AL	149	579	172	37	5	50	(19	31)	369	117	110	76	1	106	22	6	4	21	8	.72	11	.297	.396	.637
1988 Boston	AL	41	148	34	5	3	0	(0	0)	45	14	12	15	0	35	4	4	1	4	2	.67	2	.230	.315	.304
Baltimore	AL	53	177	35	8	1	1	(1	0)	48	17	9	8	0	40	0	7	0	6	4	.60	1	.198	.232	.271
9 ML YEARS		1094	3850	989	201	49	122	(58	64)	1654	629	456	535	34	699	78	60	32	208	61	.77	39	.257	.356	.430

Brian Anderson

Pitches: Left **Bats:** Both **Pos:** SP-9; RP-1 **Ht:** 6'1" **Wt:** 190 **Born:** 4/26/72 **Age:** 25

		HOW MUCH HE PITCHED						WHAT HE GAVE UP										THE RESULTS					
Year Team	Lg	G	GS	CG	GF	IP	BFP	H	R	ER	HR	SH	SF	HB	TBB	IBB	SO	WP	Bk	W	L	Pct.	ShO	Sv-Op	Hld	ERA
1996 Buffalo *	AAA	19	19	2	0	128	531	125	57	51	14	3	3	2	28	0	85	4	3	11	5	.688	0	0- -	0	3.59
1993 California	AL	4	1	0	3	11.1	45	11	5	5	1	0	0	0	2	0	4	0	0	0	0	.000	0	0-0	0	3.97
1994 California	AL	18	18	0	0	101.2	441	120	63	59	13	3	6	5	27	0	47	5	5	7	5	.583	0	0-0	0	5.22
1995 California	AL	18	17	1	0	99.2	433	110	66	65	24	5	5	3	30	2	45	1	3	6	8	.429	0	0-0	0	5.87
1996 Cleveland	AL	10	9	0	0	51.1	215	58	29	28	9	2	3	0	14	1	21	2	0	3	1	.750	0	0-0	0	4.91
4 ML YEARS		50	45	1	3	264	1134	299	163	157	47	10	14	8	73	3	117	8	8	16	14	.533	0	0-0	1	5.35

Garret Anderson

Bats: L **Throws:** L **Pos:** LF-140; RF-6; CF-3; PH-3; DH-1 **Ht:** 6'3" **Wt:** 190 **Born:** 6/30/72 **Age:** 25

Year Team	Lg	G	AB	H	2B	3B	HR	(Hm	Rd)	TB	R	RBI	TBB	IBB	SO	HBP	SH	SF	SB	CS	SB%	GDP	Avg	OBP	SLG
1994 California	AL	5	13	5	0	0	0	(0	0)	5	0	1	0	0	2	0	0	0	0	0	.00	0	.385	.385	.385
1995 California	AL	106	374	120	19	1	16	(7	9)	189	50	69	19	4	65	1	2	4	6	2	.75	8	.321	.352	.505
1996 California	AL	150	607	173	33	2	12	(7	5)	246	79	72	27	5	84	0	5	3	7	9	.44	22	.285	.314	.405
3 ML YEARS		261	994	298	52	3	28	(14	14)	440	129	142	46	9	151	1	7	7	13	11	.54	30	.300	.329	.443

Shane Andrews

Bats: Right **Throws:** Right **Pos:** 3B-123; PH-6 **Ht:** 6'1" **Wt:** 215 **Born:** 8/28/71 **Age:** 25

Year Team	Lg	G	AB	H	2B	3B	HR	(Hm	Rd)	TB	R	RBI	TBB	IBB	SO	HBP	SH	SF	SB	CS	SB%	GDP	Avg	OBP	SLG
1990 Expos	R	56	190	45	7	1	3	—	—	63	31	24	29	0	46	3	1	1	10	4	.71	7	.237	.345	.332
1991 Sumter	A	105	356	74	16	7	11	—	—	137	46	49	65	2	132	3	0	0	5	4	.56	8	.208	.335	.385
1992 Albany	A	136	453	104	18	1	25	—	—	199	76	87	107	4	174	7	0	3	8	3	.73	4	.230	.382	.439
1993 Harrisburg	AA	124	442	115	29	1	18	—	—	200	77	70	64	2	118	1	1	3	10	6	.63	8	.260	.352	.452
1994 Ottawa	AAA	137	460	117	25	2	16	—	—	194	79	85	80	5	126	5	0	5	6	5	.55	11	.254	.367	.422
1995 Montreal	NL	84	220	47	10	1	8	(2	6)	83	27	31	17	2	68	1	1	2	1	1	.50	4	.214	.271	.377
1996 Montreal	NL	127	375	85	15	2	19	(8	11)	161	43	64	35	8	119	2	0	2	3	1	.75	2	.227	.295	.429
2 ML YEARS		211	595	132	25	3	27	(10	17)	244	70	95	52	10	187	3	1	4	4	2	.67	6	.222	.286	.410

Luis Andujar

Pitches: Right **Bats:** Right **Pos:** SP-7; RP-1 **Ht:** 6'2" **Wt:** 175 **Born:** 11/22/72 **Age:** 24

		HOW MUCH HE PITCHED						WHAT HE GAVE UP										THE RESULTS					
Year Team	Lg	G	GS	CG	GF	IP	BFP	H	R	ER	HR	SH	SF	HB	TBB	IBB	SO	WP	Bk	W	L	Pct.	ShO	Sv-Op	Hld	ERA
1991 White Sox	R	10	10	1	0	62.1	255	60	27	17	0	1	2	4	10	0	52	3	1	4	4	.500	1	0- -	—	2.45
1992 South Bend	A	32	15	1	11	120.1	516	109	49	39	5	2	0	6	47	0	91	5	1	6	5	.545	1	3- -	—	2.92
1993 Sarasota	A+	18	11	2	4	86	345	67	26	19	2	7	0	3	28	0	72	1	0	6	6	.500	0	1- -	—	1.99
Birmingham	AA	6	6	0	0	39.2	169	31	9	8	3	3	1	5	18	0	48	1	0	5	0	1.000	0	0- -	—	1.82
1994 White Sox	R	2	0	0	0	6	22	3	0	0	0	1	0	0	1	0	6	0	0	1	0	1.000	0	0- -	—	0.00
Birmingham	AA	15	15	0	0	76.2	344	90	50	43	5	1	2	8	25	0	64	5	0	3	7	.300	0	0- -	—	5.05
1995 Birmingham	AA	27	27	2	0	167.1	689	147	64	53	10	1	5	7	44	0	146	3	1	14	8	.636	1	0- -	—	2.85
1996 Birmingham	R	1	1	0	0	6	22	3	0	0	0	0	1	0	3	0	3	0	0	1	0	1.000	0	0- -	—	0.00
Nashville	AAA	8	7	1	0	38	171	50	26	25	4	0	2	2	8	0	24	1	1	1	4	.200	0	0- -	—	5.92
Syracuse	AAA	2	2	0	0	12	55	17	7	3	1	1	0	0	2	0	10	0	0	0	0	.000	0	0- -	—	2.25
1995 Chicago	AL	5	5	0	0	30.1	128	26	12	11	4	0	0	1	14	2	19	0	0	2	1	.667	0	0-0	0	3.26
1996 ChA-Tor	AL	8	7	0	0	37.1	170	46	30	29	8	4	4	1	16	0	11	0	0	1	3	.250	0	0-0	0	6.99
1996 Chicago	AL	5	5	0	0	23	113	32	22	21	4	1	2	0	15	0	6	0	0	0	2	.000	0	0-0	0	8.22
Toronto	AL	3	2	0	0	14.1	57	14	8	8	4	3	2	1	1	0	5	0	0	1	1	.500	0	0-0	0	5.02
2 ML YEARS		13	12	0	0	67.2	298	72	42	40	12	1	4	2	30	2	20	0	0	3	4	.429	0	0-0	0	5.32

Eric Anthony

Bats: L **Throws:** L **Pos:** RF-34; PH-24; LF-14; CF-9   **Ht:** 6'2" **Wt:** 195 **Born:** 11/8/67 **Age:** 29

						BATTING												BASERUNNING				PERCENTAGES		
Year Team	Lg	G	AB	H	2B	3B	HR	(Hm | Rd)	TB	R	RBI	TBB	IBB	SO	HBP	SH	SF	SB	CS	SB%	GDP	Avg	OBP	SLG
1996 Indianapols *	AAA	7	21	5	1	0	2	—	—	12	4	7	7	0	8	0	0	0	0	0	.00	1	.238	.429	.571
1989 Houston	NL	25	61	11	2	0	4	(2 | 2)	25	7	7	9	2	16	0	0	0	0	0	.00	1	.180	.286	.410
1990 Houston	NL	84	239	46	8	0	10	(5 | 5)	84	26	29	29	3	78	2	1	6	5	0	1.00	4	.192	.279	.351
1991 Houston	NL	39	118	18	6	0	1	(0 | 1)	27	11	7	12	1	41	0	1	0	1	0	1.00	2	.153	.227	.229
1992 Houston	NL	137	440	105	15	1	19	(9 | 10)	179	45	80	38	5	98	1	0	4	5	4	.56	7	.239	.298	.407
1993 Houston	NL	145	486	121	19	4	15	(5 | 10)	193	70	66	49	2	88	2	0	2	3	5	.38	9	.249	.319	.397
1994 Seattle	AL	79	262	62	14	1	10	(3 | 7)	108	31	30	23	4	66	0	0	2	6	2	.75	7	.237	.297	.412
1995 Cincinnati	NL	47	134	36	6	0	5	(3 | 2)	57	19	23	13	2	30	0	0	3	2	1	.67	1	.269	.327	.425
1996 Cin-Col	NL	79	185	45	8	0	12	(4 | 8)	89	32	22	32	2	56	0	0	0	0	1	.00	3	.243	.353	.481
1996 Cincinnati	NL	47	123	30	6	0	8	(3 | 5)	60	22	13	22	2	36	0	0	0	0	1	.00	2	.244	.359	.488
Colorado	NL	32	62	15	2	0	4	(1 | 3)	29	10	9	10	0	20	0	0	0	0	0	.00	1	.242	.342	.468
8 ML YEARS		635	1925	444	78	6	76	(31 | 45)	762	241	264	205	21	473	5	3	19	22	14	.61	34	.231	.304	.396

Kevin Appier

Pitches: Right **Bats:** Right **Pos:** SP-32   **Ht:** 6'2" **Wt:** 195 **Born:** 12/6/67 **Age:** 29

		HOW MUCH HE PITCHED						WHAT HE GAVE UP										THE RESULTS					
Year Team	Lg	G	GS	CG	GF	IP	BFP	H	R	ER	HR	SH	SF	HB	TBB	IBB	SO	WP	Bk	W	L	Pct.	ShO	Sv-Op	Hld	ERA
1989 Kansas City	AL	6	5	0	0	21.2	106	34	22	22	3	0	3	0	12	1	10	0	0	1	4	.200	0	0-0		9.14
1990 Kansas City	AL	32	24	3	1	185.2	784	179	67	57	13	5	9	6	54	2	127	6	1	12	8	.600	3	0-0		2.76
1991 Kansas City	AL	34	31	6	1	207.2	881	205	97	79	13	8	6	2	61	3	158	7	1	13	10	.565	3	0-0		3.42
1992 Kansas City	AL	30	30	3	0	208.1	852	167	59	57	10	8	3	2	68	5	150	4	0	15	8	.652	0	0-0		2.46
1993 Kansas City	AL	34	34	5	0	238.2	953	183	74	68	8	3	5	1	81	3	186	5	0	18	8	.692	1	0-0		**2.56**
1994 Kansas City	AL	23	23	1	0	155	653	137	68	66	11	9	7	4	63	7	145	11	1	7	6	.538	0	0-0		3.83
1995 Kansas City	AL	31	31	4	0	201.1	832	163	90	87	14	3	3	8	80	1	185	5	0	15	10	.600	1	0-0		3.89
1996 Kansas City	AL	32	32	5	0	211.1	874	192	87	85	17	7	4	5	75	2	207	10	1	14	11	.560	1	0-0		3.62
8 ML YEARS		222	210	27	2	1429.2	5935	1260	564	521	89	43	40	28	494	24	1168	48	4	95	65	.594	9	0-0		3.28

Alex Arias

Bats: R **Throws:** R **Pos:** 3B-59; PH-31; SS-20; 1B-1; 2B-1   **Ht:** 6'3" **Wt:** 185 **Born:** 11/20/67 **Age:** 29

						BATTING												BASERUNNING				PERCENTAGES		
Year Team	Lg	G	AB	H	2B	3B	HR	(Hm	Rd)	TB	R	RBI	TBB	IBB	SO	HBP	SH	SF	SB	CS	SB%	GDP	Avg	OBP	SLG
1992 Chicago	NL	32	99	29	6	0	0	(0	0)	35	14	7	11	0	13	2	1	0	0	0	.00	4	.293	.375	.354
1993 Florida	NL	96	249	67	5	1	2	(1	1)	80	27	20	27	0	18	3	1	3	1	1	.50	5	.269	.344	.321
1994 Florida	NL	59	113	27	5	0	0	(0	0)	32	4	15	9	0	19	1	1	0	0	1	.00	5	.239	.298	.283
1995 Florida	NL	94	216	58	9	2	3	(2	1)	80	22	26	22	1	20	2	3	3	1	0	1.00	8	.269	.337	.370
1996 Florida	NL	100	224	62	11	2	3	(1	2)	86	27	26	17	1	28	3	1	1	2	0	1.00	2	.277	.335	.384
5 ML YEARS		381	901	243	36	5	8	(4	4)	313	94	94	86	2	98	11	7	8	4	2	.67	24	.270	.338	.347

George Arias

Bats: Right **Throws:** Right **Pos:** 3B-83; DH-1; PH-1   **Ht:** 5'11" **Wt:** 190 **Born:** 3/12/72 **Age:** 25

						BATTING												BASERUNNING				PERCENTAGES		
Year Team	Lg	G	AB	H	2B	3B	HR	(Hm	Rd)	TB	R	RBI	TBB	IBB	SO	HBP	SH	SF	SB	CS	SB%	GDP	Avg	OBP	SLG
1993 Cedar Rapds	A	74	253	55	13	3	9	—	—	101	31	41	31	1	65	3	1	2	6	1	.86	6	.217	.308	.399
1994 Lk Elsinore	A+	134	514	144	28	3	23	—	—	247	89	80	58	1	111	5	3	4	6	3	.67	9	.280	.356	.481
1995 Midland	AA	134	520	145	19	10	30	—	—	274	91	104	63	1	119	5	1	5	3	1	.75	11	.279	.359	.527
1996 Vancouver	AAA	59	243	82	24	0	9	—	—	133	49	55	20	2	38	3	0	2	2	1	.67	5	.337	.392	.547
1996 California	AL	84	252	60	8	1	6	(5	1)	88	19	28	16	2	50	0	0	6	2	0	1.00	6	.238	.284	.349

Andy Ashby

Pitches: Right **Bats:** Right **Pos:** SP-24   **Ht:** 6'5" **Wt:** 190 **Born:** 7/11/67 **Age:** 29

		HOW MUCH HE PITCHED						WHAT HE GAVE UP										THE RESULTS					
Year Team	Lg	G	GS	CG	GF	IP	BFP	H	R	ER	HR	SH	SF	HB	TBB	IBB	SO	WP	Bk	W	L	Pct.	ShO	Sv-Op	Hld	ERA
1991 Philadelphia	NL	8	8	0	0	42	186	41	28	28	5	1	3	3	19	0	26	6	0	1	5	.167	0	0-0		6.00
1992 Philadelphia	NL	10	8	0	0	37	171	42	31	31	6	2	2	1	21	0	24	2	0	1	3	.250	0	0-0		7.54
1993 Col-SD	NL	32	21	0	3	123	577	168	100	93	19	6	7	4	56	5	77	6	3	3	10	.231	0	1-1		6.80
1994 San Diego	NL	24	24	4	0	164.1	682	145	75	62	16	11	3	3	43	12	121	5	0	6	11	.353	0	0-0		3.40
1995 San Diego	NL	31	**31**	2	0	192.2	800	180	79	63	17	10	4	11	62	3	150	7	0	12	10	.545	2	0-0		2.94
1996 San Diego	NL	24	24	1	0	150.2	612	147	60	54	17	6	2	3	34	1	85	3	0	9	5	.643	0	0-0		3.23
1993 Colorado	NL	20	9	0	3	54	277	89	54	51	5	3	3	3	32	4	33	2	3	0	4	.000	0	1-1		8.50
San Diego	NL	12	12	0	0	69	300	79	46	42	14	3	4	1	24	1	44	4	0	3	6	.333	0	0-0		5.48
6 ML YEARS		129	116	7	3	709.2	3028	723	373	331	80	36	21	25	235	21	483	29	3	32	44	.421	2	1-1		4.20

Billy Ashley

Bats: Right **Throws:** Right **Pos:** LF-38; PH-38 **Ht:** 6'7" **Wt:** 235 **Born:** 7/11/70 **Age:** 26

Year Team	Lg	G	AB	H	2B	3B	HR	(Hm	Rd)	TB	R	RBI	TBB	IBB	SO	HBP	SH	SF	SB	CS	SB%	GDP	Avg	OBP	SLG
1996 Albuquerque *	AAA	7	23	8	1	0	1	—	—	12	6	9	7	0	9	0	0	0	2	0	1.00	0	.348	.500	.522
1992 Los Angeles	NL	29	95	21	5	0	2	(2	0)	32	6	6	5	0	34	0	0	0	0	0	.00	2	.221	.260	.337
1993 Los Angeles	NL	14	37	9	0	0	0	(0	0)	9	0	0	2	0	11	0	0	0	0	0	.00	0	.243	.282	.243
1994 Los Angeles	NL	2	6	2	1	0	0	(0	0)	3	0	0	0	0	2	0	0	0	0	0	.00	0	.333	.333	.500
1995 Los Angeles	NL	81	215	51	5	0	8	(6	2)	80	17	27	25	4	88	2	0	0	0	0	.00	8	.237	.320	.372
1996 Los Angeles	NL	71	110	22	2	1	9	(5	4)	53	18	25	21	1	44	1	0	0	0	0	.00	3	.200	.331	.482
5 ML YEARS		197	463	105	13	1	19	(13	6)	177	41	58	53	5	179	3	0	0	0	0	.00	13	.227	.308	.382

Paul Assenmacher

Pitches: Left **Bats:** Left **Pos:** RP-63 **Ht:** 6'3" **Wt:** 210 **Born:** 12/10/60 **Age:** 36

Year Team	Lg	G	GS	CG	GF	IP	BFP	H	R	ER	HR	SH	SF	HB	TBB	IBB	SO	WP	Bk	W	L	Pct.	ShO	Sv-Op	Hld	ERA
1986 Atlanta	NL	61	0	0	27	68.1	287	61	23	19	5	7	1	0	26	4	56	2	3	7	3	.700	0	7--	—	2.50
1987 Atlanta	NL	52	0	0	10	54.2	251	58	41	31	8	2	1	1	24	4	39	0	0	1	1	.500	0	2-6	10	5.10
1988 Atlanta	NL	64	0	0	32	79.1	329	72	28	27	4	8	1	1	32	11	71	7	0	8	7	.533	0	5-11	8	3.06
1989 Atl-ChN	NL	63	0	0	17	76.2	331	74	37	34	3	9	3	1	28	8	79	3	1	3	4	.429	0	0-3	13	3.99
1990 Chicago	NL	74	1	0	21	103	426	90	33	32	10	10	3	1	36	8	95	2	0	7	2	.778	0	10-20	10	2.80
1991 Chicago	NL	75	0	0	31	102.2	427	85	41	37	10	8	4	3	31	6	117	4	0	7	8	.467	0	15-24	14	3.24
1992 Chicago	NL	70	0	0	23	68	298	72	32	31	6	1	2	3	26	5	67	4	0	4	4	.500	0	8-13	20	4.10
1993 ChN-NYA		72	0	0	21	56	237	54	21	21	5	4	0	1	22	6	45	0	0	4	3	.571	0	5-17	13	3.38
1994 Chicago	AL	44	0	0	11	33	134	26	13	13	2	1	3	1	13	2	29	1	0	1	2	.333	0	1-3	**14**	3.55
1995 Cleveland	AL	47	0	0	12	38.1	160	32	13	12	3	1	2	3	12	3	40	1	0	6	2	.750	0	0-1	9	2.82
1996 Cleveland	AL	63	0	0	25	46.2	201	46	18	16	1	4	2	4	14	5	44	2	0	4	2	.667	0	1-3	13	3.09
1989 Atlanta	NL	49	0	0	14	57.2	247	55	26	23	2	7	2	1	16	7	64	3	1	1	3	.250	0	0-2	7	3.59
Chicago	NL	14	0	0	3	19	84	19	11	11	1	2	1	0	12	1	15	0	0	2	1	.667	0	0-1	6	5.21
1993 Chicago	NL	46	0	0	15	38.2	166	44	15	15	5	0	0	0	13	3	34	0	0	2	1	.667	0	0-4	12	3.49
New York	AL	26	0	0	6	17.1	71	10	6	6	0	4	0	1	9	3	11	0	0	2	2	.500	0	0-1	5	3.12
11 ML YEARS		685	1	0	230	726.2	3081	670	300	273	57	55	22	19	264	62	682	26	4	52	38	.578	0	49--	—	3.38

Pedro Astacio

Pitches: Right **Bats:** Right **Pos:** SP-32; RP-3 **Ht:** 6'2" **Wt:** 195 **Born:** 11/28/69 **Age:** 27

Year Team	Lg	G	GS	CG	GF	IP	BFP	H	R	ER	HR	SH	SF	HB	TBB	IBB	SO	WP	Bk	W	L	Pct.	ShO	Sv-Op	Hld	ERA
1992 Los Angeles	NL	11	11	4	0	82	341	80	23	18	1	3	2	2	20	4	43	1	0	5	5	.500	4	0-0	0	1.98
1993 Los Angeles	NL	31	31	3	0	186.1	777	165	80	74	14	7	8	5	68	5	122	8	9	14	9	.609	2	0-0	0	3.57
1994 Los Angeles	NL	23	23	3	0	149	625	142	77	71	18	6	5	4	47	4	108	4	0	6	8	.429	1	0-0	0	4.29
1995 Los Angeles	NL	48	11	1	7	104	436	103	53	49	12	5	3	4	29	5	80	5	0	7	8	.467	1	0-1	2	4.24
1996 Los Angeles	NL	35	32	0	0	211.2	885	207	86	81	18	11	5	9	67	9	130	6	2	9	8	.529	0	0-0	0	3.44
5 ML YEARS		148	108	11	7	733	3064	697	319	293	63	32	23	24	231	27	483	24	11	41	38	.519	8	0-1	2	3.60

Derek Aucoin

Pitches: Right **Bats:** Right **Pos:** RP-2 **Ht:** 6'7" **Wt:** 235 **Born:** 3/27/70 **Age:** 27

Year Team	Lg	G	GS	CG	GF	IP	BFP	H	R	ER	HR	SH	SF	HB	TBB	IBB	SO	WP	Bk	W	L	Pct.	ShO	Sv-Op	Hld	ERA
1989 Expos	R	7	3	0	1	23.2	106	24	10	7	2	1	0	0	12	0	27	3	1	2	1	.667	0	1--	—	2.66
1990 Jamestown	A-	8	8	1	0	36.1	152	28	20	18	3	1	1	1	18	0	27	6	0	1	3	.250	0	0--	—	4.46
1991 Sumter	A	41	4	0	8	90.1	408	85	55	43	5	4	2	10	44	3	70	6	1	3	6	.333	0	1--	—	4.28
1992 Rockford	A	39	2	0	17	69	289	48	32	23	2	1	2	4	34	2	65	6	3	3	2	.600	0	3--	—	3.00
1993 W. Palm Bch	A+	38	6	0	6	87.1	387	89	48	41	5	6	2	0	44	3	62	8	2	4	4	.500	0	1--	—	4.23
1994 W. Palm Bch	A+	7	0	0	5	7.1	26	3	0	0	0	0	0	0	2	0	10	0	0	0	0	.000	0	2--	—	0.00
Harrisburg	AA	31	0	0	12	47	208	36	19	17	4	1	0	2	29	0	48	3	0	3	4	.429	0	4--	—	3.26
1995 Harrisburg	AA	52	0	0	10	52.2	242	52	34	29	3	0	5	8	28	2	48	2	0	2	4	.333	0	1--	—	4.96
1996 Ottawa	AAA	52	0	0	24	75	351	74	37	33	6	2	2	7	53	4	69	11	1	3	5	.375	0	3--	—	3.96
1996 Montreal	NL	2	0	0	0	2.2	12	3	1	1	0	1	0	0	1	0	1	0	0	0	1	.000	0	0-0	0	3.38

Rich Aude

Bats: Right **Throws:** Right **Pos:** 1B-4; PH-3 **Ht:** 6'5" **Wt:** 215 **Born:** 7/13/71 **Age:** 25

Year Team	Lg	G	AB	H	2B	3B	HR	(Hm	Rd)	TB	R	RBI	TBB	IBB	SO	HBP	SH	SF	SB	CS	SB%	GDP	Avg	OBP	SLG
1996 Calgary *	AAA	103	394	115	29	0	17	—	—	195	69	81	26	2	69	4	0	5	4	4	.50	10	.292	.338	.495
1993 Pittsburgh	NL	13	26	3	1	0	0	(0	0)	4	1	4	1	0	7	0	0	0	0	2	.00	0	.115	.148	.154
1995 Pittsburgh	NL	42	109	27	8	0	2	(1	1)	41	10	19	6	0	20	0	0	0	1	2	.33	4	.248	.287	.376
1996 Pittsburgh	NL	7	16	4	0	0	0	(0	0)	4	0	1	0	0	8	0	0	0	0	0	.00	0	.250	.250	.250
3 ML YEARS		62	151	34	9	0	2	(1	1)	49	11	24	7	0	35	0	0	0	1	2	.33	4	.225	.259	.325

Rich Aurilia

Bats: Right **Throws:** Right **Pos:** SS-93; 2B-11; PH-6   **Ht:** 6'1" **Wt:** 170 **Born:** 9/2/71 **Age:** 25

								BATTING											BASERUNNING				PERCENTAGES		
Year Team	Lg	G	AB	H	2B	3B	HR	(Hm Rd)	TB	R	RBI	TBB	IBB	SO	HBP	SH	SF	SB	CS	SB%	GDP	Avg	OBP	SLG
1992 Butte	R+	59	202	68	11	3	3	— —	94	37	30	42	0	18	0	5	2	13	9	.59	2	.337	.447	.465
1993 Charlotte	A+	122	440	136	16	5	5	— —	177	80	56	75	4	57	3	9	7	15	18	.45	9	.309	.408	.402
1994 Tulsa	AA	129	458	107	18	6	12	— —	173	67	57	53	0	74	4	8	5	10	13	.43	8	.234	.315	.378
1995 Shreveport	AA	64	226	74	17	1	4	— —	105	29	42	27	3	26	1	5	2	10	3	.77	6	.327	.398	.465
Phoenix	AAA	71	258	72	12	0	5	— —	99	42	34	35	2	29	0	0	3	2	2	.50	4	.279	.361	.384
1996 Phoenix	AAA	7	30	13	1	0	0	— —	20	9	4	2	0	3	0	0	0	1	1	.50	1	.433	.469	.667
1995 San Francisco	NL	9	19	9	3	0	2	(0 2)	18	4	4	1	0	2	0	1	1	1	0	1.00	1	.474	.476	.947
1996 San Francisco	NL	105	318	76	7	1	3	(1 2)	94	27	26	25	2	52	1	6	2	4	1	.80	1	.239	.295	.296
2 ML YEARS		114	337	85	10	1	5	(1 4)	112	31	30	26	2	54	1	7	3	5	1	.83	2	.252	.305	.332

Brad Ausmus

Bats: Right **Throws:** Right **Pos:** C-119; PH-12   **Ht:** 5'11" **Wt:** 190 **Born:** 4/14/69 **Age:** 28

								BATTING											BASERUNNING				PERCENTAGES		
Year Team	Lg	G	AB	H	2B	3B	HR	(Hm Rd)	TB	R	RBI	TBB	IBB	SO	HBP	SH	SF	SB	CS	SB%	GDP	Avg	OBP	SLG
1993 San Diego	NL	49	160	41	8	1	5	(4 1)	66	18	12	6	0	28	0	0	0	2	0	1.00	2	.256	.283	.413
1994 San Diego	NL	101	327	82	12	1	7	(6 1)	117	45	24	30	12	63	1	6	2	5	1	.83	8	.251	.314	.358
1995 San Diego	NL	103	328	96	16	4	5	(2 3)	135	44	34	31	3	56	2	4	4	16	5	.76	6	.293	.353	.412
1996 SD-Det		125	375	83	16	0	5	(2 3)	114	46	35	39	1	72	5	6	2	4	8	.33	8	.221	.302	.304
1996 San Diego	NL	50	149	27	4	0	1	(0 1)	34	16	13	13	0	27	3	1	0	1	4	.20	4	.181	.261	.228
Detroit	AL	75	226	56	12	0	4	(2 2)	80	30	22	26	1	45	2	5	2	3	4	.43	4	.248	.328	.354
4 ML YEARS		378	1190	302	52	6	22	(14 8)	432	153	105	106	16	219	8	16	8	27	14	.66	24	.254	.317	.363

Steve Avery

Pitches: Left **Bats:** Left **Pos:** SP-23; RP-1   **Ht:** 6'4" **Wt:** 205 **Born:** 4/14/70 **Age:** 27

				HOW MUCH HE PITCHED				WHAT HE GAVE UP										THE RESULTS					
Year Team	Lg	G	GS	CG	GF	IP	BFP	H	R	ER	HR	SH	SF	HB	TBB	IBB	SO	WP	Bk	W	L	Pct.	ShO	Sv-Op	Hld	ERA
1996 Greenville *	AA	1	1	0	0	0.2	2	0	0	0	0	0	0	0	0	0	0	0	0	0	0	.000	0	0--	—	0.00
1990 Atlanta	NL	21	20	1	1	99	466	121	79	62	7	14	4	2	45	2	75	5	1	3	11	.214	1	0-0	0	5.64
1991 Atlanta	NL	35	35	3	0	210.1	868	189	89	79	21	8	4	3	65	0	137	4	1	18	8	.692	1	0-0	0	3.38
1992 Atlanta	NL	35	35	2	0	233.2	969	216	95	83	14	12	8	0	71	3	129	7	3	11	11	.500	2	0-0	0	3.20
1993 Atlanta	NL	35	35	3	0	223.1	891	216	81	73	14	8	8	0	43	5	125	3	1	18	6	.750	1	0-0	0	2.94
1994 Atlanta	NL	24	24	1	0	151.2	628	127	71	68	15	4	6	4	55	4	122	5	2	8	3	.727	0	0-0	0	4.04
1995 Atlanta	NL	29	29	3	0	173.1	724	165	92	90	22	6	4	6	52	4	141	3	0	7	13	.350	1	0-0	0	4.67
1996 Atlanta	NL	24	23	1	0	131	567	146	70	65	10	7	3	4	40	8	86	5	0	7	10	.412	0	0-0	0	4.47
7 ML YEARS		203	201	14	1	1222.1	5113	1180	577	520	103	63	37	19	371	26	815	32	8	72	62	.537	6	0-0	0	3.83

Bobby Ayala

Pitches: Right **Bats:** Right **Pos:** RP-50   **Ht:** 6'3" **Wt:** 210 **Born:** 7/8/69 **Age:** 27

				HOW MUCH HE PITCHED				WHAT HE GAVE UP										THE RESULTS					
Year Team	Lg	G	GS	CG	GF	IP	BFP	H	R	ER	HR	SH	SF	HB	TBB	IBB	SO	WP	Bk	W	L	Pct.	ShO	Sv-Op	Hld	ERA
1996 Port City *	AA	2	1	0	0	1.2	8	0	0	0	0	0	0	0	1	0	2	0	0	0	0	.000	0	0--	—	0.00
Tacoma *	AAA	1	1	0	0	1	4	0	0	0	0	0	0	0	1	0	1	0	0	0	0	.000	0	0--	—	0.00
1992 Cincinnati	NL	5	5	0	0	29	127	33	15	14	1	2	0	1	13	2	23	0	0	2	1	.667	0	0-0	0	4.34
1993 Cincinnati	NL	43	9	0	8	98	450	106	72	61	16	9	2	7	45	4	65	5	0	7	10	.412	0	3-5	6	5.60
1994 Seattle	AL	46	0	0	40	56.2	236	42	25	18	2	1	2	0	26	0	76	2	0	4	3	.571	0	18-24	0	2.86
1995 Seattle	AL	63	0	0	50	71	320	73	42	35	9	2	3	6	30	4	77	3	0	6	5	.545	0	19-27	2	4.44
1996 Seattle	AL	50	0	0	26	67.1	285	65	45	44	10	2	2	2	25	3	61	2	0	6	3	.667	0	3-6	7	5.88
5 ML YEARS		207	14	0	124	322	1418	319	199	172	38	16	9	16	139	13	302	12	0	25	22	.532	0	43-62	15	4.81

Joe Ayrault

Bats: Right **Throws:** Right **Pos:** C-7   **Ht:** 6'3" **Wt:** 190 **Born:** 10/8/71 **Age:** 25

								BATTING											BASERUNNING				PERCENTAGES		
Year Team	Lg	G	AB	H	2B	3B	HR	(Hm Rd)	TB	R	RBI	TBB	IBB	SO	HBP	SH	SF	SB	CS	SB%	GDP	Avg	OBP	SLG
1990 Braves	R	30	87	24	2	2	0	— —	30	8	12	9	0	14	1	2	0	1	1	.50	1	.276	.351	.345
1991 Pulaski	R+	55	202	52	12	0	3	— —	73	22	27	13	0	49	0	2	0	0	0	.00	4	.257	.302	.361
1992 Macon	A	90	297	77	12	0	6	— —	107	24	24	24	0	68	4	2	1	1	1	.50	7	.259	.322	.360
1993 Durham	A+	119	390	99	21	0	6	— —	138	45	52	23	0	103	7	8	3	1	4	.20	8	.254	.305	.354
1994 Greenville	AA	107	350	80	24	0	6	— —	122	38	40	19	1	74	6	4	2	2	2	.50	6	.229	.279	.349
1995 Greenville	AA	89	302	74	20	0	7	— —	115	27	42	13	5	70	3	7	3	2	4	.33	8	.245	.280	.381
1996 Richmond	AAA	98	314	72	15	0	5	— —	102	23	34	26	4	57	3	2	4	1	1	.50	12	.229	.291	.325
1996 Atlanta	NL	7	5	1	0	0	0	(0 0)	1	0	0	0	0	1	1	0	0	0	0	.00	0	.200	.333	.200

Carlos Baerga

Bats: B **Throws:** R **Pos:** 2B-101; 1B-16; 3B-6; PH-6   **Ht:** 5'11"   **Wt:** 200   **Born:** 11/4/68   **Age:** 28

											BATTING							BASERUNNING				PERCENTAGES		
Year Team	Lg	G	AB	H	2B	3B	HR	(Hm | Rd)	TB	R	RBI	TBB	IBB	SO	HBP	SH	SF	SB	CS	SB%	GDP	Avg	OBP	SLG
1990 Cleveland	AL	108	312	81	17	2	7	(3 | 4)	123	46	47	16	2	57	4	1	5	0	2	.00	4	.260	.300	.394
1991 Cleveland	AL	158	593	171	28	2	11	(2 | 9)	236	80	69	48	5	74	6	4	3	3	2	.60	12	.288	.346	.398
1992 Cleveland	AL	161	657	205	32	1	20	(9 | 11)	299	92	105	35	10	76	13	2	9	10	2	.83	15	.312	.354	.455
1993 Cleveland	AL	154	624	200	28	6	21	(8 | 13)	303	105	114	34	7	68	6	3	13	15	4	.79	17	.321	.355	.486
1994 Cleveland	AL	103	442	139	32	2	19	(8 | 11)	232	81	80	10	1	45	6	3	8	8	2	.80	10	.314	.333	.525
1995 Cleveland	AL	135	557	175	28	2	15	(7 | 8)	252	87	90	35	6	31	3	0	5	11	2	.85	15	.314	.355	.452
1996 Cle-NYN		126	507	129	28	0	12	(5 | 7)	193	59	66	21	0	27	9	2	5	1	1	.50	23	.254	.293	.381
1996 Cleveland	AL	100	424	113	25	0	10	(5 | 5)	168	54	55	16	0	25	7	2	4	1	1	.50	15	.267	.302	.396
New York	NL	26	83	16	3	0	2	(0 | 2)	25	5	11	5	0	2	2	0	1	0	0	.00	8	.193	.253	.301
7 ML YEARS		945	3692	1100	193	15	105	(42 | 63)	1638	550	571	199	31	378	47	15	48	48	15	.76	96	.298	.338	.444

Jeff Bagwell

Bats: Right **Throws:** Right **Pos:** 1B-162   **Ht:** 6'0"   **Wt:** 195   **Born:** 5/27/68   **Age:** 29

											BATTING							BASERUNNING				PERCENTAGES		
Year Team	Lg	G	AB	H	2B	3B	HR	(Hm	Rd)	TB	R	RBI	TBB	IBB	SO	HBP	SH	SF	SB	CS	SB%	GDP	Avg	OBP	SLG
1991 Houston	NL	156	554	163	26	4	15	(6	9)	242	79	82	75	5	116	13	1	7	7	4	.64	12	.294	.387	.437
1992 Houston	NL	162	586	160	34	6	18	(8	10)	260	87	96	84	13	97	12	2	13	10	6	.63	17	.273	.368	.444
1993 Houston	NL	142	535	171	37	4	20	(9	11)	276	76	88	62	6	73	3	0	9	13	4	.76	20	.320	.388	.516
1994 Houston	NL	110	400	147	32	2	39	(23	16)	300	104	116	65	14	65	4	0	10	15	4	.79	12	.368	.451	.750
1995 Houston	NL	114	448	130	29	0	21	(10	11)	222	88	87	79	12	102	6	0	6	12	5	.71	9	.290	.399	.496
1996 Houston	NL	162	568	179	48	2	31	(16	15)	324	111	120	135	20	114	10	0	6	21	7	.75	15	.315	.451	.570
6 ML YEARS		846	3091	950	206	18	144	(72	72)	1624	545	589	500	70	567	48	3	51	78	30	.72	85	.307	.406	.525

Cory Bailey

Pitches: Right **Bats:** Right **Pos:** RP-51   **Ht:** 6'1"   **Wt:** 202   **Born:** 1/24/71   **Age:** 26

			HOW MUCH HE PITCHED					WHAT HE GAVE UP										THE RESULTS					
Year Team	Lg	G	GS	CG	GF	IP	BFP	H	R	ER	HR	SH	SF	HB	TBB	IBB	SO	WP	Bk	W	L	Pct.	ShO	Sv-Op	Hld	ERA
1991 Red Sox	R	1	0	0	1	2	9	2	1	0	0	0	0	0	1	0	1	0	0	0	0	.000	0	1- -	—	0.00
Elmira	A-	28	0	0	25	39	151	19	10	8	2	1	0	3	12	0	54	2	0	2	4	.333	0	15- -	—	1.85
1992 Lynchburg	A+	49	0	0	43	66.1	272	43	20	18	3	6	2	2	30	2	87	5	0	5	7	.417	0	23- -	—	2.44
1993 Pawtucket	AAA	52	0	0	40	65.2	264	48	21	21	1	2	2	1	31	3	59	5	1	4	5	.444	0	20- -	—	2.88
1994 Pawtucket	AAA	53	0	0	43	61.1	264	44	25	22	4	4	0	1	38	2	52	7	0	4	3	.571	0	19- -	—	3.23
1995 Louisville	AAA	55	0	0	40	59.1	258	51	30	30	6	6	2	0	30	4	49	7	0	5	3	.625	0	25- -	—	4.55
1996 Louisville	AAA	22	0	0	8	34	151	29	22	22	1	3	1	0	20	5	27	4	1	2	4	.333	0	1- -	—	5.82
1993 Boston	AL	11	0	0	5	15.2	66	12	7	6	0	1	1	0	12	3	11	2	1	0	1	.000	0	0-0	0	3.45
1994 Boston	AL	5	0	0	2	4.1	24	10	6	6	2	0	0	0	3	1	4	0	0	0	1	.000	0	0-1	0	12.46
1995 St. Louis	NL	3	0	0	0	3.2	15	2	3	3	0	0	0	0	2	1	5	1	0	0	0	.000	0	0-0	0	7.36
1996 St. Louis	NL	51	0	0	12	57	251	57	21	19	1	2	1	1	30	3	38	3	0	5	2	.714	0	0-1	10	3.00
4 ML YEARS		70	0	0	19	80.2	356	81	37	34	3	3	2	1	47	8	58	6	1	5	4	.556	0	0-2	10	3.79

Roger Bailey

Pitches: Right **Bats:** Right **Pos:** RP-13; SP-11   **Ht:** 6'1"   **Wt:** 180   **Born:** 10/3/70   **Age:** 26

			HOW MUCH HE PITCHED					WHAT HE GAVE UP										THE RESULTS					
Year Team	Lg	G	GS	CG	GF	IP	BFP	H	R	ER	HR	SH	SF	HB	TBB	IBB	SO	WP	Bk	W	L	Pct.	ShO	Sv-Op	Hld	ERA
1992 Bend	A-	11	11	1	0	65.1	271	48	19	16	4	2	2	2	30	0	81	2	1	5	2	.714	0	0- -	—	2.20
1993 Central Val	A+	22	22	1	0	111.2	515	139	78	60	9	1	3	6	56	1	84	7	1	4	7	.364	1	0- -	—	4.84
1994 New Haven	AA	25	24	1	1	159	675	157	70	57	8	5	7	5	56	1	112	6	0	9	9	.500	1	0- -	—	3.23
1995 Colo. Sprng	AAA	3	3	0	0	16.2	71	15	9	5	0	0	3	2	8	0	7	0	0	0	0	.000	0	0- -	—	2.70
1996 Colo. Sprng	AAA	9	9	0	0	48.2	214	60	34	34	5	0	3	2	20	0	27	2	0	4	4	.500	0	0- -	—	6.29
1995 Colorado	NL	39	6	0	9	81.1	360	88	49	45	9	7	2	1	39	3	33	7	1	7	6	.538	0	0-0	5	4.98
1996 Colorado	NL	24	11	0	4	83.2	385	94	64	58	7	2	4	1	52	0	45	3	0	2	3	.400	0	1-1	0	6.24
2 ML YEARS		63	17	0	13	165	745	182	113	103	16	9	6	2	91	3	78	10	1	9	9	.500	0	1-1	5	5.62

Harold Baines

Bats: Left **Throws:** Left **Pos:** DH-141; PH-2   **Ht:** 6'2"   **Wt:** 195   **Born:** 3/15/59   **Age:** 38

											BATTING							BASERUNNING				PERCENTAGES		
Year Team	Lg	G	AB	H	2B	3B	HR	(Hm	Rd)	TB	R	RBI	TBB	IBB	SO	HBP	SH	SF	SB	CS	SB%	GDP	Avg	OBP	SLG
1980 Chicago	AL	141	491	125	23	6	13	(3	10)	199	55	49	19	7	65	1	2	5	2	4	.33	15	.255	.281	.405
1981 Chicago	AL	82	280	80	11	7	10	(3	7)	135	42	41	12	4	41	2	0	2	6	2	.75	6	.286	.318	.482
1982 Chicago	AL	161	608	165	29	8	25	(11	14)	285	89	105	49	10	95	0	2	9	10	3	.77	12	.271	.321	.469
1983 Chicago	AL	156	596	167	33	2	20	(12	8)	264	76	99	49	13	85	1	3	6	7	5	.58	15	.280	.333	.443
1984 Chicago	AL	147	569	173	28	10	29	(16	13)	308	72	94	54	9	75	0	1	5	1	2	.33	12	.304	.361	.541
1985 Chicago	AL	160	640	198	29	3	22	(13	9)	299	86	113	42	8	89	1	0	10	1	1	.50	23	.309	.348	.467
1986 Chicago	AL	145	570	169	29	2	21	(8	13)	265	72	88	38	9	89	2	0	8	2	1	.67	14	.296	.338	.465
1987 Chicago	AL	132	505	148	26	4	20	(12	8)	242	59	93	46	2	82	1	0	12	0	0	.00	12	.293	.352	.479
1988 Chicago	AL	158	599	166	39	1	13	(5	8)	246	55	81	67	14	109	1	0	7	0	0	.00	21	.277	.347	.411
1989 ChA-Tex	AL	146	505	156	29	1	16	(5	11)	235	73	72	73	13	79	1	0	4	0	3	.00	15	.309	.395	.465

			BATTING																		BASERUNNING				PERCENTAGES		
Year Team	Lg	G	AB	H	2B	3B	HR	(Hm	Rd)	TB	R	RBI	TBB	IBB	SO	HBP	SH	SF	SB	CS	SB%	GDP	Avg	OBP	SLG
1990 Tex-Oak	AL	135	415	118	15	1	16	(9	7)	183	52	65	67	10	80	0	0	7	0	3	.00	17	.284	.378	.441
1991 Oakland	AL	141	488	144	25	1	20	(11	9)	231	76	90	72	22	67	1	0	5	0	1	.00	12	.295	.383	.473
1992 Oakland	AL	140	478	121	18	0	16	(10	6)	187	58	76	59	6	61	0	0	6	1	3	.25	11	.253	.331	.391
1993 Baltimore	AL	118	416	130	22	0	20	(12	8)	212	64	78	57	9	52	0	1	6	0	0	.00	14	.313	.390	.510
1994 Baltimore	AL	94	326	96	12	1	16	(11	5)	158	44	54	30	6	49	1	0	0	0	0	.00	9	.294	.356	.485
1995 Baltimore	AL	127	385	115	19	1	24	(7	17)	208	60	63	70	13	45	0	0	4	0	2	.00	17	.299	.403	.540
1996 Chicago	AL	143	495	154	29	0	22	(9	13)	249	80	95	73	7	62	1	0	3	3	1	.75	20	.311	.399	.503
1989 Chicago	AL	96	333	107	20	1	13	(4	9)	168	55	56	60	13	52	1	0	3	0	1	.00	11	.321	.423	.505
Texas		50	172	49	9	0	3	(1	2)	67	18	16	13	0	27	0	0	1	0	2	.00	4	.285	.333	.390
1990 Texas	AL	103	321	93	10	1	13	(6	7)	144	41	44	47	9	63	0	0	3	0	1	.00	13	.290	.377	.449
Oakland		32	94	25	5	0	3	(3	0)	39	11	21	20	1	17	0	0	4	0	2	.00	4	.266	.381	.415
17 ML YEARS		2326	8366	2425	416	48	323	(157	166)	3906	1113	1356	877	162	1225	13	9	89	33	31	.52	245	.290	.355	.467

James Baldwin

Pitches: Right **Bats:** Right **Pos:** SP-28 **Ht:** 6'3" **Wt:** 210 **Born:** 7/15/71 **Age:** 25

		HOW MUCH HE PITCHED						WHAT HE GAVE UP												THE RESULTS						
Year Team	Lg	G	GS	CG	GF	IP	BFP	H	R	ER	HR	SH	SF	HB	TBB	IBB	SO	WP	Bk	W	L	Pct.	ShO	Sv-Op	Hld	ERA
1990 White Sox	R	9	7	0	1	37.1	164	32	29	17	1	1	2	0	18	0	32	6	3	1	6	.143	0	0--	—	4.10
1991 White Sox	R	6	6	0	0	34	132	16	8	8	0	0	1	1	16	0	48	3	1	3	1	.750	0	0--	—	2.12
Utica	A-	7	7	1	0	37.1	180	40	26	22	0	0	1	2	27	0	23	4	2	1	4	.200	0	0--	—	5.30
1992 South Bend	A	21	21	1	0	137.2	570	118	53	37	6	2	2	3	45	0	137	8	2	9	5	.643	1	0--	—	2.42
Sarasota	A+	6	6	1	0	37.2	149	31	13	12	2	3	0	1	7	0	39	1	0	1	2	.333	0	0--	—	2.87
1993 Birmingham	AA	17	17	4	0	120	491	94	48	30	6	9	3	6	43	0	107	7	2	8	5	.615	0	0--	—	2.25
Nashville	AAA	10	10	1	0	69	279	43	21	20	5	2	2	0	36	0	61	3	1	5	4	.556	0	0--	—	2.61
1994 Nashville	AAA	26	26	2	0	162	696	144	75	67	14	2	2	1	83	1	156	9	4	12	6	.667	0	0--	—	3.72
1995 Nashville	AAA	18	18	0	0	95.1	448	120	76	62	27	1	3	2	44	1	89	10	3	5	9	.357	0	0--	—	5.85
1996 Nashville	AAA	2	2	1	0	14	48	5	1	1	0	1	0	0	4	0	15	1	0	1	1	.500	0	0--	—	0.64
1995 Chicago	AL	6	4	0	0	14.2	81	32	22	21	6	0	0	0	9	1	10	1	0	0	1	.000	0	0-0	0	12.89
1996 Chicago	AL	28	28	0	0	169	719	168	88	83	24	2	2	4	57	3	127	12	1	11	6	.647	0	0-0	0	4.42
2 ML YEARS		34	32	0	0	183.2	800	200	110	104	30	2	2	4	66	4	137	13	1	11	7	.611	0	0-0	0	5.10

Brian Banks

Bats: Both **Throws:** Right **Pos:** LF-3; 1B-1; PH-1 **Ht:** 6'3" **Wt:** 200 **Born:** 9/28/70 **Age:** 26

			BATTING																		BASERUNNING				PERCENTAGES		
Year Team	Lg	G	AB	H	2B	3B	HR	(Hm	Rd)	TB	R	RBI	TBB	IBB	SO	HBP	SH	SF	SB	CS	SB%	GDP	Avg	OBP	SLG
1993 Helena	R+	12	48	19	1	1	2	—	—	28	8	8	11	0	8	0	0	1	1	2	.33	2	.396	.500	.583
Beloit	A	38	147	36	5	1	4	—	—	55	21	19	7	0	34	1	0	0	1	2	.33	1	.245	.284	.374
1994 Stockton	A+	67	246	58	1	1	4	—	—	81	29	28	38	2	46	2	3	2	3	8	.27	8	.236	.340	.329
Beloit	A	65	237	71	13	1	9	—	—	113	41	47	29	5	40	2	1	4	11	1	.92	3	.300	.375	.477
1995 El Paso	AA	127	441	136	39	10	12	—	—	231	81	78	81	6	113	3	3	8	9	9	.50	10	.308	.413	.524
1996 New Orleans	AAA	137	487	132	29	7	16	—	—	223	71	64	66	3	105	2	2	7	17	8	.68	6	.271	.356	.458
1996 Milwaukee	AL	4	7	4	2	0	1	(0	1)	9	2	2	1	0	2	0	0	0	0	0	.00	0	.571	.625	1.286

Brian Barber

Pitches: Right **Bats:** Right **Pos:** SP-1 **Ht:** 6'1" **Wt:** 175 **Born:** 3/4/73 **Age:** 24

		HOW MUCH HE PITCHED						WHAT HE GAVE UP												THE RESULTS						
Year Team	Lg	G	GS	CG	GF	IP	BFP	H	R	ER	HR	SH	SF	HB	TBB	IBB	SO	WP	Bk	W	L	Pct.	ShO	Sv-Op	Hld	ERA
1991 Johnson Cty	R+	14	13	0	0	73.1	325	62	48	44	5	1	1	5	38	0	84	4	6	4	6	.400	0	0--	—	5.40
1992 Springfield	A	8	8	0	0	50.2	215	39	21	21	7	2	0	1	24	0	56	2	1	3	4	.429	0	0--	—	3.73
St. Pete	A+	19	19	1	0	113.1	473	99	51	41	7	1	2	5	46	0	102	4	1	5	5	.500	0	0--	—	3.26
1993 Arkansas	AA	24	24	1	0	143.1	625	154	70	64	19	7	4	4	56	2	126	10	2	9	8	.529	0	0--	—	4.02
Louisville	AAA	1	1	0	0	5.2	25	4	3	3	0	1	0	0	4	0	5	0	1	0	1	.000	0	0--	—	4.76
1994 Arkansas	AA	6	6	0	0	36	152	31	15	13	4	1	0	0	16	2	54	2	0	1	3	.250	0	0--	—	3.25
Louisville	AAA	19	18	0	1	85.1	376	79	58	51	7	4	3	5	46	1	95	7	0	4	7	.364	0	1--	—	5.38
1995 Louisville	AAA	20	19	0	0	107.1	465	105	67	56	14	2	6	4	40	1	94	1	0	6	5	.545	0	0--	—	4.70
1996 Louisville	AAA	11	11	1	0	49.2	222	49	37	31	12	0	1	3	26	1	33	2	0	0	6	.000	0	0--	—	5.62
1995 St. Louis	NL	9	4	0	2	29.1	130	31	17	17	4	0	3	0	16	0	27	3	0	2	1	.667	0	0-0	0	5.22
1996 St. Louis	NL	1	1	0	0	3	20	4	5	5	0	0	2	1	6	0	1	0	0	0	0	.000	0	0-0	0	15.00
2 ML YEARS		10	5	0	2	32.1	150	35	22	22	4	0	5	1	22	0	28	3	0	2	1	.667	0	0-0	0	6.12

Bret Barberie

Bats: Both **Throws:** Right **Pos:** PH-9; 2B-6; 3B-2; SS-1 **Ht:** 5'11" **Wt:** 180 **Born:** 8/16/67 **Age:** 29

			BATTING																		BASERUNNING				PERCENTAGES		
Year Team	Lg	G	AB	H	2B	3B	HR	(Hm	Rd)	TB	R	RBI	TBB	IBB	SO	HBP	SH	SF	SB	CS	SB%	GDP	Avg	OBP	SLG
1996 Iowa *	AAA	68	210	49	8	0	5	—	—	72	26	24	31	1	23	3	0	2	3	2	.60	5	.233	.337	.343
1991 Montreal	NL	57	136	48	12	2	2	(2	0)	70	16	18	20	2	22	2	1	3	0	0	.00	4	.353	.435	.515
1992 Montreal	NL	111	285	66	11	0	1	(0	1)	80	26	24	47	3	62	8	1	2	9	5	.64	4	.232	.354	.281
1993 Florida	NL	99	375	104	16	2	5	(2	3)	139	45	33	33	2	58	7	5	3	2	4	.33	7	.277	.344	.371
1994 Florida	NL	107	372	112	20	2	5	(2	3)	151	40	31	23	3	65	9	2	0	2	1	1.00	4	.301	.356	.406
1995 Baltimore	AL	90	237	57	14	0	3	(1	1)	77	32	25	36	0	50	6	6	3	3	3	.50	6	.241	.351	.325

Year Team	Lg	G	AB	H	2B	3B	HR	(Hm	Rd)	TB	R	RBI	TBB	IBB	SO	HBP	SH	SF	SB	CS	SB%	GDP	Avg	OBP	SLG
1996 Chicago	NL	15	29	1	0	0	1	(1	0)	4	4	2	5	0	11	0	3	0	0	1	.00	0	.034	.176	.138
6 ML YEARS		479	1434	388	73	6	16	(8	8)	521	163	133	164	10	268	32	18	11	16	13	.55	25	.271	.356	.363

Tony Barron

Bats: Right **Throws:** Right **Pos:** PH-1   **Ht:** 6'0" **Wt:** 185 **Born:** 8/17/66   **Age:** 30

Year Team	Lg	G	AB	H	2B	3B	HR	(Hm	Rd)	TB	R	RBI	TBB	IBB	SO	HBP	SH	SF	SB	CS	SB%	GDP	Avg	OBP	SLG
1987 Great Falls	R+	53	171	51	13	2	3	—	—	77	33	30	13	2	49	5	1	3	5	3	.63	1	.298	.359	.450
1988 Bakersfield	A+	12	20	5	2	0	0	—	—	7	1	4	1	1	5	0	0	0	0	0	.00	1	.250	.286	.350
Salem	A-	73	261	79	6	3	9	—	—	118	54	38	25	1	75	10	6	0	36	7	.84	2	.303	.385	.452
1989 Vero Beach	A+	105	324	79	7	5	4	—	—	108	45	40	17	1	90	4	2	3	26	12	.68	9	.244	.287	.333
1990 Vero Beach	A+	111	344	102	21	3	6	—	—	147	58	60	30	1	82	7	2	5	42	7	.86	9	.297	.360	.427
1991 San Antonio	AA	73	200	47	2	2	9	—	—	80	35	31	28	2	44	3	0	1	8	3	.73	11	.235	.336	.400
1992 San Antonio	AA	28	97	39	4	1	7	—	—	66	18	22	6	1	22	2	0	1	7	3	.70	3	.402	.443	.680
Albuquerque	AAA	78	286	86	18	2	6	—	—	126	40	33	17	1	65	2	2	0	6	4	.60	15	.301	.344	.441
1993 Albuquerque	AAA	107	259	75	22	1	8	—	—	123	42	36	27	1	59	2	2	2	6	5	.55	7	.290	.359	.475
1994 Jacksonville	AA	108	402	119	19	3	18	—	—	198	60	55	26	1	85	4	1	3	18	5	.78	19	.296	.343	.493
Calgary	AAA	2	8	2	0	0	2	—	—	8	2	2	0	0	0	0	0	0	0	0	.00	1	.250	.250	1.000
1995 Tacoma	AAA	9	25	5	0	0	0	—	—	5	4	2	2	0	3	1	0	0	0	0	.00	0	.200	.286	.200
Harrisburg	AA	29	103	30	5	0	10	—	—	65	20	23	10	0	21	2	0	0	0	0	.00	8	.291	.365	.631
Ottawa	AAA	50	147	36	10	0	10	—	—	76	20	22	14	1	22	2	0	1	0	2	.00	3	.245	.317	.517
1996 Harrisburg	AA	18	67	19	3	1	5	—	—	39	12	12	6	1	19	0	0	0	1	0	1.00	1	.284	.342	.582
Ottawa	AAA	105	394	126	29	2	14	—	—	201	58	59	20	1	74	9	3	1	9	4	.69	12	.320	.366	.510
1996 Montreal	NL	1	1	0	0	0	0	(0	0)	0	0	0	0	0	1	0	0	0	0	0	.00	0	.000	.000	.000

Kimera Bartee

Bats: R **Throws:** R **Pos:** CF-95; PH-22; LF-4; DH-2; RF-2   **Ht:** 6'0" **Wt:** 175 **Born:** 7/21/72   **Age:** 24

Year Team	Lg	G	AB	H	2B	3B	HR	(Hm	Rd)	TB	R	RBI	TBB	IBB	SO	HBP	SH	SF	SB	CS	SB%	GDP	Avg	OBP	SLG
1993 Bluefield	R+	66	264	65	15	2	4	—	—	96	59	37	44	0	66	3	3	2	27	6	.82	0	.246	.358	.364
1994 Frederick	A+	130	514	150	22	4	10	—	—	210	97	57	56	1	117	7	14	4	44	9	.83	7	.292	.367	.409
1995 Orioles	R	5	21	5	0	0	1	—	—	8	5	3	3	0	2	0	0	0	1	1	.50	0	.238	.333	.381
Bowie	AA	53	218	62	9	1	3	—	—	82	45	19	23	1	45	1	3	2	22	7	.76	1	.284	.352	.376
Rochester	AAA	15	52	8	2	1	0	—	—	12	5	3	0	0	16	0	2	1	0	0	.00	0	.154	.151	.231
1996 Detroit	AL	110	217	55	6	1	1	(0	1)	66	32	14	17	0	77	0	13	0	20	10	.67	1	.253	.308	.304

Shawn Barton

Pitches: Left **Bats:** Right **Pos:** RP-7   **Ht:** 6'1" **Wt:** 195 **Born:** 5/14/63   **Age:** 34

Year Team	Lg	G	GS	CG	GF	IP	BFP	H	R	ER	HR	SH	SF	HB	TBB	IBB	SO	WP	Bk	W	L	Pct.	ShO	Sv-Op	Hld	ERA
1996 Phoenix *	AAA	44	0	0	15	49.1	213	52	27	26	1	4	0	1	19	4	27	1	0	4	4	.500	0	2- —	—	4.74
1992 Seattle	AL	14	0	0	2	12.1	50	10	5	4	1	0	0	0	7	2	4	2	0	0	1	.000	0	0-1	0	2.92
1995 San Francisco	NL	52	0	0	11	44.1	181	37	22	21	3	1	3	2	19	1	22	0	1	4	1	.800	0	1-4	10	4.26
1996 San Francisco	NL	7	0	0	2	8.1	45	19	12	9	2	1	0	0	1	0	3	1	1	0	0	.000	0	0-0	0	9.72
3 ML YEARS		73	0	0	15	65	276	66	39	34	6	3	3	2	27	3	29	3	2	4	2	.667	0	1-5	10	4.71

Richard Batchelor

Pitches: Right **Bats:** Right **Pos:** RP-11   **Ht:** 6'1" **Wt:** 195 **Born:** 4/8/67   **Age:** 30

Year Team	Lg	G	GS	CG	GF	IP	BFP	H	R	ER	HR	SH	SF	HB	TBB	IBB	SO	WP	Bk	W	L	Pct.	ShO	Sv-Op	Hld	ERA
1996 Louisville *	AAA	51	0	0	44	54.2	246	59	29	25	4	2	2	2	19	5	57	5	0	5	2	.714	0	28- —	—	4.12
1993 St. Louis	NL	9	0	0	2	10	45	14	12	9	1	1	2	0	3	1	4	0	0	0	0	.000	0	0-0	1	8.10
1996 St. Louis	NL	11	0	0	7	15	54	9	2	2	1	0	0	0	1	0	11	0	0	2	0	1.000	0	0-0	0	1.20
2 ML YEARS		20	0	0	9	25	99	23	14	11	2	1	2	0	4	1	15	0	0	2	0	1.000	0	0-0	1	3.96

Jason Bates

Bats: B **Throws:** R **Pos:** PH-38; 2B-37; SS-18; 3B-12   **Ht:** 5'11" **Wt:** 185 **Born:** 1/5/71   **Age:** 26

Year Team	Lg	G	AB	H	2B	3B	HR	(Hm	Rd)	TB	R	RBI	TBB	IBB	SO	HBP	SH	SF	SB	CS	SB%	GDP	Avg	OBP	SLG
1992 Bend	A-	70	255	73	10	3	6	—	—	107	57	31	56	1	55	5	2	4	18	4	.82	5	.286	.419	.420
1993 Colo. Sprng	AAA	122	449	120	21	2	13	—	—	184	76	62	45	4	99	10	3	3	9	8	.53	8	.267	.345	.410
1994 Colo. Sprng	AAA	125	458	131	19	5	10	—	—	190	68	76	60	4	57	4	2	5	4	6	.40	11	.286	.370	.415
1995 Colorado	NL	116	322	86	17	4	8	(4	4)	135	42	46	42	3	70	2	2	0	3	6	.33	4	.267	.355	.419
1996 Colorado	NL	88	160	33	8	1	1	(1	0)	46	19	9	23	1	34	2	1	1	2	1	.67	7	.206	.312	.288
2 ML YEARS		204	482	119	25	5	9	(5	4)	181	61	55	65	4	104	4	3	1	5	7	.42	11	.247	.341	.376

14

Miguel Batista

Pitches: Right **Bats:** Right **Pos:** RP-9   **Ht:** 6'0" **Wt:** 160 **Born:** 2/19/71 **Age:** 26

Year Team	Lg	G	GS	CG	GF	IP	BFP	H	R	ER	HR	SH	SF	HB	TBB	IBB	SO	WP	Bk	W	L	Pct.	ShO	Sv-Op	Hld	ERA
1996 Charlotte *	AAA	47	2	0	14	77	360	93	57	46	4	4	4	6	39	0	56	16	1	4	3	.571	0	4--	—	5.38
1992 Pittsburgh	NL	1	0	0	1	2	13	4	2	2	1	0	0	0	3	0	1	0	0	0	0	.000	0	0-0	0	9.00
1996 Florida	NL	9	0	0	4	11.1	49	9	8	7	0	3	0	0	7	2	6	1	0	0	0	.000	0	0-0	0	5.56
2 ML YEARS		10	0	0	5	13.1	62	13	10	9	1	3	0	0	10	2	7	1	0	0	0	.000	0	0-0	0	6.08

Tony Batista

Bats: R **Throws:** R **Pos:** 2B-52; 3B-18; PH-12; DH-4; SS-4   **Ht:** 6'0" **Wt:** 165 **Born:** 12/9/73 **Age:** 23

Year Team	Lg	G	AB	H	2B	3B	HR	(Hm	Rd)	TB	R	RBI	TBB	IBB	SO	HBP	SH	SF	SB	CS	SB%	GDP	Avg	OBP	SLG
1992 Athletics	R	45	167	41	6	2	0	—	—	51	32	22	15	0	29	2	5	0	1	0	1.00	4	.246	.315	.305
1993 Athletics	R	24	104	34	6	2	2	—	—	50	21	17	6	1	14	0	0	2	6	2	.75	1	.327	.357	.481
Tacoma	AAA	4	12	2	1	0	0	—	—	3	1	1	1	0	4	0	0	0	0	0	.00	0	.167	.286	.250
1994 Modesto	A+	119	466	131	26	3	17	—	—	214	91	68	54	1	108	4	5	2	7	7	.50	10	.281	.359	.459
1995 Huntsville	AA	120	419	107	23	1	16	—	—	180	55	61	29	0	98	2	6	3	7	8	.47	8	.255	.305	.430
1996 Edmonton	AAA	57	205	66	17	4	8	—	—	115	33	40	15	0	30	2	1	1	2	1	.67	8	.322	.372	.561
1996 Oakland	AL	74	238	71	10	2	6	(1	5)	103	38	25	19	0	49	1	0	2	7	3	.70	2	.298	.350	.433

Kim Batiste

Bats: Right **Throws:** Right **Pos:** 3B-25; PH-25; SS-7   **Ht:** 5'9" **Wt:** 170 **Born:** 3/15/68 **Age:** 29

Year Team	Lg	G	AB	H	2B	3B	HR	(Hm	Rd)	TB	R	RBI	TBB	IBB	SO	HBP	SH	SF	SB	CS	SB%	GDP	Avg	OBP	SLG
1996 San Jose *	A+	2	6	1	0	0	0	—	—	1	0	0	0	0	2	0	0	0	0	0	.00	0	.167	.167	.167
Phoenix *	AAA	42	165	49	8	3	14	—	—	105	32	44	6	3	25	1	0	1	1	1	.50	7	.297	.324	.636
1991 Philadelphia	NL	10	27	6	0	0	0	(0	0)	6	2	1	1	1	8	0	0	0	1	0	.00	0	.222	.250	.222
1992 Philadelphia	NL	44	136	28	4	0	1	(0	1)	35	9	10	4	1	18	0	2	3	0	0	.00	7	.206	.224	.257
1993 Philadelphia	NL	79	156	44	7	1	5	(1	4)	68	14	29	3	2	29	1	0	1	0	1	.00	3	.282	.298	.436
1994 Philadelphia	NL	64	209	49	6	0	1	(1	0)	58	17	13	1	0	32	1	1	2	1	1	.50	11	.234	.239	.278
1996 San Francisco	NL	54	130	27	6	0	3	(1	2)	42	17	11	5	1	33	0	0	1	3	3	.50	4	.208	.235	.323
5 ML YEARS		251	658	154	23	1	10	(3	7)	209	59	64	14	5	120	2	3	7	4	6	.40	25	.234	.250	.318

Allen Battle

Bats: Right **Throws:** Right **Pos:** CF-27; LF-24; PH-8   **Ht:** 6'0" **Wt:** 170 **Born:** 11/29/68 **Age:** 28

Year Team	Lg	G	AB	H	2B	3B	HR	(Hm	Rd)	TB	R	RBI	TBB	IBB	SO	HBP	SH	SF	SB	CS	SB%	GDP	Avg	OBP	SLG
1991 Johnson Cty	R+	17	62	24	6	1	0	—	—	32	26	7	14	0	6	1	1	0	7	1	.88	2	.387	.506	.516
Savannah	A	48	169	42	7	1	0	—	—	51	27	20	27	0	34	1	0	2	12	3	.80	0	.249	.352	.302
1992 Springfield	A	67	235	71	10	4	4	—	—	101	49	24	41	0	34	10	1	2	22	12	.65	1	.302	.424	.430
St. Pete	A+	60	222	71	9	2	1	—	—	87	34	15	35	2	38	4	4	2	21	11	.66	2	.320	.418	.392
1993 Arkansas	AA	108	390	107	24	12	3	—	—	164	71	40	45	0	75	6	2	3	20	12	.63	4	.274	.356	.421
1994 Louisville	AAA	132	520	163	44	7	6	—	—	239	104	69	59	2	82	6	1	7	23	8	.74	14	.313	.385	.460
1995 Louisville	AAA	47	164	46	12	1	3	—	—	69	28	18	28	0	32	1	5	0	7	1	.88	3	.280	.389	.421
1996 Edmonton	AAA	62	224	68	12	4	3	—	—	97	53	33	37	0	37	3	6	2	9	3	.75	5	.304	.406	.433
1995 St. Louis	NL	61	118	32	5	0	0	(0	0)	37	13	2	15	0	26	1	3	0	3	3	.50	0	.271	.358	.314
1996 Oakland	AL	47	130	25	3	0	1	(0	1)	31	20	5	17	1	26	2	1	1	10	2	.83	3	.192	.293	.238
2 ML YEARS		108	248	57	8	0	1	(0	1)	68	33	7	32	1	52	3	4	1	13	5	.72	3	.230	.324	.274

Howard Battle

Bats: Right **Throws:** Right **Pos:** PH-4; 3B-1   **Ht:** 6'0" **Wt:** 197 **Born:** 3/25/72 **Age:** 25

Year Team	Lg	G	AB	H	2B	3B	HR	(Hm	Rd)	TB	R	RBI	TBB	IBB	SO	HBP	SH	SF	SB	CS	SB%	GDP	Avg	OBP	SLG
1990 Medicne Hat	R+	61	233	62	17	1	5	—	—	96	25	32	15	2	38	2	0	0	5	2	.71	2	.266	.316	.412
1991 Myrtle Bch	A	138	520	147	33	4	20	—	—	248	82	86	49	2	88	3	0	4	15	7	.68	1	.283	.345	.477
1992 Dunedin	A+	136	520	132	27	3	17	—	—	216	76	85	49	3	89	5	1	5	6	8	.43	5	.254	.321	.415
1993 Knoxville	AA	141	520	145	21	5	7	—	—	197	66	70	45	3	94	7	1	3	12	9	.57	8	.278	.342	.378
1994 Syracuse	AAA	139	517	143	26	8	14	—	—	227	72	75	40	4	82	3	1	7	26	2	.93	15	.277	.328	.439
1995 Syracuse	AAA	118	443	111	17	4	8	—	—	160	43	48	39	2	73	3	1	2	10	11	.48	7	.251	.314	.361
1996 Scranton-WB	AAA	115	391	89	24	1	8	—	—	139	37	44	21	0	53	2	2	6	3	8	.27	15	.228	.267	.355
1995 Toronto	AL	9	15	3	0	0	0	(0	0)	3	3	0	4	0	8	0	0	0	1	0	1.00	0	.200	.368	.200
1996 Philadelphia	NL	5	5	0	0	0	0	(0	0)	0	0	0	0	0	2	0	0	0	0	0	.00	0	.000	.000	.000
2 ML YEARS		14	20	3	0	0	0	(0	0)	3	3	0	4	0	10	0	0	0	1	0	1.00	0	.150	.292	.150

Danny Bautista

Bats: R **Throws:** R **Pos:** RF-22; LF-14; PH-10; CF-2; DH-1   **Ht:** 5'11" **Wt:** 170 **Born:** 5/24/72 **Age:** 25

Year Team	Lg	G	AB	H	2B	3B	HR	(Hm	Rd)	TB	R	RBI	TBB	IBB	SO	HBP	SH	SF	SB	CS	SB%	GDP	Avg	OBP	SLG
1993 Detroit	AL	17	61	19	3	0	1	(0	1)	25	6	9	1	0	10	0	0	1	3	1	.75	1	.311	.317	.410
1994 Detroit	AL	31	99	23	4	1	1	(1	3)	41	12	15	3	0	18	0	0	0	1	2	.33	3	.232	.255	.414
1995 Detroit	AL	89	271	55	9	0	7	(3	4)	85	28	27	12	0	68	0	6	0	4	1	.80	6	.203	.237	.314
1996 Det-Atl		42	84	19	2	0	2	(1	1)	27	13	9	11	0	20	1	0	0	1	2	.33	4	.226	.323	.321
1996 Detroit	AL	25	64	16	2	0	2	(1	1)	24	12	8	9	0	15	0	0	0	1	2	.33	1	.250	.342	.375
Atlanta	NL	17	20	3	0	0	0	(0	0)	3	1	1	2	0	5	1	0	0	0	0	.00	3	.150	.261	.150
4 ML YEARS		179	515	116	18	1	14	(5	9)	178	59	60	27	0	116	1	6	1	9	6	.60	14	.225	.265	.346

Jose Bautista

Pitches: Right **Bats:** Right **Pos:** RP-36; SP-1   **Ht:** 6'2" **Wt:** 205 **Born:** 7/26/64 **Age:** 32

Year Team	Lg	G	GS	CG	GF	IP	BFP	H	R	ER	HR	SH	SF	HB	TBB	IBB	SO	WP	Bk	W	L	Pct.	ShO	Sv-Op	Hld	ERA
1996 Phoenix *	AAA	6	6	0	0	39.1	159	41	19	19	1	0	1	4	5	0	18	0	0	2	2	.500	0	0--	—	4.35
1988 Baltimore	AL	33	25	3	5	171.2	721	171	86	82	21	2	3	7	45	3	76	4	5	6	15	.286	0	0-0	0	4.30
1989 Baltimore	AL	15	10	0	4	78	325	84	46	46	17	1	1	1	15	0	30	0	0	3	4	.429	0	0-0	0	5.31
1990 Baltimore	AL	22	0	0	9	26.2	112	28	15	12	4	1	1	0	7	3	15	2	0	1	0	1.000	0	0-0	5	4.05
1991 Baltimore	AL	5	0	0	3	5.1	34	13	10	10	1	0	0	1	5	0	3	1	0	0	1	.000	0	0-0	0	16.88
1993 Chicago	NL	58	7	1	14	111.2	459	105	38	35	11	4	3	5	27	3	63	4	1	10	3	.769	0	2-2	7	2.82
1994 Chicago	NL	58	0	0	24	69.1	293	75	30	30	10	5	4	3	17	7	45	2	1	4	5	.444	0	1-4	14	3.89
1995 San Francisco	NL	52	6	0	19	100.2	451	120	77	72	24	8	5	5	26	3	45	1	2	3	8	.273	0	0-0	5	6.44
1996 San Francisco	NL	37	1	0	12	69.2	289	66	32	26	10	4	3	2	15	5	28	0	0	3	4	.429	0	0-1	2	3.36
8 ML YEARS		280	49	4	90	633	2684	662	334	313	98	25	20	24	157	24	305	14	9	30	40	.429	0	3-7	33	4.45

Trey Beamon

Bats: Left **Throws:** Right **Pos:** RF-11; PH-10; LF-5   **Ht:** 6'3" **Wt:** 195 **Born:** 2/11/74 **Age:** 23

Year Team	Lg	G	AB	H	2B	3B	HR	(Hm	Rd)	TB	R	RBI	TBB	IBB	SO	HBP	SH	SF	SB	CS	SB%	GDP	Avg	OBP	SLG
1992 Pirates	R	13	39	12	1	0	1	—	—	16	9	6	4	1	0	0	0	0	0	1	.00	0	.308	.372	.410
Welland	A-	19	69	20	5	0	3	—	—	34	15	9	8	0	9	0	0	0	4	3	.57	6	.290	.364	.493
1993 Augusta	A	104	373	101	18	6	0	—	—	131	64	45	48	2	60	6	0	4	19	6	.76	12	.271	.360	.351
1994 Carolina	AA	112	434	140	18	9	5	—	—	191	69	47	33	4	53	5	4	3	24	9	.73	8	.323	.375	.440
1995 Calgary	AAA	118	452	151	29	5	5	—	—	205	74	62	39	4	55	2	2	3	18	8	.69	7	.334	.387	.454
1996 Calgary	AAA	111	378	109	15	3	5	—	—	145	62	52	55	6	63	6	3	5	16	3	.84	12	.288	.383	.384
1996 Pittsburgh	NL	24	51	11	2	0	0	(0	0)	13	7	6	4	0	6	0	1	0	1	1	.50	0	.216	.273	.255

Rod Beck

Pitches: Right **Bats:** Right **Pos:** RP-63   **Ht:** 6'1" **Wt:** 236 **Born:** 8/3/68 **Age:** 28

Year Team	Lg	G	GS	CG	GF	IP	BFP	H	R	ER	HR	SH	SF	HB	TBB	IBB	SO	WP	Bk	W	L	Pct.	ShO	Sv-Op	Hld	ERA
1991 San Francisco	NL	31	0	0	10	52.1	214	53	22	22	4	4	2	1	13	2	38	0	0	1	1	.500	0	1-1	1	3.78
1992 San Francisco	NL	65	0	0	42	92	352	62	20	18	4	6	2	2	15	2	87	5	2	3	3	.500	0	17-23	4	1.76
1993 San Francisco	NL	76	0	0	71	79.1	309	57	20	19	11	6	3	3	13	4	86	4	0	3	1	.750	0	48-52	0	2.16
1994 San Francisco	NL	48	0	0	47	48.2	207	49	17	15	10	3	3	0	13	2	39	0	0	2	4	.333	0	28-28	0	2.77
1995 San Francisco	NL	60	0	0	52	58.2	255	60	31	29	7	4	3	2	21	3	42	2	0	5	6	.455	0	33-43	0	4.45
1996 San Francisco	NL	63	0	0	58	62	248	56	23	23	9	0	1	1	10	2	48	1	0	0	9	.000	0	35-42	0	3.34
6 ML YEARS		343	0	0	280	393	1585	337	133	126	45	23	15	9	85	15	340	12	2	14	24	.368	0	162-189	5	2.89

Rich Becker

Bats: L **Throws:** L **Pos:** CF-121; LF-15; PH-12; RF-10   **Ht:** 5'10" **Wt:** 199 **Born:** 2/1/72 **Age:** 25

Year Team	Lg	G	AB	H	2B	3B	HR	(Hm	Rd)	TB	R	RBI	TBB	IBB	SO	HBP	SH	SF	SB	CS	SB%	GDP	Avg	OBP	SLG
1993 Minnesota	AL	3	7	2	2	0	0	(0	0)	4	3	0	5	0	4	0	0	0	1	1	.50	0	.286	.583	.571
1994 Minnesota	AL	28	98	26	3	0	1	(1	0)	32	12	8	13	0	25	0	1	0	6	1	.86	2	.265	.351	.327
1995 Minnesota	AL	106	392	93	15	1	2	(1	1)	116	45	33	34	0	95	4	6	2	8	9	.47	9	.237	.303	.296
1996 Minnesota	AL	148	525	153	31	4	12	(8	4)	228	92	71	68	1	118	2	5	4	19	5	.79	14	.291	.372	.434
4 ML YEARS		285	1022	274	51	5	15	(10	5)	380	152	112	120	1	242	6	12	6	34	16	.68	25	.268	.347	.372

Robbie Beckett

Pitches: Left **Bats:** Right **Pos:** RP-5   **Ht:** 6'5" **Wt:** 225 **Born:** 7/16/72 **Age:** 24

Year Team	Lg	G	GS	CG	GF	IP	BFP	H	R	ER	HR	SH	SF	HB	TBB	IBB	SO	WP	Bk	W	L	Pct.	ShO	Sv-Op	Hld	ERA
1990 Padres	R	10	10	0	0	49.1	236	40	28	24	1	3	1	2	45	0	54	8	3	2	5	.286	0	0--	—	4.38
Riverside	A+	3	3	0	0	16.2	76	18	13	13	0	1	0	0	11	0	11	1	1	2	1	.667	0	0--	—	7.02
1991 Charlstn-SC	A	28	26	1	0	109.1	545	115	111	100	5	1	8	3	117	0	96	20	2	2	14	.125	0	0--	—	8.23

| | | HOW MUCH HE PITCHED | | | | | | WHAT HE GAVE UP | | | | | | | | | | | | THE RESULTS | | | | | | |
Year Team	Lg	G	GS	CG	GF	IP	BFP	H	R	ER	HR	SH	SF	HB	TBB	IBB	SO	WP	Bk	W	L	Pct.	ShO	Sv-Op	Hld	ERA
1992 Waterloo	A	24	24	1	0	120.2	578	77	88	64	4	1	1	6	140	0	147	20	4	4	10	.286	1	0--	—	4.77
1993 Rancho Cuca	A+	37	10	0	14	83.2	413	75	62	56	7	1	7	2	93	1	88	25	3	2	4	.333	0	4--	—	6.02
1994 Wichita	AA	33	0	0	14	40	188	30	28	26	2	4	2	1	40	0	59	10	0	1	3	.250	0	2--	—	5.85
Las Vegas	AAA	23	0	0	11	23.2	134	27	36	31	4	0	3	0	39	0	30	7	0	0	1	.000	0	0--	—	11.79
1995 Memphis	AA	36	8	2	11	86.1	400	65	57	46	3	2	3	10	73	4	98	19	0	3	4	.429	1	0--	—	4.80
1996 Portland	AA	3	3	0	0	13	66	17	9	9	1	1	2	0	13	0	7	1	0	1	0	1.000	0	0--	—	6.23
New Haven	AA	30	4	0	11	48.2	219	38	30	24	7	4	3	1	46	5	55	3	0	6	3	.667	0	0--	—	4.81
Colo. Sprng	AAA	12	0	0	4	12.1	55	6	6	3	0	1	0	1	11	0	15	2	0	0	2	.000	0	1--	—	2.19
1996 Colorado	NL	5	0	0	2	5.1	31	6	8	8	3	0	1	0	9	0	6	1	0	0	0	.000	0	0-1	0	13.50

Matt Beech

Pitches: Left **Bats:** Left **Pos:** SP-8 **Ht:** 6'2" **Wt:** 190 **Born:** 1/20/72 **Age:** 25

| | | HOW MUCH HE PITCHED | | | | | | WHAT HE GAVE UP | | | | | | | | | | | | THE RESULTS | | | | | | |
Year Team	Lg	G	GS	CG	GF	IP	BFP	H	R	ER	HR	SH	SF	HB	TBB	IBB	SO	WP	Bk	W	L	Pct.	ShO	Sv-Op	Hld	ERA
1994 Batavia	A-	4	3	0	1	18.2	80	9	4	4	0	1	0	4	12	0	27	0	0	2	1	.667	0	0--	—	1.93
Spartanburg	A	10	10	4	0	69.2	274	51	23	20	7	0	1	3	23	0	83	5	3	4	4	.500	1	0--	—	2.58
1995 Reading	AA	14	13	0	0	79	345	67	33	26	7	6	2	6	33	1	70	4	1	2	4	.333	0	0--	—	2.96
1996 Reading	AA	21	21	0	0	133.1	547	108	57	47	16	2	5	4	32	0	132	9	0	11	6	.647	0	0--	—	3.17
Scranton-WB	AAA	2	2	0	0	15	57	9	6	4	3	0	0	1	1	0	14	0	0	2	0	1.000	0	0--	—	2.40
1996 Philadelphia	NL	8	8	0	0	41.1	182	49	32	32	8	2	6	3	11	0	33	0	0	1	4	.200	0	0-0	0	6.97

Tim Belcher

Pitches: Right **Bats:** Right **Pos:** SP-35 **Ht:** 6'3" **Wt:** 220 **Born:** 10/19/61 **Age:** 35

| | | HOW MUCH HE PITCHED | | | | | | WHAT HE GAVE UP | | | | | | | | | | | | THE RESULTS | | | | | | |
Year Team	Lg	G	GS	CG	GF	IP	BFP	H	R	ER	HR	SH	SF	HB	TBB	IBB	SO	WP	Bk	W	L	Pct.	ShO	Sv-Op	Hld	ERA
1987 Los Angeles	NL	6	5	0	1	34	135	30	11	9	2	2	1	0	7	0	23	0	1	4	2	.667	0	0-0	0	2.38
1988 Los Angeles	NL	36	27	4	5	179.2	719	143	65	58	8	6	1	2	51	7	152	4	0	12	6	.667	1	4-5	0	2.91
1989 Los Angeles	NL	39	30	10	6	230	937	182	81	72	20	6	6	7	80	5	200	7	2	15	12	.556	8	1-1	1	2.82
1990 Los Angeles	NL	24	24	5	0	153	627	136	76	68	17	5	6	2	48	0	102	6	1	9	9	.500	2	0-0	0	4.00
1991 Los Angeles	NL	33	33	2	0	209.1	880	189	76	61	19	10	11	3	75	3	156	7	0	10	9	.526	1	0-0	0	2.62
1992 Cincinnati	NL	35	34	2	1	227.2	949	201	104	99	17	12	11	3	80	2	149	3	1	15	14	.517	1	0-0	0	3.91
1993 Cin-ChA		34	33	5	0	208.2	886	198	108	103	19	8	4	8	74	4	135	6	0	12	11	.522	3	0-0	0	4.44
1994 Detroit	AL	25	25	3	0	162	750	192	124	106	21	3	3	4	78	10	76	6	1	7	15	.318	0	0-0	0	5.89
1995 Seattle	AL	28	28	1	0	179.1	802	188	101	90	19	4	5	5	88	5	96	6	0	10	12	.455	0	0-0	0	4.52
1996 Kansas City	AL	35	35	4	0	238.2	1021	262	117	104	28	6	10	6	68	4	113	7	0	15	11	.577	1	0-0	0	3.92
1993 Cincinnati	AL	22	22	4	0	137	590	134	72	68	11	6	3	7	47	4	101	6	0	9	6	.600	2	0-0	0	4.47
Chicago	AL	12	11	1	0	71.2	296	64	36	35	8	2	1	1	27	0	34	0	0	3	5	.375	1	0-0	0	4.40
10 ML YEARS		295	274	36	13	1822.1	7706	1721	863	770	161	63	50	39	649	40	1202	52	6	109	101	.519	17	5-6	1	3.80

Stan Belinda

Pitches: Right **Bats:** Right **Pos:** RP-31 **Ht:** 6'3" **Wt:** 215 **Born:** 8/6/66 **Age:** 30

| | | HOW MUCH HE PITCHED | | | | | | WHAT HE GAVE UP | | | | | | | | | | | | THE RESULTS | | | | | | |
Year Team	Lg	G	GS	CG	GF	IP	BFP	H	R	ER	HR	SH	SF	HB	TBB	IBB	SO	WP	Bk	W	L	Pct.	ShO	Sv-Op	Hld	ERA
1996 Sarasota *	A+	1	1	0	0	1	9	6	5	5	0	0	0	0	1	0	1	1	0	0	1	.000	0	0--	—	45.00
Pawtucket *	AAA	6	0	0	2	7.2	30	2	2	0	0	0	0	0	0	0	7	0	0	1	0	1.000	0	0--	—	0.00
1989 Pittsburgh	NL	8	0	0	2	10.1	46	13	8	7	0	0	0	0	2	0	10	1	0	0	1	.000	0	0-0	2	6.10
1990 Pittsburgh	NL	55	0	0	17	58.1	245	48	23	23	4	2	2	1	29	3	55	1	0	3	4	.429	0	8-13	9	3.55
1991 Pittsburgh	NL	60	0	0	37	78.1	318	50	30	30	10	4	3	4	35	4	71	2	0	7	5	.583	0	16-20	6	3.45
1992 Pittsburgh	NL	59	0	0	42	71.1	299	58	26	25	8	4	6	0	29	5	57	1	0	6	4	.600	0	18-24	0	3.15
1993 Pit-KC		63	0	0	44	69.2	287	65	31	30	6	3	2	2	17	4	55	2	0	4	2	.667	0	19-23	8	3.88
1994 Kansas City	AL	37	0	0	10	49	220	47	36	28	6	0	3	5	24	3	37	1	0	2	2	.500	0	1-2	5	5.14
1995 Boston	AL	63	0	0	30	69.2	285	51	25	24	5	0	4	4	28	3	57	2	0	8	1	.889	0	10-14	17	3.10
1996 Boston	AL	31	0	0	10	28.2	139	32	21	21	3	1	0	4	20	1	18	2	0	2	1	.667	0	2-4	6	6.59
1993 Pittsburgh	NL	40	0	0	37	42.1	171	35	18	17	4	1	2	1	11	4	30	0	0	3	1	.750	0	19-22	0	3.61
Kansas City	AL	23	0	0	7	27.1	116	30	13	13	2	2	0	1	6	0	25	2	0	1	1	.500	0	0-1	8	4.28
8 ML YEARS		376	0	0	192	435.1	1839	363	201	188	42	14	20	20	184	23	360	12	0	32	20	.615	0	74-100	54	3.89

Tim Belk

Bats: Right **Throws:** Right **Pos:** 1B-6; PH-2 **Ht:** 6'3" **Wt:** 200 **Born:** 4/6/70 **Age:** 27

| | | BATTING | | | | | | | | | | | | | | | | | BASERUNNING | | | | PERCENTAGES | | |
Year Team	Lg	G	AB	H	2B	3B	HR	(Hm	Rd)	TB	R	RBI	TBB	IBB	SO	HBP	SH	SF	SB	CS	SB%	GDP	Avg	OBP	SLG
1992 Billings	R+	73	273	78	13	0	12	—	—	127	60	56	35	0	33	4	0	6	15	2	.88	6	.286	.368	.465
1993 Winston-Sal	A+	134	509	156	23	3	14	—	—	227	89	65	48	3	76	6	2	2	9	7	.56	9	.306	.372	.446
1994 Indianapols	AAA	6	18	2	1	0	0	—	—	3	1	0	1	0	5	0	1	0	0	1	.00	1	.111	.158	.167
Chattanooga	AA	118	411	127	35	3	10	—	—	198	64	86	60	5	41	0	0	11	13	8	.62	7	.309	.392	.482
1995 Indianapols	AAA	57	193	58	11	0	4	—	—	81	30	18	16	0	30	2	1	0	2	5	.29	9	.301	.360	.420
1996 Indianapols	AAA	120	436	125	27	3	15	—	—	203	63	63	27	1	72	2	1	6	5	2	.71	7	.287	.327	.466
1996 Cincinnati	NL	7	15	3	0	0	0	(0	0)	3	2	0	1	0	2	0	0	0	0	0	.00	0	.200	.250	.200

David Bell

Bats: R **Throws:** R **Pos:** 3B-45; 2B-20; PH-7; SS-1   **Ht:** 5'10" **Wt:** 170 **Born:** 9/14/72 **Age:** 24

					BATTING														BASERUNNING				PERCENTAGES		
Year Team	Lg	G	AB	H	2B	3B	HR	(Hm	Rd)	TB	R	RBI	TBB	IBB	SO	HBP	SH	SF	SB	CS	SB%	GDP	Avg	OBP	SLG
1990 Indians	R	30	111	29	5	1	0	—	—	36	18	13	10	1	8	4	0	1	1	1	.50	5	.261	.341	.324
Burlington	R+	12	42	7	1	1	0	—	—	10	4	2	2	0	5	1	0	1	2	1	.67	1	.167	.217	.238
1991 Columbus	A	136	491	113	23	1	5	—	—	153	47	63	37	2	49	5	3	7	3	2	.60	22	.230	.287	.312
1992 Kinston	A+	123	464	117	17	2	6	—	—	156	52	47	54	1	66	1	2	7	2	4	.33	13	.252	.327	.336
1993 Canton-Akrn	AA	129	483	141	20	2	9	—	—	192	69	60	43	0	54	3	2	6	3	4	.43	12	.292	.350	.398
1994 Charlotte	AAA	134	481	141	17	4	18	—	—	220	66	88	41	5	54	9	1	7	2	5	.29	9	.293	.355	.457
1995 Buffalo	AAA	70	254	69	11	1	8	—	—	106	34	34	22	0	37	4	1	3	0	3	.00	4	.272	.336	.417
Louisville	AAA	18	76	21	3	1	1	—	—	29	9	9	2	1	10	3	1	0	4	0	1.00	2	.276	.321	.382
1996 Louisville	AAA	42	136	24	5	1	0	—	—	31	9	7	7	1	15	0	0	0	1	2	.33	4	.176	.217	.228
1995 Cle-StL		41	146	36	7	2	2	(1	1)	53	13	19	4	0	25	2	0	1	1	2	.33	0	.247	.275	.363
1996 St. Louis	NL	62	145	31	6	0	1	(1	0)	40	12	9	10	2	22	1	0	1	1	1	.50	3	.214	.268	.276
1995 Cleveland	AL	2	2	0	0	0	0	(0	0)	0	0	0	0	0	0	0	0	0	0	0	.00	0	.000	.000	.000
St. Louis	NL	39	144	36	7	2	2	(1	1)	53	13	19	4	0	25	2	0	1	1	2	.33	0	.250	.278	.368
2 ML YEARS		103	291	67	13	2	3	(2	1)	93	25	28	14	2	47	3	0	2	2	3	.40	3	.230	.271	.320

Derek Bell

Bats: Right **Throws:** Right **Pos:** RF-157; CF-2; PH-1   **Ht:** 6'2" **Wt:** 215 **Born:** 12/11/68 **Age:** 28

					BATTING														BASERUNNING				PERCENTAGES		
Year Team	Lg	G	AB	H	2B	3B	HR	(Hm	Rd)	TB	R	RBI	TBB	IBB	SO	HBP	SH	SF	SB	CS	SB%	GDP	Avg	OBP	SLG
1991 Toronto	AL	18	28	4	0	0	0	(0	0)	4	5	1	6	0	5	1	0	0	3	2	.60	0	.143	.314	.143
1992 Toronto	AL	61	161	39	6	3	2	(2	0)	57	23	15	15	1	34	5	2	1	7	2	.78	6	.242	.324	.354
1993 San Diego	NL	150	542	142	19	2	21	(12	9)	226	73	72	23	5	122	12	0	6	26	5	.84	7	.262	.303	.417
1994 San Diego	NL	108	434	135	20	0	14	(8	6)	197	54	54	29	5	88	1	0	2	24	8	.75	14	.311	.354	.454
1995 Houston	NL	112	452	151	21	2	8	(3	5)	200	63	86	33	2	71	8	0	6	27	9	.75	10	.334	.385	.442
1996 Houston	NL	158	627	165	40	3	17	(8	9)	262	84	113	40	8	123	8	0	9	29	3	.91	18	.263	.311	.418
6 ML YEARS		607	2244	636	106	9	62	(33	29)	946	302	341	146	21	443	35	2	26	116	29	.80	55	.283	.333	.422

Jay Bell

Bats: Right **Throws:** Right **Pos:** SS-151; PH-1   **Ht:** 6'0" **Wt:** 182 **Born:** 12/11/65 **Age:** 31

					BATTING														BASERUNNING				PERCENTAGES		
Year Team	Lg	G	AB	H	2B	3B	HR	(Hm	Rd)	TB	R	RBI	TBB	IBB	SO	HBP	SH	SF	SB	CS	SB%	GDP	Avg	OBP	SLG
1986 Cleveland	AL	5	14	5	2	0	1	(0	1)	10	3	4	2	0	3	0	0	0	0	0	.00	0	.357	.438	.714
1987 Cleveland	AL	38	125	27	9	1	2	(1	1)	44	14	13	8	0	31	1	3	0	2	0	1.00	0	.216	.269	.352
1988 Cleveland	AL	73	211	46	5	1	2	(2	0)	59	23	21	21	0	53	1	1	2	4	2	.67	3	.218	.289	.280
1989 Pittsburgh	NL	78	271	70	13	3	2	(1	1)	95	33	27	19	0	47	1	10	2	5	3	.63	9	.258	.307	.351
1990 Pittsburgh	NL	159	583	148	28	7	7	(1	6)	211	93	52	65	0	109	3	39	6	10	6	.63	14	.254	.329	.362
1991 Pittsburgh	NL	157	608	164	32	8	16	(7	9)	260	96	67	52	1	99	4	30	5	10	6	.63	15	.270	.330	.428
1992 Pittsburgh	NL	159	632	167	36	6	9	(5	4)	242	87	55	55	0	103	4	19	2	7	5	.58	12	.264	.326	.383
1993 Pittsburgh	NL	154	604	187	32	9	9	(3	6)	264	102	51	77	6	122	6	13	6	16	10	.62	16	.310	.392	.437
1994 Pittsburgh	NL	110	424	117	35	4	9	(3	6)	187	68	45	49	1	82	3	8	3	2	0	1.00	15	.276	.353	.441
1995 Pittsburgh	NL	138	530	139	28	4	13	(8	5)	214	79	55	55	1	110	4	3	1	2	5	.29	13	.262	.336	.404
1996 Pittsburgh	NL	151	527	132	29	3	13	(7	6)	206	65	71	54	5	108	5	6	6	6	4	.60	10	.250	.323	.391
11 ML YEARS		1222	4529	1202	249	46	83	(38	45)	1792	663	461	457	14	867	32	132	26	64	41	.61	107	.265	.335	.396

Albert Belle

Bats: Right **Throws:** Right **Pos:** LF-152; DH-6   **Ht:** 6'2" **Wt:** 210 **Born:** 8/25/66 **Age:** 30

					BATTING														BASERUNNING				PERCENTAGES		
Year Team	Lg	G	AB	H	2B	3B	HR	(Hm	Rd)	TB	R	RBI	TBB	IBB	SO	HBP	SH	SF	SB	CS	SB%	GDP	Avg	OBP	SLG
1989 Cleveland	AL	62	218	49	8	4	7	(3	4)	86	22	37	12	0	55	2	0	2	2	2	.50	4	.225	.269	.394
1990 Cleveland	AL	9	23	4	0	0	1	(1	0)	7	1	3	1	0	6	0	1	0	0	0	.00	1	.174	.208	.304
1991 Cleveland	AL	123	461	130	31	2	28	(8	20)	249	60	95	25	2	99	5	0	5	3	1	.75	24	.282	.323	.540
1992 Cleveland	AL	153	585	152	23	1	34	(15	19)	279	81	112	52	5	128	4	1	8	8	2	.80	18	.260	.320	.477
1993 Cleveland	AL	159	594	172	36	3	38	(20	18)	328	93	129	76	13	96	8	1	14	23	12	.66	18	.290	.370	.552
1994 Cleveland	AL	106	412	147	35	2	36	(21	15)	294	90	101	58	9	71	5	1	4	9	6	.60	5	.357	.438	.714
1995 Cleveland	AL	143	546	173	52	1	50	(25	25)	377	121	126	73	5	80	6	0	4	5	2	.71	24	.317	.401	.690
1996 Cleveland	AL	158	602	187	38	3	48	(22	26)	375	124	148	99	15	87	7	0	7	11	0	1.00	20	.311	.410	.623
8 ML YEARS		913	3441	1014	223	16	242	(115	127)	1995	592	751	396	49	622	37	4	44	61	25	.71	114	.295	.369	.580

Rafael Belliard

Bats: Right **Throws:** Right **Pos:** SS-63; PH-17; 2B-15   **Ht:** 5'6" **Wt:** 160 **Born:** 10/24/61 **Age:** 35

					BATTING														BASERUNNING				PERCENTAGES		
Year Team	Lg	G	AB	H	2B	3B	HR	(Hm	Rd)	TB	R	RBI	TBB	IBB	SO	HBP	SH	SF	SB	CS	SB%	GDP	Avg	OBP	SLG
1982 Pittsburgh	NL	9	2	1	0	0	0	(0	0)	1	3	0	0	0	0	0	0	0	1	0	1.00	0	.500	.500	.500
1983 Pittsburgh	NL	4	1	0	0	0	0	(0	0)	0	1	0	0	0	1	0	0	0	0	0	.00	0	.000	.000	.000
1984 Pittsburgh	NL	20	22	5	0	0	0	(0	0)	5	3	0	0	0	1	0	0	0	4	1	.80	0	.227	.227	.227
1985 Pittsburgh	NL	17	20	4	0	0	0	(0	0)	4	1	1	0	0	5	0	0	0	0	0	.00	0	.200	.200	.200
1986 Pittsburgh	NL	117	309	72	5	2	0	(0	0)	81	33	31	26	6	54	3	11	1	12	2	.86	8	.233	.298	.262

Year Team	Lg	G	AB	H	2B	3B	HR	(Hm	Rd)	TB	R	RBI	TBB	IBB	SO	HBP	SH	SF	SB	CS	SB%	GDP	Avg	OBP	SLG
1987 Pittsburgh	NL	81	203	42	4	3	1	(0	1)	55	26	15	20	6	25	3	2	1	5	1	.83	4	.207	.286	.271
1988 Pittsburgh	NL	122	286	61	0	4	0	(0	0)	69	28	11	26	3	47	4	5	0	7	1	.88	10	.213	.288	.241
1989 Pittsburgh	NL	67	154	33	4	0	0	(0	0)	37	10	8	8	2	22	0	3	0	5	2	.71	1	.214	.253	.240
1990 Pittsburgh	NL	47	54	11	3	0	0	(0	0)	14	10	6	5	0	13	1	1	0	1	2	.33	2	.204	.283	.259
1991 Atlanta	NL	149	353	88	9	2	0	(0	0)	101	36	27	22	2	63	2	7	1	3	1	.75	4	.249	.296	.286
1992 Atlanta	NL	144	285	60	6	1	0	(0	0)	68	20	14	14	4	43	3	13	0	0	1	.00	6	.211	.255	.239
1993 Atlanta	NL	91	79	18	5	0	0	(0	0)	23	6	6	4	0	13	3	3	0	0	0	.00	1	.228	.291	.291
1994 Atlanta	NL	46	120	29	7	1	0	(0	0)	38	9	9	2	1	29	2	2	1	0	2	.00	4	.242	.264	.317
1995 Atlanta	NL	75	180	40	2	1	0	(0	0)	44	12	7	6	2	28	2	4	0	2	2	.50	4	.222	.255	.244
1996 Atlanta	NL	87	142	24	7	0	0	(0	0)	31	9	3	2	0	22	0	3	1	3	1	.75	6	.169	.179	.218
15 ML YEARS		1076	2210	488	52	14	1	(0	1)	571	207	138	135	26	366	23	54	5	43	16	.73	50	.221	.272	.258

Esteban Beltre

Bats: R Throws: R Pos: 3B-13; 2B-8; SS-6; PH-3; DH-1 **Ht: 5'10"** **Wt: 171** **Born: 12/26/67** **Age: 29**

Year Team	Lg	G	AB	H	2B	3B	HR	(Hm	Rd)	TB	R	RBI	TBB	IBB	SO	HBP	SH	SF	SB	CS	SB%	GDP	Avg	OBP	SLG
1996 Scrnton-WB *	AAA	4	15	2	0	0	0	—	—	2	1	1	0	0	1	0	0	0	0	0	.00	2	.133	.133	.133
Richmond *	AAA	10	28	7	3	0	0	—	—	10	3	0	1	0	2	0	0	0	0	0	.00	0	.250	.276	.357
1991 Chicago	AL	8	6	1	0	0	0	(0	0)	1	0	0	1	0	1	0	0	0	1	0	1.00	0	.167	.286	.167
1992 Chicago	AL	49	110	21	2	0	1	(1	0)	26	21	10	3	0	18	0	2	1	1	0	1.00	3	.191	.211	.236
1994 Texas	AL	48	131	37	5	0	0	(0	0)	42	12	12	16	0	25	0	5	1	2	5	.29	3	.282	.358	.321
1995 Texas	AL	54	92	20	8	0	0	(0	0)	28	7	7	4	0	15	0	3	0	0	0	.00	1	.217	.250	.304
1996 Boston	AL	27	62	16	2	0	0	(0	0)	18	6	6	4	0	14	0	1	1	1	0	1.00	1	.258	.299	.290
5 ML YEARS		186	401	95	17	0	1	(1	0)	115	46	35	28	0	73	0	11	3	5	5	.50	8	.237	.285	.287

Marvin Benard

Bats: L Throws: L Pos: CF-102; RF-38; PH-6; LF-5 **Ht: 5'9"** **Wt: 180** **Born: 1/20/70** **Age: 27**

Year Team	Lg	G	AB	H	2B	3B	HR	(Hm	Rd)	TB	R	RBI	TBB	IBB	SO	HBP	SH	SF	SB	CS	SB%	GDP	Avg	OBP	SLG
1992 Everett	A-	64	161	38	10	2	1	—	—	55	31	17	24	0	39	6	1	0	17	3	.85	1	.236	.356	.342
1993 Clinton	A	112	349	105	14	2	5	—	—	138	84	50	56	1	66	4	2	0	42	10	.81	1	.301	.403	.395
1994 Shreveport	AA	125	454	143	32	3	4	—	—	193	66	48	31	5	58	4	7	4	24	13	.65	14	.315	.361	.425
1995 Phoenix	AAA	111	378	115	14	6	6	—	—	159	70	32	50	3	66	5	5	3	10	13	.43	2	.304	.390	.421
1996 Phoenix	AAA	4	19	7	0	0	0	—	—	7	2	4	2	0	2	0	0	0	1	0	1.00	0	.368	.429	.368
1995 San Francisco	NL	13	34	13	2	0	1	(0	1)	18	5	4	1	0	7	0	0	0	1	0	1.00	1	.382	.400	.529
1996 San Francisco	NL	135	488	121	17	4	5	(2	3)	161	89	27	59	2	84	4	6	1	25	11	.69	8	.248	.333	.330
2 ML YEARS		148	522	134	19	4	6	(2	4)	179	94	31	60	2	91	4	6	1	26	11	.70	9	.257	.337	.343

Alan Benes

Pitches: Right **Bats: Right** **Pos: SP-32; RP-2** **Ht: 6'5"** **Wt: 215** **Born: 1/21/72** **Age: 25**

	HOW MUCH HE PITCHED						WHAT HE GAVE UP												THE RESULTS					
Year Team	Lg	G	GS	CG	GF	IP	BFP	H	R	ER	HR	SH	SF	HB	TBB	IBB	SO	WP	Bk	W	L	Pct.	ShO	Sv-Op	Hld	ERA
1993 Glens Falls	A-	7	7	0	0	37	162	39	20	15	2	0	1	2	14	0	29	2	1	0	4	.000	0	0--		3.65
1994 Savannah	A	4	4	0	0	24.1	95	21	5	4	1	0	0	1	7	0	24	1	0	2	0	1.000	0	0--		1.48
St. Pete	A+	11	11	0	0	78.1	299	55	18	14	0	3	0	2	15	0	69	4	1	7	1	.875	0	0--		1.61
Arkansas	AA	13	13	1	0	87.2	341	58	38	29	8	1	2	4	26	0	75	3	1	7	2	.778	0	0--		2.98
Louisville	AAA	2	2	1	0	15.1	61	10	5	5	1	0	0	0	4	0	16	3	0	1	0	1.000	0	0--		2.93
1995 Louisville	AAA	11	11	2	0	56	215	37	16	15	5	0	0	1	14	1	54	2	0	4	2	.667	1	0--		2.41
1995 St. Louis	NL	3	3	0	0	16	76	24	15	15	2	1	0	1	9	0	20	3	0	1	2	.333	0	0-0	0	8.44
1996 St. Louis	NL	34	32	3	1	191	840	192	120	104	27	15	9	7	87	3	131	5	1	13	10	.565	0	0-0	0	4.90
2 ML YEARS		37	35	3	1	207	916	216	135	119	29	16	9	8	91	3	151	8	1	14	12	.538	0	0-0	0	5.17

Andy Benes

Pitches: Right **Bats: Right** **Pos: SP-34; RP-2** **Ht: 6'6"** **Wt: 245** **Born: 8/20/67** **Age: 29**

	HOW MUCH HE PITCHED						WHAT HE GAVE UP												THE RESULTS					
Year Team	Lg	G	GS	CG	GF	IP	BFP	H	R	ER	HR	SH	SF	HB	TBB	IBB	SO	WP	Bk	W	L	Pct.	ShO	Sv-Op	Hld	ERA
1989 San Diego	NL	10	10	0	0	66.2	280	51	28	26	7	6	2	1	31	0	66	0	3	6	3	.667	0	0-0	0	3.51
1990 San Diego	NL	32	31	2	1	192.1	811	177	87	77	18	5	6	1	69	5	140	2	5	10	11	.476	0	0-0	0	3.60
1991 San Diego	NL	33	33	4	0	223	908	194	76	75	23	5	4	4	59	7	167	3	4	15	11	.577	1	0-0	0	3.03
1992 San Diego	NL	34	34	2	0	231.1	961	230	90	86	14	19	6	5	61	6	169	1	1	13	14	.481	2	0-0	0	3.35
1993 San Diego	NL	34	34	4	0	230.2	968	200	111	97	23	10	6	4	86	7	179	14	2	15	15	.500	2	0-0	0	3.78
1994 San Diego	NL	25	25	2	0	172.1	717	155	82	74	20	11	1	1	51	2	189	4	0	6	14	.300	2	0-0	0	3.86
1995 SD-Sea		31	31	1	0	181.2	809	176	100	96	18	4	8	6	78	5	171	6	0	4	7	.364	0	0-0	0	4.76
1996 St. Louis	NL	36	34	3	1	230.1	963	215	107	98	28	2	6	6	77	7	160	6	0	18	10	.643	1	1-1	0	3.83
1995 San Diego	NL	19	19	1	0	118.2	518	121	65	55	10	3	4	4	45	3	126	3	0	4	7	.364	0	0-0	0	4.17
Seattle	AL	12	12	0	0	63	291	72	42	41	8	1	4	2	33	2	45	2	0	7	2	.778	0	0-0	0	5.86
8 ML YEARS		235	232	18	2	1528.1	6417	1415	688	629	151	62	39	28	512	39	1241	35	15	94	87	.519	9	1-1	0	3.70

Armando Benitez

Pitches: Right **Bats:** Right **Pos:** RP-18 **Ht:** 6'4" **Wt:** 220 **Born:** 11/3/72 **Age:** 24

			HOW MUCH HE PITCHED						WHAT HE GAVE UP										THE RESULTS					
Year Team	Lg	G	GS	CG	GF	IP	BFP	H	R	ER	HR	SH	SF	HB	TBB	IBB	SO	WP	Bk	W	L	Pct.	ShO	Sv-Op	Hld	ERA
1996 Orioles *	R	1	0	0	1	2	7	1	0	0	0	0	0	0	0	0	5	0	0	1	0	1.000	0	0- --	—	0.00
Bowie *	AA	4	4	0	0	6	23	7	3	3	0	0	0	0	0	0	8	0	0	0	0	.000	0	0- --	—	4.50
Rochester *	AAA	2	0	0	0	4	17	3	1	1	0	0	0	0	1	0	5	1	0	0	0	.000	0	0- --	—	2.25
1994 Baltimore	AL	3	0	0	1	10	42	8	1	1	0	0	0	1	4	0	14	0	0	0	0	.000	0	0-0	0	0.90
1995 Baltimore	AL	44	0	0	18	47.2	221	37	33	30	8	2	3	5	37	2	56	3	1	1	5	.167	0	2-5	6	5.66
1996 Baltimore	AL	18	0	0	8	14.1	56	7	6	6	2	0	1	0	6	0	20	1	0	1	0	1.000	0	4-5	1	3.77
3 ML YEARS		65	0	0	27	72	319	52	40	37	10	2	4	6	47	2	90	4	1	2	5	.286	0	6-10	7	4.63

Yamil Benitez

Bats: Right **Throws:** Right **Pos:** PH-8; LF-3; RF-1 **Ht:** 6'2" **Wt:** 195 **Born:** 5/10/72 **Age:** 25

					BATTING													BASERUNNING				PERCENTAGES		
Year Team	Lg	G	AB	H	2B	3B	HR	(Hm	Rd)	TB	R	RBI	TBB	IBB	SO	HBP	SH	SF	SB	CS	SB%	GDP	Avg	OBP	SLG
1990 Expos	R	22	83	19	1	0	1	—	—	23	6	5	8	0	18	0	0	0	0	0	.00	1	.229	.297	.277
1991 Expos	R	54	197	47	9	5	5	—	—	81	20	38	12	1	55	1	1	5	10	5	.67	3	.239	.279	.411
1992 Albany	A	23	79	13	3	2	1	—	—	23	6	6	5	1	49	0	0	0	0	2	.00	1	.165	.214	.291
Jamestown	A-	44	162	44	6	6	3	—	—	71	24	23	14	0	52	2	1	0	19	1	.95	5	.272	.337	.438
1993 Burlington	A	111	411	112	21	5	15	—	—	188	70	61	29	1	99	3	6	3	18	7	.72	8	.273	.323	.457
1994 Harrisburg	AA	126	475	123	18	4	17	—	—	200	58	91	36	2	134	2	1	4	18	15	.55	12	.259	.311	.421
1995 Ottawa	AAA	127	474	123	24	6	18	—	—	213	66	69	44	3	128	2	2	2	14	6	.70	10	.259	.324	.449
1996 Ottawa	AAA	114	439	122	20	2	23	—	—	215	56	81	28	5	120	1	0	6	11	4	.73	5	.278	.319	.490
1995 Montreal	NL	14	39	15	2	1	2	(1	1)	25	8	7	1	0	7	0	0	0	0	2	.00	1	.385	.400	.641
1996 Montreal	NL	11	12	2	0	0	0	(0	0)	2	0	2	0	0	4	0	0	0	0	0	.00	0	.167	.167	.167
2 ML YEARS		25	51	17	2	1	2	(1	1)	27	8	9	1	0	11	0	0	0	0	2	.00	1	.333	.346	.529

Mike Benjamin

Bats: Right **Throws:** Right **Pos:** SS-31; PH-4; 2B-1 **Ht:** 6'0" **Wt:** 169 **Born:** 11/22/65 **Age:** 31

					BATTING													BASERUNNING				PERCENTAGES		
Year Team	Lg	G	AB	H	2B	3B	HR	(Hm	Rd)	TB	R	RBI	TBB	IBB	SO	HBP	SH	SF	SB	CS	SB%	GDP	Avg	OBP	SLG
1996 Clearwater *	A+	8	23	4	1	0	0	—	—	5	3	0	3	0	4	0	0	0	1	0	1.00	1	.174	.269	.217
Scrnton-WB *	AAA	4	13	5	2	0	0	—	—	7	2	4	3	2	0	0	0	1	0	0	.00	1	.385	.471	.538
1989 San Francisco	NL	14	6	1	0	0	0	(0	0)	1	6	0	0	0	1	0	0	0	0	0	.00	0	.167	.167	.167
1990 San Francisco	NL	22	56	12	3	1	2	(2	0)	23	7	3	1	0	10	0	0	0	1	0	1.00	2	.214	.254	.411
1991 San Francisco	NL	54	106	13	3	0	2	(0	2)	22	12	8	7	2	26	2	3	2	3	0	1.00	1	.123	.188	.208
1992 San Francisco	NL	40	75	13	2	1	1	(0	1)	20	4	3	4	1	15	0	3	0	1	0	1.00	1	.173	.215	.267
1993 San Francisco	NL	63	146	29	7	0	4	(3	1)	48	22	16	9	2	23	4	6	0	0	0	.00	3	.199	.264	.329
1994 San Francisco	NL	38	62	16	5	1	1	(1	0)	26	9	9	5	1	16	3	5	0	5	0	1.00	1	.258	.343	.419
1995 San Francisco	NL	68	186	41	6	0	3	(1	2)	56	19	12	8	3	51	1	7	0	11	1	.92	3	.220	.256	.301
1996 Philadelphia	NL	35	103	23	5	1	4	(0	4)	42	13	13	12	5	21	2	1	0	3	1	.75	2	.223	.316	.408
8 ML YEARS		334	740	148	31	4	17	(7	10)	238	92	64	48	15	163	12	25	2	24	2	.92	13	.200	.259	.322

Erik Bennett

Pitches: Right **Bats:** Right **Pos:** RP-24 **Ht:** 6'2" **Wt:** 205 **Born:** 9/13/68 **Age:** 28

					HOW MUCH HE PITCHED				WHAT HE GAVE UP										THE RESULTS					
Year Team	Lg	G	GS	CG	GF	IP	BFP	H	R	ER	HR	SH	SF	HB	TBB	IBB	SO	WP	Bk	W	L	Pct.	ShO	Sv-Op	Hld	ERA
1989 Bend	A-	15	15	2	0	96	422	96	58	37	4	3	2	3	36	0	96	8	6	6	8	.429	0	0- --	—	3.47
1990 Quad City	A	18	18	3	0	108.1	453	91	48	36	9	5	6	4	37	0	100	2	4	7	7	.500	1	0- --	—	2.99
1991 Palm Spring	A+	8	8	1	0	43	192	41	15	12	2	3	0	3	27	0	31	0	0	2	3	.400	0	0- --	—	2.51
1992 Quad City	A	8	8	1	0	57.1	238	46	20	17	0	3	5	4	22	0	59	3	1	3	3	.500	1	0- --	—	2.67
Palm Spring	A+	6	6	1	0	42	171	27	19	17	0	2	1	4	15	0	33	2	1	4	2	.667	0	0- --	—	3.64
Midland	AA	7	7	0	0	46	195	47	22	20	3	3	2	7	16	0	36	1	0	1	3	.250	0	0- --	—	3.91
1993 Midland	AA	11	11	0	0	69.1	308	87	57	50	12	2	6	6	17	1	33	1	0	5	4	.556	0	0- --	—	6.49
Vancouver	AAA	18	12	0	1	80.1	353	101	57	54	10	1	0	4	21	0	51	3	0	6	6	.500	0	1- --	—	6.05
1994 Vancouver	AAA	45	1	0	14	89.2	375	71	32	28	9	2	4	10	28	2	83	8	2	1	4	.200	0	3- --	—	2.81
1995 Tucson	AAA	42	1	0	16	73.1	316	71	41	36	6	4	5	5	32	4	63	4	1	9	1	.900	0	3- --	—	4.42
Vancouver	AAA	42	1	0	16	73.1	316	71	41	36	6	0	5	5	32	4	63	4	1	9	1	.900	0	3- --	—	4.42
1996 Salt Lake	AAA	17	0	0	4	24	114	27	17	17	4	0	0	2	14	1	10	0	0	3	1	.750	0	0- --	—	6.38
1995 California	AL	1	0	0	1	0	0	0	0	0	0	0	0	0	0	0	0	0	0	0	0	.000	0	0-0	0	0.00
1996 Minnesota	AL	24	0	0	10	27.1	130	33	24	24	7	3	1	2	16	1	13	1	0	2	0	1.000	0	1-1	2	7.90
2 ML YEARS		25	0	0	11	27.2	131	33	24	24	7	3	1	2	16	1	13	1	0	2	0	1.000	0	1-1	2	7.81

Gary Bennett

Bats: Right **Throws:** Right **Pos:** C-5; PH-1 **Ht:** 6'0" **Wt:** 190 **Born:** 4/17/72 **Age:** 25

					BATTING													BASERUNNING				PERCENTAGES		
Year Team	Lg	G	AB	H	2B	3B	HR	(Hm	Rd)	TB	R	RBI	TBB	IBB	SO	HBP	SH	SF	SB	CS	SB%	GDP	Avg	OBP	SLG
1990 Martinsvlle	R+	16	52	14	2	1	0	—	—	18	3	10	4	0	15	0	0	1	0	1	.00	0	.269	.316	.346
1991 Martinsvlle	R+	41	136	32	7	0	1	—	—	42	15	16	17	0	26	5	1	1	0	1	.00	5	.235	.340	.309
1992 Batavia	A-	47	146	30	2	0	0	—	—	32	22	12	15	0	27	2	3	0	2	1	.67	2	.205	.288	.219

					BATTING															BASERUNNING				PERCENTAGES		
Year Team	Lg	G	AB	H	2B	3B	HR	(Hm	Rd)	TB	R	RBI	TBB	IBB	SO	HBP	SH	SF		SB	CS	SB%	GDP		Avg	OBP	SLG
1993 Spartanburg	A	42	126	32	4	1	0	—	—	38	18	15	12	0	22	1	2	1		0	2	.00	2		.254	.321	.302
Clearwater	A+	17	55	18	0	0	1	—	—	21	5	6	3	0	10	1	2	0		0	1	.00	0		.327	.373	.382
1994 Clearwater	A+	19	55	13	3	0	0	—	—	16	6	10	8	0	6	0	0	1		0	0	.00	1		.236	.328	.291
Reading	AA	63	208	48	9	0	3	—	—	66	13	22	14	0	26	0	3	3		0	1	.00	6		.231	.276	.317
1995 Reading	AA	86	271	64	11	0	4	—	—	87	27	40	22	1	36	3	3	2		0	0	.00	12		.236	.299	.321
Scranton-WB	AAA	7	20	3	0	0	0	—	—	3	1	1	2	1	2	0	1	0		0	0	.00	0		.150	.227	.150
1996 Scranton-WB	AAA	91	286	71	15	1	8	—	—	112	37	37	24	2	43	3	3	3		1	0	1.00	10		.248	.310	.392
1995 Philadelphia	NL	1	1	0	0	0	0	(0	0)	0	0	0	0	0	1	0	0	0		0	0	.00	0		.000	.000	.000
1996 Philadelphia	NL	6	16	4	0	0	0	(0	0)	4	0	1	2	1	6	0	0	0		0	0	.00	0		.250	.333	.250
2 ML YEARS		7	17	4	0	0	0	(0	0)	4	0	1	2	1	7	0	0	0		0	0	.00	0		.235	.316	.235

Jason Bere

Pitches: Right **Bats:** Right **Pos:** SP-5   **Ht:** 6'3" **Wt:** 215 **Born:** 5/26/71 **Age:** 26

		HOW MUCH HE PITCHED						WHAT HE GAVE UP										THE RESULTS						
Year Team	Lg	G	GS	CG	GF	IP	BFP	H	R	ER	HR	SH	SF	HB	TBB	IBB	SO	WP	Bk	W	L	Pct.	ShO	Sv-Op	Hld	ERA
1996 White Sox *	R	1	1	0	0	3	14	3	2	2	0	0	0	0	1	0	3	0	0	0	1	.000	0	0--	—	6.00
Hickory *	A	1	1	0	0	5	18	3	0	0	0	0	0	0	0	0	5	1	0	1	0	1.000	0	0--	—	0.00
Birmingham *	AA	1	1	0	0	4.1	21	4	2	2	2	0	0	0	4	0	5	1	0	0	0	.000	0	0--	—	4.15
Nashville *	AAA	3	3	0	0	12.2	48	9	2	2	1	0	0	0	4	0	15	0	0	0	0	.000	0	0--	—	1.42
1993 Chicago	AL	24	24	1	0	142.2	610	109	60	55	12	4	2	5	81	0	129	8	0	12	5	.706	0	0-0	0	3.47
1994 Chicago	AL	24	24	0	0	141.2	608	119	65	60	17	4	4	1	80	0	127	2	0	12	2	.857	0	0-0	0	3.81
1995 Chicago	AL	27	27	1	0	137.2	668	151	120	110	21	4	7	6	106	6	110	8	0	8	15	.348	0	0-0	0	7.19
1996 Chicago	AL	5	5	0	0	16.2	93	26	19	19	3	1	1	0	18	1	19	2	0	0	1	.000	0	0-0	0	10.26
4 ML YEARS		80	80	2	0	438.2	1979	405	264	244	53	13	14	12	285	7	385	20	0	32	23	.582	0	0-0	0	5.01

Sean Bergman

Pitches: Right **Bats:** Right **Pos:** RP-27; SP-14   **Ht:** 6'4" **Wt:** 230 **Born:** 4/11/70 **Age:** 27

		HOW MUCH HE PITCHED						WHAT HE GAVE UP										THE RESULTS						
Year Team	Lg	G	GS	CG	GF	IP	BFP	H	R	ER	HR	SH	SF	HB	TBB	IBB	SO	WP	Bk	W	L	Pct.	ShO	Sv-Op	Hld	ERA
1993 Detroit	AL	9	6	1	1	39.2	189	47	29	25	6	3	2	1	23	3	19	3	1	1	4	.200	0	0-0	0	5.67
1994 Detroit	AL	3	3	0	0	17.2	82	22	11	11	2	0	1	0	7	0	12	1	0	2	1	.667	0	0-0	0	5.61
1995 Detroit	AL	28	28	1	0	135.1	630	169	95	77	19	5	3	4	67	8	86	13	0	7	10	.412	1	0-0	0	5.12
1996 San Diego	NL	41	14	0	11	113.1	482	119	63	55	14	8	4	2	33	3	85	7	2	6	8	.429	0	0-0	1	4.37
4 ML YEARS		81	51	2	12	306	1383	357	198	168	41	16	10	8	130	14	202	24	3	16	23	.410	1	0-0	1	4.94

Geronimo Berroa

Bats: R **Throws:** R **Pos:** DH-91; RF-54; LF-17; PH-5   **Ht:** 6'0" **Wt:** 195 **Born:** 3/18/65 **Age:** 32

					BATTING																BASERUNNING				PERCENTAGES		
Year Team	Lg	G	AB	H	2B	3B	HR	(Hm	Rd)	TB	R	RBI	TBB	IBB	SO	HBP	SH	SF		SB	CS	SB%	GDP		Avg	OBP	SLG
1989 Atlanta	NL	81	136	36	4	0	2	(1	1)	46	7	9	7	1	32	0	0	0		1	1	.00	2		.265	.301	.338
1990 Atlanta	NL	7	4	0	0	0	0	(0	0)	0	0	0	1	1	1	0	0	0		0	0	.00	0		.000	.200	.000
1992 Cincinnati	NL	13	15	4	1	0	0	(0	0)	5	2	0	2	0	1	1	0	0		0	1	.00	1		.267	.389	.333
1993 Florida	NL	14	34	4	1	0	0	(0	0)	5	3	0	2	0	7	0	0	0		0	0	.00	2		.118	.167	.147
1994 Oakland	AL	96	340	104	18	2	13	(4	9)	165	55	65	41	0	62	3	0	7		7	2	.78	5		.306	.379	.485
1995 Oakland	AL	141	546	152	22	3	22	(10	12)	246	87	88	63	2	98	1	0	6		7	4	.64	12		.278	.351	.451
1996 Oakland	AL	153	586	170	32	1	36	(21	15)	312	101	106	47	0	122	4	0	6		0	3	.00	16		.290	.344	.532
7 ML YEARS		505	1661	470	78	6	73	(36	37)	779	255	268	163	4	323	9	0	19		14	11	.56	38		.283	.347	.469

Sean Berry

Bats: Right **Throws:** Right **Pos:** 3B-110; PH-22   **Ht:** 5'11" **Wt:** 200 **Born:** 3/22/66 **Age:** 31

					BATTING																BASERUNNING				PERCENTAGES		
Year Team	Lg	G	AB	H	2B	3B	HR	(Hm	Rd)	TB	R	RBI	TBB	IBB	SO	HBP	SH	SF		SB	CS	SB%	GDP		Avg	OBP	SLG
1990 Kansas City	AL	8	23	5	1	1	0	(0	0)	8	2	4	2	0	5	0	0	0		0	0	.00	0		.217	.280	.348
1991 Kansas City	AL	31	60	8	3	0	0	(0	0)	11	5	1	5	0	23	1	0	0		0	0	.00	1		.133	.212	.183
1992 Montreal	NL	24	57	19	1	0	1	(0	1)	23	5	4	1	0	11	0	0	0		2	1	.67	1		.333	.345	.404
1993 Montreal	NL	122	299	78	15	2	14	(5	9)	139	50	49	41	6	70	2	3	6		12	2	.86	4		.261	.348	.465
1994 Montreal	NL	103	320	89	19	2	11	(4	7)	145	43	41	32	7	50	3	2	2		14	0	1.00	7		.278	.347	.453
1995 Montreal	NL	103	314	100	22	1	14	(5	9)	166	38	55	25	1	53	2	2	5		3	8	.27	5		.318	.367	.529
1996 Houston	NL	132	431	121	38	1	17	(4	13)	212	55	95	23	1	58	9	2	4		12	6	.67	11		.281	.328	.492
7 ML YEARS		523	1504	420	99	7	57	(18	39)	704	198	249	129	15	270	17	9	17		43	17	.72	29		.279	.340	.468

Mike Bertotti

Pitches: Left **Bats:** Left **Pos:** RP-13; SP-2   **Ht:** 6'1" **Wt:** 185 **Born:** 1/18/70 **Age:** 27

		HOW MUCH HE PITCHED						WHAT HE GAVE UP										THE RESULTS						
Year Team	Lg	G	GS	CG	GF	IP	BFP	H	R	ER	HR	SH	SF	HB	TBB	IBB	SO	WP	Bk	W	L	Pct.	ShO	Sv-Op	Hld	ERA
1991 Utica	A-	14	5	0	3	37.1	186	38	33	24	2	1	3	2	36	0	33	9	0	3	4	.429	0	0--	—	5.79
1992 South Bend	A	11	0	0	5	19.1	86	12	8	8	1	1	1	1	22	0	17	1	1	0	3	.000	0	1--	—	3.72

	HOW MUCH HE PITCHED							WHAT HE GAVE UP													THE RESULTS						
Year Team	Lg	G	GS	CG	GF	IP	BFP	H	R	ER	HR	SH	SF	HB	TBB	IBB	SO	WP	Bk	W	L	Pct.	ShO	Sv-Op	Hld	ERA
Utica	A-	17	1	0	5	33.1	164	36	28	23	2	0	1	2	31	0	23	7	1	2	2	.500	0	1--	—	6.21
1993 Hickory	A	9	9	2	0	59.2	248	42	19	14	2	4	0	1	29	1	77	2	3	3	3	.500	0	0--	—	2.11
South Bend	A	17	16	2	0	111	466	93	51	43	5	6	6	6	44	2	108	7	1	5	7	.417	2	0--	—	3.49
1994 Pr. William	A+	16	15	2	0	104.2	435	90	48	41	13	2	1	3	43	0	103	8	1	7	6	.538	1	0--	—	3.53
Birmingham	AA	10	10	1	0	68.1	273	55	25	22	1	2	3	0	21	1	44	5	0	4	3	.571	1	0--	—	2.90
1995 Nashville	AAA	7	6	0	1	32	154	41	34	31	8	0	1	3	17	0	35	0	0	2	3	.400	0	0--	—	8.72
Birmingham	AA	19	18	1	1	95	433	101	72	66	12	0	5	5	53	0	88	8	0	4	10	.286	0	0--	—	6.25
1996 Nashville	AAA	28	9	1	5	82.1	365	80	43	40	10	5	4	2	42	3	73	3	0	5	3	.625	0	1--	—	4.37
1995 Chicago	AL	4	4	0	0	14.1	80	23	20	20	6	0	3	3	11	0	15	2	1	1	1	.500	0	0-0	0	12.56
1996 Chicago	AL	15	2	0	4	28	130	28	18	16	3	0	1	0	20	3	19	4	0	2	0	1.000	0	0-1	2	5.14
2 ML YEARS		19	6	0	4	42.1	210	51	38	36	11	0	4	3	31	3	34	6	1	3	1	.750	0	0-1	2	7.65

Andres Berumen

Pitches: Right **Bats:** Right **Pos:** RP-3   **Ht:** 6'2" **Wt:** 205 **Born:** 4/5/71 **Age:** 26

	HOW MUCH HE PITCHED							WHAT HE GAVE UP													THE RESULTS						
Year Team	Lg	G	GS	CG	GF	IP	BFP	H	R	ER	HR	SH	SF	HB	TBB	IBB	SO	WP	Bk	W	L	Pct.	ShO	Sv-Op	Hld	ERA
1989 Royals	R	12	10	0	0	49	223	57	29	26	2	2	2	4	17	1	24	6	0	2	4	.333	0	1--	—	4.78
1990 Royals	R	5	4	0	1	22.2	95	24	9	6	0	0	1	0	8	1	18	0	0	0	2	.000	0	1--	—	2.38
Baseball Cy	A+	9	9	1	0	44	197	30	27	21	0	2	5	4	28	0	35	2	1	3	5	.375	1	0--	—	4.30
1991 Baseball Cy	A+	7	7	0	0	37	161	34	18	17	0	1	0	4	18	0	24	5	0	0	5	.000	0	0--	—	4.14
Appleton	A	13	13	0	0	56.1	254	55	33	22	0	3	4	3	26	0	49	2	1	2	6	.250	0	0--	—	3.51
1992 Appleton	A	46	0	0	38	57.2	245	50	25	17	3	1	3	1	23	2	52	3	0	5	2	.714	0	13--	—	2.65
1993 High Desert	A+	14	13	1	0	92	396	85	45	37	8	0	4	7	36	1	74	6	1	9	2	.818	0	0--	—	3.62
Wichita	AA	7	7	0	0	26.2	120	35	17	17	2	1	1	1	11	2	17	3	0	3	1	.750	0	1--	—	5.74
1994 Las Vegas	AAA	43	6	0	14	75.2	375	93	70	55	5	2	2	5	57	1	49	6	1	4	7	.364	0	1--	—	6.54
1995 Las Vegas	AAA	3	0	0	0	3.1	16	4	2	2	0	0	0	1	2	0	3	0	0	0	0	.000	0	0--	—	5.40
Rancho Cuca	A+	7	0	0	1	10.2	44	10	4	4	1	0	0	3	3	0	14	0	0	0	1	.000	0	1--	—	3.38
1996 Las Vegas	AAA	50	0	0	20	70.2	342	73	53	48	4	4	3	6	58	9	59	17	0	4	7	.364	0	1--	—	6.11
1995 San Diego	NL	37	0	0	17	44.1	207	37	29	28	3	1	3	3	36	3	42	6	0	2	3	.400	0	1-4	5	5.68
1996 San Diego	NL	3	0	0	1	3.1	16	3	2	2	1	0	0	1	2	1	4	0	0	0	0	.000	0	0-0	0	5.40
2 ML YEARS		40	0	0	18	47.2	223	40	31	30	4	1	3	4	38	4	46	6	0	2	3	.400	0	1-4	5	5.66

Brian Bevil

Pitches: Right **Bats:** Right **Pos:** RP-2; SP-1   **Ht:** 6'3" **Wt:** 190 **Born:** 9/5/71 **Age:** 25

	HOW MUCH HE PITCHED							WHAT HE GAVE UP													THE RESULTS						
Year Team	Lg	G	GS	CG	GF	IP	BFP	H	R	ER	HR	SH	SF	HB	TBB	IBB	SO	WP	Bk	W	L	Pct.	ShO	Sv-Op	Hld	ERA
1991 Royals	R	13	12	2	1	65.1	262	56	20	14	1	0	1	2	19	0	70	3	3	5	3	.625	0	0--	—	1.93
1992 Appleton	A	26	26	4	0	156	646	129	67	59	17	5	4	5	63	0	168	9	0	9	7	.563	2	0--	—	3.40
1993 Wilmington	A+	12	12	2	0	74.1	286	46	21	19	2	2	2	4	23	0	61	4	0	7	1	.875	0	0--	—	2.30
Memphis	AA	6	6	0	0	33	146	36	17	16	4	2	2	0	14	0	26	3	0	3	3	.500	0	0--	—	4.36
1994 Memphis	AA	17	17	0	0	100	408	75	42	39	6	3	5	3	40	0	78	12	0	5	4	.556	0	0--	—	3.51
1995 Omaha	AAA	6	6	0	0	22	119	40	31	23	7	1	0	3	14	1	10	2	0	1	3	.250	0	0--	—	9.41
1996 Wichita	AA	13	13	2	0	75.2	301	56	22	17	4	1	3	2	26	0	74	6	0	9	2	.818	0	0--	—	2.02
Omaha	AAA	12	12	0	0	67.2	289	62	36	31	10	0	0	5	19	0	73	6	0	7	5	.583	0	0--	—	4.12
1996 Kansas City	AL	3	1	0	1	11	44	9	7	7	2	0	1	0	5	0	7	0	0	1	0	1.000	0	0-0	1	5.73

Dante Bichette

Bats: Right **Throws:** Right **Pos:** RF-138; LF-19; PH-3   **Ht:** 6'3" **Wt:** 235 **Born:** 11/18/63 **Age:** 33

	BATTING																	BASERUNNING				PERCENTAGES		
Year Team	Lg	G	AB	H	2B	3B	HR	(Hm Rd)	TB	R	RBI	TBB	IBB	SO	HBP	SH	SF	SB	CS	SB%	GDP	Avg	OBP	SLG
1988 California	AL	21	46	12	2	0	0	(0 0)	14	1	8	0	0	7	0	0	4	0	0	.00	0	.261	.240	.304
1989 California	AL	48	138	29	7	0	3	(2 1)	45	13	15	6	0	24	0	0	2	3	0	1.00	3	.210	.240	.326
1990 California	AL	109	349	89	15	1	15	(8 7)	151	40	53	16	1	79	3	1	2	5	2	.71	9	.255	.292	.433
1991 Milwaukee	AL	134	445	106	18	3	15	(6 9)	175	53	59	22	4	107	1	1	6	14	8	.64	9	.238	.272	.393
1992 Milwaukee	AL	112	387	111	27	2	5	(3 2)	157	37	41	16	3	74	3	2	3	18	7	.72	13	.287	.318	.406
1993 Colorado	NL	141	538	167	43	5	21	(11 10)	283	93	89	28	2	99	7	0	8	14	8	.64	7	.310	.348	.526
1994 Colorado	NL	116	484	147	33	2	27	(15 12)	265	74	95	19	3	70	4	0	2	21	8	.72	17	.304	.334	.540
1995 Colorado	NL	139	579	197	38	2	40	(31 9)	359	102	128	22	5	96	4	0	7	13	9	.59	16	.340	.364	.620
1996 Colorado	NL	159	633	198	39	3	31	(22 9)	336	114	141	45	4	105	6	0	10	31	12	.72	18	.313	.359	.531
9 ML YEARS		979	3599	1056	222	18	157	(98 59)	1785	527	629	174	22	661	28	4	44	119	54	.69	92	.293	.327	.496

Mike Bielecki

Pitches: Right **Bats:** Right **Pos:** RP-35; SP-5   **Ht:** 6'3" **Wt:** 200 **Born:** 7/31/59 **Age:** 37

	HOW MUCH HE PITCHED							WHAT HE GAVE UP													THE RESULTS						
Year Team	Lg	G	GS	CG	GF	IP	BFP	H	R	ER	HR	SH	SF	HB	TBB	IBB	SO	WP	Bk	W	L	Pct.	ShO	Sv-Op	Hld	ERA
1984 Pittsburgh	NL	4	0	0	1	4.1	17	4	0	0	0	1	0	0	1	0	1	1	0	0	0	.000	0	0--	—	0.00
1985 Pittsburgh	NL	12	7	0	1	45.2	211	45	26	23	5	4	0	1	31	1	22	1	1	2	3	.400	0	0--	—	4.53
1986 Pittsburgh	NL	31	27	0	0	148.2	667	149	87	77	10	7	6	2	83	3	83	7	5	6	11	.353	0	0--	—	4.66
1987 Pittsburgh	NL	8	8	2	0	45.2	192	43	25	24	6	5	1	0	12	0	25	3	0	2	3	.400	0	0-0	0	4.73

Year Team	Lg	G	GS	CG	GF	IP	BFP	H	R	ER	HR	SH	SF	HB	TBB	IBB	SO	WP	Bk	W	L	Pct.	ShO	Sv-Op	Hld	ERA
1988 Chicago	NL	19	5	0	7	48.1	215	55	22	18	4	1	4	0	16	1	33	3	3	2	2	.500	0	0-0	1	3.35
1989 Chicago	NL	33	33	4	0	212.1	882	187	82	74	16	9	3	0	81	8	147	9	4	18	7	.720	3	0-0	0	3.14
1990 Chicago	NL	36	29	0	6	168	749	188	101	92	13	16	4	5	70	11	103	11	0	8	11	.421	0	1-1	0	4.93
1991 ChN-Atl	NL	41	25	0	9	173.2	727	171	91	86	18	10	6	2	56	6	75	6	0	13	11	.542	0	0-1	0	4.46
1992 Atlanta	NL	19	14	1	0	80.2	336	77	27	23	2	3	2	1	27	1	62	4	0	2	4	.333	1	0-0	1	2.57
1993 Cleveland	AL	13	13	0	0	68.2	317	90	47	45	8	0	2	2	23	3	38	1	0	4	5	.444	0	0-0	0	5.90
1994 Atlanta	NL	19	1	0	7	27	115	28	12	12	2	1	0	1	12	1	18	0	1	2	0	1.000	0	0-0	0	4.00
1995 California	AL	22	11	0	2	75.1	334	80	56	50	15	2	5	3	31	1	45	3	0	4	6	.400	0	0-0	0	5.97
1996 Atlanta	NL	40	5	0	8	75.1	317	63	24	22	8	0	3	0	33	6	71	2	0	4	3	.571	0	2-2	3	2.63
1991 Chicago	NL	39	25	0	8	172	718	169	91	86	18	10	6	2	54	6	72	6	0	13	11	.542	0	0-1	0	4.50
Atlanta		2	0	0	1	1.2	9	2	0	0	0	0	0	0	2	0	3	0	0	0	0	.000	0	0-0	0	0.00
13 ML YEARS		297	178	7	41	1173.2	5079	1180	600	546	107	59	37	18	475	42	723	50	15	67	66	.504	4	3--	—	4.19

Craig Biggio

Bats: Right **Throws:** Right **Pos:** 2B-162 **Ht:** 5'11" **Wt:** 180 **Born:** 12/14/65 **Age:** 31

Year Team	Lg	G	AB	H	2B	3B	HR	(Hm	Rd)	TB	R	RBI	TBB	IBB	SO	HBP	SH	SF	SB	CS	SB%	GDP	Avg	OBP	SLG
1988 Houston	NL	50	123	26	6	1	3	(1	2)	43	14	5	7	2	29	0	1	0	6	1	.86	1	.211	.254	.350
1989 Houston	NL	134	443	114	21	2	13	(6	7)	178	64	60	49	8	64	6	6	5	21	3	.88	7	.257	.336	.402
1990 Houston	NL	150	555	153	24	2	4	(2	2)	193	53	42	53	1	79	3	9	1	25	11	.69	11	.276	.342	.348
1991 Houston	NL	149	546	161	23	4	4	(0	4)	204	79	46	53	3	71	2	5	3	19	6	.76	2	.295	.358	.374
1992 Houston	NL	162	613	170	32	3	6	(3	3)	226	96	39	94	9	95	7	5	2	38	15	.72	5	.277	.378	.369
1993 Houston	NL	155	610	175	41	5	21	(8	13)	289	98	64	77	7	93	10	4	5	15	17	.47	10	.287	.373	.474
1994 Houston	NL	114	437	139	44	5	6	(4	2)	211	88	56	62	1	58	8	2	2	39	4	.91	5	.318	.411	.483
1995 Houston	NL	141	553	167	30	2	22	(6	16)	267	123	77	80	1	85	22	11	7	33	8	.80	6	.302	.406	.483
1996 Houston	NL	162	605	174	24	4	15	(7	8)	251	113	75	75	0	72	27	8	8	25	7	.78	10	.288	.386	.415
9 ML YEARS		1217	4485	1279	245	28	94	(37	57)	1862	728	464	550	32	646	85	51	33	221	72	.75	57	.285	.371	.415

Willie Blair

Pitches: Right **Bats:** Right **Pos:** RP-60 **Ht:** 6'1" **Wt:** 185 **Born:** 12/18/65 **Age:** 31

Year Team	Lg	G	GS	CG	GF	IP	BFP	H	R	ER	HR	SH	SF	HB	TBB	IBB	SO	WP	Bk	W	L	Pct.	ShO	Sv-Op	Hld	ERA
1990 Toronto	AL	27	6	0	8	68.2	297	66	33	31	4	0	4	1	28	4	43	3	0	3	5	.375	0	0-0	1	4.06
1991 Cleveland	AL	11	5	0	1	36	168	58	27	27	7	1	2	1	10	0	13	1	0	2	3	.400	0	0-1	0	6.75
1992 Houston	NL	29	8	0	1	78.2	331	74	47	35	5	4	3	2	25	2	48	2	0	5	7	.417	0	0-0	1	4.00
1993 Colorado	NL	46	18	1	5	146	664	184	90	77	20	10	8	3	42	4	84	6	1	6	10	.375	0	0-0	3	4.75
1994 Colorado	NL	47	1	0	13	77.2	365	98	57	50	9	3	1	4	39	3	68	4	0	0	5	.000	0	3-6	2	5.79
1995 San Diego	NL	40	12	0	1	114	485	112	60	55	11	8	2	2	45	3	83	4	0	7	5	.583	0	1-5	3	4.34
1996 San Diego	NL	60	0	0	17	88	377	80	52	45	13	4	3	7	29	5	67	2	0	2	6	.250	0	1-5	3	4.60
7 ML YEARS		260	50	1	56	609	2687	672	366	320	69	30	23	20	218	21	406	22	1	25	41	.379	0	4-12	13	4.73

Jeff Blauser

Bats: Right **Throws:** Right **Pos:** SS-79; PH-4 **Ht:** 6'1" **Wt:** 180 **Born:** 11/8/65 **Age:** 31

Year Team	Lg	G	AB	H	2B	3B	HR	(Hm	Rd)	TB	R	RBI	TBB	IBB	SO	HBP	SH	SF	SB	CS	SB%	GDP	Avg	OBP	SLG
1987 Atlanta	NL	51	165	40	6	3	2	(1	1)	58	11	15	18	1	34	3	1	0	7	3	.70	4	.242	.328	.352
1988 Atlanta	NL	18	67	16	3	1	2	(2	0)	27	7	7	2	0	11	1	3	0	0	1	.00	1	.239	.268	.403
1989 Atlanta	NL	142	456	123	24	2	12	(5	7)	187	63	46	38	2	101	1	8	4	5	2	.71	7	.270	.325	.410
1990 Atlanta	NL	115	386	104	24	3	8	(3	5)	158	46	39	35	1	70	5	3	0	3	5	.38	4	.269	.338	.409
1991 Atlanta	NL	129	352	91	14	3	11	(7	4)	144	49	54	54	4	59	2	4	3	5	6	.45	4	.259	.358	.409
1992 Atlanta	NL	123	343	90	19	3	14	(5	9)	157	61	46	46	2	82	4	7	3	5	5	.50	2	.262	.354	.458
1993 Atlanta	NL	161	597	182	29	2	15	(4	11)	260	110	73	85	0	109	16	5	7	16	6	.73	13	.305	.401	.436
1994 Atlanta	NL	96	380	98	21	4	6	(3	3)	145	56	45	38	0	64	5	5	6	1	3	.25	11	.258	.329	.382
1995 Atlanta	NL	115	431	91	16	2	12	(7	5)	147	60	31	57	2	107	12	2	2	8	5	.62	6	.211	.319	.341
1996 Atlanta	NL	83	265	65	14	1	10	(4	6)	111	48	35	40	3	54	6	0	1	6	0	1.00	7	.245	.356	.419
10 ML YEARS		1033	3442	900	170	24	92	(41	51)	1394	511	391	413	15	691	55	38	27	56	36	.61	59	.261	.347	.405

Ron Blazier

Pitches: Right **Bats:** Right **Pos:** RP-27 **Ht:** 6'5" **Wt:** 205 **Born:** 7/30/71 **Age:** 25

Year Team	Lg	G	GS	CG	GF	IP	BFP	H	R	ER	HR	SH	SF	HB	TBB	IBB	SO	WP	Bk	W	L	Pct.	ShO	Sv-Op	Hld	ERA
1990 Princeton	R+	14	13	1	1	78.2	331	79	46	39	10	1	3	1	29	1	45	3	1	3	5	.375	0	0--	—	4.46
1991 Batavia	A-	24	8	0	8	72.1	312	81	40	37	11	2	1	9	17	3	77	2	1	7	5	.583	0	2--	—	4.60
1992 Spartanburg	A	30	21	2	6	159.2	640	141	55	47	10	2	5	5	32	0	149	4	0	14	7	.667	0	0--	—	2.65
1993 Clearwater	A+	27	23	1	1	155.1	663	171	80	68	8	4	4	6	40	5	86	1	1	9	8	.529	0	0--	—	3.94
1994 Clearwater	A+	29	29	0	0	173.1	715	177	73	65	15	4	6	9	36	1	122	0	2	13	5	.722	0	0--	—	3.38
1995 Reading	AA	56	3	0	17	106.2	431	93	44	39	11	5	2	0	31	7	102	2	1	4	5	.444	0	1--	—	3.29
1996 Scranton-WB	AAA	33	0	0	23	42	168	33	15	12	1	1	2	1	9	2	38	1	0	4	0	1.000	0	12--	—	2.57
1996 Philadelphia	NL	27	0	0	9	38.1	173	49	30	25	2	4	1	0	10	3	25	3	0	3	1	.750	0	0-0	—	5.87

Mike Blowers

Bats: R **Throws:** R **Pos:** 3B-90; 1B-6; SS-1; PH-1   **Ht:** 6'2"   **Wt:** 210   **Born:** 4/24/65   **Age:** 32

								BATTING													BASERUNNING				PERCENTAGES		
Year Team	Lg	G	AB	H	2B	3B	HR	(Hm	Rd)	TB	R	RBI	TBB	IBB	SO	HBP	SH	SF	SB	CS	SB%	GDP	Avg	OBP	SLG
1989 New York	AL	13	38	10	0	0	0	(0	0)	10	2	3	3	0	13	0	0	0	0	0	.00	1	.263	.317	.263
1990 New York	AL	48	144	27	4	0	5	(1	4)	46	16	21	12	1	50	1	0	0	1	0	1.00	3	.188	.255	.319
1991 New York	AL	15	35	7	0	0	1	(0	1)	10	3	1	4	0	13	0	0	0	0	0	.00	1	.200	.282	.286
1992 Seattle	AL	31	73	14	3	0	1	(0	1)	20	7	2	6	0	20	0	1	0	0	0	.00	3	.192	.253	.274
1993 Seattle	AL	127	379	106	23	3	15	(8	7)	180	55	57	44	3	98	2	3	1	1	5	.17	12	.280	.357	.475
1994 Seattle	AL	85	270	78	13	0	9	(3	6)	118	37	49	25	2	60	1	1	3	2	2	.50	12	.289	.348	.437
1995 Seattle	AL	134	439	113	24	1	23	(17	6)	208	59	96	53	0	128	1	0	3	2	1	.67	18	.257	.335	.474
1996 Los Angeles	NL	92	317	84	19	2	6	(4	2)	125	31	38	37	2	77	1	0	3	0	0	.00	11	.265	.341	.394
8 ML YEARS		545	1695	439	86	6	60	(33	27)	717	210	267	184	8	449	5	5	10	6	8	.43	61	.259	.332	.423

Jaime Bluma

Pitches: Right   **Bats:** Right   **Pos:** RP-17   **Ht:** 5'11"   **Wt:** 195   **Born:** 5/18/72   **Age:** 25

		HOW MUCH HE PITCHED						WHAT HE GAVE UP												THE RESULTS						
Year Team	Lg	G	GS	CG	GF	IP	BFP	H	R	ER	HR	SH	SF	HB	TBB	IBB	SO	WP	Bk	W	L	Pct.	ShO	Sv-Op	Hld	ERA
1994 Eugene	A-	26	0	0	23	36.1	133	19	5	4	0	1	1	0	6	0	35	0	0	2	1	.667	0	12--	—	0.99
Wilmington	A+	7	0	0	7	9.2	34	7	2	1	0	0	0	0	0	0	5	0	0	4	0	1.000	0	2--	—	0.93
1995 Omaha	AAA	18	0	0	10	23.2	101	21	13	8	1	3	3	0	14	4	12	3	0	0	0	.000	0	4--	—	3.04
1996 Omaha	AAA	52	0	0	47	57.2	251	57	22	20	7	0	2	1	20	3	40	5	2	1	2	.333	0	25--	—	3.12
1996 Kansas City	AL	17	0	0	10	20	82	18	9	8	2	2	1	2	4	1	14	1	0	0	0	.000	0	5-5	2	3.60

Doug Bochtler

Pitches: Right   **Bats:** Right   **Pos:** RP-63   **Ht:** 6'3"   **Wt:** 200   **Born:** 7/5/70   **Age:** 26

		HOW MUCH HE PITCHED						WHAT HE GAVE UP												THE RESULTS						
Year Team	Lg	G	GS	CG	GF	IP	BFP	H	R	ER	HR	SH	SF	HB	TBB	IBB	SO	WP	Bk	W	L	Pct.	ShO	Sv-Op	Hld	ERA
1989 Expos	R	9	9	1	0	47.2	209	46	22	17	0	2	2	0	20	1	45	3	1	2	2	.500	0	0--	—	3.21
1990 Rockford	A	25	25	1	0	139	602	142	82	54	3	4	6	8	54	2	109	6	5	9	12	.429	1	0--	—	3.50
1991 W. Palm Bch	A+	26	24	7	1	160.1	647	148	63	52	6	6	2	6	54	2	109	7	0	12	9	.571	2	0--	—	2.92
1992 Harrisburg	AA	13	13	2	0	77.2	310	50	25	20	1	2	2	0	36	1	89	4	0	6	5	.545	1	0--	—	2.32
1993 Central Val	A+	8	8	0	0	47.2	205	40	23	18	2	1	0	1	28	0	43	2	0	3	1	.750	0	0--	—	3.40
Colo. Sprng	AAA	12	11	0	0	50.2	239	71	41	39	3	2	2	1	26	1	38	2	0	1	4	.200	0	0--	—	6.93
Las Vegas	AAA	7	7	1	0	39.2	177	52	26	23	2	1	1	0	11	1	30	1	0	0	5	.000	0	0--	—	5.22
1994 Las Vegas	AAA	22	20	2	1	100.1	458	116	67	58	11	5	3	3	48	2	86	10	0	3	7	.300	0	0--	—	5.20
1995 Las Vegas	AAA	18	2	0	7	36	161	31	18	17	5	1	2	1	26	6	32	2	0	2	3	.400	0	1--	—	4.25
1995 San Diego	NL	34	0	0	11	45.1	181	38	18	18	5	2	1	0	19	0	45	1	0	4	4	.500	0	0--	—	3.57
1996 San Diego	NL	63	0	0	17	65.2	278	45	25	22	6	5	2	1	39	8	68	8	2	2	4	.333	0	3-7	20	3.02
2 ML YEARS		97	0	0	28	111	459	83	43	40	11	7	3	1	58	8	113	9	2	6	8	.429	0	4-11	28	3.24

Brian Boehringer

Pitches: Right   **Bats:** Both   **Pos:** RP-12; SP-3   **Ht:** 6'2"   **Wt:** 190   **Born:** 1/8/70   **Age:** 27

		HOW MUCH HE PITCHED						WHAT HE GAVE UP												THE RESULTS						
Year Team	Lg	G	GS	CG	GF	IP	BFP	H	R	ER	HR	SH	SF	HB	TBB	IBB	SO	WP	Bk	W	L	Pct.	ShO	Sv-Op	Hld	ERA
1991 White Sox	R	5	1	0	2	12.1	54	14	9	9	1	0	1	0	5	0	10	3	1	1	1	.500	0	0--	—	6.57
Utica	A-	4	4	0	0	19	78	14	8	5	0	0	0	2	8	0	19	0	2	1	1	.500	0	0--	—	2.37
1992 White Sox	R	2	2	0	0	12	47	9	3	2	0	0	1	0	2	0	8	0	0	1	1	.500	0	0--	—	1.50
South Bend	A	15	15	2	0	86.1	381	87	52	42	5	3	3	6	40	0	59	6	4	6	7	.462	0	0--	—	4.38
1993 Sarasota	A+	18	17	3	0	119	495	103	47	37	2	3	6	1	51	2	92	2	2	10	4	.714	0	0--	—	2.80
Birmingham	AA	7	7	1	0	40.2	173	41	20	16	3	1	1	2	14	0	29	1	1	2	1	.667	0	0--	—	3.54
1994 Albany-Colo	AA	27	27	5	0	171.2	722	165	85	69	10	7	10	4	57	1	145	7	5	10	11	.476	1	0--	—	3.62
1995 Columbus	AAA	17	17	3	0	104	439	101	39	32	6	3	3	4	31	1	58	9	0	8	6	.571	0	0--	—	2.77
1996 Columbus	AAA	25	25	3	0	153	664	155	79	68	13	2	5	11	56	1	132	4	1	11	7	.611	1	0--	—	4.00
1995 New York	AL	7	3	0	0	17.2	99	24	27	27	5	0	1	0	22	1	10	3	0	0	3	.000	0	0-1	0	13.75
1996 New York	AL	15	3	0	1	46.1	205	46	28	28	6	3	3	1	21	2	37	1	0	2	4	.333	0	0-1	4	5.44
2 ML YEARS		22	6	0	1	64	304	70	55	55	11	3	4	2	43	3	47	4	0	2	7	.222	0	0-2	4	7.73

Joe Boever

Pitches: Right   **Bats:** Right   **Pos:** RP-13   **Ht:** 6'1"   **Wt:** 205   **Born:** 10/4/60   **Age:** 36

		HOW MUCH HE PITCHED						WHAT HE GAVE UP												THE RESULTS						
Year Team	Lg	G	GS	CG	GF	IP	BFP	H	R	ER	HR	SH	SF	HB	TBB	IBB	SO	WP	Bk	W	L	Pct.	ShO	Sv-Op	Hld	ERA
1996 Carolina *	AA	1	0	0	1	1	3	0	0	0	0	0	0	0	0	0	1	0	0	0	0	.000	0	0--	—	0.00
Calgary *	AAA	44	0	0	12	83.2	341	78	24	20	1	5	0	0	19	2	66	2	0	12	1	.923	0	4--	—	2.15
1985 St. Louis	NL	13	0	0	5	16.1	69	17	8	8	3	1	1	0	4	1	20	1	0	0	0	.000	0	0--	—	4.41
1986 St. Louis	NL	11	0	0	4	21.2	93	19	5	4	2	0	0	0	11	0	8	1	0	0	1	.000	0	0--	—	1.66
1987 Atlanta	NL	14	0	0	10	18.1	93	29	15	15	4	1	1	0	12	1	18	1	0	1	0	1.000	0	0-0	0	7.36
1988 Atlanta	NL	16	0	0	13	20.1	70	12	4	4	1	2	0	1	7	0	7	0	0	0	2	.000	0	1-1	0	1.77
1989 Atlanta	NL	66	0	0	53	82.1	349	78	37	36	6	5	0	1	34	5	68	5	0	4	11	.267	0	21-30	3	3.94
1990 Atl-Phi	NL	67	0	0	34	88.1	388	77	35	33	6	3	3	2	51	12	75	3	2	3	6	.333	0	14-19	5	3.36

Year Team	Lg	G	GS	CG	GF	IP	BFP	H	R	ER	HR	SH	SF	HB	TBB	IBB	SO	WP	Bk	W	L	Pct.	ShO	Sv-Op	Hld	ERA
		HOW MUCH HE PITCHED						**WHAT HE GAVE UP**												**THE RESULTS**						
1991 Philadelphia	NL	68	0	0	27	98.1	431	90	45	42	10	3	6	0	54	11	89	6	1	3	5	.375	0	0-2	6	3.84
1992 Houston	NL	**81**	0	0	26	111.1	479	103	38	31	3	10	4	4	45	9	67	4	0	3	6	.333	0	2-6	7	2.51
1993 Oak-Det	AL	61	0	0	22	102.1	449	101	50	41	9	5	7	4	44	7	63	1	0	6	3	.667	0	3-5	9	3.61
1994 Detroit	AL	46	0	0	27	81.1	349	80	40	36	12	4	2	2	37	12	49	4	0	9	2	.818	0	3-6	2	3.98
1995 Detroit	AL	60	0	0	27	98.2	463	128	74	70	17	7	8	3	44	12	71	1	1	5	7	.417	0	3-6	4	6.39
1996 Pittsburgh	NL	13	0	0	9	15	68	17	11	9	2	2	0	1	6	0	6	3	0	0	2	.000	0	2-3	1	5.40
1990 Atlanta	NL	33	0	0	21	42.1	198	40	23	22	6	2	2	0	35	10	35	2	0	1	3	.250	0	8-12	2	4.68
Philadelphia		34	0	0	13	46	190	37	12	11	0	2	2	0	16	2	40	1	2	2	3	.400	0	6-7	3	2.15
1993 Oakland	AL	42	0	0	19	79.1	353	87	40	34	8	2	3	4	33	4	49	1	0	4	2	.667	0	0-1	4	3.86
Detroit	AL	19	0	0	3	23	96	14	10	7	1	3	4	0	11	3	14	0	0	2	1	.667	0	3-4	5	2.74
12 ML YEARS		516	0	0	257	754.1	3301	751	362	329	75	44	31	16	343	70	541	30	4	34	45	.430	0	49--		3.93

Tim Bogar

Bats: R **Throws:** R **Pos:** PH-33; 1B-32; 3B-25; SS-19; 2B-8   **Ht:** 6'2" **Wt:** 198 **Born:** 10/28/66   **Age:** 30

Year Team	Lg	G	AB	H	2B	3B	HR	(Hm	Rd)	TB	R	RBI	TBB	IBB	SO	HBP	SH	SF	SB	CS	SB%	GDP	Avg	OBP	SLG
					BATTING														**BASERUNNING**				**PERCENTAGES**		
1993 New York	NL	78	205	50	13	0	3	(1	2)	72	19	25	14	2	29	3	1	1	0	1	.00	2	.244	.300	.351
1994 New York	NL	50	52	8	0	0	2	(0	2)	14	5	5	4	1	11	0	2	1	0	1	1.00	1	.154	.211	.269
1995 New York	NL	78	145	42	7	0	1	(0	1)	52	17	21	9	0	25	0	2	1	1	0	1.00	2	.290	.329	.359
1996 New York	NL	91	89	19	4	0	0	(0	0)	23	17	6	8	0	20	2	3	2	1	3	.25	0	.213	.287	.258
4 ML YEARS		297	491	119	24	0	6	(1	5)	161	58	57	35	3	85	5	8	5	3	4	.43	5	.242	.297	.328

Wade Boggs

Bats: Left   **Throws:** Right   **Pos:** 3B-123; PH-7; DH-4   **Ht:** 6'2" **Wt:** 197 **Born:** 6/15/58   **Age:** 39

Year Team	Lg	G	AB	H	2B	3B	HR	(Hm	Rd)	TB	R	RBI	TBB	IBB	SO	HBP	SH	SF	SB	CS	SB%	GDP	Avg	OBP	SLG
					BATTING														**BASERUNNING**				**PERCENTAGES**		
1982 Boston	AL	104	338	118	14	1	5	(4	1)	149	51	44	35	4	21	0	4	4	1	0	1.00	9	.349	.406	.441
1983 Boston	AL	153	582	210	44	7	5	(2	3)	283	100	74	92	2	36	1	3	7	3	5	.60	15	**.361**	**.444**	.486
1984 Boston	AL	158	625	203	31	4	6	(5	1)	260	109	55	89	6	44	0	8	4	3	2	.60	13	.325	.407	.416
1985 Boston	AL	161	653	**240**	42	3	8	(6	2)	312	107	78	96	5	61	4	3	2	2	1	.67	20	**.368**	**.450**	.478
1986 Boston	AL	149	580	207	47	2	8	(3	5)	282	107	71	**105**	14	44	0	4	4	0	0	.00	11	**.357**	**.453**	.486
1987 Boston	AL	147	551	200	40	6	24	(10	14)	324	108	89	105	**19**	48	2	1	8	1	3	.25	10	**.363**	**.461**	.588
1988 Boston	AL	155	584	214	**45**	6	5	(4	1)	286	**128**	58	**125**	**18**	34	3	0	7	2	3	.40	23	**.366**	**.476**	.490
1989 Boston	AL	156	621	205	**51**	7	3	(4	3)	279	**113**	54	107	**19**	51	7	0	7	2	6	.25	19	.330	**.430**	.449
1990 Boston	AL	155	619	187	44	5	6	(3	3)	259	89	63	87	**19**	68	1	0	6	0	5	.00	13	.302	.386	.418
1991 Boston	AL	144	546	181	42	2	8	(6	2)	251	93	51	89	**25**	32	0	0	6	1	2	.33	16	.332	.421	.460
1992 Boston	AL	143	514	133	22	4	7	(4	3)	184	62	50	74	**19**	31	4	0	6	1	3	.25	13	.259	.353	.358
1993 New York	AL	143	560	169	26	1	2	(1	1)	203	83	59	74	4	49	0	1	9	0	1	.00	10	.302	.378	.363
1994 New York	AL	97	366	125	19	1	11	(6	5)	179	61	55	61	3	29	1	2	4	2	1	.67	10	.342	.433	.489
1995 New York	AL	126	460	149	22	4	5	(4	1)	194	76	63	74	5	50	0	0	7	1	1	.50	13	.324	.412	.422
1996 New York	AL	132	501	156	29	2	2	(2	0)	195	80	41	67	7	32	0	1	5	1	2	.33	10	.311	.389	.389
15 ML YEARS		2123	8100	2697	518	55	105	(62	43)	3640	1367	905	1280	169	630	23	27	86	20	32	.38	206	.333	.422	.449

Brian Bohanon

Pitches: Left   **Bats:** Left   **Pos:** RP-20   **Ht:** 6'3" **Wt:** 220 **Born:** 8/1/68   **Age:** 28

Year Team	Lg	G	GS	CG	GF	IP	BFP	H	R	ER	HR	SH	SF	HB	TBB	IBB	SO	WP	Bk	W	L	Pct.	ShO	Sv-Op	Hld	ERA
		HOW MUCH HE PITCHED						**WHAT HE GAVE UP**												**THE RESULTS**						
1996 Syracuse *	AAA	31	0	0	10	58.1	245	56	29	25	4	2	2	6	17	2	38	2	0	4	3	.571	0	0--		3.86
1990 Texas	AL	11	6	0	1	34	158	40	30	25	6	0	3	2	18	0	15	1	0	0	3	.000	0	0-0	0	6.62
1991 Texas	AL	11	11	1	0	61.1	273	66	35	33	4	2	5	2	23	0	34	3	1	4	3	.571	0	0-0	0	4.84
1992 Texas	AL	18	7	0	3	45.2	220	57	38	32	7	0	2	1	25	0	29	2	0	1	1	.500	0	0-0	0	6.31
1993 Texas	AL	36	8	0	1	92.2	418	107	54	49	8	2	5	4	46	3	45	10	0	4	4	.500	0	0-1	1	4.76
1994 Texas	AL	11	5	0	1	37.1	169	51	31	30	7	1	0	1	8	1	26	5	0	2	2	.500	0	0-0	0	7.23
1995 Detroit	AL	52	10	0	7	105.2	474	121	68	65	10	0	5	4	41	5	63	3	0	1	1	.500	0	1-1	10	5.54
1996 Toronto	AL	20	0	0	6	22	112	27	19	19	4	0	2	2	19	4	17	2	0	0	1	.000	0	1-1	2	7.77
7 ML YEARS		159	47	1	22	398.2	1824	469	275	253	46	5	22	16	180	13	229	26	1	12	15	.444	0	2-3	13	5.71

Barry Bonds

Bats: Left   **Throws:** Left   **Pos:** LF-149; PH-7; CF-6   **Ht:** 6'1" **Wt:** 190 **Born:** 7/24/64   **Age:** 32

Year Team	Lg	G	AB	H	2B	3B	HR	(Hm	Rd)	TB	R	RBI	TBB	IBB	SO	HBP	SH	SF	SB	CS	SB%	GDP	Avg	OBP	SLG
					BATTING														**BASERUNNING**				**PERCENTAGES**		
1986 Pittsburgh	NL	113	413	92	26	3	16	(9	7)	172	72	48	65	2	102	2	2	2	36	7	.84	4	.223	.330	.416
1987 Pittsburgh	NL	150	551	144	34	9	25	(12	13)	271	99	59	54	3	88	3	0	3	32	10	.76	4	.261	.329	.492
1988 Pittsburgh	NL	144	538	152	30	5	24	(14	10)	264	97	58	72	14	82	2	0	6	17	11	.61	3	.283	.368	.491
1989 Pittsburgh	NL	159	580	144	34	6	19	(7	12)	247	96	58	93	22	93	1	1	4	32	10	.76	9	.248	.351	.426
1990 Pittsburgh	NL	151	519	156	32	3	33	(14	19)	293	104	114	93	15	83	3	0	6	52	13	.80	5	.301	.406	**.565**
1991 Pittsburgh	NL	153	510	149	28	5	25	(12	13)	262	95	116	107	25	73	4	0	13	43	13	.77	8	.292	**.410**	.514
1992 Pittsburgh	NL	140	473	147	36	5	34	(15	19)	295	**109**	103	**127**	**32**	69	5	0	7	39	8	.83	9	.311	**.456**	**.624**
1993 San Francisco	NL	159	539	181	38	4	**46**	(21	**25**)	365	**129**	**123**	126	**43**	79	2	0	7	29	12	.71	11	.336	**.458**	**.677**
1994 San Francisco	NL	112	391	122	18	1	37	(15	22)	253	89	81	**74**	18	43	6	0	3	29	9	.76	3	.312	.426	.647

BATTING

Year Team	Lg	G	AB	H	2B	3B	HR	Hm	Rd	TB	R	RBI	TBB	IBB	SO	HBP	SH	SF	SB	CS	SB%	GDP	Avg	OBP	SLG
1995 San Francisco	NL	144	506	149	30	7	33	(16	17)	292	109	104	120	22	83	5	0	4	31	10	.76	12	.294	.431	.577
1996 San Francisco	NL	158	517	159	27	3	42	(23	19)	318	122	129	151	30	76	1	0	6	40	7	.85	11	.308	.461	.615
11 ML YEARS		1583	5537	1595	333	51	334	(158	176)	3032	1121	993	1082	226	871	34	3	57	380	110	.78	82	.288	.404	.548

Ricky Bones

Pitches: Right **Bats:** Right **Pos:** SP-24; RP-12   **Ht:** 6'0" **Wt:** 193 **Born:** 4/7/69 **Age:** 28

| | | HOW MUCH HE PITCHED | | | | | | WHAT HE GAVE UP | | | | | | | | | | | | THE RESULTS | | | | | | |
Year Team	Lg	G	GS	CG	GF	IP	BFP	H	R	ER	HR	SH	SF	HB	TBB	IBB	SO	WP	Bk	W	L	Pct.	ShO	Sv-Op	Hld	ERA
1991 San Diego	NL	11	11	0	0	54	234	57	33	29	3	0	4	0	18	0	31	4	0	4	6	.400	0	0-0	0	4.83
1992 Milwaukee	AL	31	28	0	0	163.1	705	169	90	83	27	2	5	9	48	0	65	3	2	9	10	.474	0	0-0	0	4.57
1993 Milwaukee	AL	32	31	3	1	203.2	883	222	122	110	28	5	7	8	63	3	63	6	1	11	11	.500	0	0-0	0	4.86
1994 Milwaukee	AL	24	24	4	0	170.2	708	166	76	65	17	4	5	3	45	1	57	8	0	10	9	.526	1	0-0	0	3.43
1995 Milwaukee	AL	32	31	3	0	200.1	877	218	108	103	26	3	11	4	83	2	77	5	2	10	12	.455	0	0-0	0	4.63
1996 Mil-NYA	AL	36	24	0	2	152	699	184	115	105	30	5	5	10	68	2	63	2	0	7	14	.333	0	0-0	0	6.22
1996 Milwaukee	AL	32	23	0	2	145	658	170	104	94	28	4	4	9	62	2	59	2	0	7	14	.333	0	0-0	3	5.83
New York	AL	4	1	0	0	7	41	14	11	11	2	1	1	1	6	0	4	0	0	0	0	.000	0	0-0	0	14.14
6 ML YEARS		166	149	10	3	944	4106	1016	544	495	131	19	37	34	325	8	356	28	5	51	62	.451	1	0-0	3	4.72

Bobby Bonilla

Bats: B **Throws:** R **Pos:** RF-108; DH-44; 1B-9; 3B-4; PH-1   **Ht:** 6'4" **Wt:** 240 **Born:** 2/23/63 **Age:** 34

BATTING

Year Team	Lg	G	AB	H	2B	3B	HR	Hm	Rd	TB	R	RBI	TBB	IBB	SO	HBP	SH	SF	SB	CS	SB%	GDP	Avg	OBP	SLG
1986 ChA-Pit		138	426	109	16	4	3	(2	1)	142	55	43	62	3	88	2	5	1	8	5	.62	9	.256	.352	.333
1987 Pittsburgh	NL	141	466	140	33	3	15	(7	8)	224	58	77	39	4	64	2	0	8	3	5	.38	8	.300	.351	.481
1988 Pittsburgh	NL	159	584	160	32	7	24	(9	15)	278	87	100	85	19	82	4	0	8	3	5	.38	4	.274	.366	.476
1989 Pittsburgh	NL	163	616	173	37	10	24	(13	11)	302	96	86	76	20	93	1	0	5	8	8	.50	10	.281	.358	.490
1990 Pittsburgh	NL	160	625	175	39	7	32	(13	19)	324	112	120	45	9	103	1	0	15	4	3	.57	11	.280	.322	.518
1991 Pittsburgh	NL	157	577	174	44	6	18	(9	9)	284	102	100	90	8	67	2	0	11	2	4	.33	14	.302	.391	.492
1992 New York	NL	128	438	109	23	0	19	(5	14)	189	62	70	66	10	73	1	0	1	4	3	.57	11	.249	.348	.432
1993 New York	NL	139	502	133	21	3	34	(18	16)	262	81	87	72	11	96	0	0	3	3	3	.50	12	.265	.352	.522
1994 New York	NL	108	403	117	24	1	20	(8	12)	203	60	67	55	9	101	0	0	2	1	3	.25	10	.290	.374	.504
1995 NYN-Bal		141	554	182	37	8	28	(14	14)	319	96	99	54	10	79	2	0	4	0	5	.00	22	.329	.388	.576
1996 Baltimore	AL	159	595	171	27	5	28	(9	19)	292	107	116	75	7	85	5	0	17	1	3	.25	13	.287	.363	.491
1986 Chicago	AL	75	234	63	10	2	2	(2	0)	83	27	26	33	2	49	1	2	1	4	1	.80	4	.269	.361	.355
Pittsburgh	NL	63	192	46	6	2	1	(0	1)	59	28	17	29	1	39	1	3	0	4	4	.50	5	.240	.342	.307
1995 New York	NL	80	317	103	25	4	18	(7	11)	190	49	53	31	10	48	1	0	2	0	3	.00	11	.325	.385	.599
Baltimore	AL	61	237	79	12	4	10	(7	3)	129	47	46	23	0	31	1	0	2	0	2	.00	11	.333	.392	.544
11 ML YEARS		1593	5786	1643	333	54	245	(107	138)	2819	916	965	719	110	931	20	5	80	37	47	.44	124	.284	.361	.487

Bret Boone

Bats: Right **Throws:** Right **Pos:** 2B-141; PH-1   **Ht:** 5'10" **Wt:** 180 **Born:** 4/6/69 **Age:** 28

BATTING

Year Team	Lg	G	AB	H	2B	3B	HR	Hm	Rd	TB	R	RBI	TBB	IBB	SO	HBP	SH	SF	SB	CS	SB%	GDP	Avg	OBP	SLG
1992 Seattle	AL	33	129	25	4	0	4	(2	2)	41	15	15	4	0	34	1	1	0	1	1	.50	4	.194	.224	.318
1993 Seattle	AL	76	271	68	12	2	12	(7	5)	120	31	38	17	1	52	4	6	4	2	3	.40	6	.251	.301	.443
1994 Cincinnati	NL	108	381	122	25	2	12	(5	7)	187	59	68	24	1	74	8	5	6	3	4	.43	10	.320	.368	.491
1995 Cincinnati	NL	138	513	137	34	2	15	(6	9)	220	63	68	41	0	84	6	5	5	5	1	.83	14	.267	.326	.429
1996 Cincinnati	NL	142	520	121	21	3	12	(7	5)	184	56	69	31	0	100	3	5	9	3	2	.60	9	.233	.275	.354
5 ML YEARS		497	1814	473	96	9	55	(27	28)	752	224	258	117	2	344	22	22	24	14	11	.56	43	.261	.310	.415

Josh Booty

Bats: Right **Throws:** Right **Pos:** PH-2; 3B-1   **Ht:** 6'3" **Wt:** 210 **Born:** 4/29/75 **Age:** 22

BATTING

Year Team	Lg	G	AB	H	2B	3B	HR	Hm	Rd	TB	R	RBI	TBB	IBB	SO	HBP	SH	SF	SB	CS	SB%	GDP	Avg	OBP	SLG
1994 Marlins	R	10	36	8	0	0	1	—	—	11	5	2	5	0	8	0	1	0	1	1	1.00	2	.222	.317	.306
Elmira	A-	4	16	4	1	0	0	—	—	5	1	1	0	0	4	0	0	0	0	0	.00	0	.250	.250	.313
1995 Kane County	A	31	109	11	2	0	1	—	—	16	6	6	11	0	45	0	0	1	1	0	1.00	1	.101	.182	.147
Elmira	A-	74	287	63	18	1	6	—	—	101	33	37	19	0	85	5	0	2	4	4	.50	12	.220	.278	.352
1996 Kane County	A	128	475	98	25	1	21	—	—	188	62	87	46	0	195	1	1	6	2	3	.40	11	.206	.275	.396
1996 Florida	NL	2	2	1	0	0	0	(0	0)	1	1	0	0	0	2	0	0	0	0	0	.00	0	.500	.500	.500

Pedro Borbon

Pitches: Left **Bats:** Left **Pos:** RP-43   **Ht:** 6'1" **Wt:** 205 **Born:** 11/15/67 **Age:** 29

| | | HOW MUCH HE PITCHED | | | | | | WHAT HE GAVE UP | | | | | | | | | | | | THE RESULTS | | | | | | |
Year Team	Lg	G	GS	CG	GF	IP	BFP	H	R	ER	HR	SH	SF	HB	TBB	IBB	SO	WP	Bk	W	L	Pct.	ShO	Sv-Op	Hld	ERA
1996 Greenville *	AA	1	0	0	1	1	3	0	0	0	0	0	0	0	0	0	0	0	0	0	0	.000	0	0--	—	0.00
1992 Atlanta	NL	2	0	0	0	1.1	7	2	1	1	0	0	0	0	1	1	1	0	0	0	1	.000	0	0-0	0	6.75

Year Team	Lg	G	GS	CG	GF	IP	BFP	H	R	ER	HR	SH	SF	HB	TBB	IBB	SO	WP	Bk	W	L	Pct.	ShO	Sv-Op	Hld	ERA
		HOW MUCH HE PITCHED						**WHAT HE GAVE UP**												**THE RESULTS**						
1993 Atlanta	NL	3	0	0	0	1.2	11	3	4	4	0	1	0	0	3	0	2	0	0	0	0	.000	0	0-0	0	21.60
1995 Atlanta	NL	41	0	0	19	32	143	29	12	11	2	3	1	1	17	4	33	0	1	2	2	.500	0	2-4	6	3.09
1996 Atlanta	NL	43	0	0	19	36	140	26	12	11	1	4	0	1	7	0	31	0	0	3	0	1.000	0	1-1	4	2.75
4 ML YEARS		89	0	0	40	71	301	60	29	27	3	8	1	2	28	5	67	0	1	5	3	.625	0	3-5	10	3.42

Pat Borders

Bats: Right **Throws:** Right **Pos:** C-66; PH-9; DH-1; 1B-1   **Ht:** 6'2" **Wt:** 195 **Born:** 5/14/63 **Age:** 34

Year Team	Lg	G	AB	H	2B	3B	HR	(Hm	Rd)	TB	R	RBI	TBB	IBB	SO	HBP	SH	SF	SB	CS	SB%	GDP	Avg	OBP	SLG
		BATTING																	**BASERUNNING**				**PERCENTAGES**		
1988 Toronto	AL	56	154	42	6	3	5	(2	3)	69	15	21	3	0	24	0	2	1	0	0	.00	5	.273	.285	.448
1989 Toronto	AL	94	241	62	11	1	3	(1	2)	84	22	29	11	2	45	1	1	2	2	1	.67	7	.257	.290	.349
1990 Toronto	AL	125	346	99	24	2	15	(10	5)	172	36	49	18	2	57	0	1	3	0	1	.00	17	.286	.319	.497
1991 Toronto	AL	105	291	71	17	0	5	(2	3)	103	22	36	11	1	45	1	6	3	0	0	.00	8	.244	.271	.354
1992 Toronto	AL	138	480	116	26	2	13	(7	6)	185	47	53	33	3	75	2	1	5	1	1	.50	11	.242	.290	.385
1993 Toronto	AL	138	488	124	30	0	9	(6	3)	181	38	55	20	2	66	2	7	3	2	2	.50	18	.254	.285	.371
1994 Toronto	AL	85	295	73	13	1	3	(3	0)	97	24	26	15	0	50	0	1	0	1	1	.50	7	.247	.284	.329
1995 KC-Hou		63	178	37	8	1	4	(1	3)	59	15	13	9	2	29	0	0	0	0	0	.00	1	.208	.246	.331
1996 StL-Cal-ChA		76	220	61	7	0	5	(3	2)	83	15	18	9	0	43	0	0	2	0	0	.00	4	.277	.306	.377
1995 Kansas City	AL	52	143	33	8	1	4	(1	3)	55	14	13	7	1	22	0	0	0	0	0	.00	1	.231	.267	.385
Houston	NL	11	35	4	0	0	0	(0	0)	4	1	0	2	1	7	0	0	0	0	0	.00	0	.114	.162	.114
1996 St. Louis	NL	26	69	22	3	0	0	(0	0)	25	3	4	1	0	14	0	0	1	0	0	.00	1	.319	.329	.362
California	AL	19	57	13	3	0	2	(2	0)	22	6	8	3	0	11	0	0	1	0	0	.00	0	.228	.267	.386
Chicago	AL	31	94	26	1	0	3	(1	2)	36	6	6	5	0	18	0	0	0	0	0	.00	3	.277	.313	.383
9 ML YEARS		880	2693	685	142	10	62	(35	27)	1033	234	300	129	12	434	6	24	17	6	8	.43	80	.254	.288	.384

Mike Bordick

Bats: Right **Throws:** Right **Pos:** SS-155; PH-1   **Ht:** 5'11" **Wt:** 175 **Born:** 7/21/65 **Age:** 31

Year Team	Lg	G	AB	H	2B	3B	HR	(Hm	Rd)	TB	R	RBI	TBB	IBB	SO	HBP	SH	SF	SB	CS	SB%	GDP	Avg	OBP	SLG
		BATTING																	**BASERUNNING**				**PERCENTAGES**		
1990 Oakland	AL	25	14	1	0	0	0	(0	0)	1	0	0	1	0	4	0	0	0	0	0	.00	0	.071	.133	.071
1991 Oakland	AL	90	235	56	5	1	0	(0	0)	63	21	21	14	0	37	3	12	1	3	4	.43	3	.238	.289	.268
1992 Oakland	AL	154	504	151	19	4	3	(3	0)	187	62	48	40	2	59	9	14	5	12	6	.67	10	.300	.358	.371
1993 Oakland	AL	159	546	136	21	2	3	(2	1)	170	60	48	60	2	58	11	10	6	10	5	.50	9	.249	.332	.311
1994 Oakland	AL	114	391	99	18	4	2	(1	1)	131	38	37	38	1	44	3	3	5	7	2	.78	9	.253	.320	.335
1995 Oakland	AL	126	428	113	13	0	8	(2	6)	150	46	44	35	2	48	5	7	3	11	3	.79	8	.264	.325	.350
1996 Oakland	AL	155	525	126	18	4	5	(2	3)	167	46	54	52	0	59	1	4	5	5	6	.45	8	.240	.307	.318
7 ML YEARS		823	2643	682	94	15	21	(10	11)	869	273	252	240	7	309	32	50	25	48	31	.61	47	.258	.324	.329

Toby Borland

Pitches: Right **Bats:** Right **Pos:** RP-69   **Ht:** 6'6" **Wt:** 193 **Born:** 5/29/69 **Age:** 28

Year Team	Lg	G	GS	CG	GF	IP	BFP	H	R	ER	HR	SH	SF	HB	TBB	IBB	SO	WP	Bk	W	L	Pct.	ShO	Sv-Op	Hld	ERA
		HOW MUCH HE PITCHED						**WHAT HE GAVE UP**												**THE RESULTS**						
1994 Philadelphia	NL	24	0	0	7	34.1	144	31	10	9	1	0	4	14	3	26	4	0	1	0	1.000	0	1-1	0	2.36
1995 Philadelphia	NL	50	0	0	18	74	339	81	37	31	3	3	2	5	37	7	59	12	0	1	3	.250	0	6-9	11	3.77
1996 Philadelphia	NL	69	0	0	11	90.2	399	83	51	41	9	4	1	3	43	3	76	10	0	7	3	.700	0	0-2	10	4.07
3 ML YEARS		143	0	0	36	199	882	195	98	81	13	8	3	12	94	13	161	26	0	9	6	.600	0	7-12	21	3.66

Joe Borowski

Pitches: Right **Bats:** Right **Pos:** RP-22   **Ht:** 6'2" **Wt:** 225 **Born:** 5/4/71 **Age:** 26

Year Team	Lg	G	GS	CG	GF	IP	BFP	H	R	ER	HR	SH	SF	HB	TBB	IBB	SO	WP	Bk	W	L	Pct.	ShO	Sv-Op	Hld	ERA
		HOW MUCH HE PITCHED						**WHAT HE GAVE UP**												**THE RESULTS**						
1990 White Sox	R	12	11	0	0	61.1	286	74	47	38	1	2	2	2	25	0	67	2	2	2	8	.200	0	0--	—	5.58
1991 Kane County	A	49	0	0	28	81	344	60	26	23	2	4	4	3	43	2	76	4	0	7	2	.778	0	13--	—	2.56
1992 Frederick	A+	48	0	0	36	80.1	362	71	40	33	3	5	6	3	50	3	85	2	0	5	6	.455	0	10--	—	3.70
1993 Frederick	A+	42	2	0	27	62.1	280	61	30	25	5	2	2	3	37	0	70	8	0	1	1	.500	0	11--	—	3.61
Bowie	AA	9	0	0	5	17.2	75	11	0	0	0	3	0	0	11	3	17	0	1	3	0	1.000	0	0--	—	0.00
1994 Bowie	AA	49	0	0	37	66	277	52	14	14	3	4	1	0	28	3	73	4	0	3	4	.429	0	14--	—	1.91
1995 Bowie	AA	16	0	0	14	20.2	83	16	9	9	2	2	0	0	7	1	32	1	0	2	2	.500	0	7--	—	3.92
Rochester	AAA	44	0	0	36	56.1	232	48	25	25	5	5	1	0	25	3	64	2	0	3	5	.375	0	13--	—	3.99
1996 Richmond	AAA	34	0	0	19	53.1	224	42	25	22	4	4	4	0	30	1	40	1	0	1	5	.167	0	7--	—	3.71
1995 Baltimore	AL	6	0	0	3	7.1	30	5	1	1	0	0	0	0	4	0	3	0	0	0	0	.000	0	0-0	0	1.23
1996 Atlanta	NL	22	0	0	8	26	121	33	15	14	4	5	0	1	13	4	15	1	0	2	4	.333	0	0-0	1	4.85
2 ML YEARS		28	0	0	11	33.1	151	38	16	15	4	5	0	1	17	4	18	1	0	2	4	.333	0	0-0	1	4.05

Chris Bosio

Pitches: Right **Bats:** Right **Pos:** SP-9; RP-9 **Ht:** 6'3" **Wt:** 235 **Born:** 4/3/63 **Age:** 34

Year Team	Lg	G	GS	CG	GF	IP	BFP	H	R	ER	HR	SH	SF	HB	TBB	IBB	SO	WP	Bk	W	L	Pct.	ShO	Sv-Op	Hld	ERA
1996 Tacoma *	AAA	2	1	0	0	4	13	2	0	0	0	0	0	0	0	0	3	0	0	0	0	.000	0	0--	—	0.00
Lancaster *	A+	2	2	0	0	8	31	6	3	1	0	0	2	0	0	0	7	0	0	0	0	.000	0	0--	—	1.13
Everett *	A-	1	1	0	0	4	15	3	1	1	0	0	0	0	0	0	8	0	0	0	0	.000	0	0--	—	2.25
1986 Milwaukee	AL	10	4	0	3	34.2	154	41	27	27	9	1	0	0	13	0	29	2	1	0	4	.000	0	0--	—	7.01
1987 Milwaukee	AL	46	19	2	8	170	734	187	102	99	18	3	3	1	50	3	150	14	2	11	8	.579	1	2-5	3	5.24
1988 Milwaukee	AL	38	22	9	15	182	766	190	80	68	13	7	9	2	38	6	84	1	2	7	15	.318	1	6-6	0	3.36
1989 Milwaukee	AL	33	33	8	0	234.2	969	225	90	77	16	5	5	6	48	1	173	4	2	15	10	.600	2	0-0	0	2.95
1990 Milwaukee	AL	20	20	4	0	132.2	557	131	67	59	15	4	4	3	38	1	76	7	0	4	9	.308	1	0-0	0	4.00
1991 Milwaukee	AL	32	32	5	0	204.2	840	187	80	74	15	2	6	8	58	0	117	5	0	14	10	.583	1	0-0	0	3.25
1992 Milwaukee	AL	33	33	4	0	231.1	937	223	100	93	21	6	5	4	44	1	120	8	2	16	6	.727	2	0-0	0	3.62
1993 Seattle	AL	29	24	3	2	164.1	678	138	75	63	14	7	4	6	59	3	119	5	0	9	9	.500	1	1-2	1	3.45
1994 Seattle	AL	19	19	4	0	125	546	137	72	60	15	3	6	2	40	3	67	4	0	4	10	.286	0	0-0	0	4.32
1995 Seattle	AL	31	31	0	0	170	766	211	98	93	18	5	11	5	69	3	85	10	0	10	8	.556	0	0-0	0	4.92
1996 Seattle	AL	18	9	0	4	60.2	278	72	44	40	8	3	6	4	24	1	39	1	0	4	4	.500	0	0-0	0	5.93
11 ML YEARS		309	246	39	32	1710	7225	1742	835	753	162	46	59	41	481	22	1059	61	9	94	93	.503	9	9--	—	3.96

Shawn Boskie

Pitches: Right **Bats:** Right **Pos:** SP-28; RP-9 **Ht:** 6'3" **Wt:** 200 **Born:** 3/28/67 **Age:** 30

Year Team	Lg	G	GS	CG	GF	IP	BFP	H	R	ER	HR	SH	SF	HB	TBB	IBB	SO	WP	Bk	W	L	Pct.	ShO	Sv-Op	Hld	ERA
1990 Chicago	NL	15	15	1	0	97.2	415	99	42	40	8	8	2	1	31	3	49	3	2	5	6	.455	0	0-0	0	3.69
1991 Chicago	NL	28	20	0	2	129	582	150	78	75	14	8	6	5	52	4	62	1	1	4	9	.308	0	0-0	0	5.23
1992 Chicago	NL	23	18	0	2	91.2	393	96	55	51	14	9	4	4	36	3	39	5	1	5	11	.313	0	0-0	0	5.01
1993 Chicago	NL	39	2	0	10	65.2	277	63	30	25	7	4	1	7	21	2	39	5	0	5	3	.625	0	0-3	6	3.43
1994 ChN-Phi-Sea		22	15	1	1	90.2	394	92	58	51	15	2	3	3	30	3	61	7	0	4	7	.364	0	0-1	0	5.06
1995 California	AL	20	20	1	0	111.2	494	127	73	70	16	4	6	7	25	0	51	4	0	7	7	.500	0	0-0	0	5.64
1996 California	AL	37	28	1	1	189.1	860	226	126	112	40	6	4	13	67	7	133	10	0	12	11	.522	0	0-0	0	5.32
1994 Chicago	NL	2	0	0	0	3.2	14	3	0	0	0	0	0	0	0	0	2	1	0	0	0	.000	0	0-0	0	0.00
Philadelphia	NL	18	14	1	1	84.1	367	85	56	49	14	2	3	2	29	2	59	6	0	4	6	.400	0	0-1	0	5.23
Seattle	AL	2	1	0	0	2.2	13	4	2	2	1	0	0	1	1	1	0	0	0	0	1	.000	0	0-0	0	6.75
7 ML YEARS		184	118	4	16	775.2	3415	853	462	424	114	41	28	40	262	22	434	35	4	42	54	.438	0	0-4	7	4.92

Ricky Bottalico

Pitches: Right **Bats:** Left **Pos:** RP-61 **Ht:** 6'1" **Wt:** 208 **Born:** 8/26/69 **Age:** 27

Year Team	Lg	G	GS	CG	GF	IP	BFP	H	R	ER	HR	SH	SF	HB	TBB	IBB	SO	WP	Bk	W	L	Pct.	ShO	Sv-Op	Hld	ERA
1994 Philadelphia	NL	3	0	0	3	3	13	3	0	0	0	0	0	0	1	0	3	0	0	0	0	.000	0	0-0	0	0.00
1995 Philadelphia	NL	62	0	0	20	87.2	350	50	25	24	7	3	1	4	42	3	87	1	0	5	3	.625	0	1-5	20	2.46
1996 Philadelphia	NL	61	0	0	56	67.2	269	47	24	24	6	4	2	2	23	2	74	3	0	4	5	.444	0	34-38	0	3.19
3 ML YEARS		126	0	0	79	158.1	632	100	49	48	13	7	3	6	66	5	164	4	0	9	8	.529	0	35-43	20	2.73

Kent Bottenfield

Pitches: Right **Bats:** Right **Pos:** RP-48 **Ht:** 6'3" **Wt:** 237 **Born:** 11/14/68 **Age:** 28

Year Team	Lg	G	GS	CG	GF	IP	BFP	H	R	ER	HR	SH	SF	HB	TBB	IBB	SO	WP	Bk	W	L	Pct.	ShO	Sv-Op	Hld	ERA
1996 Iowa *	AAA	28	0	0	26	24.2	99	19	9	6	0	0	0	0	8	1	14	1	0	1	2	.333	0	18--	—	2.19
1992 Montreal	NL	10	4	0	2	32.1	135	26	9	8	1	1	2	1	11	1	14	0	0	1	2	.333	0	1-1	1	2.23
1993 Mon-Col	NL	37	25	1	2	159.2	710	179	102	90	24	21	4	6	71	3	63	4	1	5	10	.333	0	0-0	0	5.07
1994 Col-SF	NL	16	1	0	3	26.1	121	33	18	18	2	1	0	2	10	0	15	2	0	3	1	.750	0	1-1	0	6.15
1996 Chicago	NL	48	0	0	10	61.2	258	59	25	18	3	5	0	3	19	4	33	2	0	3	5	.375	0	1-3	4	2.63
1993 Montreal	NL	23	11	0	2	83	373	93	49	38	11	11	1	5	33	2	33	4	1	2	5	.286	0	0-0	0	4.12
Colorado		14	14	1	0	76.2	337	86	53	52	13	10	3	1	38	1	30	0	0	3	5	.375	0	0-0	0	6.10
1994 Colorado		15	1	0	3	24.2	112	28	16	16	1	1	0	2	10	0	15	2	0	3	1	.750	0	1-1	0	5.84
San Francisco	NL	1	0	0	0	1.2	9	5	2	2	1	0	0	0	0	0	0	0	0	0	0	.000	0	0-0	0	10.80
4 ML YEARS		111	30	1	17	280	1224	297	154	134	30	28	6	12	111	8	125	8	1	12	18	.400	0	3-5	5	4.31

Steve Bourgeois

Pitches: Right **Bats:** Right **Pos:** RP-10; SP-5 **Ht:** 6'1" **Wt:** 220 **Born:** 8/4/74 **Age:** 22

Year Team	Lg	G	GS	CG	GF	IP	BFP	H	R	ER	HR	SH	SF	HB	TBB	IBB	SO	WP	Bk	W	L	Pct.	ShO	Sv-Op	Hld	ERA
1993 Everett	A-	15	15	0	0	77	337	62	44	36	7	0	3	7	44	0	77	4	1	5	3	.625	0	0--	—	4.21
1994 Clinton	A	20	20	0	0	106.1	464	97	57	43	16	4	2	7	54	0	88	11	0	8	5	.615	0	0--	—	3.64
San Jose	A+	7	7	0	0	36.2	167	40	22	22	4	1	1	1	22	0	27	5	0	4	0	1.000	0	0--	—	5.40
1995 Phoenix	AAA	6	5	0	0	34.2	153	38	18	13	2	0	0	2	13	0	23	4	1	1	1	.500	0	0--	—	3.38
1996 Phoenix	AAA	20	18	2	0	97	435	112	50	39	6	2	4	6	42	1	65	5	0	8	6	.571	0	0--	—	3.62
1996 San Francisco	NL	15	5	0	4	40	198	60	35	28	4	2	2	4	21	4	17	4	0	1	3	.250	0	0-0	0	6.30

Rafael Bournigal

Bats: Right **Throws:** Right **Pos:** 2B-64; SS-23; PH-14 **Ht:** 5'11" **Wt:** 165 **Born:** 5/12/66 **Age:** 31

		BATTING																	BASERUNNING				PERCENTAGES		
Year Team	Lg	G	AB	H	2B	3B	HR	(Hm	Rd)	TB	R	RBI	TBB	IBB	SO	HBP	SH	SF	SB	CS	SB%	GDP	Avg	OBP	SLG
1992 Los Angeles	NL	10	20	3	1	0	0	(0	0)	4	1	0	1	0	2	1	0	0	0	0	.00	0	.150	.227	.200
1993 Los Angeles	NL	8	18	9	1	0	0	(0	0)	10	0	3	0	0	2	0	0	0	0	0	.00	0	.500	.500	.556
1994 Los Angeles	NL	40	116	26	3	1	0	(0	0)	31	2	11	9	1	5	2	5	0	0	0	.00	4	.224	.291	.267
1996 Oakland	AL	88	252	61	14	2	0	(0	0)	79	33	32	16	0	19	1	8	0	4	3	.57	6	.242	.290	.313
4 ML YEARS		146	406	99	19	3	0	(0	0)	124	36	32	26	1	28	4	13	0	4	3	.57	10	.244	.296	.305

Brent Bowers

Bats: Left **Throws:** Right **Pos:** LF-21; PH-2 **Ht:** 6'3" **Wt:** 200 **Born:** 5/2/71 **Age:** 26

		BATTING																	BASERUNNING				PERCENTAGES		
Year Team	Lg	G	AB	H	2B	3B	HR	(Hm	Rd)	TB	R	RBI	TBB	IBB	SO	HBP	SH	SF	SB	CS	SB%	GDP	Avg	OBP	SLG
1989 Medicne Hat	R+	54	207	46	2	2	0	—	—	52	16	13	19	0	55	0	0	1	6	2	.75	5	.222	.286	.251
1990 Medicne Hat	R+	60	212	58	7	3	3	—	—	80	30	27	31	0	35	1	1	0	19	8	.70	2	.274	.369	.377
1991 Myrtle Bch	A	120	402	101	8	4	2	—	—	123	53	44	31	1	76	2	9	4	35	12	.74	11	.251	.305	.306
1992 Dunedin	A+	128	524	133	10	3	3	—	—	158	74	46	34	0	99	3	8	1	31	15	.67	4	.254	.302	.302
1993 Knoxville	AA	141	577	143	23	4	5	—	—	189	63	43	21	1	121	3	13	0	36	19	.65	5	.248	.278	.328
1994 Knoxville	AA	127	472	129	18	11	4	—	—	181	52	49	20	4	75	1	7	2	15	8	.65	8	.273	.303	.383
1995 Syracuse	AAA	111	305	77	16	5	5	—	—	118	38	26	10	0	57	1	1	1	5	1	.83	3	.252	.278	.387
1996 Bowie	AA	58	228	71	11	1	9	—	—	111	37	25	17	2	40	2	3	0	10	4	.71	1	.311	.364	.487
Rochester	AAA	49	206	67	8	4	4	—	—	95	40	19	14	0	41	0	3	0	9	3	.75	1	.325	.368	.461
1996 Baltimore	AL	21	39	12	2	0	0	(0	0)	14	6	3	0	0	7	0	0	0	0	0	.00	1	.308	.308	.359

Marshall Boze

Pitches: Right **Bats:** Right **Pos:** RP-25 **Ht:** 6'1" **Wt:** 214 **Born:** 5/23/71 **Age:** 26

		HOW MUCH HE PITCHED						WHAT HE GAVE UP												THE RESULTS						
Year Team	Lg	G	GS	CG	GF	IP	BFP	H	R	ER	HR	SH	SF	HB	TBB	IBB	SO	WP	Bk	W	L	Pct.	ShO	Sv-Op	Hld	ERA
1990 Brewers	R	15	0	0	5	20.2	104	28	22	17	0	0	0	3	13	1	17	3	0	1	0	1.000	0	3- -	—	7.40
1991 Beloit	A	3	1	0	2	6.1	34	8	4	4	0	0	0	0	7	0	4	0	1	0	1	.000	0	0- -	—	5.68
Helena	R+	16	1	0	1	56	271	59	49	43	3	2	3	3	47	0	64	6	2	3	3	.500	0	0- -	—	6.91
1992 Beloit	A	26	22	4	4	146.1	635	117	59	46	6	6	2	12	82	4	126	18	1	13	7	.650	1	0- -	—	2.83
1993 Stockton	A+	14	14	0	0	88.1	379	82	36	26	4	2	4	7	41	2	54	6	0	7	2	.778	0	0- -	—	2.65
El Paso	AA	13	13	1	0	86.1	357	78	36	26	5	0	3	4	32	2	48	6	0	10	3	.769	0	0- -	—	2.71
1994 New Orleans	AAA	29	29	2	0	171.1	746	182	101	90	18	9	4	10	74	2	81	16	1	6	10	.375	0	0- -	—	4.73
1995 New Orleans	AAA	23	19	1	1	111.2	495	134	65	53	10	2	2	2	45	1	47	6	1	3	9	.250	0	1- -	—	4.27
1996 New Orleans	AAA	25	2	0	12	38.2	180	35	22	21	6	3	1	2	29	5	32	2	0	4	3	.571	0	3- -	—	4.89
1996 Milwaukee	AL	25	0	0	8	32.1	165	47	29	28	5	3	1	6	25	4	19	3	0	0	2	.000	0	1-2	6	7.79

Terry Bradshaw

Bats: Left **Throws:** Right **Pos:** PH-9; LF-4; CF-3; RF-1 **Ht:** 6'0" **Wt:** 195 **Born:** 2/3/69 **Age:** 28

		BATTING																	BASERUNNING				PERCENTAGES		
Year Team	Lg	G	AB	H	2B	3B	HR	(Hm	Rd)	TB	R	RBI	TBB	IBB	SO	HBP	SH	SF	SB	CS	SB%	GDP	Avg	OBP	SLG
1990 Hamilton	A-	68	236	55	5	1	3	—	—	71	37	13	24	1	60	1	2	1	15	3	.83	4	.233	.305	.301
1991 Savannah	A	132	443	105	17	1	7	—	—	145	90	42	99	1	117	10	4	5	64	15	.81	6	.237	.384	.327
1993 St. Pete	A+	125	461	134	25	6	5	—	—	186	84	51	82	1	60	7	7	5	43	17	.72	8	.291	.402	.403
1994 Arkansas	AA	114	425	119	25	8	10	—	—	190	65	52	50	4	69	7	2	4	13	10	.57	5	.280	.362	.447
Louisville	AAA	22	80	20	4	0	4	—	—	36	16	8	6	0	10	2	1	0	5	1	.83	2	.250	.318	.450
1995 Louisville	AAA	111	389	110	24	8	8	—	—	174	65	42	53	0	60	3	7	1	20	7	.74	4	.283	.372	.447
1996 Louisville	AAA	102	389	118	23	1	12	—	—	179	56	44	42	1	64	2	0	2	21	9	.70	6	.303	.372	.460
1995 St. Louis	NL	19	44	10	1	1	0	(0	0)	13	6	2	2	0	10	0	0	0	1	2	.33	0	.227	.261	.295
1996 St. Louis	NL	15	21	7	1	0	0	(0	0)	8	4	3	3	0	2	0	1	0	1	1	.50	0	.333	.417	.381
2 ML YEARS		34	65	17	2	1	0	(0	0)	21	10	5	5	0	12	0	1	0	2	3	.40	0	.262	.314	.323

Darren Bragg

Bats: L **Throws:** R **Pos:** LF-55; CF-52; RF-45; PH-13 **Ht:** 5'9" **Wt:** 180 **Born:** 9/7/69 **Age:** 27

		BATTING																	BASERUNNING				PERCENTAGES		
Year Team	Lg	G	AB	H	2B	3B	HR	(Hm	Rd)	TB	R	RBI	TBB	IBB	SO	HBP	SH	SF	SB	CS	SB%	GDP	Avg	OBP	SLG
1996 Tacoma *	AAA	20	71	20	8	0	3	—	—	37	17	8	14	0	14	2	0	0	1	0	1.00	1	.282	.414	.521
1994 Seattle	AL	8	19	3	1	0	0	(0	0)	4	4	2	2	1	5	0	0	0	0	0	.00	0	.158	.238	.211
1995 Seattle	AL	52	145	34	5	1	3	(1	2)	50	20	12	18	1	37	4	1	2	9	0	1.00	2	.234	.331	.345
1996 Sea-Bos	AL	127	417	109	26	2	10	(7	3)	169	74	47	69	6	74	4	2	7	14	9	.61	5	.261	.366	.405
1996 Seattle	AL	69	195	53	12	1	7	(4	3)	88	36	25	33	4	35	2	1	4	8	5	.62	2	.272	.376	.451
Boston	AL	58	222	56	14	1	3	(3	0)	81	38	22	36	2	39	2	1	3	6	4	.60	3	.252	.357	.365
3 ML YEARS		187	581	146	32	3	13	(8	5)	223	98	61	89	8	116	8	3	9	23	9	.72	7	.251	.354	.384

Mark Brandenburg

Pitches: Right **Bats:** Right **Pos:** RP-55   **Ht:** 6'0" **Wt:** 180 **Born:** 7/14/70 **Age:** 26

		HOW MUCH HE PITCHED						WHAT HE GAVE UP										THE RESULTS						
Year Team	Lg	G	GS	CG	GF	IP	BFP	H	R	ER	HR	SH	SF	HB	TBB	IBB	SO	WP	Bk	W	L	Pct.	ShO	Sv-Op	Hld	ERA
1992 Butte	R+	24	1	0	16	62	268	70	32	28	3	1	1	5	14	1	78	1	0	7	1	.875	0	2--	—	4.06
1993 Charlstn-SC	A	44	0	0	18	80	320	62	23	13	2	4	2	3	22	6	67	0	0	6	3	.667	0	4--	—	1.46
1994 Charlotte	A+	25	0	0	15	41.1	159	23	5	4	1	2	1	2	15	4	44	0	0	0	2	.000	0	5--	—	0.87
Tulsa	AA	37	0	0	26	62	248	50	17	12	2	2	2	1	12	6	63	0	0	5	4	.556	0	8--	—	1.74
1995 Okla. City	AAA	35	0	0	15	58	235	52	16	13	2	3	1	2	15	5	51	0	2	0	5	.000	0	2--	—	2.02
1995 Texas	AL	11	0	0	5	27.1	123	36	18	18	5	0	1	1	7	1	21	0	1	0	1	.000	0	0-0	1	5.93
1996 Tex-Bos	AL	55	0	0	13	76	338	76	35	29	8	3	4	3	33	2	66	0	1	5	5	.500	0	0-2	12	3.43
1996 Texas	AL	26	0	0	8	47.2	215	48	22	17	3	3	2	2	25	1	37	0	1	1	3	.250	0	0-1	2	3.21
Boston	AL	29	0	0	5	28.1	123	28	13	12	5	0	2	1	8	1	29	0	0	4	2	.667	0	0-1	10	3.81
2 ML YEARS		66	0	0	18	103.1	461	112	53	47	13	3	5	4	40	3	87	0	2	5	6	.455	0	0-2	13	4.09

Jeff Branson

Bats: L **Throws:** R **Pos:** 3B-64; SS-38; 2B-31; PH-24   **Ht:** 6'0" **Wt:** 180 **Born:** 1/26/67 **Age:** 30

		BATTING															BASERUNNING				PERCENTAGES		
Year Team	Lg	G	AB	H	2B	3B	HR	(Hm | Rd)	TB	R	RBI	TBB	IBB	SO	HBP	SH	SF	SB	CS	SB%	GDP	Avg	OBP	SLG
1992 Cincinnati	NL	72	115	34	7	1	0	(0 | 0)	43	12	15	5	2	16	0	2	1	0	1	.00	4	.296	.322	.374
1993 Cincinnati	NL	125	381	92	15	1	3	(2 | 1)	118	40	22	19	2	73	0	8	4	4	1	.80	4	.241	.275	.310
1994 Cincinnati	NL	58	109	31	4	1	6	(1 | 5)	55	18	16	5	2	16	0	2	0	0	0	.00	4	.284	.316	.505
1995 Cincinnati	NL	122	331	86	18	2	12	(9 | 3)	144	43	45	44	14	69	2	1	6	2	1	.67	5	.260	.345	.435
1996 Cincinnati	NL	129	311	76	16	4	9	(5 | 4)	127	34	37	31	4	67	1	7	3	2	0	1.00	9	.244	.312	.408
5 ML YEARS		506	1247	319	60	9	30	(17 | 13)	487	147	135	104	24	241	3	20	14	8	3	.73	30	.256	.311	.391

Jeff Brantley

Pitches: Right **Bats:** Right **Pos:** RP-66   **Ht:** 5'10" **Wt:** 190 **Born:** 9/5/63 **Age:** 33

		HOW MUCH HE PITCHED						WHAT HE GAVE UP										THE RESULTS						
Year Team	Lg	G	GS	CG	GF	IP	BFP	H	R	ER	HR	SH	SF	HB	TBB	IBB	SO	WP	Bk	W	L	Pct.	ShO	Sv-Op	Hld	ERA
1988 San Francisco	NL	9	1	0	2	20.2	88	22	13	13	2	1	0	1	6	1	11	0	1	0	1	.000	0	1-1	0	5.66
1989 San Francisco	NL	59	0	0	15	97.1	422	101	50	44	10	7	3	2	37	8	69	3	2	7	1	.875	0	0-1	11	4.07
1990 San Francisco	NL	55	0	0	32	86.2	361	77	18	15	3	2	2	3	33	6	61	0	3	5	3	.625	0	19-24	8	1.56
1991 San Francisco	NL	67	0	0	39	95.1	411	78	27	26	8	4	4	5	52	10	81	6	0	5	2	.714	0	15-19	12	2.45
1992 San Francisco	NL	56	4	0	32	91.2	381	67	32	30	8	7	3	3	45	5	86	3	1	7	7	.500	0	7-9	3	2.95
1993 San Francisco	NL	53	12	0	9	113.2	496	112	60	54	19	5	5	7	46	2	76	3	1	5	6	.455	0	0-3	10	4.28
1994 Cincinnati	NL	50	0	0	35	65.1	262	46	20	18	6	5	1	0	28	5	63	1	0	6	6	.500	0	15-21	1	2.48
1995 Cincinnati	NL	56	0	0	49	70.1	283	53	22	22	11	2	3	1	20	3	62	2	2	3	2	.600	0	28-32	0	2.82
1996 Cincinnati	NL	66	0	0	61	71	288	54	21	19	7	4	5	0	28	6	76	2	0	1	2	.333	0	44-49	0	2.41
9 ML YEARS		471	18	0	274	712	2992	610	263	241	74	37	26	22	295	46	585	20	13	39	30	.565	0	129-159	45	3.05

Brent Brede

Bats: Left **Throws:** Left **Pos:** RF-7; PH-3   **Ht:** 6'4" **Wt:** 190 **Born:** 9/13/71 **Age:** 25

		BATTING															BASERUNNING				PERCENTAGES		
Year Team	Lg	G	AB	H	2B	3B	HR	(Hm | Rd)	TB	R	RBI	TBB	IBB	SO	HBP	SH	SF	SB	CS	SB%	GDP	Avg	OBP	SLG
1990 Elizabethtn	R+	46	143	35	5	0	0	—	—	40	39	14	30	0	29	0	0	1	14	0	1.00	4	.245	.374	.280
1991 Kenosha	A	53	156	30	3	2	0	—	—	37	12	10	16	0	31	0	5	3	4	5	.44	8	.192	.263	.237
Elizabethtn	R+	68	253	61	13	0	3	—	—	83	24	36	30	2	48	1	2	4	13	4	.76	7	.241	.319	.328
1992 Kenosha	A	110	363	88	15	0	0	—	—	103	44	29	53	1	77	4	4	3	10	12	.45	8	.242	.343	.284
1993 Fort Myers	A+	53	182	60	10	1	0	—	—	72	27	27	32	3	19	1	2	0	8	4	.67	6	.330	.433	.396
1994 Fort Myers	A+	116	419	110	21	4	2	—	—	145	49	45	63	3	60	0	3	1	18	4	.82	7	.263	.358	.346
1995 New Britain	AA	134	449	123	28	2	3	—	—	164	71	39	69	2	82	3	6	5	14	6	.70	13	.274	.371	.365
1996 Salt Lake	AAA	132	483	168	38	8	11	—	—	255	102	86	87	9	87	3	4	5	14	6	.70	4	.348	.446	.528
1996 Minnesota	AL	10	20	6	0	1	0	(0 | 0)	8	2	2	1	0	5	0	0	0	0	0	.00	1	.300	.333	.400

Billy Brewer

Pitches: Left **Bats:** Left **Pos:** RP-4   **Ht:** 6'1" **Wt:** 175 **Born:** 4/15/68 **Age:** 29

		HOW MUCH HE PITCHED						WHAT HE GAVE UP										THE RESULTS						
Year Team	Lg	G	GS	CG	GF	IP	BFP	H	R	ER	HR	SH	SF	HB	TBB	IBB	SO	WP	Bk	W	L	Pct.	ShO	Sv-Op	Hld	ERA
1996 Albuquerque *	AAA	31	0	0	12	31.2	141	28	13	11	5	1	0	0	22	6	33	3	3	2	2	.500	0	2--	—	3.13
Columbus *	AAA	13	4	0	6	25	122	27	21	20	4	0	2	2	19	0	27	3	1	0	2	.000	0	0--	—	7.20
1993 Kansas City	AL	46	0	0	14	39	157	31	16	15	6	1	1	0	20	4	28	2	1	2	2	.500	0	0-2	5	3.46
1994 Kansas City	AL	50	0	0	17	38.2	171	28	11	11	4	2	2	2	16	1	25	3	0	4	1	.800	0	3-7	12	2.56
1995 Kansas City	AL	48	0	0	13	45.1	209	54	28	28	9	1	0	2	20	1	31	5	1	2	4	.333	0	0-4	7	5.56
1996 New York	AL	4	0	0	1	5.2	32	7	6	6	0	0	0	0	8	0	8	0	0	1	0	1.000	0	0-0	0	9.53
4 ML YEARS		148	0	0	45	128.2	555	120	61	60	19	4	3	4	64	6	92	10	2	9	7	.563	0	3-13	24	4.20

John Briscoe

Pitches: Right **Bats:** Right **Pos:** RP-17 **Ht:** 6'3" **Wt:** 190 **Born:** 9/22/67 **Age:** 29

Year Team	Lg	G	GS	CG	GF	IP	BFP	H	R	ER	HR	SH	SF	HB	TBB	IBB	SO	WP	Bk	W	L	Pct.	ShO	Sv-Op	Hld	ERA
1996 Edmonton *	AAA	30	1	0	10	54.2	256	69	33	29	6	2	2	2	23	3	62	5	1	5	2	.714	0	1--	—	4.77
1991 Oakland	AL	11	0	0	9	14	62	12	11	11	3	0	1	0	10	0	9	3	0	0	0	.000	0	0-0	0	7.07
1992 Oakland	AL	2	2	0	0	7	40	12	6	5	0	1	0	0	9	0	4	2	0	0	1	.000	0	0-0	0	6.43
1993 Oakland	AL	17	0	0	6	24.2	122	26	25	22	2	0	2	0	26	3	24	5	0	1	0	1.000	0	0-0	0	8.03
1994 Oakland	AL	37	0	0	8	49.1	210	31	24	22	7	1	1	1	39	2	45	8	1	4	2	.667	0	1-2	9	4.01
1995 Oakland	AL	16	0	0	7	18.1	99	25	17	17	4	2	2	2	21	1	19	1	0	0	1	.000	0	0-0	0	8.35
1996 Oakland	AL	17	0	0	8	26.1	116	18	11	11	2	2	2	0	24	2	14	3	0	0	1	.000	0	1-2	1	3.76
6 ML YEARS		100	2	0	38	139.2	649	124	94	88	18	6	8	3	129	8	115	22	1	5	5	.500	0	2-4	10	5.67

Jorge Brito

Bats: Right **Throws:** Right **Pos:** C-8; PH-1 **Ht:** 6'1" **Wt:** 190 **Born:** 6/22/66 **Age:** 31

Year Team	Lg	G	AB	H	2B	3B	HR	(Hm	Rd)	TB	R	RBI	TBB	IBB	SO	HBP	SH	SF	SB	CS	SB%	GDP	Avg	OBP	SLG
1986 Medford	A-	21	59	9	2	0	0	—	—	11	4	5	4	0	17	2	0	1	0	2	.00	3	.153	.227	.186
1987 Medford	A-	40	110	20	1	0	1	—	—	24	7	15	12	0	54	1	1	2	0	0	.00	3	.182	.264	.218
1988 Modesto	A+	96	300	65	15	0	5	—	—	95	38	27	47	0	104	8	3	3	0	0	.00	6	.217	.335	.317
1989 Modesto	A+	16	54	13	2	0	1	—	—	18	8	6	5	0	14	1	1	0	0	0	.00	2	.241	.317	.333
Tacoma	AAA	5	15	3	1	0	0	—	—	4	2	0	2	0	6	0	0	0	0	1	.00	2	.200	.294	.267
Huntsville	AA	24	73	16	2	2	0	—	—	22	13	8	20	0	23	0	2	0	1	1	.50	2	.219	.387	.301
Madison	A	43	143	30	4	1	3	—	—	45	20	14	22	1	46	2	1	0	1	0	1.00	9	.210	.323	.315
1990 Huntsville	AA	57	164	44	6	1	2	—	—	58	17	20	30	1	49	3	3	1	0	1	.00	6	.268	.389	.354
1991 Tacoma	AAA	22	73	17	2	0	1	—	—	22	6	3	4	0	20	0	0	0	0	0	.00	6	.233	.273	.301
Huntsville	AA	65	203	41	11	0	1	—	—	55	26	23	28	0	50	4	2	1	0	1	.00	6	.202	.309	.271
1992 Tacoma	AAA	18	35	5	2	0	0	—	—	7	4	1	2	0	17	0	0	0	0	0	.00	0	.143	.189	.200
Huntsville	AA	33	72	15	2	0	2	—	—	23	10	6	13	0	21	1	3	0	2	0	1.00	1	.208	.337	.319
1993 Huntsville	AA	18	36	10	3	0	4	—	—	25	6	11	1	0	10	2	0	1	0	0	.00	0	.278	.449	.694
1994 New Haven	AA	63	200	46	11	1	5	—	—	74	18	25	18	3	59	2	1	2	1	0	1.00	6	.230	.297	.370
Colo. Sprng	AAA	21	64	24	5	0	3	—	—	38	13	19	7	1	14	0	1	0	0	0	.00	3	.375	.437	.594
1995 Colo. Sprng	AAA	32	96	22	4	1	2	—	—	34	9	15	2	0	20	1	1	2	0	0	.00	2	.229	.248	.354
1996 Colo. Sprng	AAA	53	159	54	17	0	7	—	—	92	32	31	24	1	37	4	0	1	0	0	.00	7	.340	.436	.579
1995 Colorado	NL	18	51	11	3	0	0	(0	0)	14	5	7	2	0	17	1	1	0	1	0	1.00	1	.216	.259	.275
1996 Colorado	NL	8	14	1	0	0	0	(0	0)	1	1	0	1	0	8	2	1	0	0	0	.00	0	.071	.235	.071
2 ML YEARS		26	65	12	3	0	0	(0	0)	15	6	7	3	0	25	3	2	0	1	0	1.00	1	.185	.254	.231

Tilson Brito

Bats: R **Throws:** R **Pos:** 2B-18; SS-5; PH-4; DH-2 **Ht:** 6'0" **Wt:** 175 **Born:** 5/28/72 **Age:** 25

Year Team	Lg	G	AB	H	2B	3B	HR	(Hm	Rd)	TB	R	RBI	TBB	IBB	SO	HBP	SH	SF	SB	CS	SB%	GDP	Avg	OBP	SLG
1992 Blue Jays	R	54	189	58	10	4	3	—	—	85	36	36	22	1	22	6	0	5	16	8	.67	5	.307	.387	.450
Knoxville	AA	7	24	5	1	2	0	—	—	10	2	2	0	0	9	0	0	0	0	0	.00	0	.208	.208	.417
1993 Dunedin	A+	126	465	125	21	3	6	—	—	170	80	44	59	0	60	10	10	3	27	16	.63	8	.269	.361	.366
1994 Knoxville	AA	139	476	127	17	7	5	—	—	173	61	57	35	2	68	8	9	7	33	12	.73	7	.267	.323	.363
1995 Syracuse	AAA	90	327	79	16	3	7	—	—	122	49	32	29	0	69	4	2	1	17	8	.68	6	.242	.310	.373
1996 Syracuse	AAA	108	400	111	22	8	10	—	—	179	63	54	38	1	65	5	3	4	11	10	.52	8	.278	.345	.448
1996 Toronto	AL	26	80	19	7	0	1	(1	0)	29	10	7	10	0	18	3	2	0	1	1	.50	0	.238	.344	.363

Doug Brocail

Pitches: Right **Bats:** Left **Pos:** RP-19; SP-4 **Ht:** 6'5" **Wt:** 235 **Born:** 5/16/67 **Age:** 30

Year Team	Lg	G	GS	CG	GF	IP	BFP	H	R	ER	HR	SH	SF	HB	TBB	IBB	SO	WP	Bk	W	L	Pct.	ShO	Sv-Op	Hld	ERA
1996 Jackson *	AA	2	2	0	0	4	15	1	0	0	0	0	0	1	1	0	5	0	0	0	0	.000	0	0--	—	0.00
Tucson *	AAA	5	1	0	0	7.1	34	12	6	6	1	1	0	0	1	0	4	0	0	0	1	.000	0	0--	—	7.36
1992 San Diego	NL	3	3	0	0	14	64	17	10	10	2	2	0	0	5	0	15	0	0	0	0	.000	0	0-0	0	6.43
1993 San Diego	NL	24	24	0	0	128.1	571	143	75	65	16	10	8	4	42	4	70	4	1	4	13	.235	0	0-0	0	4.56
1994 San Diego	NL	12	0	0	4	17	78	21	13	11	1	1	1	2	5	3	11	1	1	0	0	.000	0	0-1	0	5.82
1995 Houston	NL	36	7	0	12	77.1	339	87	40	36	10	1	1	4	22	2	39	1	1	6	4	.600	0	1-1	0	4.19
1996 Houston	NL	23	4	0	4	53	231	58	31	27	7	3	2	2	23	1	34	0	0	1	5	.167	0	0-0	1	4.58
5 ML YEARS		98	38	0	20	289.2	1283	326	169	149	36	17	12	12	97	10	169	6	3	11	22	.333	0	1-2	1	4.63

Rico Brogna

Bats: Left **Throws:** Left **Pos:** 1B-52; PH-5 **Ht:** 6'2" **Wt:** 205 **Born:** 4/18/70 **Age:** 27

Year Team	Lg	G	AB	H	2B	3B	HR	(Hm	Rd)	TB	R	RBI	TBB	IBB	SO	HBP	SH	SF	SB	CS	SB%	GDP	Avg	OBP	SLG
1992 Detroit	AL	9	26	5	1	0	1	(1	0)	9	3	3	3	0	5	0	0	0	0	0	.00	0	.192	.276	.346
1994 New York	NL	39	131	46	11	2	7	(2	5)	82	16	20	6	0	29	0	1	0	1	0	1.00	6	.351	.380	.626
1995 New York	NL	134	495	143	27	2	22	(13	9)	240	72	76	39	7	111	2	2	2	0	0	.00	10	.289	.342	.485
1996 New York	NL	55	188	48	10	1	7	(5	2)	81	18	30	19	1	50	0	0	4	0	0	.00	4	.255	.318	.431

Year Team	Lg	G	AB	H	2B	3B	HR	(Hm	Rd)	TB	R	RBI	TBB	IBB	SO	HBP	SH	SF	SB	CS	SB%	GDP	Avg	OBP	SLG
							BATTING												BASERUNNING				PERCENTAGES		
4 ML YEARS		237	840	242	49	5	37	(21	16)	412	109	129	67	8	195	2	3	6	1	0	1.00	16	.288	.340	.490

Jerry Brooks

Bats: Right **Throws:** Right **Pos:** PH-5; RF-2; 1B-1   **Ht:** 6'0" **Wt:** 195 **Born:** 3/23/67 **Age:** 30

Year Team	Lg	G	AB	H	2B	3B	HR	(Hm	Rd)	TB	R	RBI	TBB	IBB	SO	HBP	SH	SF	SB	CS	SB%	GDP	Avg	OBP	SLG
1996 Charlotte *	AAA	136	466	134	29	2	34	—	—	269	72	107	32	3	78	2	0	2	5	5	.50	17	.288	.335	.577
1993 Los Angeles	NL	9	9	2	1	0	1	(0	1)	6	2	1	0	0	2	0	0	0	0	0	.00	0	.222	.222	.667
1996 Florida	NL	8	5	2	0	1	0	(0	0)	4	2	3	1	0	1	1	0	0	0	0	.00	0	.400	.571	.800
2 ML YEARS		17	14	4	1	1	1	(0	1)	10	4	4	1	0	3	1	0	0	0	0	.00	0	.286	.375	.714

Scott Brosius

Bats: R **Throws:** R **Pos:** 3B-109; 1B-10; LF-3; CF-2; PH-1   **Ht:** 6'1" **Wt:** 185 **Born:** 8/15/66 **Age:** 30

Year Team	Lg	G	AB	H	2B	3B	HR	(Hm	Rd)	TB	R	RBI	TBB	IBB	SO	HBP	SH	SF	SB	CS	SB%	GDP	Avg	OBP	SLG
1996 Edmonton *	AAA	3	8	5	1	0	0	—	—	6	5	0	3	0	1	0	0	0	0	0	.00	0	.625	.727	.750
1991 Oakland	AL	36	68	16	5	0	2	(1	1)	27	9	4	3	0	11	0	1	0	3	1	.75	2	.235	.268	.397
1992 Oakland	AL	38	87	19	2	0	4	(1	3)	33	13	13	3	1	13	2	0	1	3	0	1.00	0	.218	.258	.379
1993 Oakland	AL	70	213	53	10	1	6	(3	3)	83	26	25	14	0	37	1	3	2	6	0	1.00	6	.249	.296	.390
1994 Oakland	AL	96	324	77	14	1	14	(9	5)	135	31	49	24	0	57	2	4	6	2	6	.25	7	.238	.289	.417
1995 Oakland	AL	123	389	102	19	2	17	(12	5)	176	69	46	41	0	67	8	1	4	4	2	.67	5	.262	.342	.452
1996 Oakland	AL	114	428	130	25	0	22	(15	7)	221	73	71	59	4	85	7	1	5	7	2	.78	11	.304	.393	.516
6 ML YEARS		477	1509	397	75	4	65	(41	24)	675	221	208	144	5	270	20	10	18	25	11	.69	31	.263	.332	.447

Scott Brow

Pitches: Right **Bats:** Right **Pos:** RP-17; SP-1   **Ht:** 6'3" **Wt:** 200 **Born:** 3/17/69 **Age:** 28

		HOW MUCH HE PITCHED						WHAT HE GAVE UP												THE RESULTS						
Year Team	Lg	G	GS	CG	GF	IP	BFP	H	R	ER	HR	SH	SF	HB	TBB	IBB	SO	WP	Bk	W	L	Pct.	ShO	Sv-Op	Hld	ERA
1996 Syracuse *	AAA	18	11	0	2	76.2	331	84	49	42	6	0	3	0	26	1	52	1	0	5	4	.556	0	0--	—	4.93
1993 Toronto	AL	6	3	0	1	18	83	19	15	14	2	1	2	1	10	1	7	0	0	1	1	.500	0	0-0	0	6.00
1994 Toronto	AL	18	0	0	9	29	141	34	27	19	4	1	2	1	19	2	15	6	0	0	3	.000	0	2-2	0	5.90
1996 Toronto	AL	18	1	0	9	38.2	180	45	25	24	5	1	1	0	25	1	23	2	1	1	0	1.000	0	0-1	0	5.59
3 ML YEARS		42	4	0	19	85.2	404	98	67	55	11	3	5	2	54	4	45	8	1	2	4	.333	0	2-3	0	5.78

Brant Brown

Bats: Left **Throws:** Left **Pos:** 1B-18; PH-14   **Ht:** 6'3" **Wt:** 205 **Born:** 6/22/71 **Age:** 26

Year Team	Lg	G	AB	H	2B	3B	HR	(Hm	Rd)	TB	R	RBI	TBB	IBB	SO	HBP	SH	SF	SB	CS	SB%	GDP	Avg	OBP	SLG
1992 Peoria	A	70	248	68	14	0	3	—	—	91	28	27	24	2	49	1	3	5	3	4	.43	4	.274	.335	.367
1993 Daytona	A+	75	266	91	8	7	3	—	—	122	26	33	11	0	38	1	4	0	8	7	.53	5	.342	.371	.459
Orlando	AA	28	110	35	11	3	4	—	—	64	17	23	6	1	18	4	0	1	2	1	.67	2	.318	.372	.582
1994 Orlando	AA	127	470	127	30	6	5	—	—	184	54	37	37	3	86	5	2	0	11	15	.42	10	.270	.330	.391
1995 Orlando	AA	121	446	121	27	4	6	—	—	174	67	53	39	2	77	3	11	3	8	5	.62	6	.271	.332	.390
1996 Iowa	AAA	94	342	104	25	3	10	—	—	165	48	43	19	1	65	3	0	0	6	6	.50	10	.304	.346	.482
1996 Chicago	NL	29	69	21	1	0	5	(3	2)	37	11	9	2	1	17	1	0	1	3	3	.50	1	.304	.329	.536

Kevin Brown

Pitches: Right **Bats:** Right **Pos:** SP-32   **Ht:** 6'4" **Wt:** 195 **Born:** 3/14/65 **Age:** 32

		HOW MUCH HE PITCHED						WHAT HE GAVE UP												THE RESULTS						
Year Team	Lg	G	GS	CG	GF	IP	BFP	H	R	ER	HR	SH	SF	HB	TBB	IBB	SO	WP	Bk	W	L	Pct.	ShO	Sv-Op	Hld	ERA
1986 Texas	AL	1	1	0	0	5	19	6	2	2	0	0	0	0	0	0	4	0	0	1	0	1.000	0	0--	—	3.60
1988 Texas	AL	4	4	1	0	23.1	110	33	15	11	2	1	0	1	8	0	12	1	0	1	1	.500	0	0-0	0	4.24
1989 Texas	AL	28	28	7	0	191	798	167	81	71	10	3	6	4	70	2	104	7	2	12	9	.571	0	0-0	0	3.35
1990 Texas	AL	26	26	6	0	180	757	175	84	72	13	2	7	3	60	3	88	9	2	12	10	.545	2	0-0	0	3.60
1991 Texas	AL	33	33	0	0	210.2	934	233	116	103	17	6	4	13	90	5	96	12	3	9	12	.429	0	0-0	0	4.40
1992 Texas	AL	35	35	11	0	265.2	1108	262	117	98	11	7	8	10	76	2	173	8	2	21	11	.656	1	0-0	0	3.32
1993 Texas	AL	34	34	12	0	233	1001	228	105	93	14	5	3	16	74	5	142	8	1	15	12	.556	3	0-0	0	3.59
1994 Texas	AL	26	25	3	1	170	760	218	109	91	18	2	7	6	50	3	123	7	0	7	9	.438	0	0-0	0	4.82
1995 Baltimore	AL	26	26	3	0	172.1	706	155	73	69	10	5	2	9	48	1	117	3	0	10	9	.526	1	0-0	0	3.60
1996 Florida	NL	32	32	5	0	233	906	187	60	49	8	4	4	16	33	2	159	6	1	17	11	.607	3	0-0	0	1.89
10 ML YEARS		245	244	48	1	1684	7099	1664	762	659	103	35	41	77	509	23	1018	61	11	105	84	.556	10	0--	—	3.52

Kevin L. Brown

Bats: Right **Throws:** Right **Pos:** C-2; DH-1; PH-1   **Ht:** 6'2" **Wt:** 200 **Born:** 4/21/73 **Age:** 24

Year Team	Lg	G	AB	H	2B	3B	HR	(Hm	Rd)	TB	R	RBI	TBB	IBB	SO	HBP	SH	SF	SB	CS	SB%	GDP	Avg	OBP	SLG
1994 Hudson Vall	A-	68	232	57	19	1	6	—	—	96	33	32	23	0	86	4	0	6	0	1	.00	4	.246	.317	.414
1995 Charlotte	A+	107	355	94	25	1	11	—	—	154	48	57	50	0	96	9	1	4	2	3	.40	9	.265	.366	.434
Okla. City	AAA	3	10	4	1	0	0	—	—	5	1	0	2	0	4	0	0	0	0	0	.00	0	.400	.500	.500
1996 Tulsa	AA	128	460	121	27	1	26	—	—	228	77	86	73	0	150	11	0	6	0	3	.00	5	.263	.373	.496
1996 Texas	AL	3	4	0	0	0	0	(0	0)	0	1	1	2	0	2	1	0	1	0	0	.00	0	.000	.375	.000

Jacob Brumfield

Bats: R **Throws:** R **Pos:** CF-61; RF-37; PH-21; LF-18; DH-5   **Ht:** 6'0" **Wt:** 185 **Born:** 5/27/65 **Age:** 32

Year Team	Lg	G	AB	H	2B	3B	HR	(Hm	Rd)	TB	R	RBI	TBB	IBB	SO	HBP	SH	SF	SB	CS	SB%	GDP	Avg	OBP	SLG
1992 Cincinnati	NL	24	30	4	0	0	0	(0	0)	4	6	2	2	1	4	1	0	0	6	0	1.00	0	.133	.212	.133
1993 Cincinnati	NL	103	272	73	17	3	6	(1	5)	114	40	23	21	4	47	1	3	2	20	8	.71	1	.268	.321	.419
1994 Cincinnati	NL	68	122	38	10	2	4	(3	1)	64	36	11	15	0	18	0	2	2	6	3	.67	3	.311	.381	.525
1995 Pittsburgh	NL	116	402	109	23	2	4	(4	0)	148	64	26	37	0	71	5	0	1	22	12	.65	3	.271	.339	.368
1996 Pit-Tor		119	388	99	28	2	14	(8	6)	173	63	60	29	2	75	4	1	4	15	4	.79	14	.255	.311	.446
1996 Pittsburgh	NL	29	80	20	9	0	2	(0	2)	35	11	8	5	1	17	0	0	1	3	1	.75	4	.250	.291	.438
Toronto	AL	90	308	79	19	2	12	(8	4)	138	52	52	24	1	58	4	1	3	12	3	.80	10	.256	.316	.448
5 ML YEARS		430	1214	323	78	9	28	(16	12)	503	209	122	104	7	215	11	6	9	69	27	.72	21	.266	.327	.414

Jim Bruske

Pitches: Right **Bats:** Right **Pos:** RP-11   **Ht:** 6'1" **Wt:** 185 **Born:** 10/7/64 **Age:** 32

		HOW MUCH HE PITCHED						WHAT HE GAVE UP										THE RESULTS						
Year Team	Lg	G	GS	CG	GF	IP	BFP	H	R	ER	HR	SH	SF	HB	TBB	IBB	SO	WP	Bk	W	L	Pct.	ShO	Sv-Op	Hld	ERA
1986 Batavia	A-	1	0	0	1	1	7	1	2	2	0	0	0	0	3	0	3	2	0	0	0	.000	0	0- -	—	18.00
1989 Canton-Akrn	AA	2	0	0	2	2	11	3	3	3	0	0	0	0	2	0	1	1	0	0	0	.000	0	0- -	—	13.50
1990 Canton-Akrn	AA	32	13	3	6	118	511	118	53	43	6	2	3	4	42	2	62	5	0	9	3	.750	2	0- -	—	3.28
1991 Canton-Akrn	AA	17	11	0	3	80.1	337	73	36	31	3	0	1	2	27	3	35	2	0	5	2	.714	0	1- -	—	3.47
Colo. Sprng	AAA	7	1	0	3	25.2	100	19	9	7	3	0	1	0	8	0	13	1	1	4	0	1.000	0	2- -	—	2.45
1992 Colo. Sprng	AAA	7	0	0	1	17.2	83	24	11	9	2	0	0	2	6	1	8	2	0	2	0	1.000	0	0- -	—	4.58
Jackson	AA	13	9	1	1	61.2	258	54	23	18	2	2	2	4	14	1	48	1	1	4	3	.571	0	0- -	—	2.63
1993 Jackson	AA	15	15	1	0	97.1	391	86	34	25	6	1	1	2	22	1	83	2	0	9	5	.643	0	0- -	—	2.31
Tucson	AAA	12	9	0	1	66.2	290	77	36	28	4	2	1	0	18	2	42	3	0	4	2	.667	0	1- -	—	3.78
1994 Tucson	AAA	7	7	0	0	39	170	47	22	18	2	1	0	1	8	0	25	2	0	3	1	.750	0	0- -	—	4.15
1995 Albuquerque	AAA	43	6	0	13	114	492	128	54	52	6	4	4	3	41	2	99	3	0	7	5	.583	0	4- -	—	4.11
1996 Albuquerque	AAA	36	0	0	21	62	270	63	34	28	3	3	4	3	21	6	51	1	0	5	2	.714	0	4- -	—	4.06
1995 Los Angeles	NL	9	0	0	3	10	45	12	7	5	0	0	0	1	4	0	5	1	0	0	0	.000	0	1-1	0	4.50
1996 Los Angeles	NL	11	0	0	5	12.2	58	17	8	8	2	0	0	1	3	1	12	1	0	0	0	.000	0	0-0	0	5.68
2 ML YEARS		20	0	0	8	22.2	103	29	15	13	2	0	0	2	7	1	17	2	0	0	0	.000	0	1-1	0	5.16

Damon Buford

Bats: R **Throws:** R **Pos:** RF-44; PH-29; CF-25; LF-14; DH-3   **Ht:** 5'10" **Wt:** 170 **Born:** 6/12/70 **Age:** 27

Year Team	Lg	G	AB	H	2B	3B	HR	(Hm	Rd)	TB	R	RBI	TBB	IBB	SO	HBP	SH	SF	SB	CS	SB%	GDP	Avg	OBP	SLG
1993 Baltimore	AL	53	79	18	5	0	2	(0	2)	29	18	9	9	0	19	1	1	0	2	2	.50	1	.228	.315	.367
1994 Baltimore	AL	4	2	1	0	0	0	(0	0)	1	2	0	0	0	1	0	0	0	0	0	.00	0	.500	.500	.500
1995 Bal-NYN		68	168	34	5	0	4	(2	2)	51	30	14	25	0	35	5	3	3	10	8	.56	3	.202	.318	.304
1996 Texas	AL	90	145	41	9	0	6	(3	3)	68	30	20	15	0	34	0	1	1	8	5	.62	3	.283	.348	.469
1995 Baltimore	AL	24	32	2	0	0	0	(0	0)	2	6	2	6	0	7	0	3	1	3	1	.75	0	.063	.205	.063
New York	NL	44	136	32	5	0	4	(2	2)	49	24	12	19	0	28	5	0	2	7	7	.50	3	.235	.346	.360
4 ML YEARS		215	394	94	19	0	12	(5	7)	149	80	43	49	0	89	6	5	4	20	15	.57	7	.239	.329	.378

Jay Buhner

Bats: Right **Throws:** Right **Pos:** RF-142; DH-8   **Ht:** 6'3" **Wt:** 210 **Born:** 8/13/64 **Age:** 32

Year Team	Lg	G	AB	H	2B	3B	HR	(Hm	Rd)	TB	R	RBI	TBB	IBB	SO	HBP	SH	SF	SB	CS	SB%	GDP	Avg	OBP	SLG
1987 New York	AL	7	22	5	2	0	0	(0	0)	7	0	1	1	0	6	0	0	0	0	0	.00	1	.227	.261	.318
1988 NYA-Sea	AL	85	261	56	13	1	13	(8	5)	110	36	38	28	1	93	6	1	3	1	1	.50	5	.215	.302	.421
1989 Seattle	AL	58	204	56	15	1	9	(7	2)	100	27	33	19	0	55	2	0	1	1	4	.20	5	.275	.341	.490
1990 Seattle	AL	51	163	45	12	0	7	(2	5)	78	16	33	17	1	50	4	0	1	2	2	.50	6	.276	.357	.479
1991 Seattle	AL	137	406	99	14	4	27	(14	13)	202	64	77	53	5	117	6	2	4	0	1	.00	10	.244	.337	.498
1992 Seattle	AL	152	543	132	16	3	25	(9	16)	229	69	79	71	2	146	6	1	8	0	6	.00	12	.243	.333	.422
1993 Seattle	AL	158	563	153	28	3	27	(13	14)	268	91	98	100	11	144	2	2	8	2	5	.29	12	.272	.379	.476
1994 Seattle	AL	101	358	100	23	4	21	(8	13)	194	74	68	66	3	63	5	2	5	0	1	.00	7	.279	.394	.542
1995 Seattle	AL	126	470	123	23	0	40	(21	19)	266	86	121	60	7	120	1	2	6	0	1	.00	15	.262	.343	.566
1996 Seattle	AL	150	564	153	29	0	44	(21	23)	314	107	138	84	5	159	9	0	10	0	1	.00	11	.271	.369	.557
1988 New York	AL	25	69	13	0	0	3	(1	2)	22	8	13	3	0	25	0	1	0	0	0	.00	1	.188	.250	.319
Seattle	AL	60	192	43	13	1	10	(7	3)	88	28	25	25	1	68	6	0	3	1	1	.50	4	.224	.320	.458

	BATTING																	BASERUNNING				PERCENTAGES		
Year Team	Lg	G	AB	H	2B	3B	HR	(Hm | Rd)	TB	R	RBI	TBB	IBB	SO	HBP	SH	SF	SB	CS	SB%	GDP	Avg	OBP	SLG
10 ML YEARS		1025	3554	922	175	16	213	(103 | 110)	1768	570	686	499	35	953	41	10	46	6	22	.21	79	.259	.353	.497

Scott Bullett

Bats: L **Throws:** L **Pos:** PH-68; LF-28; RF-22; CF-11   **Ht:** 6'2" **Wt:** 220 **Born:** 12/25/68 **Age:** 28

	BATTING																	BASERUNNING				PERCENTAGES		
Year Team	Lg	G	AB	H	2B	3B	HR	(Hm | Rd)	TB	R	RBI	TBB	IBB	SO	HBP	SH	SF	SB	CS	SB%	GDP	Avg	OBP	SLG
1996 Orlando *	AA	3	11	2	0	0	0	—	—	2	2	0	1	0	2	0	0	0	2	0	1.00	0	.182	.250	.182
1991 Pittsburgh	NL	11	4	0	0	0	0	(0 | 0)	0	2	0	0	0	3	1	0	0	1	1	.50	0	.000	.200	.000
1993 Pittsburgh	NL	23	55	11	0	2	0	(0 | 0)	15	2	4	3	0	15	0	0	1	3	2	.60	1	.200	.237	.273
1995 Chicago	NL	104	150	41	5	7	3	(2 | 1)	69	19	22	12	2	30	1	1	0	8	3	.73	4	.273	.331	.460
1996 Chicago	NL	109	165	35	5	0	3	(2 | 1)	49	26	16	10	0	54	0	1	1	7	3	.70	2	.212	.256	.297
4 ML YEARS		247	374	87	10	9	6	(4 | 2)	133	49	42	25	2	102	2	2	2	19	9	.68	7	.233	.283	.356

Jim Bullinger

Pitches: Right **Bats:** Right **Pos:** SP-20; RP-17   **Ht:** 6'2" **Wt:** 190 **Born:** 8/21/65 **Age:** 31

	HOW MUCH HE PITCHED						WHAT HE GAVE UP											THE RESULTS					
Year Team	Lg	G	GS	CG	GF	IP	BFP	H	R	ER	HR	SH	SF	HB	TBB	IBB	SO	WP	Bk	W	L	Pct.	ShO	Sv-Op	Hld	ERA
1992 Chicago	NL	39	9	1	15	85	380	72	49	44	9	9	4	4	54	6	36	4	0	2	8	.200	0	7-7	4	4.66
1993 Chicago	NL	15	0	0	6	16.2	75	18	9	8	1	0	1	0	9	0	10	0	0	1	0	1.000	0	1-1	3	4.32
1994 Chicago	NL	33	10	1	10	100	412	87	43	40	6	3	3	1	34	2	72	4	1	6	2	.750	0	2-2	1	3.60
1995 Chicago	NL	24	24	1	0	150	665	152	80	69	14	12	5	9	65	7	93	5	1	12	8	.600	1	0-0	0	4.14
1996 Chicago	NL	37	20	1	6	129.1	598	144	101	94	15	8	5	8	68	5	90	7	0	6	10	.375	1	1-1	0	6.54
5 ML YEARS		148	63	4	37	481	2130	473	282	255	45	32	18	22	230	20	301	20	2	27	28	.491	2	11-11	8	4.77

Dave Burba

Pitches: Right **Bats:** Right **Pos:** SP-33; RP-1   **Ht:** 6'4" **Wt:** 240 **Born:** 7/7/66 **Age:** 30

	HOW MUCH HE PITCHED						WHAT HE GAVE UP											THE RESULTS					
Year Team	Lg	G	GS	CG	GF	IP	BFP	H	R	ER	HR	SH	SF	HB	TBB	IBB	SO	WP	Bk	W	L	Pct.	ShO	Sv-Op	Hld	ERA
1990 Seattle	AL	6	0	0	2	8	35	8	6	4	0	2	0	1	2	0	4	0	0	0	0	.000	0	0-0	0	4.50
1991 Seattle	AL	22	2	0	11	36.2	153	34	16	15	6	0	0	0	14	3	16	1	0	2	2	.500	0	1-1	0	3.68
1992 San Francisco	NL	23	11	0	4	70.2	318	80	43	39	4	2	4	2	31	2	47	1	1	2	7	.222	0	0-0	0	4.97
1993 San Francisco	NL	54	5	0	9	95.1	408	95	49	45	14	6	3	3	37	5	88	4	0	10	3	.769	0	0-0	10	4.25
1994 San Francisco	NL	57	0	0	13	74	322	59	39	36	5	3	1	6	45	3	84	3	0	3	6	.333	0	0-3	11	4.38
1995 SF-Cin	NL	52	9	1	7	106.2	451	90	50	47	9	4	1	0	51	3	96	5	0	10	4	.714	1	0-1	5	3.97
1996 Cincinnati	NL	34	33	0	0	195	849	179	96	83	18	5	12	4	97	9	148	9	1	11	13	.458	0	0-0	0	3.83
1995 San Francisco	NL	37	0	0	7	43.1	191	38	26	24	5	3	1	0	25	2	46	2	0	4	2	.667	0	0-1	5	4.98
Cincinnati		15	9	1	0	63.1	260	52	24	23	4	1	0	0	26	1	50	3	0	6	2	.750	1	0-0	0	3.27
7 ML YEARS		248	60	1	46	586.1	2536	545	299	269	56	22	21	14	277	25	483	23	2	38	35	.521	1	1-5	26	4.13

John Burke

Pitches: Right **Bats:** Both **Pos:** RP-11   **Ht:** 6'4" **Wt:** 215 **Born:** 2/9/70 **Age:** 27

	HOW MUCH HE PITCHED						WHAT HE GAVE UP											THE RESULTS					
Year Team	Lg	G	GS	CG	GF	IP	BFP	H	R	ER	HR	SH	SF	HB	TBB	IBB	SO	WP	Bk	W	L	Pct.	ShO	Sv-Op	Hld	ERA
1992 Bend	A-	10	10	0	0	41	173	38	13	11	3	1	0	0	18	0	32	0	3	2	0	1.000	0	0- --	—	2.41
1993 Central Val	A+	20	20	2	0	119	521	104	62	42	5	7	2	3	64	0	114	8	1	7	8	.467	0	0- --	—	3.18
Colo. Sprng	AAA	8	8	0	0	48.2	206	44	22	17	0	3	2	2	23	0	38	1	0	3	2	.600	0	0- --	—	3.14
1994 Colo. Sprng	AAA	8	8	0	3	11	72	16	25	24	0	0	1	2	22	0	6	5	0	0	0	.000	0	0- --	—	19.64
Asheville	A	4	4	0	0	17	61	5	3	2	1	0	0	0	5	0	16	1	0	0	1	.000	0	0- --	—	1.06
1995 Colo. Sprng	AAA	19	17	0	1	87	376	79	46	44	7	2	3	1	48	0	65	5	1	7	1	.875	0	1- --	—	4.55
1996 Salem	A+	3	3	0	0	12	54	10	12	8	1	1	0	0	9	0	12	4	0	0	1	.000	0	0- --	—	6.00
Colo. Sprng	AAA	24	9	0	10	63.2	293	75	46	42	3	1	5	2	28	0	54	5	0	2	4	.333	0	1- --	—	5.94
1996 Colorado	NL	11	0	0	3	15.2	75	21	13	13	3	0	1	0	7	0	19	1	0	2	1	.667	0	0-0	1	7.47

John Burkett

Pitches: Right **Bats:** Right **Pos:** SP-34   **Ht:** 6'3" **Wt:** 215 **Born:** 11/28/64 **Age:** 32

	HOW MUCH HE PITCHED						WHAT HE GAVE UP											THE RESULTS					
Year Team	Lg	G	GS	CG	GF	IP	BFP	H	R	ER	HR	SH	SF	HB	TBB	IBB	SO	WP	Bk	W	L	Pct.	ShO	Sv-Op	Hld	ERA
1987 San Francisco	NL	3	0	0	1	6	28	7	4	3	2	1	0	1	3	0	5	0	0	0	0	.000	0	0-0	0	4.50
1990 San Francisco	NL	33	32	2	1	204	857	201	92	86	18	6	5	4	61	7	118	3	3	14	7	.667	0	1-1	0	3.79
1991 San Francisco	NL	36	34	3	0	206.2	890	223	103	96	19	8	8	10	60	2	131	5	0	12	11	.522	1	0-0	1	4.18
1992 San Francisco	NL	32	32	3	0	189.2	799	194	96	81	13	11	4	4	45	6	107	0	0	13	9	.591	1	0-0	0	3.84
1993 San Francisco	NL	34	34	2	0	231.2	942	224	100	94	18	8	4	11	40	4	145	1	2	22	7	.759	1	0-0	0	3.65
1994 San Francisco	NL	25	25	0	0	159.1	676	176	72	64	14	12	5	7	36	7	85	2	0	6	8	.429	0	0-0	0	3.62
1995 Florida	NL	30	30	4	0	188.1	810	208	95	90	22	10	0	6	57	5	126	2	1	14	14	.500	1	0-0	0	4.30
1996 Fla-Tex		34	34	2	0	222.2	934	229	117	105	19	12	6	5	58	4	155	0	0	11	12	.478	1	0-0	0	4.24
1996 Florida	NL	24	24	1	0	154	645	154	84	74	15	11	4	3	42	2	108	0	0	6	10	.375	0	0-0	0	4.32
Texas	AL	10	10	1	0	68.2	289	75	33	31	4	1	2	2	16	2	47	0	0	5	2	.714	1	0-0	0	4.06

34

		HOW MUCH HE PITCHED			WHAT HE GAVE UP		THE RESULTS	
Year Team	Lg	G GS CG GF	IP	BFP	H R ER HR SH SF HB	TBB IBB SO WP Bk	W L Pct. ShO Sv-Op Hld	ERA
8 ML YEARS		227 221 16 2	1408.1	5936	1462 679 619 125 68 32 48	360 35 872 13 6	92 68 .575 4 1-1 1	3.96

Ellis Burks

Bats: Right **Throws:** Right **Pos:** LF-129; CF-32; PH-6   **Ht:** 6'2" **Wt:** 198 **Born:** 9/11/64 **Age:** 32

		BATTING										BASERUNNING	PERCENTAGES
Year Team	Lg	G AB H	2B 3B HR	(Hm Rd)	TB	R RBI	TBB IBB	SO HBP SH SF				SB CS SB% GDP	Avg OBP SLG
1987 Boston	AL	133 558 152	30 2 20	(11 9)	246	94 59	41 0	98 2 4 1				27 6 .82 1	.272 .324 .441
1988 Boston	AL	144 540 159	37 5 18	(8 10)	260	93 92	62 1	89 3 4 6				25 9 .74 8	.294 .367 .481
1989 Boston	AL	97 399 121	19 6 12	(6 6)	188	73 61	36 2	52 5 2 4				21 5 .81 8	.303 .365 .471
1990 Boston	AL	152 588 174	33 8 21	(10 11)	286	89 89	48 4	82 1 2 2				9 11 .45 18	.296 .349 .486
1991 Boston	AL	130 474 119	33 3 14	(8 6)	200	56 56	39 2	81 6 2 3				6 11 .35 7	.251 .314 .422
1992 Boston	AL	66 235 60	8 3 8	(4 4)	98	35 30	25 2	48 1 0 2				5 2 .71 5	.255 .327 .417
1993 Chicago	AL	146 499 137	24 4 17	(7 10)	220	75 74	60 2	97 4 3 8				6 9 .40 11	.275 .352 .441
1994 Colorado	NL	42 149 48	8 3 13	(7 6)	101	33 24	16 3	39 0 0 0				3 1 .75 3	.322 .388 .678
1995 Colorado	NL	103 278 74	10 6 14	(8 6)	138	41 49	39 0	72 2 1 1				7 3 .70 7	.266 .359 .496
1996 Colorado	NL	156 613 211	45 8 40	(23 17)	**392**	142 128	61 2	114 6 3 2				32 6 .84 19	.344 .408 **.639**
10 ML YEARS		1169 4333 1255	247 48 177	(92 85)	2129	731 662	427 18	772 30 21 29				141 63 .69 87	.290 .355 .491

Jeromy Burnitz

Bats: L **Throws:** R **Pos:** PH-35; RF-29; DH-15; CF-13; LF-10   **Ht:** 6'0" **Wt:** 190 **Born:** 4/15/69 **Age:** 28

		BATTING										BASERUNNING	PERCENTAGES
Year Team	Lg	G AB H	2B 3B HR	(Hm Rd)	TB	R RBI	TBB IBB	SO HBP SH SF				SB CS SB% GDP	Avg OBP SLG
1993 New York	NL	86 263 64	10 6 13	(6 7)	125	49 38	38 4	66 1 2 2				3 6 .33 2	.243 .339 .475
1994 New York	NL	45 143 34	4 0 3	(2 1)	47	26 15	23 0	45 1 1 0				1 1 .50 2	.238 .347 .329
1995 Cleveland	AL	9 7 4	1 0 0	(0 0)	5	4 0	0 0	0 0 0 0				1 0 .00 0	.571 .571 .714
1996 Cle-Mil	AL	94 200 53	14 0 9	(5 4)	94	38 40	33 2	47 4 0 2				4 1 .80 4	.265 .377 .470
1996 Cleveland	AL	71 128 36	10 0 7	(4 3)	67	30 26	25 1	31 2 0 0				2 1 .67 3	.281 .406 .523
Milwaukee		23 72 17	4 0 2	(1 1)	27	8 14	8 1	16 2 0 2				2 0 1.00 1	.236 .321 .375
4 ML YEARS		234 613 155	29 6 25	(13 12)	271	117 93	94 6	158 6 3 4				8 8 .50 8	.253 .356 .442

Terry Burrows

Pitches: Left **Bats:** Left **Pos:** RP-8   **Ht:** 6'1" **Wt:** 185 **Born:** 11/28/68 **Age:** 28

		HOW MUCH HE PITCHED			WHAT HE GAVE UP		THE RESULTS	
Year Team	Lg	G GS CG GF	IP	BFP	H R ER HR SH SF HB	TBB IBB SO WP Bk	W L Pct. ShO Sv-Op Hld	ERA
1996 Nw Orleans *	AAA	18 0 0 9	28.2	108	19 9 8 1 0 1 0	8 0 17 1 1	3 0 1.000 0 6-- —	2.51
Columbus *	AAA	23 0 0 5	22.2	102	24 16 15 1 1 1 2	11 0 20 1 0	1 0 1.000 0 0-- —	5.96
1994 Texas	AL	1 0 0 0	1	5	1 1 1 1 0 0 0	1 0 0 0 0	0 0 .000 0 0-0 —	9.00
1995 Texas	AL	28 3 0 6	44.2	207	60 37 32 11 0 0 2	19 0 22 4 0	2 2 .500 0 1-3 6	6.45
1996 Milwaukee	AL	8 0 0 4	12.2	58	12 4 4 2 1 0 1	10 0 5 0 0	1 0 1.000 0 0-0 0	2.84
3 ML YEARS		37 3 0 10	58.1	270	73 42 37 14 1 0 3	30 0 27 4 0	3 2 .667 0 1-3 6	5.71

Mike Busby

Pitches: Right **Bats:** Right **Pos:** SP-1   **Ht:** 6'4" **Wt:** 210 **Born:** 12/27/72 **Age:** 24

		HOW MUCH HE PITCHED			WHAT HE GAVE UP		THE RESULTS	
Year Team	Lg	G GS CG GF	IP	BFP	H R ER HR SH SF HB	TBB IBB SO WP Bk	W L Pct. ShO Sv-Op Hld	ERA
1991 Cardinals	R	11 11 0 0	59	267	67 35 23 1 0 2 2	29 0 71 3 1	4 3 .571 0 0-- —	3.51
1992 Savannah	A	28 28 1 0	149.2	665	145 96 61 11 1 7 17	67 0 84 16 1	4 13 .235 0 0-- —	3.67
1993 Savannah	A	23 21 1 0	143.2	579	116 49 39 8 6 4 10	31 0 125 5 2	12 2 .857 1 0-- —	2.44
1994 St. Pete	A+	26 26 1 0	151.2	663	166 82 75 11 8 5 14	49 1 89 5 2	6 13 .316 0 0-- —	4.45
1995 Louisville	AAA	6 6 1 0	38.1	154	28 18 14 2 2 2 3	11 0 26 2 0	2 2 .500 0 0-- —	3.29
1996 Louisville	AAA	14 14 0 0	72	343	89 56 51 11 3 1 6	44 1 53 7 2	2 5 .286 0 0-- —	6.38
1996 St. Louis	NL	1 1 0 0	4	28	9 13 8 4 1 0 1	4 0 4 0 0	0 1 .000 0 0-0 0	18.00

Mike Busch

Bats: Right **Throws:** Right **Pos:** 3B-23; PH-17; 1B-1   **Ht:** 6'5" **Wt:** 220 **Born:** 7/7/68 **Age:** 28

		BATTING										BASERUNNING	PERCENTAGES
Year Team	Lg	G AB H	2B 3B HR	(Hm Rd)	TB	R RBI	TBB IBB	SO HBP SH SF				SB CS SB% GDP	Avg OBP SLG
1990 Great Falls	R+	61 220 72	18 2 13	— —	133	48 47	39 2	50 3 0 3				3 2 .60 8	.327 .430 .605
1991 Bakersfield	A+	21 72 20	3 1 4	— —	37	13 16	12 0	21 0 0 1				0 1 .00 1	.278 .376 .514
1992 San Antonio	AA	115 416 99	14 2 18	— —	171	58 51	36 2	111 4 0 3				3 2 .60 7	.238 .303 .411
1993 Albuquerque	AAA	122 431 122	32 4 22	— —	228	87 70	53 4	89 8 0 5				1 2 .33 12	.283 .368 .529
1994 Albuquerque	AAA	126 460 121	23 3 27	— —	231	73 83	50 0	101 4 0 1				2 3 .40 8	.263 .340 .502
1995 Albuquerque	AAA	121 443 119	32 1 18	— —	207	68 62	42 3	103 7 0 0				2 2 .50 12	.269 .341 .467
1996 Albuquerque	AAA	38 142 43	6 1 12	— —	87	30 36	22 4	45 2 0 0				0 1 .00 1	.303 .404 .613
1995 Los Angeles	NL	13 17 4	0 0 3	(0 3)	13	3 6	0 0	7 0 0 0				0 0 .00 0	.235 .235 .765
1996 Los Angeles	NL	38 83 18	4 0 4	(1 3)	34	8 17	5 0	33 0 0 2				0 0 .00 2	.217 .261 .410
2 ML YEARS		51 100 22	4 0 7	(1 6)	47	11 23	5 0	40 0 0 2				0 0 .00 2	.220 .257 .470

35

Brett Butler

Bats: Left **Throws:** Left **Pos:** CF-34   **Ht:** 5'10" **Wt:** 161 **Born:** 6/15/57 **Age:** 40

Year Team	Lg	G	AB	H	2B	3B	HR	(Hm	Rd)	TB	R	RBI	TBB	IBB	SO	HBP	SH	SF	SB	CS	SB%	GDP	Avg	OBP	SLG
1981 Atlanta	NL	40	126	32	2	3	0	(0	0)	40	17	4	19	0	17	0	0	0	9	1	.90	0	.254	.352	.317
1982 Atlanta	NL	89	240	52	2	0	0	(0	0)	54	35	7	25	0	35	0	3	0	21	8	.72	1	.217	.291	.225
1983 Atlanta	NL	151	549	154	21	13	5	(4	1)	216	84	37	54	3	56	2	3	5	39	23	.63	5	.281	.344	.393
1984 Cleveland	AL	159	602	162	25	9	3	(1	2)	214	108	49	86	1	62	4	11	6	52	22	.70	6	.269	.361	.355
1985 Cleveland	AL	152	591	184	28	14	5	(1	4)	255	106	50	63	2	42	1	8	3	47	20	.70	8	.311	.377	.431
1986 Cleveland	AL	161	587	163	17	14	4	(0	4)	220	92	51	70	1	65	4	17	5	32	15	.68	8	.278	.356	.375
1987 Cleveland	AL	137	522	154	25	8	9	(4	5)	222	91	41	91	0	55	1	2	2	33	16	.67	3	.295	.399	.425
1988 San Francisco	NL	157	568	163	27	9	6	(1	5)	226	109	43	97	4	64	4	8	2	43	20	.68	2	.287	.393	.398
1989 San Francisco	NL	154	594	168	22	4	4	(2	2)	210	100	36	59	2	69	3	13	3	31	16	.66	4	.283	.349	.354
1990 San Francisco	NL	160	622	192	20	9	3	(3	0)	239	108	44	90	1	62	6	7	7	51	19	.73	3	.309	.397	.384
1991 Los Angeles	NL	161	615	182	13	5	2	(2	0)	211	112	38	108	4	79	1	4	2	38	28	.58	3	.296	.401	.343
1992 Los Angeles	NL	157	553	171	14	11	3	(1	2)	214	86	39	95	2	67	3	24	1	41	21	.66	4	.309	.413	.391
1993 Los Angeles	NL	156	607	181	21	10	1	(0	1)	225	80	42	86	1	69	5	14	4	39	19	.67	6	.298	.387	.371
1994 Los Angeles	NL	111	417	131	13	9	8	(2	6)	186	79	33	68	0	52	2	7	2	27	8	.77	2	.314	.411	.446
1995 NYN-LA	NL	129	513	154	18	9	1	(0	1)	193	78	38	67	2	51	0	10	6	32	8	.80	5	.300	.377	.376
1996 Los Angeles	NL	34	131	35	1	0	1	(0	0)	38	22	8	9	0	22	1	1	3	8	3	.73	1	.267	.313	.290
1995 New York	NL	90	367	114	13	7	1	(0	1)	144	54	25	43	2	42	0	6	2	21	7	.75	4	.311	.381	.392
Los Angeles	NL	39	146	40	5	2	0	(0	0)	49	24	13	24	0	9	0	4	4	11	1	.92	1	.274	.368	.336
16 ML YEARS		2108	7837	2278	269	128	54	(21	33)	2965	1307	560	1087	23	867	37	132	51	543	247	.69	61	.291	.377	.378

Paul Byrd

Pitches: Right **Bats:** Right **Pos:** RP-38   **Ht:** 6'1" **Wt:** 185 **Born:** 12/3/70 **Age:** 26

Year Team	Lg	G	GS	CG	GF	IP	BFP	H	R	ER	HR	SH	SF	HB	TBB	IBB	SO	WP	Bk	W	L	Pct.	ShO	Sv-Op	Hld	ERA
1991 Kinston	A+	14	11	0	0	62.2	263	40	27	22	7	3	3	0	36	0	62	6	7	4	3	.571	0	0--	—	3.16
1992 Canton-Akrn	AA	24	24	4	0	152.1	654	122	68	51	4	5	4	4	75	2	118	10	0	14	6	.700	0	0--	—	3.01
1993 Canton-Akrn	AA	2	1	0	1	10	41	7	4	4	1	0	1	0	3	0	8	1	0	0	0	.000	0	0--	—	3.60
Charlotte	AAA	14	14	1	0	81	351	80	43	35	9	1	3	6	30	0	54	4	1	7	4	.636	1	0--	—	3.89
1994 Canton-Akrn	AA	21	20	4	0	139.1	594	135	70	59	10	5	5	2	52	3	106	1	2	5	9	.357	1	0--	—	3.81
Charlotte	AAA	9	4	0	2	36.2	149	33	19	16	5	3	3	0	11	1	15	3	0	2	2	.500	0	1--	—	3.93
1995 Norfolk	AAA	22	10	1	10	87	341	71	29	27	6	0	1	5	21	0	61	1	0	3	5	.375	0	6--	—	2.79
1996 Norfolk	AAA	5	0	0	1	7.2	32	4	3	3	0	0	4	1	8	0	0	2	0	1.000		0	1--	—	3.52
1995 New York	NL	17	0	0	6	22	91	18	6	5	1	0	2	1	7	1	26	1	0	2	0	1.000	0	0-0	3	2.05
1996 New York	NL	38	0	0	14	46.2	204	48	22	22	7	1	1	0	21	4	31	3	0	1	2	.333	0	0-2	3	4.24
2 ML YEARS		55	0	0	20	68.2	295	66	28	27	8	1	3	1	28	5	57	4	2	3	2	.600	0	0-2	6	3.54

Miguel Cairo

Bats: Right **Throws:** Right **Pos:** 2B-9   **Ht:** 6'0" **Wt:** 160 **Born:** 5/4/74 **Age:** 23

Year Team	Lg	G	AB	H	2B	3B	HR	(Hm	Rd)	TB	R	RBI	TBB	IBB	SO	HBP	SH	SF	SB	CS	SB%	GDP	Avg	OBP	SLG
1992 Dodgers	R	21	76	23	5	2	0	—	—	32	10	9	2	0	6	2	2	1	1	0	1.00	1	.303	.333	.421
Vero Beach	A+	36	125	28	0	0	0	—	—	28	7	7	11	0	12	0	3	1	5	3	.63	3	.224	.285	.224
1993 Vero Beach	A+	89	343	108	10	1	1	—	—	123	49	23	26	0	22	7	10	0	23	16	.59	2	.315	.375	.359
1994 Bakersfield	A+	133	533	155	23	4	2	—	—	192	76	48	34	3	37	6	15	4	44	23	.66	9	.291	.338	.360
1995 San Antonio	AA	107	435	121	20	1	1	—	—	146	53	41	26	0	31	5	4	4	33	16	.67	5	.278	.323	.336
1996 Syracuse	AAA	120	465	129	14	4	3	—	—	160	71	48	26	1	44	8	5	5	27	9	.75	5	.277	.323	.344
1996 Toronto	AL	9	27	6	2	0	0	(0	0)	8	5	1	2	0	9	1	0	0	0	0	.00	1	.222	.300	.296

Mike Cameron

Bats: R **Throws:** R **Pos:** RF-5; CF-4; PH-3; LF-2; DH-1   **Ht:** 6'2" **Wt:** 190 **Born:** 1/8/73 **Age:** 24

Year Team	Lg	G	AB	H	2B	3B	HR	(Hm	Rd)	TB	R	RBI	TBB	IBB	SO	HBP	SH	SF	SB	CS	SB%	GDP	Avg	OBP	SLG
1991 White Sox	R	44	136	30	3	0	0	—	—	33	21	11	17	0	29	4	1	0	13	2	.87	3	.221	.325	.243
1992 Utica	A-	28	87	24	1	4	2	—	—	39	15	12	11	0	26	0	1	1	3	7	.30	0	.276	.354	.448
South Bend	A	35	114	26	8	1	1	—	—	39	19	9	10	0	37	4	3	1	2	3	.40	0	.228	.310	.342
1993 South Bend	A	122	411	98	14	5	0	—	—	122	52	30	27	0	101	6	2	5	19	10	.66	8	.238	.292	.297
1994 Pr. William	A+	131	468	116	15	17	6	—	—	183	86	48	60	2	101	8	2	0	22	10	.69	6	.248	.343	.391
1995 Birmingham	AA	107	350	87	20	5	11	—	—	150	64	60	54	0	104	6	5	4	21	12	.64	9	.249	.355	.429
1996 Birmingham	AA	123	473	142	34	12	28	—	—	284	120	77	71	6	117	12	3	4	39	15	.72	5	.300	.402	.600
1995 Chicago	AL	28	38	7	2	0	1	(0	1)	12	4	2	3	0	15	0	3	0	0	0	.00	0	.184	.244	.316
1996 Chicago	AL	11	11	1	0	0	0	(0	0)	1	1	0	1	0	3	0	0	0	0	0	.00	0	.091	.167	.091
2 ML YEARS		39	49	8	2	0	1	(0	1)	13	5	2	4	0	18	0	3	0	0	0	.00	0	.163	.226	.265

Ken Caminiti

Bats: Both **Throws:** Right **Pos:** 3B-145; PH-3   **Ht:** 6'0" **Wt:** 200 **Born:** 4/21/63 **Age:** 34

															BATTING				BASERUNNING				PERCENTAGES		
Year Team	Lg	G	AB	H	2B	3B	HR	(Hm	Rd)	TB	R	RBI	TBB	IBB	SO	HBP	SH	SF	SB	CS	SB%	GDP	Avg	OBP	SLG
1987 Houston	NL	63	203	50	7	1	3	(2	1)	68	10	23	12	1	44	0	2	1	0	0	.00	6	.246	.287	.335
1988 Houston	NL	30	83	15	2	0	1	(0	1)	20	5	7	5	0	18	0	0	1	0	0	.00	3	.181	.225	.241
1989 Houston	NL	161	585	149	31	3	10	(3	7)	216	71	72	51	9	93	3	3	4	4	1	.80	8	.255	.316	.369
1990 Houston	NL	153	541	131	20	2	4	(2	2)	167	52	51	48	7	97	0	3	4	9	4	.69	15	.242	.302	.309
1991 Houston	NL	152	574	145	30	3	13	(9	4)	220	65	80	46	7	85	5	3	4	4	5	.44	18	.253	.312	.383
1992 Houston	NL	135	506	149	31	2	13	(7	6)	223	68	62	44	13	68	1	2	4	10	4	.71	14	.294	.350	.441
1993 Houston	NL	143	543	142	31	0	13	(5	8)	212	75	75	49	10	88	0	1	3	8	5	.62	15	.262	.321	.390
1994 Houston	NL	111	406	115	28	2	18	(6	12)	201	63	75	43	13	71	2	0	3	4	3	.57	8	.283	.352	.495
1995 San Diego	NL	143	526	159	33	0	26	(16	10)	270	74	94	69	8	94	1	0	6	12	5	.71	11	.302	.380	.513
1996 San Diego	NL	146	546	178	37	2	40	(20	20)	339	109	130	78	16	99	4	0	10	11	5	.69	15	.326	.408	.621
10 ML YEARS		1237	4513	1233	250	15	141	(70	71)	1936	592	669	445	84	757	16	14	40	62	32	.66	113	.273	.338	.429

Mike Campbell

Pitches: Right **Bats:** Right **Pos:** RP-8; SP-5   **Ht:** 6'3" **Wt:** 215 **Born:** 2/17/64 **Age:** 33

		HOW MUCH HE PITCHED						WHAT HE GAVE UP											THE RESULTS						
Year Team	Lg	G	GS	CG	GF	IP	BFP	H	R	ER	HR	SH	SF	HB	TBB	IBB	SO	WP	Bk	W	L	Pct.	ShO	Sv-Op	Hld	ERA
1996 Iowa *	AAA	16	16	1	0	95.2	381	75	31	29	8	4	4	1	23	2	87	2	1	8	2	.800	1	0- -	—	2.73
1987 Seattle	AL	9	9	1	0	49.1	215	41	29	26	9	2	3	2	25	2	35	1	1	1	4	.200	0	0-0	0	4.74
1988 Seattle	AL	20	20	2	0	114.2	507	128	81	75	18	2	5	0	43	1	63	4	4	6	10	.375	0	0-0	0	5.89
1989 Seattle	AL	5	5	0	0	21	103	28	22	17	4	0	0	0	10	0	6	0	0	1	2	.333	0	0-0	0	7.29
1992 Texas	AL	1	0	0	0	3.2	15	3	4	4	1	0	0	0	2	0	2	0	0	0	1	.000	0	0-0	0	9.82
1994 San Diego	NL	3	2	0	0	8.1	43	13	12	12	5	1	0	0	5	0	10	0	0	1	1	.500	0	0-1	0	12.96
1996 Chicago	NL	13	5	0	4	36.1	147	29	19	18	7	2	1	0	10	0	19	0	0	3	1	.750	0	0-1	0	4.46
6 ML YEARS		51	41	3	4	233.1	1030	242	167	152	44	7	9	2	95	3	135	5	5	12	19	.387	0	0-1	—	5.86

Casey Candaele

Bats: B **Throws:** R **Pos:** PH-14; 2B-11; 3B-3; SS-1   **Ht:** 5'9" **Wt:** 165 **Born:** 1/12/61 **Age:** 36

															BATTING				BASERUNNING				PERCENTAGES		
Year Team	Lg	G	AB	H	2B	3B	HR	(Hm	Rd)	TB	R	RBI	TBB	IBB	SO	HBP	SH	SF	SB	CS	SB%	GDP	Avg	OBP	SLG
1996 Buffalo *	AAA	94	392	122	22	2	6	(—	—)	166	66	37	27	2	35	1	3	3	3	5	.38	3	.311	.355	.423
1986 Montreal	NL	30	104	24	4	1	0	(0	0)	30	9	6	5	0	15	0	0	1	3	5	.38	3	.231	.264	.288
1987 Montreal	NL	138	449	122	23	4	1	(1	0)	156	62	23	38	3	28	2	4	2	7	10	.41	5	.272	.330	.347
1988 Mon-Hou	NL	57	147	25	8	1	0	(0	0)	35	11	5	11	1	17	0	3	0	1	1	.50	7	.170	.228	.238
1990 Houston	NL	130	262	75	8	6	3	(1	2)	104	30	22	31	5	42	1	4	0	7	5	.58	4	.286	.364	.397
1991 Houston	NL	151	461	121	20	7	4	(1	3)	167	44	50	40	7	49	0	1	3	9	3	.75	5	.262	.319	.362
1992 Houston	NL	135	320	68	12	1	1	(1	0)	85	19	18	24	3	36	3	7	6	7	1	.88	5	.213	.269	.266
1993 Houston	NL	75	121	29	8	0	1	(0	1)	40	18	7	10	0	14	0	0	0	2	3	.40	6	.240	.298	.331
1996 Cleveland	AL	24	44	11	2	0	1	(0	1)	16	8	4	1	0	9	0	0	0	0	0	.00	0	.250	.267	.364
1988 Montreal	NL	36	116	20	5	1	0	(0	0)	27	9	4	10	1	11	0	2	0	1	0	1.00	7	.172	.238	.233
Houston	NL	21	31	5	3	0	0	(0	0)	8	2	1	1	0	6	0	1	0	0	1	.00	0	.161	.188	.258
8 ML YEARS		740	1908	475	85	20	11	(4	7)	633	201	135	160	19	210	6	19	12	36	28	.56	29	.249	.307	.332

Tom Candiotti

Pitches: Right **Bats:** Right **Pos:** SP-27; RP-1   **Ht:** 6'2" **Wt:** 221 **Born:** 8/31/57 **Age:** 39

		HOW MUCH HE PITCHED						WHAT HE GAVE UP											THE RESULTS						
Year Team	Lg	G	GS	CG	GF	IP	BFP	H	R	ER	HR	SH	SF	HB	TBB	IBB	SO	WP	Bk	W	L	Pct.	ShO	Sv-Op	Hld	ERA
1996 San Bernrdo *	A+	2	2	0	0	9	41	11	6	5	0	0	0	1	4	0	10	1	1	0	1	.000	0	0- -	—	5.00
1983 Milwaukee	AL	10	8	2	1	55.2	233	62	21	20	4	0	2	2	16	0	21	0	0	4	4	.500	0	0- -	—	3.23
1984 Milwaukee	AL	8	6	0	0	32.1	147	38	21	19	5	0	0	0	10	0	23	1	0	2	2	.500	0	0- -	—	5.29
1986 Cleveland	AL	36	34	17	1	252.1	1078	234	112	100	18	3	9	8	106	0	167	12	4	16	12	.571	3	0- -	—	3.57
1987 Cleveland	AL	32	32	7	0	201.2	888	193	132	107	28	8	10	4	93	2	111	13	2	7	18	.280	2	0-0	0	4.78
1988 Cleveland	AL	31	31	11	0	216.2	903	225	86	79	15	12	5	6	53	3	137	5	7	14	8	.636	1	0-0	0	3.28
1989 Cleveland	AL	31	31	4	0	206	847	188	80	71	10	6	4	4	55	5	124	4	8	13	10	.565	0	0-0	0	3.10
1990 Cleveland	AL	31	29	3	1	202	856	207	92	82	23	4	3	6	55	1	128	9	3	15	11	.577	1	0-0	0	3.65
1991 Cle-Tor	AL	34	34	6	0	238	981	202	82	70	12	4	11	6	73	1	167	11	0	13	13	.500	0	0-0	0	2.65
1992 Los Angeles	NL	32	30	6	1	203.2	839	177	78	68	13	20	6	3	63	5	152	9	2	11	15	.423	2	0-0	0	3.00
1993 Los Angeles	NL	33	32	2	0	213.2	898	192	86	74	12	15	9	6	71	1	155	6	0	8	10	.444	0	0-0	0	3.12
1994 Los Angeles	NL	23	22	5	0	153	652	149	77	70	9	8	5	5	54	2	102	9	0	7	7	.500	0	0-0	0	4.12
1995 Los Angeles	NL	30	30	1	0	190.1	812	187	93	74	18	7	5	9	58	2	141	7	0	7	14	.333	1	0-0	0	3.50
1996 Los Angeles	NL	28	27	1	0	152.1	657	172	91	76	18	8	5	3	43	3	79	3	1	9	11	.450	0	0-0	0	4.49
1991 Cleveland	AL	15	15	3	0	108.1	442	88	35	27	6	1	7	2	28	0	86	6	0	7	6	.538	0	0-0	0	2.24
Toronto	AL	19	19	3	0	129.2	539	114	47	43	6	3	4	4	45	1	81	5	0	6	7	.462	0	0-0	0	2.98
13 ML YEARS		359	346	65	4	2317.2	9791	2226	1051	910	185	96	77	62	750	25	1507	89	27	126	135	.483	11	0- -	—	3.53

John Cangelosi

Bats: Both **Throws:** Left **Pos:** LF-53; PH-38; CF-29 **Ht:** 5'8" **Wt:** 160 **Born:** 3/10/63 **Age:** 34

Year Team	Lg	G	AB	H	2B	3B	HR	(Hm	Rd)	TB	R	RBI	TBB	IBB	SO	HBP	SH	SF	SB	CS	SB%	GDP	Avg	OBP	SLG
1985 Chicago	AL	5	2	0	0	0	0	(0	0)	0	2	0	0	0	1	1	1	0	0	0	.00	0	.000	.333	.000
1986 Chicago	AL	137	438	103	16	3	2	(1	1)	131	65	32	71	0	61	7	6	3	50	17	.75	5	.235	.349	.299
1987 Pittsburgh	NL	104	182	50	8	3	4	(2	2)	76	44	18	46	1	33	3	1	1	21	6	.78	3	.275	.427	.418
1988 Pittsburgh	NL	75	118	30	4	1	0	(0	0)	36	18	8	17	0	16	1	3	0	9	4	.69	0	.254	.353	.305
1989 Pittsburgh	NL	112	160	35	4	2	0	(0	0)	43	19	9	35	2	20	3	1	2	11	8	.58	1	.219	.365	.269
1990 Pittsburgh	NL	58	76	15	2	0	0	(0	0)	17	13	1	11	0	12	1	2	0	7	2	.78	2	.197	.307	.224
1992 Texas	AL	73	85	16	2	0	1	(0	1)	21	12	6	18	0	16	0	3	0	6	5	.55	0	.188	.330	.247
1994 New York	NL	62	111	28	4	0	0	(0	0)	32	14	4	19	1	20	2	3	0	5	1	.83	1	.252	.371	.288
1995 Houston	NL	90	201	64	5	2	2	(2	0)	79	46	18	48	2	42	4	2	1	21	5	.81	3	.318	.457	.393
1996 Houston	NL	108	262	69	11	4	1	(1	0)	91	49	16	44	0	41	5	1	1	17	9	.65	6	.263	.378	.347
10 ML YEARS		824	1635	410	56	15	10	(6	4)	526	281	112	309	6	262	27	23	8	147	57	.72	19	.251	.377	.322

Jay Canizaro

Bats: Right **Throws:** Right **Pos:** 2B-35; SS-7; PH-3 **Ht:** 5'9" **Wt:** 170 **Born:** 7/4/73 **Age:** 23

Year Team	Lg	G	AB	H	2B	3B	HR	(Hm	Rd)	TB	R	RBI	TBB	IBB	SO	HBP	SH	SF	SB	CS	SB%	GDP	Avg	OBP	SLG
1993 Giants	R	49	180	47	10	6	3	—	—	78	34	41	22	1	40	0	0	3	12	3	.80	4	.261	.337	.433
1994 San Jose	A+	126	464	117	16	2	15	—	—	182	77	69	46	1	98	5	0	3	12	6	.67	7	.252	.324	.392
1995 Shreveport	AA	126	440	129	25	7	12	—	—	204	83	60	58	4	98	6	4	5	16	9	.64	9	.293	.379	.464
1996 Phoenix	AAA	102	363	95	21	2	7	—	—	141	50	64	46	2	77	4	1	5	14	4	.78	7	.262	.347	.388
1996 San Francisco	NL	43	120	24	4	1	2	(1	1)	36	11	8	9	0	38	1	1	1	0	2	.00	5	.200	.260	.300

Jose Canseco

Bats: R **Throws:** R **Pos:** DH-84; LF-10; RF-2; PH-2 **Ht:** 6'4" **Wt:** 240 **Born:** 7/2/64 **Age:** 32

Year Team	Lg	G	AB	H	2B	3B	HR	(Hm	Rd)	TB	R	RBI	TBB	IBB	SO	HBP	SH	SF	SB	CS	SB%	GDP	Avg	OBP	SLG
1996 Pawtucket *	AAA	2	5	1	0	0	0	—	—	1	0	0	0	0	3	0	0	0	0	0	.00	0	.200	.200	.200
1985 Oakland	AL	29	96	29	3	0	5	(4	1)	47	16	13	4	0	31	0	0	0	1	1	.50	1	.302	.330	.490
1986 Oakland	AL	157	600	144	29	1	33	(14	19)	274	85	117	65	1	175	8	0	9	15	7	.68	12	.240	.318	.457
1987 Oakland	AL	159	630	162	35	3	31	(16	15)	296	81	113	50	2	157	2	0	9	15	3	.83	16	.257	.310	.470
1988 Oakland	AL	158	610	187	34	0	42	(16	26)	347	120	124	78	10	128	10	1	6	40	16	.71	15	.307	.391	.569
1989 Oakland	AL	65	227	61	9	1	17	(8	9)	123	40	57	23	4	69	2	0	6	6	3	.67	4	.269	.333	.542
1990 Oakland	AL	131	481	132	14	2	37	(18	19)	261	83	101	72	8	158	5	0	5	19	10	.66	9	.274	.371	.543
1991 Oakland	AL	154	572	152	32	1	44	(16	28)	318	115	122	78	8	152	9	0	6	26	6	.81	16	.266	.359	.556
1992 Oak-Tex	AL	119	439	107	15	0	26	(15	11)	200	74	87	63	2	128	6	0	4	6	7	.46	16	.244	.344	.456
1993 Texas	AL	60	231	59	14	1	10	(6	4)	105	30	46	16	2	62	3	0	3	6	6	.50	6	.255	.308	.455
1994 Texas	AL	111	429	121	19	2	31	(17	14)	237	88	90	69	8	114	5	0	2	15	8	.65	20	.282	.386	.552
1995 Boston	AL	102	396	121	25	1	24	(10	14)	220	64	81	42	4	93	7	0	5	4	0	1.00	9	.306	.378	.556
1996 Boston	AL	96	360	104	22	1	28	(17	11)	212	68	82	63	3	82	6	0	3	3	1	.75	7	.289	.400	.589
1992 Oakland	AL	97	366	90	11	0	22	(12	10)	167	66	72	48	1	104	3	0	4	5	7	.42	15	.246	.335	.456
Texas	AL	22	73	17	4	0	4	(3	1)	33	8	15	15	1	24	3	0	0	1	0	1.00	1	.233	.385	.452
12 ML YEARS		1341	5071	1379	251	13	328	(157	171)	2640	864	1033	623	52	1349	63	0	58	156	68	.70	131	.272	.355	.521

Dan Carlson

Pitches: Right **Bats:** Right **Pos:** RP-5 **Ht:** 6'1" **Wt:** 185 **Born:** 1/26/70 **Age:** 27

Year Team	Lg	G	GS	CG	GF	IP	BFP	H	R	ER	HR	SH	SF	HB	TBB	IBB	SO	WP	Bk	W	L	Pct.	ShO	Sv-Op	Hld	ERA
1990 Everett	A-	17	11	0	3	62.1	279	60	42	37	1	5	4	1	33	1	77	9	5	2	6	.250	0	0--	—	5.34
1991 Clinton	A	27	27	5	0	181.1	740	149	69	62	11	3	3	2	76	0	164	18	5	16	7	.696	3	0--	—	3.08
1992 Shreveport	AA	27	27	4	0	186	765	166	85	66	15	5	3	1	60	3	157	4	0	15	9	.625	1	0--	—	3.19
1993 Phoenix	AAA	13	12	0	0	70	320	79	54	51	12	2	1	5	32	1	48	0	0	5	6	.455	0	0--	—	6.56
Shreveport	AA	15	15	2	0	100.1	397	86	30	25	9	4	4	0	26	3	81	5	0	7	4	.636	1	0--	—	2.24
1994 Phoenix	AAA	31	22	0	2	151.1	665	173	80	78	21	3	9	1	55	1	117	10	0	13	6	.684	0	1--	—	4.64
1995 Phoenix	AAA	23	22	2	1	132.2	582	138	67	63	11	7	7	3	66	0	93	6	1	9	5	.643	0	0--	—	4.27
1996 Phoenix	AAA	33	15	2	3	146.2	604	135	61	56	18	5	5	2	46	0	123	3	0	13	6	.684	0	1--	—	3.44
1996 San Francisco	NL	5	0	0	3	10	46	13	6	3	2	0	2	0	2	0	4	0	0	1	0	1.000	0	0-0	0	2.70

Rafael Carmona

Pitches: Right **Bats:** Left **Pos:** RP-52; SP-1 **Ht:** 6'2" **Wt:** 185 **Born:** 10/2/72 **Age:** 24

Year Team	Lg	G	GS	CG	GF	IP	BFP	H	R	ER	HR	SH	SF	HB	TBB	IBB	SO	WP	Bk	W	L	Pct.	ShO	Sv-Op	Hld	ERA
1993 Bellingham	A-	23	0	0	9	35.2	159	33	19	15	1	5	1	1	14	1	30	4	0	2	3	.400	0	0--	—	3.79
1994 Riverside	A+	50	0	0	48	67.1	264	48	22	21	3	1	0	4	19	1	63	3	0	8	2	.800	0	21--	—	2.81
1995 Tacoma	AAA	8	8	1	0	48	212	52	29	27	6	1	2	3	19	1	37	1	3	4	3	.571	1	0--	—	5.06
Port City	AA	23	8	1	15	63	271	63	34	30	6	2	3	4	22	1	54	3	3	4	5	.500	1	4--	—	4.29
1996 Tacoma	AAA	4	1	0	2	6.1	29	5	1	1	1	0	0	0	5	0	9	0	1	0	0	.000	0	0--	—	1.42

		HOW MUCH HE PITCHED			WHAT HE GAVE UP				THE RESULTS				
Year Team	Lg	G GS CG GF	IP	BFP	H R ER	HR SH SF HB	TBB IBB	SO	WP	Bk	W L	Pct.	ShO	Sv-Op	Hld	ERA
1995 Seattle	AL	15 3 0 6	47.2	230	55 31 30	9 1 5 2	34 1	28	3	1	2 4	.333	0	1-2	0	5.66
1996 Seattle	AL	53 1 0 15	90.1	415	95 47 43	11 7 2 3	55 9	62	4	0	8 3	.727	0	1-5	8	4.28
2 ML YEARS		68 4 0 21	138	645	150 78 73	20 8 7 5	89 10	90	7	1	10 7	.588	0	2-7	8	4.76

Cris Carpenter

Pitches: Right **Bats:** Right **Pos:** RP-8   **Ht:** 6'1" **Wt:** 198 **Born:** 4/5/65 **Age:** 32

		HOW MUCH HE PITCHED			WHAT HE GAVE UP						THE RESULTS				
Year Team	Lg	G GS CG GF	IP	BFP	H R ER	HR SH SF HB	TBB IBB	SO	WP	Bk	W L	Pct.	ShO	Sv-Op	Hld	ERA
1996 Nw Orleans *	AAA	40 0 0 17	50	201	46 16 14	4 1 1 2	7 3	41	0	0	1 0	1.000	0	8--	—	2.52
1988 St. Louis	NL	8 8 1 0	47.2	203	56 27 25	3 1 4 1	9 2	24	1	0	2 3	.400	0	0-0	0	4.72
1989 St. Louis	NL	36 5 0 10	68	303	70 30 24	4 4 4 2	26 9	35	1	0	4 4	.500	0	0-2	2	3.18
1990 St. Louis	NL	4 0 0 1	8	32	5 4 4	2 0 0 0	2 1	6	0	0	0 0	.000	0	0-0	0	4.50
1991 St. Louis	NL	59 0 0 19	66	266	53 31 31	6 3 2 0	20 9	47	1	0	10 4	.714	0	0-0	12	4.23
1992 St. Louis	NL	73 0 0 21	88	355	69 29 29	10 8 3 4	27 8	46	5	0	5 4	.556	0	1-8	7	2.97
1993 Fla-Tex		56 0 0 17	69.1	293	64 30 27	5 2 4 4	25 3	53	7	0	4 2	.667	0	1-4	14	3.50
1994 Texas	AL	47 0 0 16	59	263	69 35 33	7 3 3 0	20 7	39	1	0	2 5	.286	0	5-11	5	5.03
1996 Milwaukee	AL	8 0 0 2	8.1	39	12 8 7	1 0 1 0	2 0	2	0	0	0 0	.000	0	0-0	0	7.56
1993 Florida	NL	29 0 0 9	37.1	154	29 15 12	1 1 1 2	13 2	26	5	0	0 1	.000	0	0-2	3	2.89
Texas	AL	27 0 0 8	32	139	35 15 15	4 1 3 2	12 1	27	2	0	4 1	.800	0	1-2	11	4.22
8 ML YEARS		291 13 1 86	414.1	1754	398 194 180	38 21 21 11	131 39	252	16	0	27 22	.551	0	7-25	40	3.91

Chuck Carr

Bats: Both **Throws:** Right **Pos:** CF-27   **Ht:** 5'10" **Wt:** 165 **Born:** 8/10/68 **Age:** 28

		BATTING													BASERUNNING				PERCENTAGES		
Year Team	Lg	G	AB	H	2B	3B	HR	(Hm	Rd)	TB	R	RBI	TBB	IBB	SO	HBP	SH	SF	SB	CS	SB%	GDP	Avg	OBP	SLG
1996 New Orleans *	AAA	4	13	5	1	0	0	—	—	6	2	1	2	0	1	0	0	0	2	1	1.00	0	.385	.467	.462
1990 New York	NL	4	2	0	0	0	0	(0	0)	0	0	0	0	0	2	0	0	0	1	0	1.00	0	.000	.000	.000
1991 New York	NL	12	11	2	0	0	0	(0	0)	2	1	1	0	0	2	0	0	0	1	0	1.00	0	.182	.182	.182
1992 St. Louis	NL	22	64	14	3	0	0	(0	0)	17	8	3	9	0	6	0	3	0	10	2	.83	0	.219	.315	.266
1993 Florida	NL	142	551	147	19	2	4	(3	1)	182	75	41	49	0	74	2	7	4	58	22	.73	6	.267	.327	.330
1994 Florida	NL	106	433	114	19	2	2	(1	1)	143	61	30	22	1	71	5	6	2	32	8	.80	5	.263	.305	.330
1995 Florida	NL	105	308	70	20	0	2	(1	1)	96	54	20	46	1	49	2	7	2	25	11	.69	2	.227	.330	.312
1996 Milwaukee	AL	27	106	29	6	1	1	(0	1)	40	18	11	6	0	21	0	1	0	5	4	.56	1	.274	.310	.377
7 ML YEARS		418	1475	376	67	5	9	(5	4)	480	217	106	132	2	225	9	23	9	132	47	.74	14	.255	.318	.325

Giovanni Carrara

Pitches: Right **Bats:** Right **Pos:** RP-14; SP-5   **Ht:** 6'2" **Wt:** 230 **Born:** 3/4/68 **Age:** 29

		HOW MUCH HE PITCHED			WHAT HE GAVE UP						THE RESULTS				
Year Team	Lg	G GS CG GF	IP	BFP	H R ER	HR SH SF HB	TBB IBB	SO	WP	Bk	W L	Pct.	ShO	Sv-Op	Hld	ERA
1991 St. Cathrns	A-	15 13 2 0	89.2	363	66 26 16	5 0 4 8	21 0	83	4	2	5 2	.714	2	0--	—	1.61
1992 Dunedin	A+	5 4 0 1	23.1	101	22 13 12	1 0 0 2	11 0	16	4	0	0 1	.000	0	0--	—	4.63
Myrtle Bch	A	22 16 1 2	100.1	416	86 40 35	12 0 2 4	36 0	100	9	3	11 7	.611	1	0--	—	3.14
1993 Dunedin	A+	27 24 1 1	140.2	601	136 69 54	14 4 4 4	59 0	108	10	0	6 11	.353	0	0--	—	3.45
1994 Knoxville	AA	26 26 1 0	164.1	705	158 85 71	16 2 7 7	59 0	96	9	0	13 7	.650	0	0--	—	3.89
1995 Syracuse	AAA	21 21 0 0	131.2	565	116 72 58	11 3 2 4	56 2	81	3	0	7 7	.500	0	0--	—	3.96
1996 Syracuse	AAA	9 6 1 1	37.2	159	37 16 15	2 0 1 0	12 1	28	1	0	4 4	.500	0	0--	—	3.58
Indianapols	AAA	9 6 1 2	47.2	177	26 5 4	2 0 1 3	9 0	45	0	1	4 1	1.000	1	1--	—	0.76
1995 Toronto	AL	12 7 1 2	48.2	229	64 46 39	10 1 2 1	25 1	27	1	0	2 4	.333	0	0-0	0	7.21
1996 Tor-Cin		19 5 0 4	38	188	54 36 34	11 1 0 2	25 3	23	1	0	1 1	.500	0	0-1	0	8.05
1996 Toronto	AL	11 0 0 3	15	76	23 19 19	5 0 0 0	12 2	10	1	0	0 1	.000	0	0-1	0	11.40
Cincinnati	NL	8 5 0 1	23	112	31 17 15	6 1 0 2	13 1	13	0	0	1 0	1.000	0	0-0	0	5.87
2 ML YEARS		31 12 1 6	86.2	417	118 82 73	21 2 2 3	50 4	50	2	0	3 5	.375	0	0-1	0	7.58

Hector Carrasco

Pitches: Right **Bats:** Right **Pos:** RP-56   **Ht:** 6'2" **Wt:** 180 **Born:** 10/22/69 **Age:** 27

		HOW MUCH HE PITCHED			WHAT HE GAVE UP						THE RESULTS				
Year Team	Lg	G GS CG GF	IP	BFP	H R ER	HR SH SF HB	TBB IBB	SO	WP	Bk	W L	Pct.	ShO	Sv-Op	Hld	ERA
1996 Indianapols *	AAA	13 2 0 4	21	97	18 7 5	1 2 0 1	13 1	17	2	0	0 1	.000	0	0--	—	2.14
1994 Cincinnati	NL	45 0 0 29	56.1	237	42 17 14	3 5 0 2	30 1	41	3	1	5 6	.455	0	6-8	3	2.24
1995 Cincinnati	NL	64 0 0 28	87.1	391	86 45 40	1 2 6 2	46 5	64	15	0	2 7	.222	0	5-9	11	4.12
1996 Cincinnati	NL	56 0 0 10	74.1	325	58 37 31	6 4 4 1	45 5	59	8	1	4 3	.571	0	0-2	15	3.75
3 ML YEARS		165 0 0 67	218	953	186 99 85	10 11 10 5	121 11	164	26	2	11 16	.407	0	11-19	29	3.51

Mark Carreon

Bats: R **Throws:** L **Pos:** 1B-107; PH-7; CF-4; LF-3; RF-3; DH-2   **Ht:** 6'0" **Wt:** 195 **Born:** 7/9/63 **Age:** 33

		BATTING													BASERUNNING				PERCENTAGES		
Year Team	Lg	G	AB	H	2B	3B	HR	(Hm | Rd)	TB	R	RBI	TBB	IBB	SO	HBP	SH	SF	SB	CS	SB%	GDP	Avg	OBP	SLG
1987 New York	NL	9	12	3	0	0	0	(0 | 0)	3	0	1	1	0	1	0	0	0	0	1	.00	0	.250	.308	.250

39

Year Team	Lg	G	AB	H	2B	3B	HR	(Hm Rd)	TB	R	RBI	TBB	IBB	SO	HBP	SH	SF	SB	CS	SB%	GDP	Avg	OBP	SLG
								BATTING										BASERUNNING				PERCENTAGES		
1988 New York	NL	7	9	5	2	0	1	(0 1)	10	5	1	2	0	1	0	0	0	0	0	.00	0	.556	.636	1.111
1989 New York	NL	68	133	41	6	0	6	(4 2)	65	20	16	12	0	17	1	0	0	2	3	.40	1	.308	.370	.489
1990 New York	NL	82	188	47	12	0	10	(1 9)	89	30	26	15	0	29	2	0	0	1	0	1.00	1	.250	.312	.473
1991 New York	NL	106	254	66	6	0	4	(3 1)	84	18	21	12	2	26	2	1	1	2	1	.67	13	.260	.297	.331
1992 Detroit	AL	101	336	78	11	1	10	(5 5)	121	34	41	22	2	57	1	1	4	3	1	.75	12	.232	.278	.360
1993 San Francisco	NL	78	150	49	9	1	7	(2 5)	81	22	33	13	2	16	1	0	5	1	0	1.00	8	.327	.373	.540
1994 San Francisco	NL	51	100	27	4	0	3	(2 1)	40	8	20	7	0	20	2	0	2	0	0	.00	1	.270	.324	.400
1995 San Francisco	NL	117	396	119	24	0	17	(7 10)	194	53	65	23	1	37	4	0	3	0	1	.00	7	.301	.343	.490
1996 SF-Cle		119	434	122	34	3	11	(5 6)	195	56	65	33	2	42	6	0	2	3	4	.43	10	.281	.339	.449
1996 San Francisco	NL	81	292	76	22	3	9	(4 5)	131	40	51	22	2	33	3	0	2	2	3	.40	6	.260	.317	.449
Cleveland	AL	38	142	46	12	0	2	(1 1)	64	16	14	11	0	9	3	0	0	1	1	.50	4	.324	.385	.451
10 ML YEARS		738	2012	557	108	5	69	(29 40)	882	246	289	140	9	246	19	2	17	12	11	.52	53	.277	.327	.438

Joe Carter

Bats: Right **Throws:** Right **Pos:** LF-115; 1B-41; DH-15 **Ht:** 6'3" **Wt:** 215 **Born:** 3/7/60 **Age:** 37

Year Team	Lg	G	AB	H	2B	3B	HR	(Hm Rd)	TB	R	RBI	TBB	IBB	SO	HBP	SH	SF	SB	CS	SB%	GDP	Avg	OBP	SLG
								BATTING										BASERUNNING				PERCENTAGES		
1983 Chicago	NL	23	51	9	1	1	0	(0 0)	12	6	1	0	0	21	0	1	0	1	0	1.00	1	.176	.176	.235
1984 Cleveland	AL	66	244	67	6	1	13	(9 4)	114	32	41	11	0	48	1	0	1	2	4	.33	2	.275	.307	.467
1985 Cleveland	AL	143	489	128	27	0	15	(5 10)	200	64	59	25	2	74	2	3	4	24	6	.80	9	.262	.298	.409
1986 Cleveland	AL	162	663	200	36	9	29	(14 15)	341	108	121	32	3	95	5	1	8	29	7	.81	8	.302	.335	.514
1987 Cleveland	AL	149	588	155	27	2	32	(9 23)	282	83	106	27	6	105	9	1	4	31	6	.84	8	.264	.304	.480
1988 Cleveland	AL	157	621	168	36	6	27	(16 11)	297	85	98	35	6	82	7	1	6	27	5	.84	6	.271	.314	.478
1989 Cleveland	AL	162	651	158	32	4	35	(16 19)	303	84	105	39	8	112	8	2	5	13	5	.72	6	.243	.292	.465
1990 San Diego	NL	162	634	147	27	1	24	(12 12)	248	79	115	48	18	93	7	0	8	22	6	.79	12	.232	.290	.391
1991 Toronto	AL	162	638	174	42	3	33	(23 10)	321	89	108	49	12	112	10	0	9	20	9	.69	6	.273	.330	.503
1992 Toronto	AL	158	622	164	30	7	34	(21 13)	310	97	119	36	4	109	11	1	13	12	5	.71	14	.264	.309	.498
1993 Toronto	AL	155	603	153	33	5	33	(21 12)	295	92	121	47	5	113	9	0	10	8	3	.73	10	.254	.312	.489
1994 Toronto	AL	111	435	118	25	2	27	(18 9)	228	70	103	33	6	64	2	0	13	11	0	1.00	6	.271	.317	.524
1995 Toronto	AL	139	558	141	23	0	25	(13 12)	239	70	76	37	5	87	3	0	5	12	1	.92	11	.253	.300	.428
1996 Toronto	AL	157	625	158	35	7	30	(14 16)	297	84	107	44	2	106	7	0	6	7	6	.54	12	.253	.306	.475
14 ML YEARS		1906	7422	1940	380	48	357	(191 166)	3487	1043	1280	463	77	1221	81	10	92	219	63	.78	111	.261	.308	.470

Raul Casanova

Bats: Both **Throws:** Right **Pos:** C-22; DH-3; PH-2 **Ht:** 5'11" **Wt:** 200 **Born:** 8/23/72 **Age:** 24

Year Team	Lg	G	AB	H	2B	3B	HR	(Hm Rd)	TB	R	RBI	TBB	IBB	SO	HBP	SH	SF	SB	CS	SB%	GDP	Avg	OBP	SLG
								BATTING										BASERUNNING				PERCENTAGES		
1990 Mets	R	23	65	5	0	0	0	— —	5	4	1	4	0	16	0	0	0	0	1	.00	2	.077	.130	.077
1991 Mets	R	32	111	27	4	2	0	— —	35	19	9	12	0	22	2	1	1	3	0	1.00	4	.243	.325	.315
Kingsport	R+	5	18	1	0	0	0	— —	1	0	0	1	0	10	0	0	0	0	0	.00	0	.056	.105	.056
1992 Columbia	A	5	18	3	0	0	0	— —	3	2	1	1	0	4	0	0	0	0	0	.00	0	.167	.211	.167
Kingsport	R+	42	137	37	9	1	4	— —	60	25	27	26	2	25	4	0	0	3	1	.75	7	.270	.401	.438
1993 Waterloo	A	76	227	58	12	0	6	— —	88	32	30	21	2	46	1	5	0	0	1	.00	5	.256	.321	.388
1994 Rancho Cuca	A+	123	471	160	27	2	23	— —	260	83	120	43	2	97	9	0	3	1	4	.20	16	.340	.403	.552
1995 Memphis	AA	89	306	83	18	0	12	— —	137	42	44	25	2	51	4	0	8	4	1	.80	7	.271	.330	.448
1996 Jacksonvlle	AA	8	30	10	2	0	4	— —	24	5	9	2	0	7	0	0	0	0	0	.00	0	.333	.375	.800
Toledo	AAA	49	161	44	11	0	8	— —	79	23	28	20	0	24	2	1	4	0	1	.00	11	.273	.353	.491
1996 Detroit	AL	25	85	16	1	0	4	(1 3)	29	6	9	9	0	18	0	0	0	0	0	.00	6	.188	.242	.341

Larry Casian

Pitches: Left **Bats:** Right **Pos:** RP-35 **Ht:** 6'0" **Wt:** 175 **Born:** 10/28/65 **Age:** 31

Year Team	Lg	G	GS	CG	GF	IP	BFP	H	R	ER	HR	SH	SF	HB	TBB	IBB	SO	WP	Bk	W	L	Pct.	ShO	Sv-Op	Hld	ERA
		HOW MUCH HE PITCHED						WHAT HE GAVE UP												THE RESULTS						
1996 Iowa *	AAA	24	0	0	5	47.1	187	37	13	9	1	1	0	0	11	4	32	2	0	3	2	.600	0	1--	—	1.71
1990 Minnesota	AL	5	3	0	1	22.1	90	26	9	8	2	0	1	0	4	0	11	0	0	2	1	.667	0	0-0	0	3.22
1991 Minnesota	AL	15	0	0	4	18.1	87	28	16	15	4	0	0	1	7	2	6	2	0	0	0	.000	0	0-0	2	7.36
1992 Minnesota	AL	6	0	0	1	6.2	28	7	2	2	0	0	0	0	1	0	2	0	0	1	0	1.000	0	0-0	1	2.70
1993 Minnesota	AL	54	0	0	8	56.2	241	59	23	19	1	3	3	1	14	2	31	2	0	5	3	.625	0	1-3	15	3.02
1994 Min-Cle	AL	40	0	0	10	49	231	73	43	40	12	7	2	2	16	3	20	1	0	1	5	.167	0	1-1	6	7.35
1995 Chicago	NL	42	0	0	5	23.1	107	23	6	5	1	1	2	0	15	6	11	2	0	1	0	1.000	0	0-3	4	1.93
1996 Chicago	NL	35	0	0	4	24	90	14	5	5	2	2	1	1	11	3	15	1	0	1	0	.500	0	0-1	5	1.88
1994 Minnesota	AL	33	0	0	8	40.2	188	57	34	32	11	6	2	2	12	2	18	0	0	1	3	.250	0	1-1	5	7.08
Cleveland	AL	7	0	0	2	8.1	43	16	9	8	1	1	0	0	4	1	2	1	0	0	2	.000	0	0-0	1	8.64
7 ML YEARS		197	3	0	33	200.1	874	230	104	94	22	13	9	5	68	16	96	8	0	11	10	.524	0	2-8	33	4.22

Pedro Castellano

Bats: Right **Throws:** Right **Pos:** PH-8; 2B-3; 3B-1; LF-1 **Ht:** 6'1" **Wt:** 180 **Born:** 3/11/70 **Age:** 27

Year Team	Lg	G	AB	H	2B	3B	HR	(Hm Rd)	TB	R	RBI	TBB	IBB	SO	HBP	SH	SF	SB	CS	SB%	GDP	Avg	OBP	SLG
								BATTING										BASERUNNING				PERCENTAGES		
1996 Colo. Sprng *	AAA	94	362	122	30	3	13	— —	197	56	59	40	4	46	4	0	3	0	2	.00	8	.337	.406	.544

Year Team	Lg	G	AB	H	2B	3B	HR	(Hm	Rd)	TB	R	RBI	TBB	IBB	SO	HBP	SH	SF	SB	CS	SB%	GDP	Avg	OBP	SLG
1993 Colorado	NL	34	71	13	2	0	3	(1	2)	24	12	7	8	0	16	0	0	0	1	1	.50	1	.183	.266	.338
1995 Colorado	NL	4	5	0	0	0	0	(0	0)	0	0	0	2	0	3	0	0	0	0	0	.00	0	.000	.286	.000
1996 Colorado	NL	13	17	2	0	0	0	(0	0)	2	1	2	3	1	6	1	0	0	0	0	.00	0	.118	.286	.118
3 ML YEARS		51	93	15	2	0	3	(1	2)	26	13	9	13	1	25	1	0	0	1	1	.50	1	.161	.271	.280

Vinny Castilla

Bats: Right **Throws:** Right **Pos:** 3B-160; PH-2   **Ht:** 6'1" **Wt:** 200 **Born:** 7/4/67 **Age:** 29

Year Team	Lg	G	AB	H	2B	3B	HR	(Hm	Rd)	TB	R	RBI	TBB	IBB	SO	HBP	SH	SF	SB	CS	SB%	GDP	Avg	OBP	SLG
1991 Atlanta	NL	12	5	1	0	0	0	(0	0)	1	1	0	0	0	2	0	1	0	0	0	.00	0	.200	.200	.200
1992 Atlanta	NL	9	16	4	1	0	0	(0	0)	5	1	1	1	1	4	1	0	0	0	0	.00	0	.250	.333	.313
1993 Colorado	NL	105	337	86	9	7	9	(5	4)	136	36	30	13	4	45	2	0	5	2	5	.29	10	.255	.283	.404
1994 Colorado	NL	52	130	43	11	1	3	(1	2)	65	16	18	7	1	23	0	1	3	2	1	.67	3	.331	.357	.500
1995 Colorado	NL	139	527	163	34	2	32	(23	9)	297	82	90	30	2	87	4	4	6	2	8	.20	15	.309	.347	.564
1996 Colorado	NL	160	629	191	34	0	40	(27	13)	345	97	113	35	7	88	5	0	4	7	2	.78	20	.304	.343	.548
6 ML YEARS		477	1644	488	89	10	84	(56	28)	849	233	252	86	15	249	12	6	18	13	16	.45	48	.297	.333	.516

Alberto Castillo

Bats: Right **Throws:** Right **Pos:** C-6   **Ht:** 6'0" **Wt:** 184 **Born:** 2/10/70 **Age:** 27

Year Team	Lg	G	AB	H	2B	3B	HR	(Hm	Rd)	TB	R	RBI	TBB	IBB	SO	HBP	SH	SF	SB	CS	SB%	GDP	Avg	OBP	SLG
1987 Kingsport	R+	7	9	1	0	0	0	—	—	1	1	0	5	0	3	0	1	0	1	0	1.00	0	.111	.429	.111
1988 Mets	R	22	68	18	4	0	0	—	—	22	7	10	4	0	4	2	2	3	2	0	1.00	3	.265	.312	.324
Kingsport	R+	24	75	22	3	0	1	—	—	28	7	14	15	1	14	0	1	1	0	1	.00	1	.293	.407	.373
1989 Kingsport	R+	27	74	19	4	0	3	—	—	32	15	12	11	1	14	1	0	0	2	1	.67	2	.257	.360	.432
Pittsfield	A-	34	123	29	8	0	1	—	—	40	13	13	7	0	26	1	2	2	2	0	1.00	3	.236	.278	.325
1990 Columbia	A	30	103	24	4	3	1	—	—	37	8	14	10	0	21	0	2	2	1	1	.50	2	.233	.296	.359
Pittsfield	A-	58	185	41	8	1	4	—	—	63	19	24	28	2	35	5	1	2	3	3	.50	7	.222	.336	.341
St. Lucie	A+	3	11	4	0	0	1	—	—	7	4	3	1	0	1	0	0	0	0	0	.00	2	.364	.417	.636
1991 Columbia	A	90	267	74	20	3	3	—	—	109	35	47	43	0	44	5	6	4	6	6	.50	6	.277	.382	.408
1992 St. Lucie	A+	60	162	33	6	0	3	—	—	48	11	17	16	0	37	2	3	2	0	0	.00	0	.204	.280	.296
1993 St. Lucie	A+	105	333	86	21	0	5	—	—	122	37	42	28	1	46	3	2	7	2	3	.40	5	.258	.315	.366
1994 Binghamton	AA	90	315	78	14	0	7	—	—	113	33	42	41	0	46	0	3	1	1	3	.25	11	.248	.333	.359
1995 Norfolk	AAA	69	217	58	13	1	4	—	—	85	23	31	26	0	32	1	3	2	2	3	.40	6	.267	.346	.392
1996 Norfolk	AAA	113	341	71	12	1	11	—	—	118	34	39	39	1	67	4	7	3	2	2	.50	3	.208	.295	.346
1995 New York	NL	13	29	3	0	0	0	(0	0)	3	2	0	3	0	9	1	0	0	1	0	1.00	0	.103	.212	.103
1996 New York	NL	6	11	4	0	0	0	(0	0)	4	1	0	0	0	4	0	0	0	0	0	.00	0	.364	.364	.364
2 ML YEARS		19	40	7	0	0	0	(0	0)	7	3	0	3	0	13	1	0	0	1	0	1.00	0	.175	.250	.175

Frank Castillo

Pitches: Right **Bats:** Right **Pos:** SP-33   **Ht:** 6'1" **Wt:** 200 **Born:** 4/1/69 **Age:** 28

		HOW MUCH HE PITCHED						WHAT HE GAVE UP										THE RESULTS						
Year Team	Lg	G	GS	CG	GF	IP	BFP	H	R	ER	HR	SH	SF	HB	TBB	IBB	SO	WP	Bk	W	L	Pct.	ShO	Sv-Op	Hld	ERA
1991 Chicago	NL	18	18	4	0	111.2	467	107	56	54	5	6	3	6	33	2	73	5	1	6	7	.462	0	0-0	0	4.35
1992 Chicago	NL	33	33	0	0	205.1	856	179	91	79	19	11	5	6	63	6	135	11	0	10	11	.476	0	0-0	0	3.46
1993 Chicago	NL	29	25	2	0	141.1	614	162	83	76	20	10	3	9	39	4	84	5	3	5	8	.385	0	0-0	0	4.84
1994 Chicago	NL	4	4	1	0	23	96	25	13	11	3	1	0	0	5	0	19	0	0	2	1	.667	0	0-0	0	4.30
1995 Chicago	NL	29	29	2	0	188	795	179	75	67	22	11	3	6	52	4	135	3	1	11	10	.524	2	0-0	0	3.21
1996 Chicago	NL	33	33	1	0	182.1	789	209	112	107	28	4	5	8	46	4	139	2	1	7	16	.304	1	0-0	0	5.28
6 ML YEARS		146	142	10	0	851.2	3617	861	430	394	97	43	19	29	238	20	585	26	6	41	53	.436	3	0-0	0	4.16

Luis Castillo

Bats: Both **Throws:** Right **Pos:** 2B-41   **Ht:** 5'11" **Wt:** 155 **Born:** 9/12/75 **Age:** 21

Year Team	Lg	G	AB	H	2B	3B	HR	(Hm	Rd)	TB	R	RBI	TBB	IBB	SO	HBP	SH	SF	SB	CS	SB%	GDP	Avg	OBP	SLG
1994 Marlins	R	57	216	57	8	0	0	—	—	65	49	16	37	0	36	1	2	2	31	12	.72	1	.264	.371	.301
1995 Kane County	A	89	340	111	4	4	0	—	—	123	71	23	55	1	50	0	4	1	41	18	.69	1	.326	.419	.362
1996 Portland	AA	109	420	133	15	7	1	—	—	165	83	35	66	4	68	2	6	1	51	28	.65	2	.317	.411	.393
1996 Florida	NL	41	164	43	2	1	1	(0	1)	50	26	8	14	0	46	0	2	0	17	4	.81	0	.262	.320	.305

Tony Castillo

Pitches: Left **Bats:** Left **Pos:** RP-55   **Ht:** 5'10" **Wt:** 190 **Born:** 3/1/63 **Age:** 34

		HOW MUCH HE PITCHED						WHAT HE GAVE UP										THE RESULTS						
Year Team	Lg	G	GS	CG	GF	IP	BFP	H	R	ER	HR	SH	SF	HB	TBB	IBB	SO	WP	Bk	W	L	Pct.	ShO	Sv-Op	Hld	ERA
1988 Toronto	AL	14	0	0	6	15	54	10	5	5	2	0	2	0	2	0	14	0	0	1	0	1.000	0	0-0	1	3.00
1989 Tor-Atl		29	0	0	9	27	127	31	19	17	0	3	4	1	14	6	15	3	0	1	2	.333	0	1-1	6	5.67
1990 Atlanta	NL	52	3	0	7	76.2	337	93	41	36	5	4	4	1	20	3	64	2	2	5	1	.833	0	1-2	3	4.23

		HOW MUCH HE PITCHED						WHAT HE GAVE UP												THE RESULTS						
Year Team	Lg	G	GS	CG	GF	IP	BFP	H	R	ER	HR	SH	SF	HB	TBB	IBB	SO	WP	Bk	W	L	Pct.	ShO	Sv-Op	Hld	ERA
1991 Atl-NYN	NL	17	3	0	6	32.1	148	40	16	12	4	2	1	0	11	1	18	0	0	2	1	.667	0	0-0	1	3.34
1993 Toronto	AL	51	0	0	10	50.2	211	44	19	19	4	5	2	0	22	5	28	1	0	3	2	.600	0	0-1	13	3.38
1994 Toronto	AL	41	0	0	8	68	291	66	22	19	7	3	3	3	28	1	43	0	0	5	2	.714	0	1-4	13	2.51
1995 Toronto	AL	55	0	0	31	72.2	298	64	27	26	7	3	5	3	24	1	38	0	0	1	5	.167	0	13-21	5	3.22
1996 Tor-ChA	AL	55	0	0	13	95	398	95	45	38	10	3	5	3	24	2	57	3	0	5	4	.556	0	2-6	9	3.60
1989 Toronto	AL	17	0	0	8	17.2	86	23	14	12	0	2	4	1	10	5	10	3	0	1	1	.500	0	1-1	2	6.11
Atlanta	NL	12	0	0	4	9.1	41	8	5	5	0	1	0	0	4	1	5	0	0	0	0	.000	0	0-0	4	4.82
1991 Atlanta	NL	7	0	0	5	8.2	44	13	9	7	3	1	0	0	5	0	8	0	0	1	1	.500	0	0-0	0	7.27
New York	NL	10	3	0	1	23.2	104	27	7	5	1	1	1	0	6	1	10	0	0	1	0	1.000	0	0-0	1	1.90
1996 Toronto	AL	40	0	0	7	72.1	304	72	38	34	9	3	2	2	20	1	48	2	0	2	3	.400	0	1-2	6	4.23
Chicago	AL	15	0	0	6	22.2	94	23	7	4	1	0	3	1	4	1	9	1	0	3	1	.750	0	1-4	3	1.59
8 ML YEARS		314	6	0	90	437.1	1864	443	194	172	39	23	26	11	145	19	277	9	2	23	17	.575	0	18-35	51	3.54

Juan Castro

Bats: R **Throws:** R **Pos:** SS-30; 3B-23; PH-16; 2B-9; LF-1   **Ht:** 5'10" **Wt:** 163 **Born:** 6/20/72   **Age:** 25

		BATTING															BASERUNNING				PERCENTAGES		
Year Team	Lg	G	AB	H	2B	3B	HR	(Hm	Rd)	TB	R	RBI	TBB	IBB	SO	HBP	SH	SF	SB	CS	SB%	GDP	Avg	OBP	SLG
1991 Great Falls	R+	60	217	60	4	2	1	—	—	71	36	27	33	1	31	0	3	2	7	6	.54	2	.276	.369	.327
1992 Bakersfield	A+	113	446	116	15	4	4	—	—	151	56	42	37	2	64	1	20	7	14	11	.56	7	.260	.314	.339
1993 San Antonio	AA	118	424	117	23	8	7	—	—	177	55	41	30	3	40	2	17	3	12	11	.52	14	.276	.325	.417
1994 San Antonio	AA	123	445	128	25	4	4	—	—	173	55	44	31	2	66	1	10	2	4	7	.36	9	.288	.334	.389
1995 Albuquerque	AAA	104	341	91	18	4	3	—	—	126	51	43	20	3	42	0	7	0	4	4	.50	11	.267	.307	.370
1996 Albuquerque	AAA	17	56	21	4	2	1	—	—	32	12	8	6	0	7	1	0	0	1	1	.50	0	.375	.444	.571
1995 Los Angeles	NL	11	4	1	0	0	0	(0	0)	1	0	0	1	0	1	0	0	0	0	0	.00	0	.250	.400	.250
1996 Los Angeles	NL	70	132	26	5	3	0	(0	0)	37	16	5	10	0	27	0	4	0	1	0	1.00	3	.197	.254	.280
2 ML YEARS		81	136	27	5	3	0	(0	0)	38	16	5	11	0	28	0	4	0	1	0	1.00	3	.199	.259	.279

Andujar Cedeno

Bats: Right **Throws:** Right **Pos:** SS-100; PH-5; 3B-4   **Ht:** 6'1" **Wt:** 170 **Born:** 8/21/69   **Age:** 27

		BATTING															BASERUNNING				PERCENTAGES		
Year Team	Lg	G	AB	H	2B	3B	HR	(Hm | Rd)	TB	R	RBI	TBB	IBB	SO	HBP	SH	SF	SB	CS	SB%	GDP	Avg	OBP	SLG
1990 Houston	NL	7	8	0	0	0	0	(0 | 0)	0	0	0	0	0	5	0	0	0	0	0	.00	0	.000	.000	.000
1991 Houston	NL	67	251	61	13	2	9	(4 | 5)	105	27	36	9	1	74	1	1	2	4	3	.57	3	.243	.270	.418
1992 Houston	NL	71	220	38	13	2	2	(2 | 0)	61	15	13	14	2	71	3	0	0	2	0	1.00	1	.173	.232	.277
1993 Houston	NL	149	505	143	24	4	11	(6 | 5)	208	69	56	49	9	97	3	4	5	9	7	.56	17	.283	.346	.412
1994 Houston	NL	98	342	90	26	0	9	(4 | 5)	143	38	49	29	15	79	0	1	5	1	1	.50	5	.263	.334	.418
1995 San Diego	NL	120	390	82	16	2	6	(3 | 3)	120	42	31	28	7	92	5	0	1	5	3	.63	12	.210	.271	.308
1996 SD-Det-Hou		104	335	71	6	3	10	(8 | 2)	113	30	38	15	2	70	1	3	1	5	3	.63	15	.212	.247	.337
1996 San Diego	NL	49	154	36	2	1	3	(2 | 1)	49	10	18	9	2	32	1	0	0	3	2	.60	7	.234	.279	.318
Detroit	AL	52	179	35	4	2	7	(6 | 1)	64	19	20	4	0	37	0	3	0	2	1	.67	8	.196	.213	.358
Houston	NL	3	2	0	0	0	0	(0 | 0)	0	1	0	2	0	1	0	0	1	0	0	.00	0	.000	.500	.000
7 ML YEARS		616	2051	485	98	13	47	(28 | 19)	750	221	223	143	36	488	21	8	10	26	17	.60	53	.236	.292	.366

Domingo Cedeno

Bats: B **Throws:** R **Pos:** 2B-64; PH-16; SS-7; 3B-6; DH-1   **Ht:** 6'0" **Wt:** 170 **Born:** 11/4/68   **Age:** 28

		BATTING															BASERUNNING				PERCENTAGES		
Year Team	Lg	G	AB	H	2B	3B	HR	(Hm | Rd)	TB	R	RBI	TBB	IBB	SO	HBP	SH	SF	SB	CS	SB%	GDP	Avg	OBP	SLG
1993 Toronto	AL	15	46	8	0	0	0	(0 | 0)	8	5	7	1	0	10	0	2	1	1	0	1.00	1	.174	.188	.174
1994 Toronto	AL	47	97	19	2	3	0	(0 | 0)	27	14	10	10	0	31	0	3	4	1	2	.33	1	.196	.261	.278
1995 Toronto	AL	51	161	38	6	1	4	(1 | 3)	58	18	14	10	0	35	2	1	0	0	1	.00	3	.236	.289	.360
1996 Tor-ChA	AL	89	301	82	12	2	2	(0 | 2)	104	46	20	15	0	64	2	8	3	6	3	.67	7	.272	.308	.346
1996 Toronto	AL	77	282	79	10	2	2	(0 | 2)	99	44	17	15	0	60	2	7	1	5	3	.63	6	.280	.320	.351
Chicago	AL	12	19	3	2	0	0	(0 | 0)	5	2	3	0	0	4	0	1	2	1	0	1.00	1	.158	.143	.263
4 ML YEARS		202	605	147	20	6	6	(1 | 5)	197	83	51	36	0	140	4	14	8	8	6	.57	13	.243	.286	.326

Roger Cedeno

Bats: B **Throws:** R **Pos:** CF-50; PH-30; LF-20; RF-4   **Ht:** 6'1" **Wt:** 165 **Born:** 8/16/74   **Age:** 22

		BATTING															BASERUNNING				PERCENTAGES		
Year Team	Lg	G	AB	H	2B	3B	HR	(Hm	Rd)	TB	R	RBI	TBB	IBB	SO	HBP	SH	SF	SB	CS	SB%	GDP	Avg	OBP	SLG
1992 Great Falls	R+	69	256	81	6	5	2	—	—	103	60	27	51	3	53	2	4	2	40	9	.82	4	.316	.431	.402
1993 San Antonio	AA	122	465	134	13	8	4	—	—	175	70	30	45	2	90	1	4	1	28	20	.58	5	.288	.352	.376
Albuquerque	AAA	6	18	4	1	1	0	—	—	7	1	4	3	0	3	0	0	0	1	0	1.00	0	.222	.333	.389
1994 Albuquerque	AAA	104	383	123	18	5	4	—	—	163	84	49	51	0	57	0	3	7	30	13	.70	4	.321	.395	.426
1995 Albuquerque	AAA	99	367	112	19	9	2	—	—	155	67	44	53	2	56	2	4	3	23	18	.56	5	.305	.393	.422
1996 Albuquerque	AAA	33	125	28	2	3	1	—	—	39	16	10	15	1	22	0	2	0	6	5	.55	2	.224	.307	.312
1995 Los Angeles	NL	40	42	10	2	0	0	(0	0)	12	4	3	3	0	10	0	1	0	1	0	1.00	1	.238	.283	.286
1996 Los Angeles	NL	86	211	52	11	1	2	(0	2)	71	26	18	24	0	47	1	2	0	5	1	.83	0	.246	.326	.336
2 ML YEARS		126	253	62	13	1	2	(0	2)	83	30	21	27	0	57	1	3	0	6	1	.86	1	.245	.319	.328

Norm Charlton

Pitches: Left   **Bats:** Both   **Pos:** RP-70   **Ht:** 6'3"   **Wt:** 205   **Born:** 1/6/63   **Age:** 34

		HOW MUCH HE PITCHED						WHAT HE GAVE UP									THE RESULTS					
Year Team	Lg	G	GS	CG	GF	IP	BFP	H	R	ER	HR	SH	SF	HB	TBB	IBB	SO	WP	Bk	W	L	Pct.	ShO	Sv-Op	Hld	ERA
1988 Cincinnati	NL	10	10	0	0	61.1	259	60	27	27	6	1	2	2	20	2	39	3	2	4	5	.444	0	0-0	—	3.96
1989 Cincinnati	NL	69	0	0	27	95.1	393	67	38	31	5	9	2	2	40	7	98	2	4	8	3	.727	0	0-1	8	2.93
1990 Cincinnati	NL	56	16	1	13	154.1	650	131	53	47	10	7	2	2	70	4	117	9	1	12	9	.571	1	2-3	9	2.74
1991 Cincinnati	NL	39	11	0	10	108.1	438	92	37	35	6	7	1	6	34	4	77	11	0	3	5	.375	0	1-4	3	2.91
1992 Cincinnati	NL	64	0	0	46	81.1	341	79	39	27	7	7	3	3	26	4	90	8	0	4	2	.667	0	26-34	7	2.99
1993 Seattle	AL	34	0	0	29	34.2	141	22	12	9	4	0	1	0	17	0	48	6	0	1	3	.250	0	18-21	1	2.34
1995 Phi-Sea		55	0	0	27	69.2	284	46	31	26	4	4	2	4	31	3	70	6	1	4	6	.400	0	14-16	12	3.36
1996 Seattle	AL	70	0	0	50	75.2	323	68	37	34	7	3	2	1	38	1	73	9	0	4	7	.364	0	20-27	8	4.04
1995 Philadelphia	NL	25	0	0	5	22	102	23	19	18	2	1	1	3	15	3	12	1	0	2	5	.286	0	0-1	3	7.36
Seattle	AL	30	0	0	22	47.2	182	23	12	8	2	3	1	1	16	0	58	5	1	2	1	.667	0	14-15	9	1.51
8 ML YEARS		397	37	1	202	680.2	2829	565	274	236	49	38	15	22	276	25	612	54	8	40	40	.500	1	81-106	48	3.12

Raul Chavez

Bats: Right   **Throws:** Right   **Pos:** C-2; PH-1   **Ht:** 5'11"   **Wt:** 175   **Born:** 3/18/73   **Age:** 24

								BATTING									BASERUNNING				PERCENTAGES		
Year Team	Lg	G	AB	H	2B	3B	HR	(Hm | Rd)	TB	R	RBI	TBB	IBB	SO	HBP	SH	SF	SB	CS	SB%	GDP	Avg	OBP	SLG
1990 Astros	R	48	155	50	8	1	0	—	—	60	23	23	7	0	12	2	2	1	5	3	.63	7	.323	.358	.387
1991 Burlington	A	114	420	108	17	0	3	—	—	134	54	41	25	1	64	10	3	4	1	4	.20	13	.257	.312	.319
1992 Asheville	A	95	348	99	22	1	2	—	—	129	37	40	16	1	39	4	1	4	1	0	1.00	11	.284	.320	.371
1993 Osceola	A+	58	197	45	5	1	0	—	—	52	13	16	8	0	19	1	1	1	1	1	.50	12	.228	.261	.264
1994 Jackson	AA	89	251	55	7	0	1	—	—	65	17	22	17	3	41	2	2	1	1	0	1.00	5	.219	.273	.259
1995 Jackson	AA	58	188	54	8	0	4	—	—	74	16	25	8	1	17	3	4	2	0	4	.00	7	.287	.323	.394
Tucson	AAA	32	103	27	5	0	0	—	—	32	14	10	8	0	13	2	1	1	0	1	.00	7	.262	.325	.311
1996 Ottawa	AAA	60	198	49	10	0	2	—	—	65	15	24	11	0	31	1	4	0	0	2	.00	1	.247	.290	.328
1996 Montreal	NL	3	5	1	0	0	0	(0 | 0)	1	1	0	1	0	1	0	0	0	0	1	1.00	1	.200	.333	.200

Bobby Chouinard

Pitches: Right   **Bats:** Right   **Pos:** SP-11; RP-2   **Ht:** 6'1"   **Wt:** 172   **Born:** 5/1/72   **Age:** 25

				HOW MUCH HE PITCHED						WHAT HE GAVE UP										THE RESULTS				
Year Team	Lg	G	GS	CG	GF	IP	BFP	H	R	ER	HR	SH	SF	HB	TBB	IBB	SO	WP	Bk	W	L	Pct.	ShO	Sv-Op	Hld	ERA
1990 Bluefield	R+	10	10	2	0	56	237	61	34	23	10	1	2	1	14	0	30	2	2	2	5	.286	1	0--	—	3.70
1991 Kane County	A	6	6	1	0	33	147	45	24	17	3	0	3	2	5	0	17	3	1	2	4	.333	0	0--	—	4.64
Bluefield	R+	6	6	0	0	33.2	150	44	19	13	1	0	2	2	11	0	31	1	2	5	1	.833	0	0--	—	3.48
1992 Kane County	A	26	26	9	0	181.2	735	151	60	42	4	9	7	6	38	3	112	13	5	10	14	.417	2	0--	—	2.08
1993 Modesto	A+	24	24	1	0	145.2	623	154	75	69	15	3	8	4	56	1	82	4	1	8	10	.444	0	0--	—	4.26
1994 Modesto	A+	29	20	0	0	145.2	599	147	53	42	5	8	2	8	32	1	74	5	1	12	5	.706	0	3--	—	2.59
1995 Huntsville	AA	29	29	1	0	166.2	694	155	81	67	10	9	1	4	50	5	106	4	0	14	8	.636	1	0--	—	3.62
1996 Edmonton	AAA	15	15	0	0	84.1	344	70	32	26	7	1	2	1	24	2	45	1	0	10	2	.833	0	0--	—	2.77
1996 Oakland	AL	13	11	0	0	59	278	75	41	40	8	3	3	3	32	3	32	0	0	4	2	.667	0	0-0	0	6.10

Jason Christiansen

Pitches: Left   **Bats:** Right   **Pos:** RP-33   **Ht:** 6'5"   **Wt:** 230   **Born:** 9/21/69   **Age:** 27

				HOW MUCH HE PITCHED						WHAT HE GAVE UP										THE RESULTS				
Year Team	Lg	G	GS	CG	GF	IP	BFP	H	R	ER	HR	SH	SF	HB	TBB	IBB	SO	WP	Bk	W	L	Pct.	ShO	Sv-Op	Hld	ERA
1991 Pirates	R	6	0	0	4	8	29	4	0	0	0	0	0	0	1	0	8	0	0	1	0	1.000	0	1--	—	0.00
Welland	A-	8	1	0	1	21.1	85	15	9	6	1	0	0	1	12	1	17	5	0	0	1	.000	0	0--	—	2.53
1992 Augusta	A	10	0	0	4	20	73	12	4	4	0	3	0	0	8	0	21	1	0	1	0	1.000	0	0--	—	1.80
Salem	A+	38	0	0	15	50	212	47	20	18	7	3	1	1	22	2	59	0	1	3	1	.750	0	2--	—	3.24
1993 Salem	A+	57	0	0	22	71.1	287	48	30	25	5	5	1	4	24	2	70	2	0	1	1	.500	0	4--	—	3.15
Carolina	AA	2	0	0	1	2.2	12	3	0	0	0	0	0	0	1	0	2	0	0	0	0	.000	0	0--	—	0.00
1994 Carolina	AA	28	0	0	9	38.2	158	30	10	9	2	3	1	1	14	1	43	2	0	2	1	.667	0	2--	—	2.09
Buffalo	AAA	33	0	0	12	33.2	132	19	9	9	3	1	2	0	16	0	39	1	0	3	1	.750	0	0--	—	2.41
1996 Calgary	AAA	2	2	0	0	11	40	9	4	4	1	1	0	0	1	0	10	0	0	1	0	1.000	0	0--	—	3.27
1995 Pittsburgh	NL	63	0	0	13	56.1	255	49	28	26	5	6	3	3	34	9	53	4	1	1	3	.250	0	0-4	12	4.15
1996 Pittsburgh	NL	33	0	0	9	44.1	205	56	34	33	7	2	3	1	19	2	38	4	1	3	3	.500	0	0-2	2	6.70
2 ML YEARS		96	0	0	22	100.2	460	105	62	59	12	8	6	4	53	11	91	8	2	4	6	.400	0	0-6	14	5.27

Mike Christopher

Pitches: Right   **Bats:** Right   **Pos:** RP-13   **Ht:** 6'5"   **Wt:** 220   **Born:** 11/3/63   **Age:** 33

				HOW MUCH HE PITCHED						WHAT HE GAVE UP										THE RESULTS				
Year Team	Lg	G	GS	CG	GF	IP	BFP	H	R	ER	HR	SH	SF	HB	TBB	IBB	SO	WP	Bk	W	L	Pct.	ShO	Sv-Op	Hld	ERA
1996 Toledo *	AAA	39	0	0	38	39	168	50	21	17	5	1	0	0	5	1	40	5	0	4	1	.800	0	22--	—	3.92
1991 Los Angeles	NL	3	0	0	2	4	15	2	0	0	0	0	0	0	3	0	2	0	0	0	0	.000	0	0-0	1	0.00
1992 Cleveland	AL	10	0	0	4	18	79	17	8	6	2	1	1	0	10	1	13	2	0	0	0	.000	0	0-0	1	3.00
1993 Cleveland	AL	9	0	0	3	11.2	51	14	6	5	3	0	0	0	2	1	8	0	0	0	0	.000	0	0-0	1	3.86
1995 Detroit	AL	36	0	0	11	61.1	262	71	28	26	8	1	4	2	14	2	34	5	0	4	0	1.000	0	1-2	5	3.82

43

		HOW MUCH HE PITCHED		WHAT HE GAVE UP		THE RESULTS	
Year Team	Lg	G GS CG GF	IP BFP	H R ER HR SH SF HB	TBB IBB SO WP Bk	W L Pct. ShO Sv-Op Hld	ERA
1996 Detroit	AL	13 0 0 3	30 149	47 36 31 12 0 4 0	11 2 19 1 0	1 1 .500 0 0-0 0	9.30
5 ML YEARS		71 0 0 23	125 556	151 78 68 25 2 7 2	40 6 76 8 0	5 1 .833 0 1-2 7	4.90

Archi Cianfrocco

B: R T: R Pos: 1B-33; PH-23; 3B-11; SS-10; RF-7; 2B-6; C-1; LF-1   **Ht:** 6'5"   **Wt:** 215   **Born:** 10/6/66   **Age:** 30

		BATTING														BASERUNNING				PERCENTAGES		
Year Team	Lg	G	AB	H	2B	3B	HR	(Hm Rd)	TB	R	RBI	TBB	IBB	SO	HBP	SH	SF	SB	CS	SB%	GDP	Avg	OBP	SLG
1992 Montreal	NL	86	232	56	5	2	6	(3 3)	83	25	30	11	0	66	1	1	2	3	0	1.00	2	.241	.276	.358
1993 Mon-SD	NL	96	296	72	11	2	12	(6 6)	123	30	48	17	1	69	3	2	5	2	0	1.00	9	.243	.287	.416
1994 San Diego	NL	59	146	32	8	0	4	(3 1)	52	9	13	3	0	39	4	1	2	2	0	1.00	2	.219	.252	.356
1995 San Diego	NL	51	118	31	7	0	5	(1 4)	53	22	31	11	1	28	2	0	1	0	2	.00	3	.263	.333	.449
1996 San Diego	NL	79	192	54	13	3	2	(0 2)	79	21	32	8	0	56	2	0	1	1	0	1.00	4	.281	.315	.411
1993 Montreal	NL	12	17	4	1	0	1	(0 1)	8	3	1	0	0	5	0	0	0	0	0	.00	0	.235	.235	.471
San Diego	NL	84	279	68	10	2	11	(6 5)	115	27	47	17	1	64	3	2	5	2	0	1.00	9	.244	.289	.412
5 ML YEARS		371	984	245	44	7	29	(13 16)	390	107	154	50	2	258	12	4	11	8	2	.80	20	.249	.290	.396

Jeff Cirillo

Bats: R **Throws:** R **Pos:** 3B-154; PH-6; DH-3; 1B-2; 2B-1   **Ht:** 6'2"   **Wt:** 188   **Born:** 9/23/69   **Age:** 27

		BATTING														BASERUNNING				PERCENTAGES		
Year Team	Lg	G	AB	H	2B	3B	HR	(Hm Rd)	TB	R	RBI	TBB	IBB	SO	HBP	SH	SF	SB	CS	SB%	GDP	Avg	OBP	SLG
1994 Milwaukee	AL	39	126	30	9	0	3	(1 2)	48	17	12	11	0	16	2	0	0	0	1	.00	4	.238	.309	.381
1995 Milwaukee	AL	125	328	91	19	4	9	(6 3)	145	57	39	47	0	42	4	1	4	7	2	.78	8	.277	.371	.442
1996 Milwaukee	AL	158	566	184	46	5	15	(6 9)	285	101	83	58	0	69	7	6	6	4	9	.31	14	.325	.391	.504
3 ML YEARS		322	1020	305	74	9	27	(13 14)	478	175	134	116	0	127	13	7	10	11	12	.48	26	.299	.374	.469

Dave Clark

Bats: Left   **Throws:** Right   **Pos:** PH-55; LF-35; RF-28   **Ht:** 6'2"   **Wt:** 209   **Born:** 9/3/62   **Age:** 34

		BATTING														BASERUNNING				PERCENTAGES		
Year Team	Lg	G	AB	H	2B	3B	HR	(Hm Rd)	TB	R	RBI	TBB	IBB	SO	HBP	SH	SF	SB	CS	SB%	GDP	Avg	OBP	SLG
1986 Cleveland	AL	18	58	16	1	0	3	(1 2)	26	10	9	7	0	11	0	2	1	1	0	1.00	1	.276	.348	.448
1987 Cleveland	AL	29	87	18	5	0	3	(1 2)	32	11	12	2	0	24	0	0	0	1	0	1.00	4	.207	.225	.368
1988 Cleveland	AL	63	156	41	4	1	3	(2 1)	56	11	18	17	2	28	0	0	2	0	2	.00	8	.263	.333	.359
1989 Cleveland	AL	102	253	60	12	0	8	(4 4)	96	21	29	30	5	63	0	1	1	0	2	.00	7	.237	.317	.379
1990 Chicago	NL	84	171	47	4	2	5	(3 2)	70	22	20	8	1	40	0	0	2	7	1	.88	4	.275	.304	.409
1991 Kansas City	AL	11	10	2	0	0	0	(0 0)	2	1	1	1	0	1	0	0	0	0	0	.00	0	.200	.273	.200
1992 Pittsburgh	NL	23	33	7	0	0	2	(2 0)	13	3	7	6	0	8	0	0	1	0	0	.00	1	.212	.325	.394
1993 Pittsburgh	NL	110	277	75	11	2	11	(8 3)	123	43	46	38	5	58	1	0	2	1	0	1.00	10	.271	.358	.444
1994 Pittsburgh	NL	86	223	66	11	1	10	(7 3)	109	37	46	22	0	48	0	1	3	2	2	.50	5	.296	.355	.489
1995 Pittsburgh	NL	77	196	55	6	0	4	(2 2)	73	30	24	24	1	38	1	0	2	3	3	.50	9	.281	.359	.372
1996 Pit-LA	NL	107	226	61	12	2	8	(6 2)	101	28	36	34	3	53	0	0	1	2	1	.67	6	.270	.364	.447
1996 Pittsburgh	NL	92	211	58	12	2	8	(6 2)	98	28	35	31	3	51	0	0	1	2	1	.67	6	.275	.366	.464
Los Angeles	NL	15	15	3	0	0	0	(0 0)	3	0	1	3	0	2	0	0	0	0	0	.00	0	.200	.333	.200
11 ML YEARS		710	1690	448	66	8	57	(36 21)	701	217	248	189	17	372	2	4	14	17	11	.61	54	.265	.337	.415

Mark Clark

Pitches: Right   **Bats:** Right   **Pos:** SP-32   **Ht:** 6'5"   **Wt:** 225   **Born:** 5/12/68   **Age:** 29

		HOW MUCH HE PITCHED		WHAT HE GAVE UP		THE RESULTS	
Year Team	Lg	G GS CG GF	IP BFP	H R ER HR SH SF HB	TBB IBB SO WP Bk	W L Pct. ShO Sv-Op Hld	ERA
1991 St. Louis	NL	7 2 0 1	22.1 93	17 10 10 3 0 3 0	11 0 13 2 0	1 1 .500 0 0-0 1	4.03
1992 St. Louis	NL	20 20 1 0	113.1 488	117 59 56 12 7 4 0	36 2 44 4 0	3 10 .231 1 0-0 0	4.45
1993 Cleveland	AL	26 15 1 1	109.1 454	119 55 52 18 1 1 1	25 1 57 1 0	7 5 .583 0 0-0 2	4.28
1994 Cleveland	AL	20 20 4 0	127.1 540	133 61 54 14 2 7 4	40 0 60 9 1	11 3 .786 1 0-0 0	3.82
1995 Cleveland	AL	22 21 2 0	124.2 552	143 77 73 13 3 6 4	42 0 68 8 0	9 7 .563 0 0-0 0	5.27
1996 New York	NL	32 32 2 0	212.1 883	217 98 81 20 8 4 3	48 8 142 6 2	14 11 .560 0 0-0 0	3.43
6 ML YEARS		127 110 10 2	709.1 3010	746 360 326 80 21 25 12	202 11 384 30 3	45 37 .549 2 0-0 3	4.14

Phil Clark

Bats: Right   **Throws:** Right   **Pos:** PH-2; DH-1; 1B-1; 3B-1   **Ht:** 6'0"   **Wt:** 200   **Born:** 5/6/68   **Age:** 29

		BATTING														BASERUNNING				PERCENTAGES		
Year Team	Lg	G	AB	H	2B	3B	HR	(Hm Rd)	TB	R	RBI	TBB	IBB	SO	HBP	SH	SF	SB	CS	SB%	GDP	Avg	OBP	SLG
1996 Pawtucket *	AAA	97	369	120	36	2	12	— —	196	57	69	17	4	32	10	0	3	3	6	.33	10	.325	.368	.531
1992 Detroit	AL	23	54	22	4	0	1	(0 1)	29	3	5	6	1	9	0	1	0	1	0	1.00	2	.407	.467	.537
1993 San Diego	NL	102	240	75	17	0	9	(6 3)	119	33	33	8	2	31	5	1	2	2	0	1.00	2	.313	.345	.496
1994 San Diego	NL	61	149	32	6	0	5	(4 1)	53	14	20	5	1	17	3	0	3	1	2	.33	7	.215	.250	.356
1995 San Diego	NL	75	97	21	3	0	2	(1 1)	30	12	7	8	1	18	1	0	2	0	2	.00	3	.216	.278	.309
1996 Boston	AL	3	3	0	0	0	0	(0 0)	0	0	0	0	0	1	0	0	0	0	0	.00	1	.000	.000	.000
5 ML YEARS		264	543	150	30	0	17	(11 6)	231	62	65	27	5	76	9	2	7	4	4	.50	9	.276	.317	.425

Terry Clark

Pitches: Right **Bats:** Right **Pos:** RP-17   **Ht:** 6'2" **Wt:** 195 **Born:** 10/10/60 **Age:** 36

Year Team	Lg	G	GS	CG	GF	IP	BFP	H	R	ER	HR	SH	SF	HB	TBB	IBB	SO	WP	Bk	W	L	Pct.	ShO	Sv-Op	Hld	ERA
1996 Omaha *	AAA	16	2	0	4	45.2	190	42	15	13	5	1	2	4	13	1	36	1	0	3	1	.750	0	2--	—	2.56
1988 California	AL	15	15	2	0	94	410	120	54	53	8	2	5	0	31	6	39	5	2	6	6	.500	1	0-0	0	5.07
1989 California	AL	4	2	0	2	11	48	13	8	6	0	2	1	0	3	0	7	2	1	0	2	.000	0	0-0	0	4.91
1990 Houston	NL	1	1	0	0	4	25	9	7	6	0	1	0	0	3	0	2	0	0	0	0	.000	0	0-0	0	13.50
1995 Atl-Bal		41	0	0	13	42.2	184	43	17	17	3	4	1	1	20	5	20	2	0	2	5	.286	0	1-1	7	3.59
1996 KC-Hou		17	0	0	8	23.2	124	44	25	23	4	0	0	1	9	2	17	4	0	1	3	.250	0	0-0	1	8.75
1995 Atlanta	NL	3	0	0	1	3.2	18	3	2	2	0	0	0	0	5	0	2	1	0	0	0	.000	0	0-0	0	4.91
Baltimore	AL	38	0	0	12	39	166	40	15	15	3	4	1	1	15	5	18	1	0	2	5	.286	0	1-1	7	3.46
1996 Kansas City	AL	12	0	0	5	17.1	87	28	15	15	0	0	0	0	7	1	12	3	0	1	1	.500	0	0-0	1	7.79
Houston	NL	5	0	0	3	6.1	37	16	10	8	4	0	0	1	2	1	5	1	0	0	2	.000	0	0-0	0	11.37
5 ML YEARS		78	18	2	23	175.1	791	229	111	105	15	9	7	2	66	13	85	13	3	9	16	.360	1	1-1	8	5.39

Tony Clark

Bats: Both **Throws:** Right **Pos:** 1B-86; DH-12; PH-2   **Ht:** 6'7" **Wt:** 245 **Born:** 6/15/72 **Age:** 25

Year Team	Lg	G	AB	H	2B	3B	HR	(Hm	Rd)	TB	R	RBI	TBB	IBB	SO	HBP	SH	SF	SB	CS	SB%	GDP	Avg	OBP	SLG
1990 Bristol	R+	25	73	12	2	0	1	—	—	17	2	8	6	0	28	1	0	0	0	0	.00	0	.164	.238	.233
1992 Niagara Fal	A-	27	85	26	9	0	5	—	—	50	12	17	9	0	34	0	0	0	1	0	1.00	6	.306	.372	.588
1993 Lakeland	A+	36	117	31	4	1	1	—	—	40	14	22	18	2	32	0	2	2	0	1	.00	1	.265	.358	.342
1994 Trenton	AA	107	394	110	25	0	21	—	—	198	50	86	40	5	113	1	0	2	0	4	.00	9	.279	.346	.503
Toledo	AAA	25	92	24	4	0	2	—	—	34	10	13	12	1	25	0	0	2	2	0	1.00	1	.261	.340	.370
1995 Toledo	AAA	110	405	98	17	2	14	—	—	161	50	63	52	1	129	3	0	3	0	2	.00	8	.242	.330	.398
1996 Toledo	AAA	55	194	58	7	1	14	—	—	109	42	36	31	0	58	0	0	0	1	1	.50	3	.299	.396	.562
1995 Detroit	AL	27	101	24	5	1	3	(0	3)	40	10	11	8	0	30	0	0	0	0	0	.00	2	.238	.294	.396
1996 Detroit	AL	100	376	94	14	0	27	(17	10)	189	56	72	29	1	127	0	0	6	0	1	.00	7	.250	.299	.503
2 ML YEARS		127	477	118	19	1	30	(17	13)	229	66	83	37	1	157	0	0	6	0	1	.00	9	.247	.298	.480

Will Clark

Bats: Left **Throws:** Left **Pos:** 1B-117; PH-1   **Ht:** 6'1" **Wt:** 200 **Born:** 3/13/64 **Age:** 33

Year Team	Lg	G	AB	H	2B	3B	HR	(Hm	Rd)	TB	R	RBI	TBB	IBB	SO	HBP	SH	SF	SB	CS	SB%	GDP	Avg	OBP	SLG
1996 Tulsa *	AA	3	9	2	0	0	0	—	—	2	3	0	2	0	0	0	0	0	0	0	.00	0	.222	.364	.222
1986 San Francisco	NL	111	408	117	27	2	11	(7	4)	181	66	41	34	10	76	3	9	4	4	7	.36	3	.287	.343	.444
1987 San Francisco	NL	150	529	163	29	5	35	(22	13)	307	89	91	49	11	98	5	3	2	5	17	.23	2	.308	.371	.580
1988 San Francisco	NL	162	575	162	31	6	29	(14	15)	292	102	109	100	27	129	4	0	10	9	1	.90	9	.282	.386	.508
1989 San Francisco	NL	159	588	196	38	9	23	(9	14)	321	104	111	74	14	103	5	0	8	8	3	.73	6	.333	.407	.546
1990 San Francisco	NL	154	600	177	25	5	19	(8	11)	269	91	95	62	9	97	3	0	13	8	2	.80	7	.295	.357	.448
1991 San Francisco	NL	148	565	170	32	7	29	(17	12)	303	84	116	51	12	91	2	0	4	4	2	.67	5	.301	.359	.536
1992 San Francisco	NL	144	513	154	40	1	16	(11	5)	244	69	73	73	23	82	4	0	11	12	7	.63	5	.300	.384	.476
1993 San Francisco	NL	132	491	139	27	2	14	(5	9)	212	82	73	63	6	68	6	1	6	2	2	.50	10	.283	.367	.432
1994 Texas	AL	110	389	128	24	2	13	(9	4)	195	73	80	71	11	59	3	0	6	5	1	.83	5	.329	.431	.501
1995 Texas	AL	123	454	137	27	3	16	(10	6)	218	85	92	68	6	50	4	0	11	0	1	.00	7	.302	.389	.480
1996 Texas	AL	117	436	124	25	1	13	(9	4)	190	69	72	64	5	67	5	0	7	2	1	.67	10	.284	.377	.436
11 ML YEARS		1510	5548	1667	325	43	218	(121	97)	2732	914	953	709	134	920	44	13	82	59	44	.57	69	.300	.379	.492

Royce Clayton

Bats: Right **Throws:** Right **Pos:** SS-113; PH-16   **Ht:** 6'0" **Wt:** 183 **Born:** 1/2/70 **Age:** 27

Year Team	Lg	G	AB	H	2B	3B	HR	(Hm	Rd)	TB	R	RBI	TBB	IBB	SO	HBP	SH	SF	SB	CS	SB%	GDP	Avg	OBP	SLG
1991 San Francisco	NL	9	26	3	1	0	0	(0	0)	4	0	2	1	0	6	0	0	0	0	0	.00	1	.115	.148	.154
1992 San Francisco	NL	98	321	72	7	4	4	(3	1)	99	31	24	26	3	63	0	3	2	8	4	.67	11	.224	.281	.308
1993 San Francisco	NL	153	549	155	21	5	6	(5	1)	204	54	70	38	2	91	5	8	7	11	10	.52	16	.282	.331	.372
1994 San Francisco	NL	108	385	91	14	6	3	(1	2)	126	38	30	30	2	74	3	3	2	23	3	.88	7	.236	.295	.327
1995 San Francisco	NL	138	509	124	29	3	5	(2	3)	174	56	58	38	1	109	3	4	3	24	9	.73	7	.244	.298	.342
1996 St. Louis	NL	129	491	136	20	4	6	(6	0)	182	64	35	33	4	89	1	2	4	33	15	.69	13	.277	.321	.371
6 ML YEARS		635	2281	581	92	22	24	(17	7)	789	243	219	166	12	432	12	20	18	99	41	.71	55	.255	.306	.346

Roger Clemens

Pitches: Right **Bats:** Right **Pos:** SP-34   **Ht:** 6'4" **Wt:** 230 **Born:** 8/4/62 **Age:** 34

Year Team	Lg	G	GS	CG	GF	IP	BFP	H	R	ER	HR	SH	SF	HB	TBB	IBB	SO	WP	Bk	W	L	Pct.	ShO	Sv-Op	Hld	ERA
1984 Boston	AL	21	20	5	0	133.1	575	146	67	64	13	2	3	2	29	3	126	4	0	9	4	.692	1	0--	—	4.32
1985 Boston	AL	15	15	3	0	98.1	407	83	38	36	5	1	2	3	37	0	74	1	3	7	5	.583	1	0--	—	3.29
1986 Boston	AL	33	33	10	0	254	997	179	77	70	21	4	6	4	67	0	238	11	3	24	4	.857	1	0--	—	2.48
1987 Boston	AL	36	36	18	0	281.2	1157	248	100	93	19	6	4	9	83	4	256	4	3	20	9	.690	7	0-0	0	2.97
1988 Boston	AL	35	35	14	0	264	1063	217	93	86	17	6	3	6	62	4	291	4	7	18	12	.600	8	0-0	0	2.93

45

HOW MUCH HE PITCHED								WHAT HE GAVE UP												THE RESULTS						
Year Team	Lg	G	GS	CG	GF	IP	BFP	H	R	ER	HR	SH	SF	HB	TBB	IBB	SO	WP	Bk	W	L	Pct.	ShO	Sv-Op	Hld	ERA
1989 Boston	AL	35	35	8	0	253.1	1044	215	101	88	20	9	5	8	93	5	230	7	0	17	11	.607	3	0-0	0	3.13
1990 Boston	AL	31	31	7	0	228.1	920	193	59	49	7	7	5	7	54	3	209	8	0	21	6	.778	4	0-0	0	1.93
1991 Boston	AL	35	35	13	0	271.1	1077	219	93	79	15	6	8	5	65	12	241	6	0	18	10	.643	4	0-0	0	2.62
1992 Boston	AL	32	32	11	0	246.2	989	203	80	66	11	5	5	9	62	5	208	3	0	18	11	.621	5	0-0	0	2.41
1993 Boston	AL	29	29	2	0	191.2	808	175	99	95	17	5	7	11	67	4	160	3	1	11	14	.440	1	0-0	0	4.46
1994 Boston	AL	24	24	3	0	170.2	692	124	62	54	15	2	5	4	71	1	168	4	0	9	7	.563	1	0-0	0	2.85
1995 Boston	AL	23	23	0	0	140	623	141	70	65	15	2	3	14	60	0	132	9	0	10	5	.667	0	0-0	0	4.18
1996 Boston	AL	34	34	6	0	242.2	1032	216	106	98	19	4	7	4	106	2	257	1	0	10	13	.435	2	0-0	0	3.63
13 ML YEARS		383	382	100	0	2776	11384	2359	1045	943	194	59	63	86	856	43	2590	72	18	192	111	.634	38	0--	—	3.06

Brad Clontz

Pitches: Right **Bats:** Right **Pos:** RP-81 **Ht:** 6'1" **Wt:** 180 **Born:** 4/25/71 **Age:** 26

HOW MUCH HE PITCHED								WHAT HE GAVE UP												THE RESULTS						
Year Team	Lg	G	GS	CG	GF	IP	BFP	H	R	ER	HR	SH	SF	HB	TBB	IBB	SO	WP	Bk	W	L	Pct.	ShO	Sv-Op	Hld	ERA
1992 Pulaski	R+	4	0	0	3	5.2	23	3	1	1	0	0	0	2	2	0	7	1	0	0	0	.000	0	1--	—	1.59
Macon	A	17	0	0	14	23	103	19	14	10	2	2	1	3	10	0	18	1	0	2	1	.667	0	2--	—	3.91
1993 Durham	A+	51	0	0	38	75.1	325	69	32	23	5	8	0	4	26	1	79	6	0	1	7	.125	0	10--	—	2.75
1994 Greenville	AA	39	0	0	38	45	178	32	13	6	5	3	1	1	10	2	49	2	0	1	2	.333	0	27--	—	1.20
Richmond	AAA	24	0	0	22	25.2	101	19	6	6	1	0	1	0	9	2	21	0	0	0	0	.000	0	11--	—	2.10
1995 Atlanta	NL	59	0	0	14	69	295	71	29	28	5	3	2	4	22	4	55	0	0	8	1	.889	0	4-6	6	3.65
1996 Atlanta	NL	81	0	0	11	80.2	350	78	53	51	11	5	4	2	33	8	49	0	1	6	3	.667	0	1-6	17	5.69
2 ML YEARS		140	0	0	25	149.2	645	149	82	79	16	8	6	6	55	12	104	0	1	14	4	.778	0	5-12	23	4.75

Alan Cockrell

Bats: Right **Throws:** Right **Pos:** PH-9; RF-1 **Ht:** 6'2" **Wt:** 212 **Born:** 12/5/62 **Age:** 34

BATTING																		BASERUNNING				PERCENTAGES		
Year Team	Lg	G	AB	H	2B	3B	HR	(Hm	Rd)	TB	R	RBI	TBB	IBB	SO	HBP	SH	SF	SB	CS	SB%	GDP	Avg	OBP	SLG
1984 Everett	A-	2	8	3	0	0	0	—	—	3	1	3	1	0	2	0	0	0	0	0	.00	0	.375	.444	.375
Fresno	A+	61	214	46	6	0	1	—	—	55	20	32	28	0	66	5	0	0	0	1	.00	10	.215	.317	.257
1985 Shreveport	AA	126	455	115	25	3	11	—	—	179	53	68	54	2	137	3	3	2	12	3	.80	16	.253	.335	.393
1986 Shreveport	AA	124	438	113	31	3	14	—	—	192	66	78	61	3	126	3	3	3	4	2	.67	11	.258	.350	.438
1987 Phoenix	AAA	129	432	111	23	5	11	—	—	177	82	72	69	4	131	3	5	4	7	3	.70	9	.257	.360	.410
1988 Phoenix	AAA	102	347	105	16	2	8	—	—	149	65	39	48	1	93	1	1	1	3	3	.50	6	.303	.388	.429
Portland	AAA	18	63	15	1	1	2	—	—	24	9	8	5	0	25	0	0	0	1	0	1.00	0	.238	.294	.381
1989 Portland	AAA	127	433	116	15	3	11	—	—	170	60	61	57	0	127	2	5	6	8	5	.62	11	.268	.351	.393
1990 Portland	AAA	6	23	5	1	1	0	—	—	8	2	1	0	0	5	1	0	0	1	0	1.00	0	.217	.250	.348
Colo. Sprng	AAA	113	352	116	23	4	17	—	—	198	75	70	50	2	68	2	0	3	5	3	.63	12	.330	.413	.563
1991 Calgary	AAA	117	435	126	27	2	11	—	—	190	77	81	45	1	74	4	1	3	7	4	.64	17	.290	.359	.437
1992 Colo. Sprng	AAA	82	259	61	6	2	7	—	—	92	31	38	22	1	51	4	2	2	0	2	.00	6	.236	.303	.355
1993 Charlotte	AAA	96	275	76	12	2	8	—	—	116	31	39	23	0	59	2	2	3	0	0	.00	9	.276	.333	.422
1994 New Haven	AA	12	43	13	4	0	1	—	—	20	6	8	3	1	6	1	0	1	2	0	1.00	1	.302	.354	.465
Colo. Sprng	AAA	84	271	83	15	2	13	—	—	141	50	60	29	0	58	4	1	1	1	1	.50	6	.306	.380	.520
1995 Colo. Sprng	AAA	106	355	111	22	1	12	—	—	171	58	58	30	3	65	2	1	0	3	0	.00	8	.313	.370	.482
1996 Colo. Sprng	AAA	109	357	107	25	3	14	—	—	180	55	60	52	3	88	1	0	4	1	2	.33	14	.300	.386	.504
1996 Colorado	NL	9	8	2	1	0	0	(0	0)	3	0	2	0	0	4	0	0	1	0	0	.00	0	.250	.222	.375

Greg Colbrunn

Bats: Right **Throws:** Right **Pos:** 1B-134; PH-8 **Ht:** 6'0" **Wt:** 200 **Born:** 7/26/69 **Age:** 27

BATTING																		BASERUNNING				PERCENTAGES		
Year Team	Lg	G	AB	H	2B	3B	HR	(Hm	Rd)	TB	R	RBI	TBB	IBB	SO	HBP	SH	SF	SB	CS	SB%	GDP	Avg	OBP	SLG
1992 Montreal	NL	52	168	45	8	0	2	(1	1)	59	12	18	6	1	34	2	0	4	3	2	.60	1	.268	.294	.351
1993 Montreal	NL	70	153	39	9	0	4	(2	2)	60	15	23	6	1	33	1	1	3	4	2	.67	1	.255	.282	.392
1994 Florida	NL	47	155	47	10	0	6	(3	3)	75	17	31	9	0	27	2	0	2	1	1	.50	3	.303	.345	.484
1995 Florida	NL	138	528	146	22	1	23	(12	11)	239	70	89	22	4	69	6	0	4	11	3	.79	15	.277	.311	.453
1996 Florida	NL	141	511	146	26	2	16	(7	9)	224	60	69	25	1	76	14	0	5	4	5	.44	22	.286	.333	.438
5 ML YEARS		448	1515	423	75	3	51	(25	26)	657	174	230	68	7	239	25	1	18	23	13	.64	42	.279	.317	.434

Alex Cole

Bats: Left **Throws:** Left **Pos:** CF-24; PH-4 **Ht:** 6'0" **Wt:** 184 **Born:** 8/17/65 **Age:** 31

BATTING																		BASERUNNING				PERCENTAGES		
Year Team	Lg	G	AB	H	2B	3B	HR	(Hm	Rd)	TB	R	RBI	TBB	IBB	SO	HBP	SH	SF	SB	CS	SB%	GDP	Avg	OBP	SLG
1996 Pawtucket *	AAA	82	304	90	14	8	4	—	—	132	57	39	50	0	47	2	4	2	11	7	.61	3	.296	.397	.434
1990 Cleveland	AL	63	227	68	5	4	0	(0	0)	81	43	13	28	0	38	1	0	0	40	9	.82	2	.300	.379	.357
1991 Cleveland	AL	122	387	114	17	3	0	(0	0)	137	58	21	58	2	47	1	4	2	27	17	.61	4	.295	.386	.354
1992 Cle-Pit		105	302	77	4	7	0	(0	0)	95	44	15	28	1	67	1	1	2	16	6	.73	4	.255	.318	.315
1993 Colorado	NL	126	348	89	9	4	0	(0	0)	106	50	24	43	3	58	2	4	2	30	13	.70	1	.256	.339	.305
1994 Minnesota	AL	105	345	102	15	5	4	(2	2)	139	68	23	44	2	60	1	6	2	29	8	.78	5	.296	.375	.403
1995 Minnesota	AL	28	79	27	3	2	1	(0	1)	37	10	14	8	0	15	1	2	0	1	3	.25	0	.342	.409	.468
1996 Boston	AL	24	72	16	5	1	0	(0	0)	23	13	7	8	0	11	0	0	2	5	3	.63	2	.222	.296	.319
1992 Cleveland	AL	41	97	20	1	0	0	(0	0)	21	11	5	10	0	21	1	0	1	9	2	.82	2	.206	.284	.216

		BATTING																BASERUNNING				PERCENTAGES		
Year Team	Lg	G	AB	H	2B	3B	HR	(Hm Rd)	TB	R	RBI	TBB	IBB	SO	HBP	SH	SF	SB	CS	SB%	GDP	Avg	OBP	SLG
Pittsburgh	NL	64	205	57	3	7	0	(0 0)	74	33	10	18	1	46	0	1	1	7	4	.64	2	.278	.335	.361
7 ML YEARS		573	1760	493	58	26	5	(2 3)	618	286	117	217	8	296	7	19	9	148	59	.71	25	.280	.360	.351

Vince Coleman

Bats: Both **Throws:** Right **Pos:** LF-20; PH-15 **Ht:** 6'1" **Wt:** 185 **Born:** 9/22/61 **Age:** 35

		BATTING																BASERUNNING				PERCENTAGES		
Year Team	Lg	G	AB	H	2B	3B	HR	(Hm Rd)	TB	R	RBI	TBB	IBB	SO	HBP	SH	SF	SB	CS	SB%	GDP	Avg	OBP	SLG
1996 Indianapols *	AAA	7	26	2	0	0	0	— —	2	2	1	1	0	5	0	0	0	0	0	.00	0	.077	.111	.077
Vancouver *	AAA	21	87	18	2	1	0	— —	22	9	5	9	0	15	0	0	0	4	1	.80	0	.207	.281	.253
1985 St. Louis	NL	151	636	170	20	10	1	(1 0)	213	107	40	50	1	115	0	5	1	110	25	.81	3	.267	.320	.335
1986 St. Louis	NL	154	600	139	13	8	0	(0 0)	168	94	29	60	0	98	2	3	5	107	14	.88	4	.232	.301	.280
1987 St. Louis	NL	151	623	180	14	10	3	(3 0)	223	121	43	70	0	126	3	5	1	109	22	.83	7	.289	.363	.358
1988 St. Louis	NL	153	616	160	20	10	3	(2 1)	209	77	38	49	4	111	1	8	5	81	27	.75	4	.260	.313	.339
1989 St. Louis	NL	145	563	143	21	9	2	(1 1)	188	94	28	50	0	90	2	7	2	65	10	.87	4	.254	.316	.334
1990 St. Louis	NL	124	497	145	18	9	6	(5 1)	199	73	39	35	1	88	2	4	1	77	17	.82	6	.292	.340	.400
1991 New York	NL	72	278	71	7	5	1	(0 1)	91	45	17	39	0	47	0	1	0	37	14	.73	3	.255	.347	.327
1992 New York	NL	71	229	63	11	1	2	(2 0)	82	37	21	27	3	41	2	2	1	24	9	.73	1	.275	.355	.358
1993 New York	NL	92	373	104	14	8	2	(2 0)	140	64	25	21	1	58	0	3	2	38	13	.75	2	.279	.316	.375
1994 Kansas City	AL	104	438	105	14	12	2	(1 1)	149	61	33	29	0	72	1	4	5	50	8	.86	2	.240	.285	.340
1995 KC-Sea	AL	115	455	131	23	6	5	(3 2)	181	66	29	37	2	80	2	5	1	42	16	.72	8	.288	.343	.398
1996 Cincinnati	NL	33	84	13	1	1	1	(1 0)	19	10	4	9	0	31	0	1	0	12	2	.86	0	.155	.237	.226
1995 Kansas City	AL	75	293	84	13	4	4	(2 2)	117	39	20	27	1	48	1	2	1	26	9	.74	7	.287	.348	.399
Seattle	AL	40	162	47	10	2	1	(1 0)	64	27	9	10	1	32	1	3	0	16	7	.70	1	.290	.335	.395
12 ML YEARS		1365	5392	1424	176	89	28	(21 7)	1862	849	346	476	12	957	15	48	24	752	177	.81	44	.264	.324	.345

David Cone

Pitches: Right **Bats:** Left **Pos:** SP-11 **Ht:** 6'1" **Wt:** 190 **Born:** 1/2/63 **Age:** 34

		HOW MUCH HE PITCHED						WHAT HE GAVE UP												THE RESULTS						
Year Team	Lg	G	GS	CG	GF	IP	BFP	H	R	ER	HR	SH	SF	HB	TBB	IBB	SO	WP	Bk	W	L	Pct.	ShO	Sv-Op	Hld	ERA
1996 Norwich *	AA	2	2	0	0	10	38	9	3	1	1	0	0	0	1	0	13	0	0	0	0	.000	0	0--	—	0.90
1986 Kansas City	AL	11	0	0	5	22.2	108	29	14	14	2	0	0	1	13	1	21	3	0	0	0	.000	0	0--	—	5.56
1987 New York	NL	21	13	1	3	99.1	420	87	46	41	11	4	3	5	44	1	68	2	4	5	6	.455	0	1-1	2	3.71
1988 New York	NL	35	28	8	0	231.1	936	178	67	57	10	11	5	4	80	7	213	10	10	20	3	.870	4	0-0	1	2.22
1989 New York	NL	34	33	7	0	219.2	910	183	92	86	20	6	4	4	74	6	190	14	4	14	8	.636	2	0-0	0	3.52
1990 New York	NL	31	30	6	1	211.2	860	177	84	76	21	4	6	1	65	1	233	10	4	14	10	.583	2	0-0	0	3.23
1991 New York	NL	34	34	5	0	232.2	966	204	95	85	13	13	7	5	73	2	241	17	1	14	14	.500	2	0-0	0	3.29
1992 NYN-Tor		35	34	7	0	249.2	1055	201	91	78	15	6	9	12	111	7	261	12	1	17	10	.630	5	0-0	0	2.81
1993 Kansas City	AL	34	34	6	0	254	1060	205	102	94	20	7	9	10	114	2	191	14	2	11	14	.440	1	0-0	0	3.33
1994 Kansas City	AL	23	23	4	0	171.2	690	130	60	56	15	1	5	7	54	0	132	5	1	16	5	.762	3	0-0	0	2.94
1995 Tor-NYA	AL	30	30	6	0	229.1	954	195	95	91	24	2	3	6	88	2	191	11	1	18	8	.692	2	0-0	0	3.57
1996 New York	AL	11	11	1	0	72	295	50	25	23	3	1	5	2	34	0	71	4	1	7	2	.778	0	0-0	0	2.88
1992 New York	NL	27	27	7	0	196.2	831	162	75	63	12	6	6	9	82	5	214	9	1	13	7	.650	5	0-0	0	2.88
Toronto	AL	8	7	0	0	53	224	39	16	15	3	0	3	3	29	2	47	3	0	4	3	.571	0	0-0	0	2.55
1995 Toronto	AL	17	17	5	0	130.1	537	113	53	49	12	2	2	5	41	2	102	6	1	9	6	.600	2	0-0	0	3.38
New York	AL	13	13	1	0	99	417	82	42	42	12	0	1	1	47	0	89	5	0	9	2	.818	0	0-0	0	3.82
11 ML YEARS		299	270	51	9	1994	8254	1639	771	701	154	55	56	57	750	29	1812	102	29	136	80	.630	21	1--	—	3.16

Jeff Conine

Bats: Right **Throws:** Right **Pos:** LF-128; 1B-48; PH-1 **Ht:** 6'1" **Wt:** 220 **Born:** 6/27/66 **Age:** 31

		BATTING																BASERUNNING				PERCENTAGES		
Year Team	Lg	G	AB	H	2B	3B	HR	(Hm Rd)	TB	R	RBI	TBB	IBB	SO	HBP	SH	SF	SB	CS	SB%	GDP	Avg	OBP	SLG
1990 Kansas City	AL	9	20	5	2	0	0	(0 0)	7	3	2	2	0	5	0	0	0	0	0	.00	1	.250	.318	.350
1992 Kansas City	AL	28	91	23	5	2	0	(0 0)	32	10	9	8	1	23	0	0	0	0	0	.00	1	.253	.313	.352
1993 Florida	NL	162	595	174	24	3	12	(5 7)	240	75	79	52	2	135	5	0	6	2	2	.50	14	.292	.351	.403
1994 Florida	NL	115	451	144	27	6	18	(8 10)	237	60	82	40	4	92	1	0	4	1	2	.33	8	.319	.373	.525
1995 Florida	NL	133	483	146	26	2	25	(12 12)	251	72	105	66	5	94	1	0	12	2	2	1.00	13	.302	.379	.520
1996 Florida	NL	157	597	175	32	2	26	(15 11)	289	84	95	62	1	121	4	0	7	1	4	.20	17	.293	.360	.484
6 ML YEARS		604	2237	667	116	15	81	(41 40)	1056	304	372	230	13	470	11	0	29	6	8	.43	54	.298	.362	.472

Dennis Cook

Pitches: Left **Bats:** Left **Pos:** RP-60 **Ht:** 6'3" **Wt:** 190 **Born:** 10/4/62 **Age:** 34

		HOW MUCH HE PITCHED						WHAT HE GAVE UP												THE RESULTS						
Year Team	Lg	G	GS	CG	GF	IP	BFP	H	R	ER	HR	SH	SF	HB	TBB	IBB	SO	WP	Bk	W	L	Pct.	ShO	Sv-Op	Hld	ERA
1988 San Francisco	NL	4	4	1	0	22	86	9	8	7	1	0	3	0	11	1	13	1	0	2	1	.667	1	0-0	—	2.86
1989 SF-Phi	NL	23	18	2	1	121	499	110	59	50	18	5	2	2	38	6	67	4	2	7	8	.467	1	0-0	1	3.72
1990 Phi-LA	NL	47	16	2	4	156	663	155	74	68	20	7	7	2	56	9	64	6	3	9	4	.692	1	1-2	4	3.92
1991 Los Angeles	NL	20	1	0	5	17.2	86	12	3	1	0	1	2	0	7	1	8	0	0	1	0	1.000	0	0-1	1	0.51
1992 Cleveland	AL	32	25	1	1	158	669	156	79	67	29	3	3	2	50	2	96	4	5	5	7	.417	0	0-0	0	3.82
1993 Cleveland	AL	25	6	0	2	54	233	62	36	34	9	3	2	2	16	1	34	0	1	5	5	.500	0	0-2	2	5.67

Year Team	Lg	G	GS	CG	GF	IP	BFP	H	R	ER	HR	SH	SF	HB	TBB	IBB	SO	WP	Bk	W	L	Pct.	ShO	Sv-Op	Hld	ERA
1994 Chicago	AL	38	0	0	8	33	143	29	17	13	4	3	0	0	14	3	26	0	1	3	1	.750	0	0-1	3	3.55
1995 Cle-Tex	AL	46	1	0	10	57.2	255	63	32	29	9	4	5	2	26	3	53	1	0	0	2	.000	0	2-2	6	4.53
1996 Texas	AL	60	0	0	9	70.1	298	53	34	32	2	3	5	7	35	7	64	0	0	5	2	.714	0	0-2	11	4.09
1989 San Francisco	NL	2	2	1	0	15	58	13	3	3	1	0	0	0	5	0	9	1	0	1	0	1.000	0	0-0	0	1.80
Philadelphia	NL	21	16	1	1	106	441	97	56	47	17	5	2	2	33	6	58	3	2	6	8	.429	1	0-0	1	3.99
1990 Philadelphia	NL	42	13	2	4	141.2	594	132	61	56	13	5	5	2	54	9	58	6	4	8	3	.727	1	1-2	3	3.56
Los Angeles	NL	5	3	0	0	14.1	69	23	13	12	7	2	2	0	2	0	6	0	0	1	1	.500	0	0-0	1	7.53
1995 Cleveland	AL	11	0	0	1	12.2	62	16	9	9	3	1	0	1	10	2	13	0	0	0	0	.000	0	0-0	1	6.39
Texas	AL	35	1	0	9	45	193	47	23	20	6	3	5	1	16	1	40	1	0	0	2	.000	0	2-2	5	4.00
9 ML YEARS		295	71	6	40	689.2	2915	649	342	301	92	29	29	17	253	33	425	16	12	37	30	.552	3	3-10	28	3.93

Steve Cooke

Pitches: Left **Bats:** Right **Pos:** RP-3   **Ht:** 6'6" **Wt:** 236 **Born:** 1/14/70 **Age:** 27

Year Team	Lg	G	GS	CG	GF	IP	BFP	H	R	ER	HR	SH	SF	HB	TBB	IBB	SO	WP	Bk	W	L	Pct.	ShO	Sv-Op	Hld	ERA
1996 Carolina *	AA	12	12	0	0	53.2	240	56	34	26	3	4	1	3	26	3	45	3	1	1	5	.167	0	0--	—	4.36
1992 Pittsburgh	NL	11	0	0	8	23	91	22	9	9	2	0	0	0	4	1	10	0	0	2	0	1.000	0	1-1	1	3.52
1993 Pittsburgh	NL	32	32	3	0	210.2	882	207	101	91	22	13	6	3	59	4	132	3	3	10	10	.500	1	0-0	0	3.89
1994 Pittsburgh	NL	25	23	2	1	134.1	590	157	79	75	21	9	3	5	46	7	74	3	0	4	11	.267	0	0-0	0	5.02
1996 Pittsburgh	NL	3	0	0	1	8.1	41	11	7	7	1	0	0	0	5	0	7	1	0	0	0	.000	0	0-0	0	7.56
4 ML YEARS		71	55	5	10	376.1	1604	397	196	182	46	22	10	8	114	12	223	7	3	16	21	.432	1	1-1	1	4.35

Ron Coomer

Bats: R **Throws:** R **Pos:** 1B-57; PH-29; RF-23; 3B-9; DH-3   **Ht:** 5'11" **Wt:** 195 **Born:** 11/18/66 **Age:** 30

Year Team	Lg	G	AB	H	2B	3B	HR	(Hm	Rd)	TB	R	RBI	TBB	IBB	SO	HBP	SH	SF	SB	CS	SB%	GDP	Avg	OBP	SLG
1990 Huntsville	AA	66	194	43	7	0	3	—	—	59	22	27	21	1	40	1	4	3	3	1	.75	5	.222	.297	.304
1991 Birmingham	AA	137	505	129	27	5	13	—	—	205	81	76	59	1	78	1	6	8	0	3	.00	21	.255	.330	.406
1992 Vancouver	AAA	86	262	62	10	0	9	—	—	99	29	40	16	3	36	0	6	3	3	0	1.00	14	.237	.277	.378
1993 Birmingham	AA	69	262	85	18	0	13	—	—	142	44	50	15	3	43	0	0	2	1	1	.50	8	.324	.358	.542
Nashville	AAA	59	211	66	19	0	13	—	—	124	34	51	10	1	29	1	0	3	1	2	.33	5	.313	.342	.588
1994 Albuquerque	AAA	127	535	181	34	6	22	—	—	293	89	123	26	4	62	2	0	7	4	3	.57	12	.338	.367	.548
1995 Albuquerque	AAA	85	323	104	23	2	16	—	—	179	54	76	18	1	28	0	0	4	5	2	.71	16	.322	.357	.554
1995 Minnesota	AL	37	101	26	3	1	5	(2	3)	46	15	19	9	0	11	1	0	0	0	1	.00	9	.257	.324	.455
1996 Minnesota	AL	95	233	69	12	1	12	(5	7)	119	34	41	17	1	24	0	0	3	3	0	1.00	10	.296	.340	.511
2 ML YEARS		132	334	95	15	2	17	(7	10)	165	49	60	26	1	35	1	0	3	3	1	.75	19	.284	.335	.494

Scott Cooper

Bats: Left **Throws:** Right **Pos:** 3B   **Ht:** 6'3" **Wt:** 215 **Born:** 10/13/67 **Age:** 29

Year Team	Lg	G	AB	H	2B	3B	HR	(Hm	Rd)	TB	R	RBI	TBB	IBB	SO	HBP	SH	SF	SB	CS	SB%	GDP	Avg	OBP	SLG
1990 Boston	AL	2	1	0	0	0	0	(0	0)	0	0	0	0	0	1	0	0	0	0	0	.00	0	.000	.000	.000
1991 Boston	AL	14	35	16	4	2	0	(0	0)	24	6	7	2	0	2	0	0	0	0	0	.00	0	.457	.486	.686
1992 Boston	AL	123	337	93	21	0	5	(2	3)	129	34	33	37	0	33	0	2	2	1	1	.50	8	.276	.346	.383
1993 Boston	AL	156	526	147	29	3	9	(3	6)	209	67	63	58	15	81	5	4	3	5	2	.71	8	.279	.355	.397
1994 Boston	AL	104	369	104	16	4	13	(9	4)	167	49	53	30	2	65	1	1	5	0	3	.00	6	.282	.333	.453
1995 St. Louis	NL	118	374	86	18	2	3	(1	2)	117	29	40	49	3	85	3	0	4	0	3	.00	9	.230	.321	.313
6 ML YEARS		517	1642	446	88	11	30	(15	15)	646	185	196	176	20	267	9	7	14	6	9	.40	28	.272	.343	.393

Rocky Coppinger

Pitches: Right **Bats:** Right **Pos:** SP-22; RP-1   **Ht:** 6'5" **Wt:** 250 **Born:** 3/19/74 **Age:** 23

Year Team	Lg	G	GS	CG	GF	IP	BFP	H	R	ER	HR	SH	SF	HB	TBB	IBB	SO	WP	Bk	W	L	Pct.	ShO	Sv-Op	Hld	ERA
1994 Bluefield	R+	14	13	0	1	73.1	302	51	24	20	5	0	3	2	40	0	88	5	0	4	3	.571	0	0--	—	2.45
1995 Frederick	A+	11	11	2	0	68.2	272	46	16	12	3	3	1	0	24	0	91	1	0	7	1	.875	1	0--	—	1.57
Rochester	AAA	5	5	0	0	34.2	140	23	5	4	2	0	2	1	17	0	19	0	0	3	0	1.000	0	0--	—	1.04
1996 Rochester	AAA	12	12	0	0	73	315	65	36	34	6	1	2	0	39	1	81	4	1	6	4	.600	0	0--	—	4.19
1996 Baltimore	AL	23	22	0	1	125	548	126	76	72	25	2	5	2	60	1	104	4	0	10	6	.625	0	0-0	0	5.18

Joey Cora

Bats: Both **Throws:** Right **Pos:** 2B-140; PH-23; 3B-1   **Ht:** 5'8" **Wt:** 162 **Born:** 5/14/65 **Age:** 32

Year Team	Lg	G	AB	H	2B	3B	HR	(Hm	Rd)	TB	R	RBI	TBB	IBB	SO	HBP	SH	SF	SB	CS	SB%	GDP	Avg	OBP	SLG
1987 San Diego	NL	77	241	57	7	2	0	(0	0)	68	23	13	28	1	26	1	5	1	15	11	.58	4	.237	.317	.282
1989 San Diego	NL	12	19	6	1	0	0	(0	0)	7	5	1	1	0	0	0	0	0	1	0	1.00	0	.316	.350	.368
1990 San Diego	NL	51	100	27	3	0	0	(0	0)	30	12	2	6	1	9	0	0	0	8	3	.73	1	.270	.311	.300
1991 Chicago	AL	100	228	55	2	3	0	(0	0)	63	37	18	20	0	21	5	8	3	11	6	.65	1	.241	.313	.276
1992 Chicago	AL	68	122	30	7	1	0	(0	0)	39	27	9	22	1	13	4	2	3	10	3	.77	2	.246	.371	.320

Year Team	Lg	G	AB	H	2B	3B	HR	(Hm	Rd)	TB	R	RBI	TBB	IBB	SO	HBP	SH	SF	SB	CS	SB%	GDP	Avg	OBP	SLG
					BATTING														**BASERUNNING**				**PERCENTAGES**		
1993 Chicago	AL	153	579	155	15	13	2	(0	2)	202	95	51	67	0	63	9	19	4	20	8	.71	14	.268	.351	.349
1994 Chicago	AL	90	312	86	13	4	2	(2	0)	113	55	30	38	0	32	2	11	5	8	4	.67	8	.276	.353	.362
1995 Seattle	AL	120	427	127	19	2	3	(1	2)	159	64	39	37	0	31	6	13	4	18	7	.72	8	.297	.359	.372
1996 Seattle	AL	144	530	154	37	6	6	(2	4)	221	90	45	35	1	32	7	6	5	5	5	.50	9	.291	.340	.417
9 ML YEARS		815	2558	697	104	31	13	(5	8)	902	408	208	254	4	227	34	64	25	96	47	.67	47	.272	.343	.353

Archie Corbin

Pitches: Right **Bats:** Right **Pos:** RP-18   **Ht:** 6'4" **Wt:** 190 **Born:** 12/30/67 **Age:** 29

Year Team	Lg	G	GS	CG	GF	IP	BFP	H	R	ER	HR	SH	SF	HB	TBB	IBB	SO	WP	Bk	W	L	Pct.	ShO	Sv-Op	Hld	ERA
						HOW MUCH HE PITCHED				**WHAT HE GAVE UP**												**THE RESULTS**				
1996 Rochester *	AAA	20	0	0	10	43.2	197	44	25	23	5	1	1	4	25	0	47	4	0	0	2	.000	0	1--	—	4.74
1991 Kansas City	AL	2	0	0	2	2.1	12	3	1	1	0	0	0	0	2	0	1	0	1	0	0	.000	0	0-0	0	3.86
1996 Baltimore	AL	18	0	0	5	27.1	123	22	7	7	2	0	1	1	22	0	20	2	0	2	0	1.000	0	0-0	3	2.30
2 ML YEARS		20	0	0	7	29.2	135	25	8	8	2	0	1	1	24	0	21	2	1	2	0	1.000	0	0-0	3	2.43

Wil Cordero

Bats: R **Throws:** R **Pos:** 2B-37; DH-13; PH-9; 1B-1   **Ht:** 6'2" **Wt:** 195 **Born:** 10/3/71 **Age:** 25

Year Team	Lg	G	AB	H	2B	3B	HR	(Hm	Rd)	TB	R	RBI	TBB	IBB	SO	HBP	SH	SF	SB	CS	SB%	GDP	Avg	OBP	SLG
					BATTING														**BASERUNNING**				**PERCENTAGES**		
1996 Red Sox *	R	3	10	3	0	0	1	—	—	6	1	3	0	0	2	0	0	1	0	0	.00	1	.300	.273	.600
Pawtucket *	AAA	4	10	3	1	0	1	—	—	7	2	2	2	0	3	0	0	0	0	0	.00	1	.300	.417	.700
1992 Montreal	NL	45	126	38	4	1	2	(1	1)	50	17	8	9	0	31	1	1	0	0	0	.00	3	.302	.353	.397
1993 Montreal	NL	138	475	118	32	2	10	(8	2)	184	56	58	34	8	60	7	4	1	12	3	.80	12	.248	.308	.387
1994 Montreal	NL	110	415	122	30	3	15	(5	10)	203	65	63	41	3	62	6	2	3	16	3	.84	8	.294	.363	.489
1995 Montreal	NL	131	514	147	35	2	10	(2	8)	216	64	49	36	4	88	9	1	4	9	5	.64	11	.286	.341	.420
1996 Boston	AL	59	198	57	14	0	3	(2	1)	80	29	37	11	4	31	2	1	1	2	1	.67	8	.288	.330	.404
5 ML YEARS		483	1728	482	115	8	40	(18	22)	733	231	215	131	19	272	25	9	9	39	12	.76	42	.279	.337	.424

Francisco Cordova

Pitches: Right **Bats:** Right **Pos:** RP-53; SP-6   **Ht:** 5'11" **Wt:** 163 **Born:** 4/26/72 **Age:** 25

Year Team	Lg	G	GS	CG	GF	IP	BFP	H	R	ER	HR	SH	SF	HB	TBB	IBB	SO	WP	Bk	W	L	Pct.	ShO	Sv-Op	Hld	ERA
						HOW MUCH HE PITCHED				**WHAT HE GAVE UP**												**THE RESULTS**				
1996 Pittsburgh	NL	59	6	0	41	99	414	103	49	45	11	1	0	2	20	6	95	2	1	4	7	.364	0	12-18	3	4.09

Marty Cordova

Bats: Right **Throws:** Right **Pos:** LF-145; PH-1   **Ht:** 6'0" **Wt:** 193 **Born:** 7/10/69 **Age:** 27

Year Team	Lg	G	AB	H	2B	3B	HR	(Hm	Rd)	TB	R	RBI	TBB	IBB	SO	HBP	SH	SF	SB	CS	SB%	GDP	Avg	OBP	SLG
					BATTING														**BASERUNNING**				**PERCENTAGES**		
1989 Elizabethtn	R+	38	148	42	2	3	8	—	—	74	32	29	14	1	29	3	0	0	2	1	.67	7	.284	.358	.500
1990 Kenosha	A	81	269	58	7	5	7	—	—	96	35	25	28	0	73	5	0	1	6	3	.67	5	.216	.300	.357
1991 Visalia	A+	71	189	40	6	1	7	—	—	69	31	19	17	0	46	2	2	0	2	3	.40	3	.212	.284	.365
1992 Visalia	A+	134	513	175	31	6	28	—	—	302	103	131	76	5	99	3	5	5	13	5	.72	20	.341	.431	.589
1993 Nashville	AA	138	508	127	30	5	19	—	—	224	83	77	64	3	153	13	0	3	10	5	.67	10	.250	.347	.441
1994 Salt Lake	AAA	103	385	138	25	4	19	—	—	228	69	66	39	0	63	8	0	2	17	6	.74	9	.358	.426	.592
1995 Minnesota	AL	137	512	142	27	4	24	(16	8)	249	81	84	52	1	111	10	0	5	20	7	.74	10	.277	.352	.486
1996 Minnesota	AL	145	569	176	46	1	16	(10	6)	272	97	111	53	4	96	8	0	9	11	5	.69	18	.309	.371	.478
2 ML YEARS		282	1081	318	73	5	40	(26	14)	521	178	195	105	5	207	18	0	14	31	12	.72	28	.294	.362	.482

Rheal Cormier

Pitches: Left **Bats:** Left **Pos:** SP-27; RP-6   **Ht:** 5'10" **Wt:** 187 **Born:** 4/23/67 **Age:** 30

Year Team	Lg	G	GS	CG	GF	IP	BFP	H	R	ER	HR	SH	SF	HB	TBB	IBB	SO	WP	Bk	W	L	Pct.	ShO	Sv-Op	Hld	ERA
						HOW MUCH HE PITCHED				**WHAT HE GAVE UP**												**THE RESULTS**				
1991 St. Louis	NL	11	10	2	1	67.2	281	74	35	31	5	1	3	2	8	1	38	2	1	4	5	.444	0	0-0	0	4.12
1992 St. Louis	NL	31	30	3	1	186	772	194	83	76	15	11	3	5	33	2	117	4	2	10	10	.500	0	0-0	0	3.68
1993 St. Louis	NL	38	21	1	4	145.1	619	163	80	70	18	10	4	4	27	3	75	6	0	7	6	.538	0	0-0	0	4.33
1994 St. Louis	NL	7	7	0	0	39.2	169	40	24	24	6	1	2	3	7	0	26	2	0	3	2	.600	0	0-0	0	5.45
1995 Boston	AL	48	12	0	3	115	488	131	60	52	12	6	2	3	31	2	69	4	0	7	5	.583	0	0-2	9	4.07
1996 Montreal	NL	33	27	1	1	159.2	674	165	80	74	16	4	8	9	41	3	100	8	0	7	10	.412	1	0-0	0	4.17
6 ML YEARS		168	107	7	10	713.1	3003	767	362	327	72	33	22	26	147	11	425	26	3	38	38	.500	1	0-2	9	4.13

Jim Corsi

Pitches: Right **Bats:** Right **Pos:** RP-57   **Ht:** 6'1" **Wt:** 220 **Born:** 9/9/61 **Age:** 35

Year Team	Lg	G	GS	CG	GF	IP	BFP	H	R	ER	HR	SH	SF	HB	TBB	IBB	SO	WP	Bk	W	L	Pct.	ShO	Sv-Op	Hld	ERA
						HOW MUCH HE PITCHED				**WHAT HE GAVE UP**												**THE RESULTS**				
1996 Modesto *	A+	1	1	0	0	1	3	0	0	0	0	0	0	0	0	0	2	0	0	0	0	.000	0	0--	—	0.00

Year Team	Lg	G	GS	CG	GF	IP	BFP	H	R	ER	HR	SH	SF	HB	TBB	IBB	SO	WP	Bk	W	L	Pct.	ShO	Sv-Op	Hld	ERA
1988 Oakland	AL	11	1	0	7	21.1	89	20	10	9	1	3	3	0	6	1	10	1	1	0	1	.000	0	0-0	0	3.80
1989 Oakland	AL	22	0	0	14	38.1	149	26	8	8	2	2	2	1	10	0	21	0	0	1	2	.333	0	0-0	2	1.88
1991 Houston	NL	47	0	0	15	77.2	322	76	37	32	6	3	2	0	23	5	53	1	1	0	5	.000	0	0-3	6	3.71
1992 Oakland	AL	32	0	0	16	44	185	44	12	7	2	4	2	0	18	2	19	0	0	4	2	.667	0	0-0	4	1.43
1993 Florida	NL	15	0	0	6	20.1	97	28	15	15	1	3	1	0	10	3	7	0	0	0	2	.000	0	0-0	1	6.64
1995 Oakland	AL	38	0	0	7	45	187	31	14	11	2	5	1	2	26	1	26	0	0	2	4	.333	0	2-4	13	2.20
1996 Oakland	AL	57	0	0	19	73.2	312	71	33	33	6	9	2	3	34	4	43	1	0	6	0	1.000	0	3-6	10	4.03
7 ML YEARS		222	1	0	84	320.1	1341	296	129	115	20	29	13	6	127	16	179	3	2	13	16	.448	0	5-13	34	3.23

Tim Crabtree

Pitches: Right **Bats:** Right **Pos:** RP-53 **Ht:** 6'4" **Wt:** 195 **Born:** 10/13/69 **Age:** 27

Year Team	Lg	G	GS	CG	GF	IP	BFP	H	R	ER	HR	SH	SF	HB	TBB	IBB	SO	WP	Bk	W	L	Pct.	ShO	Sv-Op	Hld	ERA
1992 St. Cathrns	A-	12	12	2	0	69	279	45	19	12	1	1	0	7	22	0	47	6	0	6	3	.667	0	0--	—	1.57
Knoxville	AA	3	3	1	0	19	78	14	8	2	0	1	0	2	4	0	13	0	0	2	0	.000	0	0--	—	0.95
1993 Knoxville	AA	27	27	2	0	158.2	707	178	93	72	11	10	7	10	59	0	67	7	3	9	14	.391	2	0--	—	4.08
1994 Syracuse	AAA	51	9	0	15	108	474	125	58	50	5	4	2	2	49	6	58	4	0	2	6	.250	0	2--	—	4.17
1995 Syracuse	AAA	26	0	0	16	31.2	148	38	25	19	1	1	1	1	12	2	22	5	1	0	2	.000	0	5--	—	5.40
1995 Toronto	AL	31	0	0	19	32	141	30	16	11	1	0	1	2	13	0	21	2	0	0	2	.000	0	0-2	1	3.09
1996 Toronto	AL	53	0	0	21	67.1	284	59	26	19	4	2	2	3	22	4	57	3	0	5	3	.625	0	1-5	17	2.54
2 ML YEARS		84	0	0	40	99.1	425	89	42	30	5	2	3	5	35	4	78	5	0	5	5	.500	0	1-7	18	2.72

Carlos Crawford

Pitches: Right **Bats:** Right **Pos:** SP-1 **Ht:** 6'1" **Wt:** 190 **Born:** 10/4/71 **Age:** 25

Year Team	Lg	G	GS	CG	GF	IP	BFP	H	R	ER	HR	SH	SF	HB	TBB	IBB	SO	WP	Bk	W	L	Pct.	ShO	Sv-Op	Hld	ERA
1990 Indians	R	10	9	0	0	53.2	257	68	43	26	0	0	2	8	25	0	39	6	4	2	3	.400	0	0--	—	4.36
1991 Burlington	R+	13	13	2	0	80.1	325	62	28	22	3	2	2	9	14	0	80	6	3	6	3	.667	1	0--	—	2.46
1992 Columbus	A	28	28	6	0	188.1	805	167	78	61	7	5	4	12	85	4	127	3	2	10	11	.476	3	0--	—	2.92
1993 Kinston	A+	28	28	4	0	165	703	158	87	67	11	10	4	10	46	0	124	8	4	7	9	.438	1	0--	—	3.65
1994 Canton-Akrn	AA	26	25	3	0	175	734	164	83	67	15	3	7	6	59	2	99	8	2	12	6	.667	0	0--	—	3.45
1995 Canton-Akrn	AA	8	8	2	0	51.2	212	47	19	15	1	1	0	1	15	0	36	2	0	2	2	.500	0	0--	—	2.61
1996 Scranton-WB	AAA	28	25	3	3	158.2	695	169	87	80	15	5	5	4	63	5	89	3	2	9	10	.474	1	0--	—	4.54
1996 Philadelphia	NL	1	1	0	0	3.2	22	7	10	2	1	1	0	1	2	0	4	0	0	0	1	.000	0	0-0	0	4.91

Doug Creek

Pitches: Left **Bats:** Left **Pos:** RP-63 **Ht:** 5'10" **Wt:** 205 **Born:** 3/1/69 **Age:** 28

Year Team	Lg	G	GS	CG	GF	IP	BFP	H	R	ER	HR	SH	SF	HB	TBB	IBB	SO	WP	Bk	W	L	Pct.	ShO	Sv-Op	Hld	ERA
1991 Hamilton	A-	9	5	0	1	38.2	169	39	22	22	2	0	3	3	18	0	45	3	0	3	2	.600	0	1--	—	5.12
Savannah	A	5	5	0	0	28.1	117	24	14	14	2	0	1	1	17	0	32	1	0	2	1	.667	0	0--	—	4.45
1992 Springfield	A	6	6	0	0	38.1	155	32	11	11	4	1	0	0	13	1	43	0	1	4	1	.800	0	0--	—	2.58
St. Pete	A+	13	13	0	0	73.1	300	57	31	23	5	0	4	1	37	1	63	4	1	5	4	.556	0	0--	—	2.82
1993 Arkansas	AA	25	25	1	0	147.2	620	142	75	66	15	5	5	3	48	1	128	10	1	11	10	.524	1	0--	—	4.02
Louisville	AAA	2	2	0	0	14	60	10	5	5	0	2	0	1	9	0	9	2	0	0	0	.000	0	0--	—	3.21
1994 Louisville	AAA	7	7	0	0	26.1	132	37	26	25	2	0	2	1	23	0	16	2	1	1	4	.200	0	0--	—	8.54
Arkansas	AA	17	17	1	0	92	405	96	54	45	8	11	4	3	36	0	65	7	1	3	10	.231	0	0--	—	4.40
1995 Arkansas	AA	26	0	0	11	34.1	143	24	12	11	4	3	0	3	16	2	50	1	0	4	2	.667	0	1--	—	2.88
Louisville	AAA	52	0	0	16	65	275	44	24	22	5	3	0	4	37	2	79	5	0	7	4	.636	0	1--	—	3.05
1995 St. Louis	NL	6	0	0	1	6.2	24	2	0	0	0	0	0	0	3	0	10	0	0	0	0	.000	0	0-0	0	0.00
1996 San Francisco	NL	63	0	0	15	48.1	220	45	41	35	11	1	0	2	32	2	38	2	0	0	2	.000	0	0-1	7	6.52
2 ML YEARS		69	0	0	16	55	244	47	41	35	11	1	0	2	35	2	48	2	0	0	2	.000	0	0-1	7	5.73

Felipe Crespo

Bats: B **Throws:** R **Pos:** 2B-10; 3B-6; PH-6; 1B-2 **Ht:** 5'11" **Wt:** 195 **Born:** 3/5/73 **Age:** 24

			BATTING															BASERUNNING				PERCENTAGES		
Year Team	Lg	G	AB	H	2B	3B	HR	(Hm | Rd)	TB	R	RBI	TBB	IBB	SO	HBP	SH	SF	SB	CS	SB%	GDP	Avg	OBP	SLG
1991 Medicne Hat	R+	49	184	57	11	4	4	—	—	88	40	31	25	0	31	3	2	1	6	4	.60	2	.310	.397	.478
1992 Myrtle Bch	A	81	263	74	14	3	1	—	—	97	43	29	58	2	38	4	2	5	7	7	.50	1	.281	.412	.369
1993 Dunedin	A+	96	345	103	16	8	6	—	—	153	51	39	47	3	40	4	5	2	18	5	.78	9	.299	.387	.443
1994 Knoxville	AA	129	502	135	30	4	8	—	—	197	74	49	57	3	95	2	4	1	20	8	.71	5	.269	.345	.392
1995 Syracuse	AAA	88	347	102	20	5	13	—	—	171	56	41	41	4	56	2	1	1	12	7	.63	5	.294	.371	.493
1996 Dunedin	A+	9	34	11	1	0	2	—	—	18	3	6	2	1	3	0	0	0	1	3	.25	1	.324	.361	.529
Syracuse	AAA	98	355	100	25	4	8	—	—	149	53	58	56	2	39	9	2	4	10	11	.48	7	.282	.389	.420
1996 Toronto	AL	22	49	9	4	0	0	(0 | 0)	13	6	4	12	0	13	3	0	0	1	0	1.00	0	.184	.375	.265

Fausto Cruz

Bats: Right **Throws:** Right **Pos:** 2B-8; SS-4; DH-1; PH-1   **Ht:** 5'10" **Wt:** 165 **Born:** 5/1/72 **Age:** 25

Year Team	Lg	G	AB	H	2B	3B	HR	(Hm	Rd)	TB	R	RBI	TBB	IBB	SO	HBP	SH	SF	SB	CS	SB%	GDP	Avg	OBP	SLG
1996 Toledo *	AAA	107	384	96	18	2	12	—	—	154	49	59	33	0	81	1	2	2	11	10	.52	7	.250	.310	.401
1994 Oakland	AL	17	28	3	0	0	0	(0	0)	3	2	0	4	0	6	0	0	0	0	0	.00	0	.107	.219	.107
1995 Oakland	AL	8	23	5	0	0	0	(0	0)	5	0	5	3	0	5	0	2	2	1	1	.50	1	.217	.286	.217
1996 Detroit	AL	14	38	9	2	0	0	(0	0)	11	5	0	1	0	11	0	1	0	0	0	.00	1	.237	.256	.289
3 ML YEARS		39	89	17	2	0	0	(0	0)	19	7	5	8	0	22	0	3	2	1	1	.50	2	.191	.253	.213

Jacob Cruz

Bats: Left **Throws:** Left **Pos:** RF-17; PH-10; LF-6   **Ht:** 6'1" **Wt:** 175 **Born:** 1/28/73 **Age:** 24

Year Team	Lg	G	AB	H	2B	3B	HR	(Hm	Rd)	TB	R	RBI	TBB	IBB	SO	HBP	SH	SF	SB	CS	SB%	GDP	Avg	OBP	SLG
1994 San Jose	A+	31	118	29	7	0	0	—	—	36	14	12	9	0	22	2	2	2		2	.00	6	.246	.305	.305
1995 Shreveport	AA	127	458	136	33	1	13	—	—	210	88	77	57	6	72	8	4	2	9	8	.53	15	.297	.383	.459
1996 Phoenix	AAA	121	435	124	26	4	7	—	—	179	60	75	62	5	77	10	2	11	5	9	.36	16	.285	.378	.411
1996 San Francisco	NL	33	77	18	3	0	3	(3	0)	30	10	10	12	0	24	2	1	0		1	.00	2	.234	.352	.390

John Cummings

Pitches: Left **Bats:** Left **Pos:** RP-25   **Ht:** 6'3" **Wt:** 200 **Born:** 5/10/69 **Age:** 28

Year Team	Lg	G	GS	CG	GF	IP	BFP	H	R	ER	HR	SH	SF	HB	TBB	IBB	SO	WP	Bk	W	L	Pct	ShO	Sv-Op	Hld	ERA
1996 Albuquerque *	AAA	27	9	0	8	78.1	342	91	47	36	5	4	3		28	1	49	3	0	2	6	.250	0	2- --		4.14
1993 Seattle	AL	10	8	1	0	46.1	207	59	34	31	6	0	2	2	16	2	19	1	1	0	6	.000	0	0-0	0	6.02
1994 Seattle	AL	17	8	0	2	64	285	66	43	40	7	1	3	0	37	2	33	3	1	2	4	.333	0	0-0	0	5.63
1995 Sea-LA		39	0	0	11	44.1	195	46	24	20	3	3	0		17	6	25	5	1	3	1	.750	0	0-0	6	4.06
1996 LA-Det		25	0	0	8	37	182	48	27	22	4	3	2		22	4	29	1	0	3	4	.429	0	0-1	5	5.35
1995 Seattle	AL	4	0	0	0	5.1	30	8	8	7	0	1	2		7	2	4	4	1	0	0	.000	0	0-0	0	11.81
Los Angeles	NL	35	0	0	11	39	165	38	16	13	3	2	1		10	4	21	1	0	3	1	.750	0	0-0	6	3.00
1996 Los Angeles	NL	4	0	0	1	5.1	30	12	7	4	1	1	1		2	1	5	0	0	0	1	.000	0	0-0	0	6.75
Detroit	AL	21	0	0	8	31.2	152	36	20	18	3	2	2		20	3	24	1	0	3	3	.500	0	0-1	5	5.12
4 ML YEARS		91	16	1	21	191.2	869	219	128	113	20	7	10	4	92	14	106	10	3	8	15	.348	0	0-1	7	5.31

Midre Cummings

Bats: Left **Throws:** Right **Pos:** CF-11; RF-10; PH-4   **Ht:** 6'0" **Wt:** 203 **Born:** 10/14/71 **Age:** 25

Year Team	Lg	G	AB	H	2B	3B	HR	(Hm	Rd)	TB	R	RBI	TBB	IBB	SO	HBP	SH	SF	SB	CS	SB%	GDP	Avg	OBP	SLG
1996 Calgary *	AAA	97	368	112	24	3	8	—	—	166	60	55	21	3	60	1	4	3	6	4	.60	6	.304	.341	.451
1993 Pittsburgh	NL	13	36	4	1	0	0	(0	0)	5	5	3	4	0	9	0	0	1	0	0	.00	1	.111	.195	.139
1994 Pittsburgh	NL	24	86	21	4	0	1	(1	0)	28	11	12	4	0	18	1	0	1	0	0	.00	0	.244	.283	.326
1995 Pittsburgh	NL	59	152	37	7	1	2	(1	1)	52	13	15	13	3	30	0	1	0	1	0	1.00	2	.243	.303	.342
1996 Pittsburgh	NL	24	85	19	3	1	3	(2	1)	33	11	7	0	0	16	0	1	1	0	0	1.00	0	.224	.221	.388
4 ML YEARS		120	359	81	15	2	6	(4	2)	118	40	37	21	3	73	1	2	3	1	0	1.00	3	.226	.268	.329

Chad Curtis

Bats: Right **Throws:** Right **Pos:** CF-120; LF-48; PH-13   **Ht:** 5'10" **Wt:** 175 **Born:** 11/6/68 **Age:** 28

Year Team	Lg	G	AB	H	2B	3B	HR	(Hm	Rd)	TB	R	RBI	TBB	IBB	SO	HBP	SH	SF	SB	CS	SB%	GDP	Avg	OBP	SLG
1992 California	AL	139	441	114	16	2	10	(5	5)	164	59	46	51	2	71	6	5	4	43	18	.70	10	.259	.341	.372
1993 California	AL	152	583	166	25	3	6	(3	3)	215	94	59	70	2	89	4	7	7	48	24	.67	16	.285	.361	.369
1994 California	AL	114	453	116	23	4	11	(8	3)	180	67	50	37	0	69	5	7	4	25	11	.69	10	.256	.317	.397
1995 Detroit	AL	144	586	157	29	3	21	(11	10)	255	96	67	70	3	93	7	0	6	27	15	.64	12	.268	.349	.435
1996 Det-LA		147	504	127	25	1	12	(3	9)	190	85	46	70	0	88	1	6	6	18	11	.62	15	.252	.341	.377
1996 Detroit	AL	104	400	105	20	1	10	(2	8)	157	65	37	53	0	73	1	6	6	16	10	.62	14	.263	.346	.393
Los Angeles	NL	43	104	22	5	0	2	(1	1)	33	20	9	17	0	15	0	0	0	2	1	.67	1	.212	.322	.317
5 ML YEARS		696	2567	680	118	13	60	(30	30)	1004	401	268	298	7	410	23	25	28	161	79	.67	63	.265	.343	.391

Milt Cuyler

Bats: B **Throws:** R **Pos:** CF-30; RF-22; PH-9; DH-1   **Ht:** 5'10" **Wt:** 185 **Born:** 10/7/68 **Age:** 28

Year Team	Lg	G	AB	H	2B	3B	HR	(Hm	Rd)	TB	R	RBI	TBB	IBB	SO	HBP	SH	SF	SB	CS	SB%	GDP	Avg	OBP	SLG
1990 Detroit	AL	19	51	13	3	1	0	(0	0)	18	8	8	5	0	10	0	2	1	1	2	.33	1	.255	.316	.353
1991 Detroit	AL	154	475	122	15	7	3	(1	2)	160	77	33	52	0	92	5	12	2	41	10	.80	4	.257	.335	.337
1992 Detroit	AL	89	291	70	11	1	3	(1	2)	92	39	28	10	0	62	4	8	0	8	5	.62	4	.241	.275	.316
1993 Detroit	AL	82	249	53	11	7	0	(0	0)	78	46	19	19	0	53	3	4	1	13	2	.87	2	.213	.276	.313
1994 Detroit	AL	48	116	28	3	1	1	(1	0)	36	20	11	13	0	21	1	2	2	5	3	.63	3	.241	.318	.310
1995 Detroit	AL	41	88	18	1	4	0	(0	0)	27	15	5	8	0	16	0	2	0	2	1	.67	0	.205	.271	.307
1996 Boston	AL	50	110	22	1	2	2	(0	0)	33	19	12	13	0	19	3	7	1	7	3	.70	1	.200	.299	.300

Year Team		BATTING																	BASERUNNING				PERCENTAGES		
Year Team	Lg	G	AB	H	2B	3B	HR	(Hm	Rd)	TB	R	RBI	TBB	IBB	SO	HBP	SH	SF	SB	CS	SB%	GDP	Avg	OBP	SLG
7 ML YEARS		483	1380	326	45	23	9	(3	6)	444	224	116	120	0	273	16	37	7	77	26	.75	15	.236	.303	.322

Jeff D'Amico

Pitches: Right **Bats:** Right **Pos:** SP-17   **Ht:** 6'7" **Wt:** 250 **Born:** 12/27/75 **Age:** 21

Year Team		HOW MUCH HE PITCHED						WHAT HE GAVE UP										THE RESULTS						
Year Team	Lg	G	GS	CG	GF	IP	BFP	H	R	ER	HR	SH	SF	HB	TBB	IBB	SO	WP	Bk	W	L	Pct.	ShO	Sv-Op	Hld	ERA
1995 Beloit	A	21	20	3	0	132	523	102	40	35	7	3	2	4	31	2	119	6	1	13	3	.813	1	0--	—	2.39
1996 El Paso	AA	13	13	3	0	96	387	89	42	34	10	0	2	2	13	0	76	0	1	5	4	.556	0	0--	—	3.19
1996 Milwaukee	AL	17	17	0	0	86	367	88	53	52	21	3	3	0	31	0	53	1	1	6	6	.500	0	0-0	0	5.44

Omar Daal

Pitches: Left **Bats:** Left **Pos:** RP-58; SP-6   **Ht:** 6'3" **Wt:** 185 **Born:** 3/1/72 **Age:** 25

Year Team		HOW MUCH HE PITCHED						WHAT HE GAVE UP										THE RESULTS						
Year Team	Lg	G	GS	CG	GF	IP	BFP	H	R	ER	HR	SH	SF	HB	TBB	IBB	SO	WP	Bk	W	L	Pct.	ShO	Sv-Op	Hld	ERA
1993 Los Angeles	NL	47	0	0	12	35.1	155	36	20	20	5	2	2	0	21	3	19	1	2	2	3	.400	0	0-1	7	5.09
1994 Los Angeles	NL	24	0	0	5	13.2	55	12	5	5	1	1	0	0	5	0	9	1	1	0	0	.000	0	0-0	3	3.29
1995 Los Angeles	NL	28	0	0	20	100	29	16	16	1	1	1	1	15	4	11	0	1	4	0	1.000	0	0-1	4	7.20
1996 Montreal	NL	64	6	0	9	87.1	366	74	40	39	10	2	2	1	37	3	82	1	1	4	5	.444	0	0-4	9	4.02
4 ML YEARS		163	6	0	26	156.1	676	151	81	80	17	6	5	2	78	10	121	3	5	10	8	.556	0	0-6	23	4.61

Johnny Damon

Bats: L **Throws:** L **Pos:** CF-89; RF-63; PH-8; DH-1   **Ht:** 6'2" **Wt:** 190 **Born:** 11/5/73 **Age:** 23

Year Team		BATTING																	BASERUNNING				PERCENTAGES		
Year Team	Lg	G	AB	H	2B	3B	HR	(Hm	Rd)	TB	R	RBI	TBB	IBB	SO	HBP	SH	SF	SB	CS	SB%	GDP	Avg	OBP	SLG
1992 Royals	R	50	192	67	12	9	4	—	—	109	58	24	31	1	21	4	4	0	23	6	.79	1	.349	.449	.568
Baseball Cy	A+	1	1	0	0	0	0	—	—	0	0	0	0	0	0	0	0	0	0	0	.00	0	.000	.000	.000
1993 Rockford	A	127	511	148	25	13	5	—	—	214	82	50	51	1	83	6	3	3	59	18	.77	4	.290	.359	.419
1994 Wilmington	A+	119	472	149	25	13	6	—	—	218	96	75	62	6	55	8	5	7	44	9	.83	4	.316	.399	.462
1995 Wichita	AA	111	423	145	15	9	16	—	—	226	83	54	67	13	35	2	10	1	26	15	.63	3	.343	.434	.534
1995 Kansas City	AL	47	188	53	11	5	3	(1	2)	83	32	23	12	0	22	1	2	3	7	0	1.00	2	.282	.324	.441
1996 Kansas City	AL	145	517	140	22	5	6	(3	3)	190	61	50	31	3	64	3	10	5	25	5	.83	4	.271	.313	.368
2 ML YEARS		192	705	193	33	10	9	(4	5)	273	93	73	43	3	86	4	12	8	32	5	.86	6	.274	.316	.387

Danny Darwin

Pitches: Right **Bats:** Right **Pos:** SP-25; RP-9   **Ht:** 6'3" **Wt:** 202 **Born:** 10/25/55 **Age:** 41

Year Team		HOW MUCH HE PITCHED						WHAT HE GAVE UP										THE RESULTS						
Year Team	Lg	G	GS	CG	GF	IP	BFP	H	R	ER	HR	SH	SF	HB	TBB	IBB	SO	WP	Bk	W	L	Pct.	ShO	Sv-Op	Hld	ERA
1978 Texas	AL	3	1	0	2	9	36	11	4	4	0	0	1	0	1	0	8	0	0	1	0	1.000	0	0--	—	4.00
1979 Texas	AL	20	6	1	4	78	313	50	36	35	5	3	6	5	30	2	58	0	1	4	4	.500	0	0--	—	4.04
1980 Texas	AL	53	2	0	35	110	468	98	37	32	4	5	7	2	50	7	104	3	0	13	4	.765	0	8--	—	2.62
1981 Texas	AL	22	22	6	0	146	601	115	67	59	12	8	3	6	57	5	98	1	0	9	9	.500	2	0--	—	3.64
1982 Texas	AL	56	1	0	41	89	394	95	38	34	6	10	5	2	37	8	61	2	1	10	8	.556	0	7--	—	3.44
1983 Texas	AL	28	26	9	0	183	780	175	86	71	9	7	7	3	62	3	92	2	0	8	13	.381	2	0--	—	3.49
1984 Texas	AL	35	32	5	2	223.2	955	249	110	98	19	3	3	4	54	2	123	3	0	8	12	.400	1	0--	—	3.94
1985 Milwaukee	AL	39	29	11	8	217.2	919	212	112	92	34	7	9	4	65	4	125	6	0	8	18	.308	1	2--	—	3.80
1986 Mil-Hou		39	22	6	6	184.2	759	170	81	65	16	6	9	4	44	1	120	7	1	11	10	.524	1	0--	—	3.17
1987 Houston	NL	33	30	3	0	195.2	833	184	87	78	17	8	3	5	69	12	134	3	1	9	10	.474	1	0-0	1	3.59
1988 Houston	NL	44	20	3	9	192	804	189	86	82	20	10	9	7	48	9	129	1	2	8	13	.381	0	3-3	3	3.84
1989 Houston	NL	68	0	0	26	122	482	92	34	32	8	8	5	2	33	9	104	2	3	11	4	.733	0	7-11	8	2.36
1990 Houston	NL	48	17	3	14	162.2	646	136	42	40	11	4	2	4	31	4	109	0	2	11	4	.733	0	2-4	0	**2.21**
1991 Boston	AL	12	12	0	0	68	292	71	39	39	15	1	2	4	15	1	42	2	0	3	6	.333	0	0-0	—	5.16
1992 Boston	AL	51	15	2	21	161.1	688	159	76	71	11	7	5	5	53	9	124	5	0	9	9	.500	0	3-6	1	3.96
1993 Boston	AL	34	34	2	0	229.1	919	196	93	83	31	6	9	3	49	8	130	5	1	15	11	.577	1	0-0	—	3.26
1994 Boston	AL	13	13	0	0	75.2	350	101	56	53	13	1	5	1	24	6	54	0	0	7	5	.583	0	0-0	—	6.30
1995 Tor-Tex	AL	20	15	1	0	99	448	131	87	82	25	3	5	4	31	3	58	2	0	3	10	.231	0	0-0	0	7.45
1996 Pit-Hou	NL	34	25	0	1	164.2	677	160	79	69	16	8	7	12	27	3	96	3	3	10	11	.476	0	0-2	1	3.77
1986 Milwaukee	AL	27	14	5	4	130.1	537	120	62	51	13	5	6	3	35	1	80	5	0	6	8	.429	1	0--	—	3.52
Houston	NL	12	8	1	2	54.1	222	50	19	14	3	1	3	0	9	0	40	2	1	5	2	.714	0	0--	—	2.32
1995 Toronto	AL	13	11	1	0	65	303	91	60	55	13	3	5	3	24	2	36	1	0	1	8	.111	0	0-0	0	7.62
Texas	AL	7	4	0	0	34	145	40	27	27	12	0	0	1	7	1	22	1	0	2	2	.500	0	0-0	0	7.15
1996 Pittsburgh	NL	19	19	0	0	122.1	493	117	48	41	9	5	4	6	16	0	69	3	3	7	9	.438	0	0-0	0	3.02
Houston	NL	15	6	0	1	42.1	184	43	31	28	7	3	3	6	11	3	27	0	0	3	2	.600	0	0-2	1	5.95
19 ML YEARS		652	322	52	169	2711.1	11364	2594	1248	1119	272	105	102	76	780	96	1769	47	15	158	161	.495	9	32--	—	3.71

52

Jeff Darwin

Pitches: Right **Bats:** Right **Pos:** RP-22   **Ht:** 6'3" **Wt:** 180 **Born:** 7/6/69 **Age:** 27

Year Team	Lg	G	GS	CG	GF	IP	BFP	H	R	ER	HR	SH	SF	HB	TBB	IBB	SO	WP	Bk	W	L	Pct.	ShO	Sv-Op	Hld	ERA
1996 Nashville *	AAA	25	6	0	11	63.1	256	52	31	25	8	0	1	1	17	1	33	5	0	5	2	.714	0	3--	—	3.55
1994 Seattle	AL	2	0	0	1	4	22	7	6	6	1	0	0	1	3	1	1	0	0	0	0	.000	0	0-0	0	13.50
1996 Chicago	AL	22	0	0	9	30.2	124	26	10	10	5	1	0	2	9	1	15	0	0	0	1	.000	0	0-1	2	2.93
2 ML YEARS		24	0	0	10	34.2	146	33	16	16	6	1	0	3	12	2	16	0	0	0	1	.000	0	0-1	2	4.15

Doug Dascenzo

Bats: Both **Throws:** Left **Pos:** PH-15; RF-9; CF-1   **Ht:** 5'8" **Wt:** 160 **Born:** 6/30/64 **Age:** 33

Year Team	Lg	G	AB	H	2B	3B	HR	(Hm	Rd)	TB	R	RBI	TBB	IBB	SO	HBP	SH	SF	SB	CS	SB%	GDP	Avg	OBP	SLG
1996 Las Vegas *	AAA	86	320	91	17	3	0	—	—	114	48	20	32	2	38	2	10	2	15	13	.54	6	.284	.351	.356
1988 Chicago	NL	26	75	16	3	0	0	(0	0)	19	9	4	9	1	4	0	1	0	6	1	.86	2	.213	.298	.253
1989 Chicago	NL	47	139	23	1	0	1	(0	1)	27	20	12	13	0	13	0	3	2	6	3	.67	2	.165	.234	.194
1990 Chicago	NL	113	241	61	9	5	1	(1	0)	83	27	26	21	2	18	1	5	3	15	6	.71	3	.253	.312	.344
1991 Chicago	NL	118	239	61	11	0	1	(0	1)	75	40	18	24	2	26	2	6	1	14	7	.67	3	.255	.327	.314
1992 Chicago	NL	139	376	96	13	4	0	(0	0)	117	37	20	27	2	32	0	4	2	6	8	.43	3	.255	.304	.311
1993 Texas	AL	76	146	29	5	1	2	(0	2)	42	20	10	8	0	22	0	3	1	2	0	1.00	1	.199	.239	.288
1996 San Diego	NL	21	9	1	0	0	0	(0	0)	1	3	0	1	0	2	0	0	0	0	1	.00	0	.111	.200	.111
7 ML YEARS		540	1225	287	42	10	5	(1	4)	364	156	90	103	7	117	3	22	9	49	26	.65	14	.234	.293	.297

Darren Daulton

Bats: Left **Throws:** Right **Pos:** LF-5   **Ht:** 6'2" **Wt:** 207 **Born:** 1/3/62 **Age:** 35

Year Team	Lg	G	AB	H	2B	3B	HR	(Hm	Rd)	TB	R	RBI	TBB	IBB	SO	HBP	SH	SF	SB	CS	SB%	GDP	Avg	OBP	SLG
1996 Clearwater *	A+	1	1	0	0	0	0	—	—	0	1	0	0	0	0	1	0	0	0	0	.00	0	.000	.500	.000
1983 Philadelphia	NL	2	3	1	0	0	0	(0	0)	1	1	0	1	0	1	0	0	0	0	0	.00	0	.333	.500	.333
1985 Philadelphia	NL	36	103	21	3	1	4	(0	4)	38	14	11	16	0	37	0	0	0	3	0	1.00	1	.204	.311	.369
1986 Philadelphia	NL	49	138	31	4	0	8	(4	4)	59	18	21	38	3	41	1	2	2	2	3	.40	1	.225	.391	.428
1987 Philadelphia	NL	53	129	25	6	0	3	(1	2)	40	10	13	16	1	37	0	4	1	0	0	.00	4	.194	.281	.310
1988 Philadelphia	NL	58	144	30	6	0	1	(0	1)	39	13	12	17	1	26	0	0	2	2	1	.67	4	.208	.288	.271
1989 Philadelphia	NL	131	368	74	12	2	8	(2	6)	114	29	44	52	8	58	2	1	1	2	1	.67	4	.201	.303	.310
1990 Philadelphia	NL	143	459	123	30	1	12	(5	7)	191	62	57	72	9	72	2	3	4	7	1	.88	6	.268	.367	.416
1991 Philadelphia	NL	89	285	56	12	0	12	(8	4)	104	36	42	41	4	66	2	2	5	5	0	1.00	4	.196	.297	.365
1992 Philadelphia	NL	145	485	131	32	5	27	(17	10)	254	80	109	88	11	103	6	0	6	11	2	.85	3	.270	.385	.524
1993 Philadelphia	NL	147	510	131	35	4	24	(10	14)	246	90	105	117	12	111	2	0	8	5	0	1.00	2	.257	.392	.482
1994 Philadelphia	NL	69	257	77	17	1	15	(7	8)	141	43	56	33	2	43	1	0	1	4	1	.80	4	.300	.380	.549
1995 Philadelphia	NL	98	342	85	19	3	9	(7	2)	137	44	55	55	2	52	5	0	2	3	0	1.00	4	.249	.359	.401
1996 Philadelphia	NL	5	12	2	0	0	0	(0	0)	2	3	0	7	0	5	0	0	0	0	0	.00	1	.167	.500	.167
13 ML YEARS		1025	3235	787	176	17	123	(61	62)	1366	443	525	553	53	652	22	12	32	44	9	.83	31	.243	.355	.422

Chili Davis

Bats: Both **Throws:** Right **Pos:** DH-143; PH-2   **Ht:** 6'3" **Wt:** 217 **Born:** 1/17/60 **Age:** 37

Year Team	Lg	G	AB	H	2B	3B	HR	(Hm	Rd)	TB	R	RBI	TBB	IBB	SO	HBP	SH	SF	SB	CS	SB%	GDP	Avg	OBP	SLG
1981 San Francisco	NL	8	15	2	0	0	0	(0	0)	2	1	0	1	0	2	0	0	0	2	0	1.00	1	.133	.188	.133
1982 San Francisco	NL	154	641	167	27	6	19	(6	13)	263	86	76	45	2	115	2	7	6	24	13	.65	13	.261	.308	.410
1983 San Francisco	NL	137	486	113	21	2	11	(7	4)	171	54	59	55	6	108	0	3	9	10	12	.45	9	.233	.305	.352
1984 San Francisco	NL	137	499	157	21	6	21	(7	14)	253	87	81	42	6	74	1	2	2	12	8	.60	13	.315	.368	.507
1985 San Francisco	NL	136	481	130	25	2	13	(7	6)	198	53	56	62	12	74	0	1	7	15	7	.68	16	.270	.349	.412
1986 San Francisco	NL	153	526	146	28	3	13	(7	6)	219	71	70	84	23	96	1	2	5	16	13	.55	11	.278	.375	.416
1987 San Francisco	NL	149	500	125	22	1	24	(9	15)	221	80	76	72	15	109	2	0	4	16	9	.64	8	.250	.344	.442
1988 California	AL	158	600	161	29	3	21	(11	10)	259	81	93	56	14	118	0	1	10	9	10	.47	13	.268	.326	.432
1989 California	AL	154	560	152	24	1	22	(6	16)	244	81	90	61	12	109	0	3	6	3	0	1.00	21	.271	.340	.436
1990 California	AL	113	412	109	17	1	12	(10	2)	164	58	58	61	4	89	0	0	3	1	2	.33	14	.265	.357	.398
1991 Minnesota	AL	153	534	148	34	1	29	(14	15)	271	84	93	95	13	117	1	0	4	5	6	.45	9	.277	.385	.507
1992 Minnesota	AL	138	444	128	27	2	12	(6	6)	195	63	66	73	11	76	3	0	9	4	5	.44	11	.288	.386	.439
1993 California	AL	153	573	139	32	0	27	(13	14)	252	74	112	71	12	135	1	0	6	4	1	.80	18	.243	.327	.440
1994 California	AL	108	392	122	18	1	26	(14	12)	220	72	84	69	11	84	1	0	6	3	2	.60	12	.311	.410	.561
1995 California	AL	119	424	135	23	0	20	(11	9)	218	81	86	89	12	79	0	0	9	3	3	.50	12	.318	.429	.514
1996 California	AL	145	530	155	24	0	28	(15	13)	263	73	95	86	11	99	0	1	6	5	2	.71	18	.292	.387	.496
16 ML YEARS		2115	7617	2089	372	29	298	(143	155)	3413	1099	1195	1022	164	1484	12	20	86	132	93	.59	199	.274	.357	.448

Eric Davis

Bats: R **Throws:** R **Pos:** CF-115; LF-14; PH-8; 1B-1   **Ht:** 6'3" **Wt:** 190 **Born:** 5/29/62 **Age:** 35

Year Team	Lg	G	AB	H	2B	3B	HR	(Hm	Rd)	TB	R	RBI	TBB	IBB	SO	HBP	SH	SF	SB	CS	SB%	GDP	Avg	OBP	SLG
1984 Cincinnati	NL	57	174	39	10	1	10	(3	7)	81	33	30	24	0	48	1	0	1	10	2	.83	1	.224	.320	.466
1985 Cincinnati	NL	56	122	30	3	3	8	(1	7)	63	26	18	7	0	39	0	2	0	16	3	.84	1	.246	.287	.516

BATTING																				BASERUNNING				PERCENTAGES		
Year Team	Lg	G	AB	H	2B	3B	HR	(Hm	Rd)	TB	R	RBI	TBB	IBB	SO	HBP	SH	SF	SB	CS	SB%	GDP	Avg	OBP	SLG
1986 Cincinnati	NL	132	415	115	15	3	27	(12	15)	217	97	71	68	5	100	1	0	3	80	11	.88	6	.277	.378	.523
1987 Cincinnati	NL	129	474	139	23	4	37	(17	20)	281	120	100	84	8	134	1	0	3	50	6	.89	6	.293	.399	.593
1988 Cincinnati	NL	135	472	129	18	3	26	(14	12)	231	81	93	65	10	124	3	0	3	35	3	.92	11	.273	.363	.489
1989 Cincinnati	NL	131	462	130	14	2	34	(15	19)	250	74	101	68	12	116	1	0	11	21	7	.75	16	.281	.367	.541
1990 Cincinnati	NL	127	453	118	26	2	24	(13	11)	220	84	86	60	6	100	2	0	3	21	3	.88	7	.260	.347	.486
1991 Cincinnati	NL	89	285	67	10	0	11	(5	6)	110	39	33	48	5	92	5	0	2	14	2	.88	4	.235	.353	.386
1992 Los Angeles	NL	76	267	61	8	1	5	(1	4)	86	21	32	36	2	71	3	0	2	19	1	.95	9	.228	.325	.322
1993 LA-Det		131	451	107	18	1	20	(10	10)	187	71	68	55	7	106	1	0	4	35	7	.83	12	.237	.319	.415
1994 Detroit	AL	37	120	22	4	0	3	(3	0)	35	19	13	18	0	45	0	0	0	5	0	1.00	4	.183	.290	.292
1996 Detroit	AL	129	415	119	20	0	26	(8	18)	217	81	83	70	3	121	6	1	4	23	9	.72	8	.287	.394	.523
1993 Los Angeles	NL	108	376	88	17	0	14	(7	7)	147	57	53	41	6	88	1	0	4	33	5	.87	8	.234	.308	.391
Detroit	AL	23	75	19	1	1	6	(3	3)	40	14	15	14	1	18	0	0	0	2	2	.50	4	.253	.371	.533
12 ML YEARS		1229	4110	1076	169	20	231	(102	129)	1978	746	728	603	58	1096	24	3	36	329	54	.86	85	.262	.357	.481

Russ Davis

Bats: Right **Throws:** Right **Pos:** 3B-51; PH-2 **Ht:** 6'0" **Wt:** 195 **Born:** 9/13/69 **Age:** 27

BATTING																				BASERUNNING				PERCENTAGES		
Year Team	Lg	G	AB	H	2B	3B	HR	(Hm	Rd)	TB	R	RBI	TBB	IBB	SO	HBP	SH	SF	SB	CS	SB%	GDP	Avg	OBP	SLG
1994 New York	AL	4	14	2	0	0	0	(0	0)	2	0	1	0	0	4	0	0	0	0	0	.00	1	.143	.143	.143
1995 New York	AL	40	98	27	5	2	2	(2	0)	42	14	12	10	0	26	1	0	0	0	0	.00	0	.276	.349	.429
1996 Seattle	AL	51	167	39	9	0	5	(3	2)	63	24	18	17	1	50	2	4	0	2	0	1.00	1	.234	.312	.377
3 ML YEARS		95	279	68	14	2	7	(5	2)	107	38	31	27	1	80	3	4	0	2	0	1.00	2	.244	.317	.384

Tim Davis

Pitches: Left **Bats:** Left **Pos:** RP-40 **Ht:** 5'11" **Wt:** 165 **Born:** 7/14/70 **Age:** 26

HOW MUCH HE PITCHED							WHAT HE GAVE UP											THE RESULTS						
Year Team	Lg	G	GS	CG	GF	IP	BFP	H	R	ER	HR	SH	SF	HB	TBB	IBB	SO	WP	Bk	W	L	Pct.	ShO	Sv-Op	Hld	ERA
1996 Everett *	A-	1	1	0	0	2	7	0	0	0	0	0	0	0	1	0	5	0	0	0	0	.000	0	0--	—	0.00
Tacoma *	AAA	8	1	0	1	17	78	19	12	10	1	3	1	0	10	2	19	1	0	0	1	.000	0	0--	—	5.29
1994 Seattle	AL	42	1	0	12	49.1	225	57	25	22	4	3	3	1	25	5	28	6	0	2	2	.500	0	2-4	5	4.01
1995 Seattle	AL	5	5	0	0	24	117	30	21	17	2	0	1	0	18	2	19	0	0	2	1	.667	0	0-0	0	6.38
1996 Seattle	AL	40	0	0	4	42.2	187	43	21	19	4	1	1	2	17	1	34	0	0	2	2	.500	0	0-0	5	4.01
3 ML YEARS		87	6	0	16	116	529	130	67	58	10	4	5	3	60	8	81	6	0	6	5	.545	0	2-4	10	4.50

Scott Davison

Pitches: Right **Bats:** Right **Pos:** RP-5 **Ht:** 6'0" **Wt:** 190 **Born:** 10/16/70 **Age:** 26

HOW MUCH HE PITCHED							WHAT HE GAVE UP											THE RESULTS						
Year Team	Lg	G	GS	CG	GF	IP	BFP	H	R	ER	HR	SH	SF	HB	TBB	IBB	SO	WP	Bk	W	L	Pct.	ShO	Sv-Op	Hld	ERA
1994 Bellingham	A-	13	0	0	11	15	66	11	5	3	0	1	0	1	6	1	21	3	2	0	1	.000	0	7--	—	1.80
Appleton	A	4	0	0	2	7.1	30	7	4	3	0	0	2	0	2	0	7	0	2	0	1	.000	0	0--	—	3.68
Calgary	AAA	11	0	0	3	14.2	67	20	10	10	1	0	0	1	6	0	17	2	1	0	1	.000	0	0--	—	6.14
1995 Tacoma	AAA	8	3	0	2	22	91	21	14	13	1	1	1	0	4	0	12	1	1	1	1	.500	0	0--	—	5.32
Port City	AA	42	3	0	30	62.2	247	43	18	17	2	7	3	1	20	1	62	3	1	3	1	.750	0	10--	—	2.44
1996 Tacoma	AAA	17	0	0	16	23	90	13	2	1	0	1	0	1	6	1	23	3	0	1	1	.500	0	9--	—	0.39
1995 Seattle	AL	3	0	0	3	4.1	21	7	3	3	1	0	0	1	1	0	3	0	0	0	0	.000	0	0-0	0	6.23
1996 Seattle	AL	5	0	0	3	9	40	11	9	9	1	0	0	0	3	0	9	0	0	0	0	.000	0	0-0	0	9.00
2 ML YEARS		8	0	0	6	13.1	61	18	12	12	2	0	0	1	4	0	12	0	0	0	0	.000	0	0-0	0	8.10

Andre Dawson

Bats: Right **Throws:** Right **Pos:** PH-36; LF-6 **Ht:** 6'3" **Wt:** 197 **Born:** 7/10/54 **Age:** 42

BATTING																				BASERUNNING				PERCENTAGES		
Year Team	Lg	G	AB	H	2B	3B	HR	(Hm	Rd)	TB	R	RBI	TBB	IBB	SO	HBP	SH	SF	SB	CS	SB%	GDP	Avg	OBP	SLG
1976 Montreal	NL	24	85	20	4	1	0	(0	0)	26	9	7	5	1	13	0	2	0	1	2	.33	0	.235	.278	.306
1977 Montreal	NL	139	525	148	26	9	19	(7	12)	249	64	65	34	4	93	2	1	4	21	7	.75	6	.282	.326	.474
1978 Montreal	NL	157	609	154	24	8	25	(12	13)	269	84	72	30	3	128	12	4	5	28	11	.72	7	.253	.299	.442
1979 Montreal	NL	155	639	176	24	12	25	(13	12)	299	90	92	27	5	115	6	8	4	35	10	.78	10	.275	.309	.468
1980 Montreal	NL	151	577	178	41	7	17	(7	10)	284	96	87	44	7	69	6	1	10	34	9	.79	9	.308	.358	.492
1981 Montreal	NL	103	394	119	21	3	24	(9	15)	218	71	64	35	14	50	7	0	5	26	4	.87	6	.302	.365	.553
1982 Montreal	NL	148	608	183	37	7	23	(9	14)	303	107	83	34	4	96	8	4	6	39	10	.80	8	.301	.343	.498
1983 Montreal	NL	159	633	189	36	10	32	(10	22)	341	104	113	38	12	81	9	0	18	25	11	.69	14	.299	.338	.539
1984 Montreal	NL	138	533	132	23	6	17	(6	11)	218	73	86	41	2	80	2	1	6	13	5	.72	12	.248	.301	.409
1985 Montreal	NL	139	529	135	27	2	23	(11	12)	235	65	91	29	8	92	4	1	7	13	4	.76	12	.255	.295	.444
1986 Montreal	NL	130	496	141	32	2	20	(11	9)	237	65	78	37	11	79	6	1	6	18	12	.60	13	.284	.338	.478
1987 Chicago	NL	153	621	178	24	2	49	(27	22)	353	90	137	32	7	103	7	0	2	11	3	.79	15	.287	.328	.568
1988 Chicago	NL	157	591	179	31	8	24	(12	12)	298	78	79	37	12	73	4	1	7	12	4	.75	15	.303	.344	.504
1989 Chicago	NL	118	416	105	18	6	21	(6	15)	198	62	77	35	13	62	1	0	7	8	5	.62	16	.252	.307	.476
1990 Chicago	NL	147	529	164	28	5	27	(14	13)	283	72	100	42	21	65	2	0	8	16	2	.89	12	.310	.358	.535
1991 Chicago	NL	149	563	153	21	4	31	(22	9)	275	69	104	22	3	80	5	0	5	4	5	.44	10	.272	.302	.488
1992 Chicago	NL	143	542	150	27	2	22	(13	9)	247	60	90	30	8	70	4	0	6	6	2	.75	13	.277	.316	.456
1993 Boston	AL	121	461	126	29	1	13	(8	5)	196	44	67	17	4	49	13	0	7	2	1	.67	12	.273	.313	.425

54

Year Team	Lg	G	AB	H	2B	3B	HR	(Hm	Rd)	TB	R	RBI	TBB	IBB	SO	HBP	SH	SF	SB	CS	SB%	GDP	Avg	OBP	SLG
1994 Boston	AL	75	292	70	18	0	16	(7	9)	136	34	48	9	3	53	4	0	1	2	2	.50	15	.240	.271	.466
1995 Florida	NL	79	226	58	10	3	8	(1	7)	98	30	37	9	1	45	8	0	3	0	0	.00	7	.257	.305	.434
1996 Florida	NL	42	58	16	2	0	2	(2	0)	24	6	14	2	0	13	1	0	0	0	0	.00	1	.276	.311	.414
21 ML YEARS		2627	9927	2774	503	98	438	(207	231)	4787	1373	1591	589	143	1509	111	24	118	314	109	.74	217	.279	.323	.482

Steve Decker

Bats: R **Throws:** R **Pos:** C-40; PH-24; 1B-3; 3B-2   **Ht:** 6'3" **Wt:** 220 **Born:** 10/25/65 **Age:** 31

Year Team	Lg	G	AB	H	2B	3B	HR	(Hm	Rd)	TB	R	RBI	TBB	IBB	SO	HBP	SH	SF	SB	CS	SB%	GDP	Avg	OBP	SLG
1996 Colo. Sprng *	AAA	7	25	10	1	0	0	—	—	11	4	3	4	1	3	1	0	0	0	0	.00	1	.400	.500	.440
1990 San Francisco	NL	15	54	16	2	0	3	(1	2)	27	5	8	1	0	10	0	1	0	0	0	.00	1	.296	.309	.500
1991 San Francisco	NL	79	233	48	7	1	5	(4	1)	72	11	24	16	1	44	3	2	4	0	1	.00	7	.206	.262	.309
1992 San Francisco	NL	15	43	7	1	0	0	(0	0)	8	3	1	6	0	7	1	0	0	0	0	.00	0	.163	.280	.186
1993 Florida	NL	8	15	0	0	0	0	(0	0)	0	0	1	3	0	3	0	0	1	0	0	.00	2	.000	.158	.000
1995 Florida	NL	51	133	30	2	1	3	(2	1)	43	12	13	19	1	22	0	0	2	1	0	1.00	1	.226	.318	.323
1996 SF-Col	NL	67	147	36	3	0	2	(1	1)	45	24	20	18	4	29	0	4	2	1	0	1.00	3	.245	.323	.306
1996 San Francisco	NL	57	122	28	1	0	1	(0	1)	32	16	12	15	4	26	0	3	2	0	0	.00	3	.230	.309	.262
Colorado	NL	10	25	8	2	0	1	(1	0)	13	8	8	3	0	3	0	1	0	1	0	1.00	0	.320	.393	.520
6 ML YEARS		235	625	137	15	2	13	(8	5)	195	55	67	63	6	115	1	7	9	2	1	.67	14	.219	.291	.312

Rob Deer

Bats: Right **Throws:** Right **Pos:** RF-17; PH-11; LF-1   **Ht:** 6'3" **Wt:** 225 **Born:** 9/29/60 **Age:** 36

Year Team	Lg	G	AB	H	2B	3B	HR	(Hm	Rd)	TB	R	RBI	TBB	IBB	SO	HBP	SH	SF	SB	CS	SB%	GDP	Avg	OBP	SLG
1996 Las Vegas *	AAA	84	259	58	14	2	20	—	—	136	43	47	56	2	118	1	0	1	5	1	.83	7	.224	.363	.525
1984 San Francisco	NL	13	24	4	0	0	3	(2	1)	13	5	3	7	0	10	1	0	0	1	1	.50	0	.167	.375	.542
1985 San Francisco	NL	78	162	30	5	1	8	(5	3)	61	22	20	23	0	71	0	0	2	0	1	.00	0	.185	.283	.377
1986 Milwaukee	AL	134	466	108	17	3	33	(19	14)	230	75	86	72	3	179	3	2	3	5	2	.71	4	.232	.336	.494
1987 Milwaukee	AL	134	474	113	15	2	28	(11	17)	216	71	80	86	6	186	5	0	1	12	4	.75	4	.238	.360	.456
1988 Milwaukee	AL	135	492	124	24	0	23	(12	11)	217	71	85	51	4	153	7	0	5	9	5	.64	4	.252	.328	.441
1989 Milwaukee	AL	130	466	98	18	2	26	(15	11)	198	72	65	60	5	158	4	0	2	4	8	.33	8	.210	.305	.425
1990 Milwaukee	AL	134	440	92	15	1	27	(11	16)	190	57	69	64	6	147	4	0	3	2	3	.40	0	.209	.313	.432
1991 Detroit	AL	134	448	80	14	2	25	(12	13)	173	64	64	89	1	175	0	0	2	1	3	.25	3	.179	.314	.386
1992 Detroit	AL	110	393	97	20	1	32	(13	19)	215	66	64	51	1	131	3	0	1	4	2	.67	8	.247	.337	.547
1993 Det-Bos	AL	128	466	98	17	1	21	(12	9)	180	66	55	58	1	169	5	0	3	5	2	.71	6	.210	.303	.386
1996 San Diego	NL	25	50	9	3	0	4	(3	1)	24	9	9	14	0	30	0	0	0	0	0	.00	0	.180	.359	.480
1993 Detroit	AL	90	323	70	11	0	14	(9	5)	123	48	39	38	1	120	3	0	3	3	2	.60	4	.217	.302	.381
Boston	AL	38	143	28	6	1	7	(3	4)	57	18	16	20	0	49	2	0	0	2	0	1.00	2	.196	.303	.399
11 ML YEARS		1155	3881	853	148	13	230	(115	115)	1717	578	600	575	27	1409	32	2	22	43	31	.58	38	.220	.324	.442

Alex Delgado

Bats: R **Throws:** R **Pos:** C-14; PH-12; LF-5; 3B-4; RF-2; 1B-1; 2B-1   **Ht:** 6'0" **Wt:** 160 **Born:** 1/11/71 **Age:** 26

Year Team	Lg	G	AB	H	2B	3B	HR	(Hm	Rd)	TB	R	RBI	TBB	IBB	SO	HBP	SH	SF	SB	CS	SB%	GDP	Avg	OBP	SLG
1988 R.S./Mrnrs	R	34	111	39	10	0	0	—	—	49	11	22	6	0	5	1	3	2	2	4	.33	1	.351	.383	.441
1989 Winter Havn	A+	78	285	64	7	0	0	—	—	71	27	16	17	0	30	1	5	0	7	3	.70	9	.225	.271	.249
1990 New Britain	AA	7	18	1	1	0	0	—	—	2	3	0	2	0	5	0	0	0	0	0	.00	1	.056	.150	.111
Winter Havn	A+	89	303	68	9	2	1	—	—	84	37	25	37	0	37	3	5	3	10	4	.71	7	.224	.312	.277
1991 Lynchburg	A+	61	179	38	8	0	0	—	—	46	21	17	16	0	19	2	1	1	2	1	.67	6	.212	.283	.257
1992 Winter Havn	A+	56	167	35	2	0	2	—	—	43	11	12	16	0	11	1	4	1	1	1	.50	6	.210	.281	.257
1993 Ft. Laud	A+	63	225	57	9	0	2	—	—	72	26	25	9	1	21	5	7	1	2	2	.50	4	.253	.296	.320
New Britain	AA	33	87	16	2	0	1	—	—	21	10	9	4	0	11	4	4	2	1	1	.50	1	.184	.247	.241
1994 Red Sox	R	7	24	4	1	0	0	—	—	5	3	7	2	1	2	2	0	1	0	0	.00	0	.167	.276	.208
New Britain	AA	40	140	36	3	0	2	—	—	45	16	12	4	0	21	2	1	1	1	1	.50	7	.257	.286	.321
1995 Pawtucket	AAA	44	107	27	3	0	5	—	—	45	14	12	6	0	12	1	0	0	0	0	.00	4	.252	.298	.421
Trenton	AA	23	72	24	1	0	3	—	—	34	13	14	9	0	8	3	1	1	0	0	.00	2	.333	.424	.472
1996 Trenton	AA	21	81	18	4	0	3	—	—	31	7	14	9	1	8	1	1	1	1	0	1.00	0	.222	.304	.383
Pawtucket	AAA	27	88	19	3	0	1	—	—	25	15	6	7	0	11	0	0	0	0	0	.00	5	.216	.274	.284
1996 Boston	AL	26	20	5	0	0	0	(0	0)	5	5	1	3	0	1	0	0	1	0	0	.00	0	.250	.348	.250

Carlos Delgado

Bats: Left **Throws:** Right **Pos:** DH-108; 1B-27; PH-4   **Ht:** 6'3" **Wt:** 206 **Born:** 6/25/72 **Age:** 25

Year Team	Lg	G	AB	H	2B	3B	HR	(Hm	Rd)	TB	R	RBI	TBB	IBB	SO	HBP	SH	SF	SB	CS	SB%	GDP	Avg	OBP	SLG
1993 Toronto	AL	2	1	0	0	0	0	(0	0)	0	0	0	1	0	0	0	0	0	0	0	.00	0	.000	.500	.000
1994 Toronto	AL	43	130	28	2	0	9	(5	4)	57	17	24	25	4	46	3	0	1	1	1	.50	5	.215	.352	.438
1995 Toronto	AL	37	91	15	3	0	3	(2	1)	27	7	11	6	0	26	0	0	2	0	0	.00	1	.165	.212	.297
1996 Toronto	AL	138	488	132	28	2	25	(12	13)	239	68	92	58	2	139	9	0	8	0	0	.00	13	.270	.353	.490
4 ML YEARS		220	710	175	33	2	37	(19	18)	323	92	127	90	6	211	12	0	11	1	1	.50	19	.246	.337	.455

Wilson Delgado

Bats: Both **Throws:** Right **Pos:** SS-6 | **Ht:** 5'11" **Wt:** 165 **Born:** 7/15/75 **Age:** 21

Year Team	Lg	G	AB	H	2B	3B	HR	(Hm	Rd)	TB	R	RBI	TBB	IBB	SO	HBP	SH	SF	SB	CS	SB%	GDP	Avg	OBP	SLG
								BATTING											BASERUNNING				PERCENTAGES		
1996 San Francisco	NL	6	22	8	0	0	0	(0	0)	8	3	2	1	0	5	2	0	0	1	0	1.00	0	.364	.440	.364

Rich DeLucia

Pitches: Right **Bats:** Right **Pos:** RP-56 | **Ht:** 6'0" **Wt:** 185 **Born:** 10/7/64 **Age:** 32

Year Team	Lg	G	GS	CG	GF	IP	BFP	H	R	ER	HR	SH	SF	HB	TBB	IBB	SO	WP	Bk	W	L	Pct.	ShO	Sv-Op	Hld	ERA
		HOW MUCH HE PITCHED						WHAT HE GAVE UP												THE RESULTS						
1996 San Jose *	A+	5	4	0	0	7.1	28	5	2	2	0	0	0	0	3	0	11	0	0	0	0	.000	0	0--	—	2.45
1990 Seattle	AL	5	5	1	0	36	144	30	9	8	2	2	0	0	9	0	20	0	0	1	2	.333	0	0-0	0	2.00
1991 Seattle	AL	32	31	0	0	182	779	176	107	103	31	5	14	4	78	4	98	10	0	12	13	.480	0	0-0	0	5.09
1992 Seattle	AL	30	11	0	6	83.2	382	100	55	51	13	2	2	2	35	1	66	1	0	3	6	.333	0	1-3	3	5.49
1993 Seattle	AL	30	1	0	11	42.2	195	46	24	22	5	1	1	1	23	3	48	1	0	3	6	.333	0	0-4	6	4.64
1994 Cincinnati	NL	8	0	0	2	10.2	47	9	6	5	4	0	0	0	5	0	15	1	0	0	0	.000	0	0-0	0	4.22
1995 St. Louis	NL	56	1	0	8	82.1	342	63	38	31	9	5	2	3	36	2	76	5	0	8	7	.533	0	0-1	9	3.39
1996 San Francisco	NL	56	0	0	20	61.2	279	62	44	40	8	4	2	3	31	6	55	7	0	3	6	.333	0	0-2	11	5.84
7 ML YEARS		217	49	1	47	499	2168	486	283	260	72	19	21	13	217	16	378	28	0	30	40	.429	0	1-10	29	4.69

Delino DeShields

Bats: Left **Throws:** Right **Pos:** 2B-154; PH-3 | **Ht:** 6'1" **Wt:** 175 **Born:** 1/15/69 **Age:** 28

Year Team	Lg	G	AB	H	2B	3B	HR	(Hm	Rd)	TB	R	RBI	TBB	IBB	SO	HBP	SH	SF	SB	CS	SB%	GDP	Avg	OBP	SLG
								BATTING											BASERUNNING				PERCENTAGES		
1990 Montreal	NL	129	499	144	28	6	4	(3	1)	196	69	45	66	3	96	4	1	2	42	22	.66	10	.289	.375	.393
1991 Montreal	NL	151	563	134	15	4	10	(3	7)	187	83	51	95	2	151	2	8	5	56	23	.71	6	.238	.347	.332
1992 Montreal	NL	135	530	155	19	8	7	(1	6)	211	82	56	54	4	108	3	9	3	46	15	.75	10	.292	.359	.398
1993 Montreal	NL	123	481	142	17	7	2	(2	0)	179	75	29	72	3	64	3	4	2	43	10	.81	6	.295	.389	.372
1994 Los Angeles	NL	89	320	80	11	3	2	(1	1)	103	51	33	54	0	53	0	1	1	27	7	.79	9	.250	.357	.322
1995 Los Angeles	NL	127	425	109	18	3	8	(2	6)	157	66	37	63	4	83	1	3	1	39	14	.74	6	.256	.353	.369
1996 Los Angeles	NL	154	581	130	12	8	5	(3	2)	173	75	41	53	7	124	1	2	5	48	11	.81	12	.224	.288	.298
7 ML YEARS		908	3399	894	120	39	38	(15	23)	1206	501	292	457	23	679	14	28	19	301	102	.75	59	.263	.351	.355

Elmer Dessens

Pitches: Right **Bats:** Right **Pos:** RP-12; SP-3 | **Ht:** 6'0" **Wt:** 190 **Born:** 1/13/72 **Age:** 25

Year Team	Lg	G	GS	CG	GF	IP	BFP	H	R	ER	HR	SH	SF	HB	TBB	IBB	SO	WP	Bk	W	L	Pct.	ShO	Sv-Op	Hld	ERA
		HOW MUCH HE PITCHED						WHAT HE GAVE UP												THE RESULTS						
1995 Carolina	AA	27	27	1	0	152	638	170	62	42	10	11	4	3	21	3	68	7	0	15	8	.652	0	0--	—	2.49
1996 Calgary	AAA	6	6	0	0	34.1	150	40	14	12	5	2	1	1	15	1	15	2	1	2	2	.500	0	0--	—	3.15
Carolina	AA	5	1	0	2	11.2	55	15	8	7	1	0	0	1	4	0	7	0	0	0	1	.000	0	0--	—	5.40
1996 Pittsburgh	NL	15	3	0	1	25	112	40	23	23	2	3	1	0	4	0	13	0	0	0	0	.000	0	0-0	3	8.28

Cesar Devarez

Bats: Right **Throws:** Right **Pos:** C-10; PH-1 | **Ht:** 5'10" **Wt:** 175 **Born:** 9/22/69 **Age:** 27

Year Team	Lg	G	AB	H	2B	3B	HR	(Hm	Rd)	TB	R	RBI	TBB	IBB	SO	HBP	SH	SF	SB	CS	SB%	GDP	Avg	OBP	SLG
								BATTING											BASERUNNING				PERCENTAGES		
1989 Bluefield	R+	12	42	9	4	0	0	—	—	13	3	7	1	0	5	0	0	0	0	0	.00	3	.214	.233	.310
1990 Wausau	A	56	171	34	4	1	3	—	—	49	7	19	7	0	28	0	2	0	2	3	.40	3	.199	.230	.287
1991 Frederick	A+	74	235	59	13	2	3	—	—	85	25	29	14	0	28	4	2	1	2	2	.50	9	.251	.303	.362
1992 Hagerstown	AA	110	319	72	8	1	2	—	—	88	20	32	17	0	49	6	2	2	2	5	.29	3	.226	.276	.276
1993 Frederick	A+	38	124	36	8	0	2	—	—	50	15	16	12	1	18	1	1	0	1	4	.20	2	.290	.358	.403
Bowie	AA	57	174	39	7	1	0	—	—	48	14	15	5	0	21	2	2	2	5	1	.83	6	.224	.251	.276
1994 Bowie	AA	73	249	78	13	4	6	—	—	117	43	48	8	1	25	1	3	4	7	2	.78	10	.313	.332	.470
1995 Rochester	AAA	67	240	60	12	1	1	—	—	77	32	21	7	0	25	0	1	1	2	2	.50	8	.250	.270	.321
1996 Rochester	AAA	67	223	64	9	1	4	—	—	87	24	27	9	0	26	1	2	4	5	1	.83	7	.287	.312	.390
1995 Baltimore	AL	6	4	0	0	0	0	(0	0)	0	0	0	0	0	0	0	0	1	0	0	.00	0	.000	.000	.000
1996 Baltimore	AL	10	18	2	0	1	0	(0	0)	3	0	3	1	0	3	0	0	0	0	0	.00	0	.111	.158	.222
2 ML YEARS		16	22	2	0	1	0			3	0	3	1	0	3	0	0	1	0	0	.00	0	.091	.130	.182

Mike Devereaux

Bats: R **Throws:** R **Pos:** RF-62; LF-35; CF-30; PH-22; DH-10 | **Ht:** 6'0" **Wt:** 195 **Born:** 4/10/63 **Age:** 34

Year Team	Lg	G	AB	H	2B	3B	HR	(Hm	Rd)	TB	R	RBI	TBB	IBB	SO	HBP	SH	SF	SB	CS	SB%	GDP	Avg	OBP	SLG
								BATTING											BASERUNNING				PERCENTAGES		
1987 Los Angeles	NL	19	54	12	3	0	0	(0	0)	15	7	4	3	0	10	0	1	0	3	1	.75	0	.222	.263	.278
1988 Los Angeles	NL	30	43	5	1	0	0	(0	0)	6	4	2	2	0	10	0	0	0	0	1	.00	0	.116	.156	.140
1989 Baltimore	AL	122	391	104	14	3	8	(4	4)	148	55	46	36	0	60	2	2	3	22	11	.67	9	.266	.329	.379
1990 Baltimore	AL	108	367	88	18	1	12	(6	6)	144	48	49	28	0	48	0	4	4	13	12	.52	10	.240	.291	.392
1991 Baltimore	AL	149	608	158	27	10	19	(10	9)	262	82	59	47	2	115	2	4	4	16	9	.64	13	.260	.313	.431
1992 Baltimore	AL	156	653	180	29	11	24	(14	10)	303	76	107	44	1	94	4	0	9	10	8	.56	14	.276	.321	.464

Year Team	Lg	G	AB	H	2B	3B	HR	(Hm	Rd)	TB	R	RBI	TBB	IBB	SO	HBP	SH	SF	SB	CS	SB%	GDP	Avg	OBP	SLG
1993 Baltimore	AL	131	527	132	31	3	14	(8	6)	211	72	75	43	0	99	1	2	4	3	3	.50	13	.250	.306	.400
1994 Baltimore	AL	85	301	61	8	2	9	(5	4)	100	35	33	22	0	72	1	2	4	1	2	.33	6	.203	.256	.332
1995 ChA-Atl		121	388	116	24	1	11	(5	6)	175	55	63	27	3	62	0	0	3	8	6	.57	11	.299	.342	.451
1996 Baltimore	AL	127	323	74	11	2	8	(5	3)	113	49	34	34	0	53	2	2	2	8	2	.80	8	.229	.305	.350
1995 Chicago	AL	92	333	102	21	1	10	(4	6)	155	48	55	25	3	51	0	0	3	6	6	.50	10	.306	.352	.465
Atlanta	NL	29	55	14	3	0	1	(1	0)	20	7	8	2	0	11	0	0	0	2	0	1.00	1	.255	.281	.364
10 ML YEARS		1048	3655	930	166	33	105	(57	48)	1477	483	472	286	6	623	12	20	33	84	55	.60	82	.254	.308	.404

Mark Dewey

Pitches: Right **Bats:** Right **Pos:** RP-78 **Ht:** 6'0" **Wt:** 216 **Born:** 1/3/65 **Age:** 32

		HOW MUCH HE PITCHED						WHAT HE GAVE UP											THE RESULTS						
Year Team	Lg	G	GS	CG	GF	IP	BFP	H	R	ER	HR	SH	SF	HB	TBB	IBB	SO	WP	Bk	W	L	Pct.	ShO	Sv-Op	Hld	ERA
1990 San Francisco	NL	14	0	0	5	22.2	92	22	7	7	1	2	0	0	5	1	11	0	1	1	1	.500	0	0-1	1	2.78
1992 New York	NL	20	0	0	6	33.1	143	37	16	16	2	1	0	0	10	2	24	0	1	1	0	1.000	0	0-0	1	4.32
1993 Pittsburgh	NL	21	0	0	17	26.2	108	14	8	7	0	3	3	3	10	1	14	0	0	1	2	.333	0	7-12	6	2.36
1994 Pittsburgh	NL	45	0	0	18	51.1	226	61	22	21	4	2	1	3	19	3	30	0	0	2	1	.667	0	1-2	10	3.68
1995 San Francisco	NL	27	0	0	5	31.2	137	30	12	11	2	1	1	0	17	6	32	1	0	1	0	1.000	0	0-0	5	3.13
1996 San Francisco	NL	78	0	0	19	83.1	360	79	40	39	9	3	4	5	41	9	57	4	0	6	3	.667	0	0-5	7	4.21
6 ML YEARS		205	0	0	70	249	1066	243	105	101	18	12	9	11	102	22	168	5	2	12	7	.632	0	8-20	24	3.65

Alex Diaz

Bats: B **Throws:** R **Pos:** LF-19; PH-13; CF-5; RF-5; DH-1 **Ht:** 5'11" **Wt:** 180 **Born:** 10/5/68 **Age:** 28

		BATTING																	BASERUNNING				PERCENTAGES		
Year Team	Lg	G	AB	H	2B	3B	HR	(Hm	Rd)	TB	R	RBI	TBB	IBB	SO	HBP	SH	SF	SB	CS	SB%	GDP	Avg	OBP	SLG
1996 Tacoma *	AAA	44	176	43	5	0	0	—	—	48	19	7	7	0	20	0	3	1	5	6	.45	9	.244	.272	.273
1992 Milwaukee	AL	22	9	1	0	0	0	(0	0)	1	5	1	0	0	0	0	0	0	3	2	.60	0	.111	.111	.111
1993 Milwaukee	AL	32	69	22	2	0	0	(0	0)	24	9	1	0	0	12	0	3	0	5	3	.63	3	.319	.319	.348
1994 Milwaukee	AL	79	187	47	5	7	1	(0	1)	69	17	17	10	1	19	0	3	3	5	5	.50	5	.251	.285	.369
1995 Seattle	AL	103	270	67	14	0	3	(3	0)	90	44	27	13	2	27	2	5	2	18	8	.69	3	.248	.286	.333
1996 Seattle	AL	38	79	19	2	0	1	(1	0)	24	11	5	2	0	8	2	0	1	6	3	.67	2	.241	.274	.304
5 ML YEARS		274	614	156	23	7	5	(4	1)	208	86	51	25	3	66	4	11	6	37	21	.64	13	.254	.285	.339

Einar Diaz

Bats: Right **Throws:** Right **Pos:** C-4 **Ht:** 5'10" **Wt:** 165 **Born:** 12/28/72 **Age:** 24

		BATTING																	BASERUNNING				PERCENTAGES		
Year Team	Lg	G	AB	H	2B	3B	HR	(Hm	Rd)	TB	R	RBI	TBB	IBB	SO	HBP	SH	SF	SB	CS	SB%	GDP	Avg	OBP	SLG
1992 Burlington	R+	52	178	37	3	0	1	—	—	43	19	14	20	0	9	3	2	2	2	3	.40	4	.208	.296	.242
1993 Burlington	R+	60	231	69	15	3	5	—	—	105	40	33	8	0	7	4	2	4	7	3	.70	5	.299	.328	.455
Columbus	A	1	5	0	0	0	0	—	—	0	0	0	0	0	0	0	0	0	0	0	.00	0	.000	.000	.000
1994 Columbus	A	120	491	137	23	2	16	—	—	212	67	71	17	0	34	21	1	1	4	4	.50	18	.279	.330	.432
1995 Kinston	A+	104	373	98	21	0	6	—	—	137	46	43	12	2	29	8	1	4	3	6	.33	6	.263	.297	.367
1996 Canton-Akrn	AA	104	395	111	26	2	3	—	—	150	47	35	12	0	22	9	1	1	3	2	.60	11	.281	.317	.380
1996 Cleveland	AL	4	1	0	0	0	0	(0	0)	0	0	0	0	0	0	0	0	0	0	0	.00	0	.000	.000	.000

Jason Dickson

Pitches: Right **Bats:** Left **Pos:** SP-7 **Ht:** 6'0" **Wt:** 190 **Born:** 3/30/73 **Age:** 24

		HOW MUCH HE PITCHED						WHAT HE GAVE UP											THE RESULTS						
Year Team	Lg	G	GS	CG	GF	IP	BFP	H	R	ER	HR	SH	SF	HB	TBB	IBB	SO	WP	Bk	W	L	Pct.	ShO	Sv-Op	Hld	ERA
1994 Boise	A-	9	7	0	1	44.1	190	40	22	19	3	1	0	2	18	1	37	3	2	3	1	.750	0	1--	—	3.86
1995 Cedar Rapds	A	25	25	9	0	173	708	151	71	55	12	4	3	8	45	0	134	7	2	14	6	.700	1	0--	—	2.86
1996 Midland	AA	8	8	3	0	55.1	228	55	27	22	3	2	0	0	10	0	40	3	0	5	2	.714	1	0--	—	3.58
Vancouver	AAA	18	18	7	0	130.1	553	134	73	55	9	2	4	5	40	1	70	4	4	7	11	.389	0	0--	—	3.80
1996 California	AL	7	7	0	0	43.1	192	52	22	22	6	2	1	1	18	1	20	1	1	1	4	.200	0	0-0	—	4.57

Mike Difelice

Bats: Right **Throws:** Right **Pos:** C-4 **Ht:** 6'2" **Wt:** 205 **Born:** 5/28/69 **Age:** 28

		BATTING																	BASERUNNING				PERCENTAGES		
Year Team	Lg	G	AB	H	2B	3B	HR	(Hm	Rd)	TB	R	RBI	TBB	IBB	SO	HBP	SH	SF	SB	CS	SB%	GDP	Avg	OBP	SLG
1991 Hamilton	A-	43	157	33	5	0	4	—	—	50	10	15	9	0	40	1	0	0	1	5	.17	3	.210	.257	.318
1992 Hamilton	A-	18	58	20	3	0	2	—	—	29	11	9	4	1	7	1	1	0	2	0	1.00	0	.345	.397	.500
St. Pete	A+	17	53	12	3	0	0	—	—	15	0	4	3	0	11	0	0	2	0	0	.00	3	.226	.259	.283
1993 Springfield	A	8	20	7	1	0	0	—	—	8	5	3	2	0	3	1	0	0	1	0	1.00	0	.350	.435	.400
St. Pete	A+	30	97	22	2	0	0	—	—	24	5	8	11	1	13	1	2	2	1	0	1.00	1	.227	.306	.247
1994 Arkansas	AA	71	200	50	11	2	2	—	—	71	19	15	12	0	48	2	1	2	0	1	.00	9	.250	.296	.355
1995 Arkansas	AA	62	176	47	10	1	1	—	—	62	14	24	23	0	29	3	2	1	0	2	.00	13	.267	.360	.352
Louisville	AAA	21	63	17	4	0	0	—	—	21	8	3	5	0	11	0	0	0	1	0	1.00	4	.270	.324	.333
1996 Louisville	AAA	79	246	70	13	0	9	—	—	110	25	33	20	1	43	1	0	2	0	3	.00	15	.285	.338	.447
1996 St. Louis	NL	4	7	2	1	0	0	(0	0)	3	0	2	0	0	1	0	0	0	0	0	.00	0	.286	.286	.429

Jerry DiPoto

Pitches: Right   **Bats:** Right   **Pos:** RP-57   **Ht:** 6'2"   **Wt:** 200   **Born:** 5/24/68   **Age:** 29

| | | HOW MUCH HE PITCHED | | | | | | WHAT HE GAVE UP | | | | | | | | | | | | THE RESULTS | | | | | | |
Year Team	Lg	G	GS	CG	GF	IP	BFP	H	R	ER	HR	SH	SF	HB	TBB	IBB	SO	WP	Bk	W	L	Pct.	ShO	Sv-Op	Hld	ERA
1993 Cleveland	AL	46	0	0	26	56.1	247	57	21	15	0	3	2	1	30	7	41	0	0	4	4	.500	0	11-17	6	2.40
1994 Cleveland	AL	7	0	0	1	15.2	79	26	14	14	1	0	4	1	10	0	9	0	0	0	0	.000	0	0-0	1	8.04
1995 New York	NL	58	0	0	26	78.2	330	77	41	33	2	6	3	4	29	8	49	3	1	4	6	.400	0	2-6	8	3.78
1996 New York	NL	57	0	0	21	77.1	364	91	44	36	5	7	4	3	45	8	52	3	3	7	2	.778	0	0-5	3	4.19
4 ML YEARS		168	0	0	74	228	1020	251	120	98	8	16	13	9	114	23	151	6	4	15	12	.556	0	13-28	18	3.87

Gary DiSarcina

Bats: Right   **Throws:** Right   **Pos:** SS-150   **Ht:** 6'2"   **Wt:** 190   **Born:** 11/19/67   **Age:** 29

| | | BATTING | | | | | | | | | | | | | | | | BASERUNNING | | | | PERCENTAGES | | |
Year Team	Lg	G	AB	H	2B	3B	HR	(Hm Rd)	TB	R	RBI	TBB	IBB	SO	HBP	SH	SF	SB	CS	SB%	GDP	Avg	OBP	SLG
1989 California	AL	2	0	0	0	0	0	(0 0)	0	0	0	0	0	0	0	0	0	0	0	.00	0	.000	.000	.000
1990 California	AL	18	57	8	1	1	0	(0 0)	11	8	0	3	0	10	0	1	0	1	0	1.00	3	.140	.183	.193
1991 California	AL	18	57	12	2	0	0	(0 0)	14	5	3	3	0	4	2	2	0	0	0	.00	0	.211	.274	.246
1992 California	AL	157	518	128	19	4	3	(2 1)	156	48	42	20	0	50	7	5	3	9	7	.56	15	.247	.283	.301
1993 California	AL	126	416	99	20	1	3	(2 1)	130	44	45	15	0	38	6	5	3	5	7	.42	13	.238	.273	.313
1994 California	AL	112	389	101	14	2	3	(2 1)	128	53	33	18	0	28	2	10	2	3	7	.30	10	.260	.294	.329
1995 California	AL	99	362	111	28	6	5	(1 4)	166	61	41	20	0	25	2	7	3	7	4	.64	10	.307	.344	.459
1996 California	AL	150	536	137	26	4	5	(2 3)	186	62	48	21	0	36	2	16	1	2	1	.67	16	.256	.286	.347
8 ML YEARS		682	2335	596	110	14	19	(9 10)	791	281	212	100	0	191	21	46	12	27	26	.51	67	.255	.291	.339

Glenn Dishman

Pitches: Left   **Bats:** Right   **Pos:** RP-6; SP-1   **Ht:** 6'1"   **Wt:** 195   **Born:** 11/5/70   **Age:** 26

| | | HOW MUCH HE PITCHED | | | | | | WHAT HE GAVE UP | | | | | | | | | | | | THE RESULTS | | | | | | |
Year Team	Lg	G	GS	CG	GF	IP	BFP	H	R	ER	HR	SH	SF	HB	TBB	IBB	SO	WP	Bk	W	L	Pct.	ShO	Sv-Op	Hld	ERA
1993 Spokane	A-	12	12	6	0	77.2	307	59	25	19	3	2	1	5	13	0	79	3	1	6	3	.667	2	0--	—	2.20
Rancho Cuca	A+	2	2	0	0	11.1	52	14	9	9	0	0	0	1	5	0	6	1	1	0	1	.000	0	0--	—	7.15
1994 Wichita	AA	27	27	1	0	169.1	693	156	73	53	6	8	3	3	42	2	165	4	1	11	8	.579	0	0--	—	2.82
Las Vegas	AAA	2	2	0	0	13	50	15	7	5	1	0	2	0	1	0	12	0	0	1	1	.500	0	0--	—	3.46
1995 Las Vegas	AAA	14	14	3	0	106	430	91	37	30	12	4	1	0	20	2	64	3	1	6	3	.667	1	0--	—	2.55
1996 Las Vegas	AAA	26	26	3	0	155	669	177	103	96	11	3	9	3	43	5	115	7	1	6	8	.429	1	0--	—	5.57
1995 San Diego	NL	19	16	0	1	97	421	104	60	54	11	6	3	4	34	1	43	3	1	4	8	.333	0	0-0	—	5.01
1996 SD-Phi	NL	7	1	0	4	9.1	42	12	8	8	2	0	1	0	3	0	3	1	0	0	0	.000	0	0-0	—	7.71
1996 San Diego	NL	3	0	0	2	2.1	11	3	2	2	0	0	0	0	1	0	1	1	0	0	0	.000	0	0-0	—	7.71
Philadelphia	NL	4	1	0	2	7	31	9	6	6	2	0	1	0	2	0	3	0	1	0	0	.000	0	0-0	—	7.71
2 ML YEARS		26	17	0	5	106.1	463	116	68	62	13	6	4	4	37	1	46	4	1	4	8	.333	0	0-0	—	5.25

John Doherty

Pitches: Right   **Bats:** Right   **Pos:** RP-3   **Ht:** 6'4"   **Wt:** 215   **Born:** 6/11/67   **Age:** 30

| | | HOW MUCH HE PITCHED | | | | | | WHAT HE GAVE UP | | | | | | | | | | | | THE RESULTS | | | | | | |
Year Team	Lg	G	GS	CG	GF	IP	BFP	H	R	ER	HR	SH	SF	HB	TBB	IBB	SO	WP	Bk	W	L	Pct.	ShO	Sv-Op	Hld	ERA
1996 Trenton *	AA	4	4	0	0	24.1	95	20	8	5	0	1	1	3	2	0	14	0	0	1	1	.500	0	0--	—	1.85
Pawtucket *	AAA	19	7	0	5	50.1	235	79	39	37	4	1	0	4	8	0	13	1	0	1	4	.200	0	1--	—	6.62
1992 Detroit	AL	47	11	0	9	116	491	131	61	50	4	3	2	4	25	5	37	5	0	7	4	.636	0	3-4	10	3.88
1993 Detroit	AL	32	31	3	1	184.2	780	205	104	91	19	5	4	5	48	7	63	4	1	14	11	.560	2	0-0	0	4.44
1994 Detroit	AL	18	17	2	1	101.1	454	139	75	73	13	5	7	3	26	6	28	4	0	6	7	.462	0	0-0	0	6.48
1995 Detroit	AL	48	2	0	18	113	499	130	66	64	10	3	2	6	37	10	46	0	0	5	9	.357	0	6-9	5	5.10
1996 Boston	AL	3	0	0	1	6.1	34	8	10	4	1	0	0	1	4	0	3	0	0	0	0	.000	0	0-0	0	5.68
5 ML YEARS		148	61	5	30	521.1	2258	613	316	282	47	16	15	19	140	28	177	13	1	32	31	.508	2	9-13	15	4.87

Brian Dorsett

Bats: Right   **Throws:** Right   **Pos:** C-15; PH-4   **Ht:** 6'4"   **Wt:** 222   **Born:** 4/9/61   **Age:** 36

| | | BATTING | | | | | | | | | | | | | | | | BASERUNNING | | | | PERCENTAGES | | |
Year Team	Lg	G	AB	H	2B	3B	HR	(Hm Rd)	TB	R	RBI	TBB	IBB	SO	HBP	SH	SF	SB	CS	SB%	GDP	Avg	OBP	SLG
1996 Iowa *	AAA	9	29	6	2	0	1	(— —)	11	2	2	2	0	4	0	0	0	0	0	.00	0	.207	.207	.379
1987 Cleveland	AL	5	11	3	0	0	1	(1 0)	6	2	3	0	0	3	1	0	0	0	0	.00	0	.273	.333	.545
1988 California	AL	7	11	1	0	0	0	(0 0)	1	0	2	1	0	5	0	0	0	0	0	.00	0	.091	.167	.091
1989 New York	AL	8	22	8	1	0	0	(0 0)	9	3	4	1	0	3	0	0	0	0	0	.00	0	.364	.391	.409
1990 New York	AL	14	35	5	2	0	0	(0 0)	7	2	0	2	0	4	0	0	0	0	2	.00	0	.143	.189	.200
1991 San Diego	NL	11	12	1	0	0	0	(0 0)	1	0	0	0	0	3	0	0	0	0	0	.00	0	.083	.083	.083
1993 Cincinnati	NL	25	63	16	4	0	2	(2 0)	26	7	12	3	0	14	0	0	0	0	1	.00	0	.254	.288	.413
1994 Cincinnati	NL	76	216	53	8	0	5	(2 3)	76	21	26	21	7	33	1	1	2	0	0	.00	10	.245	.313	.352
1996 Chicago	NL	17	41	5	0	0	1	(0 1)	8	3	3	4	0	8	0	0	0	0	0	.00	0	.122	.196	.195
8 ML YEARS		163	411	92	15	0	9	(5 4)	134	38	51	32	7	73	2	1	3	0	0	.00	15	.224	.281	.326

David Doster

Bats: Right **Throws:** Right **Pos:** 2B-24; PH-16; 3B-1   **Ht:** 5'10" **Wt:** 185 **Born:** 10/8/70 **Age:** 26

Year Team	Lg	G	AB	H	2B	3B	HR	(Hm	Rd)	TB	R	RBI	TBB	IBB	SO	HBP	SH	SF	SB	CS	SB%	GDP	Avg	OBP	SLG
1993 Spartanburg	A	60	223	61	15	0	3	—	—	85	34	20	25	1	36	3	6	1	1	0	1.00	5	.274	.353	.381
Clearwater	A+	9	28	10	3	1	0	—	—	15	4	2	2	0	2	0	0	0	0	0	.00	1	.357	.400	.536
1994 Clearwater	A+	131	480	135	42	4	13	—	—	224	76	74	54	3	71	11	3	8	12	7	.63	12	.281	.362	.467
1995 Reading	AA	139	551	146	39	3	21	—	—	254	84	79	51	2	61	7	8	4	11	7	.61	11	.265	.333	.461
1996 Scranton-WB	AAA	88	322	83	20	0	7	—	—	124	37	48	26	1	54	2	3	5	7	3	.70	8	.258	.313	.385
1996 Philadelphia	NL	39	105	28	8	0	1	(1	0)	39	14	8	7	0	21	0	1	0	0	0	.00	1	.267	.313	.371

Jim Dougherty

Pitches: Right **Bats:** Right **Pos:** RP-12   **Ht:** 6'0" **Wt:** 210 **Born:** 3/8/68 **Age:** 29

Year Team	Lg	G	GS	CG	GF	IP	BFP	H	R	ER	HR	SH	SF	HB	TBB	IBB	SO	WP	Bk	W	L	Pct.	ShO	Sv-Op	Hld	ERA
1991 Asheville	A	61	0	0	48	82	324	63	17	14	0	7	0	3	24	6	76	0	2	3	1	.750	0	27--	—	1.54
1992 Osceola	A+	57	0	0	52	81	325	66	21	14	1	4	2	2	22	4	77	0	1	5	2	.714	0	31--	—	1.56
1993 Jackson	AA	52	0	0	50	53	207	39	15	11	3	0	0	1	21	0	55	0	0	2	2	.500	0	36--	—	1.87
1994 Tucson	AAA	55	0	0	48	59	276	70	32	27	9	1	1	2	30	6	49	4	0	5	4	.556	0	21--	—	4.12
1995 Tucson	AAA	8	0	0	3	11	46	11	4	4	1	0	0	0	5	0	12	0	1	1	0	1.000	0	1--	—	3.27
1996 Tucson	AAA	46	0	0	23	61.2	269	65	35	24	0	1	1	2	27	3	53	2	1	4	3	.571	0	1--	—	3.50
1995 Houston	NL	56	0	0	11	67.2	294	76	37	37	7	3	3	3	25	1	49	1	0	8	4	.667	0	0-2	5	4.92
1996 Houston	NL	12	0	0	2	13	64	14	14	13	2	1	1	1	11	1	6	0	0	0	2	.000	0	0-1	1	9.00
2 ML YEARS		68	0	0	13	80.2	358	90	51	50	9	4	4	4	36	2	55	1	0	8	6	.571	0	0-3	6	5.58

Doug Drabek

Pitches: Right **Bats:** Right **Pos:** SP-30   **Ht:** 6'1" **Wt:** 185 **Born:** 7/25/62 **Age:** 34

Year Team	Lg	G	GS	CG	GF	IP	BFP	H	R	ER	HR	SH	SF	HB	TBB	IBB	SO	WP	Bk	W	L	Pct.	ShO	Sv-Op	Hld	ERA
1986 New York	AL	27	21	0	2	131.2	561	126	64	60	13	5	2	3	50	1	76	2	0	7	8	.467	0	0--	—	4.10
1987 Pittsburgh	NL	29	28	1	0	176.1	721	165	86	76	22	3	4	0	46	2	120	5	1	11	12	.478	1	0-0	0	3.88
1988 Pittsburgh	NL	33	32	3	0	219.1	880	194	83	75	21	7	5	6	50	4	127	4	1	15	7	.682	1	0-0	0	3.08
1989 Pittsburgh	NL	35	34	8	1	244.1	994	215	83	76	21	13	7	3	69	3	123	3	0	14	12	.538	5	0-0	0	2.80
1990 Pittsburgh	NL	33	33	9	0	231.1	918	190	78	71	15	10	3	3	56	2	131	6	0	22	6	.786	3	0-0	0	2.76
1991 Pittsburgh	NL	35	35	5	0	234.2	977	245	92	80	16	12	6	3	62	6	142	5	0	15	14	.517	2	0-0	0	3.07
1992 Pittsburgh	NL	34	34	10	0	256.2	1021	218	84	79	17	8	4	4	54	8	177	11	1	15	11	.577	4	0-0	0	2.77
1993 Houston	NL	34	34	7	0	237.2	991	242	108	100	18	14	8	3	60	12	157	12	0	9	18	.333	2	0-0	0	3.79
1994 Houston	NL	23	23	6	0	164.2	657	132	58	52	14	5	6	2	45	2	121	2	0	12	6	.667	2	0-0	0	2.84
1995 Houston	NL	31	31	2	0	185	797	205	104	98	18	4	3	8	54	4	143	8	1	10	9	.526	1	0-0	0	4.77
1996 Houston	NL	30	30	1	0	175.1	786	208	102	89	21	12	8	7	60	5	137	9	0	7	9	.438	0	0-0	0	4.57
11 ML YEARS		344	335	52	3	2257	9303	2140	942	856	196	93	60	44	606	49	1454	67	4	137	112	.550	21	0--	—	3.41

Darren Dreifort

Pitches: Right **Bats:** Right **Pos:** RP-19   **Ht:** 6'2" **Wt:** 205 **Born:** 5/18/72 **Age:** 25

Year Team	Lg	G	GS	CG	GF	IP	BFP	H	R	ER	HR	SH	SF	HB	TBB	IBB	SO	WP	Bk	W	L	Pct.	ShO	Sv-Op	Hld	ERA
1996 Albuquerque *	AAA	18	18	0	0	86.1	387	88	49	40	6	3	2	6	52	3	75	6	2	5	6	.455	0	0--	—	4.17
1994 Los Angeles	NL	27	0	0	15	29	148	45	21	20	0	3	0	4	15	3	22	1	0	0	5	.000	0	6-9	3	6.21
1996 Los Angeles	NL	19	0	0	5	23.2	106	23	13	13	2	3	1	0	12	4	24	2	1	1	4	.200	0	0-2	1	4.94
2 ML YEARS		46	0	0	20	52.2	254	68	34	33	2	6	1	4	27	7	46	3	1	1	9	.100	0	6-11	4	5.64

Mariano Duncan

Bats: R **Throws:** R **Pos:** 2B-104; PH-4; 3B-3; DH-2; LF-2; RF-1   **Ht:** 6'0" **Wt:** 185 **Born:** 3/13/63 **Age:** 34

Year Team	Lg	G	AB	H	2B	3B	HR	(Hm	Rd)	TB	R	RBI	TBB	IBB	SO	HBP	SH	SF	SB	CS	SB%	GDP	Avg	OBP	SLG
1996 Columbus *	AAA	2	5	1	0	0	0	—	—	1	0	2	0	0	2	0	0	1	0	0	.00	0	.200	.167	.200
1985 Los Angeles	NL	142	562	137	24	6	6	(1	5)	191	74	39	38	4	113	3	13	4	38	8	.83	9	.244	.293	.340
1986 Los Angeles	NL	109	407	93	7	0	8	(2	6)	124	47	30	30	1	78	2	5	1	48	13	.79	6	.229	.284	.305
1987 Los Angeles	NL	76	261	56	8	1	6	(3	3)	84	31	18	17	1	62	2	6	1	11	1	.92	4	.215	.267	.322
1989 LA-Cin	NL	94	258	64	15	2	3	(2	1)	92	32	21	8	0	51	5	2	0	9	5	.64	3	.248	.284	.357
1990 Cincinnati	NL	125	435	133	22	11	10	(5	5)	207	67	55	24	4	67	4	4	4	13	7	.65	10	.306	.345	.476
1991 Cincinnati	NL	100	333	86	7	4	12	(10	2)	137	46	40	12	0	57	3	5	3	5	4	.56	0	.258	.288	.411
1992 Philadelphia	NL	142	574	153	40	3	8	(3	5)	223	71	50	17	0	108	5	5	4	23	3	.88	15	.267	.292	.389
1993 Philadelphia	NL	124	496	140	26	4	11	(5	6)	207	68	73	12	0	88	4	4	2	6	5	.55	13	.282	.304	.417
1994 Philadelphia	NL	88	347	93	22	1	8	(6	2)	141	49	48	11	1	72	4	2	4	10	2	.83	10	.268	.306	.406
1995 Phi-Cin	NL	81	265	76	14	2	6	(3	3)	112	36	36	5	0	62	1	1	5	1	3	.25	7	.287	.297	.423
1996 New York	AL	109	400	136	34	3	8	(5	3)	200	62	56	9	1	77	1	2	5	4	3	.57	10	.340	.352	.500
1989 Los Angeles	NL	49	84	21	5	1	0	(0	0)	28	9	8	0	0	15	2	1	0	3	3	.50	1	.250	.267	.333
Cincinnati	NL	45	174	43	10	1	3	(2	1)	64	23	13	8	0	36	3	1	0	6	2	.75	2	.247	.292	.368
1995 Philadelphia	NL	52	196	56	12	1	3	(1	2)	79	20	23	0	0	43	1	1	3	1	2	.33	6	.286	.285	.403
Cincinnati	NL	29	69	20	2	1	3	(2	1)	33	16	13	5	0	19	0	0	2	0	1	.00	1	.290	.329	.478

59

Year Team	Lg	G	AB	H	2B	3B	HR	(Hm	Rd)	TB	R	RBI	TBB	IBB	SO	HBP	SH	SF	SB	CS	SB%	GDP	Avg	OBP	SLG
11 ML YEARS		1190	4338	1167	219	37	86	(45	41)	1718	583	466	189	12	835	34	49	33	168	54	.76	87	.269	.303	.396

Todd Dunn

Bats: Right **Throws:** Right **Pos:** RF-4; LF-1; CF-1; PH-1 **Ht:** 6'5" **Wt:** 220 **Born:** 7/29/70 **Age:** 26

Year Team	Lg	G	AB	H	2B	3B	HR	(Hm	Rd)	TB	R	RBI	TBB	IBB	SO	HBP	SH	SF	SB	CS	SB%	GDP	Avg	OBP	SLG
1993 Helena	R+	43	150	46	11	2	10	—	—	91	33	42	22	1	52	6	1	2	5	2	.71	2	.307	.411	.607
1994 Beloit	A	129	429	94	13	2	23	—	—	180	72	63	50	3	131	6	4	4	18	8	.69	6	.219	.307	.420
1995 Stockton	A+	67	249	73	20	2	7	—	—	118	44	40	19	2	67	2	1	1	14	3	.82	5	.293	.347	.474
1996 El Paso	AA	98	359	122	24	5	19	—	—	213	72	78	45	1	84	2	2	4	13	4	.76	11	.340	.412	.593
1996 Milwaukee	AL	6	10	3	1	0	0	(0	0)	4	2	1	0	0	3	0	0	0	0	0	.00	1	.300	.300	.400

Shawon Dunston

Bats: Right **Throws:** Right **Pos:** SS-78; PH-4 **Ht:** 6'1" **Wt:** 180 **Born:** 3/21/63 **Age:** 34

Year Team	Lg	G	AB	H	2B	3B	HR	(Hm	Rd)	TB	R	RBI	TBB	IBB	SO	HBP	SH	SF	SB	CS	SB%	GDP	Avg	OBP	SLG
1985 Chicago	NL	74	250	65	12	4	4	(3	1)	97	40	18	19	3	42	0	1	2	11	3	.79	3	.260	.310	.388
1986 Chicago	NL	150	581	145	37	3	17	(10	7)	239	66	68	21	5	114	3	4	2	13	11	.54	5	.250	.278	.411
1987 Chicago	NL	95	346	85	18	3	5	(3	2)	124	40	22	10	1	68	1	0	2	12	3	.80	6	.246	.267	.358
1988 Chicago	NL	155	575	143	23	6	9	(5	4)	205	69	56	16	8	108	2	4	2	30	9	.77	6	.249	.271	.357
1989 Chicago	NL	138	471	131	20	6	9	(3	6)	190	52	60	30	15	86	1	6	4	19	11	.63	7	.278	.320	.403
1990 Chicago	NL	146	545	143	22	8	17	(7	10)	232	73	66	15	1	87	3	4	6	25	5	.83	9	.262	.283	.426
1991 Chicago	NL	142	492	128	22	7	12	(7	5)	200	59	50	23	5	64	4	4	11	21	6	.78	9	.260	.292	.407
1992 Chicago	NL	18	73	23	3	1	0	(0	0)	28	8	2	3	0	13	0	0	0	2	3	.40	1	.315	.342	.384
1993 Chicago	NL	7	10	4	2	0	0	(0	0)	6	3	2	0	0	1	0	0	0	0	0	.00	0	.400	.400	.600
1994 Chicago	NL	88	331	92	19	0	11	(2	9)	144	38	35	16	3	48	2	5	2	3	8	.27	4	.278	.313	.435
1995 Chicago	NL	127	477	141	30	6	14	(8	6)	225	58	69	10	3	75	6	7	3	10	5	.67	8	.296	.317	.472
1996 San Francisco	NL	82	287	86	12	2	5	(3	2)	117	27	25	13	0	40	1	5	1	8	0	1.00	8	.300	.331	.408
12 ML YEARS		1222	4438	1186	220	46	103	(51	52)	1807	533	473	176	44	746	23	40	35	154	64	.71	65	.267	.296	.407

Mike Durant

Bats: Right **Throws:** Right **Pos:** C-37; PH-6 **Ht:** 6'2" **Wt:** 200 **Born:** 9/14/69 **Age:** 27

Year Team	Lg	G	AB	H	2B	3B	HR	(Hm	Rd)	TB	R	RBI	TBB	IBB	SO	HBP	SH	SF	SB	CS	SB%	GDP	Avg	OBP	SLG
1991 Kenosha	A	66	217	44	10	0	2	—	—	60	27	20	25	0	35	3	2	1	20	5	.80	4	.203	.293	.276
1992 Visalia	A+	119	418	119	18	2	6	—	—	159	61	57	55	0	35	5	3	8	19	15	.56	10	.285	.368	.380
1993 Nashville	AA	123	437	106	23	1	8	—	—	155	58	57	44	1	68	6	4	3	16	4	.80	2	.243	.318	.355
1994 Salt Lake	AAA	103	343	102	24	4	4	—	—	146	67	51	35	0	47	4	5	0	9	3	.75	7	.297	.369	.426
1995 Salt Lake	AAA	85	295	74	15	3	2	—	—	101	40	23	20	0	31	2	3	2	11	7	.61	13	.251	.301	.342
1996 Salt Lake	AAA	31	101	29	7	0	1	—	—	39	21	12	11	1	21	4	1	0	7	2	.78	3	.287	.379	.386
1996 Minnesota	AL	40	81	17	3	0	0	(0	0)	20	15	5	10	0	15	0	4	1	3	0	1.00	2	.210	.293	.247

Ray Durham

Bats: Both **Throws:** Right **Pos:** 2B-150; PH-7; DH-3 **Ht:** 5'8" **Wt:** 170 **Born:** 11/30/71 **Age:** 25

Year Team	Lg	G	AB	H	2B	3B	HR	(Hm	Rd)	TB	R	RBI	TBB	IBB	SO	HBP	SH	SF	SB	CS	SB%	GDP	Avg	OBP	SLG
1990 White Sox	R	35	116	31	3	3	0	—	—	40	18	13	15	0	35	4	0	1	22	9	.71	0	.267	.368	.345
1991 Utica	A-	39	142	36	2	7	0	—	—	52	29	17	25	0	43	2	2	1	12	1	.92	0	.254	.366	.366
White Sox	R	6	23	7	1	0	0	—	—	8	3	4	3	0	5	0	0	0	5	1	.83	0	.304	.385	.348
1992 White Sox	R	5	13	7	2	0	0	—	—	9	3	2	3	0	1	0	0	0	1	0	1.00	0	.538	.625	.692
Sarasota	A+	57	202	55	6	3	0	—	—	67	37	7	32	0	36	10	5	0	28	8	.78	2	.272	.398	.332
1993 Birmingham	AA	137	528	143	22	10	3	—	—	194	83	37	42	2	100	14	5	5	39	25	.61	5	.271	.338	.367
1994 Nashville	AAA	133	527	156	33	12	16	—	—	261	89	66	46	7	91	12	3	4	34	11	.76	5	.296	.363	.495
1995 Chicago	AL	125	471	121	27	6	7	(1	6)	181	68	51	31	2	83	6	5	4	18	5	.78	8	.257	.309	.384
1996 Chicago	AL	156	557	153	33	5	10	(3	7)	226	79	65	58	4	95	10	7	7	30	4	**.88**	6	.275	.350	.406
2 ML YEARS		281	1028	274	60	11	17	(4	13)	407	147	116	89	6	178	16	12	11	48	9	.84	14	.267	.331	.396

Jermaine Dye

Bats: R **Throws:** R **Pos:** RF-71; LF-25; PH-7; CF-4 **Ht:** 6'4" **Wt:** 210 **Born:** 1/28/74 **Age:** 23

Year Team	Lg	G	AB	H	2B	3B	HR	(Hm	Rd)	TB	R	RBI	TBB	IBB	SO	HBP	SH	SF	SB	CS	SB%	GDP	Avg	OBP	SLG
1993 Braves	R	31	124	43	14	0	0	—	—	57	17	27	5	0	13	5	0	1	5	0	1.00	5	.347	.375	.460
Danville	R+	25	94	26	6	1	2	—	—	40	6	12	8	1	10	0	0	2	4	1	.80	2	.277	.327	.426
1994 Macon	A	135	506	151	41	1	15	—	—	239	73	98	33	1	82	8	0	8	19	10	.66	10	.298	.346	.472
1995 Greenville	AA	104	403	115	26	4	15	—	—	194	50	71	27	2	74	1	2	4	4	8	.33	9	.285	.329	.481
1996 Richmond	AAA	36	142	33	7	1	6	—	—	60	25	19	5	0	25	1	0	0	3	0	1.00	3	.232	.264	.423
1996 Atlanta	NL	98	292	82	16	0	12	(4	8)	134	32	37	8	0	67	3	0	3	1	4	.20	11	.281	.304	.459

Mike Dyer

Pitches: Right **Bats:** Right **Pos:** RP-69; SP-1   **Ht:** 6'3" **Wt:** 200 **Born:** 9/8/66 **Age:** 30

		HOW	MUCH	HE	PITCHED			WHAT	HE	GAVE	UP								THE	RESULTS			
Year Team	Lg	G	GS	CG	GF	IP	BFP	H	R	ER	HR	SH	SF	HB	TBB	IBB	SO	WP	Bk	W	L	Pct.	ShO	Sv-Op	Hld	ERA
1989 Minnesota	AL	16	12	1	0	71	317	74	43	38	2	5	2	2	37	0	37	1	1	4	7	.364	0	0-0	1	4.82
1994 Pittsburgh	NL	14	0	0	7	15.1	74	15	12	10	1	1	2	3	12	4	13	0	1	1	1	.500	0	4-6	1	5.87
1995 Pittsburgh	NL	55	0	0	15	74.2	327	81	40	36	9	3	1	5	30	3	53	4	1	4	5	.444	0	0-2	6	4.34
1996 Montreal	NL	70	1	0	20	75.2	334	79	40	37	7	6	4	5	34	4	51	4	0	5	5	.500	0	2-6	8	4.40
4 ML YEARS		155	13	1	42	236.2	1052	249	135	121	19	15	9	15	113	11	154	9	3	14	18	.438	0	6-14	16	4.60

Lenny Dykstra

Bats: Left **Throws:** Left **Pos:** CF-39; PH-5   **Ht:** 5'10" **Wt:** 188 **Born:** 2/10/63 **Age:** 34

				BATTING															BASERUNNING				PERCENTAGES		
Year Team	Lg	G	AB	H	2B	3B	HR	(Hm	Rd)	TB	R	RBI	TBB	IBB	SO	HBP	SH	SF	SB	CS	SB%	GDP	Avg	OBP	SLG
1985 New York	NL	83	236	60	9	3	1	(0	1)	78	40	19	30	0	24	1	4	2	15	5	.88	4	.254	.338	.331
1986 New York	NL	147	431	127	27	7	8	(4	4)	192	77	45	58	1	55	0	7	2	31	7	.82	4	.295	.377	.445
1987 New York	NL	132	431	123	37	3	10	(7	3)	196	86	43	40	3	67	4	4	0	27	7	.79	1	.285	.352	.455
1988 New York	NL	126	429	116	19	3	8	(3	5)	165	57	33	30	2	43	3	2	2	30	8	.79	3	.270	.321	.385
1989 NYN-Phi	NL	146	511	121	32	4	7	(5	2)	182	66	32	60	1	53	3	5	5	30	12	.71	7	.237	.318	.356
1990 Philadelphia	NL	149	590	192	35	3	9	(6	3)	260	106	60	89	14	48	7	2	3	33	5	.87	5	.325	.418	.441
1991 Philadelphia	NL	63	246	73	13	5	3	(3	0)	105	48	12	37	1	20	1	0	0	24	4	.86	1	.297	.391	.427
1992 Philadelphia	NL	85	345	104	18	0	6	(5	1)	140	53	39	40	4	32	3	0	4	30	5	.86	1	.301	.375	.406
1993 Philadelphia	NL	161	637	194	44	6	19	(12	7)	307	143	66	129	9	64	2	0	5	37	12	.76	5	.305	.420	.482
1994 Philadelphia	NL	84	315	86	26	5	5	(3	2)	137	68	24	68	11	44	2	0	1	15	4	.79	3	.273	.404	.435
1995 Philadelphia	NL	62	254	67	15	1	2	(2	0)	90	37	18	33	2	28	3	0	2	10	5	.67	1	.264	.353	.354
1996 Philadelphia	NL	40	134	35	6	3	3	(1	2)	56	21	13	26	2	25	1	1	1	3	1	.75	1	.261	.387	.418
1989 New York	NL	56	159	43	12	1	3	(2	1)	66	27	13	23	0	15	2	4	4	13	1	.93	2	.270	.362	.415
Philadelphia	NL	90	352	78	20	3	4	(3	1)	116	39	19	37	1	38	1	1	1	17	11	.61	5	.222	.299	.330
12 ML YEARS		1278	4559	1298	281	43	81	(51	30)	1908	802	404	640	50	503	31	25	27	285	72	.80	39	.285	.375	.419

Damion Easley

Bats: R **Throws:** R **Pos:** SS-21; 2B-17; PH-7; 3B-5; DH-3; CF-2   **Ht:** 5'11" **Wt:** 185 **Born:** 11/11/69 **Age:** 27

				BATTING															BASERUNNING				PERCENTAGES		
Year Team	Lg	G	AB	H	2B	3B	HR	(Hm	Rd)	TB	R	RBI	TBB	IBB	SO	HBP	SH	SF	SB	CS	SB%	GDP	Avg	OBP	SLG
1996 Midland *	AA	4	14	6	2	0	0	—	—	8	1	2	0	0	0	0	0	0	1	0	1.00	0	.429	.429	.571
Vancouver *	AAA	12	48	15	2	1	2	—	—	25	13	8	9	0	6	1	0	1	4	1	.80	0	.313	.424	.521
1992 California	AL	47	151	39	5	0	1	(1	0)	47	14	12	8	0	26	3	2	1	9	5	.64	2	.258	.307	.311
1993 California	AL	73	230	72	13	2	2	(0	2)	95	33	22	28	2	35	3	1	2	6	6	.50	5	.313	.392	.413
1994 California	AL	88	316	68	16	1	6	(4	2)	104	41	30	29	0	48	4	4	2	4	5	.44	8	.215	.288	.329
1995 California	AL	114	357	77	14	2	4	(1	3)	107	35	35	32	1	47	6	6	4	5	2	.71	11	.216	.288	.300
1996 Cal-Det	AL	49	112	30	2	0	4	(1	3)	44	14	17	10	0	25	1	5	1	3	1	.75	0	.268	.331	.393
1996 California	AL	28	45	7	1	0	2	(1	1)	14	4	7	6	0	12	0	3	0	0	0	.00	0	.156	.255	.311
Detroit	AL	21	67	23	1	0	2	(0	2)	30	10	10	4	0	13	1	2	1	3	1	.75	0	.343	.384	.448
5 ML YEARS		371	1166	286	50	5	17	(7	10)	397	137	116	107	3	181	17	18	10	27	19	.59	26	.245	.315	.340

Angel Echevarria

Bats: Right **Throws:** Right **Pos:** PH-18; RF-7; LF-4   **Ht:** 6'3" **Wt:** 219 **Born:** 5/25/71 **Age:** 26

				BATTING															BASERUNNING				PERCENTAGES		
Year Team	Lg	G	AB	H	2B	3B	HR	(Hm	Rd)	TB	R	RBI	TBB	IBB	SO	HBP	SH	SF	SB	CS	SB%	GDP	Avg	OBP	SLG
1992 Bend	A-	57	205	46	4	1	5	—	—	67	24	30	19	1	54	2	0	0	8	1	.89	5	.224	.296	.327
1993 Central Val	A+	104	358	97	16	2	6	—	—	135	45	52	44	0	74	5	5	3	6	5	.55	7	.271	.356	.377
1994 Central Val	A+	50	192	58	8	1	6	—	—	86	28	35	9	0	25	4	0	3	2	2	.50	6	.302	.341	.448
New Haven	AA	58	205	52	6	0	8	—	—	82	25	32	15	1	46	2	0	2	2	4	.33	8	.254	.308	.400
1995 New Haven	AA	124	453	136	30	1	21	—	—	231	78	100	56	3	93	8	0	7	8	3	.73	8	.300	.382	.510
1996 Colo. Sprng	AAA	110	415	140	19	2	16	—	—	211	67	74	38	3	81	3	0	1	4	3	.57	4	.337	.393	.508
1996 Colorado	NL	26	21	6	0	0	0	(0	0)	6	2	6	2	0	5	1	0	2	0	0	.00	0	.286	.346	.286

Dennis Eckersley

Pitches: Right **Bats:** Right **Pos:** RP-63   **Ht:** 6'2" **Wt:** 195 **Born:** 10/3/54 **Age:** 42

		HOW	MUCH	HE	PITCHED			WHAT	HE	GAVE	UP								THE	RESULTS			
Year Team	Lg	G	GS	CG	GF	IP	BFP	H	R	ER	HR	SH	SF	HB	TBB	IBB	SO	WP	Bk	W	L	Pct.	ShO	Sv-Op	Hld	ERA
1975 Cleveland	AL	34	24	6	5	187	794	147	61	54	16	6	7	7	90	8	152	4	2	13	7	.650	2	2- -	—	2.60
1976 Cleveland	AL	36	30	9	3	199	821	155	82	76	13	10	4	5	78	2	200	6	1	13	12	.520	3	1- -	—	3.44
1977 Cleveland	AL	33	33	12	0	247	1006	214	100	97	31	11	6	7	54	11	191	3	0	14	13	.519	3	0- -	—	3.53
1978 Boston	AL	35	35	16	0	268	1121	258	99	89	30	7	8	7	71	8	162	3	0	20	8	.714	3	0- -	—	2.99
1979 Boston	AL	33	33	17	0	247	1018	234	89	82	29	10	6	6	59	4	150	1	1	17	10	.630	2	0- -	—	2.99
1980 Boston	AL	30	30	8	0	198	818	188	101	94	25	7	4	2	44	7	121	0	0	12	14	.462	0	0- -	—	4.27
1981 Boston	AL	23	23	8	0	154	649	160	82	73	9	6	5	3	35	2	79	0	0	9	8	.529	2	0- -	—	4.27
1982 Boston	AL	33	33	11	0	224.1	926	228	101	93	31	4	4	2	43	3	127	1	0	13	13	.500	3	0- -	—	3.73
1983 Boston	AL	28	28	2	0	176.1	787	223	119	110	27	1	5	6	39	4	77	1	0	9	13	.409	0	0- -	—	5.61

61

Year Team	Lg	G	GS	CG	GF	IP	BFP	H	R	ER	HR	SH	SF	HB	TBB	IBB	SO	WP	Bk	W	L	Pct.	ShO	Sv-Op	Hld	ERA
						HOW MUCH HE PITCHED					WHAT HE GAVE UP									THE RESULTS						
1984 Bos-ChN		33	33	4	0	225	932	223	97	90	21	11	9	5	49	9	114	3		14	12	.538	0	0--	—	3.60
1985 Chicago	NL	25	25	6	0	169.1	664	145	61	58	15	6	2	3	19	4	117	0	3	11	7	.611	2	0--	—	3.08
1986 Chicago	NL	33	32	1	0	201	862	226	109	102	21	13	10	3	43	3	137	2	5	6	11	.353	0	0--	—	4.57
1987 Oakland	AL	54	2	0	33	115.2	460	99	41	39	11	3	3	3	17	3	113	1	0	6	8	.429	0	16-20	2	3.03
1988 Oakland	AL	60	0	0	53	72.2	279	52	20	19	5	1	3	1	11	2	70	0	2	4	2	.667	0	**45-53**	1	2.35
1989 Oakland	AL	51	0	0	46	57.2	206	32	10	10	5	0	4	1	3	0	55	0		4	0	1.000	0	33-39	1	1.56
1990 Oakland	AL	63	0	0	61	73.1	262	41	9	5	2	0	1	0	4	1	73	0	0	4	2	.667	0	48-50	0	0.61
1991 Oakland	AL	67	0	0	59	76	299	60	26	25	11	1	0	1	9	3	87	1	0	5	4	.556	0	43-51	0	2.96
1992 Oakland	AL	69	0	0	**65**	80	309	62	17	17	5	3	0	1	11	6	93	0	0	7	1	.875	0	**51-54**	0	1.91
1993 Oakland	AL	64	0	0	52	67	276	67	32	31	7	2	2	2	13	4	80	0	0	2	4	.333	0	36-46	0	4.16
1994 Oakland	AL	45	0	0	39	44.1	193	49	26	21	5	1	0	1	13	2	47	0	0	5	4	.556	0	19-25	0	4.26
1995 Oakland	AL	52	0	0	48	50.1	212	53	29	27	5	4	3	1	11	0	40	0	1	4	6	.400	0	29-38	0	4.83
1996 St. Louis	NL	63	0	0	53	60	251	65	26	22	8	1	3	4	6	2	49	0	0	0	0	.000	0	30-34	4	3.30
1984 Boston	AL	9	9	2	0	64.2	270	71	38	36	10	3	3	1	13	2	33	2	0	4	4	.500	0	0--	—	5.01
Chicago	NL	24	24	2	0	160.1	662	152	59	54	11	8	6	4	36	7	81	1	2	10	8	.556	0	0--	—	3.03
22 ML YEARS		964	361	100	517	3193	13145	2981	1337	1234	332	105	92	71	722	88	2334	26	16	192	165	.538	20	353--	—	3.48

Ken Edenfield

Pitches: Right **Bats:** Right **Pos:** RP-2   **Ht:** 6'1" **Wt:** 165 **Born:** 3/18/67 **Age:** 30

Year Team	Lg	G	GS	CG	GF	IP	BFP	H	R	ER	HR	SH	SF	HB	TBB	IBB	SO	WP	Bk	W	L	Pct.	ShO	Sv-Op	Hld	ERA
						HOW MUCH HE PITCHED					WHAT HE GAVE UP									THE RESULTS						
1990 Boise	A-	31	0	0	24	54.1	225	38	15	10	1	5	1	4	20	3	57	2	0	8	4	.667	0	9--	—	1.66
1991 Quad City	A	47	0	0	40	87	356	69	30	25	3	5	3	4	30	2	106	5	1	8	5	.615	0	15--	—	2.59
1992 Palm Spring	A+	13	0	0	13	18.1	70	12	1	1	0	0	0	0	7	0	20	0	0	0	0	.000	0	7--	—	0.49
Midland	AA	31	0	0	17	49.2	225	60	35	33	5	3	2	4	24	3	43	4	0	1	5	.167	0	2--	—	5.98
1993 Midland	AA	48	3	1	19	93.2	404	93	56	48	10	2	5	8	35	5	84	14	2	5	8	.385	0	4--	—	4.61
Vancouver	AAA	2	0	0	2	3.2	13	1	0	0	0	0	0	0	1	0	5	0	0	0	0	.000	0	0--	—	0.00
1994 Vancouver	AAA	51	0	0	28	87.2	368	69	38	33	7	3	4	9	36	3	84	12	0	9	4	.692	0	4--	—	3.39
1995 Vancouver	AAA	33	0	0	4	60	259	56	24	23	2	3	3	5	25	2	44	5	0	7	2	.778	0	4--	—	3.45
1996 Vancouver	AAA	19	0	0	7	32	139	26	13	10	1	3	2	1	20	5	18	2	1	2	4	.333	0	0--	—	2.81
Columbus	AAA	33	0	0	13	42.1	172	32	12	11	1	4	0	4	15	1	28	2	0	4	1	.800	0	3--	—	2.34
1995 California	AL	7	0	0	3	12.2	56	15	7	6	1	0	1	0	5	0	6	3	0	0	0	.000	0	0-0	1	4.26
1996 California	AL	2	0	0	0	4.1	26	10	5	5	2	0	0	1	2	0	4	0	0	0	0	.000	0	0-0	0	10.38
2 ML YEARS		9	0	0	3	17	82	25	12	11	3	0	1	1	7	0	10	3	0	0	0	.000	0	0-0	1	5.82

Jim Edmonds

Bats: Left **Throws:** Left **Pos:** CF-111; PH-6; DH-1   **Ht:** 6'1" **Wt:** 190 **Born:** 6/27/70 **Age:** 27

Year Team	Lg	G	AB	H	2B	3B	HR	(Hm	Rd)	TB	R	RBI	TBB	IBB	SO	HBP	SH	SF	SB	CS	SB%	GDP	Avg	OBP	SLG
						BATTING													BASERUNNING				PERCENTAGES		
1996 Lk Elsinore *	A+	5	15	6	2	0	1	(—	—)	11	4	4	1	1	1	1	0	0	0	2	.00	0	.400	.471	.733
1993 California	AL	18	61	15	4	1	0	(0	0)	21	5	4	2	1	16	0	0	0	0	2	.00	1	.246	.270	.344
1994 California	AL	94	289	79	13	1	5	(3	2)	109	35	37	30	3	72	1	1	1	4	2	.67	3	.273	.343	.377
1995 California	AL	141	558	162	30	4	33	(16	17)	299	120	107	51	4	130	5	1	5	1	4	.20	10	.290	.352	.536
1996 California	AL	114	431	131	28	3	27	(17	10)	246	73	66	46	2	101	4	0	2	4	0	1.00	8	.304	.375	.571
4 ML YEARS		367	1339	387	75	9	65	(36	29)	675	233	214	129	10	319	10	2	8	9	8	.53	22	.289	.354	.504

Robert Eenhoorn

Bats: R **Throws:** R **Pos:** 2B-12; SS-4; 3B-2; PH-1   **Ht:** 6'3" **Wt:** 185 **Born:** 2/9/68 **Age:** 29

Year Team	Lg	G	AB	H	2B	3B	HR	(Hm	Rd)	TB	R	RBI	TBB	IBB	SO	HBP	SH	SF	SB	CS	SB%	GDP	Avg	OBP	SLG
						BATTING													BASERUNNING				PERCENTAGES		
1996 Columbus *	AAA	55	172	58	14	1	1	(—	—)	77	28	16	21	0	18	1	3	3	7	2	.78	3	.337	.406	.448
1994 New York	AL	3	4	2	1	0	0	(0	0)	3	1	0	0	0	0	0	0	0	0	0	.00	0	.500	.500	.750
1995 New York	AL	5	14	2	1	0	0	(0	0)	3	1	2	1	0	3	0	0	0	0	0	.00	0	.143	.200	.214
1996 NYA-Cal	AL	18	29	5	0	0	0	(0	0)	5	3	2	2	0	5	0	0	1	0	0	.00	0	.172	.212	.172
1996 New York	AL	12	14	1	0	0	0	(0	0)	1	2	2	2	0	3	0	0	1	0	0	.00	0	.071	.167	.071
California	AL	6	15	4	0	0	0	(0	0)	4	1	0	0	0	2	0	0	0	0	0	.00	0	.267	.267	.267
3 ML YEARS		26	47	9	2	0	0	(0	0)	11	5	4	3	0	8	0	0	2	0	0	.00	0	.191	.231	.234

Mark Eichhorn

Pitches: Right **Bats:** Right **Pos:** RP-24   **Ht:** 6'3" **Wt:** 210 **Born:** 11/21/60 **Age:** 36

Year Team	Lg	G	GS	CG	GF	IP	BFP	H	R	ER	HR	SH	SF	HB	TBB	IBB	SO	WP	Bk	W	L	Pct.	ShO	Sv-Op	Hld	ERA
						HOW MUCH HE PITCHED					WHAT HE GAVE UP									THE RESULTS						
1996 Lk Elsinore *	A+	12	4	0	1	15.1	62	15	9	8	1	2	1	0	2	0	21	0	0	1	0	1.000	0	0--	—	4.70
1982 Toronto	AL	7	7	0	0	38	171	40	28	23	4	1	2	0	14	1	16	3	0	0	3	.000	0	0--	—	5.45
1986 Toronto	AL	69	0	0	38	157	612	105	32	30	8	9	2	7	45	14	166	2	1	14	6	.700	0	10--	—	1.72
1987 Toronto	AL	**89**	0	0	27	127.2	540	110	47	45	14	7	4	6	52	13	96	3	1	10	6	.625	0	4-6	8	3.17
1988 Toronto	AL	37	0	0	17	66.2	302	79	32	31	3	8	1	6	27	4	28	3	6	0	3	.000	0	1-1	2	4.19
1989 Atlanta	NL	45	0	0	13	68.1	286	70	36	33	6	7	4	1	19	8	49	0	1	5	5	.500	0	0-2	8	4.35
1990 California	AL	60	0	0	40	84.2	374	98	36	29	4	4	4	6	23	0	69	2	0	2	5	.286	0	13-16	4	3.08

Year Team	Lg	G	GS	CG	GF	IP	BFP	H	R	ER	HR	SH	SF	HB	TBB	IBB	SO	WP	Bk	W	L	Pct.	ShO	Sv-Op	Hld	ERA
1991 California	AL	70	0	0	23	81.2	311	63	21	18	2	5	3	2	13	1	49	0	0	3	3	.500	0	1-4	25	1.98
1992 Cal-Tor	AL	65	0	0	26	87.2	372	86	34	30	3	3	5	2	25	8	61	9	1	4	4	.500	0	2-6	5	3.08
1993 Toronto	AL	54	0	0	16	72.2	309	76	26	22	3	3	2	3	22	7	47	2	0	3	1	.750	0	0-2	5	2.72
1994 Baltimore	AL	43	0	0	20	71	290	62	19	17	1	4	4	5	19	4	35	1	0	6	5	.545	0	1-5	10	2.15
1996 California	AL	24	0	0	6	30.1	135	36	17	17	3	3	2	2	11	3	24	0	1	1	2	.333	0	0-2	5	5.04
1992 California	AL	42	0	0	19	56.2	237	51	19	15	2	2	3	0	18	8	42	3	1	2	4	.333	0	2-6	3	2.38
Toronto	AL	23	0	0	7	31	135	35	15	15	1	1	2	2	7	0	19	6	0	2	0	1.000	0	0-0	2	4.35
11 ML YEARS		563	7	0	226	885.2	3702	825	328	295	49	52	33	40	270	63	640	25	11	48	43	.527	0	32--	—	3.00

Joey Eischen

Pitches: Left **Bats:** Left **Pos:** RP-52 **Ht:** 6'1" **Wt:** 190 **Born:** 5/25/70 **Age:** 27

Year Team	Lg	G	GS	CG	GF	IP	BFP	H	R	ER	HR	SH	SF	HB	TBB	IBB	SO	WP	Bk	W	L	Pct.	ShO	Sv-Op	Hld	ERA
1994 Montreal	NL	1	0	0	0	0.2	7	4	4	4	0	0	0	1	0	0	1	0	0	0	0	.000	0	0-0	0	54.00
1995 Los Angeles	NL	17	0	0	8	20.1	95	19	9	7	1	0	0	2	11	1	15	1	0	0	0	.000	0	0-0	1	3.10
1996 LA-Det		52	0	0	14	68.1	308	75	36	32	7	3	2	4	34	7	51	4	0	1	2	.333	0	0-2	2	4.21
1996 Los Angeles	NL	28	0	0	11	43.1	198	48	25	23	4	3	1	4	20	4	36	1	0	1	0	.000	0	0-0	1	4.78
Detroit	AL	24	0	0	3	25	110	27	11	9	3	0	1	0	14	3	15	3	0	1	1	.500	0	0-2	1	3.24
3 ML YEARS		70	0	0	22	89.1	410	98	49	43	8	3	2	7	45	8	67	5	0	1	2	.333	0	0-2	3	4.33

Jim Eisenreich

Bats: L **Throws:** L **Pos:** RF-50; LF-43; PH-25; CF-3 **Ht:** 5'11" **Wt:** 195 **Born:** 4/18/59 **Age:** 38

Year Team	Lg	G	AB	H	2B	3B	HR	(Hm	Rd)	TB	R	RBI	TBB	IBB	SO	HBP	SH	SF	SB	CS	SB%	GDP	Avg	OBP	SLG
1982 Minnesota	AL	34	99	30	6	0	2	(1	1)	42	10	9	11	0	13	1	0	0	0	0	.00	1	.303	.378	.424
1983 Minnesota	AL	2	7	2	1	0	0	(0	0)	3	1	0	1	0	1	0	0	0	0	0	.00	0	.286	.375	.429
1984 Minnesota	AL	12	32	7	1	0	0	(0	0)	8	1	3	2	1	4	0	0	0	2	0	1.00	1	.219	.250	.250
1987 Kansas City	AL	44	105	25	8	2	4	(3	1)	49	10	21	7	2	13	0	0	3	1	1	.50	2	.238	.278	.467
1988 Kansas City	AL	82	202	44	8	1	1	(0	1)	57	26	19	6	1	31	0	0	2	9	3	.75	2	.218	.236	.282
1989 Kansas City	AL	134	475	139	33	7	9	(4	5)	213	64	59	37	9	44	0	3	4	27	8	.77	8	.293	.341	.448
1990 Kansas City	AL	142	496	139	29	7	5	(2	3)	197	61	51	42	2	51	1	2	4	12	14	.46	7	.280	.335	.397
1991 Kansas City	AL	135	375	113	22	3	2	(2	0)	147	47	47	20	1	35	1	3	6	5	3	.63	10	.301	.333	.392
1992 Kansas City	AL	113	353	95	13	3	2	(1	1)	120	31	28	24	4	36	0	0	3	11	6	.65	6	.269	.313	.340
1993 Philadelphia	NL	153	362	115	17	4	7	(3	4)	161	51	54	26	5	36	1	3	2	5	0	1.00	6	.318	.363	.445
1994 Philadelphia	NL	104	290	87	15	4	4	(3	1)	122	42	43	33	3	31	1	3	2	6	2	.75	8	.300	.371	.421
1995 Philadelphia	NL	129	377	119	22	2	10	(5	5)	175	46	55	38	4	44	1	2	5	10	0	1.00	7	.316	.375	.464
1996 Philadelphia	NL	113	338	122	24	3	3	(1	2)	161	45	41	31	9	32	1	0	3	11	1	.92	7	.361	.413	.476
13 ML YEARS		1197	3511	1037	199	36	49	(25	24)	1455	435	430	278	41	371	7	18	38	99	38	.72	65	.295	.345	.414

Cal Eldred

Pitches: Right **Bats:** Right **Pos:** SP-15 **Ht:** 6'4" **Wt:** 236 **Born:** 11/24/67 **Age:** 29

Year Team	Lg	G	GS	CG	GF	IP	BFP	H	R	ER	HR	SH	SF	HB	TBB	IBB	SO	WP	Bk	W	L	Pct.	ShO	Sv-Op	Hld	ERA
1996 Nw Orleans *	AAA	6	6	0	0	32.1	135	24	12	12	2	0	0	1	17	0	30	1	0	2	2	.500	0	0--	—	3.34
1991 Milwaukee	AL	3	3	0	0	16	73	20	9	8	2	0	0	0	6	0	10	0	0	2	0	1.000	0	0-0	0	4.50
1992 Milwaukee	AL	14	14	2	0	100.1	394	76	21	20	4	1	0	2	23	0	62	0	0	11	2	.846	1	0-0	0	1.79
1993 Milwaukee	AL	36	36	8	0	258	1087	232	120	115	32	5	12	10	91	5	180	2	0	16	16	.500	1	0-0	0	4.01
1994 Milwaukee	AL	25	25	6	0	179	769	158	96	93	23	5	7	4	84	0	98	2	0	11	11	.500	0	0-0	0	4.68
1995 Milwaukee	AL	4	4	0	0	23.2	104	24	10	9	4	1	0	1	10	0	18	1	1	1	1	.500	0	0-0	0	3.42
1996 Milwaukee	AL	15	15	0	0	84.2	363	82	43	42	8	0	4	4	38	0	50	1	0	4	4	.500	0	0-0	0	4.46
6 ML YEARS		97	97	16	0	661.2	2790	592	299	287	73	12	23	21	252	5	418	9	1	45	34	.570	2	0-0	0	3.90

Robert Ellis

Pitches: Right **Bats:** Right **Pos:** RP-3 **Ht:** 6'5" **Wt:** 220 **Born:** 12/15/70 **Age:** 26

Year Team	Lg	G	GS	CG	GF	IP	BFP	H	R	ER	HR	SH	SF	HB	TBB	IBB	SO	WP	Bk	W	L	Pct.	ShO	Sv-Op	Hld	ERA
1991 Utica	A-	15	15	1	0	87.2	407	87	66	45	4	6	5	6	61	0	66	13	0	3	9	.250	1	0--	—	4.62
1992 White Sox	R	1	1	0	0	5	24	10	6	6	0	0	0	0	1	0	4	0	0	1	0	1.000	0	0--	—	10.80
South Bend	A	18	18	1	0	123	481	90	46	32	3	4	2	4	35	0	97	7	2	6	5	.545	1	0--	—	2.34
1993 Sarasota	A+	15	15	8	0	104	414	81	37	29	3	4	3	3	31	1	79	6	1	7	8	.467	2	0--	—	2.51
Birmingham	AA	12	12	2	0	81.1	336	68	33	28	2	1	1	4	21	0	77	6	0	6	3	.667	1	0--	—	3.10
1994 Nashville	AAA	19	19	1	0	105	483	126	77	71	19	5	6	2	55	1	76	1	4	4	10	.286	0	0--	—	6.09
1995 Nashville	AAA	4	4	0	0	20.2	85	16	7	5	2	0	1	1	10	0	9	1	1	1	1	.500	0	0--	—	2.18
1996 Nashville	AAA	19	13	1	2	70.1	327	78	49	47	6	5	3	7	45	3	35	8	0	3	8	.273	0	0--	—	6.01
Birmingham	AA	2	2	0	0	7.1	35	6	9	9	1	1	1	1	8	0	8	1	0	0	1	.000	0	0--	—	11.05
Vancouver	AAA	7	7	1	0	44.1	186	30	19	16	2	2	0	0	28	0	29	5	0	2	3	.400	0	0--	—	3.25
1996 California	AL	3	0	0	3	5	19	0	0	0	0	0	0	0	4	0	1	1	0	0	0	.000	0	0-0	0	0.00

Kevin Elster

Bats: Right **Throws:** Right **Pos:** SS-157   **Ht:** 6'2" **Wt:** 200 **Born:** 8/3/64 **Age:** 32

Year Team	Lg	G	AB	H	2B	3B	HR	(Hm	Rd)	TB	R	RBI	TBB	IBB	SO	HBP	SH	SF	SB	CS	SB%	GDP	Avg	OBP	SLG
1986 New York	NL	19	30	5	1	0	0	(0	0)	6	3	0	3	1	8	0	0	0	0	0	.00	0	.167	.242	.200
1987 New York	NL	5	10	4	2	0	0	(0	0)	6	1	1	0	0	1	0	0	0	0	0	.00	1	.400	.400	.600
1988 New York	NL	149	406	87	11	1	9	(6	3)	127	41	37	35	12	47	3	6	0	2	0	1.00	5	.214	.282	.313
1989 New York	NL	151	458	106	25	2	10	(5	5)	165	52	55	34	11	77	2	6	8	4	3	.57	13	.231	.283	.360
1990 New York	NL	92	314	65	20	1	9	(2	7)	114	36	45	30	2	54	1	1	6	2	0	1.00	4	.207	.274	.363
1991 New York	NL	115	348	84	16	2	6	(3	3)	122	33	36	40	6	53	1	1	4	2	3	.40	4	.241	.318	.351
1992 New York	NL	6	18	4	0	0	0	(0	0)	4	0	0	0	0	2	0	0	0	0	0	.00	1	.222	.222	.222
1994 New York	AL	7	20	0	0	0	0	(0	0)	0	0	0	1	0	6	0	1	0	0	0	.00	0	.000	.048	.000
1995 NYA-Phi		36	70	13	5	1	1	(1	0)	23	11	9	8	1	19	1	2	1	0	0	.00	1	.186	.272	.329
1996 Texas	AL	157	515	130	32	2	24	(9	15)	238	79	99	52	1	138	2	2	16	4	1	.80	8	.252	.317	.462
1995 New York	AL	10	17	2	1	0	0	(0	0)	3	1	0	1	0	5	0	0	0	0	0	.00	0	.118	.167	.176
Philadelphia	NL	26	53	11	4	1	1	(1	0)	20	10	9	7	1	14	1	2	1	0	0	.00	1	.208	.302	.377
10 ML YEARS		737	2189	498	112	9	59	(26	33)	805	256	282	203	34	405	10	33	31	14	7	.67	37	.228	.292	.368

Alan Embree

Pitches: Left **Bats:** Left **Pos:** RP-24   **Ht:** 6'2" **Wt:** 190 **Born:** 1/23/70 **Age:** 27

Year Team	Lg	G	GS	CG	GF	IP	BFP	H	R	ER	HR	SH	SF	HB	TBB	IBB	SO	WP	Bk	W	L	Pct.	ShO	Sv-Op	Hld	ERA
1990 Burlington	R+	15	15	0	0	81.2	351	87	36	24	3	1	3	0	30	0	58	5	4	4	4	.500	0	0--	—	2.64
1991 Columbus	A	27	26	3	0	155.1	651	125	80	62	4	5	3	4	77	1	137	7	0	10	8	.556	1	0--	—	3.59
1992 Kinston	A+	15	15	1	0	101	418	89	48	37	10	3	1	2	32	0	115	6	3	10	5	.667	0	0--	—	3.30
Canton-Akrn	AA	12	12	0	0	79	316	61	24	20	2	3	1	2	28	1	56	2	1	7	2	.778	0	0--	—	2.28
1993 Canton-Akrn	AA	1	1	0	0	5.1	20	3	2	2	0	0	0	0	3	0	4	0	0	0	0	.000	0	0--	—	3.38
1994 Canton-Akrn	AA	30	27	2	1	157	698	183	106	96	15	2	6	4	64	3	81	8	1	9	16	.360	1	0--	—	5.50
1995 Buffalo	AAA	30	0	0	19	40.2	170	31	10	4	0	1	2	1	19	2	56	0	0	3	4	.429	0	5--	—	0.89
1996 Buffalo	AAA	20	0	0	15	34.1	142	26	16	15	1	0	3	1	14	0	46	5	0	4	1	.800	0	5--	—	3.93
1992 Cleveland	AL	4	4	0	0	18	81	19	14	14	3	0	2	1	8	0	12	1	1	0	2	.000	0	0-0	0	7.00
1995 Cleveland	AL	23	0	0	8	24.2	111	23	16	14	2	2	2	0	16	0	23	1	0	3	2	.600	0	1-1	6	5.11
1996 Cleveland	AL	24	0	0	2	31	141	30	26	22	10	1	3	0	21	3	33	3	0	1	1	.500	0	0-0	1	6.39
3 ML YEARS		51	4	0	10	73.2	333	72	56	50	15	3	7	1	45	3	68	5	1	4	5	.444	0	1-1	7	6.11

Angelo Encarnacion

Bats: Right **Throws:** Right **Pos:** C-7   **Ht:** 5'8" **Wt:** 177 **Born:** 4/18/73 **Age:** 24

Year Team	Lg	G	AB	H	2B	3B	HR	(Hm	Rd)	TB	R	RBI	TBB	IBB	SO	HBP	SH	SF	SB	CS	SB%	GDP	Avg	OBP	SLG
1991 Welland	A-	50	181	46	3	2	0	—	—	53	21	15	5	0	27	1	0	0	4	3	.57	5	.254	.278	.293
1992 Augusta	A	94	314	80	14	3	1	—	—	103	39	29	25	1	37	1	4	2	2	4	.33	5	.255	.310	.328
1993 Salem	A+	70	238	61	12	1	3	—	—	84	20	24	13	1	27	0	0	1	1	4	.20	5	.256	.294	.353
Buffalo	AAA	3	9	3	0	0	0	—	—	3	1	2	0	0	0	0	0	0	0	0	.00	0	.333	.333	.333
1994 Carolina	AA	67	227	66	17	0	3	—	—	92	26	32	11	1	28	2	0	4	2	2	.50	4	.291	.324	.405
1995 Calgary	AAA	21	80	20	3	0	1	—	—	26	8	6	1	1	12	0	0	0	1	0	1.00	2	.250	.259	.325
1996 Calgary	AAA	75	263	84	18	0	4	—	—	114	38	31	10	2	19	3	0	2	6	2	.75	10	.319	.344	.433
1995 Pittsburgh	NL	58	159	36	7	2	2	(2	0)	53	18	10	13	5	28	0	3	0	1	1	.50	3	.226	.285	.333
1996 Pittsburgh	NL	7	22	7	2	0	0	(0	0)	9	3	1	0	0	5	0	0	0	0	0	.00	0	.318	.318	.409
2 ML YEARS		65	181	43	9	2	2	(2	0)	62	21	11	13	5	33	0	3	0	1	1	.50	3	.238	.289	.343

John Ericks

Pitches: Right **Bats:** Right **Pos:** RP-24; SP-4   **Ht:** 6'7" **Wt:** 251 **Born:** 9/16/67 **Age:** 29

Year Team	Lg	G	GS	CG	GF	IP	BFP	H	R	ER	HR	SH	SF	HB	TBB	IBB	SO	WP	Bk	W	L	Pct.	ShO	Sv-Op	Hld	ERA
1988 Johnson Cty	R+	9	9	1	0	41	174	27	20	17	1	1	2	0	27	0	41	5	4	3	2	.600	0	0--	—	3.73
1989 Savannah	A	28	28	1	0	167.1	695	90	59	38	4	4	5	9	101	0	211	11	2	11	10	.524	0	0--	—	2.04
1990 St. Pete	A+	4	4	0	0	23	88	16	5	4	0	0	1	0	6	0	25	1	1	2	1	.667	0	0--	—	1.57
Arkansas	AA	4	4	1	0	15.1	83	17	19	16	2	0	2	1	19	0	19	3	1	1	2	.333	1	0--	—	9.39
1991 Arkansas	AA	25	25	1	0	139.2	630	138	94	74	6	5	4	7	84	3	103	15	3	5	14	.263	0	0--	—	4.77
1992 Arkansas	AA	13	13	1	0	75	316	69	36	34	4	4	3	3	29	1	71	6	0	2	6	.250	0	0--	—	4.08
1994 Salem	A+	17	5	0	0	52.1	219	42	22	18	4	1	2	3	20	0	71	3	0	4	2	.667	0	1--	—	3.10
Carolina	AA	11	11	0	0	57	234	42	22	17	2	2	1	3	19	0	64	5	0	2	4	.333	0	0--	—	2.68
1995 Calgary	AAA	5	5	0	0	29	116	20	8	8	2	1	0	0	13	0	25	3	0	2	1	.667	0	0--	—	2.48
1996 Calgary	AAA	14	4	0	5	30	131	31	15	14	3	1	2	1	15	1	40	2	1	1	2	.333	0	1--	—	4.20
1995 Pittsburgh	NL	19	18	1	0	106	472	108	59	54	7	5	5	2	50	4	80	11	1	3	9	.250	0	0-0	0	4.58
1996 Pittsburgh	NL	28	4	0	13	46.2	213	56	35	30	11	1	1	0	19	2	46	2	0	4	5	.444	0	8-10	1	5.79
2 ML YEARS		47	22	1	13	152.2	685	164	94	84	18	6	6	2	69	6	126	13	1	7	14	.333	0	8-10	1	4.95

Scott Erickson

Pitches: Right **Bats:** Right **Pos:** SP-34   **Ht:** 6'4" **Wt:** 230 **Born:** 2/2/68 **Age:** 29

		HOW MUCH HE PITCHED						WHAT HE GAVE UP										THE RESULTS					
Year Team	Lg	G	GS	CG	GF	IP	BFP	H	R	ER	HR	SH	SF	HB	TBB	IBB	SO	WP	Bk	W	L	Pct.	ShO	Sv-Op	Hld	ERA
1990 Minnesota	AL	19	17	1	1	113	485	108	49	36	9	5	2	5	51	4	53	3	0	8	4	.667	0	0-0	0	2.87
1991 Minnesota	AL	32	32	5	0	204	851	189	80	72	13	5	7	6	71	3	108	4	0	20	8	.714	3	0-0	0	3.18
1992 Minnesota	AL	32	32	5	0	212	888	197	86	80	18	9	7	8	83	3	101	6	1	13	12	.520	3	0-0	0	3.40
1993 Minnesota	AL	34	34	1	0	218.2	976	266	138	126	17	10	13	10	71	1	116	5	0	8	19	.296	0	0-0	0	5.19
1994 Minnesota	AL	23	23	2	0	144	654	173	95	87	15	3	4	9	59	0	104	10	0	8	11	.421	1	0-0	0	5.44
1995 Min-Bal	AL	32	31	7	1	196.1	836	213	108	105	18	3	3	5	67	0	106	3	2	13	10	.565	2	0-0	0	4.81
1996 Baltimore	AL	34	34	6	0	222.1	968	262	137	124	21	5	5	11	66	4	100	1	0	13	12	.520	0	0-0	0	5.02
1995 Minnesota	AL	15	15	0	0	87.2	390	102	61	58	11	2	1	4	32	0	45	1	0	4	6	.400	0	0-0	0	5.95
Baltimore	AL	17	16	7	1	108.2	446	111	47	47	7	1	2	1	35	0	61	2	2	9	4	.692	2	0-0	0	3.89
7 ML YEARS		206	203	27	2	1310.1	5658	1408	693	630	111	40	41	54	468	15	688	32	3	83	76	.522	9	0-0	0	4.33

Darin Erstad

Bats: L **Throws:** L **Pos:** CF-36; LF-11; PH-10; RF-1   **Ht:** 6'2" **Wt:** 210 **Born:** 6/4/74 **Age:** 23

		BATTING																BASERUNNING				PERCENTAGES		
Year Team	Lg	G	AB	H	2B	3B	HR	(Hm	Rd)	TB	R	RBI	TBB	IBB	SO	HBP	SH	SF	SB	CS	SB%	GDP	Avg	OBP	SLG
1995 Angels	R	4	18	10	1	0	0	—	—	11	2	1	1	0	1	0	0	0	1	0	1.00	0	.556	.579	.611
Lk Elsinore	A+	25	113	41	7	3	5	—	—	69	24	24	6	0	22	0	0	1	3	0	1.00	2	.363	.392	.611
1996 Vancouver	AAA	85	351	107	22	5	6	—	—	157	63	41	44	4	53	3	1	2	11	6	.65	5	.305	.385	.447
1996 California	AL	57	208	59	5	1	4	(1	3)	78	34	20	17	1	29	0	1	1	3	3	.50	3	.284	.333	.375

Vaughn Eshelman

Pitches: Left **Bats:** Left **Pos:** RP-29; SP-10   **Ht:** 6'3" **Wt:** 210 **Born:** 5/22/69 **Age:** 28

		HOW MUCH HE PITCHED						WHAT HE GAVE UP										THE RESULTS					
Year Team	Lg	G	GS	CG	GF	IP	BFP	H	R	ER	HR	SH	SF	HB	TBB	IBB	SO	WP	Bk	W	L	Pct.	ShO	Sv-Op	Hld	ERA
1991 Bluefield	R+	3	3	0	0	14	59	10	4	1	1	0	1	0	9	0	15	1	0	1	0	1.000	0	0- –	–	0.64
Kane County	A	11	11	2	0	77.2	319	57	23	20	3	3	1	3	35	0	90	2	2	5	3	.625	1	0- –	–	2.32
1993 Frederick	A+	24	24	2	0	143.1	608	128	70	62	10	4	3	7	59	0	122	7	1	7	10	.412	1	0- –	–	3.89
1994 Bowie	AA	27	25	2	0	166.1	713	175	81	74	13	7	3	3	60	1	133	6	0	11	9	.550	2	0- –	–	4.00
1995 Trenton	AA	2	2	0	0	7	25	3	1	0	0	0	0	1	0	0	7	0	0	0	1	.000	0	0- –	–	0.00
1996 Pawtucket	AAA	7	7	1	0	43.2	190	40	21	21	6	3	0	3	19	1	28	1	0	1	2	.333	0	0- –	–	4.33
1995 Boston	AL	23	14	0	4	81.2	356	86	47	44	3	0	3	1	36	0	41	4	0	6	3	.667	0	0-0	1	4.85
1996 Boston	AL	39	10	0	1	87.2	428	112	79	69	13	3	5	2	58	4	59	4	0	6	3	.667	0	0-0	8	7.08
2 ML YEARS		62	24	0	5	169.1	784	198	126	113	16	3	8	3	94	4	100	8	0	12	6	.667	0	0-0	9	6.01

Alvaro Espinoza

Bats: R **Throws:** R **Pos:** 3B-58; SS-23; 1B-19; 2B-7; PH-7; DH-1   **Ht:** 6'0" **Wt:** 190 **Born:** 2/19/62 **Age:** 35

		BATTING																BASERUNNING				PERCENTAGES		
Year Team	Lg	G	AB	H	2B	3B	HR	(Hm	Rd)	TB	R	RBI	TBB	IBB	SO	HBP	SH	SF	SB	CS	SB%	GDP	Avg	OBP	SLG
1984 Minnesota	AL	1	0	0	0	0	0	(0	0)	0	0	0	0	0	0	0	0	0	0	0	.00	0	.000	.000	.000
1985 Minnesota	AL	32	57	15	2	0	0	(0	0)	17	5	9	1	0	9	1	3	0	0	1	.00	2	.263	.288	.298
1986 Minnesota	AL	37	42	9	1	0	0	(0	0)	10	4	1	1	0	10	0	2	0	0	1	.00	0	.214	.233	.238
1988 New York	AL	3	3	0	0	0	0	(0	0)	0	0	0	0	0	0	0	0	0	0	0	.00	0	.000	.000	.000
1989 New York	AL	146	503	142	23	1	0	(0	0)	167	51	41	14	1	60	1	23	3	3	3	.50	14	.282	.301	.332
1990 New York	AL	150	438	98	12	2	2	(0	2)	120	31	20	16	0	54	5	11	2	1	2	.33	13	.224	.258	.274
1991 New York	AL	148	480	123	23	2	5	(0	5)	165	51	33	16	0	57	2	9	2	4	1	.80	10	.256	.282	.344
1993 Cleveland	AL	129	263	73	15	0	4	(3	1)	100	34	27	8	0	36	1	8	3	2	2	.50	7	.278	.298	.380
1994 Cleveland	AL	90	231	55	13	0	1	(1	0)	71	27	19	6	0	33	1	4	2	1	3	.25	7	.238	.258	.307
1995 Cleveland	AL	66	143	36	4	0	2	(0	2)	46	15	17	2	0	16	1	2	2	0	2	.00	5	.252	.264	.322
1996 Cle-NYN		107	246	66	11	4	8	(3	5)	109	31	27	10	0	37	3	8	2	1	3	.25	8	.268	.303	.443
1996 Cleveland	AL	59	112	25	4	2	4	(1	3)	45	12	11	6	0	18	3	3	1	1	1	.50	4	.223	.279	.402
New York	NL	48	134	41	7	2	4	(2	2)	64	19	16	4	0	19	0	5	1	0	2	.00	4	.306	.324	.478
11 ML YEARS		909	2406	617	104	9	22	(9	13)	805	249	194	74	1	312	15	70	16	12	18	.40	64	.256	.281	.335

Bobby Estalella

Bats: Right **Throws:** Right **Pos:** C-4; PH-3   **Ht:** 6'1" **Wt:** 195 **Born:** 8/23/74 **Age:** 22

		BATTING																BASERUNNING				PERCENTAGES		
Year Team	Lg	G	AB	H	2B	3B	HR	(Hm	Rd)	TB	R	RBI	TBB	IBB	SO	HBP	SH	SF	SB	CS	SB%	GDP	Avg	OBP	SLG
1993 Martinsvlle	R+	35	122	36	11	0	3	—	—	56	14	19	14	2	24	2	0	0	0	1	.00	6	.295	.377	.459
Clearwater	A+	11	35	8	0	0	0	—	—	8	4	4	2	0	3	0	0	0	0	0	.00	1	.229	.270	.229
1994 Spartanburg	A	86	299	65	19	1	9	—	—	113	34	41	31	0	85	1	1	4	0	0	.00	5	.217	.290	.378
Clearwater	A+	13	46	12	1	0	2	—	—	19	3	9	3	0	17	0	2	1	0	0	.00	1	.261	.300	.413
1995 Clearwater	A+	117	404	105	24	1	15	—	—	176	61	58	56	2	76	2	3	4	0	3	.00	12	.260	.350	.436
Reading	AA	10	34	8	1	0	2	—	—	15	5	9	1	1	7	1	0	0	0	0	.00	1	.235	.333	.441
1996 Reading	AA	111	365	89	14	2	23	—	—	176	48	72	67	5	104	5	1	4	2	4	.33	7	.244	.365	.482
Scranton-WB	AAA	11	36	9	3	0	3	—	—	21	7	8	5	0	10	0	0	0	0	0	.00	1	.250	.341	.583
1996 Philadelphia	NL	7	17	6	0	0	2	(0	2)	12	5	4	1	0	6	0	0	0	1	0	1.00	0	.353	.389	.706

Shawn Estes

Pitches: Left **Bats:** Right **Pos:** SP-11   **Ht:** 6'2" **Wt:** 185 **Born:** 2/18/73 **Age:** 24

		HOW MUCH HE PITCHED					WHAT HE GAVE UP												THE RESULTS					
Year Team	Lg	G	GS	CG	GF	IP	BFP	H	R	ER	HR	SH	SF	HB	TBB	IBB	SO	WP	Bk	W	L	Pct.	ShO	Sv-Op	Hld	ERA
1991 Bellingham	A-	9	9	0	0	34	185	27	33	26	2	2	3	1	55	0	35	6	10	1	3	.250	0	0--	—	6.88
1992 Bellingham	A-	15	15	0	0	77	354	84	55	37	6	2	2	3	45	0	77	10	3	3	3	.500	0	0--	—	4.32
1993 Appleton	A	19	18	0	0	83.1	418	108	85	67	3	1	3	7	52	1	65	19	2	5	9	.357	0	0--	—	7.24
1994 Mariners	R	5	5	0	0	20	86	16	9	7	0	1	0	1	6	0	31	7	0	0	3	.000	0	0--	—	3.15
Appleton	A	5	4	0	1	19.2	92	19	13	10	1	2	1	2	17	0	28	4	0	0	2	.000	0	0--	—	4.58
1995 Wisconsin	A	2	2	0	0	10	38	5	1	1	0	0	1	0	5	0	11	2	1	0	0	.000	0	0--	—	0.90
Burlington	A	6	6	0	0	25.1	110	18	9	8	2	0	1	2	17	0	33	4	1	0	0	.000	0	0--	—	2.84
Shreveport	AA	4	4	0	0	22.1	90	14	5	5	1	0	1	3	10	0	18	3	0	2	0	1.000	0	0--	—	2.01
San Jose	A+	19	18	0	0	97.1	391	64	27	25	4	0	5	6	44	0	112	14	1	7	2	.778	0	0--	—	2.31
1996 Phoenix	AAA	18	18	0	0	110.1	446	92	43	42	7	2	0	2	38	1	95	4	0	9	3	.750	0	0--	—	3.43
1995 San Francisco	NL	3	3	0	0	17.1	76	16	14	13	2	0	1	0	5	0	14	4	0	0	3	.000	0	0-0	—	6.75
1996 San Francisco	NL	11	11	0	0	70	305	63	30	28	3	5	0	2	39	3	60	4	0	3	5	.375	0	0-0	—	3.60
2 ML YEARS		14	14	0	0	87.1	381	79	44	41	5	5	0	3	44	3	74	8	0	3	8	.273	0	0-0	—	4.23

Tony Eusebio

Bats: Right **Throws:** Right **Pos:** C-48; PH-15   **Ht:** 6'2" **Wt:** 210 **Born:** 4/27/67 **Age:** 30

		BATTING																	BASERUNNING				PERCENTAGES		
Year Team	Lg	G	AB	H	2B	3B	HR	(Hm	Rd)	TB	R	RBI	TBB	IBB	SO	HBP	SH	SF	SB	CS	SB%	GDP	Avg	OBP	SLG
1996 Tucson *	AAA	15	53	22	4	0	0	—	—	26	8	14	2	1	7	0	0	0	0	0	.00	0	.415	.436	.491
1991 Houston	NL	10	19	2	1	0	0	(0	0)	3	4	0	6	0	8	0	0	0	0	0	.00	1	.105	.320	.158
1994 Houston	NL	55	159	47	9	1	5	(1	4)	73	18	30	8	0	33	0	2	5	0	1	.00	4	.296	.320	.459
1995 Houston	NL	113	368	110	21	1	6	(5	1)	151	46	58	31	1	59	3	1	5	0	2	.00	12	.299	.354	.410
1996 Houston	NL	58	152	41	7	2	1	(1	0)	55	15	19	18	2	20	0	0	0	0	1	.00	5	.270	.343	.362
4 ML YEARS		236	698	200	38	4	12	(7	5)	282	83	107	63	3	120	3	3	12	0	4	.00	22	.287	.343	.404

Carl Everett

Bats: B **Throws:** R **Pos:** PH-54; RF-37; CF-15; LF-8   **Ht:** 6'0" **Wt:** 190 **Born:** 6/3/71 **Age:** 26

		BATTING																	BASERUNNING				PERCENTAGES		
Year Team	Lg	G	AB	H	2B	3B	HR	(Hm	Rd)	TB	R	RBI	TBB	IBB	SO	HBP	SH	SF	SB	CS	SB%	GDP	Avg	OBP	SLG
1993 Florida	NL	11	19	2	0	0	0	(0	0)	2	0	0	1	0	9	0	0	0	1	0	1.00	0	.105	.150	.105
1994 Florida	NL	16	51	11	1	0	2	(2	0)	18	7	6	3	0	15	0	0	0	4	0	1.00	0	.216	.259	.353
1995 New York	NL	79	289	75	13	1	12	(9	3)	126	48	54	39	2	67	2	1	0	2	5	.29	11	.260	.352	.436
1996 New York	NL	101	192	46	8	1	1	(1	0)	59	29	16	21	2	53	4	1	1	6	0	1.00	4	.240	.326	.307
4 ML YEARS		207	551	134	22	2	15	(12	3)	205	84	76	64	4	144	6	2	1	13	5	.72	15	.243	.328	.372

Jorge Fabregas

Bats: Left **Throws:** Right **Pos:** C-89; DH-1; PH-1   **Ht:** 6'3" **Wt:** 214 **Born:** 3/13/70 **Age:** 27

		BATTING																	BASERUNNING				PERCENTAGES		
Year Team	Lg	G	AB	H	2B	3B	HR	(Hm	Rd)	TB	R	RBI	TBB	IBB	SO	HBP	SH	SF	SB	CS	SB%	GDP	Avg	OBP	SLG
1996 Vancouver *	AAA	10	37	11	3	0	0	—	—	14	4	5	4	1	4	1	1	0	0	0	.00	1	.297	.381	.378
1994 California	AL	43	127	36	3	0	0	(0	0)	39	12	16	7	1	18	0	1	0	2	1	.67	5	.283	.321	.307
1995 California	AL	73	227	56	10	0	1	(0	0)	69	24	22	17	0	28	0	3	1	0	2	.00	9	.247	.298	.304
1996 California	AL	90	254	73	6	0	2	(1	1)	85	18	26	17	3	27	0	3	5	0	1	.00	7	.287	.326	.335
3 ML YEARS		206	608	165	19	0	3	(2	1)	193	54	64	41	4	73	0	7	6	2	4	.33	21	.271	.315	.317

Rikkert Faneyte

Bats: Right **Throws:** Right **Pos:** CF-4; DH-2; LF-2; PH-2   **Ht:** 6'1" **Wt:** 170 **Born:** 5/31/69 **Age:** 28

		BATTING																	BASERUNNING				PERCENTAGES		
Year Team	Lg	G	AB	H	2B	3B	HR	(Hm	Rd)	TB	R	RBI	TBB	IBB	SO	HBP	SH	SF	SB	CS	SB%	GDP	Avg	OBP	SLG
1996 Okla. City *	AAA	93	364	86	15	0	11	—	—	134	53	44	34	1	65	5	5	5	14	9	.61	7	.236	.306	.368
1993 San Francisco	NL	7	15	2	0	0	0	(0	0)	2	2	0	2	0	4	0	0	0	0	0	.00	0	.133	.235	.133
1994 San Francisco	NL	19	26	3	3	0	0	(0	0)	6	1	4	3	0	11	0	0	0	0	0	.00	1	.115	.207	.231
1995 San Francisco	NL	46	86	17	4	1	0	(0	0)	23	7	4	11	0	27	0	1	0	1	0	1.00	2	.198	.289	.267
1996 Texas	AL	8	5	1	0	0	0	(0	0)	1	0	1	0	0	0	0	0	3	0	0	.00	0	.200	.200	.200
4 ML YEARS		80	132	23	7	1	0	(0	0)	32	10	9	16	0	42	0	1	3	1	0	1.00	3	.174	.264	.242

Mike Farmer

Pitches: Left **Bats:** Right **Pos:** SP-4; RP-3   **Ht:** 6'1" **Wt:** 193 **Born:** 7/3/68 **Age:** 28

		HOW MUCH HE PITCHED						WHAT HE GAVE UP												THE RESULTS					
Year Team	Lg	G	GS	CG	GF	IP	BFP	H	R	ER	HR	SH	SF	HB	TBB	IBB	SO	WP	Bk	W	L	Pct.	ShO	Sv-Op	Hld	ERA
1992 Clearwater	A+	11	9	1	2	53	209	33	16	11	1	1	1	1	13	1	41	2	5	3	3	.500	1	0--	—	1.87
1993 Reading	AA	22	18	0	3	102	455	125	62	57	18	5	5	1	34	2	64	8	4	5	10	.333	0	0--	—	5.03
1994 Central Val	A+	14	3	0	4	28.2	125	28	17	15	4	1	1	3	11	1	28	4	1	1	4	.200	0	1--	—	4.71
New Haven	AA	10	0	0	4	14	54	7	2	1	1	1	0	0	5	0	13	0	0	0	0	.000	0	2--	—	1.29

		HOW MUCH HE PITCHED						WHAT HE GAVE UP												THE RESULTS						
Year Team	Lg	G	GS	CG	GF	IP	BFP	H	R	ER	HR	SH	SF	HB	TBB	IBB	SO	WP	Bk	W	L	Pct.	ShO	Sv-Op	Hld	ERA
1995 New Haven	AA	40	12	0	7	110.1	475	117	63	60	8	6	2	5	35	4	77	5	3	10	5	.667	0	0--	—	4.89
1996 Colo. Sprng	AAA	9	9	2	0	57.1	245	51	27	21	4	2	3	2	25	2	28	2	0	3	3	.500	1	0--	—	3.30
1996 Colorado	NL	7	4	0	1	28	127	32	25	24	8	2	0	0	13	0	16	1	0	0	1	.000	0	0-0	0	7.71

John Farrell

Pitches: Right **Bats:** Right **Pos:** SP-2 **Ht:** 6'4" **Wt:** 210 **Born:** 8/4/62 **Age:** 34

		HOW MUCH HE PITCHED						WHAT HE GAVE UP												THE RESULTS						
Year Team	Lg	G	GS	CG	GF	IP	BFP	H	R	ER	HR	SH	SF	HB	TBB	IBB	SO	WP	Bk	W	L	Pct.	ShO	Sv-Op	Hld	ERA
1996 Buffalo *	AAA	4	4	0	0	27	106	20	11	11	2	0	1	2	7	0	14	0	0	3	0	1.000	0	0--	—	3.67
Toledo *	AAA	6	6	1	0	30	135	38	29	27	8	1	1	3	9	0	21	2	0	2	4	.333	0	0--	—	8.10
1987 Cleveland	AL	10	9	1	1	69	297	68	29	26	7	3	1	5	22	1	28	1	1	5	1	.833	0	0-0	0	3.39
1988 Cleveland	AL	31	30	4	0	210.1	895	216	106	99	15	9	6	9	67	3	92	2	3	14	10	.583	0	0-0	0	4.24
1989 Cleveland	AL	31	31	7	0	208	895	196	97	84	14	8	6	7	71	4	132	4	0	9	14	.391	2	0-0	0	3.63
1990 Cleveland	AL	17	17	1	0	96.2	418	108	49	46	10	5	2	1	33	1	44	1	0	4	5	.444	0	0-0	0	4.28
1993 California	AL	21	17	0	1	90.2	420	110	74	74	22	2	2	7	44	3	45	3	0	3	12	.200	0	0-0	0	7.35
1994 California	AL	3	3	0	0	13	61	16	14	13	2	0	0	1	8	0	10	0	0	1	2	.333	0	0-0	0	9.00
1995 Cleveland	AL	1	0	0	0	4.2	21	7	4	2	0	1	1	0	0	0	4	0	0	0	0	.000	0	0-0	0	3.86
1996 Detroit	AL	2	2	0	0	6.1	33	11	10	10	2	0	0	1	5	0	0	1	0	0	2	.000	0	0-0	0	14.21
8 ML YEARS		116	109	13	2	698.2	3040	732	383	354	72	28	18	31	250	12	355	12	4	36	46	.439	2	0-0	0	4.56

Sal Fasano

Bats: Right **Throws:** Right **Pos:** C-51 **Ht:** 6'2" **Wt:** 220 **Born:** 8/10/71 **Age:** 25

		BATTING																	BASERUNNING				PERCENTAGES		
Year Team	Lg	G	AB	H	2B	3B	HR	(Hm	Rd)	TB	R	RBI	TBB	IBB	SO	HBP	SH	SF	SB	CS	SB%	GDP	Avg	OBP	SLG
1993 Eugene	A-	49	176	47	11	1	10	—	—	90	25	36	19	2	49	6	0	2	4	3	.57	1	.267	.355	.511
1994 Rockford	A	97	345	97	16	1	25	—	—	190	61	81	33	4	66	16	0	5	8	3	.73	10	.281	.366	.551
Wilmington	A+	23	90	29	7	0	7	—	—	57	15	32	13	0	24	0	0	0	0	0	.00	3	.322	.408	.633
1995 Wilmington	A+	23	88	20	2	1	2	—	—	30	12	7	5	0	16	1	0	0	0	0	.00	4	.227	.277	.341
Wichita	AA	87	317	92	18	2	20	—	—	174	60	66	27	1	61	16	0	2	3	6	.33	8	.290	.373	.549
1996 Omaha	AAA	29	104	24	4	0	4	—	—	40	12	15	6	0	21	1	0	1	0	1	.00	3	.231	.277	.385
1996 Kansas City	AL	51	143	29	2	0	6	(1	5)	49	20	19	14	0	25	2	1	0	1	1	.50	3	.203	.283	.343

Jeff Fassero

Pitches: Left **Bats:** Left **Pos:** SP-34 **Ht:** 6'1" **Wt:** 195 **Born:** 1/5/63 **Age:** 34

		HOW MUCH HE PITCHED						WHAT HE GAVE UP												THE RESULTS						
Year Team	Lg	G	GS	CG	GF	IP	BFP	H	R	ER	HR	SH	SF	HB	TBB	IBB	SO	WP	Bk	W	L	Pct.	ShO	Sv-Op	Hld	ERA
1991 Montreal	NL	51	0	0	30	55.1	223	39	17	15	1	6	0	1	17	1	42	4	0	2	5	.286	0	8-11	7	2.44
1992 Montreal	NL	70	0	0	22	85.2	368	81	35	27	1	5	2	2	34	6	63	7	1	8	7	.533	0	1-7	12	2.84
1993 Montreal	NL	56	15	1	10	149.2	616	119	50	38	7	7	4	0	54	0	140	5	0	12	5	.706	0	1-3	6	2.29
1994 Montreal	NL	21	21	1	0	138.2	569	119	54	46	13	7	2	1	40	4	119	6	0	8	6	.571	0	0-0	0	2.99
1995 Montreal	NL	30	30	1	0	189	833	207	102	91	15	**19**	7	2	74	3	164	7	1	13	14	.481	0	0-0	0	4.33
1996 Montreal	NL	34	34	5	0	231.2	967	217	95	85	20	16	5	3	55	3	222	5	2	15	11	.577	1	0-0	0	3.30
6 ML YEARS		262	100	8	62	850	3576	782	353	302	57	60	20	9	274	17	750	34	4	58	48	.547	1	10-21	25	3.20

Felix Fermin

Bats: Right **Throws:** Right **Pos:** 2B-6; PH-6; SS-2 **Ht:** 5'11" **Wt:** 170 **Born:** 10/9/63 **Age:** 33

		BATTING																	BASERUNNING				PERCENTAGES		
Year Team	Lg	G	AB	H	2B	3B	HR	(Hm	Rd)	TB	R	RBI	TBB	IBB	SO	HBP	SH	SF	SB	CS	SB%	GDP	Avg	OBP	SLG
1996 Columbus *	AAA	7	19	4	0	0	0	—	—	4	3	3	3	0	1	2	0	1	0	0	.00	1	.211	.360	.211
Iowa *	AAA	39	119	34	4	1	0	—	—	40	8	8	3	0	7	0	1	0	1	0	1.00	5	.286	.303	.336
1987 Pittsburgh	NL	23	68	17	0	0	0	(0	0)	17	6	4	4	1	9	1	2	0	0	0	.00	3	.250	.301	.250
1988 Pittsburgh	NL	43	87	24	0	2	0	(0	0)	28	9	2	8	1	10	3	1	1	3	1	.75	3	.276	.354	.322
1989 Cleveland	AL	156	484	115	9	1	0	(0	0)	126	50	21	41	0	27	4	**32**	1	6	4	.60	15	.238	.302	.260
1990 Cleveland	AL	148	414	106	13	2	1	(1	0)	126	47	40	26	0	22	0	13	5	3	3	.50	13	.256	.297	.304
1991 Cleveland	AL	129	424	111	13	2	0	(0	0)	128	30	31	26	0	27	3	13	3	5	4	.56	17	.262	.307	.302
1992 Cleveland	AL	79	215	58	7	2	0	(0	0)	69	27	13	18	1	10	1	9	2	0	0	.00	7	.270	.326	.321
1993 Cleveland	AL	140	480	126	16	2	2	(0	2)	152	48	45	24	1	14	4	5	1	4	5	.44	12	.263	.303	.317
1994 Seattle	AL	101	379	120	21	0	1	(0	1)	144	52	35	11	0	22	4	12	5	4	4	.50	9	.317	.338	.380
1995 Seattle	AL	73	200	39	6	0	0	(0	0)	45	21	15	6	0	6	4	8	1	2	0	1.00	7	.195	.232	.225
1996 Chicago	NL	11	16	2	1	0	0	(0	0)	3	4	1	2	0	0	0	1	0	0	0	.00	2	.125	.222	.188
10 ML YEARS		903	2767	718	86	11	4	(1	3)	838	294	207	166	4	147	24	96	19	27	21	.56	88	.259	.305	.303

Alex Fernandez

Pitches: Right **Bats:** Right **Pos:** SP-35 **Ht:** 6'1" **Wt:** 215 **Born:** 8/13/69 **Age:** 27

		HOW MUCH HE PITCHED						WHAT HE GAVE UP												THE RESULTS						
Year Team	Lg	G	GS	CG	GF	IP	BFP	H	R	ER	HR	SH	SF	HB	TBB	IBB	SO	WP	Bk	W	L	Pct.	ShO	Sv-Op	Hld	ERA
1990 Chicago	AL	13	13	3	0	87.2	378	89	40	37	6	5	0	3	34	0	61	1	0	5	5	.500	0	0-0	0	3.80

		HOW MUCH HE PITCHED						WHAT HE GAVE UP										THE RESULTS					
Year Team	Lg	G	GS	CG	GF	IP	BFP	H	R	ER	HR	SH	SF	HB	TBB	IBB	SO	WP	Bk	W	L	Pct.	ShO	Sv-Op	Hld	ERA
1991 Chicago	AL	34	32	2	1	191.2	827	186	100	96	16	7	11	2	88	2	145	4	1	9	13	.409	0	0-0	1	4.51
1992 Chicago	AL	29	29	4	0	187.2	804	199	100	89	21	6	4	8	50	3	95	3	0	8	11	.421	2	0-0	0	4.27
1993 Chicago	AL	34	34	3	0	247.1	1004	221	95	86	27	9	3	6	67	5	169	8	0	18	9	.667	1	0-0	0	3.13
1994 Chicago	AL	24	24	4	0	170.1	712	163	83	73	25	4	6	1	50	4	122	3	1	11	7	.611	3	0-0	0	3.86
1995 Chicago	AL	30	30	5	0	203.2	858	200	98	86	19	4	6	0	65	7	159	3	0	12	8	.600	2	0-0	0	3.80
1996 Chicago	AL	35	35	6	0	258	1071	248	110	99	34	5	7	7	72	4	200	5	0	16	10	.615	1	0-0	1	3.45
7 ML YEARS		199	197	27	1	1346.1	5654	1306	626	566	148	40	37	27	426	25	951	27	2	79	63	.556	9	0-0	1	3.78

Osvaldo Fernandez

Pitches: Right **Bats:** Right **Pos:** SP-28; RP-2   **Ht:** 6'2" **Wt:** 190 **Born:** 11/4/68 **Age:** 28

		HOW MUCH HE PITCHED						WHAT HE GAVE UP										THE RESULTS					
Year Team	Lg	G	GS	CG	GF	IP	BFP	H	R	ER	HR	SH	SF	HB	TBB	IBB	SO	WP	Bk	W	L	Pct.	ShO	Sv-Op	Hld	ERA
1996 San Francisco	NL	30	28	2	1	171.2	760	193	95	88	20	12	5	10	57	4	106	6	2	7	13	.350	0	0-0	0	4.61

Sid Fernandez

Pitches: Left **Bats:** Left **Pos:** SP-11   **Ht:** 6'1" **Wt:** 230 **Born:** 10/12/62 **Age:** 34

		HOW MUCH HE PITCHED						WHAT HE GAVE UP										THE RESULTS					
Year Team	Lg	G	GS	CG	GF	IP	BFP	H	R	ER	HR	SH	SF	HB	TBB	IBB	SO	WP	Bk	W	L	Pct.	ShO	Sv-Op	Hld	ERA
1996 Clearwater *	A+	1	1	0	0	3	9	0	0	0	0	0	0	0	0	0	5	0	0	0	0	.000	0	0--	—	0.00
1983 Los Angeles	NL	2	1	0	0	6	33	7	4	4	0	0	0	1	7	0	9	0	0	0	1	.000	0	0--	—	6.00
1984 New York	NL	15	15	0	0	90	371	74	40	35	8	5	5	0	34	3	62	1	4	6	6	.500	0	0--	—	3.50
1985 New York	NL	26	26	3	0	170.1	685	108	56	53	14	4	3	2	80	3	180	3	2	9	9	.500	0	0--	—	2.80
1986 New York	NL	32	31	2	1	204.1	855	161	82	80	13	9	7	2	91	1	200	6	0	16	6	.727	1	1--	—	3.52
1987 New York	NL	28	27	3	0	156	665	130	75	66	16	3	6	8	67	8	134	2	0	12	8	.600	1	0-0	0	3.81
1988 New York	NL	31	31	1	0	187	751	127	69	63	15	2	7	6	70	1	189	4	0	12	10	.545	1	0-0	0	3.03
1989 New York	NL	35	32	6	0	219.1	883	157	73	69	21	4	4	6	75	3	198	1	3	14	5	.737	2	0-0	1	2.83
1990 New York	NL	30	30	2	0	179.1	735	130	79	69	18	7	6	5	67	4	181	1	0	9	14	.391	1	0-0	0	3.46
1991 New York	NL	8	8	0	0	44	177	36	18	14	4	5	1	0	9	0	31	0	0	1	3	.250	0	0-0	0	2.86
1992 New York	NL	32	32	5	0	214.2	865	162	67	65	12	12	11	4	67	4	193	0	0	14	11	.560	2	0-0	0	2.73
1993 New York	NL	18	18	1	0	119.2	469	82	42	39	17	3	1	3	36	0	81	2	0	5	6	.455	1	0-0	0	2.93
1994 Baltimore	AL	19	19	2	0	115.1	494	109	66	66	27	4	3	2	46	2	95	1	0	6	6	.500	0	0-0	0	5.15
1995 Bal-Phi		19	18	0	1	92.2	400	84	51	47	20	2	1	1	38	2	110	0	1	6	5	.545	0	0-0	0	4.56
1996 Philadelphia	NL	11	11	0	0	63	264	50	25	24	5	2	2	1	26	2	77	1	0	3	6	.333	0	0-0	0	3.43
1995 Baltimore	AL	8	7	0	1	28	137	36	26	23	9	1	1	0	17	2	31	0	1	0	4	.000	0	0-0	0	7.39
Philadelphia	NL	11	11	0	0	64.2	263	48	25	24	11	1	0	1	21	0	79	0	1	6	1	.857	0	0-0	0	3.34
14 ML YEARS		306	299	25	2	1861.2	7647	1417	747	694	190	62	57	41	713	33	1740	22	19	113	96	.541	9	1--	—	3.36

Tony Fernandez

Bats: Both **Throws:** Right **Pos:** SS/2B   **Ht:** 6'2" **Wt:** 175 **Born:** 6/30/62 **Age:** 35

		BATTING																BASERUNNING				PERCENTAGES		
Year Team	Lg	G	AB	H	2B	3B	HR	(Hm	Rd)	TB	R	RBI	TBB	IBB	SO	HBP	SH	SF	SB	CS	SB%	GDP	Avg	OBP	SLG
1983 Toronto	AL	15	34	9	1	1	0	(0	0)	12	5	2	2	0	2	1	1	0	0	1	.00	1	.265	.324	.353
1984 Toronto	AL	88	233	63	5	3	3	(1	2)	83	29	19	17	0	15	0	2	2	5	7	.42	3	.270	.317	.356
1985 Toronto	AL	161	564	163	31	10	2	(1	1)	220	71	51	43	2	41	2	7	2	13	6	.68	12	.289	.340	.390
1986 Toronto	AL	163	687	213	33	9	10	(4	6)	294	91	65	27	0	52	4	5	4	25	12	.68	8	.310	.338	.428
1987 Toronto	AL	146	578	186	29	8	5	(1	4)	246	90	67	51	3	48	5	4	4	32	12	.73	14	.322	.379	.426
1988 Toronto	AL	154	648	186	41	4	5	(2	3)	250	76	70	45	3	65	4	3	4	15	5	.75	9	.287	.335	.386
1989 Toronto	AL	140	573	147	25	9	11	(2	9)	223	64	64	29	1	51	3	2	10	22	6	.79	9	.257	.291	.389
1990 Toronto	AL	161	635	175	27	17	4	(2	2)	248	84	66	71	4	70	7	2	6	26	13	.67	17	.276	.352	.391
1991 San Diego	NL	145	558	152	27	5	4	(3	1)	201	81	38	55	0	74	0	7	1	23	9	.72	12	.272	.337	.360
1992 San Diego	NL	155	622	171	32	4	4	(3	1)	223	84	37	56	4	62	4	9	3	20	20	.50	6	.275	.337	.359
1993 NYN-Tor		142	526	147	23	11	5	(1	4)	207	65	64	56	3	45	1	8	3	21	10	.68	16	.279	.348	.394
1994 Cincinnati	NL	104	366	102	18	6	8	(3	5)	156	50	50	44	8	40	5	4	3	12	7	.63	5	.279	.361	.426
1995 New York	AL	108	384	94	20	2	5	(3	2)	133	57	45	42	4	40	4	3	5	6	6	.50	14	.245	.322	.346
1993 New York	NL	48	173	39	5	2	1	(0	1)	51	20	14	25	0	19	1	3	2	6	2	.75	3	.225	.323	.295
Toronto		94	353	108	18	9	4	(1	3)	156	45	50	31	3	26	0	5	1	15	8	.65	13	.306	.361	.442
13 ML YEARS		1682	6408	1808	312	89	66	(25	41)	2496	847	638	538	32	605	40	57	47	220	114	.66	126	.282	.339	.390

Mike Fetters

Pitches: Right **Bats:** Right **Pos:** RP-61   **Ht:** 6'4" **Wt:** 224 **Born:** 12/19/64 **Age:** 32

		HOW MUCH HE PITCHED						WHAT HE GAVE UP										THE RESULTS					
Year Team	Lg	G	GS	CG	GF	IP	BFP	H	R	ER	HR	SH	SF	HB	TBB	IBB	SO	WP	Bk	W	L	Pct.	ShO	Sv-Op	Hld	ERA
1989 California	AL	1	0	0	0	3.1	16	5	4	3	1	0	0	0	1	0	4	2	0	0	0	.000	0	0-0	0	8.10
1990 California	AL	26	2	0	10	67.2	291	77	33	31	9	1	0	2	20	0	35	3	0	1	1	.500	0	1-1	1	4.12
1991 California	AL	19	4	0	8	44.2	206	53	29	24	4	1	0	3	28	2	24	4	0	2	5	.286	0	0-1	0	4.84
1992 Milwaukee	AL	50	0	0	11	62.2	243	38	15	13	3	5	2	7	24	2	43	4	1	5	1	.833	0	2-5	8	1.87
1993 Milwaukee	AL	45	0	0	14	59.1	246	59	29	22	4	5	5	2	22	4	23	0	0	3	3	.500	0	0-0	8	3.34
1994 Milwaukee	AL	42	0	0	31	46	202	41	16	13	0	2	3	1	27	5	31	3	1	1	4	.200	0	17-20	1	2.54
1995 Milwaukee	AL	40	0	0	34	34.2	163	40	16	13	3	2	1	0	20	4	33	5	0	0	3	.000	0	22-27	2	3.38

		HOW MUCH HE PITCHED			WHAT HE GAVE UP		THE RESULTS	
Year Team	Lg	G GS CG GF	IP	BFP	H R ER HR SH SF HB	TBB IBB SO WP Bk	W L Pct. ShO Sv-Op Hld	ERA
1996 Milwaukee	AL	61 0 0 55	61.1	268	65 28 23 4 0 4 1	26 4 53 5 0	3 3 .500 0 32-38 1	3.38
8 ML YEARS		284 6 0 163	379.2	1635	378 170 142 28 16 15 16	168 21 246 26 2	15 20 .429 0 74-92 23	3.37

Cecil Fielder

Bats: Right **Throws:** Right **Pos:** 1B-80; DH-79; PH-1   **Ht:** 6'3" **Wt:** 250 **Born:** 9/21/63 **Age:** 33

		BATTING																BASERUNNING				PERCENTAGES		
Year Team	Lg	G	AB	H	2B	3B	HR	(Hm	Rd)	TB	R	RBI	TBB	IBB	SO	HBP	SH	SF	SB	CS	SB%	GDP	Avg	OBP	SLG
1985 Toronto	AL	30	74	23	4	0	4	(2	2)	39	6	16	6	0	16	0	0	1	0	0	.00	2	.311	.358	.527
1986 Toronto	AL	34	83	13	2	0	4	(0	4)	27	7	13	6	0	27	1	0	0	0	0	.00	3	.157	.222	.325
1987 Toronto	AL	82	175	47	7	1	14	(10	4)	98	30	32	20	2	48	1	0	1	0	1	.00	6	.269	.345	.560
1988 Toronto	AL	74	174	40	6	1	9	(6	3)	75	24	23	14	0	53	1	0	1	0	1	.00	6	.230	.289	.431
1990 Detroit	AL	159	573	159	25	1	51	(25	26)	339	104	132	90	11	182	5	0	5	0	1	.00	15	.277	.377	.592
1991 Detroit	AL	162	624	163	25	0	44	(27	17)	320	102	133	78	12	151	6	0	4	0	0	.00	17	.261	.347	.513
1992 Detroit	AL	155	594	145	22	0	35	(18	17)	272	80	124	73	8	151	2	0	7	0	0	.00	14	.244	.325	.458
1993 Detroit	AL	154	573	153	23	0	30	(20	10)	266	80	117	90	15	125	4	0	5	0	1	.00	22	.267	.368	.464
1994 Detroit	AL	109	425	110	16	2	28	(12	16)	214	67	90	50	4	110	2	0	4	0	0	.00	17	.259	.337	.504
1995 Detroit	AL	136	494	120	18	1	31	(16	15)	233	70	82	75	8	116	5	0	5	0	1	.00	17	.243	.346	.472
1996 Det-NYA	AL	160	591	149	20	0	39	(18	21)	286	85	117	87	12	139	5	0	5	2	0	1.00	18	.252	.350	.484
1996 Detroit	AL	107	391	97	12	0	26	(9	17)	187	55	80	63	8	91	3	0	3	2	0	1.00	11	.248	.354	.478
New York	AL	53	200	52	8	0	13	(9	4)	99	30	37	24	4	48	2	0	2	0	0	.00	7	.260	.342	.495
11 ML YEARS		1255	4380	1122	168	6	289	(154	135)	2169	655	879	589	72	1118	32	0	37	2	5	.29	137	.256	.346	.495

Chuck Finley

Pitches: Left **Bats:** Left **Pos:** SP-35   **Ht:** 6'6" **Wt:** 214 **Born:** 11/26/62 **Age:** 34

		HOW MUCH HE PITCHED			WHAT HE GAVE UP			THE RESULTS		
Year Team	Lg	G GS CG GF	IP	BFP	H R ER HR SH SF HB	TBB IBB SO WP Bk	W L Pct. ShO	Sv-Op	Hld	ERA
1986 California	AL	25 0 0 7	46.1	198	40 17 17 2 4 0 1	23 1 37 2 0	3 1 .750 0	0--	—	3.30
1987 California	AL	35 3 0 17	90.2	405	102 54 47 7 2 2 3	43 3 63 4 3	2 7 .222 0	0-2	0	4.67
1988 California	AL	31 31 2 0	194.1	831	191 95 90 15 7 10 6	82 7 111 5 8	9 15 .375 0	0-0	0	4.17
1989 California	AL	29 29 9 0	199.2	827	171 64 57 13 7 3 2	82 0 156 4 2	16 9 .640 1	0-0	0	2.57
1990 California	AL	32 32 7 0	236	962	210 77 63 17 12 3 2	81 3 177 9 0	18 9 .667 2	0-0	0	2.40
1991 California	AL	34 34 4 0	227.1	955	205 102 96 23 4 3 8	101 1 171 6 3	18 9 .667 2	0-0	0	3.80
1992 California	AL	31 31 4 0	204.1	885	212 99 90 24 10 10 3	98 2 124 6 0	7 12 .368 1	0-0	0	3.96
1993 California	AL	35 35 13 0	251.1	1065	243 108 88 22 11 7 6	82 1 187 8 1	16 14 .533 2	0-0	0	3.15
1994 California	AL	25 25 7 0	183.1	774	178 95 88 21 9 6 3	71 0 148 10 0	10 10 .500 2	0-0	0	4.32
1995 California	AL	32 32 2 0	203	880	192 106 95 20 4 5 7	93 1 195 13 1	15 12 .556 1	0-0	0	4.21
1996 California	AL	35 35 4 0	238	1037	241 124 110 27 7 9 11	94 5 215 17 2	15 16 .484 1	0-0	0	4.16
11 ML YEARS		344 287 52 24	2074.1	8819	1985 941 841 191 77 58 52	850 24 1584 84 20	129 114 .531 12	0--	—	3.65

Steve Finley

Bats: Left **Throws:** Left **Pos:** CF-160; PH-3   **Ht:** 6'2" **Wt:** 180 **Born:** 3/12/65 **Age:** 32

		BATTING																	BASERUNNING				PERCENTAGES		
Year Team	Lg	G	AB	H	2B	3B	HR	(Hm	Rd)	TB	R	RBI	TBB	IBB	SO	HBP	SH	SF	SB	CS	SB%	GDP	Avg	OBP	SLG
1989 Baltimore	AL	81	217	54	5	2	2	(0	2)	69	35	25	15	1	30	1	6	2	17	3	.85	3	.249	.298	.318
1990 Baltimore	AL	142	464	119	16	4	3	(1	2)	152	46	37	32	3	53	2	10	5	22	9	.71	8	.256	.304	.328
1991 Houston	NL	159	596	170	28	10	8	(0	8)	242	84	54	42	5	65	2	10	6	34	18	.65	8	.285	.331	.406
1992 Houston	NL	162	607	177	29	13	5	(5	0)	247	84	55	58	6	63	3	16	2	44	9	.83	10	.292	.355	.407
1993 Houston	NL	142	545	145	15	13	8	(1	7)	210	69	44	28	1	65	3	6	3	19	6	.76	8	.266	.304	.385
1994 Houston	NL	94	373	103	16	5	11	(4	7)	162	64	33	28	0	52	1	4	3	13	7	.65	3	.276	.329	.434
1995 San Diego	NL	139	562	167	23	8	10	(4	6)	236	104	44	59	5	62	3	4	2	36	12	.75	8	.297	.366	.420
1996 San Diego	NL	161	655	195	45	9	30	(15	15)	348	126	95	56	5	88	4	1	5	22	8	.73	20	.298	.354	.531
8 ML YEARS		1080	4019	1130	177	64	77	(30	47)	1666	612	387	318	26	478	20	66	26	207	72	.74	68	.281	.335	.415

John Flaherty

Bats: Right **Throws:** Right **Pos:** C-118; PH-5   **Ht:** 6'1" **Wt:** 200 **Born:** 10/21/67 **Age:** 29

		BATTING																	BASERUNNING				PERCENTAGES		
Year Team	Lg	G	AB	H	2B	3B	HR	(Hm	Rd)	TB	R	RBI	TBB	IBB	SO	HBP	SH	SF	SB	CS	SB%	GDP	Avg	OBP	SLG
1992 Boston	AL	35	66	13	2	0	0	(0	0)	15	3	2	3	0	7	0	1	1	0	0	.00	0	.197	.229	.227
1993 Boston	AL	13	25	3	2	0	0	(0	0)	5	3	2	2	0	6	1	1	1	0	0	.00	0	.120	.214	.200
1994 Detroit	AL	34	40	6	1	0	0	(0	0)	7	2	4	1	0	11	0	2	1	0	1	.00	1	.150	.167	.175
1995 Detroit	AL	112	354	86	22	1	11	(6	5)	143	39	40	18	0	47	3	8	2	0	0	.00	8	.243	.284	.404
1996 Det-SD		119	416	118	24	0	13	(8	5)	181	40	64	17	2	61	3	4	4	3	3	.50	13	.284	.314	.435
1996 Detroit	AL	47	152	38	12	0	4	(2	2)	62	18	23	8	1	25	1	3	1	1	0	1.00	5	.250	.290	.408
San Diego	NL	72	264	80	12	0	9	(6	3)	119	22	41	9	1	36	2	1	3	2	3	.40	8	.303	.327	.451
5 ML YEARS		313	901	226	51	1	24	(14	10)	351	87	112	41	2	132	7	16	8	3	4	.43	22	.251	.286	.390

Huck Flener

Pitches: Left **Bats:** Both **Pos:** SP-11; RP-4   **Ht:** 5'11" **Wt:** 175 **Born:** 2/25/69 **Age:** 28

		HOW MUCH HE PITCHED					WHAT HE GAVE UP								THE RESULTS					
Year Team	Lg	G	GS	CG	GF	IP	BFP	H	R	ER	HR	SH	SF	HB	TBB	IBB	SO	WP	Bk	W	L	Pct.	ShO	Sv-Op	Hld	ERA
1996 Syracuse *	AAA	14	14	0	0	86.2	350	73	27	22	3	3	3	3	23	1	62	2	3	7	3	.700	0	0- -		2.28
1993 Toronto	AL	6	0	0	1	6.2	30	7	3	3	0	0	0	0	4	1	2	1	0	0	0	.000	0	0-0	2	4.05
1996 Toronto	AL	15	11	0	0	70.2	309	68	40	36	9	0	4	1	33	1	44	1	0	3	2	.600	0	0-0		4.58
2 ML YEARS		21	11	0	1	77.1	339	75	43	39	9	0	4	1	37	2	46	2	0	3	2	.600	0	0-0	2	4.54

Darrin Fletcher

Bats: Left **Throws:** Right **Pos:** C-112; PH-22   **Ht:** 6'1" **Wt:** 200 **Born:** 10/3/66 **Age:** 30

		BATTING															BASERUNNING				PERCENTAGES		
Year Team	Lg	G	AB	H	2B	3B	HR	(Hm | Rd)	TB	R	RBI	TBB	IBB	SO	HBP	SH	SF	SB	CS	SB%	GDP	Avg	OBP	SLG
1989 Los Angeles	NL	5	8	4	0	0	1	(1 | 0)	7	1	2	1	0	0	0	0	0	0	0	.00	0	.500	.556	.875
1990 LA-Phi	NL	11	23	3	1	0	0	(0 | 0)	4	3	1	1	0	6	0	0	0	0	0	.00	0	.130	.167	.174
1991 Philadelphia	NL	46	136	31	8	0	1	(1 | 0)	42	5	12	5	0	15	0	1	0	0	1	.00	2	.228	.255	.309
1992 Montreal	NL	83	222	54	10	2	2	(0 | 2)	74	13	26	14	3	28	2	2	4	0	2	.00	8	.243	.289	.333
1993 Montreal	NL	133	396	101	20	1	9	(5 | 4)	150	33	60	34	2	40	6	5	4	0	0	.00	7	.255	.320	.379
1994 Montreal	NL	94	285	74	18	1	10	(4 | 6)	124	28	57	25	4	23	3	0	12	0	0	.00	6	.260	.314	.435
1995 Montreal	NL	110	350	100	21	1	11	(3 | 8)	156	42	45	32	1	23	4	1	2	0	1	.00	15	.286	.351	.446
1996 Montreal	NL	127	394	105	22	0	12	(7 | 5)	163	41	57	27	4	42	6	1	3	0	0	.00	13	.266	.321	.414
1990 Los Angeles	NL	2	1	0	0	0	0	(0 | 0)	0	0	0	0	0	1	0	0	0	0	0	.00	0	.000	.000	.000
Philadelphia	NL	9	22	3	1	0	0	(0 | 0)	4	3	1	1	0	5	0	0	0	0	0	.00	0	.136	.174	.182
8 ML YEARS		609	1814	472	100	5	46	(21 | 25)	720	166	260	139	14	177	21	10	25	0	4	.00	51	.260	.316	.397

Paul Fletcher

Pitches: Right **Bats:** Right **Pos:** RP-1   **Ht:** 6'1" **Wt:** 193 **Born:** 1/14/67 **Age:** 30

		HOW MUCH HE PITCHED						WHAT HE GAVE UP										THE RESULTS						
Year Team	Lg	G	GS	CG	GF	IP	BFP	H	R	ER	HR	SH	SF	HB	TBB	IBB	SO	WP	Bk	W	L	Pct.	ShO	Sv-Op	Hld	ERA
1988 Martinsville	R+	15	14	1	1	69.1	320	81	44	36	4	1	3	4	33	0	61	3	1	1	3	.250	0	1- -	—	4.67
1989 Batavia	A-	14	14	3	0	82.1	339	77	41	30	13	2	2	3	28	0	58	3	1	7	5	.583	0	0- -	—	3.28
1990 Spartanburg	A	9	9	1	0	49.1	207	46	24	18	3	1	1	2	18	0	53	7	1	2	4	.333	0	0- -	—	3.28
Clearwater	A+	20	18	2	1	117.1	498	104	56	44	3	6	6	13	49	0	106	7	2	5	8	.385	0	1- -	—	3.38
1991 Clearwater	A+	14	4	0	5	29.1	119	22	6	4	1	1	2	0	8	1	27	2	0	0	1	.000	0	1- -	—	1.23
Reading	AA	21	19	3	1	120.2	517	111	56	47	12	3	1	5	56	3	90	6	1	7	9	.438	1	0- -	—	3.51
1992 Reading	AA	22	20	2	0	127	521	103	45	40	10	1	1	5	47	2	103	4	1	9	4	.692	1	0- -	—	2.83
Scranton-WB	AAA	4	4	0	0	22.2	85	17	8	7	1	0	0	1	2	0	26	2	0	3	0	1.000	0	0- -	—	2.78
1993 Scranton-WB	AAA	34	19	2	5	140	625	146	99	88	21	4	4	9	60	3	116	21	0	4	12	.250	1	1- -	—	5.66
1994 Scranton-WB	AAA	42	13	0	7	138.1	604	144	78	72	12	4	1	6	54	0	92	6	0	4	9	.308	1	3- -	—	4.68
1995 Scranton-WB	AAA	52	0	0	7	61	257	45	33	21	7	7	3	1	28	4	48	8	0	4	1	.800	0	2- -	—	3.10
1996 Edmonton	AAA	38	0	0	5	83.1	349	66	28	25	8	2	1	2	41	6	76	3	0	4	6	.400	0	1- -	—	2.70
1993 Philadelphia	NL	1	0	0	0	0.1	1	0	0	0	0	0	0	0	0	0	0	1	0	0	0	.000	0	0-0	0	0.00
1995 Philadelphia	NL	10	0	0	1	13.1	64	15	8	8	2	1	1	1	9	2	10	2	0	1	0	1.000	0	0-0	1	5.40
1996 Oakland	AL	1	0	0	0	1.1	10	6	3	3	0	0	0	1	1	0	0	0	0	0	0	.000	0	0-0	0	20.25
3 ML YEARS		12	0	0	1	15	75	21	11	11	2	1	1	2	10	2	10	3	0	1	0	1.000	0	0-0	1	6.60

Bryce Florie

Pitches: Right **Bats:** Right **Pos:** RP-54   **Ht:** 5'11" **Wt:** 190 **Born:** 5/21/70 **Age:** 27

		HOW MUCH HE PITCHED						WHAT HE GAVE UP										THE RESULTS						
Year Team	Lg	G	GS	CG	GF	IP	BFP	H	R	ER	HR	SH	SF	HB	TBB	IBB	SO	WP	Bk	W	L	Pct.	ShO	Sv-Op	Hld	ERA
1994 San Diego	NL	9	0	0	4	9.1	37	8	1	1	0	0	1	0	3	0	8	1	0	0	0	.000	0	0-0	0	0.96
1995 San Diego	NL	47	0	0	10	68.2	290	49	30	23	8	5	1	4	38	3	68	7	2	2	2	.500	0	1-4	9	3.01
1996 SD-Mil		54	0	0	16	68.1	312	65	40	36	4	1	3	6	40	5	63	6	1	2	3	.400	0	0-3	8	4.74
1996 San Diego	NL	39	0	0	11	49.1	222	45	24	22	1	0	1	6	27	3	51	3	1	2	2	.500	0	0-1	4	4.01
Milwaukee	AL	15	0	0	5	19	90	20	16	14	3	1	2	0	13	2	12	3	0	0	1	.000	0	0-2	4	6.63
3 ML YEARS		110	0	0	30	146.1	639	122	71	60	12	6	5	10	81	8	139	14	3	4	5	.444	0	1-7	17	3.69

Cliff Floyd

Bats: L **Throws:** R **Pos:** LF-69; PH-44; CF-16; RF-7; 1B-2   **Ht:** 6'4" **Wt:** 235 **Born:** 12/5/72 **Age:** 24

		BATTING															BASERUNNING				PERCENTAGES		
Year Team	Lg	G	AB	H	2B	3B	HR	(Hm | Rd)	TB	R	RBI	TBB	IBB	SO	HBP	SH	SF	SB	CS	SB%	GDP	Avg	OBP	SLG
1996 Ottawa *	AAA	20	76	23	3	1	1	—		31	7	8	7	1	20	1	0	0	2	2	.50	0	.303	.369	.408
1993 Montreal	NL	10	31	7	0	0	1	(0 | 1)	10	3	2	1	0	9	0	0	0	0	0	.00	0	.226	.226	.323
1994 Montreal	NL	100	334	94	19	4	4	(2 | 2)	133	43	41	24	0	63	3	2	3	10	3	.77	3	.281	.332	.398
1995 Montreal	NL	29	69	9	1	0	1	(1 | 0)	13	6	8	7	0	22	1	1	0	3	0	1.00	1	.130	.221	.188
1996 Montreal	NL	117	227	55	15	4	6	(3 | 3)	96	29	26	29	1	52	5	1	3	7	1	.88	3	.242	.337	.423
4 ML YEARS		256	661	165	35	8	12	(6 | 6)	252	81	77	60	1	146	9	4	6	20	4	.83	7	.250	.318	.381

Chad Fonville

Bats: B **Throws:** R **Pos:** PH-40; 2B-23; SS-20; LF-19; CF-18; 3B-2   **Ht:** 5'6" **Wt:** 155 **Born:** 3/5/71 **Age:** 26

				BATTING															BASERUNNING				PERCENTAGES		
Year Team	Lg	G	AB	H	2B	3B	HR	(Hm	Rd)	TB	R	RBI	TBB	IBB	SO	HBP	SH	SF	SB	CS	SB%	GDP	Avg	OBP	SLG
1992 Everett	A-	63	260	71	9	1	1	—	—	85	56	33	31	1	39	3	1	0	36	14	.72	2	.273	.357	.327
1993 Clinton	A	120	447	137	16	10	1	—	—	176	80	44	40	2	48	9	5	2	52	16	.76	0	.306	.373	.394
1994 San Jose	A+	68	283	87	9	6	0	—	—	108	58	26	34	0	34	4	5	0	22	8	.73	5	.307	.389	.382
1996 Albuquerque	AAA	25	96	23	1	0	0	—	—	24	17	5	8	0	13	0	4	2	7	0	1.00	0	.240	.292	.250
1995 Mon-LA	NL	102	320	89	6	1	0	(0	0)	97	43	16	23	1	42	1	6	0	20	7	.74	3	.278	.328	.303
1996 Los Angeles	NL	103	201	41	4	1	0	(0	0)	47	34	13	17	1	31	0	3	0	7	2	.78	1	.204	.266	.234
1995 Montreal	NL	14	12	4	0	0	0	(0	0)	4	2	0	0	0	3	0	0	0	0	2	.00	0	.333	.333	.333
Los Angeles	NL	88	308	85	6	1	0	(0	0)	93	41	16	23	1	39	1	6	0	20	5	.80	3	.276	.328	.302
2 ML YEARS		205	521	130	10	2	0	(0	0)	144	77	29	40	2	73	1	9	0	27	9	.75	4	.250	.304	.276

Brook Fordyce

Bats: Right **Throws:** Right **Pos:** C-4   **Ht:** 6'1" **Wt:** 185 **Born:** 5/7/70 **Age:** 27

				BATTING															BASERUNNING				PERCENTAGES		
Year Team	Lg	G	AB	H	2B	3B	HR	(Hm	Rd)	TB	R	RBI	TBB	IBB	SO	HBP	SH	SF	SB	CS	SB%	GDP	Avg	OBP	SLG
1989 Kingsport	R+	69	226	74	15	0	9	—	—	116	45	38	30	1	26	1	3	2	10	6	.63	3	.327	.405	.513
1990 Columbia	A	104	372	117	29	1	10	—	—	178	45	54	39	0	42	0	1	2	4	1	.80	18	.315	.378	.478
1991 St. Lucie	A+	115	406	97	19	3	7	—	—	143	42	55	37	2	51	4	0	6	4	5	.44	7	.239	.305	.352
1992 Binghamton	AA	118	425	118	30	0	11	—	—	181	59	61	37	1	78	4	3	6	1	2	.33	13	.278	.337	.426
1993 Norfolk	AAA	116	409	106	21	2	2	—	—	137	33	40	26	3	62	5	3	6	2	2	.50	10	.259	.307	.335
1994 Norfolk	AAA	66	229	60	13	3	3	—	—	88	26	32	19	1	26	1	2	1	1	0	1.00	9	.262	.320	.384
1995 Buffalo	AAA	58	176	44	13	0	0	—	—	57	18	9	14	0	20	2	3	0	1	0	1.00	1	.250	.313	.324
1996 Indianapols	AAA	107	374	103	20	3	16	—	—	177	48	64	25	3	56	1	1	4	2	1	.67	5	.275	.319	.473
1995 New York	NL	4	2	1	1	0	0	(0	0)	2	1	0	1	0	0	0	0	0	0	0	.00	0	.500	.667	1.000
1996 Cincinnati	NL	4	7	2	1	0	0	(0	0)	3	0	1	3	0	1	0	0	0	0	0	.00	0	.286	.500	.429
2 ML YEARS		8	9	3	2	0	0	(0	0)	5	1	1	4	0	1	0	0	0	0	0	.00	0	.333	.538	.556

Tony Fossas

Pitches: Left **Bats:** Left **Pos:** RP-65   **Ht:** 6'0" **Wt:** 198 **Born:** 9/23/57 **Age:** 39

		HOW MUCH HE PITCHED						WHAT HE GAVE UP												THE RESULTS					
Year Team	Lg	G	GS	CG	GF	IP	BFP	H	R	ER	HR	SH	SF	HB	TBB	IBB	SO	WP	Bk	W	L	Pct.	ShO	Sv-Op	Hld	ERA
1988 Texas	AL	5	0	0	1	5.2	28	11	3	3	0	0	0	0	2	0	0	1	0	0	0	.000	0	0-0	0	4.76
1989 Milwaukee	AL	51	0	0	16	61	256	57	27	24	3	7	3	1	22	7	42	1	3	2	2	.500	0	1-3	13	3.54
1990 Milwaukee	AL	32	0	0	9	29.1	146	44	23	21	5	2	1	0	10	2	24	0	0	2	3	.400	0	0-2	8	6.44
1991 Boston	AL	64	0	0	18	57	244	49	27	22	3	5	0	3	28	9	29	2	0	3	2	.600	0	1-2	18	3.47
1992 Boston	AL	60	0	0	17	29.2	129	31	9	8	1	3	0	1	14	3	19	0	0	1	2	.333	0	2-3	14	2.43
1993 Boston	AL	71	0	0	19	40	175	38	28	23	4	0	1	2	15	4	39	1	1	1	1	.500	0	0-2	13	5.18
1994 Boston	AL	44	0	0	14	34	151	35	18	18	6	2	0	1	15	1	31	1	0	2	0	1.000	0	1-1	9	4.76
1995 St. Louis	NL	58	0	0	20	36.2	145	28	6	6	1	2	1	1	10	3	40	1	0	3	0	1.000	0	0-0	19	1.47
1996 St. Louis	NL	65	0	0	11	47	209	43	19	14	7	1	1	0	21	3	36	3	0	0	4	.000	0	2-7	15	2.68
9 ML YEARS		450	0	0	125	340.1	1483	336	160	139	30	22	9	9	137	32	260	10	4	14	14	.500	0	7-20	109	3.68

Kevin Foster

Pitches: Right **Bats:** Right **Pos:** SP-16; RP-1   **Ht:** 6'1" **Wt:** 170 **Born:** 1/13/69 **Age:** 28

		HOW MUCH HE PITCHED						WHAT HE GAVE UP												THE RESULTS					
Year Team	Lg	G	GS	CG	GF	IP	BFP	H	R	ER	HR	SH	SF	HB	TBB	IBB	SO	WP	Bk	W	L	Pct.	ShO	Sv-Op	Hld	ERA
1996 Iowa *	AAA	18	18	3	0	115	484	106	56	55	23	2	2	0	46	2	87	6	1	7	6	.538	1	0- --	—	4.30
1993 Philadelphia	NL	2	1	0	0	6.2	40	13	11	11	3	0	0	0	7	0	6	2	0	0	1	.000	0	0-0	0	14.85
1994 Chicago	NL	13	13	0	0	81	337	70	31	26	7	1	1	1	35	1	75	1	1	3	4	.429	0	0-0	0	2.89
1995 Chicago	NL	30	28	0	1	167.2	703	149	90	84	32	4	6	6	65	4	146	2	2	12	11	.522	0	0-0	0	4.51
1996 Chicago	NL	17	16	1	0	87	386	98	63	60	16	5	4	2	35	3	53	2	0	7	6	.538	0	0-0	0	6.21
4 ML YEARS		62	58	1	1	342.1	1466	330	195	181	58	10	11	9	142	8	280	7	3	22	22	.500	0	0-0	0	4.76

Andy Fox

Bats: L **Throws:** R **Pos:** 2B-72; 3B-31; PH-28; SS-9; DH-3; RF-1   **Ht:** 6'4" **Wt:** 205 **Born:** 1/12/71 **Age:** 26

				BATTING															BASERUNNING				PERCENTAGES		
Year Team	Lg	G	AB	H	2B	3B	HR	(Hm	Rd)	TB	R	RBI	TBB	IBB	SO	HBP	SH	SF	SB	CS	SB%	GDP	Avg	OBP	SLG
1989 Yankees	R	40	141	35	9	2	3	—	—	57	26	25	31	1	29	2	0	2	6	1	.86	1	.248	.386	.404
1990 Greensboro	A	134	455	99	19	4	9	—	—	153	68	55	92	5	132	4	1	7	26	5	.84	14	.218	.353	.336
1991 Pr. William	A+	126	417	96	22	2	10	—	—	152	60	46	81	3	104	6	1	9	15	13	.54	7	.230	.357	.365
1992 Pr. William	A+	125	473	113	18	3	7	—	—	158	75	42	54	1	81	6	4	0	28	14	.67	7	.239	.325	.334
1993 Albany-Colo	AA	65	236	65	16	1	3	—	—	92	44	24	32	1	54	0	2	2	12	6	.67	1	.275	.362	.390
1994 Albany-Colo	AA	121	472	105	20	3	11	—	—	164	75	43	62	3	102	2	4	1	22	13	.63	4	.222	.315	.347
1995 Norwich	AA	44	175	36	3	5	5	—	—	64	23	17	19	0	36	0	1	1	8	1	.89	3	.206	.282	.366
Columbus	AAA	82	302	105	16	6	9	—	—	160	61	37	43	4	41	4	2	3	22	4	.85	5	.348	.432	.530
1996 New York	AL	113	189	37	4	0	3	(1	2)	50	26	13	20	0	28	1	9	0	11	3	.79	2	.196	.276	.265

John Franco

Pitches: Left   **Bats:** Left   **Pos:** RP-51   **Ht:** 5'10"   **Wt:** 185   **Born:** 9/17/60   **Age:** 36

Year Team	Lg	G	GS	CG	GF	IP	BFP	H	R	ER	HR	SH	SF	HB	TBB	IBB	SO	WP	Bk	W	L	Pct.	ShO	Sv-Op	Hld	ERA
1984 Cincinnati	NL	54	0	0	30	79.1	335	74	28	23	3	4	4	2	36	4	55	2	0	6	2	.750	0	4- --	—	2.61
1985 Cincinnati	NL	67	0	0	33	99	407	83	27	24	5	11	1	1	40	8	61	4	0	12	3	.800	0	12- --	—	2.18
1986 Cincinnati	NL	74	0	0	52	101	429	90	40	33	7	8	3	2	44	12	84	4	2	6	6	.500	0	29- --	—	2.94
1987 Cincinnati	NL	68	0	0	60	82	344	76	26	23	6	5	2	0	27	6	61	1	0	8	5	.615	0	32-41	0	2.52
1988 Cincinnati	NL	70	0	0	61	86	336	60	18	15	3	5	1	0	27	3	46	1	2	6	6	.500	0	39-42	1	1.57
1989 Cincinnati	NL	60	0	0	50	80.2	345	77	35	28	3	7	3	0	36	8	60	3	2	4	8	.333	0	32-39	1	3.12
1990 New York	NL	55	0	0	48	67.2	287	66	22	19	4	3	1	0	21	2	56	7	2	5	3	.625	0	33-39	0	2.53
1991 New York	NL	52	0	0	48	55.1	247	61	27	18	2	3	0	1	18	4	45	6	0	5	9	.357	0	30-35	0	2.93
1992 New York	NL	31	0	0	30	33	128	24	6	6	1	0	2	0	11	2	20	0	0	6	2	.750	0	15-17	1	1.64
1993 New York	NL	35	0	0	30	36.1	172	46	24	21	6	4	1	1	19	3	29	5	0	4	3	.571	0	10-17	0	5.20
1994 New York	NL	47	0	0	43	50	216	47	20	15	5	2	2	1	19	0	42	1	0	1	4	.200	0	30-36	0	2.70
1995 New York	NL	48	0	0	41	51.2	213	48	17	14	4	4	1	0	17	2	41	0	0	5	3	.625	0	29-36	0	2.44
1996 New York	NL	51	0	0	44	54	235	54	15	11	2	6	0	0	21	0	48	2	0	4	3	.571	0	28-36	0	1.83
13 ML YEARS		712	0	0	570	876	3694	806	305	250	48	62	20	8	336	54	648	36	8	72	57	.558	0	323- --	—	2.57

Julio Franco

Bats: Right   **Throws:** Right   **Pos:** 1B-97; DH-13; PH-3   **Ht:** 6'1"   **Wt:** 190   **Born:** 8/23/61   **Age:** 35

Year Team	Lg	G	AB	H	2B	3B	HR	(Hm	Rd)	TB	R	RBI	TBB	IBB	SO	HBP	SH	SF	SB	CS	SB%	GDP	Avg	OBP	SLG
1982 Philadelphia	NL	16	29	8	1	0	0	(0	0)	9	3	3	2	1	4	0	1	0	0	2	.00	1	.276	.323	.310
1983 Cleveland	AL	149	560	153	24	8	8	(6	2)	217	68	80	27	1	50	2	3	6	32	12	.73	21	.273	.306	.388
1984 Cleveland	AL	160	658	188	22	5	3	(1	2)	229	82	79	43	1	68	6	1	10	19	10	.66	23	.286	.331	.348
1985 Cleveland	AL	160	636	183	33	4	6	(3	3)	242	97	90	54	2	74	4	0	9	13	9	.59	26	.288	.343	.381
1986 Cleveland	AL	149	599	183	30	5	10	(4	6)	253	80	74	32	1	66	0	0	5	10	7	.59	28	.306	.338	.422
1987 Cleveland	AL	128	495	158	24	3	8	(5	3)	212	86	52	57	2	56	3	0	5	32	9	.78	23	.319	.389	.428
1988 Cleveland	AL	152	613	186	23	6	10	(3	7)	251	88	54	56	4	72	2	1	4	25	11	.69	17	.303	.361	.409
1989 Texas	AL	150	548	173	31	5	13	(9	4)	253	80	92	66	11	69	1	0	6	21	3	.88	27	.316	.386	.462
1990 Texas	AL	157	582	172	27	1	11	(4	7)	234	96	69	82	3	83	2	2	2	31	10	.76	12	.296	.383	.402
1991 Texas	AL	146	589	201	27	3	15	(7	8)	279	108	78	65	8	78	3	0	2	36	9	.80	13	.341	.408	.474
1992 Texas	AL	35	107	25	7	0	2	(2	0)	38	19	8	15	2	17	0	1	0	1	1	.50	3	.234	.328	.355
1993 Texas	AL	144	532	154	31	3	14	(6	8)	233	85	84	62	4	95	1	5	7	9	3	.75	16	.289	.360	.438
1994 Chicago	AL	112	433	138	19	2	20	(10	10)	221	72	98	62	4	75	5	0	5	8	1	.89	14	.319	.406	.510
1996 Cleveland	AL	112	432	139	20	1	14	(7	7)	203	72	76	61	2	82	3	0	3	8	8	.50	14	.322	.407	.470
14 ML YEARS		1770	6813	2061	319	46	134	(67	67)	2874	1036	937	684	46	889	32	14	64	245	95	.72	238	.303	.366	.422

Matt Franco

Bats: Left   **Throws:** Right   **Pos:** 3B-8; PH-6; 1B-2   **Ht:** 6'2"   **Wt:** 200   **Born:** 8/19/69   **Age:** 27

Year Team	Lg	G	AB	H	2B	3B	HR	(Hm	Rd)	TB	R	RBI	TBB	IBB	SO	HBP	SH	SF	SB	CS	SB%	GDP	Avg	OBP	SLG
1987 Wytheville	R+	62	202	50	10	1	1	—	—	65	25	21	26	1	41	0	0	0	4	1	.80	3	.248	.333	.322
1988 Wytheville	R+	20	79	31	9	1	0	—	—	42	14	16	7	1	5	0	0	0	0	1	.00	3	.392	.442	.532
Geneva	A-	44	164	42	2	0	3	—	—	53	19	21	19	3	13	0	0	1	2	0	1.00	7	.256	.332	.323
1989 Charlstn-WV	A	109	377	102	16	1	5	—	—	135	42	48	57	0	40	0	5	4	2	2	.50	10	.271	.363	.358
Peoria	A	16	58	13	4	0	0	—	—	17	4	9	5	0	5	1	0	1	0	1	.00	1	.224	.292	.293
1990 Peoria	A	123	443	125	33	2	6	—	—	180	52	65	43	2	39	1	1	2	4	4	.50	19	.282	.346	.406
1991 Winston-Sal	A+	104	307	66	12	1	4	—	—	92	47	40	46	2	41	2	2	6	4	1	.80	6	.215	.316	.300
1992 Charlotte	AA	108	343	97	18	3	2	—	—	127	35	31	26	1	46	1	0	3	3	3	.50	4	.283	.332	.370
1993 Orlando	AA	68	237	75	20	1	7	—	—	118	31	37	29	2	30	2	1	2	3	6	.33	2	.316	.393	.498
Iowa	AAA	62	199	58	17	4	5	—	—	98	24	29	16	3	30	1	0	3	1	1	.50	7	.291	.342	.492
1994 Iowa	AAA	128	437	121	32	4	11	—	—	194	63	71	52	5	66	2	2	5	3	3	.50	7	.277	.353	.444
1995 Iowa	AAA	121	455	128	28	5	6	—	—	184	51	58	37	5	44	0	1	6	1	1	.50	11	.281	.331	.404
1996 Norfolk	AAA	133	508	164	40	2	7	—	—	229	74	81	36	3	55	1	1	9	5	2	.71	10	.323	.365	.451
1995 Chicago	NL	16	17	5	1	0	0	(0	0)	6	3	1	0	0	4	0	0	0	0	0	.00	0	.294	.294	.353
1996 New York	NL	14	31	6	1	0	1	(0	1)	10	3	2	1	0	5	1	0	1	0	0	.00	1	.194	.235	.323
2 ML YEARS		30	48	11	2	0	1	(0	1)	16	6	3	1	0	9	1	0	1	0	0	.00	1	.229	.255	.333

Lou Frazier

Bats: B   **Throws:** R   **Pos:** PH-15; LF-12; DH-11; CF-3; 2B-1   **Ht:** 6'2"   **Wt:** 175   **Born:** 1/26/65   **Age:** 32

Year Team	Lg	G	AB	H	2B	3B	HR	(Hm	Rd)	TB	R	RBI	TBB	IBB	SO	HBP	SH	SF	SB	CS	SB%	GDP	Avg	OBP	SLG
1996 Okla. City *	AAA	58	208	51	8	3	3	—	—	74	28	16	14	2	42	1	3	1	13	4	.76	3	.245	.295	.356
1993 Montreal	NL	112	189	54	7	1	1	(1	0)	66	27	16	16	0	24	0	5	1	17	2	.89	3	.286	.340	.349
1994 Montreal	NL	76	140	38	3	1	0	(0	0)	43	25	14	18	0	23	1	4	0	20	4	.83	1	.271	.358	.307
1995 Mon-Tex		84	162	33	4	0	0	(0	0)	37	25	11	15	0	32	4	3	1	13	1	.93	3	.204	.286	.228
1996 Texas	AL	30	50	13	2	1	0	(0	0)	17	5	5	8	0	10	1	1	0	4	2	.67	2	.260	.373	.340
1995 Montreal	NL	35	63	12	2	0	0	(0	0)	14	6	3	8	0	12	2	0	1	4	1	1.00	1	.190	.297	.222
Texas	AL	49	99	21	2	0	0	(0	0)	23	19	8	7	0	20	2	3	0	9	1	.90	2	.212	.278	.232
4 ML YEARS		302	541	138	16	3	1	(1	0)	163	82	46	57	0	89	6	10	2	54	9	.86	9	.255	.332	.301

Marvin Freeman

Pitches: Right **Bats:** Right **Pos:** SP-24; RP-3   **Ht:** 6'7" **Wt:** 222 **Born:** 4/10/63 **Age:** 34

			HOW MUCH HE PITCHED					WHAT HE GAVE UP									THE RESULTS						
Year Team	Lg	G	GS	CG	GF	IP	BFP	H	R	ER	HR	SH	SF	HB	TBB	IBB	SO	WP	Bk	W	L	Pct.	ShO	Sv-Op	Hld	ERA
1986 Philadelphia	NL	3	3	0	0	16	61	6	4	4	0	0	1	0	10	0	8	1	0	2	0	1.000	0	0- -	0	2.25
1988 Philadelphia	NL	11	11	0	0	51.2	249	55	36	35	2	5	1	1	43	2	37	3	1	2	3	.400	0	0-0	0	6.10
1989 Philadelphia	NL	1	1	0	0	3	16	2	2	2	0	0	0	0	5	0	0	0	1	0	0	.000	0	0-0	0	6.00
1990 Phi-Atl	NL	25	3	0	5	48	207	41	24	23	5	2	0	5	17	2	38	4	0	1	2	.333	0	1-1	1	4.31
1991 Atlanta	NL	34	0	0	6	48	190	37	19	16	2	1	1	2	13	1	34	4	0	1	0	1.000	0	1-1	9	3.00
1992 Atlanta	NL	58	0	0	15	64.1	276	61	26	23	7	2	1	1	29	7	41	4	0	7	5	.583	0	3-6	16	3.22
1993 Atlanta	NL	21	0	0	5	23.2	103	24	16	16	1	0	0	1	10	2	25	3	0	2	0	1.000	0	0-0	0	6.08
1994 Colorado	NL	19	18	0	0	112.2	465	113	39	35	10	4	1	5	23	2	67	4	0	10	2	.833	0	0-0	0	2.80
1995 Colorado	NL	22	18	0	0	94.2	437	122	64	62	15	7	3	2	41	1	61	5	1	3	7	.300	0	0-1	0	5.89
1996 Col-ChA	NL	27	24	0	0	131.2	600	155	103	90	21	9	3	6	58	1	72	13	1	7	9	.438	0	0-1	1	6.15
1990 Philadelphia	NL	16	3	0	4	32.1	147	34	21	20	5	1	0	3	14	2	26	4	0	0	2	.000	0	1-1	1	5.57
Atlanta	NL	9	0	0	1	15.2	60	7	3	3	0	1	0	2	3	0	12	0	0	1	0	1.000	0	0-0	0	1.72
1996 Colorado	NL	26	23	0	0	129.2	588	151	100	87	21	9	3	6	57	1	71	13	1	7	9	.438	0	0-1	1	6.04
Chicago	AL	1	1	0	0	2	12	4	3	3	0	0	0	0	1	0	1	0	0	0	0	.000	0	0-0	0	13.50
10 ML YEARS		221	78	0	32	593.2	2604	616	333	306	63	30	11	23	249	18	383	41	4	35	28	.556	0	5- -	—	4.64

Steve Frey

Pitches: Left **Bats:** Left **Pos:** RP-31   **Ht:** 5'9" **Wt:** 170 **Born:** 7/29/63 **Age:** 33

			HOW MUCH HE PITCHED					WHAT HE GAVE UP									THE RESULTS						
Year Team	Lg	G	GS	CG	GF	IP	BFP	H	R	ER	HR	SH	SF	HB	TBB	IBB	SO	WP	Bk	W	L	Pct.	ShO	Sv-Op	Hld	ERA
1996 Scrnton-WB *	AAA	10	0	0	2	13.1	57	11	8	8	1	1	0	0	8	0	9	0	0	2	2	.500	0	0- -		5.40
1989 Montreal	NL	20	0	0	11	21.1	103	29	15	13	4	0	2	1	11	1	15	1	1	3	2	.600	0	0-0	1	5.48
1990 Montreal	NL	51	0	0	21	55.2	236	44	15	13	4	3	2	1	29	6	29	0	0	8	2	.800	0	9-9	5	2.10
1991 Montreal	NL	31	0	0	5	39.2	182	43	31	22	3	3	2	1	23	4	21	3	1	0	1	.000	0	1-2	4	4.99
1992 California	AL	51	0	0	20	45.1	193	39	18	18	6	2	3	2	22	3	24	1	0	4	2	.667	0	4-5	4	3.57
1993 California	AL	55	0	0	28	48.1	212	41	20	16	1	4	1	3	26	1	22	3	0	2	3	.400	0	13-16	7	2.98
1994 San Francisco	NL	44	0	0	12	31	137	37	17	17	6	1	4	2	15	3	20	1	0	1	0	1.000	0	0-3	6	4.94
1995 SF-Sea-Phi	NL	31	0	0	7	28.1	121	26	14	10	2	5	2	1	10	2	14	0	0	0	4	.000	0	1-1	4	3.18
1996 Philadelphia	NL	31	0	0	12	34.1	151	38	19	18	4	4	2	0	18	3	12	0	0	0	1	.000	0	0-0	4	4.72
1995 San Francisco	NL	9	0	0	1	6.1	29	7	6	3	1	1	1	0	2	0	5	0	0	0	0	.000	0	0-0	0	4.26
Seattle	AL	13	0	0	3	11.1	56	16	7	6	0	3	1	1	6	1	7	0	0	0	3	.000	0	0-0	2	4.76
Philadelphia	NL	9	0	0	3	10.2	36	3	1	1	1	1	0	0	2	1	2	0	0	0	1	.000	0	1-1	2	0.84
8 ML YEARS		314	0	0	116	304	1335	297	149	127	30	20	18	11	154	23	157	9	2	18	15	.545	0	28-36	35	3.76

Todd Frohwirth

Pitches: Right **Bats:** Right **Pos:** RP-4   **Ht:** 6'4" **Wt:** 205 **Born:** 9/28/62 **Age:** 34

			HOW MUCH HE PITCHED					WHAT HE GAVE UP									THE RESULTS						
Year Team	Lg	G	GS	CG	GF	IP	BFP	H	R	ER	HR	SH	SF	HB	TBB	IBB	SO	WP	Bk	W	L	Pct.	ShO	Sv-Op	Hld	ERA
1996 Vancouver *	AAA	9	0	0	8	14	55	11	5	5	1	1	2	1	3	0	13	1	0	0	1	.000	0	2- -	—	3.21
Rochester *	AAA	9	0	0	3	16	61	11	8	8	2	0	0	0	5	1	16	1	0	0	2	.000	0	0- -	—	4.50
1987 Philadelphia	NL	10	0	0	2	11	43	12	0	0	0	0	0	0	2	0	9	0	0	1	0	1.000	0	0-0	0	0.00
1988 Philadelphia	NL	12	0	0	6	12	62	16	11	11	2	1	1	0	11	6	11	1	0	1	2	.333	0	0-1	0	8.25
1989 Philadelphia	NL	45	0	0	11	62.2	258	56	26	25	4	3	1	3	18	0	39	1	1	1	0	1.000	0	0-0	6	3.59
1990 Philadelphia	NL	5	0	0	0	1	12	3	2	2	0	0	0	0	6	2	1	1	0	0	0	.000	0	0-0	1	18.00
1991 Baltimore	AL	51	0	0	10	96.1	372	64	24	20	2	4	1	1	29	3	77	1	0	7	3	.700	0	3-5	10	1.87
1992 Baltimore	AL	65	0	0	23	106	444	97	33	29	4	7	1	3	41	4	58	1	0	4	3	.571	0	4-7	15	2.46
1993 Baltimore	AL	70	0	0	30	96.1	411	91	47	41	7	7	2	3	44	8	50	1	0	6	7	.462	0	3-7	14	3.83
1994 Boston	AL	22	0	0	8	26.2	141	40	36	32	3	4	0	2	17	2	13	1	0	0	3	.000	0	1-1	2	10.80
1996 California	AL	4	0	0	2	5.2	33	10	11	7	1	0	1	1	4	0	1	0	0	0	0	.000	0	0-0	0	11.12
9 ML YEARS		284	0	0	92	417.2	1776	389	190	167	23	26	7	13	172	25	259	7	1	20	19	.513	0	11-22	48	3.60

Jeff Frye

B: R **T:** R **Pos:** 2B-100; SS-3; PH-3; LF-2; RF-2; DH-1; CF-1   **Ht:** 5'9" **Wt:** 165 **Born:** 8/31/66 **Age:** 30

					BATTING														BASERUNNING			PERCENTAGES		
Year Team	Lg	G	AB	H	2B	3B	HR	(Hm	Rd)	TB	R	RBI	TBB	IBB	SO	HBP	SH	SF	SB	CS	SB%	GDP	Avg	OBP	SLG
1996 Okla. City *	AAA	49	181	43	10	0	1			56	25	18	24	1	21	3	2	1	10	1	.91	5	.238	.335	.309
1992 Texas	AL	67	199	51	9	1	1	(0	1)	65	24	12	16	0	27	3	11	1	1	3	.25	2	.256	.320	.327
1994 Texas	AL	57	205	67	20	3	0	(0	0)	93	37	18	29	0	23	1	5	3	6	1	.86	1	.327	.408	.454
1995 Texas	AL	90	313	87	15	2	4	(2	2)	118	38	29	24	0	45	5	8	4	3	3	.50	7	.278	.335	.377
1996 Boston	AL	105	419	120	27	2	4	(3	1)	163	74	41	54	0	57	5	5	3	18	4	.82	6	.286	.372	.389
4 ML YEARS		319	1136	325	71	8	9	(5	4)	439	173	100	123	0	152	14	29	11	28	11	.72	16	.286	.360	.386

Travis Fryman

Bats: Right **Throws:** Right **Pos:** 3B-128; SS-29   **Ht:** 6'1" **Wt:** 195 **Born:** 3/25/69 **Age:** 28

					BATTING														BASERUNNING			PERCENTAGES		
Year Team	Lg	G	AB	H	2B	3B	HR	(Hm	Rd)	TB	R	RBI	TBB	IBB	SO	HBP	SH	SF	SB	CS	SB%	GDP	Avg	OBP	SLG
1990 Detroit	AL	66	232	69	11	1	9	(5	4)	109	32	27	17	0	51	1	1	0	3	3	.50	3	.297	.348	.470

73

Year Team	Lg	G	AB	H	2B	3B	HR	(Hm	Rd)	TB	R	RBI	TBB	IBB	SO	HBP	SH	SF	SB	CS	SB%	GDP	Avg	OBP	SLG
1991 Detroit	AL	149	557	144	36	3	21	(8	13)	249	65	91	40	0	149	3	6	6	12	5	.71	13	.259	.309	.447
1992 Detroit	AL	161	659	175	31	4	20	(9	11)	274	87	96	45	1	144	6	5	6	8	4	.67	13	.266	.316	.416
1993 Detroit	AL	151	607	182	37	5	22	(13	9)	295	98	97	77	1	128	4	1	6	9	4	.69	8	.300	.379	.486
1994 Detroit	AL	114	464	122	34	5	18	(10	8)	220	66	85	45	1	128	5	1	13	2	2	.50	6	.263	.326	.474
1995 Detroit	AL	144	567	156	21	5	15	(9	6)	232	79	81	63	4	100	3	0	7	4	2	.67	18	.275	.347	.409
1996 Detroit	AL	157	616	165	32	3	22	(10	12)	269	90	100	57	2	118	4	1	10	4	3	.57	18	.268	.329	.437
7 ML YEARS		942	3702	1013	202	26	127	(64	63)	1648	517	577	344	9	818	26	15	48	42	23	.65	79	.274	.336	.445

Mike Fyhrie

Pitches: Right **Bats:** Right **Pos:** RP-2 　　　　　　**Ht:** 6'2" **Wt:** 190 **Born:** 12/9/69 **Age:** 27

		HOW MUCH HE PITCHED						WHAT HE GAVE UP											THE RESULTS						
Year Team	Lg	G	GS	CG	GF	IP	BFP	H	R	ER	HR	SH	SF	HB	TBB	IBB	SO	WP	Bk	W	L	Pct.	ShO	Sv-Op	Hld	ERA
1991 Eugene	A-	21	0	0	13	39.1	176	41	17	11	0	3	0	1	19	1	45	1	2	2	1	.667	0	5- --	—	2.52
1992 Baseball Cy	A+	26	26	2	0	162	670	148	65	45	6	10	6	7	37	1	92	4	6	7	13	.350	0	0- --	—	2.50
1993 Wilmington	A+	5	5	0	0	29.1	124	32	15	12	3	0	2	0	8	0	19	1	0	3	2	.600	0	0- --	—	3.68
Memphis	AA	22	22	3	0	131.1	579	143	59	52	11	0	4	9	59	0	59	7	1	11	4	.733	0	0- --	—	3.56
1994 Omaha	AAA	18	16	0	0	85	379	100	57	54	13	2	4	6	33	1	37	0	0	6	5	.545	0	0- --	—	5.72
Memphis	AA	11	11	0	0	67	279	67	29	24	4	1	2	5	17	1	38	1	0	2	5	.286	0	0- --	—	3.22
1995 Omaha	AAA	14	11	0	2	60.2	259	71	34	30	7	0	2	4	14	0	39	0	0	3	4	.429	0	0- --	—	4.45
1996 Norfolk	AAA	27	27	2	0	169	678	150	61	57	16	2	2	5	33	1	103	8	2	15	6	.714	2	0- --	—	3.04
1996 New York	NL	2	0	0	0	2.1	14	4	4	4	0	0	0	0	3	0	1	0	0	0	1	.000	0	0-0	0	15.43

Gary Gaetti

Bats: Right **Throws:** Right **Pos:** 3B-133; 1B-14; PH-1 　　　　**Ht:** 6'0" **Wt:** 200 **Born:** 8/19/58 **Age:** 38

Year Team	Lg	G	AB	H	2B	3B	HR	(Hm	Rd)	TB	R	RBI	TBB	IBB	SO	HBP	SH	SF	SB	CS	SB%	GDP	Avg	OBP	SLG
1981 Minnesota	AL	9	26	5	0	0	2	(1	1)	11	4	3	0	0	6	0	0	0	0	0	.00	1	.192	.192	.423
1982 Minnesota	AL	145	508	117	25	4	25	(15	10)	225	59	84	37	2	107	3	4	13	0	4	.00	1	.230	.280	.443
1983 Minnesota	AL	157	584	143	30	3	21	(7	14)	242	81	78	54	2	121	4	0	8	7	1	.88	18	.245	.309	.414
1984 Minnesota	AL	162	588	154	29	4	5	(2	3)	206	55	65	44	1	81	4	3	5	11	5	.69	9	.262	.315	.350
1985 Minnesota	AL	160	560	138	31	0	20	(10	10)	229	71	63	37	3	89	7	3	1	13	5	.72	15	.246	.301	.409
1986 Minnesota	AL	157	596	171	34	1	34	(16	18)	309	91	108	52	4	108	6	1	6	14	15	.48	18	.287	.347	.518
1987 Minnesota	AL	154	584	150	36	2	31	(18	13)	283	95	109	37	7	92	3	1	3	10	7	.59	25	.257	.303	.485
1988 Minnesota	AL	133	468	141	29	2	28	(9	19)	258	66	88	36	5	85	5	1	6	7	4	.64	10	.301	.353	.551
1989 Minnesota	AL	130	498	125	11	4	19	(10	9)	201	63	75	25	5	87	3	1	9	6	2	.75	12	.251	.286	.404
1990 Minnesota	AL	154	577	132	27	5	16	(7	9)	217	61	85	36	1	101	3	1	8	6	1	.86	22	.229	.274	.376
1991 California	AL	152	586	144	22	1	18	(12	6)	222	58	66	33	3	104	8	2	5	5	5	.50	13	.246	.293	.379
1992 California	AL	130	456	103	13	2	12	(8	4)	156	41	48	21	4	79	6	0	3	3	1	.75	9	.226	.267	.342
1993 Cal-KC	AL	102	331	81	20	1	14	(6	8)	145	40	50	21	0	87	8	2	7	1	3	.25	5	.245	.300	.438
1994 Kansas City	AL	90	327	94	15	3	12	(5	7)	151	53	57	19	3	63	2	1	3	0	2	.00	9	.287	.328	.462
1995 Kansas City	AL	137	514	134	27	0	35	(16	19)	266	76	96	47	6	91	8	3	6	3	3	.50	7	.261	.329	.518
1996 St. Louis	NL	141	522	143	27	4	23	(13	10)	247	71	80	35	6	97	8	4	5	2	2	.50	10	.274	.326	.473
1993 California	AL	20	50	9	2	0	0	(0	0)	11	3	4	5	0	12	0	0	1	1	0	1.00	3	.180	.250	.220
Kansas City	AL	82	281	72	18	1	14	(6	8)	134	37	46	16	0	75	8	2	6	0	3	.00	2	.256	.309	.477
16 ML YEARS		2113	7725	1975	376	36	315	(155	160)	3368	985	1155	534	52	1398	78	27	88	88	60	.59	199	.256	.307	.436

Greg Gagne

Bats: Right **Throws:** Right **Pos:** SS-127; PH-1 　　　　**Ht:** 5'11" **Wt:** 180 **Born:** 11/12/61 **Age:** 35

Year Team	Lg	G	AB	H	2B	3B	HR	(Hm	Rd)	TB	R	RBI	TBB	IBB	SO	HBP	SH	SF	SB	CS	SB%	GDP	Avg	OBP	SLG
1996 Albuquerque *	AAA	4	11	3	1	0	0	—	—	4	1	1	1	0	1	1	0	0	0	1	.00	1	.273	.385	.364
1983 Minnesota	AL	10	27	3	1	0	0	(0	0)	4	2	3	0	0	6	0	0	2	0	0	.00	0	.111	.103	.148
1984 Minnesota	AL	2	1	0	0	0	0	(0	0)	0	0	0	0	0	0	0	0	0	0	0	.00	0	.000	.000	.000
1985 Minnesota	AL	114	293	66	15	3	2	(0	2)	93	37	23	20	0	57	3	3	3	10	4	.71	5	.225	.279	.317
1986 Minnesota	AL	156	472	118	22	6	12	(10	2)	188	63	54	30	0	108	6	13	3	12	10	.55	4	.250	.301	.398
1987 Minnesota	AL	137	437	116	28	7	10	(7	3)	188	68	40	25	0	84	4	10	2	6	6	.50	3	.265	.310	.430
1988 Minnesota	AL	149	461	109	20	6	14	(5	9)	183	70	48	27	2	110	7	11	1	15	7	.68	13	.236	.288	.397
1989 Minnesota	AL	149	460	125	29	7	9	(5	4)	195	69	48	17	0	80	2	7	5	11	4	.73	10	.272	.298	.424
1990 Minnesota	AL	138	388	91	22	3	7	(3	4)	140	38	38	24	0	76	1	8	2	8	5	.62	5	.235	.280	.361
1991 Minnesota	AL	139	408	108	23	3	8	(3	5)	161	52	42	26	0	72	3	5	5	11	9	.55	15	.265	.310	.395
1992 Minnesota	AL	146	439	108	23	0	7	(1	6)	152	53	39	19	0	83	2	12	1	6	7	.46	11	.246	.280	.346
1993 Kansas City	AL	159	540	151	32	3	10	(3	7)	219	66	57	33	1	93	0	4	4	10	12	.45	7	.280	.319	.406
1994 Kansas City	AL	107	375	97	23	3	7	(2	5)	147	39	51	27	0	79	4	7	2	10	17	.37	8	.259	.314	.392
1995 Kansas City	AL	120	430	110	25	4	6	(2	4)	161	58	49	38	2	60	2	7	5	3	5	.38	11	.256	.316	.374
1996 Los Angeles	NL	128	428	109	13	2	10	(3	7)	156	48	55	50	11	93	2	4	3	4	2	.67	6	.255	.333	.364
14 ML YEARS		1654	5159	1311	276	47	102	(44	58)	1987	663	547	336	16	1001	36	86	37	106	91	.54	98	.254	.302	.385

Andres Galarraga

Bats: Right **Throws:** Right **Pos:** 1B-159; 3B-1; PH-1   **Ht:** 6'3" **Wt:** 235 **Born:** 6/18/61 **Age:** 36

Year Team	Lg	G	AB	H	2B	3B	HR	(Hm	Rd)	TB	R	RBI	TBB	IBB	SO	HBP	SH	SF	SB	CS	SB%	GDP	Avg	OBP	SLG
1985 Montreal	NL	24	75	14	1	0	2	(0	2)	21	9	4	3	0	18	1	0	1	1	2	.33	1	.187	.228	.280
1986 Montreal	NL	105	321	87	13	0	10	(4	6)	130	39	42	30	5	79	3	1	1	6	5	.55	8	.271	.338	.405
1987 Montreal	NL	147	551	168	40	3	13	(7	6)	253	72	90	41	13	127	10	0	4	7	10	.41	11	.305	.361	.459
1988 Montreal	NL	157	609	184	42	8	29	(14	15)	329	99	92	39	9	153	10	0	3	13	4	.76	12	.302	.352	.540
1989 Montreal	NL	152	572	147	30	1	23	(13	10)	248	76	85	48	10	158	13	0	3	12	5	.71	12	.257	.327	.434
1990 Montreal	NL	155	579	148	29	0	20	(6	14)	237	65	87	40	8	169	4	0	5	10	1	.91	14	.256	.306	.409
1991 Montreal	NL	107	375	82	13	2	9	(3	6)	126	34	33	23	5	86	2	0	0	5	6	.45	6	.219	.268	.336
1992 St. Louis	NL	95	325	79	14	2	10	(4	6)	127	38	39	11	0	69	8	0	3	5	4	.56	8	.243	.282	.391
1993 Colorado	NL	120	470	174	35	4	22	(13	9)	283	71	98	24	12	73	6	0	6	2	4	.33	9	.370	.403	.602
1994 Colorado	NL	103	417	133	21	0	31	(16	15)	247	77	85	19	8	93	8	0	5	8	3	.73	10	.319	.356	.592
1995 Colorado	NL	143	554	155	29	3	31	(18	13)	283	89	106	32	6	146	13	0	5	12	2	.86	14	.280	.331	.511
1996 Colorado	NL	159	626	190	39	3	47	(32	15)	376	119	150	40	3	157	17	0	8	18	8	.69	6	.304	.357	.601
12 ML YEARS		1467	5474	1561	306	26	247	(130	117)	2660	788	911	350	79	1328	95	1	43	99	54	.65	110	.285	.336	.486

Mike Gallego

Bats: R **Throws:** R **Pos:** 2B-43; 3B-7; PH-4; SS-1   **Ht:** 5'8" **Wt:** 175 **Born:** 10/31/60 **Age:** 36

Year Team	Lg	G	AB	H	2B	3B	HR	(Hm	Rd)	TB	R	RBI	TBB	IBB	SO	HBP	SH	SF	SB	CS	SB%	GDP	Avg	OBP	SLG
1996 St. Pete *	A+	14	51	15	0	0	0	—	—	15	7	5	7	1	4	1	0	0	0	0	.00	2	.294	.390	.294
1985 Oakland	AL	76	77	16	5	1	1	(0	1)	26	13	9	12	0	14	1	2	1	1	1	.50	2	.208	.319	.338
1986 Oakland	AL	20	37	10	2	0	0	(0	0)	12	2	4	1	0	6	0	2	0	0	2	.00	0	.270	.289	.324
1987 Oakland	AL	72	124	31	6	0	2	(0	2)	43	18	14	12	0	21	1	5	1	0	1	.00	5	.250	.319	.347
1988 Oakland	AL	129	277	58	8	0	2	(2	0)	72	38	20	34	0	53	1	8	0	2	3	.40	6	.209	.298	.260
1989 Oakland	AL	133	357	90	14	2	3	(2	1)	117	45	30	35	0	43	6	8	3	7	5	.58	10	.252	.327	.328
1990 Oakland	AL	140	389	80	13	2	3	(1	2)	106	36	34	35	0	50	1	17	2	5	5	.50	13	.206	.277	.272
1991 Oakland	AL	159	482	119	15	4	12	(6	6)	178	67	49	67	3	84	5	10	3	6	9	.40	8	.247	.343	.369
1992 New York	AL	53	173	44	7	1	3	(1	2)	62	24	14	20	0	22	4	3	1	0	1	.00	5	.254	.343	.358
1993 New York	AL	119	403	114	20	1	10	(5	5)	166	63	54	50	0	65	4	3	5	3	2	.60	16	.283	.364	.412
1994 New York	AL	89	306	73	17	1	6	(2	4)	110	39	41	38	1	46	4	5	4	0	1	.00	4	.239	.327	.359
1995 Oakland	AL	43	120	28	0	0	0	(0	0)	28	11	8	9	0	24	1	2	0	0	1	.00	3	.233	.292	.233
1996 St. Louis	NL	51	143	30	2	0	0	(0	0)	32	12	4	12	1	31	1	3	0	0	0	.00	0	.210	.276	.224
12 ML YEARS		1084	2888	693	109	12	42	(19	23)	952	368	281	325	1	459	32	68	20	24	31	.44	72	.240	.322	.330

Ron Gant

Bats: Right **Throws:** Right **Pos:** LF-116; PH-6   **Ht:** 6'0" **Wt:** 200 **Born:** 3/2/65 **Age:** 32

Year Team	Lg	G	AB	H	2B	3B	HR	(Hm	Rd)	TB	R	RBI	TBB	IBB	SO	HBP	SH	SF	SB	CS	SB%	GDP	Avg	OBP	SLG
1987 Atlanta	NL	21	83	22	4	0	2	(1	1)	32	9	9	1	0	11	0	1	1	4	2	.67	3	.265	.271	.386
1988 Atlanta	NL	146	563	146	28	8	19	(7	12)	247	85	60	46	4	118	3	2	4	19	10	.66	7	.259	.317	.439
1989 Atlanta	NL	75	260	46	8	3	9	(5	4)	87	26	25	20	0	63	1	2	2	9	6	.60	0	.177	.237	.335
1990 Atlanta	NL	152	575	174	34	3	32	(18	14)	310	107	84	50	0	86	1	1	4	33	16	.67	8	.303	.357	.539
1991 Atlanta	NL	154	561	141	35	3	32	(18	14)	278	101	105	71	8	104	5	0	5	34	15	.69	6	.251	.338	.496
1992 Atlanta	NL	153	544	141	22	6	17	(10	7)	226	74	80	45	5	101	7	0	6	32	10	.76	10	.259	.321	.415
1993 Atlanta	NL	157	606	166	27	4	36	(17	19)	309	113	117	67	2	117	2	0	7	26	9	.74	14	.274	.345	.510
1995 Cincinnati	NL	119	410	113	19	4	29	(12	17)	227	79	88	74	5	108	3	1	5	23	8	.74	11	.276	.386	.554
1996 St. Louis	NL	122	419	103	14	2	30	(17	13)	211	74	82	73	5	98	3	1	4	13	4	.76	9	.246	.359	.504
9 ML YEARS		1099	4021	1052	191	33	206	(105	101)	1927	668	650	447	29	806	25	8	38	193	80	.71	68	.262	.336	.479

Rich Garces

Pitches: Right **Bats:** Right **Pos:** RP-37   **Ht:** 6'0" **Wt:** 215 **Born:** 5/18/71 **Age:** 26

Year Team		G	GS	CG	GF	IP	BFP	H	R	ER	HR	SH	SF	HB	TBB	IBB	SO	WP	Bk	W	L	Pct.	ShO	Sv-Op	Hld	ERA
1996 Pawtucket *	AAA	10	0	0	4	15.2	58	10	4	4	2	0	0	0	5	0	13	1	0	4	0	1.000	0	0--	—	2.30
1990 Minnesota	AL	5	0	0	3	5.2	24	4	2	1	0	0	0	0	4	0	1	0	0	0	0	.000	0	2-2	0	1.59
1993 Minnesota	AL	3	0	0	1	4	18	4	2	0	0	0	0	0	2	0	3	0	0	0	0	.000	0	0-0	0	0.00
1995 ChN-Fla	NL	18	0	0	7	24.1	108	25	15	12	1	1	0	0	11	2	22	0	0	0	2	.000	0	0-1	1	4.44
1996 Boston	AL	37	0	0	9	44	205	42	26	24	5	0	5	0	33	5	55	0	0	3	2	.600	0	0-2	4	4.91
1995 Chicago	NL	11	0	0	4	11	46	11	6	4	0	0	0	0	3	0	6	0	0	0	0	.000	0	0-0	0	3.27
Florida	NL	11	0	0	3	13.1	62	14	9	8	1	1	0	0	8	2	16	0	0	0	2	.000	0	0-1	1	5.40
4 ML YEARS		63	0	0	20	78	355	75	45	37	6	1	5	0	50	7	81	0	0	3	4	.429	0	2-5	5	4.27

Carlos Garcia

Bats: R **Throws:** R **Pos:** 2B-77; SS-19; 3B-14; PH-3   **Ht:** 6'1" **Wt:** 205 **Born:** 10/15/67 **Age:** 29

Year Team	Lg	G	AB	H	2B	3B	HR	(Hm	Rd)	TB	R	RBI	TBB	IBB	SO	HBP	SH	SF	SB	CS	SB%	GDP	Avg	OBP	SLG
1996 Calgary *	AAA	2	6	2	0	1	0	—	—	4	0	0	0	0	0	0	0	0	0	0	.00	0	.333	.333	.667
1990 Pittsburgh	NL	4	4	2	0	0	0	(0	0)	2	1	0	0	0	2	0	0	0	0	0	.00	0	.500	.500	.500

Year Team	Lg	G	AB	H	2B	3B	HR	(Hm	Rd)	TB	R	RBI	TBB	IBB	SO	HBP	SH	SF	SB	CS	SB%	GDP	Avg	OBP	SLG
1991 Pittsburgh	NL	12	24	6	0	2	0	(0	0)	10	2	1	1	0	8	0	0	0	0	0	.00	1	.250	.280	.417
1992 Pittsburgh	NL	22	39	8	1	0	0	(0	0)	9	4	4	0	0	9	0	1	2	0	0	.00	1	.205	.195	.231
1993 Pittsburgh	NL	141	546	147	25	5	12	(7	5)	218	77	47	31	2	67	9	6	5	18	11	.62	9	.269	.316	.399
1994 Pittsburgh	NL	98	412	114	15	2	6	(4	2)	151	49	28	16	2	67	4	1	1	18	9	.67	6	.277	.309	.367
1995 Pittsburgh	NL	104	367	108	24	2	6	(4	2)	154	41	50	25	5	55	2	5	3	8	4	.67	4	.294	.340	.420
1996 Pittsburgh	NL	101	390	111	18	4	6	(3	3)	155	66	44	23	3	58	4	3	2	16	6	.73	3	.285	.329	.397
7 ML YEARS		482	1782	496	83	15	30	(18	12)	699	240	174	96	12	266	19	16	13	60	30	.67	24	.278	.320	.392

Karim Garcia

Bats: Left **Throws:** Left **Pos:** PH-1   **Ht:** 6'0" **Wt:** 172 **Born:** 10/29/75 **Age:** 21

Year Team	Lg	G	AB	H	2B	3B	HR	(Hm	Rd)	TB	R	RBI	TBB	IBB	SO	HBP	SH	SF	SB	CS	SB%	GDP	Avg	OBP	SLG
1993 Bakersfield	A+	123	460	111	20	9	19	—	—	206	61	54	37	4	109	2	0	2	5	3	.63	5	.241	.299	.448
1994 Vero Beach	A+	121	452	120	28	10	21	—	—	231	72	84	37	4	112	1	0	6	8	3	.73	7	.265	.319	.511
1995 Albuquerque	AAA	124	474	151	26	10	20	—	—	257	88	91	38	5	102	2	2	3	12	6	.67	12	.319	.369	.542
1996 San Antonio	AA	35	129	32	6	1	5	—	—	55	21	22	9	0	38	0	0	1	1	1	.50	1	.248	.297	.426
Albuquerque	AAA	84	327	97	17	10	13	—	—	173	54	58	29	8	67	1	0	3	4	4	.60	9	.297	.353	.529
1995 Los Angeles	NL	13	20	4	0	0	0	(0	0)	4	1	0	0	0	4	0	0	0	0	0	.00	0	.200	.200	.200
1996 Los Angeles	NL	1	1	0	0	0	0	(0	0)	0	0	0	0	0	1	0	0	0	0	0	.00	0	.000	.000	.000
2 ML YEARS		14	21	4	0	0	0	(0	0)	4	1	0	0	0	5	0	0	0	0	0	.00	0	.190	.190	.190

Ramon Garcia

Pitches: Right **Bats:** Right **Pos:** RP-35; SP-2   **Ht:** 6'2" **Wt:** 200 **Born:** 12/9/69 **Age:** 27

Year Team	Lg	G	GS	CG	GF	IP	BFP	H	R	ER	HR	SH	SF	HB	TBB	IBB	SO	WP	Bk	W	L	Pct.	ShO	Sv-Op	Hld	ERA
1996 Nw Orleans *	AAA	11	5	0	2	38.1	155	31	10	8	2	2	2	2	12	0	32	0	1	2	1	.667	0	0- -	0	1.88
1991 Chicago	AL	16	15	0	0	78.1	332	79	50	47	13	3	2	2	31	2	40	0	2	4	4	.500	0	0-0	0	5.40
1996 Milwaukee	AL	37	2	0	14	75.2	326	84	58	56	17	1	5	6	21	3	40	2	1	4	4	.500	0	4-7	6	6.66
2 ML YEARS		53	17	0	14	154	658	163	108	103	30	4	7	8	52	5	80	2	3	8	8	.500	0	4-7	6	6.02

Nomar Garciaparra

Bats: R **Throws:** R **Pos:** SS-22; PH-2; DH-1; 2B-1   **Ht:** 6'0" **Wt:** 167 **Born:** 7/23/73 **Age:** 23

Year Team	Lg	G	AB	H	2B	3B	HR	(Hm	Rd)	TB	R	RBI	TBB	IBB	SO	HBP	SH	SF	SB	CS	SB%	GDP	Avg	OBP	SLG
1994 Sarasota	A+	28	105	31	8	1	1	—	—	44	20	16	10	0	6	1	3	2	5	2	.71	2	.295	.356	.419
1995 Trenton	AA	125	513	137	20	8	8	—	—	197	77	47	50	3	42	8	4	6	35	12	.74	10	.267	.338	.384
1996 Red Sox	R	5	14	4	2	1	0	—	—	8	4	5	1	1	0	1	0	0	0	0	.00	1	.286	.375	.571
Pawtucket	AAA	43	172	59	15	2	16	—	—	126	40	46	14	0	21	1	0	0	3	1	.75	6	.343	.387	.733
1996 Boston	AL	24	87	21	2	3	4	(3	1)	41	11	16	4	0	14	0	1	1	5	0	1.00	0	.241	.272	.471

Mark Gardner

Pitches: Right **Bats:** Right **Pos:** SP-28; RP-2   **Ht:** 6'1" **Wt:** 205 **Born:** 3/1/62 **Age:** 35

Year Team	Lg	G	GS	CG	GF	IP	BFP	H	R	ER	HR	SH	SF	HB	TBB	IBB	SO	WP	Bk	W	L	Pct.	ShO	Sv-Op	Hld	ERA
1996 San Jose *	A+	1	1	0	0	5.2	21	4	2	2	0	1	0	0	0	0	7	0	0	0	0	.000	0	0- -	0	3.18
1989 Montreal	NL	7	4	0	1	26.1	117	26	16	15	2	0	0	2	11	1	21	0	0	0	3	.000	0	0-0	0	5.13
1990 Montreal	NL	27	26	3	1	152.2	642	129	62	58	13	4	7	9	61	5	135	2	4	7	9	.438	3	0-0	0	3.42
1991 Montreal	NL	27	27	0	0	168.1	692	139	78	72	17	7	2	4	75	1	107	2	1	9	11	.450	0	0-0	0	3.85
1992 Montreal	NL	33	30	0	1	179.2	778	179	91	87	15	12	7	9	60	2	132	2	0	12	10	.545	0	0-0	0	4.36
1993 Kansas City	AL	17	16	0	0	91.2	387	92	65	63	17	1	7	4	36	0	54	2	0	4	6	.400	0	0-0	0	6.19
1994 Florida	NL	20	14	0	3	92.1	391	97	53	50	14	4	5	1	30	2	57	3	1	4	4	.500	0	0-0	0	4.87
1995 Florida	NL	39	11	1	7	102.1	456	109	60	51	14	7	0	5	43	5	87	3	1	5	5	.500	1	1-1	0	4.49
1996 San Francisco	NL	30	28	4	0	179.1	782	200	105	88	28	6	5	8	57	3	145	2	0	12	7	.632	0	0-0	1	4.42
8 ML YEARS		200	156	8	13	992.2	4245	971	530	484	120	41	33	42	373	19	738	16	7	53	55	.491	5	1-1	5	4.39

Webster Garrison

Bats: Right **Throws:** Right **Pos:** 2B-3; 1B-1; PH-1   **Ht:** 5'11" **Wt:** 193 **Born:** 8/24/65 **Age:** 31

Year Team	Lg	G	AB	H	2B	3B	HR	(Hm	Rd)	TB	R	RBI	TBB	IBB	SO	HBP	SH	SF	SB	CS	SB%	GDP	Avg	OBP	SLG
1984 Florence	A	129	502	120	14	0	0	—	—	134	80	33	57	0	44	1	2	2	16	7	.70	9	.239	.317	.267
1985 Kinston	A+	129	449	91	14	1	1	—	—	110	40	30	42	0	76	3	2	5	22	5	.81	6	.203	.273	.245
1986 Florence	A	105	354	85	10	0	3	—	—	104	47	40	56	3	53	2	0	3	4	7	.36	7	.240	.345	.294
Knoxville	AA	5	6	0	0	0	0	—	—	0	0	0	2	0	2	0	0	0	1	0	1.00	0	.000	.000	.000
1987 Dunedin	A+	128	477	135	14	4	0	—	—	157	70	44	57	0	53	0	0	2	27	9	.75	12	.283	.356	.329
1988 Knoxville	AA	138	534	136	24	5	0	—	—	170	61	40	53	0	74	1	2	4	42	15	.74	7	.255	.321	.318
1989 Knoxville	AA	54	203	55	6	2	4	—	—	77	38	14	33	0	38	0	4	1	18	6	.75	5	.271	.371	.379
Syracuse	AAA	50	151	43	7	1	0	—	—	52	18	9	18	1	25	2	4	0	3	2	.60	5	.285	.368	.344
1990 Syracuse	AAA	37	101	20	5	1	0	—	—	27	12	5	14	0	20	0	3	1	0	3	.00	3	.198	.293	.267

Year Team	Lg	G	AB	H	2B	3B	HR	(Hm	Rd)	TB	R	RBI	TBB	IBB	SO	HBP	SH	SF	SB	CS	SB%	GDP	Avg	OBP	SLG
1991 Tacoma	AAA	75	237	51	11	2	2	—	—	72	28	28	26	0	34	2	7	2	4	0	1.00	6	.215	.296	.304
Huntsville	AA	31	110	29	9	0	2	—	—	44	18	10	16	0	21	1	0	1	5	2	.71	1	.264	.359	.400
1992 Tacoma	AAA	33	116	28	5	1	2	—	—	41	15	17	2	0	12	0	1	2	1	1	.50	5	.241	.250	.353
Huntsville	AA	91	348	96	25	4	8	—	—	153	50	61	30	0	59	0	3	5	8	6	.57	12	.276	.329	.440
1993 Tacoma	AAA	138	544	165	29	5	7	—	—	225	91	73	58	2	64	2	2	5	17	9	.65	17	.303	.369	.414
1994 Colo. Sprng	AAA	128	514	155	32	5	13	—	—	236	94	68	46	2	65	0	1	4	18	5	.78	11	.302	.356	.459
1995 Colo. Sprng	AAA	126	460	135	32	6	12	—	—	215	83	77	46	2	74	3	3	6	12	4	.75	9	.293	.357	.467
1996 Huntsville	AA	47	178	50	12	2	7	—	—	87	28	31	22	0	33	1	0	1	1	1	.50	4	.281	.361	.489
Edmonton	AAA	80	294	89	18	0	10	—	—	137	56	49	41	2	47	0	1	2	2	1	.67	11	.303	.386	.466
1996 Oakland	AL	5	9	0	0	0	0	(0	0)	0	0	0	1	0	1	0	0	0	0	0	.00	0	.000	.100	.000

Brent Gates

Bats: Both **Throws:** Right **Pos:** 2B-64; PH-1　　**Ht:** 6'1" **Wt:** 180 **Born:** 3/14/70 **Age:** 27

Year Team	Lg	G	AB	H	2B	3B	HR	(Hm	Rd)	TB	R	RBI	TBB	IBB	SO	HBP	SH	SF	SB	CS	SB%	GDP	Avg	OBP	SLG
1993 Oakland	AL	139	535	155	29	2	7	(4	3)	209	64	69	56	4	75	4	6	8	7	3	.70	17	.290	.357	.391
1994 Oakland	AL	64	233	66	11	1	2	(0	2)	85	29	24	21	1	32	1	3	6	3	0	1.00	3	.283	.337	.365
1995 Oakland	AL	136	524	133	24	4	5	(3	2)	180	60	56	46	2	84	0	4	11	3	3	.50	15	.254	.308	.344
1996 Oakland	AL	64	247	65	19	2	2	(1	1)	94	26	30	18	0	35	2	5	2	1	1	.50	9	.263	.316	.381
4 ML YEARS		403	1539	419	83	9	16	(8	8)	568	179	179	141	7	226	7	18	27	14	7	.67	49	.272	.331	.369

Jason Giambi

Bats: L **Throws:** R **Pos:** 1B-45; LF-44; 3B-39; DH-12; PH-4; RF-1　　**Ht:** 6'2" **Wt:** 200 **Born:** 1/8/71 **Age:** 26

Year Team	Lg	G	AB	H	2B	3B	HR	(Hm	Rd)	TB	R	RBI	TBB	IBB	SO	HBP	SH	SF	SB	CS	SB%	GDP	Avg	OBP	SLG
1992 Sou. Oregon	A-	13	41	13	3	0	3	—	—	25	9	13	9	1	6	0	0	0	1	1	.50	0	.317	.440	.610
1993 Modesto	A+	89	313	91	16	2	12	—	—	147	72	60	73	7	47	10	1	3	2	3	.40	12	.291	.436	.470
1994 Huntsville	AA	56	193	43	9	0	6	—	—	70	31	30	27	2	31	2	3	4	0	0	.00	8	.223	.319	.363
Tacoma	AAA	52	176	56	20	0	4	—	—	88	28	38	25	2	32	0	0	8	1	0	1.00	4	.318	.388	.500
1995 Edmonton	AAA	55	190	65	26	1	3	—	—	102	34	41	34	4	26	2	0	3	0	0	.00	4	.342	.441	.537
1995 Oakland	AL	54	176	45	7	0	6	(3	3)	70	27	25	28	0	31	3	1	2	2	1	.67	4	.256	.364	.398
1996 Oakland	AL	140	536	156	40	1	20	(6	14)	258	84	79	51	3	95	5	1	5	0	1	.00	15	.291	.355	.481
2 ML YEARS		194	712	201	47	1	26	(9	17)	328	111	104	79	3	126	8	2	7	2	2	.50	19	.282	.357	.461

Steve Gibralter

Bats: Right **Throws:** Right **Pos:** LF-1; CF-1　　**Ht:** 6'0" **Wt:** 190 **Born:** 10/9/72 **Age:** 24

Year Team	Lg	G	AB	H	2B	3B	HR	(Hm	Rd)	TB	R	RBI	TBB	IBB	SO	HBP	SH	SF	SB	CS	SB%	GDP	Avg	OBP	SLG
1990 Reds	R	52	174	45	11	3	4	—	—	74	26	27	23	1	30	3	3	1	8	2	.80	5	.259	.353	.425
1991 Charlstn-WV	A	140	544	145	36	7	6	—	—	213	72	71	31	2	117	5	2	6	11	13	.46	14	.267	.309	.392
1992 Cedar Rapds	A	137	529	162	32	3	19	—	—	257	92	99	51	4	99	12	1	3	12	9	.57	8	.306	.378	.486
1993 Chattanooga	AA	132	477	113	25	3	11	—	—	177	65	47	20	2	108	7	3	4	7	12	.37	6	.237	.276	.371
1994 Chattanooga	AA	133	460	124	28	3	14	—	—	200	71	63	47	0	114	9	4	5	10	8	.56	5	.270	.345	.435
1995 Indianapols	AAA	79	263	83	19	3	18	—	—	162	49	63	25	3	70	4	1	2	2	2	.00	4	.316	.381	.616
1996 Indianapols	AAA	126	447	114	29	3	11	—	—	180	58	54	26	6	114	2	1	3	2	3	.40	10	.255	.297	.403
1995 Cincinnati	NL	4	3	1	0	0	0	(0	0)	1	0	0	0	0	0	0	0	0	0	0	.00	0	.333	.333	.333
1996 Cincinnati	NL	2	2	0	0	0	0	(0	0)	0	0	0	0	0	2	0	0	0	0	0	.00	0	.000	.000	.000
2 ML YEARS		6	5	1	0	0	0	(0	0)	1	0	0	0	0	2	0	0	0	0	0	.00	0	.200	.200	.200

Paul Gibson

Pitches: Left **Bats:** Right **Pos:** RP-4　　**Ht:** 6'1" **Wt:** 195 **Born:** 1/4/60 **Age:** 37

Year Team	Lg	G	GS	CG	GF	IP	BFP	H	R	ER	HR	SH	SF	HB	TBB	IBB	SO	WP	Bk	W	L	Pct.	ShO	Sv-Op	Hld	ERA
1996 Columbus *	AAA	9	0	0	2	7.2	38	8	6	6	3	1	0	0	9	1	4	0	0	1	0	1.000	0	0--	—	7.04
1988 Detroit	AL	40	1	0	18	92	390	83	33	30	4	5	3	1	34	8	50	3	1	4	2	.667	0	0-2	1	2.93
1989 Detroit	AL	45	13	0	16	132	573	129	71	68	11	7	5	6	57	12	77	4	1	4	8	.333	0	0-2	2	4.64
1990 Detroit	AL	61	0	0	17	97.1	422	99	36	33	10	4	5	1	44	12	56	1	1	5	4	.556	0	3-6	9	3.05
1991 Detroit	AL	68	0	0	28	96	432	112	51	49	10	2	2	3	48	8	52	4	0	5	7	.417	0	8-13	10	4.59
1992 New York	NL	43	1	0	12	62	273	70	37	36	7	3	1	0	25	0	49	1	0	0	1	.000	0	0-0	5	5.23
1993 NYN-NYA		28	0	0	10	44	184	45	21	17	5	0	3	0	11	0	37	1	0	3	1	.750	0	0-1	1	3.48
1994 New York	AL	30	0	0	15	29	130	26	17	16	5	0	2	1	17	3	21	1	1	1	1	.500	0	0-2	0	4.97
1996 New York	AL	4	0	0	2	4.1	19	6	3	3	1	0	0	0	0	0	3	0	0	0	0	.000	0	0-0	0	6.23
1993 New York	NL	8	0	0	1	8.2	42	14	6	5	1	0	0	0	2	0	12	1	0	1	1	.500	0	0-1	1	5.19
New York	AL	20	0	0	9	35.1	142	31	15	12	4	0	3	0	9	0	25	0	0	2	1	1.000	0	0-0	0	3.06
8 ML YEARS		319	15	0	118	556.2	2423	570	269	252	55	19	23	13	236	43	345	15	4	22	24	.478	0	11-26	28	4.07

Benji Gil

Bats: Right Throws: Right Pos: SS-5   Ht: 6'2" Wt: 182 Born: 10/6/72 Age: 24

Year Team	Lg	G	AB	H	2B	3B	HR	(Hm	Rd)	TB	R	RBI	TBB	IBB	SO	HBP	SH	SF	SB	CS	SB%	GDP	Avg	OBP	SLG
1996 Charlotte *	A+	11	31	8	6	0	1	—	—	17	2	7	3	0	7	0	0	0	0	0	.00	0	.258	.324	.548
Okla. City *	AAA	84	292	65	15	1	6	—	—	100	32	28	21	0	90	0	2	4	4	6	.40	10	.223	.277	.342
1993 Texas	AL	22	57	7	0	0	0	(0	0)	7	3	2	5	0	22	0	4	0	1	2	.33	1	.123	.194	.123
1995 Texas	AL	130	415	91	20	3	9	(5	4)	144	36	46	26	0	147	1	10	2	2	4	.33	5	.219	.266	.347
1996 Texas	AL	5	5	2	0	0	0	(0	0)	2	0	1	1	0	1	0	1	0	0	1	.00	0	.400	.500	.400
3 ML YEARS		157	477	100	20	3	9	(5	4)	153	39	49	32	0	170	1	15	2	3	7	.30	5	.210	.260	.321

Brian Giles

Bats: L Throws: L Pos: DH-21; PH-17; LF-11; RF-5   Ht: 5'11" Wt: 195 Born: 1/21/71 Age: 26

Year Team	Lg	G	AB	H	2B	3B	HR	(Hm	Rd)	TB	R	RBI	TBB	IBB	SO	HBP	SH	SF	SB	CS	SB%	GDP	Avg	OBP	SLG
1989 Burlington	R+	36	129	40	7	0	0	—	—	47	18	20	11	2	19	1	0	1	6	3	.67	0	.310	.366	.364
1990 Watertown	A-	70	246	71	15	2	1	—	—	93	44	23	48	1	23	0	0	1	10	8	.56	3	.289	.403	.378
1991 Kinston	A+	125	394	122	14	0	4	—	—	148	70	47	68	2	70	2	3	3	19	7	.73	5	.310	.411	.376
1992 Canton-Akrn	AA	23	74	16	4	0	0	—	—	20	6	3	10	1	10	0	0	0	3	1	.75	4	.216	.310	.270
Kinston	A+	42	140	37	5	1	3	—	—	53	28	18	30	1	21	1	0	0	3	5	.38	5	.264	.398	.379
1993 Canton-Akrn	AA	123	425	139	16	6	8	—	—	191	64	64	57	4	43	4	7	3	18	12	.60	9	.327	.409	.449
1994 Charlotte	AAA	128	434	136	18	3	16	—	—	208	74	58	55	10	61	2	1	4	8	5	.62	5	.313	.390	.479
1995 Buffalo	AAA	123	413	128	18	8	15	—	—	207	67	67	54	4	40	8	5	6	7	3	.70	3	.310	.395	.501
1996 Buffalo	AAA	83	318	100	17	6	20	—	—	189	65	64	42	6	29	2	1	3	1	0	1.00	4	.314	.395	.594
1995 Cleveland	AL	6	9	5	0	0	1	(0	1)	8	6	3	0	0	1	0	0	0	0	0	.00	0	.556	.556	.889
1996 Cleveland	AL	51	121	43	14	1	5	(2	3)	74	26	27	19	4	13	0	0	3	3	0	1.00	6	.355	.434	.612
2 ML YEARS		57	130	48	14	1	6	(2	4)	82	32	30	19	4	14	0	0	3	3	0	1.00	6	.369	.441	.631

Bernard Gilkey

Bats: Right Throws: Right Pos: LF-151; PH-2   Ht: 6'0" Wt: 200 Born: 9/24/66 Age: 30

Year Team	Lg	G	AB	H	2B	3B	HR	(Hm	Rd)	TB	R	RBI	TBB	IBB	SO	HBP	SH	SF	SB	CS	SB%	GDP	Avg	OBP	SLG
1990 St. Louis	NL	18	64	19	5	2	1	(0	1)	31	11	3	8	0	5	0	0	0	6	1	.86	1	.297	.375	.484
1991 St. Louis	NL	81	268	58	7	2	5	(2	3)	84	28	20	39	0	33	1	1	2	14	8	.64	14	.216	.316	.313
1992 St. Louis	NL	131	384	116	19	4	7	(3	4)	164	56	43	39	1	52	1	3	4	18	12	.60	5	.302	.364	.427
1993 St. Louis	NL	137	557	170	40	5	16	(7	9)	268	99	70	56	2	66	4	0	5	15	10	.60	16	.305	.370	.481
1994 St. Louis	NL	105	380	96	22	1	6	(0	6)	138	52	45	39	2	65	10	0	2	15	8	.65	6	.253	.336	.363
1995 St. Louis	NL	121	480	143	33	4	17	(5	12)	235	73	69	42	3	70	5	1	3	12	6	.67	17	.298	.358	.490
1996 New York	NL	153	571	181	44	3	30	(14	16)	321	108	117	73	7	125	4	0	8	17	9	.65	18	.317	.393	.562
7 ML YEARS		746	2704	783	170	21	82	(31	51)	1241	427	367	296	15	416	25	5	24	97	54	.64	77	.290	.362	.459

Ed Giovanola

Bats: L Throws: R Pos: SS-25; PH-18; 3B-6; 2B-5   Ht: 5'10" Wt: 170 Born: 3/4/69 Age: 28

Year Team	Lg	G	AB	H	2B	3B	HR	(Hm	Rd)	TB	R	RBI	TBB	IBB	SO	HBP	SH	SF	SB	CS	SB%	GDP	Avg	OBP	SLG
1990 Idaho Falls	R+	25	98	38	6	0	0	—	—	44	25	13	17	0	9	0	2	1	6	2	.75	0	.388	.474	.449
Sumter	A	35	119	29	4	0	0	—	—	33	20	8	34	1	17	0	3	0	8	6	.57	0	.244	.412	.277
1991 Durham	A+	101	299	76	9	0	6	—	—	103	50	27	57	1	39	2	0	3	18	11	.62	6	.254	.374	.344
1992 Greenville	AA	75	270	72	5	0	5	—	—	92	39	30	29	2	40	0	1	2	4	1	.80	1	.267	.336	.341
1993 Greenville	AA	120	384	108	21	5	5	—	—	154	70	43	84	3	49	2	4	6	6	7	.46	11	.281	.408	.401
1994 Greenville	AA	25	84	20	6	1	4	—	—	40	13	16	10	1	12	0	1	0	2	0	1.00	0	.238	.319	.476
Richmond	AAA	98	344	97	16	2	6	—	—	135	48	30	31	5	49	3	5	2	7	4	.64	5	.282	.345	.392
1995 Richmond	AAA	99	321	103	18	2	4	—	—	137	45	36	55	3	37	1	4	4	8	7	.53	10	.321	.417	.427
1996 Richmond	AAA	62	210	62	15	1	3	—	—	88	29	16	37	3	34	1	4	0	2	6	.25	2	.295	.403	.419
1995 Atlanta	NL	13	14	1	0	0	0	(0	0)	1	2	0	3	0	5	0	0	0	0	0	.00	1	.071	.235	.071
1996 Atlanta	NL	43	82	19	2	0	0	(0	0)	21	10	7	8	0	13	1	2	1	1	0	1.00	3	.232	.304	.256
2 ML YEARS		56	96	20	2	0	0	(0	0)	22	12	7	11	0	18	1	2	1	1	0	1.00	4	.208	.294	.229

Joe Girardi

Bats: Right Throws: Right Pos: C-120; PH-8; DH-2   Ht: 5'11" Wt: 195 Born: 10/14/64 Age: 32

Year Team	Lg	G	AB	H	2B	3B	HR	(Hm	Rd)	TB	R	RBI	TBB	IBB	SO	HBP	SH	SF	SB	CS	SB%	GDP	Avg	OBP	SLG
1989 Chicago	NL	59	157	39	10	0	1	(0	1)	52	15	14	11	5	26	2	1	1	2	1	.67	4	.248	.304	.331
1990 Chicago	NL	133	419	113	24	2	1	(1	0)	144	36	38	17	11	50	3	4	4	8	3	.73	13	.270	.300	.344
1991 Chicago	NL	21	47	9	2	0	0	(0	0)	11	3	6	6	1	6	0	1	0	0	0	.00	0	.191	.283	.234
1992 Chicago	NL	91	270	73	3	1	1	(1	0)	81	19	12	19	3	38	1	0	1	0	2	.00	6	.270	.320	.300
1993 Colorado	NL	86	310	90	14	5	3	(2	1)	123	35	31	24	0	41	3	12	1	6	6	.50	8	.290	.346	.397
1994 Colorado	NL	93	330	91	9	4	4	(1	3)	120	47	34	21	1	48	2	6	5	3	3	.50	13	.276	.321	.364
1995 Colorado	NL	125	462	121	17	2	8	(6	2)	166	63	55	29	0	76	2	12	1	3	3	.50	15	.262	.308	.359
1996 New York	AL	124	422	124	22	3	2	(1	1)	158	55	45	30	1	55	5	11	3	13	4	.76	11	.294	.346	.374
8 ML YEARS		732	2417	660	101	17	20	(12	8)	855	273	235	157	22	340	18	47	13	35	22	.61	70	.273	.321	.354

Brian Givens

Pitches: Left **Bats:** Right **Pos:** SP-4 **Ht:** 6'6" **Wt:** 220 **Born:** 11/6/65 **Age:** 31

Year Team	Lg	G	GS	CG	GF	IP	BFP	H	R	ER	HR	SH	SF	HB	TBB	IBB	SO	WP	Bk	W	L	Pct.	ShO	Sv-Op	Hld	ERA
1984 Kingsport	R+	14	10	0	2	44.1	227	41	36	32	2	0	1	3	52	0	51	20	1	4	1	.800	0	0--	—	6.50
1985 Little Fall	A-	11	11	3	0	73.2	315	54	28	24	1	4	2	2	43	0	81	2	0	3	4	.429	1	0--	—	2.93
Columbia	A	3	3	1	0	21.1	88	15	7	7	2	0	0	0	13	0	25	6	0	1	2	.333	0	0--	—	2.95
1986 Columbia	A	27	27	2	0	172	753	147	89	72	8	2	3	4	100	1	189	21	0	8	7	.533	1	0--	—	3.77
1987 Tidewater	AAA	1	1	0	0	3.2	25	9	10	10	0	0	0	0	6	0	3	2	0	0	1	.000	0	0--	—	24.55
Lynchburg	A+	21	20	3	0	112.1	523	112	79	58	8	5	2	4	69	0	96	19	2	6	8	.429	0	0--	—	4.65
1988 Jackson	AA	26	26	4	0	164.1	689	140	78	69	6	13	5	1	68	2	156	14	11	6	14	.300	3	0--	—	3.78
1989 St. Lucie	A+	1	1	0	0	5	25	7	6	0	1	0	0	0	1	0	8	0	0	1	0	.000	0	0--	—	0.00
Jackson	AA	13	13	2	0	85	382	76	39	32	4	1	4	3	55	5	68	11	1	3	5	.375	0	0--	—	3.39
1990 Tidewater	AAA	15	15	0	0	83	376	99	45	38	9	4	1	2	39	0	53	9	0	4	6	.400	0	0--	—	4.12
Calgary	AAA	2	2	0	0	5.2	29	7	8	8	1	0	0	0	8	0	4	1	0	0	1	.000	0	0--	—	12.71
1991 San Bernrdo	A+	1	1	0	0	5	20	4	2	1	0	1	0	0	1	0	4	0	0	1	0	1.000	0	0--	—	1.80
Calgary	AAA	3	3	0	0	14.2	65	16	8	8	1	1	0	1	6	0	8	4	1	1	0	1.000	0	0--	—	4.91
1992 Memphis	AA	7	0	0	1	8.1	38	5	5	3	0	1	0	0	7	0	9	1	0	0	0	.000	0	0--	—	3.24
1993 Royals	R	4	4	0	0	8	31	7	3	3	0	0	0	0	1	0	11	0	0	0	1	.000	0	0--	—	3.38
Memphis	AA	14	4	0	7	35.1	154	37	22	18	4	2	3	1	11	0	29	3	0	1	3	.250	0	2--	—	4.58
1994 Birmingham	AA	36	13	1	8	110	480	103	57	45	8	4	1	8	52	6	111	11	0	4	7	.364	1	1--	—	3.68
1995 New Orleans	AAA	16	11	2	1	77.2	320	67	28	22	2	2	3	0	33	1	75	2	2	7	4	.636	1	0--	—	2.55
1996 New Orleans	AAA	29	22	3	1	137	591	124	60	46	11	4	3	3	57	1	117	7	0	10	9	.526	2	1--	—	3.02
1995 Milwaukee	AL	19	19	0	0	107.1	481	116	71	59	11	1	1	3	54	0	73	3	2	5	7	.417	0	0-0	0	4.95
1996 Milwaukee	AL	4	4	0	0	14	81	32	22	20	3	0	1	0	7	0	10	0	0	1	3	.250	0	0-0	0	12.86
2 ML YEARS		23	23	0	0	121.1	562	148	93	79	14	1	2	3	61	0	83	3	2	6	10	.375	0	0-0	0	5.86

Doug Glanville

Bats: R **Throws:** R **Pos:** PH-24; LF-19; CF-9; RF-8 **Ht:** 6'2" **Wt:** 170 **Born:** 8/25/70 **Age:** 26

Year Team	Lg	G	AB	H	2B	3B	HR	(Hm	Rd)	TB	R	RBI	TBB	IBB	SO	HBP	SH	SF	SB	CS	SB%	GDP	Avg	OBP	SLG
1991 Geneva	A-	36	152	46	8	0	2	—	—	60	29	12	11	0	25	1	3	1	17	3	.85	1	.303	.352	.395
1992 Winston-Sal	A+	120	485	125	18	4	4	—	—	163	72	36	40	0	78	4	9	2	32	9	.78	6	.258	.318	.336
1993 Daytona	A+	61	239	70	10	1	2	—	—	88	47	21	28	0	24	3	4	0	18	15	.55	2	.293	.374	.368
Orlando	AA	73	295	78	14	4	9	—	—	127	42	40	12	0	40	2	6	5	15	7	.68	1	.264	.293	.431
1994 Orlando	AA	130	483	127	22	2	5	—	—	168	53	52	24	4	49	5	10	7	26	20	.57	7	.263	.301	.348
1995 Iowa	AAA	112	419	113	16	2	4	—	—	145	48	37	16	0	64	3	7	4	13	9	.59	4	.270	.296	.346
1996 Iowa	AAA	90	373	115	23	3	3	—	—	153	53	34	12	1	35	2	7	3	15	10	.60	2	.308	.331	.410
1996 Chicago	NL	49	83	20	5	1	1	(1	0)	30	10	10	3	0	11	0	2	1	2	0	1.00	0	.241	.264	.361

Tom Glavine

Pitches: Left **Bats:** Left **Pos:** SP-36 **Ht:** 6'1" **Wt:** 185 **Born:** 3/25/66 **Age:** 31

Year Team	Lg	G	GS	CG	GF	IP	BFP	H	R	ER	HR	SH	SF	HB	TBB	IBB	SO	WP	Bk	W	L	Pct.	ShO	Sv-Op	Hld	ERA
1987 Atlanta	NL	9	9	0	0	50.1	238	55	34	31	5	2	3	3	33	4	20	1	1	2	4	.333	0	0-0	0	5.54
1988 Atlanta	NL	34	34	1	0	195.1	844	201	111	99	12	17	11	8	63	7	84	2	2	7	17	.292	0	0-0	0	4.56
1989 Atlanta	NL	29	29	6	0	186	766	172	88	76	20	11	4	2	40	3	90	2	0	14	8	.636	4	0-0	0	3.68
1990 Atlanta	NL	33	33	1	0	214.1	929	232	111	102	18	21	2	1	78	10	129	8	1	10	12	.455	0	0-0	0	4.28
1991 Atlanta	NL	34	34	9	0	246.2	989	201	83	70	17	7	6	2	69	6	192	10	2	20	11	.645	1	0-0	0	2.55
1992 Atlanta	NL	33	33	7	0	225	919	197	81	69	6	7	2	6	70	7	129	5	0	20	8	.714	5	0-0	0	2.76
1993 Atlanta	NL	36	36	4	0	239.1	1014	236	91	85	16	10	2	2	90	7	120	4	0	22	6	.786	2	0-0	0	3.20
1994 Atlanta	NL	25	25	2	0	165.1	731	173	76	73	10	9	6	1	70	10	140	8	1	13	9	.591	0	0-0	0	3.97
1995 Atlanta	NL	29	29	3	0	198.2	822	182	76	68	9	7	5	5	66	0	127	3	0	16	7	.696	1	0-0	0	3.08
1996 Atlanta	NL	36	36	1	0	235.1	994	222	91	78	14	15	2	0	85	7	181	4	0	15	10	.600	0	0-0	0	2.98
10 ML YEARS		298	298	34	0	1956.1	8246	1871	842	751	127	101	47	26	664	61	1212	47	7	139	92	.602	13	0-0	0	3.45

Jerry Goff

Bats: Left **Throws:** Right **Pos:** C-1 **Ht:** 6'3" **Wt:** 207 **Born:** 4/12/64 **Age:** 33

Year Team	Lg	G	AB	H	2B	3B	HR	(Hm	Rd)	TB	R	RBI	TBB	IBB	SO	HBP	SH	SF	SB	CS	SB%	GDP	Avg	OBP	SLG
1996 Tucson *	AAA	96	275	65	14	2	9	—	—	110	39	52	55	9	97	2	0	1	1	0	1.00	1	.236	.366	.400
1990 Montreal	NL	52	119	27	1	0	3	(0	3)	37	14	7	21	4	36	0	1	0	0	2	.00	0	.227	.343	.311
1992 Montreal	NL	3	3	0	0	0	0	(0	0)	0	0	0	0	0	3	0	0	0	0	0	.00	0	.000	.000	.000
1993 Pittsburgh	NL	14	37	11	2	0	2	(2	0)	19	5	6	8	1	9	0	1	0	0	0	.00	0	.297	.422	.514
1994 Pittsburgh	NL	8	25	2	0	0	0	(0	0)	2	0	1	0	0	11	0	1	0	0	0	.00	0	.080	.080	.080
1995 Houston	NL	12	26	4	2	0	1	(1	0)	9	2	3	4	0	13	0	0	0	0	0	.00	0	.154	.267	.346
1996 Houston	NL	1	4	2	0	0	1	(0	1)	5	1	2	2	0	1	0	0	0	0	0	.00	0	.500	.500	1.250
6 ML YEARS		90	214	46	5	0	7	(3	4)	72	22	19	33	5	73	0	3	0	0	2	.00	2	.215	.320	.336

Greg Gohr

Pitches: Right **Bats:** Right **Pos:** SP-16; RP-16   **Ht:** 6'3" **Wt:** 205 **Born:** 10/29/67 **Age:** 29

		HOW MUCH HE PITCHED						WHAT HE GAVE UP											THE RESULTS							
Year Team	Lg	G	GS	CG	GF	IP	BFP	H	R	ER	HR	SH	SF	HB	TBB	IBB	SO	WP	Bk	W	L	Pct.	ShO	Sv-Op	Hld	ERA
1996 Toledo *	AAA	2	2	0	0	12	57	17	10	10	1	0	1	0	5	0	15	2	0	0	0	.000	0	0--	—	7.50
1993 Detroit	AL	16	0	0	9	22.2	108	26	15	15	1	1	1	2	14	2	23	1	0	0	0	.000	0	0-1	1	5.96
1994 Detroit	AL	8	6	0	1	34	159	36	19	17	3	0	1	0	21	1	21	2	1	2	2	.500	0	0-0	0	4.50
1995 Detroit	AL	10	0	0	1	10.1	41	9	1	1	0	1	0	0	3	0	12	1	0	1	0	1.000	0	0-0	3	0.87
1996 Det-Cal	AL	32	16	0	7	115.2	546	163	96	93	31	1	4	3	44	2	75	6	0	5	9	.357	0	1-1	0	7.24
1996 Detroit	AL	17	16	0	0	91.2	434	129	76	73	24	1	3	3	34	2	60	6	0	4	8	.333	0	0-0	0	7.17
California	AL	15	0	0	7	24	112	34	20	20	7	0	1	0	10	0	15	0	0	1	1	.500	0	1-1	0	7.50
4 ML YEARS		66	22	0	18	182.2	854	234	131	126	35	3	6	5	82	5	131	10	1	8	11	.421	0	1-2	4	6.21

Chris Gomez

Bats: Right **Throws:** Right **Pos:** SS-136; PH-2   **Ht:** 6'1" **Wt:** 188 **Born:** 6/16/71 **Age:** 26

					BATTING														BASERUNNING				PERCENTAGES		
Year Team	Lg	G	AB	H	2B	3B	HR	(Hm	Rd)	TB	R	RBI	TBB	IBB	SO	HBP	SH	SF	SB	CS	SB%	GDP	Avg	OBP	SLG
1993 Detroit	AL	46	128	32	7	1	0	(0	0)	41	11	11	9	0	17	1	3	0	2	2	.50	2	.250	.304	.320
1994 Detroit	AL	84	296	76	19	0	8	(5	3)	119	32	53	33	0	64	3	3	1	5	3	.63	8	.257	.336	.402
1995 Detroit	AL	123	431	96	20	2	11	(5	6)	153	49	50	41	0	96	3	3	4	4	1	.80	13	.223	.292	.355
1996 Det-SD		137	456	117	21	1	4	(2	2)	152	53	45	57	1	84	7	6	2	3	3	.50	16	.257	.347	.333
1996 Detroit	AL	48	128	31	5	0	1	(1	0)	39	21	16	18	0	20	1	3	0	1	1	.50	5	.242	.340	.305
San Diego	NL	89	328	86	16	1	3	(1	2)	113	32	29	39	1	64	6	3	2	2	2	.50	11	.262	.349	.345
4 ML YEARS		390	1311	321	67	4	23	(12	11)	465	145	159	140	1	261	14	15	7	14	9	.61	39	.245	.323	.355

Leo Gomez

Bats: R **Throws:** R **Pos:** 3B-124; PH-20; 1B-8; SS-1   **Ht:** 6'0" **Wt:** 208 **Born:** 3/2/67 **Age:** 30

					BATTING														BASERUNNING				PERCENTAGES		
Year Team	Lg	G	AB	H	2B	3B	HR	(Hm	Rd)	TB	R	RBI	TBB	IBB	SO	HBP	SH	SF	SB	CS	SB%	GDP	Avg	OBP	SLG
1990 Baltimore	AL	12	39	9	0	0	0	(0	0)	9	3	1	8	0	7	0	1	0	0	0	.00	2	.231	.362	.231
1991 Baltimore	AL	118	391	91	17	2	16	(7	9)	160	40	45	40	0	82	2	5	7	1	1	.50	11	.233	.302	.409
1992 Baltimore	AL	137	468	124	24	0	17	(6	11)	199	62	64	63	4	78	8	5	8	2	3	.40	14	.265	.356	.425
1993 Baltimore	AL	71	244	48	7	0	10	(7	3)	85	30	25	32	1	60	3	3	2	0	1	.00	2	.197	.295	.348
1994 Baltimore	AL	84	285	78	20	0	15	(11	4)	143	46	56	43	0	55	3	0	4	0	0	.00	5	.274	.366	.502
1995 Baltimore	AL	53	127	30	5	0	4	(3	1)	47	16	12	18	1	23	0	1	0	0	1	.00	0	.236	.336	.370
1996 Chicago	NL	136	362	86	19	0	17	(10	7)	156	44	56	53	0	94	7	3	2	1	4	.20	8	.238	.344	.431
7 ML YEARS		611	1916	466	92	2	79	(44	35)	799	241	259	255	6	399	25	17	25	4	10	.29	42	.243	.336	.417

Rene Gonzales

Bats: R **Throws:** R **Pos:** 1B-23; 3B-15; SS-10; PH-7; 2B-5; LF-1   **Ht:** 6'3" **Wt:** 220 **Born:** 9/3/61 **Age:** 35

					BATTING														BASERUNNING				PERCENTAGES		
Year Team	Lg	G	AB	H	2B	3B	HR	(Hm	Rd)	TB	R	RBI	TBB	IBB	SO	HBP	SH	SF	SB	CS	SB%	GDP	Avg	OBP	SLG
1996 Okla. City *	AAA	42	154	40	8	2	3	—	—	61	21	13	26	2	23	2	2	2	1	1	.50	5	.260	.370	.396
1984 Montreal	NL	29	30	7	1	0	0	(0	0)	8	5	2	2	0	5	1	0	0	0	0	.00	0	.233	.303	.267
1986 Montreal	NL	11	26	3	0	0	0	(0	0)	3	1	0	2	0	7	0	0	0	0	2	.00	0	.115	.179	.115
1987 Baltimore	AL	37	60	16	2	1	1	(1	0)	23	14	7	3	0	11	0	2	0	1	0	1.00	0	.267	.302	.383
1988 Baltimore	AL	92	237	51	6	0	2	(1	1)	63	13	15	13	0	32	3	5	2	2	0	1.00	5	.215	.263	.266
1989 Baltimore	AL	71	166	36	4	0	1	(0	1)	43	16	11	12	0	30	0	6	1	5	3	.63	6	.217	.268	.259
1990 Baltimore	AL	67	103	22	3	1	1	(1	0)	30	13	12	12	0	14	0	6	0	1	2	.33	3	.214	.296	.291
1991 Toronto	AL	71	118	23	3	0	1	(1	0)	29	16	6	12	0	22	4	6	1	0	0	.00	5	.195	.289	.246
1992 California	AL	104	329	91	17	1	7	(6	1)	131	47	38	41	1	46	4	5	1	7	4	.64	17	.277	.363	.398
1993 California	AL	118	335	84	17	0	2	(1	1)	107	34	31	49	2	45	1	2	2	5	5	.50	12	.251	.346	.319
1994 Cleveland	AL	22	23	8	1	1	1	(0	1)	14	6	5	5	0	3	0	1	1	2	0	1.00	0	.348	.448	.609
1995 California	AL	30	18	6	1	0	1	(0	1)	10	1	3	0	0	4	0	0	0	0	0	.00	1	.333	.333	.556
1996 Texas	AL	51	92	20	4	0	2	(1	1)	30	19	5	10	0	11	0	0	2	0	0	.00	3	.217	.288	.326
12 ML YEARS		703	1537	367	59	4	19	(12	7)	491	185	135	161	3	230	13	33	10	23	16	.59	54	.239	.314	.319

Alex Gonzalez

Bats: Right **Throws:** Right **Pos:** SS-147   **Ht:** 6'0" **Wt:** 182 **Born:** 4/8/73 **Age:** 24

					BATTING														BASERUNNING				PERCENTAGES		
Year Team	Lg	G	AB	H	2B	3B	HR	(Hm	Rd)	TB	R	RBI	TBB	IBB	SO	HBP	SH	SF	SB	CS	SB%	GDP	Avg	OBP	SLG
1994 Toronto	AL	15	53	8	3	1	0	(0	0)	13	7	1	4	0	17	1	1	0	3	1	1.00	2	.151	.224	.245
1995 Toronto	AL	111	367	89	19	4	10	(8	2)	146	51	42	44	1	114	1	9	4	4	4	.50	7	.243	.322	.398
1996 Toronto	AL	147	527	124	30	5	14	(3	11)	206	64	64	45	0	127	5	7	3	16	4	.73	12	.235	.300	.391
3 ML YEARS		273	947	221	52	10	24	(11	13)	365	122	107	93	1	258	7	17	7	23	10	.70	21	.233	.305	.385

Juan Gonzalez

Bats: Right **Throws:** Right **Pos:** RF-102; DH-32 **Ht:** 6'3" **Wt:** 220 **Born:** 10/16/69 **Age:** 27

Year Team	Lg	G	AB	H	2B	3B	HR	(Hm	Rd)	TB	R	RBI	TBB	IBB	SO	HBP	SH	SF	SB	CS	SB%	GDP	Avg	OBP	SLG
1989 Texas	AL	24	60	9	3	0	1	(1	0)	15	6	7	6	0	17	0	2	0	0	0	.00	4	.150	.227	.250
1990 Texas	AL	25	90	26	7	1	4	(3	1)	47	11	12	2	0	18	2	0	1	0	1	.00	2	.289	.316	.522
1991 Texas	AL	142	545	144	34	1	27	(7	20)	261	78	102	42	7	118	5	0	3	4	4	.50	10	.264	.321	.479
1992 Texas	AL	155	584	152	24	2	43	(19	24)	309	77	109	35	1	143	5	0	8	0	1	.00	16	.260	.304	.529
1993 Texas	AL	140	536	166	33	1	46	(24	22)	339	105	118	37	7	99	13	0	1	1	1	.80	12	.310	.368	**.632**
1994 Texas	AL	107	422	116	18	4	19	(6	13)	199	57	85	30	10	66	7	0	4	6	4	.60	18	.275	.330	.472
1995 Texas	AL	90	352	104	20	2	27	(15	12)	209	57	82	17	3	66	0	0	5	0	0	.00	15	.295	.324	.594
1996 Texas	AL	134	541	170	33	2	47	(23	24)	348	89	144	45	12	82	3	0	3	2	0	1.00	10	.314	.368	.643
8 ML YEARS		817	3130	887	172	13	214	(98	116)	1727	480	659	214	40	609	35	2	25	16	11	.59	87	.283	.334	.552

Luis Gonzalez

Bats: Left **Throws:** Right **Pos:** LF-139; PH-11; 1B-2 **Ht:** 6'2" **Wt:** 185 **Born:** 9/3/67 **Age:** 29

Year Team	Lg	G	AB	H	2B	3B	HR	(Hm	Rd)	TB	R	RBI	TBB	IBB	SO	HBP	SH	SF	SB	CS	SB%	GDP	Avg	OBP	SLG
1990 Houston	NL	12	21	4	2	0	0	(0	0)	6	1	0	2	1	5	0	0	0	0	0	.00	0	.190	.261	.286
1991 Houston	NL	137	473	120	28	9	13	(4	9)	205	51	69	40	4	101	8	1	4	10	7	.59	9	.254	.320	.433
1992 Houston	NL	122	387	94	19	3	10	(4	6)	149	40	55	24	3	52	2	1	2	7	7	.50	6	.243	.289	.385
1993 Houston	NL	154	540	162	34	3	15	(8	7)	247	82	72	47	7	83	10	3	10	20	9	.69	9	.300	.361	.457
1994 Houston	NL	112	392	107	29	4	8	(3	5)	168	57	67	49	6	57	3	0	6	15	13	.54	10	.273	.353	.429
1995 Hou-ChN	NL	133	471	130	29	8	13	(6	7)	214	69	69	57	8	63	6	1	6	6	8	.43	16	.276	.357	.454
1996 Chicago	NL	146	483	131	30	4	15	(6	9)	214	70	79	61	8	49	4	1	6	9	6	.60	13	.271	.354	.443
1995 Houston	NL	56	209	54	10	4	6	(1	5)	90	35	35	18	3	30	3	1	3	1	3	.25	8	.258	.322	.431
Chicago	NL	77	262	76	19	4	7	(5	2)	124	34	34	39	5	33	3	0	3	5	5	.50	8	.290	.384	.473
7 ML YEARS		816	2767	748	171	31	74	(31	43)	1203	370	411	280	37	410	33	7	34	67	50	.57	63	.270	.341	.435

Dwight Gooden

Pitches: Right **Bats:** Right **Pos:** SP-29 **Ht:** 6'3" **Wt:** 210 **Born:** 11/16/64 **Age:** 32

Year Team	Lg	G	GS	CG	GF	IP	BFP	H	R	ER	HR	SH	SF	HB	TBB	IBB	SO	WP	Bk	W	L	Pct.	ShO	Sv-Op	Hld	ERA
1984 New York	NL	31	31	7	0	218	879	161	72	63	7	3	2	2	73	3	**276**	3	**7**	17	9	.654	3	0--	--	2.60
1985 New York	NL	35	35	**16**	0	**276.2**	1065	198	51	47	13	6	2	2	69	4	**268**	6	2	**24**	4	.857	8	0--	--	**1.53**
1986 New York	NL	33	33	12	0	250	1020	197	92	79	17	10	8	4	80	3	200	4	4	17	6	.739	2	0--	--	2.84
1987 New York	NL	25	25	7	0	179.2	730	162	68	64	11	5	5	2	53	2	148	1	1	15	7	.682	3	0-0	0	3.21
1988 New York	NL	34	34	10	0	248.1	1024	242	98	88	8	10	6	6	57	4	175	5	5	18	9	.667	3	0-0	0	3.19
1989 New York	NL	19	17	0	1	118.1	497	93	42	38	9	4	3	2	47	2	101	7	5	9	4	.692	0	1-1	0	2.89
1990 New York	NL	34	34	2	0	232.2	983	229	106	99	10	10	7	7	70	3	223	6	3	19	7	.731	1	0-0	0	3.83
1991 New York	NL	27	27	3	0	190	789	185	80	76	12	5	4	3	56	2	150	5	2	13	7	.650	1	0-0	0	3.60
1992 New York	NL	31	31	3	0	206	863	197	93	84	11	10	7	3	70	7	145	3	1	10	13	.435	0	0-0	0	3.67
1993 New York	NL	29	29	7	0	208.2	866	188	89	80	16	11	7	9	61	1	149	5	2	12	15	.444	2	0-0	0	3.45
1994 New York	NL	7	7	0	0	41.1	182	46	32	29	9	3	0	1	15	1	40	2	0	3	4	.429	0	0-0	0	6.31
1996 New York	AL	29	29	1	0	170.2	756	169	101	95	19	1	5	9	88	2	126	9	1	11	7	.611	1	0-0	--	5.01
12 ML YEARS		334	332	68	1	2340.1	9654	2067	924	842	142	78	56	50	739	35	2001	56	33	168	92	.646	24	1--	--	3.24

Curtis Goodwin

Bats: L **Throws:** L **Pos:** CF-28; PH-11; LF-9; RF-6 **Ht:** 5'11" **Wt:** 180 **Born:** 9/30/72 **Age:** 24

Year Team	Lg	G	AB	H	2B	3B	HR	(Hm	Rd)	TB	R	RBI	TBB	IBB	SO	HBP	SH	SF	SB	CS	SB%	GDP	Avg	OBP	SLG
1991 Orioles	R	48	151	39	5	0	0	—	—	44	32	9	38	0	25	1	5	0	26	5	.84	3	.258	.411	.291
1992 Kane County	A	134	542	153	7	5	1	—	—	173	85	42	38	0	106	2	14	0	52	18	.74	1	.282	.332	.319
1993 Frederick	A+	138	555	156	15	10	2	—	—	197	98	42	52	0	90	1	7	1	61	15	.80	8	.281	.343	.355
1994 Bowie	AA	142	597	171	18	8	2	—	—	211	105	37	40	0	78	3	13	2	59	10	.86	7	.286	.333	.353
1995 Rochester	AAA	36	140	37	3	3	0	—	—	46	24	7	12	0	15	1	3	0	17	3	.85	4	.264	.327	.329
1996 Indianapols	AAA	91	337	88	19	4	2	—	—	121	57	30	54	2	67	1	5	1	40	12	.77	2	.261	.364	.359
1995 Baltimore	AL	87	289	76	11	3	1	(0	1)	96	40	24	15	0	53	2	7	3	22	4	.85	5	.263	.301	.332
1996 Cincinnati	NL	49	136	31	3	0	0	(0	0)	34	20	5	19	0	34	0	1	0	15	6	.71	1	.228	.323	.250
2 ML YEARS		136	425	107	14	3	1	(0	1)	130	60	29	34	0	87	2	8	3	37	10	.79	6	.252	.308	.306

Tom Goodwin

Bats: L **Throws:** R **Pos:** CF-81; LF-75; PH-9; DH-5 **Ht:** 6'1" **Wt:** 175 **Born:** 7/27/68 **Age:** 28

Year Team	Lg	G	AB	H	2B	3B	HR	(Hm	Rd)	TB	R	RBI	TBB	IBB	SO	HBP	SH	SF	SB	CS	SB%	GDP	Avg	OBP	SLG
1991 Los Angeles	NL	16	7	1	0	0	0	(0	0)	1	3	0	0	0	0	0	0	0	1	1	.50	0	.143	.143	.143
1992 Los Angeles	NL	57	73	17	1	1	0	(0	0)	20	15	3	6	0	10	0	0	0	7	3	.70	2	.233	.291	.274
1993 Los Angeles	NL	30	17	5	1	0	0	(0	0)	6	6	1	1	0	4	0	0	0	1	2	.33	1	.294	.333	.353
1994 Kansas City	AL	2	2	0	0	0	0	(0	0)	0	0	0	0	0	1	0	0	0	0	0	.00	0	.000	.000	.000
1995 Kansas City	AL	133	480	138	16	3	4	(2	2)	172	72	28	38	0	72	5	**14**	0	50	18	.74	1	.288	.346	.358
1996 Kansas City	AL	143	524	148	14	4	1	(0	0)	173	80	35	39	0	79	2	**21**	1	66	**22**	.75	3	.282	.334	.330

							BATTING												BASERUNNING				PERCENTAGES		
Year Team	Lg	G	AB	H	2B	3B	HR	(Hm	Rd)	TB	R	RBI	TBB	IBB	SO	HBP	SH	SF	SB	CS	SB%	GDP	Avg	OBP	SLG
6 ML YEARS		381	1103	309	32	8	5	(2	3)	372	176	67	84	0	166	7	35	1	125	46	.73	11	.280	.335	.337

Tom Gordon

Pitches: Right **Bats:** Right **Pos:** SP-34 **Ht:** 5'9" **Wt:** 180 **Born:** 11/18/67 **Age:** 29

			HOW MUCH HE PITCHED						WHAT HE GAVE UP										THE RESULTS					
Year Team	Lg	G	GS	CG	GF	IP	BFP	H	R	ER	HR	SH	SF	HB	TBB	IBB	SO	WP	Bk	W	L	Pct.	ShO	Sv-Op	Hld	ERA
1988 Kansas City	AL	5	2	0	0	15.2	67	16	9	9	1	0	0	0	7	0	18	0	0	0	2	.000	0	0-0	2	5.17
1989 Kansas City	AL	49	16	1	16	163	677	122	67	66	10	4	4	1	86	4	153	12	0	17	9	.654	1	1-7	3	3.64
1990 Kansas City	AL	32	32	6	0	195.1	858	192	99	81	17	8	2	3	99	4	175	11	0	12	11	.522	1	0-0	0	3.73
1991 Kansas City	AL	45	14	1	11	158	684	129	76	68	16	5	3	4	87	6	167	5	0	9	14	.391	0	1-4	4	3.87
1992 Kansas City	AL	40	11	0	13	117.2	516	116	67	60	9	2	6	4	55	4	98	5	2	6	10	.375	0	0-2	0	4.59
1993 Kansas City	AL	48	14	2	18	155.2	651	125	65	62	11	6	6	1	77	5	143	17	0	12	6	.667	0	1-6	2	3.58
1994 Kansas City	AL	24	24	0	0	155.1	675	136	79	75	15	3	8	3	87	3	126	12	1	11	7	.611	0	0-0	0	4.35
1995 Kansas City	AL	31	31	2	0	189	843	204	110	93	12	7	11	4	89	4	119	9	0	12	12	.500	0	0-0	0	4.43
1996 Boston	AL	34	34	4	0	215.2	998	249	143	**134**	28	2	11	4	105	5	171	6	1	12	9	.571	1	0-0	0	5.59
9 ML YEARS		308	178	16	58	1365.1	5969	1289	715	648	119	37	51	24	692	32	1170	77	4	91	80	.532	3	3-19	11	4.27

Mark Grace

Bats: Left **Throws:** Left **Pos:** 1B-141; PH-2 **Ht:** 6'2" **Wt:** 190 **Born:** 6/28/64 **Age:** 33

							BATTING												BASERUNNING				PERCENTAGES		
Year Team	Lg	G	AB	H	2B	3B	HR	(Hm	Rd)	TB	R	RBI	TBB	IBB	SO	HBP	SH	SF	SB	CS	SB%	GDP	Avg	OBP	SLG
1988 Chicago	NL	134	486	144	23	4	7	(0	7)	196	65	57	60	5	43	0	0	4	3	3	.50	12	.296	.371	.403
1989 Chicago	NL	142	510	160	28	3	13	(8	5)	233	74	79	80	13	42	0	3	3	14	7	.67	13	.314	.405	.457
1990 Chicago	NL	157	589	182	32	1	9	(4	5)	243	72	82	59	5	54	5	1	8	15	6	.71	10	.309	.372	.413
1991 Chicago	NL	160	**619**	169	28	5	8	(5	3)	231	87	58	70	7	53	3	4	7	3	4	.43	6	.273	.346	.373
1992 Chicago	NL	158	603	185	37	5	9	(4	5)	259	72	79	72	8	36	4	2	8	6	1	.86	14	.307	.380	.430
1993 Chicago	NL	155	594	193	39	4	14	(5	9)	282	86	98	71	14	32	1	1	9	8	4	.67	**25**	.325	.393	.475
1994 Chicago	NL	106	403	120	23	3	6	(5	1)	167	55	44	48	5	41	0	0	3	0	1	.00	10	.298	.370	.414
1995 Chicago	NL	143	552	180	**51**	3	16	(4	12)	285	97	92	65	9	46	2	1	7	6	2	.75	10	.326	.395	.516
1996 Chicago	NL	142	547	181	39	1	9	(4	5)	249	88	75	62	8	41	1	0	6	2	3	.40	18	.331	.396	.455
9 ML YEARS		1297	4903	1514	300	29	91	(40	51)	2145	696	664	587	74	388	16	12	55	57	31	.65	118	.309	.381	.437

Mike Grace

Pitches: Right **Bats:** Right **Pos:** SP-12 **Ht:** 6'4" **Wt:** 220 **Born:** 6/20/70 **Age:** 27

				HOW MUCH HE PITCHED						WHAT HE GAVE UP									THE RESULTS					
Year Team	Lg	G	GS	CG	GF	IP	BFP	H	R	ER	HR	SH	SF	HB	TBB	IBB	SO	WP	Bk	W	L	Pct.	ShO	Sv-Op	Hld	ERA
1991 Batavia	A-	6	6	0	0	32.1	123	20	9	5	3	2	0	1	14	1	36	1	2	1	2	.333	0	0--	—	1.39
Spartanburg	A	6	6	0	0	33.1	127	24	7	7	1	2	1	0	9	0	23	1	0	3	1	.750	0	0--	—	1.89
1992 Spartanburg	A	6	6	0	0	27.1	114	25	16	15	3	0	0	1	8	0	21	2	0	0	1	.000	0	0--	—	4.94
1994 Spartanburg	A	15	15	0	0	80.1	345	84	50	43	6	4	1	8	20	1	45	2	0	5	5	.500	0	0--	—	4.82
1995 Scranton-WB	AAA	2	2	1	0	17	68	17	3	3	0	0	0	0	2	0	13	2	0	2	0	1.000	0	0--	—	1.59
Reading	AA	26	26	3	0	164.1	674	154	68	61	13	5	0	6	37	0	131	5	2	15	6	.714	0	0--	—	3.34
1995 Philadelphia	NL	2	2	0	0	11.1	47	10	4	4	0	1	0	0	4	0	7	0	0	1	1	.500	0	0-0	0	3.18
1996 Philadelphia	NL	12	12	1	0	80	323	72	33	31	9	4	0	1	16	1	49	0	1	7	2	.778	1	0-0	0	3.49
2 ML YEARS		14	14	1	0	91.1	370	82	37	35	9	5	0	1	20	1	56	0	1	8	3	.727	1	0-0	0	3.45

Tony Graffanino

Bats: Right **Throws:** Right **Pos:** 2B-18; PH-8 **Ht:** 6'1" **Wt:** 175 **Born:** 6/6/72 **Age:** 25

							BATTING												BASERUNNING				PERCENTAGES		
Year Team	Lg	G	AB	H	2B	3B	HR	(Hm	Rd)	TB	R	RBI	TBB	IBB	SO	HBP	SH	SF	SB	CS	SB%	GDP	Avg	OBP	SLG
1990 Pulaski	R+	42	131	27	5	1	0	—	—	34	23	11	26	0	17	2	1	1	6	3	.67	3	.206	.344	.260
1991 Idaho Falls	R+	66	274	95	16	4	4	—	—	131	53	57	27	0	37	3	2	2	19	4	.83	2	.347	.408	.478
1992 Macon	A	112	400	96	15	5	10	—	—	151	50	31	50	1	84	8	4	4	9	6	.60	6	.240	.333	.378
1993 Durham	A+	123	459	126	30	5	15	—	—	211	78	69	45	1	78	4	2	4	24	11	.69	10	.275	.342	.460
1994 Greenville	AA	124	440	132	28	3	7	—	—	187	66	52	50	7	53	2	7	3	29	7	.81	6	.300	.372	.425
1995 Richmond	AAA	50	179	34	6	0	4	—	—	52	20	17	15	0	49	1	1	2	2	2	.50	4	.190	.254	.291
1996 Richmond	AAA	96	353	100	29	2	7	—	—	154	57	33	34	2	72	3	5	1	11	7	.61	3	.283	.350	.436
1996 Atlanta	NL	22	46	8	1	1	0	(0	0)	11	7	2	4	0	13	1	0	0	0	0	.00	0	.174	.250	.239

Jeff Granger

Pitches: Left **Bats:** Right **Pos:** RP-15 **Ht:** 6'4" **Wt:** 200 **Born:** 12/16/71 **Age:** 25

				HOW MUCH HE PITCHED						WHAT HE GAVE UP									THE RESULTS					
Year Team	Lg	G	GS	CG	GF	IP	BFP	H	R	ER	HR	SH	SF	HB	TBB	IBB	SO	WP	Bk	W	L	Pct.	ShO	Sv-Op	Hld	ERA
1993 Eugene	A-	8	7	0	0	36	146	28	17	12	2	1	0	1	10	1	56	1	0	3	3	.500	0	0--	—	3.00
1994 Memphis	AA	25	25	0	0	139.2	615	155	72	60	8	3	3	0	61	0	112	14	3	7	7	.500	0	0--	—	3.87
1995 Wichita	AA	18	18	0	0	95.2	439	122	76	63	9	3	4	1	40	0	81	10	0	4	7	.364	0	0--	—	5.93
1996 Omaha	AAA	45	0	0	25	77	314	65	24	20	10	2	2	2	29	2	68	3	0	5	3	.625	0	4--	—	2.34

		HOW MUCH HE PITCHED						WHAT HE GAVE UP												THE RESULTS					
Year Team	Lg	G	GS	CG	GF	IP	BFP	H	R	ER	HR	SH	SF	HB	TBB	IBB	SO	WP	Bk	W	L	Pct.	ShO	Sv-Op	Hld	ERA
1993 Kansas City	AL	1	0	0	0	1	8	3	3	3	0	0	0	0	2	0	1	0	0	0	0	.000	0	0-0	0	27.00
1994 Kansas City	AL	2	2	0	0	9.1	47	13	8	7	2	0	1	0	6	0	3	0	0	0	1	.000	0	0-0	1	6.75
1996 Kansas City	AL	15	0	0	5	16.1	80	21	13	12	3	0	1	2	10	0	11	2	0	0	0	.000	0	0-0	1	6.61
3 ML YEARS		18	2	0	5	26.2	135	37	24	22	5	0	2	2	18	0	15	2	0	0	1	.000	0	0-0	1	7.43

Danny Graves

Pitches: Right   **Bats:** Right   **Pos:** RP-15   **Ht:** 5'11" **Wt:** 200 **Born:** 8/7/73   **Age:** 23

		HOW MUCH HE PITCHED						WHAT HE GAVE UP												THE RESULTS					
Year Team	Lg	G	GS	CG	GF	IP	BFP	H	R	ER	HR	SH	SF	HB	TBB	IBB	SO	WP	Bk	W	L	Pct.	ShO	Sv-Op	Hld	ERA
1995 Canton-Akrn	AA	17	0	0	17	23.1	82	10	1	0	0	4	0	1	2	0	11	0	0	1	0	1.000	0	10--	—	0.00
Buffalo	AAA	3	0	0	3	3	16	5	4	1	0	0	0	0	1	0	2	1	0	0	0	.000	0	0--	—	3.00
1996 Buffalo	AAA	43	0	0	32	79	308	57	14	13	1	5	3	2	24	2	46	1	0	4	3	.571	0	19--	—	1.48
1996 Cleveland	AL	15	0	0	5	29.2	129	29	18	15	2	0	1	0	10	0	22	1	0	2	0	1.000	0	0-1	0	4.55

Craig Grebeck

Bats: R   **Throws:** R   **Pos:** 2B-29; PH-21; SS-2; 3B-1   **Ht:** 5'7" **Wt:** 150 **Born:** 12/29/64   **Age:** 32

		BATTING															BASERUNNING				PERCENTAGES		
Year Team	Lg	G	AB	H	2B	3B	HR	(Hm | Rd)	TB	R	RBI	TBB	IBB	SO	HBP	SH	SF	SB	CS	SB%	GDP	Avg	OBP	SLG
1990 Chicago	AL	59	119	20	3	1	1	(1 | 0)	28	7	9	8	0	24	2	3	3	0	0	.00	2	.168	.227	.235
1991 Chicago	AL	107	224	63	16	3	6	(3 | 3)	103	37	31	38	0	40	1	4	1	1	3	.25	3	.281	.386	.460
1992 Chicago	AL	88	287	77	21	2	3	(2 | 1)	111	24	35	30	0	34	3	10	3	0	3	.00	5	.268	.341	.387
1993 Chicago	AL	72	190	43	5	0	1	(0 | 1)	51	25	12	26	0	26	0	7	0	1	2	.33	9	.226	.319	.268
1994 Chicago	AL	35	97	30	5	0	0	(0 | 0)	35	17	5	12	0	5	1	3	0	0	0	.00	1	.309	.391	.361
1995 Chicago	AL	53	154	40	12	0	1	(0 | 1)	55	19	18	21	0	23	3	4	0	0	0	.00	4	.260	.360	.357
1996 Florida	NL	50	95	20	1	0	1	(0 | 1)	24	8	9	4	1	14	1	1	2	0	0	.00	2	.211	.245	.253
7 ML YEARS		464	1166	293	63	6	13	(6 | 7)	407	137	119	139	1	166	11	32	9	2	8	.20	26	.251	.334	.349

Shawn Green

Bats: L   **Throws:** L   **Pos:** RF-127; PH-17; CF-2; DH-1   **Ht:** 6'4" **Wt:** 190 **Born:** 11/10/72   **Age:** 24

		BATTING															BASERUNNING				PERCENTAGES		
Year Team	Lg	G	AB	H	2B	3B	HR	(Hm	Rd)	TB	R	RBI	TBB	IBB	SO	HBP	SH	SF	SB	CS	SB%	GDP	Avg	OBP	SLG
1993 Toronto	AL	3	6	0	0	0	0	(0	0)	0	0	0	0	0	1	0	0	0	0	0	.00	0	.000	.000	.000
1994 Toronto	AL	14	33	3	1	0	0	(0	0)	4	1	1	1	0	8	0	0	0	1	0	1.00	1	.091	.118	.121
1995 Toronto	AL	121	379	109	31	4	15	(5	10)	193	52	54	20	3	68	3	0	3	1	2	.33	4	.288	.326	.509
1996 Toronto	AL	132	422	118	32	3	11	(7	4)	189	52	45	33	3	75	8	0	2	5	1	.83	9	.280	.342	.448
4 ML YEARS		270	840	230	64	7	26	(12	14)	386	105	100	54	6	152	11	0	5	7	3	.70	14	.274	.324	.460

Charlie Greene

Bats: Right   **Throws:** Right   **Pos:** C-1; PH-1   **Ht:** 6'1" **Wt:** 177 **Born:** 1/23/71   **Age:** 26

		BATTING															BASERUNNING				PERCENTAGES		
Year Team	Lg	G	AB	H	2B	3B	HR	(Hm	Rd)	TB	R	RBI	TBB	IBB	SO	HBP	SH	SF	SB	CS	SB%	GDP	Avg	OBP	SLG
1991 Padres	R	49	183	52	15	1	5	—	—	84	27	39	16	0	23	3	2	6	6	1	.86	7	.284	.341	.459
1992 Charlstn-SC	A	98	298	55	9	1	1	—	—	69	22	24	11	0	60	5	3	2	1	2	.33	7	.185	.225	.232
1993 Waterloo	A	84	213	38	8	0	2	—	—	52	19	20	13	0	33	3	6	3	0	0	.00	5	.178	.233	.244
1994 Binghamton	AA	30	106	18	4	0	0	—	—	22	13	2	6	1	18	1	0	1	0	0	.00	3	.170	.219	.208
St. Lucie	A+	69	224	57	4	0	0	—	—	61	23	21	9	0	31	4	4	1	0	1	.00	4	.254	.294	.272
1995 Binghamton	AA	100	346	82	13	0	2	—	—	101	26	34	15	4	47	5	3	4	2	1	.67	10	.237	.276	.292
Norfolk	AAA	27	88	17	3	0	0	—	—	20	6	4	3	0	28	0	1	0	0	1	.00	1	.193	.220	.227
1996 Binghamton	AA	100	336	82	17	0	2	—	—	105	35	27	17	0	52	2	0	4	2	0	1.00	8	.244	.277	.313
1996 New York	NL	2	1	0	0	0	0	(0	0)	0	0	0	0	0	0	0	0	0	0	0	.00	0	.000	.000	.000

Todd Greene

Bats: Right   **Throws:** Right   **Pos:** C-26; PH-7; DH-1   **Ht:** 5'10" **Wt:** 200 **Born:** 5/8/71   **Age:** 26

		BATTING															BASERUNNING				PERCENTAGES		
Year Team	Lg	G	AB	H	2B	3B	HR	(Hm	Rd)	TB	R	RBI	TBB	IBB	SO	HBP	SH	SF	SB	CS	SB%	GDP	Avg	OBP	SLG
1993 Boise	A-	76	305	82	15	3	15	—	—	148	55	71	34	6	44	9	0	3	4	3	.57	3	.269	.356	.485
1994 Lk Elsinore	A+	133	524	158	39	2	35	—	—	306	98	124	64	12	96	4	0	6	10	3	.77	12	.302	.378	.584
1995 Midland	AA	82	318	104	19	1	26	—	—	203	59	57	17	4	55	5	1	5	3	5	.38	3	.327	.365	.638
Vancouver	AAA	43	168	42	3	1	14	—	—	89	28	35	11	2	36	4	0	2	1	0	1.00	3	.250	.308	.530
1996 Vancouver	AAA	60	223	68	18	0	5	—	—	101	27	33	16	0	36	1	0	5	2	0	.00	6	.305	.347	.453
1996 California	AL	29	79	15	1	0	2	(1	1)	22	9	9	4	0	11	1	0	0	2	0	1.00	4	.190	.238	.278

Tommy Greene

Pitches: Right **Bats:** Right **Pos:** SP/RP   **Ht:** 6'5" **Wt:** 222 **Born:** 4/6/67 **Age:** 30

		HOW MUCH HE PITCHED						WHAT HE GAVE UP											THE RESULTS					
Year Team	Lg	G	GS	CG	GF	IP	BFP	H	R	ER	HR	SH	SF	HB	TBB	IBB	SO	WP	Bk	W	L	Pct.	ShO	Sv-Op	Hld	ERA
1989 Atlanta	NL	4	4	1	0	26.1	103	22	12	12	5	1	2	0	6	1	17	1	0	1	2	.333	1	0-0	0	4.10
1990 Atl-Phi	NL	15	9	0	1	51.1	227	50	31	29	8	5	0	1	26	1	21	1	0	3	3	.500	0	0-0	0	5.08
1991 Philadelphia	NL	36	27	3	3	207.2	857	177	85	78	19	9	11	3	66	4	154	9	1	13	7	.650	2	0-0	0	3.38
1992 Philadelphia	NL	13	12	0	0	64.1	298	75	39	38	5	4	2	0	34	2	39	1	0	3	3	.500	0	0-0	0	5.32
1993 Philadelphia	NL	31	30	7	0	200	834	175	84	76	12	9	9	3	62	3	167	15	0	16	4	.800	2	0-0	0	3.42
1994 Philadelphia	NL	7	7	0	0	35.2	164	37	20	18	5	5	1	0	22	0	22	8	0	2	0	1.000	0	0-0	0	4.54
1995 Philadelphia	NL	11	6	0	3	33.2	167	45	32	31	4	2	1	3	20	0	24	3	1	0	5	.000	0	0-0	0	8.29
1990 Atlanta	NL	5	2	0	0	12.1	61	14	11	11	3	2	0	1	9	0	4	0	0	1	0	1.000	0	0-0	0	8.03
Philadelphia	NL	10	7	0	1	39	166	36	20	18	5	3	0	0	17	1	17	1	0	2	3	.400	0	0-0	0	4.15
7 ML YEARS		117	95	11	7	619	2650	581	303	282	60	35	26	10	236	11	450	32	2	38	24	.613	5	0-0	0	4.10

Willie Greene

Bats: L **Throws:** R **Pos:** 3B-74; PH-38; LF-9; 1B-2; SS-1; RF-1   **Ht:** 5'11" **Wt:** 192 **Born:** 9/23/71 **Age:** 25

		BATTING																BASERUNNING				PERCENTAGES		
Year Team	Lg	G	AB	H	2B	3B	HR	(Hm	Rd)	TB	R	RBI	TBB	IBB	SO	HBP	SH	SF	SB	CS	SB%	GDP	Avg	OBP	SLG
1992 Cincinnati	NL	29	93	25	5	2	2	(2	0)	40	10	13	10	0	23	0	0	1	0	2	.00	1	.269	.337	.430
1993 Cincinnati	NL	15	50	8	1	1	2	(2	0)	17	7	5	2	0	19	0	0	1	0	0	.00	1	.160	.189	.340
1994 Cincinnati	NL	16	37	8	2	0	0	(0	0)	10	5	3	6	1	14	0	0	1	0	0	.00	1	.216	.318	.270
1995 Cincinnati	NL	8	19	2	0	0	0	(0	0)	2	1	0	3	0	7	0	0	0	0	0	.00	1	.105	.227	.105
1996 Cincinnati	NL	115	287	70	5	5	19	(11	8)	142	48	63	36	6	88	0	1	1	0	1	.00	5	.244	.327	.495
5 ML YEARS		183	486	113	13	8	23	(15	8)	211	71	84	57	7	151	0	1	4	0	3	.00	9	.233	.311	.434

Mike Greenwell

Bats: L **Throws:** R **Pos:** LF-75; PH-3; CF-1; RF-1   **Ht:** 6'0" **Wt:** 205 **Born:** 7/18/63 **Age:** 33

		BATTING																BASERUNNING				PERCENTAGES		
Year Team	Lg	G	AB	H	2B	3B	HR	(Hm	Rd)	TB	R	RBI	TBB	IBB	SO	HBP	SH	SF	SB	CS	SB%	GDP	Avg	OBP	SLG
1996 Pawtucket *	AAA	3	11	3	0	0	2	—	—	9	3	2	1	0	0	0	0	0	0	0	.00	0	.273	.333	.818
1985 Boston	AL	17	31	10	1	0	4	(1	3)	23	7	8	3	1	4	0	0	0	1	0	1.00	0	.323	.382	.742
1986 Boston	AL	31	35	11	2	0	0	(0	0)	13	4	4	5	0	7	0	0	0	0	0	.00	1	.314	.400	.371
1987 Boston	AL	125	412	135	31	6	19	(8	11)	235	71	89	35	1	40	6	0	3	5	4	.56	7	.328	.386	.570
1988 Boston	AL	158	590	192	39	8	22	(12	10)	313	86	119	87	18	38	9	0	7	16	8	.67	11	.325	.416	.531
1989 Boston	AL	145	578	178	36	0	14	(6	8)	256	87	95	56	15	44	3	0	4	13	5	.72	21	.308	.370	.443
1990 Boston	AL	159	610	181	30	6	14	(6	8)	265	71	73	65	12	43	4	0	3	8	7	.53	19	.297	.367	.434
1991 Boston	AL	147	544	163	26	6	9	(5	4)	228	76	83	43	6	35	3	1	7	15	5	.75	11	.300	.350	.419
1992 Boston	AL	49	180	42	2	0	2	(0	2)	50	16	18	18	1	19	2	0	2	2	3	.40	8	.233	.307	.278
1993 Boston	AL	146	540	170	38	6	13	(6	7)	259	77	72	54	12	46	4	2	3	5	4	.56	17	.315	.379	.480
1994 Boston	AL	95	327	88	25	1	11	(10	1)	148	60	45	38	6	26	4	0	5	2	2	.50	12	.269	.348	.453
1995 Boston	AL	120	481	143	25	4	15	(6	9)	221	67	76	38	4	35	2	0	4	9	5	.64	18	.297	.349	.459
1996 Boston	AL	77	295	87	20	1	7	(4	3)	130	35	44	18	3	27	2	0	3	4	0	1.00	11	.295	.336	.441
12 ML YEARS		1269	4623	1400	275	38	130	(64	66)	2141	657	726	460	79	364	39	4	41	80	43	.65	136	.303	.368	.463

Rusty Greer

Bats: L **Throws:** L **Pos:** LF-136; PH-2; DH-1; 1B-1; CF-1   **Ht:** 6'0" **Wt:** 190 **Born:** 1/21/69 **Age:** 28

		BATTING																BASERUNNING				PERCENTAGES		
Year Team	Lg	G	AB	H	2B	3B	HR	(Hm	Rd)	TB	R	RBI	TBB	IBB	SO	HBP	SH	SF	SB	CS	SB%	GDP	Avg	OBP	SLG
1994 Texas	AL	80	277	87	16	1	10	(3	7)	135	36	46	46	2	46	2	2	4	0	0	.00	3	.314	.410	.487
1995 Texas	AL	131	417	113	21	2	13	(7	6)	177	58	61	55	1	66	1	2	3	3	1	.75	9	.271	.355	.424
1996 Texas	AL	139	542	180	41	6	18	(9	9)	287	96	100	62	4	86	3	0	10	9	0	1.00	9	.332	.397	.530
3 ML YEARS		350	1236	380	78	9	41	(19	22)	599	190	207	163	7	198	6	4	17	12	1	.92	21	.307	.386	.485

Ken Griffey Jr

Bats: Left **Throws:** Left **Pos:** CF-137; DH-5   **Ht:** 6'3" **Wt:** 205 **Born:** 11/21/69 **Age:** 27

		BATTING																BASERUNNING				PERCENTAGES		
Year Team	Lg	G	AB	H	2B	3B	HR	(Hm	Rd)	TB	R	RBI	TBB	IBB	SO	HBP	SH	SF	SB	CS	SB%	GDP	Avg	OBP	SLG
1989 Seattle	AL	127	455	120	23	0	16	(10	6)	191	61	61	44	8	83	2	1	4	16	7	.70	4	.264	.329	.420
1990 Seattle	AL	155	597	179	28	7	22	(8	14)	287	91	80	63	12	81	2	0	4	16	11	.59	12	.300	.366	.481
1991 Seattle	AL	154	548	179	42	1	22	(16	6)	289	76	100	71	21	82	1	4	9	18	6	.75	10	.327	.399	.527
1992 Seattle	AL	142	565	174	39	4	27	(16	11)	302	83	103	44	15	67	5	0	3	10	5	.67	15	.308	.361	.535
1993 Seattle	AL	156	582	180	38	3	45	(21	24)	359	113	109	96	25	91	6	0	7	17	9	.65	14	.309	.408	.617
1994 Seattle	AL	111	433	140	24	4	40	(18	22)	292	94	90	56	19	73	2	0	2	11	3	.79	9	.323	.402	.674
1995 Seattle	AL	72	260	67	7	0	17	(13	4)	125	52	42	52	6	53	0	0	2	4	2	.67	4	.258	.379	.481
1996 Seattle	AL	140	545	165	26	2	49	(26	23)	342	125	140	78	13	104	7	1	7	16	1	.94	7	.303	.392	.628
8 ML YEARS		1057	3985	1204	227	21	238	(128	110)	2187	695	725	504	119	634	25	6	38	108	44	.71	75	.302	.381	.549

Jason Grimsley

Pitches: Right **Bats:** Right **Pos:** SP-20; RP-15 **Ht:** 6'3" **Wt:** 180 **Born:** 8/7/67 **Age:** 29

			HOW MUCH HE PITCHED					WHAT HE GAVE UP									THE RESULTS					
Year Team	Lg	G	GS	CG	GF	IP	BFP	H	R	ER	HR	SH	SF	HB	TBB	IBB	SO	WP	Bk	W	L	Pct.	ShO	Sv-Op	Hld	ERA
1996 Vancouver *	AAA	2	2	1	0	15	55	8	2	2	0	1	1	1	3	0	11	0	1	2	0	1.000	0	0--	—	1.20
1989 Philadelphia	NL	4	4	0	0	18.1	91	19	13	12	2	1	0	0	19	1	7	2	0	1	3	.250	0	0-0	0	5.89
1990 Philadelphia	NL	11	11	0	0	57.1	255	47	21	21	1	2	1	2	43	0	41	6	1	3	2	.600	0	0-0	0	3.30
1991 Philadelphia	NL	12	12	0	0	61	272	54	34	33	4	3	2	0	41	3	42	14	0	1	7	.125	0	0-0	0	4.87
1993 Cleveland	AL	10	6	0	1	42.1	194	52	26	25	3	1	0	1	20	1	27	2	0	3	4	.429	0	0-0	1	5.31
1994 Cleveland	AL	14	13	1	0	82.2	368	91	47	42	7	4	2	6	34	1	59	6	1	5	2	.714	0	0-0	0	4.57
1995 Cleveland	AL	15	2	0	2	34	165	37	24	23	4	1	2	2	32	1	25	7	0	0	0	.000	0	1-1	0	6.09
1996 California	AL	35	20	2	4	130.1	620	150	110	99	14	4	5	13	74	5	82	11	0	5	7	.417	1	0-0	0	6.84
7 ML YEARS		101	68	3	7	426	1965	450	275	255	35	16	12	27	263	12	283	48	2	18	25	.419	1	1-1	1	5.39

Marquis Grissom

Bats: Right **Throws:** Right **Pos:** CF-158; PH-1 **Ht:** 5'11" **Wt:** 190 **Born:** 4/17/67 **Age:** 30

								BATTING										BASERUNNING				PERCENTAGES		
Year Team	Lg	G	AB	H	2B	3B	HR	(Hm	Rd)	TB	R	RBI	TBB	IBB	SO	HBP	SH	SF	SB	CS	SB%	GDP	Avg	OBP	SLG
1989 Montreal	NL	26	74	19	2	0	1	(0	1)	24	16	2	12	0	21	0	1	0	1	0	1.00	1	.257	.360	.324
1990 Montreal	NL	98	288	74	14	2	3	(2	1)	101	42	29	27	2	40	0	4	1	22	2	.92	3	.257	.320	.351
1991 Montreal	NL	148	558	149	23	9	6	(3	3)	208	73	39	34	0	89	1	4	0	76	17	.82	8	.267	.310	.373
1992 Montreal	NL	159	653	180	39	6	14	(8	6)	273	99	66	42	6	81	5	3	4	78	13	.86	12	.276	.322	.418
1993 Montreal	NL	157	630	188	27	2	19	(9	10)	276	104	95	52	6	76	3	0	8	53	10	.84	9	.298	.351	.438
1994 Montreal	NL	110	475	137	25	4	11	(4	7)	203	96	45	41	4	66	1	0	4	36	6	.86	10	.288	.344	.427
1995 Atlanta	NL	139	551	142	23	3	12	(5	7)	207	80	42	47	4	61	3	1	4	29	9	.76	8	.258	.317	.376
1996 Atlanta	NL	158	671	207	32	10	23	(11	12)	328	106	74	41	4	73	3	4	4	28	11	.72	12	.308	.349	.489
8 ML YEARS		995	3900	1096	185	36	89	(42	47)	1620	616	392	296	28	507	16	17	25	323	68	.83	63	.281	.332	.415

Buddy Groom

Pitches: Left **Bats:** Left **Pos:** RP-71; SP-1 **Ht:** 6'2" **Wt:** 200 **Born:** 7/10/65 **Age:** 31

				HOW MUCH HE PITCHED					WHAT HE GAVE UP									THE RESULTS					
Year Team	Lg	G	GS	CG	GF	IP	BFP	H	R	ER	HR	SH	SF	HB	TBB	IBB	SO	WP	Bk	W	L	Pct.	ShO	Sv-Op	Hld	ERA
1992 Detroit	AL	12	7	0	3	38.2	177	48	28	25	4	3	2	0	22	4	15	0	1	0	5	.000	0	1-2	0	5.82
1993 Detroit	AL	19	3	0	8	36.2	170	48	25	25	4	2	4	2	13	5	15	2	1	0	2	.000	0	0-0	1	6.14
1994 Detroit	AL	40	0	0	10	32	139	31	14	14	4	0	3	2	13	2	27	0	0	0	1	.000	0	1-1	11	3.94
1995 Det-Fla		37	4	0	11	55.2	274	81	47	46	8	2	2	2	32	4	35	3	0	2	5	.286	0	1-3	0	7.44
1996 Oakland	AL	72	1	0	16	77.1	341	85	37	33	8	2	0	3	34	3	57	5	0	5	0	1.000	0	2-4	10	3.84
1995 Detroit	AL	23	4	0	6	40.2	203	55	35	34	6	2	2	2	26	4	23	3	0	1	3	.250	0	1-3	0	7.52
Florida	NL	14	0	0	5	15	71	26	12	12	2	0	0	0	6	0	12	0	0	1	2	.333	0	0-0	0	7.20
5 ML YEARS		180	15	0	48	240.1	1101	293	151	143	28	9	11	9	114	18	149	10	2	7	13	.350	0	5-10	22	5.36

Kevin Gross

Pitches: Right **Bats:** Right **Pos:** SP-19; RP-9 **Ht:** 6'5" **Wt:** 227 **Born:** 6/8/61 **Age:** 36

				HOW MUCH HE PITCHED					WHAT HE GAVE UP									THE RESULTS					
Year Team	Lg	G	GS	CG	GF	IP	BFP	H	R	ER	HR	SH	SF	HB	TBB	IBB	SO	WP	Bk	W	L	Pct.	ShO	Sv-Op	Hld	ERA
1996 Okla. City *	AAA	1	1	0	0	4	18	6	4	3	0	0	2	0	3	0	3	0	0	0	0	.000	0	0--	—	6.75
1983 Philadelphia	NL	17	17	1	0	96	418	100	46	38	13	2	1	3	35	3	66	4	1	4	6	.400	1	0--	—	3.56
1984 Philadelphia	NL	44	14	1	9	129	566	140	66	59	8	9	3	5	44	4	84	4	4	8	5	.615	0	1--	—	4.12
1985 Philadelphia	NL	38	31	6	0	205.2	873	194	86	78	11	7	5	7	81	6	151	2	4	15	13	.536	2	0--	—	3.41
1986 Philadelphia	NL	37	36	7	0	241.2	1040	240	115	108	28	8	5	8	94	2	154	2	1	12	12	.500	2	0--	—	4.02
1987 Philadelphia	NL	34	33	3	1	200.2	878	205	107	97	26	8	6	10	87	7	110	3	7	9	16	.360	1	0-0	0	4.35
1988 Philadelphia	NL	33	33	5	0	231.2	989	209	101	95	18	9	4	11	89	5	162	5	7	12	14	.462	1	0-0	0	3.69
1989 Montreal	NL	31	31	4	0	201.1	867	188	105	98	20	10	3	6	88	6	158	5	5	11	12	.478	0	0-0	0	4.38
1990 Montreal	NL	31	26	2	3	163.1	712	171	86	83	9	6	9	4	65	7	111	4	1	9	12	.429	1	0-0	0	4.57
1991 Los Angeles	NL	46	10	0	16	115.2	509	123	55	46	10	6	4	2	50	6	95	3	0	10	11	.476	0	3-6	4	3.58
1992 Los Angeles	NL	34	30	4	0	204.2	856	182	82	72	11	14	6	4	77	10	158	4	2	8	13	.381	3	0-0	2	3.17
1993 Los Angeles	NL	33	32	3	1	202.1	892	224	110	93	15	11	6	5	74	7	150	2	5	13	13	.500	0	0-0	0	4.14
1994 Los Angeles	NL	25	23	1	2	157.1	665	162	64	63	11	4	1	2	43	2	124	4	1	9	7	.563	0	1-1	0	3.60
1995 Texas	AL	31	30	4	0	183.2	825	200	124	113	27	5	7	8	89	8	106	5	0	9	15	.375	0	0-0	0	5.54
1996 Texas	AL	28	19	1	4	129.1	580	151	78	75	19	3	8	4	50	2	78	4	0	11	8	.579	0	0-0	2	5.22
14 ML YEARS		462	365	42	36	2462.1	10670	2489	1225	1118	226	102	68	78	966	75	1707	51	34	140	157	.471	14	5--	—	4.09

Mark Grudzielanek

Bats: Right **Throws:** Right **Pos:** SS-153 **Ht:** 6'1" **Wt:** 185 **Born:** 6/30/70 **Age:** 27

								BATTING										BASERUNNING				PERCENTAGES		
Year Team	Lg	G	AB	H	2B	3B	HR	(Hm	Rd)	TB	R	RBI	TBB	IBB	SO	HBP	SH	SF	SB	CS	SB%	GDP	Avg	OBP	SLG
1991 Jamestown	A-	72	275	72	9	3	2	—	—	93	44	32	18	0	42	3	3	3	14	4	.78	6	.262	.311	.338
1992 Rockford	A	128	496	122	12	5	5	—	—	159	64	54	22	1	59	5	0	0	25	4	.86	10	.246	.285	.321
1993 W. Palm Bch	A+	86	300	80	11	6	1	—	—	106	41	34	14	0	42	7	0	0	17	10	.63	6	.267	.315	.353
1994 Harrisburg	AA	122	488	157	37	3	11	—	—	233	92	66	43	2	66	8	5	5	32	10	.76	15	.322	.382	.477
1995 Ottawa	AAA	49	181	54	9	1	1	—	—	68	26	22	10	0	17	4	2	4	12	1	.92	6	.298	.342	.376

85

		BATTING												BASERUNNING				PERCENTAGES		
Year Team	Lg	G	AB	H	2B	3B	HR	(Hm Rd)	TB	R	RBI	TBB	IBB	SO	HBP	SH	SF	SB	CS	SB%	GDP	Avg	OBP	SLG
1995 Montreal	NL	78	269	66	12	2	1	(1 0)	85	27	20	14	4	47	7	3	0	8	3	.73	7	.245	.300	.316
1996 Montreal	NL	153	657	201	34	4	6	(5 1)	261	99	49	26	3	83	9	1	3	33	7	.83	10	.306	.340	.397
2 ML YEARS		231	926	267	46	6	7	(6 1)	346	126	69	40	7	130	16	4	3	41	10	.80	17	.288	.328	.374

Ken Grundt

Pitches: Left **Bats:** Left **Pos:** RP-1 **Ht:** 6'4" **Wt:** 195 **Born:** 8/26/69 **Age:** 27

		HOW MUCH HE PITCHED						WHAT HE GAVE UP												THE RESULTS					
Year Team	Lg	G	GS	CG	GF	IP	BFP	H	R	ER	HR	SH	SF	HB	TBB	IBB	SO	WP	Bk	W	L	Pct.	ShO	Sv-Op	Hld	ERA
1991 Everett	A-	29	0	0	15	54	231	55	27	14	3	3	0	3	16	5	58	3	0	4	5	.444	0	4--	—	2.33
1992 Clinton	A	40	0	0	28	57.2	226	39	11	4	2	3	0	1	11	2	59	1	0	5	3	.625	0	16--	—	0.62
San Jose	A+	11	0	0	5	17.2	70	9	3	2	1	2	0	2	7	1	17	0	0	1	0	1.000	0	3--	—	1.02
1993 Giants	R	4	0	0	4	17	51	5	1	1	0	0	0	0	0	0	2	0	0	0	0	.000	0	0--	—	2.25
1994 Sioux Falls	IND	26	0	0	10	44	189	44	15	8	2	0	0	1	21	0	35	1	0	3	3	.500	0	2--	—	1.64
1995 Asheville	A	20	0	0	11	30.1	111	18	1	1	0	1	1	1	7	1	38	2	0	0	0	.000	0	1--	—	0.30
Colo. Sprng	AAA	9	0	0	1	5.2	30	9	5	3	0	0	0	0	4	0	5	0	0	0	0	.000	0	0--	—	4.76
1996 Trenton	AA	12	0	0	3	12.2	48	6	0	0	0	1	0	0	6	0	13	1	0	1	0	1.000	0	0--	—	0.00
Pawtucket	AAA	44	0	0	16	64.1	274	72	32	30	4	3	2	1	16	0	46	5	0	9	4	.692	0	2--	—	4.20
1996 Boston	AL	1	0	0	0	0.1	2	1	1	1	0	0	0	0	0	0	0	0	0	0	0	.000	0	0-0	0	27.00

Eddie Guardado

Pitches: Left **Bats:** Right **Pos:** RP-83 **Ht:** 6'0" **Wt:** 193 **Born:** 10/2/70 **Age:** 26

		HOW MUCH HE PITCHED						WHAT HE GAVE UP												THE RESULTS					
Year Team	Lg	G	GS	CG	GF	IP	BFP	H	R	ER	HR	SH	SF	HB	TBB	IBB	SO	WP	Bk	W	L	Pct.	ShO	Sv-Op	Hld	ERA
1993 Minnesota	AL	19	16	0	2	94.2	426	123	68	65	13	3	1	1	36	2	46	0	0	3	8	.273	0	0-0	0	6.18
1994 Minnesota	AL	4	4	0	0	17	81	26	16	16	3	1	2	0	4	0	8	0	0	0	2	.000	0	0-0	0	8.47
1995 Minnesota	AL	51	5	0	10	91.1	410	99	54	52	13	6	5	0	45	2	71	5	1	4	9	.308	0	2-5	5	5.12
1996 Minnesota	AL	83	0	0	17	73.2	313	61	45	43	12	6	4	3	33	4	74	3	0	6	5	.545	0	4-7	18	5.25
4 ML YEARS		157	25	0	29	276.2	1230	309	183	176	41	14	14	4	118	8	199	8	1	13	24	.351	0	6-12	23	5.73

Mark Gubicza

Pitches: Right **Bats:** Right **Pos:** SP-19 **Ht:** 6'5" **Wt:** 230 **Born:** 8/14/62 **Age:** 34

		HOW MUCH HE PITCHED						WHAT HE GAVE UP												THE RESULTS					
Year Team	Lg	G	GS	CG	GF	IP	BFP	H	R	ER	HR	SH	SF	HB	TBB	IBB	SO	WP	Bk	W	L	Pct.	ShO	Sv-Op	Hld	ERA
1984 Kansas City	AL	29	29	4	0	189	800	172	90	85	13	4	9	5	75	0	111	3	1	10	14	.417	2	0--	—	4.05
1985 Kansas City	AL	29	28	0	0	177.1	760	160	88	80	14	1	6	5	77	0	99	12	0	14	10	.583	0	0--	—	4.06
1986 Kansas City	AL	35	24	3	2	180.2	765	155	77	73	8	4	8	5	84	2	118	15	0	12	6	.667	2	0--	—	3.64
1987 Kansas City	AL	35	35	10	0	241.2	1036	231	114	107	18	6	11	6	120	3	166	14	1	13	18	.419	2	0-0	0	3.98
1988 Kansas City	AL	35	35	8	0	269.2	1111	237	94	81	11	3	6	6	83	3	183	12	4	20	8	.714	4	0-0	0	2.70
1989 Kansas City	AL	36	36	8	0	255	1060	252	100	86	10	4	4	5	63	8	173	9	0	15	11	.577	2	0-0	0	3.04
1990 Kansas City	AL	16	16	2	0	94	409	101	48	47	5	6	4	4	38	4	71	2	1	4	7	.364	0	0-0	0	4.50
1991 Kansas City	AL	26	26	0	0	133	601	168	90	84	10	3	5	6	42	1	89	5	0	9	12	.429	0	0-0	0	5.68
1992 Kansas City	AL	18	18	2	0	111.1	470	110	47	46	8	5	3	1	36	3	81	5	1	7	6	.538	1	0-0	0	3.72
1993 Kansas City	AL	49	6	0	12	104.1	474	128	61	54	2	6	6	2	43	8	80	12	0	5	8	.385	0	2-3	8	4.66
1994 Kansas City	AL	22	22	0	0	130	561	158	74	65	11	5	5	0	26	5	59	9	2	7	9	.438	0	0-0	0	4.50
1995 Kansas City	AL	33	33	3	0	213.1	898	222	97	89	21	9	6	6	62	2	81	4	1	12	14	.462	2	0-0	0	3.75
1996 Kansas City	AL	19	19	2	0	119.1	512	132	70	68	22	5	7	7	34	0	55	5	0	4	12	.250	1	0-0	0	5.13
13 ML YEARS		382	327	42	14	2218.2	9457	2226	1050	965	153	65	82	58	783	39	1366	107	11	132	135	.494	16	2--	—	3.91

Vladimir Guerrero

Bats: Right **Throws:** Right **Pos:** RF-7; CF-1; PH-1 **Ht:** 6'2" **Wt:** 195 **Born:** 2/9/76 **Age:** 21

		BATTING															BASERUNNING				PERCENTAGES		
Year Team	Lg	G	AB	H	2B	3B	HR	(Hm Rd)	TB	R	RBI	TBB	IBB	SO	HBP	SH	SF	SB	CS	SB%	GDP	Avg	OBP	SLG
1994 Expos	R	37	137	43	13	3	5	— —	77	24	25	11	0	18	2	0	3	0	7	.00	0	.314	.366	.562
1995 Albany	A	110	421	140	21	10	16	— —	229	77	63	30	3	45	7	0	4	12	7	.63	8	.333	.383	.544
1996 W. Palm Bch	A+	20	80	29	8	0	5	— —	52	16	18	3	0	10	1	0	1	2	2	.50	1	.363	.388	.650
Harrisburg	AA	118	417	150	32	8	19	— —	255	84	78	51	13	42	9	0	2	17	10	.63	8	.360	.438	.612
1996 Montreal	NL	9	27	5	0	0	1	(0 1)	8	2	1	0	0	3	0	0	0	0	0	.00	1	.185	.185	.296

Wilton Guerrero

Bats: Right **Throws:** Right **Pos:** PH-5 **Ht:** 5'11" **Wt:** 155 **Born:** 10/24/74 **Age:** 22

		BATTING															BASERUNNING				PERCENTAGES		
Year Team	Lg	G	AB	H	2B	3B	HR	(Hm Rd)	TB	R	RBI	TBB	IBB	SO	HBP	SH	SF	SB	CS	SB%	GDP	Avg	OBP	SLG
1993 Great Falls	R+	66	256	76	5	1	0	— —	83	44	21	24	1	33	3	5	0	20	8	.71	5	.297	.364	.324
1994 Vero Beach	A+	110	402	118	11	4	1	— —	140	55	32	29	0	71	1	10	2	23	20	.53	2	.294	.341	.348
1995 San Antonio	AA	95	382	133	13	6	0	— —	158	53	26	26	3	63	1	4	1	21	22	.49	10	.348	.390	.414
Albuquerque	AAA	14	49	16	1	1	0	— —	19	10	2	1	1	7	0	2	0	2	3	.40	1	.327	.340	.388
1996 Albuquerque	AAA	98	425	146	17	12	2	— —	193	79	38	26	2	48	1	11	0	26	15	.63	6	.344	.383	.454
1996 Los Angeles	NL	5	2	0	0	0	0	(0 0)	0	1	0	0	0	2	0	0	0	0	0	.00	0	.000	.000	.000

Lee Guetterman

Pitches: Left **Bats:** Left **Pos:** RP-17   **Ht:** 6'8" **Wt:** 230 **Born:** 11/22/58 **Age:** 38

Year Team	Lg	G	GS	CG	GF	IP	BFP	H	R	ER	HR	SH	SF	HB	TBB	IBB	SO	WP	Bk	W	L	Pct.	ShO	Sv-Op	Hld	ERA
1996 Tacoma *	AAA	25	0	0	11	28.2	121	27	14	12	2	3	0	2	10	0	28	2	0	2	2	.500	0	0--	—	3.77
1984 Seattle	AL	3	0	0	1	4.1	22	9	2	2	0	0	0	0	2	0	2	1	0	0	0	.000	0	0--	—	4.15
1986 Seattle	AL	41	4	1	8	76	353	108	67	62	7	3	5	4	30	3	38	2	0	0	4	.000	0	0--	—	7.34
1987 Seattle	AL	25	17	2	3	113.1	483	117	60	48	13	2	5	2	35	2	42	3	0	11	4	.733	1	0-0	0	3.81
1988 New York	AL	20	2	0	7	40.2	177	49	21	21	2	1	1	1	14	0	15	2	0	1	2	.333	0	0-1	3	4.65
1989 New York	AL	70	0	0	38	103	412	98	31	28	6	4	2	0	26	9	51	4	0	5	5	.500	0	13-13	12	2.45
1990 New York	AL	64	0	0	21	93	376	80	37	35	6	8	3	0	26	7	48	1	1	11	7	.611	0	2-7	12	3.39
1991 New York	AL	64	0	0	37	88	376	91	42	36	6	4	4	3	25	5	35	4	0	3	4	.429	0	6-9	8	3.68
1992 NYA-NYN		58	0	0	22	66	310	92	52	52	10	2	5	1	27	8	20	4	0	4	5	.444	0	2-3	9	7.09
1993 St. Louis	NL	40	0	0	14	46	192	41	18	15	1	1	2	2	16	5	19	1	0	3	3	.500	0	1-4	4	2.93
1995 Seattle	AL	23	0	0	3	17	85	21	13	13	1	1	0	3	11	0	11	0	0	0	0	.000	0	1-2	5	6.88
1996 Seattle	AL	17	0	0	1	11	50	11	8	5	0	0	2	0	10	2	6	0	0	2	0	.000	0	0-0	5	4.09
1992 New York	AL	15	0	0	7	22.2	114	35	24	24	5	0	2	0	13	3	5	1	0	1	1	.500	0	0-0	2	9.53
New York	NL	43	0	0	15	43.1	196	57	28	28	5	2	3	1	14	5	15	3	0	3	4	.429	0	2-3	7	5.82
11 ML YEARS		425	23	3	155	658.1	2836	717	351	317	52	26	27	16	222	41	287	22	1	38	36	.514	1	25--	—	4.33

Ozzie Guillen

Bats: Left **Throws:** Right **Pos:** SS-146; PH-9; LF-2   **Ht:** 5'11" **Wt:** 164 **Born:** 1/20/64 **Age:** 33

Year Team	Lg	G	AB	H	2B	3B	HR	(Hm	Rd)	TB	R	RBI	TBB	IBB	SO	HBP	SH	SF	SB	CS	SB%	GDP	Avg	OBP	SLG
1985 Chicago	AL	150	491	134	21	9	1	(1	0)	176	71	33	12	1	36	1	8	1	7	4	.64	5	.273	.291	.358
1986 Chicago	AL	159	547	137	19	4	2	(1	1)	170	58	47	12	1	52	1	12	5	8	4	.67	14	.250	.265	.311
1987 Chicago	AL	149	560	156	22	7	2	(2	0)	198	64	51	22	2	52	1	13	5	25	8	.76	10	.279	.303	.354
1988 Chicago	AL	156	566	148	16	7	0	(0	0)	178	58	39	25	3	40	2	10	3	25	13	.66	14	.261	.294	.314
1989 Chicago	AL	155	597	151	20	8	1	(0	1)	190	63	54	15	3	48	0	11	3	36	17	.68	8	.253	.270	.318
1990 Chicago	AL	160	516	144	21	4	1	(1	0)	176	61	58	26	8	37	1	15	5	13	17	.43	6	.279	.312	.341
1991 Chicago	AL	154	524	143	20	3	3	(1	2)	178	52	49	11	1	38	0	13	7	21	15	.58	7	.273	.284	.340
1992 Chicago	AL	12	40	8	4	0	0	(0	0)	12	5	7	1	0	5	0	1	1	1	0	1.00	1	.200	.214	.300
1993 Chicago	AL	134	457	128	23	4	4	(3	1)	171	44	50	10	0	41	0	13	6	5	4	.56	6	.280	.292	.374
1994 Chicago	AL	100	365	105	9	5	1	(0	1)	127	46	39	14	2	35	0	7	4	5	4	.56	5	.288	.311	.348
1995 Chicago	AL	122	415	103	20	3	1	(1	0)	132	50	41	13	1	25	0	4	1	6	7	.46	11	.248	.270	.318
1996 Chicago	AL	150	499	131	24	8	4	(0	4)	183	62	45	10	0	27	0	12	7	6	5	.55	10	.263	.273	.367
12 ML YEARS		1601	5577	1488	219	62	20	(10	10)	1891	634	513	171	22	436	6	119	51	158	98	.62	97	.267	.287	.339

Eric Gunderson

Pitches: Left **Bats:** Right **Pos:** RP-28   **Ht:** 6'0" **Wt:** 190 **Born:** 3/29/66 **Age:** 31

Year Team	Lg	G	GS	CG	GF	IP	BFP	H	R	ER	HR	SH	SF	HB	TBB	IBB	SO	WP	Bk	W	L	Pct.	ShO	Sv-Op	Hld	ERA
1996 Pawtucket *	AAA	26	1	0	3	33.2	144	38	15	13	2	0	1	0	9	1	34	3	0	2	1	.667	0	2--	—	3.48
1990 San Francisco	NL	7	4	0	1	19.2	94	24	14	12	2	1	0	0	11	1	14	0	0	1	2	.333	0	0-0	0	5.49
1991 San Francisco	NL	2	0	0	1	3.1	18	6	4	2	0	0	0	0	1	0	2	0	0	0	0	.000	0	1-1	0	5.40
1992 Seattle	AL	9	0	0	4	9.1	45	12	12	9	1	0	2	1	5	3	2	0	2	2	1	.667	0	0-0	0	8.68
1994 New York	NL	14	0	0	3	9	31	5	0	0	0	0	0	0	4	0	4	0	0	0	0	.000	0	0-0	2	0.00
1995 NYN-Bos		49	0	0	8	36.2	161	38	17	17	2	2	2	3	17	4	28	1	0	3	2	.600	0	0-3	6	4.17
1996 Boston	AL	28	0	0	2	17.1	82	21	17	16	5	0	2	2	8	2	7	3	0	0	0	.000	0	0-0	8	8.31
1995 New York	NL	30	0	0	7	24.1	103	25	10	10	2	0	1	1	8	3	19	1	0	1	1	.500	0	0-3	0	3.70
Boston	AL	19	0	0	1	12.1	58	13	7	7	0	2	1	2	9	1	9	0	0	2	1	.667	0	0-0	6	5.11
6 ML YEARS		109	4	0	19	95.1	431	106	64	56	10	3	6	6	46	10	57	4	2	6	6	.500	0	1-4	11	5.29

Mark Guthrie

Pitches: Left **Bats:** Right **Pos:** RP-66   **Ht:** 6'4" **Wt:** 207 **Born:** 9/22/65 **Age:** 31

Year Team	Lg	G	GS	CG	GF	IP	BFP	H	R	ER	HR	SH	SF	HB	TBB	IBB	SO	WP	Bk	W	L	Pct.	ShO	Sv-Op	Hld	ERA
1989 Minnesota	AL	13	8	0	2	57.1	254	66	32	29	7	1	5	1	21	1	38	1	0	2	4	.333	0	0-0	0	4.55
1990 Minnesota	AL	24	21	3	0	144.2	603	154	65	61	8	6	0	1	39	3	101	9	0	7	9	.438	1	0-0	0	3.79
1991 Minnesota	AL	41	12	0	13	98	432	116	52	47	11	4	3	1	41	2	72	7	0	7	5	.583	0	2-2	5	4.32
1992 Minnesota	AL	54	0	0	15	75	303	59	27	24	7	4	2	0	23	7	76	2	0	2	3	.400	0	5-7	19	2.88
1993 Minnesota	AL	22	0	0	2	21	94	20	11	11	2	1	2	0	16	2	15	1	3	2	1	.667	0	0-1	8	4.71
1994 Minnesota	AL	50	2	0	13	51.1	234	65	43	35	8	2	6	2	18	2	38	7	0	4	2	.667	0	1-3	12	6.14
1995 Min-LA		60	0	0	14	62	272	66	33	29	6	4	0	2	25	5	67	5	1	5	5	.500	0	0-2	15	4.21
1996 Los Angeles	NL	66	0	0	16	73	302	65	21	18	3	4	4	1	22	2	56	1	0	3	4	.400	0	1-3	12	2.22
1995 Minnesota	AL	36	0	0	7	42.1	181	47	22	21	5	2	0	1	16	3	48	3	1	5	3	.625	0	0-2	10	4.46
Los Angeles	NL	24	0	0	7	19.2	91	19	11	8	1	2	0	1	9	2	19	2	0	0	2	.000	0	0-0	5	3.66
8 ML YEARS		330	43	3	75	582.1	2494	611	284	254	52	26	22	8	205	24	463	33	4	31	32	.492	1	9-18	71	3.93

Ricky Gutierrez

Bats: R **Throws:** R **Pos:** SS-74; PH-9; 3B-6; 2B-5   **Ht:** 6'1" **Wt:** 175 **Born:** 5/23/70 **Age:** 27

Year Team	Lg	G	AB	H	2B	3B	HR	(Hm	Rd)	TB	R	RBI	TBB	IBB	SO	HBP	SH	SF	SB	CS	SB%	GDP	Avg	OBP	SLG
1993 San Diego	NL	133	438	110	10	5	5	(5	0)	145	76	26	50	2	97	5	1	1	4	3	.57	7	.251	.334	.331
1994 San Diego	NL	90	275	66	11	2	1	(1	0)	84	27	28	32	1	54	2	2	3	2	6	.25	8	.240	.321	.305
1995 Houston	NL	52	156	43	6	0	0	(0	0)	49	22	12	10	3	33	1	1	1	5	0	1.00	4	.276	.321	.314
1996 Houston	NL	89	218	62	8	1	1	(1	0)	75	28	15	23	3	42	3	4	1	6	1	.86	4	.284	.359	.344
4 ML YEARS		364	1087	281	35	8	7	(7	0)	353	153	81	115	9	226	11	8	6	17	10	.63	23	.259	.334	.325

Juan Guzman

Pitches: Right **Bats:** Right **Pos:** SP-27   **Ht:** 5'11" **Wt:** 195 **Born:** 10/28/66 **Age:** 30

Year Team	Lg	G	GS	CG	GF	IP	BFP	H	R	ER	HR	SH	SF	HB	TBB	IBB	SO	WP	Bk	W	L	Pct.	ShO	Sv-Op	Hld	ERA
1991 Toronto	AL	23	23	1	0	138.2	574	98	53	46	6	2	5	4	66	0	123	10	0	10	3	.769	0	0-0	0	2.99
1992 Toronto	AL	28	28	1	0	180.2	733	135	56	53	6	5	3	1	72	2	165	14	0	16	5	.762	0	0-0	0	2.64
1993 Toronto	AL	33	33	2	0	221	963	211	107	98	17	5	9	3	110	2	194	26	1	14	3	.824	1	0-0	0	3.99
1994 Toronto	AL	25	25	2	0	147.1	671	165	102	93	20	1	6	3	76	1	124	13	1	12	11	.522	0	0-0	0	5.68
1995 Toronto	AL	24	24	3	0	135.1	619	151	101	95	13	3	2	3	73	6	94	8	0	4	14	.222	0	0-0	0	6.32
1996 Toronto	AL	27	27	4	0	187.2	756	158	68	61	20	2	2	7	53	3	165	7	0	11	8	.579	1	0-0	0	2.93
6 ML YEARS		160	160	13	0	1010.2	4316	918	487	446	82	18	27	21	450	14	865	78	4	67	44	.604	2	0-0	0	3.97

Chris Gwynn

Bats: L **Throws:** L **Pos:** PH-60; RF-24; LF-5; 1B-1   **Ht:** 6'0" **Wt:** 220 **Born:** 10/13/64 **Age:** 32

Year Team	Lg	G	AB	H	2B	3B	HR	(Hm	Rd)	TB	R	RBI	TBB	IBB	SO	HBP	SH	SF	SB	CS	SB%	GDP	Avg	OBP	SLG
1987 Los Angeles	NL	17	32	7	1	0	0	(0	0)	8	2	2	1	0	7	0	1	0	0	0	.00	0	.219	.242	.250
1988 Los Angeles	NL	12	11	2	0	0	0	(0	0)	2	1	0	1	0	2	0	0	0	0	0	.00	0	.182	.250	.182
1989 Los Angeles	NL	32	68	16	4	1	0	(0	0)	22	8	7	2	0	9	0	2	1	1	0	1.00	1	.235	.254	.324
1990 Los Angeles	NL	101	141	40	2	1	5	(0	5)	59	19	22	7	2	28	0	0	3	0	1	.00	2	.284	.311	.418
1991 Los Angeles	NL	94	139	35	5	1	5	(3	2)	57	18	22	10	1	23	1	1	3	1	0	1.00	5	.252	.301	.410
1992 Kansas City	AL	34	84	24	3	2	1	(0	1)	34	10	7	3	0	10	0	1	2	0	0	.00	1	.286	.303	.405
1993 Kansas City	AL	103	287	86	14	4	1	(0	1)	111	36	25	24	5	34	1	2	2	0	1	.00	4	.300	.354	.387
1994 Los Angeles	NL	58	71	19	0	0	3	(0	3)	28	9	13	7	0	7	0	0	0	0	2	.00	7	.268	.333	.394
1995 Los Angeles	NL	67	84	18	3	2	1	(1	0)	28	8	10	6	1	23	1	0	1	0	0	.00	5	.214	.272	.333
1996 San Diego	NL	81	90	16	4	0	1	(0	1)	23	8	10	10	0	28	0	0	0	0	0	.00	0	.178	.260	.256
10 ML YEARS		599	1007	263	36	11	17	(4	13)	372	119	118	71	9	171	3	7	12	2	4	.33	24	.261	.308	.369

Tony Gwynn

Bats: Left **Throws:** Left **Pos:** RF-111; PH-6   **Ht:** 5'11" **Wt:** 220 **Born:** 5/9/60 **Age:** 37

Year Team	Lg	G	AB	H	2B	3B	HR	(Hm	Rd)	TB	R	RBI	TBB	IBB	SO	HBP	SH	SF	SB	CS	SB%	GDP	Avg	OBP	SLG
1982 San Diego	NL	54	190	55	12	2	1	(0	1)	74	33	17	14	0	16	0	4	1	8	3	.73	5	.289	.337	.389
1983 San Diego	NL	86	304	94	12	2	1	(0	1)	113	34	37	23	5	21	0	4	3	7	4	.64	9	.309	.355	.372
1984 San Diego	NL	158	606	213	21	10	5	(3	2)	269	88	71	59	13	23	2	6	2	33	18	.65	15	.351	.410	.444
1985 San Diego	NL	154	622	197	29	5	6	(3	3)	254	90	46	45	4	33	2	1	1	14	11	.56	17	.317	.364	.408
1986 San Diego	NL	160	642	211	33	7	14	(8	6)	300	107	59	52	11	35	3	2	2	37	9	.80	20	.329	.381	.467
1987 San Diego	NL	157	589	218	36	13	7	(5	2)	301	119	54	82	26	35	3	2	4	56	12	.82	13	.370	.447	.511
1988 San Diego	NL	133	521	163	22	5	7	(3	4)	216	64	70	51	13	40	0	4	2	26	11	.70	11	.313	.373	.415
1989 San Diego	NL	158	604	203	27	7	4	(3	1)	256	82	62	56	16	30	1	11	7	40	16	.71	12	.336	.389	.424
1990 San Diego	NL	141	573	177	29	10	4	(2	2)	238	79	72	44	20	23	1	7	4	17	8	.68	13	.309	.357	.415
1991 San Diego	NL	134	530	168	27	11	4	(1	3)	229	69	62	34	8	19	0	0	5	8	8	.50	11	.317	.355	.432
1992 San Diego	NL	128	520	165	27	3	6	(4	2)	216	77	41	46	12	16	0	0	3	3	6	.33	13	.317	.371	.415
1993 San Diego	NL	122	489	175	41	3	7	(3	4)	243	70	59	36	11	19	1	1	7	14	1	.93	18	.358	.398	.497
1994 San Diego	NL	110	419	165	35	1	12	(4	8)	238	79	64	48	16	19	2	1	5	5	0	1.00	20	.394	.454	.568
1995 San Diego	NL	135	535	197	33	1	9	(5	4)	259	82	90	35	10	15	1	0	6	17	5	.77	20	.368	.404	.484
1996 San Diego	NL	116	451	159	27	2	3	(2	1)	199	67	50	39	12	17	1	1	6	11	4	.73	17	.353	.400	.441
15 ML YEARS		1946	7595	2560	411	82	90	(47	43)	3405	1140	854	664	177	361	17	44	58	296	116	.72	214	.337	.389	.448

John Habyan

Pitches: Right **Bats:** Right **Pos:** RP-19   **Ht:** 6'2" **Wt:** 195 **Born:** 1/29/64 **Age:** 33

Year Team	Lg	G	GS	CG	GF	IP	BFP	H	R	ER	HR	SH	SF	HB	TBB	IBB	SO	WP	Bk	W	L	Pct.	ShO	Sv-Op	Hld	ERA
1996 Colo. Sprng *	AAA	1	1	0	0	4	15	2	2	2	1	0	0	0	1	0	4	0	0	0	0	.000	0	0- -		4.50
Ottawa *	AAA	7	0	0	2	7.1	29	7	2	2	1	0	0	0	2	0	8	0	0	0	1	.000	0	1- -		2.45
1985 Baltimore	AL	2	0	0	1	2.2	12	3	1	0	0	0	0	0	0	0	2	0	0	1	0	1.000	0	0- -		0.00
1986 Baltimore	AL	6	5	0	1	26.1	117	24	17	13	3	2	1	0	18	2	14	1	0	1	3	.250	0	0- -		4.44
1987 Baltimore	AL	27	13	0	4	116.1	493	110	67	62	20	4	4	2	40	1	64	3	0	6	7	.462	0	1-1	0	4.80
1988 Baltimore	AL	7	0	0	1	14.2	68	22	10	7	2	0	4	1	4	0	4	1	1	1	0	1.000	0	0-0	0	4.30
1990 New York	AL	6	0	0	1	8.2	37	10	2	2	0	4	0	1	4	0	6	0	0	0	0	.000	0	0-1		2.08

	HOW MUCH HE PITCHED						WHAT HE GAVE UP										THE RESULTS					
Year Team	Lg	G	GS	CG	GF	IP	BFP	H	R	ER	HR	SH	SF	HB	TBB	IBB	SO	WP	Bk	W	L	Pct.	ShO	Sv-Op	Hld	ERA
1991 New York	AL	66	0	0	16	90	349	73	28	23	2	2	1	2	20	2	70	1	2	4	2	.667	0	2-4	20	2.30
1992 New York	AL	56	0	0	20	72.2	316	84	32	31	6	5	3	2	21	5	44	2	1	5	6	.455	0	7-12	16	3.84
1993 NYA-KC	AL	48	0	0	23	56.1	239	59	27	26	6	0	2	0	20	4	39	0	2	2	1	.667	0	1-3	7	4.15
1994 St. Louis	NL	52	0	0	10	47.1	204	50	17	17	2	2	0	0	20	8	46	4	0	1	0	1.000	0	1-3	10	3.23
1995 StL-Cal	NL	59	0	0	16	73.1	311	68	34	28	2	6	3	2	27	4	60	4	3	4	4	.500	0	0-2	12	3.44
1996 Colorado	NL	19	0	0	5	24	116	34	19	19	4	2	1	1	14	1	25	5	1	1	1	.500	0	0-0	1	7.13
1993 New York	AL	36	0	0	21	42.1	181	45	20	19	5	0	2	0	16	2	29	0	2	2	1	.667	0	1-3	6	4.04
Kansas City	AL	12	0	0	2	14	58	14	7	7	1	0	0	0	4	2	10	0	0	0	0	.000	0	0-0	1	4.50
1995 St. Louis	NL	31	0	0	9	40.2	165	32	18	13	0	4	1	1	15	4	35	2	3	3	2	.600	0	0-1	3	2.88
California	AL	28	0	0	7	32.2	146	36	16	15	2	2	2	1	12	0	25	2	0	1	2	.333	0	0-1	9	4.13
11 ML YEARS		348	18	0	98	532.1	2262	537	254	228	47	23	17	10	186	27	372	22	10	26	24	.520	0	12- –	—	3.85

Dave Hajek

Bats: Right **Throws:** Right **Pos:** PH-4; 3B-3; 2B-2   **Ht:** 5'10" **Wt:** 165 **Born:** 10/14/67 **Age:** 29

	BATTING																BASERUNNING				PERCENTAGES		
Year Team	Lg	G	AB	H	2B	3B	HR	(Hm | Rd)	TB	R	RBI	TBB	IBB	SO	HBP	SH	SF	SB	CS	SB%	GDP	Avg	OBP	SLG
1990 Asheville	A	135	498	155	28	0	6	—	—	201	86	60	61	1	50	2	6	10	43	24	.64	16	.311	.382	.404
1991 Osceola	A+	63	232	61	9	4	0	—	—	78	35	20	23	0	30	1	4	1	8	5	.62	5	.263	.331	.336
Jackson	AA	37	94	18	6	0	0	—	—	24	10	9	7	2	12	0	1	1	2	0	1.00	1	.191	.245	.255
1992 Osceola	A+	5	18	2	1	0	0	—	—	3	3	1	1	0	1	0	0	0	1	0	1.00	0	.111	.158	.167
Jackson	AA	103	326	88	12	3	1	—	—	109	36	18	31	2	25	0	10	3	8	3	.73	5	.270	.331	.334
1993 Jackson	AA	110	332	97	20	2	5	—	—	136	50	27	17	2	14	2	1	3	6	5	.55	10	.292	.328	.410
1994 Tucson	AAA	129	484	157	29	5	7	—	—	217	71	70	29	5	23	2	5	5	12	7	.63	10	.324	.362	.448
1995 Tucson	AAA	131	502	164	37	4	4	—	—	221	99	79	39	7	27	2	5	6	12	7	.63	11	.327	.373	.440
1996 Tucson	AAA	121	508	161	31	5	4	—	—	214	81	64	25	5	36	1	1	4	9	6	.60	17	.317	.348	.421
1995 Houston	NL	5	2	0	0	0	0	(0 | 0)	0	0	0	1	0	1	0	0	2	1	0	1.00	0	.000	.333	.000
1996 Houston	NL	8	10	3	1	0	0	(0 | 0)	4	3	0	2	0	0	0	0	0	0	0		3	.300	.417	.400
2 ML YEARS		13	12	3	1	0	0	(0 | 0)	4	3	0	3	0	1	0	0	2	1	0	1.00	3	.250	.400	.333

Chip Hale

Bats: L **Throws:** R **Pos:** PH-69; 2B-14; DH-10; 1B-6; 3B-3; RF-3   **Ht:** 5'11" **Wt:** 186 **Born:** 12/2/64 **Age:** 32

	BATTING																BASERUNNING				PERCENTAGES		
Year Team	Lg	G	AB	H	2B	3B	HR	(Hm | Rd)	TB	R	RBI	TBB	IBB	SO	HBP	SH	SF	SB	CS	SB%	GDP	Avg	OBP	SLG
1989 Minnesota	AL	28	67	14	3	0	0	(0 | 0)	17	6	4	1	0	6	0	1	2	0	0	.00	0	.209	.214	.254
1990 Minnesota	AL	1	2	0	0	0	0	(0 | 0)	0	0	2	0	0	1	0	0	2	0	0	.00	0	.000	.000	.000
1993 Minnesota	AL	69	186	62	6	1	3	(1 | 2)	79	25	27	18	0	17	6	2	1	2	1	.67	2	.333	.408	.425
1994 Minnesota	AL	67	118	31	9	0	1	(0 | 1)	43	13	11	16	1	14	1	1	2	0	2	.00	2	.263	.350	.364
1995 Minnesota	AL	69	103	27	4	0	2	(0 | 2)	37	10	18	11	1	20	0	0	6	0	0	.00	6	.262	.333	.359
1996 Minnesota	AL	85	87	24	5	0	1	(0 | 1)	32	8	16	10	2	6	0	0	1	0	0	.00	4	.276	.347	.368
6 ML YEARS		319	563	158	27	1	7	(1 | 6)	208	62	78	56	4	64	7	4	8	2	3	.40	14	.281	.349	.369

Darren Hall

Pitches: Right **Bats:** Right **Pos:** RP-9   **Ht:** 6'3" **Wt:** 205 **Born:** 7/14/64 **Age:** 32

	HOW MUCH HE PITCHED						WHAT HE GAVE UP										THE RESULTS					
Year Team	Lg	G	GS	CG	GF	IP	BFP	H	R	ER	HR	SH	SF	HB	TBB	IBB	SO	WP	Bk	W	L	Pct.	ShO	Sv-Op	Hld	ERA
1996 Yakima *	A-	2	2	0	0	3	13	5	2	1	0	0	0	0	0	0	4	0	0	0	1	.000	0	0- –	—	3.00
1994 Toronto	AL	30	0	0	28	31.2	131	26	12	12	3	1	0	1	14	1	28	1	0	2	3	.400	0	17-20	1	3.41
1995 Toronto	AL	17	0	0	11	16.1	77	21	9	8	2	0	0	0	9	0	11	0	0	0	2	.000	0	3-4	2	4.41
1996 Los Angeles	NL	9	0	0	3	12	53	13	9	8	2	0	0	0	5	0	12	0	0	0	2	.000	0	0-1	2	6.00
3 ML YEARS		56	0	0	42	60	261	60	30	28	7	1	0	1	28	1	51	1	0	2	7	.222	0	20-25	5	4.20

Mel Hall

Bats: Left **Throws:** Left **Pos:** PH-22; LF-3; RF-1   **Ht:** 6'1" **Wt:** 214 **Born:** 9/16/60 **Age:** 36

	BATTING																BASERUNNING				PERCENTAGES		
Year Team	Lg	G	AB	H	2B	3B	HR	(Hm | Rd)	TB	R	RBI	TBB	IBB	SO	HBP	SH	SF	SB	CS	SB%	GDP	Avg	OBP	SLG
1996 Nashville *	AAA	4	15	4	0	0	1	—	—	7	1	1	1	0	1	0	0	0	0	0	.00	0	.267	.313	.467
1981 Chicago	NL	10	11	1	0	0	1	(1 | 0)	4	1	2	1	0	4	0	0	0	0	0	.00	0	.091	.167	.364
1982 Chicago	NL	24	80	21	3	2	0	(0 | 0)	28	6	4	5	1	17	2	0	1	0	1	.00	0	.263	.318	.350
1983 Chicago	NL	112	410	116	23	5	17	(6 | 11)	200	60	56	42	6	101	3	1	2	6	6	.50	4	.283	.352	.488
1984 ChN-Cle		131	407	108	24	4	11	(7 | 4)	173	68	52	47	8	78	2	0	7	3	2	.60	5	.265	.339	.425
1985 Cleveland	AL	23	66	21	6	0	0	(0 | 0)	27	7	12	8	0	12	0	0	1	1	0	.00	2	.318	.387	.409
1986 Cleveland	AL	140	442	131	29	2	18	(8 | 10)	218	68	77	33	8	65	0	0	3	6	2	.75	8	.296	.346	.493
1987 Cleveland	AL	142	485	136	21	1	18	(8 | 10)	213	57	76	20	6	68	1	0	4	5	4	.56	7	.280	.309	.439
1988 Cleveland	AL	150	515	144	32	4	6	(3 | 3)	202	69	71	28	12	50	0	0	2	7	3	.70	8	.280	.312	.392
1989 New York	AL	113	361	94	9	0	17	(11 | 6)	154	54	58	21	4	37	0	1	8	0	0	.00	7	.260	.295	.427
1990 New York	AL	113	360	93	23	2	12	(3 | 9)	156	41	46	6	2	46	0	0	3	0	0	.00	7	.258	.272	.433
1991 New York	AL	141	492	140	23	2	19	(13 | 6)	224	67	80	26	6	40	3	0	6	0	1	.00	9	.285	.321	.455
1992 New York	AL	152	583	163	36	3	15	(7 | 8)	250	67	81	29	4	53	1	0	9	4	2	.67	13	.280	.310	.429
1996 San Francisco	NL	25	25	3	0	0	0	(0 | 0)	3	3	5	1	0	4	0	0	0	0	0	.00	0	.120	.148	.120
1984 Chicago	NL	48	150	42	11	3	4	(3 | 1)	71	25	22	13	2	23	2	0	2	5	1	.67	2	.280	.329	.473

						BATTING														BASERUNNING				PERCENTAGES		
Year Team	Lg	G	AB	H	2B	3B	HR	(Hm	Rd)	TB	R	RBI	TBB	IBB	SO	HBP	SH	SF	SB	CS	SB%	GDP	Avg	OBP	SLG
Cleveland	AL	83	257	66	13	1	7	(4	3)	102	43	30	35	5	55	2	0	5	1	1	.50	3	.257	.344	.397
13 ML YEARS		1276	4237	1171	229	25	134	(67	67)	1852	568	620	267	57	575	16	4	51	31	22	.58	69	.276	.318	.437

Bob Hamelin

Bats: Left **Throws:** Left **Pos:** DH-47; 1B-33; PH-13 **Ht:** 6'0" **Wt:** 235 **Born:** 11/29/67 **Age:** 29

						BATTING														BASERUNNING				PERCENTAGES		
Year Team	Lg	G	AB	H	2B	3B	HR	(Hm	Rd)	TB	R	RBI	TBB	IBB	SO	HBP	SH	SF	SB	CS	SB%	GDP	Avg	OBP	SLG
1996 Omaha *	AAA	4	16	5	1	1	0	—	—	8	4	0	1	0	4	0	0	0	1	0	1.00	0	.313	.353	.500
1993 Kansas City	AL	16	49	11	3	0	2	(1	1)	20	2	5	6	0	15	0	0	0	0	0	.00	2	.224	.309	.408
1994 Kansas City	AL	101	312	88	25	1	24	(13	11)	187	64	65	56	3	62	1	0	5	4	3	.57	4	.282	.388	.599
1995 Kansas City	AL	72	208	35	7	1	7	(3	4)	65	20	25	26	1	56	6	0	1	0	1	.00	6	.168	.278	.313
1996 Kansas City	AL	89	239	61	14	1	9	(2	7)	104	31	40	54	2	58	2	0	4	5	2	.71	7	.255	.391	.435
4 ML YEARS		278	808	195	49	3	42	(19	23)	376	117	135	142	6	191	9	0	10	9	6	.60	19	.241	.357	.465

Darryl Hamilton

Bats: Left **Throws:** Right **Pos:** CF-147; PH-3 **Ht:** 6'1" **Wt:** 185 **Born:** 12/3/64 **Age:** 32

						BATTING														BASERUNNING				PERCENTAGES		
Year Team	Lg	G	AB	H	2B	3B	HR	(Hm	Rd)	TB	R	RBI	TBB	IBB	SO	HBP	SH	SF	SB	CS	SB%	GDP	Avg	OBP	SLG
1988 Milwaukee	AL	44	103	19	4	0	1	(1	0)	26	14	11	12	0	9	1	0	1	7	3	.70	2	.184	.274	.252
1990 Milwaukee	AL	89	156	46	5	0	1	(1	0)	54	27	18	9	0	12	0	3	0	10	3	.77	2	.295	.333	.346
1991 Milwaukee	AL	122	405	126	15	6	1	(0	1)	156	64	57	33	2	38	0	7	3	16	6	.73	10	.311	.361	.385
1992 Milwaukee	AL	128	470	140	19	7	5	(1	4)	188	67	62	45	0	42	1	4	7	41	14	.75	10	.298	.356	.400
1993 Milwaukee	AL	135	520	161	21	1	9	(5	4)	211	74	48	45	5	62	3	4	1	21	13	.62	9	.310	.367	.406
1994 Milwaukee	AL	36	141	37	10	1	1	(0	1)	52	23	13	15	1	17	0	2	1	3	0	1.00	2	.262	.331	.369
1995 Milwaukee	AL	112	398	108	20	6	5	(3	2)	155	54	44	47	3	35	3	8	3	11	1	.92	9	.271	.350	.389
1996 Texas	AL	148	627	184	29	4	6	(2	4)	239	94	51	54	4	66	2	7	6	15	5	.75	15	.293	.348	.381
8 ML YEARS		814	2820	821	123	25	29	(13	16)	1081	417	304	260	15	281	10	35	22	124	45	.73	59	.291	.351	.383

Joey Hamilton

Pitches: Right **Bats:** Right **Pos:** SP-33; RP-1 **Ht:** 6'4" **Wt:** 230 **Born:** 9/9/70 **Age:** 26

		HOW MUCH HE PITCHED						WHAT HE GAVE UP												THE RESULTS					
Year Team	Lg	G	GS	CG	GF	IP	BFP	H	R	ER	HR	SH	SF	HB	TBB	IBB	SO	WP	Bk	W	L	Pct.	ShO	Sv-Op	Hld	ERA
1994 San Diego	NL	16	16	1	0	108.2	447	98	46	36	7	4	2	6	29	3	61	6	0	9	6	.600	1	0-0	0	2.98
1995 San Diego	NL	31	30	2	1	204.1	850	189	89	70	17	12	4	11	56	5	123	2	0	6	9	.400	2	0-0	0	3.08
1996 San Diego	NL	34	33	3	0	211.2	908	206	100	98	19	6	5	9	83	3	184	14	1	15	9	.625	1	0-0	1	4.17
3 ML YEARS		81	79	6	1	524.2	2205	493	229	204	43	22	11	26	168	11	368	22	1	30	24	.556	4	0-0	1	3.50

Chris Hammond

Pitches: Left **Bats:** Left **Pos:** RP-29; SP-9 **Ht:** 6'1" **Wt:** 195 **Born:** 1/21/66 **Age:** 31

		HOW MUCH HE PITCHED						WHAT HE GAVE UP												THE RESULTS					
Year Team	Lg	G	GS	CG	GF	IP	BFP	H	R	ER	HR	SH	SF	HB	TBB	IBB	SO	WP	Bk	W	L	Pct.	ShO	Sv-Op	Hld	ERA
1996 Brevard Cty *	A+	1	1	0	0	4	14	3	0	0	0	0	0	0	0	0	8	1	0	0	0	.000	0	0--	—	0.00
Charlotte *	AAA	1	1	0	0	5	20	5	4	4	0	0	0	0	3	0	3	0	0	1	0	1.000	0	0--	—	7.20
1990 Cincinnati	NL	3	3	0	0	11.1	56	13	9	8	2	1	0	0	12	1	4	1	3	0	2	.000	0	0-0	0	6.35
1991 Cincinnati	NL	20	18	0	0	99.2	425	92	51	45	4	6	1	2	48	3	50	3	0	7	7	.500	0	0-0	0	4.06
1992 Cincinnati	NL	28	26	0	1	147.1	627	149	75	69	13	5	3	3	55	6	79	6	0	7	10	.412	0	0-0	0	4.21
1993 Florida	NL	32	32	1	0	191	826	207	106	99	18	10	2	1	66	2	108	10	5	11	12	.478	1	0-0	0	4.66
1994 Florida	NL	13	13	1	0	73.1	312	79	30	25	5	5	2	1	23	1	40	3	4	4	4	.500	1	0-0	0	3.07
1995 Florida	NL	25	24	3	0	161	683	157	73	68	17	7	7	9	47	2	126	3	1	9	6	.600	2	0-0	0	3.80
1996 Florida	NL	38	9	0	5	81	368	104	65	59	14	3	4	4	27	3	50	1	0	5	8	.385	0	0-0	5	6.56
7 ML YEARS		159	125	5	6	764.2	3297	801	409	373	73	37	19	20	278	18	457	27	9	43	49	.467	3	0-0	5	4.39

Jeffrey Hammonds

Bats: R **Throws:** R **Pos:** LF-64; RF-11; PH-3; DH-1; CF-1 **Ht:** 6'0" **Wt:** 195 **Born:** 3/5/71 **Age:** 26

						BATTING														BASERUNNING				PERCENTAGES		
Year Team	Lg	G	AB	H	2B	3B	HR	(Hm	Rd)	TB	R	RBI	TBB	IBB	SO	HBP	SH	SF	SB	CS	SB%	GDP	Avg	OBP	SLG
1996 Rochester *	AAA	34	125	34	4	2	3	—	—	51	24	19	19	0	19	1	0	3	3	1	.75	2	.272	.365	.408
1993 Baltimore	AL	33	105	32	8	0	3	(2	1)	49	10	19	2	1	16	0	1	2	4	0	1.00	3	.305	.312	.467
1994 Baltimore	AL	68	250	74	18	2	8	(6	2)	120	45	31	17	1	39	2	0	5	5	0	1.00	4	.296	.339	.480
1995 Baltimore	AL	57	178	43	9	1	4	(2	2)	66	18	23	9	0	30	1	1	2	4	2	.67	3	.242	.279	.371
1996 Baltimore	AL	71	248	56	10	1	9	(3	6)	95	38	27	23	1	53	4	6	1	3	3	.50	7	.226	.301	.383
4 ML YEARS		229	781	205	45	4	24	(13	11)	330	111	100	51	3	138	7	8	10	16	5	.76	16	.262	.310	.423

Mike Hampton

Pitches: Left **Bats:** Right **Pos:** SP-27   **Ht:** 5'10" **Wt:** 180 **Born:** 9/9/72 **Age:** 24

		HOW MUCH HE PITCHED						WHAT HE GAVE UP												THE RESULTS						
Year Team	Lg	G	GS	CG	GF	IP	BFP	H	R	ER	HR	SH	SF	HB	TBB	IBB	SO	WP	Bk	W	L	Pct.	ShO	Sv-Op	Hld	ERA
1993 Seattle	AL	13	3	0	2	17	95	28	20	18	3	1	1	0	17	3	8	1	1	1	3	.250	0	1-1	2	9.53
1994 Houston	NL	44	0	0	7	41.1	181	46	19	17	4	0	0	2	16	1	24	5	1	2	1	.667	0	0-1	10	3.70
1995 Houston	NL	24	24	0	0	150.2	641	141	73	56	13	11	5	4	49	3	115	3	1	9	8	.529	0	0-0		3.35
1996 Houston	NL	27	27	2	0	160.1	691	175	79	64	12	10	3	3	49	1	101	7	2	10	10	.500	1	0-0		3.59
4 ML YEARS		108	54	2	9	369.1	1608	390	191	155	32	22	9	9	131	8	248	16	5	22	22	.500	1	1-2	12	3.78

Lee Hancock

Pitches: Left **Bats:** Left **Pos:** RP-13   **Ht:** 6'4" **Wt:** 220 **Born:** 6/27/67 **Age:** 30

		HOW MUCH HE PITCHED						WHAT HE GAVE UP												THE RESULTS						
Year Team	Lg	G	GS	CG	GF	IP	BFP	H	R	ER	HR	SH	SF	HB	TBB	IBB	SO	WP	Bk	W	L	Pct.	ShO	Sv-Op	Hld	ERA
1988 Bellingham	A-	16	16	2	0	100.1	411	83	37	29	3	2	3	2	31	0	102	5	2	6	5	.545	0	0- -	—	2.60
1989 San Bernrdo	A+	26	26	5	0	173	720	131	69	50	5	5	3	5	82	2	119	11	2	12	7	.632	0	0- -	—	2.60
1990 Williamsprt	AA	7	7	0	0	47	193	39	20	14	2	0	1	0	20	1	27	1	0	3	2	.600	0	0- -	—	2.68
Harrisburg	AA	20	19	3	0	117.2	513	106	51	45	4	5	0	1	57	1	65	8	4	6	7	.462	1	0- -	—	3.44
Buffalo	AAA	1	0	0	0	0	1	0	0	0	0	0	0	0	1	0	0	0	0	0	0	.000	0	0- -	—	0.00
1991 Carolina	AA	37	11	0	10	98	420	93	48	41	3	5	3	2	42	4	66	8	0	4	7	.364	0	4- -	—	3.77
1992 Buffalo	AAA	10	0	0	7	9	38	9	2	2	0	1	0	0	3	1	5	2	1	0	2	.000	0	0- -	—	2.00
Carolina	AA	23	0	0	6	40.1	166	32	13	10	2	0	0	0	14	4	40	6	0	1	1	.500	0	0- -	—	2.23
1993 Carolina	AA	25	11	0	3	99.2	409	87	42	28	3	2	1	4	32	2	85	5	0	7	3	.700	0	0- -	—	2.53
Buffalo	AAA	11	11	0	0	66	278	73	38	36	4	4	3	0	14	0	30	2	0	2	6	.250	0	0- -	—	4.91
1994 Buffalo	AAA	37	7	0	8	86.2	371	103	35	33	8	0	3	1	23	3	39	1	0	4	5	.444	0	1- -	—	3.43
1995 Calgary	AAA	34	17	1	5	113.2	510	146	78	64	9	5	0	4	27	2	49	4	1	6	10	.375	0	0- -	—	5.07
1996 Calgary	AAA	9	1	0	3	15	58	9	3	3	0	0	0	0	5	2	9	1	0	0	0	.000	0	0- -	—	1.80
Phoenix	AAA	17	3	0	6	35.1	159	42	19	17	0	4	1	0	12	0	19	4	0	0	2	.000	0	0- -	—	4.33
1995 Pittsburgh	NL	11	0	0	3	14	54	10	3	3	0	0	0	0	2	0	6	2	0	0	0	.000	0	0-0	0	1.93
1996 Pittsburgh	NL	13	0	0	3	18.1	89	21	18	13	5	1	0	2	10	3	13	1	0	0	0	.000	0	0-0	1	6.38
2 ML YEARS		24	0	0	6	32.1	143	31	21	16	5	1	0	2	12	3	19	3	0	0	0	.000	0	0-0	1	4.45

Ryan Hancock

Pitches: Right **Bats:** Right **Pos:** RP-7; SP-4   **Ht:** 6'2" **Wt:** 220 **Born:** 11/11/71 **Age:** 25

		HOW MUCH HE PITCHED						WHAT HE GAVE UP												THE RESULTS						
Year Team	Lg	G	GS	CG	GF	IP	BFP	H	R	ER	HR	SH	SF	HB	TBB	IBB	SO	WP	Bk	W	L	Pct.	ShO	Sv-Op	Hld	ERA
1993 Boise	A-	3	3	0	0	16.1	69	14	9	6	1	1	0	0	8	1	18	0	0	1	0	1.000	0	0- -	—	3.31
1994 Lk Elsinore	A+	18	18	3	0	116.1	494	113	62	49	10	1	5	5	36	1	95	0	2	9	6	.600	1	0- -	—	3.79
Midland	AA	8	8	0	0	48	219	63	34	31	1	1	1	6	11	0	35	0	2	3	4	.429	0	0- -	—	5.81
1995 Midland	AA	28	28	5	0	175.2	764	222	107	89	17	5	4	8	45	1	79	7	3	12	9	.571	1	0- -	—	4.56
1996 Vancouver	AAA	19	11	1	1	80.1	347	69	38	33	7	7	0	5	38	0	65	1	1	4	6	.400	0	0- -	—	3.70
1996 California	AL	11	4	0	4	27.2	130	34	23	23	2	0	0	2	17	1	19	2	0	4	1	.800	0	0-0	0	7.48

Chris Haney

Pitches: Left **Bats:** Left **Pos:** SP-35   **Ht:** 6'3" **Wt:** 195 **Born:** 11/16/68 **Age:** 28

		HOW MUCH HE PITCHED						WHAT HE GAVE UP												THE RESULTS						
Year Team	Lg	G	GS	CG	GF	IP	BFP	H	R	ER	HR	SH	SF	HB	TBB	IBB	SO	WP	Bk	W	L	Pct.	ShO	Sv-Op	Hld	ERA
1991 Montreal	NL	16	16	0	0	84.2	387	94	49	38	6	6	1	1	43	1	51	9	0	3	7	.300	0	0-0	0	4.04
1992 Mon-KC		16	13	2	2	80	339	75	43	41	11	0	6	4	26	2	54	5	1	4	6	.400	2	0-0	0	4.61
1993 Kansas City	AL	23	23	1	0	124	556	141	87	83	13	3	4	3	53	2	65	6	1	9	9	.500	1	0-0	0	6.02
1994 Kansas City	AL	6	6	0	0	28.1	127	36	25	23	2	3	4	1	11	1	18	2	0	2	2	.500	0	0-0	0	7.31
1995 Kansas City	AL	16	13	1	0	81.1	338	78	35	33	7	1	4	2	33	0	31	2	0	3	4	.429	0	0-0	2	3.65
1996 Kansas City	AL	35	35	4	0	228	988	267	136	119	29	5	8	6	51	0	115	8	0	10	14	.417	1	0-0	0	4.70
1992 Montreal	NL	9	6	1	2	38	165	40	25	23	6	0	3	4	10	0	27	5	1	2	3	.400	1	0-0	0	5.45
Kansas City	AL	7	7	1	0	42	174	35	18	18	5	0	3	0	16	2	27	0	0	2	3	.400	1	0-0	0	3.86
6 ML YEARS		112	106	8	2	626.1	2735	691	375	337	68	18	27	17	217	6	334	32	2	31	42	.425	4	0-0	2	4.84

Todd Haney

Bats: R **Throws:** R **Pos:** PH-25; 2B-23; 3B-4; SS-3   **Ht:** 5'9" **Wt:** 165 **Born:** 7/30/65 **Age:** 31

		BATTING																	BASERUNNING			PERCENTAGES		
Year Team	Lg	G	AB	H	2B	3B	HR	(Hm	Rd)	TB	R	RBI	TBB	IBB	SO	HBP	SH	SF	SB	CS	SB%	GDP	Avg	OBP	SLG
1996 Iowa *	AAA	66	240	59	13	0	2	—	—	78	20	19	19	0	24	0	6	2	3	1	.75	6	.246	.299	.325
1992 Montreal	NL	7	10	3	1	0	0	(0	0)	4	0	1	0	0	0	1	1	0	0	0	.00	0	.300	.300	.400
1994 Chicago	NL	17	37	6	0	0	1	(0	1)	9	6	2	3	0	3	1	1	1	2	1	.67	0	.162	.238	.243
1995 Chicago	NL	25	73	30	8	0	2	(1	1)	44	11	6	7	0	11	0	1	0	0	0	.00	0	.411	.463	.603
1996 Chicago	NL	49	82	11	1	0	0	(0	0)	12	11	3	7	0	15	0	2	1	1	0	1.00	2	.134	.200	.146
4 ML YEARS		98	202	50	10	0	3	(1	2)	69	28	12	17	0	29	1	5	2	3	1	.75	2	.248	.306	.342

Greg Hansell

Pitches: Right **Bats:** Right **Pos:** RP-50 **Ht:** 6'5" **Wt:** 215 **Born:** 3/12/71 **Age:** 26

Year Team	Lg	G	GS	CG	GF	IP	BFP	H	R	ER	HR	SH	SF	HB	TBB	IBB	SO	WP	Bk	W	L	Pct.	ShO	Sv-Op	Hld	ERA
1989 Red Sox	R	10	8	0	2	57	246	51	23	16	1	3	1	4	23	0	44	3	3	3	2	.600	0	2--	—	2.53
1990 Winter Havn	A+	21	21	2	0	115.1	502	95	63	46	8	4	4	9	64	0	79	4	4	7	10	.412	1	0--	—	3.59
St. Lucie	A+	6	6	0	0	38	168	34	22	11	0	1	1	3	15	0	16	3	0	2	4	.333	0	0--	—	2.61
1991 Bakersfield	A+	25	25	0	0	150.2	625	142	56	48	5	10	2	5	42	1	132	3	0	14	5	.737	0	0--	—	2.87
1992 Albuquerque	AAA	13	13	0	0	68.2	321	84	46	40	9	1	1	1	35	3	38	4	0	1	5	.167	0	0--	—	5.24
San Antonio	AA	14	14	0	0	92.1	380	80	40	29	6	2	1	3	33	2	64	1	2	6	4	.600	0	0--	—	2.83
1993 Albuquerque	AAA	26	20	0	3	101.1	478	131	86	78	9	1	4	3	60	1	60	10	0	5	10	.333	0	0--	—	6.93
1994 Albuquerque	AAA	47	6	0	19	123.1	498	109	44	41	4	3	4	6	31	3	101	8	0	10	2	.833	0	8--	—	2.99
1995 Salt Lake	AAA	15	6	0	3	48.1	218	64	35	33	2	2	1	2	10	2	32	3	1	4	2	.667	0	1--	—	6.14
Albuquerque	AAA	15	6	0	3	48.1	218	64	35	33	5	2	1	2	10	2	32	3	1	4	2	.667	0	1--	—	6.14
1995 Los Angeles	NL	20	0	0	7	19.1	93	29	17	16	5	1	1	2	6	1	13	0	0	0	1	.000	0	0-1	1	7.45
1996 Minnesota	AL	50	0	0	23	74.1	329	83	48	47	14	3	2	2	31	1	46	9	1	3	0	1.000	0	3-4	3	5.69
2 ML YEARS		70	0	0	30	93.2	422	112	65	63	19	4	3	4	37	2	59	9	1	3	1	.750	0	3-5	4	6.05

Dave Hansen

Bats: Left **Throws:** Right **Pos:** PH-58; 3B-19; 1B-8 **Ht:** 6'0" **Wt:** 195 **Born:** 11/24/68 **Age:** 28

Year Team	Lg	G	AB	H	2B	3B	HR	(Hm	Rd)	TB	R	RBI	TBB	IBB	SO	HBP	SH	SF	SB	CS	SB%	GDP	Avg	OBP	SLG
1990 Los Angeles	NL	5	7	1	0	0	0	(0	0)	1	0	1	0	0	3	0	0	0	0	0	.00	0	.143	.143	.143
1991 Los Angeles	NL	53	56	15	4	0	1	(0	1)	22	3	5	2	0	12	0	0	0	1	0	1.00	2	.268	.293	.393
1992 Los Angeles	NL	132	341	73	11	0	6	(1	5)	102	30	22	34	3	49	1	0	2	0	2	.00	9	.214	.286	.299
1993 Los Angeles	NL	84	105	38	3	0	4	(2	2)	53	13	30	21	3	13	0	0	1	0	1	.00	3	.362	.465	.505
1994 Los Angeles	NL	40	44	15	3	0	0	(0	0)	18	3	5	5	0	5	0	0	0	0	0	.00	4	.341	.408	.409
1995 Los Angeles	NL	100	181	52	10	0	1	(0	1)	65	19	14	28	4	28	1	0	1	0	0	.00	4	.287	.384	.359
1996 Los Angeles	NL	80	104	23	1	0	0	(0	0)	24	7	6	11	1	22	0	0	0	0	0	.00	4	.221	.293	.231
7 ML YEARS		494	838	217	32	0	12	(3	9)	285	75	83	101	11	132	2	0	5	1	3	.25	19	.259	.338	.340

Erik Hanson

Pitches: Right **Bats:** Right **Pos:** SP-35 **Ht:** 6'6" **Wt:** 215 **Born:** 5/18/65 **Age:** 32

Year Team	Lg	G	GS	CG	GF	IP	BFP	H	R	ER	HR	SH	SF	HB	TBB	IBB	SO	WP	Bk	W	L	Pct.	ShO	Sv-Op	Hld	ERA
1988 Seattle	AL	6	6	0	0	41.2	168	35	17	15	4	3	0	1	12	1	36	2	2	2	3	.400	0	0-0	0	3.24
1989 Seattle	AL	17	17	1	0	113.1	465	103	44	40	7	4	1	5	32	1	75	3	0	9	5	.643	0	0-0	0	3.18
1990 Seattle	AL	33	33	5	0	236	964	205	88	85	15	5	6	2	68	6	211	10	1	18	9	.667	1	0-0	0	3.24
1991 Seattle	AL	27	27	2	0	174.2	744	182	82	74	16	2	8	2	56	2	143	14	1	8	8	.500	1	0-0	0	3.81
1992 Seattle	AL	31	30	6	0	186.2	809	209	110	100	14	8	9	7	57	1	112	6	0	8	17	.320	1	0-0	0	4.82
1993 Seattle	AL	31	30	7	0	215	898	215	91	83	17	10	4	6	60	6	163	8	0	11	12	.478	0	0-0	0	3.47
1994 Cincinnati	NL	22	21	0	1	122.2	519	137	60	56	10	5	4	3	23	3	101	8	1	5	5	.500	0	0-0	0	4.11
1995 Boston	AL	29	29	1	0	186.2	800	187	94	88	17	6	8	1	59	0	139	5	0	15	5	.750	1	0-0	0	4.24
1996 Toronto	AL	35	35	4	0	214.2	955	243	143	129	26	4	5	2	102	2	156	13	0	13	17	.433	1	0-0	0	5.41
9 ML YEARS		231	228	26	1	1491.1	6322	1516	729	670	126	47	45	28	469	22	1136	69	5	89	81	.524	5	0-0	0	4.04

Jason Hardtke

Bats: Both **Throws:** Right **Pos:** 2B-18; PH-5 **Ht:** 5'10" **Wt:** 175 **Born:** 9/15/71 **Age:** 25

Year Team	Lg	G	AB	H	2B	3B	HR	(Hm	Rd)	TB	R	RBI	TBB	IBB	SO	HBP	SH	SF	SB	CS	SB%	GDP	Avg	OBP	SLG
1990 Burlington	R+	39	142	38	7	0	4	—	—	57	18	16	23	0	19	2	0	0	11	1	.92	3	.268	.377	.401
1991 Columbus	A	139	534	155	26	8	12	—	—	233	104	81	75	5	48	7	6	6	22	4	.85	6	.290	.381	.436
1992 Kinston	A+	6	19	4	0	0	0	—	—	4	3	1	4	0	4	0	0	0	0	0	.00	0	.211	.348	.211
Waterloo	A	110	411	125	27	4	8	—	—	184	75	47	38	3	33	5	1	5	9	7	.56	9	.304	.366	.448
High Desert	A+	10	41	11	1	0	2	—	—	18	9	8	4	0	4	1	0	1	1	1	.50	1	.268	.340	.439
1993 Rancho Cuca	A+	130	523	167	38	7	11	—	—	252	98	85	61	2	54	2	2	6	7	8	.47	12	.319	.389	.482
1994 Wichita	AA	75	255	60	15	1	5	—	—	92	26	29	21	1	44	0	2	4	1	2	.33	4	.235	.289	.361
Rancho Cuca	A+	4	13	4	0	0	0	—	—	4	2	0	9	0	2	0	0	0	1	1	.00	0	.308	.438	.308
1995 Norfolk	AAA	4	7	2	1	0	0	—	—	3	1	0	2	0	0	0	0	0	1	1	.50	0	.286	.444	.429
Binghamton	AA	121	455	130	42	4	4	—	—	192	65	52	66	1	58	4	2	9	6	8	.43	7	.286	.375	.422
1996 Binghamton	AA	35	137	36	11	0	3	—	—	56	23	16	16	1	16	0	1	0	0	1	.00	3	.263	.340	.409
Norfolk	AAA	71	257	77	17	2	9	—	—	125	49	35	29	1	29	0	0	2	4	6	.40	4	.300	.368	.486
1996 New York	NL	19	57	11	5	0	0	(0	0)	16	3	6	2	0	12	1	0	0	0	0	.00	1	.193	.233	.281

Tim Harikkala

Pitches: Right **Bats:** Right **Pos:** SP-1 **Ht:** 6'2" **Wt:** 185 **Born:** 7/15/71 **Age:** 25

Year Team	Lg	G	GS	CG	GF	IP	BFP	H	R	ER	HR	SH	SF	HB	TBB	IBB	SO	WP	Bk	W	L	Pct.	ShO	Sv-Op	Hld	ERA
1992 Bellingham	A-	15	2	0	2	33.1	145	37	15	10	2	3	2	0	16	0	18	1	2	2	0	1.000	0	1--	—	2.70
1993 Bellingham	A-	4	0	0	0	8	30	3	1	1	0	0	1	0	2	0	12	0	0	1	0	1.000	0	0--	—	1.13

Year Team	Lg	G	GS	CG	GF	IP	BFP	H	R	ER	HR	SH	SF	HB	TBB	IBB	SO	WP	Bk	W	L	Pct.	ShO	Sv-Op	Hld	ERA
Appleton	A	15	4	0	5	38.2	175	50	30	28	3	2	1	2	12	2	33	4	3	3	3	.500	0	0--	—	6.52
1994 Appleton	A	13	13	3	0	93.2	373	69	31	20	6	2	3	5	24	0	63	5	0	8	3	.727	0	0--	—	1.92
Riverside	A+	4	4	0	0	29	108	16	6	2	1	0	1	0	10	0	30	1	0	4	0	1.000	0	0--	—	0.62
Jacksonville	AA	9	9	0	0	54.1	245	70	30	24	4	1	3	1	19	0	22	4	0	4	1	.800	0	0--	—	3.98
1995 Tacoma	AAA	25	24	4	0	146.1	638	151	78	69	13	3	4	2	55	3	73	7	0	5	12	.294	1	0--	—	4.24
1996 Tacoma	AAA	27	27	1	0	158.1	715	204	98	85	12	3	6	5	48	2	115	5	1	8	12	.400	1	0--	—	4.83
1995 Seattle	AL	1	0	0	1	3.1	18	7	6	6	1	0	0	0	1	0	1	0	0	0	0	.000	0	0-0	0	16.20
1996 Seattle	AL	1	1	0	0	4.1	20	4	6	6	1	0	1	0	2	0	1	0	0	0	0	.000	0	0-0	0	12.46
2 ML YEARS		2	1	0	1	7.2	38	11	12	12	2	0	1	1	3	0	2	0	0	0	1	.000	0	0-0	0	14.09

Pete Harnisch

Pitches: Right Bats: Right Pos: SP-31   Ht: 6'0" Wt: 207 Born: 9/23/66 Age: 30

Year Team	Lg	G	GS	CG	GF	IP	BFP	H	R	ER	HR	SH	SF	HB	TBB	IBB	SO	WP	Bk	W	L	Pct.	ShO	Sv-Op	Hld	ERA
1996 St. Lucie *	A+	2	2	0	0	13	49	11	4	4	1	0	0	0	0	0	12	0	0	1	0	1.000	0	0--	—	2.77
1988 Baltimore	AL	2	2	0	0	13	61	13	8	8	1	2	0	0	9	1	10	1	0	0	2	.000	0	0-0	0	5.54
1989 Baltimore	AL	18	17	2	1	103.1	468	97	55	53	10	4	5	5	64	3	70	5	1	5	9	.357	0	0-0	0	4.62
1990 Baltimore	AL	31	31	3	0	188.2	821	189	96	91	17	6	5	1	86	5	122	2	2	11	11	.500	0	0-0	0	4.34
1991 Houston	NL	33	33	4	0	216.2	900	169	71	65	14	9	7	5	83	3	172	5	2	12	9	.571	2	0-0	0	2.70
1992 Houston	NL	34	34	0	0	206.2	859	182	92	85	18	5	5	5	64	3	164	4	1	9	10	.474	0	0-0	0	3.70
1993 Houston	NL	33	33	5	0	217.2	896	171	84	72	20	9	4	6	79	5	185	3	1	16	9	.640	4	0-0	0	2.98
1994 Houston	NL	17	17	1	0	95	419	100	59	57	13	3	2	3	39	1	62	2	0	8	5	.615	0	0-0	0	5.40
1995 New York	NL	18	18	0	1	110	462	111	55	45	13	4	6	3	24	4	82	0	1	2	8	.200	0	0-0	0	3.68
1996 New York	NL	31	31	2	0	194.2	839	195	103	91	30	13	9	7	61	5	114	7	3	8	12	.400	1	0-0	0	4.21
9 ML YEARS		217	216	17	1	1345.2	5725	1227	623	567	136	55	43	35	509	30	981	29	11	71	75	.486	7	0-0	0	3.79

Lenny Harris

B: L T: R Pos: PH-58; 3B-24; LF-23; RF-18; 1B-16; 2B-8; CF-1   Ht: 5'10" Wt: 210 Born: 10/28/64 Age: 32

Year Team	Lg	G	AB	H	2B	3B	HR	(Hm	Rd)	TB	R	RBI	TBB	IBB	SO	HBP	SH	SF	SB	CS	SB%	GDP	Avg	OBP	SLG
1988 Cincinnati	NL	16	43	16	1	0	0	(0	0)	17	7	8	5	0	4	0	1	1	4	1	.80	0	.372	.420	.395
1989 Cin-LA	NL	115	335	79	10	1	3	(1	2)	100	36	26	20	0	33	2	1	0	14	9	.61	14	.236	.283	.299
1990 Los Angeles	NL	137	431	131	16	4	2	(0	2)	161	61	29	29	2	31	1	3	1	15	10	.60	8	.304	.348	.374
1991 Los Angeles	NL	145	429	123	16	1	3	(1	2)	150	59	38	37	5	32	5	12	2	12	3	.80	16	.287	.349	.350
1992 Los Angeles	NL	135	347	94	11	0	0	(0	0)	105	28	30	24	3	24	1	6	2	19	7	.73	10	.271	.318	.303
1993 Los Angeles	NL	107	160	38	6	1	2	(0	2)	52	20	11	15	4	15	0	1	0	3	1	.75	4	.238	.303	.325
1994 Cincinnati	NL	66	100	31	3	1	0	(0	0)	36	13	14	5	0	13	0	0	1	7	2	.78	6	.310	.340	.360
1995 Cincinnati	NL	101	197	41	8	3	2	(0	2)	61	32	16	14	0	20	0	3	1	10	1	.91	6	.208	.259	.310
1996 Cincinnati	NL	125	302	86	17	2	5	(2	3)	122	33	32	21	1	31	1	6	3	14	6	.70	3	.285	.330	.404
1989 Cincinnati	NL	61	188	42	4	0	2	(0	2)	52	17	11	9	0	20	1	1	0	10	6	.63	5	.223	.263	.277
Los Angeles	NL	54	147	37	6	1	1	(1	0)	48	19	15	11	0	13	1	0	0	4	3	.57	9	.252	.308	.327
9 ML YEARS		947	2344	639	88	13	17	(4	13)	804	289	204	170	15	203	10	33	12	98	40	.71	61	.273	.323	.343

Pep Harris

Pitches: Right Bats: Right Pos: RP-8; SP-3   Ht: 6'2" Wt: 185 Born: 9/23/72 Age: 24

Year Team	Lg	G	GS	CG	GF	IP	BFP	H	R	ER	HR	SH	SF	HB	TBB	IBB	SO	WP	Bk	W	L	Pct.	ShO	Sv-Op	Hld	ERA
1991 Burlington	R+	13	13	0	0	65.2	292	67	30	24	7	4	2	3	31	0	47	5	0	4	3	.571	0	0--	—	3.29
1992 Columbus	A	18	17	0	0	90.2	400	88	51	37	10	3	6	2	51	1	57	11	0	7	4	.636	0	0--	—	3.67
1993 Columbus	A	26	17	0	4	119	510	113	67	56	7	4	1	4	44	0	82	6	0	7	8	.467	0	0--	—	4.24
1994 Kinston	A+	27	0	0	20	32.2	140	21	14	7	1	0	0	2	16	0	37	2	0	4	1	.800	0	8--	—	1.93
Canton-Akrn	AA	24	0	0	22	20.1	86	9	5	5	0	1	0	2	13	2	15	1	0	2	0	1.000	0	12--	—	2.21
1995 Buffalo	AAA	14	0	0	3	32.2	141	32	11	9	2	0	0	0	15	0	18	0	0	2	1	.667	0	0--	—	2.48
1996 Midland	AA	6	6	0	0	39	177	47	27	23	2	1	0	2	9	1	28	0	0	2	2	.500	0	0--	—	5.31
Vancouver	AAA	18	18	1	0	118.1	517	135	67	60	12	6	2	3	46	0	61	2	2	9	3	.750	0	0--	—	4.56
1996 California	AL	11	3	0	0	32.1	146	31	16	14	2	3	0	1	17	2	20	4	0	2	0	1.000	0	0-0	2	3.90

Reggie Harris

Pitches: Right Bats: Right Pos: RP-4   Ht: 6'1" Wt: 190 Born: 8/12/68 Age: 28

Year Team	Lg	G	GS	CG	GF	IP	BFP	H	R	ER	HR	SH	SF	HB	TBB	IBB	SO	WP	Bk	W	L	Pct.	ShO	Sv-Op	Hld	ERA
1996 Trenton *	AA	33	0	0	30	37	144	17	6	6	2	0	3	0	19	2	43	1	1	2	1	.667	0	17--	—	1.46
1990 Oakland	AL	16	1	0	9	41.1	168	25	16	16	5	1	2	2	21	1	31	2	0	1	1	1.000	0	0-0	0	3.48
1991 Oakland	AL	2	0	0	0	3	15	5	4	4	0	0	1	0	3	1	2	2	0	0	0	.000	0	0-0	0	12.00
1996 Boston	AL	4	0	0	1	4.1	24	7	6	6	2	0	0	1	5	0	4	0	0	0	0	.000	0	0-1	0	12.46
3 ML YEARS		22	1	0	11	48.2	207	37	26	26	7	1	3	3	29	2	37	4	0	1	1	1.000	0	0-1	0	4.81

Dean Hartgraves

Pitches: Left **Bats:** Right **Pos:** RP-39 | **Ht:** 6'0" **Wt:** 185 **Born:** 8/12/66 **Age:** 30

Year Team	Lg	G	GS	CG	GF	IP	BFP	H	R	ER	HR	SH	SF	HB	TBB	IBB	SO	WP	Bk	W	L	Pct.	ShO	Sv-Op	Hld	ERA
1987 Auburn	A-	23	0	0	12	31.2	157	31	24	14	1	3	0	1	27	4	42	1	0	0	5	.000	0	2--	—	3.98
1988 Asheville	A	34	13	2	7	118.1	523	131	70	59	9	2	8	5	47	2	83	8	5	5	9	.357	1	0--	—	4.49
1989 Asheville	A	19	19	4	0	120.1	542	140	66	55	6	5	3	4	49	2	87	5	3	5	8	.385	0	0--	—	4.11
Osceola	A+	7	6	1	0	39.2	165	36	20	13	0	2	2	2	12	0	21	4	0	3	3	.500	1	0--	—	2.95
1990 Columbus	AA	33	14	0	6	99.2	454	108	66	52	8	7	4	3	48	1	64	6	0	8	8	.500	0	0--	—	4.70
1991 Jackson	AA	19	9	3	5	74	302	60	25	22	3	6	4	2	25	3	44	4	0	6	5	.545	0	0--	—	2.68
Tucson	AAA	16	3	1	4	43.2	189	47	17	15	2	2	3	0	20	1	18	2	0	3	0	1.000	1	0--	—	3.09
1992 Tucson	AAA	5	1	0	0	8	61	26	24	22	1	0	0	0	9	0	6	4	0	0	1	.000	0	0--	—	24.75
Jackson	AA	22	22	3	0	146.2	585	127	54	45	7	4	1	3	40	1	92	9	1	9	6	.600	2	0--	—	2.76
1993 Tucson	AAA	23	10	0	2	77.2	369	90	65	55	7	2	6	4	40	0	42	5	0	1	6	.143	0	0--	—	6.37
1994 Tucson	AAA	47	4	0	16	97.2	429	106	64	55	11	3	4	1	36	2	54	4	0	7	2	.778	0	3--	—	5.07
1995 Tucson	AAA	14	0	0	9	21.1	91	21	5	6	0	0	1	1	5	2	15	0	1	3	2	.600	0	5--	—	2.11
1996 Tucson	AAA	18	0	0	9	19	79	17	6	4	1	0	1	0	8	1	13	1	0	2	1	.667	0	4--	—	1.89
Richmond	AAA	4	0	0	1	8.2	32	4	2	2	1	0	1	1	2	0	8	0	0	0	0	.000	0	0--	—	2.08
1995 Houston	NL	40	0	0	11	36.1	150	30	14	13	2	1	1	0	16	2	24	1	0	2	0	1.000	0	0-3	4	3.22
1996 Hou-Atl	NL	39	0	0	9	37.2	167	34	21	20	4	1	2	2	23	3	30	2	0	1	0	1.000	0	0-0	6	4.78
1996 Houston	NL	19	0	0	5	19	89	18	11	11	1	1	1	1	16	3	16	2	0	0	0	.000	0	0-0	4	5.21
Atlanta	NL	20	0	0	4	18.2	78	16	10	9	3	0	1	1	7	0	14	0	0	1	0	1.000	0	0-0	2	4.34
2 ML YEARS		79	0	0	20	74	317	64	35	33	6	2	3	2	39	5	54	3	0	3	0	1.000	0	0-3	10	4.01

Bryan Harvey

Pitches: Right **Bats:** Right **Pos:** RP | **Ht:** 6'2" **Wt:** 212 **Born:** 6/2/63 **Age:** 34

Year Team	Lg	G	GS	CG	GF	IP	BFP	H	R	ER	HR	SH	SF	HB	TBB	IBB	SO	WP	Bk	W	L	Pct.	ShO	Sv-Op	Hld	ERA
1987 California	AL	3	0	0	2	5	22	6	0	0	0	0	0	0	3	0	3	3	0	0	0	.000	0	0-0	0	0.00
1988 California	AL	50	0	0	38	76	303	59	22	18	4	3	3	1	20	6	67	4	1	7	5	.583	0	17-23	1	2.13
1989 California	AL	51	0	0	42	55	245	36	21	21	6	5	2	0	41	1	78	5	0	3	3	.500	0	25-32	0	3.44
1990 California	AL	54	0	0	47	64.1	267	45	24	23	4	4	4	0	35	6	82	7	1	4	4	.500	0	25-31	1	3.22
1991 California	AL	67	0	0	**63**	78.2	309	51	20	14	6	3	2	1	17	3	101	2	2	2	4	.333	0	**46-52**	0	1.60
1992 California	AL	25	0	0	22	28.2	122	22	12	9	4	2	3	0	11	1	34	4	0	0	4	.000	0	13-16	0	2.83
1993 Florida	NL	59	0	0	54	69	264	45	14	13	4	3	6	0	13	2	73	0	1	1	5	.167	0	45-49	0	1.70
1994 Florida	NL	12	0	0	10	10.1	47	12	6	6	1	0	0	0	4	0	10	0	0	0	0	.000	0	6-6	0	5.23
1995 Florida	NL	1	0	0	0	3	13	2	3	3	1	0	0	0	1	0	0	0	0	0	0	.000	0	0-0	0	0.00
9 ML YEARS		322	0	0	278	387	1582	278	122	107	30	20	20	2	144	19	448	25	5	17	25	.405	0	177-209	2	2.49

Bill Haselman

Bats: Right **Throws:** Right **Pos:** C-69; PH-9; DH-2; 1B-2 | **Ht:** 6'3" **Wt:** 223 **Born:** 5/25/66 **Age:** 31

Year Team	Lg	G	AB	H	2B	3B	HR	(Hm	Rd)	TB	R	RBI	TBB	IBB	SO	HBP	SH	SF	SB	CS	SB%	GDP	Avg	OBP	SLG
1990 Texas	AL	7	13	2	0	0	0	(0	0)	2	0	3	1	0	5	0	0	0	0	0	.00	0	.154	.214	.154
1992 Seattle	AL	8	19	5	0	0	0	(0	0)	5	1	0	0	0	7	0	0	0	0	0	.00	1	.263	.263	.263
1993 Seattle	AL	58	137	35	8	0	5	(3	2)	58	21	16	12	0	19	1	2	2	2	1	.67	5	.255	.316	.423
1994 Seattle	AL	38	83	16	7	1	1	(1	0)	28	11	8	3	0	11	1	1	0	1	0	1.00	3	.193	.230	.337
1995 Boston	AL	64	152	37	6	1	5	(3	2)	60	22	23	17	0	30	2	0	3	0	2	.00	4	.243	.322	.395
1996 Boston	AL	77	237	65	13	1	8	(5	3)	104	33	34	19	3	52	1	0	0	4	2	.67	13	.274	.331	.439
6 ML YEARS		252	641	160	34	3	19	(12	7)	257	88	84	52	3	124	5	3	5	7	5	.58	25	.250	.309	.401

Scott Hatteberg

Bats: Left **Throws:** Right **Pos:** C-10; PH-3 | **Ht:** 6'1" **Wt:** 195 **Born:** 12/14/69 **Age:** 27

Year Team	Lg	G	AB	H	2B	3B	HR	(Hm	Rd)	TB	R	RBI	TBB	IBB	SO	HBP	SH	SF	SB	CS	SB%	GDP	Avg	OBP	SLG
1991 Winter Havn	A+	56	191	53	7	3	1	(Hm	—)	69	21	24	22	4	22	0	2	2	1	2	.33	6	.277	.349	.361
Lynchburg	A+	8	25	5	1	0	0	—	—	6	4	3	7	0	6	0	0	0	0	0	.00	0	.200	.375	.240
1992 New Britain	AA	103	297	69	13	2	1	—	—	89	28	30	41	2	49	2	1	3	1	3	.25	6	.232	.327	.300
1993 New Britain	AA	68	227	63	10	2	7	—	—	98	35	28	42	3	38	1	1	0	1	3	.25	6	.278	.393	.432
Pawtucket	AAA	18	53	10	0	0	1	—	—	13	6	2	6	0	12	1	2	0	0	0	.00	5	.189	.283	.245
1994 New Britain	AA	20	68	18	4	1	1	—	—	27	6	9	7	1	9	0	0	1	0	2	.00	4	.265	.329	.397
Pawtucket	AAA	78	238	56	14	0	7	—	—	91	26	19	32	1	49	3	2	1	2	1	.67	14	.235	.332	.382
1995 Pawtucket	AAA	85	251	68	15	1	7	—	—	106	36	27	40	2	39	4	1	3	2	0	1.00	8	.271	.376	.422
1996 Pawtucket	AAA	90	287	77	16	0	12	—	—	129	52	49	58	0	66	2	1	1	1	1	.50	6	.268	.391	.449
1995 Boston	AL	2	2	1	0	0	0	(0	0)	1	1	0	0	0	0	0	0	0	0	0	.00	1	.500	.500	.500
1996 Boston	AL	10	11	2	1	0	0	(0	0)	3	3	0	3	0	2	0	0	0	0	0	.00	2	.182	.357	.273
2 ML YEARS		12	13	3	1	0	0	(0	0)	4	4	0	3	0	2	0	0	0	0	0	.00	3	.231	.375	.308

Ryan Hawblitzel

Pitches: Right **Bats:** Right **Pos:** RP-8   **Ht:** 6'2" **Wt:** 185 **Born:** 4/30/71 **Age:** 26

		HOW MUCH HE PITCHED						WHAT HE GAVE UP										THE RESULTS					
Year Team	Lg	G	GS	CG	GF	IP	BFP	H	R	ER	HR	SH	SF	HB	TBB	IBB	SO	WP	Bk	W	L	Pct.	ShO	Sv-Op	Hld	ERA
1990 Huntington	R+	14	14	2	0	75.2	322	72	38	33	8	0	0	6	25	0	71	2	0	6	5	.545	1	0--	—	3.93
1991 Winston-Sal	A+	20	20	5	0	134	552	110	40	34	7	5	7	7	47	0	103	8	1	15	2	.882	2	0--	—	2.28
Charlotte	AA	5	5	1	0	33.2	141	31	14	12	2	5	2	3	12	3	25	0	0	1	2	.333	1	0--	—	3.21
1992 Charlotte	AA	28	28	3	0	174.2	727	180	84	73	18	5	5	4	38	3	119	8	0	12	8	.600	1	0--	—	3.76
1993 Colo. Sprng	AAA	29	28	2	0	165.1	764	221	129	113	16	10	9	4	49	0	90	3	0	8	13	.381	0	0--	—	6.15
1994 Colo. Sprng	AAA	28	28	3	0	163	732	200	119	111	21	6	2	10	53	2	103	5	0	10	10	.500	1	0--	—	6.13
1995 Colo. Sprng	AAA	21	14	0	1	83	352	88	47	42	7	3	5	3	17	1	40	2	0	5	3	.625	0	0--	—	4.55
1996 Colo. Sprng	AAA	26	18	0	5	117	501	131	76	65	17	4	4	5	27	2	75	2	0	7	6	.538	0	1--	—	5.00
1996 Colorado	NL	8	0	0	3	15	69	18	12	10	2	0	1	0	6	0	7	1	0			.000	0	0-0	0	6.00

LaTroy Hawkins

Pitches: Right **Bats:** Right **Pos:** SP-6; RP-1   **Ht:** 6'5" **Wt:** 193 **Born:** 12/21/72 **Age:** 24

		HOW MUCH HE PITCHED						WHAT HE GAVE UP										THE RESULTS					
Year Team	Lg	G	GS	CG	GF	IP	BFP	H	R	ER	HR	SH	SF	HB	TBB	IBB	SO	WP	Bk	W	L	Pct.	ShO	Sv-Op	Hld	ERA
1991 Twins	R	11	11	0	0	55	251	62	34	29	2	0	1	3	26	0	47	6	3	4	3	.571	0	0--	—	4.75
1992 Twins	R	6	6	1	0	36.1	161	36	19	13	1	0	0	3	10	0	35	3	2	3	2	.600	0	0--	—	3.22
Elizabethtn	R+	5	5	1	0	26.2	115	21	12	10	2	0	0	0	11	0	36	0	1	0	1	.000	0	0--	—	3.38
1993 Fort Wayne	A	26	23	4	1	157.1	619	110	53	36	5	4	4	4	41	0	179	8	2	15	5	.750	3	0--	—	2.06
1994 Fort Myers	A+	6	6	1	0	38.2	153	32	10	10	1	2	0	2	6	0	36	0	0	4	0	1.000	1	0--	—	2.33
Nashville	AA	11	11	1	0	73.1	297	50	23	19	2	3	1	3	28	0	53	2	1	9	2	.818	0	0--	—	2.33
Salt Lake	AAA	12	12	1	0	81.2	353	92	42	37	8	2	2	5	33	0	37	4	2	5	4	.556	0	0--	—	4.08
1995 Salt Lake	AAA	22	22	4	0	144.1	601	150	63	57	7	5	2	1	40	1	74	6	1	9	7	.563	1	0--	—	3.55
1996 Salt Lake	AAA	20	20	4	0	137.2	563	138	66	60	11	0	4	3	31	3	99	6	0	9	8	.529	1	0--	—	3.92
1995 Minnesota	AL	6	6	1	0	27	131	39	29	26	3	0	3	1	12	0	9	1	1	2	3	.400	0	0-0	0	8.67
1996 Minnesota	AL	7	6	0	1	26.1	124	42	24	24	8	1	1	0	9	0	24	1	1	1	1	.500	0	0-0	0	8.20
2 ML YEARS		13	12	1	1	53.1	255	81	53	50	11	1	4	1	21	0	33	2	2	3	4	.429	0	0-0	0	8.44

Charlie Hayes

Bats: Right **Throws:** Right **Pos:** 3B-143; PH-11   **Ht:** 6'0" **Wt:** 224 **Born:** 5/29/65 **Age:** 32

		BATTING																BASERUNNING				PERCENTAGES		
Year Team	Lg	G	AB	H	2B	3B	HR	(Hm | Rd)	TB	R	RBI	TBB	IBB	SO	HBP	SH	SF	SB	CS	SB%	GDP	Avg	OBP	SLG
1988 San Francisco	NL	7	11	1	0	0	0	(0 | 0)	1	0	0	0	0	3	0	0	0	0	0	.00	0	.091	.091	.091
1989 SF-Phi	NL	87	304	78	15	1	8	(3 | 5)	119	26	43	11	1	50	0	2	3	3	1	.75	6	.257	.280	.391
1990 Philadelphia	NL	152	561	145	20	0	10	(3 | 7)	195	56	57	28	3	91	2	0	6	4	4	.50	12	.258	.293	.348
1991 Philadelphia	NL	142	460	106	23	1	12	(6 | 6)	167	34	53	16	3	75	1	2	1	3	3	.50	13	.230	.257	.363
1992 New York	AL	142	509	131	19	2	18	(7 | 11)	208	52	66	28	0	100	3	4	5	3	5	.38	12	.257	.297	.409
1993 Colorado	NL	157	573	175	45	2	25	(17 | 8)	299	89	98	43	6	82	5	1	8	11	6	.65	25	.305	.355	.522
1994 Colorado	NL	113	423	122	23	4	10	(4 | 6)	183	46	50	36	4	71	3	0	1	3	6	.33	11	.288	.348	.433
1995 Philadelphia	NL	141	529	146	30	3	11	(6 | 5)	215	58	85	50	2	88	4	0	6	5	1	.83	22	.276	.340	.406
1996 Pit-NYA	NL	148	526	133	24	2	12	(5 | 7)	197	58	75	37	4	90	0	3	3	6	0	1.00	17	.253	.300	.375
1989 San Francisco	NL	3	5	1	0	0	0	(0 | 0)	1	0	0	0	0	1	0	0	0	0	0	.00	0	.200	.200	.200
Philadelphia	NL	84	299	77	15	1	8	(3 | 5)	118	26	43	11	1	49	0	2	3	3	1	.75	6	.258	.281	.395
1996 Pittsburgh	NL	128	459	114	21	2	10	(5 | 5)	169	51	62	36	4	78	0	2	3	6	0	1.00	16	.248	.301	.368
New York	AL	20	67	19	3	0	2	(0 | 2)	28	7	13	1	0	12	0	1	0	0	0	.00	1	.284	.294	.418
9 ML YEARS		1089	3896	1037	199	15	106	(51 | 55)	1584	419	527	249	23	650	18	11	34	38	26	.59	118	.266	.311	.407

Jimmy Haynes

Pitches: Right **Bats:** Right **Pos:** RP-15; SP-11   **Ht:** 6'3" **Wt:** 180 **Born:** 9/5/72 **Age:** 24

		HOW MUCH HE PITCHED						WHAT HE GAVE UP										THE RESULTS					
Year Team	Lg	G	GS	CG	GF	IP	BFP	H	R	ER	HR	SH	SF	HB	TBB	IBB	SO	WP	Bk	W	L	Pct.	ShO	Sv-Op	Hld	ERA
1991 Orioles	R	14	8	1	4	62	256	44	27	11	0	1	3	6	21	0	67	6	1	3	2	.600	0	2--	—	1.60
1992 Kane County	A	24	24	4	0	144	616	131	66	41	2	4	9	4	45	0	141	12	7	7	11	.389	0	0--	—	2.56
1993 Frederick	A+	27	27	2	0	172.1	707	139	73	58	13	2	3	1	61	1	174	20	4	12	8	.600	1	0--	—	3.03
1994 Rochester	AAA	3	3	0	0	13.1	68	20	12	10	3	0	1	1	6	0	14	0	0	1	0	1.000	0	0--	—	6.75
Bowie	AA	25	25	5	0	173.2	705	154	67	56	16	6	4	3	46	1	177	8	3	13	8	.619	1	0--	—	2.90
1995 Rochester	AAA	26	25	3	0	167	691	162	77	61	16	4	7	0	49	0	140	6	1	12	8	.600	1	0--	—	3.29
1996 Rochester	AAA	5	5	0	0	28.2	130	31	19	18	5	1	0	0	18	0	24	1	1	1	1	.500	0	0--	—	5.65
1995 Baltimore	AL	4	3	0	0	24	94	11	6	6	2	1	0	0	12	1	22	0	0	2	1	.667	0	0-0	0	2.25
1996 Baltimore	AL	26	11	0	8	89	435	122	84	82	14	4	5	2	58	1	65	5	0	3	6	.333	0	1-1	0	8.29
2 ML YEARS		30	14	0	8	113	529	133	90	88	16	5	5	2	70	2	87	5	0	5	7	.417	0	1-1	0	7.01

Bronson Heflin

Pitches: Right **Bats:** Right **Pos:** RP-3   **Ht:** 6'3" **Wt:** 200 **Born:** 8/29/71 **Age:** 25

		HOW MUCH HE PITCHED						WHAT HE GAVE UP										THE RESULTS					
Year Team	Lg	G	GS	CG	GF	IP	BFP	H	R	ER	HR	SH	SF	HB	TBB	IBB	SO	WP	Bk	W	L	Pct.	ShO	Sv-Op	Hld	ERA
1994 Batavia	A-	14	13	1	0	83	353	85	38	33	5	5	0	6	20	0	71	11	2	6	5	.545	0	0--	—	3.58

			HOW MUCH HE PITCHED						WHAT HE GAVE UP										THE RESULTS						
Year Team	Lg	G	GS	CG	GF	IP	BFP	H	R	ER	HR	SH	SF	HB	TBB	IBB	SO	WP	Bk	W	L	Pct.	ShO	Sv-Op	Hld	ERA
1995 Reading	AA	1	0	0	1	1	4	0	0	0	0	0	0	0	1	0	2	0	0	0	0	.000	0	0--	—	0.00
1996 Reading	AA	25	0	0	12	29.1	139	37	20	17	3	2	0	2	15	2	27	2	0	2	2	.500	0	1--	—	5.22
Scranton-WB	AAA	30	0	0	27	38	140	25	11	11	0	0	3	1	3	1	23	1	0	4	0	1.000	0	12--	—	2.61
1996 Philadelphia	NL	3	0	0	2	6.2	34	11	7	5	1	0	1	0	3	0	4	0	0	0	0	.000	0	0-0	0	6.75

Rick Helling

Pitches: Right Bats: Right Pos: SP-6; RP-5   **Ht: 6'3" Wt: 215 Born: 12/15/70 Age: 26**

			HOW MUCH HE PITCHED						WHAT HE GAVE UP										THE RESULTS						
Year Team	Lg	G	GS	CG	GF	IP	BFP	H	R	ER	HR	SH	SF	HB	TBB	IBB	SO	WP	Bk	W	L	Pct.	ShO	Sv-Op	Hld	ERA
1996 Okla. City *	AAA	23	22	2	1	140	574	124	54	46	10	3	5	7	38	1	157	4	2	12	4	.750	1	0--	—	2.96
1994 Texas	AL	9	9	1	0	52	228	62	34	34	14	0	0	0	18	0	25	4	1	3	2	.600	1	0-0	0	5.88
1995 Texas	AL	3	3	0	0	12.1	62	17	11	9	2	0	2	2	8	0	5	0	0	0	2	.000	0	0-0	0	6.57
1996 Tex-Fla		11	6	0	2	48	198	37	23	23	9	1	1	0	16	0	42	1	1	3	3	.500	0	0-0	1	4.31
1996 Texas	AL	6	2	0	2	20.1	92	23	17	17	7	0	1	0	9	0	16	1	0	1	2	.333	0	0-0	0	7.52
Florida	NL	5	4	0	0	27.2	106	14	6	6	2	1	0	0	7	0	26	0	1	2	1	.667	0	0-0	1	1.95
3 ML YEARS		23	18	1	2	112.1	488	116	68	66	25	1	3	2	42	0	72	5	2	6	7	.462	1	0-0	1	5.29

Rickey Henderson

Bats: R Throws: L Pos: LF-114; PH-19; RF-17; CF-10   **Ht: 5'10" Wt: 190 Born: 12/25/58 Age: 38**

							BATTING												BASERUNNING				PERCENTAGES		
Year Team	Lg	G	AB	H	2B	3B	HR	(Hm	Rd)	TB	R	RBI	TBB	IBB	SO	HBP	SH	SF	SB	CS	SB%	GDP	Avg	OBP	SLG
1979 Oakland	AL	89	351	96	13	3	1	(1	0)	118	49	26	34	0	39	2	8	3	33	11	.75	4	.274	.338	.336
1980 Oakland	AL	158	591	179	22	4	9	(3	6)	236	111	53	117	7	54	5	6	3	100	26	.79	6	.303	.420	.399
1981 Oakland	AL	108	423	135	18	7	6	(5	1)	185	89	35	64	4	68	2	0	4	56	22	.72	7	.319	.408	.437
1982 Oakland	AL	149	536	143	24	4	10	(5	5)	205	119	51	116	1	94	2	0	2	130	42	.76	5	.267	.398	.382
1983 Oakland	AL	145	513	150	25	7	9	(5	4)	216	105	48	103	8	80	4	1	1	108	19	.85	11	.292	.414	.421
1984 Oakland	AL	142	502	147	27	4	16	(7	9)	230	113	58	86	1	81	5	1	3	66	18	.79	7	.293	.399	.458
1985 New York	AL	143	547	172	28	5	24	(8	16)	282	146	72	99	1	65	3	0	5	80	10	.89	8	.314	.419	.516
1986 New York	AL	153	608	160	31	5	28	(13	15)	285	130	74	89	2	81	2	0	2	87	18	.83	12	.263	.358	.469
1987 New York	AL	95	358	104	17	3	17	(10	7)	178	78	37	80	1	52	2	0	0	41	8	.84	10	.291	.423	.497
1988 New York	AL	140	554	169	30	2	6	(2	4)	221	118	50	82	1	54	3	2	6	93	13	.88	6	.305	.394	.399
1989 NYA-Oak	AL	150	541	148	26	3	12	(7	5)	216	113	57	126	5	68	3	0	1	77	14	.85	8	.274	.411	.399
1990 Oakland	AL	136	489	159	33	3	28	(8	20)	282	119	61	97	2	60	4	0	2	65	10	.87	13	.325	.439	.577
1991 Oakland	AL	134	470	126	17	1	18	(8	10)	199	105	57	98	7	73	7	0	3	58	18	.76	7	.268	.400	.423
1992 Oakland	AL	117	396	112	18	3	15	(10	5)	181	77	46	95	5	56	6	0	3	48	11	.81	5	.283	.426	.457
1993 Oak-Tor	AL	134	481	139	22	2	21	(10	11)	228	114	59	120	7	65	4	1	4	53	8	.87	9	.289	.432	.474
1994 Oakland	AL	87	296	77	13	0	6	(4	2)	108	66	20	72	1	45	1	0	5	22	7	.76	0	.260	.411	.365
1995 Oakland	AL	112	407	122	31	1	9	(3	6)	182	67	54	72	2	66	4	1	3	32	10	.76	8	.300	.407	.447
1996 San Diego	NL	148	465	112	17	2	9	(6	3)	160	110	29	125	2	90	10	0	2	37	15	.71	5	.241	.410	.344
1989 New York	AL	65	235	58	13	1	3	(1	2)	82	41	22	56	0	29	1	0	1	25	8	.76	0	.247	.392	.349
Oakland	AL	85	306	90	13	2	9	(6	3)	134	72	35	70	5	39	2	0	0	52	6	.90	8	.294	.425	.438
1993 Oakland	AL	90	318	104	19	1	17	(8	9)	176	77	47	85	6	46	2	0	2	31	6	.84	8	.327	.469	.553
Toronto	AL	44	163	35	3	1	4	(2	2)	52	37	12	35	1	19	2	1	2	22	2	.92	1	.215	.356	.319
18 ML YEARS		2340	8528	2450	412	59	244	(115	129)	3712	1829	887	1675	57	1191	73	23	52	1186	280	.81	131	.287	.406	.435

Mike Henneman

Pitches: Right Bats: Right Pos: RP-49   **Ht: 6'3" Wt: 210 Born: 12/11/61 Age: 35**

			HOW MUCH HE PITCHED						WHAT HE GAVE UP										THE RESULTS						
Year Team	Lg	G	GS	CG	GF	IP	BFP	H	R	ER	HR	SH	SF	HB	TBB	IBB	SO	WP	Bk	W	L	Pct.	ShO	Sv-Op	Hld	ERA
1987 Detroit	AL	55	0	0	28	96.2	399	86	36	32	8	2	3	3	30	5	75	7	0	11	3	.786	0	7-11	7	2.98
1988 Detroit	AL	65	0	0	51	91.1	364	72	23	19	7	5	2	2	24	10	58	8	1	9	6	.600	0	22-29	3	1.87
1989 Detroit	AL	60	0	0	35	90	401	84	46	37	4	7	3	5	51	15	69	0	1	11	4	.733	0	8-12	6	3.70
1990 Detroit	AL	69	0	0	53	94.1	399	90	36	32	4	5	2	3	33	12	50	3	0	8	6	.571	0	22-28	4	3.05
1991 Detroit	AL	60	0	0	50	84.1	358	81	29	27	2	5	5	0	34	8	61	5	0	10	2	.833	0	21-24	1	2.88
1992 Detroit	AL	60	0	0	53	77.1	321	75	36	34	6	3	5	0	20	10	58	7	0	2	6	.250	0	24-28	0	3.96
1993 Detroit	AL	63	0	0	50	71.2	316	69	28	21	4	5	2	2	32	8	58	4	0	5	3	.625	0	24-29	2	2.64
1994 Detroit	AL	30	0	0	23	34.2	167	43	27	20	5	2	1	0	17	7	27	5	0	1	3	.250	0	8-13	0	5.19
1995 Det-Hou		50	0	0	44	50.1	205	45	12	12	1	1	2	2	13	2	43	5	0	0	0	.000	0	26-29	1	2.15
1996 Texas	AL	49	0	0	45	42	182	41	28	27	6	4	2	0	17	5	34	4	0	0	7	.000	0	31-37	2	5.79
1995 Detroit	AL	29	0	0	26	29.1	118	24	5	5	0	1	1	0	9	1	24	2	0	0	1	.000	0	18-20	1	1.53
Houston	NL	21	0	0	18	21	87	21	7	7	1	0	2	2	4	1	19	3	0	0	1	.000	0	8-9	1	3.00
10 ML YEARS		561	0	0	432	732.2	3112	686	301	261	47	39	26	19	271	82	533	48	2	57	42	.576	0	193-240	26	3.21

Doug Henry

Pitches: Right Bats: Right Pos: RP-58   **Ht: 6'4" Wt: 205 Born: 12/10/63 Age: 33**

			HOW MUCH HE PITCHED						WHAT HE GAVE UP										THE RESULTS						
Year Team	Lg	G	GS	CG	GF	IP	BFP	H	R	ER	HR	SH	SF	HB	TBB	IBB	SO	WP	Bk	W	L	Pct.	ShO	Sv-Op	Hld	ERA
1991 Milwaukee	AL	32	0	0	25	36	137	16	4	4	1	1	2	0	14	1	28	0	0	2	1	.667	0	15-16	3	1.00
1992 Milwaukee	AL	68	0	0	56	65	277	64	34	29	6	1	2	0	24	4	52	4	0	1	4	.200	0	29-33	1	4.02

Year Team	Lg	G	GS	CG	GF	IP	BFP	H	R	ER	HR	SH	SF	HB	TBB	IBB	SO	WP	Bk	W	L	Pct.	ShO	Sv-Op	Hld	ERA
1993 Milwaukee	AL	54	0	0	41	55	260	67	37	34	7	5	4	3	25	8	38	4	0	4	4	.500	0	17-24	0	5.56
1994 Milwaukee	AL	25	0	0	7	31.1	143	32	17	16	7	1	0	1	23	1	20	3	0	2	3	.400	0	0-0	4	4.60
1995 New York	NL	51	0	0	20	67	273	48	23	22	7	3	2	1	25	6	62	6	1	3	6	.333	0	4-7	6	2.96
1996 New York	NL	58	0	0	33	75	343	82	48	39	7	3	3	1	36	6	58	6	1	2	8	.200	0	9-14	8	4.68
6 ML YEARS		288	0	0	182	329.1	1433	309	163	144	35	14	13	6	147	26	258	23	2	14	26	.350	0	74-94	22	3.94

Pat Hentgen

Pitches: Right   Bats: Right   Pos: SP-35   **Ht: 6'2"   Wt: 200   Born: 11/13/68   Age: 28**

Year Team	Lg	G	GS	CG	GF	IP	BFP	H	R	ER	HR	SH	SF	HB	TBB	IBB	SO	WP	Bk	W	L	Pct.	ShO	Sv-Op	Hld	ERA
1991 Toronto	AL	3	1	0	1	7.1	30	5	2	2	1	1	0	0	3	0	3	1	0	0	0	.000	0	0-0	0	2.45
1992 Toronto	AL	28	2	0	10	50.1	229	49	30	30	7	2	2	0	32	5	39	2	1	5	2	.714	0	0-1	1	5.36
1993 Toronto	AL	34	32	3	0	216.1	926	215	103	93	27	6	5	7	74	0	122	11	1	19	9	.679	0	0-0	0	3.87
1994 Toronto	AL	24	24	6	0	174.2	728	158	74	66	21	6	3	3	59	1	147	5	1	13	8	.619	3	0-0	0	3.40
1995 Toronto	AL	30	30	2	0	200.2	913	236	129	114	24	2	1	5	90	6	135	7	2	10	14	.417	0	0-0	0	5.11
1996 Toronto	AL	35	35	10	0	265.2	1100	238	105	95	20	5	8	5	94	3	177	8	0	20	10	.667	3	0-0	0	3.22
6 ML YEARS		154	124	21	11	915	3926	901	443	400	100	22	19	22	352	15	623	34	5	67	43	.609	6	0-1	1	3.93

Felix Heredia

Pitches: Left   Bats: Left   Pos: RP-21   **Ht: 6'0"   Wt: 165   Born: 6/18/76   Age: 21**

Year Team	Lg	G	GS	CG	GF	IP	BFP	H	R	ER	HR	SH	SF	HB	TBB	IBB	SO	WP	Bk	W	L	Pct.	ShO	Sv-Op	Hld	ERA
1993 Marlins	R	11	11	0	0	57	225	48	18	17	0	2	0	2	9	0	47	1	1	4	1	.800	0	0--	--	2.68
1994 Kane County	A	24	8	1	11	68	306	86	55	43	7	3	4	3	14	0	65	6	0	4	5	.444	0	3--	--	5.69
1995 Brevard Cty	A+	34	8	0	3	95.2	420	101	52	38	6	0	7	4	36	1	76	6	1	6	4	.600	0	1--	--	3.57
1996 Portland	AA	55	0	0	17	60	236	48	11	10	3	4	1	1	15	2	42	1	1	8	1	.889	0	5--	--	1.50
1996 Florida	NL	21	0	0	5	16.2	78	21	8	8	1	0	1	0	10	1	10	2	0	1	1	.500	0	0-0	2	4.32

Gil Heredia

Pitches: Right   Bats: Right   Pos: RP-44   **Ht: 6'1"   Wt: 210   Born: 10/26/65   Age: 31**

Year Team	Lg	G	GS	CG	GF	IP	BFP	H	R	ER	HR	SH	SF	HB	TBB	IBB	SO	WP	Bk	W	L	Pct.	ShO	Sv-Op	Hld	ERA
1996 Okla. City *	AAA	6	0	0	3	9.2	38	11	3	2	0	0	0	0	0	0	4	0	0	0	0	.000	0	0--	--	1.86
1991 San Francisco	NL	7	4	0	1	33	126	27	14	14	4	2	1	0	7	2	13	1	0	0	2	.000	0	0-0	0	3.82
1992 SF-Mon	NL	20	5	0	4	44.2	187	44	23	21	4	2	1	1	20	1	22	1	0	2	3	.400	0	0-0	1	4.23
1993 Montreal	NL	20	9	1	2	57.1	246	66	28	25	4	4	1	2	14	2	40	0	0	4	2	.667	0	2-3	1	3.92
1994 Montreal	NL	39	3	0	8	75.1	325	85	34	29	7	3	4	2	13	3	62	4	1	6	3	.667	0	0-0	5	3.46
1995 Montreal	NL	40	18	0	5	119	509	137	60	57	7	9	4	5	21	1	74	1	0	5	6	.455	0	1-3	5	4.31
1996 Texas	AL	44	0	0	21	73.1	320	91	50	48	12	1	2	1	14	2	43	2	0	2	5	.286	0	1-4	7	5.89
1992 San Francisco	NL	13	4	0	3	30	132	32	20	18	3	0	0	1	16	1	15	1	0	2	3	.400	0	0-0	0	5.40
Montreal	NL	7	1	0	1	14.2	55	12	3	3	1	2	1	0	4	0	7	0	0	0	0	.000	0	0-0	0	1.84
6 ML YEARS		170	39	1	41	402.2	1713	450	209	194	38	21	13	11	89	11	254	9	1	19	21	.475	0	4-10	15	4.34

Dustin Hermanson

Pitches: Right   Bats: Right   Pos: RP-8   **Ht: 6'2"   Wt: 195   Born: 12/21/72   Age: 24**

Year Team	Lg	G	GS	CG	GF	IP	BFP	H	R	ER	HR	SH	SF	HB	TBB	IBB	SO	WP	Bk	W	L	Pct.	ShO	Sv-Op	Hld	ERA
1994 Wichita	AA	16	0	0	14	21	82	13	1	1	0	1	0	1	6	2	30	2	1	1	0	1.000	0	8--	--	0.43
Las Vegas	AAA	7	0	0	7	7.1	33	6	5	5	1	0	1	0	5	0	6	0	0	0	0	.000	0	3--	--	6.14
1995 Las Vegas	AAA	31	0	0	22	36	174	35	23	14	5	0	0	2	29	0	42	1	1	0	1	.000	0	11--	--	3.50
1996 Las Vegas	AAA	42	0	0	35	46	208	41	20	16	3	1	0	1	27	7	54	2	1	1	4	.200	0	21--	--	3.13
1995 San Diego	NL	26	0	0	6	31.2	151	35	26	24	8	3	0	1	22	1	19	3	0	3	1	.750	0	0-0	1	6.82
1996 San Diego	NL	8	0	0	4	13.2	62	18	15	13	3	2	3	0	4	0	11	0	1	1	0	1.000	0	0-0	0	8.56
2 ML YEARS		34	0	0	10	45.1	213	53	41	37	11	5	3	1	26	1	30	3	1	4	1	.800	0	0-0	1	7.35

Carlos Hernandez

Bats: Right   Throws: Right   Pos: C-9; PH-4   **Ht: 5'11"   Wt: 215   Born: 5/24/67   Age: 30**

Year Team	Lg	G	AB	H	2B	3B	HR	(Hm	Rd)	TB	R	RBI	TBB	IBB	SO	HBP	SH	SF	SB	CS	SB%	GDP	Avg	OBP	SLG
1996 Albuquerque *	AAA	66	233	56	11	0	5	--	--	82	19	30	11	0	49	2	1	3	5	4	.56	4	.240	.277	.352
1990 Los Angeles	NL	10	20	4	1	0	0	(0	0)	5	2	1	0	0	2	0	0	0	0	0	.00	0	.200	.200	.250
1991 Los Angeles	NL	15	14	3	1	0	0	(0	0)	4	1	1	0	0	5	1	0	1	1	0	1.00	2	.214	.250	.286
1992 Los Angeles	NL	69	173	45	4	0	3	(1	2)	58	11	17	11	1	21	4	4	0	2	0	.00	8	.260	.316	.335
1993 Los Angeles	NL	50	99	25	5	0	2	(1	1)	36	6	7	2	0	11	0	1	0	0	0	.00	0	.253	.267	.364
1994 Los Angeles	NL	32	64	14	2	0	2	(0	2)	22	6	6	1	0	14	0	0	0	0	0	.00	4	.219	.231	.344
1995 Los Angeles	NL	45	94	14	1	0	2	(1	1)	21	3	8	7	0	25	1	1	0	0	0	.00	5	.149	.216	.223
1996 Los Angeles	NL	13	14	4	0	0	0	(0	0)	4	1	0	2	0	2	0	0	0	0	0	.00	0	.286	.375	.286
7 ML YEARS		234	478	109	14	0	9	(3	6)	150	30	40	23	1	80	6	2	3	1	1	.50	15	.228	.271	.314

Jose Hernandez

Bats: R **Throws:** R **Pos:** SS-87; 3B-43; PH-17; 2B-1; CF-1   **Ht:** 6'1"   **Wt:** 180   **Born:** 7/14/69   **Age:** 27

					BATTING														BASERUNNING				PERCENTAGES		
Year Team	Lg	G	AB	H	2B	3B	HR	(Hm	Rd)	TB	R	RBI	TBB	IBB	SO	HBP	SH	SF	SB	CS	SB%	GDP	Avg	OBP	SLG
1991 Texas	AL	45	98	18	2	1	0	(0	0)	22	8	4	3	0	31	0	6	0	0	1	.00	2	.184	.208	.224
1992 Cleveland	AL	3	4	0	0	0	0	(0	0)	0	0	0	0	0	2	0	0	0	0	0	.00	0	.000	.000	.000
1994 Chicago	NL	56	132	32	2	3	1	(0	1)	43	18	9	8	0	29	1	5	0	2	2	.50	4	.242	.291	.326
1995 Chicago	NL	93	245	60	11	4	13	(6	7)	118	37	40	13	3	69	0	8	2	1	0	1.00	8	.245	.281	.482
1996 Chicago	NL	131	331	80	14	1	10	(4	6)	126	52	41	24	4	97	1	5	2	4	0	1.00	10	.242	.293	.381
5 ML YEARS		328	810	190	29	9	24	(10	14)	309	115	94	48	7	228	2	24	4	7	3	.70	24	.235	.278	.381

Livan Hernandez

Pitches: Right   **Bats:** Right   **Pos:** RP-1   **Ht:** 6'2"   **Wt:** 220   **Born:** 2/20/75   **Age:** 22

		HOW MUCH HE PITCHED						WHAT HE GAVE UP									THE RESULTS					
Year Team	Lg	G	GS	CG	GF	IP	BFP	H	R	ER	HR	SH	SF	HB	TBB	IBB	SO	WP	Bk	W	L	Pct.	ShO	Sv-Op	Hld	ERA
1996 Charlotte	AAA	10	10	0	0	49	239	61	32	28	3	2	4	1	34	1	45	2	4	2	4	.333	0	0--	—	5.14
Portland	AA	15	15	0	0	93.1	380	81	48	45	14	3	0	3	34	1	95	3	1	9	2	.818	0	0--	—	4.34
1996 Florida	NL	1	0	0	0	3	13	3	0	0	0	0	0	0	2	0	2	0	0	0	0	.000	0	0-0	0	0.00

Roberto Hernandez

Pitches: Right   **Bats:** Right   **Pos:** RP-72   **Ht:** 6'4"   **Wt:** 235   **Born:** 11/11/64   **Age:** 32

		HOW MUCH HE PITCHED						WHAT HE GAVE UP									THE RESULTS					
Year Team	Lg	G	GS	CG	GF	IP	BFP	H	R	ER	HR	SH	SF	HB	TBB	IBB	SO	WP	Bk	W	L	Pct.	ShO	Sv-Op	Hld	ERA
1991 Chicago	AL	9	3	0	1	15	69	18	15	13	1	0	0	0	7	0	6	1	0	1	0	1.000	0	0-0	0	7.80
1992 Chicago	AL	43	0	0	27	71	277	45	15	13	4	0	3	4	20	1	68	2	0	7	3	.700	0	12-16	6	1.65
1993 Chicago	AL	70	0	0	67	78.2	314	66	21	20	6	2	2	0	20	1	71	2	0	3	4	.429	0	38-44	0	2.29
1994 Chicago	AL	45	0	0	43	47.2	206	44	29	26	5	0	1	1	19	1	50	1	0	4	4	.500	0	14-20	0	4.91
1995 Chicago	AL	60	0	0	57	59.2	272	63	30	26	9	4	0	3	28	4	84	1	0	3	7	.300	0	32-42	0	3.92
1996 Chicago	AL	72	0	0	61	84.2	355	65	21	18	2	2	2	0	38	5	85	6	0	6	5	.545	0	38-46	0	1.91
6 ML YEARS		299	3	0	256	356.2	1493	301	131	116	27	8	8	8	132	12	364	13	0	24	23	.511	0	134-168	6	2.93

Xavier Hernandez

Pitches: Right   **Bats:** Left   **Pos:** RP-61   **Ht:** 6'2"   **Wt:** 195   **Born:** 8/16/65   **Age:** 31

		HOW MUCH HE PITCHED						WHAT HE GAVE UP									THE RESULTS					
Year Team	Lg	G	GS	CG	GF	IP	BFP	H	R	ER	HR	SH	SF	HB	TBB	IBB	SO	WP	Bk	W	L	Pct.	ShO	Sv-Op	Hld	ERA
1986 St. Cathrns	A-	13	10	1	3	70.2	284	55	27	21	4	1	1	6	16	0	69	5	2	5	5	.500	0	0--	—	2.67
1987 St. Cathrns	A-	13	11	0	0	55	242	57	39	31	4	1	1	4	16	0	49	2	0	3	3	.500	0	0--	—	5.07
1988 Myrtle Bch	A	23	22	2	1	148	585	116	52	42	5	1	3	7	28	1	111	10	4	13	6	.684	2	0--	—	2.55
Knoxville	AA	11	11	2	0	68.1	290	73	32	22	3	2	1	3	15	0	33	2	1	4	4	.333	0	0--	—	2.90
1989 Knoxville	AA	4	4	1	0	24	112	25	11	11	0	0	1	1	11	0	17	1	0	1	1	.500	1	0--	—	4.13
Syracuse	AAA	15	15	2	0	99.1	411	95	42	39	7	4	4	2	22	0	47	4	2	5	6	.455	1	0--	—	3.53
1991 Tucson	AAA	16	3	0	8	36	151	35	16	11	1	1	3	2	9	0	34	4	2	2	1	.667	0	4--	—	2.75
1989 Toronto	AL	7	0	0	2	22.2	101	25	15	12	2	0	2	1	8	0	7	1	0	1	0	1.000	0	0-0	—	4.76
1990 Houston	NL	34	1	0	10	62.1	268	60	34	32	8	2	4	4	24	5	24	6	0	2	1	.667	0	0-1	4	4.62
1991 Houston	NL	32	6	0	8	63	285	66	34	33	6	1	1	0	32	7	55	0	0	2	7	.222	0	3-6	5	4.71
1992 Houston	NL	77	0	0	25	111	454	81	31	26	5	3	2	3	42	7	96	5	0	9	1	.900	0	7-10	8	2.11
1993 Houston	NL	72	0	0	29	96.2	389	75	37	28	6	3	3	1	28	3	101	6	0	4	5	.444	0	9-17	22	2.61
1994 New York	AL	31	0	0	14	40	187	48	27	26	7	2	2	2	21	3	37	3	0	4	4	.500	0	6-8	1	5.85
1995 Cincinnati	NL	59	0	0	19	90	391	95	47	46	8	6	2	4	31	1	84	7	0	7	2	.778	0	3-4	6	4.60
1996 Cin-Hou	NL	61	0	0	27	78	340	77	45	40	13	8	3	2	28	5	81	9	0	5	5	.500	0	6-10	7	4.62
1996 Cincinnati	NL	3	0	0	0	3.1	19	8	6	5	2	0	0	0	2	0	3	0	0	0	0	.000	0	0-0	0	13.50
Houston	NL	58	0	0	27	74.2	321	69	39	35	11	8	3	2	26	5	78	9	0	5	5	.500	0	6-10	7	4.22
8 ML YEARS		373	7	0	134	563.2	2415	527	270	243	55	25	19	17	214	31	485	37	0	34	25	.576	0	34-56	51	3.88

Jose Herrera

Bats: L **Throws:** L **Pos:** RF-92; CF-19; PH-18; DH-1   **Ht:** 6'0"   **Wt:** 165   **Born:** 8/30/72   **Age:** 24

					BATTING														BASERUNNING				PERCENTAGES		
Year Team	Lg	G	AB	H	2B	3B	HR	(Hm	Rd)	TB	R	RBI	TBB	IBB	SO	HBP	SH	SF	SB	CS	SB%	GDP	Avg	OBP	SLG
1991 Medicne Hat	R+	40	143	35	5	1	1	—	—	45	21	11	6	1	38	3	1	0	6	7	.46	0	.245	.289	.315
St. Cathrns	A-	3	9	3	1	0	0	—	—	4	3	2	1	0	2	1	0	0	0	1	.00	0	.333	.455	.444
1992 Medicne Hat	R+	72	265	72	9	2	0	—	—	85	45	21	32	1	62	6	7	0	32	8	.80	4	.272	.363	.321
1993 Hagerstown	A	95	388	123	22	5	5	—	—	170	60	42	26	1	63	7	5	4	36	20	.64	3	.317	.367	.438
Madison	A	4	14	3	0	0	0	—	—	3	1	0	0	0	6	0	1	0	1	1	.50	0	.214	.214	.214
1994 Modesto	A+	103	370	106	20	3	11	—	—	165	59	56	38	3	76	10	5	6	21	12	.64	5	.286	.363	.446
1995 Huntsville	AA	92	358	101	11	4	6	—	—	138	37	45	27	2	58	2	0	2	9	8	.53	8	.282	.334	.385
1996 Huntsville	AA	23	84	24	4	0	1	—	—	31	18	7	14	1	15	0	0	2	3	2	.60	2	.286	.380	.369
1995 Oakland	AL	33	70	17	1	2	0	(0	0)	22	9	2	6	0	11	0	0	1	1	3	.25	1	.243	.299	.314
1996 Oakland	AL	108	320	86	15	1	6	(3	3)	121	44	30	20	1	59	3	3	0	8	2	.80	5	.269	.318	.378
2 ML YEARS		141	390	103	16	3	6	(3	3)	143	53	32	26	1	70	3	3	1	9	5	.64	6	.264	.314	.367

Orel Hershiser

Pitches: Right **Bats:** Right **Pos:** SP-33   **Ht:** 6'3" **Wt:** 195 **Born:** 9/16/58 **Age:** 38

Year Team	Lg	G	GS	CG	GF	IP	BFP	H	R	ER	HR	SH	SF	HB	TBB	IBB	SO	WP	Bk	W	L	Pct.	ShO	Sv-Op	Hld	ERA
1983 Los Angeles	NL	8	0	0	4	8	37	7	6	3	1	1	0	0	6	0	5	1	0	0	0	.000	0	1- -	—	3.38
1984 Los Angeles	NL	45	20	8	10	189.2	771	160	65	56	9	2	3	4	50	8	150	8	1	11	8	.579	4	2- -	—	2.66
1985 Los Angeles	NL	36	34	9	1	239.2	953	179	72	54	8	5	4	6	68	5	157	5	0	19	3	.864	5	0- -	—	2.03
1986 Los Angeles	NL	35	35	8	0	231.1	988	213	112	99	13	14	6	5	86	11	153	12	3	14	14	.500	1	0- -	—	3.85
1987 Los Angeles	NL	37	35	10	2	264.2	1093	247	105	90	17	8	2	9	74	5	190	11	2	16	16	.500	1	1-1	—	3.06
1988 Los Angeles	NL	35	34	15	1	267	1068	208	73	67	18	9	6	4	73	10	178	6	5	23	8	.742	8	1-1	0	2.26
1989 Los Angeles	NL	35	33	8	0	256.2	1047	226	75	66	9	19	6	3	77	14	178	8	4	15	15	.500	4	0-0	0	2.31
1990 Los Angeles	NL	4	4	0	0	25.1	106	26	12	12	1	1	0	1	4	0	16	0	1	1	1	.500	0	0-0	0	4.26
1991 Los Angeles	NL	21	21	0	0	112	473	112	43	43	3	2	1	5	32	6	73	2	4	7	2	.778	0	0-0	0	3.46
1992 Los Angeles	NL	33	33	1	0	210.2	910	209	101	86	15	15	6	4	69	13	130	10	0	10	15	.400	0	0-0	0	3.67
1993 Los Angeles	NL	33	33	5	0	215.2	913	201	106	86	17	12	4	7	72	13	141	7	0	12	14	.462	1	0-0	0	3.59
1994 Los Angeles	NL	21	21	0	0	135.1	575	146	67	57	15	4	3	2	42	6	72	6	2	6	6	.500	0	0-0	0	3.79
1995 Cleveland	AL	26	26	1	0	167.1	683	151	76	72	21	3	4	5	51	1	111	3	0	16	6	.727	1	0-0	0	3.87
1996 Cleveland	AL	33	33	1	0	206	908	238	115	97	21	5	4	12	58	4	125	11	1	15	9	.625	0	0-0	0	4.24
14 ML YEARS		402	362	67	18	2529.1	10525	2323	1028	888	168	100	49	71	762	96	1679	90	23	165	117	.585	25	5- -	—	3.16

Phil Hiatt

Bats: R **Throws:** R **Pos:** 3B-3; PH-2; DH-1; LF-1; RF-1   **Ht:** 6'3" **Wt:** 200 **Born:** 5/1/69 **Age:** 28

Year Team	Lg	G	AB	H	2B	3B	HR	(Hm	Rd)	TB	R	RBI	TBB	IBB	SO	HBP	SH	SF	SB	CS	SB%	GDP	Avg	OBP	SLG
1996 Toledo *	AAA	142	555	145	27	3	42			304	99	119	50	3	180	2	0	4	17	6	.74	13	.261	.322	.548
1993 Kansas City	AL	81	238	52	12	1	7	(4	3)	87	30	36	16	0	82	7	0	2	6	3	.67	8	.218	.285	.366
1995 Kansas City	AL	52	113	23	6	0	4	(1	3)	41	11	12	9	0	37	0	2	0	1	0	1.00	3	.204	.262	.363
1996 Detroit	AL	7	21	4	0	1	0	(0	0)	6	3	1	2	0	11	0	0	0	0	0	.00	1	.190	.261	.286
3 ML YEARS		140	372	79	18	2	11	(5	6)	134	44	49	27	0	130	7	2	2	7	3	.70	12	.212	.277	.360

Bob Higginson

Bats: L **Throws:** R **Pos:** LF-63; RF-57; CF-19; PH-10; DH-4   **Ht:** 5'11" **Wt:** 195 **Born:** 8/18/70 **Age:** 26

Year Team	Lg	G	AB	H	2B	3B	HR	(Hm	Rd)	TB	R	RBI	TBB	IBB	SO	HBP	SH	SF	SB	CS	SB%	GDP	Avg	OBP	SLG
1992 Niagara Fal	A-	70	232	68	17	4	2	—	—	99	35	37	33	0	47	1	2	0	12	8	.60	4	.293	.383	.427
1993 Lakeland	A+	61	223	67	11	7	3	—	—	101	42	25	40	1	31	1	2	2	8	3	.73	6	.300	.406	.453
London	AA	63	224	69	15	4	4	—	—	104	25	35	19	0	37	0	0	3	3	4	.43	6	.308	.358	.464
1994 Toledo	AAA	137	476	131	28	3	23	—	—	234	81	67	46	3	99	5	0	3	16	8	.67	9	.275	.343	.492
1996 Toledo	AAA	3	13	4	0	1	0	—	—	6	4	1	3	0	0	0	0	0	0	0	.00	0	.308	.438	.462
1995 Detroit	AL	131	410	92	17	5	14	(10	4)	161	61	43	62	3	107	5	2	7	6	4	.60	5	.224	.329	.393
1996 Detroit	AL	130	440	141	35	0	26	(15	11)	254	75	81	65	7	66	1	3	6	6	3	.67	7	.320	.404	.577
2 ML YEARS		261	850	233	52	5	40	(25	15)	415	136	124	127	10	173	6	5	13	12	7	.63	12	.274	.367	.488

Glenallen Hill

Bats: Right **Throws:** Right **Pos:** RF-98   **Ht:** 6'2" **Wt:** 220 **Born:** 3/22/65 **Age:** 32

Year Team	Lg	G	AB	H	2B	3B	HR	(Hm	Rd)	TB	R	RBI	TBB	IBB	SO	HBP	SH	SF	SB	CS	SB%	GDP	Avg	OBP	SLG
1996 Phoenix *	AAA	5	17	6	1	0	2	(Hm	Rd)	13	4	2	0	0	3	0	0	0	1	0	1.00	0	.353	.353	.765
1989 Toronto	AL	19	52	15	0	0	1	(1	0)	18	4	7	3	0	12	0	0	0	2	1	.67	0	.288	.327	.346
1990 Toronto	AL	84	260	60	11	3	12	(7	5)	113	47	32	18	0	62	0	0	0	8	3	.73	5	.231	.281	.435
1991 Tor-Cle	AL	72	221	57	8	2	8	(5	3)	93	29	25	23	0	54	0	1	3	6	4	.60	7	.258	.324	.421
1992 Cleveland	AL	102	369	89	16	1	18	(7	11)	161	38	49	20	0	73	4	0	1	9	6	.60	11	.241	.287	.436
1993 Cle-ChN		97	261	69	14	2	15	(5	10)	132	33	47	17	1	71	1	0	4	8	3	.73	4	.264	.307	.506
1994 Chicago	NL	89	269	80	12	1	10	(3	7)	124	48	38	29	0	57	0	0	1	19	6	.76	5	.297	.365	.461
1995 San Francisco	NL	132	497	131	29	4	24	(13	11)	240	71	86	39	4	98	1	0	2	25	5	.83	11	.264	.317	.483
1996 San Francisco	NL	98	379	106	26	0	19	(9	10)	189	56	67	33	3	95	6	0	3	6	3	.67	6	.280	.344	.499
1991 Toronto	AL	35	99	25	5	2	3	(2	1)	43	14	11	7	0	24	0	0	2	2	2	.50	2	.253	.296	.434
Cleveland	AL	37	122	32	3	0	5	(1	4)	50	15	14	16	0	30	0	1	1	4	2	.67	5	.262	.345	.410
1993 Cleveland	AL	66	174	39	7	2	5	(0	5)	65	19	25	11	1	50	1	0	4	7	3	.70	2	.224	.268	.374
Chicago	NL	31	87	30	7	0	10	(5	5)	67	14	22	6	0	21	0	0	0	1	0	1.00	2	.345	.387	.770
8 ML YEARS		693	2308	607	116	13	107	(48	59)	1070	326	351	182	8	522	12	2	14	83	31	.73	49	.263	.318	.464

Ken Hill

Pitches: Right **Bats:** Right **Pos:** SP-35   **Ht:** 6'2" **Wt:** 205 **Born:** 12/14/65 **Age:** 31

Year Team	Lg	G	GS	CG	GF	IP	BFP	H	R	ER	HR	SH	SF	HB	TBB	IBB	SO	WP	Bk	W	L	Pct.	ShO	Sv-Op	Hld	ERA
1988 St. Louis	NL	4	1	0	0	14	62	16	9	8	0	0	0	0	6	0	6	1	0	0	1	.000	0	0-0	0	5.14
1989 St. Louis	NL	33	33	2	0	196.2	862	186	92	83	9	14	5	5	99	6	112	11	2	7	15	.318	1	0-0	0	3.80
1990 St. Louis	NL	17	14	1	1	78.2	343	79	49	48	7	5	5	1	33	1	58	5	0	5	6	.455	0	0-0	1	5.49
1991 St. Louis	NL	30	30	0	0	181.1	743	147	76	72	15	7	6	7	67	4	121	7	1	11	10	.524	0	0-0	0	3.57

Year Team	Lg	G	GS	CG	GF	IP	BFP	H	R	ER	HR	SH	SF	HB	TBB	IBB	SO	WP	Bk	W	L	Pct.	ShO	Sv-Op	Hld	ERA
1992 Montreal	NL	33	33	3	0	218	908	187	76	65	13	15	3	3	75	4	150	11	4	16	9	.640	3	0-0	0	2.68
1993 Montreal	NL	28	28	2	0	183.2	780	163	84	66	7	9	7	4	74	7	90	6	2	9	7	.563	0	0-0	0	3.23
1994 Montreal	NL	23	23	2	0	154.2	647	145	61	57	12	6	6	6	44	7	85	3	0	16	5	.762	1	0-0	0	3.32
1995 StL-Cle		30	29	1	0	185	817	202	107	95	21	12	3	1	77	4	98	6	0	10	8	.556	0	0-0	0	4.62
1996 Texas	AL	35	35	7	0	250.2	1061	250	110	101	19	4	7	6	95	3	170	5	4	16	10	.615	3	0-0	0	3.63
1995 St. Louis	NL	18	18	0	0	110.1	493	125	71	62	16	9	2	0	45	4	50	3	0	6	7	.462	0	0-0	0	5.06
Cleveland	AL	12	11	1	0	74.2	324	77	36	33	5	3	1	1	32	0	48	3	0	4	1	.800	0	0-0	0	3.98
9 ML YEARS		233	226	18	1	1462.2	6223	1375	664	595	103	72	43	34	570	36	890	55	13	90	71	.559	8	0-0	0	3.66

Sterling Hitchcock

Pitches: Left **Bats:** Left **Pos:** SP-35 **Ht:** 6'1" **Wt:** 192 **Born:** 4/29/71 **Age:** 26

Year Team	Lg	G	GS	CG	GF	IP	BFP	H	R	ER	HR	SH	SF	HB	TBB	IBB	SO	WP	Bk	W	L	Pct.	ShO	Sv-Op	Hld	ERA
1992 New York	AL	3	3	0	0	13	68	23	12	12	2	0	0	1	6	0	6	0	0	0	2	.000	0	0-0	0	8.31
1993 New York	AL	6	6	0	0	31	135	32	18	16	4	0	2	1	14	1	26	3	2	1	2	.333	0	0-0	0	4.65
1994 New York	AL	23	5	1	4	49.1	218	48	24	23	3	1	7	0	29	1	37	5	0	4	1	.800	0	2-2	3	4.20
1995 New York	AL	27	27	4	0	168.1	719	155	91	88	22	5	9	5	68	1	121	5	2	11	10	.524	1	0-0	0	4.70
1996 Seattle	AL	35	35	0	0	196.2	885	245	131	117	27	3	8	7	73	4	132	4	1	13	9	.591	0	0-0	0	5.35
5 ML YEARS		94	76	5	4	458.1	2025	503	276	256	58	9	26	14	190	7	322	17	5	29	24	.547	1	2-2	3	5.03

Denny Hocking

Bats: B **Throws:** R **Pos:** RF-33; PH-11; SS-6; 2B-2; DH-1; 1B-1 **Ht:** 5'10" **Wt:** 174 **Born:** 4/2/70 **Age:** 27

								BATTING												BASERUNNING				PERCENTAGES		
Year Team	Lg	G	AB	H	2B	3B	HR	(Hm	Rd)	TB	R	RBI	TBB	IBB	SO	HBP	SH	SF	SB	CS	SB%	GDP	Avg	OBP	SLG
1990 Elizabethtn	R+	54	201	59	6	2	6	—	—	87	45	30	40	1	25	6	1	2	13	4	.76	6	.294	.422	.433
1991 Kenosha	A	125	432	110	17	8	2	—	—	149	72	36	77	4	69	6	3	4	22	10	.69	6	.255	.372	.345
1992 Visalia	A+	135	550	182	34	9	7	—	—	255	117	81	72	1	77	8	2	2	38	18	.68	7	.331	.415	.464
1993 Nashville	AA	107	409	109	9	4	8	—	—	150	54	50	34	0	66	4	3	2	15	5	.75	12	.267	.327	.367
1994 Salt Lake	AAA	112	394	110	14	6	5	—	—	151	61	57	28	1	57	2	5	4	13	7	.65	6	.279	.327	.383
1995 Salt Lake	AAA	117	397	112	24	2	8	—	—	164	51	75	25	1	41	2	8	5	12	8	.60	10	.282	.324	.413
1996 Salt Lake	AAA	37	130	36	6	2	3	—	—	55	18	22	10	2	17	2	2	2	2	2	.50	4	.277	.333	.423
1993 Minnesota	AL	15	36	5	1	0	0	(0	0)	6	7	0	6	0	8	0	0	0	1	0	1.00	1	.139	.262	.167
1994 Minnesota	AL	11	31	10	3	0	0	(0	0)	13	3	2	0	0	4	0	0	0	2	0	1.00	1	.323	.323	.419
1995 Minnesota	AL	9	25	5	0	2	0	(0	0)	9	4	3	2	1	2	0	1	0	1	0	1.00	1	.200	.259	.360
1996 Minnesota	AL	49	127	25	6	0	1	(0	1)	34	16	10	8	0	24	0	1	1	3	3	.50	3	.197	.243	.268
4 ML YEARS		84	219	45	10	2	1	(0	1)	62	30	15	16	1	38	0	2	1	7	3	.70	6	.205	.258	.283

Trevor Hoffman

Pitches: Right **Bats:** Right **Pos:** RP-70 **Ht:** 6'0" **Wt:** 205 **Born:** 10/13/67 **Age:** 29

Year Team	Lg	G	GS	CG	GF	IP	BFP	H	R	ER	HR	SH	SF	HB	TBB	IBB	SO	WP	Bk	W	L	Pct.	ShO	Sv-Op	Hld	ERA
1993 Fla-SD	NL	67	0	0	26	90	391	80	43	39	10	4	5	1	39	13	79	5	0	4	6	.400	0	5-8	15	3.90
1994 San Diego	NL	47	0	0	41	56	225	39	16	16	4	1	2	0	20	6	68	3	0	4	4	.500	0	20-23	1	2.57
1995 San Diego	NL	55	0	0	51	53.1	218	48	25	23	10	0	0	0	14	3	52	1	0	7	4	.636	0	31-38	0	3.88
1996 San Diego	NL	70	0	0	62	88	348	50	23	22	6	2	2	2	31	5	111	2	0	9	5	.643	0	42-49	0	2.25
1993 Florida	NL	28	0	0	13	35.2	152	24	13	13	5	2	1	0	19	7	26	3	0	2	2	.500	0	2-3	8	3.28
San Diego	NL	39	0	0	13	54.1	239	56	30	26	5	2	4	1	20	6	53	2	0	2	4	.333	0	3-5	7	4.31
4 ML YEARS		239	0	0	180	287.1	1182	217	107	100	30	7	9	3	104	27	310	11	0	24	19	.558	0	98-118	16	3.13

Chris Hoiles

Bats: Right **Throws:** Right **Pos:** C-126; PH-4; 1B-1 **Ht:** 6'0" **Wt:** 215 **Born:** 3/20/65 **Age:** 32

								BATTING												BASERUNNING				PERCENTAGES		
Year Team	Lg	G	AB	H	2B	3B	HR	(Hm	Rd)	TB	R	RBI	TBB	IBB	SO	HBP	SH	SF	SB	CS	SB%	GDP	Avg	OBP	SLG
1989 Baltimore	AL	6	9	1	1	0	0	(0	0)	2	0	1	1	0	3	0	0	0	0	0	.00	0	.111	.200	.222
1990 Baltimore	AL	23	63	12	3	0	1	(1	0)	18	7	6	5	1	12	0	0	0	0	0	.00	0	.190	.250	.286
1991 Baltimore	AL	107	341	83	15	0	11	(5	6)	131	36	31	29	1	61	1	0	1	0	2	.00	11	.243	.304	.384
1992 Baltimore	AL	96	310	85	10	1	20	(8	12)	157	49	40	55	2	60	2	1	3	0	2	.00	8	.274	.384	.506
1993 Baltimore	AL	126	419	130	28	0	29	(16	13)	245	80	82	69	4	94	9	3	3	1	1	.50	10	.310	.416	.585
1994 Baltimore	AL	99	332	82	10	0	19	(11	8)	149	45	53	63	2	73	5	1	4	2	0	1.00	11	.247	.371	.449
1995 Baltimore	AL	114	352	88	15	1	19	(9	10)	162	53	58	67	3	80	4	0	3	1	0	1.00	11	.250	.373	.460
1996 Baltimore	AL	127	407	105	13	0	25	(13	12)	193	64	73	57	1	97	9	1	7	0	1	.00	7	.258	.356	.474
8 ML YEARS		698	2233	586	95	2	124	(63	61)	1057	334	344	346	14	480	30	6	21	4	6	.40	53	.262	.366	.473

Aaron Holbert

Bats: Right **Throws:** Right **Pos:** 2B-1 **Ht:** 6'0" **Wt:** 160 **Born:** 1/9/73 **Age:** 24

								BATTING												BASERUNNING				PERCENTAGES		
Year Team	Lg	G	AB	H	2B	3B	HR	(Hm	Rd)	TB	R	RBI	TBB	IBB	SO	HBP	SH	SF	SB	CS	SB%	GDP	Avg	OBP	SLG
1990 Johnson Cty	R+	54	176	30	4	1	1	—	—	39	27	18	24	1	33	3	1	1	3	5	.38	2	.170	.279	.222

			BATTING																BASERUNNING				PERCENTAGES		
Year Team	Lg	G	AB	H	2B	3B	HR	(Hm Rd)	TB	R	RBI	TBB	IBB	SO	HBP	SH	SF	SB	CS	SB%	GDP	Avg	OBP	SLG
1991 Springfield	A	59	215	48	5	1	1	— —	58	22	24	15	0	26	6	1	2	5	8	.38	3	.223	.290	.270
1992 Savannah	A	119	438	117	17	4	1	— —	145	53	34	40	0	57	8	6	3	62	25	.71	4	.267	.337	.331
1993 St. Pete	A+	121	457	121	18	3	2	— —	151	60	31	28	2	61	4	15	1	45	22	.67	6	.265	.312	.330
1994 Cardinals	R	5	12	2	0	0	0	— —	2	3	0	2	0	2	0	0	0	2	0	1.00	0	.167	.286	.167
Arkansas	AA	59	233	69	10	6	2	— —	97	41	19	14	0	25	2	4	1	9	7	.56	5	.296	.340	.416
1995 Louisville	AAA	112	401	103	16	4	9	— —	154	57	40	20	1	60	5	3	5	14	6	.70	10	.257	.297	.384
1996 Louisville	AAA	112	436	115	16	6	4	— —	155	54	32	21	0	61	2	5	4	20	14	.59	8	.264	.298	.356
1996 St. Louis	NL	1	3	0	0	0	0	(0 0)	0	0	0	0	0	0	0	0	0	0	0	.00	0	.000	.000	.000

Todd Hollandsworth

Bats: L Throws: L Pos: LF-122; CF-18; PH-16; RF-9   **Ht: 6'2" Wt: 193 Born: 4/20/73 Age: 24**

			BATTING																BASERUNNING				PERCENTAGES		
Year Team	Lg	G	AB	H	2B	3B	HR	(Hm Rd)	TB	R	RBI	TBB	IBB	SO	HBP	SH	SF	SB	CS	SB%	GDP	Avg	OBP	SLG
1991 Dodgers	R	6	16	5	0	0	0	— —	5	1	0	0	0	6	0	0	0	0	0	.00	1	.313	.313	.313
Yakima	A-	56	203	48	1	1	8	— —	79	34	33	27	3	57	4	0	0	11	1	.92	2	.236	.338	.389
1992 Bakersfield	A+	119	430	111	23	5	13	— —	183	70	58	50	5	113	3	0	2	27	13	.68	6	.258	.338	.426
1993 San Antonio	AA	126	474	119	24	9	17	— —	212	57	63	29	2	101	5	2	5	23	12	.66	7	.251	.298	.447
1994 Albuquerque	AAA	132	505	144	31	5	19	— —	242	80	91	46	5	96	0	1	3	15	9	.63	15	.285	.343	.479
1995 San Bernrdo	A+	1	2	1	0	0	0	— —	1	0	0	0	0	1	0	0	0	0	1	.00	0	.500	.500	.500
Albuquerque	AAA	10	38	9	2	0	2	— —	17	9	4	6	2	8	1	0	0	1	0	1.00	1	.237	.356	.447
1995 Los Angeles	NL	41	103	24	2	0	5	(3 2)	41	16	13	10	2	29	1	0	1	2	1	.67	1	.233	.304	.398
1996 Los Angeles	NL	149	478	139	26	4	12	(2 10)	209	64	59	41	1	93	2	3	2	21	6	.78	2	.291	.348	.437
2 ML YEARS		190	581	163	28	4	17	(5 12)	250	80	72	51	3	122	3	3	3	23	7	.77	3	.281	.340	.430

Dave Hollins

Bats: B Throws: R Pos: 3B-144; PH-5; DH-3; 1B-1; SS-1   **Ht: 6'1" Wt: 210 Born: 5/25/66 Age: 31**

			BATTING																BASERUNNING				PERCENTAGES		
Year Team	Lg	G	AB	H	2B	3B	HR	(Hm Rd)	TB	R	RBI	TBB	IBB	SO	HBP	SH	SF	SB	CS	SB%	GDP	Avg	OBP	SLG
1990 Philadelphia	NL	72	114	21	0	0	5	(2 3)	36	14	15	10	3	28	1	0	2	0	0	.00	1	.184	.252	.316
1991 Philadelphia	NL	56	151	45	10	2	6	(3 3)	77	18	21	17	1	26	3	0	1	1	1	.50	2	.298	.378	.510
1992 Philadelphia	NL	156	586	158	28	4	27	(14 13)	275	104	93	76	4	110	19	0	4	9	6	.60	8	.270	.369	.469
1993 Philadelphia	NL	143	543	148	30	4	18	(9 9)	240	104	93	85	5	109	5	0	7	2	3	.40	15	.273	.372	.442
1994 Philadelphia	NL	44	162	36	7	1	4	(1 3)	57	28	26	23	0	32	4	0	3	1	0	1.00	6	.222	.328	.352
1995 Phi-Bos		70	218	49	12	2	7	(5 2)	86	48	26	57	4	45	5	0	4	1	1	.50	4	.225	.391	.394
1996 Min-Sea	AL	149	516	135	29	0	16	(7 9)	212	88	78	84	7	117	13	1	2	6	6	.50	11	.262	.377	.411
1995 Philadelphia	NL	65	205	47	12	2	7	(5 2)	84	46	25	53	4	38	5	0	4	1	1	.50	4	.229	.393	.410
Boston	AL	5	13	2	0	0	0	(0 0)	2	2	1	4	0	7	0	0	0	0	0	.00	0	.154	.353	.154
1996 Minnesota	AL	121	422	102	26	0	13	(6 7)	167	71	53	71	5	102	10	0	0	6	4	.60	9	.242	.364	.396
Seattle	AL	28	94	33	3	0	3	(1 2)	45	17	25	13	2	15	3	1	2	0	2	.00	2	.351	.438	.479
7 ML YEARS		690	2290	592	116	13	83	(41 42)	983	404	352	352	24	467	50	1	23	20	17	.54	47	.259	.366	.429

Darren Holmes

Pitches: Right Bats: Right Pos: RP-62   **Ht: 6'0" Wt: 202 Born: 4/25/66 Age: 31**

		HOW MUCH HE PITCHED						WHAT HE GAVE UP												THE RESULTS						
Year Team	Lg	G	GS	CG	GF	IP	BFP	H	R	ER	HR	SH	SF	HB	TBB	IBB	SO	WP	Bk	W	L	Pct.	ShO	Sv-Op	Hld	ERA
1990 Los Angeles	NL	14	0	0	1	17.1	77	15	10	10	1	1	2	0	11	3	19	1	0	0	1	.000	0	0-0	0	5.19
1991 Milwaukee	AL	40	0	0	9	76.1	344	90	43	40	6	8	3	1	27	1	59	6	0	1	4	.200	0	3-6	3	4.72
1992 Milwaukee	AL	41	0	0	25	42.1	173	35	12	12	1	4	0	2	11	4	31	0	0	4	4	.500	0	6-8	2	2.55
1993 Colorado	NL	62	0	0	51	66.2	274	56	31	30	6	0	0	2	20	1	60	2	1	3	3	.500	0	25-29	2	4.05
1994 Colorado	NL	29	0	0	14	28.1	142	35	25	20	5	4	1	1	24	4	33	2	0	0	3	.000	0	3-8	3	6.35
1995 Colorado	NL	68	0	0	33	66.2	286	59	26	24	3	5	3	1	28	3	61	7	1	6	1	.857	0	14-18	13	3.24
1996 Colorado	NL	62	0	0	21	77	333	78	41	34	8	2	1	1	28	2	73	2	0	5	4	.556	0	1-8	7	3.97
7 ML YEARS		316	0	0	154	374.2	1629	368	188	170	30	24	10	8	149	18	336	20	2	19	20	.487	0	52-77	30	4.08

Chris Holt

Pitches: Right Bats: Right Pos: RP-4   **Ht: 6'4" Wt: 205 Born: 9/18/71 Age: 25**

		HOW MUCH HE PITCHED						WHAT HE GAVE UP												THE RESULTS						
Year Team	Lg	G	GS	CG	GF	IP	BFP	H	R	ER	HR	SH	SF	HB	TBB	IBB	SO	WP	Bk	W	L	Pct.	ShO	Sv-Op	Hld	ERA
1992 Auburn	A-	14	14	0	0	83	353	75	48	41	9	4	2	7	24	0	81	11	4	2	5	.286	0	0--	—	4.45
1993 Quad City	A	26	26	10	0	186.1	775	162	70	47	10	8	2	3	54	1	176	9	3	11	10	.524	3	0--	—	2.27
1994 Jackson	AA	26	25	5	0	167	679	169	78	64	11	6	4	9	22	2	111	5	1	10	9	.526	2	0--	—	3.45
1995 Jackson	AA	5	5	1	0	32.1	126	27	8	6	2	1	0	0	5	1	24	1	0	2	1	.500	1	0--	—	1.67
1996 Tucson	AAA	28	27	4	0	186.1	782	208	87	75	11	11	0	5	38	1	137	6	1	9	6	.600	1	0--	—	3.62
1996 Houston	NL	4	0	0	3	4.2	22	5	3	3	0	0	0	0	3	1	0	1	0	0	1	.000	0	0-0	—	5.79

Mike Holtz

Pitches: Left **Bats:** Left **Pos:** RP-30 **Ht:** 5'9" **Wt:** 175 **Born:** 10/10/72 **Age:** 24

Year Team	Lg	G	GS	CG	GF	IP	BFP	H	R	ER	HR	SH	SF	HB	TBB	IBB	SO	WP	Bk	W	L	Pct.	ShO	Sv-Op	Hld	ERA
1994 Boise	A-	22	0	0	16	35	143	22	4	2	0	0	1	2	11	2	59	3	1	0	0	.000	0	11--	—	0.51
1995 Lk Elsinore	A+	56	0	0	19	82.2	341	70	26	21	7	5	4	5	23	3	101	2	0	4	4	.500	0	3--	—	2.29
1996 Midland	AA	33	0	0	13	41	188	52	34	19	6	1	1	1	9	1	41	4	0	1	2	.333	0	2--	—	4.17
1996 California	AL	30	0	0	8	29.1	127	21	11	8	1	1	1	3	19	2	31	1	0	3	3	.500	0	0-0	5	2.45

Mark Holzemer

Pitches: Left **Bats:** Left **Pos:** RP-25 **Ht:** 6'0" **Wt:** 165 **Born:** 8/20/69 **Age:** 27

Year Team	Lg	G	GS	CG	GF	IP	BFP	H	R	ER	HR	SH	SF	HB	TBB	IBB	SO	WP	Bk	W	L	Pct.	ShO	Sv-Op	Hld	ERA
1988 Bend	A-	13	13	1	0	68.2	311	59	51	40	3	0	1	6	47	1	72	8	6	4	6	.400	1	0--	—	5.24
1989 Quad City	A	25	25	3	0	139.1	603	122	68	52	4	3	5	5	64	1	131	12	4	12	7	.632	1	0--	—	3.36
1990 Midland	AA	15	15	1	0	77	363	92	55	45	10	2	1	6	41	0	54	6	0	1	7	.125	0	0--	—	5.26
1991 Midland	AA	2	2	0	0	6.1	28	3	2	1	0	1	0	1	5	0	7	2	0	0	0	.000	0	0--	—	1.42
1992 Palm Spring	A+	5	5	2	0	30	124	23	10	10	2	1	0	3	13	0	32	0	0	3	2	.600	0	0--	—	3.00
Midland	AA	7	7	2	0	44.2	188	45	22	19	4	0	1	1	13	0	36	3	1	2	5	.286	0	0--	—	3.83
Edmonton	AAA	17	16	4	1	89	416	114	69	66	12	2	6	7	55	1	49	6	1	5	7	.417	0	0--	—	6.67
1993 Vancouver	AAA	24	23	2	0	145.2	642	158	94	78	9	6	4	4	70	2	80	5	5	9	6	.600	0	0--	—	4.82
1994 Vancouver	AAA	29	17	0	5	117.1	540	144	93	86	19	4	5	6	58	1	77	15	0	5	10	.333	0	0--	—	6.60
1995 Vancouver	AAA	28	4	0	11	54.2	228	45	18	15	2	5	0	3	24	4	35	2	0	3	2	.600	0	2--	—	2.47
1996 Lk Elsinore	A+	9	3	0	2	11.1	47	10	3	3	0	0	0	1	4	0	10	0	0	0	1	.000	0	0--	—	2.38
1993 California	AL	5	4	0	1	23.1	117	34	24	23	2	1	0	3	13	0	10	1	0	0	3	.000	0	0-0	0	8.87
1995 California	AL	12	0	0	5	8.1	45	11	6	5	1	1	0	1	7	1	5	0	0	0	1	.000	0	0-0	0	5.40
1996 California	AL	25	0	0	3	24.2	119	35	28	24	7	0	1	3	8	1	20	0	0	1	0	1.000	0	0-0	1	8.76
3 ML YEARS		42	4	0	9	56.1	281	80	58	52	10	2	1	7	28	2	35	1	0	1	4	.200	0	0-0	1	8.31

Rick Honeycutt

Pitches: Left **Bats:** Left **Pos:** RP-61 **Ht:** 6'1" **Wt:** 195 **Born:** 6/29/54 **Age:** 43

Year Team	Lg	G	GS	CG	GF	IP	BFP	H	R	ER	HR	SH	SF	HB	TBB	IBB	SO	WP	Bk	W	L	Pct.	ShO	Sv-Op	Hld	ERA
1977 Seattle	AL	10	3	0	3	29	125	26	16	14	7	0	2	3	11	2	17	2	1	0	1	.000	0	0--	—	4.34
1978 Seattle	AL	26	24	4	0	134	594	150	81	73	12	9	7	3	49	5	50	3	0	5	11	.313	1	0--	—	4.90
1979 Seattle	AL	33	28	8	2	194	839	201	103	87	22	11	6	6	67	7	83	5	1	11	12	.478	1	0--	—	4.04
1980 Seattle	AL	30	30	9	0	203	871	221	99	89	22	11	7	3	60	7	79	4	0	10	17	.370	1	0--	—	3.95
1981 Texas	AL	20	20	8	0	128	509	120	49	47	12	5	0	0	17	1	40	1	0	11	6	.647	2	0--	—	3.30
1982 Texas	AL	30	26	4	3	164	728	201	103	96	20	4	8	3	54	4	64	3	1	5	17	.227	1	0--	—	5.27
1983 Tex-LA		34	32	6	0	213.2	865	214	85	72	15	5	6	8	50	6	74	1	3	16	11	.593	2	0--	—	**3.03**
1984 Los Angeles	NL	29	28	6	0	183.2	762	180	72	58	11	6	5	2	51	11	75	1	2	10	9	.526	2	0--	—	2.84
1985 Los Angeles	NL	31	25	1	2	142	600	141	71	54	9	5	4	1	49	7	67	2	0	8	12	.400	0	1--	—	3.42
1986 Los Angeles	NL	32	28	0	2	171	713	164	71	63	9	4	1	3	45	4	100	4	1	11	9	.550	0	0--	—	3.32
1987 LA-Oak		34	24	1	1	139.1	631	158	91	73	13	3	4	4	54	4	102	5	1	3	16	.158	1	0-0	1	4.72
1988 Oakland	AL	55	0	0	17	79.2	330	74	36	31	6	3	6	3	25	2	47	3	8	3	2	.600	0	7-9	19	3.50
1989 Oakland	AL	64	0	0	24	76.2	305	56	26	20	5	5	2	1	26	3	52	6	1	2	2	.500	0	12-16	24	2.35
1990 Oakland	AL	63	0	0	13	63.1	256	46	23	19	2	2	6	1	22	2	38	1	1	2	2	.500	0	7-10	27	2.70
1991 Oakland	AL	43	0	0	7	37.2	167	37	16	15	3	2	1	2	20	3	26	0	0	2	4	.333	0	0-4	14	3.58
1992 Oakland	AL	54	0	0	7	39	169	41	19	16	2	4	1	3	10	3	32	2	0	1	4	.200	0	3-7	18	3.69
1993 Oakland	AL	52	0	0	7	41.2	174	30	18	13	2	7	4	1	20	6	21	0	0	1	4	.200	0	1-3	20	2.81
1994 Texas	AL	42	0	0	9	25	122	37	21	20	4	5	0	2	9	1	18	0	0	1	2	.333	0	1-2	11	7.20
1995 Oak-NYA	AL	52	0	0	6	45.2	180	39	16	15	6	3	1	1	10	0	21	0	0	5	1	.833	0	2-5	12	2.96
1996 St. Louis	NL	61	0	0	13	47.1	190	42	15	15	3	5	3	0	7	3	30	1	2	2	1	.667	0	4-7	19	2.85
1983 Texas	AL	25	25	5	0	174.2	693	168	59	47	9	3	6	6	37	2	56	1	2	14	8	.636	2	0--	—	2.42
Los Angeles	NL	9	7	1	0	39	172	46	26	25	6	2	0	2	13	4	18	0	1	2	3	.400	0	0--	—	5.77
1987 Los Angeles	NL	27	20	1	0	115.2	525	133	74	59	10	0	0	2	45	4	92	4	0	2	12	.143	1	0-0	1	4.59
Oakland	AL	7	4	0	1	23.2	106	25	17	14	3	1	3	2	9	0	10	1	1	1	4	.200	0	0-0	0	5.32
1995 Oakland	AL	49	0	0	6	44.2	174	37	13	12	5	3	1	1	9	0	21	0	0	5	1	.833	0	2-5	12	2.42
New York	AL	3	0	0	0	1	6	2	3	3	1	0	0	0	1	0	0	0	0	0	0	.000	0	0-0	0	27.00
20 ML YEARS		795	268	47	116	2157.2	9130	2178	1031	890	185	99	73	50	656	81	1036	44	22	109	143	.433	11	38--	—	3.71

Chris Hook

Pitches: Right **Bats:** Right **Pos:** RP-10 **Ht:** 6'5" **Wt:** 230 **Born:** 8/4/68 **Age:** 28

Year Team	Lg	G	GS	CG	GF	IP	BFP	H	R	ER	HR	SH	SF	HB	TBB	IBB	SO	WP	Bk	W	L	Pct.	ShO	Sv-Op	Hld	ERA
1989 Reds	R	14	9	0	1	51	209	43	19	18	1	1	1	4	17	0	39	4	2	4	1	.800	0	0--	—	3.18
1990 Charlstn-WV	A	30	16	0	3	119.1	537	117	65	54	3	4	3	8	62	4	87	19	1	6	5	.545	0	0--	—	4.07
1991 Charlstn-WV	A	45	0	0	19	71	306	52	26	19	1	4	1	11	40	1	79	8	0	4	1	.800	0	2--	—	2.41
1992 Cedar Rapds	A	26	25	1	1	159	664	138	59	48	2	7	5	10	53	0	144	5	6	14	8	.636	0	0--	—	2.72
1993 Chattanooga	AA	28	28	1	0	166.2	723	163	85	67	7	11	7	12	66	2	122	9	1	12	8	.600	0	0--	—	3.62
1994 Phoenix	AAA	27	11	0	8	90	401	109	48	46	6	3	4	4	29	0	57	4	1	7	2	.778	0	2--	—	4.60

102

			HOW MUCH HE PITCHED						WHAT HE GAVE UP											THE RESULTS						
Year Team	Lg	G	GS	CG	GF	IP	BFP	H	R	ER	HR	SH	SF	HB	TBB	IBB	SO	WP	Bk	W	L	Pct.	ShO	Sv-Op	Hld	ERA
1995 Phoenix	AAA	4	0	0	0	6	22	2	1	1	0	0	0	0	3	0	5	0	1	0	0	.000	0	0--	—	1.50
1996 Phoenix	AAA	32	20	0	3	128	560	139	75	68	18	7	3	6	51	1	70	9	1	7	10	.412	0	0--	—	4.78
1995 San Francisco	NL	45	0	0	14	52.1	239	55	33	32	7	3	3	3	29	3	40	2	0	5	1	.833	0	0-0	6	5.50
1996 San Francisco	NL	10	0	0	3	13.1	71	16	13	11	3	2	1	2	14	2	4	1	0	0	1	.000	0	0-0	0	7.43
2 ML YEARS		55	0	0	17	65.2	310	71	46	43	10	5	4	5	43	5	44	3	0	5	2	.714	0	0-0	6	5.89

John Hope

Pitches: Right **Bats:** Right **Pos:** SP-4; RP-1   **Ht:** 6'3" **Wt:** 206 **Born:** 12/21/70 **Age:** 26

			HOW MUCH HE PITCHED						WHAT HE GAVE UP											THE RESULTS						
Year Team	Lg	G	GS	CG	GF	IP	BFP	H	R	ER	HR	SH	SF	HB	TBB	IBB	SO	WP	Bk	W	L	Pct.	ShO	Sv-Op	Hld	ERA
1996 Calgary *	AAA	23	21	0	0	125	561	147	74	67	11	6	11	7	49	3	71	6	0	4	7	.364	0	0--	—	4.82
1993 Pittsburgh	NL	7	7	0	0	38	166	47	19	17	2	5	1	2	8	3	8	1	0	0	2	.000	0	0-0	0	4.03
1994 Pittsburgh	NL	9	0	0	1	14	64	18	12	9	1	0	0	2	4	0	6	1	0	0	0	.000	0	0-0	3	5.79
1995 Pittsburgh	NL	3	0	0	0	2.1	21	8	8	8	0	0	1	3	4	0	2	0	0	0	0	.000	0	0-0	0	30.86
1996 Pittsburgh	NL	5	4	0	0	19.1	86	17	18	15	5	2	1	2	11	1	13	2	0	1	3	.250	0	0-0	0	6.98
4 ML YEARS		24	11	0	1	73.2	337	90	57	49	8	7	3	9	27	4	29	4	0	1	5	.167	0	0-0	3	5.99

Dwayne Hosey

Bats: B **Throws:** R **Pos:** CF-20; LF-7; PH-6; DH-1   **Ht:** 5'10" **Wt:** 180 **Born:** 3/11/67 **Age:** 30

			BATTING																BASERUNNING				PERCENTAGES		
Year Team	Lg	G	AB	H	2B	3B	HR	(Hm	Rd)	TB	R	RBI	TBB	IBB	SO	HBP	SH	SF	SB	CS	SB%	GDP	Avg	OBP	SLG
1987 White Sox	R	41	129	36	2	1	1	—	—	43	26	10	18	1	22	3	0	2	19	4	.83	1	.279	.375	.333
1988 South Bend	A	95	311	71	11	0	2	—	—	88	53	24	28	2	55	5	4	2	36	15	.71	5	.228	.301	.283
Utica	A-	3	7	1	0	0	0	—	—	1	0	0	2	0	1	0	0	0	1	0	1.00	0	.143	.333	.143
1989 Madison	A	123	470	115	16	6	11	—	—	176	72	51	44	3	82	8	2	2	33	18	.65	9	.245	.319	.374
1990 Modesto	A+	113	453	133	21	5	16	—	—	212	77	61	50	5	70	8	8	2	30	23	.57	2	.294	.372	.468
1991 Huntsville	AA	28	102	25	6	0	1	—	—	34	16	7	9	1	15	1	1	1	5	4	.56	1	.245	.310	.333
Stockton	A+	85	356	97	12	7	15	—	—	168	55	62	31	1	58	3	1	9	22	8	.73	4	.272	.328	.472
1992 Wichita	AA	125	427	108	23	5	9	—	—	168	56	68	40	3	70	10	1	7	16	11	.59	3	.253	.326	.393
1993 Wichita	AA	86	326	95	19	2	18	—	—	172	52	61	25	4	44	2	0	1	13	4	.76	4	.291	.342	.528
Las Vegas	AAA	32	110	29	4	4	3	—	—	50	21	12	11	1	17	4	0	0	7	4	.64	0	.264	.332	.455
1994 Omaha	AAA	112	406	135	23	4	27	—	—	255	95	80	61	10	85	8	0	6	27	12	.69	3	.333	.424	.628
1995 Omaha	AAA	75	271	80	21	4	12	—	—	145	59	50	29	2	45	1	1	2	15	6	.71	1	.295	.363	.535
1996 Pawtucket	AAA	93	367	109	25	4	14	—	—	184	77	53	40	2	67	3	0	5	20	7	.74	3	.297	.366	.501
1995 Boston	AL	24	68	23	8	1	3	(1	2)	42	20	7	8	0	16	0	1	0	6	0	1.00	0	.338	.408	.618
1996 Boston	AL	28	78	17	2	2	1	(0	1)	26	13	3	7	0	17	0	0	0	6	3	.67	0	.218	.282	.333
2 ML YEARS		52	146	40	10	3	4	(1	3)	68	33	10	15	0	33	0	1	0	12	3	.80	0	.274	.342	.466

Tyler Houston

Bats: L **Throws:** R **Pos:** PH-37; C-27; 1B-11; 3B-10; 2B-2; LF-1   **Ht:** 6'2" **Wt:** 210 **Born:** 1/17/71 **Age:** 26

			BATTING																BASERUNNING				PERCENTAGES		
Year Team	Lg	G	AB	H	2B	3B	HR	(Hm	Rd)	TB	R	RBI	TBB	IBB	SO	HBP	SH	SF	SB	CS	SB%	GDP	Avg	OBP	SLG
1989 Idaho Falls	R+	50	176	43	11	0	4	—	—	66	30	24	25	1	41	1	0	0	4	0	1.00	4	.244	.342	.375
1990 Sumter	A	117	442	93	14	3	13	—	—	152	58	56	49	2	101	2	2	7	6	2	.75	15	.210	.288	.344
1991 Macon	A	107	351	81	16	3	8	—	—	127	41	47	39	0	70	1	1	3	10	2	.83	8	.231	.307	.362
1992 Durham	A+	117	402	91	17	1	7	—	—	131	39	38	20	0	89	1	3	5	5	6	.45	5	.226	.262	.326
1993 Greenville	AA	84	262	73	14	1	5	—	—	104	27	33	13	4	50	2	3	4	5	3	.63	12	.279	.313	.397
Richmond	AAA	13	36	5	1	1	1	—	—	11	4	3	1	0	8	0	0	0	0	1	.00	1	.139	.162	.306
1994 Richmond	AAA	97	312	76	15	2	4	—	—	107	33	33	16	1	44	0	0	5	3	3	.50	12	.244	.276	.343
1995 Richmond	AAA	103	349	89	10	3	12	—	—	141	41	42	18	3	62	4	1	2	3	5	.38	6	.255	.298	.404
1996 Atl-ChN	NL	79	142	45	9	1	3	(1	2)	65	21	27	9	1	27	0	0	0	3	2	.60	5	.317	.358	.458
1996 Atlanta	NL	33	27	6	2	1	1	(1	0)	13	3	8	1	0	9	0	0	0	0	0	.00	1	.222	.250	.481
Chicago	NL	46	115	39	7	0	2	(0	2)	52	18	19	8	1	18	0	0	0	3	2	.60	4	.339	.382	.452

Dave Howard

Bats: B **Throws:** R **Pos:** SS-135; PH-6; 2B-3; 1B-2; DH-1; CF-1   **Ht:** 6'0" **Wt:** 175 **Born:** 2/26/67 **Age:** 30

			BATTING																BASERUNNING				PERCENTAGES		
Year Team	Lg	G	AB	H	2B	3B	HR	(Hm	Rd)	TB	R	RBI	TBB	IBB	SO	HBP	SH	SF	SB	CS	SB%	GDP	Avg	OBP	SLG
1991 Kansas City	AL	94	236	51	7	0	1	(0	1)	61	20	17	16	0	45	1	9	2	3	2	.60	1	.216	.267	.258
1992 Kansas City	AL	74	219	49	6	2	1	(1	0)	62	19	18	15	0	43	0	8	2	3	4	.43	3	.224	.271	.283
1993 Kansas City	AL	15	24	8	0	1	0	(0	0)	10	5	2	2	0	5	0	2	1	1	0	1.00	0	.333	.370	.417
1994 Kansas City	AL	46	83	19	4	0	1	(0	1)	26	9	13	11	0	23	0	3	3	3	2	.60	1	.229	.309	.313
1995 Kansas City	AL	95	255	62	13	4	0	(0	0)	83	23	19	24	1	41	1	6	1	6	1	.86	7	.243	.310	.325
1996 Kansas City	AL	143	420	92	14	5	4	(3	1)	128	51	48	40	0	74	4	17	4	5	6	.45	6	.219	.291	.305
6 ML YEARS		467	1237	281	44	12	7	(4	3)	370	127	117	108	1	231	6	45	13	21	15	.58	18	.227	.290	.299

Matt Howard

Bats: Right **Throws:** Right **Pos:** 2B-30; PH-7; 3B-6   **Ht:** 5'10" **Wt:** 170 **Born:** 9/22/67 **Age:** 29

						BATTING											BASERUNNING				PERCENTAGES		
Year Team	Lg	G	AB	H	2B	3B	HR	(Hm	Rd)	TB	R	RBI	TBB	IBB	SO	HBP	SH	SF	SB	CS	SB%	GDP	Avg	OBP	SLG
1989 Great Falls	R+	59	186	62	8	2	3	—	—	83	39	34	21	0	14	9	5	2	23	8	.74	3	.333	.422	.446
1990 Bakersfield	A+	137	551	144	22	3	1	—	—	175	75	54	37	1	39	13	4	6	47	10	.82	8	.261	.320	.318
1991 Vero Beach	A+	128	441	115	21	3	3	—	—	151	79	39	56	2	49	10	14	6	50	18	.74	6	.261	.353	.342
1992 San Antonio	AA	95	345	93	12	5	2	—	—	121	40	34	28	1	38	4	16	1	18	15	.55	12	.270	.331	.351
Albuquerque	AAA	36	116	34	3	0	0	—	—	37	14	8	7	0	7	0	2	0	1	2	.33	2	.293	.344	.319
1993 Albuquerque	AAA	18	26	4	0	1	0	—	—	6	3	4	3	0	2	0	1	1	1	1	.50	1	.154	.233	.231
San Antonio	AA	41	122	35	5	1	0	—	—	42	12	5	16	1	14	3	2	0	4	5	.44	4	.287	.383	.344
1994 Albuquerque	AAA	88	267	79	12	6	1	—	—	106	44	33	14	0	13	6	4	1	15	8	.65	12	.296	.344	.397
1995 Bowie	AA	70	251	76	8	2	1	—	—	91	42	15	29	1	27	5	3	1	22	4	.85	6	.303	.385	.363
1996 Columbus	AAA	51	202	70	12	2	2	—	—	92	36	16	18	0	9	1	3	1	9	3	.75	5	.347	.401	.455
1996 New York	AL	35	54	11	1	0	1	(0	1)	15	9	9	4	0	8	0	2	1	1	0	1.00	2	.204	.228	.278

Thomas Howard

Bats: L **Throws:** R **Pos:** LF-51; CF-40; PH-33; RF-32   **Ht:** 6'2" **Wt:** 205 **Born:** 12/11/64 **Age:** 32

						BATTING											BASERUNNING				PERCENTAGES		
Year Team	Lg	G	AB	H	2B	3B	HR	(Hm	Rd)	TB	R	RBI	TBB	IBB	SO	HBP	SH	SF	SB	CS	SB%	GDP	Avg	OBP	SLG
1996 Chattanooga *	AA	8	30	10	1	0	1	—	—	14	4	2	2	0	7	0	0	0	1	1	.50	1	.333	.375	.467
Indianapolis *	AAA	1	5	2	0	0	1	—	—	5	2	2	0	0	0	0	0	0	0	0	.00	0	.400	.400	1.000
1990 San Diego	NL	20	44	12	2	0	0	(0	0)	14	4	0	0	0	11	0	1	0	0	1	.00	1	.273	.273	.318
1991 San Diego	NL	106	281	70	12	3	4	(4	0)	100	30	22	24	4	57	1	2	1	10	7	.59	4	.249	.309	.356
1992 SD-Cle		122	361	100	15	2	2	(1	1)	125	37	32	17	1	60	0	11	2	15	8	.65	4	.277	.308	.346
1993 Cle-Cin		112	319	81	15	3	7	(5	2)	123	48	36	24	0	63	0	0	5	10	7	.59	9	.254	.302	.386
1994 Cincinnati	NL	83	178	47	11	0	5	(4	1)	73	24	24	10	1	30	0	3	1	4	2	.67	2	.264	.302	.410
1995 Cincinnati	NL	113	281	85	15	2	3	(1	2)	113	42	26	20	0	37	1	1	1	17	8	.68	3	.302	.350	.402
1996 Cincinnati	NL	121	360	98	19	10	6	(1	5)	155	50	42	17	3	51	3	2	4	6	5	.55	5	.272	.307	.431
1992 San Diego	NL	5	3	1	0	0	0	(0	0)	1	1	0	0	0	0	0	1	0	0	0	.333	.333	.333
Cleveland	AL	117	358	99	15	2	2	(1	1)	124	36	32	17	1	60	0	10	2	15	8	.65	4	.277	.308	.346
1993 Cleveland	AL	74	178	42	7	0	3	(3	0)	58	26	23	12	0	42	0	0	4	5	1	.83	5	.236	.278	.326
Cincinnati	NL	38	141	39	8	3	4	(2	2)	65	22	13	12	0	21	0	0	1	5	6	.45	4	.277	.331	.461
7 ML YEARS		677	1824	493	89	20	27	(16	11)	703	235	182	112	9	309	5	20	14	62	38	.62	28	.270	.312	.385

Steve Howe

Pitches: Left **Bats:** Left **Pos:** RP-25   **Ht:** 6'2" **Wt:** 198 **Born:** 3/10/58 **Age:** 39

		HOW MUCH HE PITCHED						WHAT HE GAVE UP												THE RESULTS					
Year Team	Lg	G	GS	CG	GF	IP	BFP	H	R	ER	HR	SH	SF	HB	TBB	IBB	SO	WP	Bk	W	L	Pct.	ShO	Sv-Op	Hld	ERA
1980 Los Angeles	NL	59	0	0	36	85	359	83	33	25	1	8	3	2	22	10	39	1	0	7	9	.438	0	17--	—	2.65
1981 Los Angeles	NL	41	0	0	25	54	227	51	17	15	2	4	4	0	18	7	32	0	0	5	3	.625	0	8--	—	2.50
1982 Los Angeles	NL	66	0	0	41	99.1	393	87	27	23	4	3	10	3	17	11	49	1	0	7	5	.583	0	13--	—	2.08
1983 Los Angeles	NL	46	0	0	33	68.2	274	55	15	11	2	5	3	1	12	7	52	3	0	4	7	.364	0	18--	—	1.44
1985 LA-Min		32	0	0	19	41	198	58	33	25	3	2	5	1	12	4	21	3	0	3	4	.429	0	3--	—	5.49
1987 Texas	AL	24	0	0	15	31.1	131	33	15	15	2	2	0	3	8	1	19	2	1	3	3	.500	0	1-3	2	4.31
1991 New York	AL	37	0	0	10	48.1	189	39	12	9	1	2	1	3	7	2	34	2	0	3	1	.750	0	3-3	7	1.68
1992 New York	AL	20	0	0	10	22	79	9	7	6	1	1	1	0	3	1	12	1	0	3	0	1.000	0	6-7	5	2.45
1993 New York	AL	51	0	0	19	50.2	215	58	31	28	7	5	2	3	10	4	19	0	0	3	5	.375	0	4-7	10	4.97
1994 New York	AL	40	0	0	25	40	152	28	8	8	2	1	0	0	7	1	18	1	0	3	0	1.000	0	15-19	3	1.80
1995 New York	AL	56	0	0	49	49	230	66	29	27	7	3	2	4	17	3	28	1	0	6	3	.667	0	2-3	10	4.96
1996 New York	AL	25	0	0	4	17	76	19	12	12	1	0	0	1	6	3	5	2	1	0	1	.000	0	1-2	7	6.35
1985 Los Angeles	NL	19	0	0	14	22	104	30	17	12	2	2	2	1	5	2	11	2	0	1	1	.500	0	3--	—	4.91
Minnesota	AL	13	0	0	5	19	94	28	16	13	1	0	3	0	7	2	10	1	0	2	3	.400	0	0--	—	6.16
12 ML YEARS		497	0	0	257	606.1	2523	586	239	204	32	45	24	18	139	54	328	17	2	47	41	.534	0	91--	—	3.03

Jack Howell

Bats: L **Throws:** R **Pos:** 3B-43; PH-36; DH-4; 1B-2; 2B-1   **Ht:** 6'0" **Wt:** 190 **Born:** 8/18/61 **Age:** 35

						BATTING											BASERUNNING				PERCENTAGES		
Year Team	Lg	G	AB	H	2B	3B	HR	(Hm	Rd)	TB	R	RBI	TBB	IBB	SO	HBP	SH	SF	SB	CS	SB%	GDP	Avg	OBP	SLG
1996 Lk Elsinore *	A+	4	12	2	1	0	1	—	—	6	2	3	3	0	4	0	0	0	0	0	.00	1	.167	.333	.500
1985 California	AL	43	137	27	4	0	5	(2	3)	46	19	18	16	2	33	0	4	1	1	1	.50	1	.197	.279	.336
1986 California	AL	63	151	41	14	2	4	(1	3)	71	26	21	19	0	28	0	3	2	2	0	1.00	1	.272	.349	.470
1987 California	AL	138	449	110	18	5	23	(15	8)	207	64	64	57	4	118	2	1	2	4	3	.57	7	.245	.331	.461
1988 California	AL	154	500	127	32	2	16	(9	7)	211	59	63	46	8	130	6	4	2	2	6	.25	8	.254	.323	.422
1989 California	AL	144	474	108	19	4	20	(9	11)	195	56	52	52	9	125	3	3	1	0	3	.00	8	.228	.308	.411
1990 California	AL	105	316	72	19	1	8	(3	5)	117	35	33	46	5	61	1	1	2	3	0	1.00	8	.228	.326	.370
1991 Cal-SD		90	241	50	5	1	8	(3	5)	81	35	23	25	1	44	0	1	0	1	1	.50	2	.207	.293	.336
1996 California	AL	66	126	34	4	1	8	(4	4)	64	20	21	10	0	30	0	0	0	0	0	.00	3	.270	.324	.508
1991 California	AL	32	81	17	2	0	2	(0	2)	25	11	7	11	0	11	0	0	0	1	1	.50	2	.210	.304	.309
San Diego	NL	58	160	33	3	1	6	(3	3)	56	24	16	18	1	33	0	1	0	0	0	.00	0	.206	.287	.350
8 ML YEARS		803	2394	569	115	16	92	(46	46)	992	314	295	275	29	569	12	17	10	13	15	.46	33	.238	.318	.414

Mike Hubbard

Bats: Right   **Throws:** Right   **Pos:** C-14; PH-10   **Ht:** 6'1"   **Wt:** 195   **Born:** 2/16/71   **Age:** 26

							BATTING												BASERUNNING				PERCENTAGES		
Year Team	Lg	G	AB	H	2B	3B	HR	(Hm	Rd)	TB	R	RBI	TBB	IBB	SO	HBP	SH	SF	SB	CS	SB%	GDP	Avg	OBP	SLG
1992 Geneva	A-	50	183	44	4	4	3	—	—	65	25	25	7	0	29	3	4	4	6	4	.60	2	.240	.274	.355
1993 Daytona	A+	68	245	72	10	3	1	—	—	91	25	20	18	0	41	5	2	5	10	6	.63	4	.294	.348	.371
1994 Orlando	AA	104	357	102	13	3	11	—	—	154	52	39	29	4	58	8	2	2	7	7	.50	5	.286	.351	.431
1995 Iowa	AAA	75	254	66	6	3	5	—	—	93	28	23	26	1	60	0	6	3	6	1	.86	5	.260	.325	.366
1996 Iowa	AAA	67	232	68	12	0	7	—	—	101	38	33	10	1	56	3	3	1	2	0	1.00	5	.293	.329	.435
1995 Chicago	NL	15	23	4	0	0	0	(0	0)	4	2	1	2	0	2	0	0	0	0	0	.00	1	.174	.240	.174
1996 Chicago	NL	21	38	4	0	0	1	(1	0)	7	1	4	0	0	15	0	0	1	0	0	.00	1	.105	.103	.184
2 ML YEARS		36	61	8	0	0	1	(1	0)	11	3	5	2	0	17	0	0	1	0	0	.00	2	.131	.156	.180

Trent Hubbard

Bats: Right   **Throws:** Right   **Pos:** PH-33; CF-17; LF-11   **Ht:** 5'8"   **Wt:** 180   **Born:** 5/11/66   **Age:** 31

							BATTING												BASERUNNING				PERCENTAGES		
Year Team	Lg	G	AB	H	2B	3B	HR	(Hm	Rd)	TB	R	RBI	TBB	IBB	SO	HBP	SH	SF	SB	CS	SB%	GDP	Avg	OBP	SLG
1986 Auburn	A-	70	242	75	12	1	1	—	—	92	42	32	28	0	42	1	2	2	35	5	.88	2	.310	.381	.380
1987 Asheville	A	101	284	67	8	1	1	—	—	80	39	35	28	1	42	0	0	7	28	13	.68	4	.236	.298	.282
1988 Osceola	A+	130	446	116	15	11	3	—	—	162	68	65	61	0	72	3	1	3	44	18	.71	10	.260	.351	.363
1989 Tucson	AAA	21	50	11	2	0	0	—	—	13	3	2	1	0	10	1	0	0	3	3	.50	2	.220	.250	.260
Columbus	AA	104	348	92	7	8	3	—	—	124	55	37	43	3	53	2	4	2	28	6	.82	8	.264	.347	.356
1990 Tucson	AAA	12	27	6	2	2	0	—	—	12	5	2	3	0	6	0	0	0	1	1	.50	1	.222	.300	.444
Columbus	AA	95	335	84	14	4	4	—	—	118	39	35	37	0	51	3	8	2	17	8	.68	7	.251	.329	.352
1991 Jackson	AA	126	455	135	21	3	2	—	—	168	78	41	65	2	81	9	3	2	39	17	.70	3	.297	.394	.369
Tucson	AAA	2	4	0	0	0	0	—	—	0	0	0	0	0	0	0	0	0	0	0	.00	0	.000	.000	.000
1992 Tucson	AAA	115	420	130	16	4	2	—	—	160	69	33	45	1	68	4	9	2	34	10	.77	7	.310	.380	.381
1993 Colo. Sprng	AAA	117	439	138	24	8	7	—	—	199	83	56	47	3	57	6	5	1	33	18	.65	4	.314	.387	.453
1994 Colo. Sprng	AAA	79	320	116	22	5	8	—	—	172	78	38	44	1	40	2	2	1	28	10	.74	7	.363	.441	.538
1995 Colo. Sprng	AAA	123	480	163	29	7	12	—	—	242	102	66	61	5	59	5	2	5	37	14	.73	2	.340	.416	.504
1996 Colo. Sprng	AAA	50	188	59	15	5	6	—	—	102	41	16	28	0	14	2	0	1	6	8	.43	4	.314	.406	.543
1994 Colorado	NL	18	25	7	1	1	1	(1	0)	13	3	3	3	0	4	0	0	0	0	0	.00	1	.280	.357	.520
1995 Colorado	NL	24	58	18	4	0	3	(2	1)	31	13	9	8	0	6	0	1	0	2	1	.67	2	.310	.394	.534
1996 Col-SF	NL	55	89	19	5	2	2	(2	0)	34	15	14	11	0	27	1	0	0	2	0	1.00	3	.213	.307	.382
1996 Colorado	NL	45	60	13	5	1	1	(1	0)	23	12	12	9	0	22	1	0	0	2	0	1.00	1	.217	.329	.383
San Francisco	NL	10	29	6	0	1	1	(1	0)	11	3	2	2	0	5	0	0	0	0	0	.00	2	.207	.258	.379
3 ML YEARS		97	172	44	10	3	6	(5	1)	78	31	26	22	0	37	1	1	0	4	1	.80	6	.256	.344	.453

John Hudek

Pitches: Right   **Bats:** Both   **Pos:** RP-15   **Ht:** 6'1"   **Wt:** 200   **Born:** 8/8/66   **Age:** 30

		HOW MUCH HE PITCHED						WHAT HE GAVE UP											THE RESULTS					
Year Team	Lg	G	GS	CG	GF	IP	BFP	H	R	ER	HR	SH	SF	HB	TBB	IBB	SO	WP	Bk	W	L	Pct.	ShO	Sv-Op	Hld	ERA
1996 Kissimmee *	A+	2	1	0	0	3	14	2	0	0	0	0	0	0	2	0	3	0	0	0	0	.000	0	0- -	—	0.00
Tucson *	AAA	17	2	0	13	20.1	86	17	8	7	2	1	0	1	8	0	26	1	0	1	0	1.000	0	4- -	—	3.10
1994 Houston	NL	42	0	0	33	39.1	159	24	14	13	5	0	2	1	18	2	39	0	0	0	2	.000	0	16-18	1	2.97
1995 Houston	NL	19	0	0	16	20	83	19	12	12	3	1	0	0	5	0	29	2	0	2	2	.500	0	7-9	0	5.40
1996 Houston	NL	15	0	0	6	16	65	12	5	5	2	2	0	0	5	2	14	1	1	2	0	1.000	0	2-2	1	2.81
3 ML YEARS		76	0	0	55	75.1	307	55	31	30	10	3	2	1	28	4	82	3	1	4	4	.500	0	25-29	2	3.58

Rex Hudler

Bats: R **Throws:** R **Pos:** 2B-53; CF-14; PH-14; LF-8; DH-7; 1B-7   **Ht:** 6'0"   **Wt:** 195   **Born:** 9/2/60   **Age:** 36

							BATTING												BASERUNNING				PERCENTAGES		
Year Team	Lg	G	AB	H	2B	3B	HR	(Hm	Rd)	TB	R	RBI	TBB	IBB	SO	HBP	SH	SF	SB	CS	SB%	GDP	Avg	OBP	SLG
1984 New York	AL	9	7	1	1	0	0	(0	0)	2	2	0	1	0	5	1	0	0	0	0	.00	0	.143	.333	.286
1985 New York	AL	20	51	8	0	1	0	(0	0)	10	4	1	0	0	9	0	5	0	0	1	.00	0	.157	.173	.196
1986 Baltimore	AL	14	1	0	0	0	0	(0	0)	0	1	0	0	0	0	0	0	0	1	0	1.00	0	.000	.000	.000
1988 Montreal	NL	77	216	59	14	2	4	(1	3)	89	38	34	10	6	34	0	1	2	29	7	.81	2	.273	.303	.412
1989 Montreal	NL	92	155	38	7	0	6	(3	3)	63	21	13	6	2	23	1	0	0	15	4	.79	2	.245	.278	.406
1990 Mon-StL	NL	93	220	62	11	2	7	(2	5)	98	31	22	12	1	32	2	2	1	18	10	.64	3	.282	.323	.445
1991 St. Louis	NL	101	207	47	10	2	1	(1	0)	64	21	15	10	1	29	0	2	2	12	8	.60	1	.227	.260	.309
1992 St. Louis	NL	61	98	24	4	0	3	(2	1)	37	17	5	2	0	23	1	1	1	2	6	.25	0	.245	.265	.378
1994 California	AL	56	124	37	8	0	8	(4	4)	69	17	20	6	0	28	0	4	2	2	2	.50	7	.298	.326	.556
1995 California	AL	84	223	59	16	0	6	(4	2)	93	30	27	10	1	48	5	2	1	13	0	1.00	2	.265	.310	.417
1996 California	AL	92	302	94	20	3	16	(6	10)	168	60	40	9	0	54	3	2	1	14	5	.74	7	.311	.337	.556
1990 Montreal	NL	4	3	1	0	0	0	(0	0)	1	1	0	0	0	1	0	0	0	0	0	.00	0	.333	.333	.333
St. Louis	NL	89	217	61	11	2	7	(2	5)	97	30	22	12	1	31	2	2	1	18	10	.64	3	.281	.323	.447
11 ML YEARS		699	1604	429	91	10	51	(23	28)	693	242	157	67	11	285	13	19	10	106	43	.71	24	.267	.300	.432

105

Joe Hudson

Pitches: Right **Bats:** Right **Pos:** RP-36 **Ht:** 6'1" **Wt:** 180 **Born:** 9/29/70 **Age:** 26

Year Team	Lg	G	GS	CG	GF	IP	BFP	H	R	ER	HR	SH	SF	HB	TBB	IBB	SO	WP	Bk	W	L	Pct.	ShO	Sv-Op	Hld	ERA
1992 Elmira	A-	19	7	0	6	72	320	76	46	35	2	3	0	2	33	0	38	4	2	3	3	.500	0	6- -	—	4.38
1993 Lynchburg	A+	49	1	0	30	84.1	372	97	49	38	1	2	2	2	38	2	62	10	4	8	6	.571	0	6- -	—	4.06
1994 Sarasota	A+	30	0	0	21	48.1	215	42	20	12	0	1	1	2	27	0	33	6	0	3	1	.750	0	7- -	—	2.23
New Britain	AA	23	0	0	11	39	183	49	18	17	0	3	1	2	18	1	24	1	1	5	3	.625	0	0- -	—	3.92
1995 Trenton	AA	22	0	0	17	31.2	133	20	8	6	0	1	0	1	17	3	24	2	1	0	1	.000	0	8- -	—	1.71
1996 Pawtucket	AAA	25	0	0	15	33.1	151	29	19	13	0	0	1	0	21	0	18	4	0	1	1	.500	0	5- -	—	3.51
1995 Boston	AL	39	0	0	11	46	205	53	21	21	2	3	1	2	23	1	29	6	0	0	1	.000	0	1-4	8	4.11
1996 Boston	AL	36	0	0	16	45	214	57	35	27	4	1	2	0	32	4	19	0	0	3	5	.375	0	1-5	3	5.40
2 ML YEARS		75	0	0	27	91	419	110	56	48	6	4	3	2	55	5	48	6	0	3	6	.333	0	2-9	11	4.75

Michael Huff

Bats: R **Throws:** R **Pos:** CF-4; RF-4; 3B-3; PH-2; LF-1 **Ht:** 6'1" **Wt:** 190 **Born:** 8/11/63 **Age:** 33

Year Team	Lg	G	AB	H	2B	3B	HR	(Hm	Rd)	TB	R	RBI	TBB	IBB	SO	HBP	SH	SF	SB	CS	SB%	GDP	Avg	OBP	SLG
1996 Syracuse *	AAA	78	248	72	20	3	8	—	—	122	40	42	28	0	39	1	0	4	8	3	.73	5	.290	.359	.492
1989 Los Angeles	NL	12	25	5	1	0	1	(0	1)	9	4	2	3	0	6	1	1	0	0	1	.00	0	.200	.310	.360
1991 Cle-ChA	AL	102	243	61	10	2	3	(1	2)	84	42	25	37	2	48	6	6	2	14	4	.78	7	.251	.361	.346
1992 Chicago	AL	60	115	24	5	0	0	(0	0)	29	13	8	10	1	24	1	2	2	1	2	.33	2	.209	.273	.252
1993 Chicago	AL	43	44	8	2	0	1	(0	1)	13	4	6	9	0	15	1	1	2	1	0	1.00	1	.182	.321	.295
1994 Toronto	AL	80	207	63	15	3	3	(1	2)	93	31	25	27	2	27	3	0	0	2	1	.67	6	.304	.392	.449
1995 Toronto	AL	61	138	32	9	1	1	(0	1)	46	14	9	22	0	21	1	5	2	1	1	.50	4	.232	.337	.333
1996 Toronto	AL	11	29	5	0	1	0	(0	0)	7	1	0	5	0	5	0	0	0	0	0	.00	0	.172	.200	.241
1991 Cleveland	AL	51	146	35	6	1	2	(1	1)	49	28	10	25	0	30	4	3	1	11	2	.85	2	.240	.364	.336
Chicago	AL	51	97	26	4	1	1	(0	1)	35	14	15	12	2	18	2	3	1	3	2	.60	5	.268	.357	.361
7 ML YEARS		369	801	198	42	7	9	(2	7)	281	113	75	109	5	146	13	15	8	19	9	.68	19	.247	.344	.351

Rick Huisman

Pitches: Right **Bats:** Right **Pos:** RP-22 **Ht:** 6'3" **Wt:** 210 **Born:** 5/17/69 **Age:** 28

Year Team	Lg	G	GS	CG	GF	IP	BFP	H	R	ER	HR	SH	SF	HB	TBB	IBB	SO	WP	Bk	W	L	Pct.	ShO	Sv-Op	Hld	ERA
1990 Everett	A-	1	0	0	0	2	10	3	1	1	0	0	0	0	2	0	2	1	0	0	0	.000	0	0- -	—	4.50
Clinton	A	14	13	0	0	79	315	57	19	18	2	1	2	0	33	0	103	5	4	6	5	.545	0	0- -	—	2.05
1991 San Jose	A+	26	26	7	0	182.1	720	126	45	37	5	11	3	3	73	1	216	13	3	16	4	.800	4	0- -	—	1.83
1992 Shreveport	AA	17	16	1	0	103.1	403	79	33	27	3	2	0	5	31	1	100	3	1	7	4	.636	1	0- -	—	2.35
Phoenix	AAA	9	8	0	0	56	230	45	16	15	3	1	1	1	24	0	44	1	0	3	2	.600	0	0- -	—	2.41
1993 San Jose	A+	4	4	1	0	23.1	97	19	6	6	0	2	1	2	12	0	15	1	0	2	1	.667	0	0- -	—	2.31
Phoenix	AAA	14	14	0	0	72.1	333	78	54	48	5	1	1	1	45	0	59	8	4	3	4	.429	0	0- -	—	5.97
Tucson	AAA	2	0	0	0	3.2	18	6	5	3	0	0	0	0	1	0	4	5	0	1	0	1.000	0	0- -	—	7.36
1994 Jackson	AA	49	0	0	46	50.1	204	32	10	9	1	1	1	2	24	2	63	1	0	3	0	1.000	0	31- -	—	1.61
1995 Omaha	AAA	5	0	0	3	5	19	3	1	1	1	0	0	0	1	0	13	0	0	0	0	.000	0	1- -	—	1.80
Omaha	AAA	47	0	0	31	59.2	265	61	34	28	2	0	3	1	29	3	60	3	1	6	1	.857	0	7- -	—	4.22
1996 Omaha	AAA	27	4	0	6	57.1	243	54	32	31	9	0	1	2	24	0	50	0	1	2	4	.333	0	0- -	—	4.87
1995 Kansas City	AL	7	0	0	2	9.2	44	14	8	8	2	1	0	0	1	0	12	0	0	0	0	.000	0	0-0	—	7.45
1996 Kansas City	AL	22	0	0	5	29.1	130	25	15	15	4	2	2	0	18	2	23	0	0	2	1	.667	0	1-1	0	4.60
2 ML YEARS		29	0	0	7	39	174	39	23	23	6	3	2	0	19	2	35	0	0	2	1	.667	0	1-1	0	5.31

David Hulse

Bats: L **Throws:** L **Pos:** CF-37; PH-29; LF-24; RF-11; DH-3 **Ht:** 5'11" **Wt:** 195 **Born:** 2/25/68 **Age:** 29

Year Team	Lg	G	AB	H	2B	3B	HR	(Hm	Rd)	TB	R	RBI	TBB	IBB	SO	HBP	SH	SF	SB	CS	SB%	GDP	Avg	OBP	SLG
1996 New Orleans *	AAA	8	29	8	2	0	0	—	—	10	2	1	1	0	6	0	0	0	0	0	.00	1	.276	.300	.345
1992 Texas	AL	32	92	28	4	0	0	(0	0)	32	14	2	3	0	18	0	2	0	3	1	.75	0	.304	.326	.348
1993 Texas	AL	114	407	118	9	10	1	(0	1)	150	71	29	26	1	57	1	5	2	29	9	.76	9	.290	.333	.369
1994 Texas	AL	77	310	79	8	4	1	(1	0)	98	58	19	21	0	53	2	7	1	18	2	.90	1	.255	.305	.316
1995 Milwaukee	AL	119	339	85	11	6	3	(1	2)	117	46	47	18	2	60	0	2	5	15	3	.83	3	.251	.285	.345
1996 Milwaukee	AL	81	117	26	3	0	0	(0	0)	29	18	6	8	0	16	0	2	0	4	1	.80	2	.222	.272	.248
5 ML YEARS		423	1265	336	35	20	5	(2	3)	426	207	103	76	3	204	3	18	8	69	16	.81	15	.266	.307	.337

Todd Hundley

Bats: Both **Throws:** Right **Pos:** C-150; PH-10 **Ht:** 5'11" **Wt:** 185 **Born:** 5/27/69 **Age:** 28

Year Team	Lg	G	AB	H	2B	3B	HR	(Hm	Rd)	TB	R	RBI	TBB	IBB	SO	HBP	SH	SF	SB	CS	SB%	GDP	Avg	OBP	SLG
1990 New York	NL	36	67	14	6	0	0	(0	0)	20	8	2	6	0	18	0	1	0	0	0	.00	1	.209	.274	.299
1991 New York	NL	21	60	8	0	1	1	(1	0)	13	5	7	6	0	14	1	1	1	0	0	.00	3	.133	.221	.217
1992 New York	NL	123	358	75	17	0	7	(2	5)	113	32	32	19	4	76	4	7	2	3	0	1.00	8	.209	.256	.316
1993 New York	NL	130	417	95	17	2	11	(5	6)	149	40	53	23	7	62	2	2	4	1	1	.50	10	.228	.269	.357
1994 New York	NL	91	291	69	10	1	16	(8	8)	129	45	42	25	4	73	3	3	1	2	1	.67	3	.237	.303	.443

							BATTING											BASERUNNING				PERCENTAGES		
Year Team	Lg	G	AB	H	2B	3B	HR	(Hm Rd)	TB	R	RBI	TBB	IBB	SO	HBP	SH	SF	SB	CS	SB%	GDP	Avg	OBP	SLG
1995 New York	NL	90	275	77	11	0	15	(6 9)	133	39	51	42	5	64	5	1	3	1	0	1.00	4	.280	.382	.484
1996 New York	NL	153	540	140	32	1	41	(20 21)	297	85	112	79	15	146	3	0	2	1	3	.25	9	.259	.356	.550
7 ML YEARS		644	2008	478	93	5	91	(42 49)	854	254	299	200	35	453	18	15	13	8	5	.62	38	.238	.311	.425

Brian Hunter

Bats: R **Throws:** L **Pos:** 1B-41; LF-29; PH-23; DH-2; RF-2   **Ht:** 6'0" **Wt:** 225 **Born:** 3/4/68 **Age:** 29

							BATTING											BASERUNNING				PERCENTAGES		
Year Team	Lg	G	AB	H	2B	3B	HR	(Hm Rd)	TB	R	RBI	TBB	IBB	SO	HBP	SH	SF	SB	CS	SB%	GDP	Avg	OBP	SLG
1996 Tacoma *	AAA	25	92	32	6	1	7	— —	61	19	24	9	0	11	0	0	1	1	0	1.00	1	.348	.394	.663
1991 Atlanta	NL	97	271	68	16	1	12	(7 5)	122	32	50	17	0	48	1	0	2	0	2	.00	6	.251	.296	.450
1992 Atlanta	NL	102	238	57	13	2	14	(9 5)	116	34	41	21	3	50	0	1	8	1	2	.33	2	.239	.292	.487
1993 Atlanta	NL	37	80	11	3	1	0	(0 0)	16	4	8	2	1	15	0	0	1	0	0	.00	1	.138	.153	.200
1994 Pit-Cin	NL	85	256	60	16	1	15	(4 11)	123	34	57	17	2	56	0	0	5	0	0	.00	3	.234	.277	.480
1995 Cincinnati	NL	40	79	17	6	0	1	(0 1)	26	9	9	11	1	21	1	0	2	2	1	.67	2	.215	.312	.329
1996 Seattle	AL	75	198	53	10	0	7	(2 5)	84	21	28	15	2	43	4	1	3	0	1	.00	6	.268	.327	.424
1994 Pittsburgh	NL	76	233	53	15	1	11	(4 7)	103	28	47	15	2	55	0	0	4	0	0	.00	3	.227	.270	.442
Cincinnati	NL	9	23	7	1	0	4	(0 4)	20	6	10	2	0	1	0	0	1	0	0	.00	0	.304	.346	.870
6 ML YEARS		436	1122	266	64	5	49	(22 27)	487	134	193	83	9	233	6	2	23	3	6	.33	20	.237	.288	.434

Brian L. Hunter

Bats: Right **Throws:** Right **Pos:** CF-127; PH-9   **Ht:** 6'4" **Wt:** 180 **Born:** 3/5/71 **Age:** 26

							BATTING											BASERUNNING				PERCENTAGES		
Year Team	Lg	G	AB	H	2B	3B	HR	(Hm Rd)	TB	R	RBI	TBB	IBB	SO	HBP	SH	SF	SB	CS	SB%	GDP	Avg	OBP	SLG
1996 Tucson *	AAA	3	14	5	0	1	0	— —	7	3	1	0	0	2	0	0	1	3	0	1.00	0	.357	.333	.500
1994 Houston	NL	6	24	6	1	0	0	(0 0)	7	2	0	1	0	6	0	1	0	2	1	.67	2	.250	.280	.292
1995 Houston	NL	78	321	97	14	5	2	(0 2)	127	52	28	21	0	52	2	2	3	24	7	.77	2	.302	.346	.396
1996 Houston	NL	132	526	145	27	2	5	(1 4)	191	74	35	17	0	92	2	1	7	35	9	.80	6	.276	.297	.363
3 ML YEARS		216	871	248	42	7	7	(1 6)	325	128	63	39	0	150	4	4	10	61	17	.78	8	.285	.315	.373

Rich Hunter

Pitches: Right **Bats:** Right **Pos:** SP-14   **Ht:** 6'1" **Wt:** 185 **Born:** 9/25/74 **Age:** 22

		HOW MUCH HE PITCHED						WHAT HE GAVE UP										THE RESULTS						
Year Team	Lg	G	GS	CG	GF	IP	BFP	H	R	ER	HR	SH	SF	HB	TBB	IBB	SO	WP	Bk	W	L	Pct.	ShO	Sv-Op	Hld	ERA
1993 Martinsvlle	R+	13	9	0	1	49	254	82	61	52	9	1	6	4	27	0	36	4	1	0	6	.000	0	0--	—	9.55
1994 Martinsvlle	R+	18	0	0	8	38	153	31	19	19	3	1	2	0	9	1	39	1	0	3	2	.600	0	5--	—	4.50
1995 Clearwater	A+	9	9	0	0	58.1	242	62	23	19	3	3	2	5	7	0	46	3	3	6	0	1.000	0	0--	—	2.93
Reading	AA	3	3	0	0	22	86	14	6	5	1	0	1	0	6	0	17	2	0	3	0	1.000	0	0--	—	2.05
1996 Scranton-WB	AAA	8	7	1	0	40.1	182	39	31	30	5	4	1	3	22	0	22	3	0	2	4	.333	0	0--	—	6.69
Reading	AA	10	10	2	0	71	290	69	26	25	7	1	1	7	12	0	40	3	1	4	3	.571	0	0--	—	3.17
1996 Philadelphia	NL	14	14	0	0	69.1	322	84	54	50	10	3	4	5	33	2	32	4	0	3	7	.300	0	0-0	0	6.49

Bill Hurst

Pitches: Right **Bats:** Right **Pos:** RP-2   **Ht:** 6'7" **Wt:** 215 **Born:** 4/28/70 **Age:** 27

		HOW MUCH HE PITCHED						WHAT HE GAVE UP										THE RESULTS						
Year Team	Lg	G	GS	CG	GF	IP	BFP	H	R	ER	HR	SH	SF	HB	TBB	IBB	SO	WP	Bk	W	L	Pct.	ShO	Sv-Op	Hld	ERA
1990 Johnson Cty	R+	2	2	0	0	10.2	41	5	2	2	0	0	0	0	5	0	12	0	0	0	0	.000	0	0--	—	1.69
Savannah	A	7	7	0	0	31.2	141	22	17	12	0	0	1	1	27	1	14	8	2	2	1	.667	0	0--	—	3.41
1991 Johnson Cty	R+	2	0	0	0	1.2	8	0	2	2	0	0	0	1	2	0	2	0	0	0	0	.000	0	0--	—	10.80
1992 Hamilton	A-	3	3	0	0	14.2	64	11	7	6	1	0	0	3	4	0	9	3	1	0	1	.000	0	0--	—	3.68
1995 Brevard Cty	A+	39	4	0	29	50.2	228	33	20	17	1	3	1	8	41	4	35	4	0	1	4	.200	0	12--	—	3.02
1996 Portland	AA	45	0	0	42	49	218	45	22	12	3	1	2	1	31	0	46	6	0	2	3	.400	0	30--	—	2.20
1996 Florida	NL	2	0	0	2	2	10	3	0	0	0	0	0	0	1	0	1	1	0	0	0	.000	0	0-0	0	0.00

Edwin Hurtado

Pitches: Right **Bats:** Right **Pos:** RP-12; SP-4   **Ht:** 6'3" **Wt:** 215 **Born:** 2/1/70 **Age:** 27

		HOW MUCH HE PITCHED						WHAT HE GAVE UP										THE RESULTS						
Year Team	Lg	G	GS	CG	GF	IP	BFP	H	R	ER	HR	SH	SF	HB	TBB	IBB	SO	WP	Bk	W	L	Pct.	ShO	Sv-Op	Hld	ERA
1993 St. Cathrns	A-	15	15	3	0	101	402	69	34	28	6	1	3	4	34	0	87	3	3	10	2	.833	1	0--	—	2.50
1994 Hagerstown	A	33	16	1	9	134.1	553	118	53	44	8	0	4	1	46	0	121	5	2	11	2	.846	0	2--	—	2.95
1995 Knoxville	AA	11	11	0	0	54.2	240	54	34	27	7	1	4	0	25	0	38	4	0	2	4	.333	0	0--	—	4.45
1996 Tacoma	AAA	5	4	0	0	31.1	123	23	13	13	5	1	1	0	12	1	26	3	0	1	2	.333	0	0--	—	3.73
1995 Toronto	AL	14	10	1	0	77.2	345	81	50	47	11	2	3	5	40	3	33	11	0	5	2	.714	0	0-0	1	5.45
1996 Seattle	AL	16	4	0	6	47.2	223	61	42	41	10	0	5	0	30	3	36	2	0	2	5	.286	0	2-3	0	7.74
2 ML YEARS		30	14	1	6	125.1	568	142	92	88	21	2	8	5	70	6	69	13	0	7	7	.500	0	2-3	1	6.32

Butch Huskey

Bats: R **Throws:** R **Pos:** 1B-75; RF-40; 3B-6; PH-5   **Ht:** 6'3"   **Wt:** 244   **Born:** 11/10/71   **Age:** 25

Year Team		Lg	G	AB	H	2B	3B	HR	(Hm	Rd)	TB	R	RBI	TBB	IBB	SO	HBP	SH	SF	SB	CS	SB%	GDP	Avg	OBP	SLG
1993 New York		NL	13	41	6	1	0	0	(0	0)	7	2	3	1	1	13	0	0	2	0	0	.00	0	.146	.159	.171
1995 New York		NL	28	90	17	1	0	3	(2	1)	27	8	11	10	0	16	0	1	1	1	0	1.00	3	.189	.267	.300
1996 New York		NL	118	414	115	16	2	15	(9	6)	180	43	60	27	3	78	0	0	4	1	2	.33	10	.278	.319	.435
3 ML YEARS			159	545	138	18	2	18	(11	7)	214	53	74	38	4	107	0	1	7	2	2	.50	13	.253	.298	.393

Jeff Huson

Bats: L **Throws:** R **Pos:** 2B-12; PH-7; 3B-3; RF-1   **Ht:** 6'1"   **Wt:** 185   **Born:** 8/15/64   **Age:** 32

Year Team		Lg	G	AB	H	2B	3B	HR	(Hm	Rd)	TB	R	RBI	TBB	IBB	SO	HBP	SH	SF	SB	CS	SB%	GDP	Avg	OBP	SLG
1996 Frederick *		A+	4	16	7	2	0	1	—	—	12	4	1	2	0	0	0	0	0	0	0	.00	0	.438	.500	.750
Bowie *		AA	3	13	5	2	0	0	—	—	7	3	0	1	0	0	0	0	0	0	0	.00	0	.385	.429	.538
Rochester *		AAA	2	8	2	0	0	0	—	—	2	0	1	0	0	2	0	0	0	0	0	.00	1	.250	.250	.250
Colo. Sprng *		AAA	14	61	18	4	0	0	—	—	22	10	8	3	0	1	0	0	2	6	0	1.00	0	.295	.348	.361
1988 Montreal		NL	20	42	13	2	0	0	(0	0)	15	7	3	4	2	3	0	0	0	2	1	.67	2	.310	.370	.357
1989 Montreal		NL	32	74	12	5	0	0	(0	0)	17	1	2	6	3	6	0	3	0	3	0	1.00	6	.162	.225	.230
1990 Texas		AL	145	396	95	12	2	0	(0	0)	111	57	28	46	0	54	2	7	3	12	4	.75	8	.240	.320	.280
1991 Texas		AL	119	268	57	8	3	2	(1	1)	77	36	26	39	0	32	0	9	1	8	3	.73	6	.213	.312	.287
1992 Texas		AL	123	318	83	14	3	4	(0	4)	115	49	24	41	2	43	1	8	6	18	6	.75	7	.261	.342	.362
1993 Texas		AL	23	45	6	1	1	0	(0	0)	9	3	2	0	0	10	0	1	0	0	0	.00	4	.133	.133	.200
1995 Baltimore		AL	66	161	40	4	2	1	(0	1)	51	24	19	15	1	20	1	2	1	5	4	.56	4	.248	.315	.317
1996 Baltimore		AL	17	28	9	1	0	0	(0	0)	10	5	2	1	0	3	0	0	0	0	0	.00	0	.321	.333	.357
8 ML YEARS			545	1332	315	47	11	7	(1	6)	405	182	106	152	8	171	4	30	12	48	18	.73	33	.236	.314	.304

Mark Hutton

Pitches: Right   **Bats:** Right   **Pos:** RP-14; SP-11   **Ht:** 6'6"   **Wt:** 240   **Born:** 2/6/70   **Age:** 27

			HOW MUCH HE PITCHED						WHAT HE GAVE UP										THE RESULTS						
Year Team		Lg	G	GS	CG	GF	IP	BFP	H	R	ER	HR	SH	SF	HB	TBB	IBB	SO	WP	Bk	W	L	Pct.	ShO	Sv-Op	Hld	ERA
1989 Oneonta		A-	12	12	0	0	66.1	283	70	39	30	1	2	4	1	24	0	62	5	2	6	2	.750	0	0--	—	4.07
1990 Greensboro		A	21	19	0	1	81.1	394	77	78	57	2	2	3	7	62	0	72	14	1	1	10	.091	0	0--	—	6.31
1991 Ft. Laud		A+	24	24	3	0	147	606	82	54	40	5	6	1	11	65	5	117	4	4	5	8	.385	0	0--	—	2.45
Columbus		AAA	1	1	0	0	6	24	3	2	1	0	0	0	0	5	0	5	0	0	1	0	1.000	0	0--	—	1.50
1992 Albany-Colo		AA	25	25	1	0	165.1	703	146	75	66	6	2	3	11	66	1	128	2	1	13	7	.650	0	0--	—	3.59
Columbus		AAA	1	0	0	0	5	22	7	4	3	0	0	0	0	2	0	4	0	0	1	0	.000	0	0--	—	5.40
1993 Columbus		AAA	21	21	0	0	133	544	98	52	47	14	2	0	10	53	0	112	2	1	10	4	.714	0	0--	—	3.18
1994 Columbus		AAA	22	5	0	12	34.2	146	31	16	14	5	1	2	2	12	0	27	0	0	2	5	.286	0	3--	—	3.63
1995 Columbus		AAA	11	11	0	0	52.1	243	64	51	49	7	0	3	4	24	1	23	2	0	2	6	.250	0	0--	—	8.43
1996 Tampa		A+	3	2	0	0	5	18	2	1	1	0	0	0	0	1	0	6	0	0	0	0	.000	0	0--	—	1.80
Columbus		AAA	2	0	0	1	2	8	0	0	0	0	0	0	0	2	0	3	1	0	0	0	.000	0	0--	—	0.00
1993 New York		AL	7	4	0	2	22	104	24	17	14	2	2	2	1	17	0	12	0	0	1	1	.500	0	0-0	0	5.73
1994 New York		AL	2	0	0	1	3.2	16	4	3	2	0	0	0	0	0	0	1	0	0	0	0	.000	0	0-0	0	4.91
1996 NYA-Fla			25	11	0	5	86.2	374	79	42	40	9	0	3	4	36	1	56	2	0	5	3	.625	0	0-0	1	4.15
1996 New York		AL	12	2	0	0	30.1	140	32	19	17	3	0	2	1	18	1	25	0	0	0	2	.000	0	0-0	1	5.04
Florida		NL	13	9	0	0	56.1	234	47	23	23	6	0	1	3	18	0	31	2	0	5	1	.833	0	0-0	0	3.67
3 ML YEARS			34	15	0	8	112.1	494	107	62	56	11	2	5	5	53	1	69	2	0	6	4	.600	0	0-0	1	4.49

Tim Hyers

Bats: Left   **Throws:** Left   **Pos:** 1B-9; PH-8; DH-2; LF-1   **Ht:** 6'1"   **Wt:** 195   **Born:** 10/3/71   **Age:** 25

Year Team		Lg	G	AB	H	2B	3B	HR	(Hm	Rd)	TB	R	RBI	TBB	IBB	SO	HBP	SH	SF	SB	CS	SB%	GDP	Avg	OBP	SLG
1996 Toledo *		AAA	117	437	113	17	6	7	—	—	163	55	59	40	2	57	3	1	5	7	1	.88	8	.259	.322	.373
1994 San Diego		NL	52	118	30	3	0	0	(0	0)	33	13	7	9	0	15	0	2	0	3	0	1.00	1	.254	.307	.280
1995 San Diego		NL	6	5	0	0	0	0	(0	0)	0	0	0	0	0	1	0	0	0	0	0	.00	0	.000	.000	.000
1996 Detroit		AL	17	26	2	1	0	0	(0	0)	3	1	0	4	2	5	0	0	0	0	0	.00	2	.077	.200	.115
3 ML YEARS			75	149	32	4	0	0	(0	0)	36	14	7	13	2	21	0	2	0	3	0	1.00	3	.215	.278	.242

Raul Ibanez

Bats: Left   **Throws:** Right   **Pos:** DH-2; PH-2   **Ht:** 6'2"   **Wt:** 200   **Born:** 6/2/72   **Age:** 25

Year Team		Lg	G	AB	H	2B	3B	HR	(Hm	Rd)	TB	R	RBI	TBB	IBB	SO	HBP	SH	SF	SB	CS	SB%	GDP	Avg	OBP	SLG
1992 Mariners		R	33	120	37	8	2	1	—	—	52	25	16	9	1	18	2	0	0	1	2	.33	3	.308	.366	.433
1993 Appleton		A	52	157	43	9	0	5	—	—	67	26	21	24	2	31	1	1	2	0	2	.00	0	.274	.370	.427
Bellingham		A-	43	134	38	5	2	0	—	—	47	16	15	21	1	23	1	0	1	0	3	.00	0	.284	.378	.351
1994 Appleton		A	91	327	102	30	3	7	—	—	159	55	59	32	3	37	2	0	2	10	5	.67	3	.312	.375	.486
1995 Riverside		A+	95	361	120	23	9	20	—	—	221	59	108	41	1	49	2	1	9	4	3	.57	7	.332	.395	.612
1996 Port City		AA	19	76	28	8	1	1	—	—	41	12	13	8	1	7	0	0	1	3	2	.60	1	.368	.424	.539
Tacoma		AAA	111	405	115	20	3	11	—	—	174	59	47	44	2	56	2	0	5	7	7	.50	5	.284	.353	.430
1996 Seattle		AL	4	5	0	0	0	0	(0	0)	0	0	0	1	0	0	0	0	0	0	0	.00	0	.000	.167	.000

Pete Incaviglia

Bats: R **Throws:** R **Pos:** LF-77; PH-31; DH-4; RF-2   **Ht:** 6'1" **Wt:** 225 **Born:** 4/2/64   **Age:** 33

Year Team	Lg	G	AB	H	2B	3B	HR	(Hm	Rd)	TB	R	RBI	TBB	IBB	SO	HBP	SH	SF	SB	CS	SB%	GDP	Avg	OBP	SLG
1986 Texas	AL	153	540	135	21	2	30	(17	13)	250	82	88	55	2	185	4	0	7	3	2	.60	9	.250	.320	.463
1987 Texas	AL	139	509	138	26	4	27	(11	16)	253	85	80	48	1	168	1	0	5	9	3	.75	8	.271	.332	.497
1988 Texas	AL	116	418	104	19	3	22	(12	10)	195	59	54	39	3	153	7	0	3	6	4	.60	6	.249	.321	.467
1989 Texas	AL	133	453	107	27	4	21	(13	8)	205	48	81	32	0	136	6	0	4	5	7	.42	12	.236	.293	.453
1990 Texas	AL	153	529	123	27	0	24	(15	9)	222	59	85	45	5	146	9	0	4	3	4	.43	18	.233	.302	.420
1991 Detroit	AL	97	337	72	12	1	11	(6	5)	119	38	38	36	0	92	1	1	2	1	3	.25	6	.214	.290	.353
1992 Houston	NL	113	349	93	22	1	11	(6	5)	150	31	44	25	2	99	3	0	2	2	2	.50	6	.266	.319	.430
1993 Philadelphia	NL	116	368	101	16	3	24	(15	9)	195	60	89	21	1	82	6	0	7	1	1	.50	9	.274	.318	.530
1994 Philadelphia	NL	80	244	56	10	1	13	(6	7)	107	28	32	16	3	71	1	0	2	1	0	1.00	6	.230	.278	.439
1996 Phi-Bal		111	302	73	9	2	18	(6	12)	140	37	50	30	2	89	4	0	1	2	0	1.00	6	.242	.318	.464
1996 Philadelphia	NL	99	269	63	7	2	16	(6	10)	122	33	42	30	2	82	3	0	0	2	0	1.00	6	.234	.318	.454
Baltimore	AL	12	33	10	2	0	2	(0	2)	18	4	8	0	0	7	1	0	1	0	0	.00	0	.303	.314	.545
10 ML YEARS		1211	4049	1002	189	21	201	(107	94)	1836	527	641	347	19	1221	42	1	37	33	26	.56	83	.247	.311	.453

Jason Isringhausen

Pitches: Right **Bats:** Right **Pos:** SP-27   **Ht:** 6'3" **Wt:** 196 **Born:** 9/7/72   **Age:** 24

Year Team	Lg	G	GS	CG	GF	IP	BFP	H	R	ER	HR	SH	SF	HB	TBB	IBB	SO	WP	Bk	W	L	Pct.	ShO	Sv-Op	Hld	ERA
1992 Mets	R	6	6	0	0	29	133	26	19	14	0	0	0	3	17	1	25	2	0	2	4	.333	0	0--	--	4.34
Kingsport	R+	7	6	1	0	36	160	32	22	13	2	0	3	1	12	1	24	2	1	4	1	.800	1	0--	--	3.25
1993 Pittsfield	A-	15	15	2	0	90.1	375	68	45	33	7	4	6	3	28	0	104	8	0	7	4	.636	0	0--	--	3.29
1994 St. Lucie	A+	14	14	6	0	101	391	76	31	25	2	1	1	2	27	2	59	4	0	6	4	.600	3	0--	--	2.23
Binghamton	AA	14	14	2	0	92.1	368	87	35	31	6	4	5	2	23	0	69	5	1	5	4	.556	0	0--	--	3.02
1995 Binghamton	AA	6	6	1	0	41	164	26	15	13	1	0	0	3	12	0	59	6	0	2	1	.667	0	0--	--	2.85
Norfolk	AAA	18	18	4	0	128	507	90	32	28	3	2	0	5	36	0	134	10	1	11	2	.846	3	0--	--	1.97
1995 New York	NL	14	14	1	0	93	385	88	29	29	6	3	3	2	31	2	55	4	1	9	2	.818	0	0-0	0	2.81
1996 New York	NL	27	27	2	0	171.2	766	190	103	91	13	7	9	8	73	5	114	14	0	6	14	.300	0	0-0	0	4.77
2 ML YEARS		41	41	3	0	264.2	1151	278	132	120	19	10	12	10	104	7	169	18	1	15	16	.484	1	0-0	0	4.08

Damian Jackson

Bats: Right **Throws:** Right **Pos:** SS-5; PH-1   **Ht:** 5'10" **Wt:** 160 **Born:** 8/16/73   **Age:** 23

Year Team	Lg	G	AB	H	2B	3B	HR	(Hm	Rd)	TB	R	RBI	TBB	IBB	SO	HBP	SH	SF	SB	CS	SB%	GDP	Avg	OBP	SLG
1992 Burlington	R+	62	226	56	12	1	0	—	—	70	32	23	32	0	31	6	6	3	29	5	.85	1	.248	.352	.310
1993 Columbus	A	108	350	94	19	3	6	—	—	137	70	45	41	0	61	5	5	1	26	7	.79	1	.269	.353	.391
1994 Canton-Akrn	AA	138	531	143	29	5	5	—	—	197	85	46	60	2	121	5	10	5	37	16	.70	8	.269	.346	.371
1995 Canton-Akrn	AA	131	484	120	20	2	3	—	—	153	67	34	65	0	103	9	7	0	40	22	.65	6	.248	.348	.316
1996 Buffalo	AAA	133	452	116	15	1	12	—	—	169	77	49	48	0	78	7	8	6	24	7	.77	1	.257	.333	.374
1996 Cleveland	AL	5	10	3	2	0	0	(0	0)	5	2	1	1	0	4	0	0	0	0	0	.00	0	.300	.364	.500

Danny Jackson

Pitches: Left **Bats:** Right **Pos:** RP-9; SP-4   **Ht:** 6'0" **Wt:** 220 **Born:** 1/5/62   **Age:** 35

Year Team	Lg	G	GS	CG	GF	IP	BFP	H	R	ER	HR	SH	SF	HB	TBB	IBB	SO	WP	Bk	W	L	Pct.	ShO	Sv-Op	Hld	ERA
1996 St. Pete *	A+	1	1	0	0	4	14	2	0	0	0	0	0	0	0	0	3	0	0	0	0	.000	0	0--	--	0.00
Louisville *	AAA	8	8	0	1	13	56	14	6	5	2	0	1	1	5	0	10	0	0	0	0	.000	0	0--	--	3.46
1983 Kansas City	AL	4	3	0	0	19	87	26	12	11	1	1	0	0	6	0	9	0	0	1	1	.500	0	0--	--	5.21
1984 Kansas City	AL	15	11	1	3	76	338	84	41	36	4	3	0	5	35	0	40	3	2	2	6	.250	0	0--	--	4.26
1985 Kansas City	AL	32	32	4	0	208	893	209	94	79	7	5	4	6	76	2	114	4	2	14	12	.538	3	0--	--	3.42
1986 Kansas City	AL	32	27	4	3	185.2	789	177	83	66	13	10	4	4	79	1	115	7	0	11	12	.478	1	1--	--	3.20
1987 Kansas City	AL	36	34	11	1	224	981	219	115	100	11	8	7	7	109	1	152	5	0	9	18	.333	2	0-1	--	4.02
1988 Cincinnati	NL	35	35	15	0	260.2	1034	206	86	79	13	13	5	2	71	6	161	5	2	23	8	.742	6	0-0	0	2.73
1989 Cincinnati	NL	20	20	1	0	115.2	519	122	78	72	10	6	4	1	57	7	70	3	2	6	11	.353	0	0-0	0	5.60
1990 Cincinnati	NL	22	21	0	1	117.1	499	119	54	53	11	4	5	2	40	4	76	3	1	6	6	.500	0	0-0	0	3.61
1991 Chicago	NL	17	14	0	0	70.2	347	89	59	53	8	8	2	1	48	4	31	1	1	1	5	.167	0	0-0	0	6.75
1992 ChN-Pit	NL	34	34	0	0	201.1	883	211	99	86	6	17	10	4	77	6	97	2	2	8	13	.381	0	0-0	0	3.84
1993 Philadelphia	NL	32	32	2	0	210.1	919	214	105	88	12	14	8	4	80	2	120	4	0	12	11	.522	1	0-0	0	3.77
1994 Philadelphia	NL	25	25	4	0	179.1	755	183	71	65	13	14	4	3	46	1	129	2	0	14	6	.700	1	0-0	U	3.26
1995 St. Louis	NL	19	19	2	0	100.2	467	120	82	66	10	10	7	6	48	1	52	6	0	2	12	.143	0	0-0	0	5.90
1996 St. Louis	NL	13	4	0	3	36.1	154	33	18	18	3	0	1	1	16	1	27	0	0	1	1	.500	0	0-0	0	4.46
1992 Chicago	NL	19	19	0	0	113	501	117	59	53	5	11	5	3	48	3	51	1	2	4	9	.308	0	0-0	0	4.22
Pittsburgh	NL	15	15	0	0	88.1	382	94	40	33	1	6	5	1	29	3	46	1	0	4	4	.500	0	0-0	0	3.36
14 ML YEARS		336	311	44	11	2005	8665	2012	997	866	122	113	63	45	788	36	1193	45	12	110	122	.474	15	1--	--	3.89

Darrin Jackson

Bats: Right **Throws:** Right **Pos:** RF/CF   **Ht:** 6'0" **Wt:** 185 **Born:** 8/22/63 **Age:** 33

Year Team	Lg	G	AB	H	2B	3B	HR	(Hm	Rd)	TB	R	RBI	TBB	IBB	SO	HBP	SH	SF	SB	CS	SB%	GDP	Avg	OBP	SLG
1985 Chicago	NL	5	11	1	0	0	0	(0	0)	1	0	0	0	0	3	0	0	0	0	0	.00	0	.091	.091	.091
1987 Chicago	NL	7	5	4	1	0	0	(0	0)	5	2	0	0	0	0	0	0	0	0	0	.00	0	.800	.800	1.000
1988 Chicago	NL	100	188	50	11	3	6	(3	3)	85	29	20	5	1	28	1	2	1	4	1	.80	3	.266	.287	.452
1989 ChN-SD	NL	70	170	37	7	0	4	(1	3)	56	17	20	13	5	34	0	0	2	1	4	.20	2	.218	.270	.329
1990 San Diego	NL	58	113	29	3	0	3	(1	2)	41	10	9	5	1	24	0	1	1	3	0	1.00	1	.257	.286	.363
1991 San Diego	NL	122	359	94	12	1	21	(12	9)	171	51	49	27	2	66	2	3	3	5	3	.63	5	.262	.315	.476
1992 San Diego	NL	155	587	146	23	5	17	(11	6)	230	72	70	26	4	106	4	6	5	14	3	.82	21	.249	.283	.392
1993 Tor-NYN		77	263	55	9	0	6	(4	2)	82	19	26	10	0	75	0	6	1	0	2	.00	9	.209	.237	.312
1994 Chicago	AL	104	369	115	17	3	10	(4	6)	168	43	51	27	3	56	3	2	2	7	1	.88	5	.312	.362	.455
1989 Chicago	NL	45	83	19	4	0	1	(0	1)	26	7	8	6	1	17	0	0	0	1	2	.33	1	.229	.281	.313
San Diego	NL	25	87	18	3	0	3	(1	2)	30	10	12	7	4	17	0	0	2	0	2	.00	1	.207	.260	.345
1993 Toronto	AL	46	176	38	8	0	5	(4	1)	61	15	19	8	0	53	0	5	0	0	2	.00	9	.216	.250	.347
New York	NL	31	87	17	1	0	1	(0	1)	21	4	7	2	0	22	0	1	1	0	0	.00	0	.195	.211	.241
9 ML YEARS		698	2065	531	83	12	67	(36	31)	839	243	245	113	16	392	10	20	15	34	14	.71	46	.257	.297	.406

Mike Jackson

Pitches: Right **Bats:** Right **Pos:** RP-73   **Ht:** 6'2" **Wt:** 225 **Born:** 12/22/64 **Age:** 32

Year Team	Lg	G	GS	CG	GF	IP	BFP	H	R	ER	HR	SH	SF	HB	TBB	IBB	SO	WP	Bk	W	L	Pct.	ShO	Sv-Op	Hld	ERA
1986 Philadelphia	NL	9	0	0	4	13.1	54	12	5	5	2	0	0	2	4	1	3	0	0	0	0	.000	0	0--	—	3.38
1987 Philadelphia	NL	55	7	0	8	109.1	468	88	55	51	16	3	4	3	56	6	93	6	8	3	10	.231	0	1-2	6	4.20
1988 Seattle	AL	62	0	0	29	99.1	412	74	37	29	10	3	10	2	43	10	76	6	6	6	5	.545	0	4-11	10	2.63
1989 Seattle	AL	65	0	0	27	99.1	431	81	43	35	8	6	2	6	54	6	94	1	2	4	6	.400	0	7-10	9	3.17
1990 Seattle	AL	63	0	0	28	77.1	338	64	42	39	8	8	5	2	44	12	69	9	2	5	7	.417	0	3-12	13	4.54
1991 Seattle	AL	72	0	0	35	88.2	363	64	35	32	5	4	0	6	34	11	74	3	0	7	7	.500	0	14-22	9	3.25
1992 San Francisco	NL	67	0	0	24	82	346	76	35	34	7	5	2	4	33	10	80	1	0	6	6	.500	0	2-3	9	3.73
1993 San Francisco	NL	81	0	0	17	77.1	317	58	28	26	7	4	2	3	24	6	70	2	2	6	6	.500	0	1-6	34	3.03
1994 San Francisco	NL	36	0	0	12	42.1	158	23	8	7	4	4	1	2	11	0	51	0	0	3	2	.600	0	4-6	9	1.49
1995 Cincinnati	NL	40	0	0	10	49	200	38	13	13	5	1	1	1	19	1	41	1	1	6	1	.857	0	2-4	9	2.39
1996 Seattle	AL	73	0	0	23	72	302	61	32	29	11	0	1	6	24	1	70	2	0	1	1	.500	0	6-8	15	3.63
11 ML YEARS		623	7	0	217	810	3389	639	333	300	83	38	28	37	346	66	721	31	21	47	51	.480	0	44--	—	3.33

Jason Jacome

Pitches: Left **Bats:** Left **Pos:** RP-47; SP-2   **Ht:** 6'0" **Wt:** 180 **Born:** 11/24/70 **Age:** 26

Year Team	Lg	G	GS	CG	GF	IP	BFP	H	R	ER	HR	SH	SF	HB	TBB	IBB	SO	WP	Bk	W	L	Pct.	ShO	Sv-Op	Hld	ERA
1994 New York	NL	8	8	1	0	54	222	54	17	16	3	3	1	0	17	2	30	2	0	4	3	.571	1	0-0	0	2.67
1995 NYN-KC		20	19	1	0	105	474	134	76	74	18	3	4	2	36	2	50	1	1	4	10	.286	0	0-0	0	6.34
1996 Kansas City	AL	49	2	0	21	47.2	226	67	27	25	5	3	0	2	22	5	32	1	0	0	4	.000	0	1-4	6	4.72
1995 New York	NL	5	5	0	0	21	110	33	24	24	3	1	1	0	15	0	11	1	0	0	4	.000	0	0-0	0	10.29
Kansas City	AL	15	14	1	0	84	364	101	52	50	15	2	3	2	21	2	39	0	1	4	6	.400	0	0-0	0	5.36
3 ML YEARS		77	29	2	21	206.2	922	255	120	115	26	9	5	4	75	9	112	4	1	8	17	.320	1	1-4	6	5.01

John Jaha

Bats: Right **Throws:** Right **Pos:** 1B-85; DH-63; PH-3   **Ht:** 6'1" **Wt:** 222 **Born:** 5/27/66 **Age:** 31

Year Team	Lg	G	AB	H	2B	3B	HR	(Hm	Rd)	TB	R	RBI	TBB	IBB	SO	HBP	SH	SF	SB	CS	SB%	GDP	Avg	OBP	SLG
1992 Milwaukee	AL	47	133	30	3	1	2	(1	1)	41	17	10	12	1	30	2	1	4	10	0	1.00	1	.226	.291	.308
1993 Milwaukee	AL	153	515	136	21	0	19	(5	14)	214	78	70	51	4	109	8	4	4	13	9	.59	6	.264	.337	.416
1994 Milwaukee	AL	84	291	70	14	0	12	(5	7)	120	45	39	32	3	75	10	1	4	3	3	.50	8	.241	.332	.412
1995 Milwaukee	AL	88	316	99	20	2	20	(8	12)	183	59	65	36	0	66	4	0	1	2	1	.67	8	.313	.389	.579
1996 Milwaukee	AL	148	543	163	28	1	34	(17	17)	295	108	118	85	1	118	5	0	3	3	1	.75	16	.300	.398	.543
5 ML YEARS		520	1798	498	86	4	87	(36	51)	853	307	302	216	9	398	29	6	16	31	14	.69	39	.277	.361	.474

Dion James

Bats: Left **Throws:** Left **Pos:** LF-3; DH-1; RF-1; PH-1   **Ht:** 6'1" **Wt:** 185 **Born:** 11/9/62 **Age:** 34

Year Team	Lg	G	AB	H	2B	3B	HR	(Hm	Rd)	TB	R	RBI	TBB	IBB	SO	HBP	SH	SF	SB	CS	SB%	GDP	Avg	OBP	SLG
1996 Stockton *	A+	4	16	3	0	0	0	—	—	3	5	0	5	0	3	0	0	0	3	0	1.00	0	.188	.381	.188
New Orleans *	AAA	11	31	9	0	0	0	—	—	9	0	3	3	0	5	0	0	1	0	1	.00	1	.290	.343	.290
1983 Milwaukee	AL	11	20	2	0	0	0	(0	0)	2	1	1	2	0	2	0	0	0	1	0	1.00	0	.100	.182	.100
1984 Milwaukee	AL	128	387	114	19	5	1	(1	0)	146	52	30	32	1	41	3	6	3	10	10	.50	7	.295	.351	.377
1985 Milwaukee	AL	18	49	11	1	0	0	(0	0)	12	5	3	6	0	6	0	0	0	0	0	.00	0	.224	.309	.245
1987 Atlanta	NL	134	494	154	37	6	10	(5	5)	233	80	61	70	2	63	2	5	3	10	8	.56	8	.312	.397	.472
1988 Atlanta	NL	132	386	99	17	5	3	(1	2)	135	46	30	58	5	59	1	2	5	9	9	.50	12	.256	.353	.350
1989 Atl-Cle		134	415	119	18	0	5	(1	4)	152	41	40	49	6	49	1	5	1	2	7	.22	9	.287	.363	.366
1990 Cleveland	AL	87	248	68	15	2	1	(1	0)	90	28	22	27	3	21	1	3	3	5	3	.63	6	.274	.347	.363

Year Team	Lg	G	AB	H	2B	3B	HR	(Hm	Rd)	TB	R	RBI	TBB	IBB	SO	HBP	SH	SF	SB	CS	SB%	GDP	Avg	OBP	SLG
1992 New York	AL	67	145	38	8	0	3	(2	1)	55	24	17	22	0	15	1	0	2	1	0	1.00	5	.262	.359	.379
1993 New York	AL	115	343	114	21	2	7	(5	2)	160	62	36	31	1	31	2	1	1	0	0	.00	5	.332	.390	.466
1995 New York	AL	85	209	60	6	1	2	(1	1)	74	22	26	20	2	16	0	0	2	4	1	.80	5	.287	.346	.354
1996 New York	AL	6	12	2	0	0	0	(0	0)	2	1	0	1	0	2	0	0	0	1	0	1.00		.167	.231	.167
1989 Atlanta	NL	63	170	44	7	0	1	(0	1)	54	15	11	25	2	23	1	3	1	1	3	.25	4	.259	.355	.318
Cleveland	AL	71	245	75	11	0	4	(1	3)	98	26	29	24	4	26	0	2	1	4	1	.20	5	.306	.368	.400
11 ML YEARS		917	2708	781	142	21	32	(16	16)	1061	362	266	318	20	307	11	22	15	43	38	.53	56	.288	.364	.392

Mike James

Pitches: Right **Bats:** Right **Pos:** RP-69 **Ht:** 6'3" **Wt:** 185 **Born:** 8/15/67 **Age:** 29

		HOW MUCH HE PITCHED						WHAT HE GAVE UP												THE RESULTS						
Year Team	Lg	G	GS	CG	GF	IP	BFP	H	R	ER	HR	SH	SF	HB	TBB	IBB	SO	WP	Bk	W	L	Pct.	ShO	Sv-Op	Hld	ERA
1988 Great Falls	R+	14	12	0	0	67	299	61	36	28	7	3	2	3	41	0	59	2	5	7	1	.875	0	0--	—	3.76
1989 Bakersfield	A+	27	27	1	0	159.2	706	144	82	67	11	3	3	12	78	1	127	13	0	11	8	.579	1	0--	—	3.78
1990 San Antonio	AA	26	26	3	0	157	681	144	73	58	14	4	7	9	78	1	97	10	0	11	4	.733	0	0--	—	3.32
1991 San Antonio	AA	15	15	2	0	89.1	402	88	54	45	10	2	1	4	51	1	74	5	0	9	5	.643	1	0--	—	4.53
Albuquerque	AAA	13	8	0	3	45	208	51	36	33	7	0	3	2	30	0	39	5	1	1	3	.250	0	0--	—	6.60
1992 San Antonio	AA	8	8	0	0	54	214	39	16	16	3	2	0	1	20	0	52	1	1	2	1	.667	0	0--	—	2.67
Albuquerque	AAA	18	6	0	3	46.2	211	55	35	29	4	3	2	2	22	0	33	4	0	2	1	.667	0	1--	—	5.59
1993 Albuquerque	AAA	16	0	0	5	31.1	154	38	28	26	5	1	2	4	19	3	32	2	0	1	0	1.000	0	2--	—	7.47
Vero Beach	A+	30	1	0	15	60.1	271	54	37	33	2	2	2	5	33	5	60	5	1	2	3	.400	0	5--	—	4.92
1994 Vancouver	AAA	37	10	0	18	91.1	402	101	56	53	15	1	3	6	34	1	66	3	0	5	3	.625	0	8--	—	5.22
1995 Lk Elsinore	A+	5	1	0	1	5.2	26	9	6	6	1	0	0	0	3	0	8	0	0	0	0	.000	0	0--	—	9.53
1995 California	AL	46	0	0	11	55.2	237	49	27	24	6	2	0	3	26	2	36	1	0	3	0	1.000	0	1-2	3	3.88
1996 California	AL	69	0	0	23	81	353	62	27	24	7	6	5	10	42	7	65	5	0	5	5	.500	0	1-6	18	2.67
2 ML YEARS		115	0	0	34	136.2	590	111	54	48	13	8	5	13	68	9	101	6	0	8	5	.615	0	2-8	21	3.16

Marty Janzen

Pitches: Right **Bats:** Right **Pos:** SP-11; RP-4 **Ht:** 6'3" **Wt:** 200 **Born:** 5/31/73 **Age:** 24

		HOW MUCH HE PITCHED						WHAT HE GAVE UP												THE RESULTS						
Year Team	Lg	G	GS	CG	GF	IP	BFP	H	R	ER	HR	SH	SF	HB	TBB	IBB	SO	WP	Bk	W	L	Pct.	ShO	Sv-Op	Hld	ERA
1992 Yankees	R	12	11	0	0	68.2	277	55	21	18	0	3	2	5	15	0	73	3	3	7	2	.778	0	0--	—	2.36
Greensboro	A	2	0	0	2	5	20	5	2	2	0	0	0	0	1	0	5	2	0	0	0	.000	0	1--	—	3.60
1993 Yankees	R	5	5	0	0	22.1	93	20	5	3	0	0	0	1	3	0	19	0	0	1	0	1.000	0	0--	—	1.21
1994 Greensboro	A	17	17	0	0	104	431	98	57	45	8	0	0	2	25	1	92	2	2	3	7	.300	0	0--	—	3.89
1995 Norwich	AA	3	3	0	0	20	85	17	11	11	2	0	0	2	7	0	16	2	0	1	2	.333	0	0--	—	4.95
Knoxville	AA	7	7	2	0	48	188	35	14	14	2	0	2	1	14	0	44	1	1	5	1	.833	1	0--	—	2.63
1996 Syracuse	AAA	10	10	0	0	55.2	257	74	54	48	12	1	4	2	24	2	34	2	0	3	4	.429	0	0--	—	7.76
1996 Toronto	AL	15	11	0	3	73.2	344	95	65	60	16	1	3	2	38	3	47	7	0	4	6	.400	0	0-0	0	7.33

Kevin Jarvis

Pitches: Right **Bats:** Left **Pos:** SP-20; RP-4 **Ht:** 6'2" **Wt:** 200 **Born:** 8/1/69 **Age:** 27

		HOW MUCH HE PITCHED						WHAT HE GAVE UP												THE RESULTS						
Year Team	Lg	G	GS	CG	GF	IP	BFP	H	R	ER	HR	SH	SF	HB	TBB	IBB	SO	WP	Bk	W	L	Pct.	ShO	Sv-Op	Hld	ERA
1996 Indianapols *	AAA	8	8	0	0	42.2	186	45	27	24	3	0	2	1	12	0	32	3	0	4	3	.571	0	0--	—	5.06
1994 Cincinnati	NL	6	3	0	0	17.2	79	22	14	14	4	1	0	0	5	0	10	1	1	1	1	.500	0	0-0	0	7.13
1995 Cincinnati	NL	19	11	1	2	79	354	91	56	50	13	2	5	3	32	2	33	2	0	3	4	.429	1	0-0	0	5.70
1996 Cincinnati	NL	24	20	2	2	120.1	552	152	93	80	17	6	2	2	43	5	63	3	0	8	9	.471	0	0-0	0	5.98
3 ML YEARS		49	34	3	4	217	985	265	163	144	34	9	7	5	80	7	106	6	0	12	14	.462	2	0-0	0	5.97

Stan Javier

Bats: Both **Throws:** Right **Pos:** CF-53; RF-18 **Ht:** 6'0" **Wt:** 185 **Born:** 1/9/64 **Age:** 33

		BATTING																	BASERUNNING				PERCENTAGES		
Year Team	Lg	G	AB	H	2B	3B	HR	(Hm	Rd)	TB	R	RBI	TBB	IBB	SO	HBP	SH	SF	SB	CS	SB%	GDP	Avg	OBP	SLG
1996 San Jose *	A+	3	5	2	0	0	0	—	—	2	1	1	1	0	1	1	0	0	0	0	.00	0	.400	.571	.400
1984 New York	AL	7	7	1	0	0	0	(0	0)	1	1	0	0	0	1	0	0	0	0	0	.00	0	.143	.143	.143
1986 Oakland	AL	59	114	23	8	0	0	(0	0)	31	13	8	16	0	27	1	0	0	8	0	1.00	2	.202	.305	.272
1987 Oakland	AL	81	151	28	3	1	2	(1	1)	39	22	9	19	3	33	0	6	0	3	2	.60	2	.185	.276	.258
1988 Oakland	AL	125	397	102	13	3	2	(0	2)	127	49	35	32	1	63	2	6	3	20	1	.95	13	.257	.313	.320
1989 Oakland	AL	112	310	77	12	3	1	(1	0)	98	42	28	31	1	45	1	4	2	12	2	.86	6	.248	.317	.316
1990 Oak-LA		123	309	92	9	6	3	(1	2)	122	46	27	40	2	50	2	5	2	15	7	.68	6	.298	.376	.395
1991 Los Angeles	NL	121	176	36	5	3	1	(1	0)	50	21	11	16	0	36	0	3	2	7	1	.88	4	.205	.268	.284
1992 LA-Phi	NL	130	334	83	17	1	1	(0	1)	105	42	29	37	2	54	3	3	2	18	3	.86	7	.249	.327	.314
1993 California	AL	92	237	69	10	4	0	(0	0)	96	33	28	27	1	33	1	1	3	12	2	.86	7	.291	.362	.405
1994 Oakland	AL	109	419	114	23	0	10	(1	9)	167	75	44	49	1	76	2	7	3	24	7	.77	7	.272	.349	.399
1995 Oakland	AL	130	442	123	20	2	8	(3	5)	171	81	56	49	3	63	4	5	4	36	5	.88	3	.278	.353	.387
1996 San Francisco	NL	71	274	74	25	0	2	(1	1)	105	44	22	25	0	51	2	5	0	14	2	.88	4	.270	.336	.383
1990 Oakland	AL	19	33	8	0	2	0	(0	0)	12	4	3	3	0	6	0	0	0	0	0	.00	0	.242	.306	.364
Los Angeles	NL	104	276	84	9	4	3	(1	2)	110	56	24	37	2	44	0	6	2	15	7	.68	6	.304	.384	.399
1992 Los Angeles	NL	56	58	11	3	0	1	(0	0)	17	6	5	11	1	2	1	2	0	2	2	.33	0	.190	.277	.293

		BATTING																	BASERUNNING				PERCENTAGES		
Year Team	Lg	G	AB	H	2B	3B	HR	(Hm	Rd)	TB	R	RBI	TBB	IBB	SO	HBP	SH	SF	SB	CS	SB%	GDP	Avg	OBP	SLG
Philadelphia	NL	74	276	72	14	1	0	(0	0)	88	36	24	31	0	43	2	2	2	17	1	.94	4	.261	.338	.319
12 ML YEARS		1160	3170	822	145	23	33	(9	24)	1112	483	297	341	14	532	16	46	21	169	32	.84	63	.259	.332	.351

Gregg Jefferies

Bats: Both **Throws:** Right **Pos:** 1B-53; LF-51; PH-1   **Ht:** 5'10" **Wt:** 184 **Born:** 8/1/67 **Age:** 29

		BATTING																	BASERUNNING				PERCENTAGES		
Year Team	Lg	G	AB	H	2B	3B	HR	(Hm	Rd)	TB	R	RBI	TBB	IBB	SO	HBP	SH	SF	SB	CS	SB%	GDP	Avg	OBP	SLG
1996 Scrnton-WB *	AAA	4	17	2	0	1	0	—	—	4	1	0	1	0	3	0	0	0	0	0	.00	1	.118	.167	.235
1987 New York	NL	6	6	3	1	0	0	(0	0)	4	0	2	0	0	0	0	0	0	0	0	.00	0	.500	.500	.667
1988 New York	NL	29	109	35	8	2	6	(3	3)	65	19	17	8	0	10	0	0	1	5	1	.83	1	.321	.364	.596
1989 New York	NL	141	508	131	28	2	12	(7	5)	199	72	56	39	8	46	5	2	5	21	6	.78	16	.258	.314	.392
1990 New York	NL	153	604	171	40	3	15	(9	6)	262	96	68	46	2	40	5	0	4	11	2	.85	12	.283	.337	.434
1991 New York	NL	136	486	132	19	2	9	(5	4)	182	59	62	47	2	38	2	1	3	26	5	.84	12	.272	.336	.374
1992 Kansas City	AL	152	604	172	36	3	10	(3	7)	244	66	75	43	4	29	1	0	9	19	9	.68	24	.285	.329	.404
1993 St. Louis	NL	142	544	186	24	3	16	(10	6)	264	89	83	62	7	32	2	0	4	46	9	.84	15	.342	.408	.485
1994 St. Louis	NL	103	397	129	27	1	12	(7	5)	194	52	55	45	12	26	1	0	4	12	5	.71	9	.325	.391	.489
1995 Philadelphia	NL	114	480	147	31	2	11	(4	7)	215	69	56	35	5	26	0	0	6	9	5	.64	15	.306	.349	.448
1996 Philadelphia	NL	104	404	118	17	3	7	(4	3)	162	59	51	36	6	21	1	0	5	20	6	.77	9	.292	.348	.401
10 ML YEARS		1080	4142	1224	231	21	98	(52	46)	1791	581	525	361	46	268	17	3	41	169	48	.78	113	.296	.351	.432

Reggie Jefferson

Bats: L **Throws:** L **Pos:** DH-49; LF-45; PH-21; 1B-16   **Ht:** 6'4" **Wt:** 215 **Born:** 9/25/68 **Age:** 28

		BATTING																	BASERUNNING				PERCENTAGES		
Year Team	Lg	G	AB	H	2B	3B	HR	(Hm	Rd)	TB	R	RBI	TBB	IBB	SO	HBP	SH	SF	SB	CS	SB%	GDP	Avg	OBP	SLG
1991 Cin-Cle		31	108	21	3	0	3	(2	1)	33	11	13	4	0	24	0	0	1	0	0	.00	1	.194	.221	.306
1992 Cleveland	AL	24	89	30	6	2	1	(1	0)	43	8	6	1	0	17	1	0	0	0	0	.00	2	.337	.352	.483
1993 Cleveland	AL	113	366	91	11	2	10	(4	6)	136	35	34	28	7	78	5	3	1	1	3	.25	7	.249	.310	.372
1994 Seattle	AL	63	162	53	11	0	8	(4	4)	88	24	32	17	5	32	1	0	1	0	0	.00	4	.327	.392	.543
1995 Boston	AL	46	121	35	8	0	5	(1	4)	58	21	26	9	1	24	0	0	2	0	0	.00	3	.289	.333	.479
1996 Boston	AL	122	386	134	30	4	19	(12	7)	229	67	74	25	5	89	3	0	4	0	0	.00	11	.347	.388	.593
1991 Cincinnati	NL	5	7	1	0	0	0	(0	0)	1	1	1	1	0	2	0	0	0	0	0	.00	0	.143	.250	.571
Cleveland	AL	26	101	20	3	0	2	(1	1)	29	10	12	3	0	22	0	0	1	0	0	.00	1	.198	.219	.287
6 ML YEARS		399	1232	364	69	8	46	(24	22)	587	166	185	84	18	264	10	3	9	1	3	.25	30	.295	.343	.476

Robin Jennings

Bats: Left **Throws:** Left **Pos:** PH-20; RF-11   **Ht:** 6'2" **Wt:** 205 **Born:** 4/11/72 **Age:** 25

		BATTING																	BASERUNNING				PERCENTAGES		
Year Team	Lg	G	AB	H	2B	3B	HR	(Hm	Rd)	TB	R	RBI	TBB	IBB	SO	HBP	SH	SF	SB	CS	SB%	GDP	Avg	OBP	SLG
1992 Geneva	A-	72	275	82	12	2	7	—	—	119	39	47	20	5	43	2	0	0	10	3	.77	7	.298	.350	.433
1993 Peoria	A	132	474	146	29	5	3	—	—	194	65	65	46	2	73	4	5	3	11	11	.50	9	.308	.372	.409
1994 Daytona	A+	128	476	133	24	5	8	—	—	191	54	60	45	5	54	4	4	4	2	10	.17	13	.279	.344	.401
1995 Orlando	AA	132	490	145	27	7	17	—	—	237	71	79	44	5	61	4	0	5	7	14	.33	11	.296	.355	.484
1996 Iowa	AAA	86	331	94	15	6	18	—	—	175	53	56	32	1	53	1	0	3	2	0	1.00	6	.284	.346	.529
1996 Chicago	NL	31	58	13	5	0	0	(0	0)	18	7	4	3	0	9	1	0	0	1	0	1.00	1	.224	.274	.310

Marcus Jensen

Bats: Both **Throws:** Right **Pos:** C-7; PH-2   **Ht:** 6'4" **Wt:** 195 **Born:** 12/14/72 **Age:** 24

		BATTING																	BASERUNNING				PERCENTAGES		
Year Team	Lg	G	AB	H	2B	3B	HR	(Hm	Rd)	TB	R	RBI	TBB	IBB	SO	HBP	SH	SF	SB	CS	SB%	GDP	Avg	OBP	SLG
1990 Everett	A-	51	171	29	3	0	2	—	—	38	21	12	24	0	60	5	0	0	0	1	.00	3	.170	.290	.222
1991 Giants	R	48	155	44	8	3	2	—	—	64	28	30	34	3	22	5	0	4	4	2	.67	2	.284	.419	.413
1992 Clinton	A	86	264	62	14	0	4	—	—	88	35	33	54	3	87	4	1	2	4	2	.67	5	.235	.370	.333
1993 Clinton	A	104	324	85	24	2	11	—	—	146	53	56	66	5	98	4	0	4	1	2	.33	5	.262	.389	.451
1994 San Jose	A+	118	418	101	18	0	7	—	—	140	56	47	61	5	100	8	2	6	1	1	.50	9	.242	.345	.335
1995 Shreveport	AA	95	321	91	22	8	4	—	—	141	55	45	41	1	68	3	5	8	0	0	.00	4	.283	.362	.439
1996 Phoenix	AAA	120	405	107	22	4	5	—	—	152	41	53	44	4	95	3	2	4	1	1	.50	10	.264	.338	.375
1996 San Francisco	NL	9	19	4	1	0	0	(0	0)	5	4	4	8	0	7	0	0	0	0	0	.00	1	.211	.444	.263

Derek Jeter

Bats: Right **Throws:** Right **Pos:** SS-157   **Ht:** 6'3" **Wt:** 185 **Born:** 6/26/74 **Age:** 23

		BATTING																	BASERUNNING				PERCENTAGES		
Year Team	Lg	G	AB	H	2B	3B	HR	(Hm	Rd)	TB	R	RBI	TBB	IBB	SO	HBP	SH	SF	SB	CS	SB%	GDP	Avg	OBP	SLG
1992 Yankees	R	47	173	35	10	0	3	—	—	54	19	25	19	0	36	5	0	2	2	2	.50	4	.202	.296	.312
Greensboro	A	11	37	9	0	0	1	—	—	12	4	4	7	0	16	1	0	0	0	1	.00	0	.243	.378	.324
1993 Greensboro	A	128	515	152	14	11	5	—	—	203	85	71	58	1	95	11	2	4	18	9	.67	9	.295	.376	.394
1994 Tampa	A+	69	292	96	13	8	0	—	—	125	61	39	23	2	30	3	3	3	28	2	.93	4	.329	.380	.428
Albany-Colo	AA	34	122	46	7	2	2	—	—	63	17	13	15	0	16	1	3	1	12	2	.86	3	.377	.446	.516
Columbus	AAA	35	126	44	7	1	3	—	—	62	25	16	20	1	15	1	1	0	10	4	.71	6	.349	.439	.492

Year Team	Lg	G	AB	H	2B	3B	HR	(Hm	Rd)	TB	R	RBI	TBB	IBB	SO	HBP	SH	SF	SB	CS	SB%	GDP	Avg	OBP	SLG
1995 Columbus	AAA	123	486	154	27	9	2	—	—	205	96	45	61	1	56	4	2	5	20	12	.63	9	.317	.394	.422
1995 New York	AL	15	48	12	4	1	0	(0	0)	18	5	7	3	0	11	0	0	0	0	0	.00	0	.250	.294	.375
1996 New York	AL	157	582	183	25	6	10	(3	7)	250	104	78	48	1	102	9	6	9	14	7	.67	13	.314	.370	.430
2 ML YEARS		172	630	195	29	7	10	(3	7)	268	109	85	51	1	113	9	6	9	14	7	.67	13	.310	.365	.425

Doug Johns

Pitches: Left **Bats:** Right **Pos:** SP-23; RP-17 **Ht:** 6'2" **Wt:** 185 **Born:** 12/19/67 **Age:** 29

Year Team	Lg	G	GS	CG	GF	IP	BFP	H	R	ER	HR	SH	SF	HB	TBB	IBB	SO	WP	Bk	W	L	Pct.	ShO	Sv-Op	Hld	ERA
1990 Sou. Oregon	A-	6	2	0	4	11	57	13	9	7	0	0	0	0	11	1	9	2	1	0	2	.000	0	1--	—	5.73
Athletics	R	8	7	1	1	44	172	36	11	9	1	0	0	0	9	1	37	2	0	3	1	.750	0	0--	—	1.84
1991 Madison	A	38	14	1	9	128.1	549	108	59	46	5	6	2	8	54	1	104	13	0	12	6	.667	1	2--	—	3.23
1992 Reno	A+	27	26	4	1	179.1	776	194	98	65	11	7	4	1	64	3	101	5	2	13	10	.565	1	0--	—	3.26
Huntsville	AA	3	1	0	1	16	74	21	11	7	0	1	0	0	5	0	4	1	0	0	0	.000	0	0--	—	3.94
1993 Huntsville	AA	40	6	0	11	91	379	82	41	30	3	7	2	2	31	4	56	2	1	7	5	.583	0	1--	—	2.97
1994 Huntsville	AA	9	0	0	2	15	70	16	2	2	1	2	0	1	12	5	9	1	3	3	0	1.000	0	0--	—	1.20
Tacoma	AAA	22	19	2	2	134	549	114	55	43	10	4	3	7	48	0	65	2	2	9	8	.529	1	0--	—	2.89
1995 Edmonton	AAA	23	21	0	1	132	567	148	55	50	8	3	1	3	43	3	70	6	3	9	5	.643	0	0--	—	3.41
1995 Oakland	AL	11	9	1	1	54.2	229	44	32	28	5	2	1	5	26	1	25	5	1	5	3	.625	1	0-0	0	4.61
1996 Oakland	AL	40	23	1	4	158	710	187	112	105	21	2	3	6	69	5	71	9	0	6	12	.333	0	1-2	0	5.98
2 ML YEARS		51	32	2	5	212.2	939	231	144	133	26	4	4	11	95	6	96	14	1	11	15	.423	1	1-2	0	5.63

Brian Johnson

Bats: R **Throws:** R **Pos:** C-66; PH-15; 1B-1; 3B-1 **Ht:** 6'2" **Wt:** 210 **Born:** 1/8/68 **Age:** 29

Year Team	Lg	G	AB	H	2B	3B	HR	(Hm	Rd)	TB	R	RBI	TBB	IBB	SO	HBP	SH	SF	SB	CS	SB%	GDP	Avg	OBP	SLG
1994 San Diego	NL	36	93	23	4	1	3	(3	0)	38	7	16	5	0	21	0	2	1	0	0	.00	4	.247	.283	.409
1995 San Diego	NL	68	207	52	9	0	3	(1	2)	70	20	29	11	2	39	1	1	4	0	0	.00	2	.251	.287	.338
1996 San Diego	NL	82	243	66	13	1	8	(3	5)	105	18	35	4	2	36	4	2	4	0	0	.00	8	.272	.290	.432
3 ML YEARS		186	543	141	26	2	14	(7	7)	213	45	80	20	4	96	5	5	9	0	0	.00	14	.260	.288	.392

Charles Johnson

Bats: Right **Throws:** Right **Pos:** C-120; PH-2 **Ht:** 6'2" **Wt:** 215 **Born:** 7/20/71 **Age:** 25

Year Team	Lg	G	AB	H	2B	3B	HR	(Hm	Rd)	TB	R	RBI	TBB	IBB	SO	HBP	SH	SF	SB	CS	SB%	GDP	Avg	OBP	SLG
1994 Florida	NL	4	11	5	1	0	1	(1	0)	9	5	4	1	0	4	0	0	1	0	0	.00	1	.455	.462	.818
1995 Florida	NL	97	315	79	15	1	11	(3	8)	129	40	39	46	2	71	4	4	2	0	2	.00	11	.251	.351	.410
1996 Florida	NL	120	386	84	13	1	13	(9	4)	138	34	37	40	6	91	2	2	4	1	0	1.00	20	.218	.292	.358
3 ML YEARS		221	712	168	29	2	25	(13	12)	276	79	80	87	8	166	6	6	7	1	2	.33	32	.236	.321	.388

Dane Johnson

Pitches: Right **Bats:** Right **Pos:** RP-10 **Ht:** 6'5" **Wt:** 205 **Born:** 2/10/63 **Age:** 34

Year Team	Lg	G	GS	CG	GF	IP	BFP	H	R	ER	HR	SH	SF	HB	TBB	IBB	SO	WP	Bk	W	L	Pct.	ShO	Sv-Op	Hld	ERA
1996 Syracuse *	AAA	43	0	0	42	51.1	201	37	14	14	4	2	2	2	17	1	51	2	1	3	2	.600	0	22--	—	2.45
1994 Chicago	AL	15	0	0	4	12.1	61	16	9	9	2	0	1	0	11	1	7	0	0	2	1	.667	0	0-0	2	6.57
1996 Toronto	AL	10	0	0	2	9	36	5	3	3	0	0	0	0	5	0	7	0	0	0	0	.000	0	0-0	2	3.00
2 ML YEARS		25	0	0	6	21.1	97	21	12	12	2	0	1	0	16	1	14	0	0	2	1	.667	0	0-0	4	5.06

Lance Johnson

Bats: Left **Throws:** Left **Pos:** CF-157; PH-4 **Ht:** 5'11" **Wt:** 160 **Born:** 7/6/63 **Age:** 33

Year Team	Lg	G	AB	H	2B	3B	HR	(Hm	Rd)	TB	R	RBI	TBB	IBB	SO	HBP	SH	SF	SB	CS	SB%	GDP	Avg	OBP	SLG
1987 St. Louis	NL	33	59	13	2	1	0	(0	0)	17	4	7	4	1	6	0	0	0	6	1	.86	2	.220	.270	.288
1988 Chicago	AL	33	124	23	4	1	0	(0	0)	29	11	6	6	0	11	0	2	0	6	2	.75	1	.185	.223	.234
1989 Chicago	AL	50	180	54	8	2	0	(0	0)	66	28	16	17	0	24	0	2	0	16	3	.84	1	.300	.360	.367
1990 Chicago	AL	151	541	154	18	9	1	(0	1)	193	76	51	33	2	45	1	8	4	36	22	.62	12	.285	.325	.357
1991 Chicago	AL	160	588	161	14	13	0	(0	0)	201	72	49	26	2	58	1	6	3	26	11	.70	14	.274	.304	.342
1992 Chicago	AL	157	567	158	15	12	3	(2	1)	206	67	47	34	4	33	1	4	5	41	14	.75	20	.279	.318	.363
1993 Chicago	AL	147	540	168	18	14	0	(0	0)	214	75	47	36	1	33	0	3	0	35	7	.83	10	.311	.354	.396
1994 Chicago	AL	106	412	114	11	14	3	(1	2)	162	56	54	26	5	23	2	0	0	26	6	.81	8	.277	.321	.354
1995 Chicago	AL	142	607	186	18	12	10	(2	8)	258	98	57	32	2	31	1	2	3	40	6	.87	7	.306	.341	.425
1996 New York	NL	160	682	227	31	21	9	(1	8)	327	117	69	33	8	40	1	3	5	50	12	.81	8	.333	.362	.479
10 ML YEARS		1139	4300	1258	139	99	26	(6	20)	1673	604	403	247	25	304	7	30	23	282	84	.77	83	.293	.330	.389

Mark Johnson

Bats: Left   **Throws:** Left   **Pos:** 1B-100; PH-36; LF-1   **Ht:** 6'4" **Wt:** 230 **Born:** 10/17/67 **Age:** 29

Year Team	Lg	G	AB	H	2B	3B	HR	(Hm	Rd)	TB	R	RBI	TBB	IBB	SO	HBP	SH	SF	SB	CS	SB%	GDP	Avg	OBP	SLG
1990 Welland	A-	5	8	3	1	0	0	—	—	4	2	2	2	0	0	0	0	0	0	0	.00	0	.375	.500	.500
Augusta	A	43	144	36	7	0	0	—	—	43	12	19	24	2	18	0	0	2	4	2	.67	3	.250	.353	.299
1991 Augusta	A	49	139	36	7	4	2	—	—	57	23	25	29	1	14	0	1	2	4	2	.67	2	.259	.382	.410
Salem	A+	37	103	26	2	0	2	—	—	34	12	13	18	0	25	1	0	0	0	2	.00	2	.252	.369	.330
1992 Carolina	AA	122	383	89	16	1	7	—	—	128	40	45	55	4	94	3	1	0	16	11	.59	8	.232	.333	.334
1993 Carolina	AA	125	399	93	18	4	14	—	—	161	48	52	66	7	93	3	2	3	6	2	.75	8	.233	.344	.404
1994 Carolina	AA	111	388	107	20	2	23	—	—	200	69	85	67	11	89	4	0	4	6	6	.50	7	.276	.384	.515
1995 Calgary	AAA	9	23	7	4	0	2	—		17	7	7	8	1	4	1	0	0	1	0	1.00	0	.304	.467	.739
1995 Pittsburgh	NL	79	221	46	6	1	13	(7	6)	93	32	37	37	2	66	2	0	1	5	2	.71	2	.208	.304	.421
1996 Pittsburgh	NL	127	343	94	24	0	13	(10	3)	157	55	47	44	3	64	5	0	4	6	4	.60	5	.274	.361	.458
2 ML YEARS		206	564	140	30	1	26	(17	9)	250	87	75	81	5	130	7	0	5	11	6	.65	7	.248	.347	.443

Randy Johnson

Pitches: Left   **Bats:** Right   **Pos:** SP-8; RP-6   **Ht:** 6'10" **Wt:** 230 **Born:** 9/10/63 **Age:** 33

Year Team	Lg	G	GS	CG	GF	IP	BFP	H	R	ER	HR	SH	SF	HB	TBB	IBB	SO	WP	Bk	W	L	Pct.	ShO	Sv-Op	Hld	ERA
1996 Everett *	A-	1	1	0	0	2	6	0	0	0	0	0	0	0	0	0	5	0	0	0	0	.000	0	0--	—	0.00
1988 Montreal	NL	4	4	1	0	26	109	23	8	7	3	0	0	0	7	0	25	3	0	0	0	1.000	0	0-0	0	2.42
1989 Mon-Sea		29	28	2	1	160.2	715	147	100	86	13	10	13	3	96	2	130	7	7	7	13	.350	0	0-0	0	4.82
1990 Seattle	AL	33	33	5	0	219.2	944	174	103	89	26	7	6	5	120	2	194	4	2	14	11	.560	2	0-0	0	3.65
1991 Seattle	AL	33	33	2	0	201.1	889	151	96	89	15	9	8	12	152	0	228	12	2	13	10	.565	1	0-0	0	3.98
1992 Seattle	AL	31	31	6	0	210.1	922	154	104	88	13	3	8	18	144	1	241	13	1	12	14	.462	2	0-0	0	3.77
1993 Seattle	AL	35	34	10	1	255.1	1043	185	97	92	22	8	7	16	99	1	308	8	2	19	8	.704	3	1-1	0	3.24
1994 Seattle	AL	23	23	9	0	172	694	132	65	61	14	3	1	6	72	2	204	5	0	13	6	.684	4	0-0	0	3.19
1995 Seattle	AL	30	30	6	0	214.1	866	159	65	59	12	2	1	6	65	1	294	5	2	18	2	.900	3	0-0	0	2.48
1996 Seattle	AL	14	8	0	2	61.1	256	48	27	25	8	1	0	2	25	0	85	3	1	5	0	1.000	0	1-2	0	3.67
1989 Montreal	NL	7	6	0	1	29.2	143	29	25	22	2	3	4	0	26	1	26	2	0	0	0	.000	0	0-0	0	6.67
Seattle	AL	22	22	2	0	131	572	118	75	64	11	7	9	3	70	1	104	5	7	7	9	.438	0	0-0	0	4.40
9 ML YEARS		232	224	41	4	1521	6438	1173	665	596	126	43	44	68	780	9	1709	60	17	104	64	.619	15	2-3	0	3.53

John Johnstone

Pitches: Right   **Bats:** Right   **Pos:** RP-9   **Ht:** 6'3" **Wt:** 195 **Born:** 11/25/68 **Age:** 28

Year Team	Lg	G	GS	CG	GF	IP	BFP	H	R	ER	HR	SH	SF	HB	TBB	IBB	SO	WP	Bk	W	L	Pct.	ShO	Sv-Op	Hld	ERA
1996 Tucson *	AAA	45	1	0	17	55.1	249	59	27	21	2	3	2	1	22	2	70	3	0	3	3	.500	0	5--	—	3.42
1993 Florida	NL	7	0	0	3	10.2	54	16	8	7	1	0	0	0	7	0	5	1	0	0	2	.000	0	0-0	0	5.91
1994 Florida	NL	17	0	0	7	21.1	105	23	20	14	4	1	0	1	16	5	23	0	0	1	2	.333	0	0-0	3	5.91
1995 Florida	NL	4	0	0	0	4.2	23	7	2	2	1	0	0	0	2	1	3	0	0	0	0	.000	0	0-0	0	3.86
1996 Houston	NL	9	0	0	6	13	60	17	8	8	2	0	2	0	5	0	5	0	0	1	0	1.000	0	0-0	0	5.54
4 ML YEARS		37	0	0	16	49.2	242	63	38	31	8	1	2	1	30	6	36	1	0	2	4	.333	0	0-0	3	5.62

Andruw Jones

Bats: Right   **Throws:** Right   **Pos:** RF-20; CF-12; PH-4   **Ht:** 6'1" **Wt:** 185 **Born:** 4/23/77 **Age:** 20

Year Team	Lg	G	AB	H	2B	3B	HR	(Hm	Rd)	TB	R	RBI	TBB	IBB	SO	HBP	SH	SF	SB	CS	SB%	GDP	Avg	OBP	SLG
1994 Braves	R	27	95	21	5	1	2	—	—	34	22	10	16	2	19	2	0	0	5	2	.71	3	.221	.345	.358
Danville	R+	36	143	48	9	2	1	—	—	64	20	16	9	0	25	3	0	1	16	9	.64	0	.336	.385	.448
1995 Macon	A	139	537	149	41	5	25	—	—	275	104	100	70	7	122	16	0	9	56	11	.84	9	.277	.372	.512
1996 Durham	A+	66	243	76	14	3	17	—	—	147	65	43	42	3	54	3	0	1	16	4	.80	5	.313	.419	.605
Greenville	AA	38	157	58	10	1	12	—	—	106	39	37	17	0	34	1	0	1	12	4	.75	3	.369	.432	.675
Richmond	AAA	12	45	17	3	1	5	—	—	37	11	12	1	0	9	0	0	0	2	2	.50	0	.378	.391	.822
1996 Atlanta	NL	31	106	23	7	1	5	(3	2)	47	11	13	7	0	29	0	0	0	3	0	1.00	0	.217	.265	.443

Bobby Jones

Pitches: Right   **Bats:** Right   **Pos:** SP-31   **Ht:** 6'4" **Wt:** 225 **Born:** 2/10/70 **Age:** 27

Year Team	Lg	G	GS	CG	GF	IP	BFP	H	R	ER	HR	SH	SF	HB	TBB	IBB	SO	WP	Bk	W	L	Pct.	ShO	Sv-Op	Hld	ERA
1993 New York	NL	9	9	0	0	61.2	265	61	35	25	6	5	3	2	22	3	35	1	0	2	4	.333	0	0-0	0	3.65
1994 New York	NL	24	24	1	0	160	685	157	75	56	10	11	4	4	56	9	80	1	3	12	7	.632	1	0-0	0	3.15
1995 New York	NL	30	30	3	0	195.2	839	209	107	91	20	11	6	7	53	6	127	2	1	10	10	.500	1	0-0	0	4.19
1996 New York	NL	31	31	3	0	195.2	826	219	102	96	26	12	5	3	46	6	116	2	0	12	8	.600	1	0-0	0	4.42
4 ML YEARS		94	94	7	0	613	2615	646	319	268	62	39	18	16	177	24	358	6	4	36	29	.554	3	0-0	0	3.93

Chipper Jones

Bats: B **Throws:** R **Pos:** 3B-118; SS-38; PH-2; RF-1   **Ht:** 6'3" **Wt:** 200 **Born:** 4/24/72 **Age:** 25

Year Team	Lg	G	AB	H	2B	3B	HR	(Hm	Rd)	TB	R	RBI	TBB	IBB	SO	HBP	SH	SF	SB	CS	SB%	GDP	Avg	OBP	SLG
1993 Atlanta	NL	8	3	2	1	0	0	(0	0)	3	2	0	1	0	1	0	0	0	0	0	.00	0	.667	.750	1.000
1995 Atlanta	NL	140	524	139	22	3	23	(15	8)	236	87	86	73	1	99	0	1	4	8	4	.67	10	.265	.353	.450
1996 Atlanta	NL	157	598	185	32	5	30	(18	12)	317	114	110	87	0	88	0	1	7	14	1	.93	14	.309	.393	.530
3 ML YEARS		305	1125	326	55	8	53	(33	20)	556	203	196	161	1	188	0	2	11	22	5	.81	24	.290	.375	.494

Chris Jones

Bats: R **Throws:** R **Pos:** RF-44; PH-35; LF-17; CF-8; 1B-5   **Ht:** 6'2" **Wt:** 210 **Born:** 12/16/65 **Age:** 31

Year Team	Lg	G	AB	H	2B	3B	HR	(Hm	Rd)	TB	R	RBI	TBB	IBB	SO	HBP	SH	SF	SB	CS	SB%	GDP	Avg	OBP	SLG
1991 Cincinnati	NL	52	89	26	1	2	2	(0	2)	37	14	6	2	0	31	0	0	1	2	1	.67	2	.292	.304	.416
1992 Houston	NL	54	63	12	2	1	1	(1	0)	19	7	4	7	0	21	0	3	0	3	0	1.00	1	.190	.271	.302
1993 Colorado	NL	86	209	57	11	4	6	(2	4)	94	29	31	10	1	48	0	5	1	9	4	.69	6	.273	.305	.450
1994 Colorado	NL	21	40	12	2	1	0	(0	0)	16	6	2	2	1	14	0	0	0	0	1	.00	1	.300	.333	.400
1995 New York	NL	79	182	51	6	2	8	(4	4)	85	33	31	13	1	45	1	2	3	2	1	.67	2	.280	.327	.467
1996 New York	NL	89	149	36	7	0	4	(2	2)	55	22	18	12	1	42	2	0	0	1	0	1.00	3	.242	.307	.369
6 ML YEARS		381	732	194	29	10	21	(9	12)	306	111	92	46	4	201	3	10	5	17	7	.71	15	.265	.309	.418

Dax Jones

Bats: Right **Throws:** Right **Pos:** CF-29; PH-6; RF-4   **Ht:** 6'0" **Wt:** 170 **Born:** 8/4/70 **Age:** 26

Year Team	Lg	G	AB	H	2B	3B	HR	(Hm	Rd)	TB	R	RBI	TBB	IBB	SO	HBP	SH	SF	SB	CS	SB%	GDP	Avg	OBP	SLG
1991 Everett	A-	53	180	55	5	6	5	—	—	87	42	29	27	0	26	1	1	3	15	8	.65	4	.306	.393	.483
1992 Clinton	A	79	295	88	12	4	1	—	—	111	45	42	21	0	32	1	1	1	18	5	.78	6	.298	.346	.376
Shreveport	AA	19	66	20	0	2	1	—	—	27	10	7	4	0	6	1	1	2	2	0	1.00	1	.303	.342	.409
1993 Shreveport	AA	118	436	124	19	5	4	—	—	165	59	36	26	6	53	4	3	2	13	8	.62	5	.284	.329	.378
1994 Phoenix	AAA	111	399	111	25	5	4	—	—	158	55	52	21	1	42	3	3	4	16	8	.67	14	.278	.316	.396
1995 Phoenix	AAA	112	404	108	21	3	2	—	—	141	47	45	31	3	52	2	2	5	11	10	.52	8	.267	.319	.349
1996 Phoenix	AAA	74	298	92	20	6	6	—	—	142	52	41	19	1	21	1	1	0	13	8	.62	7	.309	.352	.477
1996 San Francisco	NL	34	58	10	0	2	1	(0	1)	17	7	7	8	0	12	0	0	1	2	2	.50	0	.172	.269	.293

Doug Jones

Pitches: Right **Bats:** Right **Pos:** RP-52   **Ht:** 6'2" **Wt:** 205 **Born:** 6/24/57 **Age:** 40

Year Team	Lg	G	GS	CG	GF	IP	BFP	H	R	ER	HR	SH	SF	HB	TBB	IBB	SO	WP	Bk	W	L	Pct.	ShO	Sv-Op	Hld	ERA
1996 Nw Orleans *	AAA	13	0	0	9	24	106	28	10	10	2	2	0	1	6	4	17	0	0	0	3	.000	0	6--	—	3.75
1982 Milwaukee	AL	4	0	0	2	2.2	14	5	3	3	1	0	0	0	1	0	1	0	0	0	0	.000	0	0--	—	10.13
1986 Cleveland	AL	11	0	0	5	18	79	18	5	5	0	1	1	1	6	1	12	0	0	1	0	1.000	0	1--	—	2.50
1987 Cleveland	AL	49	0	0	29	91.1	400	101	45	32	4	5	5	6	24	5	87	0	0	6	5	.545	0	8-12	1	3.15
1988 Cleveland	AL	51	0	0	46	83.1	338	69	26	21	1	3	0	2	16	3	72	2	3	3	4	.429	0	37-43	0	2.27
1989 Cleveland	AL	59	0	0	53	80.2	331	76	25	21	4	8	6	1	13	4	65	1	1	7	10	.412	0	32-41	0	2.34
1990 Cleveland	AL	66	0	0	64	84.1	331	66	26	24	5	2	2	2	22	4	55	2	0	5	5	.500	0	43-51	0	2.56
1991 Cleveland	AL	36	4	0	29	63.1	293	87	42	39	7	2	2	0	17	5	48	1	0	4	8	.333	0	7-12	0	5.54
1992 Houston	NL	80	0	0	70	111.2	440	96	29	23	5	9	0	5	17	5	93	2	1	11	8	.579	0	36-42	0	1.85
1993 Houston	NL	71	0	0	60	85.1	381	102	46	43	7	9	4	5	21	6	66	3	0	4	10	.286	0	26-34	1	4.54
1994 Philadelphia	NL	47	0	0	42	54	226	55	14	13	2	4	0	0	6	0	38	1	0	2	4	.333	0	27-29	0	2.17
1995 Baltimore	AL	52	0	0	47	46.2	211	55	30	26	6	1	0	2	16	2	42	0	0	0	4	.000	0	22-25	0	5.01
1996 ChN-Mil		52	0	0	21	64	282	72	33	30	7	7	1	2	20	6	60	1	0	7	2	.778	0	3-11	2	4.22
1996 Chicago	NL	28	0	0	13	32.1	143	41	20	18	4	1	0	1	7	4	26	0	0	2	2	.500	0	2-7	0	5.01
Milwaukee	AL	24	0	0	8	31.2	139	31	13	12	3	6	1	1	13	2	34	1	0	5	0	1.000	0	1-4	2	3.41
12 ML YEARS		578	4	0	468	785.1	3326	802	324	280	49	45	22	27	179	41	639	13	5	50	60	.455	0	242--	—	3.21

Stacy Jones

Pitches: Right **Bats:** Right **Pos:** RP-2   **Ht:** 6'6" **Wt:** 225 **Born:** 5/26/67 **Age:** 30

Year Team	Lg	G	GS	CG	GF	IP	BFP	H	R	ER	HR	SH	SF	HB	TBB	IBB	SO	WP	Bk	W	L	Pct.	ShO	Sv-Op	Hld	ERA
1996 Nw Orleans *	AAA	9	0	0	2	12.2	64	18	10	10	2	1	1	2	7	1	10	1	0	0	1	.000	0	0--	—	7.11
Birmingham *	AA	27	0	0	24	28	115	25	11	8	0	2	0	2	6	1	31	0	0	1	1	.500	0	14--	—	2.57
Nashville *	AAA	19	0	0	18	21.2	81	17	3	2	0	0	1	0	6	2	18	0	0	3	0	1.000	0	12--	—	0.83
1991 Baltimore	AL	4	1	0	0	11	49	11	6	5	1	0	1	0	5	0	10	0	0	0	0	.000	0	0-0		4.09
1996 Chicago	AL	1	0	0	0	2	7	0	0	0	0	0	0	0	1	0	1	0	0	0	0	.000	0	0-0		0.00
2 ML YEARS		6	1	0	1	13	56	11	6	5	1	0	1	0	6	0	11	0	0	0	0	.000	0	0-0		3.46

Terry Jones

Bats: Both **Throws:** Right **Pos:** PH-8; CF-4 **Ht:** 5'10" **Wt:** 165 **Born:** 2/15/71 **Age:** 26

Year Team	Lg	G	AB	H	2B	3B	HR	(Hm	Rd)	TB	R	RBI	TBB	IBB	SO	HBP	SH	SF	SB	CS	SB%	GDP	Avg	OBP	SLG
1993 Bend	A-	33	138	40	5	4	0	—	—	53	21	18	12	1	19	0	2	0	16	6	.73	0	.290	.347	.384
Central Val	A+	21	73	21	1	0	0	—	—	22	16	7	10	0	15	1	1	0	5	0	1.00	2	.288	.381	.301
1994 Central Val	A+	129	536	157	20	1	2	—	—	185	94	34	42	1	85	1	10	1	44	12	.79	12	.293	.345	.345
1995 New Haven	AA	124	472	127	12	1	1	—	—	144	78	26	39	0	104	3	3	3	51	19	.73	6	.269	.327	.305
1996 Colo. Sprng	AAA	128	497	143	7	4	0	—	—	158	75	33	37	3	80	1	4	2	26	14	.65	5	.288	.337	.318
1996 Colorado	NL	12	10	3	0	0	0	(0	0)	3	6	1	0	0	3	0	0	1	0	0	.00	0	.300	.273	.300

Todd Jones

Pitches: Right **Bats:** Left **Pos:** RP-51 **Ht:** 6'3" **Wt:** 200 **Born:** 4/24/68 **Age:** 29

Year Team	Lg	G	GS	CG	GF	IP	BFP	H	R	ER	HR	SH	SF	HB	TBB	IBB	SO	WP	Bk	W	L	Pct.	ShO	Sv-Op	Hld	ERA
1996 Tucson *	AAA	1	0	0	0	2	7	1	1	0	0	0	0	0	2	0	1	0	0	0	0	.000	0	0- -	—	0.00
1993 Houston	NL	27	0	0	8	37.1	150	28	14	13	4	2	1	1	15	2	25	1	1	1	2	.333	0	2-3	6	3.13
1994 Houston	NL	48	0	0	20	72.2	288	52	23	22	4	3	1	1	26	4	63	1	0	5	2	.714	0	5-9	8	2.72
1995 Houston	NL	68	0	0	40	99.2	442	89	38	34	8	5	4	6	52	17	96	5	0	6	5	.545	0	15-20	8	3.07
1996 Houston	NL	51	0	0	37	57.1	263	61	30	28	5	2	1	5	32	6	44	3	0	6	3	.667	0	17-23	1	4.40
4 ML YEARS		194	0	0	105	267	1143	230	105	97	20	12	7	13	125	29	228	10	1	18	12	.600	0	39-55	23	3.27

Brian Jordan

Bats: R **Throws:** R **Pos:** RF-128; CF-13; PH-7; 1B-1 **Ht:** 6'1" **Wt:** 215 **Born:** 3/29/67 **Age:** 30

Year Team	Lg	G	AB	H	2B	3B	HR	(Hm	Rd)	TB	R	RBI	TBB	IBB	SO	HBP	SH	SF	SB	CS	SB%	GDP	Avg	OBP	SLG
1992 St. Louis	NL	55	193	40	9	4	5	(3	2)	72	17	22	10	1	48	1	0	0	7	2	.78	6	.207	.250	.373
1993 St. Louis	NL	67	223	69	10	6	10	(4	6)	121	33	44	12	0	35	4	0	3	6	6	.50	6	.309	.351	.543
1994 St. Louis	NL	53	178	46	8	2	5	(4	1)	73	14	15	16	0	40	1	0	2	4	3	.57	6	.258	.320	.410
1995 St. Louis	NL	131	490	145	20	4	22	(14	8)	239	83	81	22	4	79	11	0	2	24	9	.73	5	.296	.339	.488
1996 St. Louis	NL	140	513	159	36	1	17	(3	14)	248	82	104	29	4	84	7	2	9	22	5	.81	6	.310	.349	.483
5 ML YEARS		446	1597	459	83	17	59	(28	31)	753	229	266	89	9	286	24	2	16	63	25	.72	29	.287	.331	.472

Kevin Jordan

Bats: R **Throws:** R **Pos:** 1B-30; 2B-7; PH-6; 3B-1 **Ht:** 6'1" **Wt:** 194 **Born:** 10/9/69 **Age:** 27

Year Team	Lg	G	AB	H	2B	3B	HR	(Hm	Rd)	TB	R	RBI	TBB	IBB	SO	HBP	SH	SF	SB	CS	SB%	GDP	Avg	OBP	SLG
1990 Oneonta	A-	73	276	92	13	7	4	—	—	131	47	54	23	0	31	5	0	1	19	6	.76	3	.333	.393	.475
1991 Ft. Laud	A+	121	448	122	25	5	4	—	—	169	61	53	37	4	66	11	0	6	15	3	.83	13	.272	.339	.377
1992 Pr. William	A+	112	438	136	29	8	8	—	—	205	67	63	27	3	54	3	1	5	6	4	.60	9	.311	.351	.468
1993 Albany-Colo	AA	135	513	145	33	4	16	—	—	234	87	87	41	2	53	9	0	4	8	4	.67	8	.283	.344	.456
1994 Scranton-WB	AAA	81	314	91	22	1	12	—	—	151	44	57	29	2	28	3	0	9	0	2	.00	9	.290	.348	.481
1995 Scranton-WB	AAA	106	410	127	29	4	5	—	—	179	61	60	28	0	36	8	1	4	3	0	1.00	14	.310	.361	.437
1995 Philadelphia	NL	24	54	10	1	0	2	(1	1)	17	6	6	2	1	9	1	0	0	0	0	.00	0	.185	.228	.315
1996 Philadelphia	NL	43	131	37	10	0	3	(2	1)	56	15	12	5	0	20	1	3	2	2	1	.67	3	.282	.309	.427
2 ML YEARS		67	185	47	11	0	5	(3	2)	73	21	18	7	1	29	2	3	2	2	1	.67	3	.254	.286	.395

Ricardo Jordan

Pitches: Left **Bats:** Left **Pos:** RP-26 **Ht:** 6'0" **Wt:** 180 **Born:** 6/27/70 **Age:** 27

Year Team	Lg	G	GS	CG	GF	IP	BFP	H	R	ER	HR	SH	SF	HB	TBB	IBB	SO	WP	Bk	W	L	Pct.	ShO	Sv-Op	Hld	ERA
1990 Dunedin	A	13	2	0	4	22.2	103	15	9	6	0	1	1	1	19	3	16	1	5	0	2	.000	0	0- -	—	2.38
1991 Myrtle Bch	A	29	23	3	3	144.2	606	100	58	44	3	3	4	6	79	0	152	3	5	9	8	.529	1	1- -	—	2.74
1992 Dunedin	A+	45	0	0	32	47	208	44	26	20	3	3	0	2	28	3	49	7	2	0	5	.000	0	15- -	—	3.83
1993 Dunedin	A+	15	0	0	3	24.2	104	20	13	12	0	1	1	0	15	1	24	3	0	2	0	1.000	0	1- -	—	4.38
Knoxville	AA	25	0	0	8	36.2	158	33	17	10	2	5	1	0	18	1	35	0	0	1	4	.200	0	2- -	—	2.45
1994 Knoxville	AA	53	0	0	40	64.1	273	54	25	19	2	4	2	4	23	2	70	4	0	4	3	.571	0	17- -	—	2.66
1995 Syracuse	AA	13	0	0	5	12.1	59	15	9	9	1	0	0	1	7	1	17	2	0	0	0	.000	0	0- -	—	6.57
1996 Scranton-WB	AAA	32	0	0	15	39.1	180	40	30	23	5	3	0	1	22	1	40	2	0	3	3	.500	0	1- -	—	5.26
1995 Toronto	AL	15	0	0	3	15	76	18	11	11	3	0	2	2	13	1	10	1	0	1	0	1.000	0	1-1	1	6.60
1996 Philadelphia	NL	26	0	0	2	25	103	18	6	5	0	1	1	0	12	0	17	1	0	2	2	.500	0	0-0	4	1.80
2 ML YEARS		41	0	0	5	40	179	36	17	16	3	1	3	2	25	1	27	2	0	3	2	.600	0	1-1	5	3.60

Ricky Jordan

Bats: Right **Throws:** Right **Pos:** 1B-9; PH-7; DH-2 **Ht:** 6'3" **Wt:** 205 **Born:** 5/26/65 **Age:** 32

Year Team	Lg	G	AB	H	2B	3B	HR	(Hm	Rd)	TB	R	RBI	TBB	IBB	SO	HBP	SH	SF	SB	CS	SB%	GDP	Avg	OBP	SLG
1996 Lancaster *	A+	7	31	10	1	0	1	—	—	14	7	4	2	0	5	0	0	0	0	0	.00	0	.323	.364	.452
Everett *	A-	3	14	5	1	0	0	—	—	6	2	5	1	0	4	0	0	0	0	0	.00	0	.357	.400	.429

Year Team	Lg	BATTING																BASERUNNING				PERCENTAGES		
		G	AB	H	2B	3B	HR	(Hm Rd)	TB	R	RBI	TBB	IBB	SO	HBP	SH	SF	SB	CS	SB%	GDP	Avg	OBP	SLG
Tacoma *	AAA	13	50	10	0	0	2	— —	16	3	7	5	1	6	0	0	1	0	0	.00		.200	.268	.320
1988 Philadelphia	NL	69	273	84	15	1	11	(6 5)	134	41	43	7	2	39	0	0	1	1	1	.50	5	.308	.324	.491
1989 Philadelphia	NL	144	523	149	22	3	12	(7 5)	213	63	75	23	5	62	5	0	8	4	3	.57	19	.285	.317	.407
1990 Philadelphia	NL	92	324	78	21	0	5	(2 3)	114	32	44	13	6	39	5	0	4	2	0	1.00	6	.241	.277	.352
1991 Philadelphia	NL	101	301	82	21	3	9	(5 4)	136	38	49	14	2	49	2	0	5	0	2	.00	11	.272	.304	.452
1992 Philadelphia	NL	94	276	84	19	0	4	(2 2)	115	33	34	5	0	44	0	0	3	3	0	1.00	8	.304	.313	.417
1993 Philadelphia	NL	90	159	46	4	1	5	(3 2)	67	21	18	8	1	32	1	0	2	0	0	.00	2	.289	.324	.421
1994 Philadelphia	NL	72	220	62	14	2	8	(5 3)	104	29	37	6	1	32	1	0	1	0	0	.00	7	.282	.303	.473
1996 Seattle	AL	15	28	7	0	0	1	(0 1)	10	4	4	1	0	6	1	0	1	0	0	.00	0	.250	.290	.357
8 ML YEARS		677	2104	592	116	10	55	(30 25)	893	261	304	77	17	303	15	0	25	10	6	.63	61	.281	.308	.424

Wally Joyner

Bats: Left **Throws:** Left **Pos:** 1B-119; PH-4   **Ht:** 6'2" **Wt:** 200 **Born:** 6/16/62 **Age:** 35

Year Team	Lg	BATTING																BASERUNNING				PERCENTAGES		
		G	AB	H	2B	3B	HR	(Hm Rd)	TB	R	RBI	TBB	IBB	SO	HBP	SH	SF	SB	CS	SB%	GDP	Avg	OBP	SLG
1996 Rncho Cuca *	A+	3	10	3	1	0	0	— —	4	1	2	1	0	1	0	0	0	0	0	.00	0	.300	.364	.400
1986 California	AL	154	593	172	27	3	22	(11 11)	271	82	100	57	8	58	2	10	12	5	2	.71	11	.290	.348	.457
1987 California	AL	149	564	161	33	1	34	(19 15)	298	100	117	72	12	64	5	2	10	8	2	.80	14	.285	.366	.528
1988 California	AL	158	597	176	31	2	13	(6 7)	250	81	85	55	14	51	5	0	6	8	2	.80	16	.295	.356	.419
1989 California	AL	159	593	167	30	2	16	(8 8)	249	78	79	46	7	58	6	1	5	3	2	.60	15	.282	.335	.420
1990 California	AL	83	310	83	15	0	8	(5 3)	122	35	41	41	4	34	1	1	5	2	1	.67	10	.268	.350	.394
1991 California	AL	143	551	166	34	3	21	(10 11)	269	79	96	52	4	66	1	2	5	2	0	1.00	11	.301	.360	.488
1992 Kansas City	AL	149	572	154	36	2	9	(1 8)	221	66	66	55	4	50	4	0	2	11	5	.69	19	.269	.336	.386
1993 Kansas City	AL	141	497	145	36	3	15	(4 11)	232	83	65	66	13	67	3	2	5	5	9	.36	6	.292	.375	.467
1994 Kansas City	AL	97	363	113	20	3	8	(2 6)	163	52	57	47	3	43	0	2	5	3	2	.60	12	.311	.386	.449
1995 Kansas City	AL	131	465	144	28	0	12	(6 6)	208	69	83	69	10	65	2	5	9	3	2	.60	10	.310	.394	.447
1996 San Diego	NL	121	433	120	29	1	8	(5 3)	175	59	65	69	8	71	3	1	4	5	3	.63	6	.277	.377	.404
11 ML YEARS		1485	5538	1601	319	20	166	(77 89)	2458	784	854	629	87	627	32	26	71	55	30	.65	130	.289	.361	.444

Jeff Juden

Pitches: Right **Bats:** Both **Pos:** RP-58   **Ht:** 6'8" **Wt:** 265 **Born:** 1/19/71 **Age:** 26

Year Team	Lg	HOW MUCH HE PITCHED						WHAT HE GAVE UP												THE RESULTS						
		G	GS	CG	GF	IP	BFP	H	R	ER	HR	SH	SF	HB	TBB	IBB	SO	WP	Bk	W	L	Pct.	ShO	Sv-Op	Hld	ERA
1991 Houston	NL	4	3	0	0	18	81	19	14	12	3	2	3	0	7	1	11	0	1	0	2	.000	0	0-0	0	6.00
1993 Houston	NL	2	0	0	1	5	23	4	3	3	1	0	1	0	4	1	7	0	0	0	1	.000	0	0-0	0	5.40
1994 Philadelphia	NL	6	5	0	0	27.2	121	29	25	19	4	1	2	1	12	0	22	0	2	1	4	.200	0	0-0	0	6.18
1995 Philadelphia	NL	13	10	1	0	62.2	271	53	31	28	6	5	4	5	31	0	47	4	1	2	4	.333	0	0-0	0	4.02
1996 SF-Mon	NL	58	0	0	16	74.1	318	61	35	27	8	3	3	5	34	2	61	5	0	5	0	1.000	0	0-0	3	3.27
1996 San Francisco	NL	36	0	0	9	41.2	180	39	23	19	7	1	2	1	20	2	35	3	0	4	0	1.000	0	0-0	3	4.10
Montreal	NL	22	0	0	7	32.2	138	22	12	8	1	2	1	4	14	0	26	2	0	1	0	1.000	0	0-0	0	2.20
5 ML YEARS		83	18	1	17	187.2	814	166	108	89	22	11	13	11	88	4	148	9	4	8	11	.421	0	0-0	3	4.27

Dave Justice

Bats: Left **Throws:** Left **Pos:** RF-40   **Ht:** 6'3" **Wt:** 200 **Born:** 4/14/66 **Age:** 31

Year Team	Lg	BATTING																BASERUNNING				PERCENTAGES		
		G	AB	H	2B	3B	HR	(Hm Rd)	TB	R	RBI	TBB	IBB	SO	HBP	SH	SF	SB	CS	SB%	GDP	Avg	OBP	SLG
1989 Atlanta	NL	16	51	12	3	0	1	(1 0)	18	7	3	3	1	9	1	1	0	2	1	.67	4	.235	.291	.353
1990 Atlanta	NL	127	439	124	23	2	28	(19 9)	235	76	78	64	4	92	0	0	1	11	6	.65	2	.282	.373	.535
1991 Atlanta	NL	109	396	109	25	1	21	(11 10)	199	67	87	65	9	81	3	0	5	8	8	.50	4	.275	.377	.503
1992 Atlanta	NL	144	484	124	19	5	21	(10 11)	216	78	72	79	8	85	2	0	6	2	4	.33	1	.256	.359	.446
1993 Atlanta	NL	157	585	158	15	4	40	(18 22)	301	90	120	78	12	90	3	0	4	3	5	.38	9	.270	.357	.515
1994 Atlanta	NL	104	352	110	16	2	19	(9 10)	187	61	59	69	5	45	2	0	1	2	4	.33	8	.313	.427	.531
1995 Atlanta	NL	120	411	104	17	2	24	(15 9)	197	73	78	73	5	68	2	0	5	4	2	.67	5	.253	.365	.479
1996 Atlanta	NL	40	140	45	9	0	6	(5 1)	72	23	25	21	1	22	1	0	2	1	1	.50	5	.321	.409	.514
8 ML YEARS		817	2858	786	127	16	160	(88 72)	1425	475	522	452	45	492	14	1	24	33	31	.52	35	.275	.374	.499

Scott Kamieniecki

Pitches: Right **Bats:** Right **Pos:** SP-5; RP-2   **Ht:** 6'0" **Wt:** 195 **Born:** 4/19/64 **Age:** 33

Year Team	Lg	HOW MUCH HE PITCHED						WHAT HE GAVE UP												THE RESULTS						
		G	GS	CG	GF	IP	BFP	H	R	ER	HR	SH	SF	HB	TBB	IBB	SO	WP	Bk	W	L	Pct.	ShO	Sv-Op	Hld	ERA
1996 Tampa *	A+	3	3	1	0	23	92	20	6	3	1	0	0	0	4	0	17	1	0	2	1	.667	0	0--	—	1.17
Columbus *	AAA	5	5	2	0	30.1	131	33	21	19	4	0	0	1	8	0	27	2	0	2	1	.667	0	0--	—	5.64
1991 New York	AL	9	9	0	0	55.1	239	54	24	24	8	2	1	3	22	1	34	1	0	4	4	.500	0	0-0	0	3.90
1992 New York	AL	28	28	4	0	188	804	193	100	91	13	3	5	5	74	9	88	9	1	6	14	.300	0	0-0	0	4.36
1993 New York	AL	30	20	2	4	154.1	659	163	73	70	17	3	5	3	59	7	72	2	0	10	7	.588	0	1-1	0	4.08
1994 New York	AL	22	16	1	2	117.1	509	115	53	49	13	4	3	3	59	5	71	4	0	8	6	.571	0	0-0	1	3.76
1995 New York	AL	17	16	1	1	89.2	391	83	43	40	8	1	0	3	49	1	43	4	0	7	6	.538	0	0-0	0	4.01
1996 New York	AL	7	5	0	1	22.2	120	36	30	28	6	0	0	2	19	1	15	1	0	1	2	.333	0	0-1	0	11.12
6 ML YEARS		113	94	8	7	627.1	2722	644	323	302	65	13	14	19	282	24	323	21	1	36	39	.480	0	1-2	1	4.33

Matt Karchner

Pitches: Right **Bats:** Right **Pos:** RP-50   **Ht:** 6'4" **Wt:** 210 **Born:** 6/28/67 **Age:** 30

				HOW MUCH HE PITCHED				WHAT HE GAVE UP										THE RESULTS					
Year Team	Lg	G	GS	CG	GF	IP	BFP	H	R	ER	HR	SH	SF	HB	TBB	IBB	SO	WP	Bk	W	L	Pct.	ShO	Sv-Op	Hld	ERA
1989 Eugene	A-	8	5	0	0	30	131	30	19	13	1	0	1	5	8	0	25	7	0	1	1	.500	0	0--	—	3.90
1990 Appleton	A	27	11	1	5	71	308	70	42	38	3	2	1	6	31	2	58	4	1	2	7	.222	0	0--	—	4.82
1991 Baseball Cy	A+	38	0	0	16	73	295	49	28	16	1	5	0	5	25	3	65	7	1	6	3	.667	0	5--	—	1.97
1992 Memphis	AA	33	18	2	2	141	606	161	83	70	5	6	2	11	35	0	88	8	1	8	8	.500	0	1--	—	4.47
1993 Memphis	AA	6	5	0	1	30	126	34	16	14	2	2	0	4	4	0	14	1	0	3	2	.600	0	0--	—	4.20
1994 Birmingham	AA	39	0	0	33	43	177	36	10	6	0	3	2	2	14	1	29	5	0	5	2	.714	0	6--	—	1.26
Nashville	AAA	17	0	0	11	26.1	107	18	5	4	0	4	1	1	7	2	19	1	0	4	2	.667	0	2--	—	1.37
1995 Nashville	AAA	28	0	0	21	37.1	156	39	7	6	3	5	0	0	10	5	29	2	0	3	3	.500	0	9--	—	1.45
1996 Nashville	AAA	1	0	0	0	0.2	2	0	0	0	0	0	0	0	0	0	0	0	0	0	0	.000	0	0--	—	0.00
1995 Chicago	AL	31	0	0	10	32	137	33	8	6	2	0	4	1	12	2	24	1	0	4	2	.667	0	0-0	13	1.69
1996 Chicago	AL	50	0	0	13	59.1	278	61	42	38	10	2	4	2	41	8	46	4	0	7	4	.636	0	1-9	13	5.76
2 ML YEARS		81	0	0	23	91.1	415	94	50	44	12	2	8	3	53	10	70	5	0	11	6	.647	0	1-9	26	4.34

Ron Karkovice

Bats: Right **Throws:** Right **Pos:** C-111   **Ht:** 6'1" **Wt:** 219 **Born:** 8/8/63 **Age:** 33

					BATTING														BASERUNNING				PERCENTAGES		
Year Team	Lg	G	AB	H	2B	3B	HR	(Hm	Rd)	TB	R	RBI	TBB	IBB	SO	HBP	SH	SF	SB	CS	SB%	GDP	Avg	OBP	SLG
1986 Chicago	AL	37	97	24	7	0	4	(1	3)	43	13	13	9	0	37	1	1	1	1	0	1.00	3	.247	.315	.443
1987 Chicago	AL	39	85	6	0	0	2	(1	1)	12	7	7	7	0	40	2	1	0	3	0	1.00	2	.071	.160	.141
1988 Chicago	AL	46	115	20	4	0	3	(1	2)	33	10	9	7	0	30	1	3	0	4	2	.67	1	.174	.228	.287
1989 Chicago	AL	71	182	48	9	2	3	(0	3)	70	21	24	10	0	56	2	7	2	0	0	.00	0	.264	.306	.385
1990 Chicago	AL	68	183	45	10	0	6	(0	6)	73	30	20	16	1	52	1	7	1	2	0	1.00	1	.246	.308	.399
1991 Chicago	AL	75	167	41	13	0	5	(0	5)	69	25	22	15	1	42	1	9	1	0	0	.00	2	.246	.310	.413
1992 Chicago	AL	123	342	81	12	1	13	(5	8)	134	39	50	30	1	89	3	4	2	10	4	.71	3	.237	.302	.392
1993 Chicago	AL	128	403	92	17	1	20	(6	14)	171	60	54	29	1	126	6	11	4	2	2	.50	12	.228	.287	.424
1994 Chicago	AL	77	207	44	9	1	11	(6	5)	88	33	29	36	2	68	0	2	3	0	3	.00	0	.213	.325	.425
1995 Chicago	AL	113	323	70	14	1	13	(5	8)	125	44	51	39	0	84	5	9	6	2	3	.40	5	.217	.306	.387
1996 Chicago	AL	111	355	78	22	0	10	(5	5)	130	44	38	24	2	93	1	7	2	0	0	.00	7	.220	.270	.366
11 ML YEARS		888	2459	549	117	6	90	(30	60)	948	326	317	222	8	717	23	61	22	24	14	.63	36	.223	.291	.386

Scott Karl

Pitches: Left **Bats:** Left **Pos:** SP-32   **Ht:** 6'2" **Wt:** 195 **Born:** 8/9/71 **Age:** 25

				HOW MUCH HE PITCHED				WHAT HE GAVE UP										THE RESULTS					
Year Team	Lg	G	GS	CG	GF	IP	BFP	H	R	ER	HR	SH	SF	HB	TBB	IBB	SO	WP	Bk	W	L	Pct.	ShO	Sv-Op	Hld	ERA
1992 Helena	R+	9	9	1	0	61.2	245	54	13	10	2	1	1	2	16	0	57	5	1	7	0	1.000	1	0--	—	1.46
1993 El Paso	AA	27	27	4	0	180	732	172	67	49	9	6	3	6	35	0	95	6	7	13	8	.619	2	0--	—	2.45
1994 El Paso	AA	8	8	3	0	54.2	219	44	21	18	2	2	1	6	15	1	51	3	0	5	1	.833	0	0--	—	2.96
New Orleans	AAA	15	13	2	0	89	375	92	38	38	10	3	4	2	33	1	54	2	0	5	5	.500	0	0--	—	3.84
1995 New Orleans	AAA	8	6	1	1	46.1	191	47	18	17	3	0	1	2	12	2	29	1	0	3	4	.429	1	0--	—	3.30
1995 Milwaukee	AL	25	18	1	3	124	548	141	65	57	10	3	3	3	50	6	59	0	0	6	7	.462	0	0-0	1	4.14
1996 Milwaukee	AL	32	32	3	0	207.1	905	220	124	112	29	2	7	11	72	0	121	5	1	13	9	.591	1	0-0	0	4.86
2 ML YEARS		57	50	4	3	331.1	1453	361	189	169	39	5	10	14	122	6	180	5	1	19	16	.543	1	0-0	1	4.59

Eric Karros

Bats: Right **Throws:** Right **Pos:** 1B-154   **Ht:** 6'4" **Wt:** 222 **Born:** 11/4/67 **Age:** 29

					BATTING														BASERUNNING				PERCENTAGES		
Year Team	Lg	G	AB	H	2B	3B	HR	(Hm	Rd)	TB	R	RBI	TBB	IBB	SO	HBP	SH	SF	SB	CS	SB%	GDP	Avg	OBP	SLG
1991 Los Angeles	NL	14	14	1	1	0	0	(0	0)	2	0	1	1	0	6	0	0	0	0	0	.00	0	.071	.133	.143
1992 Los Angeles	NL	149	545	140	30	1	20	(6	14)	232	63	88	37	3	103	2	0	5	2	4	.33	15	.257	.304	.426
1993 Los Angeles	NL	158	619	153	27	2	23	(13	10)	253	74	80	34	1	82	2	0	3	0	1	.00	17	.247	.287	.409
1994 Los Angeles	NL	111	406	108	21	1	14	(5	9)	173	51	46	29	1	53	2	0	11	2	0	1.00	13	.266	.310	.426
1995 Los Angeles	NL	143	551	164	29	3	32	(19	13)	295	83	105	61	4	115	4	0	4	4	4	.50	14	.298	.369	.535
1996 Los Angeles	NL	154	608	158	29	1	34	(16	18)	291	84	111	53	2	121	1	0	8	8	0	1.00	27	.260	.316	.479
6 ML YEARS		729	2743	724	137	8	123	(59	64)	1246	355	431	215	11	480	11	0	31	16	9	.64	86	.264	.317	.454

Greg Keagle

Pitches: Right **Bats:** Right **Pos:** RP-20; SP-6   **Ht:** 6'2" **Wt:** 195 **Born:** 6/28/71 **Age:** 26

				HOW MUCH HE PITCHED				WHAT HE GAVE UP										THE RESULTS					
Year Team	Lg	G	GS	CG	GF	IP	BFP	H	R	ER	HR	SH	SF	HB	TBB	IBB	SO	WP	Bk	W	L	Pct.	ShO	Sv-Op	Hld	ERA
1993 Spokane	A-	15	15	1	0	83	368	80	37	30	2	4	4	7	40	2	77	4	4	3	3	.500	0	0--	—	3.25
1994 Rancho Cuca	A+	14	14	1	0	92	377	62	23	21	2	1	3	5	41	1	91	1	0	11	1	.917	1	0--	—	2.05
Wichita	AA	13	13	0	0	70.1	321	84	53	49	5	5	2	2	32	1	57	3	1	3	9	.250	0	0--	—	6.27
1995 Rancho Cuca	A+	2	2	0	0	14	59	14	9	7	1	0	1	2	2	0	11	1	0	0	0	.000	0	0--	—	4.50
Las Vegas	AAA	14	13	0	1	75.2	351	76	47	36	3	6	5	6	42	2	49	2	0	7	6	.538	0	0--	—	4.28
1996 Toledo	AAA	6	6	0	0	27	135	42	32	30	7	1	2	4	11	0	24	0	1	2	3	.400	0	0--	—	10.00
1996 Detroit	AL	26	6	0	5	87.2	435	104	76	72	13	2	7	9	68	5	70	2	0	3	6	.333	0	0-0	0	7.39

Mike Kelly

Bats: R **Throws:** R **Pos:** CF-10; LF-6; PH-3; RF-1   **Ht:** 6'4" **Wt:** 195 **Born:** 6/2/70 **Age:** 27

								BATTING												BASERUNNING				PERCENTAGES		
Year Team	Lg	G	AB	H	2B	3B	HR	(Hm	Rd)	TB	R	RBI	TBB	IBB	SO	HBP	SH	SF	SB	CS	SB%	GDP	Avg	OBP	SLG
1996 Indianapols *	AAA	88	292	61	10	1	8	—	—	97	43	30	30	0	80	3	1	3	13	2	.87	2	.209	.287	.332
1994 Atlanta	NL	30	77	21	10	1	2	(0	2)	39	14	9	2	0	17	1	0	0	0	1	.00	1	.273	.300	.506
1995 Atlanta	NL	97	137	26	6	1	3	(0	3)	43	26	17	11	0	49	2	2	1	7	3	.70	2	.190	.258	.314
1996 Cincinnati	NL	19	49	9	4	0	1	(0	1)	16	5	7	9	0	11	2	0	0	4	0	1.00	2	.184	.333	.327
3 ML YEARS		146	263	56	20	2	6	(0	6)	98	45	33	22	0	77	5	2	1	11	4	.73	5	.213	.285	.373

Pat Kelly

Bats: Right **Throws:** Right **Pos:** 2B-10; PH-6; DH-3   **Ht:** 6'0" **Wt:** 182 **Born:** 10/14/67 **Age:** 29

								BATTING												BASERUNNING				PERCENTAGES		
Year Team	Lg	G	AB	H	2B	3B	HR	(Hm	Rd)	TB	R	RBI	TBB	IBB	SO	HBP	SH	SF	SB	CS	SB%	GDP	Avg	OBP	SLG
1996 Yankees *	R	5	17	6	2	0	1	—	—	11	7	1	3	0	2	1	0	0	3	0	1.00	0	.353	.476	.647
Tampa *	A+	6	22	6	0	0	1	—	—	9	6	2	1	0	7	1	0	0	0	0	.00	0	.273	.333	.409
Columbus *	AAA	8	37	14	1	1	2	—	—	23	6	7	2	0	11	0	0	1	3	0	1.00	0	.378	.400	.622
Norwich *	AA	4	17	5	2	1	0	—	—	9	3	0	0	0	2	0	0	0	1	0	1.00	0	.294	.294	.529
1991 New York	AL	96	298	72	12	4	3	(3	0)	101	35	23	15	0	52	5	2	2	12	1	.92	5	.242	.288	.339
1992 New York	AL	106	318	72	22	2	7	(3	4)	119	38	27	25	1	72	10	6	3	8	5	.62	6	.226	.301	.374
1993 New York	AL	127	406	111	24	1	7	(4	3)	158	49	51	24	0	68	5	10	6	14	11	.56	9	.273	.317	.389
1994 New York	AL	93	286	80	21	2	3	(1	2)	114	35	41	19	1	51	5	14	5	6	5	.55	10	.280	.330	.399
1995 New York	AL	89	270	64	12	1	4	(1	3)	90	32	29	23	0	65	5	10	2	8	3	.73	5	.237	.307	.333
1996 New York	AL	13	21	3	0	0	0	(0	0)	3	4	2	2	0	9	0	0	0	0	1	.00	1	.143	.217	.143
6 ML YEARS		524	1599	402	91	10	24	(12	12)	585	193	173	108	2	317	30	42	18	48	26	.65	36	.251	.308	.366

Roberto Kelly

Bats: R **Throws:** R **Pos:** RF-54; CF-40; LF-6; PH-6; DH-2   **Ht:** 6'2" **Wt:** 202 **Born:** 10/1/64 **Age:** 32

								BATTING												BASERUNNING				PERCENTAGES		
Year Team	Lg	G	AB	H	2B	3B	HR	(Hm	Rd)	TB	R	RBI	TBB	IBB	SO	HBP	SH	SF	SB	CS	SB%	GDP	Avg	OBP	SLG
1987 New York	AL	23	52	14	3	0	1	(0	1)	20	12	7	5	0	15	0	1	1	9	3	.75	0	.269	.328	.385
1988 New York	AL	38	77	19	4	1	1	(1	0)	28	9	7	3	0	15	0	3	1	5	2	.71	0	.247	.272	.364
1989 New York	AL	137	441	133	18	3	9	(2	7)	184	65	48	41	3	89	6	8	0	35	12	.74	9	.302	.369	.417
1990 New York	AL	162	641	183	32	4	15	(5	10)	268	85	61	33	0	148	4	4	4	42	17	.71	7	.285	.323	.418
1991 New York	AL	126	486	130	22	2	20	(11	9)	216	68	69	45	2	77	5	2	5	32	9	.78	14	.267	.333	.444
1992 New York	AL	152	580	158	31	2	10	(6	4)	223	81	66	41	4	96	4	1	6	28	5	.85	19	.272	.322	.384
1993 Cincinnati	NL	78	320	102	17	3	9	(4	5)	152	44	35	17	0	43	2	0	3	21	5	.81	10	.319	.354	.475
1994 Cin-Atl	NL	110	434	127	23	3	9	(4	5)	183	73	45	35	1	71	3	0	3	19	11	.63	8	.293	.347	.422
1995 Mon-LA	NL	136	504	140	23	2	7	(2	5)	188	58	57	22	6	79	6	0	7	19	10	.66	14	.278	.312	.373
1996 Minnesota	AL	98	322	104	17	4	6	(3	3)	147	41	47	23	0	53	7	0	5	10	2	.83	17	.323	.375	.457
1994 Cincinnati	NL	47	179	54	8	0	3	(1	2)	71	29	21	11	1	35	3	0	1	9	8	.53	3	.302	.351	.397
Atlanta	NL	63	255	73	15	3	6	(3	3)	112	44	24	24	0	36	0	0	2	10	3	.77	5	.286	.345	.439
1995 Montreal	NL	24	95	26	4	0	1	(0	1)	33	11	9	7	1	14	2	0	0	4	3	.57	4	.274	.337	.347
Los Angeles	NL	112	409	114	19	2	6	(2	4)	155	47	48	15	5	65	4	0	7	15	7	.68	10	.279	.306	.379
10 ML YEARS		1060	3857	1110	190	24	87	(38	49)	1609	536	442	265	16	686	37	19	35	220	76	.74	98	.288	.337	.417

Jason Kendall

Bats: Right **Throws:** Right **Pos:** C-129; PH-4   **Ht:** 6'0" **Wt:** 181 **Born:** 6/26/74 **Age:** 23

								BATTING												BASERUNNING				PERCENTAGES		
Year Team	Lg	G	AB	H	2B	3B	HR	(Hm	Rd)	TB	R	RBI	TBB	IBB	SO	HBP	SH	SF	SB	CS	SB%	GDP	Avg	OBP	SLG
1992 Pirates	R	33	111	29	2	0	0	—	—	31	7	10	8	1	9	2	0	2	2	2	.50	3	.261	.317	.279
1993 Augusta	A	102	366	101	17	4	1	—	—	129	43	40	22	1	30	7	0	5	8	5	.62	7	.276	.325	.352
1994 Salem	A+	101	371	118	19	2	7	—	—	162	68	66	47	1	21	13	0	7	14	3	.82	15	.318	.406	.437
Carolina	AA	13	47	11	2	0	0	—	—	13	6	6	2	0	3	2	0	0	0	0	.00	0	.234	.294	.277
1995 Carolina	AA	117	429	140	26	1	8	—	—	192	87	71	56	5	22	14	1	8	10	7	.59	10	.326	.414	.448
1996 Pittsburgh	NL	130	414	124	23	5	3	(2	1)	166	54	42	35	11	30	15	3	4	5	2	.71	7	.300	.372	.401

Jeff Kent

Bats: R **Throws:** R **Pos:** 3B-95; 1B-20; 2B-9; DH-5; PH-2   **Ht:** 6'1" **Wt:** 185 **Born:** 3/7/68 **Age:** 29

								BATTING												BASERUNNING				PERCENTAGES		
Year Team	Lg	G	AB	H	2B	3B	HR	(Hm	Rd)	TB	R	RBI	TBB	IBB	SO	HBP	SH	SF	SB	CS	SB%	GDP	Avg	OBP	SLG
1992 Tor-NYN		102	305	73	21	2	11	(4	7)	131	52	50	27	0	76	7	0	4	2	3	.40	5	.239	.312	.430
1993 New York	NL	140	496	134	24	0	21	(9	12)	221	65	80	30	2	88	8	6	4	4	4	.50	11	.270	.320	.446
1994 New York	NL	107	415	121	24	5	14	(10	4)	197	53	68	23	3	84	10	1	3	1	4	.20	7	.292	.341	.475
1995 New York	NL	125	472	131	22	3	20	(11	9)	219	65	65	29	3	89	8	1	6	3	3	.50	9	.278	.327	.464
1996 NYN-Cle		128	437	124	27	1	12	(4	8)	189	61	55	31	1	78	2	1	6	6	4	.60	8	.284	.330	.432
1992 Toronto	AL	65	192	46	13	1	8	(2	6)	85	36	35	20	0	47	6	0	4	2	1	.67	4	.240	.324	.443
New York	NL	37	113	27	8	1	3	(2	1)	46	16	15	7	0	29	1	0	0	0	2	.00	2	.239	.289	.407
1996 New York	NL	89	335	97	20	1	9	(2	7)	146	45	39	21	1	56	1	1	3	4	3	.57	7	.290	.331	.436
Cleveland	AL	39	102	27	7	0	3	(2	1)	43	16	16	10	0	22	1	0	3	2	1	.67	1	.265	.328	.422
5 ML YEARS		602	2125	583	118	11	78	(38	40)	957	296	318	140	9	415	35	9	21	16	18	.47	40	.274	.327	.450

Jimmy Key

Pitches: Left **Bats:** Right **Pos:** SP-30   **Ht:** 6'1" **Wt:** 185 **Born:** 4/22/61 **Age:** 36

		HOW MUCH HE PITCHED						WHAT HE GAVE UP										THE RESULTS					
Year Team	Lg	G	GS	CG	GF	IP	BFP	H	R	ER	HR	SH	SF	HB	TBB	IBB	SO	WP	Bk	W	L	Pct.	ShO	Sv-Op	Hld	ERA
1996 Tampa *	A+	2	2	0	0	13	53	10	4	4	1	0	0	0	1	0	11	0	0	0	0	.000	0	0--	—	2.77
Yankees *	R	1	1	0	0	5	21	3	2	0	0	0	0	1	0	0	10	0	0	1	0	1.000	0	0--	—	0.00
1984 Toronto	AL	63	0	0	24	62	285	70	37	32	8	6	1	1	32	8	44	3	1	4	5	.444	0	10--	—	4.65
1985 Toronto	AL	35	32	3	0	212.2	856	188	77	71	22	5	5	2	50	1	85	6	1	14	6	.700	0	0--	—	3.00
1986 Toronto	AL	36	35	4	0	232	959	222	98	92	24	10	6	3	74	1	141	3	0	14	11	.560	2	0--	—	3.57
1987 Toronto	AL	36	36	8	0	261	1033	210	93	80	24	11	3	2	66	6	161	8	5	17	8	.680	1	0-0	0	**2.76**
1988 Toronto	AL	21	21	2	0	131.1	551	127	55	48	13	4	3	5	30	2	65	1	0	12	5	.706	2	0-0	0	3.29
1989 Toronto	AL	33	33	5	0	216	886	226	99	93	18	9	9	3	27	2	118	4	1	13	14	.481	1	0-0	0	3.88
1990 Toronto	AL	27	27	0	0	154.2	636	169	79	73	20	5	6	1	22	2	88	0	1	13	7	.650	0	0-0	0	4.25
1991 Toronto	AL	33	33	2	0	209.1	877	207	84	71	12	10	5	3	44	3	125	1	0	16	12	.571	2	0-0	0	3.05
1992 Toronto	AL	33	33	4	0	216.2	900	205	88	85	24	2	7	4	59	0	117	5	0	13	13	.500	2	0-0	0	3.53
1993 New York	AL	34	34	4	0	236.2	948	219	84	79	26	6	9	1	43	1	173	3	0	18	6	.750	2	0-0	0	3.00
1994 New York	AL	25	**25**	1	0	168	710	177	68	61	10	4	2	3	52	0	97	8	1	**17**	4	.810	0	0-0	0	3.27
1995 New York	AL	5	5	0	0	30.1	134	40	20	19	3	3	1	0	6	1	14	1	0	1	2	.333	0	0-0	0	5.64
1996 New York	AL	30	30	0	0	169.1	715	171	93	88	21	7	5	2	58	1	116	2	0	12	11	.522	0	0-0	0	4.68
13 ML YEARS		411	344	33	24	2300	9490	2231	975	892	225	82	62	30	563	28	1344	45	10	164	104	.612	12	10--	—	3.49

Brian Keyser

Pitches: Right **Bats:** Right **Pos:** RP-28   **Ht:** 6'1" **Wt:** 180 **Born:** 10/31/66 **Age:** 30

		HOW MUCH HE PITCHED						WHAT HE GAVE UP										THE RESULTS					
Year Team	Lg	G	GS	CG	GF	IP	BFP	H	R	ER	HR	SH	SF	HB	TBB	IBB	SO	WP	Bk	W	L	Pct.	ShO	Sv-Op	Hld	ERA
1989 Utica	A-	14	13	2	0	93.2	374	79	37	31	6	2	2	4	22	0	70	5	3	4	4	.500	0	0--	—	2.98
1990 Sarasota	A+	38	10	2	13	115.2	475	107	54	47	5	5	4	6	40	1	83	6	3	6	7	.462	1	2--	—	3.66
1991 Sarasota	A+	27	14	2	9	129	527	110	40	33	5	8	3	6	45	8	94	3	3	6	7	.462	1	2--	—	2.30
Birmingham	AA	3	3	0	0	18	78	19	10	10	2	0	1	0	9	0	9	0	1	0	0	.000	0	0--	—	5.00
1992 Birmingham	AA	28	27	7	1	183.1	754	173	86	76	12	1	7	4	60	1	99	9	0	9	10	.474	3	0--	—	3.73
1993 Birmingham	AA	2	2	1	0	11	50	15	9	7	0	1	1	0	5	0	8	0	0	0	2	.000	0	0--	—	5.73
Nashville	AAA	30	18	2	4	121.2	511	142	70	63	8	2	4	1	27	4	44	4	1	9	5	.643	0	1--	—	4.66
1994 Birmingham	AA	1	1	0	0	6	23	4	1	1	1	0	0	1	1	0	5	0	0	0	0	.000	0	0--	—	1.50
Nashville	AAA	37	10	2	15	135.2	556	123	49	42	9	7	5	3	36	4	76	9	0	9	5	.643	1	2--	—	2.79
1995 Nashville	AAA	10	10	2	0	72.1	273	49	23	19	4	3	3	1	9	0	40	1	0	2	4	.333	1	0--	—	2.36
1996 Nashville	AAA	6	6	2	0	44.2	178	38	11	10	2	2	3	0	13	1	22	0	0	3	3	.500	1	0--	—	2.01
1995 Chicago	AL	23	10	0	0	92.1	404	114	53	51	10	0	2	2	27	1	48	1	1	5	6	.455	0	0-1	2	4.97
1996 Chicago	AL	28	0	0	10	59.2	275	78	35	33	3	6	3	0	28	8	19	2	0	1	2	.333	0	1-2	1	4.98
2 ML YEARS		51	10	0	10	152	679	192	88	84	13	6	5	2	55	9	67	3	1	6	8	.429	0	1-3	3	4.97

Mark Kiefer

Pitches: Right **Bats:** Right **Pos:** RP-7   **Ht:** 6'4" **Wt:** 194 **Born:** 11/13/68 **Age:** 28

		HOW MUCH HE PITCHED						WHAT HE GAVE UP										THE RESULTS					
Year Team	Lg	G	GS	CG	GF	IP	BFP	H	R	ER	HR	SH	SF	HB	TBB	IBB	SO	WP	Bk	W	L	Pct.	ShO	Sv-Op	Hld	ERA
1996 Nw Orleans *	AAA	22	10	1	3	72.2	310	60	40	35	15	3	3	3	33	1	66	4	0	3	6	.333	0	0--	—	4.33
Omaha *	AAA	8	7	0	0	45.2	196	49	31	25	7	2	1	2	9	0	33	0	0	3	2	.600	0	0--	—	4.93
1993 Milwaukee	AL	6	0	0	4	9.1	37	3	0	0	0	0	0	1	5	0	7	0	0	0	0	.000	0	1-2	0	0.00
1994 Milwaukee	AL	7	0	0	1	10.2	52	15	12	10	4	0	2	0	8	0	8	0	0	1	0	1.000	0	0-0	3	8.44
1995 Milwaukee	AL	24	0	0	7	49.2	209	37	20	19	6	0	0	0	27	2	41	4	0	4	1	.800	0	0-0	2	3.44
1996 Milwaukee	AL	7	0	0	2	10	48	15	9	9	1	1	0	0	5	1	5	1	1	0	0	.000	0	0-0	1	8.10
4 ML YEARS		44	0	0	14	79.2	346	70	41	38	11	1	3	1	45	3	61	5	1	5	1	.833	0	1-2	6	4.29

Brooks Kieschnick

Bats: Left **Throws:** Right **Pos:** PH-20; RF-5; LF-4   **Ht:** 6'4" **Wt:** 225 **Born:** 6/6/72 **Age:** 25

		BATTING																	BASERUNNING			PERCENTAGES		
Year Team	Lg	G	AB	H	2B	3B	HR	(Hm	Rd)	TB	R	RBI	TBB	IBB	SO	HBP	SH	SF	SB	CS	SB%	GDP	Avg	OBP	SLG
1993 Cubs	R	3	9	2	1	0	0	—	—	3	0	0	0	0	1	0	0	0	0	0	.00	0	.222	.222	.333
Daytona	A+	6	22	4	2	0	0	—	—	6	1	2	1	0	4	0	0	0	0	1	.00	1	.182	.217	.273
Orlando	AA	25	91	31	8	0	2	—	—	45	12	10	7	1	19	0	0	0	1	2	.33	0	.341	.388	.495
1994 Orlando	AA	126	468	132	25	3	14	—	—	205	57	55	33	3	78	4	0	4	3	5	.38	10	.282	.332	.438
1995 Iowa	AAA	138	505	149	30	1	23	—	—	250	61	73	58	7	91	4	0	3	2	3	.40	11	.295	.370	.495
1996 Iowa	AAA	117	441	114	20	1	18	—	—	190	47	64	37	4	108	0	0	2	0	1	.00	8	.259	.315	.431
1996 Chicago	NL	25	29	10	2	0	1	(0	1)	15	6	6	3	0	8	0	0	0	0	0	.00	0	.345	.406	.517

Darryl Kile

Pitches: Right **Bats:** Right **Pos:** SP-33; RP-2   **Ht:** 6'5" **Wt:** 185 **Born:** 12/2/68 **Age:** 28

		HOW MUCH HE PITCHED						WHAT HE GAVE UP										THE RESULTS					
Year Team	Lg	G	GS	CG	GF	IP	BFP	H	R	ER	HR	SH	SF	HB	TBB	IBB	SO	WP	Bk	W	L	Pct.	ShO	Sv-Op	Hld	ERA
1991 Houston	NL	37	22	0	5	153.2	689	144	81	63	16	9	5	6	84	4	100	5	4	7	11	.389	0	0-1	0	3.69
1992 Houston	NL	22	22	2	0	125.1	554	124	61	55	8	5	6	4	63	4	90	3	4	5	10	.333	0	0-0	0	3.95

		HOW MUCH HE PITCHED						WHAT HE GAVE UP												THE RESULTS						
Year Team	Lg	G	GS	CG	GF	IP	BFP	H	R	ER	HR	SH	SF	HB	TBB	IBB	SO	WP	Bk	W	L	Pct.	ShO	Sv-Op	Hld	ERA
1993 Houston	NL	32	26	4	0	171.2	733	152	73	67	12	5	7	15	69	1	141	9	3	15	8	.652	2	0-0	0	3.51
1994 Houston	NL	24	24	0	0	147.2	664	153	84	75	13	14	2	9	82	6	105	10	0	9	6	.600	0	0-0	0	4.57
1995 Houston	NL	25	21	0	1	127	570	114	81	70	5	7	3	12	73	2	113	11	1	4	12	.250	0	0-0	0	4.96
1996 Houston	NL	35	33	4	1	219	975	233	113	102	16	10	9	16	97	8	219	13	3	12	11	.522	0	0-0	0	4.19
6 ML YEARS		175	148	10	7	944.1	4185	920	493	432	70	50	32	62	468	25	768	51	15	52	58	.473	2	0-1	0	4.12

Jeff King

Bats: R **Throws:** R **Pos:** 1B-92; 2B-71; 3B-17; PH-6   **Ht:** 6'1" **Wt:** 184 **Born:** 12/26/64   **Age:** 32

		BATTING															BASERUNNING				PERCENTAGES		
Year Team	Lg	G	AB	H	2B	3B	HR	(Hm | Rd)	TB	R	RBI	TBB	IBB	SO	HBP	SH	SF	SB	CS	SB%	GDP	Avg	OBP	SLG
1989 Pittsburgh	NL	75	215	42	13	3	5	(3 | 2)	76	31	19	20	1	34	2	2	4	4	2	.67	3	.195	.266	.353
1990 Pittsburgh	NL	127	371	91	17	1	14	(9 | 5)	152	46	53	21	1	50	1	2	7	3	3	.50	12	.245	.283	.410
1991 Pittsburgh	NL	33	109	26	1	1	4	(3 | 1)	41	16	18	14	3	15	1	0	1	3	1	.75	3	.239	.328	.376
1992 Pittsburgh	NL	130	480	111	21	2	14	(6 | 8)	178	56	65	27	3	56	2	8	5	4	6	.40	8	.231	.272	.371
1993 Pittsburgh	NL	158	611	180	35	3	9	(4 | 5)	248	82	98	59	4	54	4	1	8	8	6	.57	17	.295	.356	.406
1994 Pittsburgh	NL	94	339	89	23	0	5	(2 | 3)	127	36	42	30	1	38	0	2	7	3	2	.60	7	.263	.316	.375
1995 Pittsburgh	NL	122	445	118	27	2	18	(7 | 11)	203	61	87	55	5	63	1	0	8	7	4	.64	10	.265	.342	.456
1996 Pittsburgh	NL	155	591	160	36	4	30	(14 | 16)	294	91	111	70	3	95	2	1	8	15	1	.94	17	.271	.346	.497
8 ML YEARS		894	3161	817	173	16	99	(48 | 51)	1319	419	493	296	21	405	13	16	48	47	25	.65	77	.258	.320	.417

Mike Kingery

Bats: L **Throws:** L **Pos:** CF-64; PH-44; RF-16; LF-5   **Ht:** 6'0" **Wt:** 185 **Born:** 3/29/61   **Age:** 36

		BATTING															BASERUNNING				PERCENTAGES		
Year Team	Lg	G	AB	H	2B	3B	HR	(Hm | Rd)	TB	R	RBI	TBB	IBB	SO	HBP	SH	SF	SB	CS	SB%	GDP	Avg	OBP	SLG
1986 Kansas City	AL	62	209	54	8	5	3	(1 | 2)	81	25	14	12	2	30	0	0	2	7	3	.70	4	.258	.296	.388
1987 Seattle	AL	120	354	99	25	4	9	(5 | 4)	159	38	52	27	0	43	2	1	6	7	9	.44	4	.280	.329	.449
1988 Seattle	AL	57	123	25	6	0	1	(1 | 0)	34	21	9	19	1	23	1	1	1	3	1	.75	1	.203	.313	.276
1989 Seattle	AL	31	76	17	3	0	2	(2 | 0)	26	14	6	7	0	14	0	0	1	1	1	.50	2	.224	.286	.342
1990 San Francisco	NL	105	207	61	7	1	0	(0 | 0)	70	24	24	12	0	19	1	5	1	6	1	.86	1	.295	.335	.338
1991 San Francisco	NL	91	110	20	2	2	0	(0 | 0)	26	13	8	15	1	21	0	0	0	1	0	1.00	3	.182	.280	.236
1992 Oakland	AL	12	28	3	0	0	0	(0 | 0)	3	3	1	1	0	3	0	0	0	0	0	.00	1	.107	.138	.107
1994 Colorado	NL	105	301	105	27	8	4	(0 | 4)	160	56	41	30	2	26	2	5	8	5	7	.42	8	.349	.402	.532
1995 Colorado	NL	119	350	94	18	4	8	(4 | 4)	144	66	37	45	1	40	0	6	1	13	5	.72	7	.269	.351	.411
1996 Pittsburgh	NL	117	276	68	12	2	3	(2 | 1)	93	32	27	23	2	29	1	1	3	2	1	.67	5	.246	.304	.337
10 ML YEARS		819	2034	546	108	26	30	(15 | 15)	796	292	219	191	9	248	7	19	23	45	28	.62	36	.268	.330	.391

Gene Kingsale

Bats: Both **Throws:** Right **Pos:** CF-2; PH-1   **Ht:** 6'3" **Wt:** 170 **Born:** 8/20/76   **Age:** 20

		BATTING															BASERUNNING				PERCENTAGES		
Year Team	Lg	G	AB	H	2B	3B	HR	(Hm	Rd)	TB	R	RBI	TBB	IBB	SO	HBP	SH	SF	SB	CS	SB%	GDP	Avg	OBP	SLG
1994 Orioles	R	50	168	52	2	3	0	—	—	60	26	9	18	0	24	2	1	1	15	8	.65	1	.310	.381	.357
1995 Bluefield	R+	47	171	54	11	2	0	—	—	69	45	16	27	0	31	5	4	2	20	8	.71	0	.316	.420	.404
1996 Frederick	A+	49	166	45	6	4	0	—	—	59	26	9	19	1	32	6	3	2	23	4	.85	1	.271	.363	.355
1996 Baltimore	AL	3	0	0	0	0	0	(0	0)	0	0	0	0	0	0	0	0	0	0	0	.00	0	.000	.000	.000

Wayne Kirby

Bats: L **Throws:** R **Pos:** CF-53; PH-26; LF-10; RF-10; DH-3   **Ht:** 5'10" **Wt:** 190 **Born:** 1/22/64   **Age:** 33

		BATTING															BASERUNNING				PERCENTAGES		
Year Team	Lg	G	AB	H	2B	3B	HR	(Hm | Rd)	TB	R	RBI	TBB	IBB	SO	HBP	SH	SF	SB	CS	SB%	GDP	Avg	OBP	SLG
1991 Cleveland	AL	21	43	9	2	0	0	(0 | 0)	11	4	5	2	0	6	0	1	1	1	2	.33	2	.209	.239	.256
1992 Cleveland	AL	21	18	3	1	0	1	(0 | 1)	7	9	1	3	0	2	0	0	0	0	3	.00	1	.167	.286	.389
1993 Cleveland	AL	131	458	123	19	5	6	(4 | 2)	170	71	60	37	2	58	3	7	6	17	5	.77	8	.269	.323	.371
1994 Cleveland	AL	78	191	56	6	0	5	(3 | 2)	77	33	23	13	0	30	1	4	2	11	4	.73	1	.293	.341	.403
1995 Cleveland	AL	101	188	39	10	2	1	(0 | 1)	56	29	14	13	0	32	1	1	2	10	3	.77	4	.207	.260	.298
1996 Cle-LA		92	204	55	11	1	1	(0 | 1)	71	26	12	19	1	19	1	1	4	4	3	.57	4	.270	.333	.348
1996 Cleveland	AL	27	16	4	1	0	0	(0 | 0)	5	3	1	2	0	2	0	0	0	0	1	.00	1	.250	.333	.313
Los Angeles	NL	65	188	51	10	1	1	(0 | 1)	66	23	11	17	1	17	1	1	4	4	2	.67	3	.271	.333	.351
6 ML YEARS		444	1102	285	49	8	14	(7 | 7)	392	172	115	87	3	147	6	12	10	43	20	.68	20	.259	.314	.356

Ryan Klesko

Bats: Left **Throws:** Left **Pos:** LF-144; PH-9; 1B-2   **Ht:** 6'3" **Wt:** 220 **Born:** 6/12/71   **Age:** 26

		BATTING															BASERUNNING				PERCENTAGES		
Year Team	Lg	G	AB	H	2B	3B	HR	(Hm | Rd)	TB	R	RBI	TBB	IBB	SO	HBP	SH	SF	SB	CS	SB%	GDP	Avg	OBP	SLG
1992 Atlanta	NL	13	14	0	0	0	0	(0 | 0)	0	0	1	0	0	5	1	0	0	0	0	.00	0	.000	.067	.000
1993 Atlanta	NL	22	17	6	1	0	2	(2 | 0)	13	3	5	3	1	4	0	0	0	0	0	.00	0	.353	.450	.765
1994 Atlanta	NL	92	245	68	13	3	17	(7 | 10)	138	42	47	26	3	48	1	0	4	1	0	1.00	8	.278	.344	.563
1995 Atlanta	NL	107	329	102	25	2	23	(15 | 8)	200	48	70	47	10	72	2	0	3	5	4	.56	8	.310	.396	.608
1996 Atlanta	NL	153	528	149	21	4	34	(20 | 14)	280	90	93	68	10	129	2	0	4	6	3	.67	10	.282	.364	.530

Year Team	Lg	G	AB	H	2B	3B	HR	(Hm	Rd)	TB	R	RBI	TBB	IBB	SO	HBP	SH	SF	SB	CS	SB%	GDP	Avg	OBP	SLG
5 ML YEARS		387	1133	325	60	9	76	(44	32)	631	183	216	144	24	258	6	0	11	12	7	.63	26	.287	.367	.557

Scott Klingenbeck

Pitches: Right **Bats:** Right **Pos:** RP-7; SP-3   **Ht:** 6'2" **Wt:** 205 **Born:** 2/3/71 **Age:** 26

Year Team	Lg	G	GS	CG	GF	IP	BFP	H	R	ER	HR	SH	SF	HB	TBB	IBB	SO	WP	Bk	W	L	Pct.	ShO	Sv-Op	Hld	ERA
1996 Salt Lake *	AAA	22	22	5	0	150.2	635	159	64	52	8	4	6	3	41	2	100	9	1	9	3	.750	2	0--	—	3.11
1994 Baltimore	AL	1	1	0	0	7	31	6	4	3	1	0	1	1	4	1	5	0	0	1	0	1.000	0	0-0	0	3.86
1995 Bal-Min	AL	24	9	0	4	79.2	373	101	65	63	22	3	1	4	42	0	42	7	0	2	4	.333	0	0-0	0	7.12
1996 Minnesota	AL	10	3	0	2	28.2	137	42	28	25	5	1	1	1	10	0	15	1	0	1	1	.500	0	0-1	0	7.85
1995 Baltimore	AL	6	5	0	0	31.1	137	32	17	17	6	0	0	0	18	0	15	2	0	2	2	.500	0	0-0	0	4.88
Minnesota	AL	18	4	0	4	48.1	236	69	48	46	16	3	1	4	24	0	27	5	0	0	2	.000	0	0-0	0	8.57
3 ML YEARS		35	13	0	6	115.1	541	149	97	91	28	4	3	6	56	1	62	8	0	4	5	.444	0	0-1	0	7.10

Joe Klink

Pitches: Left **Bats:** Left **Pos:** RP-3   **Ht:** 5'11" **Wt:** 175 **Born:** 2/3/62 **Age:** 35

Year Team	Lg	G	GS	CG	GF	IP	BFP	H	R	ER	HR	SH	SF	HB	TBB	IBB	SO	WP	Bk	W	L	Pct.	ShO	Sv-Op	Hld	ERA
1996 Tacoma *	AAA	7	0	0	3	6.2	32	9	3	3	0	1	1	1	3	0	4	0	0	1	0	1.000	0	0--	—	4.05
1987 Minnesota	AL	12	0	0	5	23	116	37	18	17	4	1	1	0	11	0	17	1	0	0	1	.000	0	0-0	1	6.65
1990 Oakland	AL	40	0	0	19	39.2	165	34	9	9	1	1	0	0	18	0	19	3	1	0	0	.000	0	1-1	4	2.04
1991 Oakland	AL	62	0	0	10	62	266	60	30	30	4	8	0	5	21	5	34	4	0	10	3	.769	0	2-4	16	4.35
1993 Florida	NL	59	0	0	10	37.2	168	37	22	21	0	2	3	0	24	4	22	1	2	0	2	.000	0	0-0	5	5.02
1996 Seattle	AL	3	0	0	1	2.1	11	3	1	1	1	0	0	0	1	0	2	0	0	0	0	.000	0	0-0	0	3.86
5 ML YEARS		176	0	0	45	164.2	726	171	80	78	10	12	4	5	75	9	94	9	3	10	6	.625	0	3-5	30	4.26

Brent Knackert

Pitches: Right **Bats:** Right **Pos:** RP-8   **Ht:** 6'3" **Wt:** 195 **Born:** 8/1/69 **Age:** 27

Year Team	Lg	G	GS	CG	GF	IP	BFP	H	R	ER	HR	SH	SF	HB	TBB	IBB	SO	WP	Bk	W	L	Pct.	ShO	Sv-Op	Hld	ERA
1996 Trenton *	AA	11	0	0	10	13	50	6	2	2	0	2	0	0	6	1	21	2	0	0	0	.000	0	10--	—	1.38
Pawtucket *	AAA	19	5	0	4	47	209	48	32	27	11	0	2	2	26	0	34	4	0	2	3	.400	0	2--	—	5.17
1990 Seattle	AL	24	2	0	6	37.1	186	50	28	27	5	1	2	2	21	2	28	3	0	1	1	.500	0	0-0	1	6.51
1996 Boston	AL	8	0	0	2	10	53	16	12	10	1	0	1	0	7	1	5	1	0	0	0	.000	0	0-0	0	9.00
2 ML YEARS		32	2	0	8	47.1	239	66	40	37	6	1	3	2	28	3	33	4	0	1	2	.333	0	0-0	1	7.04

Chuck Knoblauch

Bats: Right **Throws:** Right **Pos:** 2B-151; DH-1; PH-1   **Ht:** 5'9" **Wt:** 181 **Born:** 7/7/68 **Age:** 28

Year Team	Lg	G	AB	H	2B	3B	HR	(Hm	Rd)	TB	R	RBI	TBB	IBB	SO	HBP	SH	SF	SB	CS	SB%	GDP	Avg	OBP	SLG
1991 Minnesota	AL	151	565	159	24	6	1	(1	0)	198	78	50	59	0	40	4	1	5	25	5	.83	8	.281	.351	.350
1992 Minnesota	AL	155	600	178	19	6	2	(0	2)	215	104	56	88	1	60	5	2	12	34	13	.72	8	.297	.384	.358
1993 Minnesota	AL	153	602	167	27	4	2	(2	0)	208	82	41	65	1	44	9	4	5	29	11	.73	11	.277	.354	.346
1994 Minnesota	AL	109	445	139	45	3	5	(1	4)	205	85	51	41	2	56	10	0	3	35	6	.85	13	.312	.381	.461
1995 Minnesota	AL	136	538	179	34	8	11	(4	7)	262	107	63	78	3	95	10	0	3	46	18	.72	15	.333	.424	.487
1996 Minnesota	AL	153	578	197	35	14	13	(7	6)	299	140	72	98	6	74	19	0	9	45	14	.76	9	.341	.448	.517
6 ML YEARS		857	3328	1019	184	41	34	(15	19)	1387	596	333	429	13	369	57	7	34	214	67	.76	64	.306	.391	.417

Randy Knorr

Bats: Right **Throws:** Right **Pos:** C-33; PH-4   **Ht:** 6'2" **Wt:** 215 **Born:** 11/12/68 **Age:** 28

Year Team	Lg	G	AB	H	2B	3B	HR	(Hm	Rd)	TB	R	RBI	TBB	IBB	SO	HBP	SH	SF	SB	CS	SB%	GDP	Avg	OBP	SLG
1996 Syracuse *	AAA	12	36	10	5	0	0	(—	—)	15	1	5	5	1	8	0	1	0	0	0	.00	0	.278	.366	.417
1991 Toronto	AL	3	1	0	0	0	0	(0	0)	0	0	0	1	0	1	0	0	0	0	0	.00	0	.000	.500	.000
1992 Toronto	AL	8	19	5	0	0	0	(0	1)	8	1	2	1	1	5	0	0	0	0	0	.00	0	.263	.300	.421
1993 Toronto	AL	39	101	25	3	2	4	(2	2)	44	11	20	9	0	29	1	0	2	0	0	.00	2	.248	.309	.436
1994 Toronto	AL	40	124	30	2	0	7	(4	3)	53	20	19	10	0	35	1	0	1	0	0	.00	7	.242	.301	.427
1995 Toronto	AL	45	132	28	8	0	3	(2	1)	45	18	16	11	0	28	0	1	0	0	0	.00	5	.212	.273	.341
1996 Houston	NL	37	87	17	5	0	1	(1	0)	25	7	7	5	2	18	1	0	1	0	1	.00	1	.195	.245	.287
6 ML YEARS		172	464	105	18	2	16	(9	7)	175	57	64	37	3	116	2	3	2	0	1	.00	15	.226	.285	.377

Kevin Koslofski

Bats: L **Throws:** R **Pos:** CF-14; LF-6; PH-5; RF-2; DH-1   **Ht:** 5'8" **Wt:** 175 **Born:** 9/24/66 **Age:** 30

Year Team	Lg	G	AB	H	2B	3B	HR	(Hm	Rd)	TB	R	RBI	TBB	IBB	SO	HBP	SH	SF	SB	CS	SB%	GDP	Avg	OBP	SLG
1996 New Orleans *	AAA	75	238	55	8	3	4	(—	—)	81	39	25	31	1	64	2	2	2	5	2	.71	5	.231	.322	.340

		BATTING																BASERUNNING				PERCENTAGES		
Year Team	Lg	G	AB	H	2B	3B	HR	(Hm Rd)	TB	R	RBI	TBB	IBB	SO	HBP	SH	SF	SB	CS	SB%	GDP	Avg	OBP	SLG
1992 Kansas City	AL	55	133	33	0	2	3	(1 2)	46	20	13	12	0	23	1	3	1	2	1	.67	2	.248	.313	.346
1993 Kansas City	AL	15	26	7	0	0	1	(0 1)	10	4	2	4	0	5	1	1	0	0	1	.00	1	.269	.387	.385
1994 Kansas City	AL	2	4	1	0	0	0	(0 0)	1	2	0	2	1	1	0	0	0	0	0	.00	0	.250	.500	.250
1996 Milwaukee	AL	25	42	9	3	2	0	(0 0)	16	5	6	4	1	12	1	0	0	0	0	.00	0	.214	.298	.381
4 ML YEARS		97	205	50	3	4	4	(1 3)	73	31	21	22	2	41	3	4	1	2	2	.50	4	.244	.325	.356

Chad Kreuter

Bats: B **Throws:** R **Pos:** C-38; PH-20; 1B-2; DH-1   **Ht:** 6'2"   **Wt:** 200   **Born:** 8/26/64   **Age:** 32

		BATTING																BASERUNNING				PERCENTAGES		
Year Team	Lg	G	AB	H	2B	3B	HR	(Hm Rd)	TB	R	RBI	TBB	IBB	SO	HBP	SH	SF	SB	CS	SB%	GDP	Avg	OBP	SLG
1988 Texas	AL	16	51	14	2	1	1	(0 1)	21	3	5	7	0	13	0	0	0	0	0	.00	1	.275	.362	.412
1989 Texas	AL	87	158	24	3	0	5	(2 3)	42	16	9	27	0	40	0	6	1	0	1	.00	4	.152	.274	.266
1990 Texas	AL	22	22	1	1	0	0	(0 0)	2	2	2	8	0	9	0	1	1	0	0	.00	0	.045	.290	.091
1991 Texas	AL	3	4	0	0	0	0	(0 0)	0	0	0	0	0	1	0	0	0	0	0	.00	0	.000	.000	.000
1992 Detroit	AL	67	190	48	9	0	2	(2 0)	63	22	16	20	1	38	0	3	2	0	1	.00	8	.253	.321	.332
1993 Detroit	AL	119	374	107	23	3	15	(9 6)	181	59	51	49	4	92	3	2	3	2	1	.67	5	.286	.371	.484
1994 Detroit	AL	65	170	38	8	0	1	(1 0)	49	17	19	28	0	36	0	2	4	0	1	.00	0	.224	.327	.288
1995 Seattle	AL	26	75	17	5	0	1	(0 1)	25	12	8	5	0	22	2	1	0	0	0	.00	0	.227	.293	.333
1996 Chicago	AL	46	114	25	8	0	3	(2 1)	42	14	18	13	0	29	2	2	1	0	0	.00	5	.219	.308	.368
9 ML YEARS		451	1158	274	59	4	28	(16 12)	425	145	128	157	5	280	7	17	12	2	4	.33	23	.237	.328	.367

Rick Krivda

Pitches: Left   **Bats:** Right   **Pos:** SP-11; RP-11   **Ht:** 6'1"   **Wt:** 180   **Born:** 1/19/70   **Age:** 27

		HOW MUCH HE PITCHED						WHAT HE GAVE UP										THE RESULTS					
Year Team	Lg	G	GS	CG	GF	IP	BFP	H	R	ER	HR	SH	SF	HB	TBB	IBB	SO	WP	Bk	W	L	Pct.	ShO	Sv-Op	Hld	ERA
1991 Bluefield	R+	15	6	3	0	2	67	265	48	20	14	0	2	0	4	24	0	79	1	4	7	1	.875	0	1--	—	1.88
1992 Kane County	A	18	18	2	0	121.2	502	108	53	41	6	0	3	1	41	0	124	5	1	12	5	.706	0	0--	—	3.03
Frederick	A+	9	9	1	0	57.1	236	51	23	19	7	0	0	1	15	0	64	1	1	5	1	.833	1	0--	—	2.98
1993 Bowie	AA	22	22	0	0	125.2	522	114	46	43	10	2	1	2	50	0	108	1	2	7	5	.583	0	0--	—	3.08
Rochester	AAA	5	5	0	0	33.1	133	20	7	7	2	1	0	1	16	0	23	1	0	3	0	1.000	0	0--	—	1.89
1994 Rochester	AAA	28	26	3	2	163	688	149	75	64	12	1	6	4	73	4	122	9	1	9	10	.474	2	0--	—	3.53
1995 Rochester	AAA	16	16	1	0	101.2	429	96	44	36	11	6	4	2	32	0	74	3	3	6	5	.545	1	0--	—	3.19
1996 Rochester	AAA	8	8	0	0	44	191	51	24	21	6	0	1	1	15	0	34	2	2	3	1	.750	0	0--	—	4.30
1995 Baltimore	AL	13	13	1	0	75.1	319	76	40	38	9	0	4	4	25	1	53	0	2	2	7	.222	0	0--	0	4.54
1996 Baltimore	AL	22	11	0	4	81.2	359	89	48	45	14	2	2	1	39	2	54	3	1	3	5	.375	0	0-0	1	4.96
2 ML YEARS		35	24	1	4	157	678	165	88	83	23	2	6	5	64	3	107	5	3	5	12	.294	0	0-0	1	4.76

Kerry Lacy

Pitches: Right   **Bats:** Right   **Pos:** RP-11   **Ht:** 6'2"   **Wt:** 215   **Born:** 8/7/72   **Age:** 24

		HOW MUCH HE PITCHED						WHAT HE GAVE UP										THE RESULTS					
Year Team	Lg	G	GS	CG	GF	IP	BFP	H	R	ER	HR	SH	SF	HB	TBB	IBB	SO	WP	Bk	W	L	Pct.	ShO	Sv-Op	Hld	ERA
1991 Butte	R+	24	2	0	6	48	221	47	34	30	5	0	2	6	36	0	45	15	4	2	1	.667	0	1--	—	5.63
1992 Gastonia	A	49	0	0	32	55.2	262	55	35	24	2	2	0	1	42	2	57	9	2	3	7	.300	0	17--	—	3.88
1993 Charlstn-SC	A	58	0	0	57	60	267	49	25	21	1	3	5	5	32	5	54	6	2	0	6	.000	0	36--	—	3.15
Charlotte	A+	4	0	0	3	4.2	21	2	2	1	0	0	0	1	3	0	3	1	0	0	0	.000	0	2--	—	1.93
1994 Tulsa	AA	41	0	0	35	63.2	270	49	30	26	4	3	2	3	37	4	46	3	1	2	6	.250	0	12--	—	3.68
1995 Okla. City	AAA	1	0	0	1	2.1	7	0	0	0	0	0	0	0	0	0	1	0	0	0	0	.000	0	1--	—	0.00
1996 Tulsa	AA	2	0	0	2	4	15	3	0	0	0	1	0	2	0	0	1	0	0	0	0	.000	0	2--	—	0.00
Okla. City	AAA	37	0	0	28	56	232	48	21	18	2	2	0	0	15	2	31	2	0	3	3	.500	0	6--	—	2.89
Pawtucket	AAA	7	0	0	6	8	26	1	0	0	0	0	0	0	2	0	8	0	0	0	0	.000	0	4--	—	0.00
1996 Boston	AL	11	0	0	3	10.2	54	15	5	4	2	0	0	0	8	0	9	0	0	2	0	1.000	0	0-2	1	3.38

Tom Lampkin

Bats: Left   **Throws:** Right   **Pos:** C-53; PH-18   **Ht:** 5'11"   **Wt:** 185   **Born:** 3/4/64   **Age:** 33

		BATTING																BASERUNNING				PERCENTAGES		
Year Team	Lg	G	AB	H	2B	3B	HR	(Hm Rd)	TB	R	RBI	TBB	IBB	SO	HBP	SH	SF	SB	CS	SB%	GDP	Avg	OBP	SLG
1996 San Jose *	A+	2	7	2	0	1	0	— —	4	2	2	1	0	2	0	0	0	0	0	.00	0	.286	.375	.571
1988 Cleveland	AL	4	4	0	0	0	0	(0 0)	0	0	0	1	0	0	0	0	0	0	0	.00	1	.000	.200	.000
1990 San Diego	NL	26	63	14	0	1	1	(1 0)	19	4	4	4	1	9	0	0	0	0	1	.00	2	.222	.269	.302
1991 San Diego	NL	38	58	11	3	1	0	(0 0)	16	4	3	3	0	9	0	1	0	0	0	.00	0	.190	.230	.276
1992 San Diego	NL	9	17	4	0	0	0	(0 0)	4	3	0	6	0	1	1	0	0	2	0	1.00	0	.235	.458	.235
1993 Milwaukee	AL	73	162	32	8	0	4	(1 3)	52	22	25	20	3	26	0	2	4	7	3	.70	2	.198	.280	.321
1995 San Francisco	NL	65	76	21	2	0	1	(1 0)	26	8	9	9	1	8	1	0	1	2	0	1.00	1	.276	.360	.342
1996 San Francisco	NL	66	177	41	8	0	6	(5 1)	67	26	29	20	2	22	5	0	2	1	5	.17	2	.232	.324	.379
7 ML YEARS		281	557	123	21	2	12	(8 4)	184	67	70	63	7	75	7	2	6	12	9	.57	8	.221	.305	.330

Mark Langston

Pitches: Left **Bats:** Right **Pos:** SP-18 **Ht:** 6'2" **Wt:** 184 **Born:** 8/20/60 **Age:** 36

		HOW MUCH HE PITCHED						WHAT HE GAVE UP										THE RESULTS						
Year Team	Lg	G	GS	CG	GF	IP	BFP	H	R	ER	HR	SH	SF	HB	TBB	IBB	SO	WP	Bk	W	L	Pct.	ShO	Sv-Op	Hld	ERA
1996 Lk Elsinore *	A+	1	1	0	0	4	13	3	0	0	0	0	0	0	0	0	5	0	0	0	0	.000	0	0- -	—	0.00
1984 Seattle	AL	35	33	5	0	225	965	188	99	85	16	13	7	8	118	5	204	4	2	17	10	.630	2	0- -	—	3.40
1985 Seattle	AL	24	24	2	0	126.2	577	122	85	77	22	3	2	2	91	1	72	3	3	7	14	.333	0	0- -	—	5.47
1986 Seattle	AL	37	36	9	1	239.1	1057	234	142	129	30	5	8	4	123	1	245	10	3	12	14	.462	0	0- -	—	4.85
1987 Seattle	AL	35	35	14	0	272	1152	242	132	116	30	12	6	5	114	0	262	9	2	19	13	.594	3	0-0	0	3.84
1988 Seattle	AL	35	35	9	0	261.1	1078	222	108	97	32	6	5	3	110	2	235	7	4	15	11	.577	3	0-0	0	3.34
1989 Sea-Mon		34	34	8	0	250	1037	198	87	76	16	9	7	4	112	6	235	6	4	16	14	.533	5	0-0	0	2.74
1990 California	AL	33	33	5	0	223	950	215	120	109	13	6	6	5	104	1	195	8	0	10	17	.370	1	0-0	0	4.40
1991 California	AL	34	34	7	0	246.1	992	190	89	82	30	4	6	2	96	3	183	6	0	19	8	.704	0	0-0	0	3.00
1992 California	AL	32	32	9	0	229	941	206	103	93	14	4	5	6	74	2	174	5	0	13	14	.481	2	0-0	0	3.66
1993 California	AL	35	35	7	0	256.1	1039	220	100	91	22	3	8	1	85	2	196	10	2	16	11	.593	0	0-0	0	3.20
1994 California	AL	18	18	2	0	119.1	517	121	67	62	19	3	8	0	54	1	109	6	0	7	8	.467	1	0-0	0	4.68
1995 California	AL	31	31	2	0	200.1	859	212	109	103	21	11	3	3	64	1	142	5	1	15	7	.682	1	0-0	0	4.63
1996 California	AL	18	18	2	0	123.1	518	116	68	66	18	0	2	2	45	0	83	4	0	6	5	.545	0	0-0	0	4.82
1989 Seattle	AL	10	10	2	0	73.1	297	60	30	29	3	0	3	4	19	0	60	1	2	4	5	.444	1	0-0	—	3.56
Montreal	NL	24	24	6	0	176.2	740	138	57	47	13	9	4	0	93	6	175	5	2	12	9	.571	4	0-0	0	2.39
13 ML YEARS		401	398	81	1	2772	11682	2486	1309	1186	283	79	73	45	1190	26	2335	83	21	172	146	.541	18	0- -	—	3.85

Ray Lankford

Bats: Left **Throws:** Left **Pos:** CF-144; PH-7 **Ht:** 5'11" **Wt:** 200 **Born:** 6/5/67 **Age:** 30

		BATTING																BASERUNNING				PERCENTAGES		
Year Team	Lg	G	AB	H	2B	3B	HR	(Hm	Rd)	TB	R	RBI	TBB	IBB	SO	HBP	SH	SF	SB	CS	SB%	GDP	Avg	OBP	SLG
1990 St. Louis	NL	39	126	36	10	1	3	(2	1)	57	12	12	13	0	27	0	0	0	8	2	.80	1	.286	.353	.452
1991 St. Louis	NL	151	566	142	23	15	9	(4	5)	222	83	69	41	1	114	1	4	3	44	20	.69	4	.251	.301	.392
1992 St. Louis	NL	153	598	175	40	6	20	(13	7)	287	87	86	72	6	147	5	2	5	42	24	.64	5	.293	.371	.480
1993 St. Louis	NL	127	407	97	17	3	7	(6	1)	141	64	45	81	7	111	3	1	3	14	14	.50	5	.238	.366	.346
1994 St. Louis	NL	109	416	111	25	5	19	(8	11)	203	89	57	58	3	113	4	0	4	11	10	.52	0	.267	.359	.488
1995 St. Louis	NL	132	483	134	35	2	25	(16	9)	248	81	82	63	6	110	2	0	5	24	8	.75	10	.277	.360	.513
1996 St. Louis	NL	149	545	150	36	8	21	(8	13)	265	100	86	79	10	133	3	1	7	35	7	.83	12	.275	.366	.486
7 ML YEARS		860	3141	845	186	40	104	(57	47)	1423	516	437	407	33	755	18	8	27	178	85	.68	37	.269	.353	.453

Mike Lansing

Bats: Right **Throws:** Right **Pos:** 2B-159; SS-2 **Ht:** 6'0" **Wt:** 180 **Born:** 4/3/68 **Age:** 29

		BATTING																BASERUNNING				PERCENTAGES		
Year Team	Lg	G	AB	H	2B	3B	HR	(Hm	Rd)	TB	R	RBI	TBB	IBB	SO	HBP	SH	SF	SB	CS	SB%	GDP	Avg	OBP	SLG
1993 Montreal	NL	141	491	141	29	1	3	(1	2)	181	64	45	46	2	56	5	10	3	23	5	.82	16	.287	.352	.369
1994 Montreal	NL	106	394	105	21	2	5	(3	2)	145	44	35	30	3	37	7	2	2	12	8	.60	10	.266	.328	.368
1995 Montreal	NL	127	467	119	30	2	10	(4	6)	183	47	62	28	2	65	3	1	3	27	4	.87	14	.255	.299	.392
1996 Montreal	NL	159	641	183	40	2	11	(3	8)	260	99	53	44	1	85	10	9	1	23	8	.74	19	.285	.341	.406
4 ML YEARS		533	1993	548	120	7	29	(11	18)	769	254	195	148	8	243	25	22	9	85	25	.77	59	.275	.331	.386

Andy Larkin

Pitches: Right **Bats:** Right **Pos:** SP-1 **Ht:** 6'4" **Wt:** 175 **Born:** 6/27/74 **Age:** 23

		HOW MUCH HE PITCHED						WHAT HE GAVE UP										THE RESULTS						
Year Team	Lg	G	GS	CG	GF	IP	BFP	H	R	ER	HR	SH	SF	HB	TBB	IBB	SO	WP	Bk	W	L	Pct.	ShO	Sv-Op	Hld	ERA
1992 Marlins	R	14	4	0	2	41.1	187	41	26	24	0	1	1	7	19	0	20	4	0	1	2	.333	0	2- -	—	5.23
1993 Elmira	A-	14	14	4	0	88	368	74	43	29	1	1	3	12	23	0	89	9	1	5	7	.417	1	0- -	—	2.97
1994 Kane County	A	21	21	3	0	140	577	125	53	44	6	3	3	19	27	0	125	4	0	9	7	.563	1	0- -	—	2.83
1995 Portland	AA	9	9	0	0	40	160	29	16	15	5	4	0	6	11	2	23	1	0	1	2	.333	0	0- -	—	3.38
1996 Brevard Cty	A+	6	6	0	0	27.2	126	34	20	13	0	0	1	7	7	0	18	3	0	0	4	.000	0	0- -	—	4.23
Portland	AA	8	8	0	0	49.1	195	45	18	17	6	2	0	2	10	0	40	3	0	4	1	.800	0	0- -	—	3.10
1996 Florida	NL	1	1	0	0	5	22	3	1	1	0	0	0	0	4	0	2	0	0	0	0	.000	0	0-0	0	1.80

Barry Larkin

Bats: Right **Throws:** Right **Pos:** SS-151; PH-4 **Ht:** 6'0" **Wt:** 195 **Born:** 4/28/64 **Age:** 33

		BATTING																BASERUNNING				PERCENTAGES		
Year Team	Lg	G	AB	H	2B	3B	HR	(Hm	Rd)	TB	R	RBI	TBB	IBB	SO	HBP	SH	SF	SB	CS	SB%	GDP	Avg	OBP	SLG
1986 Cincinnati	NL	41	159	45	4	3	3	(3	0)	64	27	19	9	1	21	0	0	1	8	0	1.00	2	.283	.320	.403
1987 Cincinnati	NL	125	439	107	16	2	12	(6	6)	163	64	43	36	3	52	5	5	3	21	6	.78	8	.244	.306	.371
1988 Cincinnati	NL	151	588	174	32	5	12	(9	3)	252	91	56	41	3	24	8	10	5	40	7	.85	7	.296	.347	.429
1989 Cincinnati	NL	97	325	111	14	4	4	(1	3)	145	47	36	20	5	23	2	2	8	10	5	.67	7	.342	.375	.446
1990 Cincinnati	NL	158	614	185	25	6	7	(4	3)	243	85	67	49	3	49	7	7	4	30	5	.86	14	.301	.358	.396
1991 Cincinnati	NL	123	464	140	27	4	20	(16	4)	235	88	69	55	1	64	3	3	2	24	6	.80	7	.302	.378	.506
1992 Cincinnati	NL	140	533	162	32	6	12	(8	4)	242	76	78	63	6	58	4	2	7	15	4	.79	13	.304	.377	.454
1993 Cincinnati	NL	100	384	121	20	3	8	(4	4)	171	57	51	51	6	33	1	1	3	14	1	.93	13	.315	.394	.445
1994 Cincinnati	NL	110	427	119	23	5	9	(3	6)	179	78	52	64	3	58	0	5	5	26	2	.93	6	.279	.369	.419
1995 Cincinnati	NL	131	496	158	29	6	15	(8	7)	244	98	66	61	2	49	3	3	4	51	5	.91	6	.319	.394	.492

Year Team	Lg	G	AB	H	2B	3B	HR	(Hm	Rd)	TB	R	RBI	TBB	IBB	SO	HBP	SH	SF	SB	CS	SB%	GDP	Avg	OBP	SLG
1996 Cincinnati	NL	152	517	154	32	4	33	(14	19)	293	117	89	96	3	52	7	0	7	36	10	.78	20	.298	.410	.567
11 ML YEARS		1328	4946	1476	254	48	135	(76	59)	2231	828	626	545	38	483	40	38	49	275	51	.84	103	.298	.369	.451

Matt Lawton

Bats: L **Throws:** R **Pos:** RF-60; CF-18; PH-9; DH-1; LF-1   **Ht:** 5'10" **Wt:** 196 **Born:** 11/3/71   **Age:** 25

Year Team	Lg	G	AB	H	2B	3B	HR	(Hm	Rd)	TB	R	RBI	TBB	IBB	SO	HBP	SH	SF	SB	CS	SB%	GDP	Avg	OBP	SLG
1992 Twins	R	53	173	45	8	3	2	—	—	65	39	26	27	0	27	9	1	7	20	1	.95	2	.260	.375	.376
1993 Fort Wayne	A	111	340	97	21	3	9	—	—	151	50	38	65	3	43	8	0	2	23	15	.61	8	.285	.410	.444
1994 Fort Myers	A+	122	446	134	30	1	7	—	—	187	79	51	80	3	64	2	2	3	42	19	.69	7	.300	.407	.419
1995 New Britain	AA	114	412	111	19	5	13	—	—	179	75	54	56	1	70	12	2	3	26	9	.74	8	.269	.371	.434
1996 Salt Lake	AAA	53	212	63	16	1	7	—	—	102	40	33	26	0	34	3	0	2	2	4	.33	2	.297	.379	.481
1995 Minnesota	AL	21	60	19	4	1	1	(1	0)	28	11	12	7	0	11	3	0	0	1	1	.50	1	.317	.414	.467
1996 Minnesota	AL	79	252	65	7	1	6	(1	5)	92	34	42	28	1	28	4	0	2	4	4	.50	6	.258	.339	.365
2 ML YEARS		100	312	84	11	2	7	(2	5)	120	45	54	35	1	39	7	0	2	5	5	.50	7	.269	.354	.385

Phil Leftwich

Pitches: Right **Bats:** Right **Pos:** SP-2   **Ht:** 6'5" **Wt:** 205 **Born:** 5/19/69   **Age:** 28

Year Team	Lg	G	GS	CG	GF	IP	BFP	H	R	ER	HR	SH	SF	HB	TBB	IBB	SO	WP	Bk	W	L	Pct.	ShO	Sv-Op	Hld	ERA
1996 Vancouver *	AAA	19	19	3	0	110	477	113	75	63	14	3	6	8	41	1	87	7	0	6	6	.500	0	0--	—	5.15
Midland *	AA	6	6	1	0	40.1	154	33	14	13	4	1	0	4	4	0	33	1	0	4	2	.667	0	0--	—	2.90
1993 California	AL	12	12	1	0	80.2	343	81	35	34	5	3	1	3	27	1	31	1	0	4	6	.400	0	0-0	0	3.79
1994 California	AL	20	20	1	0	114	499	127	75	72	16	2	4	3	42	2	67	3	1	5	10	.333	0	0-0	0	5.68
1996 California	AL	2	2	0	0	7.1	35	12	9	6	1	0	0	0	3	0	4	0	0	0	1	.000	0	0-0	0	7.36
3 ML YEARS		34	34	2	0	202	877	220	119	112	22	5	5	6	72	3	102	4	1	9	17	.346	0	0-0	0	4.99

Dave Leiper

Pitches: Left **Bats:** Left **Pos:** RP-33   **Ht:** 6'1" **Wt:** 175 **Born:** 6/18/62   **Age:** 35

Year Team	Lg	G	GS	CG	GF	IP	BFP	H	R	ER	HR	SH	SF	HB	TBB	IBB	SO	WP	Bk	W	L	Pct.	ShO	Sv-Op	Hld	ERA
1996 Ottawa *	AAA	25	0	0	19	32.2	125	29	7	7	3	3	0	6	3	26	1	0	3	1	.750	0	6--	—	1.93
1984 Oakland	AL	8	0	0	2	7	39	12	7	7	2	0	0	0	5	0	3	1	0	1	0	1.000	0	0--	—	9.00
1986 Oakland	AL	33	0	0	9	31.2	136	28	17	17	3	2	3	2	18	4	15	2	0	2	2	.500	0	1--	—	4.83
1987 Oak-SD		57	0	0	7	68.1	291	65	36	30	8	4	4	1	23	0	43	3	1	3	1	.750	0	2-5	16	3.95
1988 San Diego	NL	35	0	0	10	54	217	45	19	13	1	3	5	0	14	5	33	2	0	3	0	1.000	0	1-1	3	2.17
1989 San Diego	NL	22	0	0	11	28.2	143	40	19	16	2	1	0	2	20	4	7	2	1	0	1	.000	0	0-0	1	5.02
1994 Oakland	AL	26	0	0	8	18.2	75	13	4	4	0	3	2	1	6	1	14	0	0	0	0	.000	0	1-1	3	1.93
1995 Oak-Mon	AL	50	0	0	10	44.2	191	39	18	16	5	2	0	1	19	1	22	0	1	1	3	.250	0	2-3	7	3.22
1996 Phi-Mon	NL	33	0	0	8	25	120	40	21	20	4	3	0	0	9	2	13	2	0	2	1	.667	0	0-3	3	7.20
1987 Oakland	AL	45	0	0	6	52.1	224	49	28	22	6	2	4	1	18	0	33	3	0	2	1	.667	0	1-4	16	3.78
San Diego	NL	12	0	0	1	16	67	16	8	8	2	2	0	0	5	0	10	0	1	1	0	1.000	0	1-1	0	4.50
1995 Oakland	AL	24	0	0	3	22.2	103	23	10	9	3	0	0	1	13	1	10	0	0	1	1	.500	0	0-0	2	3.57
Montreal	NL	26	0	0	7	22	88	16	8	7	2	2	0	0	6	0	12	0	1	0	2	.000	0	2-3	5	2.86
1996 Philadelphia	NL	26	0	0	8	21	97	31	16	15	4	1	0	0	7	2	10	2	0	2	0	1.000	0	0-0	3	6.43
Montreal	NL	7	0	0	0	4	23	9	5	5	0	2	0	0	2	0	3	0	0	0	1	.000	0	0-0	0	11.25
8 ML YEARS		264	0	0	65	278	1212	282	141	123	25	18	14	7	114	17	150	12	3	12	8	.600	0	7--	—	3.98

Al Leiter

Pitches: Left **Bats:** Left **Pos:** SP-33   **Ht:** 6'3" **Wt:** 215 **Born:** 10/12/65   **Age:** 31

Year Team	Lg	G	GS	CG	GF	IP	BFP	H	R	ER	HR	SH	SF	HB	TBB	IBB	SO	WP	Bk	W	L	Pct.	ShO	Sv-Op	Hld	ERA
1987 New York	AL	4	4	0	0	22.2	104	24	16	16	2	1	0	0	15	0	28	4	0	2	2	.500	0	0-0	0	6.35
1988 New York	AL	14	14	0	0	57.1	251	49	27	25	7	1	0	5	33	0	60	1	4	4	4	.500	0	0-0	0	3.92
1989 NYA-Tor	AL	5	5	0	0	33.1	154	32	23	21	2	1	1	2	23	0	26	2	1	1	2	.333	0	0-0	0	5.67
1990 Toronto	AL	4	0	0	2	6.1	22	1	0	0	0	0	0	0	2	0	5	0	0	0	0	.000	0	0-0	0	0.00
1991 Toronto	AL	3	0	0	1	1.2	13	3	5	5	0	1	0	0	5	0	1	0	0	0	0	.000	0	0-0	0	27.00
1992 Toronto	AL	1	0	0	0	1	7	1	1	1	0	0	0	0	2	0	0	0	0	0	0	.000	0	0-0	0	9.00
1993 Toronto	AL	34	12	1	4	105	454	93	52	48	8	3	3	4	56	2	66	2	2	9	6	.600	1	2-3	3	4.11
1994 Toronto	AL	20	20	1	0	111.2	516	125	68	63	6	3	8	2	65	3	100	7	5	6	7	.462	0	0-0	0	5.08
1995 Toronto	AL	28	28	2	0	183	805	162	80	74	15	6	4	6	108	1	153	14	0	11	11	.500	1	0-0	0	3.64
1996 Florida	NL	33	33	2	0	215.1	896	153	74	70	14	7	3	11	119	3	200	5	0	16	12	.571	1	0-0	0	2.93
1989 New York	AL	4	4	0	0	26.2	123	23	20	18	1	1	1	2	21	0	22	1	1	1	2	.333	0	0-0	0	6.08
Toronto	AL	1	1	0	0	6.2	31	9	3	3	1	0	0	0	2	0	4	1	0	0	0	.000	0	0-0	0	4.05
10 ML YEARS		146	116	6	7	737.1	3222	643	346	323	54	23	19	30	428	9	639	35	12	49	44	.527	3	2-3	3	3.94

Mark Leiter

Pitches: Right **Bats:** Right **Pos:** SP-34; RP-1   **Ht:** 6'3" **Wt:** 210 **Born:** 4/13/63 **Age:** 34

Year Team	Lg	G	GS	CG	GF	IP	BFP	H	R	ER	HR	SH	SF	HB	TBB	IBB	SO	WP	Bk	W	L	Pct.	ShO	Sv-Op	Hld	ERA
1990 New York	AL	8	3	0	2	26.1	119	33	20	20	5	2	1	2	9	0	21	0	0	1	1	.500	0	0-0	0	6.84
1991 Detroit	AL	38	15	1	7	134.2	578	125	66	63	16	5	6	6	50	4	103	2	0	9	7	.563	0	1-2	2	4.21
1992 Detroit	AL	35	14	1	7	112	475	116	57	52	9	2	8	3	43	5	75	3	0	8	5	.615	0	0-0	3	4.18
1993 Detroit	AL	27	13	1	4	106.2	471	111	61	56	17	3	5	3	44	5	70	5	0	6	6	.500	0	0-1	1	4.73
1994 California	AL	40	7	0	15	95.1	425	99	56	50	13	4	4	9	35	6	71	2	0	4	7	.364	0	2-3	3	4.72
1995 San Francisco	NL	30	29	7	0	195.2	817	185	91	83	19	10	6	17	55	4	129	9	3	10	12	.455	1	0-0	0	3.82
1996 SF-Mon	NL	35	34	2	0	205	904	219	128	112	37	12	6	16	69	8	164	6	4	8	12	.400	0	0-0	0	4.92
1996 San Francisco	NL	23	22	1	0	135.1	602	151	93	78	25	7	3	9	50	7	118	2	3	4	10	.286	0	0-0	0	5.19
Montreal	NL	12	12	1	0	69.2	302	68	35	34	12	5	3	7	19	1	46	4	1	4	2	.667	0	0-0	0	4.39
7 ML YEARS		213	115	12	35	875.2	3789	888	479	436	116	38	36	56	305	32	633	27	7	46	50	.479	1	3-6	9	4.48

Scott Leius

Bats: R **Throws:** R **Pos:** 3B-8; 1B-7; PH-7; 2B-6; DH-1   **Ht:** 6'3" **Wt:** 200 **Born:** 9/24/65 **Age:** 31

Year Team	Lg	G	AB	H	2B	3B	HR	(Hm	Rd)	TB	R	RBI	TBB	IBB	SO	HBP	SH	SF	SB	CS	SB%	GDP	Avg	OBP	SLG
1996 Buffalo *	AAA	35	123	33	3	1	4	—	—	50	22	17	12	1	16	2	0	1	0	0	.00	4	.268	.341	.407
1990 Minnesota	AL	14	25	6	1	0	1	(0	1)	10	4	4	2	0	2	0	1	0	0	0	.00	2	.240	.296	.400
1991 Minnesota	AL	109	199	57	7	2	5	(2	3)	83	35	20	30	1	35	0	5	1	5	5	.50	4	.286	.378	.417
1992 Minnesota	AL	129	409	102	18	2	2	(2	0)	130	50	35	34	0	61	1	5	0	6	5	.55	10	.249	.309	.318
1993 Minnesota	AL	10	18	3	0	0	0	(0	0)	3	4	2	2	0	4	0	0	2	0	0	.00	1	.167	.227	.167
1994 Minnesota	AL	97	350	86	16	1	14	(7	7)	146	57	49	37	0	58	1	1	2	2	4	.33	9	.246	.318	.417
1995 Minnesota	AL	117	372	92	16	5	4	(2	2)	130	51	45	49	3	54	2	0	4	2	1	.67	14	.247	.335	.349
1996 Cleveland	AL	27	43	6	4	0	1	(0	1)	13	3	3	2	0	8	0	1	0	0	0	.00	1	.140	.178	.302
7 ML YEARS		503	1416	352	62	10	27	(13	14)	515	204	158	156	4	222	4	13	9	15	15	.50	41	.249	.323	.364

Mark Lemke

Bats: Both **Throws:** Right **Pos:** 2B-133; PH-3   **Ht:** 5'9" **Wt:** 167 **Born:** 8/13/65 **Age:** 31

Year Team	Lg	G	AB	H	2B	3B	HR	(Hm	Rd)	TB	R	RBI	TBB	IBB	SO	HBP	SH	SF	SB	CS	SB%	GDP	Avg	OBP	SLG
1988 Atlanta	NL	16	58	13	4	0	0	(0	0)	17	8	2	4	0	5	0	2	0	0	2	.00	1	.224	.274	.293
1989 Atlanta	NL	14	55	10	2	1	2	(1	1)	20	4	10	5	0	7	0	0	0	0	1	.00	1	.182	.250	.364
1990 Atlanta	NL	102	239	54	13	0	0	(0	0)	67	22	21	21	3	22	0	4	2	0	1	.00	6	.226	.286	.280
1991 Atlanta	NL	136	269	63	11	2	2	(2	0)	84	36	23	29	2	27	0	6	4	1	2	.33	9	.234	.305	.312
1992 Atlanta	NL	155	427	97	7	4	6	(4	2)	130	38	26	50	11	39	0	12	2	0	3	.00	9	.227	.307	.304
1993 Atlanta	NL	151	493	124	19	2	7	(3	4)	168	52	49	65	13	50	0	5	6	1	2	.33	21	.252	.335	.341
1994 Atlanta	NL	104	350	103	15	0	3	(2	1)	127	40	31	38	12	37	0	6	0	0	3	.00	11	.294	.363	.363
1995 Atlanta	NL	116	399	101	16	5	5	(3	2)	142	42	38	44	4	40	0	7	3	2	2	.50	17	.253	.325	.356
1996 Atlanta	NL	135	498	127	17	0	5	(3	2)	159	64	37	53	1	48	0	5	6	5	2	.71	9	.255	.323	.319
9 ML YEARS		929	2788	692	104	14	30	(18	12)	914	306	237	309	46	275	0	47	23	9	18	.33	84	.248	.321	.328

Patrick Lennon

Bats: Right **Throws:** Right **Pos:** LF-11; PH-5; DH-1   **Ht:** 6'2" **Wt:** 200 **Born:** 4/27/68 **Age:** 29

Year Team	Lg	G	AB	H	2B	3B	HR	(Hm	Rd)	TB	R	RBI	TBB	IBB	SO	HBP	SH	SF	SB	CS	SB%	GDP	Avg	OBP	SLG
1996 Edmonton *	AAA	68	251	82	16	2	12	—	—	138	37	42	28	2	82	2	0	0	3	3	.50	9	.327	.399	.550
1991 Seattle	AL	9	8	1	1	0	0	(0	0)	2	2	1	3	0	1	0	0	0	0	0	.00	0	.125	.364	.250
1992 Seattle	AL	1	2	0	0	0	0	(0	0)	0	0	0	0	0	0	0	0	0	0	0	.00	0	.000	.000	.000
1996 Kansas City	AL	14	30	7	3	0	0	(0	0)	10	5	1	7	0	10	0	0	0	0	0	.00	0	.233	.378	.333
3 ML YEARS		24	40	8	4	0	0	(0	0)	12	7	2	10	0	11	0	0	0	0	0	.00	0	.200	.360	.300

Brian Lesher

Bats: R **Throws:** L **Pos:** LF-14; RF-14; PH-5; 1B-1   **Ht:** 6'5" **Wt:** 205 **Born:** 3/5/71 **Age:** 26

Year Team	Lg	G	AB	H	2B	3B	HR	(Hm	Rd)	TB	R	RBI	TBB	IBB	SO	HBP	SH	SF	SB	CS	SB%	GDP	Avg	OBP	SLG
1992 Sou. Oregon	A-	46	136	26	7	1	3	—	—	44	21	18	12	0	35	2	0	1	3	7	.30	3	.191	.265	.324
1993 Madison	A	119	394	108	13	5	5	—	—	146	63	47	46	0	102	9	6	6	20	9	.69	13	.274	.358	.371
1994 Modesto	A+	117	393	114	21	0	14	—	—	177	76	68	81	5	84	8	0	8	11	11	.50	8	.290	.414	.450
1995 Huntsville	AA	127	471	123	23	2	19	—	—	207	78	71	64	2	110	2	0	1	7	8	.47	7	.261	.351	.439
1996 Edmonton	AAA	109	414	119	29	2	18	—	—	206	57	75	36	0	108	7	2	3	6	5	.55	9	.287	.352	.498
1996 Oakland	AL	26	82	19	3	0	5	(2	3)	37	11	16	5	0	17	1	1	1	0	0	.00	2	.232	.281	.451

Curt Leskanic

Pitches: Right **Bats:** Right **Pos:** RP-70   **Ht:** 6'0" **Wt:** 180 **Born:** 4/2/68 **Age:** 29

		HOW MUCH HE PITCHED						WHAT HE GAVE UP										THE RESULTS						
Year Team	Lg	G	GS	CG	GF	IP	BFP	H	R	ER	HR	SH	SF	HB	TBB	IBB	SO	WP	Bk	W	L	Pct.	ShO	Sv-Op	Hld	ERA
1996 Colo. Sprng *	AAA	3	0	0	2	3	14	5	1	1	0	0	0	0	1	0	2	0	0	0	0	.000	0	0- -	—	3.00
1993 Colorado	NL	18	8	0	1	57	260	59	40	34	7	5	4	2	27	1	30	8	2	1	5	.167	0	0-0	0	5.37
1994 Colorado	NL	8	3	0	2	22.1	98	27	14	14	2	2	0	0	10	0	17	2	0	1	1	.500	0	0-0	0	5.64
1995 Colorado	NL	76	0	0	27	98	406	83	38	37	7	3	2	0	33	1	107	6	1	6	3	.667	0	10-16	19	3.40
1996 Colorado	NL	70	0	0	32	73.2	334	82	51	51	12	3	3	2	38	1	76	6	2	7	5	.583	0	6-10	9	6.23
4 ML YEARS		172	11	0	62	251	1098	251	143	136	28	13	9	4	108	3	230	22	5	15	14	.517	0	16-26	28	4.88

Al Levine

Pitches: Right **Bats:** Left **Pos:** RP-16   **Ht:** 6'3" **Wt:** 180 **Born:** 5/22/68 **Age:** 29

		HOW MUCH HE PITCHED						WHAT HE GAVE UP										THE RESULTS						
Year Team	Lg	G	GS	CG	GF	IP	BFP	H	R	ER	HR	SH	SF	HB	TBB	IBB	SO	WP	Bk	W	L	Pct.	ShO	Sv-Op	Hld	ERA
1991 Utica	A-	16	12	2	3	85	361	75	43	30	2	4	2	4	26	0	83	8	1	6	4	.600	1	1- -	—	3.18
1992 South Bend	A	23	23	2	0	156.2	650	151	67	49	6	6	2	8	36	1	131	9	1	9	5	.643	0	0- -	—	2.81
Sarasota	A+	3	2	0	0	15.2	68	17	11	7	1	3	2	0	5	1	11	0	1	0	2	.000	0	0- -	—	4.02
1993 Sarasota	A+	27	26	5	0	161.1	696	169	87	66	6	11	3	7	50	3	129	11	3	11	8	.579	1	0- -	—	3.68
1994 Birmingham	AA	18	18	1	0	114.1	501	117	50	42	7	2	3	14	44	1	94	3	0	5	9	.357	0	0- -	—	3.31
Nashville	AAA	8	4	0	1	24	116	34	23	21	2	1	3	2	11	0	24	0	0	0	2	.000	0	0- -	—	7.88
1995 Nashville	AAA	3	3	0	0	14	69	20	10	8	1	0	0	0	7	0	14	3	0	0	2	.000	0	0- -	—	5.14
1996 Nashville	AAA	43	0	0	28	61.2	267	58	27	25	4	2	2	3	24	6	45	1	0	4	5	.444	0	12- -	—	3.65
1996 Chicago	AL	16	0	0	5	18.1	85	22	14	11	1	0	1	1	7	1	12	0	0	0	1	.000	0	0-1	0	5.40

Jesse Levis

Bats: Left **Throws:** Right **Pos:** C-90; PH-33; DH-6   **Ht:** 5'9" **Wt:** 180 **Born:** 4/14/68 **Age:** 29

		BATTING															BASERUNNING				PERCENTAGES		
Year Team	Lg	G	AB	H	2B	3B	HR	(Hm | Rd)	TB	R	RBI	TBB	IBB	SO	HBP	SH	SF	SB	CS	SB%	GDP	Avg	OBP	SLG
1992 Cleveland	AL	28	43	12	4	0	1	(0 | 1)	19	2	3	0	0	5	0	0	0	0	0	.00	1	.279	.279	.442
1993 Cleveland	AL	31	63	11	2	0	0	(0 | 0)	13	7	4	2	0	10	0	1	1	0	0	.00	0	.175	.197	.206
1994 Cleveland	AL	1	1	1	0	0	0	(0 | 0)	1	0	0	0	0	0	0	0	0	0	0	.00	0	1.000	1.000	1.000
1995 Cleveland	AL	12	18	6	2	0	0	(0 | 0)	8	1	3	1	0	0	0	1	2	0	0	.00	0	.333	.333	.444
1996 Milwaukee	AL	104	233	55	6	1	1	(0 | 1)	66	27	21	38	0	15	2	1	0	0	0	.00	7	.236	.348	.283
5 ML YEARS		176	358	85	14	1	2	(0 | 2)	107	37	31	41	0	30	2	3	3	0	0	.00	9	.237	.317	.299

Darren Lewis

Bats: Right **Throws:** Right **Pos:** CF-137; PH-16; LF-1   **Ht:** 6'0" **Wt:** 189 **Born:** 8/28/67 **Age:** 29

		BATTING															BASERUNNING				PERCENTAGES		
Year Team	Lg	G	AB	H	2B	3B	HR	(Hm | Rd)	TB	R	RBI	TBB	IBB	SO	HBP	SH	SF	SB	CS	SB%	GDP	Avg	OBP	SLG
1990 Oakland	AL	25	35	8	0	0	0	(0 | 0)	8	4	1	7	0	4	1	3	0	2	0	1.00	2	.229	.372	.229
1991 San Francisco	NL	72	222	55	5	3	1	(0 | 1)	69	41	15	36	0	30	2	7	0	13	7	.65	1	.248	.358	.311
1992 San Francisco	NL	100	320	74	8	1	1	(1 | 0)	87	38	18	29	0	46	1	10	2	28	8	.78	3	.231	.295	.272
1993 San Francisco	NL	136	522	132	17	7	2	(2 | 0)	169	84	48	30	0	40	7	12	1	46	15	.75	4	.253	.302	.324
1994 San Francisco	NL	114	451	116	15	9	2	(4 | 0)	161	70	29	53	0	50	4	4	1	30	13	.70	6	.257	.340	.357
1995 SF-Cin	NL	132	472	118	13	3	1	(1 | 0)	140	66	24	34	0	57	8	12	1	32	18	.64	9	.250	.311	.297
1996 Chicago	AL	141	337	77	12	2	4	(0 | 4)	105	55	53	45	1	40	3	15	5	21	5	.81	9	.228	.321	.312
1995 San Francisco	NL	74	309	78	10	3	1	(1 | 0)	97	47	16	17	0	37	6	7	1	21	7	.75	6	.252	.303	.314
Cincinnati	NL	58	163	40	3	0	0	(0 | 0)	43	19	8	17	0	20	2	5	0	11	11	.50	3	.245	.324	.264
7 ML YEARS		720	2359	580	70	25	13	(8 | 5)	739	358	188	234	1	267	26	63	10	172	66	.72	34	.246	.320	.313

Mark Lewis

Bats: Right **Throws:** Right **Pos:** 2B-144; DH-1   **Ht:** 6'1" **Wt:** 185 **Born:** 11/30/69 **Age:** 27

		BATTING															BASERUNNING				PERCENTAGES		
Year Team	Lg	G	AB	H	2B	3B	HR	(Hm | Rd)	TB	R	RBI	TBB	IBB	SO	HBP	SH	SF	SB	CS	SB%	GDP	Avg	OBP	SLG
1991 Cleveland	AL	84	314	83	15	1	0	(0 | 0)	100	29	30	15	0	45	0	2	5	2	2	.50	12	.264	.293	.318
1992 Cleveland	AL	122	413	109	21	0	5	(2 | 3)	145	44	30	25	1	69	3	1	4	4	5	.44	12	.264	.308	.351
1993 Cleveland	AL	14	52	13	2	0	1	(1 | 0)	18	6	5	0	0	7	0	1	0	3	0	1.00	1	.250	.250	.346
1994 Cleveland	AL	20	73	15	5	0	1	(1 | 0)	23	6	8	2	0	13	0	1	0	1	0	1.00	1	.205	.227	.315
1995 Cincinnati	NL	81	171	58	13	1	3	(1 | 2)	82	25	30	21	2	33	0	0	2	0	3	.00	1	.339	.407	.480
1996 Detroit	AL	145	545	147	30	3	11	(8 | 3)	216	69	55	42	0	109	5	4	3	6	1	.86	12	.270	.326	.396
6 ML YEARS		466	1568	425	86	5	21	(13 | 8)	584	179	158	105	3	276	8	9	14	16	11	.59	40	.271	.317	.372

Richie Lewis

Pitches: Right **Bats:** Right **Pos:** RP-72   **Ht:** 5'10" **Wt:** 175 **Born:** 1/25/66 **Age:** 31

		HOW MUCH HE PITCHED						WHAT HE GAVE UP										THE RESULTS						
Year Team	Lg	G	GS	CG	GF	IP	BFP	H	R	ER	HR	SH	SF	HB	TBB	IBB	SO	WP	Bk	W	L	Pct.	ShO	Sv-Op	Hld	ERA
1996 Toledo *	AAA	2	0	0	0	4	13	1	1	1	0	0	0	1	0	4	0	0	0	0	.000	0	0- -	—	2.25

<table>

Year Team	Lg	G	GS	CG	GF	IP	BFP	H	R	ER	HR	SH	SF	HB	TBB	IBB	SO	WP	Bk	W	L	Pct.	ShO	Sv-Op	Hld	ERA
1992 Baltimore	AL	2	2	0	0	6.2	40	13	8	8	1	0	1	0	7	0	4	0	0	1	1	.500	0	0-0	0	10.80
1993 Florida	NL	57	0	0	14	77.1	341	68	37	28	7	8	4	1	43	6	65	9	1	6	3	.667	0	0-2	3	3.26
1994 Florida	NL	45	0	0	9	54	261	62	44	34	7	3	1	1	38	9	45	10	1	1	4	.200	0	0-0	4	5.67
1995 Florida	NL	21	1	0	6	36	152	30	15	15	9	2	0	1	15	5	32	1	2	0	1	.000	0	0-0	0	3.75
1996 Detroit	AL	72	0	0	19	90.1	412	78	45	42	9	5	10	4	65	9	78	14	2	4	6	.400	0	2-6	6	4.18
5 ML YEARS		197	3	0	48	264.1	1206	251	149	127	33	18	16	7	168	29	224	34	6	12	15	.444	0	2-8	13	4.32

</table>

Jim Leyritz

B: R **T:** R **Pos:** C-55; DH-13; 3B-13; PH-8; 1B-5; LF-3; 2B-2   **Ht:** 6'0" **Wt:** 195 **Born:** 12/27/63 **Age:** 33

<table>

							BATTING										BASERUNNING				PERCENTAGES		
Year Team	Lg	G	AB	H	2B	3B	HR	(Hm | Rd)	TB	R	RBI	TBB	IBB	SO	HBP	SH	SF	SB	CS	SB%	GDP	Avg	OBP	SLG
1990 New York	AL	92	303	78	13	1	5	(1 | 4)	108	28	25	27	1	51	7	1	1	2	3	.40	11	.257	.331	.356
1991 New York	AL	32	77	14	3	0	0	(0 | 0)	17	8	4	13	0	15	0	1	0	0	1	.00	0	.182	.300	.221
1992 New York	AL	63	144	37	6	0	7	(3 | 4)	64	17	26	14	1	22	6	0	3	0	1	.00	2	.257	.341	.444
1993 New York	AL	95	259	80	14	0	14	(6 | 8)	136	43	53	37	3	59	8	0	1	0	0	.00	12	.309	.410	.525
1994 New York	AL	75	249	66	12	0	17	(4 | 13)	129	47	58	35	1	61	6	0	3	0	0	.00	9	.265	.365	.518
1995 New York	AL	77	264	71	12	0	7	(3 | 4)	104	37	37	37	2	73	8	0	1	1	1	.50	4	.269	.374	.394
1996 New York	AL	88	265	70	10	0	7	(3 | 4)	101	23	40	30	3	68	9	2	3	2	0	1.00	11	.264	.355	.381
7 ML YEARS		522	1561	416	70	1	57	(20 | 37)	659	203	243	193	11	349	44	4	12	5	6	.45	49	.266	.361	.422

</table>

Jon Lieber

Pitches: Right **Bats:** Left **Pos:** RP-36; SP-15   **Ht:** 6'3" **Wt:** 220 **Born:** 4/2/70 **Age:** 27

<table>

						HOW MUCH HE PITCHED						WHAT HE GAVE UP					THE RESULTS						
Year Team	Lg	G	GS	CG	GF	IP	BFP	H	R	ER	HR	SH	SF	HB	TBB	IBB	SO	WP	Bk	W	L	Pct.	ShO	Sv-Op	Hld	ERA
1994 Pittsburgh	NL	17	17	1	0	108.2	460	116	62	45	12	3	3	1	25	3	71	2	3	6	7	.462	0	0-0	0	3.73
1995 Pittsburgh	NL	21	12	0	3	72.2	327	103	56	51	7	5	6	4	14	0	45	3	0	4	7	.364	0	0-1	3	6.32
1996 Pittsburgh	NL	51	15	0	6	142	600	156	70	63	19	7	2	3	28	2	94	0	0	9	5	.643	0	1-4	9	3.99
3 ML YEARS		89	44	1	9	323.1	1387	375	188	159	38	15	11	8	67	5	210	5	3	19	19	.500	0	1-5	12	4.43

</table>

Mike Lieberthal

Bats: Right **Throws:** Right **Pos:** C-43; PH-8   **Ht:** 6'0" **Wt:** 178 **Born:** 1/18/72 **Age:** 25

<table>

							BATTING										BASERUNNING				PERCENTAGES		
Year Team	Lg	G	AB	H	2B	3B	HR	(Hm | Rd)	TB	R	RBI	TBB	IBB	SO	HBP	SH	SF	SB	CS	SB%	GDP	Avg	OBP	SLG
1994 Philadelphia	NL	24	79	21	3	1	1	(1 | 0)	29	6	5	3	0	5	1	1	0	0	0	.00	4	.266	.301	.367
1995 Philadelphia	NL	16	47	12	2	0	0	(0 | 0)	14	1	4	5	0	5	0	2	0	0	0	.00	1	.255	.327	.298
1996 Philadelphia	NL	50	166	42	8	0	7	(4 | 3)	71	21	23	10	0	30	2	0	4	0	0	.00	4	.253	.297	.428
3 ML YEARS		90	292	75	13	1	8	(5 | 3)	114	28	32	18	0	40	3	3	4	0	0	.00	9	.257	.303	.390

</table>

Derek Lilliquist

Pitches: Left **Bats:** Left **Pos:** RP-5   **Ht:** 5'10" **Wt:** 195 **Born:** 2/20/66 **Age:** 31

<table>

						HOW MUCH HE PITCHED						WHAT HE GAVE UP					THE RESULTS						
Year Team	Lg	G	GS	CG	GF	IP	BFP	H	R	ER	HR	SH	SF	HB	TBB	IBB	SO	WP	Bk	W	L	Pct.	ShO	Sv-Op	Hld	ERA
1996 Indianapolis *	AAA	47	0	0	17	52	208	47	17	15	3	5	0	2	7	1	51	0	0	4	1	.800	0	1--	—	2.60
1989 Atlanta	NL	32	30	0	0	165.2	718	202	87	73	16	8	3	2	34	5	79	4	3	8	10	.444	0	0-1	1	3.97
1990 Atl-SD	NL	28	18	1	3	122	537	136	74	72	16	9	5	3	42	5	63	2	3	5	11	.313	1	0-0	0	5.31
1991 San Diego	NL	6	2	0	1	14.70	75	25	14	14	3	0	0	0	4	1	7	0	0	0	2	.000	0	0-0	0	8.79
1992 Cleveland	AL	71	0	0	22	61.2	239	39	13	12	5	5	4	2	18	6	47	2	0	5	3	.625	0	6-11	15	1.75
1993 Cleveland	AL	56	2	0	28	64	271	64	20	16	5	6	2	1	19	5	40	1	0	4	4	.500	0	10-13	11	2.25
1994 Cleveland	AL	36	0	0	12	29.1	127	34	17	16	6	3	3	1	8	1	15	0	0	1	3	.250	0	1-3	4	4.91
1995 Boston	AL	28	0	0	6	23	103	27	17	16	7	2	3	0	9	2	9	1	0	2	1	.667	0	0-3	1	6.26
1996 Cincinnati	NL	5	0	0	3	3.2	15	5	3	3	1	1	0	0	0	0	1	0	0	0	0	.000	0	0-1	0	7.36
1990 Indianapolis	NL	12	11	0	1	61.2	279	75	45	43	10	6	4	1	19	4	34	0	2	2	8	.200	0	0-0	0	6.28
San Diego	NL	16	7	1	2	60.1	258	61	29	29	6	3	1	2	23	1	29	2	1	3	3	.500	1	0-0	0	4.33
8 ML YEARS		262	52	1	75	483.2	2080	532	245	222	59	34	20	9	134	25	261	10	6	25	34	.424	1	17-32	32	4.13

</table>

Jose Lima

Pitches: Right **Bats:** Right **Pos:** RP-35; SP-4   **Ht:** 6'2" **Wt:** 205 **Born:** 9/30/72 **Age:** 24

<table>

						HOW MUCH HE PITCHED						WHAT HE GAVE UP					THE RESULTS						
Year Team	Lg	G	GS	CG	GF	IP	BFP	H	R	ER	HR	SH	SF	HB	TBB	IBB	SO	WP	Bk	W	L	Pct.	ShO	Sv-Op	Hld	ERA
1996 Toledo *	AAA	12	12	0	0	69	303	93	53	52	11	1	1	0	12	0	57	2	0	5	4	.556	0	0--	—	6.78
1994 Detroit	AL	3	1	0	1	6.2	34	11	10	10	2	0	0	0	3	1	7	1	0	0	1	.000	0	0-0	0	13.50
1995 Detroit	AL	15	15	0	0	73.2	320	85	52	50	10	2	1	4	18	4	37	5	0	3	9	.250	0	0-0	0	6.11
1996 Detroit	AL	39	4	0	15	72.2	329	87	48	46	13	5	3	5	22	4	59	3	0	5	6	.455	0	3-7	6	5.70
3 ML YEARS		57	20	0	16	153	683	183	110	106	25	7	4	9	43	9	103	9	0	8	16	.333	0	3-7	6	6.24

</table>

Doug Linton

Pitches: Right **Bats:** Right **Pos:** SP-18; RP-3   **Ht:** 6'1" **Wt:** 190 **Born:** 9/2/65 **Age:** 31

Year Team	Lg	G	GS	CG	GF	IP	BFP	H	R	ER	HR	SH	SF	HB	TBB	IBB	SO	WP	Bk	W	L	Pct.	ShO	Sv-Op	Hld	ERA
1996 Omaha *	AAA	4	4	0	0	22.2	99	26	13	12	1	0	1	2	7	0	14	2	0	1	1	.500	0	0- -	—	4.76
1992 Toronto	AL	8	3	0	2	24	116	31	23	23	5	1	2	0	17	0	16	2	0	1	3	.250	0	0-0	0	8.63
1993 Tor-Cal	AL	23	1	0	6	36.2	178	46	30	30	8	0	3	1	23	1	23	2	0	2	1	.667	0	0-1	0	7.36
1994 New York	NL	32	3	0	8	50.1	241	74	27	25	4	3	1	0	20	3	29	2	0	6	2	.750	0	0-0	0	4.47
1995 Kansas City	AL	7	2	0	0	22.1	98	22	21	18	4	0	0	2	10	1	13	0	0	0	1	.000	0	0-0	0	7.25
1996 Kansas City	AL	21	18	0	0	104	452	111	65	58	13	6	2	8	26	1	87	3	1	7	9	.438	0	0-0	1	5.02
1993 Toronto	AL	4	1	0	0	11	55	11	8	8	0	0	2	1	9	0	4	0	0	0	1	.000	0	0-0	0	6.55
California	AL	19	0	0	6	25.2	123	35	22	22	8	0	1	0	14	1	19	2	0	2	0	1.000	0	0-1	0	7.71
5 ML YEARS		91	27	0	16	237.1	1085	284	166	154	34	10	8	11	96	6	168	9	1	16	16	.500	0	0-1	1	5.84

Felipe Lira

Pitches: Right **Bats:** Right **Pos:** SP-32   **Ht:** 6'0" **Wt:** 170 **Born:** 4/26/72 **Age:** 25

Year Team	Lg	G	GS	CG	GF	IP	BFP	H	R	ER	HR	SH	SF	HB	TBB	IBB	SO	WP	Bk	W	L	Pct.	ShO	Sv-Op	Hld	ERA
1990 Bristol	R+	13	10	2	2	78.1	318	70	26	21	4	0	1	3	16	1	71	4	2	5	5	.500	1	1- -	—	2.41
Lakeland	A+	1	0	0	0	1.2	11	3	1	1	0	0	1	0	3	0	4	0	0	0	0	.000	0	0- -	—	5.40
1991 Fayetteville	A	15	13	0	2	73.1	315	79	43	38	8	4	2	1	19	0	56	6	4	5	5	.500	0	1- -	—	4.66
1992 Lakeland	A+	32	8	2	2	109	442	95	36	29	6	3	1	7	16	1	84	4	0	11	5	.688	1	1- -	—	2.39
1993 London	AA	22	22	3	0	162	641	157	63	57	16	5	3	6	39	2	122	8	1	10	4	.714	0	0- -	—	3.38
Toledo	AAA	5	5	0	0	31.1	135	32	18	16	5	0	3	1	11	1	23	0	1	1	2	.333	0	0- -	—	4.60
1994 Toledo	AAA	26	26	1	0	151.1	669	171	91	79	19	4	9	6	45	4	110	16	0	7	12	.368	1	0- -	—	4.70
1995 Detroit	AL	37	22	0	7	146.1	635	151	74	70	17	4	9	8	56	7	89	5	1	9	13	.409	0	1-3	1	4.31
1996 Detroit	AL	32	32	3	0	194.2	850	204	123	113	30	5	11	10	66	2	113	7	0	6	14	.300	2	0-0	0	5.22
2 ML YEARS		69	54	3	7	341	1485	355	197	183	47	9	20	18	122	9	202	12	1	15	27	.357	2	1-3	1	4.83

Nelson Liriano

Bats: B **Throws:** R **Pos:** PH-71; 2B-36; 3B-9; SS-5   **Ht:** 5'10" **Wt:** 181 **Born:** 6/3/64 **Age:** 33

Year Team	Lg	G	AB	H	2B	3B	HR	(Hm	Rd)	TB	R	RBI	TBB	IBB	SO	HBP	SH	SF	SB	CS	SB%	GDP	Avg	OBP	SLG
1987 Toronto	AL	37	158	38	6	2	2	(1	1)	54	29	10	16	2	22	0	1	2	13	2	.87	3	.241	.310	.342
1988 Toronto	AL	99	276	73	6	2	3	(0	3)	92	36	23	11	0	40	2	5	1	12	5	.71	4	.264	.297	.333
1989 Toronto	AL	132	418	110	26	3	5	(3	2)	157	51	53	43	0	51	2	10	5	16	7	.70	10	.263	.331	.376
1990 Tor-Min	AL	103	355	83	12	9	1	(1	0)	116	46	28	38	0	44	1	4	2	8	7	.53	8	.234	.308	.327
1991 Kansas City	AL	10	22	9	0	0	0	(0	0)	9	5	1	0	0	2	0	1	0	1	0	.00	0	.409	.409	.409
1993 Colorado	NL	48	151	46	6	3	2	(0	2)	64	28	15	18	2	22	0	5	1	6	4	.60	5	.305	.376	.424
1994 Colorado	NL	87	255	65	17	5	3	(2	1)	101	39	31	42	5	44	0	3	3	2	2	.00	4	.255	.357	.396
1995 Pittsburgh	NL	107	259	74	12	1	5	(2	3)	103	29	38	24	3	34	2	1	3	2	2	.50	2	.286	.347	.398
1996 Pittsburgh	NL	112	217	58	14	2	3	(0	3)	85	23	30	14	2	22	0	0	3	2	0	1.00	5	.267	.308	.392
1990 Toronto	AL	50	170	36	7	2	1	(1	0)	50	16	15	16	0	20	1	1	1	3	5	.38	5	.212	.282	.294
Minnesota	AL	53	185	47	5	7	0	(0	0)	66	30	13	22	0	24	0	3	1	5	2	.71	3	.254	.332	.357
9 ML YEARS		735	2111	556	99	27	24	(9	15)	781	286	229	206	14	281	7	31	18	59	30	.66	38	.263	.328	.370

Pat Listach

Bats: B **Throws:** R **Pos:** CF-66; 2B-12; PH-8; SS-7; LF-2; DH-1   **Ht:** 5'9" **Wt:** 180 **Born:** 9/12/67 **Age:** 29

Year Team	Lg	G	AB	H	2B	3B	HR	(Hm	Rd)	TB	R	RBI	TBB	IBB	SO	HBP	SH	SF	SB	CS	SB%	GDP	Avg	OBP	SLG
1996 Beloit *	A	1	5	2	0	0	0			2	2	0	0	0	1	0	0	0	0	0	.00	0	.400	.400	.400
1992 Milwaukee	AL	149	579	168	19	6	1	(0	1)	202	93	47	55	0	124	1	12	2	54	18	.75	3	.290	.352	.349
1993 Milwaukee	AL	98	356	87	15	1	3	(0	3)	113	50	30	37	0	70	3	5	2	18	9	.67	7	.244	.319	.317
1994 Milwaukee	AL	16	54	16	3	0	0	(0	0)	19	8	2	3	0	8	0	0	0	2	1	.67	1	.296	.333	.352
1995 Milwaukee	AL	101	334	73	8	2	0	(0	0)	85	35	25	25	0	61	2	7	1	13	3	.81	6	.219	.276	.254
1996 Milwaukee	AL	87	317	76	16	2	1	(1	0)	99	51	33	36	0	51	1	6	2	25	5	.83	2	.240	.317	.312
5 ML YEARS		451	1640	420	61	11	5	(1	4)	518	237	137	156	0	314	7	30	7	112	36	.76	19	.256	.322	.316

Scott Livingstone

Bats: Left **Throws:** Right **Pos:** PH-68; 1B-22; 3B-16   **Ht:** 6'0" **Wt:** 190 **Born:** 7/15/65 **Age:** 31

Year Team	Lg	G	AB	H	2B	3B	HR	(Hm	Rd)	TB	R	RBI	TBB	IBB	SO	HBP	SH	SF	SB	CS	SB%	GDP	Avg	OBP	SLG
1991 Detroit	AL	44	127	37	5	0	2	(1	1)	48	19	11	10	0	25	0	1	1	2	1	.67	4	.291	.341	.378
1992 Detroit	AL	117	354	100	21	0	4	(2	2)	133	43	46	21	0	36	0	3	4	1	3	.25	8	.282	.319	.376
1993 Detroit	AL	98	304	89	10	2	2	(1	1)	109	39	39	19	1	32	0	1	6	1	3	.25	4	.293	.328	.359
1994 Det-SD	AL	72	203	54	13	1	2	(1	1)	75	11	11	7	0	26	0	0	1	2	2	.50	5	.266	.289	.369
1995 San Diego	NL	99	196	66	15	0	5	(1	4)	96	26	32	15	1	22	0	1	0	2	1	.67	3	.337	.380	.490
1996 San Diego	NL	102	172	51	4	1	2	(0	2)	63	20	20	9	0	22	0	0	0	0	1	.00	6	.297	.331	.366
1994 Detroit	AL	15	23	5	1	0	0	(0	0)	6	0	1	1	0	4	0	0	0	0	0	.00	0	.217	.250	.261
San Diego	NL	57	180	49	12	1	2	(1	1)	69	11	10	6	0	22	0	0	1	2	2	.50	5	.272	.289	.383
6 ML YEARS		532	1356	397	68	4	17	(6	11)	524	158	159	81	3	163	0	5	14	8	11	.42	26	.293	.329	.386

129

Graeme Lloyd

Pitches: Left **Bats:** Left **Pos:** RP-65   **Ht:** 6'7" **Wt:** 234 **Born:** 4/9/67 **Age:** 30

Year Team	Lg	G	GS	CG	GF	IP	BFP	H	R	ER	HR	SH	SF	HB	TBB	IBB	SO	WP	Bk	W	L	Pct.	ShO	Sv-Op	Hld	ERA
1993 Milwaukee	AL	55	0	0	12	63.2	269	64	24	20	5	1	2	3	13	3	31	4	0	3	4	.429	0	0-4	6	2.83
1994 Milwaukee	AL	43	0	0	21	47	203	49	28	27	4	1	2	3	15	6	31	2	0	2	3	.400	0	3-6	3	5.17
1995 Milwaukee	AL	33	0	0	14	32	127	28	16	16	4	1	4	0	8	2	13	3	0	0	5	.000	0	4-6	9	4.50
1996 Mil-NYA	AL	65	0	0	15	56.2	252	61	30	27	4	5	3	1	22	4	30	4	0	2	6	.250	0	0-5	17	4.29
1996 Milwaukee	AL	52	0	0	15	51	217	49	19	16	3	5	1	1	17	3	24	0	0	2	4	.333	0	0-3	15	2.82
New York	AL	13	0	0	0	5.2	35	12	11	11	1	0	2	0	5	1	6	4	0	0	2	.000	0	0-2	2	17.47
4 ML YEARS		196	0	0	62	199.1	851	202	98	90	17	8	11	7	58	15	105	13	0	7	18	.280	0	7-21	35	4.06

Esteban Loaiza

Pitches: Right **Bats:** Right **Pos:** SP-10   **Ht:** 6'4" **Wt:** 190 **Born:** 12/31/71 **Age:** 25

Year Team	Lg	G	GS	CG	GF	IP	BFP	H	R	ER	HR	SH	SF	HB	TBB	IBB	SO	WP	Bk	W	L	Pct.	ShO	Sv-Op	Hld	ERA
1991 Pirates	R	11	11	1	0	51.2	220	48	17	13	0	0	2	5	14	0	41	1	0	5	1	.833	1	0--	—	2.26
1992 Augusta	A	26	25	3	0	143.1	613	134	72	62	7	2	3	10	60	0	123	7	4	10	8	.556	0	0--	—	3.89
1993 Salem	A+	17	17	3	0	109	462	113	53	41	7	2	4	4	30	0	61	8	0	6	7	.462	0	0--	—	3.39
Carolina	AA	7	7	1	0	43	176	39	18	18	5	0	2	0	12	1	40	3	0	2	1	.667	0	0--	—	3.77
1994 Carolina	AA	24	24	3	0	154.1	647	169	69	65	15	5	3	5	30	0	115	1	1	10	5	.667	0	0--	—	3.79
1996 Calgary	AAA	12	11	1	0	69.1	288	61	34	31	5	3	6	3	25	2	38	0	0	3	4	.429	1	0--	—	4.02
1995 Pittsburgh	NL	32	31	1	0	172.2	762	205	115	99	21	10	9	5	55	3	85	6	1	8	9	.471	0	0-0	—	5.16
1996 Pittsburgh	NL	10	10	1	0	52.2	236	65	32	29	11	3	1	2	19	2	32	0	0	2	3	.400	1	0-0	—	4.96
2 ML YEARS		42	41	2	0	225.1	998	270	147	128	32	13	10	7	74	5	117	6	1	10	12	.455	1	0-0	—	5.11

Keith Lockhart

Bats: L **Throws:** R **Pos:** 2B-84; 3B-55; PH-24; DH-1   **Ht:** 5'10" **Wt:** 170 **Born:** 11/10/64 **Age:** 32

Year Team	Lg	G	AB	H	2B	3B	HR	(Hm	Rd)	TB	R	RBI	TBB	IBB	SO	HBP	SH	SF	SB	CS	SB%	GDP	Avg	OBP	SLG
1994 San Diego	NL	27	43	9	0	0	2	(2	0)	15	4	6	4	0	10	1	1	1	1	0	1.00	2	.209	.286	.349
1995 Kansas City	AL	94	274	88	19	3	6	(3	3)	131	41	33	14	2	21	4	1	7	8	1	.89	2	.321	.355	.478
1996 Kansas City	AL	138	433	118	33	3	7	(3	4)	178	49	55	30	4	40	2	1	5	11	6	.65	7	.273	.319	.411
3 ML YEARS		259	750	215	52	6	15	(9	6)	324	94	94	48	6	71	7	3	13	20	7	.74	11	.287	.330	.432

Kenny Lofton

Bats: Left **Throws:** Left **Pos:** CF-153; PH-1   **Ht:** 6'0" **Wt:** 180 **Born:** 5/31/67 **Age:** 30

Year Team	Lg	G	AB	H	2B	3B	HR	(Hm	Rd)	TB	R	RBI	TBB	IBB	SO	HBP	SH	SF	SB	CS	SB%	GDP	Avg	OBP	SLG
1991 Houston	NL	20	74	15	1	0	0	(0	0)	16	9	0	5	0	19	0	0	0	2	1	.67	0	.203	.253	.216
1992 Cleveland	AL	148	576	164	15	8	5	(3	2)	210	96	42	68	3	54	2	4	1	66	12	.85	7	.285	.362	.365
1993 Cleveland	AL	148	569	185	28	8	1	(1	0)	232	116	42	81	6	83	1	2	1	70	14	.83	8	.325	.408	.408
1994 Cleveland	AL	112	459	160	32	9	12	(10	2)	246	105	57	52	5	56	2	4	6	60	12	.83	5	.349	.412	.536
1995 Cleveland	AL	118	481	149	22	13	7	(4	3)	218	93	53	40	6	49	1	4	3	54	15	.78	6	.310	.362	.453
1996 Cleveland	AL	154	662	210	35	4	14	(7	7)	295	132	67	61	3	82	0	7	6	75	17	.82	7	.317	.372	.446
6 ML YEARS		700	2821	883	133	42	39	(26	13)	1217	551	261	307	23	343	6	21	20	327	71	.82	33	.313	.379	.431

Rich Loiselle

Pitches: Right **Bats:** Right **Pos:** SP-3; RP-2   **Ht:** 6'5" **Wt:** 225 **Born:** 1/12/72 **Age:** 25

Year Team	Lg	G	GS	CG	GF	IP	BFP	H	R	ER	HR	SH	SF	HB	TBB	IBB	SO	WP	Bk	W	L	Pct.	ShO	Sv-Op	Hld	ERA
1991 Pirates	R	12	12	0	0	61.1	285	72	40	24	1	1	3	3	26	0	47	4	3	2	3	.400	0	0--	—	3.52
1992 Charlstn-SC	A	19	19	2	0	97	407	93	51	40	2	0	1	3	42	0	64	2	0	4	8	.333	2	0--	—	3.71
1993 Waterloo	A	10	10	1	0	59.1	254	55	28	26	3	2	1	4	29	1	47	6	0	1	5	.167	1	0--	—	3.94
Rancho Cuca	A+	14	14	1	0	82.2	380	109	64	53	5	3	3	5	34	1	53	1	0	5	8	.385	0	0--	—	5.77
1994 Rancho Cuca	A+	27	27	0	0	156.2	704	160	81	69	12	7	6	1	76	2	120	12	0	9	10	.474	0	0--	—	3.96
1995 Las Vegas	AAA	8	7	1	0	27.1	131	36	27	22	5	1	0	2	9	0	16	0	0	2	2	.500	1	0--	—	7.24
1996 Jackson	AA	16	16	2	0	98.2	429	107	46	38	6	0	1	4	27	0	65	3	0	7	4	.636	0	0--	—	3.47
Tucson	AAA	5	5	1	0	33.1	145	28	20	9	1	0	0	1	11	0	31	0	0	2	2	.500	1	0--	—	2.43
Calgary	AAA	8	8	0	0	50.2	234	64	28	23	3	3	0	3	16	1	41	0	0	2	2	.500	0	0--	—	4.09
1996 Pittsburgh	NL	5	3	0	0	20.2	90	22	8	7	3	0	0	0	8	1	9	3	0	1	0	1.000	0	0-0	1	3.05

Kevin Lomon

Pitches: Right **Bats:** Right **Pos:** RP-6   **Ht:** 6'1" **Wt:** 195 **Born:** 11/20/71 **Age:** 25

Year Team	Lg	G	GS	CG	GF	IP	BFP	H	R	ER	HR	SH	SF	HB	TBB	IBB	SO	WP	Bk	W	L	Pct.	ShO	Sv-Op	Hld	ERA
1991 Pulaski	R+	10	5	1	1	44	168	17	9	3	0	0	1	4	13	0	70	4	6	6	0	1.000	1	1--	—	0.61
Macon	A	1	0	0	1	5	17	2	1	1	0	0	0	0	1	0	2	0	0	0	0	1.000	0	0--	—	1.80

Year Team	Lg	G	GS	CG	GF	IP	BFP	H	R	ER	HR	SH	SF	HB	TBB	IBB	SO	WP	Bk	W	L	Pct.	ShO	Sv-Op	Hld	ERA
1992 Durham	A+	27	27	0	0	135	609	147	83	74	13	5	3	11	63	1	113	16	3	8	9	.471	0	0--	—	4.93
1993 Durham	A+	14	14	1	0	85	358	80	36	35	6	0	1	2	30	1	68	5	3	4	2	.667	0	0--	—	3.71
Greenville	AA	13	13	1	0	79.1	338	76	41	34	4	3	3	4	31	2	68	4	0	3	4	.429	1	0--	—	3.86
1994 Richmond	AAA	28	26	0	0	147	628	159	69	63	12	1	2	3	53	2	97	9	0	10	8	.556	0	0--	—	3.86
1995 Richmond	AAA	32	3	0	8	60	261	62	23	20	2	4	4	0	32	4	52	4	0	1	2	.333	0	1--	—	3.00
1996 Richmond	AAA	26	26	2	0	141.1	607	151	82	68	11	5	4	4	44	2	102	6	1	9	8	.529	0	0--	—	4.33
1995 New York	NL	6	0	0	1	9.1	47	17	8	7	0	0	0	0	5	1	6	0	0	0	1	.000	0	0-0	0	6.75
1996 Atlanta	NL	6	0	0	1	7.1	31	7	4	4	0	0	0	0	3	0	1	0	1	0	0	.000	0	0-0	0	4.91
2 ML YEARS		12	0	0	2	16.2	78	24	12	11	0	0	0	0	8	1	7	0	1	0	1	.000	0	0-0	0	5.94

Albie Lopez

Pitches: Right **Bats:** Right **Pos:** SP-10; RP-3 **Ht:** 6'2" **Wt:** 185 **Born:** 8/18/71 **Age:** 25

Year Team	Lg	G	GS	CG	GF	IP	BFP	H	R	ER	HR	SH	SF	HB	TBB	IBB	SO	WP	Bk	W	L	Pct.	ShO	Sv-Op	Hld	ERA
1996 Buffalo *	AAA	17	17	2	0	104.2	444	90	54	45	13	1	3	10	40	0	89	1	3	10	2	.833	0	0--	—	3.87
1993 Cleveland	AL	9	9	0	0	49.2	222	49	34	33	7	1	1	1	32	1	25	0	0	3	1	.750	0	0-0	0	5.98
1994 Cleveland	AL	4	4	1	0	17	76	20	11	8	3	0	0	1	6	0	18	3	0	1	2	.333	1	0-0	0	4.24
1995 Cleveland	AL	6	2	0	0	23	92	17	8	8	4	0	1	1	7	1	22	2	0	0	0	.000	0	0-0	0	3.13
1996 Cleveland	AL	13	10	0	0	62	282	80	47	44	14	0	1	2	22	1	45	2	0	5	4	.556	0	0-0	0	6.39
4 ML YEARS		32	25	1	0	151.2	672	166	100	93	28	1	3	5	67	3	110	7	0	9	7	.563	1	0-0	0	5.52

Javy Lopez

Bats: Right **Throws:** Right **Pos:** C-135; PH-6 **Ht:** 6'3" **Wt:** 200 **Born:** 11/5/70 **Age:** 26

Year Team	Lg	G	AB	H	2B	3B	HR	(Hm	Rd)	TB	R	RBI	TBB	IBB	SO	HBP	SH	SF	SB	CS	SB%	GDP	Avg	OBP	SLG
1992 Atlanta	NL	9	16	6	2	0	0	(0	0)	8	3	2	0	0	1	0	0	0	0	0	.00	0	.375	.375	.500
1993 Atlanta	NL	8	16	6	1	1	1	(0	1)	12	1	2	0	0	2	1	0	0	0	0	.00	0	.375	.412	.750
1994 Atlanta	NL	80	277	68	9	0	13	(4	9)	116	27	35	17	0	61	5	2	2	0	2	.00	12	.245	.299	.419
1995 Atlanta	NL	100	333	105	11	4	14	(8	6)	166	37	51	14	0	57	2	0	3	0	1	.00	13	.315	.344	.498
1996 Atlanta	NL	138	489	138	19	1	23	(10	13)	228	56	69	28	3	84	3	1	5	1	6	.14	17	.282	.322	.466
5 ML YEARS		335	1131	323	42	6	51	(22	29)	530	124	159	59	5	205	11	3	10	1	9	.10	42	.286	.325	.469

Luis Lopez

Bats: B **Throws:** R **Pos:** SS-35; 2B-22; PH-13; 3B-2 **Ht:** 5'11" **Wt:** 175 **Born:** 9/4/70 **Age:** 26

Year Team	Lg	G	AB	H	2B	3B	HR	(Hm	Rd)	TB	R	RBI	TBB	IBB	SO	HBP	SH	SF	SB	CS	SB%	GDP	Avg	OBP	SLG
1996 Las Vegas *	AAA	18	68	14	3	0	1	—	—	20	4	12	2	0	15	0	1	0	0	0	.00	0	.206	.229	.294
1993 San Diego	NL	17	43	5	1	0	0	(0	0)	6	1	1	0	0	8	0	0	1	0	0	.00	0	.116	.114	.140
1994 San Diego	NL	77	235	65	16	1	2	(2	0)	89	29	20	15	2	39	3	2	2	3	2	.60	7	.277	.325	.379
1996 San Diego	NL	63	139	25	3	0	2	(1	1)	34	10	11	9	1	35	1	1	1	0	0	.00	7	.180	.233	.245
3 ML YEARS		157	417	95	20	1	4	(3	1)	129	40	32	24	3	82	4	3	4	3	2	.60	14	.228	.274	.309

Mark Loretta

Bats: R **Throws:** R **Pos:** 2B-28; 3B-23; SS-21; PH-7 **Ht:** 6'0" **Wt:** 175 **Born:** 8/14/71 **Age:** 25

Year Team	Lg	G	AB	H	2B	3B	HR	(Hm	Rd)	TB	R	RBI	TBB	IBB	SO	HBP	SH	SF	SB	CS	SB%	GDP	Avg	OBP	SLG
1993 Helena	R+	6	28	9	1	0	1	—	—	13	5	8	1	0	4	1	0	0	0	0	.00	0	.321	.367	.464
Stockton	A+	53	201	73	4	1	4	—	—	91	36	31	22	0	17	2	2	2	8	2	.80	6	.363	.427	.453
1994 El Paso	AA	77	302	95	13	6	0	—	—	120	50	38	27	0	33	2	9	5	8	5	.62	12	.315	.369	.397
New Orleans	AAA	43	138	29	7	0	1	—	—	39	16	14	12	0	13	3	3	3	2	1	.67	2	.210	.282	.283
1995 New Orleans	AAA	127	479	137	22	5	7	—	—	190	48	79	34	1	47	9	5	7	8	9	.47	12	.286	.340	.397
1996 New Orleans	AAA	19	71	18	5	1	0	—	—	25	10	11	9	0	8	2	1	2	1	1	.50	1	.254	.345	.352
1995 Milwaukee	AL	19	50	13	3	0	1	(0	1)	19	13	3	4	0	7	1	0	1	1	1	.50	1	.260	.327	.380
1996 Milwaukee	AL	73	154	43	3	0	1	(0	1)	49	20	13	14	0	15	0	2	0	2	1	.67	7	.279	.339	.318
2 ML YEARS		92	204	56	6	0	2	(0	2)	68	33	16	18	0	22	1	2	1	3	2	.60	8	.275	.336	.333

Torey Lovullo

B: B **T:** R **Pos:** 1B-42; PH-28; 3B-11; DH-4; 2B-2; SS-1; LF-1 **Ht:** 6'0" **Wt:** 185 **Born:** 7/25/65 **Age:** 31

Year Team	Lg	G	AB	H	2B	3B	HR	(Hm	Rd)	TB	R	RBI	TBB	IBB	SO	HBP	SH	SF	SB	CS	SB%	GDP	Avg	OBP	SLG
1996 Edmonton *	AAA	26	93	26	4	0	4	—	—	42	18	19	18	1	12	1	1	0	0	0	.00	3	.280	.398	.452
1988 Detroit	AL	12	21	8	1	1	1	(0	1)	14	2	2	1	0	2	1	0	0	0	0	.00	0	.381	.409	.667
1989 Detroit	AL	29	87	10	2	0	1	(0	1)	15	8	4	14	0	20	0	1	2	0	0	.00	3	.115	.233	.172
1991 New York	AL	22	51	9	2	0	0	(0	0)	11	0	2	5	1	7	0	3	0	0	0	.00	0	.176	.250	.216
1993 California	AL	116	367	92	20	0	6	(4	2)	130	42	30	36	1	49	1	3	2	7	6	.54	8	.251	.318	.354
1994 Seattle	AL	36	72	16	5	0	2	(2	0)	27	9	7	9	1	13	0	0	0	1	0	1.00	2	.222	.309	.375
1996 Oakland	AL	65	82	18	4	0	3	(0	3)	31	15	9	11	0	17	2	3	1	1	2	.33	0	.220	.323	.378
6 ML YEARS		280	680	153	34	1	13	(6	7)	228	76	54	76	3	108	3	11	5	9	8	.53	14	.225	.304	.335

Eric Ludwick

Pitches: Right **Bats:** Right **Pos:** RP-5; SP-1 **Ht:** 6'5" **Wt:** 220 **Born:** 12/14/71 **Age:** 25

Year Team	Lg	G	GS	CG	GF	IP	BFP	H	R	ER	HR	SH	SF	HB	TBB	IBB	SO	WP	Bk	W	L	Pct.	ShO	Sv-Op	Hld	ERA
1993 Pittsfield	A-	10	10	1	0	51	219	51	27	18	0	3	1	0	18	0	40	4	2	4	4	.500	0	0--	—	3.18
1994 St. Lucie	A+	27	27	3	0	150.1	671	162	102	76	6	1	12	6	77	1	77	3	5	7	13	.350	0	0--	—	4.55
1995 Norfolk	AAA	4	3	0	0	20	88	22	15	13	3	0	0	1	7	0	9	1	0	1	1	.500	0	0--	—	5.85
1996 Louisville	AAA	11	11	0	0	60.1	253	55	24	19	4	2	2	1	24	2	73	0	0	3	4	.429	0	0--	—	2.83
1996 St. Louis	NL	6	1	0	2	10	45	11	11	10	4	0	1	1	3	0	12	0	0	0	1	.000	0	0-0	0	9.00

Rob Lukachyk

Bats: Left **Throws:** Right **Pos:** PH-2 **Ht:** 6'0" **Wt:** 175 **Born:** 7/24/68 **Age:** 28

Year Team	Lg	G	AB	H	2B	3B	HR	(Hm	Rd)	TB	R	RBI	TBB	IBB	SO	HBP	SH	SF	SB	CS	SB%	GDP	Avg	OBP	SLG
1987 White Sox	R	17	54	12	1	1	0	—	—	15	6	7	9	2	13	0	0	0	5	1	.83	1	.222	.333	.278
1988 Utica	A-	71	227	64	10	8	7	—	—	111	42	48	31	1	48	3	2	1	9	6	.60	2	.282	.374	.489
1989 South Bend	A	122	430	125	16	4	3	—	—	158	60	63	35	7	78	2	5	6	18	15	.55	5	.291	.342	.367
1990 Sarasota	A+	118	428	104	23	9	4	—	—	157	56	36	31	4	88	2	4	4	17	8	.68	6	.243	.295	.367
1991 Sarasota	A+	125	399	108	27	2	9	—	—	166	63	49	63	4	100	15	9	2	22	8	.73	2	.271	.388	.416
1992 Stockton	A+	105	359	99	21	14	15	—	—	193	77	81	53	3	86	9	0	5	44	15	.75	0	.276	.378	.538
1993 New Orleans	AAA	8	24	4	1	0	2	—	—	11	5	6	3	0	6	0	2	0	0	0	.00	0	.167	.259	.458
El Paso	AA	113	362	96	24	7	9	—	—	161	58	63	52	3	75	7	2	5	8	10	.44	10	.265	.364	.445
1994 Bowie	AA	108	371	107	19	6	10	—	—	168	68	54	47	9	60	5	1	5	33	6	.85	5	.288	.371	.453
1995 Toledo	AAA	104	346	88	24	7	7	—	—	147	43	26	33	0	75	2	3	2	8	5	.62	5	.254	.320	.425
1996 Harrisburg	AA	27	92	30	6	0	5	—	—	51	22	24	12	0	18	0	1	1	4	1	.80	1	.326	.400	.554
Ottawa	AAA	70	246	65	15	4	9	—	—	115	38	39	13	1	54	3	2	2	10	2	.83	4	.264	.307	.467
1996 Montreal	NL	2	2	0	0	0	0	(0	0)	0	0	0	0	0	1	0	0	0	0	0	.00	0	.000	.000	.000

Matt Luke

Bats: Left **Throws:** Left **Pos:** DH-1; PH-1 **Ht:** 6'5" **Wt:** 220 **Born:** 2/26/71 **Age:** 26

Year Team	Lg	G	AB	H	2B	3B	HR	(Hm	Rd)	TB	R	RBI	TBB	IBB	SO	HBP	SH	SF	SB	CS	SB%	GDP	Avg	OBP	SLG
1992 Oneonta	A-	69	271	67	11	7	2	—	—	98	30	34	19	3	32	2	0	3	4	1	.80	9	.247	.298	.362
1993 Greensboro	A	135	549	157	37	5	21	—	—	267	83	47	79	7	0	6	6	1	11	3	.79	9	.286	.346	.486
1994 Albany-Colo	AA	63	236	67	11	2	8	—	—	106	34	40	28	0	50	2	3	1	6	4	.60	6	.284	.363	.449
Tampa	A+	57	222	68	11	2	16	—	—	131	52	42	28	2	27	1	0	1	4	1	.80	7	.306	.385	.590
1995 Norwich	AA	93	365	95	17	5	8	—	—	146	48	53	20	2	68	2	3	4	5	4	.56	6	.260	.299	.400
Columbus	AAA	23	77	23	4	1	3	—	—	38	11	12	2	0	12	1	1	0	1	1	.50	3	.299	.325	.494
1996 Tampa	A+	2	7	2	0	0	0	—	—	2	1	1	1	0	1	0	0	0	0	0	.00	0	.286	.375	.286
Columbus	AAA	74	264	74	14	2	19	—	—	149	46	70	17	0	52	6	1	5	1	1	.50	9	.280	.332	.564
1996 New York	AL	1	0	0	0	0	0	(0	0)	0	0	0	0	0	0	0	0	0	0	0	.00	0	.000	.000	.000

Curt Lyons

Pitches: Right **Bats:** Right **Pos:** SP-3 **Ht:** 6'5" **Wt:** 240 **Born:** 10/17/74 **Age:** 22

Year Team	Lg	G	GS	CG	GF	IP	BFP	H	R	ER	HR	SH	SF	HB	TBB	IBB	SO	WP	Bk	W	L	Pct.	ShO	Sv-Op	Hld	ERA
1992 Princeton	R+	11	11	0	0	55.1	240	61	36	17	4	1	2	4	17	0	33	6	1	5	3	.625	0	0--	—	2.77
1993 Billings	R+	15	12	2	0	84	353	89	35	28	3	2	2	3	20	0	64	10	0	7	3	.700	0	0--	—	3.00
1994 Charlstn-WV	A	12	11	0	0	65.1	276	64	30	28	2	1	1	8	22	0	55	12	0	3	6	.333	0	0--	—	3.86
Princeton	R+	4	4	0	0	27.1	104	16	9	6	0	1	0	2	2	0	28	2	0	1	1	.500	0	0--	—	1.98
1995 Winston-Sal	A+	26	26	0	0	160.1	672	139	66	53	10	6	2	15	67	3	122	9	3	9	9	.500	0	0--	—	2.98
1996 Chattanooga	AA	24	24	1	0	141.2	577	113	48	38	8	1	1	10	52	0	176	6	0	13	4	.765	0	0--	—	2.41
1996 Cincinnati	NL	3	3	0	0	16	70	17	8	8	1	0	0	1	7	0	14	0	0	2	0	1.000	0	0-0	0	4.50

John Mabry

Bats: L **Throws:** R **Pos:** 1B-146; RF-13; PH-2; LF-1   **Ht:** 6'4" **Wt:** 205 **Born:** 10/17/70 **Age:** 26

Year Team	Lg	G	AB	H	2B	3B	HR	(Hm	Rd)	TB	R	RBI	TBB	IBB	SO	HBP	SH	SF	SB	CS	SB%	GDP	Avg	OBP	SLG
1994 St. Louis	NL	6	23	7	3	0	0	(0	0)	10	2	3	2	0	4	0	0	0	0	0	.00	0	.304	.360	.435
1995 St. Louis	NL	129	388	119	21	1	5	(2	3)	157	35	41	24	5	45	2	0	4	0	3	.00	6	.307	.347	.405
1996 St. Louis	NL	151	543	161	30	2	13	(3	10)	234	63	74	37	11	84	3	3	5	3	2	.60	21	.297	.342	.431
3 ML YEARS		286	954	287	54	3	18	(5	13)	401	100	118	63	16	133	5	3	9	3	5	.38	27	.301	.344	.420

Bob MacDonald

Pitches: Left **Bats:** Left **Pos:** RP-20   **Ht:** 6'3" **Wt:** 204 **Born:** 4/27/65 **Age:** 32

Year Team	Lg	G	GS	CG	GF	IP	BFP	H	R	ER	HR	SH	SF	HB	TBB	IBB	SO	WP	Bk	W	L	Pct.	ShO	Sv-Op	Hld	ERA
1996 Norfolk *	AAA	27	0	0	5	31.2	135	27	14	11	3	1	3	1	12	1	36	0	0	4	1	.800	0	0--	—	3.13
1990 Toronto	AL	4	0	0	1	2.1	8	0	0	0	0	0	0	0	2	0	0	0	0	0	0	.000	0	0-0	0	0.00
1991 Toronto	AL	45	0	0	10	53.2	231	51	19	17	5	2	2	0	25	4	24	1	1	3	3	.500	0	0-4	5	2.85
1992 Toronto	AL	27	0	0	9	47.1	204	50	24	23	4	1	1	1	16	3	26	0	0	1	0	1.000	0	0-0	2	4.37
1993 Detroit	AL	68	0	0	24	65.2	293	67	42	39	8	4	5	1	33	5	39	3	1	3	3	.500	0	3-6	16	5.35
1995 New York	AL	33	0	0	5	46.1	202	50	25	25	7	2	0	1	22	0	41	0	0	1	1	.500	0	0-1	4	4.86
1996 New York	NL	20	0	0	6	19	79	16	10	9	2	1	0	0	9	0	12	1	0	0	2	.000	0	0-0	3	4.26
6 ML YEARS		197	0	0	55	234.1	1017	234	120	113	26	10	9	3	107	12	142	6	2	8	9	.471	0	3-11	30	4.34

Mike Macfarlane

Bats: Right **Throws:** Right **Pos:** C-99; DH-9; PH-9   **Ht:** 6'1" **Wt:** 210 **Born:** 4/12/64 **Age:** 33

Year Team	Lg	G	AB	H	2B	3B	HR	(Hm	Rd)	TB	R	RBI	TBB	IBB	SO	HBP	SH	SF	SB	CS	SB%	GDP	Avg	OBP	SLG
1987 Kansas City	AL	8	19	4	1	0	0	(0	0)	5	0	3	2	0	2	0	0	0	0	0	.00	0	.211	.286	.263
1988 Kansas City	AL	70	211	56	15	0	4	(2	2)	83	25	26	21	2	37	1	1	2	0	0	.00	5	.265	.332	.393
1989 Kansas City	AL	69	157	35	6	0	2	(0	2)	47	13	19	7	0	27	2	0	1	0	0	.00	8	.223	.263	.299
1990 Kansas City	AL	124	400	102	24	4	6	(1	5)	152	37	58	25	2	69	7	1	6	1	0	1.00	9	.255	.306	.380
1991 Kansas City	AL	84	267	74	18	2	13	(6	7)	135	34	41	17	0	52	6	1	4	1	0	1.00	4	.277	.330	.506
1992 Kansas City	AL	129	402	94	28	3	17	(7	10)	179	51	48	30	2	89	15	1	2	1	5	.17	8	.234	.310	.445
1993 Kansas City	AL	117	388	106	27	0	20	(7	13)	193	55	67	40	2	83	16	1	6	2	5	.29	8	.273	.360	.497
1994 Kansas City	AL	92	314	80	17	3	14	(9	5)	145	53	47	35	1	71	18	0	3	1	0	1.00	9	.255	.359	.462
1995 Boston	AL	115	364	82	18	1	15	(7	8)	147	45	51	38	0	78	14	0	4	2	1	.67	9	.225	.319	.404
1996 Kansas City	AL	112	379	104	24	2	19	(9	10)	189	58	54	31	5	57	7	0	2	3	3	.50	4	.274	.339	.499
10 ML YEARS		920	2901	737	178	15	110	(48	62)	1275	371	414	246	14	565	86	5	30	11	14	.44	65	.254	.328	.440

Robert Machado

Bats: Right **Throws:** Right **Pos:** C-4   **Ht:** 6'1" **Wt:** 205 **Born:** 6/3/73 **Age:** 24

Year Team	Lg	G	AB	H	2B	3B	HR	(Hm	Rd)	TB	R	RBI	TBB	IBB	SO	HBP	SH	SF	SB	CS	SB%	GDP	Avg	OBP	SLG
1991 White Sox	R	38	126	31	4	1	0	—	—	37	11	15	6	0	21	6	0	1	2	1	.67	2	.246	.309	.294
1992 Utica	A-	45	161	44	13	1	2	—	—	65	16	20	5	0	26	0	0	1	1	5	.17	3	.273	.294	.404
1993 South Bend	A	75	281	86	14	3	2	—	—	112	34	33	19	0	59	4	2	4	1	2	.33	6	.306	.354	.399
1994 Pr. William	A+	93	312	81	17	1	11	—	—	133	45	47	27	0	68	4	2	1	0	1	.00	10	.260	.326	.426
1995 Nashville	AAA	16	49	7	3	0	1	—	—	13	7	5	7	0	12	0	0	0	0	1	.00	1	.143	.250	.265
Pr. William	A+	83	272	69	14	0	6	—	—	101	37	31	40	5	47	7	2	1	0	0	.00	6	.254	.363	.371
1996 Birmingham	AA	87	309	74	16	0	6	—	—	108	35	28	20	1	56	3	10	1	1	4	.20	9	.239	.291	.350
1996 Chicago	AL	4	6	4	1	0	0	(0	0)	5	1	2	0	0	0	0	0	0	0	0	.00	1	.667	.667	.833

Shane Mack

Bats: Right **Throws:** Right **Pos:** LF/CF/DH   **Ht:** 6'0" **Wt:** 190 **Born:** 12/7/63 **Age:** 33

Year Team	Lg	G	AB	H	2B	3B	HR	(Hm	Rd)	TB	R	RBI	TBB	IBB	SO	HBP	SH	SF	SB	CS	SB%	GDP	Avg	OBP	SLG
1987 San Diego	NL	105	238	57	11	3	4	(2	2)	86	28	25	18	0	47	3	6	2	4	6	.40	11	.239	.299	.361
1988 San Diego	NL	56	119	29	3	0	0	(0	0)	32	13	12	14	0	21	3	3	1	5	1	.83	2	.244	.336	.269
1990 Minnesota	AL	125	313	102	10	4	8	(5	3)	144	50	44	29	1	69	5	6	0	13	4	.76	7	.326	.392	.460
1991 Minnesota	AL	143	442	137	27	8	18	(4	14)	234	79	74	34	1	79	6	2	5	13	9	.59	11	.310	.363	.529
1992 Minnesota	AL	156	600	189	31	6	16	(10	6)	280	101	75	64	1	106	15	11	2	26	14	.65	8	.315	.394	.467
1993 Minnesota	AL	128	503	139	30	4	10	(3	7)	207	66	61	41	1	76	4	3	2	15	5	.75	13	.276	.335	.412
1994 Minnesota	AL	81	303	101	21	2	15	(8	7)	171	55	61	32	1	61	6	1	5	4	1	.80	11	.333	.402	.564
7 ML YEARS		794	2518	754	133	27	71	(32	39)	1154	392	352	232	5	449	42	32	17	80	40	.67	63	.299	.366	.458

Greg Maddux

Pitches: Right **Bats:** Right **Pos:** SP-35   **Ht:** 6'0" **Wt:** 175 **Born:** 4/14/66 **Age:** 31

		HOW MUCH HE PITCHED						WHAT HE GAVE UP												THE RESULTS						
Year Team	Lg	G	GS	CG	GF	IP	BFP	H	R	ER	HR	SH	SF	HB	TBB	IBB	SO	WP	Bk	W	L	Pct.	ShO	Sv-Op	Hld	ERA
1986 Chicago	NL	6	5	1	1	31	144	44	20	19	3	1	0	1	11	2	20	2	0	2	4	.333	0	0--	0	5.52
1987 Chicago	NL	30	27	1	2	155.2	701	181	111	97	17	7	1	4	74	13	101	4	7	6	14	.300	1	0-0	0	5.61
1988 Chicago	NL	34	34	9	0	249	1047	230	97	88	13	11	2	9	81	16	140	3	6	18	8	.692	3	0-0	0	3.18
1989 Chicago	NL	35	35	7	0	238.1	1002	222	90	78	13	18	6	6	82	13	135	5	3	19	12	.613	1	0-0	0	2.95
1990 Chicago	NL	35	35	8	0	237	1011	242	116	84	11	18	5	4	71	10	144	3	3	15	15	.500	2	0-0	0	3.46
1991 Chicago	NL	37	37	7	0	263	1070	232	113	98	18	16	3	6	66	9	198	6	3	15	11	.577	2	0-0	0	3.35
1992 Chicago	NL	35	35	9	0	268	1061	201	68	65	7	15	3	14	70	7	199	5	0	20	11	.645	4	0-0	0	2.18
1993 Atlanta	NL	36	36	8	0	267	1064	228	85	70	14	15	7	6	52	7	197	5	1	20	10	.667	1	0-0	0	2.36
1994 Atlanta	NL	25	25	10	0	202	774	150	44	35	4	6	5	6	31	3	156	3	1	16	6	.727	3	0-0	0	1.56
1995 Atlanta	NL	28	28	10	0	209.2	785	147	39	38	8	9	1	4	23	3	181	1	0	19	2	.905	3	0-0	0	1.63
1996 Atlanta	NL	35	35	5	0	245	978	225	85	74	11	8	5	3	28	11	172	4	0	15	11	.577	1	0-0	0	2.72
11 ML YEARS		336	332	75	3	2365.2	9637	2102	868	753	119	124	38	63	589	94	1643	41	24	165	104	.613	21	0--	0	2.86

Mike Maddux

Pitches: Right **Bats:** Left **Pos:** RP-16; SP-7   **Ht:** 6'2" **Wt:** 185 **Born:** 8/27/61 **Age:** 35

		HOW MUCH HE PITCHED						WHAT HE GAVE UP												THE RESULTS						
Year Team	Lg	G	GS	CG	GF	IP	BFP	H	R	ER	HR	SH	SF	HB	TBB	IBB	SO	WP	Bk	W	L	Pct.	ShO	Sv-Op	Hld	ERA
1996 Pawtucket *	AAA	3	3	0	0	14	56	13	5	5	2	1	0	0	2	0	9	0	0	2	0	1.000	0	0--	—	3.21
1986 Philadelphia	NL	16	16	0	0	78	351	88	56	47	6	3	3	3	34	4	44	4	2	3	7	.300	0	0--	—	5.42
1987 Philadelphia	NL	7	2	0	0	17	72	17	5	5	0	0	0	0	5	0	15	1	0	2	0	1.000	0	0-0	0	2.65
1988 Philadelphia	NL	25	11	0	4	88.2	380	91	41	37	6	7	3	5	34	4	59	4	2	4	3	.571	0	0-0	0	3.76
1989 Philadelphia	NL	16	4	2	1	43.2	191	52	29	25	3	3	1	2	14	3	26	3	1	1	3	.250	0	1-1	2	5.15
1990 Los Angeles	NL	11	2	0	3	20.2	88	24	15	15	3	0	1	1	4	0	11	2	0	0	1	.000	0	0-0	0	6.53
1991 San Diego	NL	64	1	0	27	98.2	388	78	30	27	4	5	2	1	27	3	57	5	0	7	2	.778	0	5-7	9	2.46
1992 San Diego	NL	50	1	0	14	79.2	330	71	25	21	2	2	3	0	24	4	60	4	1	2	2	.500	0	5-9	8	2.37
1993 New York	NL	58	0	0	31	75	320	67	34	30	3	7	6	4	27	7	57	4	1	3	8	.273	0	5-11	3	3.60
1994 New York	NL	27	0	0	12	44	186	45	25	25	7	0	2	0	13	4	32	2	0	2	1	.667	0	2-4	1	5.11
1995 Pit-Bos		44	4	0	7	98.2	409	100	49	45	5	1	1	2	18	4	69	6	0	5	1	.833	0	1-1	6	4.10
1996 Boston	AL	23	7	0	2	64.1	295	76	37	32	12	3	2	5	27	2	32	1	0	3	2	.600	0	0-0	0	4.48
1995 Pittsburgh	NL	8	0	0	1	9	42	14	9	9	0	0	0	0	3	1	4	1	0	1	0	1.000	0	0-0	2	9.00
Boston	AL	36	4	0	6	89.2	367	86	40	36	5	1	1	2	15	3	65	5	0	4	1	.800	0	1-1	4	3.61
11 ML YEARS		341	48	2	101	708.1	3010	709	346	309	51	31	24	23	227	35	462	36	7	32	30	.516	0	19--	—	3.93

Calvin Maduro

Pitches: Right **Bats:** Right **Pos:** SP-2; RP-2   **Ht:** 6'0" **Wt:** 175 **Born:** 9/5/74 **Age:** 22

		HOW MUCH HE PITCHED						WHAT HE GAVE UP												THE RESULTS						
Year Team	Lg	G	GS	CG	GF	IP	BFP	H	R	ER	HR	SH	SF	HB	TBB	IBB	SO	WP	Bk	W	L	Pct.	ShO	Sv-Op	Hld	ERA
1992 Orioles	R	13	12	1	0	71.1	289	56	29	18	2	2	3	1	26	0	66	4	3	1	4	.200	0	0--	—	2.27
1993 Bluefield	R+	14	14	3	0	91	378	90	46	40	4	0	2	3	17	0	83	4	1	9	4	.692	0	0--	—	3.96
1994 Frederick	A+	27	26	0	1	152.1	636	132	86	72	18	3	3	4	59	0	137	10	4	9	8	.529	0	0--	—	4.25
1995 Bowie	AA	7	7	0	0	35.1	165	39	28	20	3	1	2	0	27	0	26	3	0	0	6	.000	0	0--	—	5.09
1996 Bowie	AA	19	19	4	0	124.1	507	116	50	45	8	4	1	2	36	0	87	4	2	9	7	.563	3	0--	—	3.26
Rochester	AAA	8	8	0	0	43.2	197	49	25	23	8	1	1	3	18	0	40	2	0	3	5	.375	0	0--	—	4.74
1996 Philadelphia	NL	4	2	0	0	15.1	62	13	6	6	1	1	0	2	8	0	11	1	0	0	1	.000	0	0-0	0	3.52

Dave Magadan

Bats: Left **Throws:** Right **Pos:** 3B-51; PH-25; 1B-10   **Ht:** 6'3" **Wt:** 210 **Born:** 9/30/62 **Age:** 34

		BATTING																	BASERUNNING				PERCENTAGES		
Year Team	Lg	G	AB	H	2B	3B	HR	(Hm	Rd)	TB	R	RBI	TBB	IBB	SO	HBP	SH	SF	SB	CS	SB%	GDP	Avg	OBP	SLG
1996 Daytona *	A+	7	20	6	1	0	0	(--	--)	7	5	3	7	0	2	0	0	0	0	0	.00	1	.300	.481	.350
Iowa *	AAA	3	9	2	1	0	0	(--	--)	3	0	1	1	0	2	0	0	0	0	0	.00	0	.222	.300	.333
1986 New York	NL	10	18	8	0	0	0	(0	0)	8	3	3	3	0	1	0	0	0	0	0	.00	0	.444	.524	.444
1987 New York	NL	85	192	61	13	1	3	(2	1)	85	21	24	22	2	22	0	1	1	0	0	.00	5	.318	.386	.443
1988 New York	NL	112	314	87	15	0	1	(1	0)	105	39	35	60	4	39	2	1	3	0	1	.00	9	.277	.393	.334
1989 New York	NL	127	374	107	22	3	4	(3	1)	147	47	41	49	6	37	1	1	4	1	0	1.00	2	.286	.367	.393
1990 New York	NL	144	451	148	28	6	6	(2	4)	206	74	72	74	4	55	2	4	10	2	1	.67	11	.328	.417	.457
1991 New York	NL	124	418	108	23	0	4	(2	2)	143	58	51	83	3	50	2	7	7	1	1	.50	5	.258	.378	.342
1992 New York	NL	99	321	91	9	1	3	(2	1)	111	33	28	56	3	44	0	2	0	1	0	1.00	6	.283	.390	.346
1993 Fla-Sea		137	455	124	23	0	5	(3	2)	162	49	50	80	7	63	1	2	6	2	1	.67	12	.273	.378	.356
1994 Florida	NL	74	211	58	7	0	1	(1	0)	68	30	17	39	0	25	1	0	3	0	0	.00	8	.275	.386	.322
1995 Houston	NL	127	348	109	24	0	2	(0	2)	139	44	51	71	9	56	0	1	2	2	1	.67	9	.313	.428	.399
1996 Chicago	NL	78	169	43	10	0	3	(2	1)	62	23	17	29	3	23	0	1	2	0	0	.00	3	.254	.360	.367
1993 Florida	NL	66	227	65	12	0	1	(1	0)	89	22	29	44	4	30	1	0	3	0	1	.00	3	.286	.400	.392
Seattle	AL	71	228	59	11	0	1	(0	1)	73	27	21	36	3	33	0	2	3	2	0	1.00	9	.259	.356	.320
11 ML YEARS		1117	3271	944	174	11	32	(18	14)	1236	421	389	566	41	415	9	20	38	9	7	.56	71	.289	.391	.378

Wendell Magee

Bats: R **Throws:** R **Pos:** CF-18; RF-18; LF-6; PH-1   **Ht:** 6'0" **Wt:** 220 **Born:** 8/3/72 **Age:** 24

Year Team	Lg	G	AB	H	2B	3B	HR	(Hm	Rd)	TB	R	RBI	TBB	IBB	SO	HBP	SH	SF	SB	CS	SB%	GDP	Avg	OBP	SLG
1994 Batavia	A-	63	229	64	12	4	2	—	—	90	42	35	16	1	24	4	1	2	10	2	.83	5	.279	.335	.393
1995 Clearwater	A+	96	388	137	24	5	6	—	—	189	67	46	33	3	40	4	1	5	7	10	.41	15	.353	.405	.487
Reading	AA	39	136	40	9	1	3	—	—	60	17	21	21	1	17	0	0	4	3	4	.43	3	.294	.379	.441
1996 Reading	AA	71	270	79	15	5	6	—	—	122	38	30	24	1	40	1	0	0	10	6	.63	8	.293	.353	.452
Scranton-WB	AAA	44	155	44	9	2	10	—	—	87	31	32	21	0	31	0	0	2	3	1	.75	2	.284	.365	.561
1996 Philadelphia	NL	38	142	29	7	0	2	(2	0)	42	9	14	9	0	33	0	0	0	0	0	.00	2	.204	.252	.296

Mike Magnante

Pitches: Left **Bats:** Left **Pos:** RP-38   **Ht:** 6'1" **Wt:** 195 **Born:** 6/17/65 **Age:** 32

Year Team	Lg	G	GS	CG	GF	IP	BFP	H	R	ER	HR	SH	SF	HB	TBB	IBB	SO	WP	Bk	W	L	Pct.	ShO	Sv-Op	Hld	ERA
1996 Omaha *	AAA	1	0	0	1	3	12	3	1	0	0	0	0	0	0	0	6	0	0	1	0	1.000	0	0--	—	0.00
1991 Kansas City	AL	38	0	0	10	55	236	55	19	15	3	2	1	0	23	3	42	1	0	0	1	.000	0	0-0	2	2.45
1992 Kansas City	AL	44	12	0	11	89.1	403	115	53	49	5	5	7	2	35	5	31	2	0	4	9	.308	0	0-3	4	4.94
1993 Kansas City	AL	7	6	0	0	35.1	145	37	16	16	3	1	1	1	11	1	16	1	0	1	2	.333	0	0-0	0	4.08
1994 Kansas City	AL	36	1	0	10	47	211	55	27	24	7	2	3	0	16	1	21	3	0	2	3	.400	0	0-0	6	4.60
1995 Kansas City	AL	28	0	0	7	44.2	190	45	23	21	6	2	2	2	16	1	28	2	0	1	1	.500	0	0-1	5	4.23
1996 Kansas City	AL	38	0	0	9	54	238	58	38	34	5	0	4	4	24	1	32	3	0	2	2	.500	0	0-1	5	5.67
6 ML YEARS		191	19	0	47	325.1	1423	365	176	159	27	12	18	9	125	12	170	12	0	10	18	.357	0	0-5	22	4.40

Joe Magrane

Pitches: Left **Bats:** Right **Pos:** RP-11; SP-8   **Ht:** 6'6" **Wt:** 230 **Born:** 7/2/64 **Age:** 32

Year Team	Lg	G	GS	CG	GF	IP	BFP	H	R	ER	HR	SH	SF	HB	TBB	IBB	SO	WP	Bk	W	L	Pct.	ShO	Sv-Op	Hld	ERA
1996 Nashville	AAA	21	1	0	8	26.1	115	29	17	16	5	0	1	0	8	0	26	2	0	1	1	.500	0	1--	—	5.47
1987 St. Louis	NL	27	26	4	0	170.1	722	157	75	67	9	9	3	10	60	6	101	9	7	9	7	.563	2	0-0	0	3.54
1988 St. Louis	NL	24	24	4	0	165.1	677	133	57	40	6	8	4	2	51	4	100	8	8	5	9	.357	3	0-0	0	2.18
1989 St. Louis	NL	34	33	9	1	234.2	971	219	81	76	5	14	8	6	72	7	127	14	5	18	9	.667	3	0-0	0	2.91
1990 St. Louis	NL	31	31	3	0	203.1	855	204	86	81	10	8	6	8	59	7	100	11	1	10	17	.370	2	0-0	0	3.59
1992 St. Louis	NL	5	5	0	0	31.1	143	34	15	14	3	1	2		15	0	20	4	0	1	2	.333	0	0-0	0	4.02
1993 StL-Cal		30	28	0	2	164	708	175	95	85	19	10	10	5	58	3	62	8	0	11	12	.478	0	0-0	0	4.66
1994 California	AL	20	11	1	4	74	357	89	63	60	10	3	6	5	51	0	33	7	0	2	6	.250	0	0-0	0	7.30
1996 Chicago	AL	19	8	0	3	53.2	252	70	45	41	10	1	3	3	25	1	21	3	0	1	5	.167	0	0-0	5	6.88
1993 St. Louis	NL	22	20	0	2	116	499	127	68	64	15	6	7	5	37	3	38	4	0	8	10	.444	0	0-0	0	4.97
California	AL	8	8	0	0	48	209	48	27	21	4	4	3	0	21	0	24	4	0	3	2	.600	0	0-0	0	3.94
8 ML YEARS		190	166	21	10	1096.2	4685	1081	517	464	79	53	38	42	391	28	564	64	21	57	67	.460	10	0-0	5	3.81

Pat Mahomes

Pitches: Right **Bats:** Right **Pos:** RP-26; SP-5   **Ht:** 6'4" **Wt:** 212 **Born:** 8/9/70 **Age:** 26

Year Team	Lg	G	GS	CG	GF	IP	BFP	H	R	ER	HR	SH	SF	HB	TBB	IBB	SO	WP	Bk	W	L	Pct.	ShO	Sv-Op	Hld	ERA
1996 Salt Lake *	AAA	22	2	0	20	33.2	143	32	14	14	0	1	0	2	12	0	41	1	0	3	1	.750	0	7--	—	3.74
1992 Minnesota	AL	14	13	0	1	69.2	302	73	41	39	5	0	3	1	37	0	44	2	1	3	4	.429	0	0-0	0	5.04
1993 Minnesota	AL	12	5	0	4	37.1	173	47	34	32	8	1	3	1	16	0	23	3	0	1	5	.167	0	0-0	0	7.71
1994 Minnesota	AL	21	21	0	0	120	517	121	68	63	22	1	4	1	62	1	53	3	0	9	5	.643	0	0-0	0	4.73
1995 Minnesota	AL	47	7	0	16	94.2	423	100	74	67	22	3	2	2	47	1	67	6	0	4	10	.286	0	3-7	9	6.37
1996 Min-Bos	AL	31	5	0	10	57.1	271	72	46	44	13	2	2	0	33	0	36	2	0	3	4	.429	0	2-2	4	6.91
1996 Minnesota	AL	20	5	0	5	45	220	63	38	36	10	0	2	0	27	0	30	2	0	1	4	.200	0	0-0	3	7.20
Boston	AL	11	0	0	5	12.1	51	9	8	8	3	2	0	0	6	0	6	0	0	2	0	1.000	0	2-2	1	5.84
5 ML YEARS		125	51	0	31	379	1686	413	263	245	70	7	14	4	195	2	223	16	1	20	28	.417	0	5-9	13	5.82

Jose Malave

Bats: Right **Throws:** Right **Pos:** RF-30; PH-10; LF-8   **Ht:** 6'2" **Wt:** 212 **Born:** 5/31/71 **Age:** 26

Year Team	Lg	G	AB	H	2B	3B	HR	(Hm	Rd)	TB	R	RBI	TBB	IBB	SO	HBP	SH	SF	SB	CS	SB%	GDP	Avg	OBP	SLG
1990 Elmira	A-	13	29	4	1	0	0	—	—	5	4	3	2	0	12	0	0	1	1	0	1.00	0	.138	.188	.172
1991 Red Sox	R	37	146	47	4	2	2	—	—	61	24	28	10	0	23	1	0	3	6	0	1.00	3	.322	.363	.418
1992 Winter Havn	A+	8	25	4	0	0	0	—	—	4	1	0	0	0	11	0	1	0	0	0	.00	0	.160	.160	.160
Elmira	A-	65	268	87	9	1	12	—	—	134	44	46	14	3	48	3	0	1	8	3	.73	2	.325	.364	.500
1993 Lynchburg	A+	82	312	94	27	1	8	—	—	147	42	54	36	3	54	3	0	5	2	3	.40	8	.301	.374	.471
1994 New Britain	AA	122	465	139	37	7	24	—	—	262	87	92	52	1	81	4	0	7	4	7	.36	12	.299	.369	.563
1995 Pawtucket	AAA	91	318	86	12	1	23	—	—	169	55	57	30	1	67	2	0	0	0	1	.00	4	.270	.337	.531
1996 Pawtucket	AAA	41	155	42	6	0	8	—	—	72	30	29	12	1	37	2	0	1	0	0	.67	5	.271	.329	.465
1996 Boston	AL	41	102	24	3	0	4	(1	3)	39	12	17	12	0	25	1	0	0	0	0	.00	0	.235	.257	.382

Matt Mantei

Pitches: Right **Bats:** Right **Pos:** RP-14 **Ht:** 6'1" **Wt:** 181 **Born:** 7/7/73 **Age:** 23

Year Team	Lg	G	GS	CG	GF	IP	BFP	H	R	ER	HR	SH	SF	HB	TBB	IBB	SO	WP	Bk	W	L	Pct.	ShO	Sv-Op	Hld	ERA
1991 Mariners	R	17	5	0	4	40.1	202	54	40	30	0	2	3	1	28	2	28	7	8	1	5	.167	0	0--	—	6.69
1992 Mariners	R	3	3	0	0	16	68	18	10	10	1	0	0	0	5	0	19	0	0	1	1	.500	0	0--	—	5.63
1993 Bellingham	A-	26	0	0	21	25.2	120	26	19	17	2	4	0	1	15	0	34	4	0	1	1	.500	0	12--	—	5.96
1994 Appleton	A	48	0	0	43	48	201	42	14	11	2	2	2	1	21	3	70	6	0	5	1	.833	0	26--	—	2.06
1995 Charlotte	AAA	6	0	0	1	7	27	1	3	2	1	0	1	1	5	0	10	0	0	0	1	.000	0	0--	—	2.57
Portland	AA	14	0	0	5	18.1	75	11	6	5	1	1	1	2	10	0	25	0	0	1	1	.500	0	1--	—	2.45
1996 Charlotte	AAA	7	0	0	6	7.2	36	6	4	4	1	0	1	0	7	0	8	3	0	0	2	.000	0	2--	—	4.70
1995 Florida	NL	12	0	0	3	13.1	64	12	8	7	1	1	1	0	13	0	15	1	0	0	1	.000	0	0-0	—	4.73
1996 Florida	NL	14	0	0	1	18.1	89	13	13	13	2	1	0	0	21	1	25	2	0	1	0	1.000	0	0-1	0	6.38
2 ML YEARS		26	0	0	4	31.2	153	25	21	20	3	2	1	0	34	1	40	3	0	1	1	.500	0	0-1	0	5.68

Jeff Manto

Bats: R **Throws:** R **Pos:** 3B-26; PH-8; 2B-4; SS-4; DH-2; 1B-1; LF-1 **Ht:** 6'3" **Wt:** 210 **Born:** 8/23/64 **Age:** 32

Year Team	Lg	G	AB	H	2B	3B	HR	(Hm	Rd)	TB	R	RBI	TBB	IBB	SO	HBP	SH	SF	SB	CS	SB%	GDP	Avg	OBP	SLG
1996 Pawtucket *	AAA	12	45	11	5	0	2	—	—	22	6	6	5	0	8	1	0	0	1	0	1.00	1	.244	.333	.489
Trenton *	AA	6	21	6	0	0	0	—	—	6	3	5	1	0	5	1	0	1	0	0	.00	1	.286	.333	.286
1990 Cleveland	AL	30	76	17	5	1	2	(1	1)	30	12	14	21	1	18	0	0	0	0	1	.00	0	.224	.392	.395
1991 Cleveland	AL	47	128	27	7	0	2	(0	2)	40	15	13	14	0	22	4	1	1	2	0	1.00	3	.211	.306	.313
1993 Philadelphia	NL	8	18	1	0	0	0	(0	0)	1	0	0	0	0	3	1	0	0	0	0	.00	0	.056	.105	.056
1995 Baltimore	AL	89	254	65	9	0	17	(12	5)	125	31	38	24	0	69	2	0	0	0	3	.00	6	.256	.325	.492
1996 Bos-Sea	AL	43	102	20	6	1	3	(3	0)	37	15	10	17	0	24	1	0	0	0	1	.00	2	.196	.317	.363
1996 Boston	AL	22	48	10	3	1	2	(2	0)	21	8	6	8	0	12	1	0	0	0	0	.00	0	.208	.333	.438
Seattle	AL	21	54	10	3	0	1	(1	0)	16	7	4	9	0	12	0	0	0	0	1	.00	2	.185	.302	.296
5 ML YEARS		217	578	130	27	2	24	(16	8)	233	73	75	76	1	136	8	1	1	2	5	.29	11	.225	.323	.403

Barry Manuel

Pitches: Right **Bats:** Right **Pos:** RP-53 **Ht:** 5'11" **Wt:** 185 **Born:** 8/12/65 **Age:** 31

Year Team	Lg	G	GS	CG	GF	IP	BFP	H	R	ER	HR	SH	SF	HB	TBB	IBB	SO	WP	Bk	W	L	Pct.	ShO	Sv-Op	Hld	ERA
1987 Rangers	R	1	0	0	0	1	7	3	2	2	0	0	0	0	1	0	1	2	0	0	0	.000	0	0--	—	18.00
Charlotte	A+	13	5	0	3	30	138	33	24	22	2	1	2	3	18	0	19	4	0	1	2	.333	0	0--	—	6.60
1988 Charlotte	A+	37	0	0	22	60.1	259	47	24	17	4	6	1	4	32	0	55	8	3	4	3	.571	0	4--	—	2.54
1989 Tulsa	AA	11	11	0	0	49.1	237	49	44	41	5	3	6	9	39	0	40	3	3	3	4	.429	0	0--	—	7.48
Charlotte	A+	15	14	0	0	76.1	330	77	43	40	6	4	3	8	30	0	51	6	1	4	7	.364	0	0--	—	4.72
1990 Charlotte	A+	57	0	0	56	56.1	238	39	23	18	2	4	2	3	30	2	60	1	0	1	5	.167	0	36--	—	2.88
1991 Tulsa	AA	56	0	0	48	68.1	300	63	29	25	5	4	2	5	34	1	45	0	1	2	7	.222	0	25--	—	3.29
1992 Okla. City	AAA	27	0	0	22	27.1	143	32	24	16	1	1	2	2	26	0	11	1	0	1	8	.111	0	5--	—	5.27
Tulsa	AA	16	1	0	8	27	122	28	12	12	4	0	0	1	16	0	28	0	0	2	0	1.000	0	2--	—	4.00
1993 Charlotte	A+	3	0	0	1	4.2	20	6	0	0	0	0	0	0	2	0	4	0	0	0	0	.000	0	0--	—	0.00
Okla. City	AAA	21	0	0	10	23.2	109	29	21	21	1	0	1	0	16	1	19	3	0	2	2	.500	0	2--	—	7.99
Rochester	AAA	9	0	0	2	19.2	77	14	8	8	2	1	1	1	7	0	11	0	0	1	1	.500	0	0--	—	3.66
1994 Rochester	AAA	35	20	1	10	139.2	629	161	87	85	21	2	7	3	58	2	107	7	1	11	8	.579	0	4--	—	5.48
1995 Ottawa	AAA	35	22	1	8	127.1	554	125	71	65	4	4	9	14	50	1	85	6	2	5	12	.294	0	1--	—	4.59
1991 Texas	AL	8	0	0	5	16	58	7	2	2	0	0	3	0	6	0	5	2	0	1	0	1.000	0	0-0	0	1.13
1992 Texas	AL	3	0	0	0	5.2	25	6	3	3	2	0	0	1	1	0	9	0	0	1	1	.500	0	0-0	0	4.76
1996 Montreal	NL	53	0	0	7	86	360	70	34	31	10	6	2	7	26	4	62	4	0	4	1	.800	0	0-0	2	3.24
3 ML YEARS		64	0	0	12	107.2	443	83	39	36	12	6	5	8	33	4	76	6	0	6	1	.857	0	0-0	2	3.01

Kirt Manwaring

Bats: Right **Throws:** Right **Pos:** C-86 **Ht:** 5'11" **Wt:** 203 **Born:** 7/15/65 **Age:** 31

Year Team	Lg	G	AB	H	2B	3B	HR	(Hm	Rd)	TB	R	RBI	TBB	IBB	SO	HBP	SH	SF	SB	CS	SB%	GDP	Avg	OBP	SLG
1996 Phoenix *	AAA	4	11	2	0	0	0	—	—	2	1	1	2	0	0	0	0	0	0	0	.00	0	.182	.308	.182
1987 San Francisco	NL	6	7	1	0	0	0	(0	0)	1	0	0	0	0	1	1	0	0	0	0	.00	1	.143	.250	.143
1988 San Francisco	NL	40	116	29	7	0	1	(0	1)	39	12	15	2	0	21	3	1	1	0	1	.00	1	.250	.279	.336
1989 San Francisco	NL	85	200	42	4	2	0	(0	0)	50	14	18	11	1	28	4	7	1	2	1	.67	5	.210	.264	.250
1990 San Francisco	NL	8	13	2	0	1	0	(0	0)	4	0	1	0	0	3	0	0	0	0	0	.00	0	.154	.154	.308
1991 San Francisco	NL	67	178	40	9	0	0	(0	0)	49	16	19	9	0	22	3	7	2	1	1	.50	2	.225	.271	.275
1992 San Francisco	NL	109	349	85	10	5	4	(1	3)	117	24	26	29	0	42	5	6	0	2	1	.67	12	.244	.311	.335
1993 San Francisco	NL	130	432	119	15	1	5	(3	2)	151	48	49	41	13	76	6	5	2	1	3	.25	14	.275	.345	.350
1994 San Francisco	NL	97	316	79	17	1	1	(0	1)	101	30	29	25	3	50	3	4	3	1	1	.50	10	.250	.308	.320
1995 San Francisco	NL	118	379	95	15	2	4	(4	0)	126	21	36	27	6	72	10	4	2	1	0	1.00	6	.251	.314	.332
1996 SF-Hou	NL	86	227	52	9	0	1	(1	0)	64	14	18	19	1	40	5	2	2	0	2	.00	4	.229	.300	.282
1996 San Francisco	NL	49	145	34	6	0	1	(1	0)	43	9	14	16	1	24	3	1	2	0	0	.00	2	.234	.319	.297
Houston	NL	37	82	18	3	0	0	(0	0)	21	5	4	3	0	16	2	1	0	0	2	.00	2	.220	.264	.256
10 ML YEARS		746	2217	544	86	12	16	(9	7)	702	179	211	163	24	355	40	36	15	8	9	.47	57	.245	.307	.317

Oreste Marrero

Bats: Left **Throws:** Left **Pos:** PH-10; 1B-1 **Ht:** 6'0" **Wt:** 195 **Born:** 10/31/69 **Age:** 27

Year Team	Lg	G	AB	H	2B	3B	HR	(Hm	Rd)	TB	R	RBI	TBB	IBB	SO	HBP	SH	SF	SB	CS	SB%	GDP	Avg	OBP	SLG
1996 Albuquerque *	AAA	121	441	125	29	1	13	—	—	195	50	76	36	1	119	1	0	4	2	6	.25	12	.283	.336	.442
1993 Montreal	NL	32	81	17	5	1	1	(1	0)	27	10	4	14	0	16	0	0	0	1	3	.25	0	.210	.326	.333
1996 Los Angeles	NL	10	8	3	1	0	0	(0	0)	4	2	1	1	0	3	0	0	0	0	0	.00	0	.375	.444	.500
2 ML YEARS		42	89	20	6	1	1	(1	0)	31	12	5	15	0	19	0	0	0	1	3	.25	0	.225	.337	.348

Al Martin

Bats: Left **Throws:** Left **Pos:** LF-142; CF-26; PH-6 **Ht:** 6'2" **Wt:** 210 **Born:** 11/24/67 **Age:** 29

Year Team	Lg	G	AB	H	2B	3B	HR	(Hm	Rd)	TB	R	RBI	TBB	IBB	SO	HBP	SH	SF	SB	CS	SB%	GDP	Avg	OBP	SLG
1992 Pittsburgh	NL	12	12	2	0	1	0	(0	0)	4	1	2	0	0	5	0	0	1	0	0	.00	0	.167	.154	.333
1993 Pittsburgh	NL	143	480	135	26	8	18	(15	3)	231	85	64	42	5	122	1	2	3	16	9	.64	5	.281	.338	.481
1994 Pittsburgh	NL	82	276	79	12	4	9	(6	3)	126	48	33	34	3	56	2	0	1	15	6	.71	3	.286	.367	.457
1995 Pittsburgh	NL	124	439	124	25	3	13	(8	5)	194	70	41	44	6	92	2	1	0	20	11	.65	5	.282	.351	.442
1996 Pittsburgh	NL	155	630	189	40	1	18	(8	10)	285	101	72	54	2	116	2	1	7	38	12	.76	8	.300	.354	.452
5 ML YEARS		516	1837	529	103	17	58	(37	21)	840	305	212	174	16	391	7	4	12	89	38	.70	21	.288	.350	.457

Norberto Martin

Bats: R **Throws:** R **Pos:** PH-27; SS-24; DH-19; 2B-10; 3B-3 **Ht:** 5'10" **Wt:** 164 **Born:** 12/10/66 **Age:** 30

Year Team	Lg	G	AB	H	2B	3B	HR	(Hm	Rd)	TB	R	RBI	TBB	IBB	SO	HBP	SH	SF	SB	CS	SB%	GDP	Avg	OBP	SLG
1996 Nashville *	AAA	17	68	14	3	0	2	—	—	23	9	8	4	0	10	1	1	1	1	0	1.00	1	.206	.257	.338
1993 Chicago	AL	8	14	5	0	0	0	(0	0)	5	3	2	1	0	1	0	0	0	0	0	.00	0	.357	.400	.357
1994 Chicago	AL	45	131	36	7	1	1	(0	1)	48	19	16	9	0	16	0	3	2	4	2	.67	2	.275	.317	.366
1995 Chicago	AL	72	160	43	7	4	2	(1	1)	64	17	17	3	0	25	1	2	3	5	0	1.00	5	.269	.281	.400
1996 Chicago	AL	70	140	49	7	0	1	(0	1)	59	30	14	6	0	17	0	4	1	10	2	.83	4	.350	.374	.421
4 ML YEARS		195	445	133	21	5	4	(1	3)	176	69	49	19	0	59	1	9	6	19	4	.83	11	.299	.325	.396

Dave Martinez

Bats: L **Throws:** L **Pos:** CF-73; RF-73; 1B-23; PH-22; LF-3 **Ht:** 5'10" **Wt:** 175 **Born:** 9/26/64 **Age:** 32

Year Team	Lg	G	AB	H	2B	3B	HR	(Hm	Rd)	TB	R	RBI	TBB	IBB	SO	HBP	SH	SF	SB	CS	SB%	GDP	Avg	OBP	SLG
1986 Chicago	NL	53	108	15	1	1	1	(1	0)	21	13	7	6	0	22	1	0	1	4	2	.67	1	.139	.190	.194
1987 Chicago	NL	142	459	134	18	8	8	(5	3)	192	70	36	57	4	96	2	1	1	16	8	.67	4	.292	.372	.418
1988 ChN-Mon	NL	138	447	114	13	6	6	(2	4)	157	51	46	38	8	94	2	2	5	23	9	.72	3	.255	.313	.351
1989 Montreal	NL	126	361	99	16	7	3	(1	2)	138	41	27	27	2	57	0	7	1	23	4	.85	1	.274	.324	.382
1990 Montreal	NL	118	391	109	13	5	11	(5	6)	165	60	39	24	2	48	1	3	2	13	11	.54	2	.279	.321	.422
1991 Montreal	NL	124	396	117	18	5	7	(3	4)	166	47	42	20	3	54	3	5	3	16	7	.70	3	.295	.332	.419
1992 Cincinnati	NL	135	393	100	20	5	3	(3	0)	139	47	31	42	4	54	0	6	4	12	8	.60	6	.254	.323	.354
1993 San Francisco	NL	91	241	58	12	1	5	(1	4)	87	28	27	27	3	39	0	0	0	6	3	.67	5	.241	.317	.361
1994 San Francisco	NL	97	235	58	9	3	4	(1	3)	85	23	27	21	1	22	2	2	0	3	4	.43	6	.247	.314	.362
1995 Chicago	AL	118	303	93	16	4	5	(2	3)	132	49	37	32	2	41	1	9	4	8	2	.80	6	.307	.371	.436
1996 Chicago	AL	146	440	140	20	8	10	(3	7)	206	85	53	52	1	52	3	2	1	15	7	.68	4	.318	.393	.468
1988 Chicago	NL	75	256	65	10	1	4	(2	2)	89	27	34	21	5	46	2	0	4	7	3	.70	2	.254	.311	.348
Montreal	NL	63	191	49	3	5	2	(0	2)	68	24	12	17	3	48	0	2	1	16	6	.73	1	.257	.316	.356
11 ML YEARS		1288	3774	1037	156	53	63	(27	36)	1488	514	372	346	30	579	15	37	22	139	65	.68	47	.275	.336	.394

Dennis Martinez

Pitches: Right **Bats:** Right **Pos:** SP-20 **Ht:** 6'1" **Wt:** 180 **Born:** 5/14/55 **Age:** 42

Year Team	Lg	G	GS	CG	GF	IP	BFP	H	R	ER	HR	SH	SF	HB	TBB	IBB	SO	WP	Bk	W	L	Pct.	ShO	Sv-Op	Hld	ERA
1976 Baltimore	AL	4	2	1	1	28	106	23	8	8	1	1	0	0	8	0	18	1	0	1	2	.333	0	0--	—	2.57
1977 Baltimore	AL	42	13	5	19	167	709	157	86	76	10	8	8	8	64	5	107	5	0	14	7	.667	0	4--	—	4.10
1978 Baltimore	AL	40	38	15	0	276	1140	257	121	108	20	8	7	3	93	4	142	8	0	16	11	.593	2	0--	—	3.52
1979 Baltimore	AL	40	**39**	**18**	0	292	**1206**	279	129	119	28	12	**12**	1	78	1	132	9	2	15	16	.484	3	0--	—	3.67
1980 Baltimore	AL	25	12	2	8	100	428	103	44	44	12	1	3	2	44	6	42	0	1	6	4	.600	0	1--	—	3.96
1981 Baltimore	AL	25	24	9	0	179	753	173	84	66	10	2	5	2	62	1	88	6	1	**14**	5	.737	2	0--	—	3.32
1982 Baltimore	AL	40	39	10	0	252	1093	262	123	118	30	11	7	7	87	2	111	7	1	16	12	.571	2	0--	—	4.21
1983 Baltimore	AL	32	25	4	3	153	688	209	108	94	21	3	5	2	45	0	71	2	0	7	16	.304	0	0--	—	5.53
1984 Baltimore	AL	34	20	2	4	141.2	599	145	81	79	26	0	5	5	37	2	77	13	0	6	9	.400	0	0--	—	5.02
1985 Baltimore	AL	33	31	3	1	180	789	203	110	103	29	0	**11**	9	63	3	68	4	1	13	11	.542	1	0--	—	5.15
1986 Bal-Mon	AL	23	15	1	2	104.2	449	114	57	55	11	8	2	3	30	4	65	3	2	3	6	.333	1	0--	—	4.73
1987 Montreal	NL	22	22	2	0	144.2	599	133	59	53	9	4	3	6	40	2	84	4	2	11	4	**.733**	1	0-0	0	3.30
1988 Montreal	NL	34	34	9	0	235.1	968	215	94	71	21	2	6	6	55	3	120	5	**10**	15	13	.536	2	0-0	0	2.72
1989 Montreal	NL	34	33	5	1	232	950	227	88	82	21	8	2	7	49	4	142	5	2	16	7	.696	2	0-0	0	3.18
1990 Montreal	NL	32	32	7	0	226	908	191	80	74	16	11	3	6	49	9	156	1	1	10	11	.476	2	0-0	0	2.95
1991 Montreal	NL	31	31	**9**	0	222	905	187	70	59	9	7	3	4	62	3	123	3	0	14	11	.560	**5**	0-0	0	**2.39**

		HOW MUCH HE PITCHED						WHAT HE GAVE UP												THE RESULTS					
Year Team	Lg	G	GS	CG	GF	IP	BFP	H	R	ER	HR	SH	SF	HB	TBB	IBB	SO	WP	Bk	W	L	Pct.	ShO	Sv-Op	Hld	ERA
1992 Montreal	NL	32	32	6	0	226.1	900	172	75	62	12	12	5	9	60	3	147	2	0	16	11	.593	0	0-0	0	2.47
1993 Montreal	NL	35	34	2	1	224.2	945	211	110	96	27	10	4	11	64	7	138	2	4	15	9	.625	0	1-1	0	3.85
1994 Cleveland	AL	24	24	7	0	176.2	730	166	75	69	14	3	5	7	44	2	92	4	3	11	6	.647	3	0-0	0	3.52
1995 Cleveland	AL	28	28	3	0	187	771	174	71	64	17	4	4	12	46	2	99	3	0	12	5	.706	2	0-0	0	3.08
1996 Cleveland	AL	20	20	1	0	112	483	122	63	56	12	2	3	2	37	2	48	0	0	9	6	.600	1	0-0	0	4.50
1986 Baltimore	AL	4	0	0	1	6.2	33	11	5	5	0	0	1	0	2	0	2	1	0	0	0	.000	0	0- --	0	6.75
Montreal	NL	19	15	1	1	98	416	103	52	50	11	8	1	3	28	4	63	2	2	3	6	.333	1	0- --	—	4.59
21 ML YEARS		630	548	121	40	3860	16119	3723	1736	1556	356	117	103	112	1117	65	2070	87	30	240	182	.569	29	6- --	—	3.63

Edgar Martinez

Bats: Right **Throws:** Right **Pos:** DH-134; 1B-4; 3B-2   **Ht:** 5'11" **Wt:** 200 **Born:** 1/2/63 **Age:** 34

		BATTING															BASERUNNING				PERCENTAGES		
Year Team	Lg	G	AB	H	2B	3B	HR	(Hm | Rd)	TB	R	RBI	TBB	IBB	SO	HBP	SH	SF	SB	CS	SB%	GDP	Avg	OBP	SLG
1987 Seattle	AL	13	43	16	5	2	0	(0 | 0)	25	6	5	2	0	5	1	0	0	0	0	.00	0	.372	.413	.581
1988 Seattle	AL	14	32	9	4	0	0	(0 | 0)	13	0	5	4	0	7	0	1	1	0	0	.00	0	.281	.351	.406
1989 Seattle	AL	65	171	41	5	0	2	(0 | 2)	52	20	20	17	1	26	3	2	3	2	1	.67	3	.240	.314	.304
1990 Seattle	AL	144	487	147	27	2	11	(3 | 8)	211	71	49	74	3	62	5	1	3	1	4	.20	13	.302	.397	.433
1991 Seattle	AL	150	544	167	35	1	14	(8 | 6)	246	98	52	84	9	72	8	2	4	0	3	.00	19	.307	.405	.452
1992 Seattle	AL	135	528	181	46	3	18	(11 | 7)	287	100	73	54	2	61	4	1	5	14	4	.78	15	.343	.404	.544
1993 Seattle	AL	42	135	32	7	0	4	(1 | 3)	51	20	13	28	1	19	0	1	1	0	0	.00	4	.237	.366	.378
1994 Seattle	AL	89	326	93	23	1	13	(4 | 9)	157	47	51	53	3	42	3	2	3	6	2	.75	2	.285	.387	.482
1995 Seattle	AL	145	511	182	52	0	29	(16 | 13)	321	121	113	116	19	87	8	0	4	4	3	.57	11	.356	.479	.628
1996 Seattle	AL	139	499	163	52	2	26	(14 | 12)	297	121	103	123	12	84	8	0	4	3	3	.50	15	.327	.464	.595
10 ML YEARS		936	3276	1031	256	11	117	(57 | 60)	1660	604	484	555	50	465	40	10	28	30	20	.60	82	.315	.417	.507

Manny Martinez

Bats: R **Throws:** R **Pos:** RF-13; CF-5; PH-5; LF-3   **Ht:** 6'2" **Wt:** 169 **Born:** 10/3/70 **Age:** 26

		BATTING															BASERUNNING				PERCENTAGES		
Year Team	Lg	G	AB	H	2B	3B	HR	(Hm | Rd)	TB	R	RBI	TBB	IBB	SO	HBP	SH	SF	SB	CS	SB%	GDP	Avg	OBP	SLG
1990 Sou. Oregon	A-	66	244	60	5	0	2	—	—	71	35	17	16	0	59	5	1	0	6	4	.60	5	.246	.306	.291
1991 Modesto	A+	125	502	136	32	3	3	—	—	183	73	55	34	2	80	7	7	3	26	19	.58	7	.271	.324	.365
1992 Modesto	A+	121	495	125	23	1	9	—	—	177	70	45	39	3	75	4	12	5	17	13	.57	7	.253	.309	.358
1993 San Bernrdo	A+	109	459	148	26	3	11	—	—	213	88	52	41	2	60	5	6	4	28	21	.57	10	.322	.381	.464
Tacoma	AAA	20	59	18	2	0	1	—	—	23	9	6	4	0	12	0	1	0	2	3	.40	2	.305	.349	.390
1994 Tacoma	AAA	137	536	137	25	5	9	—	—	199	76	60	28	3	72	10	9	5	18	10	.64	14	.256	.302	.371
1995 Iowa	AAA	122	397	115	17	8	8	—	—	172	63	49	20	0	64	3	7	2	11	8	.58	3	.290	.327	.433
1996 Tacoma	AAA	66	277	87	15	1	4	—	—	116	54	24	23	1	41	2	3	3	14	10	.58	6	.314	.367	.419
Scranton-WB	AAA	17	67	14	1	1	0	—	—	17	8	5	4	0	17	1	0	0	3	0	1.00	0	.209	.264	.254
1996 Sea-Phi		22	53	12	2	3	0	(0 | 0)	20	5	3	4	0	16	1	1	0	4	1	.80	2	.226	.293	.377
1996 Seattle	AL	9	17	4	2	1	0	(0 | 0)	8	3	3	3	0	5	0	0	0	2	0	1.00	1	.235	.350	.471
Philadelphia	NL	13	36	8	0	2	0	(0 | 0)	12	2	0	1	0	11	1	1	0	2	1	.67	1	.222	.263	.333

Pablo Martinez

Bats: Both **Throws:** Right **Pos:** PH-3; SS-1   **Ht:** 5'10" **Wt:** 155 **Born:** 6/29/69 **Age:** 28

		BATTING															BASERUNNING				PERCENTAGES		
Year Team	Lg	G	AB	H	2B	3B	HR	(Hm | Rd)	TB	R	RBI	TBB	IBB	SO	HBP	SH	SF	SB	CS	SB%	GDP	Avg	OBP	SLG
1989 Spokane	A-	2	8	2	0	0	0	—	—	2	3	0	0	0	0	0	0	0	1	0	1.00	1	.250	.250	.250
Padres	R	45	178	42	3	1	0	—	—	47	31	12	22	1	25	2	0	0	29	4	.88	1	.236	.327	.264
Charlstn-SC	A	31	80	14	2	0	0	—	—	16	13	4	11	0	21	0	3	1	0	1	.00	2	.175	.272	.200
1990 Charlstn-SC	A	136	453	100	12	6	0	—	—	124	51	33	41	0	104	4	7	2	16	10	.62	6	.221	.290	.274
1991 Charlstn-SC	A	121	442	118	17	6	3	—	—	156	62	36	42	1	64	0	6	2	39	19	.67	8	.267	.329	.353
1992 High Desert	A+	126	427	102	8	4	0	—	—	118	60	39	50	0	74	1	2	4	19	14	.58	16	.239	.317	.276
1993 Wichita	AA	45	130	36	5	1	2	—	—	49	19	14	11	1	24	1	1	1	8	5	.62	2	.277	.336	.377
Las Vegas	AAA	76	251	58	4	1	2	—	—	70	24	20	18	3	46	3	10	2	8	2	.80	5	.231	.288	.279
1994 Norfolk	AAA	34	80	12	1	0	0	—	—	13	8	5	4	0	22	0	3	0	1	1	.50	0	.150	.190	.163
Binghamton	AA	13	48	9	2	2	0	—	—	15	3	4	5	0	12	0	2	0	0	1	.00	3	.188	.264	.313
St. Lucie	A+	49	177	42	5	0	1	—	—	50	19	10	13	0	29	0	3	1	7	7	.50	4	.237	.288	.282
1995 Greenville	AA	120	462	118	22	4	5	—	—	163	70	29	37	0	89	2	8	1	12	12	.50	7	.255	.313	.353
Richmond	AAA	14	48	11	0	2	0	—	—	15	5	4	2	0	7	0	0	0	1	1	.50	3	.229	.260	.313
1996 Greenville	AA	9	37	12	2	2	1	—	—	21	7	11	2	0	6	0	1	1	3	0	1.00	1	.324	.350	.568
Richmond	AAA	77	263	71	12	3	1	—	—	92	29	18	12	0	58	1	11	1	14	7	.67	3	.270	.303	.350
1996 Atlanta	NL	4	2	1	0	0	0	(0 | 0)	1	1	0	0	0	0	0	0	0	0	1	.00	0	.500	.500	.500

Pedro Martinez

Pitches: Right **Bats:** Right **Pos:** SP-33   **Ht:** 5'11" **Wt:** 170 **Born:** 10/25/71 **Age:** 25

		HOW MUCH HE PITCHED						WHAT HE GAVE UP												THE RESULTS					
Year Team	Lg	G	GS	CG	GF	IP	BFP	H	R	ER	HR	SH	SF	HB	TBB	IBB	SO	WP	Bk	W	L	Pct.	ShO	Sv-Op	Hld	ERA
1992 Los Angeles	NL	2	1	0	1	8	31	6	2	2	0	0	0	0	1	0	8	0	0	0	1	.000	0	0-0	0	2.25
1993 Los Angeles	NL	65	2	0	20	107	444	76	34	31	5	0	5	4	57	4	119	3	1	10	5	.667	0	2-3	14	2.61

Year Team	Lg	G	GS	CG	GF	IP	BFP	H	R	ER	HR	SH	SF	HB	TBB	IBB	SO	WP	Bk	W	L	Pct.	ShO	Sv-Op	Hld	ERA
1994 Montreal	NL	24	23	1	1	144.2	584	115	58	55	11	2	3	11	45	3	142	6	0	11	5	.688	1	1-1	0	3.42
1995 Montreal	NL	30	30	2	0	194.2	784	158	79	76	21	7	3	11	66	1	174	5	2	14	10	.583	2	0-0	0	3.51
1996 Montreal	NL	33	33	4	0	216.2	901	189	100	89	19	9	6	3	70	3	222	6	0	13	10	.565	1	0-0	0	3.70
5 ML YEARS		154	89	7	22	671	2744	544	273	253	56	18	17	29	239	11	665	20	3	48	31	.608	4	3-4	14	3.39

Pedro A. Martinez

Pitches: Left **Bats:** Right **Pos:** RP-9 **Ht:** 6'2" **Wt:** 185 **Born:** 9/29/68 **Age:** 28

		HOW MUCH HE PITCHED						WHAT HE GAVE UP												THE RESULTS						
Year Team	Lg	G	GS	CG	GF	IP	BFP	H	R	ER	HR	SH	SF	HB	TBB	IBB	SO	WP	Bk	W	L	Pct.	ShO	Sv-Op	Hld	ERA
1996 Norfolk *	AAA	34	0	0	7	56.2	236	45	29	19	4	5	1	2	20	1	37	1	0	4	4	.500	0	2- -	—	3.02
1993 San Diego	NL	32	0	0	9	37	148	23	11	10	4	0	0	1	13	1	32	0	0	3	1	.750	0	0-1	3	2.43
1994 San Diego	NL	48	1	0	18	68.1	308	52	31	22	4	9	1	1	49	9	52	2	1	3	2	.600	0	3-5	3	2.90
1995 Houston	NL	25	0	0	3	20.2	109	29	18	17	3	2	1	0	16	1	17	0	1	0	0	.000	0	0-0	3	7.40
1996 NYN-Cin	NL	9	0	0	0	10	51	13	9	7	2	1	1	0	8	4	9	0	0	0	0	.000	0	0-0	1	6.30
1996 New York	NL	5	0	0	0	7	36	8	7	5	1	1	1	0	7	4	6	0	0	0	0	.000	0	0-0	0	6.43
Cincinnati	NL	4	0	0	0	3	15	5	2	2	1	0	0	0	1	0	3	0	0	0	0	.000	0	0-0	1	6.00
4 ML YEARS		114	1	0	30	136	616	117	69	56	13	12	3	4	86	15	110	2	2	6	3	.667	0	3-6	10	3.71

Ramon Martinez

Pitches: Right **Bats:** Left **Pos:** SP-27; RP-1 **Ht:** 6'4" **Wt:** 186 **Born:** 3/22/68 **Age:** 29

		HOW MUCH HE PITCHED						WHAT HE GAVE UP												THE RESULTS						
Year Team	Lg	G	GS	CG	GF	IP	BFP	H	R	ER	HR	SH	SF	HB	TBB	IBB	SO	WP	Bk	W	L	Pct.	ShO	Sv-Op	Hld	ERA
1996 San Antonio *	AA	1	1	0	0	2.2	11	0	0	0	0	0	0	0	3	0	1	0	0	0	0	.000	0	0- -	—	0.00
Vero Beach *	A+	1	1	0	0	7	28	5	1	0	0	0	0	0	0	0	10	0	0	1	0	1.000	0	0- -	—	0.00
1988 Los Angeles	NL	9	6	0	0	35.2	151	27	17	15	0	4	0	0	22	1	23	1	0	1	3	.250	0	0-0	1	3.79
1989 Los Angeles	NL	15	15	2	0	98.2	410	79	39	35	11	4	0	5	41	1	89	1	0	6	4	.600	2	0-0	0	3.19
1990 Los Angeles	NL	33	33	12	0	234.1	950	191	89	76	22	7	5	4	67	5	223	3	3	20	6	.769	3	0-0	0	2.92
1991 Los Angeles	NL	33	33	6	0	220.1	916	190	89	80	18	8	4	7	69	4	150	6	0	17	13	.567	4	0-0	0	3.27
1992 Los Angeles	NL	25	25	1	0	150.2	662	141	82	71	11	12	1	5	69	4	101	9	0	8	11	.421	1	0-0	0	4.00
1993 Los Angeles	NL	32	32	4	0	211.2	918	202	88	81	15	12	5	6	104	9	127	2	2	10	12	.455	3	0-0	0	3.44
1994 Los Angeles	NL	24	24	4	0	170	718	160	83	75	18	6	8	6	56	2	119	2	0	12	7	.632	3	0-0	0	3.97
1995 Los Angeles	NL	30	30	4	0	206.1	859	176	95	84	19	7	5	5	81	5	138	3	0	17	7	.708	2	0-0	0	3.66
1996 Los Angeles	NL	28	27	2	1	168.2	732	153	76	64	12	7	6	8	86	5	134	2	1	15	6	.714	1	0-0	0	3.42
9 ML YEARS		229	225	35	1	1496.1	6316	1319	658	577	126	67	34	44	595	36	1104	29	6	106	69	.606	20	0-0	1	3.47

Sandy Martinez

Bats: Left **Throws:** Right **Pos:** C-75; PH-3 **Ht:** 6'2" **Wt:** 200 **Born:** 10/3/72 **Age:** 24

		BATTING																BASERUNNING				PERCENTAGES		
Year Team	Lg	G	AB	H	2B	3B	HR	(Hm	Rd)	TB	R	RBI	TBB	IBB	SO	HBP	SH	SF	SB	CS	SB%	GDP	Avg	OBP	SLG
1991 Dunedin	A+	12	38	7	1	0	0	—	—	8	3	3	7	0	7	1	2	0	0	0	.00	0	.184	.326	.211
Medicne Hat	R+	34	98	17	1	0	2	—	—	24	8	16	12	1	29	2	2	2	0	1	.00	2	.173	.272	.245
1992 Dunedin	A+	4	15	3	1	0	2	—	—	10	4	4	0	0	3	1	0	0	0	0	.00	1	.200	.250	.667
Medicne Hat	R+	57	206	52	15	0	4	—	—	79	27	39	14	0	62	1	0	2	0	0	.00	6	.252	.300	.383
1993 Hagerstown	A	94	338	89	16	1	9	—	—	134	41	46	19	0	71	6	0	1	1	1	.50	8	.263	.313	.396
1994 Dunedin	A+	122	450	117	14	6	7	—	—	164	50	52	22	1	79	11	3	1	1	3	.25	15	.260	.310	.364
1995 Knoxville	AA	41	144	33	8	1	2	—	—	49	14	22	6	0	34	0	0	2	0	1	.00	2	.229	.257	.340
1996 Knoxville	AA	4	16	3	0	0	0	—	—	3	2	0	0	0	5	0	0	0	0	0	.00	0	.188	.188	.188
1995 Toronto	AL	62	191	46	12	0	2	(1	1)	64	12	25	7	0	45	0	0	0	0	0	.00	1	.241	.270	.335
1996 Toronto	AL	76	229	52	9	3	3	(2	1)	76	17	18	16	0	58	4	1	1	0	0	.00	4	.227	.288	.332
2 ML YEARS		138	420	98	21	3	5	(3	2)	140	29	43	23	0	103	5	1	2	0	0	.00	5	.233	.280	.333

Tino Martinez

Bats: Left **Throws:** Right **Pos:** 1B-151; DH-3; PH-3 **Ht:** 6'2" **Wt:** 210 **Born:** 12/7/67 **Age:** 29

		BATTING																BASERUNNING				PERCENTAGES		
Year Team	Lg	G	AB	H	2B	3B	HR	(Hm	Rd)	TB	R	RBI	TBB	IBB	SO	HBP	SH	SF	SB	CS	SB%	GDP	Avg	OBP	SLG
1990 Seattle	AL	24	68	15	4	0	0	(0	0)	19	4	5	9	0	9	0	0	1	0	0	.00	0	.221	.308	.279
1991 Seattle	AL	36	112	23	2	0	4	(3	1)	37	11	9	11	0	24	0	0	2	0	0	.00	2	.205	.272	.330
1992 Seattle	AL	136	460	118	19	2	16	(10	6)	189	53	66	42	9	77	2	1	8	2	1	.67	24	.257	.316	.411
1993 Seattle	AL	109	408	108	25	1	17	(9	8)	186	48	60	45	9	56	5	3	3	0	3	.00	7	.265	.343	.456
1994 Seattle	AL	97	329	86	21	0	20	(8	12)	167	42	61	29	2	52	1	4	3	1	2	.33	9	.261	.320	.508
1995 Seattle	AL	141	519	152	35	3	31	(14	17)	286	92	111	62	15	91	4	2	6	0	0	.00	10	.293	.369	.551
1996 New York	AL	155	595	174	28	0	25	(9	16)	277	82	117	68	4	85	2	1	5	2	1	.67	18	.292	.364	.466
7 ML YEARS		698	2491	676	134	6	113	(53	60)	1161	332	429	266	39	394	14	11	28	5	7	.42	70	.271	.342	.466

John Marzano

Bats: Right **Throws:** Right **Pos:** C-39; PH-4 **Ht:** 5'11" **Wt:** 195 **Born:** 2/14/63 **Age:** 34

Year Team	Lg	G	AB	H	2B	3B	HR	(Hm	Rd)	TB	R	RBI	TBB	IBB	SO	HBP	SH	SF	SB	CS	SB%	GDP	Avg	OBP	SLG
1987 Boston	AL	52	168	41	11	0	5	(4	1)	67	20	24	7	0	41	3	2	2	0	1	.00	3	.244	.283	.399
1988 Boston	AL	10	29	4	1	0	0	(0	0)	5	3	1	1	0	3	0	0	0	0	0	.00	1	.138	.167	.172
1989 Boston	AL	7	18	8	3	0	1	(1	0)	14	5	3	0	0	2	0	1	1	0	0	.00	1	.444	.421	.778
1990 Boston	AL	32	83	20	4	0	0	(0	0)	24	8	6	5	0	10	0	2	1	0	1	.00	0	.241	.281	.289
1991 Boston	AL	49	114	30	8	0	0	(0	0)	38	10	9	1	0	16	1	1	2	0	0	.00	5	.263	.271	.333
1992 Boston	AL	19	50	4	2	1	0	(0	0)	8	4	1	2	0	12	1	1	0	0	0	.00	0	.080	.132	.160
1995 Texas	AL	2	6	2	0	0	0	(0	0)	2	1	0	0	0	0	0	0	0	0	0	.00	0	.333	.333	.333
1996 Seattle	AL	41	106	26	6	0	0	(0	0)	32	8	6	7	0	15	4	3	0	0	0	.00	2	.245	.316	.302
8 ML YEARS		212	574	135	35	1	6	(5	1)	190	59	50	23	0	99	9	10	6	0	2	.00	12	.235	.273	.331

Damon Mashore

Bats: R **Throws:** R **Pos:** LF-35; RF-15; PH-15; CF-7 **Ht:** 5'11" **Wt:** 195 **Born:** 10/31/69 **Age:** 27

Year Team	Lg	G	AB	H	2B	3B	HR	(Hm	Rd)	TB	R	RBI	TBB	IBB	SO	HBP	SH	SF	SB	CS	SB%	GDP	Avg	OBP	SLG
1991 Sou. Oregon	A-	73	264	72	17	6	6	—	—	119	48	31	34	1	94	2	2	3	15	5	.75	6	.273	.356	.451
1992 Modesto	A+	124	471	133	22	3	18	—	—	215	91	64	73	3	136	6	5	1	29	17	.63	6	.282	.385	.456
1993 Huntsville	AA	70	253	59	7	2	3	—	—	79	35	20	25	0	64	4	1	2	18	4	.82	5	.233	.310	.312
1994 Athletics	R	11	34	14	2	0	0	—	—	16	6	6	4	0	3	1	0	1	1	1	.50	3	.412	.475	.471
Huntsville	AA	59	210	47	11	2	3	—	—	71	24	21	13	1	53	0	1	3	6	1	.86	3	.224	.265	.338
1995 Edmonton	AAA	117	337	101	19	5	1	—	—	133	50	37	42	0	77	5	3	3	17	5	.77	9	.300	.382	.395
1996 Edmonton	AAA	50	183	49	9	1	8	—	—	84	32	29	19	0	48	5	2	2	6	2	.75	3	.268	.349	.459
1996 Oakland	AL	50	105	28	7	1	3	(1	2)	46	20	12	16	0	31	1	1	1	4	0	1.00	2	.267	.366	.438

Mike Matheny

Bats: Right **Throws:** Right **Pos:** C-104; PH-2; DH-1 **Ht:** 6'3" **Wt:** 205 **Born:** 9/22/70 **Age:** 26

Year Team	Lg	G	AB	H	2B	3B	HR	(Hm	Rd)	TB	R	RBI	TBB	IBB	SO	HBP	SH	SF	SB	CS	SB%	GDP	Avg	OBP	SLG
1996 New Orleans *	AAA	20	66	15	4	0	1	—	—	22	3	6	2	0	17	0	0	1	0	1	1.00	1	.227	.246	.333
1994 Milwaukee	AL	28	53	12	3	0	1	(1	0)	18	3	2	3	0	13	2	1	0	0	1	.00	1	.226	.293	.340
1995 Milwaukee	AL	80	166	41	9	1	0	(0	0)	52	13	21	12	0	28	2	1	0	2	1	.67	3	.247	.306	.313
1996 Milwaukee	AL	106	313	64	15	2	8	(5	3)	107	31	46	14	0	80	3	7	4	3	2	.60	9	.204	.243	.342
3 ML YEARS		214	532	117	27	3	9	(6	3)	177	47	69	29	0	121	7	9	4	5	4	.56	13	.220	.267	.333

T.J. Mathews

Pitches: Right **Bats:** Right **Pos:** RP-67 **Ht:** 6'2" **Wt:** 200 **Born:** 1/19/70 **Age:** 27

Year Team	Lg	G	GS	CG	GF	IP	BFP	H	R	ER	HR	SH	SF	HB	TBB	IBB	SO	WP	Bk	W	L	Pct.	ShO	Sv-Op	Hld	ERA
1992 Hamilton	A-	14	14	1	0	86.2	351	70	25	21	4	3	0	2	30	0	89	4	2	10	1	.909	0	0--	—	2.18
1993 Springfield	A	25	25	5	0	159.1	634	121	59	48	7	7	4	6	29	0	144	1	3	12	9	.571	2	0--	—	2.71
1994 St. Pete	A+	11	11	1	0	66.1	270	52	22	18	1	1	0	2	23	0	62	1	1	5	5	.500	0	0--	—	2.44
Arkansas	AA	16	16	1	0	97	395	83	37	34	8	6	2	6	24	1	93	1	0	5	5	.500	0	0--	—	3.15
1995 Louisville	AAA	32	7	0	10	66.2	298	60	35	20	2	0	3	3	27	2	50	1	0	9	4	.692	0	1--	—	2.70
1995 St. Louis	NL	23	0	0	12	29.2	120	21	7	5	1	4	0	0	11	1	28	2	0	1	1	.500	0	2-2	7	1.52
1996 St. Louis	NL	67	0	0	23	83.2	345	62	32	28	8	5	0	2	32	4	80	1	0	2	6	.250	0	6-11	9	3.01
2 ML YEARS		90	0	0	35	113.1	465	83	39	33	9	9	0	2	43	5	108	3	0	3	7	.300	0	8-13	16	2.62

Terry Mathews

Pitches: Right **Bats:** Left **Pos:** RP-71 **Ht:** 6'2" **Wt:** 225 **Born:** 10/5/64 **Age:** 32

Year Team	Lg	G	GS	CG	GF	IP	BFP	H	R	ER	HR	SH	SF	HB	TBB	IBB	SO	WP	Bk	W	L	Pct.	ShO	Sv-Op	Hld	ERA
1991 Texas	AL	34	2	0	8	57.1	236	54	24	23	5	2	0	1	18	3	51	5	0	4	0	1.000	0	1-3	2	3.61
1992 Texas	AL	40	0	0	11	42.1	199	48	29	28	4	1	3	4	31	3	26	2	1	2	4	.333	0	0-4	6	5.95
1994 Florida	NL	24	2	0	5	43	179	45	16	16	4	1	0	1	9	1	21	1	0	2	1	.667	0	0-1	3	3.35
1995 Florida	NL	57	0	0	14	82.2	332	70	32	31	9	5	1	1	27	4	72	3	0	4	4	.500	0	3-7	11	3.38
1996 Fla-Bal		71	0	0	24	73.2	326	79	40	37	10	3	1	1	34	5	62	0	0	4	6	.400	0	4-6	15	4.52
1996 Florida	NL	57	0	0	19	55	247	59	33	30	7	2	1	1	27	5	49	0	0	2	4	.333	0	4-5	11	4.91
Baltimore	AL	14	0	0	5	18.2	79	20	7	7	3	1	0	0	7	0	13	0	0	2	2	.500	0	0-1	4	3.38
5 ML YEARS		226	4	0	62	299	1272	296	141	135	32	12	5	5	119	16	232	11	1	16	15	.516	0	8-21	37	4.06

Don Mattingly

Bats: Left **Throws:** Left **Pos:** 1B/DH **Ht:** 6'0" **Wt:** 200 **Born:** 4/20/61 **Age:** 36

Year Team	Lg	G	AB	H	2B	3B	HR	(Hm	Rd)	TB	R	RBI	TBB	IBB	SO	HBP	SH	SF	SB	CS	SB%	GDP	Avg	OBP	SLG
1982 New York	AL	7	12	2	0	0	0	(0	0)	2	0	1	0	0	1	0	0	1	0	0	.00	2	.167	.154	.167
1983 New York	AL	91	279	79	15	4	4	(0	4)	114	34	32	21	5	31	1	2	2	0	0	.00	8	.283	.333	.409

					BATTING														BASERUNNING				PERCENTAGES		
Year Team	Lg	G	AB	H	2B	3B	HR	(Hm	Rd)	TB	R	RBI	TBB	IBB	SO	HBP	SH	SF	SB	CS	SB%	GDP	Avg	OBP	SLG
1984 New York	AL	153	603	**207**	**44**	2	23	(12	11)	324	91	110	41	8	33	1	8	9	1	1	.50	15	**.343**	.381	.537
1985 New York	AL	159	652	211	**48**	3	35	(22	13)	**370**	107	**145**	56	13	41	2	2	**15**	2	2	.50	15	.324	.371	.567
1986 New York	AL	162	677	**238**	**53**	2	31	(17	14)	**388**	117	113	53	11	35	1	1	10	0	0	.00	17	.352	.394	**.573**
1987 New York	AL	141	569	186	38	2	30	(17	13)	318	93	115	51	13	38	1	1	10	1	4	.20	16	.327	.378	.559
1988 New York	AL	144	599	186	37	0	18	(11	7)	277	94	88	41	14	29	3	0	8	1	0	1.00	13	.311	.353	.462
1989 New York	AL	158	631	191	37	2	23	(19	4)	301	79	113	51	18	30	1	0	10	3	0	1.00	15	.303	.351	.477
1990 New York	AL	102	394	101	16	0	5	(4	1)	132	40	42	28	13	22	3	0	3	1	0	1.00	13	.256	.308	.335
1991 New York	AL	152	587	169	35	0	9	(7	2)	231	64	68	46	11	42	4	0	9	2	0	1.00	21	.288	.339	.394
1992 New York	AL	157	640	184	40	0	14	(6	8)	266	89	86	39	7	43	1	0	6	3	0	1.00	11	.288	.327	.416
1993 New York	AL	134	530	154	27	2	17	(8	9)	236	78	86	61	9	42	2	1	3	0	0	.00	20	.291	.364	.445
1994 New York	AL	97	372	113	20	1	6	(3	3)	153	62	51	60	7	24	0	0	4	0	0	.00	8	.304	.397	.411
1995 New York	AL	128	458	132	32	2	7	(5	2)	189	59	49	40	7	35	1	0	8	0	2	.00	17	.288	.341	.413
14 ML YEARS		1785	7003	2153	442	20	222	(131	91)	3301	1007	1099	588	136	444	21	13	96	14	9	.61	191	.307	.358	.471

Brian Maxcy

Pitches: Right **Bats:** Right **Pos:** RP-2 **Ht:** 6'1" **Wt:** 170 **Born:** 5/4/71 **Age:** 26

			HOW MUCH HE PITCHED					WHAT HE GAVE UP										THE RESULTS						
Year Team	Lg	G	GS	CG	GF	IP	BFP	H	R	ER	HR	SH	SF	HB	TBB	IBB	SO	WP	Bk	W	L	Pct.	ShO	Sv-Op	Hld	ERA
1992 Bristol	R+	14	7	2	7	49.1	204	41	24	19	4	0	2	0	17	1	43	3	1	4	2	.667	2	3- -	—	3.47
1993 Fayettevlle	A	39	12	1	20	113.2	501	111	51	37	2	5	3	13	42	3	101	5	0	12	4	.750	1	9- -	—	2.93
1994 Trenton	AA	5	0	0	2	10.2	45	6	1	0	0	0	0	1	4	0	5	0	0	0	0	.000	0	1- -	—	0.00
Toledo	AAA	24	1	0	6	44.1	182	31	12	8	1	2	1	2	18	1	43	1	0	2	3	.400	0	3- -	—	1.62
1995 Toledo	AAA	20	0	0	9	25.2	120	32	20	15	3	4	0	1	11	1	11	3	0	1	3	.250	0	2- -	—	5.26
1996 Toledo	AAA	15	0	0	6	22.2	97	24	11	10	2	3	2	0	9	2	8	2	0	3	1	.750	0	1- -	—	3.97
Louisville	AAA	36	3	0	8	62	274	63	34	33	5	2	3	4	32	6	52	5	0	4	2	.667	0	1- -	—	4.79
1995 Detroit	AL	41	0	0	14	52.1	247	61	48	40	6	3	3	2	31	7	20	6	2	4	5	.444	0	0-2	2	6.88
1996 Detroit	AL	2	0	0	0	3.1	19	8	5	5	2	0	0	0	2	0	1	0	0	0	0	.000	0	0-0	0	13.50
2 ML YEARS		43	0	0	14	55.2	266	69	53	45	8	3	3	2	33	7	21	6	2	4	5	.444	0	0-2	2	7.28

Darrell May

Pitches: Left **Bats:** Left **Pos:** RP-8; SP-2 **Ht:** 6'2" **Wt:** 170 **Born:** 6/13/72 **Age:** 25

			HOW MUCH HE PITCHED					WHAT HE GAVE UP										THE RESULTS						
Year Team	Lg	G	GS	CG	GF	IP	BFP	H	R	ER	HR	SH	SF	HB	TBB	IBB	SO	WP	Bk	W	L	Pct.	ShO	Sv-Op	Hld	ERA
1992 Braves	R	12	7	0	4	53	204	34	13	8	0	2	0	2	13	0	61	2	1	4	3	.571	0	1- -	—	1.36
1993 Macon	A	17	17	0	0	104.1	404	81	29	26	6	0	0	4	22	1	111	3	0	10	4	.714	0	0- -	—	2.24
Durham	A+	9	9	0	0	51.2	213	44	18	12	4	4	2	1	16	0	47	2	1	5	2	.714	0	0- -	—	2.09
1994 Durham	A+	12	12	1	0	74.2	307	74	29	25	6	0	1	3	17	1	73	3	0	8	2	.800	0	0- -	—	3.01
Greenville	AA	11	11	1	0	63.2	265	61	25	22	4	1	2	2	17	0	42	6	0	5	3	.625	0	0- -	—	3.11
1995 Richmond	AAA	9	9	0	0	51	216	53	21	21	1	1	3	0	16	1	42	2	0	4	2	.667	0	0- -	—	3.71
Greenville	AA	24	24	0	0	142.1	593	134	65	57	19	3	8	3	36	1	121	6	0	6	10	.375	0	0- -	—	3.60
1996 Calgary	AAA	23	22	1	0	131.2	558	146	64	60	17	3	5	0	36	6	75	3	1	7	6	.538	1	0- -	—	4.10
1995 Atlanta	NL	2	0	0	1	4	21	10	5	5	0	0	1	0	0	0	1	0	0	0	0	.000	0	0-0	0	11.25
1996 Pit-Cal		10	2	0	2	11.1	60	18	13	12	6	0	2	1	6	0	6	0	0	0	1	.000	0	0-0	1	9.53
1996 Pittsburgh	NL	5	2	0	0	8.2	47	15	10	9	5	0	0	1	4	0	5	0	0	0	1	.000	0	0-0	1	9.35
California	AL	5	0	0	2	2.2	13	3	3	3	1	0	2	0	2	0	1	0	0	0	0	.000	0	0-0	0	10.13
2 ML YEARS		12	2	0	3	15.1	81	28	18	17	6	0	3	1	6	0	7	0	0	0	1	.000	0	0-0	1	9.98

Derrick May

Bats: Left **Throws:** Right **Pos:** LF-70; PH-42; RF-3 **Ht:** 6'4" **Wt:** 225 **Born:** 7/14/68 **Age:** 28

					BATTING														BASERUNNING				PERCENTAGES		
Year Team	Lg	G	AB	H	2B	3B	HR	(Hm	Rd)	TB	R	RBI	TBB	IBB	SO	HBP	SH	SF	SB	CS	SB%	GDP	Avg	OBP	SLG
1990 Chicago	NL	17	61	15	3	0	1	(1	0)	21	8	11	2	0	7	0	0	0	1	0	1.00	1	.246	.270	.344
1991 Chicago	NL	15	22	5	2	0	1	(1	0)	10	4	3	2	0	1	0	0	1	0	0	.00	1	.227	.280	.455
1992 Chicago	NL	124	351	96	11	0	8	(3	5)	131	33	45	14	4	40	3	2	1	5	3	.63	10	.274	.306	.373
1993 Chicago	NL	128	465	137	25	2	10	(3	7)	196	62	77	31	6	41	1	0	6	10	3	.77	15	.295	.336	.422
1994 Chicago	NL	100	345	98	19	2	8	(5	3)	145	43	51	30	4	34	0	1	2	3	2	.60	11	.284	.340	.420
1995 Mil-Hou		110	319	90	18	2	9	(4	5)	139	44	50	24	0	42	2	0	3	5	1	.83	5	.282	.333	.436
1996 Houston	NL	109	259	65	12	3	5	(2	3)	98	24	33	30	8	33	2	0	2	2	2	.50	3	.251	.330	.378
1995 Milwaukee	AL	32	113	28	3	1	1	(1	0)	36	15	9	5	0	18	1	0	0	0	1	.00	1	.248	.286	.319
Houston	NL	78	206	62	15	1	8	(3	5)	103	29	41	19	0	24	1	0	3	5	0	1.00	4	.301	.358	.500
7 ML YEARS		603	1822	506	90	9	42	(19	23)	740	218	270	133	22	198	8	3	16	26	11	.70	46	.278	.327	.406

Brent Mayne

Bats: Left **Throws:** Right **Pos:** PH-49; C-21 **Ht:** 6'1" **Wt:** 190 **Born:** 4/19/68 **Age:** 29

					BATTING														BASERUNNING				PERCENTAGES		
Year Team	Lg	G	AB	H	2B	3B	HR	(Hm	Rd)	TB	R	RBI	TBB	IBB	SO	HBP	SH	SF	SB	CS	SB%	GDP	Avg	OBP	SLG
1990 Kansas City	AL	5	13	3	0	0	0	(0	0)	3	2	1	0	0	3	0	0	0	0	0	.00	1	.231	.375	.231
1991 Kansas City	AL	85	231	58	8	0	3	(2	1)	75	22	31	23	4	42	0	2	3	2	4	.33	6	.251	.315	.325
1992 Kansas City	AL	82	213	48	10	0	0	(0	0)	58	16	18	11	0	26	0	2	3	0	4	.00	5	.225	.260	.272
1993 Kansas City	AL	71	205	52	9	1	2	(0	2)	69	22	22	18	7	31	1	3	0	3	2	.60	6	.254	.317	.337

Year Team	Lg	G	AB	H	2B	3B	HR	(Hm	Rd)	TB	R	RBI	TBB	IBB	SO	HBP	SH	SF	SB	CS	SB%	GDP	Avg	OBP	SLG
								BATTING											BASERUNNING				PERCENTAGES		
1994 Kansas City	AL	46	144	37	5	1	2	(1	1)	50	19	20	14	1	27	0	0	0	1	0	1.00	3	.257	.323	.347
1995 Kansas City	AL	110	307	77	18	1	1	(1	0)	100	23	27	25	1	41	3	11	1	0	1	.00	16	.251	.313	.326
1996 New York	NL	70	99	26	6	0	1	(0	1)	35	9	6	12	1	22	0	2	0	0	1	.00	4	.263	.342	.354
7 ML YEARS		469	1212	301	56	3	9	(4	5)	390	113	125	106	14	192	4	20	7	6	13	.32	40	.248	.309	.322

Greg McCarthy

Pitches: Left **Bats:** Left **Pos:** RP-10 **Ht:** 6'2" **Wt:** 215 **Born:** 10/30/68 **Age:** 28

Year Team	Lg	G	GS	CG	GF	IP	BFP	H	R	ER	HR	SH	SF	HB	TBB	IBB	SO	WP	Bk	W	L	Pct.	ShO	Sv-Op	Hld	ERA
			HOW MUCH HE PITCHED						WHAT HE GAVE UP											THE RESULTS						
1987 Utica	A-	20	0	0	13	29.2	130	14	9	3	0	0	2	2	23	2	40	1	1	4	1	.800	0	3- --	--	0.91
1988 Spartanburg	A	34	1	0	20	64.2	297	52	36	29	3	3	3	10	52	0	65	8	3	4	2	.667	0	2- --	--	4.04
1989 Spartanburg	A	24	15	2	4	112	499	90	58	52	3	3	5	9	80	0	115	8	2	5	8	.385	1	0- --	--	4.18
1990 Clearwater	A+	42	0	1	19	59.2	265	47	32	22	4	2	2	1	38	1	67	5	2	1	3	.250	0	5- --	--	3.32
1992 Kinston	A+	23	0	0	21	27.1	105	14	0	0	1	0	5	0	9	0	37	8	0	3	0	1.000	0	12- --	--	0.00
1993 Kinston	A+	9	0	0	6	10.2	51	8	4	2	0	0	0	0	13	0	14	2	0	0	0	.000	0	2- --	--	1.69
Canton-Akrn	AA	33	0	0	19	34.1	156	28	18	18	1	0	3	2	37	2	39	5	0	2	3	.400	0	6- --	--	4.72
1994 Canton-Akrn	AA	22	0	0	19	32	133	19	12	8	0	0	0	1	23	2	39	2	0	2	3	.400	0	9- --	--	2.25
Charlotte	AAA	18	0	0	11	23.1	118	17	22	18	1	1	2	6	28	1	21	5	0	1	0	1.000	0	0- --	--	6.94
1995 Birmingham	AA	38	0	0	13	44.2	195	37	28	25	4	4	2	2	29	3	48	3	1	3	3	.500	0	3- --	--	5.04
1996 Tacoma	AAA	39	0	0	14	68.1	317	58	31	25	2	3	1	5	53	2	90	11	2	4	2	.667	0	4- --	--	3.29
1996 Seattle	AL	10	0	0	1	9.2	45	8	2	2	0	1	1	4	7	0	7	0	0	0	0	.000	0	0-0	1	1.86

Dave McCarty

Bats: R **Throws:** L **Pos:** 1B-51; PH-36; RF-15; LF-5 **Ht:** 6'5" **Wt:** 213 **Born:** 11/23/69 **Age:** 27

Year Team	Lg	G	AB	H	2B	3B	HR	(Hm	Rd)	TB	R	RBI	TBB	IBB	SO	HBP	SH	SF	SB	CS	SB%	GDP	Avg	OBP	SLG
								BATTING											BASERUNNING				PERCENTAGES		
1996 Phoenix *	AAA	6	25	10	1	1	1	—	—	16	4	7	2	0	4	0	0	1	0	0	.00	0	.400	.429	.640
1993 Minnesota	AL	98	350	75	15	2	2	(2	0)	100	36	21	19	0	80	1	1	0	2	6	.25	13	.214	.257	.286
1994 Minnesota	AL	44	131	34	8	2	1	(1	0)	49	21	12	7	1	32	5	0	0	2	1	.67	3	.260	.322	.374
1995 Min-SF		37	75	17	4	1	0	(0	0)	23	11	6	4	0	22	1	0	0	1	1	.50	2	.227	.289	.307
1996 San Francisco	NL	91	175	38	3	0	6	(5	1)	59	16	24	18	0	43	2	0	2	1	1	.67	5	.217	.294	.337
1995 Minnesota	AL	25	55	12	3	1	0	(0	0)	17	10	4	4	0	18	1	0	1	0	1	.00	1	.218	.279	.309
San Francisco	NL	12	20	5	1	0	0	(0	0)	6	1	2	0	0	4	0	0	0	1	0	1.00	1	.250	.318	.300
4 ML YEARS		270	731	164	30	5	9	(8	1)	231	84	63	50	1	177	9	1	3	7	9	.44	22	.224	.281	.316

Kirk McCaskill

Pitches: Right **Bats:** Right **Pos:** RP-25; SP-4 **Ht:** 6'1" **Wt:** 205 **Born:** 4/9/61 **Age:** 36

Year Team	Lg	G	GS	CG	GF	IP	BFP	H	R	ER	HR	SH	SF	HB	TBB	IBB	SO	WP	Bk	W	L	Pct.	ShO	Sv-Op	Hld	ERA
			HOW MUCH HE PITCHED						WHAT HE GAVE UP											THE RESULTS						
1985 California	AL	30	29	6	0	189.2	807	189	105	99	23	2	5	4	64	1	102	5	0	12	12	.500	1	0- --	--	4.70
1986 California	AL	34	33	10	1	246.1	1013	207	98	92	19	6	5	5	92	1	202	10	2	17	10	.630	2	0- --	--	3.36
1987 California	AL	14	13	1	0	74.2	334	84	52	47	14	3	1	2	34	0	56	1	0	4	6	.400	1	0-0	0	5.67
1988 California	AL	23	23	4	0	146.1	635	155	78	70	9	1	6	1	61	3	98	13	2	8	6	.571	2	0-0	0	4.31
1989 California	AL	32	32	6	0	212	864	202	73	69	16	3	4	3	59	1	107	7	2	15	10	.600	4	0-0	0	2.93
1990 California	AL	29	29	2	0	174.1	738	161	77	63	9	3	1	2	72	1	78	6	1	12	11	.522	1	0-0	0	3.25
1991 California	AL	30	30	1	0	177.2	762	193	93	84	19	6	6	3	66	1	71	6	0	10	19	.345	0	0-0	0	4.26
1992 Chicago	AL	34	34	0	0	209	911	193	116	97	11	7	7	6	95	5	109	6	2	12	13	.480	0	0-0	0	4.18
1993 Chicago	AL	30	14	0	6	113.2	502	144	71	66	12	2	3	1	36	6	65	6	0	4	8	.333	0	2-2	2	5.23
1994 Chicago	AL	40	0	0	18	52.2	228	51	22	20	6	1	3	0	22	4	37	1	0	1	4	.200	0	3-6	8	3.42
1995 Chicago	AL	55	1	0	17	81	365	97	50	44	10	3	1	5	33	4	50	10	0	6	4	.600	0	2-5	8	4.89
1996 Chicago	AL	29	4	0	13	51.2	246	72	41	40	6	3	1	2	31	8	28	1	0	5	5	.500	0	0-1	2	6.97
12 ML YEARS		380	242	30	55	1729	7405	1748	876	791	154	40	45	34	665	35	1003	72	9	106	108	.495	11	7- --	--	4.12

Quinton McCracken

Bats: B **Throws:** R **Pos:** CF-85; PH-49; LF-8; RF-4 **Ht:** 5'7" **Wt:** 173 **Born:** 3/16/70 **Age:** 27

Year Team	Lg	G	AB	H	2B	3B	HR	(Hm	Rd)	TB	R	RBI	TBB	IBB	SO	HBP	SH	SF	SB	CS	SB%	GDP	Avg	OBP	SLG
								BATTING											BASERUNNING				PERCENTAGES		
1992 Bend	A-	67	232	65	13	2	0	—	—	82	37	27	25	0	39	0	7	2	18	6	.75	6	.280	.347	.353
1993 Central Val	A+	127	483	141	17	7	2	—	—	178	94	58	78	4	90	2	12	4	60	19	.76	15	.292	.390	.369
1994 New Haven	AA	136	544	151	27	4	5	—	—	201	94	39	48	4	72	4	10	4	36	19	.65	6	.278	.338	.369
1995 New Haven	AA	55	221	79	11	4	1	—	—	101	33	26	21	3	32	3	1	1	26	8	.76	2	.357	.419	.457
Colo. Sprng	AAA	61	244	88	14	6	3	—	—	123	55	28	23	3	30	1	1	2	17	6	.74	4	.361	.418	.504
1995 Colorado	NL	3	1	0	0	0	0	(0	0)	0	0	0	0	0	0	0	0	0	0	0	.00	0	.000	.000	.000
1996 Colorado	NL	124	283	82	13	6	3	(2	1)	116	50	40	32	4	62	1	12	1	17	6	.74	5	.290	.363	.410
2 ML YEARS		127	284	82	13	6	3	(2	1)	116	50	40	32	4	63	1	12	1	17	6	.74	5	.289	.362	.408

Jeff McCurry

Pitches: Right **Bats:** Right **Pos:** RP-2   **Ht:** 6'6" **Wt:** 215 **Born:** 1/21/70 **Age:** 27

Year Team	Lg	G	GS	CG	GF	IP	BFP	H	R	ER	HR	SH	SF	HB	TBB	IBB	SO	WP	Bk	W	L	Pct.	ShO	Sv-Op	Hld	ERA
1991 Pirates	R	6	1	0	0	14	68	19	10	4	0	0	1	2	4	0	8	2	1	1	0	1.000	0	0--	—	2.57
Welland	A-	9	0	0	5	15.2	70	11	4	1	0	3	0	0	10	3	18	5	1	2	1	.667	0	0--	—	0.57
1992 Augusta	A	19	0	0	13	30	142	36	14	11	1	6	1	3	15	1	34	4	1	2	1	.667	0	7--	—	3.30
Salem	A+	30	0	0	15	62.2	255	49	22	20	3	4	2	3	24	3	52	7	0	6	2	.750	0	3--	—	2.87
1993 Salem	A+	41	0	0	36	44	184	41	21	19	3	3	3	0	15	3	32	5	0	1	4	.200	0	22--	—	3.89
Carolina	AA	23	0	0	5	29	121	24	11	9	1	2	1	0	14	2	14	2	0	2	1	.667	0	0--	—	2.79
1994 Carolina	AA	48	2	0	32	81.1	350	74	35	29	7	5	1	6	30	3	60	9	1	6	5	.545	0	11--	—	3.21
1995 Calgary	AAA	3	0	0	0	5	22	3	1	1	0	0	0	2	2	0	2	0	0	0	0	.000	0	0--	—	1.80
1996 Toledo	AAA	39	0	0	13	58.2	264	66	37	31	2	0	0	1	26	2	56	9	0	1	4	.200	0	2--	—	4.76
1995 Pittsburgh	NL	55	0	0	10	61	282	82	38	34	9	4	0	5	30	4	27	2	0	1	4	.200	0	1-2	5	5.02
1996 Detroit	AL	2	0	0	1	3.1	21	9	9	9	3	0	0	0	2	0	0	0	0	0	0	.000	0	0-0	—	24.30
2 ML YEARS		57	0	0	11	64.1	303	91	47	43	12	4	0	5	32	4	27	2	0	1	4	.200	0	1-2	5	6.02

Ben McDonald

Pitches: Right **Bats:** Right **Pos:** SP-35   **Ht:** 6'7" **Wt:** 214 **Born:** 11/24/67 **Age:** 29

Year Team	Lg	G	GS	CG	GF	IP	BFP	H	R	ER	HR	SH	SF	HB	TBB	IBB	SO	WP	Bk	W	L	Pct.	ShO	Sv-Op	Hld	ERA
1989 Baltimore	AL	6	0	0	2	7.1	33	8	7	7	2	0	1	0	4	0	3	1	1	1	0	1.000	0	0-0	0	8.59
1990 Baltimore	AL	21	15	3	2	118.2	472	88	36	32	9	3	5	0	35	0	65	5	0	8	5	.615	2	0-0	0	2.43
1991 Baltimore	AL	21	21	1	0	126.1	532	126	71	68	16	2	3	1	43	2	85	3	0	6	8	.429	0	0-0	0	4.84
1992 Baltimore	AL	35	35	4	0	227	958	213	113	107	32	6	6	9	74	5	158	3	2	13	13	.500	2	0-0	0	4.24
1993 Baltimore	AL	34	34	7	0	220.1	914	185	92	83	17	7	4	5	86	4	171	7	1	13	14	.481	1	0-0	0	3.39
1994 Baltimore	AL	24	24	5	0	157.1	655	151	75	71	14	6	1	2	54	2	94	3	1	14	7	.667	1	0-0	0	4.06
1995 Baltimore	AL	14	13	1	1	80	342	67	40	37	10	0	2	3	38	3	62	4	2	3	6	.333	0	0-0	0	4.16
1996 Milwaukee	AL	35	35	2	0	221.1	951	228	104	96	25	8	7	6	67	0	146	4	0	12	10	.545	0	0-0	0	3.90
8 ML YEARS		190	177	23	5	1158.1	4857	1066	538	501	125	32	29	26	401	16	784	30	7	70	63	.526	6	0-0	0	3.89

Jack McDowell

Pitches: Right **Bats:** Right **Pos:** SP-30   **Ht:** 6'5" **Wt:** 188 **Born:** 1/16/66 **Age:** 31

Year Team	Lg	G	GS	CG	GF	IP	BFP	H	R	ER	HR	SH	SF	HB	TBB	IBB	SO	WP	Bk	W	L	Pct.	ShO	Sv-Op	Hld	ERA
1987 Chicago	AL	4	4	0	0	28	103	16	6	6	1	0	0	2	6	0	15	0	0	3	0	1.000	0	0-0	0	1.93
1988 Chicago	AL	26	26	1	0	158.2	687	147	85	70	12	6	7	7	68	5	84	11	1	5	10	.333	0	0-0	0	3.97
1990 Chicago	AL	33	33	4	0	205	866	189	93	87	20	1	5	7	77	0	165	7	1	14	9	.609	0	0-0	0	3.82
1991 Chicago	AL	35	35	15	0	253.2	1028	212	97	96	19	8	4	4	82	2	191	10	1	17	10	.630	3	0-0	0	3.41
1992 Chicago	AL	34	34	13	0	260.2	1079	247	95	92	21	8	6	7	75	9	178	6	0	20	10	.667	1	0-0	0	3.18
1993 Chicago	AL	34	34	10	0	256.2	1067	261	104	96	20	8	6	3	69	6	158	8	1	22	10	.688	4	0-0	0	3.37
1994 Chicago	AL	25	25	6	0	181	755	186	82	75	12	4	4	5	42	2	127	4	0	10	9	.526	2	0-0	0	3.73
1995 New York	AL	30	30	8	0	217.2	927	211	106	95	25	8	6	4	78	1	157	9	1	15	10	.600	2	0-0	0	3.93
1996 Cleveland	AL	30	30	5	0	192	846	214	119	109	22	10	5	4	67	2	141	5	0	13	9	.591	1	0-0	0	5.11
9 ML YEARS		251	251	62	0	1753.1	7358	1683	787	726	152	53	43	44	564	27	1216	60	5	119	77	.607	13	0-0	0	3.73

Roger McDowell

Pitches: Right **Bats:** Both **Pos:** RP-41   **Ht:** 6'1" **Wt:** 195 **Born:** 12/21/60 **Age:** 36

Year Team	Lg	G	GS	CG	GF	IP	BFP	H	R	ER	HR	SH	SF	HB	TBB	IBB	SO	WP	Bk	W	L	Pct.	ShO	Sv-Op	Hld	ERA
1985 New York	NL	62	2	0	36	127.1	516	108	43	40	9	6	2	1	37	8	70	6	2	6	5	.545	0	17--	—	2.83
1986 New York	NL	75	0	0	52	128	524	107	48	43	4	7	3	3	42	5	65	3	3	14	9	.609	0	22--	—	3.02
1987 New York	NL	56	0	0	45	88.2	384	95	41	41	7	5	5	2	28	4	32	3	1	7	5	.583	0	25-32	1	4.16
1988 New York	NL	62	0	0	41	89	378	80	31	26	1	3	5	3	31	7	46	6	1	5	5	.500	0	16-20	7	2.63
1989 NYN-Phi	NL	69	0	0	56	92	387	79	36	20	3	6	1	3	38	8	47	3	1	4	8	.333	0	23-28	2	1.96
1990 Philadelphia	NL	72	0	0	60	86.1	373	92	41	37	2	10	4	2	35	9	39	1	1	6	8	.429	0	22-28	1	3.86
1991 Phi-LA	NL	71	0	0	34	101.1	445	100	40	33	4	11	3	2	48	20	50	2	0	9	9	.500	0	10-15	10	2.93
1992 Los Angeles	NL	65	0	0	39	83.2	393	103	46	38	3	10	3	1	42	13	50	4	1	6	10	.375	0	14-22	5	4.09
1993 Los Angeles	NL	54	0	0	19	68	300	76	32	17	2	3	1	2	30	10	27	5	0	5	3	.625	0	2-3	3	2.25
1994 Los Angeles	NL	32	0	0	11	41.1	193	50	25	24	3	5	0	1	22	6	29	3	0	0	3	.000	0	0-1	0	5.23
1995 Texas	AL	64	0	0	26	85	362	86	39	38	5	6	5	6	34	7	49	1	1	7	4	.636	0	4-8	9	4.02
1996 Baltimore	AL	41	0	0	11	59.1	262	69	32	28	7	3	1	2	23	1	20	0	0	1	1	.500	0	4-6	9	4.25
1989 New York	NL	25	0	0	15	35.1	156	34	17	13	1	3	1	2	16	3	15	3	1	1	5	.167	0	4-5	2	3.31
Philadelphia	NL	44	0	0	41	56.2	231	45	15	7	2	3	0	1	22	5	32	0	0	3	3	.500	0	19-23	0	1.11
1991 Philadelphia	NL	38	0	0	16	59	271	61	28	21	1	7	1	2	32	12	28	1	0	3	6	.333	0	3-6	6	3.20
Los Angeles	NL	33	0	0	18	42.1	174	39	12	12	3	4	2	0	16	8	22	1	0	6	3	.667	0	7-9	4	2.55
12 ML YEARS		723	2	0	430	1050	4517	1045	454	385	50	75	33	28	410	98	524	37	11	70	70	.500	0	159--	—	3.30

143

Chuck McElroy

Pitches: Left **Bats:** Left **Pos:** RP-52 **Ht:** 6'0" **Wt:** 195 **Born:** 10/1/67 **Age:** 29

		HOW MUCH HE PITCHED						WHAT HE GAVE UP												THE RESULTS						
Year Team	Lg	G	GS	CG	GF	IP	BFP	H	R	ER	HR	SH	SF	HB	TBB	IBB	SO	WP	Bk	W	L	Pct.	ShO	Sv-Op	Hld	ERA
1996 Indianapols *	AAA	5	3	0	0	13.1	53	11	4	4	0	0	0	0	4	0	10	1	0	1	1	.500	0	0- -	—	2.70
1989 Philadelphia	NL	11	0	0	4	10.1	46	12	2	2	1	0	0	0	4	1	8	0	0	0	0	.000	0	0-0	0	1.74
1990 Philadelphia	NL	16	0	0	8	14	76	24	13	12	0	0	1	0	10	2	16	0	0	0	0	.000	0	0-0	0	7.71
1991 Chicago	NL	71	0	0	12	101.1	419	73	33	22	7	9	6	0	57	7	92	1	0	6	2	.750	0	3-6	10	1.95
1992 Chicago	NL	72	0	0	30	83.2	369	73	40	33	5	5	5	0	51	10	83	3	0	4	7	.364	0	6-11	3	3.55
1993 Chicago	NL	49	0	0	11	47.1	214	51	30	24	4	5	1	1	25	5	31	3	0	2	2	.500	0	0-0	4	4.56
1994 Cincinnati	NL	52	0	0	13	57.2	230	52	15	15	3	2	0	0	15	2	38	4	0	1	2	.333	0	5-11	10	2.34
1995 Cincinnati	NL	44	0	0	11	40.1	178	46	29	27	5	1	3	1	15	3	27	1	0	3	4	.429	0	0-3	3	6.02
1996 Cin-Cal		52	0	0	12	49	210	45	22	21	4	1	1	2	23	3	45	1	0	7	1	.875	0	0-2	7	3.86
1996 Cincinnati	NL	12	0	0	1	12.1	59	13	10	9	2	0	0	0	10	1	13	0	0	2	0	1.000	0	0-0	1	6.57
California	AL	40	0	0	11	36.2	151	32	12	12	2	1	1	2	13	2	32	1	0	5	1	.833	0	0-2	6	2.95
8 ML YEARS		367	0	0	101	403.2	1742	376	184	156	29	23	17	4	200	33	340	13	0	23	19	.548	0	14-33	37	3.48

Willie McGee

Bats: B **Throws:** R **Pos:** PH-45; RF-42; LF-35; CF-11; 1B-6 **Ht:** 6'1" **Wt:** 185 **Born:** 11/2/58 **Age:** 38

		BATTING																BASERUNNING				PERCENTAGES		
Year Team	Lg	G	AB	H	2B	3B	HR	(Hm Rd)	TB	R	RBI	TBB	IBB	SO	HBP	SH	SF	SB	CS	SB%	GDP	Avg	OBP	SLG
1982 St. Louis	NL	123	422	125	12	8	4	(2 2)	165	43	56	12	2	58	2	2	1	24	12	.67	9	.296	.318	.391
1983 St. Louis	NL	147	601	172	22	8	5	(4 1)	225	75	75	26	2	98	0	1	3	39	8	.83	8	.286	.314	.374
1984 St. Louis	NL	145	571	166	19	11	6	(2 4)	225	82	50	29	2	80	1	0	3	43	10	.81	12	.291	.325	.394
1985 St. Louis	NL	152	612	216	26	18	10	(3 7)	308	114	82	34	2	86	0	1	5	56	16	.78	3	.353	.384	.503
1986 St. Louis	NL	124	497	127	22	7	7	(7 0)	184	65	48	37	7	82	1	0	4	19	16	.54	8	.256	.306	.370
1987 St. Louis	NL	153	620	177	37	11	11	(6 5)	269	76	105	24	5	90	2	1	5	16	4	.80	24	.285	.312	.434
1988 St. Louis	NL	137	562	164	24	6	3	(1 2)	209	73	50	32	5	84	1	2	3	41	6	.87	10	.292	.329	.372
1989 St. Louis	NL	58	199	47	10	2	3	(1 2)	70	23	17	10	0	34	1	0	1	8	6	.57	2	.236	.275	.352
1990 StL-Oak		154	614	199	35	7	3	(1 2)	257	99	77	48	6	104	1	0	2	31	9	.78	13	.324	.373	.419
1991 San Francisco	NL	131	497	155	30	3	4	(2 2)	203	67	43	34	3	74	2	8	2	17	9	.65	11	.312	.357	.408
1992 San Francisco	NL	138	474	141	20	2	1	(0 1)	168	56	36	29	3	88	1	5	1	13	4	.76	7	.297	.339	.354
1993 San Francisco	NL	130	475	143	28	1	4	(0 4)	185	53	46	38	7	67	1	3	2	10	9	.53	12	.301	.353	.389
1994 San Francisco	NL	45	156	44	3	0	5	(2 3)	62	19	23	15	2	24	0	1	4	3	0	1.00	8	.282	.337	.397
1995 Boston	AL	67	200	57	11	3	2	(1 1)	80	32	15	9	0	41	0	5	3	5	2	.71	5	.285	.311	.400
1996 St. Louis	NL	123	309	95	15	2	5	(3 2)	129	52	41	18	2	60	2	1	1	5	2	.71	8	.307	.348	.417
1990 St. Louis	NL	125	501	168	32	5	3	(1 2)	219	76	62	38	6	86	1	0	2	28	9	.76	9	.335	.382	.437
Oakland	AL	29	113	31	3	2	0	(0 0)	38	23	15	10	0	18	0	0	0	3	0	1.00	4	.274	.333	.336
15 ML YEARS		1827	6809	2028	314	89	73	(34 39)	2739	929	764	395	48	1070	15	30	40	330	113	.74	140	.298	.336	.402

Fred McGriff

Bats: Left **Throws:** Left **Pos:** 1B-158; PH-1 **Ht:** 6'3" **Wt:** 215 **Born:** 10/31/63 **Age:** 33

		BATTING																BASERUNNING				PERCENTAGES		
Year Team	Lg	G	AB	H	2B	3B	HR	(Hm Rd)	TB	R	RBI	TBB	IBB	SO	HBP	SH	SF	SB	CS	SB%	GDP	Avg	OBP	SLG
1986 Toronto	AL	3	5	1	0	0	0	(0 0)	1	1	0	0	0	2	1	0	0	0	0	.00	0	.200	.200	.200
1987 Toronto	AL	107	295	73	16	0	20	(7 13)	149	58	43	60	4	104	1	0	0	3	2	.60	3	.247	.376	.505
1988 Toronto	AL	154	536	151	35	4	34	(18 16)	296	100	82	79	3	149	4	0	4	6	1	.86	15	.282	.376	.552
1989 Toronto	AL	161	551	148	27	3	36	(18 18)	289	98	92	119	12	132	4	1	5	7	4	.64	14	.269	.399	.525
1990 Toronto	AL	153	557	167	21	1	35	(14 21)	295	91	88	94	12	108	2	1	4	5	3	.63	7	.300	.400	.530
1991 San Diego	NL	153	528	147	19	1	31	(18 13)	261	84	106	105	26	135	2	0	7	4	1	.80	14	.278	.396	.494
1992 San Diego	NL	152	531	152	30	4	35	(21 14)	295	79	104	96	23	108	1	0	4	8	6	.57	14	.286	.394	.556
1993 SD-Atl	NL	151	557	162	29	2	37	(15 22)	306	111	101	76	6	106	2	0	5	5	3	.63	14	.291	.375	.549
1994 Atlanta	NL	113	424	135	25	1	34	(13 21)	264	81	94	50	8	76	1	0	3	7	3	.70	8	.318	.389	.623
1995 Atlanta	NL	144	528	148	27	1	27	(15 12)	258	85	93	65	6	99	5	0	6	3	6	.33	19	.280	.361	.489
1996 Atlanta	NL	159	617	182	37	1	28	(17 11)	305	81	107	68	12	116	2	0	4	7	3	.70	20	.295	.365	.494
1993 San Diego	NL	83	302	83	11	1	18	(7 11)	150	52	46	42	4	55	1	0	4	4	3	.57	7	.275	.361	.497
Atlanta	NL	68	255	79	18	1	19	(8 11)	156	59	55	34	2	51	1	0	1	1	0	1.00	5	.310	.392	.612
11 ML YEARS		1450	5129	1466	266	18	317	(156 161)	2719	869	910	812	112	1135	24	2	42	55	32	.63	128	.286	.383	.530

Mark McGwire

Bats: Right **Throws:** Right **Pos:** 1B-109; DH-18; PH-5 **Ht:** 6'5" **Wt:** 250 **Born:** 10/1/63 **Age:** 33

		BATTING																BASERUNNING				PERCENTAGES		
Year Team	Lg	G	AB	H	2B	3B	HR	(Hm Rd)	TB	R	RBI	TBB	IBB	SO	HBP	SH	SF	SB	CS	SB%	GDP	Avg	OBP	SLG
1986 Oakland	AL	18	53	10	1	0	3	(1 2)	20	10	9	4	0	18	1	0	0	0	1	.00	0	.189	.259	.377
1987 Oakland	AL	151	557	161	28	4	49	(21 28)	344	97	118	71	8	131	5	0	8	1	1	.50	6	.289	.370	.618
1988 Oakland	AL	155	550	143	22	1	32	(12 20)	263	87	99	76	4	117	4	1	4	0	0	.00	15	.260	.352	.478
1989 Oakland	AL	143	490	113	17	0	33	(12 21)	229	74	95	83	6	94	3	0	11	1	1	.50	23	.231	.339	.467
1990 Oakland	AL	156	523	123	16	0	39	(14 25)	256	87	108	110	9	116	7	1	9	2	1	.67	13	.235	.370	.489
1991 Oakland	AL	154	483	97	22	0	22	(15 7)	185	62	75	93	3	116	3	1	5	2	1	.67	13	.201	.330	.383
1992 Oakland	AL	139	467	125	22	0	42	(24 18)	273	87	104	90	12	105	5	0	10	0	1	.00	10	.268	.385	.585
1993 Oakland	AL	27	84	28	6	0	9	(5 4)	61	16	24	21	5	19	1	0	1	0	0	.00	0	.333	.467	.726
1994 Oakland	AL	47	135	34	3	0	9	(6 3)	64	26	25	37	3	40	0	0	0	0	0	.00	3	.252	.413	.474

						BATTING													BASERUNNING				PERCENTAGES		
Year Team	Lg	G	AB	H	2B	3B	HR	(Hm	Rd)	TB	R	RBI	TBB	IBB	SO	HBP	SH	SF	SB	CS	SB%	GDP	Avg	OBP	SLG
1995 Oakland	AL	104	317	87	13	0	39	(15	24)	217	75	90	88	5	77	11	0	6	1	1	.50	9	.274	.441	.685
1996 Oakland	AL	130	423	132	21	0	**52**	(24	28)	309	104	113	116	16	112	8	0	1	0	0	.00	14	.312	**.467**	**.730**
11 ML YEARS		1224	4082	1053	171	5	329	(149	180)	2221	725	860	789	70	945	48	3	54	7	8	.47	106	.258	.380	.544

Tim McIntosh

Bats: Right **Throws:** Right **Pos:** C-1; 1B-1; 3B-1   **Ht:** 5'11" **Wt:** 195 **Born:** 3/21/65 **Age:** 32

						BATTING													BASERUNNING				PERCENTAGES		
Year Team	Lg	G	AB	H	2B	3B	HR	(Hm	Rd)	TB	R	RBI	TBB	IBB	SO	HBP	SH	SF	SB	CS	SB%	GDP	Avg	OBP	SLG
1996 Columbus *	AAA	67	206	57	11	1	10	—	—	100	30	28	11	1	40	6	2	2	0	0	.00	6	.277	.329	.485
1990 Milwaukee	AL	5	5	1	0	0	1	(1	0)	4	1	1	0	0	2	0	0	0	0	0	.00	0	.200	.200	.800
1991 Milwaukee	AL	7	11	4	1	0	1	(1	0)	8	2	1	0	0	4	0	0	0	0	0	.00	0	.364	.364	.727
1992 Milwaukee	AL	35	77	14	3	0	0	(0	0)	17	7	6	3	0	9	2	1	1	1	3	.25	1	.182	.229	.221
1993 Mil-Mon		21	21	2	1	0	0	(0	0)	3	2	2	0	0	7	0	0	0	0	0	.00	0	.095	.095	.143
1996 New York	AL	3	3	0	0	0	0	(0	0)	0	0	0	0	0	0	0	0	0	0	0	.00	0	.000	.000	.000
1993 Milwaukee	AL	0	0	0	0	0	0	(0	0)	0	0	0	0	0	0	0	0	0	0	0	.00	0	.000	.000	.000
Montreal	NL	20	21	2	1	0	0	(0	0)	3	2	2	0	0	7	0	0	0	0	0	.00	0	.095	.095	.143
5 ML YEARS		71	117	21	5	0	2	(2	0)	32	12	10	3	0	22	2	1	1	1	3	.25	1	.179	.211	.274

Walt McKeel

Bats: Right **Throws:** Right **Pos:** C-1   **Ht:** 6'0" **Wt:** 200 **Born:** 1/17/72 **Age:** 25

						BATTING													BASERUNNING				PERCENTAGES		
Year Team	Lg	G	AB	H	2B	3B	HR	(Hm	Rd)	TB	R	RBI	TBB	IBB	SO	HBP	SH	SF	SB	CS	SB%	GDP	Avg	OBP	SLG
1990 Red Sox	R	13	44	11	3	0	0	—	—	14	2	6	3	0	8	0	0	1	0	2	.00	2	.250	.292	.318
1991 Red Sox	R	35	113	15	0	1	2	—	—	23	10	12	17	0	20	1	0	4	0	0	.00	5	.133	.244	.204
1992 Lynchburg	A+	96	288	64	11	0	12	—	—	111	33	33	22	0	77	3	5	1	2	1	.67	5	.222	.283	.385
1993 Lynchburg	A+	80	247	59	17	2	5	—	—	95	28	32	26	0	40	3	6	3	0	1	.00	6	.239	.315	.385
1994 Sarasota	A+	37	137	38	8	1	2	—	—	54	15	15	8	1	19	1	0	0	1	0	1.00	1	.277	.322	.394
New Britain	AA	50	164	30	6	1	1	—	—	41	10	17	7	1	35	3	1	2	0	0	.00	5	.183	.227	.250
1995 Trenton	AA	29	84	20	3	1	2	—	—	31	11	11	8	0	15	0	0	2	2	1	.67	1	.238	.298	.369
Sarasota	A+	62	198	66	14	0	8	—	—	104	26	35	25	0	28	3	0	5	6	3	.67	4	.333	.407	.525
1996 Trenton	AA	128	464	140	19	1	16	—	—	209	86	78	60	3	52	7	5	7	2	4	.33	13	.302	.385	.450
1996 Boston	AL	1	0	0	0	0	0	(0	0)	0	0	0	0	0	0	0	0	0	0	0	.00	0	.000	.000	.000

Mark McLemore

Bats: Both **Throws:** Right **Pos:** 2B-147; RF-1; PH-1   **Ht:** 5'11" **Wt:** 207 **Born:** 10/4/64 **Age:** 32

						BATTING													BASERUNNING				PERCENTAGES		
Year Team	Lg	G	AB	H	2B	3B	HR	(Hm	Rd)	TB	R	RBI	TBB	IBB	SO	HBP	SH	SF	SB	CS	SB%	GDP	Avg	OBP	SLG
1986 California	AL	5	4	0	0	0	0	(0	0)	0	0	0	1	0	2	0	1	0	0	1	.00	0	.000	.200	.000
1987 California	AL	138	433	102	13	3	3	(3	0)	130	61	41	48	0	72	0	15	3	25	8	.76	7	.236	.310	.300
1988 California	AL	77	233	56	11	2	2	(1	1)	77	38	16	25	0	28	0	5	2	13	7	.65	6	.240	.312	.330
1989 California	AL	32	103	25	3	1	0	(0	0)	30	12	14	7	0	19	1	3	1	6	1	.86	2	.243	.295	.291
1990 Cal-Cle	AL	28	60	9	2	0	0	(0	0)	11	6	2	4	0	15	0	1	0	1	0	1.00	1	.150	.203	.183
1991 Houston	NL	21	61	9	1	0	0	(0	0)	10	6	2	6	0	13	0	0	1	0	1	.00	1	.148	.221	.164
1992 Baltimore	AL	101	228	56	7	2	0	(0	0)	67	40	27	21	1	26	0	6	1	11	5	.69	6	.246	.308	.294
1993 Baltimore	AL	148	581	165	27	5	4	(2	2)	214	81	72	64	4	92	1	11	6	21	15	.58	21	.284	.353	.368
1994 Baltimore	AL	104	343	88	11	1	3	(2	1)	110	44	29	51	3	50	1	4	1	20	5	.80	7	.257	.354	.321
1995 Texas	AL	129	467	122	20	5	5	(3	2)	167	73	41	59	6	71	3	10	3	21	11	.66	10	.261	.346	.358
1996 Texas	AL	147	517	150	23	4	5	(3	2)	196	84	46	87	5	69	0	2	5	27	10	.73	16	.290	.389	.379
1990 California	AL	20	48	7	2	0	0	(0	0)	9	4	2	4	0	9	0	1	0	1	0	1.00	1	.146	.212	.188
Cleveland	AL	8	12	2	0	0	0	(0	0)	2	2	0	0	0	6	0	0	0	0	0	.00	0	.167	.167	.167
11 ML YEARS		930	3030	782	118	23	22	(14	8)	1012	445	290	373	19	457	6	58	23	145	64	.69	77	.258	.338	.334

Greg McMichael

Pitches: Right **Bats:** Right **Pos:** RP-73   **Ht:** 6'3" **Wt:** 215 **Born:** 12/1/66 **Age:** 30

			HOW MUCH HE PITCHED						WHAT HE GAVE UP										THE RESULTS						
Year Team	Lg	G	GS	CG	GF	IP	BFP	H	R	ER	HR	SH	SF	HB	TBB	IBB	SO	WP	Bk	W	L	Pct.	ShO	Sv-Op	Hld	ERA
1993 Atlanta	NL	74	0	0	40	91.2	365	68	22	21	3	4	2	0	29	4	89	6	1	2	3	.400	0	19-21	12	2.06
1994 Atlanta	NL	51	0	0	41	58.2	259	66	29	25	1	3	1	0	19	6	47	3	1	4	6	.400	0	21-31	1	3.84
1995 Atlanta	NL	67	0	0	16	80.2	337	64	27	25	8	5	0	0	32	9	74	3	0	7	2	.778	0	2-4	**20**	2.79
1996 Atlanta	NL	73	0	0	14	86.2	366	84	37	31	4	3	3	1	27	7	78	4	1	5	3	.625	0	2-8	18	3.22
4 ML YEARS		265	0	0	111	317.2	1327	282	115	102	16	15	6	1	107	26	288	16	3	18	14	.563	0	44-64	51	2.89

Billy McMillon

Bats: Left **Throws:** Left **Pos:** LF-15; PH-13   **Ht:** 5'11" **Wt:** 172 **Born:** 11/17/71 **Age:** 25

						BATTING													BASERUNNING				PERCENTAGES		
Year Team	Lg	G	AB	H	2B	3B	HR	(Hm	Rd)	TB	R	RBI	TBB	IBB	SO	HBP	SH	SF	SB	CS	SB%	GDP	Avg	OBP	SLG
1993 Elmira	A-	57	227	69	14	2	6	—	—	105	38	35	30	4	44	4	0	0	5	4	.56	3	.304	.395	.463
1994 Kane County	A	137	496	125	25	3	17	—	—	207	88	101	84	2	99	10	1	9	7	3	.70	13	.252	.366	.417

Year Team	Lg	G	AB	H	2B	3B	HR	(Hm	Rd)	TB	R	RBI	TBB	IBB	SO	HBP	SH	SF	SB	CS	SB%	GDP	Avg	OBP	SLG
1995 Portland	AA	141	518	162	29	3	14	—	—	239	92	93	96	5	90	7	1	5	15	9	.63	10	.313	.423	.461
1996 Charlotte	AAA	97	347	122	32	2	17	—	—	209	72	70	36	5	76	5	0	2	5	3	.63	8	.352	.418	.602
1996 Florida	NL	28	51	11	0	0	0	(0	0)	11	4	4	5	1	14	0	0	0	0	0	.00	1	.216	.286	.216

Brian McRae

Bats: Both **Throws:** Right **Pos:** CF-155; PH-4 **Ht:** 6'0" **Wt:** 196 **Born:** 8/27/67 **Age:** 29

Year Team	Lg	G	AB	H	2B	3B	HR	(Hm	Rd)	TB	R	RBI	TBB	IBB	SO	HBP	SH	SF	SB	CS	SB%	GDP	Avg	OBP	SLG
1990 Kansas City	AL	46	168	48	8	3	2	(1	1)	68	21	23	9	0	29	0	3	2	4	3	.57	5	.286	.318	.405
1991 Kansas City	AL	152	629	164	28	9	8	(3	5)	234	86	64	24	1	99	2	3	5	20	11	.65	12	.261	.288	.372
1992 Kansas City	AL	149	533	119	23	5	4	(2	2)	164	63	52	42	1	88	6	7	4	18	5	.78	10	.223	.285	.308
1993 Kansas City	AL	153	627	177	28	9	12	(5	7)	259	78	69	37	1	105	4	14	3	23	14	.62	8	.282	.325	.413
1994 Kansas City	AL	114	436	119	22	6	4	(2	2)	165	71	40	54	3	67	6	6	3	28	8	.78	3	.273	.359	.378
1995 Chicago	NL	137	580	167	38	7	12	(6	6)	255	92	48	47	1	92	7	3	1	27	8	.77	12	.288	.348	.440
1996 Chicago	NL	157	624	172	32	5	17	(9	8)	265	111	66	73	6	84	12	2	5	37	9	.80	11	.276	.360	.425
7 ML YEARS		908	3597	966	179	44	59	(28	31)	1410	522	362	286	13	564	37	38	23	157	58	.73	61	.269	.327	.392

Rusty Meacham

Pitches: Right **Bats:** Right **Pos:** RP-10; SP-5 **Ht:** 6'3" **Wt:** 180 **Born:** 1/27/68 **Age:** 29

Year Team	Lg	G	GS	CG	GF	IP	BFP	H	R	ER	HR	SH	SF	HB	TBB	IBB	SO	WP	Bk	W	L	Pct.	ShO	Sv-Op	Hld	ERA
1996 Omaha *	AAA	23	4	0	8	52.1	233	56	30	28	6	4	1	2	18	0	39	2	1	3	3	.500	0	2--	—	4.82
Tacoma *	AAA	7	2	0	2	19.2	78	13	7	5	0	0	0	1	5	0	20	1	0	2	1	.667	0	2--	—	2.29
1991 Detroit	AL	10	4	0	1	27.2	126	35	17	16	4	1	3	0	11	0	14	0	1	2	1	.667	0	0-0	1	5.20
1992 Kansas City	AL	64	0	0	20	101.2	412	88	39	31	5	3	9	1	21	5	64	4	0	10	4	.714	0	2-6	15	2.74
1993 Kansas City	AL	15	0	0	11	21	104	31	15	13	2	0	1	3	5	1	13	0	0	2	2	.500	0	0-0	1	5.57
1994 Kansas City	AL	36	0	0	15	50.2	213	51	23	21	7	1	4	2	12	1	36	4	0	3	3	.500	0	4-5	7	3.73
1995 Kansas City	AL	49	0	0	26	59.2	262	72	36	33	6	1	4	1	19	5	30	0	0	4	3	.571	0	2-3	7	4.98
1996 Seattle	AL	15	5	0	3	42.1	192	57	28	27	9	0	1	4	13	1	25	1	0	1	1	.500	0	1-1	0	5.74
6 ML YEARS		189	9	0	76	303	1309	334	158	141	33	6	23	11	81	13	182	9	1	22	14	.611	0	9-15	31	4.19

Pat Meares

Bats: Right **Throws:** Right **Pos:** SS-150; PH-5; CF-1 **Ht:** 6'0" **Wt:** 188 **Born:** 9/6/68 **Age:** 28

Year Team	Lg	G	AB	H	2B	3B	HR	(Hm	Rd)	TB	R	RBI	TBB	IBB	SO	HBP	SH	SF	SB	CS	SB%	GDP	Avg	OBP	SLG
1993 Minnesota	AL	111	346	87	14	3	0	(0	0)	107	33	33	7	0	52	1	4	3	4	5	.44	11	.251	.266	.309
1994 Minnesota	AL	80	229	61	12	1	2	(0	2)	81	29	24	14	0	50	2	6	3	5	1	.83	3	.266	.310	.354
1995 Minnesota	AL	116	390	105	19	4	12	(3	9)	168	57	49	15	0	68	11	4	5	10	4	.71	17	.269	.311	.431
1996 Minnesota	AL	152	517	138	26	7	8	(3	5)	202	66	67	17	1	90	9	4	7	9	4	.69	19	.267	.298	.391
4 ML YEARS		459	1482	391	71	15	22	(6	16)	558	185	173	53	1	260	23	18	18	28	14	.67	50	.264	.296	.377

Jim Mecir

Pitches: Right **Bats:** Both **Pos:** RP-26 **Ht:** 6'1" **Wt:** 195 **Born:** 5/16/70 **Age:** 27

Year Team	Lg	G	GS	CG	GF	IP	BFP	H	R	ER	HR	SH	SF	HB	TBB	IBB	SO	WP	Bk	W	L	Pct.	ShO	Sv-Op	Hld	ERA
1991 San Bernrdo	A+	14	12	0	2	70.1	314	72	40	33	3	2	3	3	37	0	48	8	4	3	5	.375	0	1--	—	4.22
1992 San Bernrdo	A+	14	11	0	1	61.2	283	72	40	32	8	1	2	5	26	0	53	5	1	4	5	.444	0	0--	—	4.67
1993 Riverside	A+	26	26	1	0	145.1	654	160	89	70	3	3	8	15	58	2	85	4	0	9	11	.450	0	0--	—	4.33
1994 Jacksonvlle	AA	46	0	0	34	80.1	343	73	28	24	5	4	2	4	35	3	53	6	0	6	5	.545	0	13--	—	2.69
1995 Tacoma	AAA	40	0	0	22	69.2	298	63	29	24	3	3	1	1	28	7	46	5	0	1	4	.200	0	8--	—	3.10
1996 Columbus	AAA	33	0	0	19	47.2	195	37	14	12	2	3	1	3	15	2	52	3	0	3	3	.500	0	7--	—	2.27
1995 Seattle	AL	2	0	0	1	4.2	21	5	1	0	2	0	3	0	2	0	3	0	0	0	0	.000	0	0-0	0	0.00
1996 New York	AL	26	0	0	10	40.1	185	42	24	23	6	5	4	0	23	4	38	6	0	1	1	.500	0	0-0	0	5.13
2 ML YEARS		28	0	0	11	45	206	47	25	23	6	5	4	0	25	4	41	6	0	1	1	.500	0	0-0	0	4.60

Miguel Mejia

Bats: R **Throws:** R **Pos:** PH-31; CF-11; RF-6; LF-5 **Ht:** 6'1" **Wt:** 155 **Born:** 3/25/75 **Age:** 22

Year Team	Lg	G	AB	H	2B	3B	HR	(Hm	Rd)	TB	R	RBI	TBB	IBB	SO	HBP	SH	SF	SB	CS	SB%	GDP	Avg	OBP	SLG
1993 Albany	A	23	79	13	0	3	0	—	—	19	11	2	4	0	22	2	2	0	7	2	.78	5	.165	.224	.241
Orioles	R	35	130	32	3	3	0	—	—	41	21	12	13	1	23	2	0	0	18	5	.78	5	.246	.324	.315
1994 Albany	A	22	58	10	1	1	0	—	—	13	6	3	5	0	20	1	1	1	5	5	.50	0	.172	.246	.224
Bluefield	R+	50	191	51	5	5	2	—	—	72	34	24	17	0	39	1	5	1	32	9	.78	2	.267	.329	.377
1995 High Desert	A+	37	119	32	6	1	0	—	—	40	14	12	14	0	17	1	2	1	16	7	.70	3	.269	.348	.336
Bluefield	R+	51	181	54	6	3	3	—	—	75	50	30	18	0	30	1	6	2	36	5	.88	5	.298	.361	.414
1996 St. Pete	A+	8	26	3	0	0	0	—	—	3	2	0	1	0	12	0	1	0	2	0	1.00	0	.115	.148	.115
1996 St. Louis	NL	45	23	2	0	0	0	(0	0)	2	10	0	0	0	10	0	0	0	5	3	.63	0	.087	.087	.087

Ramiro Mendoza

Pitches: Right **Bats:** Right **Pos:** SP-11; RP-1   **Ht:** 6'2" **Wt:** 154 **Born:** 6/15/72 **Age:** 25

		HOW	MUCH	HE	PITCHED			WHAT	HE	GAVE	UP							THE	RESULTS			
Year Team	Lg	G	GS	CG	GF	IP	BFP	H	R	ER	HR	SH	SF	HB	TBB	IBB	SO	WP	Bk	W	L	Pct.	ShO	Sv-Op	Hld	ERA
1993 Yankees	R	15	9	0	3	67.2	275	59	26	21	3	0	1	4	7	0	61	3	0	4	5	.444	0	1- -	—	2.79
Greensboro	A	2	0	0	1	3.2	18	2	1	1	0	0	0	0	5	0	3	0	0	0	1	.000	0	0- -	—	2.45
1994 Tampa	A+	22	21	1	1	134.1	560	133	54	45	7	5	3	2	35	1	110	2	3	12	6	.667	0	0- -	—	3.01
1995 Columbus	AAA	2	2	0	0	14	51	10	4	4	0	0	1	0	2	0	13	1	0	1	0	1.000	0	0- -	—	2.57
1996 Columbus	AAA	15	15	0	0	97	392	96	30	27	2	3	4	5	19	0	61	1	0	6	2	.750	0	0- -	—	2.51
1996 New York	AL	12	11	0	0	53	249	80	43	40	5	1	1	4	10	1	34	2	1	4	5	.444	0	0-0	0	6.79

Paul Menhart

Pitches: Right **Bats:** Right **Pos:** SP-6; RP-5   **Ht:** 6'2" **Wt:** 190 **Born:** 3/25/69 **Age:** 28

		HOW	MUCH	HE	PITCHED			WHAT	HE	GAVE	UP							THE	RESULTS			
Year Team	Lg	G	GS	CG	GF	IP	BFP	H	R	ER	HR	SH	SF	HB	TBB	IBB	SO	WP	Bk	W	L	Pct.	ShO	Sv-Op	Hld	ERA
1990 St. Cathrns	A-	8	8	0	0	40	180	34	27	18	2	1	1	5	19	0	38	6	2	0	5	.000	0	0- -	—	4.05
Myrtle Bch	A	5	4	1	1	30.2	113	18	5	2	1	1	0	0	5	0	18	1	0	3	0	1.000	0	0- -	—	0.59
1991 Dunedin	A+	20	20	3	0	128.1	521	114	42	38	3	2	2	3	34	0	114	4	1	10	6	.625	0	0- -	—	2.66
1992 Knoxville	AA	28	28	2	0	177.2	735	181	85	76	14	2	6	11	38	0	104	12	1	10	11	.476	1	0- -	—	3.85
1993 Syracuse	AAA	25	25	4	0	151	646	143	74	61	16	4	3	7	67	4	108	8	1	9	10	.474	0	0- -	—	3.64
1995 Syracuse	AAA	10	10	0	0	51.1	234	62	42	36	5	2	3	0	25	0	30	3	1	2	4	.333	0	0- -	—	6.31
1996 Tacoma	AAA	6	6	0	0	26	142	53	33	32	4	0	3	1	16	0	12	3	0	0	3	.000	0	0- -	—	11.08
1995 Toronto	AL	21	9	1	6	78.2	350	72	49	43	9	3	4	6	47	4	50	6	0	1	4	.200	0	0-0	0	4.92
1996 Seattle	AL	11	6	0	4	42	196	55	36	34	9	1	0	2	25	0	18	1	0	2	2	.500	0	0-0	0	7.29
2 ML YEARS		32	15	1	10	120.2	546	127	85	77	18	4	4	8	72	4	68	7	0	3	6	.333	0	0-0	0	5.74

Orlando Merced

Bats: Left **Throws:** Right **Pos:** RF-115; PH-7; 1B-1   **Ht:** 5'11" **Wt:** 183 **Born:** 11/2/66 **Age:** 30

				BATTING														BASERUNNING				PERCENTAGES		
Year Team	Lg	G	AB	H	2B	3B	HR	(Hm	Rd)	TB	R	RBI	TBB	IBB	SO	HBP	SH	SF	SB	CS	SB%	GDP	Avg	OBP	SLG
1990 Pittsburgh	NL	25	24	5	1	0	0	(0	0)	6	3	0	1	0	9	0	0	0	0	0	.00	1	.208	.240	.250
1991 Pittsburgh	NL	120	411	113	17	2	10	(5	5)	164	83	50	64	4	81	1	1	1	8	4	.67	6	.275	.373	.399
1992 Pittsburgh	NL	134	405	100	28	5	6	(4	2)	156	50	60	52	8	63	2	1	5	5	4	.56	6	.247	.332	.385
1993 Pittsburgh	NL	137	447	140	26	4	8	(3	5)	198	68	70	77	10	64	1	0	2	3	3	.50	9	.313	.414	.443
1994 Pittsburgh	NL	108	386	105	21	3	9	(4	5)	159	48	51	42	5	58	1	0	8	4	1	.80	17	.272	.343	.412
1995 Pittsburgh	NL	132	487	146	29	4	15	(8	7)	228	75	83	52	9	74	1	0	5	7	2	.78	5	.300	.365	.468
1996 Pittsburgh	NL	120	453	130	24	1	17	(9	8)	207	69	80	51	5	74	0	0	3	8	4	.67	9	.287	.357	.457
7 ML YEARS		776	2613	739	146	19	65	(33	32)	1118	396	394	339	41	423	6	2	18	35	18	.66	57	.283	.364	.428

Henry Mercedes

Bats: Right **Throws:** Right **Pos:** C-4   **Ht:** 6'1" **Wt:** 210 **Born:** 7/23/69 **Age:** 27

				BATTING														BASERUNNING				PERCENTAGES		
Year Team	Lg	G	AB	H	2B	3B	HR	(Hm	Rd)	TB	R	RBI	TBB	IBB	SO	HBP	SH	SF	SB	CS	SB%	GDP	Avg	OBP	SLG
1996 Omaha *	AAA	72	223	48	9	1	8	(—	—)	83	28	35	28	0	60	0	6	2	0	0	.00	7	.215	.300	.372
1992 Oakland	AL	9	5	4	0	1	0	(0	0)	6	1	1	0	0	1	0	0	0	0	0	.00	0	.800	.800	1.200
1993 Oakland	AL	20	47	10	2	0	0	(0	0)	12	5	3	2	0	15	1	0	0	1	1	.50	0	.213	.260	.255
1995 Kansas City	AL	23	43	11	2	0	0	(0	0)	13	7	9	8	0	13	1	1	2	0	0	.00	0	.256	.370	.302
1996 Kansas City	AL	4	4	1	0	0	0	(0	0)	1	1	0	0	0	1	0	0	0	0	0	.00	0	.250	.250	.250
4 ML YEARS		56	99	26	4	1	0	(0	0)	32	14	13	10	0	30	2	1	2	1	1	.50	0	.263	.336	.323

Jose Mercedes

Pitches: Right **Bats:** Right **Pos:** RP-11   **Ht:** 6'1" **Wt:** 199 **Born:** 3/5/71 **Age:** 26

		HOW	MUCH	HE	PITCHED			WHAT	HE	GAVE	UP							THE	RESULTS			
Year Team	Lg	G	GS	CG	GF	IP	BFP	H	R	ER	HR	SH	SF	HB	TBB	IBB	SO	WP	Bk	W	L	Pct.	ShO	Sv-Op	Hld	ERA
1996 Nw Orleans *	AAA	25	15	0	3	101	439	109	58	40	14	3	5	7	28	1	47	4	1	3	7	.300	0	1- -	—	3.56
1994 Milwaukee	AL	19	0	0	5	31	120	22	9	8	4	0	0	2	16	1	11	0	1	2	0	1.000	0	0-1	3	2.32
1995 Milwaukee	AL	5	0	0	0	7.1	42	12	9	8	1	0	2	0	8	0	6	1	0	0	1	.000	0	0-2	1	9.82
1996 Milwaukee	AL	11	0	0	4	16.2	74	20	18	17	6	0	1	0	5	0	6	2	0	0	2	.000	0	0-1	2	9.18
3 ML YEARS		35	0	0	9	55	236	54	36	33	11	0	3	2	29	1	23	3	1	2	3	.400	0	0-4	6	5.40

Kent Mercker

Pitches: Left **Bats:** Left **Pos:** SP-12; RP-12   **Ht:** 6'2" **Wt:** 195 **Born:** 2/1/68 **Age:** 29

		HOW	MUCH	HE	PITCHED			WHAT	HE	GAVE	UP							THE	RESULTS			
Year Team	Lg	G	GS	CG	GF	IP	BFP	H	R	ER	HR	SH	SF	HB	TBB	IBB	SO	WP	Bk	W	L	Pct.	ShO	Sv-Op	Hld	ERA
1996 Buffalo *	AAA	3	3	0	0	16	70	11	7	7	3	0	1	3	8	0	11	1	0	0	0	.000	0	0-0	—	3.94
1989 Atlanta	NL	2	1	0	1	4.1	26	8	6	6	0	0	0	0	6	0	4	0	0	0	0	.000	0	0-0	0	12.46
1990 Atlanta	NL	36	0	0	28	48.1	211	43	22	17	6	1	2	2	24	3	39	2	0	4	7	.364	0	7-10	6	3.17
1991 Atlanta	NL	50	4	0	28	73.1	306	56	23	21	8	3	2	1	35	3	62	4	1	5	3	.625	0	6-8	3	2.58

147

		HOW MUCH HE PITCHED						WHAT HE GAVE UP												THE RESULTS						
Year Team	Lg	G	GS	CG	GF	IP	BFP	H	R	ER	HR	SH	SF	HB	TBB	IBB	SO	WP	Bk	W	L	Pct.	ShO	Sv-Op	Hld	ERA
1992 Atlanta	NL	53	0	0	18	68.1	289	51	27	26	4	4	1	3	35	1	49	6	0	3	2	.600	0	6-9	6	3.42
1993 Atlanta	NL	43	6	0	9	66	283	52	24	21	2	0	0	2	36	3	59	5	1	3	1	.750	0	0-3	4	2.86
1994 Atlanta	NL	20	17	2	0	112.1	461	90	46	43	16	4	3	0	45	3	111	4	1	9	4	.692	1	0-0	0	3.45
1995 Atlanta	NL	29	26	0	1	143	622	140	73	66	16	8	7	3	61	2	102	6	2	7	8	.467	0	0-0	0	4.15
1996 Bal-Cle	AL	24	12	0	2	69.2	329	83	60	54	13	3	6	3	38	2	29	3	1	4	6	.400	0	0-0	2	6.98
1996 Baltimore	AL	14	12	0	0	58	283	73	56	50	12	3	4	3	35	1	22	3	1	3	6	.333	0	0-0	0	7.76
Cleveland	AL	10	0	0	2	11.2	46	10	4	4	1	0	2	0	3	1	7	0	0	1	0	1.000	0	0-0	2	3.09
8 ML YEARS		257	66	2	87	585.1	2527	523	281	254	62	22	21	14	280	17	455	30	6	35	31	.530	1	19-30	15	3.91

Jose Mesa

Pitches: Right **Bats:** Right **Pos:** RP-69 **Ht:** 6'3" **Wt:** 225 **Born:** 5/22/66 **Age:** 31

		HOW MUCH HE PITCHED						WHAT HE GAVE UP												THE RESULTS						
Year Team	Lg	G	GS	CG	GF	IP	BFP	H	R	ER	HR	SH	SF	HB	TBB	IBB	SO	WP	Bk	W	L	Pct.	ShO	Sv-Op	Hld	ERA
1987 Baltimore	AL	6	5	0	0	31.1	143	38	23	21	7	0	0	0	15	0	17	4	0	1	3	.250	0	0-0	1	6.03
1990 Baltimore	AL	7	7	0	0	46.2	202	37	20	20	2	2	2	1	27	2	24	1	1	3	2	.600	0	0-0	0	3.86
1991 Baltimore	AL	23	23	2	0	123.2	566	151	86	82	11	5	4	3	62	2	64	3	0	6	11	.353	1	0-0	0	5.97
1992 Bal-Cle	AL	28	27	1	1	160.2	700	169	86	82	14	2	5	4	70	1	62	2	0	7	12	.368	1	0-0	0	4.59
1993 Cleveland	AL	34	33	3	0	208.2	897	232	122	114	21	9	9	7	62	2	118	8	2	10	12	.455	1	0-0	0	4.92
1994 Cleveland	AL	51	0	0	22	73	315	71	33	31	3	3	4	3	26	7	63	3	0	7	5	.583	0	2-6	8	3.82
1995 Cleveland	AL	62	0	0	57	64	250	49	9	8	3	4	2	0	17	2	58	5	0	3	0	1.000	0	46-48	0	1.13
1996 Cleveland	AL	69	0	0	60	72.1	304	69	32	30	6	2	3	3	28	4	64	4	0	2	7	.222	0	39-44	0	3.73
1992 Baltimore	AL	13	12	0	1	67.2	300	77	41	39	9	0	3	2	27	1	22	2	0	3	8	.273	0	0-0	0	5.19
Cleveland	AL	15	15	1	0	93	400	92	45	43	5	2	2	2	43	0	40	0	0	4	4	.500	1	0-0	0	4.16
8 ML YEARS		280	95	6	140	780.1	3377	816	411	388	67	27	28	21	307	20	470	30	3	39	52	.429	2	87-98	9	4.48

Dan Miceli

Pitches: Right **Bats:** Right **Pos:** RP-35; SP-9 **Ht:** 6'0" **Wt:** 216 **Born:** 9/9/70 **Age:** 26

		HOW MUCH HE PITCHED						WHAT HE GAVE UP												THE RESULTS						
Year Team	Lg	G	GS	CG	GF	IP	BFP	H	R	ER	HR	SH	SF	HB	TBB	IBB	SO	WP	Bk	W	L	Pct.	ShO	Sv-Op	Hld	ERA
1996 Carolina *	AA	3	0	0	2	9	33	4	1	1	0	0	0	0	1	0	17	0	0	1	0	1.000	0	1--	—	1.00
1993 Pittsburgh	NL	9	0	0	1	5.1	25	6	3	3	0	0	0	0	3	0	4	1	0	0	0	.000	0	0-0	0	5.06
1994 Pittsburgh	NL	28	0	0	9	27.1	121	28	19	18	5	1	2	2	11	2	27	2	0	2	1	.667	0	2-3	4	5.93
1995 Pittsburgh	NL	58	0	0	51	58	264	61	30	30	7	2	4	4	28	5	56	4	0	4	4	.500	0	21-27	2	4.66
1996 Pittsburgh	NL	44	9	0	17	85.2	398	99	65	55	15	3	7	3	45	5	66	9	0	2	10	.167	0	1-1	4	5.78
4 ML YEARS		139	9	0	78	176.1	808	194	117	106	27	6	13	9	87	12	153	15	1	8	15	.348	0	24-31	10	5.41

Matt Mieske

Bats: R **Throws:** R **Pos:** RF-108; CF-10; PH-10; LF-9 **Ht:** 6'0" **Wt:** 192 **Born:** 2/13/68 **Age:** 29

		BATTING																BASERUNNING				PERCENTAGES		
Year Team	Lg	G	AB	H	2B	3B	HR	(Hm Rd)	TB	R	RBI	TBB	IBB	SO	HBP	SH	SF	SB	CS	SB%	GDP	Avg	OBP	SLG
1993 Milwaukee	AL	23	58	14	0	0	3	(1 2)	23	9	7	4	0	14	0	1	0	0	2	.00	0	.241	.290	.397
1994 Milwaukee	AL	84	259	67	13	1	10	(7 3)	112	39	38	21	0	62	3	2	1	3	5	.38	6	.259	.320	.432
1995 Milwaukee	AL	117	267	67	13	1	12	(3 9)	118	42	48	27	0	45	4	0	5	2	4	.33	8	.251	.323	.442
1996 Milwaukee	AL	127	374	104	24	3	14	(9 5)	176	46	64	26	2	76	2	1	6	1	5	.17	9	.278	.324	.471
4 ML YEARS		351	958	252	50	5	39	(20 19)	429	136	157	78	2	197	9	4	12	6	16	.27	25	.263	.321	.448

Bob Milacki

Pitches: Right **Bats:** Right **Pos:** SP-4; RP-3 **Ht:** 6'4" **Wt:** 230 **Born:** 7/28/64 **Age:** 32

		HOW MUCH HE PITCHED						WHAT HE GAVE UP												THE RESULTS						
Year Team	Lg	G	GS	CG	GF	IP	BFP	H	R	ER	HR	SH	SF	HB	TBB	IBB	SO	WP	Bk	W	L	Pct.	ShO	Sv-Op	Hld	ERA
1996 Tacoma *	AAA	23	23	5	0	164.1	653	131	66	50	12	3	1	4	39	1	117	4	1	13	3	.813	2	0--	—	2.74
1988 Baltimore	AL	3	3	1	0	25	91	9	2	2	1	0	0	0	9	0	18	0	0	2	0	1.000	1	0-0	0	0.72
1989 Baltimore	AL	37	36	3	1	243	1022	233	105	101	21	7	6	2	88	4	113	1	1	14	12	.538	2	0-0	0	3.74
1990 Baltimore	AL	27	24	1	0	135.1	594	143	73	67	18	5	5	0	61	2	60	2	1	5	8	.385	1	0-0	0	4.46
1991 Baltimore	AL	31	26	3	1	184	758	175	86	82	17	7	5	1	53	3	108	1	0	10	9	.526	1	0-0	0	4.01
1992 Baltimore	AL	23	20	0	1	115.2	525	140	78	75	16	3	3	2	44	2	51	7	1	6	8	.429	0	1-1	0	5.84
1993 Cleveland	AL	5	2	0	0	16	74	19	8	6	1	0	0	0	11	0	7	0	0	1	1	.500	0	0-0	0	3.38
1994 Kansas City	AL	10	10	0	0	55.2	254	68	43	38	6	1	4	1	20	3	17	2	0	0	5	.000	0	0-0	0	6.14
1996 Seattle	AL	7	4	0	0	21	106	30	20	16	2	0	4	0	15	3	13	0	0	1	4	.200	0	0-0	0	6.86
8 ML YEARS		143	125	8	4	795.2	3424	817	415	387	85	23	23	6	301	17	387	13	5	39	47	.453	5	1-1	0	4.38

Mike Milchin

Pitches: Left **Bats:** Left **Pos:** RP-39 **Ht:** 6'3" **Wt:** 190 **Born:** 2/28/68 **Age:** 29

		HOW MUCH HE PITCHED						WHAT HE GAVE UP												THE RESULTS						
Year Team	Lg	G	GS	CG	GF	IP	BFP	H	R	ER	HR	SH	SF	HB	TBB	IBB	SO	WP	Bk	W	L	Pct.	ShO	Sv-Op	Hld	ERA
1989 Hamilton	A-	8	8	0	0	41.1	165	35	11	10	2	0	1	2	9	0	46	0	5	1	2	.333	0	0--	—	2.18
Springfield	A	6	6	1	0	42	167	30	14	10	3	3	1	0	10	1	44	2	1	3	2	.600	0	0--	—	2.14

Year Team	Lg	G	GS	CG	GF	IP	BFP	H	R	ER	HR	SH	SF	HB	TBB	IBB	SO	WP	Bk	W	L	Pct.	ShO	Sv-Op	Hld	ERA
1990 St. Pete	A+	11	11	1	0	68.1	277	57	25	21	1	2	0	1	20	0	66	4	2	6	1	.857	1	0--	—	2.77
Arkansas	AA	17	17	4	0	102.1	444	103	62	49	8	7	5	1	47	3	75	6	1	6	8	.429	2	0--	—	4.31
1991 Arkansas	AA	6	6	1	0	35.1	142	27	13	12	1	0	0	0	8	2	38	0	1	3	2	.600	1	0--	—	3.06
Louisville	AAA	18	18	2	0	94	451	132	64	53	4	5	4	4	40	5	48	5	0	5	9	.357	1	0--	—	5.07
1992 Louisville	AAA	12	12	1	0	65.1	299	69	46	43	8	3	4	1	31	5	37	5	3	2	6	.250	0	0--	—	5.92
1993 Louisville	AAA	32	17	1	6	111.2	477	108	56	49	18	3	4	1	43	0	72	5	0	3	7	.300	0	0--	—	3.95
1995 Albuquerque	AAA	18	17	2	0	83.1	359	94	43	40	2	1	2	0	30	1	50	5	0	8	4	.667	1	0--	—	4.32
1996 Salt Lake	AAA	19	0	0	6	22	99	21	9	9	0	1	2	1	11	3	18	4	0	0	0	.000	0	2--	—	3.68
1996 Min-Bal	AL	39	0	0	7	32.2	154	44	28	27	6	3	3	0	17	2	29	1	0	3	1	.750	0	0-1	3	7.44
1996 Minnesota	AL	26	0	0	7	21.2	105	31	21	20	6	2	0	0	12	1	19	1	0	2	1	.667	0	0-1	3	8.31
Baltimore	AL	13	0	0	0	11	49	13	7	7	0	1	3	0	5	1	10	0	0	1	0	1.000	0	0-0	0	5.73

Kurt Miller

Pitches: Right **Bats:** Right **Pos:** RP-21; SP-5   **Ht:** 6'5" **Wt:** 205 **Born:** 8/24/72 **Age:** 24

Year Team	Lg	G	GS	CG	GF	IP	BFP	H	R	ER	HR	SH	SF	HB	TBB	IBB	SO	WP	Bk	W	L	Pct.	ShO	Sv-Op	Hld	ERA
1996 Charlotte *	AAA	12	12	2	0	65.2	294	77	39	34	7	8	4	1	26	2	38	4	1	3	5	.375	0	0--	—	4.66
1994 Florida	NL	4	4	0	0	20	92	26	18	18	3	0	1	2	7	0	11	0	0	1	3	.250	0	0-0	—	8.10
1996 Florida	NL	26	5	0	6	46.1	222	57	41	35	5	4	1	2	33	8	30	1	1	1	3	.250	0	0-2	0	6.80
2 ML YEARS		30	9	0	6	66.1	314	83	59	53	8	4	2	4	40	8	41	1	1	2	6	.250	0	0-2	0	7.19

Orlando Miller

Bats: Right **Throws:** Right **Pos:** SS-116; 3B-30; PH-7   **Ht:** 6'1" **Wt:** 180 **Born:** 1/13/69 **Age:** 28

							BATTING												BASERUNNING				PERCENTAGES		
Year Team	Lg	G	AB	H	2B	3B	HR	(Hm	Rd)	TB	R	RBI	TBB	IBB	SO	HBP	SH	SF	SB	CS	SB%	GDP	Avg	OBP	SLG
1994 Houston	NL	16	40	13	0	1	2	(0	2)	21	3	9	2	1	12	2	0	0	1	0	1.00	0	.325	.386	.525
1995 Houston	NL	92	324	85	20	1	5	(1	4)	122	36	36	22	8	71	5	4	0	3	4	.43	7	.262	.319	.377
1996 Houston	NL	139	468	120	26	2	15	(7	8)	195	43	58	14	4	116	10	1	3	3	7	.30	14	.256	.291	.417
3 ML YEARS		247	832	218	46	4	22	(8	14)	338	82	103	38	14	199	17	5	3	7	11	.39	21	.262	.307	.406

Travis Miller

Pitches: Left **Bats:** Right **Pos:** SP-7   **Ht:** 6'3" **Wt:** 200 **Born:** 11/2/72 **Age:** 24

Year Team	Lg	G	GS	CG	GF	IP	BFP	H	R	ER	HR	SH	SF	HB	TBB	IBB	SO	WP	Bk	W	L	Pct.	ShO	Sv-Op	Hld	ERA
1994 Fort Wayne	A	11	9	1	0	55.1	223	52	17	16	2	1	3	2	12	0	50	5	2	4	1	.800	0	0--	—	2.60
Nashville	AA	1	1	0	0	6.1	23	3	3	2	0	0	0	0	2	0	4	1	0	0	0	.000	0	0--	—	2.84
1995 New Britain	AA	28	27	1	1	162.2	723	172	93	79	17	6	3	4	65	2	151	5	0	7	9	.438	1	0--	—	4.37
1996 Salt Lake	AAA	27	27	1	0	160.1	709	187	97	86	17	2	6	7	57	1	143	6	1	8	10	.444	0	0--	—	4.83
1996 Minnesota	AL	7	7	0	0	26.1	126	45	29	27	7	1	0	0	9	0	15	0	0	1	2	.333	0	0-0	0	9.23

Trever Miller

Pitches: Left **Bats:** Right **Pos:** SP-4; RP-1   **Ht:** 6'4" **Wt:** 195 **Born:** 5/29/73 **Age:** 24

Year Team	Lg	G	GS	CG	GF	IP	BFP	H	R	ER	HR	SH	SF	HB	TBB	IBB	SO	WP	Bk	W	L	Pct.	ShO	Sv-Op	Hld	ERA
1991 Bristol	R+	13	13	0	0	54	253	60	44	34	7	3	3	2	29	0	46	9	1	2	7	.222	0	0--	—	5.67
1992 Bristol	R+	12	12	1	0	69.1	311	75	45	38	4	3	3	1	27	0	64	4	1	3	8	.273	0	0--	—	4.93
1993 Fayetteville	A	28	28	2	0	161	699	151	99	75	7	2	8	5	67	0	116	10	0	8	13	.381	0	0--	—	4.19
1994 Trenton	AA	26	26	6	0	174.1	754	198	95	85	9	10	8	3	51	0	73	3	1	7	16	.304	0	0--	—	4.39
1995 Jacksonville	AA	31	16	3	4	122.1	512	122	46	37	5	4	2	5	34	0	77	1	0	8	2	.800	2	0--	—	2.72
1996 Toledo	AAA	27	27	0	0	165.1	722	167	98	90	19	4	1	9	65	1	115	3	2	13	6	.684	0	0--	—	4.90
1996 Detroit	AL	5	4	0	0	16.2	88	28	17	17	3	2	2	2	9	0	8	0	0	0	4	.000	0	0-0	0	9.18

Ralph Milliard

Bats: Right **Throws:** Right **Pos:** 2B-24; PH-2   **Ht:** 5'11" **Wt:** 170 **Born:** 12/30/73 **Age:** 23

							BATTING												BASERUNNING				PERCENTAGES		
Year Team	Lg	G	AB	H	2B	3B	HR	(Hm	Rd)	TB	R	RBI	TBB	IBB	SO	HBP	SH	SF	SB	CS	SB%	GDP	Avg	OBP	SLG
1993 Marlins	R	53	192	45	15	0	0	—	—	60	35	25	30	0	17	6	0	1	11	5	.69	8	.234	.354	.313
1994 Kane County	A	133	515	153	34	2	8	—	—	215	97	67	68	2	63	9	4	7	10	10	.50	6	.297	.384	.417
1995 Portland	AA	128	464	124	22	3	11	—	—	185	104	40	85	3	83	14	13	4	22	10	.69	5	.267	.393	.399
1996 Charlotte	AAA	69	250	69	15	2	6	—	—	106	47	26	38	0	43	5	1	1	8	4	.67	5	.276	.381	.424
Portland	AA	6	20	4	0	1	0	—	—	6	2	2	1	0	5	0	0	0	1	0	1.00	0	.200	.238	.300
1996 Florida	NL	24	62	10	2	0	0	(0	0)	12	7	1	14	1	16	0	0	0	2	0	1.00	1	.161	.312	.194

Alan Mills

Pitches: Right **Bats:** Both **Pos:** RP-49 **Ht:** 6'1" **Wt:** 195 **Born:** 10/18/66 **Age:** 30

Year Team	Lg	G	GS	CG	GF	IP	BFP	H	R	ER	HR	SH	SF	HB	TBB	IBB	SO	WP	Bk	W	L	Pct.	ShO	Sv-Op	Hld	ERA
1990 New York	AL	36	0	0	18	41.2	200	48	21	19	4	4	1	1	33	6	24	3	0	1	5	.167	0	0-2	3	4.10
1991 New York	AL	6	2	0	3	16.1	72	16	9	8	1	0	1	0	8	0	11	2	0	1	1	.500	0	0-0	0	4.41
1992 Baltimore	AL	35	3	0	12	103.1	428	78	33	30	5	6	5	1	54	10	60	2	0	10	4	.714	0	2-3	2	2.61
1993 Baltimore	AL	45	0	0	18	100.1	421	80	39	36	14	4	6	4	51	5	68	3	0	5	4	.556	0	4-7	4	3.23
1994 Baltimore	AL	47	0	0	16	45.1	199	43	26	26	7	1	1	2	24	2	44	2	0	3	3	.500	0	2-4	14	5.16
1995 Baltimore	AL	21	0	0	1	23	118	30	20	19	4	0	1	2	18	4	16	1	0	3	0	1.000	0	0-1	1	7.43
1996 Baltimore	AL	49	0	0	23	54.2	233	40	26	26	10	3	2	1	35	2	50	6	0	3	2	.600	0	3-8	9	4.28
7 ML YEARS		239	5	0	91	384.2	1671	335	174	164	45	18	17	11	223	29	273	19	0	26	19	.578	0	11-25	33	3.84

Michael Mimbs

Pitches: Left **Bats:** Left **Pos:** SP-17; RP-4 **Ht:** 6'2" **Wt:** 190 **Born:** 2/13/69 **Age:** 28

Year Team	Lg	G	GS	CG	GF	IP	BFP	H	R	ER	HR	SH	SF	HB	TBB	IBB	SO	WP	Bk	W	L	Pct.	ShO	Sv-Op	Hld	ERA
1990 Great Falls	R+	3	0	0	0	6.2	32	4	5	3	0	0	0	2	5	0	7	0	1	0	0	.000	0	0- -	—	4.05
Yakima	A-	12	12	0	0	67.1	295	58	36	29	5	2	2	3	39	0	72	1	2	4	3	.571	0	0- -	—	3.88
1991 Vero Beach	A+	24	22	1	0	141.2	601	124	52	42	6	9	1	6	70	2	132	15	3	12	4	.750	1	0- -	—	2.67
1992 San Antonio	AA	24	22	2	2	129.2	581	132	65	61	11	10	5	3	73	1	87	7	1	10	8	.556	0	1- -	—	4.23
1993 St. Paul	IND	20	16	1	1	98.1	430	94	48	35	4	3	4	5	45	0	97	12	0	8	2	.800	0	0- -	—	3.20
1994 Harrisburg	AA	32	21	2	0	153.2	644	130	69	59	11	7	2	3	61	0	145	9	0	11	4	.733	1	0- -	—	3.46
1996 Scranton-WB	AAA	7	3	0	2	29	115	27	8	8	2	2	1	0	5	0	20	1	0	2	1	.667	0	0- -	—	2.48
1995 Philadelphia	NL	35	19	2	6	136.2	603	127	70	63	10	6	8	6	75	2	93	9	0	9	7	.563	1	1-1	0	4.15
1996 Philadelphia	NL	21	17	0	0	99.1	448	116	66	61	13	8	3	2	41	1	56	7	0	3	9	.250	0	0-0	0	5.53
2 ML YEARS		56	36	2	6	236	1051	243	136	124	23	14	11	8	116	3	149	16	0	12	16	.429	1	1-1	0	4.73

Nate Minchey

Pitches: Right **Bats:** Right **Pos:** SP-2 **Ht:** 6'7" **Wt:** 215 **Born:** 8/31/69 **Age:** 27

Year Team	Lg	G	GS	CG	GF	IP	BFP	H	R	ER	HR	SH	SF	HB	TBB	IBB	SO	WP	Bk	W	L	Pct.	ShO	Sv-Op	Hld	ERA
1996 Pawtucket *	AAA	14	13	6	0	97.1	394	89	32	32	8	2	2	0	21	0	61	6	0	7	4	.636	0	0- -	—	2.96
1993 Boston	AL	5	5	1	0	33	141	35	16	13	5	1	0	0	8	2	18	2	0	1	2	.333	0	0-0	0	3.55
1994 Boston	AL	6	5	0	0	23	121	44	26	22	1	1	3	0	14	2	15	3	1	2	3	.400	0	0-0	0	8.61
1996 Boston	AL	2	2	0	0	6	36	16	11	10	1	0	1	0	5	0	4	1	0	0	2	.000	0	0-0	0	15.00
3 ML YEARS		13	12	1	0	62	298	95	53	45	7	2	4	0	27	4	37	6	1	3	7	.300	0	0-0	0	6.53

Blas Minor

Pitches: Right **Bats:** Right **Pos:** RP-28 **Ht:** 6'3" **Wt:** 203 **Born:** 3/20/66 **Age:** 31

Year Team	Lg	G	GS	CG	GF	IP	BFP	H	R	ER	HR	SH	SF	HB	TBB	IBB	SO	WP	Bk	W	L	Pct.	ShO	Sv-Op	Hld	ERA
1996 Tacoma *	AAA	7	0	0	6	9.2	45	15	11	9	1	0	1	0	3	1	8	0	1	1	2	.333	0	1- -	—	8.38
1992 Pittsburgh	NL	1	0	0	0	2	9	3	2	1	0	0	0	0	0	0	0	0	0	0	0	.000	0	0-0	0	4.50
1993 Pittsburgh	NL	65	0	0	18	94.1	398	94	43	43	8	6	4	4	26	3	84	5	0	8	6	.571	0	2-3	7	4.10
1994 Pittsburgh	NL	17	0	0	2	19	90	27	17	17	4	2	1	1	9	2	17	0	0	0	1	.000	0	1-1	2	8.05
1995 New York	NL	35	0	0	10	46.2	192	44	21	19	6	4	0	1	13	1	43	3	0	4	2	.667	0	1-1	2	3.66
1996 NYN-Sea		28	0	0	10	51	213	50	25	24	10	0	1	0	17	2	34	3	0	0	1	.000	0	0-1	1	4.24
1996 New York	NL	17	0	0	4	25.2	104	23	11	10	4	0	1	0	6	2	20	1	0	0	0	.000	0	0-1	0	3.51
Seattle	AL	11	0	0	6	25.1	109	27	14	14	6	0	0	0	11	0	14	2	0	0	1	.000	0	0-0	1	4.97
5 ML YEARS		146	0	0	40	213	902	218	108	104	28	12	6	6	65	8	178	12	0	12	10	.545	0	4-6	12	4.39

Doug Mirabelli

Bats: Right **Throws:** Right **Pos:** C-8; PH-1 **Ht:** 6'0" **Wt:** 210 **Born:** 10/18/70 **Age:** 26

Year Team	Lg	G	AB	H	2B	3B	HR	(Hm	Rd)	TB	R	RBI	TBB	IBB	SO	HBP	SH	SF	SB	CS	SB%	GDP	Avg	OBP	SLG
1992 San Jose	A+	53	177	41	11	1	0	—	—	54	30	21	24	0	18	4	2	2	1	3	.25	7	.232	.333	.305
1993 San Jose	A+	113	371	100	19	2	1	—	—	126	58	48	72	1	55	4	2	4	0	4	.00	7	.270	.390	.340
1994 Shreveport	AA	85	255	56	8	0	4	—	—	76	23	24	36	5	48	0	2	0	3	1	.75	6	.220	.316	.298
1995 Phoenix	AAA	23	66	11	0	1	0	—	—	13	3	7	12	1	10	1	0	2	1	0	1.00	5	.167	.296	.197
Shreveport	AA	40	126	38	13	0	0	—	—	51	14	16	20	1	14	0	2	0	1	0	1.00	3	.302	.397	.405
1996 Phoenix	AAA	14	47	14	7	0	0	—	—	21	10	7	4	0	7	1	0	0	0	0	.00	1	.298	.365	.447
Shreveport	AA	115	380	112	23	0	21	—	—	198	60	70	76	0	49	6	1	1	0	1	.00	9	.295	.419	.521
1996 San Francisco	NL	9	18	4	1	0	0	(0	0)	5	2	1	3	0	4	0	0	0	0	0	.00	0	.222	.333	.278

Angel Miranda

Pitches: Left **Bats:** Left **Pos:** RP-34; SP-12 **Ht:** 6'1" **Wt:** 195 **Born:** 11/9/69 **Age:** 27

		HOW MUCH HE PITCHED						WHAT HE GAVE UP											THE RESULTS					
Year Team	Lg	G	GS	CG	GF	IP	BFP	H	R	ER	HR	SH	SF	HB	TBB	IBB	SO	WP	Bk	W	L	Pct.	ShO	Sv-Op	Hld	ERA
1993 Milwaukee	AL	22	17	2	0	120	502	100	53	44	12	3	3	2	52	4	88	4	2	4	5	.444	0	0-0	0	3.30
1994 Milwaukee	AL	8	8	1	0	46	196	39	28	27	8	1	1	0	27	0	24	1	1	2	5	.286	0	0-0	0	5.28
1995 Milwaukee	AL	30	10	0	5	74	339	83	47	43	8	1	4	0	49	2	45	5	1	4	5	.444	0	1-3	3	5.23
1996 Milwaukee	AL	46	12	0	5	109.1	503	116	68	60	12	5	8	2	69	4	78	10	0	7	6	.538	0	1-2	6	4.94
4 ML YEARS		106	47	3	10	349.1	1540	338	196	174	40	10	16	4	197	10	235	20	4	17	21	.447	0	2-5	9	4.48

Keith Mitchell

Bats: Right **Throws:** Right **Pos:** PH-7; LF-2; RF-2; CF-1 **Ht:** 5'10" **Wt:** 180 **Born:** 8/6/69 **Age:** 27

		BATTING																	BASERUNNING				PERCENTAGES		
Year Team	Lg	G	AB	H	2B	3B	HR	(Hm	Rd)	TB	R	RBI	TBB	IBB	SO	HBP	SH	SF	SB	CS	SB%	GDP	Avg	OBP	SLG
1996 Indianapolis *	AAA	112	357	107	21	3	16	—	—	182	60	66	64	2	68	1	0	6	9	1	.90	7	.300	.402	.510
1991 Atlanta	NL	48	66	21	0	0	2	(1	1)	27	11	5	8	0	12	0	0	0	3	1	.75	1	.318	.392	.409
1994 Seattle	AL	46	128	29	2	0	5	(2	3)	46	21	15	18	0	22	1	1	1	0	0	.00	2	.227	.324	.359
1996 Cincinnati	NL	11	15	4	1	0	1	(1	0)	8	2	3	1	0	3	0	0	0	0	0	.00	0	.267	.313	.533
3 ML YEARS		105	209	54	3	0	8	(4	4)	81	34	23	27	0	37	1	1	1	3	1	.75	3	.258	.345	.388

Kevin Mitchell

Bats: R **Throws:** R **Pos:** LF-32; RF-21; PH-6; DH-4; 1B-3 **Ht:** 5'11" **Wt:** 244 **Born:** 1/13/62 **Age:** 35

		BATTING																	BASERUNNING				PERCENTAGES		
Year Team	Lg	G	AB	H	2B	3B	HR	(Hm	Rd)	TB	R	RBI	TBB	IBB	SO	HBP	SH	SF	SB	CS	SB%	GDP	Avg	OBP	SLG
1996 Pawtucket *	AAA	5	16	2	0	0	0	—	—	2	1	0	1	0	5	0	0	0	0	0	.00	0	.125	.176	.125
1984 New York	NL	7	14	3	0	0	0	(0	0)	3	0	1	0	0	3	0	0	0	0	1	.00	0	.214	.214	.214
1986 New York	NL	108	328	91	22	2	12	(4	8)	153	51	43	33	0	61	1	1	1	3	3	.50	0	.277	.344	.466
1987 SD-SF	NL	131	464	130	20	2	22	(9	13)	220	68	70	48	4	88	2	0	1	9	6	.60	10	.280	.350	.474
1988 San Francisco	NL	148	505	127	25	7	19	(10	9)	223	60	80	48	7	85	5	1	7	5	5	.50	9	.251	.319	.442
1989 San Francisco	NL	154	543	158	34	6	47	(22	25)	345	100	125	87	32	115	3	0	1	3	4	.43	6	.291	.388	.635
1990 San Francisco	NL	140	524	152	24	2	35	(15	20)	285	90	93	58	9	87	2	0	5	4	7	.36	8	.290	.360	.544
1991 San Francisco	NL	113	371	95	13	1	27	(9	18)	191	52	69	43	8	57	5	0	4	2	3	.40	6	.256	.338	.515
1992 Seattle	AL	99	360	103	24	0	9	(5	4)	154	48	67	35	4	46	3	0	4	0	2	.00	4	.286	.351	.428
1993 Cincinnati	NL	93	323	110	21	3	19	(10	9)	194	56	64	25	4	48	1	0	1	1	0	1.00	14	.341	.385	.601
1994 Cincinnati	NL	95	310	101	18	1	30	(18	12)	211	57	77	59	15	62	3	0	8	2	0	1.00	12	.326	.429	.681
1996 Bos-Cin		64	206	65	15	0	8	(6	2)	104	27	39	37	2	30	1	0	0	0	0	.00	8	.316	.420	.505
1987 San Diego	NL	62	196	48	7	1	7	(2	5)	78	19	26	20	3	38	0	0	1	0	0	.00	5	.245	.313	.398
San Francisco	NL	69	268	82	13	1	15	(7	8)	142	49	44	28	1	50	2	0	0	9	6	.60	5	.306	.376	.530
1996 Boston	AL	27	92	28	4	0	2	(1	1)	38	9	13	11	0	14	1	0	0	0	0	.00	3	.304	.385	.413
Cincinnati	NL	37	114	37	11	0	6	(5	1)	66	18	26	26	2	16	0	0	0	0	0	.00	5	.325	.447	.579
11 ML YEARS		1152	3948	1135	216	24	228	(108	120)	2083	609	728	473	85	682	26	2	42	29	31	.48	83	.287	.364	.528

Larry Mitchell

Pitches: Right **Bats:** Right **Pos:** RP-7 **Ht:** 6'1" **Wt:** 219 **Born:** 10/16/71 **Age:** 25

		HOW MUCH HE PITCHED						WHAT HE GAVE UP											THE RESULTS					
Year Team	Lg	G	GS	CG	GF	IP	BFP	H	R	ER	HR	SH	SF	HB	TBB	IBB	SO	WP	Bk	W	L	Pct.	ShO	Sv-Op	Hld	ERA
1992 Martinsvlle	R+	3	3	0	0	19	77	17	8	3	0	0	0	1	6	0	18	0	0	1	0	1.000	0	0--	—	1.42
Batavia	A-	10	10	3	0	65	267	63	25	19	6	2	2	1	11	0	58	4	1	7	2	.778	1	0--	—	2.63
1993 Spartanburg	A	19	19	4	0	116.1	505	113	55	53	3	2	7	3	54	0	114	14	0	6	6	.500	2	0--	—	4.10
Clearwater	A+	9	9	1	0	57	234	50	23	19	0	5	2	0	21	1	45	4	1	4	4	.500	0	0--	—	3.00
1994 Reading	AA	30	30	2	0	165.1	737	143	91	73	5	13	8	2	103	1	128	15	0	10	13	.435	0	0--	—	3.97
1995 Reading	AA	25	24	1	1	128.1	584	136	85	79	13	2	2	4	72	4	107	7	1	6	11	.353	1	0--	—	5.54
1996 Reading	AA	34	2	0	7	57	267	55	39	33	2	4	2	1	44	2	71	3	0	3	6	.333	0	1--	—	5.21
Scranton-WB	AAA	11	0	0	2	24.2	99	19	8	7	2	1	2	0	10	0	24	1	1	1	1	.500	0	1--	—	2.55
1996 Philadelphia	NL	7	0	0	2	12	51	14	6	6	1	0	0	0	5	1	7	0	0	0	1	.000	0	0-0	0	4.50

Dave Mlicki

Pitches: Right **Bats:** Right **Pos:** RP-49; SP-2 **Ht:** 6'4" **Wt:** 205 **Born:** 6/8/68 **Age:** 29

		HOW MUCH HE PITCHED						WHAT HE GAVE UP											THE RESULTS					
Year Team	Lg	G	GS	CG	GF	IP	BFP	H	R	ER	HR	SH	SF	HB	TBB	IBB	SO	WP	Bk	W	L	Pct.	ShO	Sv-Op	Hld	ERA
1992 Cleveland	AL	4	4	0	0	21.2	101	23	14	12	3	2	0	1	16	0	16	1	0	0	2	.000	0	0-0	0	4.98
1993 Cleveland	AL	3	3	0	0	13.1	58	11	6	5	2	0	0	2	6	0	7	2	0	0	0	.000	0	0-0	0	3.38
1995 New York	NL	29	25	0	1	160.2	696	160	82	76	23	8	5	4	54	2	123	5	1	9	7	.563	0	0-0	0	4.26
1996 New York	NL	51	2	0	16	90	393	95	46	33	9	8	3	6	33	8	83	7	0	6	7	.462	0	1-3	8	3.30
4 ML YEARS		87	34	0	17	285.2	1248	289	148	126	37	18	8	13	109	10	229	15	1	15	16	.484	0	1-3	8	3.97

Brian Moehler

Pitches: Right **Bats:** Right **Pos:** SP-2 **Ht:** 6'3" **Wt:** 220 **Born:** 12/31/71 **Age:** 25

Year Team	Lg	G	GS	CG	GF	IP	BFP	H	R	ER	HR	SH	SF	HB	TBB	IBB	SO	WP	Bk	W	L	Pct.	ShO	Sv-Op	Hld	ERA
1993 Niagara Fal	A-	12	11	0	0	58.2	262	51	33	21	3	1	3	4	27	0	38	8	2	6	5	.545	0	0--	—	3.22
1994 Lakeland	A+	26	25	5	0	164.2	687	153	66	55	3	7	7	6	65	0	92	8	3	12	12	.500	2	0--	—	3.01
1995 Jacksonvlle	AA	28	27	0	1	162.1	696	176	94	87	14	3	5	6	52	1	89	15	0	8	10	.444	0	0--	—	4.82
1996 Jacksonvlle	AA	28	28	1	0	173.1	744	186	80	67	9	3	2	4	50	2	120	11	2	15	6	.714	0	0--	—	3.48
1996 Detroit	AL	2	2	0	0	10.1	51	11	10	5	1	1	0	0	8	1	2	1	0	0	1	.000	0	0-0	0	4.35

Mike Mohler

Pitches: Left **Bats:** Right **Pos:** RP-72 **Ht:** 6'2" **Wt:** 195 **Born:** 7/26/68 **Age:** 28

Year Team	Lg	G	GS	CG	GF	IP	BFP	H	R	ER	HR	SH	SF	HB	TBB	IBB	SO	WP	Bk	W	L	Pct.	ShO	Sv-Op	Hld	ERA
1993 Oakland	AL	42	9	0	4	64.1	290	57	45	40	10	5	2	2	44	4	42	0	1	1	6	.143	0	0-1	1	5.60
1994 Oakland	AL	1	1	0	0	2.1	14	2	3	2	1	0	0	0	2	0	4	0	0	0	0	.000	0	0-0	0	7.71
1995 Oakland	AL	28	0	0	6	23.2	100	16	8	8	0	1	0	0	18	1	15	1	0	1	1	.500	0	1-2	4	3.04
1996 Oakland	AL	72	0	0	30	81	352	79	36	33	9	6	4	1	41	6	64	9	0	6	3	.667	0	7-13	13	3.67
4 ML YEARS		143	10	0	40	171.1	756	154	92	83	20	12	6	3	105	11	125	10	1	8	11	.421	0	8-16	18	4.36

Izzy Molina

Bats: Right **Throws:** Right **Pos:** C-12; PH-3; DH-1 **Ht:** 6'1" **Wt:** 200 **Born:** 6/3/71 **Age:** 26

Year Team	Lg	G	AB	H	2B	3B	HR	(Hm	Rd)	TB	R	RBI	TBB	IBB	SO	HBP	SH	SF	SB	CS	SB%	GDP	Avg	OBP	SLG
1990 Athletics	R	38	122	43	12	2	0	—	—	59	19	18	9	1	21	2	1	3	5	0	1.00	6	.352	.397	.484
1991 Madison	A	95	316	89	16	1	3	—	—	116	35	45	15	1	40	6	1	4	6	4	.60	9	.282	.323	.367
1992 Reno	A+	116	436	113	17	2	10	—	—	164	71	75	39	0	57	7	7	6	8	7	.53	20	.259	.326	.376
Tacoma	AAA	10	36	7	0	1	0	—	—	9	3	5	2	0	6	0	0	1	1	0	1.00	1	.194	.237	.250
1993 Modesto	A+	125	444	116	26	5	6	—	—	170	61	69	44	0	85	3	4	11	2	8	.20	11	.261	.325	.383
1994 Huntsville	AA	116	388	84	17	2	8	—	—	129	31	50	16	0	47	5	7	7	5	1	.83	10	.216	.252	.332
1995 Edmonton	AAA	2	6	1	0	0	0	—	—	1	0	0	0	0	2	0	0	0	0	0	.00	0	.167	.167	.167
Huntsville	AA	83	301	78	16	1	8	—	—	120	38	26	26	0	62	8	0	2	3	4	.43	6	.259	.332	.399
1996 Edmonton	AAA	98	342	90	12	3	12	—	—	144	45	56	25	4	55	3	5	2	2	5	.29	9	.263	.317	.421
1996 Oakland	AL	14	25	5	2	0	0	(0	0)	7	0	1	1	0	3	0	0	0	0	0	.00	0	.200	.231	.280

Paul Molitor

Bats: Right **Throws:** Right **Pos:** DH-143; 1B-17; PH-1 **Ht:** 6'0" **Wt:** 190 **Born:** 8/22/56 **Age:** 40

Year Team	Lg	G	AB	H	2B	3B	HR	(Hm	Rd)	TB	R	RBI	TBB	IBB	SO	HBP	SH	SF	SB	CS	SB%	GDP	Avg	OBP	SLG
1978 Milwaukee	AL	125	521	142	26	4	6	(4	2)	194	73	45	19	2	54	4	7	5	30	12	.71	6	.273	.301	.372
1979 Milwaukee	AL	140	584	188	27	16	9	(3	6)	274	88	62	48	5	48	2	6	5	33	13	.72	9	.322	.372	.469
1980 Milwaukee	AL	111	450	137	29	2	9	(2	7)	197	81	37	48	4	48	3	6	5	34	7	.83	9	.304	.372	.438
1981 Milwaukee	AL	64	251	67	11	0	2	(1	1)	84	45	19	25	1	29	3	5	0	10	6	.63	3	.267	.341	.335
1982 Milwaukee	AL	160	666	201	26	8	19	(9	10)	300	136	71	69	1	93	1	10	5	41	9	.82	9	.302	.366	.450
1983 Milwaukee	AL	152	608	164	28	6	15	(9	6)	249	95	47	59	4	74	2	7	6	41	8	.84	12	.270	.333	.410
1984 Milwaukee	AL	13	46	10	1	0	0	(0	0)	11	3	6	2	0	8	0	0	1	1	0	1.00	0	.217	.245	.239
1985 Milwaukee	AL	140	576	171	28	3	10	(6	4)	235	93	48	54	6	80	1	7	4	21	7	.75	12	.297	.356	.408
1986 Milwaukee	AL	105	437	123	24	6	9	(5	4)	186	62	55	40	0	81	0	2	3	20	5	.80	9	.281	.340	.426
1987 Milwaukee	AL	118	465	164	41	5	16	(7	9)	263	114	75	69	2	67	2	5	1	45	10	.82	4	.353	.438	.566
1988 Milwaukee	AL	154	609	190	34	6	13	(9	4)	275	115	60	71	8	54	2	5	3	41	10	.80	10	.312	.384	.452
1989 Milwaukee	AL	155	615	194	35	4	11	(6	5)	270	84	56	64	4	67	4	4	9	27	11	.71	11	.315	.379	.439
1990 Milwaukee	AL	103	418	119	27	6	12	(6	6)	194	64	45	37	4	51	1	0	2	18	3	.86	7	.285	.343	.464
1991 Milwaukee	AL	158	665	216	32	13	17	(7	10)	325	133	75	77	16	62	6	0	1	19	8	.70	11	.325	.399	.489
1992 Milwaukee	AL	158	609	195	36	7	12	(4	8)	281	89	89	73	12	66	3	4	11	31	6	.84	13	.320	.389	.461
1993 Toronto	AL	160	636	211	37	5	22	(13	9)	324	121	111	77	3	71	3	1	8	22	4	.85	13	.332	.402	.509
1994 Toronto	AL	115	454	155	30	4	14	(8	6)	235	86	75	55	4	48	1	0	5	20	0	1.00	13	.341	.410	.518
1995 Toronto	AL	130	525	142	31	2	15	(6	9)	222	63	60	61	1	57	5	3	4	12	0	1.00	10	.270	.350	.423
1996 Minnesota	AL	161	660	225	41	8	9	(6	3)	309	99	113	56	7	72	3	0	9	18	6	.75	21	.341	.390	.468
19 ML YEARS		2422	9795	3014	544	105	220	(111	109)	4428	1644	1149	1004	87	1130	46	72	87	484	125	.79	182	.308	.372	.452

Raul Mondesi

Bats: Right **Throws:** Right **Pos:** RF-157 **Ht:** 5'11" **Wt:** 212 **Born:** 3/12/71 **Age:** 26

Year Team	Lg	G	AB	H	2B	3B	HR	(Hm	Rd)	TB	R	RBI	TBB	IBB	SO	HBP	SH	SF	SB	CS	SB%	GDP	Avg	OBP	SLG
1993 Los Angeles	NL	42	86	25	3	1	4	(2	2)	42	13	10	4	0	16	0	1	0	4	1	.80	1	.291	.322	.488
1994 Los Angeles	NL	112	434	133	27	8	16	(10	6)	224	63	56	16	5	78	2	0	2	11	8	.58	9	.306	.333	.516
1995 Los Angeles	NL	139	536	153	23	6	26	(13	13)	266	91	88	33	4	96	4	0	7	27	4	.87	7	.285	.328	.496
1996 Los Angeles	NL	157	634	188	40	7	24	(11	13)	314	98	88	32	9	122	5	0	2	14	7	.67	6	.297	.334	.495
4 ML YEARS		450	1690	499	93	22	70	(36	34)	846	265	242	85	18	312	11	1	11	56	20	.74	23	.295	.331	.501

Rich Monteleone

Pitches: Right **Bats:** Right **Pos:** RP-12   **Ht:** 6'2" **Wt:** 214 **Born:** 3/22/63 **Age:** 34

Year Team	Lg	G	GS	CG	GF	IP	BFP	H	R	ER	HR	SH	SF	HB	TBB	IBB	SO	WP	Bk	W	L	Pct.	ShO	Sv-Op	Hld	ERA
1996 Columbus *	AAA	21	1	0	6	35	151	42	17	14	1	1	0	0	7	2	21	0	0	4	3	.571	0	0--	0	3.60
1987 Seattle	AL	3	0	0	1	7	34	10	5	5	2	0	0	1	4	0	2	0	0	0	0	.000	0	0-0	0	6.43
1988 California	AL	3	0	0	2	4.1	20	4	0	0	0	0	0	1	1	1	3	0	1	0	0	.000	0	0-0	0	0.00
1989 California	AL	24	0	0	8	39.2	170	39	15	14	3	1	2	1	13	1	27	2	0	2	2	.500	0	0-2	1	3.18
1990 New York	AL	5	0	0	2	7.1	31	8	5	5	0	0	0	0	2	0	8	0	0	0	1	.000	0	0-0	0	6.14
1991 New York	AL	26	0	0	10	47	201	42	27	19	5	2	2	0	19	3	34	1	1	3	1	.750	0	0-0	0	3.64
1992 New York	AL	47	0	0	15	92.2	380	82	35	34	7	3	1	0	27	3	62	0	3	7	3	.700	0	0-2	7	3.30
1993 New York	AL	42	0	0	11	85.2	369	85	52	47	14	4	5	0	35	10	50	1	0	7	4	.636	0	0-1	1	4.94
1994 San Francisco	NL	39	0	0	8	45.1	189	43	18	16	6	2	4	0	13	2	16	1	2	4	3	.571	0	0-1	6	3.18
1995 California	AL	9	0	0	2	9	36	8	2	2	1	1	2	0	3	0	5	0	0	1	0	1.000	0	0-1	0	2.00
1996 California	AL	12	0	0	2	15.1	69	23	11	10	5	0	0	1	2	0	5	0	0	0	3	.000	0	0-0	1	5.87
10 ML YEARS		210	0	0	61	353.1	1499	344	170	152	43	13	16	4	119	20	212	5	8	24	17	.585	0	0-7	16	3.87

Jeff Montgomery

Pitches: Right **Bats:** Right **Pos:** RP-48   **Ht:** 5'11" **Wt:** 180 **Born:** 1/7/62 **Age:** 35

Year Team	Lg	G	GS	CG	GF	IP	BFP	H	R	ER	HR	SH	SF	HB	TBB	IBB	SO	WP	Bk	W	L	Pct.	ShO	Sv-Op	Hld	ERA
1987 Cincinnati	NL	14	1	0	6	19.1	89	25	15	14	2	0	0	0	9	1	13	1	1	2	2	.500	0	0-0	1	6.52
1988 Kansas City	AL	45	0	0	13	62.2	271	54	25	24	6	3	2	2	30	1	47	3	6	7	2	.778	0	1-3	9	3.45
1989 Kansas City	AL	63	0	0	39	92	363	66	16	14	3	1	1	2	25	4	94	6	1	7	3	.700	0	18-24	11	1.37
1990 Kansas City	AL	73	0	0	59	94.1	400	81	36	25	6	2	2	5	34	8	94	3	0	6	5	.545	0	24-34	7	2.39
1991 Kansas City	AL	67	0	0	55	90	376	83	32	29	6	6	2	2	28	2	77	6	0	4	4	.500	0	33-39	3	2.90
1992 Kansas City	AL	65	0	0	62	82.2	333	61	23	20	5	4	2	3	27	2	69	2	0	1	6	.143	0	39-46	0	2.18
1993 Kansas City	AL	69	0	0	63	87.1	347	65	22	22	3	5	1	2	23	4	66	3	0	7	5	.583	0	45-51	0	2.27
1994 Kansas City	AL	42	0	0	38	44.2	193	48	21	20	5	2	1	1	15	1	50	2	0	2	3	.400	0	27-32	0	4.03
1995 Kansas City	AL	54	0	0	46	65.2	275	60	27	25	7	5	5	2	25	4	49	1	1	2	3	.400	0	31-38	0	3.43
1996 Kansas City	AL	48	0	0	41	63.1	261	59	31	30	14	3	1	3	19	3	45	0	0	4	6	.400	0	24-34	0	4.26
10 ML YEARS		540	1	0	422	702	2908	602	248	223	57	31	17	22	235	30	604	27	9	42	39	.519	0	242-301	31	2.86

Ray Montgomery

Bats: Right **Throws:** Right **Pos:** PH-7; LF-5; RF-2; CF-1   **Ht:** 6'3" **Wt:** 195 **Born:** 8/8/69 **Age:** 27

Year Team	Lg	G	AB	H	2B	3B	HR	(Hm	Rd)	TB	R	RBI	TBB	IBB	SO	HBP	SH	SF	SB	CS	SB%	GDP	Avg	OBP	SLG
1990 Auburn	A-	61	193	45	8	1	0	—	—	55	19	13	23	1	32	1	4	1	11	5	.69	5	.233	.317	.285
1991 Burlington	A	120	433	109	24	3	3	—	—	148	60	57	37	1	66	8	11	2	17	14	.55	10	.252	.321	.342
1992 Jackson	AA	51	148	31	4	1	1	—	—	40	13	10	7	2	27	0	1	1	4	1	.80	5	.209	.244	.270
1993 Tucson	AAA	15	50	17	3	1	2	—	—	28	9	6	5	0	7	1	1	0	1	2	.33	1	.340	.411	.560
Jackson	AA	100	338	95	16	3	10	—	—	147	50	59	36	1	54	6	1	6	12	6	.67	7	.281	.355	.435
1994 Tucson	AAA	103	332	85	19	6	7	—	—	137	51	51	35	6	54	2	2	3	5	3	.63	9	.256	.328	.413
1995 Jackson	AA	35	127	38	8	1	10	—	—	78	24	24	13	2	13	5	0	1	6	3	.67	3	.299	.384	.614
Tucson	AAA	88	291	88	19	0	11	—	—	140	48	68	24	1	58	2	1	8	5	3	.63	3	.302	.351	.481
1996 Tucson	AAA	100	360	110	20	0	22	—	—	196	70	75	59	7	54	3	0	1	7	1	.88	12	.306	.407	.544
1996 Houston	NL	12	14	3	1	0	1	(1	0)	7	4	4	1	0	5	0	0	0	0	0	.00	0	.214	.267	.500

Steve Montgomery

Pitches: Right **Bats:** Right **Pos:** RP-8   **Ht:** 6'4" **Wt:** 208 **Born:** 12/25/70 **Age:** 26

Year Team	Lg	G	GS	CG	GF	IP	BFP	H	R	ER	HR	SH	SF	HB	TBB	IBB	SO	WP	Bk	W	L	Pct.	ShO	Sv-Op	Hld	ERA
1993 St. Pete	A+	14	5	0	7	40.2	161	33	14	12	2	1	2	0	9	0	34	1	0	2	1	.667	0	3--	—	2.66
Arkansas	AA	6	6	0	0	32	140	34	17	14	2	2	0	0	12	2	19	2	0	3	3	.500	0	0--	—	3.94
1994 Arkansas	AA	50	9	0	19	107	447	97	43	39	10	4	4	3	33	3	73	5	0	4	5	.444	0	2--	—	3.28
1995 Arkansas	AA	55	0	0	53	61	259	52	22	22	6	7	1	4	22	6	56	5	1	5	2	.714	0	36--	—	3.25
1996 Edmonton	AAA	37	0	0	15	56	230	51	19	18	7	2	0	1	12	1	40	1	0	2	0	1.000	0	1--	—	2.89
1996 Oakland	AL	8	0	0	0	13.2	71	18	14	14	5	0	0	0	13	2	8	3	0	1	0	1.000	0	0-0	0	9.22

Kerwin Moore

Bats: Both **Throws:** Right **Pos:** CF-18; PH-10; DH-1   **Ht:** 6'1" **Wt:** 190 **Born:** 10/29/70 **Age:** 26

Year Team	Lg	G	AB	H	2B	3B	HR	(Hm	Rd)	TB	R	RBI	TBB	IBB	SO	HBP	SH	SF	SB	CS	SB%	GDP	Avg	OBP	SLG
1988 Royals	R	53	165	29	5	0	0	—	—	34	19	14	19	1	49	2	1	0	20	3	.87	2	.176	.269	.206
1989 Baseball Cy	A+	4	11	4	0	0	1	—	—	7	3	2	1	0	2	0	0	0	0	0	.00	0	.364	.417	.636
Eugene	A-	65	226	50	9	2	2	—	—	69	44	25	36	0	75	2	1	0	20	6	.77	0	.221	.333	.305
1990 Appleton	A	128	451	100	17	7	2	—	—	137	93	36	111	2	139	3	6	1	57	19	.75	1	.222	.378	.304
1991 Baseball Cy	A+	130	485	102	14	2	1	—	—	123	67	23	77	0	141	3	5	1	61	15	.80	5	.210	.322	.254
1992 Baseball Cy	A+	66	248	59	2	1	1	—	—	66	39	10	40	1	67	2	4	1	26	9	.74	5	.238	.347	.266
Memphis	AA	58	179	42	4	3	4	—	—	64	27	17	24	0	39	0	1	1	16	4	.80	2	.235	.330	.358
1993 High Desert	A+	132	510	137	20	2	2	—	—	193	120	52	114	3	95	6	3	5	71	16	.82	3	.269	.405	.378

					BATTING													BASERUNNING				PERCENTAGES		
Year Team	Lg	G	AB	H	2B	3B	HR	(Hm | Rd)	TB	R	RBI	TBB	IBB	SO	HBP	SH	SF	SB	CS	SB%	GDP	Avg	OBP	SLG
1994 Huntsville	AA	132	494	120	16	5	5	—	—	161	97	33	96	0	99	1	5	5	54	19	.74	11	.243	.364	.326
1995 Modesto	A+	15	53	13	3	1	1	—	—	21	8	6	11	0	20	2	2	1	4	4	.50	0	.245	.388	.396
Edmonton	AAA	72	265	74	14	4	2	—	—	102	53	26	47	1	67	1	3	1	10	3	.77	3	.279	.389	.385
1996 Edmonton	AAA	119	452	104	12	11	2	—	—	144	90	32	95	2	115	2	4	5	38	12	.76	2	.230	.363	.319
1996 Oakland	AL	22	16	1	1	0	0	(0 | 0)	2	4	0	2	0	6	0	0	0	1	0	1.00	0	.063	.167	.125

Marcus Moore

Pitches: Right **Bats:** Both **Pos:** RP-23 **Ht:** 6'5" **Wt:** 195 **Born:** 11/2/70 **Age:** 26

			HOW MUCH HE PITCHED					WHAT HE GAVE UP										THE RESULTS						
Year Team	Lg	G	GS	CG	GF	IP	BFP	H	R	ER	HR	SH	SF	HB	TBB	IBB	SO	WP	Bk	W	L	Pct.	ShO	Sv-Op	Hld	ERA
1996 Indianapolis *	AAA	15	15	0	0	88.2	369	72	41	34	8	1	2	3	38	1	70	2	0	4	7	.364	0	0- -	—	3.45
1993 Colorado	NL	27	0	0	8	26.1	128	30	25	20	4	0	4	1	20	0	13	4	0	3	1	.750	0	0-2	3	6.84
1994 Colorado	NL	29	0	0	13	33.2	158	33	26	23	4	1	0	5	21	2	33	4	1	1	1	.500	0	0-0	1	6.15
1996 Cincinnati	NL	23	0	0	11	26.1	129	26	21	17	3	3	3	2	22	1	27	1	0	3	3	.500	0	2-2	1	5.81
3 ML YEARS		79	0	0	32	86.1	415	89	72	60	11	4	7	8	63	3	73	9	1	7	5	.583	0	2-4	5	6.25

Mickey Morandini

Bats: Left **Throws:** Right **Pos:** 2B-137; PH-4 **Ht:** 5'11" **Wt:** 176 **Born:** 4/22/66 **Age:** 31

					BATTING													BASERUNNING				PERCENTAGES		
Year Team	Lg	G	AB	H	2B	3B	HR	(Hm	Rd)	TB	R	RBI	TBB	IBB	SO	HBP	SH	SF	SB	CS	SB%	GDP	Avg	OBP	SLG
1990 Philadelphia	NL	25	79	19	4	0	1	(1	0)	26	9	3	6	0	19	0	2	0	3	0	1.00	1	.241	.294	.329
1991 Philadelphia	NL	98	325	81	11	4	1	(1	0)	103	38	20	29	0	45	2	6	2	13	2	.87	7	.249	.313	.317
1992 Philadelphia	NL	127	422	112	8	8	3	(2	1)	145	47	30	25	2	64	0	6	1	8	3	.73	4	.265	.305	.344
1993 Philadelphia	NL	120	425	105	19	9	3	(2	1)	151	57	33	34	2	73	5	4	2	13	2	.87	7	.247	.309	.355
1994 Philadelphia	NL	87	274	80	16	5	2	(1	1)	112	40	26	34	5	33	4	4	0	10	5	.67	4	.292	.378	.409
1995 Philadelphia	NL	127	494	140	34	7	6	(3	3)	206	65	49	42	3	80	9	4	1	9	6	.60	11	.283	.350	.417
1996 Philadelphia	NL	140	539	135	24	6	3	(2	1)	180	64	32	49	0	87	9	5	4	26	5	.84	15	.250	.321	.334
7 ML YEARS		724	2558	672	116	39	19	(12	7)	923	320	193	219	12	401	29	31	11	82	23	.78	49	.263	.327	.361

Mike Mordecai

Bats: R **Throws:** R **Pos:** PH-42; 2B-20; 3B-9; SS-6; 1B-2 **Ht:** 5'11" **Wt:** 175 **Born:** 12/13/67 **Age:** 29

					BATTING													BASERUNNING				PERCENTAGES		
Year Team	Lg	G	AB	H	2B	3B	HR	(Hm	Rd)	TB	R	RBI	TBB	IBB	SO	HBP	SH	SF	SB	CS	SB%	GDP	Avg	OBP	SLG
1996 Richmond *	AAA	3	11	2	0	0	1	—	—	5	2	2	0	0	3	0	0	1	0	0	.00	0	.182	.182	.455
1994 Atlanta	NL	4	4	1	0	0	1	(1	0)	4	1	3	1	0	0	0	0	0	0	0	.00	0	.250	.400	1.000
1995 Atlanta	NL	69	75	21	6	0	3	(1	2)	36	10	11	9	0	16	0	2	1	0	0	.00	0	.280	.353	.480
1996 Atlanta	NL	66	108	26	5	0	2	(0	2)	37	12	8	9	1	24	0	4	1	1	0	1.00	1	.241	.297	.343
3 ML YEARS		139	187	48	11	0	6	(2	4)	77	23	22	19	1	40	0	6	2	1	0	1.00	1	.257	.322	.412

Ramon Morel

Pitches: Right **Bats:** Right **Pos:** RP-29 **Ht:** 6'2" **Wt:** 193 **Born:** 8/15/74 **Age:** 22

			HOW MUCH HE PITCHED					WHAT HE GAVE UP										THE RESULTS						
Year Team	Lg	G	GS	CG	GF	IP	BFP	H	R	ER	HR	SH	SF	HB	TBB	IBB	SO	WP	Bk	W	L	Pct.	ShO	Sv-Op	Hld	ERA
1992 Pirates	R	14	2	1	7	45.2	193	49	26	22	0	1	0	1	11	0	29	4	2	2	2	.500	0	0- -	—	4.34
1993 Welland	A-	16	16	0	0	77	344	90	45	36	7	3	0	5	21	0	51	6	0	7	8	.467	0	0- -	—	4.21
1994 Augusta	A	28	27	2	0	168.2	689	157	69	53	8	2	4	12	24	0	152	20	0	10	7	.588	1	0- -	—	2.83
1995 Carolina	AA	10	10	0	0	69	281	71	31	27	4	1	2	2	10	0	34	2	0	3	3	.500	0	0- -	—	3.52
Lynchburg	A+	22	22	1	0	141.2	585	151	66	55	6	3	5	5	23	2	78	4	4	6	10	.375	1	0- -	—	3.49
1996 Carolina	AA	11	11	0	0	63.2	283	75	42	36	3	3	2	7	16	3	44	4	0	2	5	.286	0	0- -	—	5.09
1995 Pittsburgh	NL	5	0	0	0	6.1	23	6	2	2	0	1	0	0	2	1	3	0	0	0	0	.000	0	0-1	0	2.84
1996 Pittsburgh	NL	29	0	0	4	42	198	57	27	25	4	1	1	1	19	5	22	1	1	2	1	.667	0	0-0	2	5.36
2 ML YEARS		34	0	0	4	48.1	221	63	29	27	4	2	1	1	21	6	25	1	1	2	2	.500	0	0-1	2	5.03

Mike Morgan

Pitches: Right **Bats:** Right **Pos:** SP-23 **Ht:** 6'2" **Wt:** 220 **Born:** 10/8/59 **Age:** 37

			HOW MUCH HE PITCHED					WHAT HE GAVE UP										THE RESULTS						
Year Team	Lg	G	GS	CG	GF	IP	BFP	H	R	ER	HR	SH	SF	HB	TBB	IBB	SO	WP	Bk	W	L	Pct.	ShO	Sv-Op	Hld	ERA
1996 St. Pete *	A+	1	1	0	0	5.2	21	4	0	0	0	0	0	0	1	0	4	0	0	1	0	1.000	0	0- -	—	0.00
Louisville	AAA	4	4	1	0	23	106	29	18	18	2	0	0	2	11	1	10	0	0	1	3	.250	0	0- -	—	7.04
1978 Oakland	AL	3	3	1	0	12	60	19	12	10	1	1	0	0	8	0	0	0	0	0	3	.000	0	0- -	—	7.50
1979 Oakland	AL	13	13	2	0	77	368	102	57	51	7	4	4	3	50	0	17	7	0	2	10	.167	0	0- -	—	5.96
1982 New York	AL	30	23	2	2	150.1	661	167	77	73	15	2	4	2	67	5	71	6	0	7	11	.389	0	0- -	—	4.37
1983 Toronto	AL	16	4	0	2	45.1	198	48	26	26	6	0	1	0	21	0	22	3	0	0	3	.000	0	0- -	—	5.16
1985 Seattle	AL	2	2	0	0	6	33	11	8	8	2	0	0	0	5	0	2	1	0	1	1	.500	0	0- -	—	12.00
1986 Seattle	AL	37	33	9	2	216.1	951	243	122	109	24	7	3	4	86	3	116	8	1	11	17	.393	1	1- -	—	4.53
1987 Seattle	AL	34	31	8	2	207	878	245	117	107	25	8	5	5	53	3	85	11	0	12	17	.414	2	0-0	0	4.65
1988 Baltimore	AL	22	10	2	6	71.1	299	70	45	43	6	1	0	1	23	1	29	5	0	1	6	.143	0	0-1	0	5.43

		HOW MUCH HE PITCHED						WHAT HE GAVE UP												THE RESULTS						
Year Team	Lg	G	GS	CG	GF	IP	BFP	H	R	ER	HR	SH	SF	HB	TBB	IBB	SO	WP	Bk	W	L	Pct.	ShO	Sv-Op	Hld	ERA
1989 Los Angeles	NL	40	19	0	7	152.2	604	130	51	43	6	8	6	2	33	8	72	6	0	8	11	.421	0	0-1	1	2.53
1990 Los Angeles	NL	33	33	6	0	211	891	216	100	88	19	11	4	5	60	5	106	4	1	11	15	.423	4	0-0	0	3.75
1991 Los Angeles	NL	34	33	5	1	236.1	949	197	85	73	12	10	4	3	61	10	140	6	0	14	10	.583	1	1-1	0	2.78
1992 Chicago	NL	34	34	6	0	240	966	203	80	68	14	10	5	3	79	10	123	11	0	16	8	.667	1	0-0	0	2.55
1993 Chicago	NL	32	32	1	0	207.2	883	206	100	93	15	11	5	7	74	8	111	8	2	10	15	.400	1	0-0	0	4.03
1994 Chicago	NL	15	15	1	0	80.2	380	111	65	60	12	7	6	4	35	2	57	5	0	2	10	.167	0	0-0	0	6.69
1995 ChN-StL	NL	21	21	1	0	131.1	548	133	56	52	12	12	5	6	34	2	61	6	0	7	7	.500	0	0-0	0	3.56
1996 StL-Cin	NL	23	23	0	0	130.1	567	146	72	67	16	6	7	1	47	0	74	2	0	6	11	.353	0	0-0	0	4.63
1995 Chicago	NL	4	4	0	0	24.2	100	19	8	6	2	2	0	1	9	1	15	0	0	2	1	.667	0	0-0	0	2.19
St. Louis	NL	17	17	1	0	106.2	448	114	48	46	10	10	5	5	25	1	46	6	0	5	6	.455	0	0-0	0	3.88
1996 St. Louis	NL	18	18	0	0	103	452	118	63	60	14	5	6	0	40	0	55	2	0	4	8	.333	0	0-0	0	5.24
Cincinnati	NL	5	5	0	0	27.1	115	28	9	7	2	1	1	1	7	0	19	0	0	2	3	.400	0	0-0	0	2.30
16 ML YEARS		389	329	44	22	2175.1	9256	2247	1073	971	192	98	59	46	736	57	1086	89	4	108	155	.411	10	3--	—	4.02

Alvin Morman

Pitches: Left **Bats:** Left **Pos:** RP-53 **Ht:** 6'3" **Wt:** 210 **Born:** 1/6/69 **Age:** 28

		HOW MUCH HE PITCHED						WHAT HE GAVE UP												THE RESULTS						
Year Team	Lg	G	GS	CG	GF	IP	BFP	H	R	ER	HR	SH	SF	HB	TBB	IBB	SO	WP	Bk	W	L	Pct.	ShO	Sv-Op	Hld	ERA
1991 Astros	R	11	0	0	3	16.2	71	15	7	4	0	1	0	0	5	0	24	0	4	1	0	1.000	0	1--	—	2.16
Osceola	A+	3	0	0	0	6	25	5	3	1	0	1	0	0	2	0	3	1	0	0	0	.000	0	0--	—	1.50
1992 Asheville	A	57	0	0	37	75.1	313	60	17	13	3	3	1	3	26	2	70	2	0	8	0	1.000	0	15--	—	1.55
1993 Jackson	AA	19	19	0	0	97.1	392	77	35	32	7	3	2	5	28	0	101	5	1	8	2	.800	0	0--	—	2.96
1994 Tucson	AAA	58	0	0	23	74	327	84	51	42	7	5	9	2	26	4	49	3	0	3	7	.300	0	5--	—	5.11
1995 Tucson	AAA	45	0	0	10	48.1	211	50	26	21	6	5	8	0	20	1	36	2	0	5	1	.833	0	3--	—	3.91
1996 Houston	NL	53	0	0	9	42	192	43	24	23	8	2	1	0	24	6	31	3	1	4	1	.800	0	0-2	7	4.93

Russ Morman

Bats: Right **Throws:** Right **Pos:** PH-6; 1B-2 **Ht:** 6'4" **Wt:** 225 **Born:** 4/28/62 **Age:** 35

		BATTING																BASERUNNING				PERCENTAGES		
Year Team	Lg	G	AB	H	2B	3B	HR	(Hm	Rd)	TB	R	RBI	TBB	IBB	SO	HBP	SH	SF	SB	CS	SB%	GDP	Avg	OBP	SLG
1996 Charlotte *	AAA	80	289	96	18	1	18	—	—	170	59	77	29	2	51	1	0	4	2	4	.33	10	.332	.390	.588
1986 Chicago	AL	49	159	40	5	0	4	(1	3)	57	18	17	16	0	36	2	1	2	1	0	1.00	5	.252	.324	.358
1988 Chicago	AL	40	75	18	2	0	0	(0	0)	20	8	3	3	0	17	0	2	0	0	0	.00	5	.240	.269	.267
1989 Chicago	AL	37	58	13	2	0	0	(0	0)	15	5	8	6	1	16	0	2	1	1	0	1.00	1	.224	.292	.259
1990 Kansas City	AL	12	37	10	4	2	1	(0	1)	21	5	3	3	0	3	0	0	1	0	0	.00	0	.270	.317	.568
1991 Kansas City	AL	12	23	6	0	0	0	(0	0)	6	1	1	1	1	5	0	0	0	0	0	.00	0	.261	.292	.261
1994 Florida	NL	13	33	7	0	1	1	(0	1)	12	2	2	2	0	9	1	0	0	0	0	.00	5	.212	.278	.364
1995 Florida	NL	34	72	20	2	1	3	(1	2)	33	9	7	3	0	12	1	0	0	0	0	.00	5	.278	.316	.458
1996 Florida	NL	6	6	1	0	0	0	(0	0)	2	0	0	1	0	2	0	0	0	0	0	.00	1	.167	.286	.333
8 ML YEARS		203	463	115	16	4	9	(2	7)	166	48	41	35	2	100	4	5	4	2	0	1.00	17	.248	.304	.359

Hal Morris

Bats: Left **Throws:** Left **Pos:** 1B-140; PH-6 **Ht:** 6'4" **Wt:** 210 **Born:** 4/9/65 **Age:** 32

		BATTING																BASERUNNING				PERCENTAGES		
Year Team	Lg	G	AB	H	2B	3B	HR	(Hm	Rd)	TB	R	RBI	TBB	IBB	SO	HBP	SH	SF	SB	CS	SB%	GDP	Avg	OBP	SLG
1996 Indianapols *	AAA	1	4	2	1	0	0	—	—	6	1	1	0	0	1	0	0	0	0	0	.00	0	.500	.500	1.500
1988 New York	AL	15	20	2	0	0	0	(0	0)	2	1	0	0	0	9	0	0	0	0	0	.00	0	.100	.100	.100
1989 New York	AL	15	18	5	0	0	0	(0	0)	5	2	4	1	0	4	0	0	0	0	0	.00	2	.278	.316	.278
1990 Cincinnati	NL	107	309	105	22	3	7	(3	4)	154	50	36	21	4	32	1	3	2	9	3	.75	12	.340	.381	.498
1991 Cincinnati	NL	136	478	152	33	1	14	(9	5)	229	72	59	46	7	61	1	5	7	10	4	.71	4	.318	.374	.479
1992 Cincinnati	NL	115	395	107	21	3	6	(3	3)	152	41	53	45	8	53	2	2	2	6	6	.50	12	.271	.347	.385
1993 Cincinnati	NL	101	379	120	18	0	7	(2	5)	159	48	49	34	4	51	2	0	6	2	2	.50	5	.317	.371	.420
1994 Cincinnati	NL	112	436	146	30	4	10	(5	5)	214	60	78	34	8	62	5	2	6	6	2	.75	16	.335	.385	.491
1995 Cincinnati	NL	101	359	100	25	2	11	(6	5)	162	53	51	29	7	58	1	1	1	1	1	.50	10	.279	.333	.451
1996 Cincinnati	NL	142	528	165	32	4	16	(7	9)	253	82	80	50	5	76	5	5	6	7	5	.58	12	.313	.374	.479
9 ML YEARS		844	2922	902	181	17	71	(35	36)	1330	409	410	260	43	406	17	18	30	41	23	.64	73	.309	.365	.455

Julio Mosquera

Bats: Right **Throws:** Right **Pos:** C-8 **Ht:** 6'0" **Wt:** 190 **Born:** 1/29/72 **Age:** 25

		BATTING																BASERUNNING				PERCENTAGES		
Year Team	Lg	G	AB	H	2B	3B	HR	(Hm	Rd)	TB	R	RBI	TBB	IBB	SO	HBP	SH	SF	SB	CS	SB%	GDP	Avg	OBP	SLG
1993 Blue Jays	R	35	108	28	3	2	0	—	—	35	9	15	8	0	16	1	2	1	3	2	.60	3	.259	.314	.324
1994 Medicne Hat	R+	59	229	78	17	1	2	—	—	103	33	44	18	3	35	3	0	2	3	3	.50	4	.341	.393	.450
1995 Hagerstown	A	108	406	118	22	5	3	—	—	159	64	46	29	2	53	13	3	5	5	5	.50	13	.291	.353	.392
1996 Knoxville	AA	92	318	73	17	0	2	—	—	96	36	31	29	1	55	4	3	1	6	5	.55	16	.230	.301	.302
Syracuse	AAA	23	72	18	1	0	0	—	—	19	6	5	6	0	14	1	0	0	0	0	.00	0	.250	.316	.264
1996 Toronto	AL	8	22	5	2	0	0	(0	0)	7	2	2	0	0	3	1	0	0	0	1	.00	0	.227	.261	.318

Chad Mottola

Bats: Right **Throws:** Right **Pos:** RF-30; PH-6; CF-1   **Ht:** 6'3" **Wt:** 220 **Born:** 10/15/71 **Age:** 25

								BATTING										BASERUNNING				PERCENTAGES		
Year	Team	Lg	G	AB	H	2B	3B	HR	(Hm	Rd)	TB	R	RBI	TBB	IBB	SO	HBP	SH	SF	SB	CS	SB%	GDP	Avg	OBP	SLG
1992	Billings	R+	57	213	61	8	3	12	—	—	111	53	37	25	0	43	0	0	0	12	3	.80	4	.286	.361	.521
1993	Winston-Sal	A+	137	493	138	25	3	21	—	—	232	76	91	62	2	109	2	0	3	13	7	.65	9	.280	.361	.471
1994	Chattanooga	AA	118	402	97	19	1	7	—	—	139	44	41	30	1	68	1	2	2	9	12	.43	12	.241	.294	.346
1995	Chattanooga	AA	51	181	53	13	1	10	—	—	98	32	39	13	0	32	1	0	1	1	2	.33	2	.293	.342	.541
	Indianapolis	AAA	69	239	62	11	1	8	—	—	99	40	37	20	0	50	0	1	1	8	1	.89	6	.259	.315	.414
1996	Indianapols	AAA	103	362	95	24	3	9	—	—	152	45	47	21	3	93	4	0	4	9	6	.60	10	.262	.307	.420
1996	Cincinnati	NL	35	79	17	3	0	3	(1	2)	29	10	6	6	1	16	0	0	0	2	2	.50	0	.215	.271	.367

James Mouton

Bats: R **Throws:** R **Pos:** LF-79; PH-32; CF-29; RF-5   **Ht:** 5'9" **Wt:** 175 **Born:** 12/29/68 **Age:** 28

								BATTING										BASERUNNING				PERCENTAGES		
Year	Team	Lg	G	AB	H	2B	3B	HR	(Hm	Rd)	TB	R	RBI	TBB	IBB	SO	HBP	SH	SF	SB	CS	SB%	GDP	Avg	OBP	SLG
1996	Tucson *	AAA	1	4	1	0	0	0	—	—	1	1	0	1	0	0	0	0	0	0	0	.00	0	.250	.400	.250
1994	Houston	NL	99	310	76	11	0	2	(1	1)	93	43	16	27	0	69	5	2	1	24	5	.83	5	.245	.315	.300
1995	Houston	NL	104	298	78	18	2	4	(2	2)	112	42	27	25	1	59	4	3	1	25	8	.76	5	.262	.326	.376
1996	Houston	NL	122	300	79	15	1	3	(2	1)	105	40	34	38	2	55	0	2	3	21	9	.70	9	.263	.343	.350
	3 ML YEARS		325	908	233	44	3	9	(5	4)	310	125	77	90	3	183	9	7	5	70	22	.76	20	.257	.328	.341

Lyle Mouton

Bats: R **Throws:** R **Pos:** DH-28; RF-28; LF-22; PH-18   **Ht:** 6'4" **Wt:** 240 **Born:** 5/13/69 **Age:** 28

								BATTING										BASERUNNING				PERCENTAGES		
Year	Team	Lg	G	AB	H	2B	3B	HR	(Hm	Rd)	TB	R	RBI	TBB	IBB	SO	HBP	SH	SF	SB	CS	SB%	GDP	Avg	OBP	SLG
1991	Oneonta	A-	70	272	84	11	2	7	—	—	120	53	41	31	2	39	6	0	3	14	8	.64	1	.309	.388	.441
1992	Pr. William	A+	50	189	50	14	1	6	—	—	84	28	34	17	1	42	0	0	4	4	2	.67	3	.265	.319	.444
	Albany-Colo	AA	64	214	46	12	2	2	—	—	68	25	27	24	2	55	1	0	1	1	1	.50	9	.215	.296	.318
1993	Albany-Colo	AA	135	491	125	22	3	16	—	—	201	74	76	50	2	125	7	2	1	19	13	.59	13	.255	.332	.409
1994	Albany-Colo	AA	74	274	84	23	1	12	—	—	145	42	42	27	1	62	2	0	4	7	6	.54	8	.307	.368	.529
	Columbus	AAA	59	204	64	14	5	4	—	—	100	26	32	14	0	45	1	2	3	5	1	.83	1	.314	.356	.490
1995	Nashville	AAA	71	267	79	17	0	8	—	—	120	40	41	23	2	58	1	0	4	10	4	.71	9	.296	.349	.449
1995	Chicago	AL	58	179	54	16	0	5	(4	1)	85	23	27	19	0	46	2	0	1	1	0	1.00	7	.302	.373	.475
1996	Chicago	AL	87	214	63	8	1	7	(4	3)	94	25	39	22	4	50	2	0	3	3	0	1.00	3	.294	.361	.439
	2 ML YEARS		145	393	117	24	1	12	(8	4)	179	48	66	41	4	96	4	0	4	4	0	1.00	10	.298	.367	.455

Jamie Moyer

Pitches: Left **Bats:** Left **Pos:** SP-21; RP-13   **Ht:** 6'0" **Wt:** 170 **Born:** 11/18/62 **Age:** 34

			HOW MUCH HE PITCHED					WHAT HE GAVE UP										THE RESULTS					
Year	Team	Lg	G	GS	CG	GF	IP	BFP	H	R	ER	HR	SH	SF	HB	TBB	IBB	SO	WP	Bk	W	L	Pct.	ShO	Sv-Op	Hld	ERA
1986	Chicago	NL	16	16	1	0	87.1	395	107	52	49	10	3	3	3	42	1	45	3	3	7	4	.636	1	0- --	—	5.05
1987	Chicago	NL	35	33	1	1	201	899	210	127	114	28	14	7	5	97	9	147	11	2	12	15	.444	0	0-0	0	5.10
1988	Chicago	NL	34	30	3	1	202	855	212	84	78	20	14	4	4	55	7	121	4	0	9	15	.375	1	0-2	0	3.48
1989	Texas	AL	15	15	1	0	76	337	84	51	41	10	1	4	2	33	0	44	1	0	4	9	.308	0	0-0	0	4.86
1990	Texas	AL	33	10	1	6	102.1	447	115	59	53	6	1	7	4	39	4	58	1	0	2	6	.250	0	0-0	1	4.66
1991	St. Louis	NL	8	7	0	1	31.1	142	38	21	20	5	4	2	1	16	0	20	2	1	0	5	.000	0	0-0	0	5.74
1993	Baltimore	AL	25	25	3	0	152	630	154	63	58	11	3	1	6	38	2	90	1	1	12	9	.571	1	0-0	0	3.43
1994	Baltimore	AL	23	23	0	0	149	631	158	81	79	23	5	2	2	38	3	87	1	0	5	7	.417	0	0-0	0	4.77
1995	Baltimore	AL	27	18	0	3	115.2	483	117	70	67	18	5	3	3	30	0	65	0	0	8	6	.571	0	0-0	0	5.21
1996	Bos-Sea	AL	34	21	0	1	160.2	703	177	86	71	23	7	6	2	46	5	79	3	1	13	3	**.813**	0	0-0	1	3.98
1996	Boston	AL	23	10	0	1	90	405	111	50	45	14	4	3	1	27	2	50	2	1	7	1	.875	0	0-0	1	4.50
	Seattle	AL	11	11	0	0	70.2	298	66	36	26	9	3	3	1	19	3	29	1	0	6	2	.750	0	0-0	0	3.31
	10 ML YEARS		250	198	10	13	1277.1	5522	1372	694	630	154	57	39	32	434	31	756	27	8	72	79	.477	3	0- --	—	4.44

Bill Mueller

Bats: Both **Throws:** Right **Pos:** 3B-45; 2B-8; PH-4   **Ht:** 5'11" **Wt:** 175 **Born:** 3/17/71 **Age:** 26

								BATTING										BASERUNNING				PERCENTAGES		
Year	Team	Lg	G	AB	H	2B	3B	HR	(Hm	Rd)	TB	R	RBI	TBB	IBB	SO	HBP	SH	SF	SB	CS	SB%	GDP	Avg	OBP	SLG
1993	Everett	A-	58	200	60	8	2	1	—	—	75	31	24	42	1	17	3	6	2	13	6	.68	3	.300	.425	.375
1994	San Jose	A+	120	431	130	20	9	5	—	—	183	79	72	103	11	47	3	1	6	4	8	.33	15	.302	.435	.425
1995	Shreveport	AA	88	330	102	16	2	1	—	—	125	56	39	53	2	36	4	2	4	6	5	.55	9	.309	.407	.379
	Phoenix	AAA	41	172	51	13	6	2	—	—	82	23	19	19	0	31	0	6	1	0	0	.00	7	.297	.365	.477
1996	Phoenix	AAA	106	440	133	14	6	4	—	—	171	73	36	44	4	40	1	1	4	2	5	.29	11	.302	.365	.389
1996	San Francisco	NL	55	200	66	15	1	0	(0	0)	83	31	19	24	0	26	1	1	2	0	1	.00	1	.330	.401	.415

Terry Mulholland

Pitches: Left **Bats: Right** **Pos: SP-33** **Ht: 6'3"** **Wt: 212** **Born: 3/9/63** **Age: 34**

Year Team	Lg	G	GS	CG	GF	IP	BFP	H	R	ER	HR	SH	SF	HB	TBB	IBB	SO	WP	Bk	W	L	Pct.	ShO	Sv-Op	Hld	ERA
1986 San Francisco	NL	15	10	0	1	54.2	245	51	33	30	3	5	1	1	35	2	27	6	0	1	7	.125	0	0--	—	4.94
1988 San Francisco	NL	9	6	2	1	46	191	50	20	19	3	5	0	1	7	0	18	1	0	2	1	.667	1	0-0	1	3.72
1989 SF-Phi	NL	25	18	2	4	115.1	513	137	66	63	8	7	1	4	36	3	66	3	0	4	7	.364	1	0-0	0	4.92
1990 Philadelphia	NL	33	26	6	2	180.2	746	172	78	67	15	7	12	2	42	7	75	7	2	9	10	.474	1	0-1	0	3.34
1991 Philadelphia	NL	34	34	8	0	232	956	231	100	93	15	11	6	3	49	2	142	3	0	16	13	.552	3	0-0	0	3.61
1992 Philadelphia	NL	32	32	12	0	229	937	227	101	97	14	10	7	3	46	3	125	3	0	13	11	.542	2	0-0	0	3.81
1993 Philadelphia	NL	29	28	7	0	191	786	177	80	69	20	5	4	3	40	2	116	5	0	12	9	.571	2	0-0	0	3.25
1994 New York	AL	24	19	2	4	120.2	542	150	94	87	24	3	4	3	37	1	72	5	0	6	7	.462	0	0-0	0	6.49
1995 San Francisco	NL	29	24	2	1	149	666	190	112	96	25	11	6	4	38	1	65	4	0	5	13	.278	0	0-0	0	5.80
1996 Phi-Sea		33	33	3	0	202.2	871	232	112	105	22	11	8	5	49	4	86	6	0	13	11	.542	0	0-0	0	4.66
1989 San Francisco	NL	5	1	0	2	11	51	15	5	5	0	0	0	0	4	0	6	0	0	0	0	.000	0	0--	1	4.09
Philadelphia	NL	20	17	2	2	104.1	462	122	61	58	8	7	1	4	32	3	60	3	0	4	7	.364	1	0-0	0	5.00
1996 Philadelphia	NL	21	21	3	0	133.1	571	157	74	69	17	6	5	3	21	1	52	5	0	8	7	.533	0	0-0	0	4.66
Seattle	AL	12	12	0	0	69.1	300	75	38	36	5	5	3	2	28	3	34	1	0	5	4	.556	0	0-0	0	4.67
10 ML YEARS		263	230	44	14	1521	6453	1617	796	726	149	75	49	29	379	25	792	43	2	81	89	.476	10	0--	—	4.30

Sean Mulligan

Bats: Right **Throws: Right** **Pos: PH-2** **Ht: 6'2"** **Wt: 210** **Born: 4/25/70** **Age: 27**

Year Team	Lg	G	AB	H	2B	3B	HR	(Hm	Rd)	TB	R	RBI	TBB	IBB	SO	HBP	SH	SF	SB	CS	SB%	GDP	Avg	OBP	SLG
1991 Charlstn-SC	A	60	215	56	9	3	4	—	—	83	24	30	17	0	56	6	1	1	4	1	.80	5	.260	.331	.386
1992 High Desert	A+	35	118	19	4	0	4	—	—	35	14	14	11	1	38	3	0	1	0	0	.00	3	.161	.248	.297
Waterloo	A	79	278	70	13	1	5	—	—	100	24	43	20	0	62	5	2	4	1	1	1.00	10	.252	.309	.360
1993 Rancho Cuca	A+	79	268	75	10	3	6	—	—	109	29	36	34	0	33	3	0	4	1	3	.25	16	.280	.362	.407
1994 Rancho Cuca	A+	66	243	74	18	1	9	—	—	121	45	49	24	1	39	5	1	8	1	0	1.00	4	.305	.368	.498
Wichita	AA	56	208	73	14	0	1	—	—	90	29	30	11	2	25	5	0	3	2	3	.40	7	.351	.392	.433
1995 Las Vegas	AAA	101	339	93	20	1	7	—	—	136	34	43	27	2	61	8	1	3	3	0	.00	7	.274	.340	.401
1996 Las Vegas	AAA	102	358	103	24	3	19	—	—	190	55	75	30	4	68	7	0	2	1	2	.33	8	.288	.353	.531
1996 San Diego	NL	2	1	0	0	0	0	(0	0)	0	0	0	0	0	0	0	0	0	0	0	.00	0	.000	.000	.000

Bobby Munoz

Pitches: Right **Bats: Right** **Pos: SP-6** **Ht: 6'8"** **Wt: 259** **Born: 3/3/68** **Age: 29**

Year Team	Lg	G	GS	CG	GF	IP	BFP	H	R	ER	HR	SH	SF	HB	TBB	IBB	SO	WP	Bk	W	L	Pct.	ShO	Sv-Op	Hld	ERA
1996 Clearwater *	A+	2	2	0	0	14	58	15	4	3	1	0	1	0	2	0	7	0	0	1	1	.500	0	0--	—	1.93
Scrntn-WB *	AAA	8	8	0	0	50.2	207	50	24	22	6	1	1	0	7	0	34	2	0	4	2	.667	0	0--	—	3.91
Reading *	AA	4	4	0	0	27.2	113	24	13	9	3	1	0	1	8	0	29	2	1	0	1	.000	0	0--	—	2.93
1993 New York	AL	38	0	0	12	45.2	208	48	27	27	1	1	3	0	26	5	33	2	0	3	3	.500	0	0-2	6	5.32
1994 Philadelphia	NL	21	14	1	1	104.1	447	101	40	31	8	5	5	1	35	0	59	5	1	7	5	.583	0	1-2	0	2.67
1995 Philadelphia	NL	3	3	0	0	15.2	70	15	13	10	2	0	2	3	9	0	6	0	0	0	2	.000	0	0-0	0	5.74
1996 Philadelphia	NL	6	6	0	0	25.1	123	42	28	22	5	2	1	0	7	1	8	0	0	0	3	.000	0	0-0	0	7.82
4 ML YEARS		68	23	1	13	191	848	206	108	90	16	8	11	5	77	6	106	7	1	10	13	.435	0	1-4	6	4.24

Jose Munoz

Bats: B **Throws: R** **Pos: PH-8; 2B-7; DH-2; SS-2; 3B-1; LF-1** **Ht: 5'11"** **Wt: 165** **Born: 11/11/67** **Age: 29**

Year Team	Lg	G	AB	H	2B	3B	HR	(Hm	Rd)	TB	R	RBI	TBB	IBB	SO	HBP	SH	SF	SB	CS	SB%	GDP	Avg	OBP	SLG
1987 Dodgers	R	54	187	60	7	0	0	—	—	67	31	22	26	3	22	3	2	1	6	5	.55	2	.321	.410	.358
1988 Bakersfield	A+	105	347	86	6	0	0	—	—	92	35	24	42	0	54	3	5	1	7	2	.78	9	.248	.333	.265
1989 Vero Beach	A+	105	300	77	15	1	0	—	—	94	39	24	14	0	31	1	5	3	6	2	.75	11	.257	.289	.313
1990 Bakersfield	A+	14	39	7	1	0	0	—	—	8	3	6	6	0	7	0	0	0	2	1	.67	0	.179	.289	.205
Vero Beach	A+	113	397	117	18	3	2	—	—	147	57	47	34	3	43	2	8	4	28	8	.78	0	.295	.350	.370
1991 San Antonio	AA	31	123	39	6	2	0	—	—	49	25	13	12	1	14	1	3	0	4	2	.67	5	.317	.382	.398
Albuquerque	AAA	101	389	127	18	4	0	—	—	153	49	65	20	0	36	2	6	5	15	10	.60	14	.326	.358	.393
1992 Albuquerque	AAA	131	450	137	20	3	2	—	—	169	48	45	25	6	46	1	7	0	7	4	.64	22	.304	.342	.376
1993 Albuquerque	AAA	127	438	126	21	5	1	—	—	160	66	54	29	3	46	1	8	3	6	3	.67	19	.288	.331	.365
1994 Pawtucket	AAA	129	519	136	16	1	7	—	—	175	59	41	52	2	59	2	8	2	12	13	.48	16	.262	.330	.337
1995 Richmond	AAA	135	520	151	18	5	3	—	—	188	65	45	53	4	65	4	5	6	7	10	.41	18	.290	.357	.362
1996 Nashville	AAA	78	295	69	17	1	6	—	—	106	30	34	20	2	37	1	2	2	8	1	.89	10	.234	.283	.359
1996 Chicago	AL	17	27	7	0	0	0	(0	0)	7	7	1	4	0	1	0	0	0	0	0	.00	2	.259	.355	.259

Mike Munoz

Pitches: Left **Bats: Left** **Pos: RP-54** **Ht: 6'2"** **Wt: 192** **Born: 7/12/65** **Age: 31**

Year Team	Lg	G	GS	CG	GF	IP	BFP	H	R	ER	HR	SH	SF	HB	TBB	IBB	SO	WP	Bk	W	L	Pct.	ShO	Sv-Op	Hld	ERA
1996 Colo. Sprng *	AAA	10	0	0	4	13.1	52	8	3	3	0	0	1	0	6	0	13	0	0	1	1	.500	0	3--	—	2.03

			HOW MUCH HE PITCHED			WHAT HE GAVE UP				THE RESULTS			
Year Team	Lg	G GS CG GF	IP	BFP	H R ER	HR SH SF HB	TBB IBB	SO	WP	Bk	W	L	Pct.	ShO	Sv-Op	Hld	ERA
1989 Los Angeles	NL	3 0 0 1	2.2	14	5 5 5	1 0 0 0	2 0	3	0	0	0	0	.000	0	0-0	0	16.88
1990 Los Angeles	NL	8 0 0 3	5.2	24	6 2 2	0 1 0 0	3 0	2	0	0	0	1	.000	0	0-1	2	3.18
1991 Detroit	AL	6 0 0 4	9.1	46	14 10 10	0 0 1 0	5 0	3	1	0	0	0	.000	0	0-0	0	9.64
1992 Detroit	AL	65 0 0 15	48	210	44 16 16	3 4 2 0	25 6	23	2	0	1	2	.333	0	2-3	15	3.00
1993 Det-Col		29 0 0 10	21	101	25 14 11	2 3 2 0	15 4	17	2	0	2	2	.500	0	0-2	2	4.71
1994 Colorado	NL	57 0 0 8	45.2	200	37 22 19	3 2 1 0	31 5	32	2	0	4	2	.667	0	1-2	12	3.74
1995 Colorado	NL	64 0 0 19	43.2	208	54 38 36	9 2 2 1	27 0	37	5	0	2	4	.333	0	2-4	12	7.42
1996 Colorado	NL	54 0 0 7	44.2	203	55 33 33	4 3 1 1	16 2	45	0	0	2	2	.500	0	0-3	13	6.65
1993 Detroit	AL	8 0 0 3	3	19	4 2 2	1 0 0 0	6 1	1	0	0	0	1	.000	0	0-0	1	6.00
Colorado	NL	21 0 0 7	18	82	21 12 9	1 3 2 0	9 3	16	2	0	2	1	.667	0	0-2	1	4.50
8 ML YEARS		286 0 0 67	220.2	1006	240 140 132	22 15 9 2	124 17	162	12	0	11	13	.458	0	5-15	56	5.38

Pedro Munoz

Bats: Right **Throws:** Right **Pos:** DH-18; RF-14; PH-3 **Ht:** 5'10" **Wt:** 208 **Born:** 9/19/68 **Age:** 28

		BATTING												BASERUNNING				PERCENTAGES		
Year Team	Lg	G AB H	2B 3B HR	(Hm Rd)	TB	R	RBI	TBB	IBB	SO	HBP	SH	SF	SB	CS	SB%	GDP	Avg	OBP	SLG
1990 Minnesota	AL	22 85 23	4 1 0	(0 0)	29	13	5	2	0	16	0	1	2	3	0	1.00	3	.271	.281	.341
1991 Minnesota	AL	51 138 39	7 1 7	(4 3)	69	15	26	9	0	31	1	1	2	3	0	1.00	2	.283	.327	.500
1992 Minnesota	AL	127 418 113	16 3 12	(8 4)	171	44	71	17	1	90	1	0	3	4	5	.44	18	.270	.298	.409
1993 Minnesota	AL	104 326 76	11 1 13	(2 11)	128	34	38	25	2	97	3	0	0	1	2	.33	7	.233	.294	.393
1994 Minnesota	AL	75 244 72	15 2 11	(5 6)	124	35	36	19	0	67	2	0	2	0	0	.00	4	.295	.348	.508
1995 Minnesota	AL	104 376 113	17 0 18	(10 8)	184	45	58	19	0	86	3	0	2	0	3	.00	14	.301	.338	.489
1996 Oakland	AL	34 121 31	5 0 6	(2 4)	54	17	18	9	1	31	0	0	0	0	0	.00	2	.256	.308	.446
7 ML YEARS		517 1708 467	75 8 67	(31 36)	759	203	252	100	4	418	10	2	11	11	10	.52	50	.273	.315	.444

Eddie Murray

Bats: Both **Throws:** Right **Pos:** DH-149; PH-2; 1B-1 **Ht:** 6'2" **Wt:** 220 **Born:** 2/24/56 **Age:** 41

		BATTING												BASERUNNING				PERCENTAGES		
Year Team	Lg	G AB H	2B 3B HR	(Hm Rd)	TB	R	RBI	TBB	IBB	SO	HBP	SH	SF	SB	CS	SB%	GDP	Avg	OBP	SLG
1977 Baltimore	AL	160 611 173	29 2 27	(14 13)	287	81	88	48	6	104	1	0	6	0	1	.00	22	.283	.333	.470
1978 Baltimore	AL	161 610 174	32 3 27	(10 17)	293	85	95	70	7	97	1	1	8	6	5	.55	15	.285	.356	.480
1979 Baltimore	AL	159 606 179	30 2 25	(10 15)	288	90	99	72	9	78	2	1	6	10	2	.83	16	.295	.369	.475
1980 Baltimore	AL	158 621 186	36 2 32	(10 22)	322	100	116	54	10	71	2	0	6	7	2	.78	18	.300	.354	.519
1981 Baltimore	AL	99 378 111	21 2 **22**	(12 10)	202	57	**78**	40	10	43	1	0	3	2	3	.40	10	.294	.360	.534
1982 Baltimore	AL	151 550 174	30 1 32	(18 14)	302	87	110	70	**18**	82	1	0	6	7	2	.78	17	.316	.391	.549
1983 Baltimore	AL	156 582 178	30 3 33	(16 17)	313	115	111	86	13	90	3	0	9	5	1	.83	13	.306	.393	.538
1984 Baltimore	AL	**162** 588 180	26 3 29	(18 11)	299	97	110	**107**	**25**	87	2	0	8	10	2	.83	9	.306	**.410**	.509
1985 Baltimore	AL	156 583 173	37 1 31	(15 16)	305	111	124	84	12	68	2	0	8	5	2	.71	8	.297	.383	.523
1986 Baltimore	AL	137 495 151	25 1 17	(9 8)	229	61	84	78	7	49	0	0	5	3	0	1.00	17	.305	.396	.463
1987 Baltimore	AL	160 618 171	28 3 30	(14 16)	295	89	91	73	6	80	1	0	3	1	2	.33	15	.277	.352	.477
1988 Baltimore	AL	161 603 171	27 2 28	(14 14)	286	75	84	75	8	78	0	0	3	5	2	.71	20	.284	.361	.474
1989 Los Angeles	NL	160 594 147	29 1 20	(4 16)	238	66	88	87	24	85	2	0	7	7	2	.78	12	.247	.342	.401
1990 Los Angeles	NL	155 558 184	22 3 26	(12 14)	290	96	95	82	**21**	64	1	0	4	8	5	.62	19	.330	.414	.520
1991 Los Angeles	NL	153 576 150	23 1 19	(11 8)	232	69	96	55	17	74	0	0	8	10	3	.77	17	.260	.321	.403
1992 New York	NL	156 551 144	37 2 16	(7 9)	233	64	93	66	8	74	0	0	4	4	2	.67	15	.261	.336	.423
1993 New York	NL	154 610 174	28 1 27	(15 12)	285	77	100	40	6	61	0	0	9	2	2	.50	24	.285	.325	.467
1994 Cleveland	AL	108 433 110	21 1 17	(7 10)	184	57	76	31	6	53	0	0	3	8	4	.67	8	.254	.302	.425
1995 Cleveland	AL	113 436 141	21 0 21	(11 10)	225	68	82	39	5	65	0	0	5	5	1	.83	12	.323	.375	.516
1996 Cle-Bal	AL	152 566 147	21 1 22	(13 9)	236	69	79	61	6	87	0	0	10	4	0	1.00	19	.260	.327	.417
1996 Cleveland	AL	88 336 88	9 1 12	(7 5)	135	33	45	34	2	45	0	0	4	3	0	1.00	13	.262	.326	.402
Baltimore	AL	64 230 59	12 0 10	(6 4)	101	36	34	27	4	42	0	0	6	1	0	1.00	6	.257	.327	.439
20 ML YEARS		2971 11169 3218	553 35 501	(240 261)	5344	1614	1899	1318	222	1490	18	2	125	109	43	.72	306	.288	.361	.478

Glenn Murray

Bats: R **Throws:** R **Pos:** RF-24; PH-13; CF-2; LF-1 **Ht:** 6'2" **Wt:** 225 **Born:** 11/23/70 **Age:** 26

		BATTING												BASERUNNING				PERCENTAGES		
Year Team	Lg	G AB H	2B 3B HR	(Hm Rd)	TB	R	RBI	TBB	IBB	SO	HBP	SH	SF	SB	CS	SB%	GDP	Avg	OBP	SLG
1989 Expos	R	27 87 15	6 2 0	— —	25	10	7	6	0	30	2	0	1	8	1	.89	1	.172	.240	.287
Jamestown	A-	3 10 3	1 0 0	— —	4	1	1	1	0	1	0	0	0	0	0	.00	0	.300	.364	.400
1990 Jamestown	A-	53 165 37	8 4 1	— —	56	20	14	21	0	43	3	0	0	11	3	.79	3	.224	.323	.339
1991 Rockford	A	124 479 113	16 14 5	— —	172	73	60	77	3	137	2	0	8	22	19	.54	8	.236	.339	.359
1992 W. Palm Bch	A+	119 414 96	14 5 13	— —	159	79	41	75	3	150	4	2	1	26	11	.70	4	.232	.354	.384
1993 Harrisburg	AA	127 475 120	21 4 26	— —	227	82	96	56	1	111	8	0	5	16	7	.70	3	.253	.340	.478
1994 Pawtucket	AAA	130 465 104	17 1 25	— —	198	74	64	55	4	134	4	0	2	9	3	.75	10	.224	.310	.426
1995 Pawtucket	AAA	104 336 82	15 1 25	— —	172	66	66	34	1	109	11	1	5	5	6	.45	4	.244	.329	.512
1996 Scranton-WB	AAA	41 142 52	10 2 7	— —	87	31	22	22	0	29	1	0	1	7	0	1.00	1	.366	.452	.613
1996 Philadelphia	NL	38 97 19	3 0 2	(2 0)	28	8	6	7	0	36	1	0	0	1	1	.50	0	.196	.250	.289

Mike Mussina

Pitches: Right **Bats:** Right **Pos:** SP-36   **Ht:** 6'1" **Wt:** 180 **Born:** 12/8/68 **Age:** 28

Year Team	Lg	G	GS	CG	GF	IP	BFP	H	R	ER	HR	SH	SF	HB	TBB	IBB	SO	WP	Bk	W	L	Pct.	ShO	Sv-Op	Hld	ERA
1991 Baltimore	AL	12	12	2	0	87.2	349	77	31	28	7	3	2	1	21	0	52	3	1	4	5	.444	0	0-0	0	2.87
1992 Baltimore	AL	32	32	8	0	241	957	212	70	68	16	13	6	2	48	2	130	6	0	18	5	.783	4	0-0	0	2.54
1993 Baltimore	AL	25	25	3	0	167.2	693	163	84	83	20	6	4	3	44	2	117	5	0	14	6	.700	2	0-0	0	4.46
1994 Baltimore	AL	24	24	3	0	176.1	712	163	63	60	19	3	9	1	42	1	99	0	0	16	5	.762	0	0-0	0	3.06
1995 Baltimore	AL	32	32	7	0	221.2	882	187	86	81	24	2	2	1	50	4	158	2	0	19	9	.679	4	0-0	0	3.29
1996 Baltimore	AL	36	36	4	0	243.1	1039	264	137	130	31	4	4	3	69	0	204	3	0	19	11	.633	1	0-0	0	4.81
6 ML YEARS		161	161	27	0	1137.2	4632	1066	471	450	117	31	27	11	274	9	760	19	1	90	41	.687	11	0-0		3.56

Greg Myers

Bats: Left **Throws:** Right **Pos:** C-90; PH-16   **Ht:** 6'2" **Wt:** 215 **Born:** 4/14/66 **Age:** 31

Year Team	Lg	G	AB	H	2B	3B	HR	(Hm	Rd)	TB	R	RBI	TBB	IBB	SO	HBP	SH	SF	SB	CS	SB%	GDP	Avg	OBP	SLG
1987 Toronto	AL	7	9	1	0	0	0	(0	0)	1	1	0	0	0	3	0	0	0	0	0	.00	2	.111	.111	.111
1989 Toronto	AL	17	44	5	2	0	0	(0	0)	7	0	1	2	0	9	0	0	0	0	1	.00	2	.114	.152	.159
1990 Toronto	AL	87	250	59	7	1	5	(3	2)	83	33	22	22	0	33	0	1	4	0	1	.00	12	.236	.293	.332
1991 Toronto	AL	107	309	81	22	0	8	(5	3)	127	25	36	21	4	45	0	0	3	0	0	.00	13	.262	.306	.411
1992 Tor-Cal	AL	30	78	18	7	0	1	(0	1)	28	4	13	5	0	11	0	1	2	0	0	.00	2	.231	.271	.359
1993 California	AL	108	290	74	10	0	7	(4	3)	105	27	40	17	2	47	2	3	3	3	3	.50	8	.255	.298	.362
1994 California	AL	45	126	31	6	0	2	(1	1)	43	10	8	10	3	27	0	5	1	0	2	.00	3	.246	.299	.341
1995 California	AL	85	273	71	12	2	9	(6	3)	114	35	38	17	3	49	1	1	2	0	1	.00	4	.260	.304	.418
1996 Minnesota	AL	97	329	94	22	3	6	(3	3)	140	37	47	19	3	52	0	0	5	0	0	.00	11	.286	.320	.426
1992 Toronto	AL	22	61	14	6	0	1	(0	1)	23	4	13	5	0	5	0	0	2	0	0	.00	2	.230	.279	.377
California	AL	8	17	4	1	0	0	(0	0)	5	0	0	0	0	6	0	1	0	0	0	.00	0	.235	.235	.294
9 ML YEARS		583	1708	434	88	6	38	(22	16)	648	172	205	113	15	276	3	11	20	3	8	.27	57	.254	.298	.379

Jimmy Myers

Pitches: Right **Bats:** Right **Pos:** RP-11   **Ht:** 6'1" **Wt:** 190 **Born:** 4/28/69 **Age:** 28

Year Team	Lg	G	GS	CG	GF	IP	BFP	H	R	ER	HR	SH	SF	HB	TBB	IBB	SO	WP	Bk	W	L	Pct.	ShO	Sv-Op	Hld	ERA
1987 Pocatello	R+	10	2	0	4	19.2	92	29	21	19	1	1	1	1	16	1	12	5	2	0	2	.000	0	0--	—	8.69
1988 Pocatello	R+	12	12	0	0	58.1	283	72	50	35	3	1	5	1	32	1	39	7	1	4	5	.444	0	0--	—	5.40
1989 Clinton	A	32	21	0	5	137.2	592	139	71	57	6	8	5	9	58	5	63	11	0	4	12	.250	0	0--	—	3.73
1990 San Jose	A+	60	0	0	50	84	361	80	44	30	2	3	3	2	34	6	61	3	1	5	8	.385	0	25--	—	3.21
1991 Shreveport	AA	62	0	0	55	76.1	325	71	22	21	2	6	0	2	30	5	51	4	0	6	4	.600	0	24--	—	2.48
1992 Phoenix	AAA	25	0	0	19	23.2	114	32	20	15	1	2	1	0	13	5	11	0	0	0	6	.000	0	10--	—	5.70
Shreveport	AA	33	0	0	32	32	141	39	17	17	0	2	2	2	10	1	15	1	0	2	4	.333	0	18--	—	4.78
1993 Shreveport	AA	29	0	0	14	49.1	210	50	14	11	1	2	0	2	19	3	23	4	0	2	2	.500	0	1--	—	2.01
Phoenix	AAA	31	3	0	5	58.2	259	69	35	24	2	3	0	3	22	2	20	5	0	2	5	.286	0	0--	—	3.68
1994 Memphis	AA	33	2	0	12	64.1	286	68	38	35	3	7	2	4	32	4	35	7	1	4	4	.500	0	3--	—	4.90
1995 Rochester	AAA	55	0	0	28	64.2	289	72	28	22	2	3	2	1	29	1	31	1	0	4	4	.500	0	6--	—	3.06
1996 Rochester	AAA	39	0	0	35	53	220	53	19	17	1	8	0	2	12	4	21	5	0	7	5	.583	0	12--	—	2.89
1996 Baltimore	AL	11	0	0	5	14	64	18	13	11	4	0	2	0	3	1	6	1	0	0	0	.000	0	0-0	1	7.07

Mike Myers

Pitches: Left **Bats:** Left **Pos:** RP-83   **Ht:** 6'4" **Wt:** 197 **Born:** 6/26/69 **Age:** 28

Year Team	Lg	G	GS	CG	GF	IP	BFP	H	R	ER	HR	SH	SF	HB	TBB	IBB	SO	WP	Bk	W	L	Pct.	ShO	Sv-Op	Hld	ERA
1990 Everett	A-	15	14	1	0	85.1	374	91	43	37	9	1	0	5	30	0	73	7	0	4	5	.444	0	0--	—	3.90
1991 Clinton	A	11	11	1	0	65.1	263	61	23	19	3	2	2	0	18	0	59	4	3	5	3	.625	0	0--	—	2.62
Giants	R	1	0	0	0	3	16	5	5	4	0	0	0	0	2	0	2	0	0	0	1	.000	0	0--	—	12.00
1992 Clinton	A	7	7	0	0	37.2	147	28	11	5	0	1	1	2	8	0	32	4	0	1	2	.333	0	0--	—	1.19
San Jose	A+	8	8	0	0	54.2	215	43	20	14	1	1	0	2	17	0	40	3	1	5	1	.833	0	0--	—	2.30
1993 Edmonton	AAA	27	27	3	0	161.2	733	195	109	94	20	5	7	10	52	1	112	7	1	7	14	.333	0	0--	—	5.23
1994 Brevard Cty	A+	3	2	0	0	11.1	43	7	1	1	1	1	0	0	4	0	15	0	0	0	0	.000	0	0--	—	0.79
Edmonton	AAA	12	11	0	0	60	282	78	42	37	9	1	3	3	21	0	55	3	0	1	5	.167	0	0--	—	5.55
1995 Toledo	AAA	43	0	0	14	45	197	47	29	27	7	2	0	1	18	1	32	5	0	0	5	.000	0	0--	—	5.40
Charlotte	AAA	43	0	0	14	45	197	47	29	27	7	2	0	1	18	1	32	5	0	0	5	.000	0	0--	—	5.40
1995 Fla-Det		13	0	0	5	8.1	42	11	7	7	1	0	1	2	7	0	4	2	0	1	0	1.000	0	0-1	1	7.56
1996 Detroit	AL	83	0	0	25	64.2	298	70	41	36	6	2	1	4	34	8	69	2	0	1	5	.167	0	6-8	17	5.01
1995 Florida	NL	2	0	0	2	2	9	1	0	0	0	0	0	0	3	0	0	0	0	0	0	.000	0	0-0	0	0.00
Detroit	AL	11	0	0	3	6.1	33	10	7	7	1	0	1	2	4	0	4	0	0	1	0	1.000	0	0-1	1	9.95
2 ML YEARS		96	0	0	30	73	340	81	48	43	7	2	2	6	41	8	73	2	0	2	5	.286	0	6-9	18	5.30

Randy Myers

Pitches: Left **Bats:** Left **Pos:** RP-62   **Ht:** 6'1" **Wt:** 225 **Born:** 9/19/62 **Age:** 34

		HOW MUCH HE PITCHED						WHAT HE GAVE UP											THE RESULTS					
Year Team	Lg	G	GS	CG	GF	IP	BFP	H	R	ER	HR	SH	SF	HB	TBB	IBB	SO	WP	Bk	W	L	Pct.	ShO	Sv-Op	Hld	ERA
1985 New York	NL	1	0	0	1	2	7	0	0	0	0	0	0	0	1	0	2	0	0	0	0	.000	0	0--	—	0.00
1986 New York	NL	10	0	0	5	10.2	53	11	5	5	1	0	0	1	9	1	13	0	0	0	0	.000	0	0--	—	4.22
1987 New York	NL	54	0	0	18	75	314	61	36	33	6	7	6	0	30	5	92	3	0	3	6	.333	0	6-9	7	3.96
1988 New York	NL	55	0	0	44	68	261	45	15	13	5	3	2	2	17	2	69	2	0	7	3	.700	0	26-29	1	1.72
1989 New York	NL	65	0	0	47	84.1	349	62	23	22	4	6	2	0	40	4	88	3	0	7	4	.636	0	24-29	2	2.35
1990 Cincinnati	NL	66	0	0	59	86.2	353	59	24	20	6	4	3	2	38	8	98	2	1	4	6	.400	0	31-37	0	2.08
1991 Cincinnati	NL	58	12	1	18	132	575	116	61	52	8	8	6	1	80	5	108	2	1	6	13	.316	0	6-10	8	3.55
1992 San Diego	NL	66	0	0	57	79.2	348	84	38	38	7	7	5	1	34	3	66	5	0	3	6	.333	0	38-46	2	4.29
1993 Chicago	NL	73	0	0	69	75.1	313	65	26	26	7	1	2	1	26	2	86	3	0	2	4	.333	0	53-59	0	3.11
1994 Chicago	NL	38	0	0	34	40.1	174	40	18	17	3	3	1	0	16	1	32	2	0	1	5	.167	0	21-26	0	3.79
1995 Chicago	NL	57	0	0	47	55.2	240	49	25	24	7	2	3	0	28	1	59	0	0	1	2	.333	0	38-44	0	3.88
1996 Baltimore	AL	62	0	0	50	58.2	262	60	24	23	7	3	3	1	29	4	74	3	0	4	4	.500	0	31-38	2	3.53
12 ML YEARS		605	12	1	449	768.1	3249	652	295	273	61	44	32	10	348	36	787	25	2	38	53	.418	0	274--	—	3.20

Rod Myers

Bats: L **Throws:** L **Pos:** CF-15; PH-5; LF-4; RF-1   **Ht:** 6'0" **Wt:** 190 **Born:** 1/14/73 **Age:** 24

		BATTING														BASERUNNING				PERCENTAGES		
Year Team	Lg	G	AB	H	2B	3B	HR	(Hm	Rd)	TB	R	RBI	TBB	IBB	SO	HBP	SH	SF	SB	CS	SB%	GDP	Avg	OBP	SLG
1991 Royals	R	44	133	37	2	3	1	—	—	48	14	18	6	1	27	5	0	1	12	2	.86	1	.278	.331	.361
Baseball Cy	A+	4	11	2	0	0	0	—	—	2	1	0	0	0	5	0	0	0	1	1	.50	1	.182	.182	.182
1992 Appleton	A	71	218	48	10	2	4	—	—	74	31	30	39	1	67	2	4	4	25	6	.81	3	.220	.338	.339
1993 Rockford	A	129	474	123	24	5	9	—	—	184	69	68	58	6	117	5	6	4	49	16	.75	7	.259	.344	.388
1994 Wilmington	A+	126	457	120	20	4	12	—	—	184	76	65	67	3	93	6	12	1	31	11	.74	4	.263	.363	.403
1995 Wichita	AA	131	499	153	22	6	7	—	—	208	71	62	34	3	77	4	8	3	29	16	.64	7	.307	.354	.417
1996 Omaha	AAA	112	411	120	27	1	16	—	—	197	68	54	49	6	106	9	9	3	37	8	.82	6	.292	.377	.479
1996 Kansas City	AL	22	63	18	7	0	1	(1	0)	28	9	11	7	0	16	0	0	0	3	2	.60	1	.286	.357	.444

Rodney Myers

Pitches: Right **Bats:** Right **Pos:** RP-45   **Ht:** 6'1" **Wt:** 200 **Born:** 6/26/69 **Age:** 28

		HOW MUCH HE PITCHED						WHAT HE GAVE UP											THE RESULTS					
Year Team	Lg	G	GS	CG	GF	IP	BFP	H	R	ER	HR	SH	SF	HB	TBB	IBB	SO	WP	Bk	W	L	Pct.	ShO	Sv-Op	Hld	ERA
1990 Eugene	A-	6	4	0	0	22.2	98	19	9	3	2	0	1	0	13	0	17	1	1	0	2	.000	0	0--	—	1.19
1991 Appleton	A	9	4	0	0	27.2	127	22	9	8	0	1	1	1	26	0	29	1	1	1	1	.500	0	0--	—	2.60
1992 Lethbridge	R+	15	15	5	0	103.1	452	93	57	46	3	4	2	5	61	1	76	14	2	5	8	.385	0	0--	—	4.01
1993 Rockford	A	12	12	5	0	85.1	322	65	22	17	3	2	2	1	18	0	65	3	1	7	3	.700	2	0--	—	1.79
Memphis	AA	12	12	1	0	65.2	294	73	46	41	8	2	2	10	32	0	42	3	3	3	6	.333	1	0--	—	5.62
1994 Wilmington	A+	4	0	0	2	9.1	37	9	6	5	1	0	0	0	1	0	9	1	0	1	1	.500	0	1--	—	4.82
Memphis	AA	42	0	0	30	69.2	284	45	20	8	3	2	4	5	29	2	53	3	0	5	1	.833	0	9--	—	1.03
1995 Omaha	AAA	38	0	0	17	48.1	212	52	26	22	5	2	3	0	19	1	38	1	1	4	5	.444	0	2--	—	4.10
1996 Chicago	NL	45	0	0	8	67.1	298	61	38	35	6	1	5	3	38	3	50	4	1	2	1	.667	0	0-0	1	4.68

Tim Naehring

Bats: Right **Throws:** Right **Pos:** 3B-116; PH-3; 2B-1   **Ht:** 6'2" **Wt:** 203 **Born:** 2/1/67 **Age:** 30

		BATTING														BASERUNNING				PERCENTAGES		
Year Team	Lg	G	AB	H	2B	3B	HR	(Hm	Rd)	TB	R	RBI	TBB	IBB	SO	HBP	SH	SF	SB	CS	SB%	GDP	Avg	OBP	SLG
1996 Trenton *	AA	3	9	2	1	0	1	—	—	6	2	2	1	0	3	0	0	0	0	0	.00	1	.222	.300	.667
1990 Boston	AL	24	85	23	6	0	2	(2	0)	35	10	12	8	1	15	0	0	0	0	0	.00	2	.271	.333	.412
1991 Boston	AL	20	55	6	1	0	0	(0	0)	7	1	3	6	0	15	0	4	0	0	0	.00	0	.109	.197	.127
1992 Boston	AL	72	186	43	8	0	3	(0	3)	60	12	14	18	0	31	3	6	1	0	0	.00	1	.231	.308	.323
1993 Boston	AL	39	127	42	10	0	1	(0	1)	55	14	17	10	0	26	0	3	1	1	0	1.00	3	.331	.377	.433
1994 Boston	AL	80	297	82	18	1	7	(4	3)	123	41	42	30	1	56	4	7	1	1	3	.25	11	.276	.349	.414
1995 Boston	AL	126	433	133	27	2	10	(5	5)	194	61	57	77	5	66	4	4	2	0	2	.00	16	.307	.415	.448
1996 Boston	AL	116	430	124	16	0	17	(9	8)	191	77	65	49	4	63	4	2	4	2	1	.67	14	.288	.363	.444
7 ML YEARS		477	1613	453	86	3	40	(20	20)	665	216	210	198	11	272	15	26	9	4	6	.40	47	.281	.363	.412

Charles Nagy

Pitches: Right **Bats:** Left **Pos:** SP-32   **Ht:** 6'3" **Wt:** 200 **Born:** 5/5/67 **Age:** 30

		HOW MUCH HE PITCHED						WHAT HE GAVE UP											THE RESULTS					
Year Team	Lg	G	GS	CG	GF	IP	BFP	H	R	ER	HR	SH	SF	HB	TBB	IBB	SO	WP	Bk	W	L	Pct.	ShO	Sv-Op	Hld	ERA
1990 Cleveland	AL	9	8	0	1	45.2	208	58	31	30	7	1	1	1	21	1	26	1	1	2	4	.333	0	0-0	0	5.91
1991 Cleveland	AL	33	33	6	0	211.1	914	228	103	97	15	5	9	6	66	7	109	6	2	10	15	.400	1	0-0	0	4.13
1992 Cleveland	AL	33	33	10	0	252	1018	245	91	83	11	6	9	6	57	1	169	7	0	17	10	.630	3	0-0	0	2.96
1993 Cleveland	AL	9	9	1	0	48.2	223	66	38	34	6	2	1	2	13	1	30	2	0	2	6	.250	0	0-0	0	6.29
1994 Cleveland	AL	23	23	3	0	169.1	717	175	76	65	15	2	2	5	48	1	108	5	1	10	8	.556	0	0-0	0	3.45
1995 Cleveland	AL	29	29	2	0	178	771	194	95	90	20	2	5	6	61	0	139	2	0	16	6	.727	1	0-0	0	4.55
1996 Cleveland	AL	32	32	5	0	222	921	217	89	84	21	2	4	3	61	2	167	7	0	17	5	.773	0	0-0	0	3.41

		HOW MUCH HE PITCHED					WHAT HE GAVE UP												THE RESULTS						
Year Team	Lg	G	GS	CG	GF	IP	BFP	H	R	ER	HR	SH	SF	HB	TBB	IBB	SO	WP	Bk	W	L	Pct.	ShO	Sv-Op	Hld	ERA
7 ML YEARS		168	167	27	1	1127	4772	1183	523	483	95	20	31	25	327	13	748	30	4	74	54	.578	5	0-0	0	3.86

Bob Natal

Bats: Right **Throws:** Right **Pos:** C-43; PH-1   **Ht:** 5'11" **Wt:** 190 **Born:** 11/13/65 **Age:** 31

		BATTING														BASERUNNING				PERCENTAGES		
Year Team	Lg	G	AB	H	2B	3B	HR	(Hm | Rd)	TB	R	RBI	TBB	IBB	SO	HBP	SH	SF	SB	CS	SB%	GDP	Avg	OBP	SLG
1992 Montreal	NL	5	6	0	0	0	0	(0 | 0)	0	0	0	1	0	1	0	0	0	0	0	.00	1	.000	.143	.000
1993 Florida	NL	41	117	25	4	1	1	(0 | 1)	34	3	6	6	0	22	4	3	1	1	0	1.00	6	.214	.273	.291
1994 Florida	NL	10	29	8	2	0	0	(0 | 0)	10	2	2	5	0	5	0	0	0	1	0	1.00	1	.276	.382	.345
1995 Florida	NL	16	43	10	2	1	2	(2 | 0)	20	2	6	1	0	9	0	1	1	0	0	.00	0	.233	.244	.465
1996 Florida	NL	44	90	12	1	1	0	(0 | 0)	15	4	2	15	5	31	0	0	0	0	1	.00	3	.133	.257	.167
5 ML YEARS		116	285	55	9	3	3	(2 | 1)	79	11	16	28	5	68	4	4	2	2	1	.67	11	.193	.273	.277

Dan Naulty

Pitches: Right **Bats:** Right **Pos:** RP-49   **Ht:** 6'6" **Wt:** 211 **Born:** 1/6/70 **Age:** 27

		HOW MUCH HE PITCHED						WHAT HE GAVE UP												THE RESULTS						
Year Team	Lg	G	GS	CG	GF	IP	BFP	H	R	ER	HR	SH	SF	HB	TBB	IBB	SO	WP	Bk	W	L	Pct.	ShO	Sv-Op	Hld	ERA
1992 Kenosha	A	6	2	0	1	18	83	22	12	11	3	1	0	1	7	0	14	1	1	0	1	.000	0	0--	—	5.50
1993 Fort Myers	A+	7	6	0	0	30	148	41	22	19	4	1	1	6	14	1	20	3	0	0	3	.000	0	0--	—	5.70
Fort Wayne	A	18	18	3	0	116	478	101	45	42	5	3	1	2	48	0	96	7	5	8	4	.429	2	0--	—	3.26
1994 Fort Myers	A+	16	15	1	1	88.1	380	78	35	29	6	1	5	3	32	2	83	5	0	8	4	.667	0	0--	—	2.95
Nashville	AA	9	9	0	0	47.1	208	48	32	31	4	2	5	1	22	1	29	3	0	0	7	.000	0	0--	—	5.89
1995 Salt Lake	AAA	42	8	0	19	90.1	393	92	55	52	10	2	1	2	47	2	76	6	0	2	6	.250	0	4--	—	5.18
1996 Minnesota	AL	49	0	0	15	57	245	43	26	24	5	2	0	0	35	3	56	2	0	3	2	.600	0	4-9	4	3.79

Jaime Navarro

Pitches: Right **Bats:** Right **Pos:** SP-35   **Ht:** 6'4" **Wt:** 230 **Born:** 3/27/68 **Age:** 29

		HOW MUCH HE PITCHED						WHAT HE GAVE UP												THE RESULTS						
Year Team	Lg	G	GS	CG	GF	IP	BFP	H	R	ER	HR	SH	SF	HB	TBB	IBB	SO	WP	Bk	W	L	Pct.	ShO	Sv-Op	Hld	ERA
1989 Milwaukee	AL	19	17	1	1	109.2	470	119	47	38	6	5	2	1	32	3	56	3	0	7	8	.467	0	0-0	0	3.12
1990 Milwaukee	AL	32	22	3	2	149.1	654	176	83	74	11	4	5	4	41	3	75	6	5	8	7	.533	0	1-2	3	4.46
1991 Milwaukee	AL	34	34	10	0	234	1002	237	117	102	18	7	8	6	73	3	114	10	0	15	12	.556	2	0-0	0	3.92
1992 Milwaukee	AL	34	34	5	0	246	1004	224	98	91	14	9	13	6	64	4	100	6	0	17	11	.607	3	0-0	0	3.33
1993 Milwaukee	AL	35	34	5	0	214.1	955	254	135	127	21	6	17	11	73	4	114	11	0	11	12	.478	1	0-0	0	5.33
1994 Milwaukee	AL	29	10	0	2	89.2	411	115	71	66	10	2	4	4	35	4	65	3	0	4	9	.308	0	0-0	0	6.62
1995 Chicago	NL	29	29	1	0	200.1	837	194	79	73	19	2	3	3	56	7	128	1	0	14	6	.700	1	0-0	0	3.28
1996 Chicago	NL	35	35	4	0	236.2	1007	244	116	103	25	10	7	10	72	5	158	10	0	15	12	.556	1	0-0	0	3.92
8 ML YEARS		247	215	29	10	1480	6340	1563	746	674	124	45	59	45	446	33	810	50	5	91	77	.542	8	1-2	3	4.10

Denny Neagle

Pitches: Left **Bats:** Left **Pos:** SP-33   **Ht:** 6'2" **Wt:** 216 **Born:** 9/13/68 **Age:** 28

		HOW MUCH HE PITCHED						WHAT HE GAVE UP												THE RESULTS						
Year Team	Lg	G	GS	CG	GF	IP	BFP	H	R	ER	HR	SH	SF	HB	TBB	IBB	SO	WP	Bk	W	L	Pct.	ShO	Sv-Op	Hld	ERA
1991 Minnesota	AL	7	3	0	2	20	92	28	9	9	3	0	0	0	7	2	14	1	0	0	1	.000	0	0-0	0	4.05
1992 Pittsburgh	NL	55	6	0	8	86.1	380	81	46	43	9	4	3	2	43	8	77	3	2	4	6	.400	0	2-4	5	4.48
1993 Pittsburgh	NL	50	7	0	13	81.1	360	82	49	48	10	1	1	3	37	3	73	5	0	3	5	.375	0	1-1	6	5.31
1994 Pittsburgh	NL	24	24	2	0	137	587	135	80	78	18	7	6	3	49	3	122	2	0	9	10	.474	0	0-0	0	5.12
1995 Pittsburgh	NL	31	31	5	0	209.2	876	221	91	80	20	13	6	3	45	3	150	6	0	13	8	.619	1	0-0	0	3.43
1996 Pit-Atl	NL	33	33	2	0	221.1	910	226	93	86	26	10	4	3	48	2	149	3	1	16	9	.640	0	0-0	0	3.50
1996 Pittsburgh	NL	27	27	1	0	182.2	745	186	67	62	21	9	3	3	34	2	131	2	1	14	6	.700	0	0-0	0	3.05
Atlanta	NL	6	6	1	0	38.2	165	40	26	24	5	1	1	0	14	0	18	1	0	2	3	.400	0	0-0	0	5.59
6 ML YEARS		200	104	9	23	755.2	3205	773	368	344	86	35	20	14	229	21	585	20	3	45	39	.536	1	3-5	11	4.10

Jeff Nelson

Pitches: Right **Bats:** Right **Pos:** RP-73   **Ht:** 6'8" **Wt:** 235 **Born:** 11/17/66 **Age:** 30

		HOW MUCH HE PITCHED						WHAT HE GAVE UP												THE RESULTS						
Year Team	Lg	G	GS	CG	GF	IP	BFP	H	R	ER	HR	SH	SF	HB	TBB	IBB	SO	WP	Bk	W	L	Pct.	ShO	Sv-Op	Hld	ERA
1992 Seattle	AL	66	0	0	27	81	352	71	34	31	7	9	3	6	44	12	46	2	0	1	7	.125	0	6-14	6	3.44
1993 Seattle	AL	71	0	0	13	60	269	57	30	29	5	2	4	8	34	10	61	2	0	5	3	.625	0	1-11	17	4.35
1994 Seattle	AL	28	0	0	7	42.1	185	35	18	13	3	1	1	8	20	4	44	2	0	0	0	.000	0	0-0	2	2.76
1995 Seattle	AL	62	0	0	24	78.2	318	58	21	19	4	5	3	6	27	5	96	1	0	7	3	.700	0	2-4	14	2.17
1996 New York	AL	73	0	0	27	74.1	328	75	38	36	6	3	1	2	36	1	91	4	0	4	4	.500	0	2-4	10	4.36
5 ML YEARS		300	0	0	98	336.1	1452	296	141	128	25	20	12	30	161	32	338	11	0	17	17	.500	0	11-33	49	3.43

Robb Nen

Pitches: Right **Bats:** Right **Pos:** RP-75 **Ht:** 6'4" **Wt:** 190 **Born:** 11/28/69 **Age:** 27

Year Team	Lg	G	GS	CG	GF	IP	BFP	H	R	ER	HR	SH	SF	HB	TBB	IBB	SO	WP	Bk	W	L	Pct.	ShO	Sv-Op	Hld	ERA
1993 Tex-Fla		24	4	0	5	56	272	63	45	42	6	1	2	0	46	0	39	6	1	2	1	.667	0	0-0	0	6.75
1994 Florida	NL	44	0	0	28	58	228	46	20	19	6	3	1	0	17	2	60	3	2	5	5	.500	0	15-15	1	2.95
1995 Florida	NL	62	0	0	**54**	65.2	279	62	26	24	6	0	1	1	23	3	68	2	0	0	7	.000	0	23-29	0	3.29
1996 Florida	NL	75	0	0	66	83	326	67	21	18	2	5	1	1	21	6	92	4	0	5	1	.833	0	35-42	0	1.95
1993 Texas	AL	9	3	0	3	22.2	113	28	17	16	1	0	1	0	26	0	12	2	1	1	1	.500	0	0-0	0	6.35
Florida	NL	15	1	0	2	33.1	159	35	28	26	1	1	0	0	20	0	27	4	0	1	0	1.000	0	0-0	0	7.02
4 ML YEARS		205	4	0	153	262.2	1105	238	112	103	20	9	5	2	107	11	259	15	3	12	14	.462	0	73-86	1	3.53

Phil Nevin

Bats: R **Throws:** R **Pos:** 3B-24; LF-9; C-4; PH-2; DH-1 **Ht:** 6'2" **Wt:** 210 **Born:** 1/19/71 **Age:** 26

Year Team	Lg	G	AB	H	2B	3B	HR	(Hm	Rd)	TB	R	RBI	TBB	IBB	SO	HBP	SH	SF	SB	CS	SB%	GDP	Avg	OBP	SLG
1993 Tucson	AAA	123	448	128	21	3	10	—	—	185	67	93	52	1	99	3	0	7	8	1	.89	12	.286	.359	.413
1994 Tucson	AAA	118	445	117	20	1	12	—	—	175	67	79	55	2	101	1	0	4	3	2	.60	21	.263	.343	.393
1995 Tucson	AAA	62	223	65	16	0	7	—	—	102	31	41	27	1	39	1	1	0	2	3	.40	9	.291	.371	.457
Toledo	AAA	7	23	7	2	0	1	—	—	12	3	3	1	0	5	0	0	0	0	0	.00	2	.304	.333	.522
1996 Jacksonville	AA	98	344	101	18	1	24	—	—	193	77	69	60	4	83	3	0	6	6	2	.75	9	.294	.397	.561
1995 Hou-Det		47	156	28	4	1	2	(2	0)	40	13	13	18	1	40	4	1	0	1	0	1.00	5	.179	.281	.256
1996 Detroit	AL	38	120	35	5	0	8	(3	5)	64	15	19	8	0	39	1	0	1	1	0	1.00	1	.292	.338	.533
1995 Houston	NL	18	60	7	1	0	0	(0	0)	8	4	1	7	1	13	1	1	0	1	0	1.00	2	.117	.221	.133
Detroit	AL	29	96	21	3	1	2	(2	0)	32	9	12	11	0	27	3	0	0	0	0	.00	3	.219	.318	.333
2 ML YEARS		85	276	63	9	1	10	(5	5)	104	28	32	26	1	79	5	1	1	2	0	1.00	6	.228	.305	.377

Marc Newfield

Bats: R **Throws:** R **Pos:** LF-79; PH-37; RF-23; 1B-2 **Ht:** 6'4" **Wt:** 205 **Born:** 10/19/72 **Age:** 24

Year Team	Lg	G	AB	H	2B	3B	HR	(Hm	Rd)	TB	R	RBI	TBB	IBB	SO	HBP	SH	SF	SB	CS	SB%	GDP	Avg	OBP	SLG
1993 Seattle	AL	22	66	15	3	0	1	(1	0)	21	5	7	2	0	8	1	0	1	0	1	.00	2	.227	.257	.318
1994 Seattle	AL	12	38	7	1	0	1	(0	1)	11	3	4	2	0	4	0	0	0	0	0	.00	0	.184	.225	.289
1995 Sea-SD		45	140	33	8	1	4	(1	3)	55	13	21	5	1	24	1	0	0	0	0	.00	5	.236	.267	.393
1996 SD-Mil		133	370	103	26	0	12	(5	7)	165	46	57	27	2	70	6	0	7	1	2	.33	8	.278	.332	.446
1995 Seattle	AL	24	85	16	3	0	3	(0	3)	28	7	14	3	1	16	1	0	0	0	0	.00	3	.188	.225	.329
San Diego	NL	21	55	17	5	1	1	(1	0)	27	6	7	2	0	8	0	0	0	0	0	.00	2	.309	.333	.491
1996 San Diego	NL	84	191	48	11	0	5	(1	4)	74	27	26	16	1	44	2	0	3	1	1	.50	7	.251	.311	.387
Milwaukee	AL	49	179	55	15	0	7	(4	3)	91	21	31	11	1	26	4	0	4	0	1	.00	1	.307	.354	.508
4 ML YEARS		212	614	158	38	1	18	(7	11)	252	69	89	36	3	106	8	0	8	1	3	.25	17	.257	.303	.410

Warren Newson

Bats: L **Throws:** L **Pos:** RF-58; PH-23; DH-8; LF-8 **Ht:** 5'7" **Wt:** 202 **Born:** 7/3/64 **Age:** 32

Year Team	Lg	G	AB	H	2B	3B	HR	(Hm	Rd)	TB	R	RBI	TBB	IBB	SO	HBP	SH	SF	SB	CS	SB%	GDP	Avg	OBP	SLG
1991 Chicago	AL	71	132	39	5	0	4	(1	3)	56	20	25	28	1	34	0	0	0	2	2	.50	4	.295	.419	.424
1992 Chicago	AL	63	136	30	3	0	1	(1	0)	36	19	11	37	2	38	0	0	0	3	0	1.00	4	.221	.387	.265
1993 Chicago	AL	26	40	12	0	0	2	(2	0)	18	9	6	9	1	12	0	0	0	0	0	.00	2	.300	.429	.450
1994 Chicago	AL	63	102	26	5	0	2	(2	0)	37	16	7	14	1	23	0	2	0	1	0	1.00	3	.255	.345	.363
1995 ChA-Sea	AL	84	157	41	2	2	5	(4	1)	62	34	15	39	0	45	1	0	0	2	1	.67	3	.261	.411	.395
1996 Texas	AL	91	235	60	14	1	10	(6	4)	106	34	31	37	1	82	0	0	1	3	0	1.00	3	.255	.355	.451
1995 Chicago	AL	51	85	20	0	2	3	(3	0)	33	19	9	23	0	27	1	0	0	1	1	.50	2	.235	.404	.388
Seattle	AL	33	72	21	2	0	2	(1	1)	29	15	6	16	0	18	0	0	0	1	0	1.00	1	.292	.420	.403
6 ML YEARS		398	802	208	29	3	24	(15	9)	315	132	95	164	6	234	1	2	1	11	3	.79	19	.259	.385	.393

Dave Nied

Pitches: Right **Bats:** Right **Pos:** RP-5; SP-1 **Ht:** 6'2" **Wt:** 185 **Born:** 12/22/68 **Age:** 28

Year Team	Lg	G	GS	CG	GF	IP	BFP	H	R	ER	HR	SH	SF	HB	TBB	IBB	SO	WP	Bk	W	L	Pct.	ShO	Sv-Op	Hld	ERA
1996 Colo. Sprng *	AAA	16	16	0	0	62.1	334	116	92	85	16	1	3	8	32	0	53	1	0	3	8	.273	0	0--	—	12.27
Salem *	A+	7	6	1	1	42.2	183	37	25	14	3	1	1	1	18	0	42	3	0	3	3	.500	0	0--	—	2.95
1992 Atlanta	NL	6	2	0	0	23	83	10	3	3	0	1	0	0	5	0	19	0	0	3	0	1.000	0	0-0	0	1.17
1993 Colorado	NL	16	16	1	0	87	394	99	53	50	8	9	7	1	42	4	46	1	1	5	9	.357	0	0-0	0	5.17
1994 Colorado	NL	22	22	2	0	122	538	137	70	65	15	7	3	4	47	5	74	7	2	9	7	.563	1	0-0	0	4.80
1995 Colorado	NL	2	0	0	0	4.1	27	11	10	10	2	0	0	0	3	0	3	0	0	0	0	.000	0	0-0	0	20.77
1996 Colorado	NL	6	1	0	3	5.1	29	5	8	8	1	0	1	0	8	0	4	0	0	0	2	.000	0	0-0	0	13.50
5 ML YEARS		52	41	3	3	241.2	1071	262	144	136	26	17	11	5	105	9	146	8	3	17	18	.486	1	0-0	0	5.06

Melvin Nieves

Bats: B **Throws:** R **Pos:** RF-84; LF-21; DH-11; PH-5   **Ht:** 6'2"   **Wt:** 210   **Born:** 12/28/71   **Age:** 25

Year Team	Lg	G	AB	H	2B	3B	HR	(Hm	Rd)	TB	R	RBI	TBB	IBB	SO	HBP	SH	SF	SB	CS	SB%	GDP	Avg	OBP	SLG
1992 Atlanta	NL	12	19	4	1	0	0	(0	0)	5	0	1	2	0	7	0	0	0	0	0	.00	0	.211	.286	.263
1993 San Diego	NL	19	47	9	0	0	2	(2	0)	15	4	3	3	0	21	1	0	0	0	0	.00	0	.191	.255	.319
1994 San Diego	NL	10	19	5	1	0	1	(0	1)	9	2	4	3	0	10	0	0	0	0	0	.00	0	.263	.364	.474
1995 San Diego	NL	98	234	48	6	1	14	(5	9)	98	32	38	19	0	88	5	1	3	2	3	.40	9	.205	.276	.419
1996 Detroit	AL	120	431	106	23	4	24	(10	14)	209	71	60	44	2	158	6	0	3	1	2	.33	10	.246	.322	.485
5 ML YEARS		259	750	172	31	5	41	(17	24)	336	109	106	71	2	284	12	1	6	3	5	.38	19	.229	.304	.448

Dave Nilsson

Bats: L **Throws:** R **Pos:** RF-55; DH-40; 1B-24; LF-6; PH-6; C-2   **Ht:** 6'3"   **Wt:** 231   **Born:** 12/14/69   **Age:** 27

Year Team	Lg	G	AB	H	2B	3B	HR	(Hm	Rd)	TB	R	RBI	TBB	IBB	SO	HBP	SH	SF	SB	CS	SB%	GDP	Avg	OBP	SLG
1996 New Orleans *	AAA	7	26	7	1	0	1	—	—	11	3	2	4	0	3	0	0	0	0	0	.00	0	.269	.367	.423
1992 Milwaukee	AL	51	164	38	8	0	4	(1	3)	58	15	25	17	1	18	0	2	0	2	2	.50	1	.232	.304	.354
1993 Milwaukee	AL	100	296	76	10	2	7	(5	2)	111	35	40	37	5	36	0	4	3	3	6	.33	10	.257	.336	.375
1994 Milwaukee	AL	109	397	109	28	3	12	(4	8)	179	51	69	34	9	61	0	1	8	1	0	1.00	7	.275	.326	.451
1995 Milwaukee	AL	81	263	73	12	1	12	(7	5)	123	41	53	24	4	41	2	0	5	2	0	1.00	9	.278	.337	.468
1996 Milwaukee	AL	123	453	150	33	2	17	(3	14)	238	81	84	57	6	68	3	0	3	2	3	.40	4	.331	.407	.525
5 ML YEARS		464	1573	446	91	8	52	(20	32)	709	223	271	169	25	224	5	7	19	10	11	.48	31	.284	.351	.451

C.J. Nitkowski

Pitches: Left   **Bats:** Left   **Pos:** SP-8; RP-3   **Ht:** 6'3"   **Wt:** 190   **Born:** 3/3/73   **Age:** 24

Year Team	Lg	G	GS	CG	GF	IP	BFP	H	R	ER	HR	SH	SF	HB	TBB	IBB	SO	WP	Bk	W	L	Pct.	ShO	Sv-Op	Hld	ERA
1994 Chattanooga	AA	14	14	0	0	74.2	318	61	30	29	4	5	0	4	40	0	60	2	5	6	3	.667	0	0--	—	3.50
1995 Indianapolis	AAA	6	6	0	0	27.2	120	28	16	16	3	0	2	1	10	0	21	0	1	0	2	.000	0	0--	—	5.20
Chattanooga	AA	14	14	0	0	78	324	67	36	30	4	3	2	2	30	0	73	1	2	4	4	.500	0	0--	—	3.46
1996 Toledo	AAA	19	19	1	0	111	471	104	60	55	13	4	1	3	53	1	103	6	1	4	6	.400	0	0--	—	4.46
1995 Cin-Det		20	18	0	0	71.2	338	94	57	53	11	2	4	5	35	3	31	2	2	2	7	.222	0	0-1	0	6.66
1996 Detroit	AL	11	8	0	0	45.2	234	62	44	41	7	0	2	7	38	1	36	2	0	2	3	.400	0	0-0	0	8.08
1995 Cincinnati	NL	9	7	0	0	32.1	154	41	25	22	4	2	1	2	15	1	18	1	2	1	3	.250	0	0-1	0	6.12
Detroit	AL	11	11	0	0	39.1	184	53	32	31	7	0	3	3	20	2	13	1	0	1	4	.200	0	0-0	0	7.09
2 ML YEARS		31	26	0	0	117.1	572	156	101	94	18	2	6	12	73	4	67	4	2	4	10	.286	0	0-1	0	7.21

Otis Nixon

Bats: Both   **Throws:** Right   **Pos:** CF-125   **Ht:** 6'2"   **Wt:** 180   **Born:** 1/9/59   **Age:** 38

Year Team	Lg	G	AB	H	2B	3B	HR	(Hm	Rd)	TB	R	RBI	TBB	IBB	SO	HBP	SH	SF	SB	CS	SB%	GDP	Avg	OBP	SLG
1983 New York	AL	13	14	2	0	0	0	(0	0)	2	2	0	1	0	5	0	0	0	2	0	1.00	0	.143	.200	.143
1984 Cleveland	AL	49	91	14	0	0	0	(0	0)	14	16	1	8	0	11	0	3	1	12	6	.67	2	.154	.220	.154
1985 Cleveland	AL	104	162	38	4	0	3	(1	2)	51	34	9	8	0	27	0	4	0	20	11	.65	2	.235	.271	.315
1986 Cleveland	AL	105	95	25	4	1	0	(0	0)	31	33	8	13	0	12	0	2	0	23	6	.79	1	.263	.352	.326
1987 Cleveland	AL	19	17	1	0	0	0	(0	0)	1	2	1	3	0	4	0	0	0	2	3	.40	0	.059	.200	.059
1988 Montreal	NL	90	271	66	8	2	0	(0	0)	78	47	15	28	0	42	0	4	2	46	13	.78	0	.244	.312	.288
1989 Montreal	NL	126	258	56	7	2	0	(0	0)	67	41	21	33	1	36	0	2	1	37	12	.76	4	.217	.306	.260
1990 Montreal	NL	119	231	58	6	2	1	(0	1)	71	46	20	28	0	33	0	3	1	50	13	.79	2	.251	.331	.307
1991 Atlanta	NL	124	401	119	10	1	0	(0	0)	131	81	26	47	3	40	2	7	3	72	21	.77	5	.297	.371	.327
1992 Atlanta	NL	120	456	134	14	2	2	(1	1)	158	79	22	39	0	54	0	5	3	41	18	.69	4	.294	.348	.346
1993 Atlanta	NL	134	461	124	12	3	1	(1	0)	145	77	24	61	2	63	0	5	5	47	13	.78	10	.269	.351	.315
1994 Boston	AL	103	398	109	15	1	0	(0	0)	126	60	25	55	1	65	0	6	2	42	10	.81	0	.274	.360	.317
1995 Texas	AL	139	589	174	21	2	0	(0	0)	199	87	45	58	1	85	0	6	3	50	21	.70	6	.295	.357	.338
1996 Toronto	AL	125	496	142	15	1	1	(1	0)	162	87	29	71	1	68	1	7	0	54	13	.81	9	.286	.377	.327
14 ML YEARS		1370	3940	1062	116	17	8	(4	4)	1236	692	246	453	9	545	3	54	19	498	160	.76	45	.270	.344	.314

Trot Nixon

Bats: Left   **Throws:** Left   **Pos:** RF-2; PH-1   **Ht:** 6'2"   **Wt:** 196   **Born:** 4/11/74   **Age:** 23

Year Team	Lg	G	AB	H	2B	3B	HR	(Hm	Rd)	TB	R	RBI	TBB	IBB	SO	HBP	SH	SF	SB	CS	SB%	GDP	Avg	OBP	SLG
1994 Lynchburg	A+	71	264	65	12	0	12	—	—	113	33	43	44	1	53	1	3	1	10	3	.77	5	.246	.357	.428
1995 Sarasota	A+	73	264	80	11	4	5	—	—	114	43	39	45	3	46	1	0	2	7	5	.58	5	.303	.404	.432
Trenton	AA	25	94	15	3	1	2	—	—	26	9	8	7	0	20	0	2	2	2	1	.67	4	.160	.214	.277
1996 Trenton	AA	123	438	110	11	4	11	—	—	162	55	63	50	3	65	3	6	5	7	9	.44	6	.251	.329	.370
1996 Boston	AL	2	4	2	1	0	0	(0	0)	3	2	0	0	0	1	0	0	0	1	0	1.00	0	.500	.500	.750

Hideo Nomo

Pitches: Right **Bats:** Right **Pos:** SP-33   **Ht:** 6'2" **Wt:** 210 **Born:** 8/31/68 **Age:** 28

		HOW MUCH HE PITCHED						WHAT HE GAVE UP										THE RESULTS						
Year Team	Lg	G	GS	CG	GF	IP	BFP	H	R	ER	HR	SH	SF	HB	TBB	IBB	SO	WP	Bk	W	L	Pct.	ShO	Sv-Op	Hld	ERA
1995 Bakersfield	A+	1	1	0	0	5.1	24	6	2	2	0	0	0	1	1	0	6	1	0	0	1	.000	0	0- -	—	3.38
1995 Los Angeles	NL	28	28	4	0	191.1	780	124	63	54	14	11	4	5	78	2	**236**	**19**	5	13	6	.684	**3**	0-0	0	2.54
1996 Los Angeles	NL	33	33	3	0	228.1	932	180	93	81	23	12	6	2	85	6	234	12	3	16	11	.593	2	0-0	0	3.19
2 ML YEARS		61	61	7	0	419.2	1712	304	156	135	37	23	10	7	163	8	470	31	8	29	17	.630	5	0-0	0	2.90

Les Norman

Bats: R **Throws:** R **Pos:** PH-29; RF-20; LF-15; DH-7; CF-3   **Ht:** 6'1" **Wt:** 185 **Born:** 2/25/69 **Age:** 28

							BATTING											BASERUNNING				PERCENTAGES		
Year Team	Lg	G	AB	H	2B	3B	HR	(Hm	Rd)	TB	R	RBI	TBB	IBB	SO	HBP	SH	SF	SB	CS	SB%	GDP	Avg	OBP	SLG
1991 Eugene	A-	30	102	25	4	1	2	—	—	37	14	18	9	0	18	1	2	1	2	1	.67	4	.245	.310	.363
1992 Appleton	A	59	218	82	17	1	4	—	—	113	38	47	22	0	18	1	2	3	8	6	.57	5	.376	.430	.518
Memphis	AA	72	271	74	14	5	3	—	—	107	32	20	22	0	37	2	1	1	4	4	.50	2	.273	.331	.395
1993 Memphis	AA	133	484	141	32	5	17	—	—	234	78	81	50	3	88	14	7	2	11	9	.55	8	.291	.373	.483
1994 Omaha	AAA	13	38	7	3	0	1	—	—	13	4	4	6	0	11	1	1	0	0	1	.00	1	.184	.311	.342
Memphis	AA	106	383	101	19	4	13	—	—	167	53	55	36	1	44	7	3	2	7	7	.50	0	.264	.336	.436
1995 Omaha	AAA	83	313	89	19	3	9	—	—	141	46	33	18	2	48	4	3	2	5	3	.63	3	.284	.329	.450
1996 Omaha	AAA	24	77	20	6	0	1	—	—	29	8	13	6	0	8	1	0	1	0	1	.00	2	.260	.318	.377
1995 Kansas City	AL	24	40	9	0	1	0	(0	0)	11	6	4	6	0	6	0	1	0	1	0	.00	0	.225	.326	.275
1996 Kansas City	AL	54	49	6	0	0	0	(0	0)	6	9	0	6	0	14	1	0	0	1	1	.50	0	.122	.232	.122
2 ML YEARS		78	89	15	0	1	0	(0	0)	17	15	4	12	0	20	1	1	0	1	2	.33	0	.169	.275	.191

Greg Norton

Bats: Both **Throws:** Right **Pos:** SS-6; PH-4; 3B-2; DH-1   **Ht:** 6'1" **Wt:** 190 **Born:** 7/6/72 **Age:** 24

							BATTING											BASERUNNING				PERCENTAGES		
Year Team	Lg	G	AB	H	2B	3B	HR	(Hm	Rd)	TB	R	RBI	TBB	IBB	SO	HBP	SH	SF	SB	CS	SB%	GDP	Avg	OBP	SLG
1993 White Sox	R	3	9	2	0	0	0	—	—	2	1	2	1	0	1	0	0	0	0	0	.00	0	.222	.300	.222
Hickory	A	71	254	62	12	2	4	—	—	90	36	36	41	1	44	1	1	4	0	2	.00	6	.244	.347	.354
1994 South Bend	A	127	477	137	22	2	6	—	—	181	73	64	62	4	71	2	2	3	5	3	.63	7	.287	.369	.379
1995 Birmingham	AA	133	469	117	23	2	6	—	—	162	65	60	64	7	90	5	3	10	19	12	.61	10	.249	.339	.345
1996 Birmingham	AA	76	287	81	14	3	8	—	—	125	40	44	33	5	55	1	1	1	5	5	.50	5	.282	.357	.436
Nashville	AAA	43	164	47	14	2	7	—	—	86	28	26	17	3	42	0	0	2	2	3	.40	1	.287	.350	.524
1996 Chicago	AL	11	23	5	0	0	2	(0	2)	11	4	3	4	0	6	0	0	0	0	1	.00	0	.217	.333	.478

Jon Nunnally

Bats: L **Throws:** R **Pos:** RF-24; LF-7; PH-6; DH-4   **Ht:** 5'10" **Wt:** 190 **Born:** 11/9/71 **Age:** 25

							BATTING											BASERUNNING				PERCENTAGES		
Year Team	Lg	G	AB	H	2B	3B	HR	(Hm	Rd)	TB	R	RBI	TBB	IBB	SO	HBP	SH	SF	SB	CS	SB%	GDP	Avg	OBP	SLG
1992 Watertown	A-	69	246	59	10	4	5	—	—	92	39	43	32	2	55	1	0	4	12	3	.80	3	.240	.325	.374
1993 Columbus	A	125	438	110	15	2	15	—	—	174	81	56	63	0	108	3	4	6	17	11	.61	5	.251	.345	.397
1994 Kinston	A+	132	483	129	29	4	22	—	—	228	70	74	64	3	125	3	1	3	23	11	.68	5	.267	.354	.472
1996 Omaha	AAA	103	345	97	21	4	25	—	—	201	76	77	47	8	100	8	0	6	10	9	.53	2	.281	.374	.583
1995 Kansas City	AL	119	303	74	15	6	14	(6	8)	143	51	42	51	2	86	2	4	0	6	4	.60	4	.244	.357	.472
1996 Kansas City	AL	35	90	19	5	1	5	(2	3)	41	16	17	13	2	25	0	0	1	0	0	.00	0	.211	.308	.456
2 ML YEARS		154	393	93	20	7	19	(8	11)	184	67	59	64	4	111	2	4	1	6	4	.60	4	.237	.346	.468

Charlie O'Brien

Bats: Right **Throws:** Right **Pos:** C-105; PH-15   **Ht:** 6'2" **Wt:** 205 **Born:** 5/1/61 **Age:** 36

							BATTING											BASERUNNING				PERCENTAGES		
Year Team	Lg	G	AB	H	2B	3B	HR	(Hm	Rd)	TB	R	RBI	TBB	IBB	SO	HBP	SH	SF	SB	CS	SB%	GDP	Avg	OBP	SLG
1985 Oakland	AL	16	11	3	1	0	0	(0	0)	4	3	1	3	0	3	0	0	0	0	0	.00	0	.273	.429	.364
1987 Milwaukee	AL	10	35	7	3	1	0	(0	0)	12	2	0	4	0	4	0	1	0	0	1	.00	0	.200	.282	.343
1988 Milwaukee	AL	40	118	26	6	0	2	(2	0)	38	12	9	5	0	16	0	4	0	0	1	.00	3	.220	.252	.322
1989 Milwaukee	AL	62	188	44	10	0	6	(4	2)	72	22	35	21	1	11	9	8	0	0	0	.00	11	.234	.339	.383
1990 Mil-NYN		74	213	38	10	2	0	(0	0)	52	17	20	21	3	34	3	10	2	0	0	.00	5	.178	.259	.244
1991 New York	NL	69	168	31	6	0	2	(1	1)	43	16	14	17	1	25	4	0	2	0	2	.00	5	.185	.272	.256
1992 New York	NL	68	156	33	12	0	2	(1	1)	51	15	13	16	1	18	1	4	0	0	1	.00	5	.212	.289	.327
1993 New York	NL	67	188	48	11	0	4	(1	3)	71	15	23	14	1	14	2	3	1	1	1	.50	4	.255	.312	.378
1994 Atlanta	NL	51	152	37	11	0	8	(4	4)	72	24	28	15	2	24	3	1	1	0	0	.00	5	.243	.322	.474
1995 Atlanta	NL	67	198	45	7	0	9	(4	5)	79	18	23	29	2	40	6	0	0	0	1	.00	8	.227	.343	.399
1996 Toronto	AL	109	324	77	17	0	13	(8	5)	133	33	44	29	1	68	17	3	2	0	1	.00	8	.238	.331	.410
1990 Milwaukee	AL	46	145	27	7	2	0	(0	0)	38	11	11	11	1	26	2	8	0	0	0	.00	0	.186	.253	.262
New York	NL	28	68	11	3	0	0	(0	0)	14	6	9	10	2	8	1	2	2	0	0	.00	1	.162	.272	.206
11 ML YEARS		633	1751	389	94	3	46	(27	19)	627	177	210	174	12	257	45	34	8	1	8	.11	52	.222	.307	.358

Troy O'Leary

Bats: L **Throws:** L **Pos:** RF-110; LF-66; PH-20; CF-17   **Ht:** 6'0"   **Wt:** 198   **Born:** 8/4/69   **Age:** 27

Year Team	Lg	G	AB	H	2B	3B	HR	(Hm	Rd)	TB	R	RBI	TBB	IBB	SO	HBP	SH	SF	SB	CS	SB%	GDP	Avg	OBP	SLG
1993 Milwaukee	AL	19	41	12	3	0	0	(0	0)	15	3	3	5	0	9	0	3	0	0	0	.00	1	.293	.370	.366
1994 Milwaukee	AL	27	66	18	1	1	2	(0	2)	27	9	7	5	0	12	1	0	1	1	1	.50	0	.273	.329	.409
1995 Boston	AL	112	399	123	31	6	10	(5	5)	196	60	49	29	4	64	1	3	2	5	3	.63	8	.308	.355	.491
1996 Boston	AL	149	497	129	28	5	15	(10	5)	212	68	81	47	3	80	4	1	3	3	2	.60	13	.260	.327	.427
4 ML YEARS		307	1003	282	63	12	27	(15	12)	450	140	140	86	7	165	6	7	6	9	6	.60	22	.281	.340	.449

Paul O'Neill

Bats: L **Throws:** L **Pos:** RF-146; DH-3; 1B-1; PH-1   **Ht:** 6'4"   **Wt:** 215   **Born:** 2/25/63   **Age:** 34

Year Team	Lg	G	AB	H	2B	3B	HR	(Hm	Rd)	TB	R	RBI	TBB	IBB	SO	HBP	SH	SF	SB	CS	SB%	GDP	Avg	OBP	SLG
1985 Cincinnati	NL	5	12	4	1	0	0	(0	0)	5	1	1	0	0	2	0	0	0	0	0	.00	0	.333	.333	.417
1986 Cincinnati	NL	3	2	0	0	0	0	(0	0)	0	0	0	1	0	1	0	0	0	0	0	.00	0	.000	.333	.000
1987 Cincinnati	NL	84	160	41	14	1	7	(4	3)	78	24	28	18	1	29	0	0	0	2	1	.67	3	.256	.331	.488
1988 Cincinnati	NL	145	485	122	25	3	16	(12	4)	201	58	73	38	5	65	2	3	5	8	6	.57	7	.252	.306	.414
1989 Cincinnati	NL	117	428	118	24	2	15	(11	4)	191	49	74	46	8	64	2	0	4	20	5	.80	7	.276	.346	.446
1990 Cincinnati	NL	145	503	136	28	0	16	(10	6)	212	59	78	53	13	103	2	1	5	13	11	.54	12	.270	.339	.421
1991 Cincinnati	NL	152	532	136	36	0	28	(20	8)	256	71	91	73	14	107	1	0	1	12	7	.63	8	.256	.346	.481
1992 Cincinnati	NL	148	496	122	19	1	14	(6	8)	185	59	66	77	15	85	2	3	6	6	3	.67	10	.246	.346	.373
1993 New York	AL	141	498	155	34	1	20	(8	12)	251	71	75	44	5	69	2	0	3	2	4	.33	13	.311	.367	.504
1994 New York	AL	103	368	132	25	1	21	(10	11)	222	68	83	72	13	56	0	0	3	5	4	.56	16	.359	.460	.603
1995 New York	AL	127	460	138	30	4	22	(10	12)	242	82	96	71	8	76	1	0	11	1	2	.33	25	.300	.387	.526
1996 New York	AL	150	546	165	35	1	19	(7	12)	259	89	91	102	8	76	4	0	8	0	1	.00	21	.302	.411	.474
12 ML YEARS		1320	4490	1269	271	14	178	(100	78)	2102	631	756	595	90	733	16	7	46	69	44	.61	122	.283	.365	.468

Sherman Obando

Bats: Right **Throws:** Right **Pos:** PH-48; RF-47   **Ht:** 6'4"   **Wt:** 215   **Born:** 1/23/70   **Age:** 27

Year Team	Lg	G	AB	H	2B	3B	HR	(Hm	Rd)	TB	R	RBI	TBB	IBB	SO	HBP	SH	SF	SB	CS	SB%	GDP	Avg	OBP	SLG
1993 Baltimore	AL	31	92	25	2	0	3	(2	1)	36	8	15	4	0	26	1	0	0	0	0	.00	1	.272	.309	.391
1995 Baltimore	AL	16	38	10	1	0	0	(0	0)	11	0	3	2	0	12	0	0	1	1	0	1.00	0	.263	.293	.289
1996 Montreal	NL	89	178	44	9	0	8	(6	2)	77	30	22	22	1	48	1	0	1	2	0	1.00	2	.247	.332	.433
3 ML YEARS		136	308	79	12	0	11	(8	3)	124	38	40	28	1	86	2	0	2	3	0	1.00	3	.256	.321	.403

Alex Ochoa

Bats: Right **Throws:** Right **Pos:** RF-76; PH-7   **Ht:** 6'0"   **Wt:** 185   **Born:** 3/29/72   **Age:** 25

Year Team	Lg	G	AB	H	2B	3B	HR	(Hm	Rd)	TB	R	RBI	TBB	IBB	SO	HBP	SH	SF	SB	CS	SB%	GDP	Avg	OBP	SLG
1991 Orioles	R	53	179	55	8	3	1	—	—	72	26	30	16	0	14	1	3	1	11	6	.65	2	.307	.365	.402
1992 Kane County	A	133	499	147	22	7	1	—	—	186	65	59	58	5	55	7	5	7	31	17	.65	14	.295	.371	.373
1993 Frederick	A+	137	532	147	29	5	13	—	—	225	84	90	46	0	67	9	1	6	34	13	.72	15	.276	.341	.423
1994 Bowie	AA	134	519	156	25	2	14	—	—	227	77	82	49	0	67	1	5	12	28	15	.65	11	.301	.355	.437
1995 Rochester	AAA	91	336	92	18	2	8	—	—	138	41	46	26	1	50	2	1	2	17	7	.71	8	.274	.328	.411
Norfolk	AAA	34	123	38	6	2	2	—	—	54	17	15	14	0	12	0	0	1	7	3	.70	4	.309	.377	.439
1996 Norfolk	AAA	67	233	79	12	4	8	—	—	123	45	39	32	3	22	2	2	2	5	11	.31	8	.339	.420	.528
1995 New York	NL	11	37	11	1	0	0	(0	0)	12	7	0	2	0	10	0	0	0	1	0	1.00	1	.297	.333	.324
1996 New York	NL	82	282	83	19	3	4	(1	3)	120	37	33	17	0	30	2	0	3	4	3	.57	2	.294	.336	.426
2 ML YEARS		93	319	94	20	3	4	(1	3)	132	44	33	19	0	40	2	0	3	5	3	.63	3	.295	.335	.414

Jose Offerman

Bats: B **Throws:** R **Pos:** 1B-96; 2B-38; SS-37; PH-7; CF-1   **Ht:** 6'0"   **Wt:** 190   **Born:** 11/8/68   **Age:** 28

Year Team	Lg	G	AB	H	2B	3B	HR	(Hm	Rd)	TB	R	RBI	TBB	IBB	SO	HBP	SH	SF	SB	CS	SB%	GDP	Avg	OBP	SLG
1990 Los Angeles	NL	29	58	9	0	0	1	(1	0)	12	7	7	4	1	14	0	1	0	1	0	1.00	0	.155	.210	.207
1991 Los Angeles	NL	52	113	22	2	0	0	(1	0)	24	10	3	25	2	32	1	1	0	3	2	.60	5	.195	.345	.212
1992 Los Angeles	NL	149	534	139	20	8	1	(1	0)	178	67	30	57	4	98	0	5	2	23	16	.59	5	.260	.331	.333
1993 Los Angeles	NL	158	590	159	21	6	1	(1	0)	195	77	62	71	7	75	2	25	8	30	13	.70	12	.269	.346	.331
1994 Los Angeles	NL	72	243	51	8	4	1	(0	1)	70	27	25	38	4	38	0	6	2	2	1	.67	6	.210	.314	.288
1995 Los Angeles	NL	119	429	123	14	6	4	(2	2)	161	69	33	69	0	67	3	10	0	2	7	.22	5	.287	.389	.375
1996 Kansas City	AL	151	561	170	33	8	5	(1	4)	234	85	47	74	3	98	1	7	2	24	10	.71	9	.303	.384	.417
7 ML YEARS		730	2528	673	98	32	13	(6	7)	874	342	207	338	21	422	7	55	14	85	49	.63	42	.266	.353	.346

Chad Ogea

Pitches: Right   **Bats:** Right   **Pos:** SP-21; RP-8   **Ht:** 6'2"   **Wt:** 200   **Born:** 11/9/70   **Age:** 26

Year Team	Lg	G	GS	CG	GF	IP	BFP	H	R	ER	HR	SH	SF	HB	TBB	IBB	SO	WP	Bk	W	L	Pct.	ShO	Sv-Op	Hld	ERA
1996 Buffalo *	AAA	5	5	0	0	25.2	108	27	15	15	4	0	0	1	6	0	20	0	0	0	1	.000	0	0- -	—	5.26
1994 Cleveland	AL	4	1	0	0	16.1	80	21	11	11	2	0	0	1	10	2	11	0	0	0	1	.000	0	0-0	0	6.06
1995 Cleveland	AL	20	14	1	3	106.1	442	95	38	36	11	0	5	1	29	0	57	3	1	8	3	.727	0	0-0	0	3.05
1996 Cleveland	AL	29	21	1	2	146.2	620	151	82	78	22	3	3	5	42	3	101	2	0	10	6	.625	1	0-0	0	4.79
3 ML YEARS		53	36	2	5	269.1	1142	267	131	125	35	3	8	7	81	5	169	5	1	18	10	.643	1	0-0	0	4.18

John Olerud

Bats: Left   **Throws:** Left   **Pos:** 1B-101; PH-16; DH-15   **Ht:** 6'5"   **Wt:** 220   **Born:** 8/5/68   **Age:** 28

Year Team	Lg	G	AB	H	2B	3B	HR	(Hm	Rd)	TB	R	RBI	TBB	IBB	SO	HBP	SH	SF	SB	CS	SB%	GDP	Avg	OBP	SLG
1989 Toronto	AL	6	8	3	0	0	0	(0	0)	3	2	0	0	0	1	0	0	0	0	0	.00	0	.375	.375	.375
1990 Toronto	AL	111	358	95	15	1	14	(11	3)	154	43	48	57	6	75	1	1	4	0	0	.00	5	.265	.364	.430
1991 Toronto	AL	139	454	116	30	1	17	(7	10)	199	64	68	68	9	84	6	3	10	0	2	.00	12	.256	.353	.438
1992 Toronto	AL	138	458	130	28	0	16	(4	12)	206	68	66	70	11	61	1	1	7	1	0	1.00	15	.284	.375	.450
1993 Toronto	AL	158	551	200	54	2	24	(9	15)	330	109	107	114	33	65	7	0	7	0	2	.00	12	.363	.473	.599
1994 Toronto	AL	108	384	114	29	2	12	(6	6)	183	47	67	61	12	53	3	0	5	1	2	.33	11	.297	.393	.477
1995 Toronto	AL	135	492	143	32	0	8	(1	7)	199	72	54	84	10	54	4	0	1	0	0	.00	17	.291	.398	.404
1996 Toronto	AL	125	398	109	25	0	18	(9	9)	188	59	61	60	6	37	10	0	1	1	0	1.00	10	.274	.382	.472
8 ML YEARS		920	3103	910	213	6	109	(47	62)	1462	464	471	514	87	430	32	5	35	3	8	.27	82	.293	.395	.471

Omar Olivares

Pitches: Right   **Bats:** Right   **Pos:** SP-25   **Ht:** 6'1"   **Wt:** 190   **Born:** 7/6/67   **Age:** 29

Year Team	Lg	G	GS	CG	GF	IP	BFP	H	R	ER	HR	SH	SF	HB	TBB	IBB	SO	WP	Bk	W	L	Pct.	ShO	Sv-Op	Hld	ERA
1996 Toledo *	AAA	1	1	0	0	5.1	23	4	5	5	0	1	0	0	3	0	5	0	0	1	0	1.000	0	0- -	—	8.44
1990 St. Louis	NL	9	6	0	0	49.1	201	45	17	16	2	1	0	2	17	0	20	1	1	1	1	.500	0	0-0	1	2.92
1991 St. Louis	NL	28	24	0	2	167.1	688	148	72	69	13	11	2	5	61	1	91	3	1	11	7	.611	0	1-1	0	3.71
1992 St. Louis	NL	32	30	1	1	197	818	189	84	84	20	8	7	4	63	5	124	2	0	9	9	.500	0	0-0	0	3.84
1993 St. Louis	NL	58	9	0	11	118.2	537	134	60	55	10	4	4	9	54	7	63	4	3	5	3	.625	0	1-5	2	4.17
1994 St. Louis	NL	14	12	1	2	73.2	333	84	53	47	10	3	3	4	37	0	26	5	0	3	4	.429	0	1-1	0	5.74
1995 Col-Phi	NL	16	6	0	4	41.2	195	55	34	32	5	2	2	3	23	0	22	4	0	1	4	.200	0	0-0	0	6.91
1996 Detroit	AL	25	25	4	0	160	708	169	90	87	16	3	6	9	75	4	81	4	1	7	11	.389	0	0-0	0	4.89
1995 Colorado	NL	11	6	0	1	31.2	151	44	28	26	4	1	1	2	21	0	15	4	0	1	3	.250	0	0-0	0	7.39
Philadelphia	NL	5	0	0	3	10	44	11	6	6	1	1	1	1	2	0	7	0	0	0	1	.000	0	0-0	0	5.40
7 ML YEARS		182	112	6	20	807.2	3480	824	410	390	76	32	24	36	330	17	427	23	6	37	39	.487	0	3-7	3	4.35

Darren Oliver

Pitches: Left   **Bats:** Right   **Pos:** SP-30   **Ht:** 6'2"   **Wt:** 200   **Born:** 10/6/70   **Age:** 26

Year Team	Lg	G	GS	CG	GF	IP	BFP	H	R	ER	HR	SH	SF	HB	TBB	IBB	SO	WP	Bk	W	L	Pct.	ShO	Sv-Op	Hld	ERA
1996 Charlotte *	A+	2	1	0	0	12	47	8	4	4	1	0	0	2	3	0	9	0	0	0	1	.000	0	0- -	—	3.00
1993 Texas	AL	2	0	0	0	3.1	14	2	1	1	0	0	0	1	1	4	0	0	0	0	0	.000	0	0-0	0	2.70
1994 Texas	AL	43	0	0	10	50	226	40	24	19	4	6	0	6	35	4	50	2	2	4	0	1.000	0	2-3	9	3.42
1995 Texas	AL	17	7	0	2	49	222	47	25	23	3	5	1	1	32	1	39	4	0	4	2	.667	0	0-0	0	4.22
1996 Texas	AL	30	30	1	0	173.2	777	190	97	90	20	2	7	10	76	3	112	5	1	14	6	.700	1	0-0	0	4.66
4 ML YEARS		92	37	1	12	276	1239	279	147	133	28	13	8	17	144	9	205	11	3	22	8	.733	1	2-3	9	4.34

Joe Oliver

Bats: R   **Throws:** R   **Pos:** C-97; PH-14; 1B-3; LF-2; RF-1   **Ht:** 6'3"   **Wt:** 220   **Born:** 7/24/65   **Age:** 31

Year Team	Lg	G	AB	H	2B	3B	HR	(Hm	Rd)	TB	R	RBI	TBB	IBB	SO	HBP	SH	SF	SB	CS	SB%	GDP	Avg	OBP	SLG
1989 Cincinnati	NL	49	151	41	8	0	3	(1	2)	58	13	23	6	1	28	1	1	2	0	0	.00	3	.272	.300	.384
1990 Cincinnati	NL	121	364	84	23	0	8	(3	5)	131	34	52	37	15	75	2	5	1	1	1	.50	6	.231	.304	.360
1991 Cincinnati	NL	94	269	58	11	0	11	(7	4)	102	21	41	18	5	53	0	4	0	0	0	.00	14	.216	.265	.379
1992 Cincinnati	NL	143	485	131	25	1	10	(3	7)	188	42	57	35	19	75	1	6	7	2	3	.40	12	.270	.316	.388
1993 Cincinnati	NL	139	482	115	28	0	14	(7	7)	185	40	75	27	2	91	1	2	9	0	0	.00	13	.239	.276	.384
1994 Cincinnati	NL	6	19	4	0	0	1	(1	0)	7	1	5	2	1	3	0	0	0	0	0	.00	1	.211	.286	.368
1995 Milwaukee	AL	97	337	92	20	0	12	(4	8)	148	43	51	27	1	66	3	2	0	2	4	.33	11	.273	.332	.439
1996 Cincinnati	NL	106	289	70	12	1	11	(6	5)	117	31	46	28	6	54	2	3	3	2	0	1.00	8	.242	.311	.405
8 ML YEARS		755	2396	595	127	2	70	(36	34)	936	225	350	180	50	445	10	23	22	7	8	.47	68	.248	.301	.391

Gregg Olson

Pitches: Right **Bats:** Right **Pos:** RP-52 **Ht:** 6'4" **Wt:** 212 **Born:** 10/11/66 **Age:** 30

Year Team	Lg	G	GS	CG	GF	IP	BFP	H	R	ER	HR	SH	SF	HB	TBB	IBB	SO	WP	Bk	W	L	Pct.	ShO	Sv-Op	Hld	ERA
1996 Indianapols *	AAA	7	0	0	7	6.1	33	6	4	3	1	0	0	1	6	0	4	0	0	0	0	.000	0	4--		4.26
1988 Baltimore	AL	10	0	0	4	11	51	10	4	4	1	0	0	0	10	1	9	0	1	1	1	.500	0	0-1	1	3.27
1989 Baltimore	AL	64	0	0	52	85	356	57	17	16	1	4	1	1	46	10	90	9	3	5	2	.714	0	27-33	1	1.69
1990 Baltimore	AL	64	0	0	58	74.1	305	57	20	20	3	1	2	3	31	3	74	5	0	6	5	.545	0	37-42	0	2.42
1991 Baltimore	AL	72	0	0	62	73.2	319	74	28	26	1	5	1	1	29	5	72	8	1	4	6	.400	0	31-39	1	3.18
1992 Baltimore	AL	60	0	0	56	61.1	244	46	14	14	3	0	2	0	24	0	58	4	0	1	5	.167	0	36-44	0	2.05
1993 Baltimore	AL	50	0	0	45	45	188	37	9	8	1	2	2	0	18	3	44	5	0	0	2	.000	0	29-35	1	1.60
1994 Atlanta	NL	16	0	0	6	14.2	77	19	15	15	1	2	1	1	13	3	10	0	2	0	2	.000	0	1-1	1	9.20
1995 Cle-KC	AL	23	0	0	12	33	141	28	15	15	4	1	2	0	19	2	21	1	0	3	3	.500	0	3-5	2	4.09
1996 Det-Hou		52	0	0	30	52.1	243	55	30	29	7	1	1	1	35	6	37	6	0	1	0	1.000	0	8-10	1	4.99
1995 Cleveland	AL	3	0	0	2	2.2	14	5	4	4	1	0	0	0	2	0	0	0	0	0	0	.000	0	0-0	0	13.50
Kansas City		20	0	0	10	30.1	127	23	11	11	3	1	2	0	17	2	21	1	0	3	3	.500	0	3-5	2	3.26
1996 Detroit	AL	43	0	0	28	43	196	43	25	24	6	1	0	1	28	4	29	5	0	0	0	.000	0	8-10	1	5.02
Houston	NL	9	0	0	2	9.1	47	12	5	5	1	0	1	0	7	2	8	1	0	1	0	1.000	0	0-0	0	4.82
9 ML YEARS		411	0	0	325	450.1	1924	383	152	147	22	16	12	7	225	33	415	38	7	24	26	.480	0	172-210	7	2.94

Steve Ontiveros

Pitches: Right **Bats:** Right **Pos:** SP **Ht:** 6'0" **Wt:** 190 **Born:** 3/5/61 **Age:** 36

Year Team	Lg	G	GS	CG	GF	IP	BFP	H	R	ER	HR	SH	SF	HB	TBB	IBB	SO	WP	Bk	W	L	Pct.	ShO	Sv-Op	Hld	ERA
1985 Oakland	AL	39	0	0	18	74.2	284	45	17	16	4	2	2	2	19	2	36	1	0	1	3	.250	0	8--	—	1.93
1986 Oakland	AL	46	0	0	27	72.2	305	72	40	38	10	1	6	1	25	3	54	4	0	2	2	.500	0	10--	—	4.71
1987 Oakland	AL	35	22	2	6	150.2	645	141	78	67	19	6	2	4	50	3	97	4	1	10	8	.556	1	1-4	1	4.00
1988 Oakland	AL	10	10	0	0	54.2	241	57	32	28	4	5	0	0	21	1	30	5	5	3	4	.429	0	0-0	0	4.61
1989 Philadelphia	NL	6	5	0	0	30.2	134	34	15	13	2	1	0	0	15	1	12	2	0	2	1	.667	0	0-0	0	3.82
1990 Philadelphia	NL	5	0	0	1	10	43	9	3	3	1	0	0	0	3	0	6	0	0	0	0	.000	0	0-0	1	2.70
1993 Seattle	AL	14	0	0	8	18	72	18	3	2	0	1	0	0	6	2	13	1	0	0	2	.000	0	0-0	0	1.00
1994 Oakland	AL	27	13	2	5	115.1	463	93	39	34	7	2	1	6	26	1	56	5	0	6	4	.600	0	0-0	1	**2.65**
1995 Oakland	AL	22	22	2	0	129.2	558	144	75	63	12	2	6	4	38	0	77	5	0	9	6	.600	1	0-0	0	4.37
9 ML YEARS		204	72	6	65	656.1	2745	613	302	264	59	20	17	17	203	13	381	27	6	33	30	.524	2	19--	—	3.62

Mike Oquist

Pitches: Right **Bats:** Right **Pos:** RP-8 **Ht:** 6'2" **Wt:** 170 **Born:** 5/30/68 **Age:** 29

Year Team	Lg	G	GS	CG	GF	IP	BFP	H	R	ER	HR	SH	SF	HB	TBB	IBB	SO	WP	Bk	W	L	Pct.	ShO	Sv-Op	Hld	ERA
1996 Las Vegas *	AAA	27	20	2	4	140.1	586	136	56	45	12	6	6	3	44	2	110	4	0	9	4	.692	0	1--	—	2.89
1993 Baltimore	AL	5	0	0	2	11.2	50	12	5	5	0	0	0	0	4	1	8	0	0	0	0	.000	0	0-0	0	3.86
1994 Baltimore	AL	15	9	0	3	58.1	278	75	41	40	7	3	4	6	30	4	39	3	0	3	3	.500	0	0-0	0	6.17
1995 Baltimore	AL	27	0	0	2	54	255	51	27	25	6	1	4	2	41	3	27	2	0	2	1	.667	0	0-1	0	4.17
1996 San Diego	NL	8	0	0	3	7.2	30	6	2	2	0	0	0	0	4	2	4	1	0	0	0	.000	0	0-0	0	2.35
4 ML YEARS		55	9	0	10	131.2	613	144	75	72	13	4	8	8	79	10	78	6	0	5	4	.556	0	0-1	0	4.92

Rey Ordonez

Bats: Right **Throws:** Right **Pos:** SS-150; PH-3 **Ht:** 5'9" **Wt:** 159 **Born:** 11/11/72 **Age:** 24

Year Team	Lg	G	AB	H	2B	3B	HR	(Hm	Rd)	TB	R	RBI	TBB	IBB	SO	HBP	SH	SF	SB	CS	SB%	GDP	Avg	OBP	SLG
1994 St. Lucie	A+	79	314	97	21	2	2	—	—	128	47	40	14	0	28	0	1	6	11	6	.65	8	.309	.336	.408
Binghamton	AA	48	191	50	10	2	1	—	—	67	22	20	4	0	18	1	1	1	4	3	.57	2	.262	.279	.351
1995 Norfolk	AAA	125	439	94	21	4	2	—	—	129	49	50	27	2	50	3	10	7	11	13	.46	12	.214	.261	.294
1996 New York	NL	151	502	129	12	4	1	(0	1)	152	51	30	22	12	53	1	4	1	1	3	.25	12	.257	.289	.303

Jesse Orosco

Pitches: Left **Bats:** Right **Pos:** RP-66 **Ht:** 6'2" **Wt:** 205 **Born:** 4/21/57 **Age:** 40

Year Team	Lg	G	GS	CG	GF	IP	BFP	H	R	ER	HR	SH	SF	HB	TBB	IBB	SO	WP	Bk	W	L	Pct.	ShO	Sv-Op	Hld	ERA
1979 New York	NL	18	2	0	6	35	154	33	20	19	4	3	0	2	22	0	22	0	0	1	2	.333	0	0--	—	4.89
1981 New York	NL	8	0	0	4	17	69	13	4	3	2	2	0	0	6	2	18	0	1	0	1	.000	0	1--	—	1.59
1982 New York	NL	54	2	0	22	109.1	451	92	37	33	7	5	4	2	40	2	89	3	2	4	10	.286	0	4--	—	2.72
1983 New York	NL	62	0	0	42	110	432	76	27	18	3	4	3	1	38	7	84	1	2	13	7	.650	0	17--	—	1.47
1984 New York	NL	60	0	0	52	87	355	58	29	25	7	3	3	2	34	6	85	1	1	10	6	.625	0	31--	—	2.59
1985 New York	NL	54	0	0	39	79	331	66	26	24	6	1	1	0	34	7	68	4	0	8	6	.571	0	17--	—	2.73
1986 New York	NL	58	0	0	40	81	338	64	23	21	6	2	3	3	35	3	62	2	0	8	6	.571	0	21--	—	2.33
1987 New York	NL	58	0	0	41	77	335	78	41	38	5	5	4	2	31	9	78	2	0	3	9	.250	0	16-22	4	4.44
1988 Los Angeles	NL	55	0	0	21	53	229	41	18	16	4	3	2	2	30	3	43	1	0	3	2	.600	0	9-15	14	2.72
1989 Cleveland	AL	69	0	0	29	78	312	54	20	18	7	3	3	0	26	4	79	0	0	3	4	.429	0	3-7	12	2.08
1990 Cleveland	AL	55	0	0	28	64.2	289	58	35	28	9	5	3	0	38	7	55	1	0	5	4	.556	0	2-3	2	3.90

Year Team	Lg	G	GS	CG	GF	IP	BFP	H	R	ER	HR	SH	SF	HB	TBB	IBB	SO	WP	Bk	W	L	Pct.	ShO	Sv-Op	Hld	ERA
		HOW MUCH HE PITCHED						**WHAT HE GAVE UP**												**THE RESULTS**						
1991 Cleveland	AL	47	0	0	20	45.2	202	52	20	19	4	1	3	1	15	8	36	1	1	2	0	1.000	0	0-0	3	3.74
1992 Milwaukee	AL	59	0	0	14	39	158	33	15	14	5	0	2	1	13	1	40	2	0	3	1	.750	0	1-2	11	3.23
1993 Milwaukee	AL	57	0	0	27	56.2	233	47	25	20	2	1	2	3	17	3	67	3	1	3	5	.375	0	8-13	11	3.18
1994 Milwaukee	AL	40	0	0	5	39	174	32	26	22	4	0	2	2	26	2	36	0	0	3	1	.750	0	0-4	8	5.08
1995 Baltimore	AL	**65**	0	0	23	49.2	200	28	19	18	4	2	4	1	27	7	58	2	1	2	4	.333	0	3-6	15	3.26
1996 Baltimore	AL	66	0	0	10	55.2	236	42	22	21	5	2	1	2	28	4	52	2	0	3	1	.750	0	0-3	19	3.40
17 ML YEARS		885	4	0	423	1076.2	4498	867	407	357	84	47	41	26	460	75	972	25	9	74	69	.517	0	133--	—	2.98

Joe Orsulak

Bats: L **Throws:** L **Pos:** PH-65; LF-30; RF-19; CF-14; 1B-2   **Ht:** 6'1" **Wt:** 205 **Born:** 5/31/62 **Age:** 35

Year Team	Lg	G	AB	H	2B	3B	HR	(Hm	Rd)	TB	R	RBI	TBB	IBB	SO	HBP	SH	SF	SB	CS	SB%	GDP	Avg	OBP	SLG
		BATTING																	**BASERUNNING**				**PERCENTAGES**		
1983 Pittsburgh	NL	7	11	2	0	0	0	(0	0)	2	0	1	0	0	2	0	0	1	0	1	.00	0	.182	.167	.182
1984 Pittsburgh	NL	32	67	17	1	2	0	(0	0)	22	12	3	1	0	7	1	3	1	3	1	.75	0	.254	.271	.328
1985 Pittsburgh	NL	121	397	119	14	6	0	(0	0)	145	54	21	26	3	27	1	9	3	24	11	.69	5	.300	.342	.365
1986 Pittsburgh	NL	138	401	100	19	6	2	(0	2)	137	60	19	28	2	38	1	6	1	24	11	.69	4	.249	.299	.342
1988 Baltimore	AL	125	379	109	21	3	8	(3	5)	160	48	27	23	2	30	3	8	3	9	8	.53	7	.288	.331	.422
1989 Baltimore	AL	123	390	111	22	5	7	(0	7)	164	59	55	41	6	35	2	7	6	5	3	.63	8	.285	.351	.421
1990 Baltimore	AL	124	413	111	14	3	11	(9	2)	164	49	57	46	9	48	1	4	1	6	8	.43	7	.269	.343	.397
1991 Baltimore	AL	143	486	135	22	1	5	(3	2)	174	57	43	28	1	45	4	0	3	6	2	.75	9	.278	.321	.358
1992 Baltimore	AL	117	391	113	18	3	4	(2	2)	149	45	39	28	5	34	4	4	1	5	4	.56	3	.289	.342	.381
1993 New York	NL	134	409	116	15	4	8	(5	3)	163	59	35	28	1	25	2	0	2	5	4	.56	6	.284	.331	.399
1994 New York	NL	96	292	76	3	0	8	(4	4)	103	39	42	16	2	21	3	0	7	4	2	.67	11	.260	.299	.353
1995 New York	NL	108	290	82	19	2	1	(1	0)	108	41	37	19	2	35	1	1	6	1	3	.25	3	.283	.323	.372
1996 Florida	NL	120	217	48	6	1	2	(2	0)	62	23	19	16	1	38	0	0	1	1	1	.50	4	.221	.274	.286
13 ML YEARS		1388	4143	1139	174	36	56	(29	27)	1553	546	398	300	34	385	23	42	36	93	59	.61	67	.275	.325	.375

Luis Ortiz

Bats: Right **Throws:** Right **Pos:** PH-2; DH-1   **Ht:** 6'0" **Wt:** 195 **Born:** 5/25/70 **Age:** 27

Year Team	Lg	G	AB	H	2B	3B	HR	(Hm	Rd)	TB	R	RBI	TBB	IBB	SO	HBP	SH	SF	SB	CS	SB%	GDP	Avg	OBP	SLG
		BATTING																	**BASERUNNING**				**PERCENTAGES**		
1996 Okla. City *	AAA	124	501	159	25	0	14	—	—	226	70	73	22	2	36	4	0	6	0	5	.00	17	.317	.347	.451
1993 Boston	AL	9	12	3	0	0	0	(0	0)	3	0	1	0	0	2	0	0	0	0	0	.00	0	.250	.250	.250
1994 Boston	AL	7	18	3	2	0	0	(0	0)	5	3	6	1	0	5	0	1	3	0	0	.00	0	.167	.182	.278
1995 Texas	AL	41	108	25	5	2	1	(1	0)	37	10	18	6	0	18	0	0	1	0	1	.00	7	.231	.270	.343
1996 Texas	AL	3	7	2	0	1	1	(1	0)	7	1	1	0	0	1	0	0	0	0	0	.00	0	.286	.286	1.000
4 ML YEARS		60	145	33	7	3	2	(2	0)	52	14	26	7	0	26	0	1	4	0	1	.00	7	.228	.256	.359

Donovan Osborne

Pitches: Left **Bats:** Left **Pos:** SP-30   **Ht:** 6'2" **Wt:** 195 **Born:** 6/21/69 **Age:** 28

Year Team	Lg	G	GS	CG	GF	IP	BFP	H	R	ER	HR	SH	SF	HB	TBB	IBB	SO	WP	Bk	W	L	Pct.	ShO	Sv-Op	Hld	ERA
		HOW MUCH HE PITCHED						**WHAT HE GAVE UP**												**THE RESULTS**						
1996 St. Pete *	A+	1	1	0	0	6	19	2	0	0	0	0	0	0	0	0	2	0	0	1	0	1.000	0	0--	—	0.00
Louisville *	AAA	1	1	0	0	7	24	6	2	2	1	0	0	0	2	0	3	0	0	1	0	1.000	0	0--	—	2.57
1992 St. Louis	NL	34	29	0	2	179	754	193	91	75	14	7	4	2	38	2	104	6	0	11	9	.550	0	0-0	1	3.77
1993 St. Louis	NL	26	26	1	0	155.2	657	153	73	65	18	6	2	7	47	4	83	4	0	10	7	.588	0	0-0	0	3.76
1995 St. Louis	NL	19	19	0	0	113.1	477	112	58	48	17	8	3	2	34	2	82	0	0	4	6	.400	0	0-0	0	3.81
1996 St. Louis	NL	30	30	2	0	198.2	822	191	87	78	22	7	4	1	57	5	134	6	1	13	9	.591	1	0-0	0	3.53
4 ML YEARS		109	104	3	2	646.2	2710	649	309	266	71	28	13	12	176	13	403	16	1	38	31	.551	1	0-0	1	3.70

Keith Osik

Bats: Right **Throws:** Right **Pos:** C-41; PH-4; 3B-2; LF-2   **Ht:** 6'0" **Wt:** 185 **Born:** 10/22/68 **Age:** 28

Year Team	Lg	G	AB	H	2B	3B	HR	(Hm	Rd)	TB	R	RBI	TBB	IBB	SO	HBP	SH	SF	SB	CS	SB%	GDP	Avg	OBP	SLG
		BATTING																	**BASERUNNING**				**PERCENTAGES**		
1990 Welland	A-	29	97	27	4	0	1	—	—	34	13	20	11	1	12	2	1	3	2	6	.25	1	.278	.354	.351
1991 Carolina	AA	17	43	13	3	1	0	—	—	18	9	5	5	0	5	0	0	0	0	0	.00	1	.302	.375	.419
Salem	A+	87	300	81	13	1	6	—	—	114	31	35	38	0	48	3	3	2	2	3	.40	13	.270	.356	.380
1992 Carolina	AA	129	425	110	17	1	5	—	—	144	41	45	52	1	69	15	0	4	2	9	.18	12	.259	.357	.339
1993 Carolina	AA	103	371	105	21	2	10	—	—	160	47	47	30	1	47	9	4	1	0	2	.00	13	.283	.350	.431
1994 Buffalo	AAA	83	260	55	16	0	5	—	—	86	27	33	28	0	41	3	0	0	1	0	.00	5	.212	.294	.331
1995 Calgary	AAA	90	301	101	25	1	10	—	—	158	40	59	21	2	42	5	0	4	2	2	.50	5	.336	.384	.525
1996 Erie	A-	3	10	3	1	0	0	—	—	4	1	2	1	0	2	1	0	0	0	0	.00	0	.300	.417	.400
1996 Pittsburgh	NL	48	140	41	14	1	1	(0	1)	60	18	14	14	1	22	1	1	0	1	0	1.00	3	.293	.361	.429

Al Osuna

Pitches: Left   **Bats:** Right   **Pos:** RP-10   **Ht:** 6'3"   **Wt:** 200   **Born:** 8/10/65   **Age:** 31

		HOW MUCH HE PITCHED						WHAT HE GAVE UP										THE RESULTS					
Year Team	Lg	G	GS	CG	GF	IP	BFP	H	R	ER	HR	SH	SF	HB	TBB	IBB	SO	WP	Bk	W	L	Pct.	ShO	Sv-Op	Hld	ERA
1996 Rio Grande *	IND	14	14	3	0	104	427	74	39	33	11	3	2	3	42	0	115	8	2	8	2	.800	1	0--	—	2.86
Las Vegas *	AAA	11	0	0	3	15.2	64	9	6	4	2	0	0	0	5	0	17	1	0	1	0	1.000	0	0--	—	2.30
1990 Houston	NL	12	0	0	2	11.1	48	10	6	6	1	0	2	3	6	1	6	3	0	2	0	1.000	0	0-1	1	4.76
1991 Houston	NL	71	0	0	32	81.2	353	59	39	31	5	6	5	3	46	5	68	3	1	7	6	.538	0	12-21	10	3.42
1992 Houston	NL	66	0	0	17	61.2	270	52	29	29	8	5	6	1	38	5	37	3	1	6	3	.667	0	0-2	6	4.23
1993 Houston	NL	44	0	0	6	25.1	107	17	10	9	3	4	4	1	13	2	21	3	0	1	1	.500	0	2-2	11	3.20
1994 Los Angeles	NL	15	0	0	4	8.2	43	13	6	6	0	0	0	0	4	0	7	0	1	2	0	1.000	0	0-1	6	6.23
1996 San Diego	NL	10	0	0	0	4	20	5	1	1	0	0	1	1	2	1	4	1	1	0	0	.000	0	0-1	1	2.25
6 ML YEARS		218	0	0	61	192.2	841	156	91	82	17	15	18	9	109	14	143	13	3	18	10	.643	0	14-28	35	3.83

Antonio Osuna

Pitches: Right   **Bats:** Right   **Pos:** RP-73   **Ht:** 5'11"   **Wt:** 160   **Born:** 4/12/73   **Age:** 24

		HOW MUCH HE PITCHED						WHAT HE GAVE UP										THE RESULTS					
Year Team	Lg	G	GS	CG	GF	IP	BFP	H	R	ER	HR	SH	SF	HB	TBB	IBB	SO	WP	Bk	W	L	Pct.	ShO	Sv-Op	Hld	ERA
1991 Dodgers	R	8	0	0	6	11	44	8	5	1	0	0	0	0	0	0	13	2	1	0	0	.000	0	4--	—	0.82
Yakima	A-	13	0	0	11	25.1	101	18	10	9	1	1	0	4	8	0	38	1	0	0	0	.000	0	5--	—	3.20
1993 Bakersfield	A+	14	2	0	11	18.1	76	19	10	10	2	0	0	0	5	0	20	0	1	0	2	.000	0	2--	—	4.91
1994 San Antonio	AA	35	0	0	32	46	172	19	6	5	0	2	0	2	18	1	53	0	3	1	2	.333	0	19--	—	0.98
Albuquerque	AAA	6	0	0	6	6	24	5	1	0	0	0	0	1	1	0	8	1	0	0	0	.000	0	4--	—	0.00
1995 San Bernrdo	A+	5	0	0	2	7	31	3	1	1	1	1	0	2	5	0	11	3	1	0	0	.000	0	0--	—	1.29
Albuquerque	AAA	24	0	0	19	25.1	107	18	10	10	3	1	1	2	14	0	30	5	1	0	1	.000	0	11--	—	3.55
1996 Albuquerque	AAA	1	0	0	1	1	4	2	0	0	0	0	0	0	1	0	0	0	0	0	0	.000	0	0--	—	0.00
1995 Los Angeles	NL	39	0	0	8	44.2	186	39	22	22	5	2	1	1	20	2	46	1	0	2	4	.333	0	0-2	11	4.43
1996 Los Angeles	NL	73	0	0	21	84	342	65	33	28	6	7	5	2	32	12	85	3	2	9	6	.600	0	4-9	16	3.00
2 ML YEARS		112	0	0	29	128.2	528	104	55	50	11	9	6	3	52	14	131	4	2	11	10	.524	0	4-11	27	3.50

Ricky Otero

Bats: Both   **Throws:** Right   **Pos:** CF-100; PH-6   **Ht:** 5'5"   **Wt:** 150   **Born:** 4/15/72   **Age:** 25

		BATTING																BASERUNNING				PERCENTAGES		
Year Team	Lg	G	AB	H	2B	3B	HR	(Hm	Rd)	TB	R	RBI	TBB	IBB	SO	HBP	SH	SF	SB	CS	SB%	GDP	Avg	OBP	SLG
1991 Kingsport	R+	66	235	81	16	3	7	—	—	124	47	52	35	5	32	2	1	6	12	4	.75	4	.345	.424	.528
Pittsfield	A-	6	24	7	0	0	0	—	—	7	4	2	2	0	1	0	0	0	4	0	1.00	4	.292	.346	.292
1992 Columbia	A	96	353	106	24	4	8	—	—	162	57	60	38	0	53	3	4	6	39	13	.75	4	.300	.368	.459
St. Lucie	A+	40	151	48	8	4	0	—	—	64	20	19	9	1	11	2	3	2	10	5	.67	1	.318	.360	.424
1993 Binghamton	AA	124	503	133	21	10	2	—	—	180	63	54	38	2	57	7	7	4	28	15	.65	5	.264	.322	.358
1994 Binghamton	AA	128	531	156	31	9	7	—	—	226	96	57	50	1	49	3	4	4	33	16	.67	7	.294	.355	.426
1995 Norfolk	AAA	72	295	79	8	6	1	—	—	102	37	23	27	0	33	1	2	0	16	13	.55	2	.268	.331	.346
1996 Scranton-WB	AAA	46	177	53	9	8	1	—	—	81	39	9	28	1	13	0	1	2	15	6	.71	2	.299	.393	.458
1995 New York	NL	35	51	7	2	0	0	(0	0)	9	5	1	3	0	10	0	1	0	2	1	.67	1	.137	.185	.176
1996 Philadelphia	NL	104	411	112	11	7	2	(0	2)	143	54	32	34	0	30	2	0	2	16	10	.62	3	.273	.330	.348
2 ML YEARS		139	462	119	13	7	2	(0	2)	152	59	33	37	0	40	2	1	2	18	11	.62	4	.258	.314	.329

Eric Owens

Bats: R   **Throws:** R   **Pos:** LF-52; PH-36; 2B-6; 3B-5   **Ht:** 6'1"   **Wt:** 185   **Born:** 2/3/71   **Age:** 26

		BATTING																BASERUNNING				PERCENTAGES		
Year Team	Lg	G	AB	H	2B	3B	HR	(Hm	Rd)	TB	R	RBI	TBB	IBB	SO	HBP	SH	SF	SB	CS	SB%	GDP	Avg	OBP	SLG
1992 Billings	R+	67	239	72	10	3	3	—	—	97	41	26	23	0	22	0	3	0	15	4	.79	1	.301	.363	.406
1993 Winston-Sal	A+	122	487	132	25	4	10	—	—	195	74	63	53	0	69	4	4	7	20	12	.63	8	.271	.343	.400
1994 Chattanooga	AA	134	523	133	17	3	3	—	—	165	73	36	54	0	86	2	4	5	38	14	.73	10	.254	.325	.315
1995 Indianapls	AAA	108	427	134	24	4	12	—	—	210	86	63	52	2	61	1	3	2	33	12	.73	7	.314	.388	.492
1996 Indianapls	AAA	33	128	41	8	2	4	—	—	65	24	14	11	3	16	1	0	0	6	3	.67	3	.320	.379	.508
1995 Cincinnati	NL	2	2	2	0	0	0	(0	0)	2	0	1	0	0	0	0	1	0	0	0	.00	0	1.000	1.000	1.000
1996 Cincinnati	NL	88	205	41	6	0	0	(0	0)	47	26	9	23	1	38	1	1	2	16	2	.89	2	.200	.281	.229
2 ML YEARS		90	207	43	6	0	0	(0	0)	49	26	10	23	1	38	1	2	2	16	2	.89	2	.208	.288	.237

Jayhawk Owens

Bats: Right   **Throws:** Right   **Pos:** C-68; PH-14   **Ht:** 6'1"   **Wt:** 213   **Born:** 2/10/69   **Age:** 28

		BATTING																BASERUNNING				PERCENTAGES		
Year Team	Lg	G	AB	H	2B	3B	HR	(Hm	Rd)	TB	R	RBI	TBB	IBB	SO	HBP	SH	SF	SB	CS	SB%	GDP	Avg	OBP	SLG
1996 Colo. Sprng *	AAA	6	22	5	3	0	0	—	—	8	6	6	3	0	6	0	1	0	0	0	.00	1	.227	.320	.364
1993 Colorado	NL	33	86	18	5	0	3	(2	1)	32	12	6	6	1	30	2	0	0	1	0	1.00	1	.209	.277	.372
1994 Colorado	NL	6	12	3	0	1	0	(0	0)	5	4	1	3	0	3	0	0	0	0	0	.00	1	.250	.400	.417
1995 Colorado	NL	18	45	11	2	0	4	(3	1)	25	7	12	2	0	15	1	0	1	0	0	.00	0	.244	.286	.556
1996 Colorado	NL	73	180	43	9	1	4	(3	1)	66	31	17	27	0	56	1	0	2	4	1	.80	1	.239	.338	.367
4 ML YEARS		130	323	75	16	2	11	(8	3)	128	54	36	38	1	104	4	3	3	5	1	.83	3	.232	.318	.396

Alex Pacheco

Pitches: Right **Bats:** Right **Pos:** RP-5　　　　**Ht:** 6'3" **Wt:** 200 **Born:** 7/19/73 **Age:** 23

		HOW MUCH HE PITCHED						WHAT HE GAVE UP										THE RESULTS					
Year Team	Lg	G	GS	CG	GF	IP	BFP	H	R	ER	HR	SH	SF	HB	TBB	IBB	SO	WP	Bk	W	L	Pct.	ShO	Sv-Op	Hld	ERA
1990 Expos	R	6	0	0	0	8.2	41	11	7	5	0	0	0	0	4	0	5	2	1	1	0	1.000	0	0--	—	5.19
1991 Expos	R	15	4	0	3	44.1	209	56	32	25	0	1	2	1	26	0	19	6	0	3	0	1.000	0	1--	—	5.08
1992 Jamestown	A-	16	5	0	4	50.1	229	53	36	31	5	2	2	3	29	1	32	2	1	3	3	.500	0	0--	—	5.54
1993 Jamestown	A-	6	1	0	1	14	60	11	7	5	0	0	1	0	4	0	15	4	0	0	1	.000	0	0--	—	3.21
Burlington	A	13	7	0	2	43	194	47	31	20	3	2	2	3	12	0	24	3	0	3	5	.375	0	1--	—	4.19
1994 Burlington	A	37	4	0	19	68.1	302	79	51	39	6	7	2	6	22	1	69	5	0	3	8	.273	0	5--	—	5.14
W. Palm Bch	A+	9	0	0	0	12	47	9	3	3	1	0	1	0	4	0	12	2	0	1	0	1.000	0	0--	—	2.25
1995 Ottawa	AAA	4	0	0	0	8.2	35	8	6	6	2	0	0	0	5	0	4	0	0	1	0	1.000	0	0--	—	6.23
1996 Harrisburg	AA	18	0	0	4	26.1	113	26	10	8	2	1	1	1	12	1	27	0	0	5	2	.714	0	0--	—	2.73
Ottawa	AAA	33	0	0	12	41.2	191	47	32	30	6	5	1	6	18	0	34	2	0	2	2	.500	0	6--	—	6.48
1996 Montreal	NL	5	0	0	2	5.2	26	8	7	7	2	0	0	1	0	1	7	0	0	0	0	.000	0	0-0	0	11.12

Tom Pagnozzi

Bats: Right **Throws:** Right **Pos:** C-116; PH-2; 1B-1　　　**Ht:** 6'1" **Wt:** 195 **Born:** 7/30/62 **Age:** 34

		BATTING																	BASERUNNING				PERCENTAGES		
Year Team	Lg	G	AB	H	2B	3B	HR	(Hm	Rd)	TB	R	RBI	TBB	IBB	SO	HBP	SH	SF	SB	CS	SB%	GDP	Avg	OBP	SLG
1996 Louisville *	AAA	8	26	4	0	0	2	—	—	10	5	3	2	1	2	0	0	0	0	0	.00	0	.154	.241	.385
1987 St. Louis	NL	27	48	9	1	0	1	(2	0)	16	8	9	4	2	13	1	0	1	1	0	1.00	0	.188	.250	.333
1988 St. Louis	NL	81	195	55	9	0	0	(0	0)	64	17	15	11	1	32	0	2	1	0	0	.00	5	.282	.319	.328
1989 St. Louis	NL	52	80	12	2	0	0	(0	0)	14	3	3	6	2	19	1	0	1	0	0	.00	7	.150	.216	.175
1990 St. Louis	NL	69	220	61	15	0	2	(2	0)	82	20	23	14	1	37	1	0	2	1	1	.50	1	.277	.321	.373
1991 St. Louis	NL	140	459	121	24	5	2	(2	0)	161	38	57	36	6	63	4	6	5	9	13	.41	10	.264	.319	.351
1992 St. Louis	NL	139	485	121	26	3	7	(3	4)	174	33	44	28	9	64	1	6	3	2	5	.29	15	.249	.290	.359
1993 St. Louis	NL	92	330	85	15	1	7	(1	6)	123	31	41	19	6	30	1	0	5	1	0	1.00	9	.258	.296	.373
1994 St. Louis	NL	70	243	66	12	1	7	(2	5)	101	21	40	21	5	39	0	0	2	0	0	.00	3	.272	.327	.416
1995 St. Louis	NL	62	219	47	14	1	2	(1	1)	69	17	15	11	0	31	1	0	1	0	1	.00	9	.215	.254	.315
1996 St. Louis	NL	119	407	110	23	0	13	(9	4)	172	48	55	24	2	78	2	3	4	4	1	.80	9	.270	.311	.423
10 ML YEARS		851	2686	687	141	11	42	(22	20)	976	236	302	174	34	406	11	18	24	18	21	.46	65	.256	.301	.363

Lance Painter

Pitches: Left **Bats:** Left **Pos:** RP-33; SP-1　　　**Ht:** 6'1" **Wt:** 197 **Born:** 7/21/67 **Age:** 29

		HOW MUCH HE PITCHED						WHAT HE GAVE UP											THE RESULTS					
Year Team	Lg	G	GS	CG	GF	IP	BFP	H	R	ER	HR	SH	SF	HB	TBB	IBB	SO	WP	Bk	W	L	Pct.	ShO	Sv-Op	Hld	ERA
1993 Colorado	NL	10	6	1	2	39	166	52	26	26	5	1	0	0	9	0	16	2	0	2	2	.500	0	0-0	0	6.00
1994 Colorado	NL	15	14	0	1	73.2	336	91	51	50	9	3	5	1	26	2	41	3	1	4	6	.400	0	0-0	0	6.11
1995 Colorado	NL	33	1	0	7	45.1	198	55	23	22	9	0	0	2	10	0	36	4	1	3	0	1.000	0	1-1	4	4.37
1996 Colorado	NL	34	1	0	4	50.2	234	56	37	33	12	3	3	3	25	3	48	1	0	4	2	.667	0	0-1	4	5.86
4 ML YEARS		92	22	1	14	208.2	934	254	137	131	35	7	8	6	70	5	141	10	2	13	10	.565	0	1-2	8	5.65

Donn Pall

Pitches: Right **Bats:** Right **Pos:** RP-12　　　**Ht:** 6'1" **Wt:** 180 **Born:** 1/11/62 **Age:** 35

		HOW MUCH HE PITCHED						WHAT HE GAVE UP											THE RESULTS					
Year Team	Lg	G	GS	CG	GF	IP	BFP	H	R	ER	HR	SH	SF	HB	TBB	IBB	SO	WP	Bk	W	L	Pct.	ShO	Sv-Op	Hld	ERA
1996 Charlotte *	AAA	38	0	0	33	51.2	208	42	21	17	3	1	4	4	12	0	53	2	0	3	3	.500	0	17--	—	2.96
1988 Chicago	AL	17	0	0	6	28.2	130	39	11	11	1	2	1	0	8	1	16	1	0	0	2	.000	0	0-0	4	3.45
1989 Chicago	AL	53	0	0	27	87	370	90	35	32	9	8	2	8	19	3	58	4	1	4	5	.444	0	6-10	5	3.31
1990 Chicago	AL	56	0	0	11	76	306	63	33	28	7	4	2	4	24	8	39	2	0	3	5	.375	0	2-3	13	3.32
1991 Chicago	AL	51	0	0	7	71	282	59	22	19	7	4	0	3	20	3	40	2	0	7	2	.778	0	0-1	12	2.41
1992 Chicago	AL	39	0	0	12	73	323	79	43	40	9	1	3	2	27	8	27	1	2	5	2	.714	0	1-2	4	4.93
1993 ChA-Phi		47	0	0	11	76.1	320	77	32	26	6	7	1	2	14	3	40	3	1	3	3	.500	0	1-2	9	3.07
1994 NYA-ChN		28	0	0	7	39	176	51	20	16	4	0	1	1	10	0	23	2	0	1	2	.333	0	0-0	3	3.69
1996 Florida	NL	12	0	0	2	18.2	80	16	15	12	3	1	1	1	9	1	9	1	0	1	1	.500	0	0-0	1	5.79
1993 Chicago	AL	39	0	0	9	58.2	251	62	25	21	5	6	1	2	11	3	29	3	1	2	3	.400	0	1-2	8	3.22
Philadelphia	NL	8	0	0	2	17.2	69	15	7	5	1	1	0	0	3	0	11	0	1	1	0	1.000	0	0-0	1	2.55
1994 New York	AL	26	0	0	7	35	157	43	18	14	3	0	1	1	9	0	21	2	0	1	2	.333	0	0-0	3	3.60
Chicago	NL	2	0	0	0	4	19	8	2	2	1	0	0	0	1	0	2	0	0	0	0	.000	0	0-0	0	4.50
8 ML YEARS		303	0	0	83	469.2	1987	474	211	184	46	27	11	20	131	27	252	16	4	24	22	.522	0	10-18	49	3.53

Orlando Palmeiro

Bats: L **Throws:** R **Pos:** PH-22; CF-17; RF-8; LF-7; DH-4　　**Ht:** 5'11" **Wt:** 160 **Born:** 1/19/69 **Age:** 28

		BATTING																	BASERUNNING				PERCENTAGES		
Year Team	Lg	G	AB	H	2B	3B	HR	(Hm	Rd)	TB	R	RBI	TBB	IBB	SO	HBP	SH	SF	SB	CS	SB%	GDP	Avg	OBP	SLG
1991 Boise	A-	70	277	77	11	2	1	—	—	95	56	24	33	0	22	3	6	3	8	8	.50	8	.278	.358	.343
1992 Quad City	A	127	451	143	22	4	0	—	—	173	83	41	56	3	41	5	19	7	31	13	.70	5	.317	.393	.384
1993 Midland	AA	131	535	163	19	5	0	—	—	192	85	64	42	1	35	2	18	3	18	14	.56	13	.305	.356	.359
1994 Vancouver	AAA	117	458	150	28	4	1	—	—	189	79	47	58	4	46	1	4	3	21	16	.57	7	.328	.402	.413
1995 Vancouver	AAA	107	398	122	21	4	0	—	—	151	66	47	41	8	34	3	11	5	16	7	.70	11	.307	.371	.379

Year Team	Lg	G	AB	H	2B	3B	HR	(Hm	Rd)	TB	R	RBI	TBB	IBB	SO	HBP	SH	SF	SB	CS	SB%	GDP	Avg	OBP	SLG
1996 Vancouver	AAA	62	245	75	13	4	0	—	—	96	40	33	30	1	19	4	5	5	7	3	.70	4	.306	.384	.392
1995 California	AL	15	20	7	0	0	0	(0	0)	7	3	1	1	0	1	0	0	0	0	0	.00	0	.350	.381	.350
1996 California	AL	50	87	25	6	1	0	(0	0)	33	6	6	8	1	13	2	1	0	0	1	.00	1	.287	.361	.379
2 ML YEARS		65	107	32	6	1	0	(0	0)	40	9	7	9	1	14	2	1	0	0	1	.00	1	.299	.364	.374

Rafael Palmeiro

Bats: Left **Throws:** Left **Pos:** 1B-159; DH-3 **Ht:** 6'0" **Wt:** 190 **Born:** 9/24/64 **Age:** 32

Year Team	Lg	G	AB	H	2B	3B	HR	(Hm	Rd)	TB	R	RBI	TBB	IBB	SO	HBP	SH	SF	SB	CS	SB%	GDP	Avg	OBP	SLG
1986 Chicago	NL	22	73	18	4	0	3	(1	2)	31	9	12	4	0	6	1	0	0	1	1	.50	4	.247	.295	.425
1987 Chicago	NL	84	221	61	15	1	14	(5	9)	120	32	30	20	1	26	1	0	2	2	2	.50	4	.276	.336	.543
1988 Chicago	NL	152	580	178	41	5	8	(8	0)	253	75	53	38	6	34	3	2	6	12	2	.86	11	.307	.349	.436
1989 Texas	AL	156	559	154	23	4	8	(4	4)	209	76	64	63	3	48	6	2	2	4	3	.57	18	.275	.354	.374
1990 Texas	AL	154	598	191	35	6	14	(9	5)	280	72	89	40	6	59	3	2	8	3	3	.50	24	.319	.361	.468
1991 Texas	AL	159	631	203	49	3	26	(12	14)	336	115	88	68	10	72	6	2	7	4	3	.57	17	.322	.389	.532
1992 Texas	AL	159	608	163	27	4	22	(8	14)	264	84	85	72	8	83	10	5	6	2	3	.40	10	.268	.352	.434
1993 Texas	AL	160	597	176	40	2	37	(22	15)	331	124	105	73	22	85	5	2	9	22	3	.88	8	.295	.371	.554
1994 Baltimore	AL	111	436	139	32	0	23	(11	12)	240	82	76	54	1	63	2	0	6	7	3	.70	11	.319	.392	.550
1995 Baltimore	AL	143	554	172	30	2	39	(21	18)	323	89	104	62	5	65	3	0	5	3	1	.75	12	.310	.380	.583
1996 Baltimore	AL	162	626	181	40	2	39	(21	18)	342	110	142	95	12	96	3	0	8	8	0	1.00	9	.289	.381	.546
11 ML YEARS		1462	5483	1636	336	29	233	(122	111)	2729	868	848	589	74	637	43	15	59	68	24	.74	128	.298	.367	.498

Dean Palmer

Bats: Right **Throws:** Right **Pos:** 3B-154; DH-1 **Ht:** 6'1" **Wt:** 210 **Born:** 12/27/68 **Age:** 28

Year Team	Lg	G	AB	H	2B	3B	HR	(Hm	Rd)	TB	R	RBI	TBB	IBB	SO	HBP	SH	SF	SB	CS	SB%	GDP	Avg	OBP	SLG
1989 Texas	AL	16	19	2	2	0	0	(0	0)	4	0	1	0	0	12	0	0	1	0	0	.00	0	.105	.100	.211
1991 Texas	AL	81	268	50	9	2	15	(6	9)	108	38	37	32	0	98	3	1	0	0	2	.00	4	.187	.281	.403
1992 Texas	AL	152	541	124	25	0	26	(11	15)	227	74	72	62	2	154	4	2	4	10	4	.71	9	.229	.311	.420
1993 Texas	AL	148	519	127	31	2	33	(12	21)	261	88	96	53	4	154	8	0	5	11	10	.52	5	.245	.321	.503
1994 Texas	AL	93	342	84	14	2	19	(11	8)	159	50	59	26	0	89	2	0	1	3	4	.43	7	.246	.302	.465
1995 Texas	AL	36	119	40	6	0	9	(5	4)	73	30	24	21	1	21	4	0	1	1	1	.50	2	.336	.448	.613
1996 Texas	AL	154	582	163	26	2	38	(19	19)	307	98	107	59	4	145	5	0	6	2	0	1.00	15	.280	.348	.527
7 ML YEARS		680	2390	590	113	8	140	(64	76)	1139	378	396	253	11	673	26	3	18	27	21	.56	42	.247	.323	.477

Jose Paniagua

Pitches: Right **Bats:** Right **Pos:** SP-11; RP-2 **Ht:** 6'2" **Wt:** 185 **Born:** 8/20/73 **Age:** 23

		HOW MUCH HE PITCHED						WHAT HE GAVE UP									THE RESULTS						
Year Team	Lg	G	GS	CG	GF	IP	BFP	H	R	ER	HR	SH	SF	HB	TBB	IBB	SO	WP	Bk	W	L	Pct.	ShO	Sv-Op	Hld	ERA
1993 Expos	R	4	4	1	0	27	100	13	2	2	0	0	2	5	0	25	1	1	3	0	1.000	0	0--	—	0.67
1994 W. Palm Bch	A+	26	26	1	0	141	606	131	82	57	6	5	4	6	54	2	110	13	2	9	9	.500	0	0--	—	3.64
1995 Harrisburg	AA	25	25	2	0	126.1	575	140	84	75	9	5	5	12	62	0	89	8	0	7	12	.368	1	0--	—	5.34
1996 Harrisburg	AA	3	3	0	0	18	66	12	1	0	0	1	0	1	2	0	16	1	0	3	0	1.000	0	0--	—	0.00
Ottawa	AAA	15	14	2	0	85	352	72	39	30	7	2	4	3	23	0	61	4	0	9	5	.643	1	0--	—	3.18
1996 Montreal	NL	13	11	0	0	51	223	55	24	20	7	1	1	3	23	0	27	2	2	2	4	.333	0	0-0	0	3.53

Craig Paquette

Bats: R **Throws:** R **Pos:** 3B-51; LF-47; 1B-19; SS-11; PH-7; DH-6 **Ht:** 6'0" **Wt:** 190 **Born:** 3/28/69 **Age:** 28

Year Team	Lg	G	AB	H	2B	3B	HR	(Hm	Rd)	TB	R	RBI	TBB	IBB	SO	HBP	SH	SF	SB	CS	SB%	GDP	Avg	OBP	SLG
1996 Omaha *	AAA	18	63	21	3	0	4	—	—	36	9	13	8	1	14	0	0	1	1	0	1.00	3	.333	.403	.571
1993 Oakland	AL	105	393	86	20	4	12	(8	4)	150	35	46	14	2	108	0	1	1	4	2	.67	7	.219	.245	.382
1994 Oakland	AL	14	49	7	2	0	0	(0	0)	9	0	0	0	0	14	0	1	0	1	0	1.00	0	.143	.143	.184
1995 Oakland	AL	105	283	64	13	1	13	(8	5)	118	42	49	12	0	88	1	3	5	5	2	.71	5	.226	.256	.417
1996 Kansas City	AL	118	429	111	15	1	22	(12	10)	194	61	67	23	2	101	2	3	5	5	3	.63	11	.259	.296	.452
4 ML YEARS		342	1154	268	50	6	47	(28	19)	471	138	162	49	4	311	3	8	11	15	7	.68	23	.232	.263	.408

Mark Parent

Bats: Right **Throws:** Right **Pos:** C-51; PH-4; 1B-1 **Ht:** 6'5" **Wt:** 245 **Born:** 9/16/61 **Age:** 35

Year Team	Lg	G	AB	H	2B	3B	HR	(Hm	Rd)	TB	R	RBI	TBB	IBB	SO	HBP	SH	SF	SB	CS	SB%	GDP	Avg	OBP	SLG
1986 San Diego	NL	8	14	2	0	0	0	(0	0)	2	1	0	1	0	3	0	0	0	0	0	.00	1	.143	.200	.143
1987 San Diego	NL	12	25	2	0	0	0	(0	0)	2	0	2	0	0	9	0	0	0	0	0	.00	0	.080	.080	.080
1988 San Diego	NL	41	118	23	3	0	6	(4	2)	44	9	15	6	0	23	0	0	1	0	0	.00	0	.195	.232	.373
1989 San Diego	NL	52	141	27	4	0	7	(6	1)	52	12	21	8	2	34	0	1	4	1	0	1.00	5	.191	.229	.369
1990 San Diego	NL	65	189	42	11	0	3	(1	2)	62	13	16	16	3	29	0	3	0	1	0	1.00	0	.222	.283	.328
1991 Texas	AL	3	1	0	0	0	0	(0	0)	0	0	0	0	0	1	0	0	0	0	0	.00	0	.000	.000	.000
1992 Baltimore	AL	17	34	8	1	0	2	(0	2)	15	4	4	1	0	7	1	2	0	0	0	.00	0	.235	.316	.441

					BATTING														BASERUNNING				PERCENTAGES		
Year Team	Lg	G	AB	H	2B	3B	HR	(Hm	Rd)	TB	R	RBI	TBB	IBB	SO	HBP	SH	SF	SB	CS	SB%	GDP	Avg	OBP	SLG
1993 Baltimore	AL	22	54	14	2	0	4	(1	3)	28	7	12	3	0	14	0	3	1	0	0	.00	1	.259	.293	.519
1994 Chicago	NL	44	99	26	4	0	3	(0	3)	39	8	16	13	1	24	1	1	2	0	1	.00	5	.263	.348	.394
1995 Pit-ChN	NL	81	265	62	11	0	18	(7	11)	127	30	38	26	2	69	0	1	1	0	0	.00	6	.234	.302	.479
1996 Det-Bal	AL	56	137	31	7	0	9	(4	5)	65	17	23	5	0	37	0	1	1	0	0	.00	3	.226	.252	.474
1995 Pittsburgh	NL	69	233	54	9	0	15	(5	10)	108	25	33	23	2	62	0	1	0	0	0	.00	5	.232	.301	.464
Chicago	NL	12	32	8	2	0	3	(2	1)	19	5	5	3	0	7	0	0	0	0	0	.00	1	.250	.314	.594
1996 Detroit	AL	38	104	25	6	0	7	(4	3)	52	13	17	3	0	27	0	1	0	0	0	.00	2	.240	.259	.500
Baltimore	AL	18	33	6	1	0	2	(0	2)	13	4	6	2	0	10	0	1	0	0	0	.00	1	.182	.229	.394
11 ML YEARS		401	1077	237	43	0	52	(23	29)	436	101	147	81	8	250	2	12	9	2	1	.67	24	.220	.274	.405

Chan Ho Park

Pitches: Right **Bats:** Right **Pos:** RP-38; SP-10 **Ht:** 6'2" **Wt:** 195 **Born:** 6/30/73 **Age:** 24

		HOW MUCH HE PITCHED						WHAT HE GAVE UP										THE RESULTS						
Year Team	Lg	G	GS	CG	GF	IP	BFP	H	R	ER	HR	SH	SF	HB	TBB	IBB	SO	WP	Bk	W	L	Pct.	ShO	Sv-Op	Hld	ERA
1994 San Antonio	AA	20	20	0	0	101.1	446	91	52	40	4	5	3	4	57	0	100	7	2	5	7	.417	0	0--	—	3.55
1995 Albuquerque	AAA	23	22	0	0	110	487	93	64	60	10	3	2	6	76	2	101	8	2	6	7	.462	0	0--	—	4.91
1994 Los Angeles	NL	2	0	0	1	4	23	5	5	5	1	0	0	1	5	0	6	0	0	0	0	.000	0	0-0	0	11.25
1995 Los Angeles	NL	2	1	0	0	4	16	2	2	2	1	0	0	0	2	0	7	0	1	0	0	.000	0	0-0	0	4.50
1996 Los Angeles	NL	48	10	0	7	108.2	477	82	48	44	7	8	1	4	71	3	119	4	3	5	5	.500	0	0-0	4	3.64
3 ML YEARS		52	11	0	8	116.2	516	89	55	51	9	8	1	5	78	3	132	4	4	5	5	.500	0	0-0	4	3.93

Rick Parker

Bats: Right **Throws:** Right **Pos:** PH-15; CF-3; LF-1 **Ht:** 6'0" **Wt:** 185 **Born:** 3/20/63 **Age:** 34

					BATTING														BASERUNNING				PERCENTAGES		
Year Team	Lg	G	AB	H	2B	3B	HR	(Hm	Rd)	TB	R	RBI	TBB	IBB	SO	HBP	SH	SF	SB	CS	SB%	GDP	Avg	OBP	SLG
1996 Albuquerque *	AAA	50	175	53	7	3	0	—	—	66	26	23	23	1	27	3	4	2	7	6	.54	2	.303	.389	.377
1990 San Francisco	NL	54	107	26	5	0	2	(0	2)	37	19	14	10	0	15	1	3	0	6	1	.86	1	.243	.314	.346
1991 San Francisco	NL	13	14	1	0	0	0	(0	0)	1	0	1	1	0	5	0	0	0	0	0	.00	0	.071	.133	.071
1993 Houston	NL	45	45	15	3	0	0	(0	0)	18	11	4	3	0	8	0	1	0	1	2	.33	2	.333	.375	.400
1994 New York	NL	8	16	1	0	0	0	(0	0)	1	1	0	0	0	2	0	0	0	0	0	.00	0	.063	.063	.063
1995 Los Angeles	NL	27	29	8	0	0	0	(0	0)	8	3	4	2	0	4	0	2	0	1	1	.50	1	.276	.323	.276
1996 Los Angeles	NL	16	14	4	1	0	0	(0	0)	5	2	1	0	0	2	1	0	0	1	0	1.00	1	.286	.333	.357
6 ML YEARS		163	225	55	9	0	2	(0	2)	70	36	24	16	0	36	2	8	0	9	4	.69	5	.244	.300	.311

Jose Parra

Pitches: Right **Bats:** Right **Pos:** RP-22; SP-5 **Ht:** 5'11" **Wt:** 165 **Born:** 11/28/72 **Age:** 24

		HOW MUCH HE PITCHED						WHAT HE GAVE UP										THE RESULTS						
Year Team	Lg	G	GS	CG	GF	IP	BFP	H	R	ER	HR	SH	SF	HB	TBB	IBB	SO	WP	Bk	W	L	Pct.	ShO	Sv-Op	Hld	ERA
1990 Dodgers	R	10	10	1	0	57.1	228	50	22	17	1	0	3	1	18	0	50	1	1	5	3	.625	0	0--	—	2.67
1991 Great Falls	R+	14	14	1	0	64.1	298	86	58	44	5	2	7	2	18	0	55	0	4	4	6	.400	1	0--	—	6.16
1992 Bakersfield	A+	24	23	3	0	143	618	151	73	57	5	4	4	4	47	4	107	5	1	7	8	.467	0	0--	—	3.59
San Antonio	AA	3	3	0	0	14.2	74	22	12	10	0	2	1	1	7	0	7	0	1	2	0	1.000	0	0--	—	6.14
1993 San Antonio	AA	17	17	0	0	111.1	452	103	46	39	10	9	3	6	12	2	87	1	0	1	8	.111	0	0--	—	3.15
1994 Albuquerque	AAA	27	27	1	0	145	636	190	92	77	10	4	4	5	38	2	90	10	0	10	10	.500	0	0--	—	4.78
1995 Albuquerque	AAA	12	10	1	1	52.2	232	62	33	30	7	4	4	5	17	3	33	2	0	3	2	.600	1	0--	—	5.13
1996 Salt Lake	AAA	23	1	0	11	44	192	51	25	25	2	3	4	6	13	2	26	1	0	5	3	.625	0	8--	—	5.11
1995 LA-Min		20	12	0	0	72	339	93	67	57	13	0	4	3	28	1	36	3	1	1	5	.167	0	0-0	0	7.13
1996 Minnesota	AL	27	5	0	7	70	320	88	48	47	15	1	3	3	27	0	50	4	1	5	5	.500	0	0-1	0	6.04
1995 Los Angeles	NL	8	0	0	0	10.1	47	10	8	5	2	0	1	1	6	1	7	0	1	0	0	.000	0	0-0	0	4.35
Minnesota	AL	12	12	0	0	61.2	292	83	59	52	11	0	3	2	22	0	29	3	0	1	5	.167	0	0-0	0	7.59
2 ML YEARS		47	17	0	7	142	659	181	115	104	28	1	7	6	55	1	86	7	2	6	10	.375	0	0-1	0	6.59

Jeff Parrett

Pitches: Right **Bats:** Right **Pos:** RP-51 **Ht:** 6'3" **Wt:** 205 **Born:** 8/26/61 **Age:** 35

		HOW MUCH HE PITCHED						WHAT HE GAVE UP										THE RESULTS						
Year Team	Lg	G	GS	CG	GF	IP	BFP	H	R	ER	HR	SH	SF	HB	TBB	IBB	SO	WP	Bk	W	L	Pct.	ShO	Sv-Op	Hld	ERA
1986 Montreal	NL	12	0	0	6	20.1	91	19	11	11	3	0	1	0	13	0	21	2	0	0	1	.000	0	0--	—	4.87
1987 Montreal	NL	45	0	0	26	62	267	53	33	29	8	5	1	0	30	4	56	6	1	7	6	.538	0	6-11	3	4.21
1988 Montreal	NL	61	0	0	34	91.2	369	66	29	27	8	9	6	1	45	9	62	4	1	12	4	.750	0	6-10	2	2.65
1989 Philadelphia	NL	72	0	0	34	105.2	444	90	43	35	6	7	5	0	44	13	98	1	3	12	6	.667	0	6-12	6	2.98
1990 Phi-Atl	NL	67	5	0	19	108.2	479	119	62	56	11	7	5	2	55	10	86	5	1	5	10	.333	0	2-8	11	4.64
1991 Atlanta	NL	18	0	0	9	21.1	109	31	18	15	2	2	0	0	12	2	14	4	0	1	2	.333	0	1-1	0	6.33
1992 Oakland	AL	66	0	0	14	98.1	410	81	35	33	7	4	4	2	42	3	78	13	0	9	1	.900	0	0-1	19	3.02
1993 Colorado	NL	40	6	0	13	73.2	341	78	47	44	6	4	5	2	45	9	66	11	1	3	3	.500	0	1-4	1	5.38
1995 St. Louis	NL	59	0	0	17	76.2	328	71	33	31	8	5	2	1	28	5	71	7	0	4	7	.364	0	0-2	7	3.64
1996 StL-Phi	NL	51	0	0	23	66.1	288	64	25	25	2	2	2	1	31	4	64	10	0	3	3	.500	0	0-2	2	3.39
1990 Philadelphia	NL	47	5	0	14	81.2	355	92	51	47	10	3	1	1	36	8	69	3	1	4	9	.308	0	1-4	8	5.18
Atlanta	NL	20	0	0	5	27	124	27	11	9	1	4	4	1	19	2	17	2	0	1	1	.500	0	1-4	3	3.00
1996 St. Louis	NL	33	0	0	16	42.1	186	40	20	20	2	1	1	0	20	2	42	7	0	2	2	.500	0	0-2	1	4.25

Year Team	Lg	G	GS	CG	GF	IP	BFP	H	R	ER	HR	SH	SF	HB	TBB	IBB	SO	WP	Bk	W	L	Pct.	ShO	Sv-Op	Hld	ERA
				HOW MUCH HE PITCHED						**WHAT HE GAVE UP**												**THE RESULTS**				
Philadelphia	NL	18	0	0	7	24	102	24	5	5	0	1	1	0	11	2	22	3	0	1	1	.500	0	0-0	1	1.88
10 ML YEARS		491	11	0	195	724.2	3126	672	336	306	61	45	31	9	345	59	616	69	7	56	43	.566	0	22--	—	3.80

Steve Parris

Pitches: Right **Bats:** Right **Pos:** SP-4; RP-4   **Ht:** 6'0" **Wt:** 190 **Born:** 12/17/67 **Age:** 29

Year Team	Lg	G	GS	CG	GF	IP	BFP	H	R	ER	HR	SH	SF	HB	TBB	IBB	SO	WP	Bk	W	L	Pct.	ShO	Sv-Op	Hld	ERA
1989 Batavia	A-	13	10	1	1	66.2	291	69	38	29	6	3	2	4	20	1	46	4	0	3	5	.375	0	0--	—	3.92
1990 Batavia	A-	14	14	0	0	81.2	333	70	34	24	1	3	4	3	22	2	50	7	3	7	1	.875	0	0--	—	2.64
1991 Clearwater	A+	43	6	0	8	93	394	101	43	35	1	4	0	9	25	4	59	3	4	7	5	.583	0	1--	—	3.39
1992 Reading	AA	18	14	0	0	85.1	370	94	55	44	9	3	4	3	21	1	60	2	0	5	7	.417	0	0--	—	4.64
Scranton-WB	AAA	11	6	0	2	51.1	223	57	25	23	1	1	1	4	17	1	29	6	1	3	3	.500	0	1--	—	4.03
1993 Scranton-WB	AAA	3	0	0	0	5.2	30	9	9	8	3	0	0	1	3	0	4	1	0	0	0	.000	0	0--	—	12.71
Jacksonvlle	AA	7	1	0	0	13.2	64	15	9	9	3	0	1	2	6	0	5	0	0	0	1	.000	0	0--	—	5.93
1994 Salem	A+	17	7	0	1	57	247	58	24	23	7	0	2	6	21	1	48	1	0	3	3	.500	0	0--	—	3.63
1995 Carolina	AA	14	14	2	0	89.2	344	61	25	25	2	3	1	4	16	1	86	3	0	9	1	.900	2	0--	—	2.51
1996 Augusta	A	1	1	0	0	5	16	1	0	0	0	0	0	0	1	0	6	0	0	0	0	.000	0	0--	—	0.00
Carolina	AA	5	5	0	0	26.2	108	24	11	9	1	0	0	0	6	0	22	2	0	2	0	1.000	0	0--	—	3.04
1995 Pittsburgh	NL	15	15	1	0	82	360	89	49	49	12	3	2	7	33	1	61	4	0	6	6	.500	1	0-0	0	5.38
1996 Pittsburgh	NL	8	4	0	3	26.1	123	35	22	21	4	1	1	1	11	0	27	2	0	0	3	.000	0	0-0	0	7.18
2 ML YEARS		23	19	1	3	108.1	483	124	71	70	16	4	3	8	44	1	88	6	0	6	9	.400	1	0-0	0	5.82

Bob Patterson

Pitches: Left **Bats:** Right **Pos:** RP-79   **Ht:** 6'2" **Wt:** 195 **Born:** 5/16/59 **Age:** 38

Year Team	Lg	G	GS	CG	GF	IP	BFP	H	R	ER	HR	SH	SF	HB	TBB	IBB	SO	WP	Bk	W	L	Pct.	ShO	Sv-Op	Hld	ERA
1985 San Diego	NL	3	0	0	2	4	26	13	11	11	2	0	0	0	3	0	1	0	1	0	0	.000	0	0--	—	24.75
1986 Pittsburgh	NL	11	5	0	2	36.1	159	49	20	20	0	1	1	0	5	2	20	0	1	2	3	.400	0	0--	—	4.95
1987 Pittsburgh	NL	15	7	0	2	43	201	49	34	32	5	6	3	1	22	4	27	1	0	1	4	.200	0	0-0	0	6.70
1989 Pittsburgh	NL	12	3	0	2	26.2	109	23	13	12	3	1	1	0	8	2	20	0	0	4	3	.571	0	1-1	0	4.05
1990 Pittsburgh	NL	55	5	0	19	94.2	386	88	33	31	9	5	3	3	21	7	70	1	2	8	5	.615	0	5-8	8	2.95
1991 Pittsburgh	NL	54	1	0	19	65.2	270	67	32	30	7	2	2	0	15	1	57	0	0	4	3	.571	0	2-3	13	4.11
1992 Pittsburgh	NL	60	0	0	26	64.2	268	59	22	21	7	3	2	0	23	6	43	3	0	6	3	.667	0	9-13	10	2.92
1993 Texas	AL	52	0	0	29	52.2	224	59	28	28	8	1	2	1	11	0	46	0	0	2	4	.333	0	1-2	6	4.78
1994 California	AL	47	0	0	11	42	170	35	21	19	6	0	0	2	15	2	30	1	0	2	3	.400	0	1-1	10	4.07
1995 California	AL	62	0	0	20	53.1	212	48	18	18	6	2	1	1	13	3	41	0	1	5	2	.714	0	0-1	12	3.04
1996 Chicago	NL	79	0	0	27	54.2	230	46	19	19	6	2	4	1	22	7	53	1	1	3	3	.500	0	8-10	15	3.13
11 ML YEARS		450	21	0	159	537.2	2255	536	251	241	59	23	19	9	158	34	408	7	6	37	33	.529	0	27--	—	4.03

Danny Patterson

Pitches: Right **Bats:** Right **Pos:** RP-7   **Ht:** 6'0" **Wt:** 185 **Born:** 2/17/71 **Age:** 26

Year Team	Lg	G	GS	CG	GF	IP	BFP	H	R	ER	HR	SH	SF	HB	TBB	IBB	SO	WP	Bk	W	L	Pct.	ShO	Sv-Op	Hld	ERA
1990 Butte	R+	13	3	0	2	28.1	135	36	23	20	3	0	3	1	14	1	18	3	1	0	3	.000	0	1--	—	6.35
1991 Rangers	R	11	9	0	0	50	201	43	21	18	1	1	0	3	12	0	46	2	3	5	3	.625	0	0--	—	3.24
1992 Gastonia	A	23	21	3	0	105.1	447	106	47	42	9	2	2	4	33	3	84	5	13	4	6	.400	1	0--	—	3.59
1993 Charlotte	A+	47	0	0	24	68	286	55	22	19	2	5	1	1	28	4	41	5	0	5	6	.455	0	7--	—	2.51
1994 Charlotte	A+	7	0	0	4	13.2	57	13	7	7	1	0	1	0	5	0	9	1	0	1	0	1.000	0	0--	—	4.61
Tulsa	AA	30	1	0	19	44	181	35	13	8	2	3	3	1	17	1	33	5	2	1	4	.200	0	6--	—	1.64
1995 Okla. City	AAA	14	0	0	3	27.1	111	23	8	5	0	3	2	1	9	2	9	4	0	1	0	1.000	0	2--	—	1.65
1996 Okla. City	AAA	44	0	0	34	80.1	334	79	22	15	5	2	0	7	15	3	53	5	0	6	2	.750	0	10--	—	1.68
1996 Texas	AL	7	0	0	5	8.2	38	10	4	0	0	0	0	0	3	1	5	0	0	0	0	.000	0	0-0	0	0.00

Dave Pavlas

Pitches: Right **Bats:** Right **Pos:** RP-16   **Ht:** 6'7" **Wt:** 205 **Born:** 8/12/62 **Age:** 34

Year Team	Lg	G	GS	CG	GF	IP	BFP	H	R	ER	HR	SH	SF	HB	TBB	IBB	SO	WP	Bk	W	L	Pct.	ShO	Sv-Op	Hld	ERA
1985 Peoria	A	17	15	3	2	110	452	90	40	32	7	3	1	3	32	0	86	6	1	8	3	.727	1	1--	—	2.62
1986 Winston-Sal	A+	28	26	5	0	173.1	739	172	91	74	8	6	4	6	57	2	143	11	1	14	6	.700	2	0--	—	3.84
1987 Pittsfield	AA	7	7	0	0	45	199	49	25	19	6	0	3	3	17	0	27	1	1	6	1	.857	0	0--	—	3.80
Tulsa	AA	13	12	0	1	59.2	280	79	51	51	9	1	0	3	27	0	46	7	0	1	6	.143	0	0--	—	7.69
1988 Tulsa	AA	26	5	1	9	77.1	299	52	26	17	3	6	2	5	18	1	69	4	6	5	2	.714	0	2--	—	1.98
Okla. City	AAA	13	8	0	2	52.1	237	59	29	26	1	1	2	3	28	0	40	2	1	3	1	.750	0	0--	—	4.47
1989 Okla. City	AAA	29	21	4	4	143.2	652	175	89	75	7	6	7	7	67	4	94	8	1	2	14	.125	0	0--	—	4.70
1990 Iowa	AAA	53	3	0	22	99.1	421	84	38	36	4	4	3	10	48	6	96	8	1	8	3	.727	0	8--	—	3.26
1991 Iowa	AAA	61	0	0	29	97.1	418	92	49	43	5	10	5	5	43	9	54	13	0	5	6	.455	0	7--	—	3.98
1992 Iowa	AAA	12	4	0	6	37.1	166	43	20	14	5	2	0	1	8	0	34	0	0	3	3	.500	0	0--	—	3.38
1995 Columbus	AAA	48	0	0	32	58.2	233	43	19	17	2	4	1	1	20	2	51	4	0	3	3	.500	0	18--	—	2.61
1996 Columbus	AAA	57	0	0	46	77	306	64	20	17	5	1	0	0	13	1	65	3	0	8	2	.800	0	26--	—	1.99

173

Year Team	Lg	G	GS	CG	GF	IP	BFP	H	R	ER	HR	SH	SF	HB	TBB	IBB	SO	WP	Bk	W	L	Pct.	ShO	Sv-Op	Hld	ERA
1990 Chicago	NL	13	0	0	3	21.1	93	23	7	5	2	0	2	0	6	2	12	3	0	2	0	1.000	0	0-0	1	2.11
1991 Chicago	NL	1	0	0	1	1	5	3	2	2	1	1	0	0	0	0	0	0	0	0	0	.000	0	0-0	0	18.00
1995 New York	AL	4	0	0	1	5.2	24	8	2	2	0	0	0	0	0	0	3	0	0	0	0	.000	0	0-0	0	3.18
1996 New York	AL	16	0	0	8	23	97	23	7	6	0	2	0	1	7	2	18	3	0	0	0	.000	0	1-1	1	2.35
4 ML YEARS		34	0	0	13	51	219	57	18	15	3	3	2	1	13	4	33	6	0	2	0	1.000	0	1-1	2	2.65

Roger Pavlik

Pitches: Right **Bats:** Right **Pos:** SP-34 **Ht:** 6'2" **Wt:** 220 **Born:** 10/4/67 **Age:** 29

Year Team	Lg	G	GS	CG	GF	IP	BFP	H	R	ER	HR	SH	SF	HB	TBB	IBB	SO	WP	Bk	W	L	Pct.	ShO	Sv-Op	Hld	ERA
1992 Texas	AL	13	12	1	0	62	275	66	32	29	3	0	2	3	34	0	45	9	0	4	4	.500	0	0-0	0	4.21
1993 Texas	AL	26	26	2	0	166.1	712	151	67	63	18	6	4	5	80	3	131	6	1	12	6	.667	0	0-0	0	3.41
1994 Texas	AL	11	11	0	0	50.1	245	61	45	43	8	4	4	4	30	1	31	5	1	2	5	.286	0	0-0	0	7.69
1995 Texas	AL	31	31	2	0	191.2	819	174	96	93	19	4	5	4	90	5	149	10	1	10	10	.500	1	0-0	0	4.37
1996 Texas	AL	34	34	7	0	201	877	216	120	116	28	3	4	5	81	5	127	8	0	15	8	.652	0	0-0	0	5.19
5 ML YEARS		115	114	12	0	671.1	2928	668	360	344	76	17	19	21	315	14	483	38	2	43	33	.566	1	0-0	0	4.61

Dan Peltier

Bats: Left **Throws:** Left **Pos:** PH-19; 1B-13; LF-1 **Ht:** 6'1" **Wt:** 205 **Born:** 6/30/68 **Age:** 29

Year Team	Lg	G	AB	H	2B	3B	HR	(Hm	Rd)	TB	R	RBI	TBB	IBB	SO	HBP	SH	SF	SB	CS	SB%	GDP	Avg	OBP	SLG
1996 Phoenix *	AAA	70	267	76	8	3	0	—	—	90	40	27	28	3	39	1	1	2	0	2	.00	7	.285	.352	.337
1992 Texas	AL	12	24	4	0	0	0	(0	0)	4	1	2	0	0	3	0	0	0	0	0	.00	0	.167	.167	.167
1993 Texas	AL	65	160	43	7	1	1	(1	0)	55	23	17	20	0	27	1	1	1	0	4	.00	3	.269	.352	.344
1996 San Francisco	NL	31	59	15	2	0	0	(0	0)	17	3	9	7	1	9	0	0	1	0	0	.00	1	.254	.328	.288
3 ML YEARS		108	243	62	9	1	1	(1	0)	76	27	28	27	1	39	1	1	2	0	4	.00	4	.255	.330	.313

Rudy Pemberton

Bats: Right **Throws:** Right **Pos:** RF-12; PH-2; LF-1 **Ht:** 6'1" **Wt:** 185 **Born:** 12/17/69 **Age:** 27

Year Team	Lg	G	AB	H	2B	3B	HR	(Hm	Rd)	TB	R	RBI	TBB	IBB	SO	HBP	SH	SF	SB	CS	SB%	GDP	Avg	OBP	SLG
1988 Bristol	R+	6	5	0	0	0	0	—	—	0	2	0	1	0	3	2	0	0	0	0	.00	1	.000	.375	.000
1989 Bristol	R+	56	214	58	9	2	6	—	—	89	40	39	14	0	43	4	0	1	19	3	.86	3	.271	.326	.416
1990 Fayetteville	A	127	454	126	14	5	6	—	—	168	60	61	42	1	91	12	1	9	12	9	.57	12	.278	.348	.370
1991 Lakeland	A+	111	375	86	15	2	3	—	—	114	40	36	25	2	51	9	6	2	25	15	.63	5	.229	.292	.304
1992 Lakeland	A+	104	343	91	16	5	3	—	—	126	41	43	21	2	37	13	2	3	25	10	.71	4	.265	.329	.367
1993 London	AA	124	471	130	22	4	15	—	—	205	70	67	24	1	80	12	0	3	14	12	.54	11	.276	.325	.435
1994 Toledo	AAA	99	360	109	13	3	12	—	—	164	49	58	18	3	62	6	0	6	30	9	.77	6	.303	.341	.456
1995 Toledo	AAA	67	224	77	15	3	7	—	—	119	31	23	15	2	36	5	0	3	8	4	.67	5	.344	.393	.531
1996 Okla. City	AAA	17	71	18	3	0	2	—	—	27	6	11	1	0	10	1	0	1	1	4	.20	0	.254	.270	.380
Pawtucket	AAA	102	396	129	28	3	27	—	—	244	77	92	18	0	63	14	0	1	16	7	.70	12	.326	.375	.616
1995 Detroit	AL	12	30	9	3	1	0	(0	0)	14	3	3	1	0	5	1	0	0	0	0	.00	3	.300	.344	.467
1996 Boston	AL	13	41	21	8	0	1	(1	0)	32	11	10	2	0	4	2	0	0	3	1	.75	0	.512	.556	.780
2 ML YEARS		25	71	30	11	1	1	(1	0)	46	14	13	3	0	9	3	0	0	3	1	.75	3	.423	.468	.648

Alejandro Pena

Pitches: Right **Bats:** Right **Pos:** RP-4 **Ht:** 6'1" **Wt:** 200 **Born:** 6/25/59 **Age:** 38

Year Team	Lg	G	GS	CG	GF	IP	BFP	H	R	ER	HR	SH	SF	HB	TBB	IBB	SO	WP	Bk	W	L	Pct.	ShO	Sv-Op	Hld	ERA
1981 Los Angeles	NL	14	0	0	7	25	104	18	8	8	1	0	0	0	11	1	14	0	0	1	1	.500	0	2--	—	2.88
1982 Los Angeles	NL	29	0	0	11	35.2	160	37	24	19	2	2	0	1	21	7	20	1	1	0	2	.000	0	0--	—	4.79
1983 Los Angeles	NL	34	26	4	4	177	730	152	67	54	7	8	5	1	51	7	120	2	1	12	9	.571	3	1--	—	2.75
1984 Los Angeles	NL	28	28	8	0	199.1	813	186	67	55	7	6	2	3	46	7	135	5	1	12	6	.667	4	0--	—	2.48
1985 Los Angeles	NL	2	1	0	0	4.1	23	7	5	4	1	0	0	0	3	1	2	0	0	0	1	.000	0	0--	—	8.31
1986 Los Angeles	NL	24	10	0	6	70	309	74	40	38	6	3	1	1	30	5	46	1	1	1	2	.333	0	1--	—	4.89
1987 Los Angeles	NL	37	7	0	17	87.1	377	82	41	34	9	5	6	2	37	5	76	0	1	2	7	.222	0	11-11	6	3.50
1988 Los Angeles	NL	60	0	0	31	94.1	378	75	29	20	4	3	3	1	27	6	83	3	2	6	7	.462	0	12-14	9	1.91
1989 Los Angeles	NL	53	0	0	28	76	306	62	20	18	6	3	1	2	18	4	75	1	1	4	3	.571	0	5-9	5	2.13
1990 New York	NL	52	0	0	32	76	320	71	31	27	4	1	6	1	22	5	76	0	0	3	3	.500	0	5-5	6	3.20
1991 NYN-Atl	NL	59	0	0	36	82.1	331	74	23	22	6	3	4	0	22	4	62	1	2	8	1	.889	0	15-20	1	2.40
1992 Atlanta	NL	41	0	0	31	42	173	40	19	19	7	2	1	0	13	5	34	0	0	1	6	.143	0	15-18	4	4.07
1994 Pittsburgh	NL	22	0	0	15	28.2	118	22	16	16	4	0	0	1	10	2	27	2	0	3	2	.600	0	7-8	2	5.02
1995 Bos-Fla-Atl	NL	44	0	0	11	55.1	238	55	32	29	8	0	0	0	19	3	64	0	0	3	1	.750	0	0-1	11	4.72
1996 Florida	NL	4	0	0	3	4	18	4	5	2	2	0	0	0	1	0	5	0	0	0	0	.000	0	0-0	0	4.50
1991 New York	NL	44	0	0	24	63	261	63	20	19	5	2	4	0	19	4	49	1	2	6	1	.857	0	4-9	1	2.71
Atlanta	NL	15	0	0	12	19.1	70	11	3	3	1	1	0	0	3	0	13	0	0	2	0	1.000	0	11-11	0	1.40
1995 Boston	AL	17	0	0	5	24.1	117	33	23	20	5	0	0	0	12	2	25	0	0	1	1	.500	0	0-0	2	7.40
Florida	NL	13	0	0	4	18	68	11	3	3	2	0	0	0	3	1	21	0	0	2	0	1.000	0	0-1	6	1.50
Atlanta	NL	14	0	0	2	13	53	11	6	6	1	0	0	0	4	0	18	0	0	0	0	.000	0	0-0	3	4.15

			HOW MUCH HE PITCHED					WHAT HE GAVE UP													THE RESULTS						
Year Team	Lg	G	GS	CG	GF	IP	BFP	H	R	ER	HR	SH	SF	HB	TBB	IBB	SO	WP	Bk	W	L	Pct.	ShO	Sv-Op	Hld	ERA
15 ML YEARS		503	72	12	232	1057.1	4398	959	427	365	75	36	29	13	331	62	839	16	10	56	52	.519	7	74--	—	3.11

Geronimo Pena

Bats: Both **Throws:** Right **Pos:** 3B-3; PH-2; 2B-1 **Ht:** 6'1" **Wt:** 195 **Born:** 3/29/67 **Age:** 30

								BATTING										BASERUNNING				PERCENTAGES		
Year Team	Lg	G	AB	H	2B	3B	HR	(Hm	Rd)	TB	R	RBI	TBB	IBB	SO	HBP	SH	SF	SB	CS	SB%	GDP	Avg	OBP	SLG
1996 Louisville *	AAA	27	106	30	6	2	6	—	—	58	17	18	12	1	25	0	0	0	0	0	.00	3	.283	.356	.547
Buffalo *	AAA	24	89	31	9	1	4	—	—	54	15	17	12	1	27	0	0	1	0	0	.00	1	.348	.422	.607
1990 St. Louis	NL	18	45	11	2	0	0	(0	0)	13	5	2	4	0	14	1	0	1	1	1	.50	0	.244	.314	.289
1991 St. Louis	NL	104	185	45	8	3	5	(1	4)	74	38	17	18	1	45	5	1	3	15	5	.75	0	.243	.322	.400
1992 St. Louis	NL	62	203	62	12	1	7	(4	3)	97	31	31	24	0	37	5	0	4	13	8	.62	1	.305	.386	.478
1993 St. Louis	NL	74	254	65	19	2	5	(2	3)	103	34	30	25	0	71	4	4	2	13	5	.72	3	.256	.330	.406
1994 St. Louis	NL	83	213	54	13	1	11	(7	4)	102	33	34	24	1	54	6	4	1	9	1	.90	3	.254	.344	.479
1995 St. Louis	NL	32	101	27	6	1	1	(1	0)	38	20	8	16	1	30	1	4	2	3	2	.60	2	.267	.367	.376
1996 Cleveland	AL	5	9	1	0	0	1	(0	1)	4	1	2	1	0	4	0	0	0	0	0	.00	2	.111	.200	.444
7 ML YEARS		378	1010	265	60	8	30	(15	15)	431	162	124	112	3	255	22	13	13	54	22	.71	11	.262	.345	.427

Tony Pena

Bats: Right **Throws:** Right **Pos:** C-67 **Ht:** 6'0" **Wt:** 185 **Born:** 6/4/57 **Age:** 40

								BATTING										BASERUNNING				PERCENTAGES		
Year Team	Lg	G	AB	H	2B	3B	HR	(Hm	Rd)	TB	R	RBI	TBB	IBB	SO	HBP	SH	SF	SB	CS	SB%	GDP	Avg	OBP	SLG
1980 Pittsburgh	NL	8	21	9	1	1	0	(0	0)	12	1	1	0	0	4	0	0	0	0	1	.00	1	.429	.429	.571
1981 Pittsburgh	NL	66	210	63	9	1	2	(1	1)	80	16	17	8	2	23	1	2	2	1	2	.33	4	.300	.326	.381
1982 Pittsburgh	NL	138	497	147	28	4	11	(5	6)	216	53	63	17	3	57	4	3	2	2	5	.29	17	.296	.323	.435
1983 Pittsburgh	NL	151	542	163	22	3	15	(8	7)	236	51	70	31	8	73	0	6	1	6	7	.46	13	.301	.338	.435
1984 Pittsburgh	NL	147	546	156	27	2	15	(7	8)	232	77	78	36	5	79	4	4	2	12	8	.60	14	.286	.333	.425
1985 Pittsburgh	NL	147	546	136	27	2	10	(2	8)	197	53	59	29	4	67	0	7	5	12	8	.60	19	.249	.284	.361
1986 Pittsburgh	NL	144	510	147	26	2	10	(5	5)	207	56	52	53	6	69	1	0	1	9	10	.47	21	.288	.356	.406
1987 St. Louis	NL	116	384	82	13	4	5	(1	4)	118	40	44	36	9	54	1	2	2	6	1	.86	19	.214	.281	.307
1988 St. Louis	NL	149	505	133	23	1	10	(4	6)	188	55	51	33	11	60	1	3	4	6	2	.75	12	.263	.308	.372
1989 St. Louis	NL	141	424	110	17	2	4	(3	1)	143	36	37	35	19	33	2	2	1	5	3	.63	19	.259	.318	.337
1990 Boston	AL	143	491	129	19	1	7	(3	4)	171	62	56	43	3	71	1	2	3	8	6	.57	23	.263	.322	.348
1991 Boston	AL	141	464	107	23	2	5	(2	3)	149	45	48	37	1	53	4	4	3	8	3	.73	23	.231	.291	.321
1992 Boston	AL	133	410	99	21	1	1	(1	0)	125	39	38	24	0	61	1	13	2	3	2	.60	11	.241	.284	.305
1993 Boston	AL	126	304	55	11	0	4	(2	2)	78	20	19	25	0	46	2	13	1	1	3	.25	12	.181	.246	.257
1994 Cleveland	AL	40	112	33	8	1	2	(1	1)	49	18	10	9	0	11	0	3	2	0	1	.00	6	.295	.341	.438
1995 Cleveland	AL	91	263	69	15	0	5	(1	4)	99	25	28	14	1	44	1	1	0	1	0	1.00	9	.262	.302	.376
1996 Cleveland	AL	67	174	34	4	0	1	(0	1)	41	14	27	15	0	25	0	3	3	0	1	.00	8	.195	.255	.236
17 ML YEARS		1948	6403	1672	294	27	107	(46	61)	2341	661	698	445	72	830	23	68	36	80	63	.56	231	.261	.310	.366

Terry Pendleton

Bats: Both **Throws:** Right **Pos:** 3B-149; PH-5 **Ht:** 5'9" **Wt:** 195 **Born:** 7/16/60 **Age:** 36

								BATTING										BASERUNNING				PERCENTAGES		
Year Team	Lg	G	AB	H	2B	3B	HR	(Hm	Rd)	TB	R	RBI	TBB	IBB	SO	HBP	SH	SF	SB	CS	SB%	GDP	Avg	OBP	SLG
1984 St. Louis	NL	67	262	85	16	3	1	(0	1)	110	37	33	16	3	32	0	0	5	20	5	.80	7	.324	.357	.420
1985 St. Louis	NL	149	559	134	16	3	5	(3	2)	171	56	69	37	4	75	1	4	5	17	12	.59	18	.240	.285	.306
1986 St. Louis	NL	159	578	138	26	5	1	(0	1)	177	56	59	34	10	59	1	6	7	24	6	.80	12	.239	.279	.306
1987 St. Louis	NL	159	583	167	29	4	12	(5	7)	240	82	96	70	6	74	2	3	9	19	12	.61	18	.286	.360	.412
1988 St. Louis	NL	110	391	99	20	2	6	(3	3)	141	44	53	21	4	51	2	4	3	3	3	.50	9	.253	.293	.361
1989 St. Louis	NL	162	613	162	28	5	13	(8	5)	239	83	74	44	3	81	0	2	2	9	5	.64	16	.264	.313	.390
1990 St. Louis	NL	121	447	103	20	2	6	(6	0)	145	46	58	30	8	58	1	0	6	7	5	.58	12	.230	.277	.324
1991 Atlanta	NL	153	586	**187**	34	8	22	(13	9)	**303**	94	86	43	8	70	1	7	7	10	2	.83	16	**.319**	.363	.517
1992 Atlanta	NL	160	640	**199**	39	1	21	(13	8)	303	98	105	37	8	67	0	5	7	5	2	.71	16	.311	.345	.473
1993 Atlanta	NL	161	633	172	33	1	17	(9	8)	258	81	84	36	5	97	3	3	7	5	1	.83	18	.272	.311	.408
1994 Atlanta	NL	77	309	78	18	3	7	(3	4)	123	25	30	12	3	57	0	3	0	2	0	1.00	8	.252	.280	.398
1995 Florida	NL	133	513	149	32	1	14	(8	6)	225	70	78	38	7	84	2	0	4	1	2	.33	7	.290	.339	.439
1996 Fla-Atl	NL	153	568	135	26	1	11	(6	5)	196	51	75	41	6	111	3	1	5	2	3	.40	18	.238	.290	.345
1996 Florida	NL	111	406	102	20	1	7	(4	3)	145	30	58	26	5	75	3	1	5	0	2	.00	10	.251	.298	.357
Atlanta	NL	42	162	33	6	0	4	(2	2)	51	21	17	15	1	36	0	0	0	2	1	.67	8	.204	.271	.315
13 ML YEARS		1764	6682	1808	337	39	136	(77	59)	2631	823	900	459	75	916	15	37	65	124	58	.68	175	.271	.316	.394

Shannon Penn

Bats: Both **Throws:** Right **Pos:** DH-4; LF-1; PH-1 **Ht:** 5'10" **Wt:** 165 **Born:** 9/11/69 **Age:** 27

								BATTING										BASERUNNING				PERCENTAGES		
Year Team	Lg	G	AB	H	2B	3B	HR	(Hm	Rd)	TB	R	RBI	TBB	IBB	SO	HBP	SH	SF	SB	CS	SB%	GDP	Avg	OBP	SLG
1989 Rangers	R	47	147	32	2	1	0	—	—	36	19	8	20	0	27	1	0	1	17	7	.71	1	.218	.314	.245
1990 Butte	R+	60	197	64	4	2	0	—	—	72	38	18	15	0	35	1	0	2	9	4	.69	0	.325	.372	.365
1992 Niagara Fal	A-	70	253	69	9	2	3	—	—	91	47	25	28	2	58	6	3	1	31	10	.76	2	.273	.358	.360
1993 London	AA	128	493	128	12	6	0	—	—	152	78	36	54	1	95	8	7	4	53	16	.77	4	.260	.340	.308
1994 Toledo	AAA	114	444	126	14	6	2	—	—	158	63	33	30	0	96	5	4	4	45	16	.74	4	.284	.333	.356

Year Team	Lg	G	AB	H	2B	3B	HR	(Hm	Rd)	TB	R	RBI	TBB	IBB	SO	HBP	SH	SF	SB	CS	SB%	GDP	Avg	OBP	SLG
1995 Toledo	AAA	63	218	54	4	1	1	—	—	63	41	15	17	0	40	10	2	2	15	9	.63	4	.248	.328	.289
1996 Toledo	AAA	97	356	102	12	4	6	—	—	140	65	42	26	0	59	14	3	3	22	11	.67	5	.287	.356	.393
1995 Detroit	AL	3	9	3	0	0	0	(0	0)	3	0	0	1	0	2	0	0	0	0	0	.00	2	.333	.400	.333
1996 Detroit	AL	6	14	1	0	0	0	(0	0)	1	0	1	0	0	3	0	0	0	0	0	.00	0	.071	.071	.071
2 ML YEARS		9	23	4	0	0	0	(0	0)	4	0	1	1	0	5	0	0	0	0	0	.00	2	.174	.208	.174

Brad Pennington

Pitches: Left **Bats:** Left **Pos:** RP-22 **Ht:** 6'6" **Wt:** 215 **Born:** 4/14/69 **Age:** 28

Year Team	Lg	G	GS	CG	GF	IP	BFP	H	R	ER	HR	SH	SF	HB	TBB	IBB	SO	WP	Bk	W	L	Pct.	ShO	Sv-Op	Hld	ERA
1996 Lk Elsinore *	A+	2	2	0	0	3	11	0	0	0	0	0	0	0	2	0	5	0	0	0	0	.000	0	0--	—	0.00
Vancouver *	AAA	11	2	0	1	27.2	124	20	20	13	2	0	1	0	22	0	43	1	0	3	0	1.000	0	1--	—	4.23
1993 Baltimore	AL	34	0	0	16	33	158	34	25	24	7	2	1	2	25	0	39	3	0	3	2	.600	0	4-7	5	6.55
1994 Baltimore	AL	8	0	0	3	6	35	9	8	8	2	1	0	0	8	0	7	2	0	0	1	.000	0	0-1	1	12.00
1995 Bal-Cin	AL	14	0	0	4	16.1	80	12	15	12	1	0	2	1	22	1	17	4	0	0	1	.000	0	0-1	0	6.61
1996 Bos-Cal	AL	22	0	0	8	20.1	102	11	15	14	2	1	0	1	31	1	20	2	0	0	2	.000	0	0-0	1	6.20
1995 Baltimore	AL	8	0	0	2	6.2	33	3	7	6	1	0	0	0	11	1	10	1	0	0	1	.000	0	0-1	0	8.10
Cincinnati	NL	6	0	0	2	9.2	47	9	8	6	0	0	2	1	11	0	7	3	0	0	0	.000	0	0-0	0	5.59
1996 Boston	AL	14	0	0	6	13	59	6	5	4	1	0	1	0	15	1	13	1	0	0	2	.000	0	0-0	1	2.77
California	AL	8	0	0	2	7.1	43	5	10	10	1	1	0	1	16	0	7	1	0	0	0	.000	0	0-0	0	12.27
4 ML YEARS		78	0	0	31	75.2	375	66	63	58	12	3	4	3	86	2	83	11	0	3	6	.333	0	4-9	7	6.90

Troy Percival

Pitches: Right **Bats:** Right **Pos:** RP-62 **Ht:** 6'3" **Wt:** 200 **Born:** 8/9/69 **Age:** 27

Year Team	Lg	G	GS	CG	GF	IP	BFP	H	R	ER	HR	SH	SF	HB	TBB	IBB	SO	WP	Bk	W	L	Pct.	ShO	Sv-Op	Hld	ERA
1991 Boise	A-	28	0	0	20	38.1	157	23	7	6	0	1	2	2	18	1	63	9	0	2	0	1.000	0	12--	—	1.41
1992 Palm Spring	A+	11	0	0	9	10.2	45	6	7	6	0	0	3	2	8	1	16	1	1	1	1	.500	0	2--	—	5.06
Midland	AA	20	0	0	17	19	84	18	5	5	1	0	1	1	11	1	21	1	0	3	0	1.000	0	5--	—	2.37
1993 Vancouver	AAA	18	0	0	11	18.2	94	24	14	13	0	1	3	2	13	1	19	2	0	0	1	.000	0	4--	—	6.27
1994 Vancouver	AAA	49	0	0	32	61	266	63	31	28	4	6	3	7	29	5	73	6	2	1	3	.250	0	15--	—	4.13
1995 California	AL	62	0	0	16	74	284	37	19	16	6	4	1	1	26	2	94	2	2	3	2	.600	0	3-6	29	1.95
1996 California	AL	62	0	0	52	74	291	38	20	19	8	2	1	2	31	4	100	2	0	0	0	.000	0	36-39	2	2.31
2 ML YEARS		124	0	0	68	148	575	75	39	35	14	6	2	3	57	6	194	4	2	3	4	.429	0	39-45	31	2.13

Carlos Perez

Pitches: Left **Bats:** Left **Pos:** SP/RP **Ht:** 6'3" **Wt:** 195 **Born:** 1/14/71 **Age:** 26

Year Team	Lg	G	GS	CG	GF	IP	BFP	H	R	ER	HR	SH	SF	HB	TBB	IBB	SO	WP	Bk	W	L	Pct.	ShO	Sv-Op	Hld	ERA
1990 Expos	R	13	2	0	6	35.2	145	24	14	10	0	1	1	1	15	0	38	1	0	3	1	.750	0	2--	—	2.52
1991 Sumter	A	16	12	0	2	73.2	306	57	29	20	3	0	7	0	32	0	69	3	1	2	2	.500	0	0--	—	2.44
1992 Rockford	A	7	1	0	2	9.1	43	12	7	6	3	1	0	1	5	0	8	1	0	0	1	.000	0	1--	—	5.79
1993 Burlington	A	12	1	0	5	16.2	69	13	6	6	0	3	0	0	9	0	21	0	1	1	0	1.000	0	0--	—	3.24
San Bernrdo	A+	20	18	3	0	131	550	120	57	50	12	3	2	0	44	0	98	9	6	8	7	.533	0	0--	—	3.44
1994 Harrisburg	AA	12	11	2	1	79	307	55	27	17	3	2	2	1	18	0	69	5	0	7	2	.778	2	1--	—	1.94
Ottawa	AAA	17	17	3	0	119	511	130	50	44	8	5	3	3	41	2	82	4	1	7	5	.583	0	0--	—	3.33
1995 Montreal	NL	28	23	2	2	141.1	592	142	61	58	18	6	1	5	28	2	106	8	4	10	8	.556	1	0-0	1	3.69

Danny Perez

Bats: Right **Throws:** Right **Pos:** LF-2; DH-1; CF-1; PH-1 **Ht:** 5'10" **Wt:** 194 **Born:** 2/25/71 **Age:** 26

Year Team	Lg	G	AB	H	2B	3B	HR	(Hm	Rd)	TB	R	RBI	TBB	IBB	SO	HBP	SH	SF	SB	CS	SB%	GDP	Avg	OBP	SLG
1992 Helena	R+	33	104	22	3	0	1	—	—	28	12	13	10	0	17	1	1	0	3	0	1.00	5	.212	.287	.269
1993 Beloit	A	106	377	113	17	6	10	—	—	172	70	59	56	0	64	5	1	2	23	8	.74	6	.300	.395	.456
Stockton	A+	10	24	7	3	1	0	—	—	12	4	0	2	0	5	0	0	0	2	1	.67	0	.292	.346	.500
1994 Stockton	A+	9	33	9	0	0	0	—	—	9	7	3	7	0	7	0	0	0	2	2	.50	0	.273	.400	.273
El Paso	AA	115	440	143	19	17	6	—	—	214	88	73	45	1	79	5	1	3	9	5	.64	11	.325	.391	.486
1995 El Paso	AA	22	76	21	1	1	0	—	—	24	16	7	4	0	14	1	0	1	1	0	1.00	1	.276	.317	.316
New Orleans	AAA	12	34	10	1	0	0	—	—	11	5	0	5	1	9	0	0	0	0	0	.00	0	.294	.385	.324
1996 El Paso	AA	38	154	54	16	6	2	—	—	88	31	19	13	0	30	1	0	0	5	1	.83	6	.351	.405	.571
New Orleans	AAA	65	198	37	5	0	2	—	—	48	25	15	32	1	57	1	0	1	4	2	.67	2	.187	.302	.242
1996 Milwaukee	AL	4	4	0	0	0	0	(0	0)	0	0	0	0	0	0	0	0	0	0	0	.00	0	.000	.000	.000

Eddie Perez

Bats: Right **Throws:** Right **Pos:** C-54; PH-8; 1B-7 **Ht:** 6'1" **Wt:** 175 **Born:** 5/4/68 **Age:** 29

Year Team	Lg	G	AB	H	2B	3B	HR	(Hm	Rd)	TB	R	RBI	TBB	IBB	SO	HBP	SH	SF	SB	CS	SB%	GDP	Avg	OBP	SLG
1987 Braves	R	31	89	18	1	0	1	—	—	22	8	5	8	0	14	1	1	1	0	0	.00	4	.202	.273	.247

Year Team	Lg	G	AB	H	2B	3B	HR	(Hm	Rd)	TB	R	RBI	TBB	IBB	SO	HBP	SH	SF	SB	CS	SB%	GDP	Avg	OBP	SLG
1988 Burlington	A	64	186	43	8	0	4	—	—	63	14	19	10	0	33	0	2	1	1	0	1.00	6	.231	.269	.339
1989 Sumter	A	114	401	93	21	0	5	—	—	129	39	44	44	1	68	5	4	5	2	6	.25	10	.232	.312	.322
1990 Sumter	A	41	123	22	7	1	3	—	—	40	11	17	14	0	18	2	3	1	0	0	.00	7	.179	.271	.325
Durham	A+	31	93	22	1	0	3	—	—	32	9	10	1	0	12	1	0	1	0	0	.00	3	.237	.250	.344
1991 Durham	A+	91	277	75	10	1	9	—	—	114	38	41	17	2	33	3	2	3	0	3	.00	7	.271	.317	.412
Greenville	AA	1	4	1	0	0	0	—	—	1	0	0	0	0	1	0	0	0	0	0	.00	0	.250	.250	.250
1992 Greenville	AA	91	275	63	16	0	6	—	—	97	28	41	24	0	41	2	1	4	3	3	.50	11	.229	.292	.353
1993 Greenville	AA	28	84	28	6	0	6	—	—	52	15	17	2	0	8	0	0	2	1	0	1.00	4	.333	.341	.619
1994 Richmond	AAA	113	388	101	16	2	9	—	—	148	37	49	18	1	47	3	3	6	1	1	.50	4	.260	.294	.381
1995 Richmond	AAA	92	324	86	19	0	5	—	—	120	31	40	12	0	58	2	1	2	1	2	.33	12	.265	.294	.370
1995 Atlanta	NL	7	13	4	1	0	1	(0	1)	8	1	4	0	0	2	0	0	0	0	0	.00	0	.308	.308	.615
1996 Atlanta	NL	68	156	40	9	1	4	(2	2)	63	19	17	8	0	19	1	0	2	0	0	.00	6	.256	.293	.404
2 ML YEARS		75	169	44	10	1	5	(2	3)	71	20	21	8	0	21	1	0	2	0	0	.00	6	.260	.294	.420

Eduardo Perez

Bats: Right **Throws:** Right **Pos:** 1B-8; PH-8; 3B-3   **Ht:** 6'4" **Wt:** 215 **Born:** 9/11/69 **Age:** 27

Year Team	Lg	G	AB	H	2B	3B	HR	(Hm	Rd)	TB	R	RBI	TBB	IBB	SO	HBP	SH	SF	SB	CS	SB%	GDP	Avg	OBP	SLG
1996 Indianapols *	AAA	122	451	132	29	5	21	—	—	234	84	84	51	5	69	6	0	1	11	0	1.00	11	.293	.371	.519
1993 California	AL	52	180	45	6	2	4	(2	2)	67	16	30	9	0	39	2	0	1	5	4	.56	4	.250	.292	.372
1994 California	AL	38	129	27	7	0	5	(3	2)	49	10	16	12	1	29	0	1	1	3	0	1.00	5	.209	.275	.380
1995 California	AL	29	71	12	4	1	1	(0	1)	21	9	7	12	0	9	2	0	1	0	2	.00	3	.169	.302	.296
1996 Cincinnati	NL	18	36	8	0	0	3	(3	0)	17	8	5	5	1	9	0	0	0	0	0	.00	2	.222	.317	.472
4 ML YEARS		137	416	92	17	3	13	(8	5)	154	43	58	38	2	86	4	1	3	8	6	.57	14	.221	.291	.370

Melido Perez

Pitches: Right **Bats:** Right **Pos:** SP/RP   **Ht:** 6'4" **Wt:** 210 **Born:** 2/15/66 **Age:** 31

		HOW MUCH HE PITCHED						WHAT HE GAVE UP									THE RESULTS						
Year Team	Lg	G	GS	CG	GF	IP	BFP	H	R	ER	HR	SH	SF	HB	TBB	IBB	SO	WP	Bk	W	L	Pct.	ShO	Sv-Op	Hld	ERA
1987 Kansas City	AL	3	1	0	0	10.1	53	18	12	9	2	0	0	0	5	0	5	0	0	1	1	.500	0	0-0	0	7.84
1988 Chicago	AL	32	32	3	0	197	836	186	105	83	26	5	8	2	72	0	138	13	3	12	10	.545	1	0-0	0	3.79
1989 Chicago	AL	31	31	2	0	183.1	810	187	106	102	23	5	4	3	90	0	141	12	5	11	14	.440	0	0-0	0	5.01
1990 Chicago	AL	35	35	3	0	197	833	177	111	101	14	4	6	2	86	1	161	8	4	13	14	.481	3	0-0	0	4.61
1991 Chicago	AL	49	8	0	16	135.2	553	111	49	47	15	4	1	1	52	0	128	11	1	8	7	.533	0	1-5	9	3.12
1992 New York	AL	33	33	10	0	247.2	1013	212	94	79	16	6	8	5	93	5	218	13	0	13	16	.448	1	0-0	0	2.87
1993 New York	AL	25	25	0	0	163	718	173	103	94	22	4	2	1	64	5	148	3	1	6	14	.300	0	0-0	0	5.19
1994 New York	AL	22	22	1	0	151.1	632	134	74	69	16	5	3	3	58	5	109	7	1	9	4	.692	0	0-0	0	4.10
1995 New York	AL	13	12	1	1	69.1	304	70	46	43	10	1	3	1	31	2	44	4	0	5	5	.500	0	0-0	0	5.58
9 ML YEARS		243	201	20	17	1354.2	5752	1268	700	627	144	34	35	18	551	21	1092	71	15	78	85	.479	5	1-5	9	4.17

Mike Perez

Pitches: Right **Bats:** Right **Pos:** RP-24   **Ht:** 6'0" **Wt:** 200 **Born:** 10/19/64 **Age:** 32

		HOW MUCH HE PITCHED						WHAT HE GAVE UP									THE RESULTS						
Year Team	Lg	G	GS	CG	GF	IP	BFP	H	R	ER	HR	SH	SF	HB	TBB	IBB	SO	WP	Bk	W	L	Pct.	ShO	Sv-Op	Hld	ERA
1996 Iowa *	AAA	23	0	0	6	30.1	146	42	24	22	4	2	3	1	15	3	19	2	1	0	4	.000	0	0- -	—	6.53
1990 St. Louis	NL	13	0	0	7	13.2	55	12	6	6	0	0	2	0	3	0	5	0	0	1	0	1.000	0	1-2	2	3.95
1991 St. Louis	NL	14	0	0	2	17	75	19	11	11	1	1	0	1	7	2	7	0	0	0	2	.000	0	0-0	2	5.82
1992 St. Louis	NL	77	0	0	22	93	377	70	23	19	4	7	4	1	32	9	46	4	0	9	3	.750	0	0-3	9	1.84
1993 St. Louis	NL	65	0	0	25	72.2	298	65	24	20	4	5	5	1	20	1	58	2	0	7	2	.778	0	7-10	13	2.48
1994 St. Louis	NL	36	0	0	18	31	155	52	32	30	5	4	5	3	10	1	20	0	0	2	3	.400	0	12-14	6	8.71
1995 Chicago	NL	68	0	0	18	71.1	308	72	30	29	8	5	3	4	27	8	49	4	0	2	6	.250	0	2-3	16	3.66
1996 Chicago	NL	24	0	0	4	27	127	29	14	14	2	1	0	3	13	1	22	1	0	1	0	1.000	0	0-0	1	4.67
7 ML YEARS		297	0	0	96	325.2	1395	319	140	129	24	23	19	13	112	22	207	11	0	22	16	.579	0	22-32	49	3.56

Neifi Perez

Bats: Both **Throws:** Right **Pos:** SS-14; 2B-4; PH-4   **Ht:** 6'0" **Wt:** 173 **Born:** 2/2/75 **Age:** 22

Year Team	Lg	G	AB	H	2B	3B	HR	(Hm	Rd)	TB	R	RBI	TBB	IBB	SO	HBP	SH	SF	SB	CS	SB%	GDP	Avg	OBP	SLG
1993 Bend	A-	75	296	77	11	4	3	—	—	105	35	32	19	2	43	2	4	3	19	14	.58	3	.260	.306	.355
1994 Central Val	A+	134	506	121	16	7	1	—	—	154	64	35	32	1	79	2	19	5	9	7	.56	6	.239	.284	.304
1995 Colo. Sprng	AAA	11	36	10	4	0	0	—	—	14	4	2	0	0	5	0	1	0	1	1	.50	0	.278	.278	.389
New Haven	AA	116	427	108	28	3	5	—	—	157	59	43	24	2	52	2	4	1	5	2	.71	6	.253	.295	.368
1996 Colo. Sprng	AAA	133	570	180	28	12	7	—	—	253	77	72	21	4	48	2	4	10	16	13	.55	13	.316	.337	.444
1996 Colorado	NL	17	45	7	2	0	0	(0	0)	9	4	3	0	0	8	0	1	0	2	2	.50	2	.156	.156	.200

Robert Perez

Bats: R **Throws:** R **Pos:** LF-59; RF-25; PH-24; DH-2   **Ht:** 6'3" **Wt:** 205 **Born:** 6/4/69 **Age:** 28

									BATTING									BASERUNNING				PERCENTAGES		
Year Team	Lg	G	AB	H	2B	3B	HR	(Hm | Rd)	TB	R	RBI	TBB	IBB	SO	HBP	SH	SF	SB	CS	SB%	GDP	Avg	OBP	SLG
1990 St. Cathrns	A-	52	207	54	10	2	5	—	—	83	20	25	8	1	34	2	0	0	7	5	.58	7	.261	.295	.401
Myrtle Bch	A	21	72	21	2	0	1	—	—	26	8	10	3	0	9	2	0	1	2	1	.67	3	.292	.333	.361
1991 Dunedin	A+	127	480	145	28	6	4	—	—	197	50	50	22	3	72	5	7	2	8	8	.50	19	.302	.338	.410
Syracuse	AAA	4	20	4	1	0	0	—	—	5	2	1	0	0	2	0	0	0	0	0	.00	0	.200	.200	.250
1992 Knoxville	AA	139	526	137	25	5	9	—	—	199	59	59	13	0	87	2	3	7	11	10	.52	10	.260	.277	.378
1993 Syracuse	AAA	138	524	154	26	10	12	—	—	236	72	64	24	1	65	4	5	1	13	15	.46	19	.294	.329	.450
1994 Syracuse	AAA	128	510	155	28	3	10	—	—	219	63	65	27	7	76	2	4	8	4	7	.36	21	.304	.336	.429
1995 Syracuse	AAA	122	502	172	38	6	9	—	—	249	70	67	13	4	60	1	1	4	7	5	.58	17	.343	.359	.496
1994 Toronto	AL	4	8	1	0	0	0	(0 | 0)	1	0	0	0	0	1	0	0	0	0	0	.00	1	.125	.125	.125
1995 Toronto	AL	17	48	9	2	0	1	(1 | 0)	14	2	3	0	0	5	0	0	0	0	0	.00	1	.188	.188	.292
1996 Toronto	AL	86	202	66	10	0	2	(0 | 2)	82	30	21	8	0	17	1	4	1	3	0	1.00	6	.327	.354	.406
3 ML YEARS		107	258	76	12	0	3	(1 | 2)	97	32	24	8	0	23	1	4	1	3	0	1.00	8	.295	.317	.376

Tomas Perez

Bats: B **Throws:** R **Pos:** 2B-75; 3B-11; SS-5; PH-4   **Ht:** 5'11" **Wt:** 165 **Born:** 12/29/73 **Age:** 23

									BATTING									BASERUNNING				PERCENTAGES		
Year Team	Lg	G	AB	H	2B	3B	HR	(Hm	Rd)	TB	R	RBI	TBB	IBB	SO	HBP	SH	SF	SB	CS	SB%	GDP	Avg	OBP	SLG
1993 Expos	R	52	189	46	3	1	2	—	—	57	27	21	23	0	25	0	4	2	7	3	.70	5	.243	.322	.302
1994 Burlington	A	119	465	122	22	1	8	—	—	170	76	47	48	3	78	1	4	5	8	10	.44	2	.262	.329	.366
1996 Syracuse	AAA	40	123	34	10	1	1	—	—	49	15	13	7	0	19	0	3	1	8	1	.89	2	.276	.313	.398
1995 Toronto	AL	41	98	24	3	1	1	(1	0)	32	12	8	7	0	18	0	0	1	0	1	.00	6	.245	.292	.327
1996 Toronto	AL	91	295	74	13	4	1	(1	0)	98	24	19	25	0	29	1	6	1	1	2	.33	10	.251	.311	.332
2 ML YEARS		132	393	98	16	5	2	(2	0)	130	36	27	32	0	47	1	6	2	1	3	.25	16	.249	.306	.331

Yorkis Perez

Pitches: Left **Bats:** Left **Pos:** RP-64   **Ht:** 6'0" **Wt:** 180 **Born:** 9/30/67 **Age:** 29

		HOW MUCH HE PITCHED						WHAT HE GAVE UP										THE RESULTS					
Year Team	Lg	G	GS	CG	GF	IP	BFP	H	R	ER	HR	SH	SF	HB	TBB	IBB	SO	WP	Bk	W	L	Pct.	ShO	Sv-Op	Hld	ERA
1996 Charlotte *	AAA	9	0	0	1	10.2	41	6	5	5	1	0	0	0	3	0	13	0	0	3	0	1.000	0	0--	—	4.22
1991 Chicago	NL	3	0	0	0	4.1	16	2	1	1	0	0	2	0	2	0	3	2	0	1	0	1.000	0	0-1	0	2.08
1994 Florida	NL	44	0	0	11	40.2	167	33	18	16	4	2	0	1	14	3	41	4	1	3	0	1.000	0	0-2	15	3.54
1995 Florida	NL	69	0	0	11	46.2	205	35	29	27	6	2	1	2	28	4	47	2	0	2	6	.250	0	1-4	16	5.21
1996 Florida	NL	64	0	0	15	47.2	222	51	28	28	2	2	2	1	31	4	47	2	0	3	4	.429	0	0-2	10	5.29
4 ML YEARS		180	0	0	37	139.1	610	121	76	72	12	6	5	4	75	11	138	10	1	9	10	.474	0	1-9	41	4.65

Herbert Perry

Bats: Right **Throws:** Right **Pos:** 1B-5; PH-3; 3B-1   **Ht:** 6'2" **Wt:** 215 **Born:** 9/15/69 **Age:** 27

									BATTING									BASERUNNING				PERCENTAGES		
Year Team	Lg	G	AB	H	2B	3B	HR	(Hm	Rd)	TB	R	RBI	TBB	IBB	SO	HBP	SH	SF	SB	CS	SB%	GDP	Avg	OBP	SLG
1996 Buffalo *	AAA	40	151	51	7	1	5	—	—	75	21	30	7	2	19	2	1	0	4	0	1.00	0	.338	.375	.497
1994 Cleveland	AL	4	9	1	0	0	0	(0	0)	1	1	1	3	1	1	1	0	1	0	0	.00	0	.111	.357	.111
1995 Cleveland	AL	52	162	51	13	1	3	(3	0)	75	23	23	13	0	28	4	3	2	1	3	.25	5	.315	.376	.463
1996 Cleveland	AL	7	12	1	1	0	0	(0	0)	2	1	0	1	0	2	0	0	0	1	0	1.00	0	.083	.154	.167
3 ML YEARS		63	183	53	14	1	3	(3	0)	78	25	24	17	1	31	5	3	3	2	3	.40	5	.290	.361	.426

Robert Person

Pitches: Right **Bats:** Right **Pos:** RP-14; SP-13   **Ht:** 6'0" **Wt:** 185 **Born:** 10/6/69 **Age:** 27

		HOW MUCH HE PITCHED						WHAT HE GAVE UP										THE RESULTS					
Year Team	Lg	G	GS	CG	GF	IP	BFP	H	R	ER	HR	SH	SF	HB	TBB	IBB	SO	WP	Bk	W	L	Pct.	ShO	Sv-Op	Hld	ERA
1989 Burlington	R+	10	5	0	3	34	145	23	13	12	1	0	1	5	17	0	19	5	0	0	1	.000	0	1--	—	3.18
1990 Kinston	A+	4	3	0	1	16.2	74	17	6	5	0	0	1	0	9	0	7	0	0	1	0	1.000	0	0--	—	2.70
Indians	R	8	0	0	7	7.1	34	10	7	6	0	1	0	1	4	1	8	1	0	0	2	.000	0	2--	—	7.36
Watertown	A-	5	2	0	2	16.1	62	8	2	2	0	0	0	0	7	0	19	0	0	1	0	1.000	0	0--	—	1.10
1991 Kinston	A+	11	11	0	0	52	252	56	37	27	2	3	6	2	42	0	45	2	1	3	5	.375	0	0--	—	4.67
Bend	A-	2	2	0	0	10	41	6	6	4	0	0	0	1	5	0	6	1	0	1	1	.500	0	0--	—	3.60
South Bend	A	13	13	0	0	76.1	321	50	35	28	3	3	1	0	56	1	66	4	0	4	3	.571	0	0--	—	3.30
1992 Sarasota	A+	19	18	1	0	105.1	458	90	48	42	7	4	0	1	62	1	85	7	0	5	7	.417	0	0--	—	3.59
1993 High Desert	A+	28	26	4	1	169	740	184	115	88	13	4	6	4	48	0	107	9	1	12	10	.545	0	0--	—	4.69
1994 Binghamton	AA	31	23	3	4	159	649	124	68	61	18	6	4	3	68	3	130	6	0	9	6	.600	2	0--	—	3.45
1995 Norfolk	AAA	5	4	0	0	32	138	30	17	16	2	1	1	0	13	0	33	4	0	2	1	.667	0	0--	—	4.50
Binghamton	AA	31	11	1	13	98.2	401	76	44	39	6	5	2	0	38	0	98	1	0	7	5	.583	0	7--	—	3.56
1996 Norfolk	AAA	8	8	0	0	43	178	33	16	16	7	0	1	1	21	0	32	1	0	5	0	1.000	0	0--	—	3.35
1995 New York	NL	3	1	0	0	12	44	5	1	1	1	0	0	0	2	0	10	0	0	1	0	1.000	0	0-0	0	0.75
1996 New York	NL	27	13	0	1	89.2	390	86	50	45	16	1	4	2	35	3	76	3	0	4	5	.444	0	0-0	1	4.52
2 ML YEARS		30	14	0	1	101.2	434	91	51	46	17	1	4	2	37	3	86	3	0	5	5	.500	0	0-0	1	4.07

Roberto Petagine

Bats: Left   **Throws:** Left   **Pos:** 1B-40; PH-20   **Ht:** 6'1"   **Wt:** 170   **Born:** 6/2/71   **Age:** 26

Year Team	Lg	G	AB	H	2B	3B	HR	(Hm	Rd)	TB	R	RBI	TBB	IBB	SO	HBP	SH	SF	SB	CS	SB%	GDP	Avg	OBP	SLG
1996 Norfolk *	AAA	95	314	100	24	3	12	(—	—)	166	49	65	51	7	75	7	0	3	4	1	.80	3	.318	.421	.529
1994 Houston	NL	8	7	0	0	0	0	(0	0)	0	0	0	1	0	3	0	0	0	0	0	.00	0	.000	.125	.000
1995 San Diego	NL	89	124	29	8	0	3	(2	1)	46	15	17	26	2	41	0	2	0	0	0	.00	2	.234	.367	.371
1996 New York	NL	50	99	23	3	0	4	(2	2)	38	10	17	9	1	27	3	1	1	0	2	.00	4	.232	.313	.384
3 ML YEARS		147	230	52	11	0	7	(4	3)	84	25	34	36	3	71	3	3	1	0	2	.00	6	.226	.337	.365

Chris Peters

Pitches: Left   **Bats:** Left   **Pos:** SP-10; RP-6   **Ht:** 6'1"   **Wt:** 162   **Born:** 1/28/72   **Age:** 25

Year Team	Lg	G	GS	CG	GF	IP	BFP	H	R	ER	HR	SH	SF	HB	TBB	IBB	SO	WP	Bk	W	L	Pct.	ShO	Sv-Op	Hld	ERA
1993 Welland	A-	16	0	0	4	27.2	137	33	16	14	0	0	1	2	20	1	25	5	1	1	0	1.000	0	0--	—	4.55
1994 Salem	A+	3	0	0	1	3.1	16	5	5	5	2	0	0	1	1	0	2	1	0	1	0	1.000	0	0--	—	13.50
Augusta	A	54	0	0	29	60.2	268	51	34	29	1	5	2	2	33	2	83	7	0	4	5	.444	0	4--	—	4.30
1995 Carolina	AA	2	2	0	0	14	56	9	2	2	0	0	1	0	2	0	7	2	0	2	0	1.000	0	0--	—	1.29
1996 Carolina	AA	14	14	0	0	92	378	73	37	27	4	4	2	0	34	2	69	4	0	7	3	.700	0	0--	—	2.64
Calgary	AAA	4	4	0	0	27.2	102	18	3	3	0	1	1	0	8	1	16	1	0	1	1	.500	0	0--	—	0.98
1996 Pittsburgh	NL	16	10	0	0	64	283	72	43	40	9	3	3	1	25	0	28	4	0	2	4	.333	0	0-0	2	5.63

Mark Petkovsek

Pitches: Right   **Bats:** Right   **Pos:** RP-42; SP-6   **Ht:** 6'0"   **Wt:** 195   **Born:** 11/18/65   **Age:** 31

Year Team	Lg	G	GS	CG	GF	IP	BFP	H	R	ER	HR	SH	SF	HB	TBB	IBB	SO	WP	Bk	W	L	Pct.	ShO	Sv-Op	Hld	ERA
1996 St. Pete *	A+	3	0	0	0	6	25	6	3	3	0	0	1	1	0	0	5	0	0	0	0	.000	0	0--	—	4.50
Louisville *	AAA	2	1	0	0	3	16	5	4	3	0	0	0	0	1	0	4	1	0	0	1	.000	0	0--	—	9.00
1991 Texas	AL	4	1	0	1	9.1	53	21	16	15	4	0	1	0	4	0	6	2	0	0	1	.000	0	0-0	0	14.46
1993 Pittsburgh	NL	26	0	0	8	32.1	145	43	25	25	7	4	1	0	9	2	14	4	0	3	0	1.000	0	0-0	0	6.96
1995 St. Louis	NL	26	21	1	1	137.1	569	136	71	61	11	4	4	6	35	3	71	1	1	6	6	.500	1	0-0	0	4.00
1996 St. Louis	NL	48	6	0	7	88.2	377	83	37	35	9	5	1	5	35	2	45	2	1	11	2	.846	0	0-3	10	3.55
4 ML YEARS		104	28	1	17	267.2	1144	283	149	136	31	13	7	11	83	7	136	9	2	20	9	.690	1	0-3	10	4.57

Andy Pettitte

Pitches: Left   **Bats:** Left   **Pos:** SP-34; RP-1   **Ht:** 6'5"   **Wt:** 235   **Born:** 6/15/72   **Age:** 25

Year Team	Lg	G	GS	CG	GF	IP	BFP	H	R	ER	HR	SH	SF	HB	TBB	IBB	SO	WP	Bk	W	L	Pct.	ShO	Sv-Op	Hld	ERA
1991 Yankees	R	6	6	0	0	36.2	135	16	6	4	0	4	1	0	8	0	51	4	6	4	1	.800	0	0--	—	0.98
Oneonta	A-	6	6	1	0	33	150	33	18	8	1	1	2	0	16	0	32	4	0	2	2	.500	0	0--	—	2.18
1992 Greensboro	A	27	27	2	0	168	671	141	53	41	4	3	1	5	55	0	130	11	2	10	4	.714	1	0--	—	2.20
1993 Pr. William	A+	26	26	2	0	159.2	651	146	68	54	7	6	4	5	47	0	129	8	1	11	9	.550	1	0--	—	3.04
Albany-Colo	AA	1	1	0	0	5	22	5	4	2	0	0	0	0	2	0	6	0	0	1	0	1.000	0	0--	—	3.60
1994 Albany-Colo	AA	11	11	0	0	73	294	60	32	22	5	1	1	1	18	1	50	5	1	7	2	.778	0	0--	—	2.71
Columbus	AAA	16	16	3	0	96.2	401	101	40	32	3	3	4	2	21	0	61	5	0	7	2	.778	0	0--	—	2.98
1995 Columbus	AAA	2	2	0	0	11.2	38	7	0	0	0	0	0	0	0	8	1	0	0	0	0	.000	0	0--	—	0.00
1995 New York	AL	31	26	3	1	175	745	183	86	81	15	4	5	1	63	3	114	8	1	12	9	.571	0	0-0	0	4.17
1996 New York	AL	35	34	2	1	221	929	229	105	95	23	7	3	3	72	2	162	6	1	21	8	.724	0	0-0	0	3.87
2 ML YEARS		66	60	5	2	396	1674	412	191	176	38	11	8	4	135	5	276	14	2	33	17	.660	0	0-0	0	4.00

J.R. Phillips

Bats: Left   **Throws:** Left   **Pos:** 1B-21; RF-15; PH-15   **Ht:** 6'1"   **Wt:** 185   **Born:** 4/29/70   **Age:** 27

Year Team	Lg	G	AB	H	2B	3B	HR	(Hm	Rd)	TB	R	RBI	TBB	IBB	SO	HBP	SH	SF	SB	CS	SB%	GDP	Avg	OBP	SLG
1996 Scrnton-WB *	AAA	53	200	57	14	2	13	(—	—)	114	33	42	19	0	53	1	0	2	2	2	.50	9	.285	.347	.570
1993 San Francisco	NL	11	16	5	1	1	1	(0	1)	11	1	4	0	0	5	0	0	0	0	0	.00	0	.313	.313	.688
1994 San Francisco	NL	15	38	5	0	0	1	(0	1)	8	1	3	1	0	13	0	0	1	1	0	1.00	1	.132	.150	.211
1995 San Francisco	NL	92	231	45	9	0	9	(5	4)	81	27	28	19	2	69	0	2	0	1	1	.50	3	.195	.256	.351
1996 SF-Phi	NL	50	104	17	5	0	7	(4	3)	43	12	15	11	1	51	1	0	0	0	0	.00	0	.163	.250	.413
1996 San Francisco	NL	15	25	5	0	0	2	(0	2)	11	3	5	1	0	13	0	0	0	0	0	.00	0	.200	.231	.440
Philadelphia	NL	35	79	12	5	0	5	(4	1)	32	9	10	10	1	38	1	0	0	0	0	.00	1	.152	.256	.405
4 ML YEARS		168	389	72	15	1	18	(9	9)	143	41	50	31	3	138	1	2	1	2	1	.67	5	.185	.246	.368

Tony Phillips

Bats: B   **Throws:** R   **Pos:** LF-150; PH-4; 2B-2; CF-2; 1B-1   **Ht:** 5'10"   **Wt:** 175   **Born:** 4/25/59   **Age:** 38

Year Team	Lg	G	AB	H	2B	3B	HR	(Hm	Rd)	TB	R	RBI	TBB	IBB	SO	HBP	SH	SF	SB	CS	SB%	GDP	Avg	OBP	SLG
1982 Oakland	AL	40	81	17	2	2	0	(0	0)	23	11	8	12	0	26	2	5	0	2	3	.40	0	.210	.326	.284
1983 Oakland	AL	148	412	102	12	3	4	(1	3)	132	54	35	48	1	70	2	11	3	16	5	.76	5	.248	.327	.320

Year Team	Lg	G	AB	H	2B	3B	HR	(Hm	Rd)	TB	R	RBI	TBB	IBB	SO	HBP	SH	SF	SB	CS	SB%	GDP	Avg	OBP	SLG
1984 Oakland	AL	154	451	120	24	3	4	(2	2)	162	62	37	42	1	86	0	7	5	10	6	.63	5	.266	.325	.359
1985 Oakland	AL	42	161	45	12	2	4	(2	2)	73	23	17	13	0	34	0	3	1	3	2	.60	1	.280	.331	.453
1986 Oakland	AL	118	441	113	14	5	5	(3	2)	152	76	52	76	0	82	3	9	3	15	10	.60	2	.256	.367	.345
1987 Oakland	AL	111	379	91	20	0	10	(5	5)	141	48	46	57	1	76	0	2	3	7	6	.54	9	.240	.337	.372
1988 Oakland	AL	79	212	43	8	4	2	(2	0)	65	32	17	36	0	50	1	1	1	0	2	.00	6	.203	.307	.307
1989 Oakland	AL	143	451	118	15	6	4	(2	2)	157	48	47	58	2	66	3	5	7	3	8	.27	17	.262	.345	.348
1990 Detroit	AL	152	573	144	23	5	8	(4	4)	201	97	55	99	0	85	4	9	2	19	9	.68	10	.251	.364	.351
1991 Detroit	AL	146	564	160	28	4	17	(9	8)	247	87	72	79	5	95	3	3	6	10	5	.67	8	.284	.371	.438
1992 Detroit	AL	159	606	167	32	3	10	(3	7)	235	**114**	64	114	2	93	1	5	7	12	10	.55	13	.276	.387	.388
1993 Detroit	AL	151	566	177	27	0	7	(3	4)	225	113	57	**132**	5	102	4	1	4	16	11	.59	11	.313	.443	.398
1994 Detroit	AL	114	438	123	19	3	19	(12	7)	205	91	61	95	3	105	2	0	3	13	5	.72	8	.281	.409	.468
1995 California	AL	139	525	137	21	1	22	(13	14)	241	119	61	113	6	135	3	1	1	13	10	.57	5	.261	.394	.459
1996 Chicago	AL	153	581	161	29	3	12	(6	6)	232	119	63	**125**	9	132	4	1	8	13	8	.62	6	.277	.404	.399
15 ML YEARS		1849	6441	1718	286	44	133	(67	66)	2491	1094	692	1099	35	1237	32	63	54	152	100	.60	106	.267	.374	.387

Mike Piazza

Bats: Right **Throws:** Right **Pos:** C-147; PH-4 **Ht:** 6'3" **Wt:** 215 **Born:** 9/4/68 **Age:** 28

Year Team	Lg	G	AB	H	2B	3B	HR	(Hm	Rd)	TB	R	RBI	TBB	IBB	SO	HBP	SH	SF	SB	CS	SB%	GDP	Avg	OBP	SLG
1992 Los Angeles	NL	21	69	16	3	0	1	(1	0)	22	5	7	4	0	12	1	0	0	0	0	.00	1	.232	.284	.319
1993 Los Angeles	NL	149	547	174	24	2	35	(21	14)	307	81	112	46	6	86	3	0	6	3	4	.43	10	.318	.370	.561
1994 Los Angeles	NL	107	405	129	18	0	24	(13	11)	219	64	92	33	10	65	1	0	2	1	3	.25	11	.319	.370	.541
1995 Los Angeles	NL	112	434	150	17	0	32	(9	23)	263	82	93	39	10	80	1	0	1	1	1	1.00	10	.346	.400	.606
1996 Los Angeles	NL	148	547	184	16	0	36	(14	22)	308	87	105	81	21	93	1	0	2	0	3	.00	21	.336	.422	.563
5 ML YEARS		537	2002	653	78	2	128	(58	70)	1119	319	409	203	47	336	7	0	11	5	10	.33	53	.326	.388	.559

Hipolito Pichardo

Pitches: Right **Bats:** Right **Pos:** RP-57 **Ht:** 6'1" **Wt:** 185 **Born:** 8/22/69 **Age:** 27

Year Team	Lg	G	GS	CG	GF	IP	BFP	H	R	ER	HR	SH	SF	HB	TBB	IBB	SO	WP	Bk	W	L	Pct.	ShO	Sv-Op	Hld	ERA
1992 Kansas City	AL	31	24	1	0	143.2	615	148	71	63	9	4	5	3	49	1	59	3	1	9	6	.600	1	0-0	0	3.95
1993 Kansas City	AL	30	25	2	2	165	720	183	85	74	10	3	8	6	53	2	70	5	3	7	8	.467	0	0-0	1	4.04
1994 Kansas City	AL	45	0	0	19	67.2	303	82	42	37	4	4	2	7	24	5	36	5	0	5	3	.625	0	3-5	6	4.92
1995 Kansas City	AL	44	0	0	16	64	287	66	34	31	4	3	1	4	30	7	43	4	1	8	4	.667	0	1-2	7	4.36
1996 Kansas City	AL	57	0	0	28	68	294	74	41	41	5	3	2	2	26	5	43	4	0	3	5	.375	0	3-5	15	5.43
5 ML YEARS		207	49	3	65	508.1	2219	553	273	246	32	17	18	22	182	20	251	19	5	32	26	.552	1	7-12	29	4.36

Greg Pirkl

Bats: Right **Throws:** Right **Pos:** PH-4; DH-3; 1B-2 **Ht:** 6'5" **Wt:** 240 **Born:** 8/7/70 **Age:** 26

Year Team	Lg	G	AB	H	2B	3B	HR	(Hm	Rd)	TB	R	RBI	TBB	IBB	SO	HBP	SH	SF	SB	CS	SB%	GDP	Avg	OBP	SLG
1996 Tacoma *	AAA	88	348	105	22	2	21	—	—	194	50	75	14	2	58	6	0	3	1	1	.50	13	.302	.337	.557
1993 Seattle	AL	7	23	4	0	0	1	(1	0)	7	1	4	0	0	4	0	0	0	0	0	.00	1	.174	.174	.304
1994 Seattle	AL	19	53	14	3	0	6	(2	4)	35	7	11	1	1	12	1	0	0	0	0	.00	1	.264	.286	.660
1995 Seattle	AL	10	17	4	0	0	0	(0	0)	4	2	0	1	0	7	0	0	0	0	0	.00	0	.235	.278	.235
1996 Bos-Sea	AL	9	23	4	1	0	1	(0	1)	8	2	1	0	0	4	0	0	0	0	0	.00	0	.174	.174	.348
1996 Boston	AL	2	2	0	0	0	0	(0	0)	0	0	0	0	0	1	0	0	0	0	0	.00	0	.000	.000	.000
Seattle	AL	7	21	4	1	0	1	(0	1)	8	2	1	0	0	3	0	0	0	0	0	.00	1	.190	.190	.381
4 ML YEARS		45	116	26	4	0	8	(3	5)	54	12	16	2	1	27	1	0	1	0	0	.00	4	.224	.242	.466

Phil Plantier

Bats: L **Throws:** R **Pos:** LF-67; PH-6; DH-1; CF-1; RF-1 **Ht:** 5'11" **Wt:** 195 **Born:** 1/27/69 **Age:** 28

Year Team	Lg	G	AB	H	2B	3B	HR	(Hm	Rd)	TB	R	RBI	TBB	IBB	SO	HBP	SH	SF	SB	CS	SB%	GDP	Avg	OBP	SLG
1996 Edmonton *	AAA	34	122	43	7	1	9	—	—	79	25	45	12	1	25	2	0	3	1	0	1.00	1	.352	.410	.648
1990 Boston	AL	14	15	2	1	0	0	(0	0)	3	1	3	4	0	6	1	0	0	0	0	.00	1	.133	.333	.200
1991 Boston	AL	53	148	49	7	1	11	(6	5)	91	27	35	23	2	38	1	0	2	0	1	1.00	2	.331	.420	.615
1992 Boston	AL	108	349	86	19	0	7	(5	2)	126	46	30	44	8	83	2	2	5	2	3	.40	8	.246	.332	.361
1993 San Diego	NL	138	462	111	20	1	34	(16	18)	235	67	100	61	7	124	7	1	5	4	5	.44	4	.240	.335	.509
1994 San Diego	NL	96	341	75	21	0	18	(7	11)	150	44	41	36	6	91	5	1	2	3	1	.75	8	.220	.302	.440
1995 Hou-SD	NL	76	216	55	6	0	9	(1	8)	88	33	34	28	3	48	1	0	1	1	1	.50	3	.255	.339	.407
1996 Oakland	AL	73	231	49	8	1	7	(3	4)	80	29	31	28	0	56	3	0	1	2	2	.50	5	.212	.304	.346
1995 Houston	NL	22	68	17	2	0	4	(0	4)	31	12	15	11	1	19	1	0	0	0	0	.00	0	.250	.349	.456
San Diego	NL	54	148	38	4	0	5	(1	4)	57	21	19	17	2	29	0	0	1	1	1	.50	3	.257	.333	.385
7 ML YEARS		558	1762	427	82	3	86	(38	48)	773	247	274	224	26	446	20	4	16	13	12	.52	32	.242	.332	.439

Dan Plesac

Pitches: Left **Bats:** Left **Pos:** RP-73   **Ht:** 6'5" **Wt:** 215 **Born:** 2/4/62 **Age:** 35

		HOW MUCH HE PITCHED						WHAT HE GAVE UP												THE RESULTS						
Year Team	Lg	G	GS	CG	GF	IP	BFP	H	R	ER	HR	SH	SF	HB	TBB	IBB	SO	WP	Bk	W	L	Pct.	ShO	Sv-Op	Hld	ERA
1986 Milwaukee	AL	51	0	0	33	91	377	81	34	30	5	6	5	0	29	1	75	4	0	10	7	.588	0	14--		2.97
1987 Milwaukee	AL	57	0	0	47	79.1	325	63	30	23	8	1	2	3	23	1	89	6	0	5	6	.455	0	23-36	0	2.61
1988 Milwaukee	AL	50	0	0	48	52.1	211	46	14	14	2	2	0	0	12	2	52	4	6	1	2	.333	0	30-35	0	2.41
1989 Milwaukee	AL	52	0	0	51	61.1	242	47	16	16	6	0	4	0	17	1	52	0	0	3	4	.429	0	33-40	0	2.35
1990 Milwaukee	AL	66	0	0	52	69	299	67	36	34	5	2	2	3	31	6	65	2	0	3	7	.300	0	24-34	2	4.43
1991 Milwaukee	AL	45	10	0	25	92.1	402	92	49	44	12	3	7	3	39	1	61	2	1	2	7	.222	0	8-12	1	4.29
1992 Milwaukee	AL	44	4	0	13	79	330	64	28	26	5	8	4	3	35	5	54	3	1	4	4	.556	0	1-3	1	2.96
1993 Chicago	NL	57	0	0	12	62.2	276	74	37	33	10	4	3	0	21	6	47	5	2	2	1	.667	0	0-2	12	4.74
1994 Chicago	NL	54	0	0	14	54.2	235	61	30	28	9	1	1	1	13	0	53	0	0	2	3	.400	0	1-3	14	4.61
1995 Pittsburgh	NL	58	0	0	16	60.1	259	53	26	24	3	4	3	1	27	7	57	1	0	4	4	.500	0	3-5	11	3.58
1996 Pittsburgh	NL	73	0	0	30	70.1	300	67	35	32	4	2	3	0	24	6	76	4	0	6	5	.545	0	11-17	11	4.09
11 ML YEARS		607	14	0	341	772.1	3256	715	335	304	69	33	34	14	271	36	681	31	10	43	50	.462	0	148--		3.54

Eric Plunk

Pitches: Right **Bats:** Right **Pos:** RP-56   **Ht:** 6'6" **Wt:** 220 **Born:** 9/3/63 **Age:** 33

		HOW MUCH HE PITCHED						WHAT HE GAVE UP												THE RESULTS						
Year Team	Lg	G	GS	CG	GF	IP	BFP	H	R	ER	HR	SH	SF	HB	TBB	IBB	SO	WP	Bk	W	L	Pct.	ShO	Sv-Op	Hld	ERA
1986 Oakland	AL	26	15	0	2	120.1	537	91	75	71	14	2	3	5	102	2	98	9	6	4	7	.364	0	0--		5.31
1987 Oakland	AL	32	11	0	11	95	432	91	53	50	8	3	5	2	62	3	90	5	2	4	6	.400	0	2-5	1	4.74
1988 Oakland	AL	49	0	0	22	78	331	62	27	26	6	3	2	1	39	4	79	4	7	7	2	.778	0	5-9	5	3.00
1989 Oak-NYA	AL	50	7	0	11	104.1	445	82	43	38	10	3	4	1	64	2	85	10	3	8	6	.571	0	1-3	7	3.28
1990 New York	AL	47	0	0	16	72.2	310	58	27	22	6	7	0	2	43	4	67	4	2	6	3	.667	0	0-1	3	2.72
1991 New York	AL	43	8	0	6	111.2	521	128	69	59	18	6	4	1	62	1	103	6	2	2	5	.286	0	0-0	2	4.76
1992 Cleveland	AL	58	0	0	20	71.2	309	61	31	29	5	3	2	0	38	2	50	5	0	9	6	.600	0	4-8	7	3.64
1993 Cleveland	AL	70	0	0	40	71	306	61	29	22	5	4	2	0	30	4	77	6	0	4	5	.444	0	15-18	16	2.79
1994 Cleveland	AL	41	0	0	18	71	306	61	25	20	3	2	1	2	37	5	73	7	0	7	2	.778	0	3-7	8	2.54
1995 Cleveland	AL	56	0	0	22	64	263	48	19	19	5	2	2	4	27	2	71	3	0	6	2	.750	0	2-5	10	2.67
1996 Cleveland	AL	56	0	0	12	77.2	318	56	21	21	6	1	4	3	34	2	85	4	1	3	2	.600	0	2-3	15	2.43
1989 Oakland	AL	23	0	0	12	28.2	113	17	7	7	1	0	1	0	12	0	24	4	0	1	1	.500	0	1-3	5	2.20
New York	AL	27	7	0	5	75.2	332	65	36	31	9	2	4	0	52	2	61	6	3	7	5	.583	0	0-0	1	3.69
11 ML YEARS		528	41	0	186	937.1	4078	799	419	377	86	36	29	21	538	31	878	63	23	60	46	.566	0	34--		3.62

Dale Polley

Pitches: Left **Bats:** Right **Pos:** RP-32   **Ht:** 6'0" **Wt:** 185 **Born:** 8/9/64 **Age:** 32

		HOW MUCH HE PITCHED						WHAT HE GAVE UP												THE RESULTS						
Year Team	Lg	G	GS	CG	GF	IP	BFP	H	R	ER	HR	SH	SF	HB	TBB	IBB	SO	WP	Bk	W	L	Pct.	ShO	Sv-Op	Hld	ERA
1987 Pulaski	R+	13	1	0	8	25.2	103	18	7	5	1	0	1	0	9	0	37	1	0	0	2	.000	0	5--		1.75
Sumter	A	7	6	1	0	40.2	167	37	16	13	2	3	1	0	9	0	32	1	1	3	1	.750	1	0--		2.88
1988 Greenville	AA	36	16	0	10	128	531	102	56	45	18	5	3	1	49	0	67	4	2	9	6	.600	0	2--		3.16
1989 Greenville	AA	28	26	3	0	163.2	681	142	75	61	11	10	3	4	58	1	106	6	2	6	15	.286	2	0--		3.35
1990 Richmond	AAA	36	15	1	6	135	556	121	66	53	10	8	4	2	48	8	64	5	3	4	7	.364	1	0--		3.53
1991 Richmond	AAA	50	1	0	27	66.1	294	70	24	24	2	5	4	4	30	5	38	0	0	2	3	.400	0	4--		3.26
1992 Richmond	AAA	39	0	0	12	56.1	239	54	20	18	1	6	1	1	24	5	42	2	0	1	6	.143	0	2--		2.88
1993 Greenville	AA	42	0	0	18	59	238	44	28	27	8	3	0	3	21	2	66	2	1	8	1	.889	0	2--		4.12
Richmond	AAA	10	0	0	3	18.1	85	21	9	8	1	0	1	0	11	1	14	0	0	1	0	1.000	0	0--		3.93
1995 Richmond	AAA	47	0	0	22	63.1	261	51	15	11	2	2	3	2	20	5	60	2	0	3	2	.600	0	7--		1.56
1996 Columbus	AAA	31	0	0	6	31.2	130	29	11	11	1	0	0	0	9	0	29	2	0	2	2	.500	0	1--		3.13
1996 New York	AL	32	0	0	9	21.2	103	23	20	19	5	1	1	3	11	1	14	0	0	1	3	.250	0	0-0	4	7.89

Luis Polonia

Bats: L **Throws:** L **Pos:** LF-39; PH-27; DH-18; RF-2   **Ht:** 5'8" **Wt:** 160 **Born:** 12/10/64 **Age:** 32

		BATTING																	BASERUNNING				PERCENTAGES		
Year Team	Lg	G	AB	H	2B	3B	HR	(Hm Rd)	TB	R	RBI	TBB	IBB	SO	HBP	SH	SF	SB	CS	SB%	GDP	Avg	OBP	SLG
1996 Rochester *	AAA	13	50	12	2	0	0	-- --	14	9	3	7	0	8	0	0	0	5	0	1.00	1	.240	.333	.280
1987 Oakland	AL	125	435	125	16	10	4	(1 3)	173	78	49	32	1	64	0	1	1	29	7	.81	4	.287	.335	.398
1988 Oakland	AL	84	288	84	11	4	2	(1 1)	109	51	27	21	0	40	0	2	2	24	9	.73	3	.292	.338	.378
1989 Oak-NYA	AL	125	433	130	17	6	3	(1 2)	168	70	46	25	1	44	2		4	22	8	.73	13	.300	.338	.388
1990 NYA-Cal	AL	120	403	135	7	9	2	(2 0)	166	52	35	25	1	43	1	3	4	21	14	.60	9	.335	.372	.412
1991 California	AL	150	604	179	28	8	2	(1 1)	229	92	50	52	4	74	1	2	3	48	23	.68	11	.296	.352	.379
1992 California	AL	149	577	165	17	4	0	(0 0)	190	83	35	45	6	64	1	8	4	51	21	.71	18	.286	.337	.329
1993 California	AL	152	576	156	17	6	1	(0 1)	188	75	32	48	7	53	2	8	3	55	24	.70	7	.271	.328	.326
1994 New York	AL	95	350	109	21	6	1	(0 1)	145	62	36	37	1	36	4	2	1	20	12	.63	7	.311	.383	.414
1995 NYA-Atl	AL	95	291	76	16	3	2	(2 0)	104	43	17	28	1	38	0	3	4	13	4	.76	3	.261	.322	.357
1996 Bal-Atl	AL	80	206	55	4	1	2	(2 0)	67	28	16	11	0	23	1	1	2	9	7	.56	10	.267	.306	.325
1989 Oakland	AL	59	206	59	6	4	1	(0 1)	76	31	17	9	0	15	0	2	1	13	4	.76	5	.286	.315	.369
New York	AL	66	227	71	11	2	2	(1 1)	92	39	29	16	1	29	2	0	3	9	4	.69	8	.313	.359	.405
1990 New York	AL	11	22	7	0	0	0	(0 0)	7	2	3	0	0	1	0	0	1	1	0	1.00	1	.318	.304	.318
California	AL	109	381	128	7	9	2	(2 0)	159	50	32	25	1	42	1	3	3	20	14	.59	8	.336	.376	.417

Year Team	Lg	BATTING G	AB	H	2B	3B	HR	(Hm	Rd)	TB	R	RBI	TBB	IBB	SO	HBP	SH	SF	BASERUNNING SB	CS	SB%	GDP	PERCENTAGES Avg	OBP	SLG
1995 New York	AL	67	238	62	9	3	2	(2	0)	83	37	15	25	1	29	0	2	4	10	4	.71	3	.261	.326	.349
Atlanta	NL	28	53	14	7	0	0	(0	0)	21	6	2	3	0	9	0	1	0	3	0	1.00	0	.264	.304	.396
1996 Baltimore	AL	58	175	42	4	1	2	(2	0)	54	25	14	10	0	20	1	1	0	8	6	.57	10	.240	.285	.309
Atlanta	NL	22	31	13	0	0	0	(0	0)	13	3	2	1	0	3	0	0	1	1	1	.50	0	.419	.424	.419
10 ML YEARS		1175	4163	1214	154	57	19	(10	9)	1539	634	343	324	22	479	12	32	27	292	129	.69	85	.292	.342	.370

Jim Poole

Pitches: Left **Bats:** Left **Pos:** RP-67   **Ht:** 6'2" **Wt:** 203 **Born:** 4/28/66 **Age:** 31

Year Team	Lg	HOW MUCH HE PITCHED G	GS	CG	GF	IP	BFP	WHAT HE GAVE UP H	R	ER	HR	SH	SF	HB	TBB	IBB	SO	WP	Bk	THE RESULTS W	L	Pct.	ShO	Sv-Op	Hld	ERA
1990 Los Angeles	NL	16	0	0	4	10.2	46	7	5	5	1	0	0	0	8	4	6	1	0	0	0	.000	0	0-0	2	4.22
1991 Tex-Bal	AL	29	0	0	5	42	166	29	14	11	3	3	3	0	12	2	18	2	0	3	2	.600	0	1-1	4	2.36
1992 Baltimore	AL	6	0	0	1	3.1	14	3	3	0	0	0	0	0	1	0	3	0	0	0	0	.000	0	0-1	0	0.00
1993 Baltimore	AL	55	0	0	11	50.1	197	30	18	12	2	3	2	0	21	5	29	0	0	2	1	.667	0	2-3	14	2.15
1994 Baltimore	AL	38	0	0	10	20.1	100	32	15	15	4	0	3	0	11	2	18	1	0	1	0	1.000	0	0-2	10	6.64
1995 Cleveland	AL	42	0	0	9	50.1	206	40	22	21	7	1	2	2	17	0	41	2	1	3	3	.500	0	0-0	6	3.75
1996 Cle-SF		67	0	0	13	50.1	218	44	22	16	5	3	1	1	27	7	38	3	0	1	0	.857	0	0-4	10	2.86
1991 Texas	AL	5	0	0	2	6	31	10	4	3	0	0	1	0	3	0	4	0	0	0	0	.000	0	1-1	0	4.50
Baltimore	AL	24	0	0	3	36	135	19	10	8	3	3	2	0	9	2	34	2	0	3	2	.600	0	0-0	4	2.00
1996 Cleveland	AL	32	0	0	8	26.2	121	29	15	9	3	0	1	0	14	4	19	2	0	4	0	1.000	0	0-1	5	3.04
San Francisco	NL	35	0	0	5	23.2	97	15	7	7	2	3	0	1	13	3	19	1	0	1	0	.667	0	0-3	5	2.66
7 ML YEARS		253	0	0	53	227.1	947	185	99	80	22	10	11	3	97	20	173	9	1	15	7	.682	0	3-11	46	3.17

Mark Portugal

Pitches: Right **Bats:** Right **Pos:** SP-26; RP-1   **Ht:** 6'0" **Wt:** 190 **Born:** 10/30/62 **Age:** 34

Year Team	Lg	HOW MUCH HE PITCHED G	GS	CG	GF	IP	BFP	WHAT HE GAVE UP H	R	ER	HR	SH	SF	HB	TBB	IBB	SO	WP	Bk	THE RESULTS W	L	Pct.	ShO	Sv-Op	Hld	ERA
1985 Minnesota	AL	6	4	0	0	24.1	105	24	16	15	3	0	2	0	14	0	12	1	1	1	3	.250	0	0--		5.55
1986 Minnesota	AL	27	15	3	7	112.2	481	112	56	54	10	5	3	1	50	1	67	5	0	6	10	.375	0	1---		4.31
1987 Minnesota	AL	13	7	0	3	44	204	58	40	38	13	0	1	1	24	1	28	2	0	1	3	.250	0	0-1	0	7.77
1988 Minnesota	AL	26	0	0	9	57.2	242	60	30	29	11	2	3	1	17	1	31	2	2	3	3	.500	0	3-4	0	4.53
1989 Houston	NL	20	15	2	1	108	440	91	34	33	7	8	1	2	37	0	86	3	0	7	1	.875	1	0-0	1	2.75
1990 Houston	NL	32	32	1	0	196.2	831	187	90	79	21	7	6	4	67	4	136	6	0	11	10	.524	1	0-0		3.62
1991 Houston	NL	32	27	1	3	168.1	710	163	91	84	19	6	6	2	59	5	120	4	1	10	12	.455	1	1-2	1	4.49
1992 Houston	NL	18	16	1	0	101.1	405	76	32	30	7	5	1	1	41	3	62	1	1	6	3	.667	1	0-0		2.66
1993 Houston	NL	33	33	1	0	208	876	194	75	64	10	11	3	4	77	3	131	9	2	18	4	**.818**	1	0-0		2.77
1994 San Francisco	NL	21	21	1	0	137.1	580	135	68	60	17	6	4	6	45	2	87	5	0	10	8	.556	0	0-0		3.93
1995 SF-Cin	NL	31	31	1	0	181.2	775	185	91	81	17	9	1	4	56	2	96	7	0	11	10	.524	0	0-0		4.01
1996 Cincinnati	NL	27	26	1	0	156	646	146	77	69	20	7	6	2	42	2	93	6	0	8	9	.471	0	0-0		3.98
1995 San Francisco	NL	17	17	1	0	104	445	106	56	48	10	5	0	2	34	2	63	2	0	5	5	.500	0	0-0		4.15
Cincinnati	NL	14	14	0	0	77.2	330	79	35	33	7	4	1	2	22	0	33	5	0	6	5	.545	0	0-0		3.82
12 ML YEARS		286	227	12	23	1496	6295	1431	700	636	155	66	37	28	529	24	949	51	7	92	76	.548	4	5--	—	3.83

Jorge Posada

Bats: Both **Throws:** Right **Pos:** C-4; DH-3; PH-2   **Ht:** 6'2" **Wt:** 205 **Born:** 8/17/71 **Age:** 25

Year Team	Lg	BATTING G	AB	H	2B	3B	HR	(Hm	Rd)	TB	R	RBI	TBB	IBB	SO	HBP	SH	SF	BASERUNNING SB	CS	SB%	GDP	PERCENTAGES Avg	OBP	SLG
1991 Oneonta	A-	71	217	51	5	5	5	—	—	78	34	33	51	0	49	4	8	1	6	4	.60	3	.235	.388	.359
1992 Greensboro	A	101	339	94	22	4	12	—	—	160	60	58	58	2	87	6	0	3	11	6	.65	8	.277	.389	.472
1993 Pr. William	A+	118	410	106	27	2	17	—	—	188	71	61	67	4	90	6	1	6	17	5	.77	7	.259	.366	.459
Albany-Colo	AA	7	25	7	0	0	0	—	—	7	3	0	2	0	7	0	0	0	0	0	.00	1	.280	.333	.280
1994 Columbus	AAA	92	313	75	13	3	11	—	—	127	46	48	32	1	81	1	4	5	5	5	.50	3	.240	.308	.406
1995 Columbus	AAA	108	368	94	32	5	8	—	—	160	60	51	54	2	101	1	6	3	4	4	.50	14	.255	.350	.435
1996 Columbus	AAA	106	354	96	22	6	11	—	—	163	76	62	79	3	86	3	1	3	3	3	.50	13	.271	.405	.460
1995 New York	AL	1	0	0	0	0	0	(0	0)	0	0	0	0	0	0	0	0	0	0	0	.00	0	.000	.000	.000
1996 New York	AL	8	14	1	0	0	0	(0	0)	1	1	0	1	0	6	0	0	0	0	0	.00	1	.071	.133	.071
2 ML YEARS		9	14	1	0	0	0	(0	0)	1	1	0	1	0	6	0	0	0	0	0	.00	1	.071	.133	.071

Mike Potts

Pitches: Left **Bats:** Left **Pos:** RP-24   **Ht:** 5'9" **Wt:** 170 **Born:** 9/5/70 **Age:** 26

Year Team	Lg	HOW MUCH HE PITCHED G	GS	CG	GF	IP	BFP	WHAT HE GAVE UP H	R	ER	HR	SH	SF	HB	TBB	IBB	SO	WP	Bk	THE RESULTS W	L	Pct.	ShO	Sv-Op	Hld	ERA
1990 Braves	R	23	1	0	17	39	174	29	23	15	2	0	3	1	25	1	39	5	0	5	2	.714	0	4--	—	3.46
1991 Macon	A	34	11	2	5	95.1	399	64	45	37	3	2	4	1	50	1	76	13	0	8	5	.615	2	1--	—	3.49
1992 Durham	A+	30	21	0	2	127.2	547	104	75	57	4	6	6	1	71	5	123	14	0	6	8	.429	0	1--	—	4.02
1993 Greenville	AA	25	25	1	0	141.2	621	131	79	61	7	7	3	1	86	2	116	6	1	7	6	.538	0	0--	—	3.88
1994 Richmond	AAA	52	0	0	18	85.2	369	75	41	35	3	7	3	2	43	6	60	6	0	6	3	.667	0	1--	—	3.68
1995 Richmond	AAA	38	1	0	17	73.2	320	79	35	31	4	3	1	0	37	4	52	6	0	5	5	.500	0	1--	—	3.79
1996 New Orleans	AAA	11	1	0	0	16	78	23	15	12	0	2	0	1	11	0	8	1	0	0	0	.000	0	0--	—	6.75

Year Team	Lg	G	GS	CG	GF	IP	BFP	H	R	ER	HR	SH	SF	HB	TBB	IBB	SO	WP	Bk	W	L	Pct.	ShO	Sv-Op	Hld	ERA
		HOW MUCH HE PITCHED						**WHAT HE GAVE UP**												**THE RESULTS**						
1996 Milwaukee	AL	24	0	0	7	45.1	217	58	39	36	7	1	4	0	30	2	21	3	1	1	2	.333	0	1-1	2	7.15

Jay Powell

Pitches: Right **Bats:** Right **Pos:** RP-67 **Ht:** 6'4" **Wt:** 225 **Born:** 1/19/72 **Age:** 25

Year Team	Lg	G	GS	CG	GF	IP	BFP	H	R	ER	HR	SH	SF	HB	TBB	IBB	SO	WP	Bk	W	L	Pct.	ShO	Sv-Op	Hld	ERA
		HOW MUCH HE PITCHED						**WHAT HE GAVE UP**												**THE RESULTS**						
1993 Albany	A	6	6	0	0	27.2	122	29	19	14	0	1	2	0	13	0	29	4	1	0	2	.000	0	0--	—	4.55
1994 Frederick	A+	26	20	0	2	123.1	552	132	79	68	13	4	3	1	54	0	87	12	2	7	7	.500	0	1--	—	4.96
1995 Portland	AA	50	0	0	44	53	213	42	12	11	2	3	1	2	15	1	53	2	1	5	4	.556	0	24--	—	1.87
1996 Brevard Cty	A+	1	1	0	0	2	6	0	0	0	0	0	0	0	0	0	4	0	0	0	0	.000	0	0--	—	0.00
1995 Florida	NL	9	0	0	1	8.1	38	7	2	1	0	1	0	2	6	1	4	0	0	0	0	.000	0	0-0	2	1.08
1996 Florida	NL	67	0	0	16	71.1	321	71	41	36	5	2	1	4	36	1	52	3	0	4	3	.571	0	2-5	10	4.54
2 ML YEARS		76	0	0	17	79.2	359	78	43	37	5	3	1	6	42	2	56	3	0	4	3	.571	0	2-5	12	4.18

Arquimedez Pozo

Bats: R **Throws:** R **Pos:** 2B-10; 3B-10; PH-2; DH-1 **Ht:** 5'10" **Wt:** 160 **Born:** 8/24/73 **Age:** 23

Year Team	Lg	G	AB	H	2B	3B	HR	(Hm	Rd)	TB	R	RBI	TBB	IBB	SO	HBP	SH	SF	SB	CS	SB%	GDP	Avg	OBP	SLG
		BATTING																	**BASERUNNING**				**PERCENTAGES**		
1992 San Bernrdo	A+	54	199	52	8	4	3	—	—	77	33	19	20	0	41	2	1	0	13	8	.62	2	.261	.335	.387
Bellingham	A-	39	149	48	12	0	7	—	—	81	37	21	20	0	24	2	1	1	9	5	.64	1	.322	.407	.544
1993 Riverside	A+	127	515	176	44	6	13	—	—	271	98	69	56	4	56	2	1	5	10	10	.50	22	.342	.405	.526
1994 Jacksonvlle	AA	119	447	129	31	1	14	—	—	204	70	54	32	0	43	7	3	6	11	8	.58	8	.289	.341	.456
1995 Tacoma	AAA	122	450	135	14	9	10	—	—	196	57	62	26	1	31	3	1	4	3	3	.50	15	.300	.340	.436
1996 Tacoma	AAA	95	365	102	12	5	15	—	—	169	55	64	39	1	40	6	1	8	3	3	.50	11	.279	.352	.463
Pawtucket	AAA	11	37	9	1	0	1	—	—	13	6	3	0	0	6	2	0	0	0	0	.00	1	.243	.333	.351
1995 Seattle	AL	1	1	0	0	0	0	(0	0)	0	0	0	0	0	0	0	0	0	0	0	.00	0	.000	.000	.000
1996 Boston	AL	21	58	10	3	1	1	(0	1)	18	4	11	2	0	10	1	0	1	1	0	1.00	1	.172	.210	.310
2 ML YEARS		22	59	10	3	1	1	(0	1)	18	4	11	2	0	10	1	0	1	1	0	1.00	1	.169	.206	.305

Curtis Pride

Bats: L **Throws:** R **Pos:** LF-45; DH-31; PH-22; RF-5 **Ht:** 6'0" **Wt:** 200 **Born:** 12/17/68 **Age:** 28

Year Team	Lg	G	AB	H	2B	3B	HR	(Hm	Rd)	TB	R	RBI	TBB	IBB	SO	HBP	SH	SF	SB	CS	SB%	GDP	Avg	OBP	SLG
		BATTING																	**BASERUNNING**				**PERCENTAGES**		
1996 Toledo *	AAA	9	26	6	1	0	1	—	—	10	4	2	9	0	7	1	0	0	4	1	.80	1	.231	.444	.385
1993 Montreal	NL	10	9	4	1	1	1	(0	1)	10	3	5	0	0	3	0	0	0	1	0	1.00	0	.444	.444	1.111
1995 Montreal	NL	48	63	11	1	0	0	(0	0)	12	10	2	5	0	16	0	1	0	3	2	.60	2	.175	.235	.190
1996 Detroit	AL	95	267	80	17	5	10	(5	5)	137	52	31	31	1	63	0	3	0	11	6	.65	2	.300	.372	.513
3 ML YEARS		153	339	95	19	6	11	(5	6)	159	65	38	36	1	82	0	4	0	15	8	.65	4	.280	.349	.469

Ariel Prieto

Pitches: Right **Bats:** Right **Pos:** SP-21 **Ht:** 6'3" **Wt:** 225 **Born:** 10/22/69 **Age:** 27

Year Team	Lg	G	GS	CG	GF	IP	BFP	H	R	ER	HR	SH	SF	HB	TBB	IBB	SO	WP	Bk	W	L	Pct.	ShO	Sv-Op	Hld	ERA
		HOW MUCH HE PITCHED						**WHAT HE GAVE UP**												**THE RESULTS**						
1995 Palm Spring	IND	6	6	1	0	37	139	23	6	4	2	0	0	1	7	0	48	1	0	4	0	1.000	0	0--	—	0.97
1996 Modesto	A+	2	1	0	1	9	38	9	4	3	0	0	0	1	2	0	8	2	0	0	0	.000	0	1--	—	3.00
Edmonton	AAA	3	3	0	0	15.2	61	11	1	1	0	0	0	0	6	0	18	1	0	3	0	1.000	0	0--	—	0.57
1995 Oakland	AL	14	9	1	1	58	258	57	35	32	4	3	2	5	32	1	37	4	1	2	6	.250	0	0-0	0	4.97
1996 Oakland	AL	21	21	2	0	125.2	547	130	66	58	9	5	5	7	54	2	75	6	2	6	7	.462	0	0-0	0	4.15
2 ML YEARS		35	30	3	1	183.2	805	187	101	90	13	8	7	12	86	3	112	10	3	8	13	.381	0	0-0	0	4.41

Tom Prince

Bats: Right **Throws:** Right **Pos:** C-35; PH-8 **Ht:** 5'11" **Wt:** 202 **Born:** 8/13/64 **Age:** 32

Year Team	Lg	G	AB	H	2B	3B	HR	(Hm	Rd)	TB	R	RBI	TBB	IBB	SO	HBP	SH	SF	SB	CS	SB%	GDP	Avg	OBP	SLG
		BATTING																	**BASERUNNING**				**PERCENTAGES**		
1996 Albuquerque *	AAA	32	95	39	5	1	7	—	—	67	24	22	15	2	14	2	0	0	0	2	.00	1	.411	.500	.705
1987 Pittsburgh	NL	4	9	2	1	0	1	(0	1)	6	1	2	0	0	2	0	0	0	0	0	.00	0	.222	.222	.667
1988 Pittsburgh	NL	29	74	13	2	0	0	(0	0)	15	3	6	4	0	15	0	2	0	0	0	.00	5	.176	.218	.203
1989 Pittsburgh	NL	21	52	7	4	0	0	(0	0)	11	1	5	6	1	12	0	0	1	1	1	.50	1	.135	.220	.212
1990 Pittsburgh	NL	4	10	1	0	0	0	(0	0)	1	1	0	1	0	2	0	0	0	0	0	.00	0	.100	.182	.100
1991 Pittsburgh	NL	26	34	9	3	0	1	(0	1)	15	4	2	7	0	3	1	0	0	0	0	.00	3	.265	.405	.441
1992 Pittsburgh	NL	27	44	4	2	0	0	(0	0)	6	1	5	6	0	9	0	0	2	1	1	.50	2	.091	.192	.136
1993 Pittsburgh	NL	66	179	35	14	0	2	(2	0)	55	14	24	13	2	38	7	2	3	1	1	.50	5	.196	.272	.307
1994 Los Angeles	NL	3	6	2	0	0	0	(0	0)	2	2	1	1	0	3	0	0	0	0	0	.00	0	.333	.429	.333
1995 Los Angeles	NL	18	40	8	2	1	1	(0	1)	15	3	4	0	0	10	0	0	0	0	0	.00	0	.200	.273	.375
1996 Los Angeles	NL	40	64	19	6	0	1	(0	1)	28	6	11	6	2	15	2	3	2	0	0	.00	0	.297	.365	.438
10 ML YEARS		238	512	100	34	1	6	(2	4)	154	36	60	48	5	109	10	7	8	3	4	.43	16	.195	.273	.301

Chris Pritchett

Bats: Left **Throws:** Right **Pos:** 1B-5   **Ht:** 6'4" **Wt:** 185 **Born:** 1/31/70 **Age:** 27

				BATTING														BASERUNNING				PERCENTAGES		
Year Team	Lg	G	AB	H	2B	3B	HR	(Hm | Rd)	TB	R	RBI	TBB	IBB	SO	HBP	SH	SF	SB	CS	SB%	GDP	Avg	OBP	SLG
1991 Boise	A-	70	255	68	10	3	9	—	—	111	41	50	47	3	41	2	0	3	1	0	1.00	7	.267	.381	.435
1992 Quad City	A	128	448	130	19	1	13	—	—	190	79	72	71	6	88	5	2	5	9	4	.69	7	.290	.389	.424
1993 Midland	AA	127	464	141	30	6	2	—	—	191	61	66	61	2	72	2	6	7	3	7	.30	17	.308	.386	.412
1994 Midland	AA	127	460	142	25	4	6	—	—	193	86	91	92	9	87	2	3	7	5	3	.63	8	.309	.421	.420
1995 Vancouver	AAA	123	434	120	27	4	8	—	—	179	66	53	56	6	79	5	2	1	2	3	.40	7	.276	.365	.412
1996 Vancouver	AAA	130	485	143	39	1	16	—	—	232	78	73	71	11	96	6	0	6	5	4	.56	7	.295	.387	.478
1996 California	AL	5	13	2	0	0	0	(0 | 0)	2	1	1	0	0	3	0	0	0	0	0	.00	0	.154	.154	.154

Tim Pugh

Pitches: Right **Bats:** Right **Pos:** RP-28; SP-1   **Ht:** 6'6" **Wt:** 225 **Born:** 1/26/67 **Age:** 30

		HOW MUCH HE PITCHED						WHAT HE GAVE UP										THE RESULTS						
Year Team	Lg	G	GS	CG	GF	IP	BFP	H	R	ER	HR	SH	SF	HB	TBB	IBB	SO	WP	Bk	W	L	Pct.	ShO	Sv-Op	Hld	ERA
1996 Indianapols *	AAA	4	4	1	0	25.2	102	19	7	7	1	0	0	2	4	0	18	1	0	2	1	.667	1	0--	—	2.45
1992 Cincinnati	NL	7	7	0	0	45.1	187	47	15	13	2	2	1	1	13	3	18	0	0	4	2	.667	0	0-0	0	2.58
1993 Cincinnati	NL	31	27	3	3	164.1	738	200	102	96	19	6	5	7	59	1	94	3	2	10	15	.400	1	0-0	0	5.26
1994 Cincinnati	NL	10	9	1	0	47.2	227	60	37	32	5	2	5	3	26	0	24	4	0	3	3	.500	0	0-0	1	6.04
1995 Cincinnati	NL	28	12	0	4	98.1	413	100	46	42	13	2	2	1	32	2	38	3	1	6	5	.545	0	0-0	0	3.84
1996 Cin-KC		29	1	0	8	52	247	66	44	42	12	2	2	3	23	3	36	3	0	1	2	.333	0	0-0	3	7.27
1996 Cincinnati	NL	10	0	0	0	15.2	83	24	20	20	3	2	1	1	11	2	9	1	0	1	1	.500	0	0-0	3	11.49
Kansas City	AL	19	1	0	8	36.1	164	42	24	22	9	0	1	2	12	1	27	2	0	0	1	.000	0	0-0	0	5.45
5 ML YEARS		105	56	4	15	407.2	1812	473	244	225	51	14	15	15	153	9	210	13	3	24	27	.471	1	0-0	4	4.97

Harvey Pulliam

Bats: Right **Throws:** Right **Pos:** PH-8; LF-3   **Ht:** 6'0" **Wt:** 205 **Born:** 10/20/67 **Age:** 29

				BATTING														BASERUNNING				PERCENTAGES		
Year Team	Lg	G	AB	H	2B	3B	HR	(Hm	Rd)	TB	R	RBI	TBB	IBB	SO	HBP	SH	SF	SB	CS	SB%	GDP	Avg	OBP	SLG
1996 Colo. Sprng *	AAA	79	283	78	13	1	10	—	—	123	46	58	32	4	49	3	0	4	2	3	.40	12	.276	.351	.435
1991 Kansas City	AL	18	33	9	1	0	3	(2	1)	19	4	4	3	1	9	0	1	0	0	0	.00	1	.273	.333	.576
1992 Kansas City	AL	4	5	1	1	0	0	(0	0)	2	2	0	1	0	3	0	0	0	0	0	.00	0	.200	.333	.400
1993 Kansas City	AL	27	62	16	5	0	1	(0	1)	24	7	6	2	0	14	1	0	0	0	0	.00	3	.258	.292	.387
1995 Colorado	NL	5	5	2	1	0	1	(1	0)	6	1	3	0	0	2	0	0	0	0	0	.00	0	.400	.400	1.200
1996 Colorado	NL	10	15	2	0	0	0	(0	0)	2	2	0	2	0	6	0	0	0	0	0	.00	1	.133	.235	.133
5 ML YEARS		64	120	30	8	0	5	(3	2)	53	16	13	8	1	34	1	1	0	0	0	.00	5	.250	.302	.442

Bill Pulsipher

Pitches: Left **Bats:** Left **Pos:** SP   **Ht:** 6'3" **Wt:** 208 **Born:** 10/9/73 **Age:** 23

		HOW MUCH HE PITCHED						WHAT HE GAVE UP										THE RESULTS						
Year Team	Lg	G	GS	CG	GF	IP	BFP	H	R	ER	HR	SH	SF	HB	TBB	IBB	SO	WP	Bk	W	L	Pct.	ShO	Sv-Op	Hld	ERA
1992 Pittsfield	A-	14	14	0	0	95	413	88	40	30	3	0	1	3	56	0	83	16	1	6	3	.667	0	0--	—	2.84
1993 Capital Cty	A	6	6	1	0	43.1	175	34	17	10	1	2	0	1	12	0	29	1	1	2	3	.400	0	0--	—	2.08
St. Lucie	A+	13	13	3	0	96.1	374	63	27	24	2	3	1	3	39	0	102	9	1	7	3	.700	1	0--	—	2.24
1994 Binghamton	AA	28	28	5	0	201	849	179	90	72	18	7	1	3	89	2	171	9	5	14	9	.609	1	0--	—	3.22
1995 Norfolk	AAA	13	13	4	0	91.2	377	84	36	32	3	5	3	1	33	0	63	2	3	6	4	.600	2	0--	—	3.14
1995 New York	NL	17	17	2	0	126.2	530	122	58	56	11	2	1	4	45	0	81	2	1	5	7	.417	0	0-0	0	3.98

Paul Quantrill

Pitches: Right **Bats:** Left **Pos:** SP-20; RP-18   **Ht:** 6'1" **Wt:** 185 **Born:** 11/3/68 **Age:** 28

		HOW MUCH HE PITCHED						WHAT HE GAVE UP										THE RESULTS						
Year Team	Lg	G	GS	CG	GF	IP	BFP	H	R	ER	HR	SH	SF	HB	TBB	IBB	SO	WP	Bk	W	L	Pct.	ShO	Sv-Op	Hld	ERA
1992 Boston	AL	27	0	0	10	49.1	213	55	18	12	1	4	2	1	15	5	24	1	0	2	3	.400	0	1-5	3	2.19
1993 Boston	AL	49	14	1	8	138	594	151	73	60	13	4	2	2	44	14	66	0	1	6	12	.333	1	1-2	3	3.91
1994 Bos-Phi		35	1	0	9	53	236	64	31	29	7	5	3	5	15	4	28	0	2	3	3	.500	0	1-4	3	4.92
1995 Philadelphia	NL	33	29	0	1	179.1	784	212	102	93	20	9	6	6	44	3	103	0	3	11	12	.478	0	0-0	0	4.67
1996 Toronto	AL	38	20	0	7	134.1	609	172	90	81	27	5	7	2	51	3	86	1	1	5	14	.263	0	0-2	1	5.43
1994 Boston	AL	17	0	0	4	23	101	25	10	9	4	2	2	2	5	1	15	0	0	1	1	.500	0	0-2	3	3.52
Philadelphia	NL	18	1	0	5	30	135	39	21	20	3	3	1	3	10	3	13	0	2	2	2	.500	0	1-2	0	6.00
5 ML YEARS		182	64	1	35	554	2436	654	314	275	68	27	20	16	169	29	307	2	7	27	44	.380	1	3-13	10	4.47

Tom Quinlan

Bats: Right **Throws:** Right **Pos:** 3B-4; PH-1   **Ht:** 6'3" **Wt:** 214 **Born:** 3/27/68 **Age:** 29

				BATTING														BASERUNNING				PERCENTAGES		
Year Team	Lg	G	AB	H	2B	3B	HR	(Hm	Rd)	TB	R	RBI	TBB	IBB	SO	HBP	SH	SF	SB	CS	SB%	GDP	Avg	OBP	SLG
1996 Salt Lake *	AAA	121	491	139	38	1	15	—	—	224	81	81	38	2	121	15	0	8	4	8	.33	8	.283	.348	.456
1990 Toronto	AL	1	2	1	0	0	0	(0	0)	1	0	0	0	0	1	1	0	0	0	0	.00	0	.500	.667	.500
1992 Toronto	AL	13	15	1	1	0	0	(0	0)	2	2	2	2	0	9	0	0	0	0	0	.00	0	.067	.176	.133

184

Year Team	Lg	G	AB	H	2B	3B	HR	(Hm	Rd)	TB	R	RBI	TBB	IBB	SO	HBP	SH	SF	SB	CS	SB%	GDP	Avg	OBP	SLG
								BATTING											BASERUNNING				PERCENTAGES		
1994 Philadelphia	NL	24	35	7	2	0	1	(1	0)	12	6	3	3	1	13	0	1	0	0	0	.00	0	.200	.263	.343
1996 Minnesota	AL	4	6	0	0	0	0	(0	0)	0	0	0	0	0	3	0	0	0	0	0	.00	0	.000	.000	.000
4 ML YEARS		42	58	9	3	0	1	(1	0)	15	8	5	5	1	26	1	1	0	0	0	.00	0	.155	.234	.259

Rafael Quirico

Pitches: Left **Bats:** Left **Pos:** SP-1 **Ht:** 6'2" **Wt:** 212 **Born:** 9/7/69 **Age:** 27

Year Team	Lg	G	GS	CG	GF	IP	BFP	H	R	ER	HR	SH	SF	HB	TBB	IBB	SO	WP	Bk	W	L	Pct.	ShO	Sv-Op	Hld	ERA
		HOW MUCH HE PITCHED						WHAT HE GAVE UP												THE RESULTS						
1989 Yankees	R	17	7	0	1	63.2	268	61	32	27	.2	1	3	3	20	0	55	0	8	2	2	.500	0	1--	—	3.82
1990 Greensboro	A	13	13	1	0	72	325	74	60	40	4	1	2	3	30	0	52	5	10	2	6	.250	0	0--	—	5.00
Oneonta	A-	14	14	1	0	87	359	69	38	31	2	2	4	4	39	0	69	9	9	6	3	.667	0	0--	—	3.21
1991 Greensboro	A	26	26	1	0	155.1	641	103	59	39	5	1	2	7	80	0	162	12	9	12	8	.600	1	0--	—	2.26
1992 Pr. William	A+	23	23	2	0	130.2	570	128	84	46	11	8	1	1	50	1	123	7	7	6	11	.353	0	0--	—	3.17
Columbus	AAA	1	1	0	0	6	27	6	3	2	0	0	0	0	4	0	1	1	0	1	0	1.000	0	0--	—	3.00
1993 Albany-Colo	AA	36	11	0	15	94.2	403	92	46	37	15	5	1	1	33	2	79	6	1	4	10	.286	0	7--	—	3.52
Columbus	AAA	5	2	0	0	11	53	12	10	9	3	0	0	0	7	0	16	1	0	2	0	1.000	0	0--	—	7.36
1994 Columbus	AAA	37	0	0	12	63.2	289	63	41	33	6	1	2	3	36	1	49	9	1	0	4	.000	0	1--	—	4.66
1995 Columbus	AAA	20	0	0	8	23	96	15	14	12	1	0	1	3	14	0	21	5	2	0	0	.000	0	0--	—	4.70
1996 Clearwater	A+	2	2	0	0	10.1	45	13	9	9	2	0	0	1	1	0	12	0	4	1	0	1.000	0	0--	—	7.84
Reading	AA	5	5	0	0	30	124	22	6	6	2	0	2	2	11	1	23	0	1	1	0	1.000	0	0--	—	1.80
Scranton-WB	AAA	13	13	1	0	65	273	48	29	24	8	3	1	7	26	0	51	3	1	4	4	.500	0	0--	—	3.32
Norwich	AA	4	0	0	4	6.2	27	5	3	3	1	0	0	0	3	0	9	1	0	1	0	1.000	0	0--	—	4.05
1996 Philadelphia	NL	1	1	0	0	1.2	14	4	7	7	1	0	0	0	5	0	1	0	1	0	1	.000	0	0-0	0	37.80

Brian Raabe

Bats: Right **Throws:** Right **Pos:** 3B-6; PH-3; 2B-1 **Ht:** 5'9" **Wt:** 177 **Born:** 11/5/67 **Age:** 29

Year Team	Lg	G	AB	H	2B	3B	HR	(Hm	Rd)	TB	R	RBI	TBB	IBB	SO	HBP	SH	SF	SB	CS	SB%	GDP	Avg	OBP	SLG
								BATTING											BASERUNNING				PERCENTAGES		
1990 Visalia	A+	42	138	34	3	2	0	—	—	41	11	17	10	0	9	1	1	0	5	1	.83	6	.246	.302	.297
1991 Visalia	A+	85	311	80	3	1	1	—	—	88	36	22	40	0	14	4	3	2	15	5	.75	8	.257	.347	.283
1992 Miracle	A+	102	361	104	16	2	2	—	—	130	52	32	48	1	17	8	1	3	7	6	.54	3	.288	.381	.360
Orlando	AA	32	108	30	6	0	2	—	—	42	12	6	2	0	2	0	3	0	4	.00		2	.278	.291	.389
1993 Nashville	AA	134	524	150	23	2	6	—	—	195	80	52	56	1	28	10	10	4	18	8	.69	9	.286	.364	.372
1994 Salt Lake	AAA	123	474	152	26	3	3	—	—	193	78	49	50	1	11	1	0	8	9	8	.53	19	.321	.381	.407
1995 Salt Lake	AAA	112	440	134	32	6	3	—	—	187	88	60	45	2	14	3	2	7	15	0	1.00	12	.305	.368	.425
1996 Salt Lake	AAA	116	482	169	39	4	18	—	—	270	103	69	47	2	19	4	2	4	8	8	.50	12	.351	.410	.560
1995 Minnesota	AL	6	14	3	0	0	0	(0	0)	3	4	1	1	0	0	0	0	0	0	0	.00	0	.214	.267	.214
1996 Minnesota	AL	7	9	2	0	0	0	(0	0)	2	0	0	0	0	1	0	0	0	0	0	.00	0	.222	.200	.222
2 ML YEARS		13	23	5	0	0	0	(0	0)	5	4	2	1	0	1	0	0	0	0	0	.00	0	.217	.240	.217

Scott Radinsky

Pitches: Left **Bats:** Left **Pos:** RP-58 **Ht:** 6'3" **Wt:** 204 **Born:** 3/3/68 **Age:** 29

Year Team	Lg	G	GS	CG	GF	IP	BFP	H	R	ER	HR	SH	SF	HB	TBB	IBB	SO	WP	Bk	W	L	Pct.	ShO	Sv-Op	Hld	ERA
		HOW MUCH HE PITCHED						WHAT HE GAVE UP												THE RESULTS						
1996 San Bernrdo *	A+	3	0	0	0	4.1	17	2	1	1	0	0	0	0	2	0	4	0	0	0	0	.000	0	0--	—	2.08
1990 Chicago	AL	62	0	0	18	52.1	237	47	29	28	1	2	2	2	36	1	46	2	1	6	1	.857	0	4-5	10	4.82
1991 Chicago	AL	67	0	0	19	71.1	289	53	18	16	4	4	4	1	23	2	49	0	0	5	5	.500	0	8-15	15	2.02
1992 Chicago	AL	68	0	0	33	59.1	261	54	21	18	3	2	1	2	34	5	48	3	0	3	7	.300	0	15-23	16	2.73
1993 Chicago	AL	73	0	0	24	54.2	250	61	33	26	3	2	0	1	19	3	44	0	4	8	2	.800	0	4-5	12	4.28
1995 Chicago	AL	46	0	0	10	38	171	46	23	23	7	1	4	0	17	4	14	0	1	2	1	.667	0	1-3	8	5.45
1996 Los Angeles	NL	58	0	0	19	52.1	221	52	19	14	2	4	3	0	17	5	48	0	3	5	1	.833	0	1-4	7	2.41
6 ML YEARS		374	0	0	123	328	1429	313	143	125	20	15	14	6	146	20	249	5	8	29	17	.630	0	33-55	68	3.43

Brad Radke

Pitches: Right **Bats:** Right **Pos:** SP-35 **Ht:** 6'2" **Wt:** 186 **Born:** 10/27/72 **Age:** 24

Year Team	Lg	G	GS	CG	GF	IP	BFP	H	R	ER	HR	SH	SF	HB	TBB	IBB	SO	WP	Bk	W	L	Pct.	ShO	Sv-Op	Hld	ERA
		HOW MUCH HE PITCHED						WHAT HE GAVE UP												THE RESULTS						
1991 Twins	R	10	9	0	1	49.2	205	41	21	17	0	1	2	2	14	0	44	0	2	3	4	.429	0	1--	—	3.08
1992 Kenosha	A	26	25	4	1	165.2	680	149	70	54	8	7	6	8	47	1	127	4	0	10	10	.500	1	0--	—	2.93
1993 Fort Myers	A+	14	14	0	0	92	376	85	42	39	3	0	1	4	21	1	69	3	0	3	5	.375	0	0--	—	3.82
Nashville	AA	13	13	1	0	76	327	81	42	39	6	1	1	6	16	0	76	5	0	2	6	.250	0	0--	—	4.62
1994 Nashville	AA	29	28	5	0	186.1	741	167	66	55	9	4	2	5	34	0	123	8	1	12	9	.571	1	0--	—	2.66
1995 Minnesota	AL	29	28	2	0	181	772	195	112	107	32	2	9	4	47	0	75	4	0	11	14	.440	0	0-0	0	5.32
1996 Minnesota	AL	35	35	3	0	232	973	231	125	115	40	5	6	4	57	2	148	1	0	11	16	.407	1	0-0	0	4.46
2 ML YEARS		64	63	5	0	413	1745	426	237	222	72	7	15	8	104	2	223	5	0	22	30	.423	1	0-0	0	4.84

Tim Raines

Bats: Both **Throws:** Right **Pos:** LF-51; PH-9; DH-2   **Ht:** 5'8" **Wt:** 186 **Born:** 9/16/59 **Age:** 37

Year Team	Lg	G	AB	H	2B	3B	HR	(Hm	Rd)	TB	R	RBI	TBB	IBB	SO	HBP	SH	SF	SB	CS	SB%	GDP	Avg	OBP	SLG
1996 Yankees *	R	1	5	3	2	0	0	—	—	5	2	3	1	0	0	0	0	0	0	0	.00	0	.600	.667	1.000
Columbus *	AAA	4	12	3	1	0	0	—	—	4	3	0	1	0	3	0	0	0	1	0	1.00	0	.250	.308	.333
Tampa *	A+	9	36	13	2	0	2	—	—	21	9	11	8	1	3	0	0	0	0	0	.00	0	.361	.477	.583
Norwich *	AA	8	27	5	1	0	1	—	—	9	8	1	9	3	2	1	0	0	2	0	1.00	0	.185	.405	.333
1979 Montreal	NL	6	0	0	0	0	0	(0	0)	0	3	0	0	0	0	0	0	0	2	0	1.00	0	.000	.000	.000
1980 Montreal	NL	15	20	1	0	0	0	(0	0)	1	5	0	6	0	3	0	1	0	5	0	1.00	0	.050	.269	.050
1981 Montreal	NL	88	313	95	13	7	5	(3	2)	137	61	37	45	5	31	2	0	3	71	11	.87	7	.304	.391	.438
1982 Montreal	NL	156	647	179	32	8	4	(1	3)	239	90	43	75	9	83	2	6	1	78	16	.83	6	.277	.353	.369
1983 Montreal	NL	156	615	183	32	8	11	(5	6)	264	**133**	71	97	9	70	2	2	4	**90**	14	.87	12	.298	.393	.429
1984 Montreal	NL	160	622	192	**38**	9	8	(2	6)	272	106	60	87	7	69	2	3	4	75	10	.88	7	.309	.393	.437
1985 Montreal	NL	150	575	184	30	13	11	(4	7)	273	115	41	81	13	60	3	3	3	70	9	.89	3	.320	.405	.475
1986 Montreal	NL	151	580	194	35	10	9	(4	5)	276	91	62	78	9	60	2	1	3	70	9	.89	6	**.334**	**.413**	.476
1987 Montreal	NL	139	530	175	34	8	18	(9	9)	279	**123**	68	90	26	52	4	0	3	50	5	.91	9	.330	.429	.526
1988 Montreal	NL	109	429	116	19	7	12	(5	7)	185	66	48	53	14	44	2	0	4	33	7	.83	8	.270	.350	.431
1989 Montreal	NL	145	517	148	29	6	9	(6	3)	216	76	60	93	18	48	3	0	5	41	9	.82	8	.286	.395	.418
1990 Montreal	NL	130	457	131	11	5	9	(6	3)	179	65	62	70	8	43	3	0	8	49	16	.75	9	.287	.379	.392
1991 Chicago	AL	155	609	163	20	6	5	(1	4)	210	102	50	83	9	68	5	9	3	51	15	.77	7	.268	.359	.345
1992 Chicago	AL	144	551	162	22	9	7	(4	3)	223	102	54	81	4	48	0	4	8	45	6	.88	5	.294	.380	.405
1993 Chicago	AL	115	415	127	16	4	16	(7	9)	199	75	54	64	4	35	3	2	2	21	7	.75	7	.306	.401	.480
1994 Chicago	AL	101	384	102	15	5	10	(5	5)	157	80	52	61	3	43	1	4	3	13	0	1.00	10	.266	.365	.409
1995 Chicago	AL	133	502	143	25	4	12	(6	6)	212	81	67	70	3	52	3	3	3	13	2	.87	8	.285	.374	.422
1996 New York	AL	59	201	57	10	0	9	(7	2)	94	45	33	34	1	29	1	0	1	10	1	.91	5	.284	.383	.468
18 ML YEARS		2112	7967	2352	381	109	155	(75	80)	3416	1419	862	1168	142	838	38	38	61	787	137	.85	123	.295	.385	.429

Manny Ramirez

Bats: Right **Throws:** Right **Pos:** RF-149; DH-3; PH-3   **Ht:** 6'0" **Wt:** 190 **Born:** 5/30/72 **Age:** 25

Year Team	Lg	G	AB	H	2B	3B	HR	(Hm	Rd)	TB	R	RBI	TBB	IBB	SO	HBP	SH	SF	SB	CS	SB%	GDP	Avg	OBP	SLG
1993 Cleveland	AL	22	53	9	1	0	2	(0	2)	16	5	5	2	0	8	0	0	0	0	0	.00	3	.170	.200	.302
1994 Cleveland	AL	91	290	78	22	0	17	(9	8)	151	51	60	42	4	72	0	0	4	4	2	.67	6	.269	.357	.521
1995 Cleveland	AL	137	484	149	26	1	31	(12	19)	270	85	107	75	6	112	5	2	5	6	6	.50	13	.308	.402	.558
1996 Cleveland	AL	152	550	170	45	3	33	(19	14)	320	94	112	85	8	104	3	0	9	8	5	.62	18	.309	.399	.582
4 ML YEARS		402	1377	406	94	4	83	(40	43)	757	235	284	204	18	296	8	2	18	18	13	.58	40	.295	.385	.550

Joe Randa

Bats: R **Throws:** R **Pos:** 3B-92; PH-16; 2B-15; 1B-7; DH-1   **Ht:** 5'11" **Wt:** 190 **Born:** 12/18/69 **Age:** 27

Year Team	Lg	G	AB	H	2B	3B	HR	(Hm	Rd)	TB	R	RBI	TBB	IBB	SO	HBP	SH	SF	SB	CS	SB%	GDP	Avg	OBP	SLG
1991 Eugene	A-	72	275	93	20	2	11	—	—	150	53	59	46	4	30	6	0	4	6	1	.86	8	.338	.438	.545
1992 Appleton	A	72	266	80	13	0	5	—	—	108	55	43	34	0	37	6	0	6	6	2	.75	6	.301	.385	.406
Baseball Cy	A+	51	189	52	7	0	1	—	—	62	22	12	12	0	21	2	1	1	4	3	.57	4	.275	.324	.328
1993 Memphis	AA	131	505	149	31	5	11	—	—	223	74	72	39	2	64	3	0	10	8	7	.53	10	.295	.343	.442
1994 Omaha	AAA	127	455	125	27	2	10	—	—	186	65	51	30	1	49	8	5	5	5	2	.71	18	.275	.327	.409
1995 Omaha	AAA	64	233	64	10	2	8	—	—	102	33	33	22	0	33	2	1	1	2	2	.50	9	.275	.341	.438
1996 Omaha	AAA	3	9	1	0	1	0	—	—	3	1	0	1	0	1	0	0	0	0	0	.00	1	.111	.200	.333
1995 Kansas City	AL	34	70	12	2	0	1	(1	0)	17	6	5	6	0	17	0	0	0	0	1	.00	2	.171	.237	.243
1996 Kansas City	AL	110	337	102	24	1	6	(2	4)	146	36	47	26	4	47	1	2	4	13	4	.76	10	.303	.351	.433
2 ML YEARS		144	407	114	26	1	7	(3	4)	163	42	52	32	4	64	1	2	4	13	5	.72	12	.280	.331	.400

Pat Rapp

Pitches: Right **Bats:** Right **Pos:** SP-29; RP-1   **Ht:** 6'3" **Wt:** 215 **Born:** 7/13/67 **Age:** 29

Year Team	Lg	G	GS	CG	GF	IP	BFP	H	R	ER	HR	SH	SF	HB	TBB	IBB	SO	WP	Bk	W	L	Pct.	ShO	Sv-Op	Hld	ERA
1996 Charlotte *	AAA	2	2	0	0	11	58	18	12	10	3	0	0	0	4	0	9	1	0	1	1	.500	0	0--	—	8.18
1992 San Francisco	NL	3	2	0	1	10	43	8	8	8	0	2	0	1	6	1	3	0	0	0	2	.000	0	0-0	0	7.20
1993 Florida	NL	16	16	1	0	94	412	101	49	42	7	8	4	2	39	1	57	6	0	4	6	.400	0	0-0	0	4.02
1994 Florida	NL	24	23	2	1	133.1	584	132	67	57	13	8	4	7	69	3	75	5	1	7	8	.467	1	0-0	0	3.85
1995 Florida	NL	28	28	3	0	167.1	716	158	72	64	10	8	0	7	76	2	102	7	0	14	7	.667	2	0-0	0	3.44
1996 Florida	NL	30	29	0	1	162.1	728	184	95	92	12	15	8	3	91	6	86	13	0	8	**16**	.333	0	0-0	0	5.10
5 ML YEARS		101	98	6	3	567	2483	583	291	263	42	41	16	20	281	13	323	31	1	33	39	.458	3	0-0	0	4.17

Jeff Reboulet

B: R **T:** R **Pos:** SS-37; 3B-36; 2B-22; PH-19; 1B-13; RF-6; DH-3; LF-2 **Ht:** 6'0" **Wt:** 171 **Born:** 4/30/64 **Age:** 33

Year Team	Lg	G	AB	H	2B	3B	HR	(Hm	Rd)	TB	R	RBI	TBB	IBB	SO	HBP	SH	SF	SB	CS	SB%	GDP	Avg	OBP	SLG
1992 Minnesota	AL	73	137	26	7	1	1	(1	0)	38	15	16	23	0	26	1	7	0	3	2	.60	4	.190	.311	.277
1993 Minnesota	AL	109	240	62	8	0	1	(0	1)	73	33	15	35	0	37	2	5	1	5	5	.50	6	.258	.356	.304

		BATTING																	BASERUNNING				PERCENTAGES		
Year Team	Lg	G	AB	H	2B	3B	HR	(Hm Rd)	TB	R	RBI	TBB	IBB	SO	HBP	SH	SF	SB	CS	SB%	GDP	Avg	OBP	SLG
1994 Minnesota	AL	74	189	49	11	1	3	(2 1)	71	28	23	18	0	23	1	2	0	0	0	.00	6	.259	.327	.376
1995 Minnesota	AL	87	216	63	11	0	4	(1 3)	86	39	23	27	0	34	1	2	0	1	2	.33	3	.292	.373	.398
1996 Minnesota	AL	107	234	52	9	0	0	(0 0)	61	20	23	25	1	34	1	4	2	4	2	.67	10	.222	.298	.261
5 ML YEARS		450	1016	252	46	2	9	(4 5)	329	135	100	128	1	154	6	20	3	13	11	.54	25	.248	.335	.324

Jeff Reed

Bats: Left **Throws:** Right **Pos:** C-111; PH-8   **Ht:** 6'2" **Wt:** 190 **Born:** 11/12/62 **Age:** 34

		BATTING																	BASERUNNING				PERCENTAGES		
Year Team	Lg	G	AB	H	2B	3B	HR	(Hm Rd)	TB	R	RBI	TBB	IBB	SO	HBP	SH	SF	SB	CS	SB%	GDP	Avg	OBP	SLG
1984 Minnesota	AL	18	21	3	3	0	0	(0 0)	6	3	1	2	0	6	0	1	0	0	0	.00	0	.143	.217	.286
1985 Minnesota	AL	7	10	2	0	0	0	(0 0)	2	2	0	0	0	3	0	0	0	0	0	.00	0	.200	.200	.200
1986 Minnesota	AL	68	165	39	6	1	2	(1 1)	53	13	9	16	0	19	1	3	0	1	0	1.00	0	.236	.308	.321
1987 Montreal	NL	75	207	44	11	0	1	(1 0)	58	15	21	12	1	20	1	4	0	0	1	.00	8	.213	.254	.280
1988 Mon-Cin	NL	92	265	60	9	2	1	(1 0)	76	20	16	28	1	41	0	1	1	1	0	1.00	5	.226	.299	.287
1989 Cincinnati	NL	102	287	64	11	0	3	(1 2)	84	16	23	34	5	46	2	3	4	0	0	.00	6	.223	.306	.293
1990 Cincinnati	NL	72	175	44	8	1	3	(2 1)	63	12	16	24	5	26	0	5	1	0	0	.00	4	.251	.340	.360
1991 Cincinnati	NL	91	270	72	15	2	3	(1 2)	100	20	31	23	3	38	1	1	5	0	1	.00	6	.267	.321	.370
1992 Cincinnati	NL	15	25	4	0	0	0	(0 0)	4	2	2	1	1	4	0	0	0	0	0	.00	1	.160	.192	.160
1993 San Francisco	NL	66	119	31	3	0	6	(5 1)	52	10	12	16	4	22	0	0	1	0	1	.00	2	.261	.346	.437
1994 San Francisco	NL	50	103	18	3	0	1	(0 1)	24	11	7	11	4	21	0	0	0	0	0	.00	3	.175	.254	.233
1995 San Francisco	NL	66	113	30	2	0	0	(0 0)	32	12	9	20	3	17	0	1	0	0	0	.00	3	.265	.376	.283
1996 Colorado	NL	116	341	97	20	1	8	(7 1)	143	34	37	43	8	65	2	6	3	2	2	.50	8	.284	.365	.419
1988 Montreal	NL	43	123	27	3	2	0	(0 0)	34	10	9	13	1	22	0	1	1	1	0	1.00	3	.220	.292	.276
Cincinnati	NL	49	142	33	6	0	1	(1 0)	42	10	7	15	0	19	0	0	0	0	0	.00	2	.232	.306	.296
13 ML YEARS		838	2101	508	91	7	28	(19 9)	697	170	184	230	35	328	7	25	19	4	5	.44	48	.242	.316	.332

Jody Reed

Bats: Right **Throws:** Right **Pos:** 2B-145; PH-3   **Ht:** 5'9" **Wt:** 165 **Born:** 7/26/62 **Age:** 34

		BATTING																	BASERUNNING				PERCENTAGES		
Year Team	Lg	G	AB	H	2B	3B	HR	(Hm Rd)	TB	R	RBI	TBB	IBB	SO	HBP	SH	SF	SB	CS	SB%	GDP	Avg	OBP	SLG
1987 Boston	AL	9	30	9	1	1	0	(0 0)	12	4	8	4	0	0	1	0	1	1	1	.50	0	.300	.382	.400
1988 Boston	AL	109	338	99	23	1	1	(1 0)	127	60	28	45	1	21	4	11	3	1	3	.25	5	.293	.380	.376
1989 Boston	AL	146	524	151	42	2	3	(2 1)	206	76	40	73	0	44	4	13	5	4	5	.44	12	.288	.376	.393
1990 Boston	AL	155	598	173	45	0	5	(3 2)	233	70	51	75	4	65	4	11	3	4	4	.50	19	.289	.371	.390
1991 Boston	AL	153	618	175	42	2	5	(3 2)	236	87	60	60	2	53	4	11	3	6	5	.55	15	.283	.349	.382
1992 Boston	AL	143	550	136	27	1	3	(2 1)	174	64	40	62	2	44	0	10	4	7	8	.47	17	.247	.321	.316
1993 Los Angeles	NL	132	445	123	21	2	2	(0 2)	154	48	31	38	10	40	1	17	3	1	3	.25	16	.276	.333	.346
1994 Milwaukee	AL	108	399	108	22	0	2	(1 1)	136	48	37	57	1	34	2	4	3	5	4	.56	8	.271	.362	.341
1995 San Diego	NL	131	445	114	18	1	4	(4 0)	146	58	40	59	1	38	5	3	3	6	4	.60	9	.256	.348	.328
1996 San Diego	NL	146	495	121	20	0	2	(1 1)	147	45	49	59	8	53	3	5	6	2	5	.29	15	.244	.325	.297
10 ML YEARS		1232	4442	1209	261	10	27	(17 10)	1571	560	384	532	29	392	27	86	32	37	42	.47	116	.272	.351	.354

Steve Reed

Pitches: Right **Bats:** Right **Pos:** RP-70   **Ht:** 6'2" **Wt:** 212 **Born:** 3/11/66 **Age:** 31

		HOW MUCH HE PITCHED						WHAT HE GAVE UP										THE RESULTS						
Year Team	Lg	G	GS	CG	GF	IP	BFP	H	R	ER	HR	SH	SF	HB	TBB	IBB	SO	WP	Bk	W	L	Pct.	ShO	Sv-Op	Hld	ERA
1992 San Francisco	NL	18	0	0	2	15.2	63	13	5	4	2	0	0	1	3	0	11	0	0	1	0	1.000	0	0-0	1	2.30
1993 Colorado	NL	64	0	0	14	84.1	347	80	47	42	13	2	3	3	30	5	51	1	0	9	5	.643	0	3-6	9	4.48
1994 Colorado	NL	61	0	0	11	64	297	79	33	28	9	0	7	6	26	3	51	1	0	3	2	.600	0	3-10	14	3.94
1995 Colorado	NL	71	0	0	15	84	327	61	24	20	8	3	1	1	21	3	79	0	2	5	2	.714	0	3-6	11	2.14
1996 Colorado	NL	70	0	0	7	75	307	66	38	33	11	2	4	6	19	0	51	1	0	4	3	.571	0	0-6	22	3.96
5 ML YEARS		284	0	0	49	323	1341	299	147	127	43	7	15	17	99	11	243	3	2	22	12	.647	0	9-28	57	3.54

Bryan Rekar

Pitches: Right **Bats:** Right **Pos:** SP-11; RP-3   **Ht:** 6'3" **Wt:** 210 **Born:** 6/3/72 **Age:** 25

		HOW MUCH HE PITCHED						WHAT HE GAVE UP										THE RESULTS						
Year Team	Lg	G	GS	CG	GF	IP	BFP	H	R	ER	HR	SH	SF	HB	TBB	IBB	SO	WP	Bk	W	L	Pct.	ShO	Sv-Op	Hld	ERA
1993 Bend	A-	13	13	1	0	76.1	316	81	36	34	8	0	0	1	18	2	59	8	2	3	5	.375	0	0- -	—	4.01
1994 Central Val	A+	22	19	0	2	111.1	465	120	52	43	3	4	5	2	31	2	91	12	3	6	6	.500	0	0- -	—	3.48
1995 Colo. Sprng	AAA	7	7	2	0	48.1	182	29	10	8	0	1	0	2	13	0	39	3	0	4	2	.667	1	0- -	—	1.49
New Haven	AA	19	19	3	0	128.2	507	94	38	27	4	4	0	5	29	1	119	3	0	10	5	.667	2	0- -	—	1.89
1996 Colo. Sprng	AAA	19	19	0	0	123	534	138	68	61	13	2	6	3	36	1	75	9	0	8	8	.500	0	0- -	—	4.46
1995 Colorado	NL	15	14	1	0	85	375	95	51	47	11	7	4	3	24	2	60	3	2	4	6	.400	0	0-0	1	4.98
1996 Colorado	NL	14	11	0	0	58.1	289	87	61	58	11	3	3	5	26	1	25	4	0	2	4	.333	0	0-1	0	8.95
2 ML YEARS		29	25	1	0	143.1	664	182	112	105	22	10	7	8	50	3	85	7	2	6	10	.375	0	0-1	1	6.59

Desi Relaford

Bats: Both   **Throws:** Right   **Pos:** SS-9; PH-6; 2B-4   **Ht:** 5'8"   **Wt:** 155   **Born:** 9/16/73   **Age:** 23

Year Team	Lg	G	AB	H	2B	3B	HR	(Hm	Rd)	TB	R	RBI	TBB	IBB	SO	HBP	SH	SF	SB	CS	SB%	GDP	Avg	OBP	SLG
1991 Mariners	R	46	163	43	7	3	0	—	—	56	36	18	22	1	24	1	1	5	15	3	.83	0	.264	.346	.344
1992 Peninsula	A+	130	445	96	18	1	3	—	—	125	53	34	39	1	88	1	4	6	27	7	.79	1	.216	.277	.281
1993 Jacksonvlle	AA	133	472	115	16	4	8	—	—	163	49	47	50	1	103	7	6	4	16	12	.57	4	.244	.323	.345
1994 Jacksonvlle	AA	37	143	29	7	3	3	—	—	51	24	11	22	0	28	0	2	2	10	1	.91	2	.203	.305	.357
Riverside	A+	99	374	116	27	5	5	—	—	168	95	59	78	6	78	4	3	6	27	6	.82	7	.310	.429	.449
1995 Port City	AA	90	352	101	11	2	7	—	—	137	51	27	41	2	58	2	2	0	25	9	.74	4	.287	.365	.389
Tacoma	AAA	30	113	27	5	1	2	—	—	40	20	7	13	2	24	0	0	2	6	0	1.00	2	.239	.313	.354
1996 Tacoma	AAA	93	317	65	12	0	4	—	—	89	27	23	23	0	58	1	1	2	10	6	.63	7	.205	.259	.281
Scranton-WB	AAA	21	85	20	4	1	1	—	—	29	12	11	8	0	19	1	1	1	7	1	.88	0	.235	.305	.341
1996 Philadelphia	NL	15	40	7	2	0	0	(0	0)	9	2	1	3	0	9	0	1	0	1	0	1.00	1	.175	.233	.225

Mike Remlinger

Pitches: Left   **Bats:** Left   **Pos:** RP-15; SP-4   **Ht:** 6'0"   **Wt:** 195   **Born:** 3/23/66   **Age:** 31

Year Team	Lg	G	GS	CG	GF	IP	BFP	H	R	ER	HR	SH	SF	HB	TBB	IBB	SO	WP	Bk	W	L	Pct.	ShO	Sv-Op	Hld	ERA
1996 Indianapolis *	AAA	28	13	0	3	89.1	365	64	29	25	4	3	0	2	44	0	97	18	0	4	3	.571	0	0--	—	2.52
1991 San Francisco	NL	8	6	1	1	35	155	36	17	17	5	1	0	0	20	1	19	2	1	2	1	.667	1	0-0	0	4.37
1994 New York	NL	10	9	0	0	54.2	252	55	30	28	9	2	3	1	35	4	33	3	0	1	5	.167	0	0-0	1	4.61
1995 NYN-Cin	NL	7	0	0	4	6.2	34	9	6	5	1	1	0	0	5	0	7	0	0	0	1	.000	0	0-1	0	6.75
1996 Cincinnati	NL	19	4	0	2	27.1	125	24	17	17	4	3	1	3	19	2	19	2	2	0	1	.000	0	0-0	1	5.60
1995 New York	NL	5	0	0	4	5.2	27	7	5	4	1	1	0	0	2	0	6	0	0	0	1	.000	0	0-1	0	6.35
Cincinnati	NL	2	0	0	0	1	7	2	1	1	0	0	0	0	3	0	1	0	0	0	0	.000	0	0-0	0	9.00
4 ML YEARS		44	19	1	7	123.2	566	124	70	67	19	7	5	4	79	7	78	7	3	3	8	.273	1	0-1	2	4.88

Edgar Renteria

Bats: Right   **Throws:** Right   **Pos:** SS-106   **Ht:** 6'1"   **Wt:** 172   **Born:** 8/7/75   **Age:** 21

Year Team	Lg	G	AB	H	2B	3B	HR	(Hm	Rd)	TB	R	RBI	TBB	IBB	SO	HBP	SH	SF	SB	CS	SB%	GDP	Avg	OBP	SLG
1992 Marlins	R	43	163	47	8	1	0	—	—	57	25	9	8	0	29	2	2	0	10	6	.63	1	.288	.329	.350
1993 Kane County	A	116	384	78	8	0	1	—	—	89	40	35	35	0	94	0	6	3	7	8	.47	3	.203	.268	.232
1994 Brevard Cty	A+	128	439	111	15	1	0	—	—	128	46	35	35	2	56	0	2	2	6	11	.35	14	.253	.307	.292
1995 Portland	AA	135	508	147	15	7	7	—	—	197	70	68	32	2	85	2	8	8	30	11	.73	10	.289	.329	.388
1996 Charlotte	AAA	35	132	37	8	0	2	—	—	51	17	16	9	0	17	0	2	5	10	4	.71	5	.280	.326	.386
1996 Florida	NL	106	431	133	18	3	5	(2	3)	172	68	31	33	0	68	2	2	3	16	2	.89	12	.309	.358	.399

Al Reyes

Pitches: Right   **Bats:** Right   **Pos:** RP-5   **Ht:** 6'1"   **Wt:** 193   **Born:** 4/10/71   **Age:** 26

Year Team	Lg	G	GS	CG	GF	IP	BFP	H	R	ER	HR	SH	SF	HB	TBB	IBB	SO	WP	Bk	W	L	Pct.	ShO	Sv-Op	Hld	ERA
1990 W. Palm Bch	A+	16	10	0	4	57	253	58	32	30	4	3	3	2	32	2	46	5	0	5	4	.556	0	1--	—	4.74
1991 Rockford	A	3	3	0	0	11.1	50	14	8	7	1	0	0	2	2	0	10	0	0	0	1	.000	0	0--	—	5.56
1992 Albany	A	27	0	0	18	27.1	122	24	14	12	0	0	0	3	13	0	29	4	1	0	2	.000	0	4--	—	3.95
1993 Burlington	A	53	0	0	41	74	308	52	33	22	7	6	2	5	26	3	80	5	0	7	6	.538	0	11--	—	2.68
1994 Harrisburg	AA	60	0	0	53	69.1	284	68	26	25	4	2	2	2	13	0	60	2	0	2	2	.500	0	35--	—	3.25
1996 Beloit	A	13	0	0	4	19.2	81	17	7	4	1	0	0	0	6	0	22	1	1	1	0	1.000	0	0--	—	1.83
1995 Milwaukee	AL	27	0	0	13	33.1	138	19	9	9	3	1	2	3	18	2	29	0	0	1	1	.500	0	1-1	4	2.43
1996 Milwaukee	AL	5	0	0	2	5.2	27	8	5	5	1	0	0	0	2	0	2	2	0	1	0	1.000	0	0-0	0	7.94
2 ML YEARS		32	0	0	15	39	165	27	14	14	4	1	2	3	20	2	31	2	0	2	1	.667	0	1-1	4	3.23

Carlos Reyes

Pitches: Right   **Bats:** Both   **Pos:** RP-36; SP-10   **Ht:** 6'1"   **Wt:** 190   **Born:** 4/4/69   **Age:** 28

Year Team	Lg	G	GS	CG	GF	IP	BFP	H	R	ER	HR	SH	SF	HB	TBB	IBB	SO	WP	Bk	W	L	Pct.	ShO	Sv-Op	Hld	ERA
1994 Oakland	AL	27	9	0	8	78	344	71	38	36	10	2	3	2	44	1	57	3	0	0	3	.000	0	1-1	0	4.15
1995 Oakland	AL	40	1	0	19	69	306	71	43	39	10	4	0	5	28	4	48	5	0	4	6	.400	0	0-1	4	5.09
1996 Oakland	AL	46	10	0	14	122.1	550	134	71	65	19	2	8	2	61	8	78	2	1	7	10	.412	0	0-0	1	4.78
3 ML YEARS		113	20	0	41	269.1	1200	276	152	140	39	8	11	9	133	13	183	10	1	11	19	.367	0	1-2	5	4.68

Shane Reynolds

Pitches: Right   **Bats:** Right   **Pos:** SP-35   **Ht:** 6'3"   **Wt:** 210   **Born:** 3/26/68   **Age:** 29

Year Team	Lg	G	GS	CG	GF	IP	BFP	H	R	ER	HR	SH	SF	HB	TBB	IBB	SO	WP	Bk	W	L	Pct.	ShO	Sv-Op	Hld	ERA
1992 Houston	NL	8	5	0	0	25.1	122	42	22	20	2	6	1	0	6	1	10	1	1	1	3	.250	0	0-0	0	7.11
1993 Houston	NL	5	1	0	0	11	49	11	4	4	0	0	1	0	6	1	10	0	0	0	0	.000	0	0-0	0	0.82

					HOW MUCH HE PITCHED					WHAT HE GAVE UP								THE RESULTS					
Year Team	Lg	G	GS	CG	GF	IP	BFP	H	R	ER	HR	SH	SF	HB	TBB	IBB	SO	WP	Bk	W	L	Pct.	ShO	Sv-Op	Hld	ERA
1994 Houston	NL	33	14	1	5	124	517	128	46	42	10	4	0	6	21	3	110	3	2	8	5	.615	1	0-0	5	3.05
1995 Houston	NL	30	30	3	0	189.1	792	196	87	73	15	8	0	2	37	6	175	7	1	10	11	.476	2	0-0	0	3.47
1996 Houston	NL	35	35	4	0	239	981	227	103	97	20	11	7	8	44	3	204	5	1	16	10	.615	1	0-0	0	3.65
5 ML YEARS		111	85	8	5	588.2	2461	604	262	233	47	29	8	16	114	14	509	16	5	35	29	.547	4	0-0	5	3.56

Armando Reynoso

Pitches: Right   **Bats:** Right   **Pos:** SP-30   **Ht:** 6'0"   **Wt:** 204   **Born:** 5/1/66   **Age:** 31

					HOW MUCH HE PITCHED					WHAT HE GAVE UP								THE RESULTS					
Year Team	Lg	G	GS	CG	GF	IP	BFP	H	R	ER	HR	SH	SF	HB	TBB	IBB	SO	WP	Bk	W	L	Pct.	ShO	Sv-Op	Hld	ERA
1991 Atlanta	NL	6	5	0	1	23.1	103	26	18	16	4	3	0	3	10	1	10	2	0	2	1	.667	0	0-0	0	6.17
1992 Atlanta	NL	3	1	0	1	7.2	32	11	4	4	2	1	0	1	2	1	2	0	0	1	0	1.000	0	1-1	0	4.70
1993 Colorado	NL	30	30	4	0	189	830	206	101	84	22	5	8	9	63	7	117	7	6	12	11	.522	0	0-0	0	4.00
1994 Colorado	NL	9	9	1	0	52.1	226	54	30	28	5	2	2	6	22	1	25	2	2	3	4	.429	0	0-0	0	4.82
1995 Colorado	NL	20	18	0	0	93	418	116	61	55	12	8	2	5	36	3	40	2	0	7	7	.500	0	0-0	0	5.32
1996 Colorado	NL	30	30	0	0	168.2	733	195	97	93	27	3	3	9	49	0	88	4	3	8	9	.471	0	0-0	0	4.96
6 ML YEARS		98	93	5	2	534	2342	608	311	280	72	22	15	33	182	13	282	17	11	33	32	.508	0	1-1	0	4.72

Arthur Rhodes

Pitches: Left   **Bats:** Left   **Pos:** RP-26; SP-2   **Ht:** 6'2"   **Wt:** 205   **Born:** 10/24/69   **Age:** 27

					HOW MUCH HE PITCHED					WHAT HE GAVE UP								THE RESULTS					
Year Team	Lg	G	GS	CG	GF	IP	BFP	H	R	ER	HR	SH	SF	HB	TBB	IBB	SO	WP	Bk	W	L	Pct.	ShO	Sv-Op	Hld	ERA
1991 Baltimore	AL	8	8	0	0	36	174	47	35	32	4	1	3	0	23	0	23	2	0	0	3	.000	0	0-0	0	8.00
1992 Baltimore	AL	15	15	2	0	94.1	394	87	39	38	8	5	1	1	38	2	77	2	1	7	5	.583	1	0-0	0	3.63
1993 Baltimore	AL	17	17	0	0	85.2	387	91	62	62	16	2	3	1	49	1	49	0	0	5	6	.455	0	0-0	0	6.51
1994 Baltimore	AL	10	10	3	0	52.2	238	51	34	34	8	2	3	2	30	1	47	3	0	3	5	.375	2	0-0	0	5.81
1995 Baltimore	AL	19	9	0	3	75.1	336	68	53	52	13	4	0	0	48	1	77	3	1	2	5	.286	0	0-1	0	6.21
1996 Baltimore	AL	28	2	0	5	53	224	48	24	24	6	1	1	0	23	3	62	0	0	9	1	.900	0	1-1	2	4.08
6 ML YEARS		97	61	5	8	397	1753	392	251	242	53	15	11	4	211	8	335	12	2	26	25	.510	3	1-2	2	5.49

Jose Rijo

Pitches: Right   **Bats:** Right   **Pos:** SP   **Ht:** 6'3"   **Wt:** 215   **Born:** 5/13/65   **Age:** 32

					HOW MUCH HE PITCHED					WHAT HE GAVE UP								THE RESULTS					
Year Team	Lg	G	GS	CG	GF	IP	BFP	H	R	ER	HR	SH	SF	HB	TBB	IBB	SO	WP	Bk	W	L	Pct.	ShO	Sv-Op	Hld	ERA
1984 New York	AL	24	5	0	8	62.1	289	74	40	33	5	6	1	1	33	1	47	2	1	2	8	.200	0	2--	—	4.76
1985 Oakland	AL	12	9	0	1	63.2	272	57	26	25	6	5	0	1	28	2	65	0	0	6	4	.600	0	0--	—	3.53
1986 Oakland	AL	39	26	4	9	193.2	856	172	116	100	24	10	9	4	108	7	176	6	4	9	11	.450	0	1--	—	4.65
1987 Oakland	AL	21	14	1	3	82.1	394	106	67	54	10	0	3	2	41	1	67	5	2	2	7	.222	0	0-0	0	5.90
1988 Cincinnati	NL	49	19	0	12	162	653	120	47	43	7	8	5	3	63	7	160	1	4	13	8	.619	0	0-2	2	2.39
1989 Cincinnati	NL	19	19	1	0	111	464	101	39	35	6	8	6	2	48	3	86	4	3	7	6	.538	1	0-0	0	2.84
1990 Cincinnati	NL	29	29	7	0	197	801	151	59	59	10	8	1	2	78	1	152	2	5	14	8	.636	1	0-0	0	2.70
1991 Cincinnati	NL	30	30	3	0	204.1	825	165	69	57	8	4	8	3	55	4	172	2	1	15	6	.714	1	0-0	0	2.51
1992 Cincinnati	NL	33	33	2	0	211	836	185	67	60	15	9	4	3	44	1	171	2	1	15	10	.600	2	0-0	0	2.56
1993 Cincinnati	NL	36	36	2	0	257.1	1029	218	76	71	19	13	3	2	62	2	227	0	1	14	9	.609	1	0-0	0	2.48
1994 Cincinnati	NL	26	26	2	0	172.1	733	177	73	59	16	7	2	4	52	1	171	1	2	9	6	.600	0	0-0	0	3.08
1995 Cincinnati	NL	14	14	0	0	69	295	76	33	32	6	3	3	0	22	1	62	3	0	5	4	.556	0	0-0	0	4.17
12 ML YEARS		332	260	22	33	1786	7447	1602	718	628	132	76	45	27	634	31	1556	28	27	111	87	.561	4	3--	—	3.16

Billy Ripken

Bats: R   **Throws:** R   **Pos:** 2B-30; 3B-25; PH-8; 1B-1   **Ht:** 6'1"   **Wt:** 190   **Born:** 12/16/64   **Age:** 32

							BATTING											BASERUNNING				PERCENTAGES		
Year Team	Lg	G	AB	H	2B	3B	HR	(Hm	Rd)	TB	R	RBI	TBB	IBB	SO	HBP	SH	SF	SB	CS	SB%	GDP	Avg	OBP	SLG
1987 Baltimore	AL	58	234	72	9	0	2	(0	2)	87	27	20	21	0	23	0	1	1	4	1	.80	3	.308	.363	.372
1988 Baltimore	AL	150	512	106	18	1	2	(0	2)	132	52	34	33	0	63	5	6	3	8	2	.80	14	.207	.260	.258
1989 Baltimore	AL	115	318	76	11	2	2	(0	2)	97	31	26	22	0	53	0	19	5	1	2	.33	12	.239	.284	.305
1990 Baltimore	AL	129	406	118	28	1	3	(2	1)	157	48	38	28	2	43	4	17	1	5	2	.71	7	.291	.342	.387
1991 Baltimore	AL	104	287	62	11	1	0	(0	0)	75	24	14	15	0	31	0	11	2	0	1	.00	14	.216	.253	.261
1992 Baltimore	AL	111	330	76	15	0	4	(3	1)	103	35	36	18	1	26	3	10	2	2	3	.40	10	.230	.275	.312
1993 Texas	AL	50	132	25	4	0	0	(0	0)	29	12	11	11	0	19	4	5	1	0	2	.00	6	.189	.270	.220
1994 Texas	AL	32	81	25	5	0	0	(0	0)	30	9	6	3	0	11	0	1	0	1	0	1.00	2	.309	.333	.370
1995 Cleveland	AL	8	17	7	0	0	2	(1	1)	13	4	3	0	0	3	0	0	0	0	0	.00	0	.412	.412	.765
1996 Baltimore	AL	57	135	31	8	0	2	(1	1)	45	19	12	9	0	18	1	1	1	0	0	.00	4	.230	.281	.333
10 ML YEARS		814	2452	598	109	5	17	(7	10)	768	261	200	160	3	290	17	71	16	22	13	.63	72	.244	.293	.313

Cal Ripken

Bats: Right   **Throws:** Right   **Pos:** SS-158; 3B-6   **Ht:** 6'4"   **Wt:** 220   **Born:** 8/24/60   **Age:** 36

							BATTING											BASERUNNING				PERCENTAGES		
Year Team	Lg	G	AB	H	2B	3B	HR	(Hm	Rd)	TB	R	RBI	TBB	IBB	SO	HBP	SH	SF	SB	CS	SB%	GDP	Avg	OBP	SLG
1981 Baltimore	AL	23	39	5	0	0	0	(0	0)	5	1	0	1	0	8	0	0	0	0	0	.00	4	.128	.150	.128

Year Team	Lg	G	AB	H	2B	3B	HR	(Hm	Rd)	TB	R	RBI	TBB	IBB	SO	HBP	SH	SF	SB	CS	SB%	GDP	Avg	OBP	SLG
BATTING																									
1982 Baltimore	AL	160	598	158	32	5	28	(11	17)	284	90	93	46	3	95	3	2	6	3	3	.50	16	.264	.317	.475
1983 Baltimore	AL	**162**	**663**	**211**	**47**	2	27	(12	15)	343	**121**	102	58	0	97	0	0	5	0	4	.00	24	.318	.371	.517
1984 Baltimore	AL	**162**	641	195	37	7	27	(16	11)	327	103	86	71	1	89	2	0	2	2	1	.67	16	.304	.374	.510
1985 Baltimore	AL	161	642	181	32	5	26	(15	11)	301	116	110	67	1	68	1	0	8	2	3	.40	32	.282	.347	.469
1986 Baltimore	AL	162	627	177	35	1	25	(10	15)	289	98	81	70	5	60	4	2	6	4	2	.67	19	.282	.355	.461
1987 Baltimore	AL	**162**	624	157	28	3	27	(17	10)	272	97	98	81	0	77	1	0	11	3	5	.38	19	.252	.333	.436
1988 Baltimore	AL	161	575	152	25	1	23	(11	12)	248	87	81	102	7	69	2	0	**10**	2	2	.50	10	.264	.372	.431
1989 Baltimore	AL	**162**	646	166	30	0	21	(13	8)	259	80	93	57	5	72	3	0	6	3	2	.60	22	.257	.317	.401
1990 Baltimore	AL	161	600	150	28	4	21	(8	13)	249	78	84	82	18	66	5	1	7	3	1	.75	12	.250	.341	.415
1991 Baltimore	AL	**162**	650	210	46	5	34	(16	18)	**368**	99	114	53	15	46	5	0	9	6	1	.86	19	.323	.374	.566
1992 Baltimore	AL	**162**	637	160	29	1	14	(5	9)	233	72	64	14	50	7	0	7	4	3	.57	13	.251	.323	.366
1993 Baltimore	AL	**162**	641	165	26	3	24	(14	10)	269	87	90	65	19	58	6	0	6	1	4	.20	17	.257	.329	.420
1994 Baltimore	AL	112	444	140	19	3	13	(5	8)	204	71	75	32	3	41	4	0	4	1	0	1.00	17	.315	.364	.459
1995 Baltimore	AL	144	550	144	33	2	17	(10	7)	232	71	88	52	6	59	2	1	8	0	1	.00	15	.262	.324	.422
1996 Baltimore	AL	**163**	640	178	40	1	26	(10	16)	298	94	102	59	3	78	4	0	4	1	2	.33	**28**	.278	.341	.466
16 ML YEARS		2381	9217	2549	487	43	353	(173	180)	4181	1366	1369	960	100	1033	49	4	99	35	34	.51	283	.277	.345	.454

Bill Risley

Pitches: Right **Bats:** Right **Pos:** RP-25   **Ht:** 6'2" **Wt:** 230 **Born:** 5/29/67 **Age:** 30

Year Team	Lg	G	GS	CG	GF	IP	BFP	H	R	ER	HR	SH	SF	HB	TBB	IBB	SO	WP	Bk	W	L	Pct.	ShO	Sv-Op	Hld	ERA
HOW MUCH HE PITCHED								**WHAT HE GAVE UP**												**THE RESULTS**						
1996 Syracuse *	AAA	2	0	0	0	1	6	0	1	0	0	0	0	0	1	0	0	0	0	0	0	.000	0	0- --	—	0.00
St. Cathms *	A-	3	1	0	0	7	25	3	1	1	0	0	0	0	2	0	10	0	0	0	0	.000	0	0- --	—	1.29
1992 Montreal	NL	1	1	0	0	5	19	4	1	1	0	1	0	0	1	0	2	0	0	1	0	1.000	0	0-0	0	1.80
1993 Montreal	NL	2	0	0	1	3	14	2	3	2	1	1	0	1	2	0	2	0	0	0	0	.000	0	0-0	0	6.00
1994 Seattle	AL	37	0	0	7	52.1	203	31	20	20	7	0	2	0	19	4	61	2	0	9	6	.600	0	0-2	5	3.44
1995 Seattle	AL	45	0	0	5	60.1	249	55	21	21	7	2	3	1	18	1	65	2	0	2	1	.667	0	1-7	13	3.13
1996 Toronto	AL	25	0	0	11	41.2	177	33	20	18	7	1	2	0	25	0	29	1	0	1	1	.000	0	0-2	4	3.89
5 ML YEARS		110	1	0	24	162.1	662	125	65	62	22	5	7	2	65	5	159	5	0	12	8	.600	0	1-11	22	3.44

Kevin Ritz

Pitches: Right **Bats:** Right **Pos:** SP-35   **Ht:** 6'4" **Wt:** 222 **Born:** 6/8/65 **Age:** 32

Year Team	Lg	G	GS	CG	GF	IP	BFP	H	R	ER	HR	SH	SF	HB	TBB	IBB	SO	WP	Bk	W	L	Pct.	ShO	Sv-Op	Hld	ERA
HOW MUCH HE PITCHED								**WHAT HE GAVE UP**												**THE RESULTS**						
1989 Detroit	AL	12	12	1	0	74	334	75	41	36	2	1	5	1	44	5	56	6	0	4	6	.400	0	0-0	0	4.38
1990 Detroit	AL	4	4	0	0	7.1	52	14	12	9	0	3	0	0	14	2	3	3	0	0	4	.000	0	0-0	0	11.05
1991 Detroit	AL	11	5	0	3	15.1	86	17	22	20	1	1	2	2	22	1	9	0	0	0	3	.000	0	0-1	0	11.74
1992 Detroit	AL	23	11	0	4	80.1	368	88	52	50	4	1	4	3	44	4	57	7	1	2	5	.286	0	0-0	0	5.60
1994 Colorado	NL	15	15	0	0	73.2	335	88	49	46	5	4	2	4	35	4	53	6	1	5	6	.455	0	0-0	0	5.62
1995 Colorado	NL	31	28	0	3	173.1	743	171	91	81	16	8	5	6	65	3	120	6	0	11	11	.500	0	2-2	0	4.21
1996 Colorado	NL	35	35	2	0	213	966	236	**135**	**125**	24	8	4	12	105	3	105	10	1	17	11	.607	0	0-0	0	5.28
7 ML YEARS		131	110	3	10	637	2884	689	402	367	52	26	22	28	329	22	403	38	3	39	46	.459	0	2-3	0	5.19

Mariano Rivera

Pitches: Right **Bats:** Right **Pos:** RP-61   **Ht:** 6'2" **Wt:** 168 **Born:** 11/29/69 **Age:** 27

Year Team	Lg	G	GS	CG	GF	IP	BFP	H	R	ER	HR	SH	SF	HB	TBB	IBB	SO	WP	Bk	W	L	Pct.	ShO	Sv-Op	Hld	ERA
HOW MUCH HE PITCHED								**WHAT HE GAVE UP**												**THE RESULTS**						
1990 Yankees	R	22	1	1	12	52	180	17	3	1	0	2	2	2	7	0	58	2	0	5	1	.833	1	1- --	—	0.17
1991 Yankees	A	29	15	1	6	114.2	480	102	48	35	2	1	5	3	36	0	123	3	0	4	9	.308	0	0- --	—	2.75
1992 Ft. Laud	A+	10	10	3	0	59.1	217	40	17	15	5	2	1	0	5	0	42	0	0	5	3	.625	1	0- --	—	2.28
1993 Yankees	R	2	2	0	0	4	15	2	1	1	0	0	0	0	1	0	6	1	0	1	0	1.000	0	0- --	—	2.25
Greensboro	A	10	10	0	0	39.1	161	31	12	9	0	0	1	0	15	0	32	2	0	1	0	1.000	0	0- --	—	2.06
1994 Tampa	A+	7	7	0	0	36.2	148	34	12	9	2	1	1	2	12	0	27	0	0	3	0	1.000	0	0- --	—	2.21
Albany-Colo	AA	9	9	0	0	63.1	252	58	20	16	5	3	1	0	8	0	39	1	1	3	0	1.000	0	0- --	—	2.27
Columbus	AAA	6	6	1	0	31	137	34	22	20	5	0	0	0	10	0	23	0	1	4	2	.667	0	0- --	—	5.81
1995 Columbus	AAA	7	7	1	0	30	114	25	10	7	2	0	1	0	3	0	30	0	0	2	2	.500	0	0- --	—	2.10
1995 New York	AL	19	10	0	2	67	301	71	43	41	11	0	2	2	30	0	51	0	1	5	3	.625	0	0-1	0	5.51
1996 New York	AL	61	0	0	14	107.2	425	73	25	25	1	2	1	2	34	3	130	1	0	8	3	.727	0	5-8	27	2.09
2 ML YEARS		80	10	0	16	174.2	726	144	68	66	12	2	3	4	64	3	181	1	1	13	6	.684	0	5-9	27	3.40

Ruben Rivera

Bats: R **Throws:** R **Pos:** RF-19; CF-14; LF-13; PH-13   **Ht:** 6'3" **Wt:** 200 **Born:** 11/14/73 **Age:** 23

Year Team	Lg	G	AB	H	2B	3B	HR	(Hm	Rd)	TB	R	RBI	TBB	IBB	SO	HBP	SH	SF	SB	CS	SB%	GDP	Avg	OBP	SLG
BATTING																									
1992 Yankees	R	53	194	53	10	3	1	—	—	72	37	20	42	0	49	6	2	0	21	6	.78	2	.273	.417	.371
1993 Oneonta	A-	55	199	55	7	6	13	—	—	113	45	47	32	1	66	5	1	3	11	5	.69	2	.276	.385	.568
1994 Greensboro	A	105	400	115	24	3	28	—	—	229	83	81	47	1	125	8	0	2	36	5	.88	6	.288	.372	.573
Tampa	A+	34	134	35	4	3	5	—	—	60	18	20	8	0	38	1	0	0	12	5	.71	7	.261	.308	.448
1995 Norwich	AA	71	256	75	16	8	9	—	—	134	49	39	37	2	77	11	0	2	16	8	.67	4	.293	.402	.523
Columbus	AAA	48	174	47	8	2	15	—	—	104	37	35	26	0	62	3	0	1	8	4	.67	5	.270	.373	.598

190

			BATTING																BASERUNNING				PERCENTAGES		
Year Team	Lg	G	AB	H	2B	3B	HR	(Hm	Rd)	TB	R	RBI	TBB	IBB	SO	HBP	SH	SF	SB	CS	SB%	GDP	Avg	OBP	SLG
1996 Columbus	AAA	101	362	85	20	4	10			143	59	46	40	4	96	8	1	1	15	10	.60	4	.235	.324	.395
1995 New York	AL	5	1	0	0	0	0	(0	0)	0	0	0	0	0	1	0	0	0	0	0	.00	0	.000	.000	.000
1996 New York	AL	46	88	25	6	1	2	(0	2)	39	17	16	13	0	26	2	1	2	6	2	.75	1	.284	.381	.443
2 ML YEARS		51	89	25	6	1	2	(0	2)	39	17	16	13	0	27	2	1	2	6	2	.75	1	.281	.377	.438

Joe Roa

Pitches: Right   **Bats:** Right   **Pos:** RP-1   **Ht:** 6'1"   **Wt:** 194   **Born:** 10/11/71   **Age:** 25

		HOW MUCH HE PITCHED						WHAT HE GAVE UP											THE RESULTS						
Year Team	Lg	G	GS	CG	GF	IP	BFP	H	R	ER	HR	SH	SF	HB	TBB	IBB	SO	WP	Bk	W	L	Pct.	ShO	Sv-Op	Hld	ERA
1989 Braves	R	13	4	0	4	37.1	156	40	18	12	2	0	1	0	10	1	21	3	0	2	2	.500	0	0--	—	2.89
1990 Pulaski	R+	14	11	3	1	75.2	313	55	29	25	3	2	1	2	26	0	49	2	2	4	2	.667	1	0--	—	2.97
1991 Macon	A	30	18	4	2	141	556	106	46	33	6	0	3	5	33	4	96	3	0	13	3	.813	2	1--	—	2.11
1992 St. Lucie	A+	26	24	2	0	156.1	647	176	80	63	9	6	6	6	15	1	61	0	1	9	7	.563	1	0--	—	3.63
1993 Binghamton	AA	32	23	2	0	167.1	693	190	80	72	9	2	4	10	24	0	73	3	2	12	7	.632	1	0--	—	3.87
1994 Binghamton	AA	3	3	0	0	20	82	18	6	4	0	2	2	1	1	0	11	1	2	2	1	.667	0	0--	—	1.80
Norfolk	AAA	25	25	5	0	167.2	703	184	82	65	16	3	12	4	34	1	74	4	0	8	8	.500	0	0--	—	3.49
1995 Buffalo	AAA	25	24	3	1	164.2	678	168	71	64	9	2	5	7	28	1	93	1	2	17	3	.850	0	0--	—	3.50
1996 Buffalo	AAA	26	24	5	0	165.1	676	161	66	60	19	5	3	6	36	0	82	6	1	11	8	.579	0	0--	—	3.27
1995 Cleveland	AL	1	1	0	0	6	28	9	4	4	1	0	0	0	2	0	0	0	0	0	1	.000	0	0-0	0	6.00
1996 Cleveland	AL	1	0	0	0	1.2	11	4	2	2	0	0	0	0	3	0	0	0	0	0	0	.000	0	0-0	0	10.80
2 ML YEARS		2	1	0	0	7.2	39	13	6	6	1	1	0	0	5	0	0	0	0	0	1	.000	0	0-0	0	7.04

Kevin Roberson

Bats: Both   **Throws:** Right   **Pos:** PH-19; RF-9; LF-1   **Ht:** 6'4"   **Wt:** 210   **Born:** 1/29/68   **Age:** 29

			BATTING																BASERUNNING				PERCENTAGES		
Year Team	Lg	G	AB	H	2B	3B	HR	(Hm	Rd)	TB	R	RBI	TBB	IBB	SO	HBP	SH	SF	SB	CS	SB%	GDP	Avg	OBP	SLG
1996 Norfolk *	AAA	70	215	57	13	3	7	—	—	97	26	33	14	2	65	7	1	2	0	1	.00	4	.265	.328	.451
1993 Chicago	NL	62	180	34	4	1	9	(4	5)	67	23	27	12	0	48	3	0	0	0	1	.00	2	.189	.251	.372
1994 Chicago	NL	44	55	12	4	0	4	(2	2)	28	8	9	2	0	14	2	0	0	0	0	.00	3	.218	.271	.509
1995 Chicago	NL	32	38	7	1	0	4	(2	2)	20	5	6	4	0	14	1	0	0	0	1	.00	0	.184	.311	.526
1996 New York	NL	27	36	8	1	0	3	(0	3)	18	8	9	7	0	17	1	0	2	0	0	.00	1	.222	.348	.500
4 ML YEARS		165	309	61	10	1	20	(8	12)	133	44	51	27	0	93	7	0	2	0	2	.00	6	.197	.275	.430

Bip Roberts

Bats: B   **Throws:** R   **Pos:** 2B-63; DH-16; LF-8; PH-7; CF-2; RF-1   **Ht:** 5'7"   **Wt:** 165   **Born:** 10/27/63   **Age:** 33

			BATTING																BASERUNNING				PERCENTAGES		
Year Team	Lg	G	AB	H	2B	3B	HR	(Hm	Rd)	TB	R	RBI	TBB	IBB	SO	HBP	SH	SF	SB	CS	SB%	GDP	Avg	OBP	SLG
1986 San Diego	NL	101	241	61	5	2	1	(0	1)	73	34	12	14	1	29	0	2	1	14	12	.54	2	.253	.293	.303
1988 San Diego	NL	5	9	3	0	0	0	(0	0)	3	1	0	1	0	2	0	0	0	0	2	.00	0	.333	.400	.333
1989 San Diego	NL	117	329	99	15	8	3	(2	1)	139	81	25	49	0	45	1	6	2	21	11	.66	3	.301	.391	.422
1990 San Diego	NL	149	556	172	36	3	9	(4	5)	241	104	44	55	1	65	6	8	4	46	12	.79	6	.309	.375	.433
1991 San Diego	NL	117	424	119	13	3	3	(3	0)	147	66	32	37	0	71	4	4	3	26	11	.70	6	.281	.342	.347
1992 Cincinnati	NL	147	532	172	34	6	4	(3	1)	230	92	45	62	4	54	2	1	4	44	16	.73	7	.323	.393	.432
1993 Cincinnati	NL	83	292	70	13	0	1	(0	1)	86	46	18	38	1	46	3	0	3	26	6	.81	2	.240	.330	.295
1994 San Diego	NL	105	403	129	15	5	2	(1	1)	160	52	31	39	1	57	3	2	2	21	7	.75	7	.320	.383	.397
1995 San Diego	NL	73	296	90	14	0	2	(2	0)	110	40	25	17	1	36	2	1	0	20	2	.91	2	.304	.344	.372
1996 Kansas City	AL	90	339	96	21	2	0	(0	0)	121	39	52	25	8	38	2	0	6	12	9	.57	8	.283	.331	.357
10 ML YEARS		987	3421	1011	166	29	25	(15	10)	1310	555	284	337	17	443	23	24	25	230	88	.72	45	.296	.360	.383

Mike Robertson

Bats: Left   **Throws:** Left   **Pos:** PH-3; 1B-2; DH-1   **Ht:** 6'0"   **Wt:** 180   **Born:** 10/9/70   **Age:** 26

			BATTING																BASERUNNING				PERCENTAGES		
Year Team	Lg	G	AB	H	2B	3B	HR	(Hm	Rd)	TB	R	RBI	TBB	IBB	SO	HBP	SH	SF	SB	CS	SB%	GDP	Avg	OBP	SLG
1991 Utica	A-	13	54	9	2	1	0	—	—	13	6	8	5	0	10	0	0	2	2	1	.67	0	.167	.237	.241
South Bend	A	54	210	69	16	2	1	—	—	92	30	26	18	3	24	3	3	3	7	6	.54	5	.329	.385	.438
1992 Sarasota	A+	106	395	99	21	3	10	—	—	156	50	59	50	3	55	7	1	3	5	7	.42	8	.251	.343	.395
Birmingham	AA	27	90	17	8	1	1	—	—	30	6	9	10	1	19	0	1	1	0	1	.00	2	.189	.267	.333
1993 Birmingham	AA	138	511	138	31	3	11	—	—	208	73	73	59	4	97	3	0	8	10	5	.67	10	.270	.344	.407
1994 Birmingham	AA	53	196	62	20	2	3	—	—	95	32	30	31	4	34	2	0	5	6	3	.67	5	.316	.411	.485
Nashville	AAA	67	213	48	8	1	8	—	—	82	17	21	15	4	27	3	0	0	3	0	.00	4	.225	.286	.385
1995 Nashville	AAA	139	499	124	17	4	19	—	—	206	55	52	50	7	72	11	3	2	2	4	.33	9	.248	.329	.413
1996 Nashville	AAA	138	450	116	16	4	21	—	—	203	64	74	38	4	83	5	9	2	1	2	.33	10	.258	.321	.451
1996 Chicago	AL	6	7	1	0	0	0	(0	0)	1	2	0	0	0	1	0	0	0	0	0	.00	0	.143	.143	.286

Rich Robertson

Pitches: Left **Bats:** Left **Pos:** SP-31; RP-5   **Ht:** 6'4" **Wt:** 175 **Born:** 9/15/68 **Age:** 28

Year Team	Lg	G	GS	CG	GF	IP	BFP	H	R	ER	HR	SH	SF	HB	TBB	IBB	SO	WP	Bk	W	L	Pct.	ShO	Sv-Op	Hld	ERA
1993 Pittsburgh	NL	9	0	0	2	9	44	15	6	6	0	1	0	0	4	0	5	0	0	0	1	.000	0	0-1	0	6.00
1994 Pittsburgh	NL	8	0	0	1	15.2	76	20	12	12	2	1	0	0	10	4	8	0	0	0	0	.000	0	0-0	1	6.89
1995 Minnesota	AL	25	4	1	8	51.2	228	48	28	22	4	5	2	0	31	4	38	0	1	2	0	1.000	0	0-0	0	3.83
1996 Minnesota	AL	36	31	5	1	186.1	853	197	113	106	22	2	4	9	116	2	114	7	0	7	17	.292	3	0-1	1	5.12
4 ML YEARS		78	35	6	12	262.2	1201	280	159	146	28	9	7	9	161	10	165	7	1	9	18	.333	3	0-2	2	5.00

Ken Robinson

Pitches: Right **Bats:** Right **Pos:** RP-5   **Ht:** 5'9" **Wt:** 170 **Born:** 11/3/69 **Age:** 27

Year Team	Lg	G	GS	CG	GF	IP	BFP	H	R	ER	HR	SH	SF	HB	TBB	IBB	SO	WP	Bk	W	L	Pct.	ShO	Sv-Op	Hld	ERA
1991 Medicne Hat	R+	6	2	0	3	11.2	51	12	8	5	1	1	0	0	5	0	18	2	4	0	1	.000	0	0--	—	3.86
1992 Myrtle Bch	A	20	0	0	9	38.1	162	25	12	12	2	0	1	3	30	0	45	4	0	1	0	1.000	0	1--	—	2.82
1993 Hagerstown	A	40	0	0	24	71.2	314	74	43	37	6	2	4	6	31	1	65	5	1	4	7	.364	0	7--	—	4.65
1994 Hagerstown	A	10	0	0	6	19.2	78	15	8	7	1	1	2	0	4	0	27	2	0	4	1	.800	0	1--	—	3.20
Dunedin	A+	5	0	0	2	10	39	6	2	2	1	0	0	0	4	0	16	0	0	1	1	.500	0	0--	—	1.80
Syracuse	AAA	30	3	0	5	55.1	235	46	27	23	4	0	3	1	25	1	48	1	0	4	2	.667	0	3--	—	3.74
1995 Syracuse	AAA	38	0	0	12	50.1	201	37	18	18	6	2	2	2	12	2	61	2	0	5	3	.625	0	2--	—	3.22
1996 Omaha	AAA	6	0	0	0	11.1	43	7	1	1	1	0	1	0	4	0	9	1	0	2	0	1.000	0	0--	—	0.79
Syracuse	AAA	47	0	0	18	64	278	52	37	33	14	4	4	1	39	3	78	6	0	3	7	.300	0	1--	—	4.64
1995 Toronto	AL	21	0	0	9	39	167	25	21	16	7	1	2	2	22	1	31	0	0	1	2	.333	0	0-0	1	3.69
1996 Kansas City	AL	5	0	0	2	6	30	9	4	4	0	0	1	0	3	1	5	1	0	1	0	1.000	0	0-0	0	6.00
2 ML YEARS		26	0	0	11	45	197	34	25	20	7	1	3	2	25	2	36	1	0	2	2	.500	0	0-0	1	4.00

Alex Rodriguez

Bats: Right **Throws:** Right **Pos:** SS-146; PH-1   **Ht:** 6'3" **Wt:** 195 **Born:** 7/27/75 **Age:** 21

Year Team	Lg	G	AB	H	2B	3B	HR	Hm	Rd	TB	R	RBI	TBB	IBB	SO	HBP	SH	SF	SB	CS	SB%	GDP	Avg	OBP	SLG
1996 Tacoma *	AAA	2	5	1	0	0	0	—	—	1	0	0	2	1	1	0	0	0	0	0	.00	0	.200	.429	.200
1994 Seattle	AL	17	54	11	0	0	0	(0	0)	11	4	2	3	0	20	0	1	1	3	0	1.00	0	.204	.241	.204
1995 Seattle	AL	48	142	33	6	2	5	(1	4)	58	15	19	6	0	42	0	1	0	4	2	.67	0	.232	.264	.408
1996 Seattle	AL	146	601	215	54	1	36	(18	18)	379	141	123	59	1	104	4	6	7	15	4	.79	15	.358	.414	.631
3 ML YEARS		211	797	259	60	3	41	(19	22)	448	160	144	68	1	166	4	8	8	22	6	.79	15	.325	.377	.562

Frank Rodriguez

Pitches: Right **Bats:** Right **Pos:** SP-33; RP-5   **Ht:** 6'0" **Wt:** 195 **Born:** 12/11/72 **Age:** 24

Year Team	Lg	G	GS	CG	GF	IP	BFP	H	R	ER	HR	SH	SF	HB	TBB	IBB	SO	WP	Bk	W	L	Pct.	ShO	Sv-Op	Hld	ERA
1992 Lynchburg	A+	25	25	1	0	148.2	619	125	56	51	11	5	2	6	65	0	129	6	3	12	7	.632	0	0--	—	3.09
1993 New Britain	AA	28	26	4	1	170.2	722	147	79	71	17	2	2	4	78	4	151	7	3	7	11	.389	1	0--	—	3.74
1994 Pawtucket	AAA	28	28	8	0	186	789	182	95	81	18	3	4	8	60	0	160	5	0	8	13	.381	1	0--	—	3.92
1995 Pawtucket	AAA	13	2	0	8	27	109	19	12	12	2	0	0	3	8	0	18	1	0	1	1	.500	0	2--	—	4.00
1995 Bos-Min	AL	25	18	0	1	105.2	478	114	83	72	11	1	4	5	57	1	59	9	0	5	8	.385	0	0-0	1	6.13
1996 Minnesota	AL	38	33	3	4	206.2	899	218	129	116	27	6	8	5	78	1	110	2	0	13	14	.481	0	2-2	0	5.05
1995 Boston	AL	9	2	0	1	15.1	75	21	19	18	3	0	0	5	10	1	14	4	0	0	2	.000	0	0-0	1	10.57
Minnesota	AL	16	16	0	0	90.1	403	93	64	54	8	1	4	5	47	0	45	5	0	5	6	.455	0	0-0	0	5.38
2 ML YEARS		63	51	3	5	312.1	1377	332	212	188	38	7	12	10	135	2	169	11	0	18	22	.450	0	2-2	1	5.42

Henry Rodriguez

Bats: L **Throws:** L **Pos:** LF-89; 1B-51; PH-7; RF-2   **Ht:** 6'1" **Wt:** 205 **Born:** 11/8/67 **Age:** 29

Year Team	Lg	G	AB	H	2B	3B	HR	Hm	Rd	TB	R	RBI	TBB	IBB	SO	HBP	SH	SF	SB	CS	SB%	GDP	Avg	OBP	SLG
1992 Los Angeles	NL	53	146	32	7	0	3	(2	1)	48	11	14	8	0	30	0	1	1	0	0	.00	0	.219	.258	.329
1993 Los Angeles	NL	76	176	39	10	0	8	(5	3)	73	20	23	11	2	39	0	0	1	1	0	1.00	1	.222	.266	.415
1994 Los Angeles	NL	104	306	82	14	2	8	(5	3)	124	33	49	17	2	58	2	1	4	0	1	.00	9	.268	.307	.405
1995 LA-Mon	NL	45	138	33	4	1	2	(1	1)	45	13	15	11	2	28	0	0	1	0	1	.00	3	.239	.293	.326
1996 Montreal	NL	145	532	147	42	1	36	(20	16)	299	81	103	37	7	160	3	0	4	2	0	1.00	11	.276	.325	.562
1995 Los Angeles	NL	21	80	21	4	1	1	(0	1)	30	6	10	5	2	17	0	0	0	0	1	.00	3	.263	.306	.375
Montreal	NL	24	58	12	0	0	1	(1	0)	15	7	5	6	0	11	0	0	1	0	0	.00	2	.207	.277	.259
5 ML YEARS		423	1298	333	77	4	57	(33	24)	589	158	204	84	13	315	5	2	11	3	2	.60	28	.257	.302	.454

Ivan Rodriguez

Bats: Right **Throws:** Right **Pos:** C-147; DH-6; PH-5   **Ht:** 5'9" **Wt:** 205 **Born:** 11/30/71 **Age:** 25

Year Team	Lg	G	AB	H	2B	3B	HR	Hm	Rd	TB	R	RBI	TBB	IBB	SO	HBP	SH	SF	SB	CS	SB%	GDP	Avg	OBP	SLG
1991 Texas	AL	88	280	74	16	0	3	(3	0)	99	24	27	5	0	42	0	2	1	0	1	.00	10	.264	.276	.354

Year Team	Lg	G	AB	H	2B	3B	HR	(Hm	Rd)	TB	R	RBI	TBB	IBB	SO	HBP	SH	SF	SB	CS	SB%	GDP	Avg	OBP	SLG
											BATTING								**BASERUNNING**				**PERCENTAGES**		
1992 Texas	AL	123	420	109	16	1	8	(4	4)	151	39	37	24	2	73	1	7	2	0	0	.00	15	.260	.300	.360
1993 Texas	AL	137	473	129	28	4	10	(7	3)	195	56	66	29	3	70	4	5	8	8	7	.53	16	.273	.315	.412
1994 Texas	AL	99	363	108	19	1	16	(7	9)	177	56	57	31	5	42	7	0	4	6	3	.67	10	.298	.360	.488
1995 Texas	AL	130	492	149	32	2	12	(5	7)	221	56	67	16	2	48	4	0	5	0	2	.00	11	.303	.327	.449
1996 Texas	AL	153	639	192	47	3	19	(10	9)	302	116	86	38	7	55	4	0	4	5	0	1.00	15	.300	.342	.473
6 ML YEARS		730	2667	761	158	11	68	(36	32)	1145	347	340	143	19	330	20	14	24	19	13	.59	77	.285	.324	.429

Nerio Rodriguez

Pitches: Right **Bats:** Right **Pos:** RP-7; SP-1   **Ht:** 6'0" **Wt:** 165 **Born:** 3/22/73 **Age:** 24

Year Team	Lg	G	GS	CG	GF	IP	BFP	H	R	ER	HR	SH	SF	HB	TBB	IBB	SO	WP	Bk	W	L	Pct.	ShO	Sv-Op	Hld	ERA
						HOW MUCH HE PITCHED			**WHAT HE GAVE UP**												**THE RESULTS**					
1996 Frederick	A+	24	17	1	7	111.1	462	83	42	28	10	5	0	4	40	0	114	6	1	8	7	.533	0	2--	—	2.26
Rochester	AAA	2	2	0	0	15	58	10	3	3	0	0	0	0	2	0	6	2	0	1	0	1.000	0	0--	—	1.80
1996 Baltimore	AL	8	1	0	2	16.2	77	18	11	8	2	0	1	1	7	0	12	0	0	0	1	.000	0	0-0	0	4.32

Tony Rodriguez

Bats: Right **Throws:** Right **Pos:** SS-21; 3B-5; PH-3   **Ht:** 5'11" **Wt:** 178 **Born:** 8/15/70 **Age:** 26

Year Team	Lg	G	AB	H	2B	3B	HR	(Hm	Rd)	TB	R	RBI	TBB	IBB	SO	HBP	SH	SF	SB	CS	SB%	GDP	Avg	OBP	SLG
											BATTING								**BASERUNNING**				**PERCENTAGES**		
1991 Elmira	A-	77	272	70	10	2	1	— —		87	48	23	32	0	45	3	2	4	29	4	.88	6	.257	.338	.320
1992 Lynchburg	A+	128	516	115	14	4	1	— —		140	59	27	25	0	84	3	7	3	11	6	.65	11	.223	.261	.271
1993 New Britain	AA	99	355	81	16	4	0	— —		105	37	31	16	0	52	4	4	5	7	7	.50	8	.228	.266	.296
1994 Sarasota	A+	15	49	11	0	0	0	— —		11	4	5	4	0	9	0	2	0	1	0	1.00	3	.224	.283	.224
New Britain	AA	6	20	3	0	1	0	— —		5	1	0	0	0	7	0	0	0	0	0	.00	1	.150	.150	.250
Pawtucket	AAA	64	169	43	4	1	4	— —		61	16	18	5	0	22	0	7	2	3	3	.50	9	.254	.273	.361
1995 Pawtucket	AAA	96	317	85	15	2	0	— —		104	37	21	15	0	39	6	11	4	11	5	.69	8	.268	.310	.328
1996 Sarasota	A+	8	21	6	0	0	0	— —		6	0	1	0	1	2	0	0	0	0	0	.00	2	.286	.318	.286
Pawtucket	AAA	72	265	65	14	1	3	— —		90	37	28	15	1	32	3	10	0	3	1	.75	10	.245	.293	.340
1996 Boston	AL	27	67	16	1	0	1	(1	0)	20	7	9	4	0	8	1	5	0	0	0	.00	3	.239	.292	.299

Kenny Rogers

Pitches: Left **Bats:** Left **Pos:** SP-30   **Ht:** 6'1" **Wt:** 205 **Born:** 11/10/64 **Age:** 32

Year Team	Lg	G	GS	CG	GF	IP	BFP	H	R	ER	HR	SH	SF	HB	TBB	IBB	SO	WP	Bk	W	L	Pct.	ShO	Sv-Op	Hld	ERA
						HOW MUCH HE PITCHED			**WHAT HE GAVE UP**												**THE RESULTS**					
1989 Texas	AL	73	0	0	24	73.2	314	60	28	24	2	6	3	4	42	9	63	6	0	3	4	.429	0	2-5	16	2.93
1990 Texas	AL	69	3	0	46	97.2	428	93	40	34	6	7	4	1	42	5	74	5	0	10	6	.625	0	15-23	6	3.13
1991 Texas	AL	63	9	0	20	109.2	511	121	80	66	14	9	5	6	61	7	73	3	1	10	10	.500	0	5-6	11	5.42
1992 Texas	AL	81	0	0	38	78.2	337	80	32	27	7	4	1	0	26	8	70	4	1	3	6	.333	0	6-10	16	3.09
1993 Texas	AL	35	33	5	0	208.1	885	210	108	95	18	7	5	4	71	2	140	6	5	16	10	.615	0	0-0	1	4.10
1994 Texas	AL	24	24	6	0	167.1	714	169	93	83	24	3	6	3	52	1	120	3	1	11	8	.579	2	0-0	0	4.46
1995 Texas	AL	31	31	3	0	208	877	192	87	78	26	3	5	2	76	1	140	8	1	17	7	.708	1	0-0	0	3.38
1996 New York	AL	30	30	2	0	179	786	179	97	93	16	6	3	8	83	2	92	5	0	12	8	.600	0	0-0	0	4.68
8 ML YEARS		406	130	16	128	1122.1	4852	1104	565	500	113	45	32	28	453	35	772	40	9	82	59	.582	4	28-44	50	4.01

Mel Rojas

Pitches: Right **Bats:** Right **Pos:** RP-74   **Ht:** 5'11" **Wt:** 195 **Born:** 12/10/66 **Age:** 30

Year Team	Lg	G	GS	CG	GF	IP	BFP	H	R	ER	HR	SH	SF	HB	TBB	IBB	SO	WP	Bk	W	L	Pct.	ShO	Sv-Op	Hld	ERA
						HOW MUCH HE PITCHED			**WHAT HE GAVE UP**												**THE RESULTS**					
1990 Montreal	NL	23	0	0	4	40	173	34	17	16	5	2	0	2	24	4	26	2	0	3	1	.750	0	1-2	1	3.60
1991 Montreal	NL	37	0	0	13	48	200	42	21	20	4	0	2	1	13	1	37	3	0	3	3	.500	0	6-9	7	3.75
1992 Montreal	NL	68	0	0	26	100.2	399	71	17	16	2	4	2	2	34	8	70	2	0	7	1	.875	0	10-11	13	1.43
1993 Montreal	NL	66	0	0	25	88.1	378	80	39	29	6	8	6	4	30	3	48	5	0	5	8	.385	0	10-19	14	2.95
1994 Montreal	NL	58	0	0	27	84	341	71	35	31	11	2	1	4	21	0	84	3	0	3	2	.600	0	16-18	19	3.32
1995 Montreal	NL	59	0	0	48	67.2	302	69	32	31	2	2	1	7	29	4	61	6	0	1	4	.200	0	30-39	3	4.12
1996 Montreal	NL	74	0	0	64	81	326	56	30	29	5	2	4	2	28	3	92	3	0	7	4	.636	0	36-40	1	3.22
7 ML YEARS		385	0	0	208	509.2	2119	423	191	172	35	20	16	22	179	23	418	24	0	29	23	.558	0	109-138	58	3.04

Scott Rolen

Bats: Right **Throws:** Right **Pos:** 3B-37   **Ht:** 6'4" **Wt:** 195 **Born:** 4/4/75 **Age:** 22

Year Team	Lg	G	AB	H	2B	3B	HR	(Hm	Rd)	TB	R	RBI	TBB	IBB	SO	HBP	SH	SF	SB	CS	SB%	GDP	Avg	OBP	SLG
											BATTING								**BASERUNNING**				**PERCENTAGES**		
1993 Martinsvlle	R+	25	80	25	5	0	0	— —		30	8	12	10	0	15	7	0	1	3	4	.43	3	.313	.429	.375
1994 Spartanburg	A	138	513	151	34	5	14	— —		237	83	72	55	4	90	4	1	7	6	8	.43	8	.294	.363	.462
1995 Clearwater	A+	66	238	69	13	2	10	— —		116	45	39	37	1	46	5	0	3	4	0	1.00	4	.290	.392	.487
Reading	AA	20	76	22	3	0	3	— —		34	16	15	7	0	14	1	1	1	0	1	.00	1	.289	.353	.447
1996 Reading	AA	61	230	83	22	2	9	— —		136	44	42	34	3	32	5	0	5	8	3	.73	5	.361	.445	.591
Scranton-WB	AAA	45	168	46	17	0	2	— —		69	23	19	28	0	28	0	0	1	4	5	.44	9	.274	.376	.411
1996 Philadelphia	NL	37	130	33	7	0	4	(2	2)	52	10	18	13	0	27	1	0	2	0	0	.00	4	.254	.322	.400

Jose Rosado

Pitches: Left **Bats:** Left **Pos:** SP-16   **Ht:** 6'0" **Wt:** 175 **Born:** 11/9/74 **Age:** 22

| | | HOW MUCH HE PITCHED | | | | | | WHAT HE GAVE UP | | | | | | | | | | | | THE RESULTS | | | | | | |
Year Team	Lg	G	GS	CG	GF	IP	BFP	H	R	ER	HR	SH	SF	HB	TBB	IBB	SO	WP	Bk	W	L	Pct.	ShO	Sv-Op	Hld	ERA
1994 Royals	R	14	12	0	2	64.2	246	45	14	9	0	3	2	2	7	0	56	0	0	6	2	.750	0	0--	—	1.25
1995 Wilmington	A+	25	25	0	0	138	562	128	53	48	9	2	7	3	30	6	117	1	5	10	7	.588	0	0--	—	3.13
1996 Wichita	AA	2	2	0	0	13	48	10	0	0	1	0	0	0	1	0	12	0	0	2	0	1.000	0	0--	—	0.00
Omaha	AAA	15	15	1	0	96.2	399	80	38	34	16	3	1	2	38	0	82	4	1	8	3	.727	0	0--	—	3.17
1996 Kansas City	AL	16	16	2	0	106.2	441	101	39	38	7	1	4	4	26	1	64	5	1	8	6	.571	1	0-0	0	3.21

Matt Ruebel

Pitches: Left **Bats:** Left **Pos:** RP-19; SP-7   **Ht:** 6'2" **Wt:** 180 **Born:** 10/16/69 **Age:** 27

| | | HOW MUCH HE PITCHED | | | | | | WHAT HE GAVE UP | | | | | | | | | | | | THE RESULTS | | | | | | |
Year Team	Lg	G	GS	CG	GF	IP	BFP	H	R	ER	HR	SH	SF	HB	TBB	IBB	SO	WP	Bk	W	L	Pct.	ShO	Sv-Op	Hld	ERA
1991 Welland	A-	6	6	0	0	27.2	113	16	9	6	3	0	1	4	11	0	27	2	3	1	1	.500	0	0--	—	1.95
Augusta	A	8	8	2	0	47	202	43	26	20	2	1	0	2	25	0	35	3	0	3	4	.429	1	0--	—	3.83
1992 Augusta	A	12	10	1	1	64.2	268	53	26	20	1	3	0	5	19	0	65	2	1	5	2	.714	0	0--	—	2.78
Salem	A+	13	13	1	0	78.1	344	77	49	41	13	6	5	3	43	0	46	6	1	1	6	.143	0	0--	—	4.71
1993 Salem	A+	19	1	0	4	33.1	168	34	31	22	6	3	0	3	32	3	29	8	2	1	4	.200	0	0--	—	5.94
Augusta	A	23	7	1	6	63.1	276	51	28	17	2	1	3	5	34	4	50	1	0	5	5	.500	1	0--	—	2.42
1994 Carolina	AA	6	3	0	0	16.1	78	28	15	12	3	1	1	1	3	0	14	0	0	1	1	.500	0	0--	—	6.61
Salem	A+	21	13	0	0	86.1	374	87	46	33	9	2	3	7	27	0	72	4	1	6	6	.500	0	0--	—	3.44
1995 Carolina	AA	27	27	4	0	169.1	699	150	68	52	7	4	7	7	45	1	136	7	1	13	5	.722	3	0--	—	2.76
1996 Calgary	AAA	13	13	1	0	76.1	338	89	43	39	8	4	3	3	28	2	48	0	0	5	3	.625	0	0--	—	4.60
1996 Pittsburgh	NL	26	7	0	3	58.2	265	64	38	30	7	0	3	6	22	5	22	0	0	1	1	.500	0	1-1	4	4.60

Kirk Rueter

Pitches: Left **Bats:** Left **Pos:** SP-19; RP-1   **Ht:** 6'3" **Wt:** 195 **Born:** 12/1/70 **Age:** 26

| | | HOW MUCH HE PITCHED | | | | | | WHAT HE GAVE UP | | | | | | | | | | | | THE RESULTS | | | | | | |
Year Team	Lg	G	GS	CG	GF	IP	BFP	H	R	ER	HR	SH	SF	HB	TBB	IBB	SO	WP	Bk	W	L	Pct.	ShO	Sv-Op	Hld	ERA
1996 Ottawa *	AAA	3	3	1	0	15	67	21	7	7	3	1	0	0	3	0	3	0	0	1	2	.333	0	0--	—	4.20
Phoenix *	AAA	5	5	0	0	25.2	112	25	12	10	2	0	1	0	12	0	15	1	0	1	2	.333	0	0--	—	3.51
1993 Montreal	NL	14	14	1	0	85.2	341	85	33	26	5	1	0	0	18	1	31	0	0	8	0	1.000	0	0-0	0	2.73
1994 Montreal	NL	20	20	0	0	92.1	397	106	60	53	11	6	6	2	23	1	50	2	0	7	3	.700	0	0-0	0	5.17
1995 Montreal	NL	9	9	1	0	47.1	184	38	17	17	3	4	1	0	9	0	28	0	0	5	3	.625	1	0-0	0	3.23
1996 Mon-SF	NL	20	19	0	0	102	430	109	50	45	12	4	1	2	27	0	46	2	0	6	8	.429	0	0-0	0	3.97
1996 Montreal	NL	16	16	0	0	78.2	338	91	44	40	12	4	1	2	22	0	30	0	0	5	6	.455	0	0-0	0	4.58
San Francisco	NL	4	3	0	0	23.1	92	18	6	5	0	0	0	0	5	0	16	2	0	1	2	.333	0	0-0	0	1.93
4 ML YEARS		63	62	2	0	327.1	1352	338	160	141	31	15	7	5	77	2	155	4	0	26	14	.650	0			3.88

Scott Ruffcorn

Pitches: Right **Bats:** Right **Pos:** RP-2; SP-1   **Ht:** 6'4" **Wt:** 210 **Born:** 12/29/69 **Age:** 27

| | | HOW MUCH HE PITCHED | | | | | | WHAT HE GAVE UP | | | | | | | | | | | | THE RESULTS | | | | | | |
Year Team	Lg	G	GS	CG	GF	IP	BFP	H	R	ER	HR	SH	SF	HB	TBB	IBB	SO	WP	Bk	W	L	Pct.	ShO	Sv-Op	Hld	ERA
1991 White Sox	R	4	2	0	1	11.1	49	8	7	4	0	0	0	0	5	0	15	1	0	0	0	.000	0	0--	—	3.18
South Bend	A	9	9	0	0	43.2	193	35	26	19	1	2	1	2	25	0	45	1	2	1	3	.250	0	0--	—	3.92
1992 Sarasota	A+	25	24	2	0	160.1	642	122	53	39	7	4	5	3	39	0	140	3	1	14	5	.737	0	0--	—	2.19
1993 Birmingham	AA	20	20	3	0	135	563	108	47	41	6	5	0	4	52	0	141	7	0	9	4	.692	3	0--	—	2.73
Nashville	AAA	7	6	1	0	45	172	30	16	14	5	2	1	0	8	1	44	3	0	2	2	.500	0	0--	—	2.80
1994 Nashville	AAA	24	24	3	0	165.2	672	139	57	50	5	3	6	6	40	1	144	6	0	15	3	.833	3	0--	—	2.72
1995 Nashville	AAA	2	2	0	0	0.1	9	4	4	4	0	0	2	0	3	0	0	1	0	0	0	.000	0	0--	—	99.99
White Sox	R	3	3	0	0	10	46	7	4	1	0	1	0	0	5	0	7	1	0	0	0	.000	0	0--	—	0.90
Birmingham	AA	8	8	0	0	26.1	126	27	19	15	0	1	0	2	18	0	20	4	0	0	2	.000	0	0--	—	5.13
1996 Nashville	AAA	24	24	8	0	149	649	142	71	64	18	6	4	5	61	1	129	7	0	13	4	.765	5	0--	—	3.87
1993 Chicago	AL	3	2	0	1	10	46	9	11	9	2	1	1	0	10	0	12	1	0	0	2	.000	0	0-0	0	8.10
1994 Chicago	AL	2	2	0	0	6.1	39	15	11	9	1	0	1	0	4	0	3	0	0	0	0	.000	0	0-0	0	12.79
1995 Chicago	AL	4	0	0	0	8	46	10	7	7	0	1	0	2	13	0	5	0	0	0	0	.000	0	0-0	0	7.88
1996 Chicago	AL	3	1	0	1	6.1	34	10	8	8	1	1	0	0	6	0	3	2	0	0	1	.000	0	0-0	0	11.37
4 ML YEARS		12	5	0	2	30.2	165	44	37	33	4	3	2	2	34	0	13	3	0	0	5	.000	0			9.68

Bruce Ruffin

Pitches: Left **Bats:** Both **Pos:** RP-71   **Ht:** 6'2" **Wt:** 215 **Born:** 10/4/63 **Age:** 33

| | | HOW MUCH HE PITCHED | | | | | | WHAT HE GAVE UP | | | | | | | | | | | | THE RESULTS | | | | | | |
Year Team	Lg	G	GS	CG	GF	IP	BFP	H	R	ER	HR	SH	SF	HB	TBB	IBB	SO	WP	Bk	W	L	Pct.	ShO	Sv-Op	Hld	ERA
1986 Philadelphia	NL	21	21	6	0	146.1	600	138	53	40	6	2	4	4	44	6	70	0	1	9	4	.692	0	0--	—	2.46
1987 Philadelphia	NL	35	35	3	0	204.2	884	236	118	99	17	8	10	2	73	4	93	6	0	11	14	.440	1	0-0	0	4.35
1988 Philadelphia	NL	55	15	0	14	144.1	646	151	86	71	7	10	3	3	80	6	82	12	0	6	10	.375	0	3-5	8	4.43
1989 Philadelphia	NL	24	23	1	0	125.2	576	152	69	62	10	8	1	0	62	6	70	8	0	6	10	.375	0	0-0	0	4.44
1990 Philadelphia	NL	32	25	2	1	149	678	178	99	89	14	10	6	1	62	7	79	3	2	6	13	.316	0	0-0	0	5.38
1991 Philadelphia	NL	31	15	1	2	119	508	125	52	50	6	6	4	1	38	3	85	4	0	4	7	.364	1	0-0	5	3.78

| | | HOW MUCH HE PITCHED | | | | | | WHAT HE GAVE UP | | | | | | | | | | | | THE RESULTS | | | | | | |
Year Team	Lg	G	GS	CG	GF	IP	BFP	H	R	ER	HR	SH	SF	HB	TBB	IBB	SO	WP	Bk	W	L	Pct.	ShO	Sv-Op	Hld	ERA
1992 Milwaukee	AL	25	6	1	6	58	272	66	43	43	7	3	3	0	41	3	45	2	0	1	6	.143	0	0-2	1	6.67
1993 Colorado	NL	59	12	0	8	139.2	619	145	71	60	10	4	5	1	69	9	126	8	0	6	5	.545	0	2-3	5	3.87
1994 Colorado	NL	56	0	0	39	55.2	252	55	28	25	6	1	3	1	30	2	65	5	0	4	5	.444	0	16-21	5	4.04
1995 Colorado	NL	37	0	0	19	34	140	26	8	8	1	4	0	0	19	1	23	1	0	0	1	.000	0	11-12	6	2.12
1996 Colorado	NL	71	0	0	56	69.2	292	55	35	31	5	0	3	0	29	3	74	10	0	7	5	.583	0	24-29	6	4.00
11 ML YEARS		446	152	17	145	1246	5467	1327	662	578	89	56	42	10	547	50	812	59	3	60	80	.429	3	56--	—	4.17

Johnny Ruffin

Pitches: Right Bats: Right Pos: RP-49 **Ht: 6'3" Wt: 170 Born: 7/29/71 Age: 25**

| | | HOW MUCH HE PITCHED | | | | | | WHAT HE GAVE UP | | | | | | | | | | | | THE RESULTS | | | | | | |
Year Team	Lg	G	GS	CG	GF	IP	BFP	H	R	ER	HR	SH	SF	HB	TBB	IBB	SO	WP	Bk	W	L	Pct.	ShO	Sv-Op	Hld	ERA
1993 Cincinnati	NL	21	0	0	5	37.2	159	36	16	15	4	1	0	1	11	1	30	2	0	2	1	.667	0	2-3	2	3.58
1994 Cincinnati	NL	51	0	0	13	70	287	57	26	24	7	2	2	0	27	3	44	5	1	7	2	.778	0	1-3	11	3.09
1995 Cincinnati	NL	10	0	0	6	13.1	54	4	3	2	0	0	0	1	11	0	11	3	0	0	0	.000	0	0-0	1	1.35
1996 Cincinnati	NL	49	0	0	13	62.1	289	71	42	38	10	4	3	2	37	5	69	8	0	1	3	.250	0	0-1	5	5.49
4 ML YEARS		131	0	0	37	183.1	789	168	87	79	21	7	5	3	86	9	154	18	1	10	6	.625	0	3-7	15	3.88

Jeff Russell

Pitches: Right Bats: Right Pos: RP-55 **Ht: 6'3" Wt: 205 Born: 9/2/61 Age: 35**

| | | HOW MUCH HE PITCHED | | | | | | WHAT HE GAVE UP | | | | | | | | | | | | THE RESULTS | | | | | | |
Year Team	Lg	G	GS	CG	GF	IP	BFP	H	R	ER	HR	SH	SF	HB	TBB	IBB	SO	WP	Bk	W	L	Pct.	ShO	Sv-Op	Hld	ERA
1996 Charlotte *	A+	2	2	0	0	3	9	0	0	0	0	0	0	0	0	0	6	0	0	0	0	.000	0	0--	—	0.00
Tulsa *	AA	2	2	0	0	5	15	0	0	0	0	0	0	0	1	0	4	0	0	0	0	.000	0	0--	—	0.00
Okla. City *	AAA	5	1	0	4	8.2	32	8	2	1	0	0	1	0	1	0	5	0	0	1	0	1.000	0	2--	—	1.04
1983 Cincinnati	NL	10	10	2	0	68.1	282	58	30	23	7	6	5	0	22	3	40	1	1	4	5	.444	0	0--	—	3.03
1984 Cincinnati	NL	33	30	4	1	181.2	787	186	97	86	15	8	3	4	65	8	101	3	3	6	18	.250	2	0--	—	4.26
1985 Texas	AL	13	13	0	0	62	295	85	55	52	10	1	3	2	27	1	44	2	0	3	6	.333	0	0--	—	7.55
1986 Texas	AL	37	0	0	9	82	338	74	40	31	11	1	2	1	31	2	54	5	0	5	2	.714	0	2--	—	3.40
1987 Texas	AL	52	2	0	12	97.1	442	109	56	48	9	0	5	2	52	5	56	6	1	5	4	.556	0	3-4	3	4.44
1988 Texas	AL	34	24	5	1	188.2	793	183	86	80	15	4	3	6	66	3	88	5	7	10	9	.526	0	0-0		3.82
1989 Texas	AL	71	0	0	**66**	72.2	278	45	21	16	4	1	3	3	24	5	77	6	0	6	4	.600	0	**38-44**	0	1.98
1990 Texas	AL	27	0	0	22	25.1	111	23	15	12	1	3	1	0	16	5	16	2	0	1	5	.167	0	10-12	1	4.26
1991 Texas	AL	68	0	0	56	79.1	336	71	36	29	11	3	4	1	26	1	52	6	0	6	4	.600	0	30-40	3	3.29
1992 Tex-Oak	AL	59	0	0	46	66.1	276	55	14	12	3	1	2	2	25	3	48	3	0	4	3	.571	0	30-39	1	1.63
1993 Boston	AL	51	0	0	48	46.2	189	39	16	14	1	1	4	1	14	1	45	2	0	1	4	.200	0	33-37	1	2.70
1994 Bos-Cle	AL	42	0	0	36	40.2	179	43	25	23	5	0	2	1	16	2	28	1	0	1	6	.143	0	17-23	3	5.09
1995 Texas	AL	37	0	0	32	32.2	139	36	12	11	3	0	0	0	9	1	21	1	0	1	0	1.000	0	20-24	1	3.03
1996 Texas	AL	55	0	0	11	56	249	58	22	21	5	3	4	4	22	3	23	3	0	3	3	.500	0	3-6	20	3.38
1992 Texas	AL	51	0	0	42	56.2	241	51	14	12	3	1	2	2	22	3	43	3	0	2	3	.400	0	28-37	0	1.91
Oakland	AL	8	0	0	4	9.2	35	4	0	0	0	0	0	0	3	0	5	0	0	2	0	1.000	0	2-2	1	0.00
1994 Boston	AL	29	0	0	25	28	127	30	17	16	3	0	2	0	13	2	18	1	0	0	5	.000	0	12-15	3	5.14
Cleveland	AL	13	0	0	11	12.2	52	13	8	7	2	0	0	0	3	0	10	0	0	1	1	.500	0	5-8	0	4.97
14 ML YEARS		589	79	11	340	1099.2	4694	1065	525	458	100	32	41	28	415	43	693	46	12	56	73	.434	2	186--	—	3.75

Ken Ryan

Pitches: Right Bats: Right Pos: RP-62 **Ht: 6'3" Wt: 230 Born: 10/24/68 Age: 28**

| | | HOW MUCH HE PITCHED | | | | | | WHAT HE GAVE UP | | | | | | | | | | | | THE RESULTS | | | | | | |
Year Team	Lg	G	GS	CG	GF	IP	BFP	H	R	ER	HR	SH	SF	HB	TBB	IBB	SO	WP	Bk	W	L	Pct.	ShO	Sv-Op	Hld	ERA
1992 Boston	AL	7	0	0	6	7	30	4	5	5	2	1	1	0	5	0	5	0	0	0	0	.000	0	1-1	0	6.43
1993 Boston	AL	47	0	0	26	50	223	43	23	20	2	4	4	3	29	5	49	3	0	7	2	.778	0	1-4	3	3.60
1994 Boston	AL	42	0	0	26	48	202	46	14	13	1	4	0	1	17	3	32	2	0	2	3	.400	0	13-16	5	2.44
1995 Boston	AL	28	0	0	20	32.2	153	34	20	18	4	1	0	1	24	6	34	1	0	0	4	.000	0	7-10	0	4.96
1996 Philadelphia	NL	62	0	0	26	89	370	71	32	24	4	5	0	1	45	8	71	4	3	3	5	.375	0	8-13	15	2.43
5 ML YEARS		186	0	0	104	226.2	978	198	94	80	13	15	5	6	120	22	191	10	3	12	14	.462	0	30-44	23	3.18

Bret Saberhagen

Pitches: Right Bats: Right Pos: SP **Ht: 6'1" Wt: 200 Born: 4/11/64 Age: 33**

| | | HOW MUCH HE PITCHED | | | | | | WHAT HE GAVE UP | | | | | | | | | | | | THE RESULTS | | | | | | |
Year Team	Lg	G	GS	CG	GF	IP	BFP	H	R	ER	HR	SH	SF	HB	TBB	IBB	SO	WP	Bk	W	L	Pct.	ShO	Sv-Op	Hld	ERA
1984 Kansas City	AL	38	18	2	9	157.2	634	138	71	61	13	8	5	2	36	4	73	7	1	10	11	.476	1	1--	—	3.48
1985 Kansas City	AL	32	32	10	0	235.1	931	211	79	75	19	9	7	1	38	1	158	1	3	20	6	.769	1	0--	—	2.87
1986 Kansas City	AL	30	25	4	4	156	652	165	77	72	15	3	3	2	29	1	112	1	1	7	12	.368	2	0--	—	4.15
1987 Kansas City	AL	33	33	15	0	257	1048	246	99	96	27	8	5	6	53	2	163	6	1	18	10	.643	4	0-0	0	3.36
1988 Kansas City	AL	35	35	9	0	260.2	1089	271	122	110	18	8	10	4	59	5	171	9	0	14	16	.467	0	0-0	0	3.80
1989 Kansas City	AL	36	35	**12**	0	262.1	1021	209	74	63	13	9	6	2	43	6	193	8	1	23	6	.793	4	0-0	0	**2.16**
1990 Kansas City	AL	20	20	5	0	135	561	146	52	49	9	4	1	2	28	1	87	1	0	5	9	.357	0	0-0	0	3.27
1991 Kansas City	AL	28	28	7	0	196.1	789	165	76	67	12	8	3	9	45	5	136	8	1	13	8	.619	2	0-0	0	3.07
1992 New York	NL	17	15	1	0	97.2	397	84	39	38	6	3	4	0	27	1	81	1	2	3	5	.375	1	0-1	0	3.50
1993 New York	NL	19	19	4	0	139.1	556	131	55	51	11	6	6	3	17	4	93	2	2	7	7	.500	1	0-0	0	3.29

			HOW MUCH HE PITCHED							WHAT HE GAVE UP											THE RESULTS					
Year Team	Lg	G	GS	CG	GF	IP	BFP	H	R	ER	HR	SH	SF	HB	TBB	IBB	SO	WP	Bk	W	L	Pct.	ShO	Sv-Op	Hld	ERA
1994 New York	NL	24	24	4	0	177.1	696	169	58	54	13	9	5	4	13	0	143	0	0	14	4	.778	0	0-0	0	2.74
1995 NYN-Col	NL	25	25	3	0	153	658	165	78	71	21	7	3	10	33	3	100	3	0	7	6	.538	0	0-0	0	4.18
1995 New York	NL	16	16	3	0	110	452	105	45	41	13	5	3	5	20	2	71	2	0	5	5	.500	0	0-0	0	3.35
Colorado	NL	9	9	0	0	43	206	60	33	30	8	2	0	5	13	1	29	1	0	2	1	.667	0	0-0	0	6.28
12 ML YEARS		337	309	76	13	2227.2	9032	2100	880	807	177	82	60	48	421	33	1510	47	12	141	100	.585	16	1--	—	3.26

Chris Sabo

Bats: Right **Throws:** Right **Pos:** 3B-43; PH-16   **Ht:** 6'0" **Wt:** 185 **Born:** 1/19/62 **Age:** 35

					BATTING													BASERUNNING				PERCENTAGES		
Year Team	Lg	G	AB	H	2B	3B	HR	(Hm	Rd)	TB	R	RBI	TBB	IBB	SO	HBP	SH	SF	SB	CS	SB%	GDP	Avg	OBP	SLG
1996 Indianapols *	AAA	8	31	9	1	0	0	—	—	10	0	1	0	0	6	0	0	1	0	0	.00	3	.290	.281	.323
1988 Cincinnati	NL	137	538	146	40	2	11	(8	3)	223	74	44	29	1	52	6	5	4	46	14	.77	12	.271	.314	.414
1989 Cincinnati	NL	82	304	79	21	1	6	(3	3)	120	40	29	25	2	33	1	4	2	14	9	.61	2	.260	.316	.395
1990 Cincinnati	NL	148	567	153	38	2	25	(15	10)	270	95	71	61	7	58	4	1	3	25	10	.71	8	.270	.343	.476
1991 Cincinnati	NL	153	582	175	35	3	26	(15	11)	294	91	88	44	3	79	6	5	3	19	6	.76	13	.301	.354	.505
1992 Cincinnati	NL	96	344	84	19	3	12	(8	4)	145	42	43	30	1	54	1	1	6	4	5	.44	12	.244	.302	.422
1993 Cincinnati	NL	148	552	143	33	2	21	(12	9)	243	86	82	43	5	105	6	2	8	6	4	.60	10	.259	.315	.440
1994 Baltimore	AL	68	258	66	15	3	11	(3	8)	120	41	42	20	2	38	5	4	1	1	1	.50	8	.256	.320	.465
1995 ChA-StL		25	84	20	6	0	1	(1	0)	29	10	11	4	1	14	2	2	2	3	0	1.00	1	.238	.283	.345
1996 Cincinnati	NL	54	125	32	7	1	3	(3	0)	50	15	16	18	0	27	1	1	1	2	0	1.00	4	.256	.354	.400
1995 Chicago	AL	20	71	18	5	0	1	(1	0)	26	10	8	3	1	12	2	2	2	2	0	1.00	1	.254	.295	.366
St. Louis	NL	5	13	2	1	0	0	(0	0)	3	0	3	1	0	2	0	0	0	1	0	1.00	1	.154	.214	.231
9 ML YEARS		911	3354	898	214	17	116	(65	51)	1494	494	426	274	22	460	32	25	29	120	49	.71	70	.268	.326	.445

Brian Sackinsky

Pitches: Right **Bats:** Right **Pos:** RP-3   **Ht:** 6'4" **Wt:** 220 **Born:** 6/22/71 **Age:** 26

				HOW MUCH HE PITCHED							WHAT HE GAVE UP										THE RESULTS				
Year Team	Lg	G	GS	CG	GF	IP	BFP	H	R	ER	HR	SH	SF	HB	TBB	IBB	SO	WP	Bk	W	L	Pct.	ShO	Sv-Op	Hld	ERA
1992 Frederick	A+	5	3	0	0	10.1	55	20	15	15	3	0	1	0	6	0	10	4	0	0	3	.000	0	0--	—	13.06
Bluefield	R+	5	5	0	0	27.2	124	30	15	11	0	0	0	2	9	0	33	2	0	2	2	.500	0	0--	—	3.58
1993 Albany	A	9	8	0	0	50.2	217	50	29	18	2	0	4	0	16	0	41	5	0	3	4	.429	0	0--	—	3.20
Frederick	A+	18	18	1	0	121	512	117	55	43	13	3	3	2	37	2	112	17	1	6	8	.429	0	0--	—	3.20
1994 Bowie	AA	28	26	4	0	177	721	165	73	66	24	5	9	0	39	0	145	6	0	11	7	.611	0	0--	—	3.36
1995 Rochester	AAA	14	11	0	0	62.2	260	70	33	32	6	1	4	1	10	0	42	4	0	3	3	.500	0	0--	—	4.60
1996 Orioles	R	3	1	0	0	8.2	37	11	6	5	0	0	0	0	1	0	3	1	0	1	0	1.000	0	0--	—	5.19
Rochester	AAA	14	13	1	1	67.2	276	75	28	26	12	4	3	0	15	0	38	1	0	7	3	.700	0	0--	—	3.46
1996 Baltimore	AL	3	0	0	2	4.2	22	6	2	2	1	0	0	0	3	0	2	0	1	0	0	.000	0	0-0	0	3.86

A.J. Sager

Pitches: Right **Bats:** Right **Pos:** RP-13; SP-9   **Ht:** 6'4" **Wt:** 220 **Born:** 3/3/65 **Age:** 32

				HOW MUCH HE PITCHED							WHAT HE GAVE UP										THE RESULTS				
Year Team	Lg	G	GS	CG	GF	IP	BFP	H	R	ER	HR	SH	SF	HB	TBB	IBB	SO	WP	Bk	W	L	Pct.	ShO	Sv-Op	Hld	ERA
1996 Toledo *	AAA	18	2	0	6	37.2	149	38	14	11	5	0	0	1	3	0	24	0	1	1	0	1.000	0	0--	—	2.63
1994 San Diego	NL	22	3	0	4	46.2	217	62	34	31	4	6	2	2	16	5	26	0	0	1	4	.200	0	0-0	0	5.98
1995 Colorado	NL	10	0	0	2	14.2	70	19	16	12	1	2	0	0	7	1	10	0	0	0	0	.000	0	0-1	0	7.36
1996 Detroit	AL	22	9	0	1	79	347	91	46	44	10	3	3	2	29	2	52	1	0	4	5	.444	0	0-0	1	5.01
3 ML YEARS		54	12	0	7	140.1	634	172	96	87	15	11	5	4	52	8	88	1	0	5	9	.357	0	0-1	1	5.58

Roger Salkeld

Pitches: Right **Bats:** Right **Pos:** SP-19; RP-10   **Ht:** 6'5" **Wt:** 215 **Born:** 3/6/71 **Age:** 26

				HOW MUCH HE PITCHED							WHAT HE GAVE UP										THE RESULTS				
Year Team	Lg	G	GS	CG	GF	IP	BFP	H	R	ER	HR	SH	SF	HB	TBB	IBB	SO	WP	Bk	W	L	Pct.	ShO	Sv-Op	Hld	ERA
1993 Seattle	AL	3	2	0	0	14.1	61	13	4	4	0	0	0	1	4	0	13	0	0	0	0	.000	0	0-0	0	2.51
1994 Seattle	AL	13	13	0	0	59	291	76	47	47	7	0	3	1	45	1	46	2	0	2	5	.286	0	0-0	0	7.17
1996 Cincinnati	NL	29	19	1	2	116	509	114	69	67	18	10	3	6	54	2	82	7	1	8	5	.615	1	0-0	0	5.20
3 ML YEARS		45	34	1	2	189.1	861	203	120	118	25	10	6	8	103	3	141	9	1	10	10	.500	1	0-0	0	5.61

Tim Salmon

Bats: Right **Throws:** Right **Pos:** RF-153; DH-3; PH-2   **Ht:** 6'3" **Wt:** 220 **Born:** 8/24/68 **Age:** 28

					BATTING													BASERUNNING				PERCENTAGES		
Year Team	Lg	G	AB	H	2B	3B	HR	(Hm	Rd)	TB	R	RBI	TBB	IBB	SO	HBP	SH	SF	SB	CS	SB%	GDP	Avg	OBP	SLG
1992 California	AL	23	79	14	1	0	2	(1	1)	21	8	6	11	1	23	1	0	1	1	1	.50	1	.177	.283	.266
1993 California	AL	142	515	146	35	1	31	(23	8)	276	93	95	82	5	135	5	0	8	5	6	.45	6	.283	.382	.536
1994 California	AL	100	373	107	18	2	23	(12	11)	198	67	70	54	2	102	5	0	3	1	3	.25	3	.287	.382	.531
1995 California	AL	143	537	177	34	3	34	(15	19)	319	111	105	91	2	111	6	0	4	5	5	.50	9	.330	.429	.594
1996 California	AL	156	581	166	27	4	30	(18	12)	291	90	98	93	7	125	4	0	3	4	2	.67	8	.286	.386	.501
5 ML YEARS		564	2085	610	115	10	120	(69	51)	1105	369	374	331	17	496	21	0	19	16	17	.48	27	.293	.392	.530

Juan Samuel

Bats: R **Throws:** R **Pos:** DH-24; 1B-17; RF-15; PH-15; LF-8; CF-5   **Ht:** 5'11" **Wt:** 180 **Born:** 12/9/60 **Age:** 36

Year Team	Lg	G	AB	H	2B	3B	HR	(Hm	Rd)	TB	R	RBI	TBB	IBB	SO	HBP	SH	SF	SB	CS	SB%	GDP	Avg	OBP	SLG
1983 Philadelphia	NL	18	65	18	1	2	2	(1	1)	29	14	5	4	1	16	1	0	1	3	2	.60	1	.277	.324	.446
1984 Philadelphia	NL	160	701	191	36	19	15	(8	7)	310	105	69	28	2	168	7	0	1	72	15	.83	6	.272	.307	.442
1985 Philadelphia	NL	161	663	175	31	13	19	(8	11)	289	101	74	33	2	141	6	2	5	53	19	.74	8	.264	.303	.436
1986 Philadelphia	NL	145	591	157	36	12	16	(10	6)	265	90	78	26	3	142	8	1	7	42	14	.75	8	.266	.302	.448
1987 Philadelphia	NL	160	655	178	37	15	28	(15	13)	329	113	100	60	5	162	5	0	6	35	15	.70	12	.272	.335	.502
1988 Philadelphia	NL	157	629	153	32	9	12	(7	5)	239	68	67	39	6	151	12	0	5	33	10	.77	8	.243	.298	.380
1989 Phi-NYN	NL	137	532	125	16	2	11	(5	6)	178	69	48	42	2	120	11	2	2	42	12	.78	7	.235	.303	.335
1990 Los Angeles	NL	143	492	119	24	3	13	(6	7)	188	62	52	51	5	126	5	5	5	38	20	.66	8	.242	.316	.382
1991 Los Angeles	NL	153	594	161	22	6	12	(4	8)	231	74	58	49	4	133	3	10	3	23	8	.74	8	.271	.328	.389
1992 LA-KC		76	224	61	8	4	0	(0	0)	77	22	23	14	4	49	2	4	2	8	3	.73	2	.272	.318	.344
1993 Cincinnati	NL	103	261	60	10	4	4	(1	3)	90	31	26	23	3	53	3	0	2	9	7	.56	2	.230	.298	.345
1994 Detroit	AL	59	136	42	9	5	5	(4	1)	76	32	21	10	0	26	3	0	2	5	2	.71	4	.309	.364	.559
1995 Det-KC	AL	91	205	54	10	1	12	(6	6)	102	31	39	29	1	49	2	1	0	6	4	.60	3	.263	.360	.498
1996 Toronto	AL	69	188	48	8	3	8	(4	4)	86	34	26	15	0	65	3	0	1	9	1	.90	2	.255	.319	.457
1989 Philadelphia	NL	51	199	49	3	1	8	(3	5)	78	32	20	18	1	45	1	0	1	11	3	.79	2	.246	.311	.392
New York	NL	86	333	76	13	1	3	(2	1)	100	37	28	24	1	75	10	2	1	31	9	.78	5	.228	.299	.300
1992 Los Angeles	NL	47	122	32	3	1	0	(0	0)	37	7	15	7	3	22	1	4	2	2	2	.50	0	.262	.303	.303
Kansas City	AL	29	102	29	5	3	0	(0	0)	40	15	8	7	1	27	1	0	0	6	1	.86	2	.284	.336	.392
1995 Detroit	AL	76	171	48	10	1	10	(6	4)	90	28	34	24	0	38	2	1	0	5	4	.56	3	.281	.376	.526
Kansas City	AL	15	34	6	0	0	2	(0	2)	12	3	5	5	1	11	0	0	0	1	0	1.00	0	.176	.282	.353
14 ML YEARS		1632	5936	1542	280	98	157	(79	78)	2489	846	686	423	38	1401	71	25	42	378	132	.74	79	.260	.315	.419

Rey Sanchez

Bats: Right **Throws:** Right **Pos:** SS-92; PH-4   **Ht:** 5'9" **Wt:** 175 **Born:** 10/5/67 **Age:** 29

Year Team	Lg	G	AB	H	2B	3B	HR	(Hm	Rd)	TB	R	RBI	TBB	IBB	SO	HBP	SH	SF	SB	CS	SB%	GDP	Avg	OBP	SLG
1996 Iowa *	AAA	3	12	2	0	0	0	—	—	2	2	1	1	0	2	0	0	0	2	0	1.00	0	.167	.231	.167
1991 Chicago	NL	13	23	6	0	0	0	(0	0)	6	1	2	4	0	3	0	0	0	0	0	.00	0	.261	.370	.261
1992 Chicago	NL	74	255	64	14	3	1	(1	0)	87	24	19	10	1	17	3	5	2	2	1	.67	7	.251	.285	.341
1993 Chicago	NL	105	344	97	11	2	0	(0	0)	112	35	28	15	7	22	3	9	2	1	1	.50	8	.282	.316	.326
1994 Chicago	NL	96	291	83	13	1	0	(0	0)	98	26	24	20	4	29	7	4	1	2	5	.29	9	.285	.345	.337
1995 Chicago	NL	114	428	119	22	4	3	(0	3)	154	57	27	14	2	48	1	8	1	6	4	.60	9	.278	.301	.360
1996 Chicago	NL	95	289	61	9	0	1	(1	0)	73	28	12	22	6	42	3	8	2	7	1	.88	6	.211	.272	.253
6 ML YEARS		497	1630	430	69	8	5	(2	3)	530	171	112	85	20	161	17	34	9	18	12	.60	39	.264	.306	.325

Ryne Sandberg

Bats: Right **Throws:** Right **Pos:** 2B-146; PH-6   **Ht:** 6'2" **Wt:** 190 **Born:** 9/18/59 **Age:** 37

Year Team	Lg	G	AB	H	2B	3B	HR	(Hm	Rd)	TB	R	RBI	TBB	IBB	SO	HBP	SH	SF	SB	CS	SB%	GDP	Avg	OBP	SLG
1981 Philadelphia	NL	13	6	1	0	0	0	(0	0)	1	2	0	0	0	1	0	0	0	0	0	.00	0	.167	.167	.167
1982 Chicago	NL	156	635	172	33	5	7	(5	2)	236	103	54	36	3	90	4	7	5	32	12	.73	7	.271	.312	.372
1983 Chicago	NL	158	633	165	25	4	8	(4	4)	222	94	48	51	3	79	3	7	5	37	11	.77	8	.261	.316	.351
1984 Chicago	NL	156	636	200	36	19	19	(11	8)	331	114	84	52	3	101	3	5	4	32	7	.82	7	.314	.367	.520
1985 Chicago	NL	153	609	186	31	6	26	(17	9)	307	113	83	57	5	97	1	2	4	54	11	.83	10	.305	.364	.504
1986 Chicago	NL	154	627	178	28	5	14	(8	6)	258	68	76	46	6	79	0	3	6	34	11	.76	11	.284	.330	.411
1987 Chicago	NL	132	523	154	25	2	16	(8	8)	231	81	59	59	4	79	2	1	2	21	2	.91	11	.294	.367	.442
1988 Chicago	NL	155	618	163	23	8	19	(10	9)	259	77	69	54	3	91	1	1	5	25	10	.71	14	.264	.322	.419
1989 Chicago	NL	157	606	176	25	5	30	(16	14)	301	104	76	59	8	85	4	1	2	15	5	.75	9	.290	.356	.497
1990 Chicago	NL	155	615	188	30	3	40	(25	15)	344	116	100	50	8	84	1	0	9	25	7	.78	8	.306	.354	.559
1991 Chicago	NL	158	585	170	32	2	26	(15	11)	284	104	100	87	4	89	2	1	9	22	8	.73	9	.291	.379	.485
1992 Chicago	NL	158	612	186	32	8	26	(16	10)	312	100	87	68	4	73	1	0	6	17	6	.74	13	.304	.371	.510
1993 Chicago	NL	117	456	141	20	0	9	(5	4)	188	67	45	37	1	62	2	2	6	9	2	.82	12	.309	.359	.412
1994 Chicago	NL	57	223	53	9	5	5	(3	2)	87	36	24	23	0	40	1	0	0	2	3	.40	6	.238	.312	.390
1996 Chicago	NL	150	554	135	28	4	25	(12	13)	246	85	92	54	4	116	7	1	5	12	8	.60	9	.244	.316	.444
15 ML YEARS		2029	7938	2268	377	76	270	(155	115)	3607	1264	997	733	56	1166	32	31	68	337	103	.77	134	.286	.346	.454

Reggie Sanders

Bats: Right **Throws:** Right **Pos:** RF-80; PH-1   **Ht:** 6'1" **Wt:** 185 **Born:** 12/1/67 **Age:** 29

Year Team	Lg	G	AB	H	2B	3B	HR	(Hm	Rd)	TB	R	RBI	TBB	IBB	SO	HBP	SH	SF	SB	CS	SB%	GDP	Avg	OBP	SLG
1996 Indianapols *	AAA	4	12	5	2	0	0	—	—	7	3	1	1	0	4	1	0	0	0	0	.00	0	.417	.500	.583
1991 Cincinnati	NL	9	40	8	0	0	1	(0	1)	11	6	3	0	0	9	0	0	0	1	1	.50	1	.200	.200	.275
1992 Cincinnati	NL	116	385	104	26	6	12	(6	6)	178	62	36	48	2	98	4	0	1	16	7	.70	6	.270	.356	.462
1993 Cincinnati	NL	138	496	136	16	4	20	(8	12)	220	90	83	51	7	118	5	3	8	27	10	.73	10	.274	.343	.444
1994 Cincinnati	NL	107	400	105	20	8	17	(10	7)	192	66	62	41	1	114	2	1	3	21	9	.70	2	.263	.332	.480
1995 Cincinnati	NL	133	484	148	36	6	28	(9	19)	280	91	99	69	4	122	8	0	6	36	12	.75	9	.306	.397	.579
1996 Cincinnati	NL	81	287	72	17	1	14	(7	7)	133	49	33	44	4	86	2	0	1	24	8	.75	8	.251	.353	.463
6 ML YEARS		584	2092	573	115	25	92	(40	52)	1014	364	316	253	18	547	21	4	19	125	47	.73	36	.274	.355	.485

Scott Sanders

Pitches: Right **Bats:** Right **Pos:** RP-30; SP-16 **Ht:** 6'4" **Wt:** 220 **Born:** 3/25/69 **Age:** 28

		HOW MUCH HE PITCHED						WHAT HE GAVE UP											THE RESULTS					
Year Team	Lg	G	GS	CG	GF	IP	BFP	H	R	ER	HR	SH	SF	HB	TBB	IBB	SO	WP	Bk	W	L	Pct.	ShO	Sv-Op	Hld	ERA
1993 San Diego	NL	9	9	0	0	52.1	231	54	32	24	4	1	2	1	23	1	37	0	1	3	3	.500	0	0-0	0	4.13
1994 San Diego	NL	23	20	0	2	111	485	103	63	59	10	6	5	5	48	4	109	10	1	4	8	.333	0	1-1	1	4.78
1995 San Diego	NL	17	15	1	0	90	383	79	46	43	14	2	2	2	31	4	88	6	1	5	5	.500	0	0-0	1	4.30
1996 San Diego	NL	46	16	0	6	144	594	117	58	54	10	7	7	2	48	5	157	7	0	9	5	.643	0	0-0	3	3.38
4 ML YEARS		95	60	1	8	397.1	1693	353	199	180	38	16	16	10	150	14	391	23	3	21	21	.500	0	1-1	5	4.08

Scott Sanderson

Pitches: Right **Bats:** Right **Pos:** SP-4; RP-1 **Ht:** 6'5" **Wt:** 192 **Born:** 7/22/56 **Age:** 40

		HOW MUCH HE PITCHED						WHAT HE GAVE UP											THE RESULTS					
Year Team	Lg	G	GS	CG	GF	IP	BFP	H	R	ER	HR	SH	SF	HB	TBB	IBB	SO	WP	Bk	W	L	Pct.	ShO	Sv-Op	Hld	ERA
1996 Lk Elsinore *	A+	1	1	0	0	6	26	8	3	2	0	0	1	0	0	0	4	0	0	1	0	1.000	0	0- -	—	3.00
1978 Montreal	NL	10	9	1	1	61	251	52	20	17	3	3	2	1	21	0	50	2	0	4	2	.667	1	0- -	—	2.51
1979 Montreal	NL	34	24	5	3	168	696	148	69	64	16	5	7	3	54	4	138	2	3	9	8	.529	3	1- -	—	3.43
1980 Montreal	NL	33	33	7	0	211	875	206	76	73	18	11	5	3	56	3	125	6	0	16	11	.593	3	0- -	—	3.11
1981 Montreal	NL	22	22	4	0	137	560	122	50	45	10	7	4	1	31	2	77	2	0	9	7	.563	1	0- -	—	2.96
1982 Montreal	NL	32	32	7	0	224	922	212	98	86	24	9	6	3	58	5	158	2	1	12	12	.500	0	0- -	—	3.46
1983 Montreal	NL	18	16	0	1	81.1	346	98	50	42	12	1	2	0	20	0	55	0	0	6	7	.462	0	1- -	—	4.65
1984 Chicago	NL	24	24	3	0	140.2	571	140	54	49	5	6	8	2	24	3	76	3	2	8	5	.615	0	0- -	—	3.14
1985 Chicago	NL	19	19	2	0	121	480	100	49	42	13	7	7	0	27	4	80	1	0	5	6	.455	0	0- -	—	3.12
1986 Chicago	NL	37	28	1	2	169.2	697	165	85	79	21	6	5	2	37	2	124	3	1	9	11	.450	1	1- -	—	4.19
1987 Chicago	NL	32	22	0	5	144.2	631	156	72	69	23	4	5	3	50	5	106	1	0	8	9	.471	0	2-4	2	4.29
1988 Chicago	NL	11	0	0	3	15.1	62	13	9	9	1	0	3	0	3	1	6	0	0	1	2	.333	0	0-2	0	5.28
1989 Chicago	NL	37	23	2	2	146.1	611	155	69	64	16	8	3	2	31	6	86	1	3	11	9	.550	0	0-0	0	3.94
1990 Oakland	AL	34	34	2	0	206.1	885	205	99	89	27	4	8	4	66	2	128	7	1	17	11	.607	0	0-0	0	3.88
1991 New York	AL	34	34	2	0	208	837	200	95	88	22	5	5	3	29	0	130	4	1	16	10	.615	2	0-0	0	3.81
1992 New York	AL	33	33	2	0	193.1	851	220	116	106	28	3	11	4	64	5	104	4	1	12	11	.522	1	0-0	0	4.93
1993 Cal-SF		32	29	4	1	184	777	201	97	86	27	9	10	6	34	7	102	1	5	11	13	.458	1	0-0	0	4.21
1994 Chicago	AL	18	14	1	0	92	389	110	57	52	20	3	1	2	12	1	36	0	1	8	4	.667	0	0-0	0	5.09
1995 California	AL	7	7	0	0	39.1	170	48	23	18	6	1	2	2	4	1	23	0	1	1	3	.250	0	0-0	0	4.12
1996 California	AL	5	4	0	0	18	98	39	21	15	5	1	1	0	4	0	7	0	2	0	2	.000	0	0-0	0	7.50
1993 California	AL	21	21	4	0	135.1	576	153	77	67	15	6	8	5	27	5	66	1	2	7	11	.389	1	0-0	0	4.46
San Francisco	NL	11	8	0	1	48.2	201	48	20	19	12	3	2	1	7	2	36	0	3	4	2	.667	0	0-0	0	3.51
19 ML YEARS		472	407	43	18	2561	10709	2590	1209	1093	297	94	94	43	625	51	1611	39	22	163	143	.533	14	5- -	—	3.84

F.P. Santangelo

B: B **T:** R **Pos:** CF-76; LF-33; 3B-23; PH-23; RF-18; 2B-5; SS-1 **Ht:** 5'10" **Wt:** 168 **Born:** 10/24/67 **Age:** 29

		BATTING																		BASERUNNING				PERCENTAGES		
Year Team	Lg	G	AB	H	2B	3B	HR	(Hm	Rd)	TB	R	RBI	TBB	IBB	SO	HBP	SH	SF	SB	CS	SB%	GDP	Avg	OBP	SLG
1989 Jamestown	A-	2	6	3	1	0	0	—	—	4	0	0	1	0	0	0	0	0	1	0	1.00	0	.500	.571	.667
W. Palm Bch	A+	57	173	37	4	0	0	—	—	41	18	14	23	1	12	4	6	0	3	3	.50	5	.214	.320	.237
1990 W. Palm Bch	A+	116	394	109	19	2	0	—	—	132	63	38	51	2	49	5	18	2	22	7	.76	5	.277	.365	.335
1991 Harrisburg	AA	132	462	113	12	7	5	—	—	154	78	42	74	0	45	7	13	4	21	7	.75	6	.245	.355	.333
1992 Indianapolis	AAA	137	462	123	25	0	5	—	—	163	83	34	62	4	58	7	13	2	12	11	.52	9	.266	.360	.353
1993 Ottawa	AAA	131	453	124	21	2	4	—	—	161	86	45	59	4	52	14	8	4	18	8	.69	10	.274	.372	.355
1994 Ottawa	AAA	119	413	104	28	1	5	—	—	149	62	41	59	0	64	9	10	3	7	9	.44	11	.252	.355	.361
1995 Ottawa	AAA	95	267	68	15	3	2	—	—	95	37	25	32	3	22	6	6	4	7	4	.64	2	.255	.343	.356
1995 Montreal	NL	35	98	29	5	1	1	(1	0)	39	11	9	12	0	9	2	1	0	1	1	.50	0	.296	.384	.398
1996 Montreal	NL	152	393	109	20	5	7	(5	2)	160	54	56	49	4	61	11	9	5	5	2	.71	6	.277	.369	.407
2 ML YEARS		187	491	138	25	6	8	(6	2)	199	65	65	61	4	70	13	10	5	6	3	.67	6	.281	.372	.405

Benito Santiago

Bats: Right **Throws:** Right **Pos:** C-114; 1B-14; PH-12 **Ht:** 6'1" **Wt:** 185 **Born:** 3/9/65 **Age:** 32

		BATTING																		BASERUNNING				PERCENTAGES		
Year Team	Lg	G	AB	H	2B	3B	HR	(Hm	Rd)	TB	R	RBI	TBB	IBB	SO	HBP	SH	SF	SB	CS	SB%	GDP	Avg	OBP	SLG
1986 San Diego	NL	17	62	18	2	0	3	(2	1)	29	10	6	2	0	12	0	0	1	0	1	.00	0	.290	.308	.468
1987 San Diego	NL	146	546	164	33	2	18	(11	7)	255	64	79	16	2	112	5	1	4	21	12	.64	12	.300	.324	.467
1988 San Diego	NL	139	492	122	22	2	10	(3	7)	178	49	46	24	2	82	1	5	5	15	7	.68	18	.248	.282	.362
1989 San Diego	NL	129	462	109	16	3	16	(8	8)	179	50	62	26	6	89	1	3	2	11	6	.65	9	.236	.277	.387
1990 San Diego	NL	100	344	93	8	5	11	(5	6)	144	42	53	27	2	55	3	1	7	5	5	.50	4	.270	.323	.419
1991 San Diego	NL	152	580	155	22	3	17	(6	11)	234	60	87	23	5	114	4	0	7	8	10	.44	21	.267	.296	.403
1992 San Diego	NL	106	386	97	21	0	10	(8	2)	148	37	42	21	1	52	0	0	4	2	5	.29	14	.251	.287	.383
1993 Florida	NL	139	469	108	19	6	13	(6	7)	178	49	50	37	2	88	5	0	4	10	7	.59	9	.230	.291	.380
1994 Florida	NL	101	337	92	14	2	11	(4	7)	143	35	41	25	1	57	1	2	4	1	2	.33	11	.273	.322	.424
1995 Cincinnati	NL	81	266	76	20	0	11	(7	4)	129	40	44	24	1	48	4	0	2	2	2	.50	7	.286	.351	.485
1996 Philadelphia	NL	136	481	127	21	2	30	(8	22)	242	71	85	49	7	104	1	0	2	2	0	1.00	8	.264	.332	.503
11 ML YEARS		1246	4425	1161	198	25	150	(68	82)	1859	507	595	274	29	813	25	12	42	77	57	.57	113	.262	.306	.420

Rich Sauveur

Pitches: Left   **Bats:** Left   **Pos:** RP-3   **Ht:** 6'4"   **Wt:** 185   **Born:** 11/23/63   **Age:** 33

		HOW MUCH HE PITCHED						WHAT HE GAVE UP										THE RESULTS						
Year Team	Lg	G	GS	CG	GF	IP	BFP	H	R	ER	HR	SH	SF	HB	TBB	IBB	SO	WP	Bk	W	L	Pct.	ShO	Sv-Op	Hld	ERA
1996 Nashville *	AAA	61	3	0	20	73	311	63	34	30	8	2	3	3	28	4	69	3	0	4	3	.571	0	8--	—	3.70
1986 Pittsburgh	NL	3	3	0	0	12	57	17	8	8	3	1	0	2	6	0	6	0	2	0	0	.000	0	0--	—	6.00
1988 Montreal	NL	4	0	0	0	3	14	3	2	2	1	0	0	0	2	0	3	0	0	0	0	.000	0	0-0	1	6.00
1991 New York	NL	6	0	0	0	3.1	19	7	4	4	1	2	0	0	2	0	4	0	0	0	0	.000	0	0-2	2	10.80
1992 Kansas City	AL	8	0	0	2	14.1	65	15	7	7	1	0	0	2	8	1	7	0	1	0	1	.000	0	0-0	1	4.40
1996 Chicago	AL	3	0	0	0	3	15	3	5	5	1	0	0	1	5	0	1	0	0	0	0	.000	0	0-0	0	15.00
5 ML YEARS		24	3	0	2	35.2	170	45	26	26	7	3	0	5	23	1	21	0	3	0	1	.000	0	0--	—	6.56

Bob Scanlan

Pitches: Right   **Bats:** Right   **Pos:** RP-17   **Ht:** 6'8"   **Wt:** 215   **Born:** 8/9/66   **Age:** 30

		HOW MUCH HE PITCHED						WHAT HE GAVE UP										THE RESULTS						
Year Team	Lg	G	GS	CG	GF	IP	BFP	H	R	ER	HR	SH	SF	HB	TBB	IBB	SO	WP	Bk	W	L	Pct.	ShO	Sv-Op	Hld	ERA
1996 Lakeland *	A+	2	2	0	0	9	39	9	6	5	0	1	0	0	3	0	4	2	0	0	1	.000	0	0--	—	5.00
Toledo *	AAA	14	5	0	3	36	171	46	35	30	5	2	1	3	15	0	18	5	0	1	3	.250	0	0--	—	7.50
Omaha *	AAA	12	0	0	12	12.1	45	10	2	1	0	0	0	0	3	0	9	0	0	0	0	.000	0	5--	—	0.73
1991 Chicago	NL	40	13	0	16	111	482	114	60	48	5	8	6	3	40	3	44	5	1	7	8	.467	0	1-2	2	3.89
1992 Chicago	NL	69	0	0	41	87.1	360	76	32	28	4	4	2	1	30	6	42	6	4	3	6	.333	0	14-18	7	2.89
1993 Chicago	NL	70	0	0	13	75.1	323	79	41	38	6	2	6	3	28	7	44	0	2	4	5	.444	0	0-3	25	4.54
1994 Milwaukee	AL	30	12	0	9	103	441	117	53	47	11	1	2	4	28	2	65	3	1	2	6	.250	0	2-3	3	4.11
1995 Milwaukee	AL	17	14	0	1	83.1	389	101	66	61	9	0	6	7	44	3	29	3	0	4	7	.364	0	0-0	0	6.59
1996 Det-KC	AL	17	0	0	4	22.1	105	29	19	17	2	1	0	2	12	2	6	1	0	0	1	.000	0	0-1	5	6.85
1996 Detroit	AL	8	0	0	2	11	57	16	15	13	1	0	0	1	9	1	3	1	0	0	0	.000	0	0-0	0	10.64
Kansas City	AL	9	0	0	2	11.1	48	13	4	4	1	0	0	1	3	1	3	0	0	0	1	.000	0	0-1	5	3.18
6 ML YEARS		243	39	0	84	482.1	2100	516	271	239	37	16	22	20	182	23	230	18	8	20	33	.377	0	17-27	42	4.46

Steve Scarsone

Bats: R   **Throws:** R   **Pos:** 2B-74; PH-20; 3B-14; 1B-1; SS-1   **Ht:** 6'2"   **Wt:** 195   **Born:** 4/11/66   **Age:** 31

		BATTING																BASERUNNING				PERCENTAGES		
Year Team	Lg	G	AB	H	2B	3B	HR	(Hm	Rd)	TB	R	RBI	TBB	IBB	SO	HBP	SH	SF	SB	CS	SB%	GDP	Avg	OBP	SLG
1992 Phi-Bal		18	30	5	0	0	0	(0	0)	5	3	0	2	0	12	0	1	0	0	0	.00	0	.167	.219	.167
1993 San Francisco	NL	44	103	26	9	0	2	(1	1)	41	16	15	4	0	32	0	1	0	0	1	.00	4	.252	.278	.398
1994 San Francisco	NL	52	103	28	8	0	2	(0	2)	42	21	13	10	1	20	0	3	2	0	2	.00	1	.272	.330	.408
1995 San Francisco	NL	80	233	62	10	3	11	(7	4)	111	33	29	18	0	82	6	3	1	3	2	.60	2	.266	.333	.476
1996 San Francisco	NL	105	283	62	12	1	5	(4	1)	91	28	23	25	0	91	2	4	2	2	3	.40	6	.219	.286	.322
1992 Philadelphia	NL	7	13	2	0	0	0	(0	0)	2	1	0	1	0	6	0	0	0	0	0	.00	0	.154	.214	.154
Baltimore	AL	11	17	3	0	0	0	(0	0)	3	2	0	1	0	6	0	1	0	0	0	.00	0	.176	.222	.176
5 ML YEARS		299	752	183	39	4	20	(12	8)	290	101	80	59	1	237	8	19	5	5	8	.38	9	.243	.303	.386

Gene Schall

Bats: Right   **Throws:** Right   **Pos:** 1B-19; PH-10   **Ht:** 6'3"   **Wt:** 201   **Born:** 6/5/70   **Age:** 27

		BATTING																BASERUNNING				PERCENTAGES		
Year Team	Lg	G	AB	H	2B	3B	HR	(Hm	Rd)	TB	R	RBI	TBB	IBB	SO	HBP	SH	SF	SB	CS	SB%	GDP	Avg	OBP	SLG
1991 Batavia	A-	13	44	15	1	0	2	—	—	22	5	8	3	2	16	0	0	0	0	1	.00	1	.341	.383	.500
1992 Spartanburg	A	77	276	74	13	1	8	—	—	113	44	41	29	0	52	3	2	2	3	2	.60	8	.268	.342	.409
Clearwater	A+	40	133	33	4	2	4	—	—	53	16	19	14	0	29	4	1	3	1	2	.33	2	.248	.331	.398
1993 Reading	AA	82	285	93	12	4	15	—	—	158	51	60	24	0	56	10	0	3	2	1	.67	15	.326	.394	.554
Scranton-WB	AAA	40	139	33	6	1	4	—	—	53	16	16	19	1	38	7	1	1	4	2	.67	2	.237	.355	.381
1994 Scranton-WB	AAA	127	463	132	35	4	16	—	—	223	84	89	50	5	86	6	0	6	9	1	.90	11	.285	.358	.482
1995 Scranton-WB	AAA	92	320	100	25	4	12	—	—	169	52	63	49	2	54	10	0	4	3	3	.50	14	.313	.415	.528
1996 Scranton-WB	AAA	104	371	107	16	5	17	—	—	184	66	67	48	2	92	9	0	5	1	0	1.00	9	.288	.379	.496
1995 Philadelphia	NL	24	65	15	2	0	0	(0	0)	17	2	5	6	1	16	1	0	0	0	0	.00	0	.231	.306	.262
1996 Philadelphia	NL	28	66	18	5	1	2	(1	1)	31	7	10	12	0	15	1	0	0	0	0	.00	2	.273	.392	.470
2 ML YEARS		52	131	33	7	1	2	(1	1)	48	9	15	18	1	31	2	0	0	0	0	.00	3	.252	.351	.366

Curt Schilling

Pitches: Right   **Bats:** Right   **Pos:** SP-26   **Ht:** 6'4"   **Wt:** 226   **Born:** 11/14/66   **Age:** 30

		HOW MUCH HE PITCHED						WHAT HE GAVE UP										THE RESULTS						
Year Team	Lg	G	GS	CG	GF	IP	BFP	H	R	ER	HR	SH	SF	HB	TBB	IBB	SO	WP	Bk	W	L	Pct.	ShO	Sv-Op	Hld	ERA
1996 Clearwater *	A+	2	2	0	0	14	53	9	2	2	0	0	0	0	1	0	17	0	0	2	0	1.000	0	0--	—	1.29
Scrnton-WB *	AAA	2	2	0	0	13	50	9	2	2	0	0	0	0	5	0	10	1	0	2	0	1.000	0	0--	—	1.38
1988 Baltimore	AL	4	4	0	0	14.2	76	22	19	16	3	0	3	1	10	1	4	2	0	0	3	.000	0	0-0	0	9.82
1989 Baltimore	AL	5	1	0	0	8.2	38	10	6	6	2	0	0	0	3	0	6	1	0	0	0	.000	0	0-0	0	6.23
1990 Baltimore	AL	35	0	0	16	46	191	38	13	13	1	2	4	0	19	0	32	0	0	1	2	.333	0	3-9	5	2.54
1991 Houston	NL	56	0	0	34	75.2	336	79	35	32	2	5	1	0	39	7	71	4	1	3	5	.375	0	8-11	5	3.81
1992 Philadelphia	NL	42	26	10	10	226.1	895	165	67	59	11	7	8	1	59	4	147	4	0	14	11	.560	4	2-3	0	2.35
1993 Philadelphia	NL	34	34	7	0	235.1	982	234	114	105	23	4	7	4	57	6	186	9	3	16	7	.696	2	0-0	0	4.02

Year Team	Lg	G	GS	CG	GF	IP	BFP	H	R	ER	HR	SH	SF	HB	TBB	IBB	SO	WP	Bk	W	L	Pct.	ShO	Sv-Op	Hld	ERA
		HOW MUCH HE PITCHED						**WHAT HE GAVE UP**												**THE RESULTS**						
1994 Philadelphia	NL	13	13	1	0	82.1	360	87	42	41	10	6	1	3	28	3	58	3	1	2	8	.200	0	0-0	0	4.48
1995 Philadelphia	NL	17	17	1	0	116	473	96	52	46	12	5	2	3	26	2	114	0	1	7	5	.583	0	0-0	0	3.57
1996 Philadelphia	NL	26	26	8	0	183.1	732	149	69	65	16	6	4	3	50	5	182	5	0	9	10	.474	2	0-0	0	3.19
9 ML YEARS		232	121	27	60	988.1	4083	880	417	383	80	40	30	15	291	28	800	28	6	52	52	.500	8	13-23	10	3.49

Jason Schmidt

Pitches: Right **Bats:** Right **Pos:** SP-17; RP-2   **Ht:** 6'5" **Wt:** 185 **Born:** 1/29/73 **Age:** 24

Year Team	Lg	G	GS	CG	GF	IP	BFP	H	R	ER	HR	SH	SF	HB	TBB	IBB	SO	WP	Bk	W	L	Pct.	ShO	Sv-Op	Hld	ERA
		HOW MUCH HE PITCHED						**WHAT HE GAVE UP**												**THE RESULTS**						
1991 Braves	R	11	11	0	0	45.1	193	32	21	12	0	1	0	1	23	0	44	8	0	3	4	.429	0	0--	—	2.38
1992 Macon	A	7	7	0	0	24.2	119	31	18	11	2	0	1	1	19	0	33	2	2	0	3	.000	0	0--	—	4.01
Pulaski	R+	11	11	0	0	58.1	258	55	38	26	4	0	1	3	31	0	56	3	0	3	4	.429	0	0--	—	4.01
1993 Durham	A+	22	22	0	0	116.2	508	128	69	64	12	4	2	8	47	3	110	4	1	7	11	.389	0	0--	—	4.94
1994 Greenville	AA	24	24	1	0	140.2	599	135	64	57	9	6	2	8	54	1	131	4	1	8	7	.533	0	0--	—	3.65
1995 Richmond	AAA	19	19	0	0	116	484	97	40	29	2	15	1	3	48	3	95	4	1	8	6	.571	0	0--	—	2.25
1996 Greenville	AA	1	1	0	0	2	9	4	2	2	0	0	0	0	3	0	2	1	0	0	0	.000	0	0--	—	9.00
Richmond	AAA	7	7	0	0	45.2	184	36	17	13	2	1	0	0	19	1	41	4	0	3	0	1.000	0	0--	—	2.56
1995 Atlanta	NL	9	2	0	1	25	119	27	17	16	2	2	4	1	18	3	19	1	0	2	2	.500	0	0-1	0	5.76
1996 Atl-Pit	NL	19	17	1	0	96.1	445	108	67	61	10	4	9	2	53	0	74	8	1	5	6	.455	0	0-0	0	5.70
1996 Atlanta	NL	13	11	0	0	58.2	274	69	48	44	8	3	6	0	32	0	48	5	1	3	4	.429	0	0-0	0	6.75
Pittsburgh	NL	6	6	1	0	37.2	171	39	19	17	2	1	3	2	21	0	26	3	0	2	2	.500	0	0-0	0	4.06
2 ML YEARS		28	19	1	1	121.1	564	135	84	77	12	6	13	3	71	3	93	9	1	7	8	.467	0	0-1	0	5.71

Jeff Schmidt

Pitches: Right **Bats:** Right **Pos:** RP-9   **Ht:** 6'5" **Wt:** 205 **Born:** 2/21/71 **Age:** 26

Year Team	Lg	G	GS	CG	GF	IP	BFP	H	R	ER	HR	SH	SF	HB	TBB	IBB	SO	WP	Bk	W	L	Pct.	ShO	Sv-Op	Hld	ERA
		HOW MUCH HE PITCHED						**WHAT HE GAVE UP**												**THE RESULTS**						
1992 Boise	A-	11	11	0	0	52.1	236	55	41	26	4	1	0	4	18	1	41	3	4	1	6	.143	0	0--	—	4.47
1993 Cedar Rapids	A	26	25	3	0	152.1	696	166	105	83	16	9	6	16	58	3	107	11	4	3	14	.176	0	0--	—	4.90
1994 Lk Elsinore	A+	39	11	0	14	92	395	94	54	42	8	7	0	4	28	2	70	4	6	1	5	.167	0	12--	—	4.11
1995 Midland	AA	20	20	0	0	100.1	466	127	75	65	12	2	4	5	48	1	46	17	1	4	12	.250	0	0--	—	5.83
1996 Vancouver	AAA	35	0	0	30	37.2	164	29	12	12	0	2	4	2	25	0	19	7	1	0	1	.000	0	19--	—	2.87
1996 California	AL	9	0	0	1	8	42	13	9	7	2	0	1	0	8	0	2	1	0	2	0	1.000	0	0-0	—	7.88

Dick Schofield

Bats: Right **Throws:** Right **Pos:** SS-7; PH-4; 2B-2; 3B-1   **Ht:** 5'10" **Wt:** 179 **Born:** 11/21/62 **Age:** 34

Year Team	Lg	G	AB	H	2B	3B	HR	(Hm	Rd)	TB	R	RBI	TBB	IBB	SO	HBP	SH	SF	SB	CS	SB%	GDP	Avg	OBP	SLG
		BATTING																	**BASERUNNING**				**PERCENTAGES**		
1996 Lk Elsinore *	A+	2	4	1	0	0	0	(— | —)	1	1	0	1	0	1	1	0	0	0	1	0	.00	0	.250	.500	.250
1983 California	AL	21	54	11	2	0	3	(2 | 1)	22	4	4	6	0	8	1	1	0	0	0	0	.00	2	.204	.295	.407
1984 California	AL	140	400	77	10	3	4	(0	4)	105	39	21	33	0	79	6	13	0	5	2	.71	7	.193	.264	.263
1985 California	AL	147	438	96	19	3	8	(5	3)	145	50	41	35	0	70	8	12	3	11	4	.73	8	.219	.287	.331
1986 California	AL	139	458	114	17	6	13	(7	6)	182	67	57	48	2	55	5	9	9	23	5	.82	8	.249	.321	.397
1987 California	AL	134	479	120	17	3	9	(4	5)	170	52	46	37	0	63	2	10	3	19	3	.86	4	.251	.305	.355
1988 California	AL	155	527	126	11	6	6	(3	3)	167	61	34	40	0	57	9	11	2	20	5	.80	5	.239	.303	.317
1989 California	AL	91	302	69	11	2	4	(1	3)	96	42	26	28	0	47	3	11	2	9	3	.75	4	.228	.299	.318
1990 California	AL	99	310	79	8	1	1	(1	0)	92	41	18	52	3	61	2	13	2	3	4	.43	2	.255	.363	.297
1991 California	AL	134	427	96	9	3	0	(0	0)	111	44	31	50	2	69	3	7	0	8	4	.67	3	.225	.310	.260
1992 Cal-NYN		143	423	87	18	2	4	(3	1)	121	52	36	61	4	82	5	10	3	11	4	.73	11	.206	.311	.286
1993 Toronto	AL	36	110	21	1	2	0	(0	0)	26	11	5	16	0	25	0	2	0	3	0	1.00	1	.191	.294	.236
1994 Toronto	AL	95	325	83	14	1	4	(2	2)	111	38	32	34	0	62	4	8	2	7	7	.50	2	.255	.332	.342
1995 LA-Cal		21	30	6	0	0	0	(0	0)	6	1	2	5	0	5	0	2	0	0	0	.00	1	.200	.314	.200
1996 California	AL	13	16	4	0	0	0	(0	0)	4	3	0	1	0	1	0	0	0	1	0	1.00	0	.250	.294	.250
1992 California	AL	1	3	1	0	0	0	(0	0)	1	0	0	1	0	0	0	0	0	0	0	.00	0	.333	.500	.333
New York	NL	142	420	86	18	2	4	(3	1)	120	52	36	60	4	82	5	10	3	11	4	.73	11	.205	.309	.286
1995 Los Angeles	NL	9	10	1	0	0	0	(0	0)	1	0	0	1	0	3	0	0	0	0	0	.00	0	.100	.182	.100
California	AL	12	20	5	0	0	0	(0	0)	5	1	2	4	0	2	0	2	0	0	0	.00	1	.250	.375	.250
14 ML YEARS		1368	4299	989	137	32	56	(28	28)	1358	505	353	446	11	684	48	109	26	120	41	.75	59	.230	.308	.316

Pete Schourek

Pitches: Left **Bats:** Left **Pos:** SP-12   **Ht:** 6'5" **Wt:** 205 **Born:** 5/10/69 **Age:** 28

Year Team	Lg	G	GS	CG	GF	IP	BFP	H	R	ER	HR	SH	SF	HB	TBB	IBB	SO	WP	Bk	W	L	Pct.	ShO	Sv-Op	Hld	ERA
		HOW MUCH HE PITCHED						**WHAT HE GAVE UP**												**THE RESULTS**						
1991 New York	NL	35	8	1	7	86.1	385	82	49	41	7	4	4	2	43	4	67	1	0	5	4	.556	1	2-3	3	4.27
1992 New York	NL	22	21	0	0	136	578	137	60	55	9	4	4	2	44	6	60	4	2	6	8	.429	0	0-0	0	3.64
1993 New York	NL	41	18	0	6	128.1	586	168	90	85	13	3	8	3	45	7	72	1	2	5	12	.294	0	0-1	2	5.96
1994 Cincinnati	NL	22	10	0	3	81.1	354	90	39	37	11	6	2	3	29	4	69	0	0	7	2	.778	0	0-0	0	4.09
1995 Cincinnati	NL	29	29	2	0	190.1	754	158	72	68	17	4	4	8	45	3	160	1	1	18	7	.720	0	0-0	0	3.22
1996 Cincinnati	NL	12	12	0	0	67.1	304	79	48	45	7	3	4	3	24	1	54	3	0	4	5	.444	0	0-0	0	6.01

	HOW MUCH HE PITCHED						WHAT HE GAVE UP											THE RESULTS					
Year Team	Lg	G	GS	CG	GF	IP	BFP	H	R	ER	HR	SH	SF	HB	TBB	IBB	SO	WP	Bk	W	L	Pct.	ShO	Sv-Op	Hld	ERA
6 ML YEARS		161	98	3	16	689.2	2961	714	358	331	64	25	26	21	230	25	482	10	5	45	38	.542	1	2-4	5	4.32

Rick Schu

Bats: Right **Throws:** Right **Pos:** 3B-1   **Ht:** 6'0" **Wt:** 190 **Born:** 1/26/62 **Age:** 35

								BATTING											BASERUNNING				PERCENTAGES		
Year Team	Lg	G	AB	H	2B	3B	HR	(Hm	Rd)	TB	R	RBI	TBB	IBB	SO	HBP	SH	SF	SB	CS	SB%	GDP	Avg	OBP	SLG
1996 Ottawa *	AAA	116	395	107	24	3	12	—	—	173	48	54	41	5	51	9	0	4	9	3	.75	5	.271	.350	.438
1984 Philadelphia	NL	17	29	8	2	1	2	(1	1)	18	12	5	6	0	6	0	0	1	0	0	.00	0	.276	.389	.621
1985 Philadelphia	NL	112	416	105	21	4	7	(2	5)	155	54	24	38	3	78	2	1	0	8	6	.57	7	.252	.318	.373
1986 Philadelphia	NL	92	208	57	10	1	8	(1	7)	93	32	25	18	1	44	2	3	2	2	2	.50	1	.274	.335	.447
1987 Philadelphia	NL	92	196	46	6	3	7	(5	2)	79	24	23	20	1	36	2	0	1	0	2	.00	1	.235	.311	.403
1988 Baltimore	AL	89	270	69	9	4	4	(2	2)	98	22	20	21	0	49	3	0	0	6	4	.60	7	.256	.316	.363
1989 Bal-Det	AL	99	266	57	11	0	7	(3	4)	89	25	21	24	0	37	0	2	1	1	2	.33	6	.214	.278	.335
1990 California	AL	61	157	42	8	0	6	(3	3)	68	19	14	11	0	25	0	0	1	0	0	.00	4	.268	.314	.433
1991 Philadelphia	NL	17	22	2	0	0	0	(0	0)	2	1	2	1	0	7	0	0	1	0	0	.00	1	.091	.125	.091
1996 Montreal	NL	1	4	0	0	0	0	(0	0)	0	0	0	0	0	0	0	0	0	0	0	.00	0	.000	.000	.000
1989 Baltimore	AL	1	0	0	0	0	0	(0	0)	0	0	0	0	0	0	0	0	0	0	0	.00	0	.000	.000	.000
Detroit	AL	98	266	57	11	0	7	(3	4)	89	25	21	24	0	37	0	2	1	1	2	.33	6	.214	.278	.335
9 ML YEARS		580	1568	386	67	13	41	(17	24)	602	189	134	139	5	282	9	6	7	17	16	.52	27	.246	.310	.384

Carl Schutz

Pitches: Left **Bats:** Left **Pos:** RP-3   **Ht:** 5'11" **Wt:** 200 **Born:** 8/22/71 **Age:** 25

	HOW MUCH HE PITCHED						WHAT HE GAVE UP											THE RESULTS					
Year Team	Lg	G	GS	CG	GF	IP	BFP	H	R	ER	HR	SH	SF	HB	TBB	IBB	SO	WP	Bk	W	L	Pct.	ShO	Sv-Op	Hld	ERA
1993 Danville	R+	13	0	0	9	14.2	57	6	1	1	0	1	0	0	6	0	25	1	0	1	0	1.000	0	4-	—	0.61
Greenville	AA	22	0	0	16	21.1	101	17	17	12	3	2	3	1	22	1	19	2	0	2	1	.667	0	3-	—	5.06
1994 Durham	A+	53	0	0	47	53.1	240	35	30	29	6	4	1	2	46	1	81	10	0	3	3	.500	0	20-	—	4.89
1995 Greenville	AA	51	0	0	46	58.1	258	53	36	32	4	2	2	1	36	3	56	3	0	3	7	.300	0	26-	—	4.94
1996 Richmond	AAA	41	7	0	13	69.2	320	86	46	41	4	7	4	0	26	3	52	8	0	4	3	.571	0	3-	—	5.30
1996 Atlanta	NL	3	0	0	1	3.1	13	3	1	1	0	0	0	0	2	1	5	0	0	0	0	.000	0	0-0	0	2.70

Tim Scott

Pitches: Right **Bats:** Right **Pos:** RP-65   **Ht:** 6'2" **Wt:** 205 **Born:** 11/16/66 **Age:** 30

	HOW MUCH HE PITCHED						WHAT HE GAVE UP											THE RESULTS					
Year Team	Lg	G	GS	CG	GF	IP	BFP	H	R	ER	HR	SH	SF	HB	TBB	IBB	SO	WP	Bk	W	L	Pct.	ShO	Sv-Op	Hld	ERA
1991 San Diego	NL	2	0	0	0	1	5	2	2	1	0	0	0	0	0	0	1	0	0	0	0	.000	0	0-0	0	9.00
1992 San Diego	NL	34	0	0	16	37.2	173	39	24	22	4	4	1	1	21	6	30	0	1	4	1	.800	0	0-1	4	5.26
1993 SD-Mon	NL	56	0	0	18	71.2	317	69	28	24	4	3	2	4	34	2	65	2	1	7	2	.778	0	1-4	3	3.01
1994 Montreal	NL	40	0	0	8	53.1	223	51	17	16	0	0	0	2	18	3	37	1	1	5	2	.714	0	1-1	7	2.70
1995 Montreal	NL	62	0	0	15	63.1	268	52	30	28	6	4	1	6	23	2	57	4	0	2	0	1.000	0	2-5	19	3.98
1996 Mon-SF	NL	65	0	0	16	66	288	65	36	34	8	4	3	3	30	2	47	3	0	5	7	.417	0	1-5	10	4.64
1993 San Diego	NL	24	0	0	2	37.2	169	38	13	10	1	2	2	4	15	0	30	1	1	2	0	1.000	0	0-2	0	2.39
Montreal	NL	32	0	0	16	34	148	31	15	14	3	1	0	0	19	2	35	1	0	5	2	.714	0	1-2	3	3.71
1996 Montreal	NL	45	0	0	14	46.1	198	41	18	16	3	1	2	2	21	2	37	1	0	3	5	.375	0	1-3	8	3.11
San Francisco	NL	20	0	0	2	19.2	90	24	18	18	5	3	1	1	9	0	10	2	0	2	2	.500	0	0-2	2	8.24
6 ML YEARS		259	0	0	73	293	1274	278	137	125	22	15	7	16	126	15	237	10	3	23	12	.657	0	5-16	43	3.84

Kevin Sefcik

Bats: R **Throws:** R **Pos:** SS-21; 3B-20; PH-5; 2B-1   **Ht:** 5'10" **Wt:** 175 **Born:** 2/10/71 **Age:** 26

								BATTING											BASERUNNING				PERCENTAGES		
Year Team	Lg	G	AB	H	2B	3B	HR	(Hm	Rd)	TB	R	RBI	TBB	IBB	SO	HBP	SH	SF	SB	CS	SB%	GDP	Avg	OBP	SLG
1993 Batavia	A-	74	281	84	24	4	2	—	—	122	49	28	27	2	22	3	7	5	20	7	.74	5	.299	.361	.434
1994 Clearwater	A+	130	516	147	29	8	2	—	—	198	83	46	49	2	43	7	4	6	30	13	.70	7	.285	.351	.384
1995 Scranton-WB	AAA	7	26	9	6	1	0	—	—	17	5	6	3	0	1	0	0	1	1	0	.00	1	.346	.400	.654
Reading	AA	128	508	138	18	4	4	—	—	176	68	46	38	0	48	12	3	3	14	11	.56	5	.272	.335	.346
1996 Scranton-WB	AAA	45	180	60	7	5	0	—	—	77	34	19	15	0	20	3	3	2	11	3	.79	4	.333	.390	.428
1995 Philadelphia	NL	5	4	0	0	0	0	(0	0)	0	1	0	0	0	2	0	0	0	0	0	.00	0	.000	.000	.000
1996 Philadelphia	NL	44	116	33	5	3	0	(0	0)	44	10	9	9	3	16	2	1	2	3	0	1.00	4	.284	.341	.379
2 ML YEARS		49	120	33	5	3	0	(0	0)	44	11	9	9	3	18	2	1	2	3	0	1.00	4	.275	.331	.367

David Segui

Bats: Both **Throws:** Left **Pos:** 1B-114; PH-1   **Ht:** 6'1" **Wt:** 202 **Born:** 7/19/66 **Age:** 30

								BATTING											BASERUNNING				PERCENTAGES		
Year Team	Lg	G	AB	H	2B	3B	HR	(Hm	Rd)	TB	R	RBI	TBB	IBB	SO	HBP	SH	SF	SB	CS	SB%	GDP	Avg	OBP	SLG
1990 Baltimore	AL	40	123	30	7	0	2	(1	1)	43	14	15	11	2	15	1	1	0	0	0	.00	12	.244	.311	.350
1991 Baltimore	AL	86	212	59	7	0	2	(1	1)	72	15	22	12	2	19	0	3	1	1	1	.50	7	.278	.316	.340
1992 Baltimore	AL	115	189	44	9	0	1	(1	0)	56	21	17	20	3	23	0	2	0	1	0	1.00	4	.233	.306	.296
1993 Baltimore	AL	146	450	123	27	0	10	(6	4)	180	54	60	58	4	53	0	3	8	2	1	.67	18	.273	.351	.400

201

Year Team	Lg	G	AB	H	2B	3B	HR	(Hm	Rd)	TB	R	RBI	TBB	IBB	SO	HBP	SH	SF	SB	CS	SB%	GDP	Avg	OBP	SLG
																							BATTING / BASERUNNING / PERCENTAGES		
1994 New York	NL	92	336	81	17	1	10	(5	5)	130	46	43	33	6	43	1	1	3	0	0	.00	6	.241	.308	.387
1995 NYN-Mon	NL	130	456	141	25	4	12	(6	6)	210	68	58	40	5	47	3	8	3	2	7	.22	10	.309	.367	.461
1996 Montreal	NL	115	416	119	30	1	11	(6	5)	184	69	58	60	4	54	0	0	1	4	4	.50	8	.286	.375	.442
1995 New York	NL	33	73	24	3	1	2	(2	0)	35	9	11	12	1	9	1	4	2	1	3	.25	2	.329	.420	.479
Montreal	NL	97	383	117	22	3	10	(4	6)	175	59	57	28	4	38	2	4	1	1	4	.20	8	.305	.355	.457
7 ML YEARS		724	2182	597	122	6	48	(26	22)	875	287	283	234	26	254	5	18	16	10	13	.43	65	.274	.343	.401

Kevin Seitzer

Bats: R Throws: R Pos: DH-73; 1B-70; 3B-12; PH-4   Ht: 5'11" Wt: 193 Born: 3/26/62 Age: 35

Year Team	Lg	G	AB	H	2B	3B	HR	(Hm	Rd)	TB	R	RBI	TBB	IBB	SO	HBP	SH	SF	SB	CS	SB%	GDP	Avg	OBP	SLG
1986 Kansas City	AL	28	96	31	4	1	2	(1	1)	43	16	11	19	0	14	1	0	0	0	0	.00	0	.323	.440	.448
1987 Kansas City	AL	161	641	207	33	8	15	(7	8)	301	105	83	80	0	85	2	1	1	12	7	.63	18	.323	.399	.470
1988 Kansas City	AL	149	559	170	32	5	5	(4	1)	227	90	60	72	4	64	6	3	3	10	8	.56	15	.304	.388	.406
1989 Kansas City	AL	160	597	168	17	2	4	(2	2)	201	78	48	102	7	76	5	4	1	17	8	.68	16	.281	.387	.337
1990 Kansas City	AL	158	622	171	31	5	6	(5	1)	230	91	38	67	2	66	2	4	7	7	5	.58	11	.275	.346	.370
1991 Kansas City	AL	85	234	62	11	3	1	(0	1)	82	28	25	29	3	21	2	1	1	4	1	.80	4	.265	.350	.350
1992 Milwaukee	AL	148	540	146	35	1	5	(2	3)	198	74	71	57	4	44	2	7	9	13	11	.54	14	.270	.337	.367
1993 Oak-Mil	AL	120	417	112	16	2	11	(6	5)	165	45	57	44	1	48	2	3	5	7	7	.50	14	.269	.338	.396
1994 Milwaukee	AL	80	309	97	24	2	5	(4	1)	140	44	49	30	1	38	2	4	3	2	1	.67	7	.314	.375	.453
1995 Milwaukee	AL	132	492	153	33	3	5	(1	4)	207	56	69	64	2	57	6	5	3	2	0	1.00	13	.311	.395	.421
1996 Mil-Cle	AL	154	573	187	35	3	13	(5	8)	267	85	78	87	7	79	5	5	5	6	1	.86	13	.326	.416	.466
1993 Oakland	AL	73	255	65	10	2	4	(2	2)	91	24	27	27	1	33	1	2	4	4	7	.36	7	.255	.324	.457
Milwaukee	AL	47	162	47	6	0	7	(4	3)	74	21	30	17	0	15	1	1	1	3	0	1.00	7	.290	.359	.457
1996 Milwaukee	AL	132	490	155	25	3	12	(5	7)	222	74	62	73	6	68	4	5	5	6	1	.86	11	.316	.406	.453
Cleveland	AL	22	83	32	10	0	1	(0	1)	45	11	16	14	1	11	1	0	0	0	0	.00	2	.386	.480	.542
11 ML YEARS		1375	5080	1504	271	35	72	(37	35)	2061	712	589	651	31	592	35	37	39	80	49	.62	127	.296	.377	.406

Bill Selby

Bats: L Throws: R Pos: 2B-14; 3B-14; PH-13; LF-6; DH-1   Ht: 5'9" Wt: 190 Born: 6/11/70 Age: 27

Year Team	Lg	G	AB	H	2B	3B	HR	(Hm	Rd)	TB	R	RBI	TBB	IBB	SO	HBP	SH	SF	SB	CS	SB%	GDP	Avg	OBP	SLG
1992 Elmira	A-	73	275	72	16	1	10	(—	—)	120	38	41	31	6	53	2	2	2	4	4	.50	3	.262	.339	.436
1993 Lynchburg	A+	113	394	99	22	1	7	(—	—)	144	57	38	24	2	66	3	2	7	1	2	.33	6	.251	.294	.365
1994 Lynchburg	A+	97	352	109	20	2	19	(—	—)	190	58	69	28	0	62	5	2	2	1		.75	7	.310	.367	.540
New Britain	AA	35	107	28	5	0	1	(—	—)	36	15	18	15	0	16	0	0	6	0	1	.00	2	.262	.336	.336
1995 Trenton	AA	117	451	129	29	2	13	(—	—)	201	64	68	46	3	52	3	2	8	4	6	.40	14	.286	.350	.446
1996 Pawtucket	AAA	71	260	66	14	5	11	(—	—)	123	39	47	22	0	39	2	0	4	3		.00	5	.254	.313	.473
1996 Boston	AL	40	95	26	4	0	3	(0	3)	39	12	6	9	1	11	0	1	0	1	1	.50	3	.274	.337	.411

Aaron Sele

Pitches: Right Bats: Right Pos: SP-29   Ht: 6'5" Wt: 215 Born: 6/25/70 Age: 27

Year Team	Lg	G	GS	CG	GF	IP	BFP	H	R	ER	HR	SH	SF	HB	TBB	IBB	SO	WP	Bk	W	L	Pct.	ShO	Sv-Op	Hld	ERA
1996 Pawtucket *	AAA	1	1	0	0	3	13	3	2	2	0	0	0	0	1	0	4	0	0	0	0	.000	0	0--	—	6.00
1993 Boston	AL	18	18	0	0	111.2	484	100	42	34	5	2	5	7	48	2	93	5	0	7	2	.778	0	0-0	0	2.74
1994 Boston	AL	22	22	2	0	143.1	615	140	68	61	13	4	5	9	60	2	105	4	0	8	7	.533	0	0-0	0	3.83
1995 Boston	AL	6	6	0	0	32.1	146	32	14	11	3	1	1	3	14	0	21	3	0	3	1	.750	0	0-0	0	3.06
1996 Boston	AL	29	29	1	0	157.1	722	192	110	93	14	6	7	8	67	2	137	2	0	7	11	.389	0	0-0	0	5.32
4 ML YEARS		75	75	3	0	444.2	1967	464	234	199	35	13	18	27	189	6	356	14	0	25	21	.543	0	0-0		4.03

Dan Serafini

Pitches: Left Bats: Both Pos: SP-1   Ht: 6'1" Wt: 180 Born: 1/25/74 Age: 23

Year Team	Lg	G	GS	CG	GF	IP	BFP	H	R	ER	HR	SH	SF	HB	TBB	IBB	SO	WP	Bk	W	L	Pct.	ShO	Sv-Op	Hld	ERA
1992 Twins	R	8	6	0	0	29.2	130	27	16	12	0	1	1	1	15	0	33	3	1	1	0	1.000	0	0--	—	3.64
1993 Fort Wayne	A	27	27	1	0	140.2	606	117	72	57	5	2	2	6	83	0	147	12	2	10	8	.556	1	0--	—	3.65
1994 Fort Myers	A+	23	23	2	0	136.2	600	149	84	70	11	7	5	6	57	1	130	7	1	9	9	.500	1	0--	—	4.61
1995 Salt Lake	AAA	1	0	0	1	4	17	4	3	3	2	0	0	0	1	0	4	0	0	0	0	.000	0	1--	—	6.75
1996 Salt Lake	AAA	25	23	1	1	130.2	588	164	84	81	20	5	6	2	58	1	109	9	2	7	7	.500	0	0--	—	5.58
1996 Minnesota	AL	1	1	0	0	4.1	23	7	5	5	1	2	0	1	2	0	1	0	0	0	1	.000	0	0-0	0	10.38

Scott Servais

Bats: Right Throws: Right Pos: C-128; PH-3; 1B-1   Ht: 6'2" Wt: 205 Born: 6/4/67 Age: 30

Year Team	Lg	G	AB	H	2B	3B	HR	(Hm	Rd)	TB	R	RBI	TBB	IBB	SO	HBP	SH	SF	SB	CS	SB%	GDP	Avg	OBP	SLG
1991 Houston	NL	16	37	6	3	0	0	(0	0)	9	0	6	4	0	8	0	1	0	0	0	.00	0	.162	.244	.243
1992 Houston	NL	77	205	49	9	0	0	(0	0)	58	12	15	11	2	25	5	6	0	0	0	.00	7	.239	.294	.283

Year Team	Lg	G	AB	H	2B	3B	HR	(Hm	Rd)	TB	R	RBI	TBB	IBB	SO	HBP	SH	SF	SB	CS	SB%	GDP	Avg	OBP	SLG
1993 Houston	NL	85	258	63	11	0	11	(5	6)	107	24	32	22	2	45	5	3	3	0	0	.00	6	.244	.313	.415
1994 Houston	NL	78	251	49	15	1	9	(3	6)	93	27	41	10	0	44	4	7	3	0	0	.00	6	.195	.235	.371
1995 Hou-ChN	NL	80	264	70	22	0	13	(8	5)	131	38	47	32	8	52	3	2	3	2	2	.50	9	.265	.348	.496
1996 Chicago	NL	129	445	118	20	0	11	(6	5)	171	42	63	30	1	75	14	3	7	0	2	.00	18	.265	.327	.384
1995 Houston	NL	28	89	20	10	0	1	(1	0)	33	7	12	9	2	15	1	1	1	0	1	.00	4	.225	.300	.371
Chicago	NL	52	175	50	12	0	12	(7	5)	98	31	35	23	6	37	2	1	2	2	1	.67	5	.286	.371	.560
6 ML YEARS		465	1460	355	80	1	44	(22	22)	569	143	204	109	13	249	31	22	16	2	4	.33	46	.243	.306	.390

Scott Service

Pitches: Right **Bats:** Right **Pos:** RP-33; SP-1 **Ht:** 6'6" **Wt:** 226 **Born:** 2/26/67 **Age:** 30

Year Team	Lg	G	GS	CG	GF	IP	BFP	H	R	ER	HR	SH	SF	HB	TBB	IBB	SO	WP	Bk	W	L	Pct.	ShO	Sv-Op	Hld	ERA
1996 Indianapols *	AAA	35	1	0	26	48	193	34	18	16	5	2	1	1	10	2	58	2	0	1	4	.200	0	15--	—	3.00
1988 Philadelphia	NL	5	0	0	1	5.1	23	7	1	1	0	0	0	1	1	0	6	0	0	0	0	.000	0	0-0	0	1.69
1992 Montreal	NL	5	0	0	0	7	41	15	11	11	1	0	0	0	5	0	11	0	0	0	0	.000	0	0-0	1	14.14
1993 Col-Cin	NL	29	0	0	7	46	197	44	24	22	6	2	4	2	16	4	43	0	0	2	2	.500	0	2-2	3	4.30
1994 Cincinnati	NL	6	0	0	2	7.1	35	8	9	6	2	2	0	0	3	0	5	0	0	1	2	.333	0	0-0	7	7.36
1995 San Francisco	NL	28	0	0	6	31	129	18	11	11	4	3	2	2	20	4	30	3	0	3	1	.750	0	0-0	7	3.19
1996 Cincinnati	NL	34	1	0	5	48	213	51	21	21	7	4	1	6	18	4	46	5	0	1	0	1.000	0	0-0	3	3.94
1993 Colorado	NL	3	0	0	0	4.2	24	8	5	5	1	0	2	1	1	0	3	0	0	0	0	.000	0	0-0	0	9.64
Cincinnati	NL	26	0	0	7	41.1	173	36	19	17	5	2	2	1	15	4	40	0	0	2	2	.500	0	2-2	3	3.70
6 ML YEARS		107	1	0	21	144.2	638	143	77	72	20	11	7	11	63	12	141	8	0	7	5	.583	0	2-2	14	4.48

Jeff Shaw

Pitches: Right **Bats:** Right **Pos:** RP-78 **Ht:** 6'2" **Wt:** 200 **Born:** 7/7/66 **Age:** 30

Year Team	Lg	G	GS	CG	GF	IP	BFP	H	R	ER	HR	SH	SF	HB	TBB	IBB	SO	WP	Bk	W	L	Pct.	ShO	Sv-Op	Hld	ERA
1990 Cleveland	AL	12	9	0	0	48.2	219	73	38	36	11	1	3	0	20	0	25	3	0	3	4	.429	0	0-0	0	6.66
1991 Cleveland	AL	29	1	0	9	72.1	311	72	34	27	6	1	4	4	27	5	31	6	0	0	5	.000	0	1-4	0	3.36
1992 Cleveland	AL	2	1	0	1	7.2	33	7	7	7	2	2	0	0	4	0	3	0	0	0	1	.000	0	0-0	0	8.22
1993 Montreal	NL	55	8	0	13	95.2	404	91	44	44	12	5	2	7	32	2	50	2	0	2	7	.222	0	0-1	4	4.14
1994 Montreal	NL	46	0	0	15	67.1	287	67	32	29	8	2	4	2	15	2	47	5	0	5	2	.714	0	1-2	10	3.88
1995 Mon-ChA	NL	59	0	0	18	72	309	70	42	39	6	7	1	4	27	4	51	0	0	1	6	.143	0	3-5	6	4.88
1996 Cincinnati	NL	78	0	0	24	104.2	434	99	34	29	8	5	5	2	29	11	69	0	0	8	6	.571	0	4-11	22	2.49
1995 Montreal	NL	50	0	0	17	62.1	268	58	35	32	4	6	1	3	26	4	45	0	0	1	6	.143	0	3-5	5	4.62
Chicago	AL	9	0	0	1	9.2	41	12	7	7	2	1	0	1	1	0	6	0	0	0	0	.000	0	0-0	1	6.52
7 ML YEARS		281	19	0	80	468.1	2007	479	234	211	53	23	19	19	154	24	276	16	0	19	31	.380	0	9-23	42	4.05

Danny Sheaffer

Bats: R **Throws:** R **Pos:** C-47; PH-21; 3B-17; 1B-6; LF-3 **Ht:** 6'0" **Wt:** 195 **Born:** 8/2/61 **Age:** 35

Year Team	Lg	G	AB	H	2B	3B	HR	(Hm	Rd)	TB	R	RBI	TBB	IBB	SO	HBP	SH	SF	SB	CS	SB%	GDP	Avg	OBP	SLG
1987 Boston	AL	25	66	8	1	0	1	(0	1)	12	5	5	0	0	14	0	1	1	0	0	.00	2	.121	.119	.182
1989 Cleveland	AL	7	16	1	0	0	0	(0	0)	1	1	0	2	0	2	0	0	1	0	0	.00	0	.063	.167	.063
1993 Colorado	NL	82	216	60	9	1	4	(2	2)	83	26	32	8	0	15	1	2	6	2	3	.40	9	.278	.299	.384
1994 Colorado	NL	44	110	24	4	0	1	(0	1)	31	11	12	10	0	11	0	0	0	2	2	.00	2	.218	.283	.282
1995 St. Louis	NL	76	208	48	10	1	5	(2	3)	75	24	30	23	2	38	0	0	1	0	0	.00	8	.231	.306	.361
1996 St. Louis	NL	79	198	45	9	3	2	(1	1)	66	10	20	9	0	25	3	4	0	3	3	.50	13	.227	.271	.333
6 ML YEARS		313	814	186	33	5	13	(5	8)	268	77	99	52	2	105	4	8	8	5	8	.38	34	.229	.276	.329

Andy Sheets

Bats: R **Throws:** R **Pos:** 3B-25; 2B-18; SS-7; PH-7 **Ht:** 6'2" **Wt:** 180 **Born:** 11/19/71 **Age:** 25

Year Team	Lg	G	AB	H	2B	3B	HR	(Hm	Rd)	TB	R	RBI	TBB	IBB	SO	HBP	SH	SF	SB	CS	SB%	GDP	Avg	OBP	SLG
1993 Riverside	A+	52	176	34	9	1	1	—	—	48	23	12	17	1	51	0	6	4	2	2	.50	4	.193	.259	.273
Appleton	A	69	259	68	10	4	1	—	—	89	32	25	20	1	59	3	4	2	7	7	.50	3	.263	.320	.344
1994 Riverside	A+	31	100	27	5	1	2	—	—	40	17	10	16	0	22	0	1	0	6	1	.86	1	.270	.371	.400
Calgary	AAA	26	93	32	8	1	2	—	—	48	22	16	11	0	20	1	0	1	1	1	.50	7	.344	.415	.516
Jacksonvlle	AA	70	232	51	12	0	0	—	—	63	26	17	20	0	54	2	6	1	3	5	.38	4	.220	.286	.272
1995 Tacoma	AAA	132	437	128	29	9	2	—	—	181	57	47	32	2	83	0	10	4	8	3	.73	9	.293	.338	.414
1996 Tacoma	AAA	62	232	83	16	5	5	—	—	124	44	33	25	0	56	0	0	3	6	4	.60	6	.358	.415	.534
1996 Seattle	AL	47	110	21	8	0	0	(0	0)	29	18	9	10	0	41	1	2	1	2	0	1.00	2	.191	.262	.264

Gary Sheffield

Bats: Right **Throws:** Right **Pos:** RF-161; PH-1 **Ht:** 5'11" **Wt:** 190 **Born:** 11/18/68 **Age:** 28

Year Team	Lg	G	AB	H	2B	3B	HR	(Hm	Rd)	TB	R	RBI	TBB	IBB	SO	HBP	SH	SF	SB	CS	SB%	GDP	Avg	OBP	SLG
1988 Milwaukee	AL	24	80	19	1	0	4	(1	3)	32	12	12	7	0	7	0	1	1	3	1	.75	5	.238	.295	.400

Year Team	Lg	G	AB	H	2B	3B	HR	(Hm	Rd)	TB	R	RBI	TBB	IBB	SO	HBP	SH	SF	SB	CS	SB%	GDP	Avg	OBP	SLG
						BATTING														**BASERUNNING**				**PERCENTAGES**		
1989 Milwaukee	AL	95	368	91	18	0	5	(2	3)	124	34	32	27	0	33	4	3	3	10	6	.63	4	.247	.303	.337
1990 Milwaukee	AL	125	487	143	30	1	10	(3	7)	205	67	67	44	1	41	3	4	9	25	10	.71	11	.294	.350	.421
1991 Milwaukee	AL	50	175	34	12	2	2	(2	0)	56	25	22	19	1	15	3	1	5	5	5	.50	3	.194	.277	.320
1992 San Diego	NL	146	557	184	34	3	33	(23	10)	323	87	100	48	5	40	6	0	7	5	5	.45	19	.330	.385	.580
1993 SD-Fla	NL	140	494	145	20	5	20	(10	10)	235	67	73	47	6	64	9	0	5	17	5	.77	11	.294	.361	.476
1994 Florida	NL	87	322	89	16	1	27	(15	12)	188	61	78	51	11	50	6	0	5	12	6	.67	10	.276	.380	.584
1995 Florida	NL	63	213	69	8	0	16	(4	12)	125	46	46	55	8	45	4	0	2	19	4	.83	3	.324	.467	.587
1996 Florida	NL	161	519	163	33	1	42	(19	23)	324	118	120	142	19	66	10	0	6	16	9	.64	16	.314	.465	.624
1993 San Diego	NL	68	258	76	12	2	10	(6	4)	122	34	36	18	0	30	3	0	3	5	1	.83	9	.295	.344	.473
Florida	NL	72	236	69	8	3	10	(4	6)	113	33	37	29	6	34	6	0	4	12	4	.75	2	.292	.378	.479
9 ML YEARS		891	3215	937	172	13	159	(79	80)	1612	517	550	440	51	361	45	9	45	112	52	.68	82	.291	.380	.501

Keith Shepherd

Pitches: Right **Bats:** Right **Pos:** RP-13   **Ht:** 6'2" **Wt:** 215 **Born:** 1/21/68 **Age:** 29

Year Team	Lg	G	GS	CG	GF	IP	BFP	H	R	ER	HR	SH	SF	HB	TBB	IBB	SO	WP	Bk	W	L	Pct.	ShO	Sv-Op	Hld	ERA
			HOW MUCH HE PITCHED								**WHAT HE GAVE UP**											**THE RESULTS**				
1996 Rochester *	AAA	27	11	2	15	94.1	414	91	54	42	12	2	4	4	37	0	98	5	0	4	7	.364	0	9--	—	4.01
1992 Philadelphia	NL	12	0	0	6	22	91	19	10	8	0	4	3	0	6	1	10	1	0	1	1	.500	0	2-6	0	3.27
1993 Colorado	NL	14	1	0	3	19.1	85	26	16	15	4	1	1	1	4	0	7	1	0	1	3	.250	0	1-2	2	6.98
1995 Boston	AL	2	0	0	0	1	9	4	4	4	0	0	0	0	2	0	0	0	0	0	0	.000	0	0-0	0	36.00
1996 Baltimore	AL	13	0	0	6	20.2	111	31	27	20	6	1	1	0	18	1	17	0	0	0	0	.000	0	0-0	2	8.71
4 ML YEARS		41	1	0	15	63	296	80	57	47	10	6	5	1	30	2	34	2	0	2	5	.286	0	3-8	4	6.71

Craig Shipley

Bats: R **Throws:** R **Pos:** 2B-17; SS-7; PH-7; 3B-4; RF-3   **Ht:** 6'1" **Wt:** 190 **Born:** 1/7/63 **Age:** 34

Year Team	Lg	G	AB	H	2B	3B	HR	(Hm	Rd)	TB	R	RBI	TBB	IBB	SO	HBP	SH	SF	SB	CS	SB%	GDP	Avg	OBP	SLG
						BATTING														**BASERUNNING**				**PERCENTAGES**		
1996 Las Vegas *	AAA	1	2	0	0	0	0	(—	—)	0	1	0	0	0	1	0	0	0	0	0	.00	0	.000	.000	.000
Padres *	R	3	7	5	1	0	0	(—	—)	6	4	1	0	0	0	1	0	0	0	1	.00	0	.714	.750	.857
1986 Los Angeles	NL	12	27	3	1	0	0	(0	0)	4	3	4	2	1	5	1	1	0	0	0	.00	1	.111	.200	.148
1987 Los Angeles	NL	26	35	9	1	0	0	(0	0)	10	3	2	0	0	6	0	0	0	0	0	.00	2	.257	.257	.286
1989 New York	NL	4	7	1	0	0	0	(0	0)	1	3	0	0	0	1	0	0	0	0	0	.00	0	.143	.143	.143
1991 San Diego	NL	37	91	25	3	0	1	(0	1)	31	6	6	2	0	14	1	1	0	0	1	.00	1	.275	.298	.341
1992 San Diego	NL	52	105	26	6	0	0	(0	0)	32	7	7	2	1	21	0	1	0	1	1	.50	2	.248	.262	.305
1993 San Diego	NL	105	230	54	9	0	4	(2	2)	75	25	22	10	0	31	3	1	1	12	3	.80	3	.235	.275	.326
1994 San Diego	NL	81	240	80	14	4	4	(2	2)	114	32	30	9	1	28	3	4	2	6	6	.50	3	.333	.362	.475
1995 Houston	NL	92	232	61	8	1	3	(1	2)	80	23	24	8	3	28	2	1	2	6	1	.86	13	.263	.291	.345
1996 San Diego	NL	33	92	29	5	0	0	(0	0)	37	13	7	2	1	15	2	1	0	7	0	1.00	0	.315	.337	.402
9 ML YEARS		442	1059	288	47	5	13	(5	8)	384	115	102	35	7	149	12	10	7	32	12	.73	25	.272	.301	.363

Paul Shuey

Pitches: Right **Bats:** Right **Pos:** RP-42   **Ht:** 6'3" **Wt:** 215 **Born:** 9/16/70 **Age:** 26

Year Team	Lg	G	GS	CG	GF	IP	BFP	H	R	ER	HR	SH	SF	HB	TBB	IBB	SO	WP	Bk	W	L	Pct.	ShO	Sv-Op	Hld	ERA
			HOW MUCH HE PITCHED								**WHAT HE GAVE UP**											**THE RESULTS**				
1996 Buffalo *	AAA	19	0	0	14	33.1	121	14	4	3	1	0	1	0	9	2	57	1	0	3	2	.600	0	4--	—	0.81
1994 Cleveland	AL	14	0	0	11	11.2	62	14	11	11	1	0	0	0	12	1	16	4	0	0	1	.000	0	5-5	1	8.49
1995 Cleveland	AL	7	0	0	3	6.1	28	5	4	3	0	2	0	0	5	0	5	1	0	0	2	.000	0	0-0	0	4.26
1996 Cleveland	AL	42	0	0	18	53.2	225	45	19	17	6	1	3	0	26	3	44	3	1	5	2	.714	0	4-7	7	2.85
3 ML YEARS		63	0	0	32	71.2	315	64	34	31	7	3	3	0	43	4	65	8	1	5	5	.500	0	9-12	8	3.89

Terry Shumpert

Bats: R **Throws:** R **Pos:** PH-17; 3B-10; 2B-4; SS-1   **Ht:** 5'11" **Wt:** 185 **Born:** 8/16/66 **Age:** 30

Year Team	Lg	G	AB	H	2B	3B	HR	(Hm	Rd)	TB	R	RBI	TBB	IBB	SO	HBP	SH	SF	SB	CS	SB%	GDP	Avg	OBP	SLG
						BATTING														**BASERUNNING**				**PERCENTAGES**		
1996 Iowa *	AAA	72	246	68	13	4	5	(—	—)	104	45	32	24	0	44	2	4	3	13	3	.81	5	.276	.342	.423
1990 Kansas City	AL	32	91	25	6	1	0	(0	0)	33	7	8	2	0	17	1	0	2	3	3	.50	4	.275	.292	.363
1991 Kansas City	AL	144	369	80	16	4	5	(1	4)	119	45	34	30	0	75	5	10	3	17	11	.61	10	.217	.283	.322
1992 Kansas City	AL	36	94	14	5	1	1	(0	1)	24	6	11	3	0	17	0	2	0	2	2	.50	2	.149	.175	.255
1993 Kansas City	AL	8	10	1	0	0	0	(0	0)	1	0	0	2	0	2	0	0	0	1	0	1.00	0	.100	.250	.100
1994 Kansas City	AL	64	183	44	6	2	8	(2	6)	78	28	24	13	0	39	0	5	0	18	3	.86	0	.240	.289	.426
1995 Boston	AL	21	47	11	3	0	0	(0	0)	14	6	3	4	0	13	0	0	0	3	1	.75	0	.234	.294	.298
1996 Chicago	NL	27	31	7	1	0	2	(2	0)	14	5	6	2	0	11	1	0	0	1	0	.00	0	.226	.286	.452
7 ML YEARS		332	825	182	37	8	16	(5	11)	283	97	86	56	0	174	7	17	7	44	21	.68	16	.221	.274	.343

Joe Siddall

Bats: Left **Throws:** Right **Pos:** C-18; PH-1   **Ht:** 6'1" **Wt:** 200 **Born:** 10/25/67 **Age:** 29

Year Team	Lg	G	AB	H	2B	3B	HR	(Hm	Rd)	TB	R	RBI	TBB	IBB	SO	HBP	SH	SF	SB	CS	SB%	GDP	Avg	OBP	SLG
1988 Jamestown	A-	53	178	38	5	3	1	—	—	52	18	16	14	1	29	1	4	2	5	4	.56	3	.213	.272	.292
1989 Rockford	A	98	313	74	15	2	4	—	—	105	36	38	26	2	56	6	5	4	8	5	.62	3	.236	.304	.335
1990 W. Palm Bch	A+	106	348	78	12	1	0	—	—	92	29	32	20	0	55	1	10	2	6	7	.46	7	.224	.267	.264
1991 Harrisburg	AA	76	235	54	6	1	1	—	—	65	28	23	23	2	53	1	2	3	8	3	.73	7	.230	.298	.277
1992 Harrisburg	AA	95	288	68	12	0	2	—	—	86	26	27	29	1	55	3	1	3	4	4	.50	7	.236	.310	.299
1993 Ottawa	AAA	48	136	29	6	0	1	—	—	38	14	16	19	5	33	0	3	2	2	2	.50	6	.213	.306	.279
1994 Ottawa	AAA	38	110	19	2	1	3	—	—	32	9	13	10	2	21	2	7	2	1	1	.50	3	.173	.250	.291
1995 Ottawa	AAA	83	248	53	14	2	1	—	—	74	26	23	23	0	42	4	2	0	3	3	.50	6	.214	.291	.298
1996 Charlotte	AAA	65	189	53	13	1	3	—	—	77	22	20	11	1	36	3	2	0	1	2	.33	2	.280	.330	.407
1993 Montreal	NL	19	20	2	1	0	0	(0	0)	3	0	1	1	1	5	0	0	0	0	0	.00	0	.100	.143	.150
1995 Montreal	NL	7	10	3	0	0	0	(0	0)	3	4	1	3	0	3	1	0	0	0	0	.00	0	.300	.500	.300
1996 Florida	NL	18	47	7	1	0	0	(0	0)	8	0	3	2	0	8	0	0	0	0	0	.00	0	.149	.184	.170
3 ML YEARS		44	77	12	2	0	0	(0	0)	14	4	5	6	1	16	1	0	0	0	0	.00	0	.156	.226	.182

Ruben Sierra

Bats: B **Throws:** R **Pos:** DH-81; LF-36; RF-20; PH-6   **Ht:** 6'1" **Wt:** 200 **Born:** 10/6/65 **Age:** 31

Year Team	Lg	G	AB	H	2B	3B	HR	(Hm	Rd)	TB	R	RBI	TBB	IBB	SO	HBP	SH	SF	SB	CS	SB%	GDP	Avg	OBP	SLG
1986 Texas	AL	113	382	101	13	10	16	(8	8)	182	50	55	22	3	65	1	1	5	7	8	.47	8	.264	.302	.476
1987 Texas	AL	158	643	169	35	4	30	(15	15)	302	97	109	39	4	114	2	0	12	16	11	.59	18	.263	.302	.470
1988 Texas	AL	156	615	156	32	2	23	(15	8)	261	77	91	44	10	91	1	0	8	18	4	.82	15	.254	.301	.424
1989 Texas	AL	162	634	194	35	14	29	(21	8)	344	101	119	43	2	82	2	0	10	8	2	.80	7	.306	.347	.543
1990 Texas	AL	159	608	170	37	2	16	(10	6)	259	70	96	49	13	86	1	0	8	9	0	1.00	15	.280	.330	.426
1991 Texas	AL	161	661	203	44	5	25	(12	13)	332	110	116	56	7	91	0	0	9	16	4	.80	17	.307	.357	.502
1992 Tex-Oak	AL	151	601	167	34	7	17	(10	7)	266	83	87	45	12	68	0	0	10	14	4	.78	11	.278	.323	.443
1993 Oakland	AL	158	630	147	23	5	22	(9	13)	246	77	101	52	16	97	0	0	10	25	5	.83	17	.233	.288	.390
1994 Oakland	AL	110	426	114	21	1	23	(11	12)	206	71	92	23	4	64	0	0	11	8	5	.62	15	.268	.298	.484
1995 Oak-NYA	AL	126	479	126	32	0	19	(8	11)	215	73	86	46	4	76	0	0	8	5	4	.56	8	.263	.323	.449
1996 NYA-Det	AL	142	518	128	26	2	12	(4	8)	194	61	72	60	12	83	0	0	9	4	4	.50	12	.247	.320	.375
1992 Texas	AL	124	500	139	30	6	14	(8	6)	223	66	70	31	6	59	0	0	8	12	4	.75	9	.278	.315	.446
Oakland	AL	27	101	28	4	1	3	(2	1)	43	17	17	14	6	9	0	0	2	2	0	1.00	2	.277	.359	.426
1995 Oakland	AL	70	264	70	17	0	12	(3	9)	123	40	44	24	2	42	0	0	3	4	4	.50	2	.265	.323	.466
New York	AL	56	215	56	15	0	7	(5	2)	92	33	44	22	2	34	0	0	5	1	0	1.00	6	.260	.322	.428
1996 New York	AL	96	360	93	17	1	11	(4	7)	145	39	52	40	11	58	0	0	7	1	3	.25	10	.258	.327	.403
Detroit	AL	46	158	35	9	1	1	(0	1)	49	22	20	20	1	25	0	0	2	3	1	.75	2	.222	.306	.310
11 ML YEARS		1596	6197	1675	332	52	232	(123	109)	2807	870	1024	479	87	917	7	1	100	130	51	.72	143	.270	.319	.453

Jose Silva

Pitches: Right **Bats:** Right **Pos:** RP-2   **Ht:** 6'5" **Wt:** 210 **Born:** 12/19/73 **Age:** 23

Year Team	Lg	G	GS	CG	GF	IP	BFP	H	R	ER	HR	SH	SF	HB	TBB	IBB	SO	WP	Bk	W	L	Pct.	ShO	Sv-Op	Hld	ERA
1992 Blue Jays	R	12	12	0	0	59.1	231	42	23	15	1	0	1	2	18	0	78	1	2	6	4	.600	0	0--	—	2.28
1993 Hagerstown	A	24	24	0	0	142.2	581	103	50	40	6	0	4	4	62	0	161	9	1	12	5	.706	0	0--	—	2.52
1994 Dunedin	A+	8	7	0	0	43	188	41	32	18	4	2	6	0	24	0	41	5	0	0	2	.000	0	0--	—	3.77
Knoxville	AA	16	16	1	0	91.1	381	89	47	42	9	2	2	3	31	0	71	4	0	4	8	.333	1	0--	—	4.14
1995 Knoxville	AA	3	0	0	0	2	15	3	2	2	0	1	1	0	6	0	2	0	0	0	0	.000	0	0--	—	9.00
1996 Knoxville	AA	22	6	0	4	44	196	45	27	24	3	3	1	3	22	2	26	4	0	2	3	.400	0	0--	—	4.91
1996 Toronto	AL	2	0	0	0	2	11	5	3	3	1	0	0	0	0	0	0	0	0	0	0	.000	0	0-0	0	13.50

Dave Silvestri

B: R **T:** R **Pos:** 3B-47; PH-35; SS-10; 1B-1; 2B-1; LF-1; CF-1   **Ht:** 6'0" **Wt:** 196 **Born:** 9/29/67 **Age:** 29

Year Team	Lg	G	AB	H	2B	3B	HR	(Hm	Rd)	TB	R	RBI	TBB	IBB	SO	HBP	SH	SF	SB	CS	SB%	GDP	Avg	OBP	SLG
1992 New York	AL	7	13	4	0	2	0	(0	0)	8	3	1	0	0	3	0	0	0	0	0	.00	1	.308	.308	.615
1993 New York	AL	7	21	6	1	0	1	(0	1)	10	4	4	5	0	3	0	0	0	0	0	.00	1	.286	.423	.476
1994 New York	AL	12	18	2	0	1	1	(1	0)	7	3	2	4	0	9	0	0	1	0	1	.00	0	.111	.261	.389
1995 NYA-Mon		56	93	21	6	0	3	(0	3)	36	16	11	13	0	36	1	1	2	2	0	1.00	3	.226	.321	.387
1996 Montreal	NL	86	162	33	4	0	1	(0	1)	40	16	17	34	6	41	0	3	1	2	1	.67	5	.204	.340	.247
1995 New York	AL	17	21	2	0	0	1	(0	1)	5	4	4	4	0	9	1	0	1	0	0	.00	1	.095	.259	.238
Montreal	NL	39	72	19	6	0	2	(0	2)	31	12	7	9	0	27	0	1	1	2	0	1.00	2	.264	.341	.431
5 ML YEARS		168	307	66	11	3	6	(1	5)	101	42	35	56	6	92	1	4	4	4	2	.67	10	.215	.334	.329

Bill Simas

Pitches: Right **Bats:** Right **Pos:** RP-64   **Ht:** 6'3" **Wt:** 220 **Born:** 11/28/71 **Age:** 25

		HOW MUCH HE PITCHED						WHAT HE GAVE UP												THE RESULTS						
Year Team	Lg	G	GS	CG	GF	IP	BFP	H	R	ER	HR	SH	SF	HB	TBB	IBB	SO	WP	Bk	W	L	Pct.	ShO	Sv-Op	Hld	ERA
1992 Boise	A-	14	12	0	1	70.2	320	82	44	31	0	2	4	3	29	2	39	4	1	6	5	.545	0	1--	—	3.95
1993 Cedar Rapds	A	35	6	0	19	80	376	93	60	44	8	5	4	3	36	1	62	4	1	5	8	.385	0	6--	—	4.95
1994 Midland	AA	13	0	0	11	15.1	52	5	1	1	0	0	0	0	2	0	12	0	0	2	0	1.000	0	6--	—	0.59
Lk Elsinore	A+	37	0	0	27	47	194	44	17	11	2	3	2	3	10	1	34	3	2	5	2	.714	0	13--	—	2.11
1995 Nashville	AAA	7	0	0	3	11.2	50	12	5	5	0	1	0	0	3	1	12	0	0	1	1	.500	0	0--	—	3.86
Vancouver	AAA	37	0	0	27	49.2	225	56	24	20	1	2	1	4	17	3	56	1	0	7	4	.636	0	6--	—	3.62
1995 Chicago	AL	14	0	0	4	14	66	15	5	4	1	0	0	1	10	2	16	1	0	1	1	.500	0	0-0	3	2.57
1996 Chicago	AL	64	0	0	16	72.2	328	75	39	37	5	1	2	3	39	6	65	0	0	2	8	.200	0	2-8	15	4.58
2 ML YEARS		78	0	0	20	86.2	394	90	44	41	6	1	2	4	49	8	81	1	0	3	9	.250	0	2-8	18	4.26

Mike Simms

Bats: R **Throws:** R **Pos:** PH-35; LF-9; 1B-5; RF-3   **Ht:** 6'4" **Wt:** 200 **Born:** 1/12/67 **Age:** 30

		BATTING																	BASERUNNING				PERCENTAGES		
Year Team	Lg	G	AB	H	2B	3B	HR	(Hm	Rd)	TB	R	RBI	TBB	IBB	SO	HBP	SH	SF	SB	CS	SB%	GDP	Avg	OBP	SLG
1996 Tucson *	AAA	17	64	19	3	0	7			43	11	19	9	0	17	1	0	0	0	3	.00		.297	.392	.672
1990 Houston	NL	12	13	4	1	0	1	(0	1)	8	3	2	0	0	4	0	0	0	0	0	.00	1	.308	.308	.615
1991 Houston	NL	49	123	25	5	0	3	(1	2)	39	18	16	18	0	38	0	0	2	1	0	1.00	2	.203	.301	.317
1992 Houston	NL	15	24	6	1	0	1	(0	1)	10	1	3	2	0	9	1	0	0	0	0	.00	1	.250	.333	.417
1994 Houston	NL	6	12	1	1	0	0	(0	0)	2	1	0	0	0	5	0	0	0	1	0	1.00	1	.083	.083	.167
1995 Houston	NL	50	121	31	4	0	9	(5	4)	62	14	24	13	0	28	3	0	1	1	2	.33	3	.256	.341	.512
1996 Houston	NL	49	68	12	2	1	1	(0	1)	19	6	8	4	0	16	1	0	0	0	1	1.00	1	.176	.233	.279
6 ML YEARS		181	361	79	14	1	15	(7	8)	140	43	53	37	0	100	5	0	3	4	2	.67	8	.219	.298	.388

Duane Singleton

Bats: Left **Throws:** Right **Pos:** CF-15; PH-4; LF-3   **Ht:** 6'1" **Wt:** 177 **Born:** 8/6/72 **Age:** 24

		BATTING																	BASERUNNING				PERCENTAGES		
Year Team	Lg	G	AB	H	2B	3B	HR	(Hm	Rd)	TB	R	RBI	TBB	IBB	SO	HBP	SH	SF	SB	CS	SB%	GDP	Avg	OBP	SLG
1990 Brewers	R	46	134	31	6	1	1	—	—	42	30	13	41	0	39	1	1	1	5	9	.36	1	.231	.412	.313
1991 Beloit	A	101	388	112	13	7	3	—	—	148	57	44	40	7	57	3	5	2	42	17	.71	7	.289	.358	.381
1992 Salinas	A+	19	72	22	5	2	1	—	—	34	6	8	6	0	11	0	0	0	4	1	.80	0	.306	.359	.472
Stockton	A+	97	389	112	15	10	5	—	—	162	73	51	39	0	66	3	3	6	34	15	.69	7	.288	.352	.416
1993 El Paso	AA	125	456	105	21	6	2	—	—	144	52	61	34	0	90	3	2	5	23	19	.55	4	.230	.285	.316
1994 Stockton	A+	38	134	39	6	0	4	—	—	57	31	13	18	0	23	0	0	0	15	6	.71	6	.291	.375	.425
El Paso	AA	39	139	40	11	3	2	—	—	63	25	24	19	0	33	2	1	0	10	5	.67	6	.288	.381	.453
New Orleans	AAA	41	133	37	4	5	0	—	—	51	26	14	18	0	26	0	5	1	4	6	.40	1	.278	.362	.383
1995 New Orleans	AAA	106	355	95	10	4	4	—	—	125	48	29	39	2	63	3	3	1	31	15	.67	7	.268	.344	.352
1996 Toledo	AAA	88	294	65	15	6	8	—	—	116	42	30	36	4	84	1	1	3	17	7	.71	4	.221	.305	.395
1994 Milwaukee	AL	2	0	0	0	0	0	(0	0)	0	0	0	0	0	0	0	0	0	0	0	.00	0	.000	.000	.000
1995 Milwaukee	AL	13	31	2	0	0	0	(0	0)	2	0	0	1	0	10	0	0	0	1	0	1.00	0	.065	.094	.065
1996 Detroit	AL	18	56	9	1	0	0	(0	0)	10	5	3	4	0	15	1	0	0	0	2	.00	2	.161	.230	.179
3 ML YEARS		33	87	11	1	0	0	(0	0)	12	5	3	5	0	25	1	0	0	1	2	.33	2	.126	.183	.138

Mike Sirotka

Pitches: Left **Bats:** Left **Pos:** RP-11; SP-4   **Ht:** 6'1" **Wt:** 200 **Born:** 5/13/71 **Age:** 26

		HOW MUCH HE PITCHED						WHAT HE GAVE UP												THE RESULTS						
Year Team	Lg	G	GS	CG	GF	IP	BFP	H	R	ER	HR	SH	SF	HB	TBB	IBB	SO	WP	Bk	W	L	Pct.	ShO	Sv-Op	Hld	ERA
1993 White Sox	R	3	0	1	0	5	21	4	1	0	0	0	0	0	2	0	8	0	0	0	0	.000	0	0--	—	0.00
South Bend	A	7	1	0	3	10.1	50	12	8	7	3	0	0	0	6	0	12	0	1	0	1	.000	0	0--	—	6.10
1994 South Bend	A	27	27	8	0	196.2	824	183	99	67	11	9	6	3	58	1	173	7	2	12	9	.571	2	0--	—	3.07
1995 Nashville	AAA	8	8	0	0	54	217	51	21	17	4	2	3	1	13	1	34	1	0	1	5	.167	0	0--	—	2.83
Birmingham	AA	24	24	1	0	155.1	629	146	63	53	15	5	6	3	35	1	113	5	1	8	11	.421	0	0--	—	3.07
1996 Nashville	AAA	15	15	0	0	90	381	90	44	36	10	0	3	1	24	0	58	0	1	7	5	.583	1	0--	—	3.60
1995 Chicago	AL	6	6	0	0	34.1	152	39	16	16	2	1	3	0	17	0	19	2	0	1	2	.333	0	0-0	0	4.19
1996 Chicago	AL	15	4	0	2	26.1	122	34	27	21	0	2	0	0	12	0	11	1	0	1	2	.333	0	0-0	0	7.18
2 ML YEARS		21	10	0	2	60.2	274	73	43	37	2	3	3	0	29	0	30	3	0	2	4	.333	0	0-0	0	5.49

Don Slaught

Bats: Right **Throws:** Right **Pos:** C-71; PH-8; DH-2   **Ht:** 6'1" **Wt:** 185 **Born:** 9/11/58 **Age:** 38

		BATTING																	BASERUNNING				PERCENTAGES		
Year Team	Lg	G	AB	H	2B	3B	HR	(Hm	Rd)	TB	R	RBI	TBB	IBB	SO	HBP	SH	SF	SB	CS	SB%	GDP	Avg	OBP	SLG
1982 Kansas City	AL	43	115	32	6	0	3	(0	3)	47	14	8	9	0	12	0	2	0	0	1	.00	3	.278	.331	.409
1983 Kansas City	AL	83	276	86	13	4	0	(0	0)	107	21	28	11	0	27	0	1	2	3	1	.75	3	.312	.336	.388
1984 Kansas City	AL	124	409	108	27	4	4	(1	3)	155	48	42	20	4	55	2	8	7	0	0	.00	8	.264	.297	.379
1985 Texas	AL	102	343	96	17	4	8	(4	4)	145	34	35	20	1	41	6	1	0	5	4	.56	8	.280	.331	.423
1986 Texas	AL	95	314	83	17	1	13	(5	8)	141	39	46	16	0	59	5	3	3	3	2	.60	8	.264	.308	.449
1987 Texas	AL	95	237	53	15	2	8	(5	3)	96	25	16	24	3	51	1	4	0	0	3	.00	7	.224	.298	.405
1988 New York	AL	97	322	91	25	1	9	(7	2)	145	33	43	24	3	54	3	5	4	1	0	1.00	10	.283	.334	.450

BATTING / BASERUNNING / PERCENTAGES

Year Team	Lg	G	AB	H	2B	3B	HR	(Hm	Rd)	TB	R	RBI	TBB	IBB	SO	HBP	SH	SF	SB	CS	SB%	GDP	Avg	OBP	SLG
1989 New York	AL	117	350	88	21	3	5	(3	2)	130	34	38	30	3	57	5	2	5	1	1	.50	9	.251	.315	.371
1990 Pittsburgh	NL	84	230	69	18	3	4	(1	3)	105	27	29	27	2	27	3	3	4	0	1	.00	2	.300	.375	.457
1991 Pittsburgh	NL	77	220	65	17	1	1	(0	1)	87	19	29	21	1	32	3	5	1	1	0	1.00	6	.295	.363	.395
1992 Pittsburgh	NL	87	255	88	17	3	4	(2	2)	123	26	37	17	5	23	2	6	5	2	2	.50	6	.345	.384	.482
1993 Pittsburgh	NL	116	377	113	19	2	10	(1	9)	166	34	55	29	2	56	6	4	4	2	1	.67	13	.300	.356	.440
1994 Pittsburgh	NL	76	240	69	7	0	2	(1	1)	82	21	21	34	2	31	3	1	1	0	0	.00	5	.288	.381	.342
1995 Pittsburgh	NL	35	112	34	6	0	0	(0	0)	40	13	13	9	2	8	1	1	0	0	0	.00	5	.304	.361	.357
1996 Cal-ChA	AL	76	243	76	10	0	6	(3	3)	104	25	36	15	0	22	2	1	2	0	0	.00	16	.313	.355	.428
1996 California	AL	62	207	67	9	0	6	(3	3)	94	23	32	13	0	20	2	0	2	0	0	.00	12	.324	.366	.454
Chicago	AL	14	36	9	1	0	0	(0	0)	10	2	4	2	0	2	0	1	0	0	0	.00	4	.250	.250	.278
15 ML YEARS		1307	4043	1151	235	28	77	(33	44)	1673	413	476	306	28	555	42	47	38	18	15	.55	114	.285	.338	.414

Heathcliff Slocumb

Pitches: Right **Bats:** Right **Pos:** RP-75   **Ht:** 6'3" **Wt:** 220 **Born:** 6/7/66 **Age:** 31

Year Team	Lg	G	GS	CG	GF	IP	BFP	H	R	ER	HR	SH	SF	HB	TBB	IBB	SO	WP	Bk	W	L	Pct.	ShO	Sv-Op	Hld	ERA
1991 Chicago	NL	52	0	0	21	62.2	274	53	29	24	3	6	6	3	30	6	34	9	0	2	1	.667	0	1-3	6	3.45
1992 Chicago	NL	30	0	0	11	36	174	52	27	26	3	2	2	1	21	3	27	1	0	0	3	.000	0	1-1	1	6.50
1993 ChN-Cle		30	0	0	9	38	164	35	19	17	3	1	3	0	20	2	22	0	0	4	1	.800	0	0-2	3	4.03
1994 Philadelphia	NL	52	0	0	16	72.1	322	75	32	23	0	2	4	2	28	4	58	9	0	5	1	.833	0	0-5	18	2.86
1995 Philadelphia	NL	61	0	0	54	65.1	289	64	26	21	2	4	0	1	35	3	63	3	0	5	6	.455	0	32-38	3	2.89
1996 Boston	AL	75	0	0	60	83.1	368	68	31	28	2	1	3	3	55	5	88	10	0	5	5	.500	0	31-39	2	3.02
1993 Chicago	NL	10	0	0	4	10.2	42	7	5	4	0	0	1	0	4	0	4	0	0	1	0	1.000	0	0-2	2	3.38
Cleveland	AL	20	0	0	5	27.1	122	28	14	13	3	1	2	0	16	2	18	0	0	3	1	.750	0	0-2	1	4.28
6 ML YEARS		300	0	0	171	357.2	1591	347	164	139	13	16	18	10	189	23	292	32	0	21	17	.553	0	65-88	33	3.50

Aaron Small

Pitches: Right **Bats:** Right **Pos:** RP-9; SP-3   **Ht:** 6'5" **Wt:** 208 **Born:** 11/23/71 **Age:** 25

Year Team	Lg	G	GS	CG	GF	IP	BFP	H	R	ER	HR	SH	SF	HB	TBB	IBB	SO	WP	Bk	W	L	Pct.	ShO	Sv-Op	Hld	ERA
1989 Medicne Hat	R+	15	14	0	0	70.2	326	80	55	46	2	3	2	3	31	1	40	9	5	1	7	.125	0	0--	—	5.86
1990 Myrtle Bch	A	27	27	1	0	147.2	643	150	72	46	6	2	7	4	56	2	96	16	5	9	9	.500	0	0--	—	2.80
1991 Dunedin	A+	24	23	1	0	148.1	595	129	51	45	5	5	5	5	42	1	92	7	0	8	7	.533	0	0--	—	2.73
1992 Knoxville	AA	27	24	2	0	135	610	152	94	79	13	2	4	6	61	0	79	14	0	5	12	.294	1	0--	—	5.27
1993 Knoxville	AA	48	9	0	32	93	408	99	44	35	5	3	0	2	40	4	44	8	0	4	4	.500	0	16--	—	3.39
1994 Syracuse	AAA	13	0	0	6	24.1	99	19	8	6	2	2	0	1	9	2	15	2	0	3	2	.600	0	0--	—	2.22
Knoxville	AA	29	11	1	13	96.1	405	92	37	32	4	3	5	3	38	0	75	5	1	5	5	.500	1	5--	—	2.99
1995 Syracuse	AAA	1	0	0	0	1.2	9	3	1	1	1	0	0	0	1	0	2	0	0	0	0	.000	0	0--	—	5.40
Charlotte	AAA	34	0	0	17	42.1	179	39	16	14	3	0	1	2	11	1	33	3	0	2	1	.667	0	10--	—	2.98
1996 Edmonton	AAA	25	19	1	4	119.2	492	111	65	57	9	2	2	5	28	0	83	9	0	8	6	.571	1	1--	—	4.29
1994 Toronto	AL	1	0	0	1	2	13	5	2	2	0	1	0	1	2	0	0	0	0	0	0	.000	0	0-0	0	9.00
1995 Florida	NL	7	0	0	1	6.1	32	7	2	1	1	0	0	0	6	0	5	0	0	1	0	1.000	0	0-0	0	1.42
1996 Oakland	AL	12	3	0	4	28.2	144	37	28	26	3	0	1	1	22	1	17	2	0	1	3	.250	0	0-0	0	8.16
3 ML YEARS		20	3	0	6	37	189	49	32	29	5	0	2	1	30	1	22	2	0	2	3	.400	0	0-0	0	7.05

Mark Small

Pitches: Right **Bats:** Right **Pos:** RP-16   **Ht:** 6'3" **Wt:** 205 **Born:** 11/12/67 **Age:** 29

Year Team	Lg	G	GS	CG	GF	IP	BFP	H	R	ER	HR	SH	SF	HB	TBB	IBB	SO	WP	Bk	W	L	Pct.	ShO	Sv-Op	Hld	ERA
1989 Auburn	A-	10	3	0	4	19.2	87	17	13	11	3	0	1	1	11	0	23	3	0	0	1	.000	0	2--	—	5.03
1990 Asheville	A	34	0	0	16	52	252	54	36	24	2	4	3	4	37	5	34	9	0	3	4	.429	0	6--	—	4.15
1991 Osceola	A+	26	0	0	10	44.2	172	30	10	8	2	1	0	1	19	1	44	2	0	3	0	1.000	0	0--	—	1.61
1992 Osceola	A+	22	20	1	2	105	435	97	56	45	8	3	3	0	38	0	69	5	1	5	9	.357	0	0--	—	3.86
1993 Jackson	AA	51	0	0	18	84.2	361	71	34	30	8	8	3	3	41	6	64	8	2	7	2	.778	0	0--	—	3.19
1994 Jackson	AA	16	0	0	9	21	97	22	16	9	1	1	2	1	10	2	14	4	0	3	1	.750	0	3--	—	3.86
Tucson	AAA	41	0	0	12	70	321	88	48	41	9	3	3	2	34	2	30	13	0	8	5	.615	0	4--	—	5.27
1995 Tucson	AAA	51	0	0	40	66	285	74	32	30	5	1	2	1	19	2	51	6	0	3	3	.500	0	19--	—	4.09
1996 Tucson	AAA	32	0	0	20	39	166	32	17	9	3	4	0	1	18	4	36	4	1	3	3	.500	0	7--	—	2.08
1996 Houston	NL	16	0	0	4	24.1	122	33	23	16	1	0	1	1	13	3	16	1	1	0	1	.000	0	0-0	0	5.92

John Smiley

Pitches: Left **Bats:** Left **Pos:** SP-34; RP-1   **Ht:** 6'4" **Wt:** 210 **Born:** 3/17/65 **Age:** 32

Year Team	Lg	G	GS	CG	GF	IP	BFP	H	R	ER	HR	SH	SF	HB	TBB	IBB	SO	WP	Bk	W	L	Pct.	ShO	Sv-Op	Hld	ERA
1986 Pittsburgh	NL	12	0	0	2	11.2	42	4	6	5	2	0	0	0	4	0	9	0	0	1	0	1.000	0	0--	—	3.86
1987 Pittsburgh	NL	63	0	0	19	75	336	69	49	48	7	0	3	0	50	8	58	5	1	5	5	.500	0	4-6	12	5.76
1988 Pittsburgh	NL	34	32	5	0	205	835	185	81	74	15	11	8	3	46	4	129	6	6	13	11	.542	1	0-0	1	3.25
1989 Pittsburgh	NL	28	28	8	0	205.1	837	174	78	64	22	5	7	4	49	5	123	5	2	12	8	.600	0	0-0	0	2.81
1990 Pittsburgh	NL	26	25	2	0	149.1	632	161	83	77	15	5	4	2	36	1	86	2	2	9	10	.474	0	0-0	0	4.64

Year Team	Lg	G	GS	CG	GF	IP	BFP	H	R	ER	HR	SH	SF	HB	TBB	IBB	SO	WP	Bk	W	L	Pct.	ShO	Sv-Op	Hld	ERA
1991 Pittsburgh	NL	33	32	2	0	207.2	836	194	78	71	17	11	4	3	44	0	129	3	1	20	8	.714	1	0-0	0	3.08
1992 Minnesota	AL	34	34	5	0	241	970	205	93	86	17	4	9	6	65	0	163	4	0	16	9	.640	2	0-0	0	3.21
1993 Cincinnati	NL	18	18	2	0	105.2	455	117	69	66	15	10	3	2	31	0	60	2	1	3	9	.250	0	0-0	0	5.62
1994 Cincinnati	NL	24	24	1	0	158.2	672	169	80	68	18	16	0	4	37	3	112	4	2	11	10	.524	1	0-0	0	3.86
1995 Cincinnati	NL	28	27	1	0	176.2	724	173	72	68	11	17	5	4	39	3	124	5	1	12	5	.706	0	0-0	0	3.46
1996 Cincinnati	NL	35	34	2	0	217.1	889	207	100	88	20	16	7	4	54	5	171	7	1	13	14	.481	2	0-1	0	3.64
11 ML YEARS		335	254	28	21	1753.1	7226	1658	789	715	159	95	50	32	455	29	1164	43	17	115	89	.564	8	4--	—	3.67

Dwight Smith

Bats: Left **Throws:** Right **Pos:** PH-79; RF-26; LF-3   **Ht:** 5'11" **Wt:** 195 **Born:** 11/8/63 **Age:** 33

Year Team	Lg	G	AB	H	2B	3B	HR	(Hm	Rd)	TB	R	RBI	TBB	IBB	SO	HBP	SH	SF	SB	CS	SB%	GDP	Avg	OBP	SLG
1989 Chicago	NL	109	343	111	19	6	9	(5	4)	169	52	52	31	0	51	2	4	1	9	4	.69	4	.324	.382	.493
1990 Chicago	NL	117	290	76	15	0	6	(3	3)	109	34	27	28	2	46	2	0	2	11	6	.65	7	.262	.329	.376
1991 Chicago	NL	90	167	38	7	2	3	(2	1)	58	16	21	11	2	32	1	1	0	2	3	.40	2	.228	.279	.347
1992 Chicago	NL	109	217	60	10	3	3	(3	0)	85	28	24	13	0	40	1	0	2	9	8	.53	1	.276	.318	.392
1993 Chicago	NL	111	310	93	17	5	11	(6	5)	153	51	35	25	1	51	3	1	3	8	6	.57	3	.300	.355	.494
1994 Cal-Bal	AL	73	196	55	7	2	8	(2	6)	90	31	30	12	1	37	1	0	1	2	4	.33	3	.281	.324	.459
1995 Atlanta	NL	103	131	33	8	2	3	(1	2)	54	16	21	13	1	35	2	0	1	0	3	.00	2	.252	.327	.412
1996 Atlanta	NL	101	153	31	5	0	3	(2	1)	45	16	16	17	1	42	1	0	1	1	3	.25	2	.203	.285	.294
1994 California	AL	45	122	32	5	1	5	(2	3)	54	19	18	7	0	20	0	0	1	2	3	.40	1	.262	.300	.443
Baltimore	AL	28	74	23	2	1	3	(0	3)	36	12	12	5	1	17	1	0	0	0	1	.00	2	.311	.363	.486
8 ML YEARS		813	1807	497	88	20	46	(24	22)	763	244	226	150	8	334	13	6	11	42	37	.53	24	.275	.333	.422

Lee Smith

Pitches: Right **Bats:** Right **Pos:** RP-54   **Ht:** 6'6" **Wt:** 269 **Born:** 12/4/57 **Age:** 39

Year Team	Lg	G	GS	CG	GF	IP	BFP	H	R	ER	HR	SH	SF	HB	TBB	IBB	SO	WP	Bk	W	L	Pct.	ShO	Sv-Op	Hld	ERA
1996 Lk Elsinore *	A+	1	1	0	0	1	5	1	2	1	0	0	1	0	1	0	1	1	1	0	0	.000	0	0--	—	9.00
1980 Chicago	NL	18	0	0	6	22	97	21	9	7	0	1	1	0	14	5	17	0	0	2	0	1.000	0	0--	—	2.86
1981 Chicago	NL	40	1	0	12	67	280	57	31	26	2	8	2	1	31	8	50	7	1	3	6	.333	0	1--	—	3.49
1982 Chicago	NL	72	5	0	38	117	480	105	38	35	5	6	5	3	37	5	99	6	1	2	5	.286	0	17--	—	2.69
1983 Chicago	NL	66	0	0	56	103.1	413	70	23	19	5	9	2	1	41	14	91	5	2	4	10	.286	0	29--	—	1.65
1984 Chicago	NL	69	0	0	59	101	428	98	42	41	6	4	5	0	35	7	86	6	0	9	7	.563	0	33--	—	3.65
1985 Chicago	NL	65	0	0	57	97.2	397	87	35	33	9	3	1	1	32	6	112	4	0	7	4	.636	0	33--	—	3.04
1986 Chicago	NL	66	0	0	59	90.1	372	69	32	31	7	6	3	0	42	11	93	2	0	9	9	.500	0	31--	—	3.09
1987 Chicago	NL	62	0	0	55	83.2	360	84	30	29	4	4	0	0	32	5	96	4	0	4	10	.286	0	36-48	0	3.12
1988 Boston	AL	64	0	0	57	83.2	363	72	34	26	7	3	2	1	37	6	96	2	0	4	5	.444	0	29-37	1	2.80
1989 Boston	AL	64	0	0	50	70.2	290	53	30	28	6	2	2	0	33	6	96	1	0	6	1	.857	0	25-30	4	3.57
1990 Bos-StL	AL	64	0	0	53	83	344	71	24	19	3	2	3	0	29	7	87	2	0	5	5	.500	0	31-37	1	2.06
1991 St. Louis	NL	67	0	0	61	73	300	70	19	19	5	5	1	0	13	5	67	1	0	6	3	.667	0	47-53	0	2.34
1992 St. Louis	NL	70	0	0	55	75	310	62	28	26	4	2	1	0	26	4	60	2	0	4	9	.308	0	43-51	0	3.12
1993 StL-NYA		63	0	0	56	58	239	53	25	25	11	0	3	0	14	2	60	1	0	2	4	.333	0	46-53	0	3.88
1994 Baltimore	AL	41	0	0	39	38.1	160	34	16	14	6	5	2	0	11	1	42	0	0	1	4	.200	0	33-39	0	3.29
1995 California	AL	52	0	0	51	49.1	209	42	19	19	3	3	3	1	25	4	43	1	0	0	5	.000	0	37-41	0	3.47
1996 Cal-Cin		54	0	0	24	55.1	245	57	24	23	4	0	2	1	26	4	41	3	0	3	4	.429	0	2-8	8	3.74
1990 Boston	AL	11	0	0	8	14.1	64	13	4	3	0	0	0	0	9	2	17	1	0	2	1	.667	0	4-5	0	1.88
St. Louis	NL	53	0	0	45	68.2	280	58	20	16	3	2	3	0	20	5	70	1	0	3	4	.429	0	27-32	1	2.10
1993 St. Louis	NL	55	0	0	48	50	206	49	25	25	11	0	2	0	9	1	49	1	0	2	4	.333	0	43-50	0	4.50
New York		8	0	0	8	8	33	4	0	0	0	0	1	0	5	1	11	0	0	0	0	.000	0	3-3	0	0.00
1996 California	AL	11	0	0	8	11	44	8	4	3	0	0	2	0	3	0	6	1	0	0	0	.000	0	0-2	0	2.45
Cincinnati	NL	43	0	0	16	44.1	201	49	20	20	4	0	0	1	23	4	35	2	0	3	4	.429	0	2-6	8	4.06
17 ML YEARS		997	6	0	788	1268.1	5287	1105	459	420	87	63	38	9	478	100	1236	47	4	71	91	.438	0	473--	—	2.98

Mark Smith

Bats: R **Throws:** R **Pos:** LF-12; RF-8; DH-6; PH-3   **Ht:** 6'3" **Wt:** 205 **Born:** 5/7/70 **Age:** 27

Year Team	Lg	G	AB	H	2B	3B	HR	(Hm	Rd)	TB	R	RBI	TBB	IBB	SO	HBP	SH	SF	SB	CS	SB%	GDP	Avg	OBP	SLG
1991 Frederick	A+	38	148	37	5	1	4	—	—	56	20	29	9	0	24	2	0	3	2	3	.25	4	.250	.296	.378
1992 Hagerstown	AA	128	472	136	32	6	4	—	—	192	51	62	45	5	55	4	0	6	15	5	.75	17	.288	.351	.407
1993 Rochester	AAA	129	485	136	27	1	12	—	—	201	69	68	37	3	90	9	0	2	4	6	.40	9	.280	.341	.414
1994 Rochester	AAA	114	437	108	27	1	19	—	—	194	69	66	35	1	88	7	1	3	4	3	.57	13	.247	.311	.444
1995 Rochester	AAA	96	364	101	25	3	12	—	—	168	55	66	24	1	69	7	1	7	7	3	.70	8	.277	.328	.462
1996 Rochester	AAA	39	132	46	14	1	8	—	—	86	24	32	14	0	22	4	0	1	10	1	.91	0	.348	.424	.652
Frederick	A+	1	1	0	0	0	0	—	—	0	0	0	0	0	0	0	0	0	0	0	.00	0	.000	.000	.000
Bowie	AA	6	22	2	0	0	0	—	—	2	5	1	2	1	0	6	2	0	0	0	.00	1	.091	.200	.227
1994 Baltimore	AL	3	7	1	0	0	0	(0	0)	1	0	2	0	0	2	0	0	0	0	0	.00	0	.143	.143	.143
1995 Baltimore	AL	37	104	24	5	0	3	(1	2)	38	11	15	12	2	22	1	2	1	3	0	1.00	4	.231	.314	.365
1996 Baltimore	AL	27	78	19	2	0	4	(3	1)	33	9	10	3	0	20	3	0	0	0	2	.00	0	.244	.298	.423
3 ML YEARS		67	189	44	7	0	7	(4	3)	72	20	27	15	2	44	4	2	1	3	2	.60	4	.233	.301	.381

Ozzie Smith

Bats: Both **Throws:** Right **Pos:** SS-52; PH-32 **Ht:** 5'10" **Wt:** 170 **Born:** 12/26/54 **Age:** 42

					BATTING														BASERUNNING				PERCENTAGES		
Year Team	Lg	G	AB	H	2B	3B	HR	(Hm	Rd)	TB	R	RBI	TBB	IBB	SO	HBP	SH	SF	SB	CS	SB%	GDP	Avg	OBP	SLG
1978 San Diego	NL	159	590	152	17	6	1	(0	1)	184	69	46	47	0	43	0	28	3	40	12	.77	11	.258	.311	.312
1979 San Diego	NL	156	587	124	18	6	0	(0	0)	154	77	27	37	5	37	2	22	1	28	7	.80	11	.211	.260	.262
1980 San Diego	NL	158	609	140	18	5	0	(0	0)	168	67	35	71	1	49	5	23	4	57	15	.79	9	.230	.313	.276
1981 San Diego	NL	110	450	100	11	2	0	(0	0)	115	53	21	41	1	37	5	10	1	22	12	.65	8	.222	.294	.256
1982 St. Louis	NL	140	488	121	24	1	2	(0	2)	153	58	43	68	12	32	2	4	5	25	5	.83	10	.248	.339	.314
1983 St. Louis	NL	159	552	134	30	6	3	(1	2)	185	69	50	64	9	36	1	7	2	34	7	.83	10	.243	.321	.335
1984 St. Louis	NL	124	412	106	20	5	1	(1	0)	139	53	44	56	5	17	2	11	3	35	7	.83	8	.257	.347	.337
1985 St. Louis	NL	158	537	148	22	3	6	(2	4)	194	70	54	65	11	27	2	9	2	31	8	.79	13	.276	.355	.361
1986 St. Louis	NL	153	514	144	19	4	0	(0	0)	171	67	54	79	13	27	2	11	3	31	7	.82	9	.280	.376	.333
1987 St. Louis	NL	158	600	182	40	4	0	(0	0)	230	104	75	89	3	36	1	12	4	43	9	.83	9	.303	.392	.383
1988 St. Louis	NL	153	575	155	27	1	3	(2	1)	193	80	51	74	2	43	1	12	7	57	9	.86	7	.270	.350	.336
1989 St. Louis	NL	155	593	162	30	8	2	(1	1)	214	82	50	55	3	37	2	11	3	29	7	.81	10	.273	.335	.361
1990 St. Louis	NL	143	512	130	21	1	1	(0	1)	156	61	50	61	4	33	2	7	10	32	6	.84	8	.254	.330	.305
1991 St. Louis	NL	150	550	157	30	3	3	(2	1)	202	96	50	83	2	36	1	6	1	35	9	.80	8	.285	.380	.367
1992 St. Louis	NL	132	518	153	20	2	0	(0	0)	177	73	31	59	4	34	0	12	1	43	9	.83	11	.295	.367	.342
1993 St. Louis	NL	141	545	157	22	6	1	(1	0)	194	75	53	43	1	18	1	7	7	21	8	.72	11	.288	.337	.356
1994 St. Louis	NL	98	381	100	18	3	3	(1	2)	133	51	30	38	3	26	0	10	4	6	3	.67	3	.262	.326	.349
1995 St. Louis	NL	44	156	31	5	1	0	(0	0)	38	16	11	17	0	12	2	5	2	4	3	.57	6	.199	.282	.244
1996 St. Louis	NL	82	227	64	10	2	2	(2	0)	84	36	18	25	0	9	2	7	0	7	5	.58	5	.282	.358	.370
19 ML YEARS		2573	9396	2460	402	69	28	(13	15)	3084	1257	793	1072	79	589	33	214	63	580	148	.80	167	.262	.337	.328

Zane Smith

Pitches: Left **Bats:** Left **Pos:** SP-16 **Ht:** 6'1" **Wt:** 207 **Born:** 12/28/60 **Age:** 36

		HOW MUCH HE PITCHED						WHAT HE GAVE UP										THE RESULTS						
Year Team	Lg	G	GS	CG	GF	IP	BFP	H	R	ER	HR	SH	SF	HB	TBB	IBB	SO	WP	Bk	W	L	Pct.	ShO	Sv-Op	Hld	ERA
1984 Atlanta	NL	3	3	0	1	20	87	16	7	5	1	0	1	0	13	1	16	0	0	1	0	1.000	0	0- -	—	2.25
1985 Atlanta	NL	42	18	2	3	147	631	135	70	62	4	16	1	3	80	5	85	2	0	9	10	.474	2	0- -	—	3.80
1986 Atlanta	NL	38	32	3	2	204.2	889	209	109	92	8	13	6	5	105	6	139	8	0	8	16	.333	1	1- -	—	4.05
1987 Atlanta	NL	36	36	9	0	242	1035	245	130	110	19	12	5	5	91	6	130	5	1	15	10	.600	3	0-0	0	4.09
1988 Atlanta	NL	23	22	3	0	140.1	609	159	72	67	8	15	2	3	44	4	59	2	2	5	10	.333	0	0-0	0	4.30
1989 Atl-Mon	NL	48	17	0	10	147	634	141	76	57	7	15	5	3	52	7	93	4	0	1	13	.071	0	2-3	6	3.49
1990 Mon-Pit	NL	33	31	4	0	215.1	860	196	77	61	15	3	3	3	50	4	130	2	0	12	9	.571	2	0-0	0	2.55
1991 Pittsburgh	NL	35	35	6	0	228	916	234	95	81	15	7	5	2	29	3	120	1	0	16	10	.615	3	0-0	0	3.20
1992 Pittsburgh	NL	23	22	4	0	141	566	138	56	48	8	12	4	2	19	3	56	0	0	8	8	.500	2	0-0	1	3.06
1993 Pittsburgh	NL	14	14	1	0	83	353	97	43	42	5	6	0	0	22	3	32	2	0	3	7	.300	0	0-0	0	4.55
1994 Pittsburgh	NL	25	24	2	0	157	645	162	67	57	18	7	3	0	34	7	57	2	0	10	8	.556	1	0-0	0	3.27
1995 Boston	AL	24	21	0	0	110.2	484	144	78	69	7	0	5	1	23	1	47	0	1	8	8	.500	0	0-0	0	5.61
1996 Pittsburgh	NL	16	16	1	0	83.1	368	104	53	47	7	3	3	4	21	4	47	0	1	4	6	.400	0	0-0	0	5.08
1989 Atlanta	NL	17	17	0	0	99	432	102	65	49	5	10	5	2	33	3	58	3	0	1	12	.077	0	0-0	0	4.45
Montreal	NL	31	0	0	10	48	202	39	11	8	2	5	0	1	19	4	35	1	0	0	1	.000	0	2-3	6	1.50
1990 Montreal	NL	22	21	1	0	139.1	578	141	57	50	11	2	2	3	41	3	80	1	0	6	7	.462	0	0-0	0	3.23
Pittsburgh	NL	11	10	3	1	76	282	55	20	11	4	1	1	0	9	1	50	1	0	6	2	.750	2	0-0	0	1.30
13 ML YEARS		360	291	35	16	1919.1	8077	1980	933	798	122	110	42	31	583	55	1011	28	5	100	115	.465	16	3- -	—	3.74

John Smoltz

Pitches: Right **Bats:** Right **Pos:** SP-35 **Ht:** 6'3" **Wt:** 185 **Born:** 5/15/67 **Age:** 30

		HOW MUCH HE PITCHED						WHAT HE GAVE UP										THE RESULTS						
Year Team	Lg	G	GS	CG	GF	IP	BFP	H	R	ER	HR	SH	SF	HB	TBB	IBB	SO	WP	Bk	W	L	Pct.	ShO	Sv-Op	Hld	ERA
1988 Atlanta	NL	12	12	0	0	64	297	74	40	39	10	2	0	2	33	4	37	2	1	2	7	.222	0	0-0	0	5.48
1989 Atlanta	NL	29	29	5	0	208	847	160	79	68	15	10	7	2	72	2	168	8	3	12	11	.522	0	0-0	0	2.94
1990 Atlanta	NL	34	34	6	0	231.1	966	206	109	99	20	9	8	1	90	3	170	14	3	14	11	.560	2	0-0	0	3.85
1991 Atlanta	NL	36	36	5	0	229.2	947	206	101	97	16	9	9	3	77	1	148	20	2	14	13	.519	0	0-0	0	3.80
1992 Atlanta	NL	35	35	9	0	246.2	1021	206	90	78	17	7	8	5	80	5	215	17	1	15	12	.556	3	0-0	0	2.85
1993 Atlanta	NL	35	35	3	0	243.2	1028	208	104	98	23	13	4	6	100	12	208	13	1	15	11	.577	1	0-0	0	3.62
1994 Atlanta	NL	21	21	1	0	134.2	568	120	69	62	15	7	6	4	48	4	113	7	0	6	10	.375	0	0-0	0	4.14
1995 Atlanta	NL	29	29	2	0	192.2	808	166	76	68	15	13	5	4	72	8	193	13	0	12	7	.632	1	0-0	0	3.18
1996 Atlanta	NL	35	35	6	0	253.2	995	199	93	83	19	12	4	2	55	3	276	10	1	24	8	.750	2	0-0	0	2.94
9 ML YEARS		266	266	37	0	1804.1	7477	1545	761	692	150	82	51	29	627	42	1528	104	12	114	90	.559	9	0-0	0	3.45

Chris Snopek

Bats: R **Throws:** R **Pos:** 3B-27; SS-12; PH-9; DH-3 **Ht:** 6'1" **Wt:** 185 **Born:** 9/20/70 **Age:** 26

					BATTING														BASERUNNING				PERCENTAGES		
Year Team	Lg	G	AB	H	2B	3B	HR	(Hm	Rd)	TB	R	RBI	TBB	IBB	SO	HBP	SH	SF	SB	CS	SB%	GDP	Avg	OBP	SLG
1992 Utica	A-	73	245	69	15	1	2	—	—	92	49	29	52	4	44	2	1	4	14	4	.78	4	.282	.406	.376
1993 South Bend	A	22	72	28	8	1	5	—	—	53	20	18	15	0	13	3	0	2	1	1	.50	1	.389	.500	.736
Sarasota	A+	107	371	91	21	4	10	—	—	150	61	50	65	2	67	1	3	6	3	2	.60	2	.245	.354	.404
1994 Birmingham	AA	106	365	96	25	3	6	—	—	145	58	54	58	3	49	5	3	5	9	4	.69	7	.263	.367	.397
1995 Nashville	AAA	113	393	127	23	4	12	—	—	194	56	55	50	1	72	4	6	3	2	5	.29	5	.323	.402	.494

Year Team	Lg	G	AB	H	2B	3B	HR	(Hm	Rd)	TB	R	RBI	TBB	IBB	SO	HBP	SH	SF	SB	CS	SB%	GDP	Avg	OBP	SLG
1996 Nashville	AAA	40	153	38	8	0	2	(—	—)	52	18	12	21	1	24	1	1	0	2	2	.50	0	.248	.343	.340
1995 Chicago	AL	22	68	22	4	0	1	(1	0)	29	12	7	9	0	12	0	0	0	1	0	1.00	2	.324	.403	.426
1996 Chicago	AL	46	104	27	6	1	6	(3	3)	53	18	18	6	0	16	1	1	1	0	1	.00	5	.260	.304	.510
2 ML YEARS		68	172	49	10	1	7	(4	3)	82	30	25	15	0	28	1	1	1	1	1	.50	7	.285	.344	.477

J.T. Snow

Bats: Both **Throws:** Left **Pos:** 1B-154; PH-3 **Ht:** 6'2" **Wt:** 202 **Born:** 2/26/68 **Age:** 29

Year Team	Lg	G	AB	H	2B	3B	HR	(Hm	Rd)	TB	R	RBI	TBB	IBB	SO	HBP	SH	SF	SB	CS	SB%	GDP	Avg	OBP	SLG
1992 New York	AL	7	14	2	1	0	0	(0	0)	3	1	2	5	1	5	0	0	0	0	0	.00	0	.143	.368	.214
1993 California	AL	129	419	101	18	2	16	(10	6)	171	60	57	55	4	88	2	7	6	3	0	1.00	10	.241	.328	.408
1994 California	AL	61	223	49	4	0	8	(7	1)	77	22	30	19	1	48	3	2	1	0	1	.00	2	.220	.289	.345
1995 California	AL	143	544	157	22	1	24	(14	10)	253	80	102	52	4	91	3	5	2	2	1	.67	16	.289	.353	.465
1996 California	AL	155	575	148	20	1	17	(8	9)	221	69	67	56	6	96	5	2	3	1	6	.14	19	.257	.327	.384
5 ML YEARS		495	1775	457	65	4	65	(39	26)	725	232	258	187	16	328	13	16	12	6	8	.43	47	.257	.331	.408

Steve Soderstrom

Pitches: Right **Bats:** Right **Pos:** SP-3 **Ht:** 6'3" **Wt:** 205 **Born:** 4/3/72 **Age:** 25

Year Team	Lg	G	GS	CG	GF	IP	BFP	H	R	ER	HR	SH	SF	HB	TBB	IBB	SO	WP	Bk	W	L	Pct.	ShO	Sv-Op	Hld	ERA
1994 San Jose	A+	8	8	0	0	40.2	179	34	20	19	2	2	1	4	26	0	40	4	1	2	3	.400	0	0--	—	4.20
1995 Shreveport	AA	22	22	0	0	116	508	106	53	44	6	5	2	10	51	0	91	12	2	9	5	.643	0	0--	—	3.41
1996 Phoenix	AAA	29	29	0	0	171.1	728	178	94	84	13	8	4	7	58	1	80	9	5	7	8	.467	0	0--	—	4.41
1996 San Francisco	NL	3	3	0	0	13.2	63	16	11	8	1	0	2	0	6	0	9	0	0	1	0	1.000	0	0-0	0	5.27

Clint Sodowsky

Pitches: Right **Bats:** Left **Pos:** SP-7 **Ht:** 6'4" **Wt:** 200 **Born:** 7/13/72 **Age:** 24

Year Team	Lg	G	GS	CG	GF	IP	BFP	H	R	ER	HR	SH	SF	HB	TBB	IBB	SO	WP	Bk	W	L	Pct.	ShO	Sv-Op	Hld	ERA
1991 Bristol	R+	14	8	0	3	55	253	49	34	23	2	4	0	4	34	0	44	8	4	0	5	.000	0	0--	—	3.76
1992 Bristol	R+	15	6	0	2	56	243	46	35	22	3	1	2	4	29	0	48	6	1	2	2	.500	0	0--	—	3.54
1993 Fayettevlle	A	27	27	1	0	155.2	676	177	101	88	11	2	6	6	51	0	80	4	5	14	10	.583	0	0--	—	5.09
1994 Lakeland	A+	19	18	1	1	110.1	466	111	58	47	5	2	2	6	34	0	73	12	0	6	3	.667	1	0--	—	3.83
1995 Toledo	AAA	9	9	1	0	60	247	47	21	19	5	2	1	2	30	1	32	1	0	5	1	.833	0	0--	—	2.85
Jacksonvlle	AA	28	28	6	0	183.2	744	149	67	54	9	4	2	8	80	2	109	4	0	10	6	.625	3	0--	—	2.65
1996 Toledo	AAA	19	19	1	0	118.2	525	128	67	52	8	8	3	6	51	0	59	3	2	6	8	.429	0	0--	—	3.94
1995 Detroit	AL	6	6	0	0	23.1	112	24	15	13	4	1	0	0	18	0	14	1	1	2	2	.500	0	0-0	0	5.01
1996 Detroit	AL	7	7	0	0	24.1	132	40	34	32	5	1	0	3	20	0	9	3	0	1	3	.250	0	0-0	0	11.84
2 ML YEARS		13	13	0	0	47.2	244	64	49	45	9	2	0	3	38	0	23	4	1	3	5	.375	0	0-0	0	8.50

Luis Sojo

Bats: R **Throws:** R **Pos:** 2B-41; 3B-34; SS-23; PH-13 **Ht:** 5'11" **Wt:** 175 **Born:** 1/3/66 **Age:** 31

Year Team	Lg	G	AB	H	2B	3B	HR	(Hm	Rd)	TB	R	RBI	TBB	IBB	SO	HBP	SH	SF	SB	CS	SB%	GDP	Avg	OBP	SLG
1990 Toronto	AL	33	80	18	3	0	1	(0	1)	24	14	9	5	0	5	0	0	0	1	1	.50	1	.225	.271	.300
1991 California	AL	113	364	94	14	1	3	(1	2)	119	38	20	14	0	26	5	19	0	4	2	.67	12	.258	.295	.327
1992 California	AL	106	368	100	12	3	7	(2	5)	139	37	43	14	0	24	1	7	1	7	11	.39	14	.272	.299	.378
1993 Toronto	AL	19	47	8	2	0	0	(0	0)	10	5	6	4	0	2	0	2	1	0	0	.00	3	.170	.231	.213
1994 Seattle	AL	63	213	59	9	2	6	(4	2)	90	32	22	8	0	25	2	3	1	2	1	.67	2	.277	.308	.423
1995 Seattle	AL	102	339	98	18	2	7	(4	3)	141	50	39	23	0	19	1	6	1	4	2	.67	9	.289	.335	.416
1996 Sea-NYA	AL	95	287	63	10	1	1	(1	0)	78	23	21	11	0	17	1	8	1	2	2	.50	10	.220	.250	.272
1996 Seattle	AL	77	247	52	8	1	1	(1	0)	65	20	16	10	0	13	1	6	0	2	2	.50	8	.211	.244	.263
New York	AL	18	40	11	2	0	0	(0	0)	13	3	5	1	0	4	0	2	1	0	0	.00	2	.275	.286	.325
7 ML YEARS		531	1698	440	68	9	25	(12	13)	601	199	160	79	0	118	10	45	5	20	19	.51	51	.259	.295	.354

Paul Sorrento

Bats: Left **Throws:** Right **Pos:** 1B-138; PH-16 **Ht:** 6'2" **Wt:** 220 **Born:** 11/17/65 **Age:** 31

Year Team	Lg	G	AB	H	2B	3B	HR	(Hm	Rd)	TB	R	RBI	TBB	IBB	SO	HBP	SH	SF	SB	CS	SB%	GDP	Avg	OBP	SLG
1989 Minnesota	AL	14	21	5	0	0	0	(0	0)	5	2	1	5	1	4	0	0	1	0	0	.00	0	.238	.370	.238
1990 Minnesota	AL	41	121	25	4	1	5	(2	3)	46	11	13	12	0	31	1	0	1	1	1	.50	3	.207	.281	.380
1991 Minnesota	AL	26	47	12	2	0	4	(2	2)	26	6	13	4	2	11	0	0	0	0	0	.00	0	.255	.314	.553
1992 Cleveland	AL	140	458	123	24	1	18	(11	7)	203	52	60	51	7	89	1	1	3	0	3	.00	13	.269	.341	.443
1993 Cleveland	AL	148	463	119	26	1	18	(8	10)	201	75	65	58	11	121	2	0	4	3	1	.75	10	.257	.340	.434
1994 Cleveland	AL	95	322	90	14	0	14	(8	6)	146	43	62	34	6	68	0	1	3	0	1	.00	7	.280	.345	.453
1995 Cleveland	AL	104	323	76	14	0	25	(12	13)	165	50	79	51	6	71	0	0	4	1	1	.50	10	.235	.336	.511
1996 Seattle	AL	143	471	136	32	1	23	(13	10)	239	67	93	57	10	103	7	2	5	0	2	.00	10	.289	.370	.507
8 ML YEARS		711	2226	586	116	4	107	(56	51)	1031	306	386	272	43	498	11	4	21	5	9	.36	56	.263	.343	.463

Sammy Sosa

Bats: Right **Throws:** Right **Pos:** RF-124   **Ht:** 6'0" **Wt:** 190 **Born:** 11/12/68 **Age:** 28

Year Team	Lg	G	AB	H	2B	3B	HR	(Hm	Rd)	TB	R	RBI	TBB	IBB	SO	HBP	SH	SF	SB	CS	SB%	GDP	Avg	OBP	SLG
1989 Tex-ChA	AL	58	183	47	8	0	4	(1	3)	67	27	13	11	2	47	2	5	2	7	5	.58	6	.257	.303	.366
1990 Chicago	AL	153	532	124	26	10	15	(10	5)	215	72	70	33	4	150	6	2	6	32	16	.67	10	.233	.282	.404
1991 Chicago	AL	116	316	64	10	1	10	(3	7)	106	39	33	14	2	98	2	5	1	13	6	.68	5	.203	.240	.335
1992 Chicago	NL	67	262	68	7	2	8	(4	4)	103	41	25	19	1	63	4	4	2	15	7	.68	4	.260	.317	.393
1993 Chicago	NL	159	598	156	25	5	33	(23	10)	290	92	93	38	6	135	4	0	1	36	11	.77	14	.261	.309	.485
1994 Chicago	NL	105	426	128	17	6	25	(11	14)	232	59	70	25	1	92	2	1	4	22	13	.63	7	.300	.339	.545
1995 Chicago	NL	144	564	151	17	3	36	(19	17)	282	89	119	58	11	134	5	0	2	34	7	.83	8	.268	.340	.500
1996 Chicago	NL	124	498	136	21	2	40	(26	14)	282	84	100	34	6	134	5	0	4	18	5	.78	14	.273	.323	.564
1989 Texas	AL	25	84	20	3	0	1	(0	1)	26	8	3	0	0	20	0	4	0	0	2	.00	3	.238	.238	.310
Chicago	AL	33	99	27	5	0	3	(1	2)	41	19	10	11	2	27	2	1	2	7	3	.70	3	.273	.351	.414
8 ML YEARS		926	3379	874	131	29	171	(97	74)	1576	503	523	232	33	853	30	17	22	177	70	.72	68	.259	.310	.466

Steve Sparks

Pitches: Right **Bats:** Right **Pos:** SP-13; RP-7   **Ht:** 6'0" **Wt:** 180 **Born:** 7/2/65 **Age:** 31

Year Team	Lg	G	GS	CG	GF	IP	BFP	H	R	ER	HR	SH	SF	HB	TBB	IBB	SO	WP	Bk	W	L	Pct.	ShO	Sv-Op	Hld	ERA
1987 Helena	R+	10	9	2	0	57.2	256	68	44	30	8	3	1	4	20	1	47	5	0	6	3	.667	0	0--	—	4.68
1988 Beloit	A	25	24	5	0	164	688	162	80	69	8	4	2	7	51	2	96	5	5	9	13	.409	1	0--	—	3.79
1989 Stockton	A+	23	22	3	0	164	660	125	55	44	6	0	1	10	53	0	126	6	5	13	5	.722	2	0--	—	2.41
1990 El Paso	AA	7	6	0	1	30.1	143	43	24	22	4	0	1	1	15	0	17	2	0	1	2	.333	0	0--	—	6.53
Stockton	A+	19	19	5	0	129.1	549	136	63	53	4	4	3	8	31	0	77	7	1	10	7	.588	1	0--	—	3.69
1991 El Paso	AA	4	4	0	0	17	90	30	22	18	1	0	0	0	9	0	10	2	1	1	2	.333	0	0--	—	9.53
Stockton	A+	24	24	8	0	179.2	762	160	70	61	4	3	4	7	98	2	139	13	0	9	10	.474	2	0--	—	3.06
1992 El Paso	AA	28	22	3	3	140.2	613	159	99	84	11	6	10	8	50	1	79	6	3	9	8	.529	0	1--	—	5.37
1993 New Orleans	AAA	29	28	7	0	180.1	767	174	89	77	17	4	9	5	80	1	104	7	2	9	13	.409	1	0--	—	3.84
1994 New Orleans	AAA	28	27	5	0	183.2	787	183	101	91	23	2	4	11	68	0	105	14	3	10	12	.455	1	0--	—	4.46
1996 New Orleans	AAA	11	10	3	0	57.2	267	64	43	32	8	1	4	2	35	0	27	6	0	2	6	.250	0	0--	—	4.99
1995 Milwaukee	AL	33	27	3	2	202	875	210	111	104	17	5	12	3	86	1	96	5	1	9	11	.450	0	0-0	0	4.63
1996 Milwaukee	AL	20	13	1	2	88.2	406	103	66	65	19	3	1	5	52	0	21	6	0	4	7	.364	0	0-0	0	6.60
2 ML YEARS		53	40	4	4	290.2	1281	313	177	169	36	8	13	8	138	1	117	11	1	13	18	.419	0	0-0	0	5.23

Tim Spehr

Bats: Right **Throws:** Right **Pos:** C-58; PH-12; RF-1   **Ht:** 6'2" **Wt:** 200 **Born:** 7/2/66 **Age:** 30

Year Team	Lg	G	AB	H	2B	3B	HR	(Hm	Rd)	TB	R	RBI	TBB	IBB	SO	HBP	SH	SF	SB	CS	SB%	GDP	Avg	OBP	SLG
1991 Kansas City	AL	37	74	14	5	0	3	(1	2)	28	7	14	9	0	18	1	3	1	1	0	1.00	2	.189	.282	.378
1993 Montreal	NL	53	87	20	6	0	2	(0	2)	32	14	10	6	1	20	1	3	2	2	0	1.00	0	.230	.281	.368
1994 Montreal	NL	52	36	9	3	1	0	(0	0)	14	8	5	4	0	11	0	1	0	2	0	1.00	0	.250	.325	.389
1995 Montreal	NL	41	35	9	5	0	1	(0	1)	17	4	3	6	0	7	0	3	0	0	0	.00	0	.257	.366	.486
1996 Montreal	NL	63	44	4	1	0	1	(1	0)	8	4	3	3	0	15	1	1	0	1	0	1.00	1	.091	.167	.182
5 ML YEARS		246	276	56	20	1	7	(2	5)	99	37	35	28	1	71	3	11	3	6	0	1.00	3	.203	.281	.359

Bill Spiers

Bats: L **Throws:** R **Pos:** 3B-76; PH-41; 2B-7; SS-5; 1B-4; CF-1; RF-1   **Ht:** 6'2" **Wt:** 190 **Born:** 6/5/66 **Age:** 31

Year Team	Lg	G	AB	H	2B	3B	HR	(Hm	Rd)	TB	R	RBI	TBB	IBB	SO	HBP	SH	SF	SB	CS	SB%	GDP	Avg	OBP	SLG
1989 Milwaukee	AL	114	345	88	9	3	4	(1	3)	115	44	33	21	1	63	1	4	2	10	2	.83	2	.255	.298	.333
1990 Milwaukee	AL	112	363	88	15	3	2	(2	0)	115	44	36	16	0	45	1	6	3	11	6	.65	12	.242	.274	.317
1991 Milwaukee	AL	133	414	117	13	6	8	(1	7)	166	71	54	34	0	55	2	10	4	14	8	.64	9	.283	.337	.401
1992 Milwaukee	AL	12	16	5	2	0	0	(0	0)	7	2	2	1	0	4	0	1	0	1	1	.50	0	.313	.353	.438
1993 Milwaukee	AL	113	340	81	8	4	2	(2	0)	103	43	36	29	2	51	4	9	4	9	8	.53	11	.238	.302	.303
1994 Milwaukee	AL	73	214	54	10	1	0	(0	0)	66	27	17	19	1	42	1	3	0	7	1	.88	5	.252	.316	.308
1995 New York	NL	63	72	15	2	1	0	(0	0)	19	5	11	12	1	15	0	1	2	1	0	1.00	0	.208	.314	.264
1996 Houston	NL	122	218	55	10	1	6	(3	3)	85	27	26	20	4	34	2	1	1	7	0	1.00	3	.252	.320	.390
8 ML YEARS		742	1982	503	69	19	22	(9	13)	676	263	215	152	9	309	11	35	16	59	27	.69	42	.254	.308	.341

Scott Spiezio

Bats: Both **Throws:** Right **Pos:** 3B-5; DH-4   **Ht:** 6'2" **Wt:** 195 **Born:** 9/21/72 **Age:** 24

Year Team	Lg	G	AB	H	2B	3B	HR	(Hm	Rd)	TB	R	RBI	TBB	IBB	SO	HBP	SH	SF	SB	CS	SB%	GDP	Avg	OBP	SLG
1993 Sou. Oregon	A-	31	125	41	10	2	3	—	—	64	32	19	16	0	18	0	0	0	0	1	.00	1	.328	.404	.512
Modesto	A+	32	110	28	9	1	1	—	—	42	12	13	23	0	19	1	1	0	1	5	.17	1	.255	.388	.382
1994 Modesto	A+	127	453	127	32	5	14	—	—	211	84	68	88	4	72	7	3	9	5	0	1.00	15	.280	.399	.466
1995 Huntsville	AA	141	528	149	33	8	13	—	—	237	78	86	67	2	78	4	4	14	10	3	.77	10	.282	.359	.449
1996 Edmonton	AAA	140	523	137	30	4	20	—	—	235	87	91	56	6	66	4	3	5	6	5	.55	7	.262	.335	.449
1996 Oakland	AL	9	29	9	2	0	2	(1	1)	17	6	8	4	1	4	0	2	0	0	1	.00	0	.310	.394	.586

Paul Spoljaric

Pitches: Left   **Bats:** Right   **Pos:** RP-28   **Ht:** 6'3"   **Wt:** 205   **Born:** 9/24/70   **Age:** 26

Year Team	Lg	G	GS	CG	GF	IP	BFP	H	R	ER	HR	SH	SF	HB	TBB	IBB	SO	WP	Bk	W	L	Pct.	ShO	Sv-Op	Hld	ERA
1996 Syracuse *	AAA	17	0	0	9	22	91	20	9	8	2	2	1	1	6	1	24	1	0	3	0	1.000	0	4--	—	3.27
St. Cathrns *	A-	2	2	0	0	5	18	3	0	0	0	0	0	0	0	0	7	1	0	0	0	.000	0	0--	—	0.00
1994 Toronto	AL	2	1	0	0	2.1	21	5	10	10	3	0	0	0	9	1	2	0	0	0	1	.000	0	0-0	0	38.57
1996 Toronto	AL	28	0	0	12	38	163	30	17	13	6	1	1	2	19	1	38	0	0	2	2	.500	0	1-1	5	3.08
2 ML YEARS		30	1	0	12	40.1	184	35	27	23	9	1	1	2	28	2	40	0	0	2	3	.400	0	1-1	5	5.13

Jerry Spradlin

Pitches: Right   **Bats:** Both   **Pos:** RP-1   **Ht:** 6'7"   **Wt:** 240   **Born:** 6/14/67   **Age:** 30

Year Team	Lg	G	GS	CG	GF	IP	BFP	H	R	ER	HR	SH	SF	HB	TBB	IBB	SO	WP	Bk	W	L	Pct.	ShO	Sv-Op	Hld	ERA
1996 Indianapols *	AAA	49	8	0	28	100	415	94	49	37	14	3	1	4	23	3	79	3	0	6	8	.429	0	15--	—	3.33
1993 Cincinnati	NL	37	0	0	16	49	193	44	20	19	4	3	4	0	9	0	24	3	1	2	1	.667	0	2-3	0	3.49
1994 Cincinnati	NL	6	0	0	3	8	38	12	11	9	2	0	2	0	2	0	4	0	0	0	0	.000	0	0-0	0	10.13
1996 Cincinnati	NL	1	0	0	1	0.1	1	0	0	0	0	0	0	0	0	0	0	1	0	0	0	.000	0	0-0	0	0.00
3 ML YEARS		44	0	0	19	57.1	232	56	31	28	6	3	6	0	11	0	28	4	1	2	1	.667	0	2-3	0	4.40

Ed Sprague

Bats: Right   **Throws:** Right   **Pos:** 3B-148; DH-10; PH-1   **Ht:** 6'2"   **Wt:** 210   **Born:** 7/25/67   **Age:** 29

Year Team	Lg	G	AB	H	2B	3B	HR	(Hm	Rd)	TB	R	RBI	TBB	IBB	SO	HBP	SH	SF	SB	CS	SB%	GDP	Avg	OBP	SLG
1991 Toronto	AL	61	160	44	7	0	4	(3	1)	63	17	20	19	2	43	3	0	1	0	3	.00	2	.275	.361	.394
1992 Toronto	AL	22	47	11	2	0	1	(1	0)	16	6	7	3	0	7	0	0	0	0	0	.00	0	.234	.280	.340
1993 Toronto	AL	150	546	142	31	1	12	(8	4)	211	50	73	32	1	85	10	2	6	1	0	1.00	23	.260	.310	.386
1994 Toronto	AL	109	405	97	19	1	11	(6	5)	151	38	44	23	1	95	11	2	4	1	0	1.00	11	.240	.296	.373
1995 Toronto	AL	144	521	127	27	2	18	(12	6)	212	77	74	58	3	96	15	1	7	0	0	.00	19	.244	.333	.407
1996 Toronto	AL	159	591	146	35	2	36	(17	19)	293	88	101	60	3	146	12	0	7	0	0	.00	7	.247	.325	.496
6 ML YEARS		645	2270	567	121	6	82	(47	35)	946	276	319	195	10	472	51	5	25	2	3	.40	62	.250	.320	.417

Dennis Springer

Pitches: Right   **Bats:** Right   **Pos:** SP-15; RP-5   **Ht:** 5'10"   **Wt:** 185   **Born:** 2/12/65   **Age:** 32

Year Team	Lg	G	GS	CG	GF	IP	BFP	H	R	ER	HR	SH	SF	HB	TBB	IBB	SO	WP	Bk	W	L	Pct.	ShO	Sv-Op	Hld	ERA
1987 Great Falls	R+	23	5	1	13	65.2	290	70	38	21	3	4	2	2	16	2	54	4	0	4	3	.571	0	6--	—	2.88
1988 Bakersfield	A+	32	20	6	7	154	657	135	75	56	13	8	7	5	62	4	108	12	1	13	7	.650	4	2--	—	3.27
Vero Beach	A+	1	1	0	0	5.2	25	6	3	3	0	0	0	0	2	0	4	0	0	0	0	.000	0	0--	—	4.76
1989 San Antonio	AA	19	19	4	0	140	583	128	58	49	13	10	2	4	46	2	89	3	0	6	8	.429	1	0--	—	3.15
Albuquerque	AAA	8	7	0	0	41	193	58	28	22	5	1	0	0	14	0	18	1	0	4	1	.800	0	0--	—	4.83
1990 Albuquerque	AAA	2	2	0	0	6.1	37	10	4	4	1	0	0	2	7	0	2	0	0	0	0	.000	0	0--	—	5.68
San Antonio	AA	24	24	3	0	163.1	691	147	76	60	8	5	6	1	73	0	77	7	1	8	6	.571	2	0--	—	3.31
1991 San Antonio	AA	30	24	2	0	164.2	725	153	96	81	18	6	11	5	91	2	138	7	0	10	10	.500	2	0--	—	4.43
1992 San Antonio	AA	18	18	4	0	122	525	114	61	59	6	3	2	4	49	3	73	4	0	6	7	.462	0	0--	—	4.35
Albuquerque	AAA	11	11	1	0	62	269	70	45	39	7	4	1	4	22	0	36	3	0	2	7	.222	0	0--	—	5.66
1993 Albuquerque	AAA	35	18	0	5	130.2	591	173	104	87	18	5	6	2	39	1	69	7	1	3	8	.273	0	0--	—	5.99
1994 Reading	AA	24	19	2	3	135	567	125	74	51	11	8	5	1	44	1	118	14	0	5	8	.385	0	2--	—	3.40
1995 Scranton-WB	AAA	30	23	4	3	171	715	163	101	89	19	0	10	7	47	1	115	8	0	10	11	.476	0	0--	—	4.68
1996 Vancouver	AAA	16	12	6	1	109.1	437	89	35	33	9	4	0	4	36	1	78	10	1	10	3	.769	3	0--	—	2.72
1995 Philadelphia	NL	4	4	0	0	22.1	94	21	15	12	3	2	0	1	9	1	15	1	0	0	3	.000	0	0-0	0	4.84
1996 California	AL	20	15	2	3	94.2	413	91	65	58	24	0	1	6	43	0	64	1	0	5	6	.455	1	0-0	1	5.51
2 ML YEARS		24	19	2	3	117	507	112	80	70	27	2	1	7	52	1	79	2	0	5	9	.357	1	0-0	1	5.38

Russ Springer

Pitches: Right   **Bats:** Right   **Pos:** RP-44; SP-7   **Ht:** 6'4"   **Wt:** 205   **Born:** 11/7/68   **Age:** 28

Year Team	Lg	G	GS	CG	GF	IP	BFP	H	R	ER	HR	SH	SF	HB	TBB	IBB	SO	WP	Bk	W	L	Pct.	ShO	Sv-Op	Hld	ERA
1992 New York	AL	14	0	0	5	16	75	18	11	11	4	0	0	1	10	0	12	0	0	0	0	.000	0	0-0	2	6.19
1993 California	AL	14	9	1	3	60	278	73	48	48	11	1	1	3	32	1	31	6	0	1	6	.143	0	0-0	0	7.20
1994 California	AL	18	5	0	6	45.2	198	53	28	28	9	1	1	0	14	0	28	2	0	2	2	.500	0	2-3	6	5.52
1995 Cal-Phi		33	6	0	6	78.1	350	82	48	46	16	2	2	7	35	4	70	2	0	1	2	.333	0	1-2	0	5.29
1996 Philadelphia	NL	51	7	0	12	96.2	437	106	60	50	12	5	3	1	38	6	94	5	0	3	10	.231	0	0-3	6	4.66
1995 California	AL	19	6	0	3	51.2	238	60	37	35	11	1	0	5	25	1	38	1	0	1	2	.333	0	1-2	0	6.10
Philadelphia	NL	14	0	0	3	26.2	112	22	11	11	5	1	2	2	10	3	32	1	0	0	0	.000	0	0-0	0	3.71
5 ML YEARS		130	27	1	32	296.2	1338	332	195	183	48	9	7	12	129	11	235	15	0	7	20	.259	0	3-8	9	5.55

212

Scott Stahoviak

Bats: Left   **Throws:** Right   **Pos:** 1B-114; PH-17; DH-9   **Ht:** 6'5"   **Wt:** 222   **Born:** 3/6/70   **Age:** 27

				BATTING														BASERUNNING				PERCENTAGES		
Year Team	Lg	G	AB	H	2B	3B	HR	(Hm | Rd)	TB	R	RBI	TBB	IBB	SO	HBP	SH	SF	SB	CS	SB%	GDP	Avg	OBP	SLG
1993 Minnesota	AL	20	57	11	4	0	0	(0 | 0)	15	1	1	3	0	22	0	0	0	0	2	.00	2	.193	.233	.263
1995 Minnesota	AL	94	263	70	19	0	3	(1 | 2)	98	28	23	30	1	61	1	0	2	5	1	.83	3	.266	.341	.373
1996 Minnesota	AL	130	405	115	30	3	13	(8 | 5)	190	72	61	59	7	114	2	1	2	3	3	.50	9	.284	.376	.469
3 ML YEARS		244	725	196	53	3	16	(9 | 7)	303	101	85	92	8	197	3	1	4	8	6	.57	14	.270	.353	.418

Matt Stairs

Bats: L   **Throws:** R   **Pos:** RF-29; PH-18; LF-16; DH-5; 1B-1   **Ht:** 5'9"   **Wt:** 200   **Born:** 2/27/68   **Age:** 29

				BATTING														BASERUNNING				PERCENTAGES		
Year Team	Lg	G	AB	H	2B	3B	HR	(Hm | Rd)	TB	R	RBI	TBB	IBB	SO	HBP	SH	SF	SB	CS	SB%	GDP	Avg	OBP	SLG
1996 Edmonton *	AAA	51	180	62	16	1	8	—	—	104	35	41	21	0	34	0	1	6	0	0	.00	4	.344	.401	.578
1992 Montreal	NL	13	30	5	2	0	0	(0 | 0)	7	2	5	7	0	7	0	0	1	0	0	.00	1	.167	.316	.233
1993 Montreal	NL	6	8	3	1	0	0	(0 | 0)	4	1	2	0	0	1	0	0	0	0	0	.00	1	.375	.375	.500
1995 Boston	AL	39	88	23	7	1	1	(0 | 1)	35	8	17	4	0	14	1	1	1	0	1	.00	4	.261	.298	.398
1996 Oakland	AL	61	137	38	5	1	10	(5 | 5)	75	21	23	19	2	23	1	0	1	1	1	.50	1	.277	.367	.547
4 ML YEARS		119	263	69	15	2	11	(5 | 6)	121	32	47	30	2	45	2	1	3	1	2	.33	7	.262	.339	.460

Andy Stankiewicz

Bats: R   **Throws:** R   **Pos:** PH-38; 2B-19; SS-13; 3B-1   **Ht:** 5'9"   **Wt:** 165   **Born:** 8/10/64   **Age:** 32

				BATTING														BASERUNNING				PERCENTAGES		
Year Team	Lg	G	AB	H	2B	3B	HR	(Hm | Rd)	TB	R	RBI	TBB	IBB	SO	HBP	SH	SF	SB	CS	SB%	GDP	Avg	OBP	SLG
1992 New York	AL	116	400	107	22	2	2	(2 | 0)	139	52	25	38	0	42	5	7	1	9	5	.64	13	.268	.338	.348
1993 New York	AL	16	9	0	0	0	0	(0 | 0)	0	5	0	1	0	1	0	0	0	0	0	.00	0	.000	.100	.000
1994 Houston	NL	37	54	14	3	0	1	(1 | 0)	20	10	5	12	0	12	1	2	0	1	1	.50	2	.259	.403	.370
1995 Houston	NL	43	52	6	1	0	0	(0 | 0)	7	6	7	12	2	19	0	1	0	4	2	.67	1	.115	.281	.135
1996 Montreal	NL	64	77	22	5	1	0	(0 | 0)	29	12	9	6	1	12	3	1	1	1	0	1.00	1	.286	.356	.377
5 ML YEARS		276	592	149	31	3	3	(3 | 0)	195	85	46	69	3	86	9	11	2	15	8	.65	17	.252	.338	.329

Mike Stanley

Bats: Right   **Throws:** Right   **Pos:** C-105; PH-13; DH-10   **Ht:** 6'0"   **Wt:** 190   **Born:** 6/25/63   **Age:** 34

				BATTING														BASERUNNING				PERCENTAGES		
Year Team	Lg	G	AB	H	2B	3B	HR	(Hm | Rd)	TB	R	RBI	TBB	IBB	SO	HBP	SH	SF	SB	CS	SB%	GDP	Avg	OBP	SLG
1986 Texas	AL	15	30	10	3	0	1	(0 | 1)	16	4	1	3	0	7	0	0	0	1	0	1.00	0	.333	.394	.533
1987 Texas	AL	78	216	59	8	1	6	(3 | 3)	87	34	37	31	0	48	1	1	4	3	0	1.00	6	.273	.361	.403
1988 Texas	AL	94	249	57	8	0	3	(1 | 2)	74	21	27	37	0	62	0	1	5	0	0	.00	6	.229	.323	.297
1989 Texas	AL	67	122	30	3	1	1	(1 | 0)	38	9	11	12	1	29	2	1	0	1	0	1.00	5	.246	.324	.311
1990 Texas	AL	103	189	47	8	1	2	(1 | 1)	63	21	19	30	2	25	0	6	1	1	0	1.00	4	.249	.350	.333
1991 Texas	AL	95	181	45	13	1	3	(1 | 2)	69	25	25	34	0	44	2	5	1	0	0	.00	6	.249	.372	.381
1992 New York	AL	68	173	43	7	0	8	(5 | 3)	74	24	27	33	0	45	1	0	0	0	0	.00	6	.249	.372	.428
1993 New York	AL	130	423	129	17	1	26	(17 | 9)	226	70	84	57	4	85	5	0	6	1	1	.50	10	.305	.389	.534
1994 New York	AL	82	290	87	20	0	17	(8 | 9)	158	54	57	39	2	56	2	0	2	0	0	.00	10	.300	.384	.545
1995 New York	AL	118	399	107	29	1	18	(13 | 5)	192	63	83	57	1	106	5	0	9	1	1	.50	14	.268	.360	.481
1996 Boston	AL	121	397	107	20	1	24	(10 | 14)	201	73	69	69	3	62	5	0	2	2	0	1.00	5	.270	.383	.506
11 ML YEARS		971	2669	721	136	7	109	(60 | 49)	1198	398	440	402	13	569	23	14	30	10	2	.83	71	.270	.367	.449

Mike Stanton

Pitches: Left   **Bats:** Left   **Pos:** RP-81   **Ht:** 6'1"   **Wt:** 215   **Born:** 6/2/67   **Age:** 30

		HOW MUCH HE PITCHED						WHAT HE GAVE UP										THE RESULTS					
Year Team	Lg	G	GS	CG	GF	IP	BFP	H	R	ER	HR	SH	SF	HB	TBB	IBB	SO	WP	Bk	W	L	Pct.	ShO	Sv-Op	Hld	ERA
1989 Atlanta	NL	20	0	0	10	24	94	17	4	4	0	4	0	0	8	1	27	1	0	0	1	.000	0	7-8	2	1.50
1990 Atlanta	NL	7	0	0	4	7	42	16	16	14	1	1	0	1	4	2	7	1	0	0	3	.000	0	2-3	0	18.00
1991 Atlanta	NL	74	0	0	20	78	314	62	27	25	6	6	0	1	21	6	54	0	0	5	5	.500	0	7-10	15	2.88
1992 Atlanta	NL	65	0	0	23	63.2	264	59	32	29	6	1	2	2	20	2	44	3	0	5	4	.556	0	8-11	15	4.10
1993 Atlanta	NL	63	0	0	41	52	236	51	35	27	4	5	2	0	29	7	43	1	0	4	6	.400	0	27-33	5	4.67
1994 Atlanta	NL	49	0	0	15	45.2	197	41	18	18	2	2	1	3	26	3	35	1	0	3	1	.750	0	3-4	10	3.55
1995 Atl-Bos		48	0	0	22	40.1	178	48	23	19	6	2	1	1	14	2	23	2	1	2	1	.667	0	1-3	8	4.24
1996 Bos-Tex	AL	81	0	0	28	78.2	327	78	32	32	11	4	2	0	27	5	60	3	2	4	4	.500	0	1-6	22	3.66
1995 Atlanta	NL	26	0	0	10	19.1	94	31	14	12	3	2	1	1	6	2	13	1	1	1	1	.500	0	1-2	4	5.59
Boston	AL	22	0	0	12	21	84	17	9	7	3	0	0	0	8	0	10	1	0	1	0	1.000	0	0-1	4	3.00
1996 Boston	AL	59	0	0	19	56.1	239	58	24	24	9	3	2	0	23	4	46	3	2	4	3	.571	0	1-5	15	3.83
Texas	AL	22	0	0	9	22.1	88	20	8	8	2	1	0	0	4	1	14	0	0	0	1	.000	0	0-1	7	3.22
8 ML YEARS		407	0	0	163	389.1	1652	372	187	168	36	25	8	8	149	28	293	12	3	23	25	.479	0	56-78	77	3.88

Terry Steinbach

Bats: R **Throws:** R **Pos:** C-137; PH-10; DH-4; 1B-1   **Ht:** 6'1" **Wt:** 195 **Born:** 3/2/62 **Age:** 35

Year Team	Lg	G	AB	H	2B	3B	HR	(Hm	Rd)	TB	R	RBI	TBB	IBB	SO	HBP	SH	SF	SB	CS	SB%	GDP	Avg	OBP	SLG
1986 Oakland	AL	6	15	5	0	0	2	(0	2)	11	3	4	1	0	0	0	0	0	0	0	.00	0	.333	.375	.733
1987 Oakland	AL	122	391	111	16	3	16	(6	10)	181	66	56	32	2	66	9	3	3	1	2	.33	10	.284	.349	.463
1988 Oakland	AL	104	351	93	19	1	9	(6	3)	141	42	51	33	2	47	6	3	5	3	0	1.00	13	.265	.334	.402
1989 Oakland	AL	130	454	124	13	1	7	(5	2)	160	37	42	30	2	66	2	2	3	1	2	.33	14	.273	.319	.352
1990 Oakland	AL	114	379	95	15	2	9	(3	6)	141	32	57	19	1	66	4	5	3	0	1	.00	11	.251	.291	.372
1991 Oakland	AL	129	456	125	31	1	6	(1	5)	176	50	67	22	4	70	7	0	9	2	2	.50	15	.274	.312	.386
1992 Oakland	AL	128	438	122	20	1	12	(3	9)	180	48	53	45	3	58	1	0	3	2	3	.40	20	.279	.345	.411
1993 Oakland	AL	104	389	111	19	1	10	(5	5)	162	47	43	25	1	65	3	0	1	3	3	.50	13	.285	.333	.416
1994 Oakland	AL	103	369	105	21	2	11	(5	6)	163	51	57	26	4	62	0	1	6	2	1	.67	10	.285	.327	.442
1995 Oakland	AL	114	406	113	26	1	15	(9	6)	186	43	65	25	4	74	3	1	4	1	3	.25	15	.278	.322	.458
1996 Oakland	AL	145	514	140	25	1	35	(16	19)	272	79	100	49	5	115	6	0	2	0	1	.00	16	.272	.342	.529
11 ML YEARS		1199	4162	1144	205	14	132	(59	73)	1773	498	595	307	28	689	41	15	39	15	18	.45	137	.275	.328	.426

Garrett Stephenson

Pitches: Right **Bats:** Right **Pos:** RP-3   **Ht:** 6'4" **Wt:** 195 **Born:** 1/2/72 **Age:** 25

Year Team	Lg	G	GS	CG	GF	IP	BFP	H	R	ER	HR	SH	SF	HB	TBB	IBB	SO	WP	Bk	W	L	Pct.	ShO	Sv-Op	Hld	ERA
1992 Bluefield	R+	12	3	0	0	32.1	141	35	22	17	4	0	1	1	7	0	30	4	1	3	1	.750	0	0--	—	4.73
1993 Albany	A	30	24	3	3	171.1	697	142	65	54	6	1	4	5	44	0	147	3	5	16	7	.696	2	1--	—	2.84
1994 Frederick	A+	18	17	1	0	107.1	450	91	62	48	13	2	5	5	36	2	133	2	4	7	5	.583	0	0--	—	4.02
Bowie	AA	7	7	1	0	36.2	161	47	22	21	2	0	1	0	11	1	32	3	2	3	2	.600	1	0--	—	5.15
1995 Bowie	AA	29	29	1	0	175.1	743	154	87	71	23	5	7	18	47	0	139	4	2	7	10	.412	0	0--	—	3.64
1996 Rochester	AAA	23	21	3	1	121.2	515	123	66	65	13	2	5	10	44	0	86	3	2	7	6	.538	1	0--	—	4.81
1996 Baltimore	AL	3	0	0	2	6.1	35	13	9	9	1	1	0	1	3	1	3	0	0	0	1	.000	0	0-0	0	12.79

Dave Stevens

Pitches: Right **Bats:** Right **Pos:** RP-49   **Ht:** 6'3" **Wt:** 205 **Born:** 3/4/70 **Age:** 27

Year Team	Lg	G	GS	CG	GF	IP	BFP	H	R	ER	HR	SH	SF	HB	TBB	IBB	SO	WP	Bk	W	L	Pct.	ShO	Sv-Op	Hld	ERA
1994 Minnesota	AL	24	0	0	6	45	208	55	35	34	6	2	0	1	23	2	24	3	0	5	2	.714	0	0-0	1	6.80
1995 Minnesota	AL	56	0	0	34	65.2	302	74	40	37	14	4	5	1	32	1	47	2	0	5	4	.556	0	10-12	5	5.07
1996 Minnesota	AL	49	0	0	38	58	251	58	31	30	12	3	3	0	25	2	29	1	0	3	3	.500	0	11-16	0	4.66
3 ML YEARS		129	0	0	78	168.2	761	187	106	101	32	9	8	2	80	5	100	6	0	13	9	.591	0	21-28	6	5.39

Lee Stevens

Bats: Left **Throws:** Left **Pos:** 1B-18; PH-6; LF-5   **Ht:** 6'4" **Wt:** 219 **Born:** 7/10/67 **Age:** 29

Year Team	Lg	G	AB	H	2B	3B	HR	(Hm	Rd)	TB	R	RBI	TBB	IBB	SO	HBP	SH	SF	SB	CS	SB%	GDP	Avg	OBP	SLG
1996 Okla. City *	AAA	117	431	140	37	2	32	—	—	277	84	94	58	8	90	3	0	6	3	0	1.00	8	.325	.404	.643
1990 California	AL	67	248	53	10	0	7	(4	3)	84	28	32	22	3	75	0	2	3	1	1	.50	8	.214	.275	.339
1991 California	AL	18	58	17	7	0	0	(0	0)	24	8	9	6	2	12	0	1	1	1	2	.33	0	.293	.354	.414
1992 California	AL	106	312	69	19	0	7	(2	5)	109	25	37	29	6	64	1	1	2	1	4	.20	4	.221	.288	.349
1996 Texas	AL	27	78	18	2	3	3	(2	1)	35	6	12	6	0	22	1	0	1	0	0	.00	2	.231	.291	.449
4 ML YEARS		218	696	157	38	3	17	(8	9)	252	67	90	63	11	173	2	4	7	3	7	.30	14	.226	.289	.362

Todd Steverson

Bats: Right **Throws:** Right **Pos:** PH-1   **Ht:** 6'2" **Wt:** 200 **Born:** 11/15/71 **Age:** 25

Year Team	Lg	G	AB	H	2B	3B	HR	(Hm	Rd)	TB	R	RBI	TBB	IBB	SO	HBP	SH	SF	SB	CS	SB%	GDP	Avg	OBP	SLG
1992 St. Cathrns	A-	65	225	47	9	0	6	—	—	74	26	24	26	0	83	1	0	3	23	7	.77	2	.209	.290	.329
1993 Dunedin	A+	106	413	112	32	4	11	—	—	185	68	54	44	2	118	1	3	1	15	12	.56	3	.271	.342	.448
1994 Knoxville	AA	124	415	109	24	5	9	—	—	170	59	38	71	2	112	1	1	1	20	11	.65	3	.263	.371	.410
1995 Toledo	AAA	9	28	3	0	0	1	—	—	6	6	1	5	0	13	0	0	0	0	2	.00	1	.107	.242	.214
1996 Las Vegas	AAA	100	301	72	16	3	12	—	—	130	42	50	47	5	87	1	1	5	6	5	.55	8	.239	.339	.432
1995 Detroit	AL	30	42	11	0	0	2	(0	2)	17	11	6	6	0	10	0	0	2	2	0	1.00	0	.262	.340	.405
1996 San Diego	NL	1	1	0	0	0	0	(0	0)	0	0	0	0	0	1	0	0	0	0	0	.00	0	.000	.000	.000
2 ML YEARS		31	43	11	0	0	2	(0	2)	17	11	6	6	0	11	0	0	2	2	0	1.00	0	.256	.333	.395

Shannon Stewart

Bats: Right **Throws:** Right **Pos:** CF-6; PH-1   **Ht:** 6'1" **Wt:** 190 **Born:** 2/25/74 **Age:** 23

Year Team	Lg	G	AB	H	2B	3B	HR	(Hm	Rd)	TB	R	RBI	TBB	IBB	SO	HBP	SH	SF	SB	CS	SB%	GDP	Avg	OBP	SLG
1992 Blue Jays	R	50	172	40	1	0	1	—	—	44	44	11	24	0	27	3	4	2	32	5	.86	3	.233	.323	.256
1993 St. Cathrns	A-	75	301	84	15	2	3	—	—	112	53	29	33	1	43	2	3	3	25	10	.71	7	.279	.351	.372
1994 Hagerstown	A	56	225	73	10	5	4	—	—	105	39	25	23	1	39	1	2	2	15	11	.58	3	.324	.386	.467

Year Team	Lg	G	AB	H	2B	3B	HR	(Hm	Rd)	TB	R	RBI	TBB	IBB	SO	HBP	SH	SF	SB	CS	SB%	GDP	Avg	OBP	SLG
1995 Knoxville	AA	138	498	143	24	6	5	—	—	194	89	55	89	3	61	6	3	5	42	16	.72	13	.287	.398	.390
1996 Syracuse	AAA	112	420	125	26	8	6	—	—	185	77	42	54	0	61	2	5	4	35	8	.81	6	.298	.377	.440
1995 Toronto	AL	12	38	8	0	0	0	(0	0)	8	2	1	5	0	5	1	0	0	1	0	1.00		.211	.318	.211
1996 Toronto	AL	7	17	3	1	0	0	(0	0)	4	2	2	1	0	4	0	0	0	1	0	1.00	1	.176	.222	.235
2 ML YEARS		19	55	11	1	0	0	(0	0)	12	4	3	6	0	9	1	0	0	3	0	1.00	1	.200	.290	.218

Kurt Stillwell

Bats: B **Throws:** R **Pos:** 2B-21; PH-18; SS-9; 3B-6; DH-1; 1B-1   **Ht:** 5'11" **Wt:** 185 **Born:** 6/4/65   **Age:** 32

Year Team	Lg	G	AB	H	2B	3B	HR	(Hm	Rd)	TB	R	RBI	TBB	IBB	SO	HBP	SH	SF	SB	CS	SB%	GDP	Avg	OBP	SLG
1996 Okla. City *	AAA	4	17	4	0	0	0	—	—	4	1	1	0	0	2	0	0	0	0	0	.00	0	.235	.235	.235
1986 Cincinnati	NL	104	279	64	6	1	0	(0	0)	72	31	26	30	1	47	2	4	0	6	2	.75	1	.229	.309	.258
1987 Cincinnati	NL	131	395	102	20	7	4	(3	1)	148	54	33	32	2	50	2	2	2	4	6	.40	5	.258	.316	.375
1988 Kansas City	AL	128	459	115	28	5	10	(4	6)	183	63	53	47	0	76	3	6	3	6	5	.55	7	.251	.322	.399
1989 Kansas City	AL	130	463	121	20	7	7	(2	5)	176	52	54	42	2	64	3	5	3	9	6	.60	3	.261	.325	.380
1990 Kansas City	AL	144	506	126	35	4	3	(3	0)	178	60	51	39	1	60	4	4	7	0	2	.00	11	.249	.304	.352
1991 Kansas City	AL	122	385	102	17	1	6	(1	5)	139	44	51	33	5	56	1	5	4	3	4	.43	8	.265	.322	.361
1992 San Diego	NL	114	379	86	15	3	2	(1	1)	113	35	24	26	9	58	1	4	6	4	1	.80	6	.227	.274	.298
1993 SD-Cal		79	182	42	6	2	1	(1	0)	55	11	14	15	2	33	1	3	2	6	3	.67	4	.231	.290	.302
1996 Texas	AL	46	77	21	4	0	1	(1	0)	28	12	4	10	0	11	1	1	0	0	0	.00	1	.273	.364	.364
1993 San Diego	NL	57	121	26	4	0	1	(1	0)	33	9	11	11	2	22	1	2	0	4	3	.57	2	.215	.286	.273
California	AL	22	61	16	2	2	0	(0	0)	22	2	3	4	0	11	0	1	2	2	0	1.00	2	.262	.299	.361
9 ML YEARS		998	3125	779	151	30	34	(16	18)	1092	362	310	274	22	455	18	34	27	38	29	.57	50	.249	.311	.349

Kelly Stinnett

Bats: Right **Throws:** Right **Pos:** C-14; DH-1   **Ht:** 5'11" **Wt:** 195 **Born:** 2/14/70   **Age:** 27

Year Team	Lg	G	AB	H	2B	3B	HR	(Hm	Rd)	TB	R	RBI	TBB	IBB	SO	HBP	SH	SF	SB	CS	SB%	GDP	Avg	OBP	SLG
1996 New Orleans *	AAA	95	334	96	21	1	27	(Hm	Rd)	200	63	70	31	2	83	13	0	4	3	3	.50	6	.287	.366	.599
1994 New York	NL	47	150	38	6	2	2	(0	2)	54	20	14	11	1	28	5	0	1	2	0	1.00	3	.253	.323	.360
1995 New York	NL	77	196	43	8	1	4	(1	3)	65	23	18	29	3	65	6	0	0	2	0	1.00	3	.219	.338	.332
1996 Milwaukee	AL	14	26	2	0	0	0	(0	0)	2	1	0	2	0	11	1	0	0	0	0	.00	0	.077	.172	.077
3 ML YEARS		138	372	83	14	3	6	(1	5)	121	44	32	42	4	104	12	0	1	4	0	1.00	6	.223	.321	.325

Kevin Stocker

Bats: Both **Throws:** Right **Pos:** SS-119; PH-4   **Ht:** 6'1" **Wt:** 175 **Born:** 2/13/70   **Age:** 27

Year Team	Lg	G	AB	H	2B	3B	HR	(Hm	Rd)	TB	R	RBI	TBB	IBB	SO	HBP	SH	SF	SB	CS	SB%	GDP	Avg	OBP	SLG
1996 Scrnton-WB *	AAA	12	44	10	3	0	2	—	—	19	5	6	0	0	4	1	1	0	1	0	1.00	1	.227	.244	.432
1993 Philadelphia	NL	70	259	84	12	3	2	(1	1)	108	46	31	30	11	43	8	4	1	5	0	1.00	8	.324	.409	.417
1994 Philadelphia	NL	82	271	74	11	2	2	(2	0)	95	38	28	44	8	41	7	4	4	2	2	.50	3	.273	.383	.351
1995 Philadelphia	NL	125	412	90	14	3	1	(1	0)	113	42	32	43	9	75	9	10	3	6	1	.86	7	.218	.304	.274
1996 Philadelphia	NL	119	394	100	22	6	5	(0	5)	149	46	41	43	9	89	8	3	4	6	4	.60	6	.254	.336	.378
4 ML YEARS		396	1336	348	59	14	10	(4	6)	465	172	132	160	37	248	32	21	12	19	7	.73	24	.260	.351	.348

Todd Stottlemyre

Pitches: Right **Bats:** Left **Pos:** SP-33; RP-1   **Ht:** 6'3" **Wt:** 200 **Born:** 5/20/65   **Age:** 32

Year Team	Lg	G	GS	CG	GF	IP	BFP	H	R	ER	HR	SH	SF	HB	TBB	IBB	SO	WP	Bk	W	L	Pct.	ShO	Sv-Op	Hld	ERA
1988 Toronto	AL	28	16	0	2	98	443	109	70	62	15	5	3	4	46	5	67	2	3	4	8	.333	0	0-1	0	5.69
1989 Toronto	AL	27	18	0	4	127.2	545	137	56	55	11	3	7	5	44	4	63	4	1	7	7	.500	0	0-0	0	3.88
1990 Toronto	AL	33	33	4	0	203	866	214	101	98	18	3	5	8	69	4	115	6	1	13	17	.433	0	0-0	0	4.34
1991 Toronto	AL	34	34	1	0	219	921	194	97	92	21	0	8	12	75	3	116	4	0	15	8	.652	0	0-0	0	3.78
1992 Toronto	AL	28	27	6	0	174	755	175	99	87	20	2	11	10	63	4	98	7	0	12	11	.522	2	0-0	0	4.50
1993 Toronto	AL	30	28	1	0	176.2	786	204	107	95	11	5	11	3	69	5	98	7	1	11	12	.478	1	0-0	0	4.84
1994 Toronto	AL	26	19	3	5	140.2	605	149	67	66	19	4	5	7	48	2	105	0	0	7	7	.500	1	1-3	0	4.22
1995 Oakland	AL	31	31	2	0	209.2	920	228	117	106	26	4	4	6	80	7	205	11	0	14	7	.667	0	0-0	0	4.55
1996 St. Louis	NL	34	33	5	0	223.1	944	191	100	96	30	12	9	4	93	8	194	8	1	14	11	.560	2	0-0	0	3.87
9 ML YEARS		271	239	22	11	1572	6785	1601	814	757	171	38	63	59	587	42	1061	49	7	97	88	.524	6	1-4	0	4.33

Doug Strange

B: B **T:** R **Pos:** PH-46; 3B-39; DH-10; LF-10; 1B-3; 2B-3; RF-1   **Ht:** 6'1" **Wt:** 185 **Born:** 4/13/64   **Age:** 33

Year Team	Lg	G	AB	H	2B	3B	HR	(Hm	Rd)	TB	R	RBI	TBB	IBB	SO	HBP	SH	SF	SB	CS	SB%	GDP	Avg	OBP	SLG
1989 Detroit	AL	64	196	42	4	1	1	(1	0)	51	16	14	17	0	36	1	3	0	3	3	.50	6	.214	.280	.260
1991 Chicago	NL	3	9	4	1	0	0	(0	0)	5	0	1	0	0	1	0	1	0	1	0	1.00	0	.444	.455	.556
1992 Chicago	NL	52	94	15	1	0	1	(0	1)	19	7	5	10	2	15	0	2	0	1	0	1.00	2	.160	.240	.202
1993 Texas	AL	145	484	124	29	0	7	(4	3)	174	58	60	43	3	69	3	8	4	6	4	.60	12	.256	.318	.360

Year Team	Lg	G	AB	H	2B	3B	HR	(Hm Rd)	TB	R	RBI	TBB	IBB	SO	HBP	SH	SF	SB	CS	SB%	GDP	Avg	OBP	SLG
1994 Texas	AL	73	226	48	12	1	5	(3 2)	77	26	26	15	0	38	3	4	2	1	3	.25	6	.212	.268	.341
1995 Seattle	AL	74	155	42	9	2	2	(1 1)	61	19	21	10	0	25	2	1	0	0	3	.00	3	.271	.323	.394
1996 Seattle	AL	88	183	43	7	1	3	(2 1)	61	19	23	14	0	31	1	0	2	1	0	1.00	3	.235	.290	.333
7 ML YEARS		499	1347	318	63	5	19	(11 8)	448	145	150	109	5	215	11	18	9	13	13	.50	32	.236	.297	.333

Darryl Strawberry

Bats: L **Throws:** L **Pos:** DH-26; LF-26; RF-8; PH-6   **Ht:** 6'6" **Wt:** 215 **Born:** 3/12/62 **Age:** 35

Year Team	Lg	G	AB	H	2B	3B	HR	(Hm Rd)	TB	R	RBI	TBB	IBB	SO	HBP	SH	SF	SB	CS	SB%	GDP	Avg	OBP	SLG
1996 St. Paul *	IND	29	108	47	7	0	18	— —	108	31	39	22	6	16	2	0	0	4	2	.67	1	.435	.538	1.000
Columbus *	AAA	2	8	3	0	0	3	— —	12	3	5	0	0	3	0	0	0	0	0	.00	0	.375	.375	1.500
1983 New York	NL	122	420	108	15	7	26	(10 16)	215	63	74	47	9	128	4	0	2	19	6	.76	5	.257	.336	.512
1984 New York	NL	147	522	131	27	4	26	(8 18)	244	75	97	75	15	131	0	1	4	27	8	.77	8	.251	.343	.467
1985 New York	NL	111	393	109	15	4	29	(14 15)	219	78	79	73	13	96	1	0	3	26	11	.70	9	.277	.389	.557
1986 New York	NL	136	475	123	27	5	27	(11 16)	241	76	93	72	9	141	6	0	9	28	12	.70	4	.259	.358	.507
1987 New York	NL	154	532	151	32	5	39	(20 19)	310	108	104	97	13	122	7	0	4	36	12	.75	4	.284	.398	.583
1988 New York	NL	153	543	146	27	3	**39**	(21 18)	296	101	101	85	21	127	3	0	9	29	14	.67	6	.269	.366	**.545**
1989 New York	NL	134	476	107	26	1	29	(15 14)	222	69	77	61	13	105	1	0	3	11	4	.73	4	.225	.312	.466
1990 New York	NL	152	542	150	18	1	37	(24 13)	281	92	108	70	15	110	4	0	5	15	8	.65	5	.277	.361	.518
1991 Los Angeles	NL	139	505	134	22	4	28	(14 14)	248	86	99	75	4	125	1	0	3	10	8	.56	8	.265	.361	.491
1992 Los Angeles	NL	43	156	37	8	0	5	(3 2)	60	20	25	19	4	34	1	0	1	3	1	.75	2	.237	.322	.385
1993 Los Angeles	NL	32	100	14	2	0	5	(3 2)	31	12	12	16	1	19	2	0	2	1	0	1.00	1	.140	.267	.310
1994 San Francisco	NL	29	92	22	3	1	4	(2 2)	39	13	17	19	4	22	0	0	2	0	3	.00	2	.239	.363	.424
1995 New York	AL	32	87	24	4	1	3	(3 0)	39	15	13	10	1	22	2	0	0	0	0	.00	0	.276	.364	.448
1996 New York	AL	63	202	53	13	0	11	(8 3)	99	35	36	31	5	55	1	0	3	6	5	.55	3	.262	.359	.490
14 ML YEARS		1447	5045	1309	239	36	308	(156 152)	2544	843	935	750	127	1237	35	1	52	211	92	.70	61	.259	.356	.504

Tanyon Sturtze

Pitches: Right **Bats:** Right **Pos:** RP-6   **Ht:** 6'5" **Wt:** 205 **Born:** 10/12/70 **Age:** 26

Year Team	Lg	G	GS	CG	GF	IP	BFP	H	R	ER	HR	SH	SF	HB	TBB	IBB	SO	WP	Bk	W	L	Pct.	ShO	Sv-Op	Hld	ERA
1990 Athletics	R	12	10	0	1	48	232	55	41	29	2	0	2	5	26	0	30	5	2	2	5	.286	0	0- -	—	5.44
1991 Madison	A	27	27	0	0	163	685	136	77	56	5	6	6	5	58	5	88	10	5	10	5	.667	0	0- -	—	3.09
1992 Modesto	A+	25	25	1	0	151	656	143	72	63	6	5	5	4	78	1	126	5	0	7	11	.389	0	0- -	—	3.75
1993 Huntsville	AA	28	28	1	0	165.2	734	169	102	88	16	3	11	6	85	2	112	11	1	5	12	.294	1	0- -	—	4.78
1994 Huntsville	AA	17	17	1	0	103.1	435	100	40	37	5	3	4	3	39	1	63	1	0	6	3	.667	0	0- -	—	3.22
Tacoma	AAA	11	9	0	2	64.2	294	73	36	29	5	0	1	2	34	2	28	6	0	4	5	.444	0	0- -	—	4.04
1995 Iowa	AAA	23	17	1	0	86	398	108	66	65	18	5	2	5	42	1	48	6	0	4	7	.364	1	0- -	—	6.80
1996 Iowa	AAA	51	1	0	18	72.1	315	80	42	39	7	3	0	3	33	2	51	6	1	6	4	.600	0	4- -	—	4.85
1995 Chicago	NL	2	0	0	0	2	9	2	2	2	1	0	0	0	1	0	0	0	0	0	0	.000	0	0-0	0	9.00
1996 Chicago	NL	6	0	0	3	11	51	16	11	11	3	0	0	0	5	0	7	0	0	1	0	1.000	0	0-0	0	9.00
2 ML YEARS		8	0	0	3	13	60	18	13	13	4	0	0	0	6	0	7	0	0	1	0	1.000	0	0-0	0	9.00

Chris Stynes

Bats: R **Throws:** R **Pos:** LF-19; PH-11; 2B-5; DH-3; 3B-2   **Ht:** 5'9" **Wt:** 175 **Born:** 1/19/73 **Age:** 24

Year Team	Lg	G	AB	H	2B	3B	HR	(Hm Rd)	TB	R	RBI	TBB	IBB	SO	HBP	SH	SF	SB	CS	SB%	GDP	Avg	OBP	SLG
1991 Blue Jays	R	57	219	67	15	1	4	— —	96	29	39	9	0	38	1	1	0	10	3	.77	1	.306	.336	.438
1992 Myrtle Bch	A	127	489	139	36	0	7	— —	196	67	46	16	1	43	8	14	4	28	14	.67	8	.284	.315	.401
1993 Dunedin	A+	123	496	151	28	5	7	— —	210	72	48	25	2	40	3	4	4	19	9	.68	12	.304	.339	.423
1994 Knoxville	AA	136	545	173	32	4	8	— —	237	79	79	23	4	36	7	5	4	28	12	.70	12	.317	.351	.435
1995 Omaha	AAA	83	306	84	12	5	9	— —	133	51	42	27	0	24	5	4	5	4	5	.44	7	.275	.338	.435
1996 Omaha	AAA	72	284	101	22	2	10	— —	157	50	40	18	2	17	4	0	3	7	3	.70	7	.356	.398	.553
1995 Kansas City	AL	22	35	6	1	0	0	(0 0)	7	7	2	4	0	3	0	0	0	0	0	.00	3	.171	.256	.200
1996 Kansas City	AL	36	92	27	6	0	0	(0 0)	33	8	6	2	0	5	0	1	0	5	2	.71	1	.293	.309	.359
2 ML YEARS		58	127	33	7	0	0	(0 0)	40	15	8	6	0	8	0	1	0	5	2	.71	4	.260	.293	.315

Scott Sullivan

Pitches: Right **Bats:** Right **Pos:** RP-7   **Ht:** 6'4" **Wt:** 210 **Born:** 3/13/71 **Age:** 26

Year Team	Lg	G	GS	CG	GF	IP	BFP	H	R	ER	HR	SH	SF	HB	TBB	IBB	SO	WP	Bk	W	L	Pct.	ShO	Sv-Op	Hld	ERA
1993 Billings	R+	18	7	2	9	54	224	33	13	10	1	3	0	6	25	0	79	2	5	5	0	1.000	2	3- -	—	1.67
1994 Chattanooga	AA	34	13	2	16	121.1	508	101	60	46	8	2	1	6	40	1	111	5	4	11	7	.611	0	7- -	—	3.41
1995 Indianapolis	AAA	44	0	0	21	58.2	253	51	31	23	2	4	2	4	24	4	54	3	0	4	3	.571	0	1- -	—	3.53
1996 Indianapolis	AAA	53	3	0	12	108.2	452	95	38	33	10	1	2	4	37	3	77	5	0	5	2	.714	0	1- -	—	2.73
1995 Cincinnati	NL	3	0	0	1	3.2	17	4	2	2	0	1	0	0	2	0	2	0	0	0	0	.000	0	0-0	0	4.91
1996 Cincinnati	NL	7	0	0	4	8	35	7	2	2	0	1	0	1	5	0	3	1	0	0	0	.000	0	0-0	0	2.25
2 ML YEARS		10	0	0	5	11.2	52	11	4	4	0	2	0	1	7	0	5	1	0	0	0	.000	0	0-0	0	3.09

Jeff Suppan

Pitches: Right **Bats:** Right **Pos:** SP-4; RP-4 **Ht:** 6'2" **Wt:** 210 **Born:** 1/2/75 **Age:** 22

Year Team	Lg	G	GS	CG	GF	IP	BFP	H	R	ER	HR	SH	SF	HB	TBB	IBB	SO	WP	Bk	W	L	Pct.	ShO	Sv-Op	Hld	ERA
1993 Red Sox	R	10	9	2	1	57.2	239	52	20	14	0	1	0	3	16	0	64	2	0	4	3	.571	1	0--	—	2.18
1994 Sarasota	A+	27	27	4	0	174	712	153	74	63	10	6	2	6	50	0	173	9	1	13	7	.650	2	0--	—	3.26
1995 Pawtucket	AAA	7	7	0	0	45.2	191	50	29	27	9	0	1	1	9	0	32	2	0	2	3	.400	0	0--	—	5.32
Trenton	AA	22	22	1	0	144.2	600	136	64	53	14	1	4	9	35	1	120	6	0	8	5	.615	1	0--	—	3.30
1996 Pawtucket	AAA	22	22	7	0	145.1	593	130	66	52	16	0	3	6	25	0	142	9	1	10	6	.625	1	0--	—	3.22
1995 Boston	AL	8	3	0	1	22.2	100	29	15	15	4	1	1	0	5	1	19	0	0	1	2	.333	0	0-0	1	5.96
1996 Boston	AL	8	4	0	2	22.2	107	29	19	19	3	1	4	1	13	0	13	3	0	1	1	.500	0	0-0	0	7.54
2 ML YEARS		16	7	0	3	45.1	207	58	34	34	7	2	5	1	18	1	32	3	0	2	3	.400	0	0-0	1	6.75

B.J. Surhoff

Bats: L **Throws:** R **Pos:** 3B-106; LF-27; DH-10; PH-3; 1B-2 **Ht:** 6'1" **Wt:** 200 **Born:** 8/4/64 **Age:** 32

Year Team	Lg	G	AB	H	2B	3B	HR	(Hm	Rd)	TB	R	RBI	TBB	IBB	SO	HBP	SH	SF	SB	CS	SB%	GDP	Avg	OBP	SLG
1987 Milwaukee	AL	115	395	118	22	3	7	(5	2)	167	50	68	36	1	30	0	5	9	11	10	.52	13	.299	.350	.423
1988 Milwaukee	AL	139	493	121	21	0	5	(2	3)	157	47	38	31	9	49	3	11	3	21	6	.78	12	.245	.292	.318
1989 Milwaukee	AL	126	436	108	17	4	5	(3	2)	148	42	55	25	1	29	3	3	10	14	12	.54	8	.248	.287	.339
1990 Milwaukee	AL	135	474	131	21	4	6	(4	2)	178	55	59	41	5	37	1	7	7	18	7	.72	8	.276	.331	.376
1991 Milwaukee	AL	143	505	146	19	4	5	(3	2)	188	57	68	26	2	33	0	13	9	5	8	.38	21	.289	.319	.372
1992 Milwaukee	AL	139	480	121	19	1	4	(3	1)	154	63	62	46	8	41	2	5	10	14	8	.64	9	.252	.314	.321
1993 Milwaukee	AL	148	552	151	38	3	7	(4	3)	216	66	79	36	5	47	2	4	5	12	9	.57	9	.274	.318	.391
1994 Milwaukee	AL	40	134	35	11	2	5	(2	3)	65	20	22	16	0	14	0	2	2	0	1	.00	5	.261	.336	.485
1995 Milwaukee	AL	117	415	133	26	3	13	(7	6)	204	72	73	37	4	43	4	2	4	7	3	.70	7	.320	.378	.492
1996 Baltimore	AL	143	537	157	27	6	21	(12	9)	259	74	82	47	8	79	3	2	1	0	1	.00	7	.292	.352	.482
10 ML YEARS		1245	4421	1221	221	30	78	(45	33)	1736	546	606	341	43	402	18	54	60	102	65	.61	99	.276	.326	.393

Makoto Suzuki

Pitches: Right **Bats:** Right **Pos:** RP-1 **Ht:** 6'3" **Wt:** 195 **Born:** 5/31/75 **Age:** 22

Year Team	Lg	G	GS	CG	GF	IP	BFP	H	R	ER	HR	SH	SF	HB	TBB	IBB	SO	WP	Bk	W	L	Pct.	ShO	Sv-Op	Hld	ERA
1992 Salinas	A+	1	0	0	0	1	3	0	0	0	0	0	0	0	0	0	1	0	0	0	0	.000	0	0--	—	0.00
1993 San Bernrdo	A+	48	1	0	35	80.2	351	59	37	33	5	3	2	2	56	4	87	12	2	4	4	.500	0	12--	—	3.68
1994 Jacksonvlle	AA	8	0	0	1	12.2	58	15	4	4	1	0	1	0	6	0	10	0	0	1	0	1.000	0	1--	—	2.84
1995 Mariners	R	4	3	0	0	4	19	5	4	3	1	0	0	1	6	0	3	0	0	1	0	1.000	0	0--	—	6.75
Riverside	A+	10	3	0	1	11.2	58	15	8	7	1	0	1	1	6	0	9	2	0	1	1	.500	0	0--	—	5.40
1996 Port City	AA	16	16	0	0	74.1	320	69	41	39	10	2	1	2	32	0	66	0	0	3	6	.333	0	0--	—	4.72
Tacoma	AAA	13	2	0	6	22.1	110	31	19	18	7	2	0	0	12	2	14	3	0	0	3	.000	0	0--	—	7.25
1996 Seattle	AL	1	0	0	0	1.1	8	2	3	3	0	0	0	0	2	1	1	0	0	0	0	.000	0	0-0	0	20.25

Dale Sveum

Bats: Both **Throws:** Right **Pos:** 3B-10; PH-2 **Ht:** 6'3" **Wt:** 185 **Born:** 11/23/63 **Age:** 33

Year Team	Lg	G	AB	H	2B	3B	HR	(Hm	Rd)	TB	R	RBI	TBB	IBB	SO	HBP	SH	SF	SB	CS	SB%	GDP	Avg	OBP	SLG
1996 Calgary *	AAA	101	343	103	28	2	23	—	—	204	62	84	33	3	71	3	0	2	2	1	.67	2	.300	.365	.595
1986 Milwaukee	AL	91	317	78	13	2	7	(4	3)	116	35	35	32	0	63	1	5	1	4	3	.57	7	.246	.316	.366
1987 Milwaukee	AL	153	535	135	27	3	25	(9	16)	243	86	95	40	4	133	1	5	5	2	6	.25	11	.252	.303	.454
1988 Milwaukee	AL	129	467	113	14	4	9	(2	7)	162	41	51	21	0	122	1	3	3	1	0	1.00	6	.242	.274	.347
1990 Milwaukee	AL	48	117	23	7	0	1	(0	1)	33	15	12	12	0	30	2	0	2	0	1	.00	2	.197	.278	.282
1991 Milwaukee	AL	90	266	64	19	1	4	(3	1)	97	33	43	32	0	78	1	5	4	2	4	.33	8	.241	.320	.365
1992 Phi-ChA		94	249	49	13	0	4	(1	3)	74	28	28	28	4	68	0	2	5	1	1	.50	6	.197	.273	.297
1993 Oakland	AL	30	79	14	2	1	2	(0	2)	24	12	6	16	1	21	0	1	0	0	0	.00	4	.177	.316	.304
1994 Seattle	AL	10	27	5	0	0	1	(0	1)	8	3	2	2	0	10	0	0	0	0	0	.00	1	.185	.241	.296
1996 Pittsburgh	NL	12	34	12	5	0	1	(0	1)	20	9	5	6	0	6	0	0	0	0	0	.00	0	.353	.450	.588
1992 Philadelphia	NL	54	135	24	4	0	2	(0	2)	34	13	16	16	4	39	0	0	2	1	0	.00	5	.178	.264	.252
Chicago	AL	40	114	25	9	0	2	(1	1)	40	15	12	12	0	29	0	2	3	1	1	.50	1	.219	.287	.351
9 ML YEARS		657	2091	493	100	11	54	(20	34)	777	262	277	189	9	531	6	21	20	10	15	.40	43	.236	.298	.372

Dave Swartzbaugh

Pitches: Right **Bats:** Right **Pos:** SP-5; RP-1 **Ht:** 6'2" **Wt:** 210 **Born:** 2/11/68 **Age:** 29

Year Team	Lg	G	GS	CG	GF	IP	BFP	H	R	ER	HR	SH	SF	HB	TBB	IBB	SO	WP	Bk	W	L	Pct.	ShO	Sv-Op	Hld	ERA
1989 Geneva	A-	18	10	0	1	75	338	81	59	41	5	0	3	1	35	1	77	8	1	2	3	.400	1	0--	—	4.92
1990 Peoria	A	29	29	5	0	169.2	736	147	88	72	11	1	3	7	89	1	129	10	4	8	11	.421	2	0--	—	3.82
1991 Peoria	A	5	5	1	0	34.1	145	21	16	7	0	2	1	2	15	1	31	2	2	5	0	.000	0	0--	—	1.83
Winston-Sal	A+	15	15	2	0	93.2	379	71	22	19	3	5	1	1	42	1	73	4	0	10	4	.714	1	0--	—	1.83
Charlotte	AA	1	1	0	0	5.1	25	6	7	6	1	0	0	0	3	1	5	1	0	1	0	.000	0	0--	—	10.13
1992 Charlotte	AA	27	27	5	0	165	689	134	78	67	13	5	10	0	62	2	111	5	1	7	10	.412	2	0--	—	3.65

217

Year Team	Lg	G	GS	CG	GF	IP	BFP	H	R	ER	HR	SH	SF	HB	TBB	IBB	SO	WP	Bk	W	L	Pct.	ShO	Sv-Op	Hld	ERA
1993 Iowa	AAA	26	9	0	5	86.2	385	90	57	51	16	6	4	5	44	1	69	6	0	4	6	.400	0	1--	—	5.30
Orlando	AA	10	9	1	0	66	268	52	33	31	5	2	1	3	18	0	59	2	0	1	3	.250	0	0--	—	4.23
1994 Iowa	AAA	10	0	0	1	19.1	94	24	18	18	8	1	2	1	15	1	14	2	0	1	0	1.000	0	0--	—	8.38
Orlando	AA	42	1	0	11	79	327	70	36	29	7	5	3	4	19	2	70	0	0	2	4	.333	0	2--	—	3.30
1995 Orlando	AA	16	0	0	3	29	111	18	10	8	1	1	1	2	7	0	37	1	1	4	0	1.000	0	0--	—	2.48
Iowa	AAA	46	0	0	12	76	298	51	20	16	2	3	1	3	25	1	75	2	1	7	0	1.000	0	0--	—	1.89
1996 Iowa	AAA	44	13	0	11	118.1	491	106	61	51	22	5	4	3	33	1	103	5	0	8	11	.421	0	0--	—	3.88
1995 Chicago	NL	7	0	0	2	7.1	27	5	2	0	0	0	0	0	3	1	5	0	0	0	0	.000	0	0-0	0	0.00
1996 Chicago	NL	6	5	0	0	24	110	26	17	17	3	2	0	0	14	1	13	2	0	0	2	.000	0	0-0	0	6.38
2 ML YEARS		13	5	0	2	31.1	137	31	19	17	3	2	0	0	17	2	18	2	0	0	2	.000	0	0-0	0	4.88

Mark Sweeney

Bats: L **Throws:** L **Pos:** PH-48; LF-36; 1B-15; RF-7   **Ht:** 6'1" **Wt:** 195 **Born:** 10/26/69 **Age:** 27

Year Team	Lg	G	AB	H	2B	3B	HR	(Hm	Rd)	TB	R	RBI	TBB	IBB	SO	HBP	SH	SF	SB	CS	SB%	GDP	Avg	OBP	SLG
1991 Boise	A-	70	234	66	10	3	4	—		94	45	34	51	2	42	5	1	3	9	5	.64	7	.282	.416	.402
1992 Quad City	A	120	424	115	20	5	14	—		187	65	76	47	3	85	4	6	5	15	11	.58	6	.271	.346	.441
1993 Palm Spring	A+	66	245	87	18	3	3	—		120	41	47	42	6	29	2	0	3	9	6	.60	4	.355	.449	.490
Midland	AA	51	188	67	13	2	9	—		111	41	32	27	3	22	6	0	4	1	1	.50	5	.356	.444	.590
1994 Midland	AA	14	50	15	3	0	·3	—		27	13	18	10	2	10	0	1	2	1	1	.50	5	.300	.403	.540
Vancouver	AAA	103	344	98	12	3	8	—		140	59	49	59	3	50	5	1	3	3	3	.50	5	.285	.394	.407
1995 Vancouver	AAA	69	226	78	14	2	7	—		117	48	59	43	4	33	2	1	1	3	1	.75	6	.345	.452	.518
Louisville	AAA	22	76	28	8	0	2	—		42	15	22	14	1	8	2	0	2	2	0	1.00	0	.368	.468	.553
1995 St. Louis	NL	37	77	21	2	0	2	(0	2)	29	5	13	10	0	15	0	1	2	1	1	.50	3	.273	.348	.377
1996 St. Louis	NL	98	170	45	9	0	3	(0	3)	63	32	22	33	2	29	1	5	0	3	0	1.00	4	.265	.387	.371
2 ML YEARS		135	247	66	11	0	5	(0	5)	92	37	35	43	2	44	1	6	2	4	1	.80	7	.267	.375	.372

Mike Sweeney

Bats: Right **Throws:** Right **Pos:** C-26; DH-22; PH-2   **Ht:** 6'1" **Wt:** 195 **Born:** 7/22/73 **Age:** 23

Year Team	Lg	G	AB	H	2B	3B	HR	(Hm	Rd)	TB	R	RBI	TBB	IBB	SO	HBP	SH	SF	SB	CS	SB%	GDP	Avg	OBP	SLG
1991 Royals	R	38	102	22	3	0	1	—		28	8	11	11	0	9	0	0	2	0	0	.00	0	.216	.287	.275
1992 Eugene	A-	59	199	44	12	1	4	—		70	17	28	13	0	54	4	1	2	3	3	.50	0	.221	.280	.352
1993 Eugene	A-	53	175	42	10	2	6	—		74	32	29	30	0	41	3	0	1	1	0	1.00	2	.240	.359	.423
1994 Rockford	A	86	276	83	20	3	10	—		139	47	52	55	4	43	9	0	8	0	1	.00	8	.301	.427	.504
1995 Wilmington	A+	99	332	103	23	1	18	—		182	61	53	60	7	39	9	1	5	6	1	.86	4	.310	.424	.548
1996 Wichita	AA	66	235	75	18	1	14	—		137	45	51	32	1	29	2	0	4	3	2	.60	5	.319	.399	.583
Omaha	AAA	25	101	26	9	0	3	—		44	14	16	6	0	13	3	1	0	0	0	.00	0	.257	.318	.436
1995 Kansas City	AL	4	4	1	0	0	0	(0	0)	1	1	0	0	0	0	0	0	0	0	0	.00	0	.250	.250	.250
1996 Kansas City	AL	50	165	46	10	0	4	(1	3)	68	23	24	18	0	21	4	0	3	1	2	.33	7	.279	.358	.412
2 ML YEARS		54	169	47	10	0	4	(1	3)	69	24	24	18	0	21	4	0	3	1	2	.33	7	.278	.356	.408

Bill Swift

Pitches: Right **Bats:** Right **Pos:** RP-4; SP-3   **Ht:** 6'0" **Wt:** 197 **Born:** 10/27/61 **Age:** 35

Year Team	Lg	G	GS	CG	GF	IP	BFP	H	R	ER	HR	SH	SF	HB	TBB	IBB	SO	WP	Bk	W	L	Pct.	ShO	Sv-Op	Hld	ERA
1996 Salem *	A+	2	2	0	0	6	29	9	4	3	0	1	2	0	1	0	4	0	0	0	0	.000	0	0--	—	4.50
1985 Seattle	AL	23	21	0	0	120.2	532	131	71	64	8	6	3	5	48	5	55	5	3	6	10	.375	0	0--	—	4.77
1986 Seattle	AL	29	17	1	3	115.1	534	148	85	70	6	5	3	7	55	2	55	2	1	2	9	.182	0	0--	—	5.46
1988 Seattle	AL	38	24	6	4	174.2	757	199	99	89	10	5	3	8	65	3	47	6	2	8	12	.400	1	0-1	1	4.59
1989 Seattle	AL	37	16	0	7	130	551	140	72	64	7	4	3	2	38	4	45	4	1	7	3	.700	0	1-1	2	4.43
1990 Seattle	AL	55	8	0	18	128	533	135	46	34	4	5	4	7	21	6	42	8	3	6	4	.600	0	6-7	7	2.39
1991 Seattle	AL	71	0	0	30	90.1	359	74	22	20	3	2	0	1	26	4	48	2	1	1	2	.333	0	17-18	13	1.99
1992 San Francisco	NL	30	22	3	2	164.2	655	144	41	38	6	5	2	3	43	3	77	0	1	10	4	.714	2	1-1	3	**2.08**
1993 San Francisco	NL	34	34	1	0	232.2	928	195	82	73	18	4	2	6	55	5	157	4	0	21	8	.724	1	0-0	0	2.82
1994 San Francisco	NL	17	17	0	0	109.1	457	109	49	41	10	7	2	1	31	6	62	0	0	8	7	.533	0	0-0	0	3.38
1995 Colorado	NL	19	19	0	0	105.2	463	122	62	58	12	6	1	1	43	2	68	2	0	9	3	.750	0	0-0	0	4.94
1996 Colorado	NL	7	3	0	2	18.1	81	23	12	11	1	0	1	0	5	0	5	0	0	1	1	.500	0	2-2	1	5.40
11 ML YEARS		360	181	11	66	1389.2	5850	1420	641	562	84	49	24	41	430	40	661	35	12	79	63	.556	4	27--	—	3.64

Greg Swindell

Pitches: Left **Bats:** Right **Pos:** RP-15; SP-6   **Ht:** 6'3" **Wt:** 225 **Born:** 1/2/65 **Age:** 32

Year Team	Lg	G	GS	CG	GF	IP	BFP	H	R	ER	HR	SH	SF	HB	TBB	IBB	SO	WP	Bk	W	L	Pct.	ShO	Sv-Op	Hld	ERA
1986 Cleveland	AL	9	9	1	0	61.2	255	57	35	29	9	3	1	1	15	0	46	3	2	5	2	.714	0	0--	—	4.23
1987 Cleveland	AL	16	15	4	0	102.1	441	112	62	58	18	4	3	1	37	1	97	0	1	3	8	.273	1	0-0	1	5.10
1988 Cleveland	AL	33	33	12	0	242	988	234	97	86	18	9	5	1	45	3	180	5	0	18	14	.563	4	0-0	0	3.20
1989 Cleveland	AL	28	28	5	0	184.1	749	170	71	69	16	4	4	0	51	1	129	3	1	13	6	.684	2	0-0	0	3.37
1990 Cleveland	AL	34	34	3	0	214.2	912	245	110	105	27	8	6	1	47	2	135	3	2	12	9	.571	0	0-0	0	4.40

			HOW MUCH HE PITCHED					WHAT HE GAVE UP												THE RESULTS						
Year Team	Lg	G	GS	CG	GF	IP	BFP	H	R	ER	HR	SH	SF	HB	TBB	IBB	SO	WP	Bk	W	L	Pct.	ShO	Sv-Op	Hld	ERA
1991 Cleveland	AL	33	33	7	0	238	971	241	112	92	21	13	8	3	31	1	169	3	1	9	16	.360		0-0	0	3.48
1992 Cincinnati	NL	31	30	5	0	213.2	867	210	72	64	14	9	7	2	41	4	138	3	2	12	8	.600	3	0-0	0	2.70
1993 Houston	NL	31	30	1	0	190.1	818	215	98	88	24	13	3	1	40	3	124	2	2	12	13	.480	1	0-0	0	4.16
1994 Houston	NL	24	24	1	0	148.1	623	175	80	72	20	9	7	1	26	2	74	1	1	8	9	.471	0	0-0	0	4.37
1995 Houston	NL	33	26	1	3	153	659	180	86	76	21	4	8	2	39	2	96	3	0	10	9	.526	1	0-2	0	4.47
1996 Hou-Cle		21	6	0	0	51.2	237	66	46	41	13	1	2	1	19	0	36	0	0	1	4	.200	0	0-2	1	7.14
1996 Houston	NL	8	4	0	3	23	116	35	25	20	5	0	1	1	11	0	15	0	0	0	3	.000	0	0-2	0	7.83
Cleveland	AL	13	2	0	1	28.2	121	31	21	21	8	1	1	0	8	0	21	0	0	1	1	.500	0	0-0	1	6.59
11 ML YEARS		293	268	40	7	1800	7520	1905	869	780	201	77	54	14	391	19	1224	26	12	103	98	.512	12	0- -	—	3.90

Jeff Tabaka

Pitches: Left **Bats:** Right **Pos:** RP-18   **Ht:** 6'2" **Wt:** 195 **Born:** 1/17/64 **Age:** 33

			HOW MUCH HE PITCHED					WHAT HE GAVE UP												THE RESULTS						
Year Team	Lg	G	GS	CG	GF	IP	BFP	H	R	ER	HR	SH	SF	HB	TBB	IBB	SO	WP	Bk	W	L	Pct.	ShO	Sv-Op	Hld	ERA
1996 Tucson *	AAA	41	0	0	16	43	186	40	16	14	2	4	1	1	21	5	51	2	0	6	2	.750	0	4- -	—	2.93
1994 Pit-SD	NL	39	0	0	10	41	181	32	29	24	1	3	1	0	27	3	32	1	0	3	1	.750	0	1-1	1	5.27
1995 SD-Hou	NL	34	0	0	6	30.2	128	27	11	11	2	0	0	0	17	1	25	1	0	1	0	1.000	0	0-1	5	3.23
1996 Houston	NL	18	0	0	5	20.1	105	28	18	15	5	1	0	3	14	0	18	3	0	0	2	.000	0	1-1	0	6.64
1994 Pittsburgh	NL	5	0	0	2	4	24	4	8	8	1	0	0	0	8	0	2	0	0	0	0	.000	0	0-0	0	18.00
San Diego	NL	34	0	0	8	37	157	28	21	16	0	3	1	0	19	3	30	1	0	3	1	.750	0	1-1	1	3.89
1995 San Diego	NL	10	0	0	3	6.1	32	10	5	5	1	0	0	0	5	1	6	1	0	0	0	.000	0	0-1	0	7.11
Houston	NL	24	0	0	3	24.1	96	17	6	6	1	0	0	0	12	0	19	0	0	1	0	1.000	0	0-0	5	2.22
3 ML YEARS		91	0	0	21	92	414	87	58	50	8	4	1	3	58	4	75	5	0	4	3	.571	0	2-3	6	4.89

Kevin Tapani

Pitches: Right **Bats:** Right **Pos:** SP-34   **Ht:** 6'0" **Wt:** 189 **Born:** 2/18/64 **Age:** 33

			HOW MUCH HE PITCHED					WHAT HE GAVE UP												THE RESULTS						
Year Team	Lg	G	GS	CG	GF	IP	BFP	H	R	ER	HR	SH	SF	HB	TBB	IBB	SO	WP	Bk	W	L	Pct.	ShO	Sv-Op	Hld	ERA
1989 NYN-Min		8	5	0	1	40	169	39	18	17	3	1	2	0	12	1	23	0	1	2	2	.500	0	0-0	0	3.83
1990 Minnesota	AL	28	28	1	0	159.1	659	164	75	72	12	3	4	2	29	2	101	1	0	12	8	.600	1	0-0	0	4.07
1991 Minnesota	AL	34	34	4	0	244	974	225	84	81	23	9	6	2	40	0	135	3	0	16	9	.640	1	0-0	0	2.99
1992 Minnesota	AL	34	34	4	0	220	911	226	103	97	17	8	11	5	48	2	138	4	0	16	11	.593	1	0-0	0	3.97
1993 Minnesota	AL	36	35	3	0	225.2	964	243	123	111	21	3	5	6	57	1	150	4	0	12	15	.444	1	0-0	0	4.43
1994 Minnesota	AL	24	24	4	0	156	652	181	86	80	13	2	5	4	39	0	91	1	0	11	7	.611	1	0-0	0	4.62
1995 Min-LA		33	31	3	0	190.2	834	227	116	105	29	6	5	5	48	4	131	4	0	10	13	.435	1	0-0	0	4.96
1996 Chicago	AL	34	34	1	0	225.1	971	236	123	115	34	6	6	3	76	5	150	13	0	13	10	.565	0	0-0	0	4.59
1989 New York	NL	3	0	0	1	7.1	31	5	3	3	1	1	0	0	4	0	2	0	1	0	0	.000	0	0-0	0	3.68
Minnesota	AL	5	5	0	0	32.2	138	34	15	14	2	1	1	0	8	1	21	0	0	2	2	.500	0	0-0	0	3.86
1995 Minnesota	AL	20	20	3	0	133.2	579	155	79	73	21	3	3	4	34	2	88	3	0	6	11	.353	0	0-0	0	4.92
Los Angeles	NL	13	11	0	0	57	255	72	37	32	8	3	2	1	14	2	43	1	0	4	2	.667	0	0-0	0	5.05
8 ML YEARS		231	225	20	1	1461	6154	1541	728	678	152	38	44	27	349	15	919	30	4	92	75	.551	6	0-0	0	4.18

Tony Tarasco

Bats: L **Throws:** R **Pos:** RF-22; PH-6; DH-5; CF-1   **Ht:** 6'1" **Wt:** 205 **Born:** 12/9/70 **Age:** 26

			BATTING															BASERUNNING				PERCENTAGES		
Year Team	Lg	G	AB	H	2B	3B	HR	(Hm	Rd)	TB	R	RBI	TBB	IBB	SO	HBP	SH	SF	SB	CS	SB%	GDP	Avg	OBP	SLG
1996 Rochester *	AAA	29	103	27	6	0	2	—	—	39	18	9	17	2	20	0	1	1	4	4	.50	2	.262	.364	.379
Orioles *	R	3	8	3	1	0	0	—	—	4	2	3	2	1	1	0	0	1	0	0	.00	0	.375	.455	.500
Frederick *	A+	9	35	8	1	0	1	—	—	14	6	5	4	1	4	1	0	0	1	1	.00	0	.229	.325	.400
1993 Atlanta	NL	24	35	8	2	0	0	(0	0)	10	6	2	0	0	5	1	0	1	0	1	.00	1	.229	.243	.286
1994 Atlanta	NL	87	132	36	6	0	5	(2	3)	57	16	19	9	1	17	0	0	3	5	0	1.00	5	.273	.313	.432
1995 Montreal	NL	126	438	109	18	4	14	(7	7)	177	64	40	51	12	78	2	3	1	24	3	.89	2	.249	.329	.404
1996 Baltimore	AL	31	84	20	3	0	1	(1	0)	26	14	9	7	0	15	0	1	0	5	3	.63	1	.238	.297	.310
4 ML YEARS		268	689	173	29	4	20	(10	10)	270	100	70	67	13	115	3	4	5	34	7	.83	9	.251	.318	.392

Danny Tartabull

Bats: Right **Throws:** Right **Pos:** RF-122; DH-10; PH-1   **Ht:** 6'1" **Wt:** 204 **Born:** 10/30/62 **Age:** 34

			BATTING															BASERUNNING				PERCENTAGES		
Year Team	Lg	G	AB	H	2B	3B	HR	(Hm	Rd)	TB	R	RBI	TBB	IBB	SO	HBP	SH	SF	SB	CS	SB%	GDP	Avg	OBP	SLG
1984 Seattle	AL	10	20	6	1	0	2	(1	1)	13	3	7	2	0	3	1	0	1	0	0	.00	0	.300	.375	.650
1985 Seattle	AL	19	61	20	7	1	1	(0	1)	32	8	7	8	0	14	0	0	0	1	0	1.00	1	.328	.406	.525
1986 Seattle	AL	137	511	138	25	6	25	(13	12)	250	76	96	61	2	157	1	2	3	4	8	.33	10	.270	.347	.489
1987 Kansas City	AL	158	582	180	27	3	34	(15	19)	315	95	101	79	2	136	1	0	5	9	4	.69	14	.309	.390	.541
1988 Kansas City	AL	146	507	139	38	3	26	(15	11)	261	80	102	76	4	119	4	0	6	8	5	.62	10	.274	.369	.515
1989 Kansas City	AL	133	441	118	22	0	18	(9	9)	194	54	62	69	2	123	3	0	2	4	2	.67	12	.268	.369	.440
1990 Kansas City	AL	88	313	84	19	0	15	(5	10)	148	41	60	36	0	93	0	0	2	1	1	.50	9	.268	.341	.473
1991 Kansas City	AL	132	484	153	35	3	31	(13	18)	287	78	100	65	6	121	3	0	5	6	3	.67	9	.316	.397	.593
1992 New York	AL	123	421	112	19	0	25	(11	14)	206	72	85	103	14	115	0	0	2	2	2	.50	7	.266	.409	.489
1993 New York	AL	138	513	128	33	2	31	(11	20)	258	87	102	92	9	156	2	0	4	0	0	.00	8	.250	.363	.503
1994 New York	AL	104	399	102	24	1	19	(10	9)	185	68	67	66	3	111	1	0	4	1	1	.50	11	.256	.360	.464

Year Team	Lg	G	AB	H	2B	3B	HR	(Hm	Rd)	TB	R	RBI	TBB	IBB	SO	HBP	SH	SF	SB	CS	SB%	GDP	Avg	OBP	SLG
1995 NYA-Oak	AL	83	280	66	16	0	8	(3	5)	106	34	35	43	1	82	1	0	4	0	2	.00	9	.236	.335	.379
1996 Chicago	AL	132	472	120	23	3	27	(11	16)	230	58	101	64	4	128	0	0	5	1	2	.33	10	.254	.340	.487
1995 New York	AL	59	192	43	12	0	6	(2	4)	73	25	28	33	1	54	1	0	4	0	0	.00	6	.224	.335	.380
Oakland	AL	24	88	23	4	0	2	(1	1)	33	9	7	10	0	28	0	0	0	0	2	.00	3	.261	.337	.375
13 ML YEARS		1403	5004	1366	289	22	262	(117	145)	2485	754	925	764	47	1358	17	2	44	37	30	.55	110	.273	.368	.497

Jimmy Tatum

Bats: Right **Throws:** Right **Pos:** PH-4; 3B-3   **Ht:** 6'2" **Wt:** 200 **Born:** 10/9/67 **Age:** 29

Year Team	Lg	G	AB	H	2B	3B	HR	(Hm	Rd)	TB	R	RBI	TBB	IBB	SO	HBP	SH	SF	SB	CS	SB%	GDP	Avg	OBP	SLG
1996 Pawtucket *	AAA	19	66	18	2	0	5	—	—	35	11	16	7	0	12	1	0	0	2	0	1.00	3	.273	.351	.530
Las Vegas *	AAA	64	233	80	20	1	12	—	—	138	40	56	23	6	53	3	0	1	4	0	1.00	9	.343	.408	.592
1992 Milwaukee	AL	5	8	1	0	0	0	(0	0)	1	0	0	1	0	2	0	0	0	0	0	.00	0	.125	.222	.125
1993 Colorado	NL	92	98	20	5	0	1	(0	1)	28	7	12	5	0	27	1	0	2	0	0	.00	0	.204	.245	.286
1995 Colorado	NL	34	34	8	1	1	0	(0	0)	11	4	4	1	0	7	0	0	0	0	0	.00	0	.235	.257	.324
1996 Bos-SD		7	11	1	0	0	0	(0	0)	1	1	0	0	0	3	0	0	0	0	0	.00	0	.091	.091	.091
1996 Boston	AL	2	8	1	0	0	0	(0	0)	1	1	0	0	0	2	0	0	0	0	0	.00	0	.125	.125	.125
San Diego	NL	5	3	0	0	0	0	(0	0)	0	0	0	0	0	1	0	0	0	0	0	.00	0	.000	.000	.000
4 ML YEARS		138	151	30	6	1	1	(0	1)	41	12	16	7	0	39	1	0	2	0	0	.00	1	.199	.236	.272

Eddie Taubensee

Bats: Left **Throws:** Right **Pos:** C-94; PH-23   **Ht:** 6'4" **Wt:** 205 **Born:** 10/31/68 **Age:** 28

Year Team	Lg	G	AB	H	2B	3B	HR	(Hm	Rd)	TB	R	RBI	TBB	IBB	SO	HBP	SH	SF	SB	CS	SB%	GDP	Avg	OBP	SLG
1991 Cleveland	AL	26	66	16	2	1	0	(0	0)	20	5	8	5	1	16	0	0	2	0	0	.00	1	.242	.288	.303
1992 Houston	NL	104	297	66	15	0	5	(2	3)	96	23	28	31	3	78	2	0	1	2	1	.67	4	.222	.299	.323
1993 Houston	NL	94	288	72	11	1	9	(4	5)	112	26	42	21	5	44	0	1	2	1	0	1.00	8	.250	.299	.389
1994 Hou-Cin	NL	66	187	53	8	2	8	(2	6)	89	29	21	15	2	31	0	1	2	2	0	1.00	2	.283	.333	.476
1995 Cincinnati	NL	80	218	62	14	2	9	(4	5)	107	32	44	22	2	52	2	1	1	2	2	.50	2	.284	.354	.491
1996 Cincinnati	NL	108	327	95	20	0	12	(6	6)	151	46	48	26	5	64	0	1	5	3	4	.43	4	.291	.338	.462
1994 Houston	NL	5	10	1	0	0	0	(0	0)	1	0	0	0	0	3	0	0	0	0	0	.00	1	.100	.100	.100
Cincinnati	NL	61	177	52	8	2	8	(2	6)	88	29	21	15	2	28	0	1	2	2	0	1.00	1	.294	.345	.497
6 ML YEARS		478	1383	364	70	6	43	(18	25)	575	161	191	120	18	285	4	4	13	10	7	.59	21	.263	.321	.416

Jesus Tavarez

Bats: B **Throws:** R **Pos:** PH-47; CF-30; LF-25; RF-12   **Ht:** 6'0" **Wt:** 170 **Born:** 3/26/71 **Age:** 26

Year Team	Lg	G	AB	H	2B	3B	HR	(Hm	Rd)	TB	R	RBI	TBB	IBB	SO	HBP	SH	SF	SB	CS	SB%	GDP	Avg	OBP	SLG
1994 Florida	NL	17	39	7	0	0	0	(0	0)	7	4	4	1	0	5	0	1	0	1	1	.50	0	.179	.200	.179
1995 Florida	NL	63	190	55	6	2	2	(1	1)	71	31	13	16	1	27	1	3	1	7	5	.58	1	.289	.346	.374
1996 Florida	NL	98	114	25	3	0	0	(0	0)	28	14	6	7	0	18	0	3	0	5	1	.83	2	.219	.264	.246
3 ML YEARS		178	343	87	9	2	2	(1	1)	106	49	23	24	1	50	1	7	1	13	7	.65	3	.254	.304	.309

Julian Tavarez

Pitches: Right **Bats:** Right **Pos:** RP-47; SP-4   **Ht:** 6'2" **Wt:** 165 **Born:** 5/22/73 **Age:** 24

Year Team	Lg	G	GS	CG	GF	IP	BFP	H	R	ER	HR	SH	SF	HB	TBB	IBB	SO	WP	Bk	W	L	Pct.	ShO	Sv-Op	Hld	ERA
1996 Buffalo *	AAA	2	2	0	0	14	54	10	2	2	0	0	0	1	3	0	10	0	0	1	0	1.000	0	0--	—	1.29
1993 Cleveland	AL	8	7	0	0	37	172	53	29	27	7	0	1	2	13	2	19	3	1	2	2	.500	0	0-0	0	6.57
1994 Cleveland	AL	1	1	0	0	1.2	14	6	8	4	1	0	1	0	1	0	0	0	0	0	0	1.000	0	0-0	0	21.60
1995 Cleveland	AL	57	0	0	15	85	350	76	36	23	7	0	2	3	21	4	68	3	2	10	2	.833	0	0-4	19	2.44
1996 Cleveland	AL	51	4	0	13	80.2	353	101	49	48	9	5	4	1	22	5	46	1	0	4	7	.364	0	0-0	13	5.36
4 ML YEARS		117	12	0	28	204.1	889	236	122	102	24	5	8	6	57	8	133	7	3	16	12	.571	0	0-4	32	4.49

Billy Taylor

Pitches: Right **Bats:** Right **Pos:** RP-55   **Ht:** 6'8" **Wt:** 200 **Born:** 10/16/61 **Age:** 35

Year Team	Lg	G	GS	CG	GF	IP	BFP	H	R	ER	HR	SH	SF	HB	TBB	IBB	SO	WP	Bk	W	L	Pct.	ShO	Sv-Op	Hld	ERA
1996 Edmonton *	AAA	7	0	0	5	11.1	45	10	1	1	0	1	0	0	3	0	13	0	0	0	0	.000	0	4--	—	0.79
1994 Oakland	AL	41	0	0	11	46.1	195	38	24	18	4	1	1	2	18	5	48	0	0	1	3	.250	0	1-3	2	3.50
1996 Oakland	AL	55	0	0	30	60.1	261	52	30	29	5	4	3	4	25	4	67	1	0	6	3	.667	0	17-19	4	4.33
2 ML YEARS		96	0	0	41	106.2	456	90	54	47	9	5	4	6	43	9	115	1	0	7	6	.538	0	18-22	6	3.97

Amaury Telemaco

Pitches: Right **Bats:** Right **Pos:** SP-17; RP-8   **Ht:** 6'3" **Wt:** 210 **Born:** 1/19/74 **Age:** 23

Year Team	Lg	G	GS	CG	GF	IP	BFP	H	R	ER	HR	SH	SF	HB	TBB	IBB	SO	WP	Bk	W	L	Pct.	ShO	Sv-Op	Hld	ERA
1992 Huntington	R+	12	12	2	0	76.1	318	71	45	34	6	2	1	2	17	0	93	7	0	3	5	.375	0	0--	—	4.01
Peoria	A	2	1	0	0	5.2	31	9	5	5	0	0	0	1	5	0	5	0	0	0	1	.000	0	0--	—	7.94
1993 Peoria	A	23	23	3	0	143.2	602	129	69	55	9	2	6	5	54	0	133	8	0	8	11	.421	0	0--	—	3.45
1994 Daytona	A+	11	11	2	0	76.2	313	62	35	29	4	4	2	4	23	0	59	3	3	7	3	.700	0	0--	—	3.40
Orlando	AA	12	12	2	0	62.2	264	56	29	24	6	4	2	4	20	0	49	3	0	3	5	.375	0	0--	—	3.45
1995 Orlando	AA	22	22	3	0	147.2	587	112	60	54	13	8	3	4	42	3	151	7	1	8	8	.500	1	0--	—	3.29
1996 Iowa	AAA	8	8	1	0	50	205	38	19	17	5	2	2	2	18	2	42	3	0	3	1	.750	0	0--	—	3.06
1996 Chicago	NL	25	17	0	2	97.1	427	108	67	59	20	5	3	3	31	2	64	3	0	5	7	.417	0	0-0	0	5.46

Dave Telgheder

Pitches: Right **Bats:** Right **Pos:** SP-14; RP-2   **Ht:** 6'3" **Wt:** 212 **Born:** 11/11/66 **Age:** 30

Year Team	Lg	G	GS	CG	GF	IP	BFP	H	R	ER	HR	SH	SF	HB	TBB	IBB	SO	WP	Bk	W	L	Pct.	ShO	Sv-Op	Hld	ERA
1996 Edmonton *	AAA	17	17	1	0	101.1	421	102	53	47	7	0	4	2	23	1	59	1	0	8	6	.571	0	0--	—	4.17
Modesto *	A+	1	1	0	0	6	24	4	3	1	0	0	0	0	1	0	3	0	0	1	0	1.000	0	0--	—	1.50
1993 New York	NL	24	7	0	7	75.2	325	82	40	40	10	2	1	4	21	2	35	1	0	6	2	.750	0	0-0	1	4.76
1994 New York	NL	6	0	0	0	10	48	11	8	8	2	1	0	0	8	2	4	0	0	1	0	1.000	0	0-0	0	7.20
1995 New York	NL	7	4	0	2	25.2	118	34	18	16	4	3	1	0	7	3	16	0	1	1	2	.333	0	0-0	0	5.61
1996 Oakland	AL	16	14	1	1	79.1	348	92	42	41	12	3	3	1	26	1	43	2	0	4	7	.364	1	0-0	0	4.65
4 ML YEARS		53	25	1	10	190.2	839	219	108	105	28	9	5	5	62	8	98	3	1	11	12	.478	1	0-0	1	4.96

Mickey Tettleton

Bats: Both **Throws:** Right **Pos:** DH-115; 1B-23; PH-5   **Ht:** 6'2" **Wt:** 212 **Born:** 9/16/60 **Age:** 36

								BATTING											BASERUNNING				PERCENTAGES		
Year Team	Lg	G	AB	H	2B	3B	HR	(Hm	Rd)	TB	R	RBI	TBB	IBB	SO	HBP	SH	SF	SB	CS	SB%	GDP	Avg	OBP	SLG
1984 Oakland	AL	33	76	20	2	1	1	(1	0)	27	10	5	11	0	21	0	0	1	0	0	.00	3	.263	.352	.355
1985 Oakland	AL	78	211	53	12	0	3	(1	2)	74	23	15	28	0	59	2	5	0	2	2	.50	6	.251	.344	.351
1986 Oakland	AL	90	211	43	9	0	10	(4	6)	82	26	35	39	0	51	1	7	4	7	1	.88	3	.204	.325	.389
1987 Oakland	AL	82	211	41	3	0	8	(5	3)	68	19	26	30	0	65	0	5	2	1	1	.50	3	.194	.292	.322
1988 Baltimore	AL	86	283	74	11	1	11	(7	4)	120	31	37	28	2	70	2	1	2	0	1	.00	9	.261	.330	.424
1989 Baltimore	AL	117	411	106	21	2	26	(15	11)	209	72	65	73	4	117	1	1	3	2	3	.60	8	.258	.369	.509
1990 Baltimore	AL	135	444	99	21	2	15	(8	7)	169	68	51	106	3	160	5	0	4	2	4	.33	7	.223	.376	.381
1991 Detroit	AL	154	501	132	17	2	31	(15	16)	246	85	89	101	9	131	2	0	5	3	3	.50	12	.263	.387	.491
1992 Detroit	AL	157	525	125	25	0	32	(18	14)	246	82	83	122	18	137	1	0	6	0	6	.00	5	.238	.379	.469
1993 Detroit	AL	152	522	128	25	4	32	(16	16)	257	79	110	109	12	139	0	0	6	3	7	.30	5	.245	.372	.492
1994 Detroit	AL	107	339	84	18	2	17	(9	8)	157	57	51	97	10	98	5	0	3	0	1	.00	4	.248	.419	.463
1995 Texas	AL	134	429	102	19	1	32	(22	10)	219	76	78	107	5	110	7	1	3	0	0	.00	8	.238	.396	.510
1996 Texas	AL	143	491	121	26	1	24	(14	10)	221	78	83	95	8	137	3	1	9	2	1	.67	12	.246	.366	.450
13 ML YEARS		1468	4654	1128	209	16	242	(135	107)	2095	706	728	946	71	1295	29	21	47	23	29	.44	85	.242	.371	.450

Bob Tewksbury

Pitches: Right **Bats:** Right **Pos:** SP-33; RP-3   **Ht:** 6'4" **Wt:** 205 **Born:** 11/30/60 **Age:** 36

Year Team	Lg	G	GS	CG	GF	IP	BFP	H	R	ER	HR	SH	SF	HB	TBB	IBB	SO	WP	Bk	W	L	Pct.	ShO	Sv-Op	Hld	ERA
1986 New York	AL	23	20	2	0	130.1	558	144	58	48	8	4	7	5	31	0	49	3	2	9	5	.643	0	0--	—	3.31
1987 NYA-ChN		15	9	0	4	51.1	242	79	41	38	6	5	1	1	20	3	22	1	2	1	8	.111	0	0-1	0	6.66
1988 Chicago	NL	1	1	0	0	3.1	18	6	5	3	1	0	1	0	2	0	1	0	0	0	0	.000	0	0-0	0	8.10
1989 St. Louis	NL	7	4	1	2	30	125	25	12	11	2	1	1	2	10	3	17	0	0	1	0	1.000	1	0-0	0	3.30
1990 St. Louis	NL	28	20	3	1	145.1	595	151	67	56	7	5	7	3	15	3	50	2	0	10	9	.526	2	1-1	2	3.47
1991 St. Louis	NL	30	30	3	0	191	798	206	86	69	13	12	10	5	38	2	75	0	0	11	12	.478	0	0-0	0	3.25
1992 St. Louis	NL	33	32	5	1	233	915	217	63	56	15	9	7	3	20	0	91	2	0	16	5	.762	0	0-0	0	2.16
1993 St. Louis	NL	32	32	2	0	213.2	907	258	99	91	15	15	9	6	20	1	97	2	0	17	10	.630	0	0-0	0	3.83
1994 St. Louis	NL	24	24	4	0	155.2	667	190	97	92	19	12	4	3	22	1	79	1	0	12	10	.545	1	0-0	0	5.32
1995 Texas	AL	21	21	4	0	129.2	561	169	75	66	8	6	3	3	20	4	53	4	0	8	7	.533	1	0-0	0	4.58
1996 San Diego	NL	36	33	1	0	206.2	881	224	116	99	17	10	11	3	43	3	126	2	3	10	10	.500	0	0-0	0	4.31
1987 New York	AL	8	6	0	1	33.1	149	47	26	25	5	2	0	1	7	0	12	0	1	1	4	.200	0	0-0	0	6.75
Chicago	NL	7	3	0	3	18	93	32	15	13	1	3	1	0	13	3	10	1	1	0	4	.000	0	0-1	0	6.50
11 ML YEARS		250	226	25	8	1490	6267	1669	719	629	111	79	61	34	241	20	660	17	7	95	76	.556	5	1--	—	3.80

Tom Thobe

Pitches: Left **Bats:** Left **Pos:** RP-4   **Ht:** 6'6" **Wt:** 195 **Born:** 9/3/69 **Age:** 27

Year Team	Lg	G	GS	CG	GF	IP	BFP	H	R	ER	HR	SH	SF	HB	TBB	IBB	SO	WP	Bk	W	L	Pct.	ShO	Sv-Op	Hld	ERA
1993 Macon	A	43	0	0	22	70.1	299	70	25	21	0	6	1	4	16	1	55	8	0	7	5	.583	0	5--	—	2.69
1994 Greenville	AA	51	0	0	27	63.2	263	56	21	18	3	5	2	0	26	2	52	6	2	7	6	.538	0	9--	—	2.54
1995 Richmond	AAA	48	2	1	15	88	350	65	27	18	4	1	1	1	26	5	57	5	0	7	0	1.000	1	5--	—	1.84

		HOW MUCH HE PITCHED		WHAT HE GAVE UP			THE RESULTS		
Year Team	Lg	G GS CG GF	IP	BFP	H R ER	HR SH SF HB	TBB IBB	SO	WP	Bk	W L	Pct.	ShO	Sv-Op	Hld	ERA

Year Team	Lg	G	GS	CG	GF	IP	BFP	H	R	ER	HR	SH	SF	HB	TBB	IBB	SO	WP	Bk	W	L	Pct.	ShO	Sv-Op	Hld	ERA
1996 Richmond	AAA	31	6	1	9	72	345	89	60	49	6	1	5	2	37	2	40	4	0	1	8	.111	0	3--	--	6.13
1995 Atlanta	NL	3	0	0	1	3.1	17	7	4	4	0	0	0	0	0	0	2	0	0	0	0	.000	0	0-0	0	10.80
1996 Atlanta	NL	4	0	0	3	6	24	5	2	1	1	0	1	0	0	0	1	0	0	0	1	.000	0	0-0	0	1.50
2 ML YEARS		7	0	0	4	9.1	41	12	6	5	1	0	1	0	0	0	3	0	0	0	1	.000	0	0-0	0	4.82

Frank Thomas

Bats: Right **Throws:** Right **Pos:** 1B-139; PH-2 **Ht:** 6'5" **Wt:** 257 **Born:** 5/27/68 **Age:** 29

Year Team	Lg	G	AB	H	2B	3B	HR	(Hm	Rd)	TB	R	RBI	TBB	IBB	SO	HBP	SH	SF	SB	CS	SB%	GDP	Avg	OBP	SLG
1990 Chicago	AL	60	191	63	11	3	7	(2	5)	101	39	31	44	0	54	2	0	3	0	1	.00	5	.330	.454	.529
1991 Chicago	AL	158	559	178	31	2	32	(24	8)	309	104	109	138	13	112	1	0	2	1	2	.33	20	.318	.453	.553
1992 Chicago	AL	160	573	185	46	2	24	(10	14)	307	108	115	122	6	88	5	0	11	6	3	.67	19	.323	.439	.536
1993 Chicago	AL	153	549	174	36	0	41	(26	15)	333	106	128	112	23	54	2	0	13	4	2	.67	10	.317	.426	.607
1994 Chicago	AL	113	399	141	34	1	38	(22	16)	291	106	101	109	12	61	2	0	7	2	3	.40	15	.353	.487	.729
1995 Chicago	AL	145	493	152	27	0	40	(15	25)	299	102	111	136	29	74	6	0	12	3	2	.60	14	.308	.454	.606
1996 Chicago	AL	141	527	184	26	0	40	(16	24)	330	110	134	109	26	70	5	0	8	1	1	.50	25	.349	.459	.626
7 ML YEARS		930	3291	1077	211	8	222	(115	107)	1970	675	729	770	109	513	23	0	56	17	14	.55	108	.327	.452	.599

Larry Thomas

Pitches: Left **Bats:** Right **Pos:** RP-57 **Ht:** 6'1" **Wt:** 195 **Born:** 10/25/69 **Age:** 27

Year Team	Lg	G	GS	CG	GF	IP	BFP	H	R	ER	HR	SH	SF	HB	TBB	IBB	SO	WP	Bk	W	L	Pct.	ShO	Sv-Op	Hld	ERA
1991 Utica	A-	11	10	0	0	73.1	288	55	22	12	2	3	2	0	25	0	61	3	0	1	3	.250	0	0--	--	1.47
Birmingham	AA	2	0	0	2	6	28	6	3	2	0	0	0	0	4	1	2	0	0	0	0	.000	0	0--	--	3.00
1992 Sarasota	A+	8	8	0	0	55.2	220	44	14	10	1	1	0	0	7	1	50	2	0	5	0	1.000	0	0--	--	1.62
Birmingham	AA	17	17	3	0	120.2	474	102	32	26	4	4	2	1	30	2	72	5	0	8	6	.571	0	0--	--	1.94
1993 Nashville	AAA	18	18	1	0	100.2	441	114	73	67	15	3	6	1	32	4	67	4	1	4	6	.400	0	0--	--	5.99
Sarasota	A+	8	8	3	0	61.2	247	52	19	17	3	2	0	0	15	0	27	1	1	4	2	.667	2	0--	--	2.48
Birmingham	AA	1	1	0	0	7	33	9	5	4	1	0	0	1	1	1	5	0	0	0	1	.000	0	0--	--	5.14
1994 Birmingham	AA	24	24	1	0	144	642	159	96	74	17	4	6	5	53	0	77	11	2	5	10	.333	1	0--	--	4.63
1995 Birmingham	AA	35	0	0	9	40.1	156	24	9	6	0	2	2	2	15	1	47	3	0	4	1	.800	0	2--	--	1.34
1995 Chicago	AL	17	0	0	5	13.2	54	8	2	2	1	0	0	0	6	1	12	1	0	0	0	.000	0	0-0	2	1.32
1996 Chicago	AL	57	0	0	11	30.2	135	32	11	11	1	4	0	3	14	2	20	1	0	2	3	.400	0	0-2	7	3.23
2 ML YEARS		74	0	0	16	44.1	189	40	13	13	2	4	0	3	20	3	32	2	0	2	3	.400	0	0-2	9	2.64

Jim Thome

Bats: Left **Throws:** Right **Pos:** 3B-150; PH-6; DH-1 **Ht:** 6'4" **Wt:** 220 **Born:** 8/27/70 **Age:** 26

Year Team	Lg	G	AB	H	2B	3B	HR	(Hm	Rd)	TB	R	RBI	TBB	IBB	SO	HBP	SH	SF	SB	CS	SB%	GDP	Avg	OBP	SLG
1991 Cleveland	AL	27	98	25	4	2	1	(0	1)	36	7	9	5	1	16	1	0	0	1	1	.50	4	.255	.298	.367
1992 Cleveland	AL	40	117	24	3	1	2	(1	1)	35	8	12	10	2	34	2	0	2	2	0	1.00	3	.205	.275	.299
1993 Cleveland	AL	47	154	41	11	0	7	(5	2)	73	28	22	29	1	36	4	0	5	2	1	.67	3	.266	.385	.474
1994 Cleveland	AL	98	321	86	20	1	20	(10	10)	168	58	52	46	5	84	0	1	1	3	3	.50	11	.268	.359	.523
1995 Cleveland	AL	137	452	142	29	3	25	(13	12)	252	92	73	97	3	113	5	0	3	4	3	.57	8	.314	.438	.558
1996 Cleveland	AL	151	505	157	28	5	38	(18	20)	309	122	116	123	8	141	6	0	2	2	2	.50	13	.311	.450	.612
6 ML YEARS		500	1647	475	95	12	93	(47	46)	873	315	284	310	20	424	18	1	13	14	10	.58	42	.288	.404	.530

Jason Thompson

Bats: Left **Throws:** Left **Pos:** 1B-13 **Ht:** 6'4" **Wt:** 205 **Born:** 6/13/71 **Age:** 26

Year Team	Lg	G	AB	H	2B	3B	HR	(Hm	Rd)	TB	R	RBI	TBB	IBB	SO	HBP	SH	SF	SB	CS	SB%	GDP	Avg	OBP	SLG
1993 Spokane	A-	66	240	72	25	1	7	—	—	120	36	38	37	6	47	1	0	5	3	2	.60	3	.300	.389	.500
1994 Rancho Cuca	A+	68	253	91	19	2	13	—	—	153	57	63	37	4	58	3	0	3	1	1	.50	5	.360	.443	.605
Wichita	AA	63	215	56	17	2	8	—	—	101	35	46	28	2	77	3	1	1	0	1	.00	5	.260	.352	.470
1995 Memphis	AA	137	475	129	20	1	20	—	—	211	62	64	62	4	131	0	0	5	7	3	.70	7	.272	.354	.444
1996 Las Vegas	AAA	111	387	116	27	0	21	—	—	206	80	57	51	9	93	5	0	3	7	5	.58	10	.300	.386	.532
1996 San Diego	NL	13	49	11	4	0	2	(1	1)	21	4	6	1	0	14	0	0	1	0	0	.00	0	.224	.235	.429

Justin Thompson

Pitches: Left **Bats:** Left **Pos:** SP-11 **Ht:** 6'4" **Wt:** 215 **Born:** 3/8/73 **Age:** 24

Year Team	Lg	G	GS	CG	GF	IP	BFP	H	R	ER	HR	SH	SF	HB	TBB	IBB	SO	WP	Bk	W	L	Pct.	ShO	Sv-Op	Hld	ERA
1991 Bristol	R+	10	10	0	0	50	217	45	29	20	4	0	1	2	24	1	60	7	6	2	5	.286	0	0--	--	3.60
1992 Fayetteville	A	20	19	0	1	95	390	79	32	23	6	4	4	1	40	0	88	7	3	4	4	.500	0	0--	--	2.18
1993 Lakeland	A+	11	11	0	0	55.2	241	65	25	22	1	3	0	1	16	0	46	3	1	4	4	.500	0	0--	--	3.56
London	AA	14	14	1	0	83.2	376	96	51	38	9	0	4	2	37	0	72	4	1	3	6	.333	0	0--	--	4.09
1995 Lakeland	A+	6	6	0	0	24	107	30	13	13	1	0	2	1	8	0	20	0	0	2	1	.667	0	0--	--	4.88

Year Team	Lg	G	GS	CG	GF	IP	BFP	H	R	ER	HR	SH	SF	HB	TBB	IBB	SO	WP	Bk	W	L	Pct.	ShO	Sv-Op	Hld	ERA
		HOW MUCH HE PITCHED						**WHAT HE GAVE UP**												**THE RESULTS**						
1996 Fayettevlle	A	1	1	0	0	3	10	1	1	1	0	0	0	0	0	0	5	0	0	0	0	.000	0	0--	—	3.00
Visalia	A+	1	1	0	0	3	13	2	0	0	0	0	0	0	2	0	7	1	0	0	0	.000	0	0--	—	0.00
Toledo	AAA	13	13	3	0	84.1	338	74	36	32	2	1	2	1	26	0	69	2	0	6	3	.667	1	0--	—	3.42
1996 Detroit	AL	11	11	0	0	59	267	62	35	30	7	0	2	2	31	2	44	1	0	1	6	.143	0	0-0	0	4.58

Mark Thompson

Pitches: Right **Bats:** Right **Pos:** SP-28; RP-6 **Ht:** 6'2" **Wt:** 205 **Born:** 4/7/71 **Age:** 26

Year Team	Lg	G	GS	CG	GF	IP	BFP	H	R	ER	HR	SH	SF	HB	TBB	IBB	SO	WP	Bk	W	L	Pct.	ShO	Sv-Op	Hld	ERA
		HOW MUCH HE PITCHED						**WHAT HE GAVE UP**												**THE RESULTS**						
1994 Colorado	NL	2	2	0	0	9	49	16	9	9	2	0	0	1	8	0	5	0	0	1	1	.500	0	0-0	0	9.00
1995 Colorado	NL	21	5	0	0	51	240	73	42	37	7	4	4	1	22	2	30	2	0	2	3	.400	0	0-0	2	6.53
1996 Colorado	NL	34	28	3	2	169.2	763	189	109	100	25	10	3	13	74	1	99	1	1	9	11	.450	1	0-1	0	5.30
3 ML YEARS		57	35	3	5	229.2	1052	278	160	146	34	14	7	15	104	3	134	3	1	12	15	.444	1	0-1	2	5.72

Milt Thompson

Bats: Left **Throws:** Right **Pos:** PH-50; LF-18 **Ht:** 5'11" **Wt:** 190 **Born:** 1/5/59 **Age:** 38

Year Team	Lg	G	AB	H	2B	3B	HR	(Hm	Rd)	TB	R	RBI	TBB	IBB	SO	HBP	SH	SF	SB	CS	SB%	GDP	Avg	OBP	SLG
		BATTING																	**BASERUNNING**				**PERCENTAGES**		
1984 Atlanta	NL	25	99	30	1	0	2	(0	2)	37	16	4	11	1	11	0	1	0	14	2	.88	1	.303	.373	.374
1985 Atlanta	NL	73	182	55	7	2	0	(0	0)	66	17	6	7	0	36	3	1	0	9	4	.69	1	.302	.339	.363
1986 Philadelphia	NL	96	299	75	7	1	6	(4	2)	102	38	23	26	1	62	1	4	2	19	4	.83	4	.251	.311	.341
1987 Philadelphia	NL	150	527	159	26	9	7	(3	4)	224	86	43	42	2	87	0	3	3	46	10	.82	5	.302	.351	.425
1988 Philadelphia	NL	122	378	109	16	2	2	(1	1)	135	53	33	39	6	59	1	2	3	17	9	.65	8	.288	.354	.357
1989 St. Louis	NL	155	545	158	28	8	4	(2	2)	214	60	68	39	5	91	4	0	3	27	8	.77	12	.290	.340	.393
1990 St. Louis	NL	135	418	91	14	7	6	(3	3)	137	42	30	39	5	60	5	1	0	25	5	.83	4	.218	.292	.328
1991 St. Louis	NL	115	326	100	16	5	6	(4	2)	144	55	34	32	7	53	0	2	1	16	9	.64	4	.307	.368	.442
1992 St. Louis	NL	109	208	61	9	1	4	(1	3)	84	31	17	16	3	39	2	0	0	18	6	.75	3	.293	.350	.404
1993 Philadelphia	NL	129	340	89	14	2	4	(2	2)	119	42	44	40	9	57	2	3	2	9	4	.69	8	.262	.341	.350
1994 Phi-Hou	NL	96	241	66	7	0	4	(4	0)	85	34	33	24	4	30	3	1	1	9	2	.82	6	.274	.346	.353
1995 Houston	NL	92	132	29	9	0	2	(0	2)	44	14	19	14	3	37	1	2	1	4	2	.67	3	.220	.297	.333
1996 LA-Col	NL	62	66	7	2	0	0	(0	0)	9	3	3	7	0	13	0	0	0	1	1	.50	1	.106	.192	.136
1994 Philadelphia	NL	87	220	60	7	0	3	(3	0)	76	29	30	23	4	28	3	1	1	7	2	.78	5	.273	.348	.345
Houston	NL	9	21	6	0	0	1	(1	0)	9	5	3	1	0	2	0	0	0	2	0	1.00	1	.286	.318	.429
1996 Los Angeles	NL	48	51	6	1	0	0	(0	0)	7	2	1	6	0	10	0	0	0	1	1	.50	1	.118	.211	.137
Colorado	NL	14	15	1	1	0	0	(0	0)	2	1	2	1	0	3	0	0	0	0	0	.00	0	.067	.125	.133
13 ML YEARS		1359	3761	1029	156	37	47	(24	23)	1400	491	357	336	46	635	22	20	16	214	66	.76	60	.274	.335	.372

Robby Thompson

Bats: Right **Throws:** Right **Pos:** 2B-62; PH-2 **Ht:** 5'11" **Wt:** 173 **Born:** 5/10/62 **Age:** 35

Year Team	Lg	G	AB	H	2B	3B	HR	(Hm	Rd)	TB	R	RBI	TBB	IBB	SO	HBP	SH	SF	SB	CS	SB%	GDP	Avg	OBP	SLG
		BATTING																	**BASERUNNING**				**PERCENTAGES**		
1986 San Francisco	NL	149	549	149	27	3	7	(0	7)	203	73	47	42	0	112	5	18	1	12	15	.44	11	.271	.328	.370
1987 San Francisco	NL	132	420	110	26	5	10	(7	3)	176	62	44	40	3	91	8	6	0	16	11	.59	8	.262	.338	.419
1988 San Francisco	NL	138	477	126	24	6	7	(3	4)	183	66	48	40	0	111	4	14	5	14	5	.74	7	.264	.323	.384
1989 San Francisco	NL	148	547	132	26	11	13	(7	6)	219	91	50	51	0	133	13	9	0	12	2	.86	6	.241	.321	.400
1990 San Francisco	NL	144	498	122	22	3	15	(8	7)	195	67	56	34	1	96	6	8	3	14	4	.78	9	.245	.299	.392
1991 San Francisco	NL	144	492	129	24	5	19	(11	8)	220	74	48	63	2	95	6	11	1	14	7	.67	5	.262	.352	.447
1992 San Francisco	NL	128	443	115	25	1	14	(8	6)	184	54	49	43	1	75	8	7	4	5	9	.36	8	.260	.333	.415
1993 San Francisco	NL	128	340	154	30	2	19	(13	6)	245	85	65	45	0	97	7	9	4	10	4	.71	7	.312	.375	.496
1994 San Francisco	NL	35	129	27	8	2	2	(1	1)	45	13	7	15	0	32	0	5	1	3	1	.75	2	.209	.290	.349
1995 San Francisco	NL	95	336	75	15	0	8	(4	4)	114	51	23	42	1	76	4	9	0	1	2	.33	3	.223	.317	.339
1996 San Francisco	NL	63	227	48	11	1	5	(2	3)	76	35	21	24	0	69	5	3	0	2	2	.50	6	.211	.301	.335
11 ML YEARS		1304	4612	1187	238	39	119	(64	55)	1860	671	458	439	8	987	66	99	19	103	62	.62	72	.257	.329	.403

Ryan Thompson

Bats: Right **Throws:** Right **Pos:** CF-8; PH-2 **Ht:** 6'3" **Wt:** 215 **Born:** 11/4/67 **Age:** 29

Year Team	Lg	G	AB	H	2B	3B	HR	(Hm	Rd)	TB	R	RBI	TBB	IBB	SO	HBP	SH	SF	SB	CS	SB%	GDP	Avg	OBP	SLG
		BATTING																	**BASERUNNING**				**PERCENTAGES**		
1996 Buffalo *	AAA	138	540	140	26	4	21	—	—	237	79	83	21	1	119	7	2	4	12	5	.71	14	.259	.294	.439
1992 New York	NL	30	108	24	7	1	3	(3	0)	42	15	10	8	0	24	0	0	1	2	2	.50	2	.222	.274	.389
1993 New York	NL	80	288	72	19	2	11	(5	6)	128	34	26	19	4	81	3	5	1	2	7	.22	5	.250	.302	.444
1994 New York	NL	98	334	75	14	1	18	(5	13)	145	39	59	28	7	94	10	3	4	1	1	.50	8	.225	.301	.434
1995 New York	NL	75	267	67	13	0	7	(3	4)	101	39	31	19	1	77	4	0	4	3	1	.75	12	.251	.306	.378
1996 Cleveland	AL	8	22	7	0	0	1	(1	0)	10	2	5	1	0	6	0	0	0	0	0	.00	0	.318	.348	.455
5 ML YEARS		291	1019	245	53	4	40	(17	23)	426	129	131	75	12	282	17	8	10	8	11	.42	27	.240	.301	.418

Mike Timlin

Pitches: Right **Bats:** Right **Pos:** RP-59   **Ht:** 6'4" **Wt:** 210 **Born:** 3/10/66 **Age:** 31

Year Team	Lg	G	GS	CG	GF	IP	BFP	H	R	ER	HR	SH	SF	HB	TBB	IBB	SO	WP	Bk	W	L	Pct.	ShO	Sv-Op	Hld	ERA
1991 Toronto	AL	63	3	0	17	108.1	463	94	43	38	6	6	2	1	50	11	85	5	0	11	6	.647	0	3-8	9	3.16
1992 Toronto	AL	26	0	0	14	43.2	190	45	23	20	0	2	1	1	20	5	35	0	0	0	2	.000	0	1-1	1	4.12
1993 Toronto	AL	54	0	0	27	55.2	254	63	32	29	7	1	3	1	27	3	49	1	0	4	2	.667	0	1-4	9	4.69
1994 Toronto	AL	34	0	0	16	40	179	41	25	23	5	0	0	2	20	0	38	3	0	0	1	.000	0	2-4	5	5.18
1995 Toronto	AL	31	0	0	19	42	179	38	13	10	1	3	0	2	17	5	36	3	1	4	3	.571	0	5-9	4	2.14
1996 Toronto	AL	59	0	0	56	56.2	230	47	25	23	4	2	3	2	18	4	52	3	0	1	6	.143	0	31-38	2	3.65
6 ML YEARS		267	3	0	149	346.1	1495	328	161	143	23	14	9	9	152	28	295	15	1	20	20	.500	0	43-64	30	3.72

Ozzie Timmons

Bats: Right **Throws:** Right **Pos:** PH-30; LF-25; RF-22   **Ht:** 6'2" **Wt:** 220 **Born:** 9/18/70 **Age:** 26

Year Team	Lg	G	AB	H	2B	3B	HR	(Hm	Rd)	TB	R	RBI	TBB	IBB	SO	HBP	SH	SF	SB	CS	SB%	GDP	Avg	OBP	SLG
1991 Geneva	A-	73	294	65	10	1	12	—	—	113	35	47	18	0	39	2	0	4	4	3	.57	1	.221	.267	.384
1992 Charlotte	AA	36	122	26	7	0	3	—	—	42	13	13	12	0	26	1	1	0	2	2	.50	2	.213	.289	.344
Winston-Sal	A+	86	305	86	18	0	18	—	—	158	64	56	58	3	46	2	4	4	11	0	1.00	5	.282	.396	.518
1993 Orlando	AA	107	359	102	22	2	18	—	—	182	65	58	62	3	80	2	2	1	5	11	.31	6	.284	.392	.507
1994 Iowa	AAA	126	440	116	30	2	22	—	—	216	63	66	36	0	93	1	3	2	0	3	.00	12	.264	.319	.491
1996 Iowa	AAA	59	213	53	7	0	17	—	—	111	32	40	28	0	42	3	0	2	1	1	.50	9	.249	.341	.521
1995 Chicago	NL	77	171	45	10	1	8	(5	3)	81	30	28	13	2	32	0	0	1	3	0	1.00	8	.263	.314	.474
1996 Chicago	NL	65	140	28	4	0	7	(6	1)	53	18	16	15	0	30	1	0	0	1	0	1.00	1	.200	.282	.379
2 ML YEARS		142	311	73	14	1	15	(11	4)	134	48	44	28	2	62	1	1	1	4	0	1.00	9	.235	.299	.431

Lee Tinsley

Bats: Both **Throws:** Right **Pos:** CF-86; PH-34; LF-22   **Ht:** 5'10" **Wt:** 195 **Born:** 3/4/69 **Age:** 28

Year Team	Lg	G	AB	H	2B	3B	HR	(Hm	Rd)	TB	R	RBI	TBB	IBB	SO	HBP	SH	SF	SB	CS	SB%	GDP	Avg	OBP	SLG
1996 Clearwater *	A+	4	17	5	0	1	0	—	—	7	4	3	2	0	4	0	0	0	2	0	1.00	1	.294	.368	.412
1993 Seattle	AL	11	19	3	1	0	1	(0	1)	7	2	2	2	0	9	0	0	0	0	0	.00	1	.158	.238	.368
1994 Boston	AL	78	144	32	4	0	2	(1	1)	42	27	14	19	1	36	1	3	1	13	0	1.00	1	.222	.315	.292
1995 Boston	AL	100	341	97	17	1	7	(4	3)	137	61	41	39	1	74	1	9	1	18	8	.69	8	.284	.359	.402
1996 Phi-Bos		123	244	54	6	1	3	(1	2)	71	29	16	17	0	78	2	2	1	8	12	.40	6	.221	.277	.291
1996 Philadelphia	NL	31	52	7	0	0	0	(0	0)	7	1	2	4	0	22	0	1	0	2	4	.33	1	.135	.196	.135
Boston	AL	92	192	47	6	1	3	(1	2)	64	28	14	13	0	56	2	1	1	6	8	.43	5	.245	.298	.333
4 ML YEARS		312	748	186	28	2	13	(6	7)	257	119	73	77	2	197	4	14	3	39	20	.66	17	.249	.321	.344

Andy Tomberlin

Bats: L **Throws:** L **Pos:** PH-53; LF-9; RF-8; 1B-1   **Ht:** 5'11" **Wt:** 180 **Born:** 11/7/66 **Age:** 30

Year Team	Lg	G	AB	H	2B	3B	HR	(Hm	Rd)	TB	R	RBI	TBB	IBB	SO	HBP	SH	SF	SB	CS	SB%	GDP	Avg	OBP	SLG
1996 Edmonton *	AAA	17	60	17	2	1	0	—	—	21	12	5	8	0	15	2	0	0	1	0	1.00	0	.283	.386	.350
Norfolk *	AAA	38	129	42	6	1	8	—	—	74	17	18	8	1	29	2	3	0	1	3	.25	2	.326	.374	.574
1993 Pittsburgh	NL	27	42	12	0	1	1	(0	1)	17	4	5	2	0	14	1	0	0	0	0	.00	0	.286	.333	.405
1994 Boston	AL	17	36	7	0	1	1	(1	0)	12	1	1	6	0	12	0	0	0	1	0	1.00	0	.194	.310	.333
1995 Oakland	AL	46	85	18	0	0	4	(3	1)	30	15	10	5	0	22	0	2	0	4	1	.80	2	.212	.256	.353
1996 New York	NL	63	66	17	4	0	3	(2	1)	30	12	10	9	0	27	1	0	0	0	0	.00	0	.258	.355	.455
4 ML YEARS		153	229	54	4	2	9	(6	3)	89	32	26	22	0	75	2	2	0	5	1	.83	2	.236	.308	.389

Salomon Torres

Pitches: Right **Bats:** Right **Pos:** SP-7; RP-3   **Ht:** 5'11" **Wt:** 165 **Born:** 3/11/72 **Age:** 25

Year Team	Lg	G	GS	CG	GF	IP	BFP	H	R	ER	HR	SH	SF	HB	TBB	IBB	SO	WP	Bk	W	L	Pct.	ShO	Sv-Op	Hld	ERA
1996 Tacoma *	AAA	22	21	3	0	134.1	605	150	87	79	16	4	4	7	52	1	121	7	2	7	10	.412	1	0--	—	5.29
1993 San Francisco	NL	8	8	0	0	44.2	196	37	21	20	5	7	1	1	27	3	23	3	1	3	5	.375	0	0-0	0	4.03
1994 San Francisco	NL	16	14	1	2	84.1	378	95	55	51	10	4	8	7	34	2	42	4	1	2	8	.200	0	0-0	0	5.44
1995 SF-Sea		20	14	1	4	80	384	100	61	56	16	1	0	2	49	3	47	1	2	3	9	.250	0	0-0	0	6.30
1996 Seattle	AL	10	7	1	1	49	212	44	27	25	5	3	1	3	23	2	36	1	0	3	3	.500	1	0-0	0	4.59
1995 San Francisco	NL	4	1	0	2	8	40	13	8	8	4	0	0	0	7	0	2	0	0	0	1	.000	0	0-0	0	9.00
Seattle	AL	16	13	1	2	72	344	87	53	48	12	1	0	2	42	3	45	1	2	3	8	.273	0	0-0	0	6.00
4 ML YEARS		54	43	3	7	258	1170	276	164	152	36	15	10	13	133	10	148	9	4	11	25	.306	1	0-0	0	5.30

Steve Trachsel

Pitches: Right **Bats:** Right **Pos:** SP-31   **Ht:** 6'4" **Wt:** 205 **Born:** 10/31/70 **Age:** 26

		HOW MUCH HE PITCHED							WHAT HE GAVE UP										THE RESULTS					
Year Team	Lg	G	GS	CG	GF	IP	BFP	H	R	ER	HR	SH	SF	HB	TBB	IBB	SO	WP	Bk	W	L	Pct.	ShO	Sv-Op	Hld	ERA
1996 Orlando *	AA	2	2	0	0	13	51	11	6	4	0	1	0	0	0	0	12	1	0	0	1	.000	0	0- -	—	2.77
1993 Chicago	NL	3	3	0	0	19.2	78	16	10	10	4	1	1	0	3	0	14	1	0	0	2	.000	0	0-0	0	4.58
1994 Chicago	NL	22	22	1	0	146	612	133	57	52	19	3	3	3	54	4	108	6	1	9	7	.563	0	0-0	0	3.21
1995 Chicago	NL	30	29	2	0	160.2	722	174	104	92	25	12	5	0	76	8	117	2	1	7	13	.350	0	0-0	0	5.15
1996 Chicago	NL	31	31	3	0	205	845	181	82	69	30	3	3	8	62	3	132	5	2	13	9	.591	2	0-0	0	3.03
4 ML YEARS		86	85	6	0	531.1	2257	504	253	223	78	19	12	11	195	15	371	14	3	29	31	.483	2	0-0	0	3.78

Alan Trammell

Bats: R **Throws:** R **Pos:** SS-43; 2B-11; PH-11; 3B-8; LF-1   **Ht:** 6'0" **Wt:** 185 **Born:** 2/21/58 **Age:** 39

		BATTING																BASERUNNING				PERCENTAGES		
Year Team	Lg	G	AB	H	2B	3B	HR	(Hm	Rd)	TB	R	RBI	TBB	IBB	SO	HBP	SH	SF	SB	CS	SB%	GDP	Avg	OBP	SLG
1977 Detroit	AL	19	43	8	0	0	0	(0	0)	8	6	0	4	0	12	0	1	0	0	0	.00	1	.186	.255	.186
1978 Detroit	AL	139	448	120	14	6	2	(0	2)	152	49	34	45	0	56	2	6	3	3	1	.75	12	.268	.335	.339
1979 Detroit	AL	142	460	127	11	4	6	(4	2)	164	68	50	43	0	55	0	12	5	17	14	.55	6	.276	.335	.357
1980 Detroit	AL	146	560	168	21	5	9	(5	4)	226	107	65	69	2	63	3	13	7	12	12	.50	10	.300	.376	.404
1981 Detroit	AL	105	392	101	15	3	2	(2	0)	128	52	31	49	2	31	3	16	3	10	3	.77	10	.258	.342	.327
1982 Detroit	AL	157	489	126	34	3	9	(5	4)	193	66	57	52	0	47	0	9	6	19	8	.70	5	.258	.325	.395
1983 Detroit	AL	142	505	161	31	2	14	(8	6)	238	83	66	57	2	64	0	15	4	30	10	.75	7	.319	.385	.471
1984 Detroit	AL	139	555	174	34	5	14	(7	7)	260	85	69	60	2	63	3	6	2	19	13	.59	6	.314	.382	.468
1985 Detroit	AL	149	605	156	21	7	13	(7	6)	230	79	57	50	4	71	2	11	9	14	5	.74	6	.258	.312	.380
1986 Detroit	AL	151	574	159	33	7	21	(8	13)	269	107	75	59	4	57	5	11	4	25	12	.68	7	.277	.347	.469
1987 Detroit	AL	151	597	205	34	3	28	(13	15)	329	109	105	60	8	47	3	2	6	21	2	.91	11	.343	.402	.551
1988 Detroit	AL	128	466	145	24	1	15	(7	8)	216	73	69	46	8	46	4	0	7	7	4	.64	14	.311	.373	.464
1989 Detroit	AL	121	449	109	20	3	5	(2	3)	150	54	43	45	1	45	4	3	5	10	2	.83	9	.243	.314	.334
1990 Detroit	AL	146	559	170	37	1	14	(9	5)	251	71	89	68	7	55	1	3	6	12	10	.55	11	.304	.377	.449
1991 Detroit	AL	101	375	93	20	0	9	(6	3)	140	57	55	37	1	39	3	5	1	11	2	.85	7	.248	.320	.373
1992 Detroit	AL	29	102	28	7	1	1	(0	1)	40	11	11	15	0	4	1	1	1	2	2	.50	6	.275	.370	.392
1993 Detroit	AL	112	401	132	25	3	12	(6	6)	199	72	60	38	2	38	2	4	2	12	8	.60	7	.329	.388	.496
1994 Detroit	AL	76	292	78	17	1	8	(6	2)	121	38	28	16	1	35	1	2	0	3	0	1.00	8	.267	.307	.414
1995 Detroit	AL	74	223	60	12	0	2	(1	1)	78	28	23	27	4	19	0	3	2	3	1	.75	8	.269	.345	.350
1996 Detroit	AL	66	193	45	2	0	1	(1	0)	50	16	16	10	0	27	0	1	3	1	0	1.00	1	.233	.267	.259
20 ML YEARS		2293	8288	2365	412	55	185	(97	88)	3442	1231	1003	850	48	874	37	124	76	236	109	.68	156	.285	.352	.415

Ricky Trlicek

Pitches: Right **Bats:** Right **Pos:** RP-5   **Ht:** 6'2" **Wt:** 200 **Born:** 4/26/69 **Age:** 28

		HOW MUCH HE PITCHED							WHAT HE GAVE UP										THE RESULTS					
Year Team	Lg	G	GS	CG	GF	IP	BFP	H	R	ER	HR	SH	SF	HB	TBB	IBB	SO	WP	Bk	W	L	Pct.	ShO	Sv-Op	Hld	ERA
1996 Norfolk *	AAA	62	0	0	26	77	289	52	18	16	1	2	1	1	16	3	54	3	0	4	5	.444	0	10- -	—	1.87
1992 Toronto	AL	2	0	0	0	1.2	9	2	2	2	0	0	0	0	2	0	1	0	0	0	0	.000	0	0-0	0	10.80
1993 Los Angeles	NL	41	0	0	18	64	267	64	32	29	3	2	0	2	21	4	41	4	1	1	2	.333	0	1-1	1	4.08
1994 Boston	AL	12	1	0	2	22.1	113	32	21	20	5	0	0	0	16	2	7	1	2	1	1	.500	0	0-1	0	8.06
1996 New York	NL	5	0	0	2	5.1	20	3	2	2	0	2	0	1	3	1	3	0	0	0	1	.000	0	0-0	0	3.38
4 ML YEARS		60	1	0	22	93.1	409	96	57	53	8	4	0	3	42	7	52	5	3	2	4	.333	0	1-2	1	5.11

Mike Trombley

Pitches: Right **Bats:** Right **Pos:** RP-43   **Ht:** 6'2" **Wt:** 206 **Born:** 4/14/67 **Age:** 30

		HOW MUCH HE PITCHED							WHAT HE GAVE UP										THE RESULTS					
Year Team	Lg	G	GS	CG	GF	IP	BFP	H	R	ER	HR	SH	SF	HB	TBB	IBB	SO	WP	Bk	W	L	Pct.	ShO	Sv-Op	Hld	ERA
1996 Salt Lake *	AAA	24	0	0	20	36.2	145	24	12	10	3	3	0	0	10	0	38	6	0	2	2	.500	0	10- -	—	2.45
1992 Minnesota	AL	10	7	0	0	46.1	194	43	20	17	5	2	0	1	17	0	38	0	0	3	2	.600	0	0-0	0	3.30
1993 Minnesota	AL	44	10	0	8	114.1	506	131	72	62	15	3	7	3	41	4	85	5	0	6	6	.500	0	2-5	8	4.88
1994 Minnesota	AL	24	0	0	8	48.1	219	56	34	34	10	1	2	3	18	2	32	3	0	2	0	1.000	0	0-1	1	6.33
1995 Minnesota	AL	20	18	0	0	97.2	442	107	68	61	18	3	2	3	42	1	68	4	0	4	8	.333	0	0-0	0	5.62
1996 Minnesota	AL	43	0	0	19	68.2	292	61	24	23	2	0	3	5	25	8	57	4	0	5	1	.833	0	6-9	4	3.01
5 ML YEARS		141	35	0	35	375.1	1653	398	220	197	50	9	14	15	143	15	280	16	0	20	17	.541	0	8-15	13	4.72

Michael Tucker

Bats: L **Throws:** R **Pos:** RF-73; LF-28; PH-13; 1B-9; DH-4   **Ht:** 6'2" **Wt:** 185 **Born:** 6/25/71 **Age:** 26

		BATTING																BASERUNNING				PERCENTAGES		
Year Team	Lg	G	AB	H	2B	3B	HR	(Hm	Rd)	TB	R	RBI	TBB	IBB	SO	HBP	SH	SF	SB	CS	SB%	GDP	Avg	OBP	SLG
1993 Wilmington	A+	61	239	73	14	2	6	—	—	109	42	44	34	4	49	2	0	4	12	2	.86	0	.305	.391	.456
Memphis	AA	72	244	68	7	4	9	—	—	110	38	35	42	0	51	6	3	4	12	5	.71	1	.279	.392	.451
1994 Omaha	AAA	132	485	134	16	7	21	—	—	227	75	77	69	2	111	3	2	6	11	3	.79	6	.276	.366	.468
1995 Omaha	AAA	71	275	84	18	4	4	—	—	122	37	28	24	5	39	4	2	2	11	4	.73	3	.305	.367	.444
1996 Wichita	AA	6	20	9	1	3	0	—	—	16	4	7	5	0	4	0	0	1	0	0	.00	0	.450	.538	.800
1995 Kansas City	AL	62	177	46	10	0	4	(1	3)	68	23	17	18	2	51	1	2	0	2	3	.40	3	.260	.332	.384
1996 Kansas City	AL	108	339	88	18	4	12	(2	10)	150	55	53	40	1	69	7	3	4	10	4	.71	7	.260	.346	.442

Year Team	Lg	G	AB	H	2B	3B	HR	(Hm	Rd)	TB	R	RBI	TBB	IBB	SO	HBP	SH	SF	SB	CS	SB%	GDP	Avg	OBP	SLG
2 ML YEARS		170	516	134	28	4	16	(3	13)	218	78	70	63	3	120	8	5	4	12	7	.63	10	.260	.341	.422

Chris Turner

Bats: Right **Throws:** Right **Pos:** C-3; LF-1; PH-1   **Ht:** 6'3" **Wt:** 200 **Born:** 3/23/69 **Age:** 28

Year Team	Lg	G	AB	H	2B	3B	HR	(Hm	Rd)	TB	R	RBI	TBB	IBB	SO	HBP	SH	SF	SB	CS	SB%	GDP	Avg	OBP	SLG
1996 Vancouver *	AAA	113	390	100	19	1	2	—	—	127	51	47	61	2	85	5	1	4	1	3	.25	5	.256	.361	.326
1993 California	AL	25	75	21	5	0	1	(0	1)	29	9	13	9	0	16	1	0	1	1	1	.50	1	.280	.360	.387
1994 California	AL	58	149	36	7	1	1	(1	0)	48	23	12	10	0	29	1	1	2	3	0	1.00	2	.242	.290	.322
1995 California	AL	5	10	1	0	0	0	(0	0)	1	0	1	0	0	3	0	0	0	0	0	.00	0	.100	.100	.100
1996 California	AL	4	3	1	0	0	0	(0	0)	1	1	1	1	0	0	0	0	1	0	0	.00	0	.333	.400	.333
4 ML YEARS		92	237	59	12	1	2	(1	1)	79	33	27	20	0	48	2	1	4	4	1	.80	3	.249	.308	.333

Tim Unroe

Bats: R **Throws:** R **Pos:** 1B-11; 3B-3; PH-2; DH-1; LF-1   **Ht:** 6'3" **Wt:** 200 **Born:** 10/7/70 **Age:** 26

Year Team	Lg	G	AB	H	2B	3B	HR	(Hm	Rd)	TB	R	RBI	TBB	IBB	SO	HBP	SH	SF	SB	CS	SB%	GDP	Avg	OBP	SLG
1992 Helena	R+	74	266	74	13	2	16	—	—	139	61	58	47	1	91	4	1	7	3	4	.43	2	.278	.393	.523
1993 Stockton	A+	108	382	96	21	6	12	—	—	165	57	63	36	0	96	7	3	4	9	10	.47	8	.251	.324	.432
1994 El Paso	AA	126	474	147	36	7	15	—	—	242	97	103	42	2	107	5	0	9	14	6	.70	6	.310	.366	.511
1995 New Orleans	AAA	102	371	97	21	2	6	—	—	140	43	45	18	1	94	7	1	5	4	3	.57	9	.261	.304	.377
1996 New Orleans	AAA	109	404	109	26	4	25	—	—	218	72	67	36	2	121	4	0	4	8	3	.73	10	.270	.333	.540
1995 Milwaukee	AL	2	4	1	0	0	0	(0	0)	1	0	0	0	0	0	0	0	0	0	0	.00	0	.250	.250	.250
1996 Milwaukee	AL	14	16	3	0	0	0	(0	0)	3	5	0	4	0	5	0	0	0	0	1	.00	0	.188	.350	.188
2 ML YEARS		16	20	4	0	0	0	(0	0)	4	5	0	4	0	5	0	0	0	0	1	.00	0	.200	.333	.200

Tom Urbani

Pitches: Left **Bats:** Left **Pos:** RP-15; SP-4   **Ht:** 6'1" **Wt:** 190 **Born:** 1/21/68 **Age:** 29

Year Team	Lg	G	GS	CG	GF	IP	BFP	H	R	ER	HR	SH	SF	HB	TBB	IBB	SO	WP	Bk	W	L	Pct.	ShO	Sv-Op	Hld	ERA
1996 Louisville *	AAA	7	7	0	0	44	180	40	19	16	5	1	1	2	12	0	26	2	0	2	2	.500	0	0--	—	3.27
Toledo *	AAA	4	3	0	0	14	64	18	15	10	2	0	1	0	7	0	10	1	0	0	3	.000	0	0--	—	6.43
1993 St. Louis	NL	18	9	0	2	62	283	73	44	32	4	4	6	0	26	2	33	1	1	1	3	.250	0	0-1	0	4.65
1994 St. Louis	NL	20	10	0	2	80.1	354	98	48	46	12	3	2	3	21	0	43	4	1	3	7	.300	0	0-0	0	5.15
1995 St. Louis	NL	24	13	0	2	82.2	354	99	40	34	11	6	0	2	21	4	52	5	0	3	5	.375	0	0-0	1	3.70
1996 StL-Det		19	4	0	3	35.1	170	46	32	32	11	1	2	1	18	0	21	3	0	3	2	.600	0	0-0	1	8.15
1996 St. Louis	NL	3	2	0	0	11.2	53	15	10	10	3	1	1	0	4	0	1	0	0	1	0	1.000	0	0-0	0	7.71
Detroit	AL	16	2	0	3	23.2	117	31	22	22	8	0	1	2	14	0	20	3	0	2	2	.500	0	0-0	1	8.37
4 ML YEARS		81	36	0	9	260.1	1161	316	164	144	38	14	10	7	86	6	149	13	2	10	17	.370	0	0-1	2	4.98

Ugueth Urbina

Pitches: Right **Bats:** Right **Pos:** SP-17; RP-16   **Ht:** 6'2" **Wt:** 185 **Born:** 2/15/74 **Age:** 23

Year Team	Lg	G	GS	CG	GF	IP	BFP	H	R	ER	HR	SH	SF	HB	TBB	IBB	SO	WP	Bk	W	L	Pct.	ShO	Sv-Op	Hld	ERA
1991 Expos	R	10	10	0	0	63	252	58	24	16	2	0	0	4	10	0	51	2	3	3	3	.500	1	0--	—	2.29
1992 Albany	A	24	24	5	0	142.1	582	111	68	51	14	2	5	4	54	0	100	4	4	7	13	.350	2	0--	—	3.22
1993 Burlington	A	16	16	4	0	108.1	436	78	30	24	7	2	1	7	36	1	107	6	5	10	1	.909	1	0--	—	1.99
Harrisburg	AA	11	11	3	0	70	298	66	32	31	5	4	2	5	32	1	45	1	1	4	5	.444	1	0--	—	3.99
1994 Harrisburg	AA	21	21	0	0	120.2	497	96	49	44	11	4	7	3	43	0	86	6	1	9	3	.750	0	0--	—	3.28
1995 W. Palm Bch	A+	2	2	0	0	9	30	4	0	0	0	0	1	0	1	0	10	0	0	1	0	1.000	0	0--	—	0.00
Ottawa	AAA	15	13	2	0	77	303	50	26	23	1	3	2	2	27	0	66	1	0	7	2	.778	1	0--	—	2.69
1996 W. Palm Bch	A+	3	3	0	0	14	58	13	3	2	0	2	0	2	3	0	21	0	0	1	1	.500	0	0--	—	1.29
Ottawa	AAA	5	5	0	0	23.2	94	17	9	7	2	0	0	1	6	0	28	0	0	2	0	1.000	0	0--	—	2.66
1995 Montreal	NL	7	4	0	0	23.1	109	26	17	16	6	2	0	0	14	1	15	2	0	2	2	.500	0	0-0	0	6.17
1996 Montreal	NL	33	17	0	2	114	484	102	54	47	18	1	3	1	44	4	108	3	1	10	5	.667	0	0-1	6	3.71
2 ML YEARS		40	21	0	2	137.1	593	128	71	63	24	3	3	1	58	5	123	5	1	12	7	.632	0	0-1	6	4.13

Ismael Valdes

Pitches: Right **Bats:** Right **Pos:** SP-33   **Ht:** 6'3" **Wt:** 207 **Born:** 8/21/73 **Age:** 23

Year Team	Lg	G	GS	CG	GF	IP	BFP	H	R	ER	HR	SH	SF	HB	TBB	IBB	SO	WP	Bk	W	L	Pct.	ShO	Sv-Op	Hld	ERA
1994 Los Angeles	NL	21	1	0	7	28.1	115	21	10	10	2	3	0	0	10	2	28	1	2	3	1	.750	0	0-0	4	3.18
1995 Los Angeles	NL	33	27	6	1	197.2	804	168	76	67	17	10	5	1	51	5	150	1	3	13	11	.542	2	1-1	2	3.05
1996 Los Angeles	NL	33	33	0	0	225	945	219	94	83	20	7	7	3	54	10	173	1	5	15	7	.682	0	0-0	0	3.32
3 ML YEARS		87	61	6	8	451	1864	408	180	160	39	20	12	4	115	17	351	3	10	31	19	.620	2	1-1	6	3.19

Marc Valdes

Pitches: Right **Bats:** Right **Pos:** SP-8; RP-3   **Ht:** 6'0" **Wt:** 187 **Born:** 12/20/71 **Age:** 25

					HOW MUCH HE PITCHED				WHAT HE GAVE UP											THE RESULTS						
Year Team	Lg	G	GS	CG	GF	IP	BFP	H	R	ER	HR	SH	SF	HB	TBB	IBB	SO	WP	Bk	W	L	Pct.	ShO	Sv-Op	Hld	ERA
1993 Elmira	A-	3	3	0	0	9.2	46	8	9	6	0	0	0	3	7	0	15	0	0	0	2	.000	0	0--	—	5.59
1994 Kane County	A	11	11	2	0	76.1	315	62	30	25	3	4	1	8	21	0	68	3	0	7	4	.636	0	0--	—	2.95
Portland	AA	15	15	0	0	99	411	77	31	28	5	3	1	8	39	1	70	4	3	8	4	.667	0	0--	—	2.55
1995 Charlotte	AAA	27	27	3	0	170.1	728	189	98	92	19	3	5	12	59	1	104	2	1	9	13	.409	2	0--	—	4.86
1996 Portland	AA	10	10	1	0	64.1	263	60	25	19	5	1	2	3	12	2	49	2	0	6	2	.750	0	0--	—	2.66
Charlotte	AAA	8	8	1	0	51	229	66	32	29	10	3	0	6	15	1	24	3	0	2	4	.333	0	0--	—	5.12
1995 Florida	NL	3	3	0	0	7	49	17	13	11	1	1	1	1	9	0	2	1	0	0	0	.000	0	0-0	0	14.14
1996 Florida	NL	11	8	0	0	48.2	228	63	32	26	5	1	3	1	23	0	13	3	2	1	3	.250	0	0-1	0	4.81
2 ML YEARS		14	11	0	0	55.2	277	80	45	37	6	2	4	2	32	0	15	4	2	1	3	.250	0	0-1	0	5.98

Pedro Valdes

Bats: Left **Throws:** Left **Pos:** PH-8; RF-2   **Ht:** 6'1" **Wt:** 180 **Born:** 6/29/73 **Age:** 24

								BATTING										BASERUNNING				PERCENTAGES		
Year Team	Lg	G	AB	H	2B	3B	HR	(Hm	Rd)	TB	R	RBI	TBB	IBB	SO	HBP	SH	SF	SB	CS	SB%	GDP	Avg	OBP	SLG
1991 Huntington	R+	50	157	45	11	1	0	—	—	58	18	16	17	3	31	2	1	5	5	1	.83	7	.287	.354	.369
1992 Peoria	A	33	112	26	7	0	0	—	—	33	8	20	7	3	32	0	0	4	0	0	.00	1	.232	.268	.295
Geneva	A-	66	254	69	10	0	5	—	—	94	27	24	3	1	33	3	2	2	4	5	.44	2	.272	.286	.370
1993 Peoria	A	65	234	74	11	1	7	—	—	108	33	36	10	4	40	0	5	4	2	2	.50	3	.316	.339	.462
Daytona	A+	60	230	66	16	1	8	—	—	108	27	49	9	1	30	2	0	5	3	4	.43	8	.287	.313	.470
1994 Orlando	AA	116	365	103	14	4	1	—	—	128	39	37	20	3	45	2	2	1	2	6	.25	10	.282	.322	.351
1995 Orlando	AA	114	426	128	28	3	7	—	—	183	57	68	37	3	77	5	0	6	3	6	.33	7	.300	.359	.430
1996 Iowa	AAA	103	397	117	23	0	15	—	—	185	61	60	31	1	57	1	1	5	2	0	1.00	12	.295	.343	.466
1996 Chicago	NL	9	8	1	1	0	0	(0	0)	2	2	1	1	0	5	0	0	0	0	0	.00	0	.125	.222	.250

John Valentin

Bats: R **Throws:** R **Pos:** SS-118; 3B-12; PH-2; DH-1   **Ht:** 6'0" **Wt:** 180 **Born:** 2/18/67 **Age:** 30

								BATTING										BASERUNNING				PERCENTAGES		
Year Team	Lg	G	AB	H	2B	3B	HR	(Hm	Rd)	TB	R	RBI	TBB	IBB	SO	HBP	SH	SF	SB	CS	SB%	GDP	Avg	OBP	SLG
1992 Boston	AL	58	185	51	13	0	5	(1	4)	79	21	25	20	0	17	2	4	1	1	0	1.00	5	.276	.351	.427
1993 Boston	AL	144	468	130	40	3	11	(7	4)	209	50	66	49	2	77	2	16	4	3	4	.43	9	.278	.346	.447
1994 Boston	AL	84	301	95	26	2	9	(6	3)	152	53	49	42	1	38	3	5	4	3	1	.75	3	.316	.400	.505
1995 Boston	AL	135	520	155	37	2	27	(11	16)	277	108	102	81	2	67	10	4	6	20	5	.80	7	.298	.399	.533
1996 Boston	AL	131	527	156	29	3	13	(9	4)	230	84	59	63	0	59	7	2	7	9	10	.47	15	.296	.374	.436
5 ML YEARS		552	2001	587	145	10	65	(34	31)	947	316	301	255	5	258	24	31	22	36	20	.64	39	.293	.376	.473

Jose Valentin

Bats: Both **Throws:** Right **Pos:** SS-151; PH-8   **Ht:** 5'10" **Wt:** 166 **Born:** 10/12/69 **Age:** 27

								BATTING										BASERUNNING				PERCENTAGES		
Year Team	Lg	G	AB	H	2B	3B	HR	(Hm	Rd)	TB	R	RBI	TBB	IBB	SO	HBP	SH	SF	SB	CS	SB%	GDP	Avg	OBP	SLG
1992 Milwaukee	AL	4	3	0	0	0	0	(0	0)	0	1	1	0	0	0	0	0	1	0	0	.00	0	.000	.000	.000
1993 Milwaukee	AL	19	53	13	1	2	1	(1	0)	21	10	7	7	1	16	1	2	0	1	0	1.00	1	.245	.344	.396
1994 Milwaukee	AL	97	285	68	19	0	11	(8	3)	120	47	46	38	1	75	2	4	2	12	3	.80	1	.239	.330	.421
1995 Milwaukee	AL	112	338	74	23	3	11	(3	8)	136	62	49	37	0	83	0	1	4	16	8	.67	0	.219	.293	.402
1996 Milwaukee	AL	154	552	143	33	7	24	(10	14)	262	90	95	66	9	145	0	6	4	17	4	.81	4	.259	.336	.475
5 ML YEARS		386	1231	298	76	12	47	(22	25)	539	210	198	148	11	319	3	19	11	46	15	.75	6	.242	.322	.438

Fernando Valenzuela

Pitches: Left **Bats:** Left **Pos:** SP-31; RP-2   **Ht:** 5'11" **Wt:** 200 **Born:** 11/1/60 **Age:** 36

					HOW MUCH HE PITCHED				WHAT HE GAVE UP											THE RESULTS						
Year Team	Lg	G	GS	CG	GF	IP	BFP	H	R	ER	HR	SH	SF	HB	TBB	IBB	SO	WP	Bk	W	L	Pct.	ShO	Sv-Op	Hld	ERA
1980 Los Angeles	NL	10	0	0	4	18	66	8	2	0	0	1	1	0	5	0	16	0	1	2	0	1.000	0	1--	—	0.00
1981 Los Angeles	NL	25	25	11	0	192	758	140	55	53	11	9	3	1	61	4	180	4	0	13	7	.650	8	0--	—	2.48
1982 Los Angeles	NL	37	37	18	0	285	1156	247	105	91	13	19	6	2	83	12	199	4	0	19	13	.594	4	0--	—	2.87
1983 Los Angeles	NL	35	35	9	0	257	1094	245	122	107	16	27	5	3	99	10	189	12	1	15	10	.600	4	0--	—	3.75
1984 Los Angeles	NL	34	34	12	0	261	1078	218	109	88	14	11	7	2	106	4	240	11	1	12	17	.414	2	0--	—	3.03
1985 Los Angeles	NL	35	35	14	0	272.1	1109	211	92	74	14	13	8	1	101	5	208	10	1	17	10	.630	5	0--	—	2.45
1986 Los Angeles	NL	34	34	20	0	269.1	1102	226	104	94	18	15	3	1	85	5	242	13	0	21	11	.656	3	0--	—	3.14
1987 Los Angeles	NL	34	34	12	0	251	1116	254	120	111	25	18	2	4	124	4	190	14	1	14	14	.500	1	0-0	0	3.98
1988 Los Angeles	NL	23	22	3	1	142.1	626	142	71	67	11	15	5	0	76	4	64	7	1	5	8	.385	0	1-1	0	4.24
1989 Los Angeles	NL	31	31	3	0	196.2	852	185	89	75	11	7	7	2	98	6	116	6	4	10	13	.435	0	0-0	0	3.43
1990 Los Angeles	NL	33	33	5	0	204	900	223	112	104	19	11	4	0	77	4	115	13	1	13	13	.500	2	0-0	0	4.59
1991 California	AL	2	2	0	0	6.2	36	14	9	9	3	1	1	0	3	0	5	1	0	0	2	.000	0	0-0	0	12.15
1993 Baltimore	AL	32	31	5	0	178.2	768	179	104	98	18	4	7	4	79	2	78	8	0	8	10	.444	2	0-0	0	4.94
1994 Philadelphia	NL	8	7	0	0	45	182	42	16	15	8	3	2	0	7	1	19	1	0	1	2	.333	0	0-0	0	3.00
1995 San Diego	NL	29	15	0	5	90.1	395	101	53	50	16	10	2	0	34	2	57	4	0	8	3	.727	0	0-2	2	4.98
1996 San Diego	NL	33	31	0	0	171.2	741	177	78	69	17	11	4	0	67	4	95	7	0	13	8	.619	0	0-0	2	3.62

Year Team	Lg	G	GS	CG	GF	IP	BFP	H	R	ER	HR	SH	SF	HB	TBB	IBB	SO	WP	Bk	W	L	Pct.	ShO	Sv-Op	Hld	ERA
		HOW MUCH HE PITCHED						WHAT HE GAVE UP												THE RESULTS						
16 ML YEARS		435	406	112	10	2841	11979	2612	1242	1105	214	175	67	20	1105	65	2013	115	11	171	141	.548	31	2--	—	3.50

Julio Valera

Pitches: Right **Bats:** Right **Pos:** RP-29; SP-2   **Ht:** 6'2" **Wt:** 215 **Born:** 10/13/68 **Age:** 28

Year Team	Lg	G	GS	CG	GF	IP	BFP	H	R	ER	HR	SH	SF	HB	TBB	IBB	SO	WP	Bk	W	L	Pct.	ShO	Sv-Op	Hld	ERA
1996 Omaha *	AAA	6	2	0	1	15.2	72	22	13	9	0	0	0	0	5	1	9	3	1	1	3	.250	0	0--	—	5.17
1990 New York	NL	3	3	0	0	13	64	20	11	10	1	0	0	0	7	0	4	0	0	1	1	.500	0	0-0	0	6.92
1991 New York	NL	2	0	0	1	2	11	1	0	0	0	0	0	0	4	1	3	0	0	0	0	.000	0	0-0	0	0.00
1992 California	AL	30	28	4	0	188	792	188	82	78	15	6	2	2	64	5	113	5	0	8	11	.421	2	0-0	0	3.73
1993 California	AL	19	5	0	8	53	246	77	44	39	8	4	1	2	15	2	28	2	0	3	6	.333	0	4-7	5	6.62
1996 Kansas City	AL	31	2	0	7	61.1	279	75	44	44	7	2	4	2	27	3	31	1	1	3	2	.600	0	1-1	1	6.46
5 ML YEARS		85	38	4	16	317.1	1392	361	181	171	31	12	7	6	117	11	179	8	1	15	20	.429	2	5-8	3	4.85

Dave Valle

Bats: Right **Throws:** Right **Pos:** C-35; 1B-5; PH-4; DH-1   **Ht:** 6'2" **Wt:** 220 **Born:** 10/30/60 **Age:** 36

Year Team	Lg	G	AB	H	2B	3B	HR	(Hm	Rd)	TB	R	RBI	TBB	IBB	SO	HBP	SH	SF	SB	CS	SB%	GDP	Avg	OBP	SLG
								BATTING											BASERUNNING				PERCENTAGES		
1984 Seattle	AL	13	27	8	1	0	1	(1	0)	12	4	4	1	0	5	0	0	0	0	0	.00	0	.296	.321	.444
1985 Seattle	AL	31	70	11	1	0	0	(0	0)	12	2	4	1	0	17	1	1	0	0	0	.00	1	.157	.181	.171
1986 Seattle	AL	22	53	18	3	0	5	(4	1)	36	10	15	7	0	7	0	0	0	0	0	.00	2	.340	.417	.679
1987 Seattle	AL	95	324	83	16	3	12	(8	4)	141	40	53	15	2	46	3	0	4	2	1	1.00	13	.256	.292	.435
1988 Seattle	AL	93	290	67	15	2	10	(5	5)	116	29	50	18	0	38	9	3	2	0	1	.00	13	.231	.295	.400
1989 Seattle	AL	94	316	75	10	3	7	(1	6)	112	32	34	29	2	32	6	1	3	0	0	.00	13	.237	.311	.354
1990 Seattle	AL	107	308	66	15	0	7	(1	6)	102	37	33	45	0	48	7	4	0	1	2	.33	11	.214	.328	.331
1991 Seattle	AL	132	324	63	8	1	8	(0	8)	97	38	32	34	0	49	9	6	3	0	2	.00	19	.194	.286	.299
1992 Seattle	AL	124	367	88	16	1	9	(7	2)	133	39	30	27	1	58	8	7	1	0	0	.00	7	.240	.305	.362
1993 Seattle	AL	135	423	109	19	1	13	(4	9)	167	48	63	48	4	56	17	8	4	1	0	1.00	18	.258	.354	.395
1994 Bos-Mil	AL	46	112	26	8	1	2	(1	1)	42	14	10	18	2	22	2	2	0	0	1	.00	3	.232	.348	.375
1995 Texas	AL	36	75	18	3	0	0	(0	0)	21	7	5	6	0	18	1	1	0	1	0	1.00	3	.240	.305	.280
1996 Texas	AL	42	86	26	6	1	3	(3	0)	43	14	17	9	0	17	0	0	0	0	0	.00	3	.302	.368	.500
1994 Boston	AL	30	76	12	2	1	1	(0	1)	19	6	5	9	1	18	1	2	0	0	1	.00	2	.158	.256	.250
Milwaukee	AL	16	36	14	6	0	1	(1	0)	23	8	5	9	1	4	1	0	0	0	1	.00	1	.389	.522	.639
13 ML YEARS		970	2775	658	121	12	77	(32	45)	1034	314	350	258	11	413	63	33	17	5	7	.42	105	.237	.314	.373

Todd Van Poppel

Pitches: Right **Bats:** Right **Pos:** RP-22; SP-15   **Ht:** 6'5" **Wt:** 210 **Born:** 12/9/71 **Age:** 25

Year Team	Lg	G	GS	CG	GF	IP	BFP	H	R	ER	HR	SH	SF	HB	TBB	IBB	SO	WP	Bk	W	L	Pct.	ShO	Sv-Op	Hld	ERA
		HOW MUCH HE PITCHED						WHAT HE GAVE UP												THE RESULTS						
1991 Oakland	AL	1	1	0	0	4.2	21	7	5	5	1	0	0	0	2	0	6	0	0	0	0	.000	0	0-0	0	9.64
1993 Oakland	AL	16	16	0	0	84	380	76	50	47	10	1	2	2	62	0	47	3	0	6	6	.500	0	0-0	0	5.04
1994 Oakland	AL	23	23	0	0	116.2	532	108	80	79	20	4	4	3	89	2	83	3	1	7	10	.412	0	0-0	0	6.09
1995 Oakland	AL	36	14	1	10	138.1	582	125	77	75	16	3	6	4	56	1	122	4	0	4	8	.333	0	0-0	1	4.88
1996 Oak-Det	AL	37	15	1	8	99.1	491	139	107	100	24	4	7	3	62	3	53	7	0	3	9	.250	1	1-2	0	9.06
1996 Oakland	AL	28	6	0	8	63	301	86	56	54	13	3	5	2	33	3	37	4	0	1	5	.167	0	1-2	0	7.71
Detroit	AL	9	9	1	0	36.1	190	53	51	46	11	1	2	1	29	0	16	3	0	2	4	.333	1	0-0	0	11.39
5 ML YEARS		113	69	2	18	443	2006	455	319	306	71	12	19	12	271	6	311	17	1	20	33	.377	1	1-2	1	6.22

John Vander Wal

Bats: L **Throws:** L **Pos:** PH-72; LF-25; 1B-10; RF-1   **Ht:** 6'2" **Wt:** 198 **Born:** 4/29/66 **Age:** 31

Year Team	Lg	G	AB	H	2B	3B	HR	(Hm	Rd)	TB	R	RBI	TBB	IBB	SO	HBP	SH	SF	SB	CS	SB%	GDP	Avg	OBP	SLG
								BATTING											BASERUNNING				PERCENTAGES		
1991 Montreal	NL	21	61	13	4	1	1	(0	1)	22	4	8	1	0	18	0	0	0	0	0	.00	2	.213	.222	.361
1992 Montreal	NL	105	213	51	8	2	4	(2	2)	75	21	20	24	2	36	0	0	0	3	0	1.00	2	.239	.316	.352
1993 Montreal	NL	106	215	50	7	4	5	(1	4)	80	34	30	27	2	30	1	0	1	6	3	.67	4	.233	.320	.372
1994 Colorado	NL	91	110	27	3	1	5	(1	4)	47	12	15	16	0	31	0	0	1	2	1	.67	2	.245	.339	.427
1995 Colorado	NL	105	101	35	8	1	5	(2	3)	60	15	21	16	5	23	0	1	1	1	1	.50	4	.347	.432	.594
1996 Colorado	NL	104	151	38	6	2	5	(5	0)	63	20	31	19	2	38	1	0	2	2	2	.50	1	.252	.335	.417
6 ML YEARS		532	851	214	36	11	25	(11	14)	347	106	125	103	11	176	2	0	6	14	7	.67	15	.251	.332	.408

Tim VanEgmond

Pitches: Right **Bats:** Right **Pos:** SP-9; RP-3   **Ht:** 6'2" **Wt:** 180 **Born:** 5/31/69 **Age:** 28

Year Team	Lg	G	GS	CG	GF	IP	BFP	H	R	ER	HR	SH	SF	HB	TBB	IBB	SO	WP	Bk	W	L	Pct.	ShO	Sv-Op	Hld	ERA
		HOW MUCH HE PITCHED						WHAT HE GAVE UP												THE RESULTS						
1996 Pawtucket *	AAA	11	11	1	0	61.2	262	66	37	30	9	0	2	3	24	1	46	1	1	5	3	.625	0	0--	—	4.38
Nw Orleans *	AAA	7	7	0	0	48	180	28	8	8	2	2	0	1	11	0	32	1	0	5	1	.833	0	0--	—	1.50
1994 Boston	AL	7	7	1	0	38.1	173	38	27	27	7	0	3	0	21	3	22	1	0	2	3	.400	0	0-0	0	6.34

	HOW MUCH HE PITCHED						WHAT HE GAVE UP												THE RESULTS						
Year Team	Lg	G	GS	CG	GF	IP	BFP	H	R	ER	HR	SH	SF	HB	TBB	IBB	SO	WP	Bk	W	L	Pct.	ShO	Sv-Op	Hld	ERA
1995 Boston	AL	4	1	0	1	6.2	35	9	7	7	2	0	0	0	6	0	5	1	0	0	1	.000	0	0-0	0	9.45
1996 Milwaukee	AL	12	9	0	1	54.2	242	58	35	32	6	3	3	1	23	2	33	0	1	3	5	.375	0	0-0	0	5.27
3 ML YEARS		23	17	1	2	99.2	450	105	69	66	15	3	6	1	50	5	60	2	1	5	9	.357	0	0-0	0	5.96

William VanLandingham

Pitches: Right **Bats:** Right **Pos:** SP-32   **Ht:** 6'2" **Wt:** 210 **Born:** 7/16/70 **Age:** 26

	HOW MUCH HE PITCHED						WHAT HE GAVE UP												THE RESULTS						
Year Team	Lg	G	GS	CG	GF	IP	BFP	H	R	ER	HR	SH	SF	HB	TBB	IBB	SO	WP	Bk	W	L	Pct.	ShO	Sv-Op	Hld	ERA
1994 San Francisco	NL	16	14	0	1	84	363	70	37	33	4	3	1	2	43	4	56	3	3	8	2	.800	0	0-0	0	3.54
1995 San Francisco	NL	18	18	1	0	122.2	523	124	58	50	14	6	5	2	40	2	95	5	4	6	3	.667	0	0-0	0	3.67
1996 San Francisco	NL	32	32	0	0	181.2	810	196	123	109	17	7	5	3	78	6	97	7	2	9	14	.391	0	0-0	0	5.40
3 ML YEARS		66	64	1	1	388.1	1696	390	218	192	35	16	11	13	161	12	248	15	9	23	19	.548	0	0-0	0	4.45

Ben VanRyn

Pitches: Left **Bats:** Left **Pos:** RP-1   **Ht:** 6'5" **Wt:** 195 **Born:** 8/9/71 **Age:** 25

	HOW MUCH HE PITCHED						WHAT HE GAVE UP												THE RESULTS						
Year Team	Lg	G	GS	CG	GF	IP	BFP	H	R	ER	HR	SH	SF	HB	TBB	IBB	SO	WP	Bk	W	L	Pct.	ShO	Sv-Op	Hld	ERA
1990 Expos	R	10	9	0	0	51.2	205	44	13	10	0	0	0	2	15	0	56	0	0	5	3	.625	0	0--	—	1.74
1991 Sumter	A	20	20	0	0	109.1	506	122	96	79	14	3	7	6	61	0	77	10	4	2	13	.133	0	0--	—	6.50
Jamestown	A-	6	6	1	0	32.1	143	37	19	18	1	0	0	2	12	0	23	4	0	3	3	.500	0	0--	—	5.01
1992 Vero Beach	A+	26	25	1	0	137.2	583	125	58	49	4	5	8	2	54	1	108	4	5	10	7	.588	1	0--	—	3.20
1993 San Antonio	AA	21	21	1	0	134.1	557	118	43	33	5	4	1	3	38	1	144	2	4	14	4	.778	0	0--	—	2.21
Albuquerque	AAA	6	6	0	0	24.1	120	35	30	29	1	1	2	0	17	0	9	0	0	1	4	.200	0	0--	—	10.73
1994 Albuquerque	AAA	12	9	0	1	50.2	251	75	42	36	6	3	1	0	24	1	44	0	1	4	1	.800	0	0--	—	6.39
San Antonio	AA	17	17	0	0	102.1	418	93	42	34	5	3	1	0	35	0	72	2	0	8	3	.727	0	0--	—	2.99
1995 Chattanooga	AA	5	3	0	0	12.2	69	22	18	13	0	2	0	2	6	0	6	0	0	0	1	.000	0	0--	—	9.24
Vancouver	AAA	11	5	0	2	29.1	123	29	10	10	1	2	2	0	9	1	20	2	0	2	0	1.000	0	0--	—	3.07
1996 Vancouver	AAA	18	1	0	4	34.2	154	35	17	15	2	3	1	1	13	1	28	3	0	3	3	.500	0	0--	—	3.89
Louisville	AAA	19	10	0	4	66.1	288	69	43	36	9	2	3	0	27	0	42	2	0	4	6	.400	0	1--	—	4.88
1996 California	AL	1	0	0	1	.0	5	1	0	0	0	0	0	0	1	0	0	0	0	0	0	.000	0	0-0	0	0.00

Greg Vaughn

Bats: R **Throws:** R **Pos:** LF-137; PH-6; CF-3; DH-1   **Ht:** 6'0" **Wt:** 202 **Born:** 7/3/65 **Age:** 31

	BATTING																	BASERUNNING				PERCENTAGES		
Year Team	Lg	G	AB	H	2B	3B	HR	(Hm Rd)	TB	R	RBI	TBB	IBB	SO	HBP	SH	SF	SB	CS	SB%	GDP	Avg	OBP	SLG
1989 Milwaukee	AL	38	113	30	3	0	5	(1 4)	48	18	23	13	0	23	0	0	2	4	1	.80		.265	.336	.425
1990 Milwaukee	AL	120	382	84	26	2	17	(9 8)	165	51	61	33	1	91	1	7	6	7	4	.64	11	.220	.280	.432
1991 Milwaukee	AL	145	542	132	24	5	27	(16 11)	247	81	98	62	2	125	1	2	7	2	2	.50	5	.244	.319	.456
1992 Milwaukee	AL	141	501	114	18	2	23	(11 12)	205	77	78	60	1	123	5	2	5	15	15	.50	8	.228	.313	.409
1993 Milwaukee	AL	154	569	152	28	2	30	(12 18)	274	97	97	89	14	118	5	0	4	10	7	.59	6	.267	.369	.482
1994 Milwaukee	AL	95	370	94	24	1	19	(9 10)	177	59	55	51	6	93	1	0	1	9	5	.64	6	.254	.345	.478
1995 Milwaukee	AL	108	392	88	19	1	17	(8 9)	160	67	59	55	3	89	0	0	4	10	4	.71	10	.224	.317	.408
1996 Mil-SD		145	516	134	19	1	41	(22 19)	278	98	117	82	6	130	6	0	5	9	3	.75	7	.260	.365	.539
1996 Milwaukee	AL	102	375	105	16	0	31	(16 15)	214	78	95	58	4	99	4	0	5	5	2	.71	6	.280	.378	.571
San Diego	NL	43	141	29	3	1	10	(6 4)	64	20	22	24	2	31	2	0	0	4	1	.80	1	.206	.329	.454
8 ML YEARS		946	3385	828	161	14	179	(88 91)	1554	548	588	445	33	792	19	11	34	66	41	.62	53	.245	.333	.459

Mo Vaughn

Bats: Left **Throws:** Right **Pos:** 1B-146; DH-15   **Ht:** 6'1" **Wt:** 240 **Born:** 12/15/67 **Age:** 29

	BATTING																	BASERUNNING				PERCENTAGES		
Year Team	Lg	G	AB	H	2B	3B	HR	(Hm Rd)	TB	R	RBI	TBB	IBB	SO	HBP	SH	SF	SB	CS	SB%	GDP	Avg	OBP	SLG
1991 Boston	AL	74	219	57	12	0	4	(1 3)	81	21	32	26	2	43	2	0	4	2	1	.67	7	.260	.339	.370
1992 Boston	AL	113	355	83	16	2	13	(8 5)	142	42	57	47	7	67	3	0	3	3	3	.50	8	.234	.326	.400
1993 Boston	AL	152	539	160	34	1	29	(13 16)	283	86	101	79	23	130	8	0	7	4	3	.57	14	.297	.390	.525
1994 Boston	AL	111	394	122	25	1	26	(15 11)	227	65	82	57	20	112	10	0	2	4	4	.50	7	.310	.408	.576
1995 Boston	AL	140	550	165	28	3	39	(15 24)	316	98	126	68	17	150	14	0	4	11	4	.73	17	.300	.388	.575
1996 Boston	AL	161	635	207	29	1	44	(27 17)	370	118	143	95	19	154	14	0	8	2	0	1.00	17	.326	.420	.583
6 ML YEARS		751	2692	794	144	8	155	(79 76)	1419	430	541	372	88	656	51	0	28	26	15	.63	70	.295	.387	.527

Randy Velarde

Bats: R **Throws:** R **Pos:** 2B-114; 3B-28; SS-7; PH-3   **Ht:** 6'0" **Wt:** 192 **Born:** 11/24/62 **Age:** 34

	BATTING																	BASERUNNING				PERCENTAGES		
Year Team	Lg	G	AB	H	2B	3B	HR	(Hm Rd)	TB	R	RBI	TBB	IBB	SO	HBP	SH	SF	SB	CS	SB%	GDP	Avg	OBP	SLG
1987 New York	AL	8	22	4	0	0	0	(0 0)	4	1	1	0	0	6	0	0	0	0	0	.00	1	.182	.182	.182
1988 New York	AL	48	115	20	6	0	5	(2 3)	41	18	12	8	0	24	2	0	0	1	1	.50	3	.174	.240	.357
1989 New York	AL	33	100	34	4	2	2	(1 1)	48	12	11	7	0	14	1	3	0	0	3	.00	0	.340	.389	.480
1990 New York	AL	95	229	48	6	2	5	(1 4)	73	21	19	20	0	53	1	2	1	0	3	.00	6	.210	.275	.319
1991 New York	AL	80	184	45	11	1	1	(0 1)	61	19	19	18	0	43	3	5	0	3	1	.75	6	.245	.322	.332

Year Team	Lg	G	AB	H	2B	3B	HR	(Hm	Rd)	TB	R	RBI	TBB	IBB	SO	HBP	SH	SF	SB	CS	SB%	GDP	Avg	OBP	SLG
1992 New York	AL	121	412	112	24	1	7	(2	5)	159	57	46	38	1	78	2	4	5	7	2	.78	13	.272	.333	.386
1993 New York	AL	85	226	68	13	2	7	(4	3)	106	28	24	18	2	39	4	3	2	2	2	.50	12	.301	.360	.469
1994 New York	AL	77	280	78	16	1	9	(3	6)	123	47	34	22	0	61	4	2	2	4	2	.67	7	.279	.338	.439
1995 New York	AL	111	367	102	19	1	7	(2	5)	144	60	46	55	0	64	4	3	3	5	1	.83	9	.278	.375	.392
1996 California	AL	136	530	151	27	3	14	(8	6)	226	82	54	70	0	118	5	4	2	7	7	.50	7	.285	.372	.426
10 ML YEARS		794	2465	662	126	13	57	(23	34)	985	345	262	256	3	500	26	26	15	29	22	.57	64	.269	.342	.400

Robin Ventura

Bats: Left **Throws:** Right **Pos:** 3B-150; 1B-14; PH-11 **Ht:** 6'1" **Wt:** 198 **Born:** 7/14/67 **Age:** 29

Year Team	Lg	G	AB	H	2B	3B	HR	(Hm	Rd)	TB	R	RBI	TBB	IBB	SO	HBP	SH	SF	SB	CS	SB%	GDP	Avg	OBP	SLG
1989 Chicago	AL	16	45	8	3	0	0	(0	0)	11	5	7	8	0	6	1	1	3	0	0	.00	1	.178	.298	.244
1990 Chicago	AL	150	493	123	17	1	5	(2	3)	157	48	54	55	2	53	1	13	3	1	4	.20	5	.249	.324	.318
1991 Chicago	AL	157	606	172	25	1	23	(16	7)	268	92	100	80	3	67	4	8	7	2	4	.33	22	.284	.367	.442
1992 Chicago	AL	157	592	167	38	1	16	(7	9)	255	85	93	93	9	71	0	1	8	2	4	.33	14	.282	.375	.431
1993 Chicago	AL	157	554	145	27	1	22	(12	10)	240	85	94	105	16	82	3	1	6	1	6	.14	18	.262	.379	.433
1994 Chicago	AL	109	401	113	15	1	18	(8	10)	184	57	78	61	15	69	2	2	8	3	1	.75	8	.282	.373	.459
1995 Chicago	AL	135	492	145	22	0	26	(8	18)	245	79	93	75	11	98	1	1	8	4	3	.57	8	.295	.384	.498
1996 Chicago	AL	158	586	168	31	2	34	(13	21)	305	96	105	78	10	81	2	0	8	1	3	.25	18	.287	.368	.520
8 ML YEARS		1039	3769	1041	178	7	144	(66	78)	1665	547	624	555	66	527	14	27	51	14	25	.36	94	.276	.367	.442

Dario Veras

Pitches: Right **Bats:** Right **Pos:** RP-23 **Ht:** 6'1" **Wt:** 155 **Born:** 3/13/73 **Age:** 24

Year Team	Lg	G	GS	CG	GF	IP	BFP	H	R	ER	HR	SH	SF	HB	TBB	IBB	SO	WP	Bk	W	L	Pct.	ShO	Sv-Op	Hld	ERA
1993 Bakersfield	A+	7	0	0	1	13.1	61	13	11	11	1	0	1	0	8	2	11	0	0	1	0	1.000	0	2--	—	7.43
Vero Beach	A+	24	0	0	8	54.2	229	59	23	17	2	3	1	1	14	5	31	3	0	2	2	.500	0	2--	—	2.80
1994 Rancho Cuca	A+	59	0	0	13	79	332	66	28	18	7	7	0	6	25	9	56	2	0	9	2	.818	0	3--	—	2.05
1995 Memphis	AA	58	0	0	22	82.2	360	81	38	35	8	3	1	7	27	11	70	5	1	7	3	.700	0	1--	—	3.81
1996 Memphis	AA	29	0	0	8	42.2	172	38	14	11	4	1	2	1	9	2	47	2	1	3	1	.750	0	1--	—	2.32
Las Vegas	AAA	19	1	0	9	40.1	165	41	17	13	1	3	1	0	6	2	30	2	0	6	2	.750	0	1--	—	2.90
1996 San Diego	NL	23	0	0	6	29	117	24	10	9	3	1	1	1	10	4	23	1	0	3	1	.750	0	0-0	1	2.79

Quilvio Veras

Bats: Both **Throws:** Right **Pos:** 2B-67; PH-6 **Ht:** 5'9" **Wt:** 166 **Born:** 4/3/71 **Age:** 26

Year Team	Lg	G	AB	H	2B	3B	HR	(Hm	Rd)	TB	R	RBI	TBB	IBB	SO	HBP	SH	SF	SB	CS	SB%	GDP	Avg	OBP	SLG
1990 Mets	R	30	98	29	3	3	1	—	—	41	26	5	19	0	16	3	1	1	16	8	.67	1	.296	.421	.418
Kingsport	R+	24	94	36	5	0	1	—	—	44	21	14	13	1	14	1	1	0	9	5	.64	1	.383	.463	.468
1991 Kingsport	R+	64	226	76	11	4	1	—	—	98	54	16	36	0	28	7	5	0	38	11	.78	3	.336	.442	.434
Pittsfield	A-	5	15	4	0	1	0	—	—	6	3	2	5	0	1	0	0	0	2	0	1.00	0	.267	.450	.400
1992 Columbia	A	117	414	132	24	10	2	—	—	182	97	40	84	3	52	9	5	3	66	35	.65	5	.319	.441	.440
1993 Binghamton	AA	128	444	136	19	7	2	—	—	175	87	51	91	0	62	9	4	5	52	23	.69	3	.306	.430	.394
1994 Norfolk	AAA	123	457	114	22	4	0	—	—	144	71	43	59	2	56	4	6	4	40	18	.69	8	.249	.338	.315
1996 Charlotte	AAA	28	104	34	5	2	2	—	—	49	22	8	13	2	14	1	0	0	8	3	.73	1	.327	.407	.471
1995 Florida	NL	124	440	115	20	7	5	(2	3)	164	86	32	80	0	68	9	7	2	56	21	.73	7	.261	.384	.373
1996 Florida	NL	73	253	64	8	1	4	(1	3)	86	40	14	51	1	42	2	1	1	8	8	.50	3	.253	.381	.340
2 ML YEARS		197	693	179	28	8	9	(3	6)	250	126	46	131	1	110	11	8	3	64	29	.69	10	.258	.383	.361

Dave Veres

Pitches: Right **Bats:** Right **Pos:** RP-68 **Ht:** 6'2" **Wt:** 195 **Born:** 10/19/66 **Age:** 30

Year Team	Lg	G	GS	CG	GF	IP	BFP	H	R	ER	HR	SH	SF	HB	TBB	IBB	SO	WP	Bk	W	L	Pct.	ShO	Sv-Op	Hld	ERA
1994 Houston	NL	32	0	0	7	41	168	39	13	11	4	0	2	1	7	3	28	2	0	3	3	.500	0	1-1	3	2.41
1995 Houston	NL	72	0	0	15	103.1	418	89	29	26	5	6	8	4	30	6	94	4	0	5	1	.833	0	1-3	19	2.26
1996 Montreal	NL	68	0	0	22	77.2	351	85	39	36	10	3	3	6	32	2	81	3	2	6	3	.667	0	4-6	15	4.17
3 ML YEARS		172	0	0	44	222	937	213	81	73	19	9	13	11	69	11	203	9	2	14	7	.667	0	6-10	37	2.96

Randy Veres

Pitches: Right **Bats:** Right **Pos:** RP-25 **Ht:** 6'3" **Wt:** 210 **Born:** 11/25/65 **Age:** 31

Year Team	Lg	G	GS	CG	GF	IP	BFP	H	R	ER	HR	SH	SF	HB	TBB	IBB	SO	WP	Bk	W	L	Pct.	ShO	Sv-Op	Hld	ERA
1989 Milwaukee	AL	3	1	0	1	8.1	36	9	5	4	0	1	0	4	0	8	0	0	0	0	1	.000	0	0-0	0	4.32
1990 Milwaukee	AL	26	0	0	12	41.2	175	38	17	17	5	2	2	1	16	3	16	3	0	0	3	.000	0	1-1	1	3.67
1994 Chicago	NL	10	0	0	1	9.2	43	12	6	6	3	0	1	1	2	0	5	0	0	1	1	.500	0	0-2	2	5.59
1995 Florida	NL	47	0	0	15	48.2	215	46	25	21	6	5	4	1	22	7	31	2	0	4	4	.500	0	1-2	9	3.88
1996 Detroit	AL	25	0	0	11	30.1	153	38	29	28	6	1	3	2	23	4	28	2	0	0	2	.833	3	0-2	3	8.31

Year Team	Lg	G	GS	CG	GF	IP	BFP	H	R	ER	HR	SH	SF	HB	TBB	IBB	SO	WP	Bk	W	L	Pct.	ShO	Sv-Op	Hld	ERA
5 ML YEARS		111	1	0	40	138.2	622	143	82	76	20	8	11	5	67	14	88	7	0	5	13	.278	0	2-7	15	4.93

Ron Villone

Pitches: Left **Bats:** Left **Pos:** RP-44   **Ht:** 6'3" **Wt:** 235 **Born:** 1/16/70 **Age:** 27

Year Team	Lg	G	GS	CG	GF	IP	BFP	H	R	ER	HR	SH	SF	HB	TBB	IBB	SO	WP	Bk	W	L	Pct.	ShO	Sv-Op	Hld	ERA
1993 Riverside	A+	16	16	0	0	83.1	375	74	47	39	5	1	1	4	62	0	82	7	3	7	4	.636	0	0--	—	4.21
Jacksonvlle	AA	11	11	0	0	63.2	269	49	34	30	6	1	2	1	41	3	66	9	0	3	4	.429	0	0--	—	4.24
1994 Jacksonvlle	AA	41	5	0	19	79.1	360	56	37	34	7	1	4	5	68	3	94	9	0	6	7	.462	0	8--	—	3.86
1995 Tacoma	AAA	22	0	0	16	29.2	117	9	6	2	1	1	2	0	19	0	43	1	0	1	0	1.000	0	13--	—	0.61
1996 Las Vegas	AAA	23	0	0	22	22	90	13	5	4	0	2	0	2	9	0	29	2	1	2	1	.667	0	3--	—	1.64
1995 Sea-SD		38	0	0	15	45	212	44	31	29	11	3	1	1	34	0	63	3	0	2	3	.400	0	1-5	6	5.80
1996 SD-Mil		44	0	0	19	43	182	31	15	15	6	0	2	5	25	0	38	2	0	1	1	.500	0	2-3	9	3.14
1995 Seattle	AL	19	0	0	7	19.1	101	20	19	17	6	3	0	1	23	0	26	1	0	0	2	.000	0	0-3	3	7.91
San Diego	NL	19	0	0	8	25.2	111	24	12	12	5	0	1	0	11	0	37	2	0	2	1	.667	0	1-2	3	4.21
1996 San Diego	NL	21	0	0	9	18.1	78	17	6	6	2	0	0	1	7	0	19	0	0	1	1	.500	0	0-1	4	2.95
Milwaukee	AL	23	0	0	10	24.2	104	14	9	9	4	0	2	4	18	0	19	2	0	0	0	.000	0	2-2	5	3.28
2 ML YEARS		82	0	0	34	88	394	75	46	44	17	3	3	6	59	0	101	5	0	3	4	.429	0	3-8	15	4.50

Fernando Vina

Bats: Left **Throws:** Right **Pos:** 2B-137; PH-6   **Ht:** 5'9" **Wt:** 170 **Born:** 4/16/69 **Age:** 28

Year Team	Lg	G	AB	H	2B	3B	HR	(Hm	Rd)	TB	R	RBI	TBB	IBB	SO	HBP	SH	SF	SB	CS	SB%	GDP	Avg	OBP	SLG
1993 Seattle	AL	24	45	10	2	0	0	(0	0)	12	5	2	4	0	3	3	1	0	6	0	1.00	0	.222	.327	.267
1994 New York	NL	79	124	31	6	0	0	(0	0)	37	20	6	12	0	11	12	2	0	3	1	.75	4	.250	.372	.298
1995 Milwaukee	AL	113	288	74	7	7	3	(1	2)	104	46	29	22	0	28	9	4	2	6	3	.67	6	.257	.327	.361
1996 Milwaukee	AL	140	554	157	19	10	7	(3	4)	217	94	46	38	3	35	13	6	4	16	7	.70	15	.283	.342	.392
4 ML YEARS		356	1011	272	34	17	10	(4	6)	370	165	83	76	3	77	37	13	6	31	11	.74	25	.269	.341	.366

Frank Viola

Pitches: Left **Bats:** Left **Pos:** SP-6   **Ht:** 6'4" **Wt:** 210 **Born:** 4/19/60 **Age:** 37

Year Team	Lg	G	GS	CG	GF	IP	BFP	H	R	ER	HR	SH	SF	HB	TBB	IBB	SO	WP	Bk	W	L	Pct.	ShO	Sv-Op	Hld	ERA
1996 Knoxville *	AA	4	4	0	0	22	84	16	4	4	1	0	0	0	3	0	15	0	0	0	0	.000	0	0--	—	1.64
1982 Minnesota	AL	22	22	3	0	126	543	152	77	73	22	2	0	0	38	2	84	4	1	4	10	.286	1	0--	—	5.21
1983 Minnesota	AL	35	34	4	0	210	949	242	141	128	34	5	2	8	92	7	127	6	2	7	15	.318	0	0--	—	5.49
1984 Minnesota	AL	35	35	10	0	257.2	1047	225	101	92	28	1	5	4	73	1	149	6	1	18	12	.600	4	0--	—	3.21
1985 Minnesota	AL	36	36	9	0	250.2	1059	262	136	114	26	5	5	2	68	3	135	4	2	18	14	.563	0	0--	—	4.09
1986 Minnesota	AL	37	37	7	0	245.2	1053	257	136	123	37	4	5	3	83	0	191	12	0	16	13	.552	1	0--	—	4.51
1987 Minnesota	AL	36	36	7	0	251.2	1037	230	91	81	29	7	3	6	66	1	197	1	1	17	10	.630	1	0-0	0	2.90
1988 Minnesota	AL	35	35	7	0	255.1	1031	236	80	75	20	6	6	3	54	2	193	5	1	24	7	.774	2	0-0	0	2.64
1989 Min-NYN	AL	36	36	9	0	261	1082	246	115	106	22	12	6	4	74	4	211	8	1	13	17	.433	2	0-0	0	3.66
1990 New York	NL	35	35	7	0	249.2	1016	227	83	74	15	13	3	2	60	2	182	11	0	20	12	.625	3	0-0	0	2.67
1991 New York	NL	35	35	3	0	231.1	980	259	112	102	25	15	5	1	54	4	132	6	1	13	15	.464	0	0-0	0	3.97
1992 Boston	AL	35	35	6	0	238	999	214	99	91	13	7	10	7	89	3	121	12	2	13	12	.520	1	0-0	0	3.44
1993 Boston	AL	29	29	2	0	183.2	787	180	76	64	12	8	7	6	72	5	91	5	0	11	8	.579	1	0-0	0	3.14
1994 Boston	AL	6	6	0	0	31	136	34	17	16	2	2	2	0	17	0	9	2	0	1	1	.500	0	0-0	0	4.65
1995 Cincinnati	NL	3	3	0	0	14.1	64	20	11	10	3	0	1	0	3	1	4	1	0	0	1	.000	0	0-0	0	6.28
1996 Toronto	AL	6	6	0	0	30.1	150	43	28	26	6	1	3	2	21	3	18	1	0	1	3	.250	0	0-0	0	7.71
1989 Minnesota	AL	24	24	7	0	175.2	731	171	80	74	17	9	4	3	47	1	138	5	1	8	12	.400	1	0-0	0	3.79
New York	NL	12	12	2	0	85.1	351	75	35	32	5	3	2	1	27	3	73	3	0	5	5	.500	1	0-0	0	3.38
15 ML YEARS		421	420	74	0	2836.1	11933	2827	1303	1175	294	88	63	48	864	39	1844	86	12	176	150	.540	16	0--	—	3.73

Joe Vitiello

Bats: R **Throws:** R **Pos:** DH-70; 1B-9; PH-7; RF-1   **Ht:** 6'3" **Wt:** 230 **Born:** 4/11/70 **Age:** 27

Year Team	Lg	G	AB	H	2B	3B	HR	(Hm	Rd)	TB	R	RBI	TBB	IBB	SO	HBP	SH	SF	SB	CS	SB%	GDP	Avg	OBP	SLG
1991 Eugene	A-	19	64	21	2	0	6	—	—	41	16	21	11	1	18	1	0	2	1	1	.50	0	.328	.423	.641
Memphis	AA	36	128	27	4	1	0	—	—	33	15	18	23	0	36	1	0	1	0	0	.00	2	.211	.333	.258
1992 Baseball Cy	A+	115	400	113	16	1	8	—	—	155	52	65	46	1	101	7	0	8	0	5	.00	11	.283	.360	.388
1993 Memphis	AA	117	413	119	25	2	15	—	—	193	62	66	57	2	95	5	0	5	2	0	1.00	8	.288	.377	.467
1994 Omaha	AAA	98	352	121	28	3	10	—	—	185	46	61	56	1	63	7	1	3	3	2	.60	15	.344	.440	.526
1995 Omaha	AAA	59	229	64	14	2	12	—	—	118	33	42	12	0	50	6	0	2	0	1	.00	9	.279	.329	.515
1996 Omaha	AAA	36	132	37	7	0	9	—	—	71	26	31	16	1	32	3	0	1	0	0	1.00	6	.280	.368	.538
1995 Kansas City	AL	53	130	33	4	0	7	(3	4)	58	13	21	8	0	25	4	0	0	0	0	.00	4	.254	.317	.446
1996 Kansas City	AL	85	257	62	15	1	8	(3	5)	103	29	40	38	2	69	3	0	3	2	0	1.00	12	.241	.342	.401
2 ML YEARS		138	387	95	19	1	15	(6	9)	161	42	61	46	2	94	7	0	3	2	0	1.00	16	.245	.334	.416

Jose Vizcaino

Bats: B **Throws:** R **Pos:** 2B-138; PH-6; SS-4; DH-1   **Ht:** 6'1"   **Wt:** 180   **Born:** 3/26/68   **Age:** 29

								BATTING										BASERUNNING				PERCENTAGES		
Year Team	Lg	G	AB	H	2B	3B	HR	(Hm | Rd)	TB	R	RBI	TBB	IBB	SO	HBP	SH	SF	SB	CS	SB%	GDP	Avg	OBP	SLG
1989 Los Angeles	NL	7	10	2	0	0	0	(0 | 0)	2	2	0	0	0	1	0	1	0	0	0	.00	0	.200	.200	.200
1990 Los Angeles	NL	37	51	14	1	1	0	(0 | 0)	17	3	2	4	1	8	0	0	0	1	1	.50	1	.275	.327	.333
1991 Chicago	NL	93	145	38	5	0	0	(0 | 0)	43	7	10	5	0	18	0	2	2	2	1	.67	1	.262	.283	.297
1992 Chicago	NL	86	285	64	10	4	1	(0 | 1)	85	25	17	14	2	35	0	5	1	3	0	1.00	4	.225	.260	.298
1993 Chicago	NL	151	551	158	19	4	4	(1 | 3)	197	74	54	46	2	71	3	8	9	12	9	.57	9	.287	.340	.358
1994 New York	NL	103	410	105	13	3	3	(1 | 2)	133	47	33	33	3	62	2	5	6	1	11	.08	5	.256	.310	.324
1995 New York	NL	135	509	146	21	5	3	(2 | 1)	186	66	56	35	4	76	1	13	3	8	3	.73	14	.287	.332	.365
1996 NYN-Cle		144	542	161	17	8	1	(1 | 0)	197	70	45	35	0	82	3	10	3	15	7	.68	8	.297	.341	.363
1996 New York	NL	96	363	110	12	6	1	(1 | 0)	137	47	32	28	0	58	3	6	2	9	5	.64	6	.303	.356	.377
Cleveland	AL	48	179	51	5	2	0	(0 | 0)	60	23	13	7	0	24	0	4	1	6	2	.75	2	.285	.310	.335
8 ML YEARS		756	2503	688	86	25	12	(5 | 7)	860	294	217	172	12	353	9	44	24	42	32	.57	42	.275	.321	.344

Omar Vizquel

Bats: Both **Throws:** Right **Pos:** SS-150; PH-2   **Ht:** 5'9"   **Wt:** 165   **Born:** 4/24/67   **Age:** 30

								BATTING										BASERUNNING				PERCENTAGES		
Year Team	Lg	G	AB	H	2B	3B	HR	(Hm	Rd)	TB	R	RBI	TBB	IBB	SO	HBP	SH	SF	SB	CS	SB%	GDP	Avg	OBP	SLG
1989 Seattle	AL	143	387	85	7	3	1	(1	0)	101	45	20	28	0	40	1	13	1	1	4	.20	6	.220	.273	.261
1990 Seattle	AL	81	255	63	3	2	2	(0	2)	76	19	18	18	0	22	0	10	2	4	1	.80	7	.247	.295	.298
1991 Seattle	AL	142	426	98	16	4	1	(1	0)	125	42	41	45	0	37	0	8	3	7	2	.78	8	.230	.302	.293
1992 Seattle	AL	136	483	142	20	4	0	(0	0)	170	49	21	32	0	38	2	9	1	15	13	.54	14	.294	.340	.352
1993 Seattle	AL	158	560	143	14	2	2	(1	1)	167	68	31	50	2	71	4	13	3	12	14	.46	7	.255	.319	.298
1994 Cleveland	AL	69	286	78	10	1	1	(0	1)	93	39	33	23	0	23	0	11	2	13	4	.76	4	.273	.325	.325
1995 Cleveland	AL	136	542	144	28	0	6	(3	3)	190	87	56	59	0	59	1	10	10	29	11	.73	4	.266	.333	.351
1996 Cleveland	AL	151	542	161	36	1	9	(2	7)	226	98	64	56	0	42	4	12	9	35	9	.80	10	.297	.362	.417
8 ML YEARS		1016	3481	914	134	17	22	(8	14)	1148	447	284	311	2	332	12	86	32	116	58	.67	60	.263	.322	.330

Jack Voigt

Bats: Right **Throws:** Right **Pos:** LF-2; PH-2; 3B-1; RF-1   **Ht:** 6'1"   **Wt:** 175   **Born:** 5/17/66   **Age:** 31

								BATTING										BASERUNNING				PERCENTAGES		
Year Team	Lg	G	AB	H	2B	3B	HR	(Hm	Rd)	TB	R	RBI	TBB	IBB	SO	HBP	SH	SF	SB	CS	SB%	GDP	Avg	OBP	SLG
1996 Charlotte *	A+	7	27	11	3	0	1	—	—	17	7	8	3	0	3	1	0	0	0	0	.00	0	.407	.484	.630
Okla. City *	AAA	127	445	132	26	1	21	—	—	223	77	80	76	4	103	1	2	6	5	5	.50	11	.297	.396	.501
1992 Baltimore	AL	1	0	0	0	0	0	(0	0)	0	0	0	0	0	0	0	0	0	0	0	.00	0	.000	.000	.000
1993 Baltimore	AL	64	152	45	11	1	6	(5	1)	76	32	23	25	0	33	0	0	0	1	0	1.00	0	.296	.395	.500
1994 Baltimore	AL	59	141	34	5	0	3	(1	2)	48	15	20	18	1	25	1	1	2	0	0	.00	2	.241	.327	.340
1995 Bal-Tex	AL	36	63	11	3	0	2	(2	0)	20	9	8	10	0	14	0	0	1	0	0	.00	2	.175	.284	.317
1996 Texas	AL	5	9	1	0	0	0	(0	0)	1	1	0	0	0	2	0	0	0	0	0	.00	0	.111	.111	.111
1995 Baltimore	AL	3	1	1	0	0	0	(0	0)	1	1	0	0	0	0	0	0	0	0	0	.00	0	1.000	1.000	1.000
Texas	AL	33	62	10	3	0	2	(2	0)	19	8	8	10	0	14	0	0	1	0	0	.00	2	.161	.274	.306
5 ML YEARS		165	365	91	19	1	11	(8	3)	145	57	51	53	1	74	1	1	3	1	0	1.00	5	.249	.344	.397

Ed Vosberg

Pitches: Left **Bats:** Left **Pos:** RP-52   **Ht:** 6'1"   **Wt:** 190   **Born:** 9/28/61   **Age:** 35

		HOW MUCH HE PITCHED						WHAT HE GAVE UP									THE RESULTS					
Year Team	Lg	G	GS	CG	GF	IP	BFP	H	R	ER	HR	SH	SF	HB	TBB	IBB	SO	WP	Bk	W	L	Pct.	ShO	Sv-Op	Hld	ERA
1986 San Diego	NL	5	5	0	0	13.2	65	17	11	10	0	0	0	0	9	1	8	0	1	0	1	.000	0	0- —	—	6.59
1990 San Francisco	NL	18	0	0	5	24.1	104	21	16	15	3	2	0	0	12	2	12	0	0	1	1	.500	0	0-0	0	5.55
1994 Oakland	AL	16	0	0	2	13.2	56	16	7	6	2	1	0	0	5	0	12	1	1	0	2	.000	0	0-1	2	3.95
1995 Texas	AL	44	0	0	20	36	154	32	15	12	3	2	3	0	16	1	36	3	2	5	5	.500	0	4-8	5	3.00
1996 Texas	AL	52	0	0	21	44	195	51	17	16	4	2	1	0	21	4	32	1	2	1	1	.500	0	8-9	11	3.27
5 ML YEARS		135	3	0	48	131.2	574	137	66	59	13	7	4	0	63	8	100	5	6	7	10	.412	0	12- —	—	4.03

Terrell Wade

Pitches: Left **Bats:** Left **Pos:** RP-36; SP-8   **Ht:** 6'3"   **Wt:** 205   **Born:** 1/25/73   **Age:** 24

		HOW MUCH HE PITCHED						WHAT HE GAVE UP									THE RESULTS					
Year Team	Lg	G	GS	CG	GF	IP	BFP	H	R	ER	HR	SH	SF	HB	TBB	IBB	SO	WP	Bk	W	L	Pct.	ShO	Sv-Op	Hld	ERA
1991 Braves	R	10	2	0	0	23	112	17	16	16	0	1	2	0	15	0	22	3	2	2	0	1.000	0	0- —	—	6.26
1992 Idaho Falls	R+	13	11	0	0	50.1	257	59	46	36	5	4	5	2	42	0	54	5	0	1	4	.200	0	0- —	—	6.44
1993 Macon	A	14	14	0	0	83.1	336	57	16	16	1	0	1	1	36	0	121	11	0	8	2	.800	0	0- —	—	1.73
Durham	A+	5	5	0	0	33	137	26	13	12	3	0	0	1	18	0	47	0	1	2	1	.667	0	0- —	—	3.27
Greenville	AA	8	8	1	0	42	179	32	16	15	6	1	0	1	29	0	40	2	0	2	1	.667	1	0- —	—	3.21
1994 Greenville	AA	21	21	0	0	105.2	444	87	49	45	7	3	2	0	58	0	105	8	0	9	3	.750	0	0- —	—	3.83
Richmond	AAA	4	4	0	0	24	103	23	9	7	1	0	1	0	15	0	26	1	0	2	2	.500	0	0- —	—	2.63
1995 Richmond	AAA	24	23	1	0	142	600	137	76	72	10	3	5	1	63	1	124	5	1	10	9	.526	0	0- —	—	4.56
1995 Atlanta	NL	3	0	0	0	4	18	3	2	2	1	0	0	0	4	0	3	1	0	0	1	.000	0	0-0	0	4.50
1996 Atlanta	NL	44	8	0	13	69.2	305	57	28	23	9	5	1	1	47	6	79	2	0	5	0	1.000	0	1-2	4	2.97

Year Team	Lg	G	GS	CG	GF	IP	BFP	H	R	ER	HR	SH	SF	HB	TBB	IBB	SO	WP	Bk	W	L	Pct.	ShO	Sv-Op	Hld	ERA
2 ML YEARS		47	8	0	13	73.2	323	60	30	25	10	5	1	1	51	6	82	3	0	5	1	.833	0	1-2	4	3.05

Billy Wagner

Pitches: Left **Bats:** Left **Pos:** RP-37 **Ht:** 5'11" **Wt:** 180 **Born:** 6/25/71 **Age:** 26

Year Team	Lg	G	GS	CG	GF	IP	BFP	H	R	ER	HR	SH	SF	HB	TBB	IBB	SO	WP	Bk	W	L	Pct.	ShO	Sv-Op	Hld	ERA
1993 Auburn	A-	7	7	0	0	28.2	135	25	19	13	2	0	0	1	25	0	31	8	1	1	3	.250	0	0--	—	4.08
1994 Quad City	A	26	26	2	0	153	640	99	76	56	9	7	6	8	91	0	204	12	9	8	9	.471	0	0--	—	3.29
1995 Jackson	AA	12	12	0	0	70	288	49	25	20	7	1	1	4	36	1	77	4	1	2	2	.500	0	0--	—	2.57
Tucson	AAA	25	25	0	0	146.1	613	119	53	47	10	5	3	5	68	1	157	8	1	7	5	.583	0	0--	—	2.89
1996 Tucson	AAA	12	12	1	0	74	318	62	32	27	2	2	1	6	33	0	86	5	1	3	1	.750	1	0--	—	3.28
1995 Houston	NL	1	0	0	0	0.1	1	0	0	0	0	0	0	0	0	0	0	0	0	0	0	.000	0	0-0	0	0.00
1996 Houston	NL	37	0	0	20	51.2	212	28	16	14	6	7	2	3	30	2	67	1	0	2	2	.500	0	9-13	3	2.44
2 ML YEARS		38	0	0	20	52	213	28	16	14	6	7	2	3	30	2	67	1	0	2	2	.500	0	9-13	3	2.42

Matt Wagner

Pitches: Right **Bats:** Right **Pos:** SP-14; RP-1 **Ht:** 6'5" **Wt:** 215 **Born:** 4/4/72 **Age:** 25

Year Team	Lg	G	GS	CG	GF	IP	BFP	H	R	ER	HR	SH	SF	HB	TBB	IBB	SO	WP	Bk	W	L	Pct.	ShO	Sv-Op	Hld	ERA
1994 Appleton	A	15	15	1	0	32.2	129	23	8	3	2	2	0	0	8	1	48	4	2	4	2	.667	0	1--	—	0.83
1995 Tacoma	AAA	6	6	1	0	33	157	43	29	23	3	0	1	1	17	1	33	2	0	1	5	.167	0	0--	—	6.27
1996 Tacoma	AAA	15	15	0	0	93.1	384	89	30	25	8	2	2	2	30	2	82	4	1	9	2	.818	0	0--	—	2.41
1996 Seattle	AL	15	14	1	0	80	364	91	62	61	15	0	4	3	38	2	41	0	0	3	5	.375	0	0-0	0	6.86

Paul Wagner

Pitches: Right **Bats:** Right **Pos:** SP-15; RP-1 **Ht:** 6'1" **Wt:** 209 **Born:** 11/14/67 **Age:** 29

Year Team	Lg	G	GS	CG	GF	IP	BFP	H	R	ER	HR	SH	SF	HB	TBB	IBB	SO	WP	Bk	W	L	Pct.	ShO	Sv-Op	Hld	ERA
1996 Pirates *	R	1	1	0	0	3	11	2	0	0	0	0	0	0	4	0	0	0	0	0	0	.000	0	0--	—	0.00
1992 Pittsburgh	NL	6	1	0	1	13	52	9	1	1	0	0	0	0	5	0	5	1	0	2	0	1.000	0	0-0	0	0.69
1993 Pittsburgh	NL	44	17	1	9	141.1	599	143	67	67	15	6	7	1	42	2	114	12	0	8	8	.500	1	2-5	4	4.27
1994 Pittsburgh	NL	29	17	1	4	119.2	534	136	69	61	7	8	4	8	50	4	86	4	0	7	8	.467	0	0-0	2	4.59
1995 Pittsburgh	NL	33	25	3	1	165	725	174	96	88	18	7	2	7	72	7	120	8	0	5	16	.238	1	1-1	1	4.80
1996 Pittsburgh	NL	16	15	1	0	81.2	361	86	49	49	10	5	1	3	39	2	81	7	0	4	8	.333	0	0-0	0	5.40
5 ML YEARS		128	75	6	15	520.2	2271	548	287	266	50	26	14	19	208	15	406	32	0	26	40	.394	2	3-6	7	4.60

David Wainhouse

Pitches: Right **Bats:** Left **Pos:** RP-17 **Ht:** 6'2" **Wt:** 185 **Born:** 11/7/67 **Age:** 29

Year Team	Lg	G	GS	CG	GF	IP	BFP	H	R	ER	HR	SH	SF	HB	TBB	IBB	SO	WP	Bk	W	L	Pct.	ShO	Sv-Op	Hld	ERA
1989 W. Palm Bch	A+	13	13	0	0	66.1	286	75	35	30	4	3	2	8	19	0	26	6	3	1	5	.167	0	0--	—	4.07
1990 W. Palm Bch	A+	12	12	2	0	76.2	327	68	28	18	1	0	3	5	34	0	58	2	3	6	3	.667	1	0--	—	2.11
Jacksonville	AA	17	16	2	0	95.2	428	97	56	46	8	2	3	7	47	2	59	2	0	7	7	.500	0	0--	—	4.33
1991 Harrisburg	AA	33	0	0	27	52	224	49	17	15	1	2	0	4	17	2	46	3	0	2	2	.500	0	11--	—	2.60
Indianapolis	AAA	14	0	0	8	28.2	127	28	14	13	1	2	1	3	15	1	13	3	0	2	0	1.000	0	1--	—	4.08
1992 Indianapolis	AAA	44	0	0	41	46	208	48	22	21	4	2	2	2	24	6	37	4	0	5	4	.556	0	21--	—	4.11
1993 Calgary	AAA	13	0	0	10	15.2	62	10	7	7	2	2	2	1	7	1	7	2	0	0	1	.000	0	5--	—	4.02
1995 Portland	AA	17	0	0	5	25	122	39	22	20	3	0	1	1	8	1	16	1	0	2	1	.667	0	0--	—	7.20
Charlotte	AAA	30	0	0	22	28	132	35	19	14	2	1	3	1	15	3	20	6	0	3	2	.600	0	5--	—	4.50
Syracuse	AAA	47	0	0	27	53	254	74	41	34	5	1	4	2	23	4	36	7	0	5	3	.625	0	5--	—	5.77
1996 Carolina	AA	45	0	0	40	51.1	226	43	22	18	3	4	1	4	31	3	34	2	0	5	3	.625	0	25--	—	3.16
1991 Montreal	NL	2	0	0	1	2.2	14	2	2	2	0	0	1	0	4	0	1	2	0	0	1	.000	0	0-0	0	6.75
1993 Seattle	AL	3	0	0	0	2.1	20	7	7	7	1	0	0	1	5	0	2	0	0	0	0	.000	0	0-0	0	27.00
1996 Pittsburgh	NL	17	0	0	6	23.2	101	22	16	15	3	1	2	0	10	1	16	2	0	1	0	1.000	0	0-0	1	5.70
3 ML YEARS		22	0	0	7	28.2	135	31	25	24	4	1	3	1	19	1	19	4	0	1	1	.500	0	0-0	1	7.53

Tim Wakefield

Pitches: Right **Bats:** Right **Pos:** SP-32 **Ht:** 6'2" **Wt:** 206 **Born:** 8/2/66 **Age:** 30

Year Team	Lg	G	GS	CG	GF	IP	BFP	H	R	ER	HR	SH	SF	HB	TBB	IBB	SO	WP	Bk	W	L	Pct.	ShO	Sv-Op	Hld	ERA
1992 Pittsburgh	NL	13	13	4	0	92	373	76	26	22	3	6	4	1	35	1	51	3	1	8	1	.889	1	0-0	0	2.15
1993 Pittsburgh	NL	24	20	3	1	128.1	595	145	83	80	14	7	5	9	75	2	59	6	0	6	11	.353	2	0-0	0	5.61
1995 Boston	AL	27	27	6	0	195.1	804	163	76	64	22	3	7	4	68	0	119	11	0	16	8	.667	1	0-0	0	2.95
1996 Boston	AL	32	32	6	0	211.2	963	238	151	121	38	1	9	12	90	0	140	4	1	14	13	.519	0	0-0	0	5.14
4 ML YEARS		96	92	19	1	627.1	2735	622	336	287	77	17	25	31	268	3	369	24	2	44	33	.571	4	0-0	0	4.12

Matt Walbeck

Bats: Both **Throws:** Right **Pos:** C-61; PH-5 **Ht:** 5'11" **Wt:** 188 **Born:** 10/2/69 **Age:** 27

Year Team	Lg	G	AB	H	2B	3B	HR	(Hm	Rd)	TB	R	RBI	TBB	IBB	SO	HBP	SH	SF	SB	CS	SB%	GDP	Avg	OBP	SLG
1996 Fort Myers *	A+	9	33	9	1	1	0	—	—	12	4	9	4	0	2	1	0	2	0	1	.00	0	.273	.350	.364
New Britain *	AA	7	24	5	0	0	0	—	—	5	1	0	1	0	1	0	0	0	0	0	.00	1	.208	.240	.208
1993 Chicago	NL	11	30	6	2	0	1	(1	0)	11	2	6	1	0	6	0	0	0	0	0	.00	0	.200	.226	.367
1994 Minnesota	AL	97	338	69	12	1	5	(0	5)	96	31	35	17	1	37	2	1	1	1	1	.50	7	.204	.246	.284
1995 Minnesota	AL	115	393	101	18	1	1	(1	0)	124	40	44	25	2	71	1	1	2	3	1	.75	11	.257	.302	.316
1996 Minnesota	AL	63	215	48	10	0	2	(1	1)	64	25	24	9	0	34	0	1	2	3	1	.75	6	.223	.252	.298
4 ML YEARS		286	976	224	42	1	9	(3	6)	295	98	109	52	3	148	3	3	5	7	3	.70	24	.230	.269	.302

Larry Walker

Bats: Left **Throws:** Right **Pos:** CF-54; RF-33; PH-3 **Ht:** 6'3" **Wt:** 225 **Born:** 12/1/66 **Age:** 30

Year Team	Lg	G	AB	H	2B	3B	HR	(Hm	Rd)	TB	R	RBI	TBB	IBB	SO	HBP	SH	SF	SB	CS	SB%	GDP	Avg	OBP	SLG
1996 Salem *	A+	2	8	4	3	0	1	—	—	10	3	1	0	0	1	0	0	0	0	0	.00	1	.500	.500	1.250
Colo. Sprng *	AAA	3	11	4	0	0	2	—	—	10	2	8	1	0	4	0	0	1	0	0	.00	0	.364	.385	.909
1989 Montreal	NL	20	47	8	0	0	0	(0	0)	8	4	4	5	0	13	1	3	0	1	1	.50	0	.170	.264	.170
1990 Montreal	NL	133	419	101	18	3	19	(9	10)	182	59	51	49	5	112	5	3	2	21	7	.75	8	.241	.326	.434
1991 Montreal	NL	137	487	141	30	2	16	(6	10)	223	59	64	42	2	102	5	1	4	14	9	.61	7	.290	.349	.458
1992 Montreal	NL	143	528	159	31	4	23	(13	10)	267	85	93	41	10	97	6	0	8	18	6	.75	9	.301	.353	.506
1993 Montreal	NL	138	490	130	24	5	22	(13	9)	230	85	86	80	20	76	6	0	6	29	7	.81	8	.265	.371	.469
1994 Montreal	NL	103	395	127	44	2	19	(7	12)	232	76	86	47	5	74	4	0	6	15	5	.75	3	.322	.394	.587
1995 Colorado	NL	131	494	151	31	5	36	(24	12)	300	96	101	49	13	72	14	0	5	16	3	.84	13	.306	.381	.607
1996 Colorado	NL	83	272	75	18	4	18	(12	6)	155	58	58	20	2	58	9	0	3	18	2	.90	7	.276	.342	.570
8 ML YEARS		888	3132	892	196	25	153	(83	70)	1597	522	543	333	57	604	50	7	34	132	40	.77	60	.285	.359	.510

Mike Walker

Pitches: Right **Bats:** Right **Pos:** RP-20 **Ht:** 6'1" **Wt:** 205 **Born:** 10/4/66 **Age:** 30

Year Team	Lg	G	GS	CG	GF	IP	BFP	H	R	ER	HR	SH	SF	HB	TBB	IBB	SO	WP	Bk	W	L	Pct.	ShO	Sv-Op	Hld	ERA
1996 Toledo *	AAA	28	0	0	14	44.2	194	37	23	19	4	3	0	1	27	1	37	8	0	3	2	.600	0	6--	—	3.83
1988 Cleveland	AL	3	1	0	0	8.2	42	8	7	7	0	1	0	0	10	0	7	0	0	0	1	.000	0	0-0	0	7.27
1990 Cleveland	AL	18	11	0	2	75.2	350	82	49	41	6	4	2	6	42	4	34	3	1	2	6	.250	0	0-0	0	4.88
1991 Cleveland	AL	5	0	0	3	4.1	22	6	1	1	0	0	0	1	2	1	2	0	0	0	1	.000	0	0-0	0	2.08
1995 Chicago	NL	42	0	0	12	44.2	206	45	22	16	2	4	4	0	24	3	20	3	1	1	3	.250	0	1-3	4	3.22
1996 Detroit	AL	20	0	0	12	27.2	135	40	26	26	10	1	2	1	17	1	13	2	0	0	0	.000	0	1-2	3	8.46
5 ML YEARS		88	12	0	29	161	755	181	105	91	18	10	8	8	95	9	76	8	2	3	11	.214	0	2-5	7	5.09

Pete Walker

Pitches: Right **Bats:** Right **Pos:** RP-1 **Ht:** 6'2" **Wt:** 195 **Born:** 4/8/69 **Age:** 28

Year Team	Lg	G	GS	CG	GF	IP	BFP	H	R	ER	HR	SH	SF	HB	TBB	IBB	SO	WP	Bk	W	L	Pct.	ShO	Sv-Op	Hld	ERA
1990 Pittsfield	A-	16	13	1	1	80	346	74	43	37	2	0	4	3	46	0	73	1	0	5	7	.417	0	0--	—	4.16
1991 St. Lucie	A+	26	25	1	0	151.1	641	145	77	54	9	9	5	4	52	2	95	7	3	10	12	.455	0	0--	—	3.21
1992 Binghamton	AA	24	23	4	1	139.2	605	159	77	64	6	2	3	3	46	0	72	5	2	7	12	.368	0	0--	—	4.12
1993 Binghamton	AA	45	10	0	33	99.1	423	89	45	38	6	6	1	5	46	1	89	5	0	4	9	.308	0	19--	—	3.44
1994 St. Lucie	A+	3	0	0	2	4	16	3	2	1	1	0	0	0	1	0	5	0	0	0	0	.000	0	0--	—	2.25
Norfolk	AAA	37	0	0	19	47.2	207	48	22	21	3	3	2	0	24	2	42	3	0	2	4	.333	0	3--	—	3.97
1995 Norfolk	AAA	34	1	0	25	48.1	207	51	24	21	4	3	1	1	16	1	39	2	1	5	2	.714	0	8--	—	3.91
1996 Padres	R	2	2	0	0	4	17	4	1	1	0	1	0	0	0	0	5	0	0	0	1	.000	0	0--	—	2.25
Las Vegas	AAA	26	0	0	8	27.2	129	37	22	21	7	1	4	0	14	2	23	0	0	5	1	.833	0	0--	—	6.83
1995 New York	NL	13	0	0	10	17.2	79	24	9	9	3	0	1	0	5	0	23	0	0	1	0	1.000	0	0-0	1	4.58
1996 San Diego	NL	1	0	0	0	0.2	5	0	0	0	0	1	0	0	3	0	1	0	0	0	0	.000	0	0-0	0	0.00
2 ML YEARS		14	0	0	10	18.1	84	24	9	9	3	1	1	0	8	0	24	0	0	1	0	1.000	0	0-0	1	4.42

Todd Walker

Bats: L **Throws:** R **Pos:** 3B-20; 2B-4; PH-3; DH-1 **Ht:** 6'0" **Wt:** 170 **Born:** 5/25/73 **Age:** 24

Year Team	Lg	G	AB	H	2B	3B	HR	(Hm	Rd)	TB	R	RBI	TBB	IBB	SO	HBP	SH	SF	SB	CS	SB%	GDP	Avg	OBP	SLG
1994 Fort Myers	A+	46	171	52	5	2	10	—	—	91	29	34	32	0	15	0	0	4	6	3	.67	4	.304	.406	.532
1995 New Britain	AA	137	513	149	27	3	21	—	—	245	83	85	63	1	101	2	1	8	23	9	.72	13	.290	.365	.478
1996 Salt Lake	AAA	135	551	187	41	9	28	—	—	330	94	111	57	11	91	5	2	10	13	8	.62	17	.339	.400	.599
1996 Minnesota	AL	25	82	21	6	0	0	(0	0)	27	8	6	4	0	13	0	0	3	2	0	1.00	4	.256	.281	.329

Donne Wall

Pitches: Right **Bats:** Right **Pos:** SP-23; RP-3   **Ht:** 5'11" **Wt:** 180 **Born:** 7/11/67 **Age:** 29

Year Team	Lg	G	GS	CG	GF	IP	BFP	H	R	ER	HR	SH	SF	HB	TBB	IBB	SO	WP	Bk	W	L	Pct.	ShO	Sv-Op	Hld	ERA
1989 Auburn	A-	12	8	3	2	65.1	250	45	17	13	2	0	1	3	12	0	69	2	3	7	0	1.000	1	1--	—	1.79
1990 Asheville	A	28	22	1	3	132	586	149	87	76	18	5	6	9	47	1	111	10	0	6	8	.429	0	1--	—	5.18
1991 Burlington	A	16	16	3	0	106.2	421	73	30	24	4	4	2	4	21	1	102	5	0	7	5	.583	1	0--	—	2.03
Osceola	A+	12	12	4	0	77.1	295	55	22	18	3	3	2	2	11	1	62	1	0	6	3	.667	2	0--	—	2.09
1992 Osceola	A+	7	7	0	0	41	166	37	13	12	1	1	1	2	8	0	30	2	0	3	1	.750	0	0--	—	2.63
Jackson	AA	18	18	2	0	114.1	479	114	51	45	6	2	4	2	26	2	99	4	1	9	6	.600	0	0--	—	3.54
Tucson	AAA	2	2	0	0	8	35	11	1	1	0	0	0	0	1	0	2	0	0	0	0	.000	0	0--	—	1.13
1993 Tucson	AAA	25	22	0	2	131.2	567	147	73	56	11	7	4	2	35	3	89	4	3	6	4	.600	0	0--	—	3.83
1994 Tucson	AAA	26	24	2	0	148.1	634	171	87	73	9	4	9	3	35	2	84	4	0	11	8	.579	2	0--	—	4.43
1995 Tucson	AAA	28	28	0	0	177.1	732	190	72	65	5	6	4	5	32	1	119	5	1	17	6	.739	0	0--	—	3.30
1996 Tucson	AAA	8	8	0	0	52.1	224	67	30	24	2	1	3	0	6	0	36	3	0	3	3	.500	0	0--	—	4.13
1995 Houston	NL	6	5	0	0	24.1	110	33	19	15	5	0	2	0	5	0	16	1	0	3	1	.750	0	0-0	1	5.55
1996 Houston	NL	26	23	2	1	150	643	170	84	76	17	4	5	6	34	3	99	3	2	9	8	.529	1	0-0	0	4.56
2 ML YEARS		32	28	2	1	174.1	753	203	103	91	22	4	7	6	39	3	115	4	2	12	9	.571	1	0-0	1	4.70

Derek Wallace

Pitches: Right **Bats:** Right **Pos:** RP-19   **Ht:** 6'3" **Wt:** 185 **Born:** 9/1/71 **Age:** 25

Year Team	Lg	G	GS	CG	GF	IP	BFP	H	R	ER	HR	SH	SF	HB	TBB	IBB	SO	WP	Bk	W	L	Pct.	ShO	Sv-Op	Hld	ERA
1992 Peoria	A	2	0	0	1	3.2	13	3	2	2	0	1	0	0	1	0	2	0	2	0	1	.000	0	—	—	4.91
1993 Daytona	A+	14	12	0	1	79.1	342	85	50	37	6	6	2	2	23	2	34	5	11	5	6	.455	0	1--	—	4.20
Iowa	AAA	1	1	0	0	4	20	8	5	5	0	0	1	0	1	0	2	0	0	0	0	.000	0	0--	—	11.25
Orlando	AA	15	15	2	0	96.2	418	105	59	54	12	5	0	10	28	3	69	9	4	5	7	.417	0	0--	—	5.03
1994 Orlando	AA	33	12	1	19	89.1	391	95	61	57	11	3	4	10	31	3	49	6	4	2	9	.182	0	8--	—	5.74
Iowa	AAA	5	0	0	2	4.1	21	4	4	2	0	0	0	0	4	0	3	1	0	0	1	.000	0	1--	—	4.15
1995 Binghamton	AA	15	0	0	11	15.1	62	11	9	9	1	0	3	1	9	1	8	1	2	0	1	.000	0	2--	—	5.28
1996 Norfolk	AAA	49	0	0	39	57.2	227	37	20	11	4	2	2	1	17	1	52	0	1	5	2	.714	0	26--	—	1.72
1996 New York	NL	19	0	0	11	24.2	115	29	12	11	2	1	0	1	14	2	15	2	0	2	3	.400	0	3-3	0	4.01

Tim Wallach

Bats: R **Throws:** R **Pos:** 3B-91; DH-8; PH-4; 1B-3   **Ht:** 6'3" **Wt:** 207 **Born:** 9/14/57 **Age:** 39

Year Team	Lg	G	AB	H	2B	3B	HR	(Hm	Rd)	TB	R	RBI	TBB	IBB	SO	HBP	SH	SF	SB	CS	SB%	GDP	Avg	OBP	SLG
1996 San Bernrdo *	A+	5	20	6	0	0	1	--	--	9	3	6	2	0	7	0	0	0	0	0	.00	0	.300	.364	.450
1980 Montreal	NL	5	11	2	0	0	1	(0	1)	5	1	2	1	0	5	0	0	0	0	0	.00	0	.182	.250	.455
1981 Montreal	NL	71	212	50	9	1	4	(1	3)	73	19	13	15	2	37	4	0	0	0	1	.00	3	.236	.299	.344
1982 Montreal	NL	158	596	160	31	3	28	(11	17)	281	89	97	36	4	81	4	5	4	6	4	.60	15	.268	.313	.471
1983 Montreal	NL	156	581	156	33	3	19	(9	10)	252	54	70	55	8	97	6	0	5	0	3	.00	9	.269	.335	.434
1984 Montreal	NL	160	582	143	25	4	18	(14	4)	230	55	72	50	6	101	7	0	4	3	7	.30	12	.246	.311	.395
1985 Montreal	NL	155	569	148	36	3	22	(9	13)	256	70	81	38	8	79	5	0	5	9	9	.50	17	.260	.310	.450
1986 Montreal	NL	134	480	112	22	1	18	(6	12)	190	50	71	44	8	72	10	0	5	8	4	.67	16	.233	.308	.396
1987 Montreal	NL	153	593	177	42	4	26	(13	13)	305	89	123	37	5	98	7	0	7	9	5	.64	16	.298	.343	.514
1988 Montreal	NL	159	592	152	32	5	12	(3	9)	230	52	69	38	7	88	3	0	7	2	6	.25	19	.257	.302	.389
1989 Montreal	NL	154	573	159	42	0	13	(6	7)	240	76	77	58	10	81	1	0	7	3	7	.30	21	.277	.341	.419
1990 Montreal	NL	161	626	185	37	5	21	(9	12)	295	69	98	42	11	80	3	0	7	6	9	.40	12	.296	.339	.471
1991 Montreal	NL	151	577	130	22	1	13	(5	8)	193	60	73	50	8	100	6	0	4	2	4	.33	12	.225	.292	.334
1992 Montreal	NL	150	537	120	29	1	9	(4	5)	178	53	59	50	2	90	8	0	7	2	2	.50	10	.223	.296	.331
1993 Los Angeles	NL	133	477	106	19	1	12	(4	8)	163	42	62	32	2	70	3	1	9	0	0	.00	10	.222	.271	.342
1994 Los Angeles	NL	113	414	116	21	1	23	(7	16)	208	68	78	46	2	80	4	0	2	0	2	.00	12	.280	.356	.502
1995 Los Angeles	NL	97	327	87	22	2	9	(4	5)	140	24	38	27	4	69	4	0	0	0	0	.00	11	.266	.326	.428
1996 Cal-LA		102	352	82	10	1	12	(7	5)	130	37	42	30	2	79	2	0	0	1	1	.50	7	.233	.297	.369
1996 California	AL	57	190	45	7	0	8	(5	3)	76	23	20	18	2	47	1	0	0	1	0	1.00	3	.237	.306	.400
Los Angeles	NL	45	162	37	3	1	4	(2	2)	54	14	22	12	0	32	1	0	0	0	1	.00	4	.228	.286	.333
17 ML YEARS		2212	8099	2085	432	36	260	(103	157)	3369	908	1125	649	89	1307	77	6	77	51	66	.44	192	.257	.316	.416

Jerome Walton

Bats: R **Throws:** R **Pos:** LF-23; PH-13; RF-5; CF-1   **Ht:** 6'1" **Wt:** 185 **Born:** 7/8/65 **Age:** 31

Year Team	Lg	G	AB	H	2B	3B	HR	(Hm	Rd)	TB	R	RBI	TBB	IBB	SO	HBP	SH	SF	SB	CS	SB%	GDP	Avg	OBP	SLG
1996 Greenville *	AA	3	5	1	0	1	0	--	--	3	0	0	3	0	1	0	0	0	0	0	.00	0	.200	.500	.600
Richmond *	AAA	6	18	8	2	1	1	--	--	15	3	5	1	0	5	1	0	0	0	0	.00	0	.444	.500	.833
1989 Chicago	NL	116	475	139	23	3	5	(3	2)	183	64	46	27	1	77	6	2	5	24	7	.77	6	.293	.335	.385
1990 Chicago	NL	101	392	103	16	2	2	(2	0)	129	63	21	50	1	70	4	1	2	14	7	.67	4	.263	.350	.329
1991 Chicago	NL	123	270	59	13	1	5	(3	2)	89	42	17	19	0	55	3	3	3	7	3	.70	7	.219	.275	.330
1992 Chicago	NL	30	55	7	0	1	0	(0	0)	9	7	1	9	0	13	2	3	0	1	2	.33	1	.127	.273	.164
1993 California	AL	5	2	0	0	0	0	(0	0)	0	2	0	1	0	2	0	0	0	1	0	1.00	0	.000	.333	.000
1994 Cincinnati	NL	46	68	21	4	0	1	(1	0)	28	10	9	4	0	12	0	1	0	1	3	.25	2	.309	.347	.412
1995 Cincinnati	NL	102	162	47	12	1	3	(4	4)	85	32	22	17	0	25	4	3	2	10	7	.59	5	.290	.368	.525

Year Team	Lg	G	AB	H	2B	3B	HR	(Hm	Rd)	TB	R	RBI	TBB	IBB	SO	HBP	SH	SF	SB	CS	SB%	GDP	Avg	OBP	SLG
				BATTING															BASERUNNING				PERCENTAGES		
1996 Atlanta	NL	37	47	16	5	0	1	(1	0)	24	9	4	5	0	10	0	1	2	0	0	.00	1	.340	.389	.511
8 ML YEARS		560	1471	392	73	8	22	(14	8)	547	229	120	132	2	264	19	14	14	58	29	.67	21	.266	.332	.372

Turner Ward

Bats: B **Throws:** R **Pos:** RF-18; LF-15; PH-15; CF-3; DH-1   **Ht:** 6'2" **Wt:** 182 **Born:** 4/11/65 **Age:** 32

Year Team	Lg	G	AB	H	2B	3B	HR	(Hm	Rd)	TB	R	RBI	TBB	IBB	SO	HBP	SH	SF	SB	CS	SB%	GDP	Avg	OBP	SLG
				BATTING															BASERUNNING				PERCENTAGES		
1996 New Orleans *	AAA	9	23	8	1	0	1	—	—	12	4	1	7	0	4	1	0	0	0	0	.00	0	.348	.516	.522
1990 Cleveland	AL	14	46	16	2	1	1	(0	1)	23	10	10	3	0	8	0	0	0	3	0	1.00	1	.348	.388	.500
1991 Cle-Tor	AL	48	113	27	7	0	0	(0	0)	34	12	7	11	0	18	0	4	0	0	0	.00	2	.239	.306	.301
1992 Toronto	AL	18	29	10	3	0	1	(0	1)	16	7	3	4	0	4	0	0	0	1	0	1.00	1	.345	.424	.552
1993 Toronto	AL	72	167	32	4	2	4	(2	2)	52	20	28	23	2	26	1	3	4	3	3	.50	7	.192	.287	.311
1994 Milwaukee	AL	102	367	85	15	2	9	(3	6)	131	55	45	52	4	68	3	0	5	6	2	.75	9	.232	.328	.357
1995 Milwaukee	AL	44	129	34	3	1	4	(3	1)	51	19	16	14	1	21	1	1	1	6	1	.86	2	.264	.338	.395
1996 Milwaukee	AL	43	67	12	2	0	1	(2	0)	22	7	10	13	0	17	0	1	1	3	0	1.00	3	.179	.309	.328
1991 Cleveland	AL	40	100	23	7	0	0	(0	0)	30	11	5	10	0	16	0	4	0	0	0	.00	1	.230	.300	.300
Toronto	AL	8	13	4	0	0	0	(0	0)	4	1	2	1	0	2	0	0	0	0	0	.00	1	.308	.357	.308
7 ML YEARS		341	918	216	36	7	21	(10	11)	329	130	119	120	7	162	5	9	11	21	7	.75	25	.235	.324	.358

Jeff Ware

Pitches: Right **Bats:** Right **Pos:** RP-9; SP-4   **Ht:** 6'3" **Wt:** 190 **Born:** 11/11/70 **Age:** 26

Year Team	Lg	G	GS	CG	GF	IP	BFP	H	R	ER	HR	SH	SF	HB	TBB	IBB	SO	WP	Bk	W	L	Pct.	ShO	Sv-Op	Hld	ERA
			HOW MUCH HE PITCHED						WHAT HE GAVE UP											THE RESULTS					
1992 Dunedin	A+	12	12	1	0	75.1	319	64	26	22	1	3	0	3	30	0	49	7	3	5	3	.625	1	0--	—	2.63
1994 Knoxville	AA	10	10	0	0	38	175	50	32	29	5	0	2	2	16	0	31	1	0	0	7	.000	0	0--	—	6.87
1995 Syracuse	AAA	16	16	0	0	75	319	62	29	25	8	0	1	2	46	0	76	3	0	7	0	1.000	0	0--	—	3.00
1996 Syracuse	AAA	13	13	1	0	77.2	347	83	54	49	6	2	3	6	32	0	59	6	0	3	7	.300	1	0--	—	5.68
1995 Toronto	AL	5	5	0	0	26.1	124	28	18	16	2	1	0	1	21	0	18	2	0	2	1	.667	0	0-0	0	5.47
1996 Toronto	AL	13	4	0	6	32.2	163	35	34	33	6	1	0	2	31	1	11	6	1	1	5	.167	0	0-0	0	9.09
2 ML YEARS		18	9	0	6	59	287	63	52	49	8	2	0	3	52	1	29	8	1	3	6	.333	0	0-0	0	7.47

John Wasdin

Pitches: Right **Bats:** Right **Pos:** SP-21; RP-4   **Ht:** 6'2" **Wt:** 190 **Born:** 8/5/72 **Age:** 24

Year Team	Lg	G	GS	CG	GF	IP	BFP	H	R	ER	HR	SH	SF	HB	TBB	IBB	SO	WP	Bk	W	L	Pct.	ShO	Sv-Op	Hld	ERA
			HOW MUCH HE PITCHED						WHAT HE GAVE UP											THE RESULTS					
1993 Athletics	R	1	1	0	0	3	13	3	1	1	0	0	0	1	0	0	1	0	0	0	0	.000	0	0--	—	3.00
Madison	A	9	9	0	0	48.1	185	32	11	10	1	3	0	1	9	1	40	2	3	2	3	.400	0	0--	—	1.86
Modesto	A+	3	3	0	0	16.1	68	17	9	7	2	0	0	2	4	0	11	0	0	0	3	.000	0	0--	—	3.86
1994 Modesto	A+	6	4	0	2	26.2	102	17	6	5	2	0	0	2	5	0	30	0	1	3	1	.750	0	0--	—	1.69
Huntsville	AA	21	21	0	0	141.2	571	126	61	54	13	3	4	2	29	2	108	7	0	12	3	.800	0	0--	—	3.43
1995 Edmonton	AAA	29	28	2	0	174.1	744	193	117	107	26	3	11	4	38	3	111	10	1	12	8	.600	1	0--	—	5.52
1996 Edmonton	AAA	9	9	0	0	50	214	52	23	23	6	1	0	1	17	2	30	0	1	2	1	.667	0	0--	—	4.14
1995 Oakland	AL	5	2	0	3	17.1	69	14	9	9	4	0	0	1	3	0	6	0	0	1	1	.500	0	0-0	0	4.67
1996 Oakland	AL	25	21	1	0	131.1	575	145	96	87	24	3	6	4	50	5	75	2	2	8	7	.533	0	0-1	0	5.96
2 ML YEARS		30	23	1	5	148.2	644	159	105	96	28	3	6	5	53	5	81	2	2	9	8	.529	0	0-1	0	5.81

Allen Watson

Pitches: Left **Bats:** Left **Pos:** SP-29   **Ht:** 6'3" **Wt:** 195 **Born:** 11/18/70 **Age:** 26

Year Team	Lg	G	GS	CG	GF	IP	BFP	H	R	ER	HR	SH	SF	HB	TBB	IBB	SO	WP	Bk	W	L	Pct.	ShO	Sv-Op	Hld	ERA
			HOW MUCH HE PITCHED						WHAT HE GAVE UP											THE RESULTS					
1996 San Jose *	A+	2	2	0	0	6.1	25	7	1	1	0	0	0	0	0	0	12	0	0	0	0	.000	0	0--	—	1.42
1993 St. Louis	NL	16	15	0	1	86	373	90	53	44	11	6	4	3	28	2	49	2	1	6	7	.462	0	0-1	0	4.60
1994 St. Louis	NL	22	22	0	0	115.2	523	130	73	71	15	7	0	8	53	0	74	2	2	6	5	.545	0	0-0	0	5.52
1995 St. Louis	NL	21	19	0	1	114.1	491	126	68	63	17	2	1	5	41	0	49	2	2	7	9	.438	0	0-0	0	4.96
1996 San Francisco	NL	29	29	2	0	185.2	793	189	105	95	28	18	9	5	69	2	128	9	2	8	12	.400	0	0-0	0	4.61
4 ML YEARS		88	85	2	2	501.2	2180	535	299	273	71	33	14	21	191	4	300	15	7	27	33	.450	0	0-1	0	4.90

Dave Weathers

Pitches: Right **Bats:** Right **Pos:** RP-30; SP-12   **Ht:** 6'3" **Wt:** 220 **Born:** 9/25/69 **Age:** 27

Year Team	Lg	G	GS	CG	GF	IP	BFP	H	R	ER	HR	SH	SF	HB	TBB	IBB	SO	WP	Bk	W	L	Pct.	ShO	Sv-Op	Hld	ERA
			HOW MUCH HE PITCHED						WHAT HE GAVE UP											THE RESULTS					
1996 Charlotte *	AAA	1	1	0	0	2.1	14	5	2	2	0	0	1	0	3	0	0	0	0	0	0	.000	0	0--	—	7.71
Columbus *	AAA	3	3	0	0	16.2	77	20	13	10	1	0	3	2	5	0	7	2	0	0	2	.000	0	0--	—	5.40
1991 Toronto	AL	15	0	0	4	14.2	77	15	9	8	1	2	1	2	17	3	13	0	0	1	0	1.000	0	0-0	1	4.91
1992 Toronto	AL	2	0	0	0	3.1	15	5	3	3	1	0	0	0	2	0	3	0	0	0	0	.000	0	0-0	0	8.10
1993 Florida	NL	14	6	0	2	45.2	202	57	26	26	3	2	0	1	13	1	34	6	0	2	3	.400	0	0-0	0	5.12
1994 Florida	NL	24	24	0	0	135	621	166	87	79	13	12	4	4	59	9	72	7	1	8	12	.400	0	0-0	0	5.27

		HOW MUCH HE PITCHED						WHAT HE GAVE UP												THE RESULTS						
Year Team	Lg	G	GS	CG	GF	IP	BFP	H	R	ER	HR	SH	SF	HB	TBB	IBB	SO	WP	Bk	W	L	Pct.	ShO	Sv-Op	Hld	ERA
1995 Florida	NL	28	15	0	0	90.1	419	104	68	60	8	7	3	5	52	3	60	3	0	4	5	.444	0	0-0	1	5.98
1996 Fla-NYA		42	12	0	9	88.2	409	108	60	54	8	5	2	6	42	5	53	3	0	2	2	.333	0	0-0	3	5.48
1996 Florida	NL	31	8	0	8	71.1	319	85	41	36	7	5	1	4	28	4	40	2	0	2	2	.500	0	0-0	3	4.54
New York	AL	11	4	0	1	17.1	90	23	19	18	1	0	1	2	14	1	13	1	0	0	2	.000	0	0-0	0	9.35
6 ML YEARS		125	57	0	15	377.2	1745	455	253	230	34	28	10	18	185	21	235	19	1	17	24	.415	0	0-0	5	5.48

Lenny Webster

Bats: Right **Throws:** Right **Pos:** C-63; PH-17   **Ht:** 5'9" **Wt:** 195 **Born:** 2/10/65 **Age:** 32

		BATTING															BASERUNNING				PERCENTAGES		
Year Team	Lg	G	AB	H	2B	3B	HR	(Hm | Rd)	TB	R	RBI	TBB	IBB	SO	HBP	SH	SF	SB	CS	SB%	GDP	Avg	OBP	SLG
1989 Minnesota	AL	14	20	6	2	0	0	(0 | 0)	8	3	1	3	0	2	0	0	0	0	0	.00	0	.300	.391	.400
1990 Minnesota	AL	2	6	2	1	0	0	(0 | 0)	3	1	0	1	0	1	0	0	0	0	0	.00	0	.333	.429	.500
1991 Minnesota	AL	18	34	10	1	0	3	(1 | 2)	20	7	8	6	0	10	0	0	1	0	0	.00	2	.294	.390	.588
1992 Minnesota	AL	53	118	33	10	1	1	(1 | 0)	48	10	13	9	0	11	0	2	0	0	2	.00	3	.280	.331	.407
1993 Minnesota	AL	49	106	21	2	1	0	(1 | 0)	26	14	8	11	1	8	0	0	0	1	0	1.00	1	.198	.274	.245
1994 Montreal	NL	57	143	39	10	0	5	(2 | 3)	64	13	23	16	1	24	6	1	0	0	0	.00	7	.273	.370	.448
1995 Philadelphia	NL	49	150	40	9	0	4	(1 | 3)	61	18	14	16	0	27	0	1	0	0	0	.00	4	.267	.337	.407
1996 Montreal	NL	78	174	40	10	0	2	(1 | 1)	56	18	17	25	2	21	2	1	1	0	0	.00	10	.230	.332	.322
8 ML YEARS		320	751	191	45	2	16	(7 | 9)	286	84	84	87	4	104	8	5	2	1	2	.33	27	.254	.337	.381

John Wehner

B: R **T:** R **Pos:** PH-41; 3B-24; CF-13; 2B-12; LF-9; RF-8; C-1   **Ht:** 6'3" **Wt:** 206 **Born:** 6/29/67 **Age:** 30

		BATTING															BASERUNNING				PERCENTAGES		
Year Team	Lg	G	AB	H	2B	3B	HR	(Hm | Rd)	TB	R	RBI	TBB	IBB	SO	HBP	SH	SF	SB	CS	SB%	GDP	Avg	OBP	SLG
1991 Pittsburgh	NL	37	106	36	7	0	0	(0 | 0)	43	15	7	7	0	17	0	0	0	3	0	1.00	0	.340	.381	.406
1992 Pittsburgh	NL	55	123	22	6	0	0	(0 | 0)	28	11	4	12	2	22	0	2	0	3	0	1.00	4	.179	.252	.228
1993 Pittsburgh	NL	29	35	5	0	0	0	(0 | 0)	5	3	0	6	1	10	0	2	0	0	0	.00	0	.143	.268	.143
1994 Pittsburgh	NL	2	4	1	1	0	0	(0 | 0)	2	1	3	0	0	1	0	0	0	0	0	.00	0	.250	.250	.500
1995 Pittsburgh	NL	52	107	33	0	3	0	(0 | 0)	39	13	5	10	1	17	0	4	2	3	1	.75	2	.308	.361	.364
1996 Pittsburgh	NL	86	139	36	9	1	2	(1 | 1)	53	19	13	8	1	22	0	2	0	1	5	.17	3	.259	.299	.381
6 ML YEARS		261	514	133	23	4	2	(1 | 1)	170	62	32	43	5	89	0	10	2	10	6	.63	9	.259	.315	.331

Walt Weiss

Bats: Both **Throws:** Right **Pos:** SS-155; PH-3   **Ht:** 6'0" **Wt:** 175 **Born:** 11/28/63 **Age:** 33

		BATTING															BASERUNNING				PERCENTAGES		
Year Team	Lg	G	AB	H	2B	3B	HR	(Hm | Rd)	TB	R	RBI	TBB	IBB	SO	HBP	SH	SF	SB	CS	SB%	GDP	Avg	OBP	SLG
1987 Oakland	AL	16	26	12	4	0	0	(0 | 0)	16	3	1	2	0	2	0	1	0	1	2	.33	1	.462	.500	.615
1988 Oakland	AL	147	452	113	17	3	3	(0 | 3)	145	44	39	35	1	56	9	8	7	4	4	.50	9	.250	.312	.321
1989 Oakland	AL	84	236	55	11	0	3	(2 | 1)	75	30	21	21	0	39	1	5	0	6	1	.86	5	.233	.298	.318
1990 Oakland	AL	138	445	118	17	1	2	(1 | 1)	143	50	35	46	5	53	4	6	4	9	3	.75	7	.265	.337	.321
1991 Oakland	AL	40	133	30	6	1	0	(0 | 0)	38	15	13	12	0	14	0	1	2	6	0	1.00	3	.226	.286	.286
1992 Oakland	AL	103	316	67	5	2	0	(0 | 0)	76	36	21	43	1	39	1	11	4	6	3	.67	10	.212	.305	.241
1993 Florida	NL	158	500	133	14	2	1	(0 | 1)	154	50	39	79	13	73	3	5	4	7	3	.70	5	.266	.367	.308
1994 Colorado	NL	110	423	106	11	4	1	(1 | 0)	128	58	32	56	0	58	0	4	3	12	7	.63	6	.251	.336	.303
1995 Colorado	NL	137	427	111	17	3	1	(0 | 1)	137	65	25	98	8	57	5	6	1	15	3	.83	7	.260	.403	.321
1996 Colorado	NL	155	517	146	20	2	8	(5 | 3)	194	89	48	80	5	78	6	14	6	10	2	.83	8	.282	.381	.375
10 ML YEARS		1088	3475	891	122	18	19	(9 | 10)	1106	440	274	472	33	469	29	61	31	76	28	.73	61	.256	.347	.318

Bob Wells

Pitches: Right **Bats:** Right **Pos:** RP-20; SP-16   **Ht:** 6'0" **Wt:** 180 **Born:** 11/1/66 **Age:** 30

		HOW MUCH HE PITCHED						WHAT HE GAVE UP												THE RESULTS						
Year Team	Lg	G	GS	CG	GF	IP	BFP	H	R	ER	HR	SH	SF	HB	TBB	IBB	SO	WP	Bk	W	L	Pct.	ShO	Sv-Op	Hld	ERA
1994 Phi-Sea		7	0	0	2	9	38	8	2	2	0	0	0	1	4	0	6	0	0	2	0	1.000	0	0-0	2	2.00
1995 Seattle	AL	30	4	0	3	76.2	358	88	51	49	11	1	5	3	39	3	38	1	0	4	3	.571	0	0-1	0	5.75
1996 Seattle	AL	36	16	1	6	130.2	574	141	78	77	25	3	4	6	46	5	94	0	0	12	7	.632	1	0-0	1	5.30
1994 Philadelphia	NL	6	0	0	2	5	21	4	1	1	0	0	0	1	3	0	3	0	0	1	0	1.000	0	0-0	1	1.80
Seattle	AL	1	0	0	0	4	17	4	1	1	0	0	0	0	1	0	3	0	0	1	0	1.000	0	0-0	1	2.25
3 ML YEARS		73	20	1	11	216.1	970	237	131	128	36	4	9	10	89	8	138	1	0	18	10	.643	1	0-1	1	5.33

David Wells

Pitches: Left **Bats:** Left **Pos:** SP-34   **Ht:** 6'4" **Wt:** 225 **Born:** 5/20/63 **Age:** 34

		HOW MUCH HE PITCHED						WHAT HE GAVE UP												THE RESULTS						
Year Team	Lg	G	GS	CG	GF	IP	BFP	H	R	ER	HR	SH	SF	HB	TBB	IBB	SO	WP	Bk	W	L	Pct.	ShO	Sv-Op	Hld	ERA
1987 Toronto	AL	18	2	0	6	29.1	132	37	14	13	0	1	0	0	12	0	32	4	0	4	3	.571	0	1-2	3	3.99
1988 Toronto	AL	41	0	0	15	64.1	279	65	36	33	12	2	2	2	31	9	56	6	2	3	5	.375	0	4-6	4	4.62
1989 Toronto	AL	54	0	0	19	86.1	352	66	25	23	5	3	2	0	28	7	78	6	3	7	4	.636	0	2-9	8	2.40
1990 Toronto	AL	43	25	0	8	189	759	165	72	66	14	9	2	2	45	3	115	7	1	11	6	.647	0	3-3	3	3.14

Year Team	Lg	G	GS	CG	GF	IP	BFP	H	R	ER	HR	SH	SF	HB	TBB	IBB	SO	WP	Bk	W	L	Pct.	ShO	Sv-Op	Hld	ERA
1991 Toronto	AL	40	28	2	3	198.1	811	188	88	82	24	6	6	2	49	1	106	10	3	15	10	.600	0	1-2	3	3.72
1992 Toronto	AL	41	14	0	14	120	529	138	84	72	16	3	4	8	36	6	62	3	1	7	9	.438	0	2-4	3	5.40
1993 Detroit	AL	32	30	0	0	187	776	183	93	87	26	3	3	7	42	6	139	13	0	11	9	.550	0	0-0	1	4.19
1994 Detroit	AL	16	16	5	0	111.1	464	113	54	49	13	3	1	2	24	6	71	5	0	5	7	.417	1	0-0	0	3.96
1995 Det-Cin		29	29	6	0	203	839	194	88	73	23	7	3	2	53	9	133	7	2	16	8	.667	0	0-0	0	3.24
1996 Baltimore	AL	34	34	3	0	224.1	946	247	132	128	32	8	14	7	51	7	130	4	2	11	14	.440	0	0-0	0	5.14
1995 Detroit	AL	18	18	3	0	130.1	539	120	54	44	17	3	2	2	37	5	83	6	1	10	3	.769	0	0-0	0	3.04
Cincinnati	NL	11	11	3	0	72.2	300	74	34	29	6	4	1	0	16	4	50	1	1	6	5	.545	0	0-0	0	3.59
10 ML YEARS		348	178	16	65	1413	5887	1396	686	626	165	45	37	32	371	54	922	65	14	90	75	.545	1	13-26	30	3.99

Turk Wendell

Pitches: Right **Bats:** Left **Pos:** RP-70   **Ht:** 6'2" **Wt:** 195 **Born:** 5/19/67 **Age:** 30

Year Team	Lg	G	GS	CG	GF	IP	BFP	H	R	ER	HR	SH	SF	HB	TBB	IBB	SO	WP	Bk	W	L	Pct.	ShO	Sv-Op	Hld	ERA
1993 Chicago	NL	7	4	0	1	22.2	98	24	13	11	0	2	1	1	8	1	15	1	1	1	2	.333	0	0-0	0	4.37
1994 Chicago	NL	6	2	0	1	14.1	76	22	20	19	3	2	1	0	10	1	9	1	0	0	1	.000	0	0-0	0	11.93
1995 Chicago	NL	43	0	0	17	60.1	270	71	35	33	11	3	3	2	24	4	50	1	0	3	1	.750	0	0-0	3	4.92
1996 Chicago	NL	70	0	0	49	79.1	339	58	26	25	8	3	1	3	44	4	75	3	2	4	5	.444	0	18-21	6	2.84
4 ML YEARS		126	6	0	68	176.2	783	175	94	88	22	10	5	5	86	10	149	6	3	8	9	.471	0	18-21	9	4.48

Don Wengert

Pitches: Right **Bats:** Right **Pos:** SP-25; RP-11   **Ht:** 6'2" **Wt:** 205 **Born:** 11/6/69 **Age:** 27

Year Team	Lg	G	GS	CG	GF	IP	BFP	H	R	ER	HR	SH	SF	HB	TBB	IBB	SO	WP	Bk	W	L	Pct.	ShO	Sv-Op	Hld	ERA
1992 Sou. Oregon	A-	6	5	1	0	37	144	32	6	6	1	1	0	1	7	0	29	1	1	2	0	1.000	0	0--	—	1.46
Madison	A	7	7	0	0	40	176	42	20	15	2	2	0	2	17	0	29	1	0	3	4	.429	0	0--	—	3.38
1993 Madison	A	13	13	2	0	78.2	322	79	30	29	5	4	4	1	18	0	46	6	0	6	5	.545	0	0--	—	3.32
Modesto	A+	12	12	0	0	70.1	299	75	42	37	8	1	1	3	29	0	43	4	1	3	6	.333	0	0--	—	4.73
1994 Modesto	A+	10	7	0	3	42.2	174	40	15	14	1	2	1	1	11	0	52	1	0	4	1	.800	0	2--	—	2.95
Huntsville	AA	17	17	1	0	99.1	411	86	43	36	14	0	0	4	33	1	92	3	1	6	4	.600	0	0--	—	3.26
1995 Edmonton	AAA	16	6	0	4	39	178	55	32	32	5	0	1	1	16	2	20	3	0	1	5	.500	0	1--	—	7.38
1995 Oakland	AL	19	0	0	10	29.2	129	30	14	11	3	1	1	1	12	2	16	1	0	1	1	.500	0	0-0	1	3.34
1996 Oakland	AL	36	25	1	2	161.1	725	200	102	100	29	3	5	6	60	5	75	4	0	7	11	.389	1	0-0	2	5.58
2 ML YEARS		55	25	1	12	191	854	230	116	111	32	4	6	7	72	7	91	5	0	8	12	.400	1	0-0	3	5.23

David West

Pitches: Left **Bats:** Left **Pos:** SP-6; RP-1   **Ht:** 6'6" **Wt:** 247 **Born:** 9/1/64 **Age:** 32

Year Team	Lg	G	GS	CG	GF	IP	BFP	H	R	ER	HR	SH	SF	HB	TBB	IBB	SO	WP	Bk	W	L	Pct.	ShO	Sv-Op	Hld	ERA
1996 Clearwater *	A+	5	5	0	0	23	99	21	8	8	1	0	0	1	11	0	17	3	0	1	0	1.000	0	0--	—	3.13
Scrntn-WB *	AAA	2	2	0	0	12	52	14	8	7	3	0	0	0	2	0	12	2	0	1	0	1.000	0	0--	—	5.25
1988 New York	NL	2	1	0	0	6	25	6	2	2	0	0	0	0	3	0	3	0	2	1	0	1.000	0	0-0	0	3.00
1989 NYN-Min		21	7	0	4	63.2	294	73	49	48	9	2	3	3	33	3	50	2	0	3	4	.429	0	0-1	2	6.79
1990 Minnesota	AL	29	27	2	0	146.1	646	142	88	83	21	6	4	4	78	1	92	4	1	7	9	.438	0	0-0	0	5.10
1991 Minnesota	AL	15	12	0	0	71.1	305	66	37	36	13	2	3	1	28	0	52	3	0	4	4	.500	0	0-0	0	4.54
1992 Minnesota	AL	9	3	0	1	28.1	139	32	24	22	3	0	2	1	20	0	19	2	0	1	3	.250	0	0-0	0	6.99
1993 Philadelphia	NL	76	0	0	27	86.1	375	60	37	28	6	8	2	5	51	4	87	3	0	6	4	.600	0	3-9	21	2.92
1994 Philadelphia	NL	31	14	0	7	99	429	74	44	39	7	4	2	1	61	2	83	9	0	4	10	.286	0	0-2	3	3.55
1995 Philadelphia	NL	8	8	0	0	38	163	34	17	16	5	2	0	1	19	0	25	1	0	3	2	.600	0	0-0	0	3.79
1996 Philadelphia	NL	7	6	0	0	28.1	126	31	17	15	0	1	0	0	11	0	22	1	0	2	2	.500	0	0-0	0	4.76
1989 New York	NL	11	2	0	0	24.1	112	25	20	20	4	0	1	1	14	2	19	1	0	0	2	.000	0	0-0	2	7.40
Minnesota	AL	10	5	0	4	39.1	182	48	29	28	5	2	2	2	19	1	31	1	0	3	2	.600	0	0-1	0	6.41
9 ML YEARS		198	78	2	39	567.1	2502	518	315	289	64	25	16	16	304	10	433	25	4	31	38	.449	0	3-12	26	4.58

John Wetteland

Pitches: Right **Bats:** Right **Pos:** RP-62   **Ht:** 6'2" **Wt:** 215 **Born:** 8/21/66 **Age:** 30

Year Team	Lg	G	GS	CG	GF	IP	BFP	H	R	ER	HR	SH	SF	HB	TBB	IBB	SO	WP	Bk	W	L	Pct.	ShO	Sv-Op	Hld	ERA
1989 Los Angeles	NL	31	12	0	7	102.2	411	81	46	43	8	4	2	0	34	4	96	16	1	5	8	.385	0	1-1	1	3.77
1990 Los Angeles	NL	22	5	0	7	43	190	44	28	23	6	1	1	4	17	3	36	8	0	2	4	.333	0	0-1	0	4.81
1991 Los Angeles	NL	6	0	0	3	9	36	5	2	0	0	0	0	0	3	0	9	1	0	1	0	1.000	0	0-0	0	0.00
1992 Montreal	NL	67	0	0	58	83.1	347	64	27	27	6	5	1	4	36	3	99	4	0	4	4	.500	0	37-46	0	2.92
1993 Montreal	NL	70	0	0	58	85.1	344	58	17	13	3	5	1	2	28	3	113	7	0	9	3	.750	0	43-49	0	1.37
1994 Montreal	NL	52	0	0	43	63.2	261	46	22	20	5	5	4	3	21	4	68	0	0	4	6	.400	0	25-35	0	2.83
1995 New York	AL	60	0	0	56	61.1	233	40	22	20	6	1	2	0	14	2	66	1	0	1	5	.167	0	31-37	0	2.93
1996 New York	AL	62	0	0	56	63.2	265	54	22	20	9	1	2	0	21	4	69	1	0	2	3	.400	0	**43-47**	0	2.83
8 ML YEARS		370	17	0	290	512	2087	392	187	166	43	22	14	14	174	23	556	38	4	28	33	.459	0	180-216	1	2.92

Devon White

Bats: Both   **Throws:** Right   **Pos:** CF-139; PH-8   **Ht:** 6'2"   **Wt:** 190   **Born:** 12/29/62   **Age:** 34

						BATTING											BASERUNNING				PERCENTAGES		
Year Team	Lg	G	AB	H	2B	3B	HR	(Hm | Rd)	TB	R	RBI	TBB	IBB	SO	HBP	SH	SF	SB	CS	SB%	GDP	Avg	OBP	SLG
1985 California	AL	21	7	1	0	0	0	(0 | 0)	1	7	0	1	0	3	1	0	0	3	1	.75	0	.143	.333	.143
1986 California	AL	29	51	12	1	1	1	(0 | 1)	18	8	3	6	0	8	0	0	0	6	0	1.00	0	.235	.316	.353
1987 California	AL	159	639	168	33	5	24	(11 | 13)	283	103	87	39	2	135	2	14	2	32	11	.74	8	.263	.306	.443
1988 California	AL	122	455	118	22	2	11	(3 | 8)	177	76	51	23	1	84	2	5	1	17	8	.68	5	.259	.297	.389
1989 California	AL	156	636	156	18	13	12	(9 | 3)	236	86	56	31	3	129	2	7	2	44	16	.73	12	.245	.282	.371
1990 California	AL	125	443	96	17	3	11	(5 | 6)	152	57	44	44	5	116	3	10	3	21	6	.78	6	.217	.290	.343
1991 Toronto	AL	156	642	181	40	10	17	(9 | 8)	292	110	60	55	1	135	7	5	6	33	10	.77	7	.282	.342	.455
1992 Toronto	AL	153	641	159	26	7	17	(7 | 10)	250	98	60	47	0	133	5	0	3	37	4	.90	9	.248	.303	.390
1993 Toronto	AL	146	598	163	42	6	15	(10 | 5)	262	116	52	57	1	127	7	3	3	34	4	**.89**	3	.273	.341	.438
1994 Toronto	AL	100	403	109	24	6	13	(5 | 8)	184	67	49	21	3	80	5	4	2	11	3	.79	4	.270	.313	.431
1995 Toronto	AL	101	427	121	23	5	10	(4 | 6)	184	61	53	29	1	97	5	1	3	11	2	.85	5	.283	.334	.431
1996 Florida	NL	146	552	151	37	6	17	(5 | 12)	251	77	84	38	6	99	8	4	9	22	6	.79	8	.274	.325	.455
12 ML YEARS		1414	5494	1435	283	64	148	(68 | 80)	2290	866	599	391	23	1146	47	53	34	271	71	.79	67	.261	.314	.417

Rondell White

Bats: Right   **Throws:** Right   **Pos:** CF-86; PH-4   **Ht:** 6'1"   **Wt:** 205   **Born:** 2/23/72   **Age:** 25

						BATTING											BASERUNNING				PERCENTAGES		
Year Team	Lg	G	AB	H	2B	3B	HR	(Hm	Rd)	TB	R	RBI	TBB	IBB	SO	HBP	SH	SF	SB	CS	SB%	GDP	Avg	OBP	SLG
1996 W. Palm Bch *	A+	3	10	2	1	0	0	—	—	3	0	2	0	0	4	0	0	0	0	1	.00	0	.200	.200	.300
Expos *	R	3	12	3	0	0	2	—	—	9	3	4	0	0	1	0	0	0	1	0	1.00	1	.250	.250	.750
Harrisburg *	AA	5	20	7	1	0	3	—	—	17	5	6	1	0	1	0	0	0	1	1	.50	1	.350	.381	.850
1993 Montreal	NL	23	73	19	3	1	2	(1	1)	30	9	15	7	0	16	0	2	1	1	2	.33	2	.260	.321	.411
1994 Montreal	NL	40	97	27	10	1	2	(1	1)	45	16	13	9	0	18	3	0	0	1	1	.50	1	.278	.358	.464
1995 Montreal	NL	130	474	140	33	4	13	(6	7)	220	87	57	41	1	87	6	0	4	25	5	.83	11	.295	.356	.464
1996 Montreal	NL	88	334	98	19	4	6	(2	4)	143	35	41	22	0	53	2	0	1	14	6	.70	11	.293	.340	.428
4 ML YEARS		281	978	284	65	10	23	(10	13)	438	147	126	79	1	174	11	2	6	41	14	.75	25	.290	.348	.448

Wally Whitehurst

Pitches: Right   **Bats:** Right   **Pos:** SP-2   **Ht:** 6'3"   **Wt:** 200   **Born:** 4/11/64   **Age:** 33

		HOW MUCH HE PITCHED						WHAT HE GAVE UP										THE RESULTS					
Year Team	Lg	G	GS	CG	GF	IP	BFP	H	R	ER	HR	SH	SF	HB	TBB	IBB	SO	WP	Bk	W	L	Pct.	ShO	Sv-Op	Hld	ERA
1996 Ottawa *	AAA	15	5	0	5	35	152	41	17	17	2	1	1	2	13	0	35	4	0	2	4	.333	0	3- --	—	4.37
Columbus *	AAA	13	13	2	0	73	285	60	25	20	5	0	0	2	12	0	48	1	0	6	3	.667	0	0- --	—	2.47
1989 New York	NL	9	1	0	4	14	64	17	7	7	2	0	1	0	5	0	9	1	0	0	1	.000	0	0-0	1	4.50
1990 New York	NL	38	0	0	16	65.2	263	63	27	24	5	3	0	0	9	2	46	2	0	1	0	1.000	0	2-2	4	3.29
1991 New York	NL	36	20	0	6	133.1	556	142	67	62	11	6	3	4	25	3	87	3	4	7	12	.368	0	1-1	3	4.19
1992 New York	NL	44	11	0	7	97	421	99	45	39	4	6	3	4	33	5	70	2	1	3	9	.250	0	0-3	4	3.62
1993 San Diego	NL	21	19	0	1	105.2	441	109	47	45	11	5	8	3	30	5	57	5	1	4	7	.364	0	0-0	0	3.83
1994 San Diego	NL	13	13	0	0	64	294	80	37	35	8	4	0	1	26	4	43	2	0	4	7	.364	0	0-0	0	4.92
1996 New York	AL	2	2	0	0	8	36	11	6	6	1	0	0	0	2	0	1	0	0	1	1	.500	0	0-0	0	6.75
7 ML YEARS		163	66	0	34	487.2	2075	525	236	218	43	24	15	12	130	19	313	15	6	20	37	.351	0	3-6	12	4.02

Mark Whiten

Bats: B **Throws:** R **Pos:** RF-77; LF-36; PH-23; CF-8   **Ht:** 6'3"   **Wt:** 235   **Born:** 11/25/66   **Age:** 30

						BATTING											BASERUNNING				PERCENTAGES		
Year Team	Lg	G	AB	H	2B	3B	HR	(Hm | Rd)	TB	R	RBI	TBB	IBB	SO	HBP	SH	SF	SB	CS	SB%	GDP	Avg	OBP	SLG
1990 Toronto	AL	33	88	24	1	1	2	(1 | 1)	33	12	7	7	0	14	0	0	1	2	0	1.00	2	.273	.323	.375
1991 Tor-Cle	AL	116	407	99	18	7	9	(4 | 5)	158	46	45	30	2	85	3	0	5	4	3	.57	13	.243	.297	.388
1992 Cleveland	AL	148	508	129	19	4	9	(6 | 3)	183	73	43	72	10	102	2	3	3	16	12	.57	12	.254	.347	.360
1993 St. Louis	NL	152	562	142	13	4	25	(12 | 13)	238	81	99	58	9	110	2	0	4	15	8	.65	11	.253	.323	.423
1994 St. Louis	NL	92	334	98	18	2	14	(6 | 8)	162	57	53	37	9	75	1	0	2	10	5	.67	8	.293	.364	.485
1995 Bos-Phi		92	320	77	13	1	12	(5 | 7)	128	51	47	39	1	86	1	0	1	8	0	1.00	9	.241	.324	.400
1996 Phi-Atl-Sea		136	412	108	20	1	22	(9 | 13)	196	76	71	70	6	127	3	0	1	17	9	.65	12	.262	.372	.476
1991 Toronto	AL	46	149	33	4	3	2	(2 | 0)	49	12	19	11	1	35	1	0	3	0	1	.00	5	.221	.274	.329
Cleveland	AL	70	258	66	14	4	7	(2 | 5)	109	34	26	19	1	50	2	0	2	4	2	.67	8	.256	.310	.422
1995 Boston	AL	32	108	20	3	0	1	(0 | 1)	26	13	10	8	0	23	0	0	1	1	0	1.00	5	.185	.239	.241
Philadelphia	NL	60	212	57	10	1	11	(5 | 6)	102	38	37	31	1	63	1	0	0	7	0	1.00	4	.269	.365	.481
1996 Philadelphia	NL	60	182	43	8	0	7	(4 | 3)	72	33	21	33	2	62	1	0	0	13	3	.81	9	.236	.356	.396
Atlanta	NL	36	90	23	5	1	3	(1 | 2)	39	12	17	16	0	25	0	0	1	2	1	.67	2	.256	.364	.433
Seattle	AL	40	140	42	7	0	12	(4 | 8)	85	31	33	21	4	40	2	0	0	2	5	.29	1	.300	.399	.607
7 ML YEARS		769	2631	677	102	20	93	(43 | 50)	1098	396	365	313	37	599	12	3	17	72	37	.66	67	.257	.337	.417

Matt Whiteside

Pitches: Right **Bats:** Right **Pos:** RP-14 **Ht:** 6'0" **Wt:** 205 **Born:** 8/8/67 **Age:** 29

Year Team	Lg	G	GS	CG	GF	IP	BFP	H	R	ER	HR	SH	SF	HB	TBB	IBB	SO	WP	Bk	W	L	Pct.	ShO	Sv-Op	Hld	ERA
1996 Okla. City *	AAA	36	7	0	14	94	393	95	41	36	8	5	2	3	24	2	52	4	3	9	6	.600	0	0- -	—	3.45
1992 Texas	AL	20	0	0	8	28	118	26	8	6	1	0	1	0	11	2	13	2	0	1	1	.500	0	4-4	0	1.93
1993 Texas	AL	60	0	0	10	73	305	78	37	35	7	2	1	1	23	6	39	0	2	2	1	.667	0	1-5	14	4.32
1994 Texas	AL	47	0	0	16	61	272	68	40	34	6	3	2	1	28	3	37	1	0	2	2	.500	0	1-3	7	5.02
1995 Texas	AL	40	0	0	18	53	223	48	24	24	5	2	3	1	19	2	46	4	0	5	4	.556	0	3-4	7	4.08
1996 Texas	AL	14	0	0	7	32.1	148	43	24	24	8	1	2	0	11	1	15	1	0	0	1	.000	0	0-0	1	6.68
5 ML YEARS		181	0	0	59	247.1	1066	263	133	123	27	8	9	3	92	14	150	8	2	10	9	.526	0	9-16	29	4.48

Kevin Wickander

Pitches: Left **Bats:** Left **Pos:** RP-21 **Ht:** 6'3" **Wt:** 205 **Born:** 1/4/65 **Age:** 32

Year Team	Lg	G	GS	CG	GF	IP	BFP	H	R	ER	HR	SH	SF	HB	TBB	IBB	SO	WP	Bk	W	L	Pct.	ShO	Sv-Op	Hld	ERA
1996 Nw Orleans *	AAA	8	0	0	1	6.1	34	9	12	9	2	1	0	0	5	2	9	3	0	0	0	.000	0	0- -	—	12.79
1989 Cleveland	AL	2	0	0	1	2.2	15	6	1	1	0	0	0	0	2	1	0	0	0	0	0	.000	0	0-0	0	3.38
1990 Cleveland	AL	10	0	0	3	12.1	53	14	6	5	0	0	2	1	4	0	10	0	0	0	1	.000	0	0-1	1	3.65
1992 Cleveland	AL	44	0	0	10	41	187	39	14	14	1	2	2	4	28	3	38	1	1	2	0	1.000	0	1-3	7	3.07
1993 Cle-Cin		44	0	0	9	34	170	47	27	23	8	1	0	2	22	1	23	5	1	1	0	1.000	0	0-1	2	6.09
1995 Det-Mil		29	0	0	9	23.1	99	19	6	5	1	1	2	1	12	5	11	1	1	0	0	.000	0	1-3	5	1.93
1996 Milwaukee	AL	21	0	0	6	25.1	118	26	16	14	2	1	2	1	17	2	19	2	0	2	0	1.000	0	0-2	1	4.97
1993 Cleveland	AL	11	0	0	1	8.2	44	15	7	4	3	0	0	0	3	0	3	1	0	0	0	.000	0	0-0	1	4.15
Cincinnati	NL	33	0	0	8	25.1	126	32	20	19	5	1	0	2	19	1	20	4	1	1	0	1.000	0	0-1	1	6.75
1995 Detroit	AL	21	0	0	7	17.1	77	18	6	5	1	0	1	1	9	4	9	1	1	0	0	.000	0	1-3	3	2.60
Milwaukee	AL	8	0	0	2	6	22	1	0	0	0	1	1	0	3	1	2	0	0	0	0	.000	0	0-0	2	0.00
6 ML YEARS		150	0	0	38	138.2	642	151	70	62	12	5	8	8	85	12	101	9	3	5	1	.833	0	2-10	16	4.02

Bob Wickman

Pitches: Right **Bats:** Right **Pos:** RP-70 **Ht:** 6'1" **Wt:** 212 **Born:** 2/6/69 **Age:** 28

Year Team	Lg	G	GS	CG	GF	IP	BFP	H	R	ER	HR	SH	SF	HB	TBB	IBB	SO	WP	Bk	W	L	Pct.	ShO	Sv-Op	Hld	ERA
1992 New York	AL	8	8	0	0	50.1	213	51	25	23	2	1	3	2	20	0	21	3	0	6	1	.857	0	0-0	0	4.11
1993 New York	AL	41	19	1	9	140	629	156	82	72	13	4	1	5	69	7	70	2	0	14	4	.778	1	4-8	2	4.63
1994 New York	AL	53	0	0	19	70	286	54	26	24	3	0	5	1	27	3	56	2	0	5	4	.556	0	6-10	11	3.09
1995 New York	AL	63	1	0	14	80	347	77	38	36	6	4	1	5	33	3	51	2	0	2	4	.333	0	1-10	21	4.05
1996 NYA-Mil	AL	70	0	0	18	95.2	429	106	50	47	10	2	4	5	44	3	75	4	0	7	1	.875	0	0-4	10	4.42
1996 New York	AL	58	0	0	14	79	358	94	41	41	7	1	4	5	34	1	61	3	0	4	1	.800	0	0-3	6	4.67
Milwaukee	AL	12	0	0	4	16.2	71	12	9	6	3	1	0	0	10	2	14	1	0	3	0	1.000	0	0-1	4	3.24
5 ML YEARS		235	28	1	60	436	1904	444	221	202	34	11	14	18	193	16	273	13	0	34	14	.708	1	11-32	44	4.17

Chris Widger

Bats: Right **Throws:** Right **Pos:** C-7; PH-1 **Ht:** 6'3" **Wt:** 195 **Born:** 5/21/71 **Age:** 26

Year Team	Lg	G	AB	H	2B	3B	HR	(Hm	Rd)	TB	R	RBI	TBB	IBB	SO	HBP	SH	SF	SB	CS	SB%	GDP	Avg	OBP	SLG
1992 Bellingham	A-	51	166	43	7	2	5	—	—	69	28	30	22	0	36	1	0	5	8	1	.89	4	.259	.340	.416
1993 Riverside	A+	97	360	95	28	2	9	—	—	154	43	58	19	0	64	3	3	4	5	4	.56	8	.264	.303	.428
1994 Jacksonvlle	AA	116	388	101	15	3	16	—	—	170	58	59	39	4	69	5	0	2	8	7	.53	7	.260	.334	.438
1995 Tacoma	AAA	50	174	48	11	1	9	—	—	88	29	21	9	0	29	0	1	0	0	0	.00	4	.276	.311	.506
1996 Tacoma	AAA	97	352	107	20	2	13	—	—	170	42	48	27	0	62	2	2	2	7	1	.88	13	.304	.355	.483
1995 Seattle	AL	23	45	9	0	0	1	(1	0)	12	2	2	3	0	11	0	0	0	0	0	.00	0	.200	.245	.267
1996 Seattle	AL	8	11	2	0	0	0	(0	0)	2	1	0	0	0	5	1	0	0	0	0	.00	0	.182	.250	.182
2 ML YEARS		31	56	11	0	0	1	(1	0)	14	3	2	3	0	16	1	0	0	0	0	.00	0	.196	.246	.250

Marc Wilkins

Pitches: Right **Bats:** Right **Pos:** RP-45; SP-2 **Ht:** 5'11" **Wt:** 200 **Born:** 10/21/70 **Age:** 26

Year Team	Lg	G	GS	CG	GF	IP	BFP	H	R	ER	HR	SH	SF	HB	TBB	IBB	SO	WP	Bk	W	L	Pct.	ShO	Sv-Op	Hld	ERA
1992 Welland	A-	28	1	0	8	42	207	49	38	34	2	2	2	4	24	3	42	12	1	4	2	.667	0	5- -	—	7.29
1993 Augusta	A	48	5	0	14	77	360	83	52	36	4	1	2	13	31	1	73	10	0	5	6	.455	0	1- -	—	4.21
1994 Salem	A+	28	28	0	0	151	657	155	84	62	15	6	3	22	45	0	90	14	1	8	5	.615	0	0- -	—	3.70
1996 Carolina	AA	11	3	0	3	24.2	103	19	12	11	1	2	0	2	11	2	19	0	0	2	3	.400	0	0- -	—	4.01
1996 Pittsburgh	NL	47	2	0	11	75	331	75	36	32	6	3	4	6	36	6	62	5	0	4	3	.571	0	1-5	4	3.84

Rick Wilkins

Bats: Left **Throws:** Right **Pos:** C-124; PH-14; 1B-7   **Ht:** 6'2" **Wt:** 215 **Born:** 6/4/67 **Age:** 30

Year Team	Lg	G	AB	H	2B	3B	HR	(Hm	Rd)	TB	R	RBI	TBB	IBB	SO	HBP	SH	SF	SB	CS	SB%	GDP	Avg	OBP	SLG
1991 Chicago	NL	86	203	45	9	0	6	(2	4)	72	21	22	19	2	56	6	7	0	3	3	.50	3	.222	.307	.355
1992 Chicago	NL	83	244	66	9	1	8	(3	5)	101	20	22	28	7	53	0	1	1	0	2	.00	6	.270	.344	.414
1993 Chicago	NL	136	446	135	23	1	30	(10	20)	250	78	73	50	13	99	3	0	1	2	1	.67	6	.303	.376	.561
1994 Chicago	NL	100	313	71	25	2	7	(4	3)	121	44	39	40	5	86	2	1	2	4	3	.57	3	.227	.317	.387
1995 ChN-Hou	NL	65	202	41	3	0	7	(3	4)	65	30	19	46	2	61	1	0	2	0	0	.00	9	.203	.351	.322
1996 Hou-SF	NL	136	411	100	18	2	14	(6	8)	164	53	59	67	13	121	1	0	10	0	3	.00	5	.243	.344	.399
1995 Chicago	NL	50	162	31	2	0	6	(3	3)	51	24	14	36	1	51	1	0	1	0	0	.00	8	.191	.340	.315
Houston	NL	15	40	10	1	0	1	(0	1)	14	6	5	10	1	10	0	0	1	0	0	.00	1	.250	.392	.350
1996 Houston	NL	84	254	54	8	2	6	(3	3)	84	34	23	46	10	81	1	0	5	0	1	.00	4	.213	.330	.331
San Francisco	NL	52	157	46	10	0	8	(3	5)	80	19	36	21	3	40	0	0	5	0	2	.00	4	.293	.366	.510
6 ML YEARS		606	1819	458	87	6	72	(28	44)	773	246	234	250	42	476	13	9	16	9	12	.43	32	.252	.344	.425

Bernie Williams

Bats: Both **Throws:** Right **Pos:** CF-140; DH-2; PH-1   **Ht:** 6'2" **Wt:** 205 **Born:** 9/13/68 **Age:** 28

Year Team	Lg	G	AB	H	2B	3B	HR	(Hm	Rd)	TB	R	RBI	TBB	IBB	SO	HBP	SH	SF	SB	CS	SB%	GDP	Avg	OBP	SLG
1991 New York	AL	85	320	76	19	4	3	(1	2)	112	43	34	48	0	57	1	2	3	10	5	.67	4	.238	.336	.350
1992 New York	AL	62	261	73	14	2	5	(3	2)	106	39	26	29	1	36	1	2	0	7	6	.54	5	.280	.354	.406
1993 New York	AL	139	567	152	31	4	12	(5	7)	227	67	68	53	4	106	4	1	3	9	9	.50	17	.268	.333	.400
1994 New York	AL	108	408	118	29	1	12	(4	8)	185	80	57	61	2	54	3	1	2	16	9	.64	11	.289	.384	.453
1995 New York	AL	144	563	173	29	9	18	(7	11)	274	93	82	75	1	98	5	2	3	8	6	.57	12	.307	.392	.487
1996 New York	AL	143	551	168	26	7	29	(12	17)	295	108	102	82	8	72	0	1	7	17	4	.81	15	.305	.391	.535
6 ML YEARS		681	2670	760	148	27	79	(32	47)	1199	430	369	348	16	423	14	9	18	67	39	.63	64	.285	.368	.449

Brian Williams

Pitches: Right **Bats:** Right **Pos:** RP-23; SP-17   **Ht:** 6'2" **Wt:** 225 **Born:** 2/15/69 **Age:** 28

		HOW MUCH HE PITCHED						WHAT HE GAVE UP												THE RESULTS						
Year Team	Lg	G	GS	CG	GF	IP	BFP	H	R	ER	HR	SH	SF	HB	TBB	IBB	SO	WP	Bk	W	L	Pct.	ShO	Sv-Op	Hld	ERA
1996 Toledo *	AAA	3	3	1	0	19.2	87	22	13	12	1	0	0	0	9	1	21	3	1	1	2	.333	0	0--	—	5.49
1991 Houston	NL	2	2	0	0	12	49	11	5	5	2	0	0	1	4	0	4	0	0	0	1	.000	0	0-0	0	3.75
1992 Houston	NL	16	16	0	0	96.1	413	92	44	42	10	7	3	0	42	1	54	2	1	7	6	.538	0	0-0	0	3.92
1993 Houston	NL	42	5	0	12	82	357	76	48	44	7	5	3	4	38	4	56	9	2	4	4	.500	0	3-6	2	4.83
1994 Houston	NL	20	13	0	2	78.1	384	112	64	50	9	7	5	4	41	4	49	3	1	6	5	.545	0	0-0	1	5.74
1995 San Diego	NL	44	6	0	7	72	337	79	54	48	3	7	1	8	38	4	75	7	1	3	10	.231	0	0-2	7	6.00
1996 Detroit	AL	40	17	2	17	121	579	145	107	91	21	5	6	6	85	2	72	8	0	3	10	.231	1	2-4	0	6.77
6 ML YEARS		164	59	2	38	461.2	2119	515	322	280	52	31	18	23	248	15	310	29	5	23	36	.390	1	5-12	10	5.46

Eddie Williams

Bats: R **Throws:** R **Pos:** DH-52; PH-15; 1B-7; 3B-3; RF-2   **Ht:** 6'0" **Wt:** 210 **Born:** 11/1/64 **Age:** 32

Year Team	Lg	G	AB	H	2B	3B	HR	(Hm	Rd)	TB	R	RBI	TBB	IBB	SO	HBP	SH	SF	SB	CS	SB%	GDP	Avg	OBP	SLG
1986 Cleveland	AL	5	7	1	0	0	0	(0	0)	1	2	1	0	0	3	0	0	0	0	0	.00	0	.143	.143	.143
1987 Cleveland	AL	22	64	11	4	0	1	(0	1)	18	9	4	9	0	19	1	0	1	0	0	.00	2	.172	.280	.281
1988 Cleveland	AL	10	21	4	0	0	0	(0	0)	4	3	1	0	0	3	1	1	0	0	0	.00	1	.190	.227	.190
1989 Chicago	AL	66	201	55	8	0	3	(2	1)	72	25	10	18	3	31	4	3	3	1	2	.33	4	.274	.341	.358
1990 San Diego	NL	14	42	12	3	0	3	(1	2)	24	5	4	5	2	6	0	0	0	0	1	.00	1	.286	.362	.571
1994 San Diego	NL	49	175	58	11	1	11	(5	6)	104	32	42	15	1	26	3	2	1	0	0	.00	10	.331	.392	.594
1995 San Diego	NL	97	296	77	11	1	12	(4	8)	126	35	47	23	0	47	4	0	2	0	0	.00	21	.260	.320	.426
1996 Detroit	AL	77	215	43	5	0	6	(3	3)	66	22	26	18	0	50	2	0	1	0	2	.00	8	.200	.267	.307
8 ML YEARS		340	1021	261	42	2	36	(15	21)	415	133	135	88	6	185	15	6	8	1	6	.14	47	.256	.322	.406

George Williams

Bats: Both **Throws:** Right **Pos:** C-43; DH-11; PH-6   **Ht:** 5'10" **Wt:** 190 **Born:** 4/22/69 **Age:** 28

Year Team	Lg	G	AB	H	2B	3B	HR	(Hm	Rd)	TB	R	RBI	TBB	IBB	SO	HBP	SH	SF	SB	CS	SB%	GDP	Avg	OBP	SLG
1991 Sou. Oregon	A-	55	174	41	10	0	2	(Hm	—)	57	24	24	38	0	36	5	3	1	9	4	.69	5	.236	.385	.328
1992 Madison	A	115	349	106	18	2	5	—	—	143	56	42	76	6	53	8	5	1	9	5	.64	10	.304	.438	.410
1993 Huntsville	AA	124	434	128	26	2	14	—	—	200	80	77	67	0	66	14	1	6	6	3	.67	10	.295	.401	.461
1994 W. Michigan	A	63	221	67	20	1	8	—	—	113	40	48	44	3	47	8	1	0	6	3	.67	3	.303	.436	.511
1995 Edmonton	AAA	81	290	90	20	0	13	—	—	149	53	55	50	6	52	2	3	2	0	4	.00	8	.310	.413	.514
1996 Edmonton	AAA	14	57	23	5	0	1	—	—	43	10	18	6	0	11	2	0	1	0	0	.00	0	.404	.470	.754
1995 Oakland	AL	29	79	23	5	1	3	(1	2)	39	13	14	11	2	21	2	0	2	0	0	.00	1	.291	.383	.494
1996 Oakland	AL	56	132	20	5	0	3	(0	3)	34	17	10	28	1	32	3	2	1	0	0	.00	3	.152	.311	.258
2 ML YEARS		85	211	43	10	1	6	(1	5)	73	30	24	39	3	53	5	2	3	0	0	.00	4	.204	.337	.346

Gerald Williams

Bats: R **Throws:** R **Pos:** LF-70; CF-39; PH-18; RF-11; DH-2 **Ht:** 6'2" **Wt:** 190 **Born:** 8/10/66 **Age:** 30

Year Team	Lg	G	AB	H	2B	3B	HR	(Hm	Rd)	TB	R	RBI	TBB	IBB	SO	HBP	SH	SF	SB	CS	SB%	GDP	Avg	OBP	SLG
1992 New York	AL	15	27	8	2	0	3	(2	1)	19	7	6	0	0	3	0	0	0	2	0	1.00	0	.296	.296	.704
1993 New York	AL	42	67	10	2	3	0	(0	0)	18	11	6	1	0	14	2	0	1	2	0	1.00	2	.149	.183	.269
1994 New York	AL	57	86	25	8	0	4	(2	2)	45	19	13	4	0	17	0	0	1	1	3	.25	6	.291	.319	.523
1995 New York	AL	100	182	45	18	2	6	(4	2)	85	33	28	22	1	34	1	0	3	4	2	.67	4	.247	.327	.467
1996 NYA-Mil	AL	125	325	82	19	4	5	(3	2)	124	43	34	19	3	57	5	3	5	10	9	.53	8	.252	.299	.382
1996 New York	AL	99	233	63	15	4	5	(3	2)	101	37	30	15	2	39	4	1	5	7	8	.47	7	.270	.319	.433
Milwaukee	AL	26	92	19	4	0	0	(0	0)	23	6	4	4	1	18	1	2	0	3	1	.75	1	.207	.247	.250
5 ML YEARS		339	687	170	49	9	18	(11	7)	291	113	87	46	4	125	8	3	10	19	14	.58	20	.247	.298	.424

Keith Williams

Bats: Right **Throws:** Right **Pos:** PH-5; RF-3; LF-1 **Ht:** 6'0" **Wt:** 190 **Born:** 4/21/72 **Age:** 25

Year Team	Lg	G	AB	H	2B	3B	HR	(Hm	Rd)	TB	R	RBI	TBB	IBB	SO	HBP	SH	SF	SB	CS	SB%	GDP	Avg	OBP	SLG
1993 Everett	A-	75	288	87	21	5	12	—	—	154	57	49	48	4	73	3	2	0	21	7	.75	5	.302	.407	.535
1994 San Jose	A+	128	504	151	30	4	21	—	—	260	91	97	60	2	102	4	0	8	4	3	.57	8	.300	.373	.516
1995 Shreveport	AA	75	275	84	20	1	9	—	—	133	39	55	23	3	39	0	0	7	5	3	.63	5	.305	.351	.484
Phoenix	AAA	24	83	25	4	1	2	—	—	37	14	5	0	11	1	4	2	0	0	.00	4	.301	.341	.446
1996 Phoenix	AAA	108	398	109	25	3	13	—	—	179	63	63	52	4	96	0	1	5	2	2	.50	9	.274	.354	.450
1996 San Francisco	NL	9	20	5	0	0	0	(0	0)	5	0	0	0	0	6	0	0	0	0	0	.00	0	.250	.250	.250

Matt Williams

Bats: R **Throws:** R **Pos:** 3B-92; 1B-13; PH-3; SS-1 **Ht:** 6'2" **Wt:** 216 **Born:** 11/28/65 **Age:** 31

Year Team	Lg	G	AB	H	2B	3B	HR	(Hm	Rd)	TB	R	RBI	TBB	IBB	SO	HBP	SH	SF	SB	CS	SB%	GDP	Avg	OBP	SLG
1987 San Francisco	NL	84	245	46	9	2	8	(5	3)	83	28	21	16	4	68	1	3	1	4	3	.57	5	.188	.240	.339
1988 San Francisco	NL	52	156	32	6	1	8	(7	1)	64	17	19	8	0	41	2	3	1	0	1	.00	7	.205	.251	.410
1989 San Francisco	NL	84	292	59	18	1	18	(10	8)	133	31	50	14	1	72	2	1	2	1	2	.33	5	.202	.242	.455
1990 San Francisco	NL	159	617	171	27	2	33	(20	13)	301	87	**122**	33	9	138	7	2	5	7	4	.64	13	.277	.319	.488
1991 San Francisco	NL	157	589	158	24	5	34	(17	17)	294	72	98	33	6	128	6	0	7	5	5	.50	11	.268	.310	.499
1992 San Francisco	NL	146	529	120	13	5	20	(9	11)	203	58	66	39	11	109	6	0	4	7	7	.50	15	.227	.286	.384
1993 San Francisco	NL	145	579	170	33	4	38	(19	19)	325	105	110	27	4	80	4	0	9	1	3	.25	12	.294	.325	.561
1994 San Francisco	NL	112	445	119	16	3	43	(20	23)	270	74	96	33	7	87	2	0	3	1	0	1.00	11	.267	.319	.607
1995 San Francisco	NL	76	283	95	17	1	23	(9	14)	183	53	65	30	8	58	2	0	3	2	0	1.00	8	.336	.399	.647
1996 San Francisco	NL	105	404	122	16	1	22	(13	9)	206	69	85	39	9	91	6	0	6	1	2	.33	10	.302	.367	.510
10 ML YEARS		1120	4139	1092	179	25	247	(129	118)	2062	594	732	272	59	872	38	9	39	29	27	.52	97	.264	.312	.498

Mike Williams

Pitches: Right **Bats:** Right **Pos:** SP-29; RP-3 **Ht:** 6'3" **Wt:** 195 **Born:** 7/29/68 **Age:** 28

Year Team	Lg	G	GS	CG	GF	IP	BFP	H	R	ER	HR	SH	SF	HB	TBB	IBB	SO	WP	Bk	W	L	Pct.	ShO	Sv-Op	Hld	ERA
1992 Philadelphia	NL	5	5	1	0	28.2	121	29	20	17	3	1	0	0	7	0	5	0	0	1	1	.500	0	0-0	0	5.34
1993 Philadelphia	NL	17	4	0	2	51	221	50	32	30	5	1	0	0	22	2	33	2	0	1	3	.250	0	0-0	0	5.29
1994 Philadelphia	NL	12	8	0	2	50.1	222	61	31	28	7	2	3	0	20	3	29	0	0	2	4	.333	0	0-0	0	5.01
1995 Philadelphia	NL	33	8	0	7	87.2	367	78	37	32	10	5	3	3	29	2	57	7	0	3	3	.500	0	0-0	1	3.29
1996 Philadelphia	NL	32	29	0	1	167	732	188	107	101	25	6	5	6	67	6	103	**16**	1	6	14	.300	0	0-0	0	5.44
5 ML YEARS		99	54	1	12	384.2	1663	406	227	208	50	15	12	9	145	13	227	25	1	13	25	.342	0	0-0	1	4.87

Shad Williams

Pitches: Right **Bats:** Right **Pos:** RP-11; SP-2 **Ht:** 6'0" **Wt:** 198 **Born:** 3/10/71 **Age:** 26

Year Team	Lg	G	GS	CG	GF	IP	BFP	H	R	ER	HR	SH	SF	HB	TBB	IBB	SO	WP	Bk	W	L	Pct.	ShO	Sv-Op	Hld	ERA
1992 Quad City	A	27	26	7	0	179.1	748	161	81	65	14	6	6	7	55	0	152	9	1	13	11	.542	0	0--	—	3.26
1993 Midland	AA	27	27	2	0	175.2	758	192	100	92	16	6	6	3	65	1	91	9	1	7	10	.412	0	0--	—	4.71
1994 Midland	AA	5	5	1	0	32.1	112	13	4	4	1	0	0	1	4	0	29	2	0	3	0	1.000	1	0--	—	1.11
Vancouver	AAA	16	16	1	0	86	386	100	61	44	14	3	2	3	30	0	42	6	0	4	6	.400	1	0--	—	4.60
1995 Vancouver	AAA	25	25	3	0	149.2	627	142	65	56	16	3	3	4	48	2	114	7	1	9	7	.563	1	0--	—	3.37
1996 Vancouver	AAA	15	13	1	1	75	321	73	36	33	8	4	0	2	28	0	57	2	0	6	2	.750	1	0--	—	3.96
1996 California	AL	13	2	0	3	28.1	150	42	34	28	7	3	1	2	21	4	26	2	0	0	2	.000	0	0-0	0	8.89

Woody Williams

Pitches: Right **Bats:** Right **Pos:** SP-10; RP-2 **Ht:** 6'0" **Wt:** 190 **Born:** 8/19/66 **Age:** 30

Year Team	Lg	G	GS	CG	GF	IP	BFP	H	R	ER	HR	SH	SF	HB	TBB	IBB	SO	WP	Bk	W	L	Pct.	ShO	Sv-Op	Hld	ERA
1996 Dunedin *	A+	2	2	0	0	7.2	34	9	7	7	1	0	0	0	2	0	11	0	0	0	2	.000	0	0--	—	8.22

		HOW MUCH HE PITCHED						WHAT HE GAVE UP												THE RESULTS						
Year Team	Lg	G	GS	CG	GF	IP	BFP	H	R	ER	HR	SH	SF	HB	TBB	IBB	SO	WP	Bk	W	L	Pct.	ShO	Sv-Op	Hld	ERA
St. Cathrns *	A-	2	2	0	0	7.1	30	7	3	3	0	0	0	0	4	0	12	1	0	0	0	.000	0	0--	—	3.68
Syracuse *	AAA	7	7	1	0	32	123	22	5	5	3	0	0	1	7	0	33	3	1	3	1	.750	1	0--	—	1.41
1993 Toronto	AL	30	0	0	9	37	172	40	18	18	2	2	1	1	22	3	24	2	1	3	1	.750	0	0-2	4	4.38
1994 Toronto	AL	38	0	0	14	59.1	253	44	24	24	5	1	2	2	33	1	56	4	0	1	3	.250	0	0-0	5	3.64
1995 Toronto	AL	23	3	0	10	53.2	232	44	23	22	6	2	0	2	28	1	41	0	0	1	2	.333	0	0-1	1	3.69
1996 Toronto	AL	12	10	1	0	59	255	64	33	31	8	2	1	1	21	1	43	2	0	4	5	.444	0	0-0	0	4.73
4 ML YEARS		103	13	1	33	209	912	192	98	95	21	7	4	6	104	6	164	8	1	9	11	.450	0	0-3	10	4.09

Dan Wilson

Bats: Right **Throws:** Right **Pos:** C-135; PH-4 **Ht:** 6'3" **Wt:** 190 **Born:** 3/25/69 **Age:** 28

		BATTING																BASERUNNING				PERCENTAGES		
Year Team	Lg	G	AB	H	2B	3B	HR	(Hm Rd)	TB	R	RBI	TBB	IBB	SO	HBP	SH	SF	SB	CS	SB%	GDP	Avg	OBP	SLG
1992 Cincinnati	NL	12	25	9	1	0	0	(0 0)	10	2	3	3	0	8	0	0	0	0	0	.00	2	.360	.429	.400
1993 Cincinnati	NL	36	76	17	3	0	0	(0 0)	20	6	8	9	4	16	0	2	1	0	0	.00	2	.224	.302	.263
1994 Seattle	AL	91	282	61	14	2	3	(1 2)	88	24	27	10	0	57	1	8	2	1	2	.33	11	.216	.244	.312
1995 Seattle	AL	119	399	111	22	3	9	(5 4)	166	40	51	33	1	63	2	5	1	2	1	.67	12	.278	.336	.416
1996 Seattle	AL	138	491	140	24	0	18	(7 11)	218	51	83	32	2	88	3	9	5	1	2	.33	15	.285	.330	.444
5 ML YEARS		396	1273	338	64	5	30	(13 17)	502	123	172	87	7	232	6	24	9	4	5	.44	42	.266	.313	.394

Desi Wilson

Bats: Left **Throws:** Left **Pos:** 1B-33; PH-9 **Ht:** 6'7" **Wt:** 230 **Born:** 5/9/69 **Age:** 28

		BATTING																BASERUNNING				PERCENTAGES		
Year Team	Lg	G	AB	H	2B	3B	HR	(Hm Rd)	TB	R	RBI	TBB	IBB	SO	HBP	SH	SF	SB	CS	SB%	GDP	Avg	OBP	SLG
1991 Rangers	R	8	25	4	2	0	0	—	6	1	7	3	0	2	0	0	1	0	0	.00	0	.160	.241	.240
1992 Butte	R+	72	253	81	9	4	5	—	113	45	42	31	1	45	1	0	0	13	11	.54	1	.320	.396	.447
1993 Charlotte	A+	131	511	156	21	7	3	—	200	83	70	50	4	90	7	0	2	29	11	.73	18	.305	.374	.391
1994 Tulsa	AA	129	493	142	27	0	6	—	187	69	55	40	5	115	2	0	1	16	14	.53	14	.288	.343	.379
1995 Shreveport	AA	122	482	138	27	3	5	—	186	77	72	40	2	68	1	0	7	11	9	.55	18	.286	.338	.386
1996 Phoenix	AAA	113	407	138	26	7	5	—	193	56	59	18	3	80	3	0	3	15	4	.79	9	.339	.369	.474
1996 San Francisco	NL	41	118	32	2	0	2	(0 2)	40	10	12	12	2	27	0	0	0	0	2	.00	0	.271	.336	.339

Nigel Wilson

Bats: Left **Throws:** Left **Pos:** PH-6; DH-3; LF-1 **Ht:** 6'1" **Wt:** 185 **Born:** 1/12/70 **Age:** 27

		BATTING																BASERUNNING				PERCENTAGES		
Year Team	Lg	G	AB	H	2B	3B	HR	(Hm Rd)	TB	R	RBI	TBB	IBB	SO	HBP	SH	SF	SB	CS	SB%	GDP	Avg	OBP	SLG
1988 St. Cathrns	A-	40	103	21	1	2	2	—	32	12	11	12	0	32	4	1	1	8	4	.67	0	.204	.308	.311
1989 St. Cathrns	A-	42	161	35	5	2	4	—	56	17	18	11	0	50	4	1	0	8	2	.80	0	.217	.284	.348
1990 Myrtle Bch	A	110	440	120	23	9	16	—	209	77	62	30	3	71	6	2	2	22	12	.65	4	.273	.326	.475
1991 Dunedin	A+	119	455	137	18	13	12	—	217	64	55	29	4	99	9	4	7	26	11	.70	4	.301	.350	.477
1992 Knoxville	AA	137	521	143	34	7	26	—	269	85	69	33	5	137	7	2	2	13	8	.62	2	.274	.325	.516
1993 Edmonton	AAA	96	370	108	26	7	17	—	199	66	68	25	7	108	10	1	2	8	3	.73	6	.292	.351	.538
1994 Edmonton	AAA	87	314	97	24	1	12	—	159	50	62	22	3	79	10	0	4	2	3	.40	3	.309	.369	.506
1995 Indianapols	AAA	82	304	95	27	3	17	—	179	53	51	13	4	95	8	0	1	5	3	.63	2	.313	.356	.589
1996 Buffalo	AAA	128	482	144	23	6	30	—	269	88	95	50	7	117	12	1	7	4	4	.50	9	.299	.374	.558
1993 Florida	NL	7	16	0	0	0	0	(0 0)	0	0	0	0	0	11	0	0	0	0	0	.00	0	.000	.000	.000
1995 Cincinnati	NL	5	7	0	0	0	0	(0 0)	0	0	0	0	0	4	0	0	0	0	0	.00	0	.000	.000	.000
1996 Cleveland	AL	10	12	3	0	0	2	(1 1)	9	2	5	1	0	6	0	0	0	0	0	.00	0	.250	.308	.750
3 ML YEARS		22	35	3	0	0	2	(1 1)	9	2	5	1	0	21	0	0	0	0	0	.00	0	.086	.111	.257

Paul Wilson

Pitches: Right **Bats:** Right **Pos:** SP-26 **Ht:** 6'5" **Wt:** 235 **Born:** 3/28/73 **Age:** 24

		HOW MUCH HE PITCHED						WHAT HE GAVE UP												THE RESULTS						
Year Team	Lg	G	GS	CG	GF	IP	BFP	H	R	ER	HR	SH	SF	HB	TBB	IBB	SO	WP	Bk	W	L	Pct.	ShO	Sv-Op	Hld	ERA
1994 Mets	R	3	3	0	0	12	47	8	4	4	0	1	0	0	4	0	13	0	2	0	2	.000	0	0--	—	3.00
St. Lucie	A	8	8	0	0	37.1	160	32	23	21	3	0	1	3	17	1	37	0	5	0	5	.000	0	0--	—	5.06
1995 Norfolk	AAA	10	10	4	0	66.1	270	59	25	21	3	2	1	3	20	0	67	2	0	5	3	.625	2	0--	—	2.85
1996 St. Lucie	A+	2	2	0	0	8	36	6	5	3	0	0	1	0	4	0	5	0	0	0	1	.000	0	0--	—	3.38
Binghamton	AA	1	1	0	0	5	25	6	4	4	0	0	0	0	2	0	5	2	0	0	1	.000	0	0--	—	7.20
1996 New York	NL	26	26	1	0	149	677	157	102	89	15	7	3	10	71	11	109	3	3	5	12	.294	0	0-0	0	5.38

Jay Witasick

Pitches: Right **Bats:** Right **Pos:** RP-12 **Ht:** 6'4" **Wt:** 205 **Born:** 8/28/72 **Age:** 24

		HOW MUCH HE PITCHED						WHAT HE GAVE UP												THE RESULTS						
Year Team	Lg	G	GS	CG	GF	IP	BFP	H	R	ER	HR	SH	SF	HB	TBB	IBB	SO	WP	Bk	W	L	Pct.	ShO	Sv-Op	Hld	ERA
1993 Johnson Cty	R+	12	12	0	0	67.2	288	65	42	31	8	4	1	0	19	0	74	5	1	4	3	.571	0	0--	—	4.12
Savannah	A	1	1	0	0	6	27	7	3	3	0	0	0	0	2	0	8	0	0	1	0	1.000	0	0--	—	4.50
1994 Madison	A	18	18	2	0	112.1	443	74	36	29	5	5	3	2	42	0	141	5	0	10	4	.714	0	0--	—	2.32

Year Team	Lg	G	GS	CG	GF	IP	BFP	H	R	ER	HR	SH	SF	HB	TBB	IBB	SO	WP	Bk	W	L	Pct.	ShO	Sv-Op	Hld	ERA
1995 Arkansas	AA	7	7	0	0	34	161	46	29	26	4	0	0	0	16	1	26	2	0	2	4	.333	0	0- -	--	6.88
1996 Huntsville	AA	25	6	0	12	66.2	274	47	21	17	3	3	1	3	26	2	63	2	2	0	3	.000	0	4- -	--	2.30
Edmonton	AAA	6	0	0	5	8.2	39	9	4	4	1	1	1	1	6	0	9	2	0	0	0	.000	0	2- -	--	4.15
1996 Oakland	AL	12	0	0	6	13	55	12	9	9	5	0	1	0	5	0	12	2	0	1	1	.500	0	0-1	0	6.23

Bobby Witt

Pitches: Right **Bats:** Right **Pos:** SP-32; RP-1 **Ht:** 6'2" **Wt:** 205 **Born:** 5/11/64 **Age:** 33

Year Team	Lg	G	GS	CG	GF	IP	BFP	H	R	ER	HR	SH	SF	HB	TBB	IBB	SO	WP	Bk	W	L	Pct.	ShO	Sv-Op	Hld	ERA
1986 Texas	AL	31	31	0	0	157.2	741	130	104	96	18	3	9	3	143	2	174	22	3	11	9	.550	0	0- -	--	5.48
1987 Texas	AL	26	25	1	0	143	673	114	82	78	10	5	5	3	140	1	160	7	2	8	10	.444	0	0-0	0	4.91
1988 Texas	AL	22	22	13	0	174.1	736	134	83	76	13	7	6	1	101	2	148	16	8	8	10	.444	2	0-0	0	3.92
1989 Texas	AL	31	31	5	0	194.1	869	182	123	111	14	11	8	2	114	3	166	7	4	12	13	.480	1	0-0	0	5.14
1990 Texas	AL	33	32	7	1	222	954	197	98	83	12	5	6	4	110	3	221	11	2	17	10	.630	1	0-0	0	3.36
1991 Texas	AL	17	16	1	0	88.2	413	84	66	60	4	3	4	1	74	1	82	8	0	3	7	.300	1	0-0	0	6.09
1992 Tex-Oak	AL	31	31	0	0	193	848	183	99	92	16	7	10	2	114	2	125	9	1	10	14	.417	0	0-0	0	4.29
1993 Oakland	AL	35	33	5	0	220	950	226	112	103	16	9	8	3	91	5	131	8	1	14	13	.519	1	0-0	0	4.21
1994 Oakland	AL	24	24	5	0	135.2	618	151	88	76	22	2	7	5	70	4	111	6	1	8	10	.444	3	0-0	0	5.04
1995 Fla-Tex		29	29	2	0	172	748	185	87	79	12	7	5	3	68	2	141	7	0	5	11	.313	0	0-0	0	4.13
1996 Texas	AL	33	32	2	1	199.2	903	235	129	120	28	2	7	2	96	3	157	4	1	16	12	.571	0	0-0	0	5.41
1992 Texas	AL	25	25	0	0	161.1	708	152	87	80	14	5	8	2	95	1	100	6	1	9	13	.409	0	0-0	0	4.46
Oakland	AL	6	6	0	0	31.2	140	31	12	12	2	2	2	0	19	1	25	3	0	1	1	.500	0	0-0	0	3.41
1995 Florida	NL	19	19	1	0	110.2	472	104	52	48	8	5	3	2	47	1	95	2	0	2	7	.222	0	0-0	0	3.90
Texas	AL	10	10	1	0	61.1	276	81	35	31	4	2	2	1	21	1	46	5	0	3	4	.429	0	0-0	0	4.55
11 ML YEARS		312	306	41	2	1900.1	8453	1821	1071	974	165	61	75	29	1121	28	1616	105	23	112	119	.485	9	0- -	--	4.61

Mark Wohlers

Pitches: Right **Bats:** Right **Pos:** RP-77 **Ht:** 6'4" **Wt:** 207 **Born:** 1/23/70 **Age:** 27

Year Team	Lg	G	GS	CG	GF	IP	BFP	H	R	ER	HR	SH	SF	HB	TBB	IBB	SO	WP	Bk	W	L	Pct.	ShO	Sv-Op	Hld	ERA
1991 Atlanta	NL	17	0	0	4	19.2	89	17	7	7	1	2	1	2	13	3	13	0	0	3	1	.750	0	2-4	2	3.20
1992 Atlanta	NL	32	0	0	16	35.1	140	28	11	10	0	5	1	1	14	4	17	1	0	1	2	.333	0	4-6	2	2.55
1993 Atlanta	NL	46	0	0	13	48	199	37	25	24	2	5	1	1	22	3	45	0	0	6	2	.750	0	0-0	12	4.50
1994 Atlanta	NL	51	0	0	15	51	236	51	35	26	1	4	6	0	33	9	58	2	0	7	2	.778	0	1-2	1	4.59
1995 Atlanta	NL	65	0	0	49	64.2	269	51	16	15	2	2	0	1	24	3	90	4	0	7	3	.700	0	25-29	2	2.09
1996 Atlanta	NL	77	0	0	64	77.1	323	71	30	26	8	2	2	2	21	3	100	10	0	2	4	.333	0	39-44	5	3.03
6 ML YEARS		288	0	0	161	296	1256	255	124	108	14	20	11	7	127	25	323	17	0	26	14	.650	0	71-85	25	3.28

Steve Wojciechowski

Pitches: Left **Bats:** Left **Pos:** SP-15; RP-1 **Ht:** 6'2" **Wt:** 195 **Born:** 7/29/70 **Age:** 26

Year Team	Lg	G	GS	CG	GF	IP	BFP	H	R	ER	HR	SH	SF	HB	TBB	IBB	SO	WP	Bk	W	L	Pct.	ShO	Sv-Op	Hld	ERA
1991 Sou. Oregon	A-	16	11	0	1	67	311	74	45	28	4	4	2	1	29	2	50	6	1	2	5	.286	0	0- -	--	3.76
1992 Modesto	A+	14	14	0	0	66.1	282	60	32	26	2	2	3	1	27	0	53	5	2	6	3	.667	0	0- -	--	3.53
1993 Modesto	A+	14	14	1	0	84.2	341	64	29	24	3	3	2	0	36	0	52	1	1	8	2	.800	1	0- -	--	2.55
Huntsville	AA	13	13	1	0	67.2	310	91	50	40	6	1	5	2	30	1	52	5	1	4	6	.400	1	0- -	--	5.32
1994 Huntsville	AA	27	26	1	1	177	716	148	72	61	7	7	3	0	62	1	114	10	2	10	5	.667	0	0- -	--	3.10
1995 Edmonton	AAA	14	12	2	1	78	320	75	37	32	5	1	4	1	21	0	39	4	2	6	3	.667	1	0- -	--	3.69
1996 Edmonton	AAA	11	11	1	0	60.1	257	56	32	25	3	2	2	2	21	1	46	4	0	4	3	.571	1	0- -	--	3.73
1995 Oakland	AL	14	7	0	3	48.2	219	51	28	28	7	1	2	1	28	1	13	0	0	2	3	.400	0	0-0	0	5.18
1996 Oakland	AL	16	15	0	0	79.2	356	97	57	50	10	1	2	2	28	0	30	3	1	5	5	.500	0	0-0	0	5.65
2 ML YEARS		30	22	0	3	128.1	575	148	85	78	17	2	4	3	56	1	43	3	1	7	8	.467	0	0-0	0	5.47

Bob Wolcott

Pitches: Right **Bats:** Right **Pos:** SP-28; RP-2 **Ht:** 6'0" **Wt:** 190 **Born:** 9/8/73 **Age:** 23

Year Team	Lg	G	GS	CG	GF	IP	BFP	H	R	ER	HR	SH	SF	HB	TBB	IBB	SO	WP	Bk	W	L	Pct.	ShO	Sv-Op	Hld	ERA
1992 Bellingham	A-	9	7	0	2	22.1	105	25	18	17	4	0	0	2	19	0	17	3	2	0	1	.000	0	0- -	--	6.85
1993 Bellingham	A-	15	15	1	0	95.1	386	70	31	28	7	1	2	6	26	1	79	6	1	8	4	.667	0	0- -	--	2.64
1994 Calgary	AAA	1	1	0	0	6	25	6	2	2	1	0	0	0	3	0	5	0	0	0	1	.000	0	0- -	--	3.00
Riverside	A+	26	26	5	0	180.2	761	173	75	57	11	4	4	5	50	4	142	5	0	14	8	.636	1	0- -	--	2.84
1995 Port City	AA	12	12	2	0	86	320	60	26	21	8	0	3	3	13	0	53	2	0	7	3	.700	1	0- -	--	2.20
Tacoma	AAA	25	25	4	0	165.1	667	154	75	57	16	1	7	8	29	0	96	4	1	13	6	.684	2	0- -	--	3.10
1996 Lancaster	A+	1	1	0	0	6	27	9	7	7	3	0	0	0	0	0	6	0	0	1	0	1.000	0	0- -	--	10.50
Tacoma	AAA	3	3	0	0	12.1	58	17	13	10	5	0	0	1	3	0	16	1	0	0	2	.000	0	0- -	--	7.30
1995 Seattle	AL	7	6	0	0	36.2	164	43	18	18	6	0	3	2	14	0	19	0	0	3	2	.600	0	0-0	0	4.42
1996 Seattle	AL	30	28	1	0	149.1	672	179	101	95	26	5	3	7	54	5	78	3	1	7	10	.412	0	0-0	0	5.73
2 ML YEARS		37	34	1	0	186	836	222	119	113	32	5	6	9	68	5	97	3	1	10	12	.455	0	0-0	0	5.47

Tony Womack

Bats: L **Throws:** R **Pos:** PH-11; CF-5; 2B-4; RF-1   **Ht:** 5'9" **Wt:** 155 **Born:** 9/25/69 **Age:** 27

							BATTING											BASERUNNING				PERCENTAGES		
Year Team	Lg	G	AB	H	2B	3B	HR	(Hm | Rd)	TB	R	RBI	TBB	IBB	SO	HBP	SH	SF	SB	CS	SB%	GDP	Avg	OBP	SLG
1996 Calgary *	AAA	131	506	151	19	11	1	—	—	195	75	47	31	0	79	3	14	5	37	12	.76	3	.298	.339	.385
1993 Pittsburgh	NL	15	24	2	0	0	0	(0 | 0)	2	5	0	3	0	3	0	1	0	2	0	1.00	0	.083	.185	.083
1994 Pittsburgh	NL	5	12	4	0	0	0	(0 | 0)	4	4	1	2	0	3	0	0	0	0	0	.00	0	.333	.429	.333
1996 Pittsburgh	NL	17	30	10	3	1	0	(0 | 0)	15	11	7	6	0	1	1	3	0	2	0	1.00	0	.333	.459	.500
3 ML YEARS		37	66	16	3	1	0	(0 | 0)	21	20	8	11	0	7	1	4	0	4	0	1.00	0	.242	.359	.318

Brad Woodall

Pitches: Left **Bats:** Both **Pos:** RP-5; SP-3   **Ht:** 6'0" **Wt:** 175 **Born:** 6/25/69 **Age:** 28

		HOW MUCH HE PITCHED						WHAT HE GAVE UP										THE RESULTS						
Year Team	Lg	G	GS	CG	GF	IP	BFP	H	R	ER	HR	SH	SF	HB	TBB	IBB	SO	WP	Bk	W	L	Pct.	ShO	Sv-Op	Hld	ERA
1991 Idaho Falls	R+	28	0	0	23	39.1	160	29	9	6	1	2	1	0	19	1	57	7	1	4	1	.800	0	11--	—	1.37
Durham	A+	4	0	0	2	7.1	29	4	3	2	1	0	0	0	4	0	14	0	0	0	0	.000	0	0--	—	2.45
1992 Durham	A+	24	0	0	16	42.1	163	30	11	10	3	3	1	1	11	1	51	1	2	1	2	.333	0	4--	—	2.13
Greenville	AA	21	1	0	10	39.1	155	26	15	14	1	0	2	0	17	2	45	4	0	3	4	.429	0	1--	—	3.20
1993 Durham	A+	6	5	1	0	30	120	21	10	10	2	0	1	2	6	1	27	4	0	3	1	.750	1	0--	—	3.00
Greenville	AA	8	7	1	1	53.1	220	43	24	20	1	6	0	2	24	0	38	6	1	2	4	.333	0	0--	—	3.38
Richmond	AAA	10	9	0	0	57.2	246	59	32	27	6	1	2	1	16	0	45	1	0	5	3	.625	0	0--	—	4.21
1994 Richmond	AAA	27	27	4	0	185.2	750	159	62	50	14	7	0	2	49	2	137	7	0	15	6	.714	3	0--	—	2.42
1995 Richmond	AAA	13	11	0	1	65.1	279	70	39	37	5	6	0	3	17	1	44	1	0	4	4	.500	0	0--	—	5.10
1996 Richmond	AAA	21	21	5	0	133.1	555	124	59	50	10	7	3	1	36	1	74	3	0	9	7	.563	1	0--	—	3.38
1994 Atlanta	NL	1	1	0	0	6	24	5	3	3	2	0	0	0	2	0	2	0	0	0	1	.000	0	0-0	0	4.50
1995 Atlanta	NL	9	0	0	3	10.1	52	13	10	7	1	1	1	0	8	1	5	1	0	1	1	.500	0	0-0	0	6.10
1996 Atlanta	NL	8	3	0	2	19.2	91	28	19	16	4	1	2	0	4	0	20	1	0	2	2	.500	0	0-0	0	7.32
3 ML YEARS		18	4	0	5	36	167	46	32	26	7	2	3	0	14	1	27	2	0	3	4	.429	0	0-0	0	6.50

Tim Worrell

Pitches: Right **Bats:** Right **Pos:** RP-39; SP-11   **Ht:** 6'4" **Wt:** 220 **Born:** 7/5/67 **Age:** 29

		HOW MUCH HE PITCHED						WHAT HE GAVE UP										THE RESULTS						
Year Team	Lg	G	GS	CG	GF	IP	BFP	H	R	ER	HR	SH	SF	HB	TBB	IBB	SO	WP	Bk	W	L	Pct.	ShO	Sv-Op	Hld	ERA
1993 San Diego	NL	21	16	0	1	100.2	443	104	63	55	11	8	5	0	43	5	52	3	0	2	7	.222	0	0-0	1	4.92
1994 San Diego	NL	3	3	0	0	14.2	59	9	7	6	0	0	1	0	5	0	14	0	0	0	1	.000	0	0-0	0	3.68
1995 San Diego	NL	9	3	0	4	13.1	63	16	7	7	2	1	0	1	6	0	13	1	0	1	0	1.000	0	0-0	0	4.73
1996 San Diego	NL	50	11	0	8	121	510	109	45	41	9	3	1	6	39	1	99	0	0	9	7	.563	0	1-2	10	3.05
4 ML YEARS		83	30	0	13	249.2	1075	238	122	109	22	12	7	7	93	6	178	4	0	12	15	.444	0	1-2	11	3.93

Todd Worrell

Pitches: Right **Bats:** Right **Pos:** RP-72   **Ht:** 6'5" **Wt:** 227 **Born:** 9/28/59 **Age:** 37

		HOW MUCH HE PITCHED						WHAT HE GAVE UP										THE RESULTS						
Year Team	Lg	G	GS	CG	GF	IP	BFP	H	R	ER	HR	SH	SF	HB	TBB	IBB	SO	WP	Bk	W	L	Pct.	ShO	Sv-Op	Hld	ERA
1985 St. Louis	NL	17	0	0	11	21.2	88	17	7	7	2	0	2	0	7	2	17	2	0	3	0	1.000	0	5--	—	2.91
1986 St. Louis	NL	74	0	0	60	103.2	430	86	29	24	9	7	6	1	41	16	73	1	0	9	10	.474	0	36--	—	2.08
1987 St. Louis	NL	75	0	0	54	94.2	395	86	29	28	8	4	2	0	34	11	92	1	0	8	6	.571	0	33-43	6	2.66
1988 St. Louis	NL	68	0	0	54	90	366	69	32	30	7	3	5	1	34	14	78	6	2	5	9	.357	0	32-41	1	3.00
1989 St. Louis	NL	47	0	0	39	51.2	219	42	21	17	4	3	1	0	26	13	41	3	3	3	5	.375	0	20-23	3	2.96
1992 St. Louis	NL	67	0	0	14	64	256	45	15	15	4	3	0	1	25	5	64	1	1	5	3	.625	0	3-7	25	2.11
1993 Los Angeles	NL	35	0	0	22	38.2	167	46	28	26	6	3	6	0	11	1	31	1	0	1	1	.500	0	5-8	4	6.05
1994 Los Angeles	NL	38	0	0	27	42	173	37	21	20	4	1	2	1	12	1	44	1	0	6	5	.545	0	11-19	1	4.29
1995 Los Angeles	NL	59	0	0	53	62.1	249	50	15	14	4	1	2	1	19	2	61	2	0	4	1	.800	0	32-36	1	2.02
1996 Los Angeles	NL	72	0	0	67	65.1	285	70	29	22	5	2	2	2	15	1	66	4	1	4	6	.400	0	44-53	0	3.03
10 ML YEARS		552	0	0	401	634	2628	548	226	203	53	27	28	7	224	66	567	22	7	48	46	.511	0	221--	—	2.88

Craig Worthington

Bats: Right **Throws:** Right **Pos:** 3B-7; 1B-6; PH-2   **Ht:** 6'0" **Wt:** 200 **Born:** 4/17/65 **Age:** 32

							BATTING											BASERUNNING				PERCENTAGES		
Year Team	Lg	G	AB	H	2B	3B	HR	(Hm	Rd)	TB	R	RBI	TBB	IBB	SO	HBP	SH	SF	SB	CS	SB%	GDP	Avg	OBP	SLG
1996 Okla. City *	AAA	15	53	14	2	0	1	—	—	19	5	4	5	0	6	0	0	0	0	0	.00	2	.264	.328	.358
1988 Baltimore	AL	26	81	15	2	0	2	(0	2)	23	5	4	9	0	24	0	0	0	1	0	1.00	6	.185	.267	.284
1989 Baltimore	AL	145	497	123	23	0	15	(12	3)	191	57	70	61	2	114	4	3	1	1	2	.33	10	.247	.334	.384
1990 Baltimore	AL	133	425	96	17	0	8	(3	5)	137	46	44	63	2	96	3	7	3	1	2	.33	13	.226	.328	.322
1991 Baltimore	AL	31	102	23	4	0	4	(1	3)	38	11	12	12	0	14	1	1	0	0	0	.00	3	.225	.313	.373
1992 Cleveland	AL	9	24	4	0	0	0	(0	0)	4	0	2	2	0	4	0	0	0	0	1	.00	0	.167	.231	.167
1995 Cin-Tex	AL	36	86	20	5	0	3	(1	2)	34	5	8	9	0	9	0	2	0	0	0	.00	6	.233	.305	.395
1996 Texas	AL	13	19	3	0	0	1	(1	0)	6	2	4	0	0	3	0	0	0	0	0	.00	1	.158	.333	.316
1995 Cincinnati	NL	10	18	5	1	0	1	(0	1)	9	1	7	1	0	0	0	0	0	0	0	.00	0	.278	.350	.500
Texas	AL	26	68	15	4	0	2	(1	1)	25	4	6	7	0	8	0	2	0	0	0	.00	6	.221	.293	.368
7 ML YEARS		393	1234	284	50	0	33	(18	15)	433	126	144	162	4	264	8	13	6	3	6	.33	35	.230	.322	.351

Jamey Wright

Pitches: Right **Bats:** Right **Pos:** SP-15; RP-1   **Ht:** 6'5" **Wt:** 203 **Born:** 12/24/74 **Age:** 22

		HOW MUCH HE PITCHED						WHAT HE GAVE UP												THE RESULTS						
Year Team	Lg	G	GS	CG	GF	IP	BFP	H	R	ER	HR	SH	SF	HB	TBB	IBB	SO	WP	Bk	W	L	Pct.	ShO	Sv-Op	Hld	ERA
1993 Rockies	R	8	8	0	0	36	158	35	19	16	1	0	0	5	9	0	26	7	0	1	3	.250	0	0--	—	4.00
1994 Asheville	A	28	27	2	0	143.1	655	188	107	95	6	5	4	16	59	1	103	9	5	7	14	.333	0	0--	—	5.97
1995 New Haven	AA	1	1	0	0	3	20	6	6	3	0	0	0	1	3	0	0	0	0	0	1	.000	0	0--	—	9.00
1996 New Haven	AA	7	7	1	0	44.2	167	27	7	4	0	3	0	2	12	0	54	1	1	5	1	.833	1	0--	—	0.81
Colo. Sprng	AAA	9	9	0	0	59.2	246	53	20	18	3	0	1	2	22	0	40	1	0	4	2	.667	0	0--	—	2.72
1996 Colorado	NL	16	15	0	0	91.1	406	105	60	50	8	4	2	7	41	1	45	1	2	4	4	.500	0	0-0	1	4.93

Esteban Yan

Pitches: Right **Bats:** Right **Pos:** RP-4   **Ht:** 6'4" **Wt:** 230 **Born:** 6/22/74 **Age:** 23

		HOW MUCH HE PITCHED						WHAT HE GAVE UP												THE RESULTS						
Year Team	Lg	G	GS	CG	GF	IP	BFP	H	R	ER	HR	SH	SF	HB	TBB	IBB	SO	WP	Bk	W	L	Pct.	ShO	Sv-Op	Hld	ERA
1993 Danville	R+	14	14	0	0	71.1	324	73	46	24	4	3	3	5	24	1	50	3	0	4	7	.364	0	0--	—	3.03
1994 Macon	A	28	28	4	0	170.2	696	155	85	62	15	4	3	13	34	1	121	4	6	11	12	.478	3	0--	—	3.27
1995 W. Palm Bch	A+	24	21	1	1	137.2	580	139	63	47	3	7	5	10	33	0	89	8	3	6	8	.429	0	1--	—	3.07
1996 Bowie	AA	9	1	0	3	16	75	18	12	10	2	1	1	0	8	0	16	1	1	0	2	.000	0	0--	—	5.63
Rochester	AAA	22	10	0	3	71.2	306	75	37	34	6	3	4	2	18	0	61	0	0	5	4	.556	0	1--	—	4.27
1996 Baltimore	AL	4	0	0	2	9.1	42	13	7	6	3	0	0	0	3	1	7	0	0	0	0	.000	0	0-0	0	5.79

Anthony Young

Pitches: Right **Bats:** Right **Pos:** RP-28   **Ht:** 6'2" **Wt:** 220 **Born:** 1/19/66 **Age:** 31

		HOW MUCH HE PITCHED						WHAT HE GAVE UP												THE RESULTS						
Year Team	Lg	G	GS	CG	GF	IP	BFP	H	R	ER	HR	SH	SF	HB	TBB	IBB	SO	WP	Bk	W	L	Pct.	ShO	Sv-Op	Hld	ERA
1996 Tucson *	AAA	4	1	0	0	4.2	22	3	3	2	1	0	0	0	5	2	3	0	0	1	0	1.000	0	0--	—	3.86
1991 New York	NL	10	8	0	2	49.1	202	48	20	17	4	1	1	1	12	1	20	1	0	2	5	.286	0	0-0	—	3.10
1992 New York	NL	52	13	1	26	121	517	134	66	56	8	11	4	1	31	5	64	3	1	2	14	.125	0	15-20	2	4.17
1993 New York	NL	39	10	1	19	100.1	445	103	62	42	8	11	3	1	42	9	62	0	2	1	16	.059	0	3-5	2	3.77
1994 Chicago	NL	20	19	0	0	114.2	474	103	57	50	12	6	3	0	46	2	65	4	1	4	6	.400	0	0-0	—	3.92
1995 Chicago	NL	32	1	0	8	41.1	181	47	20	17	5	1	0	3	14	2	15	6	0	3	4	.429	0	2-2	3	3.70
1996 Houston	NL	28	0	0	10	33.1	158	36	18	17	4	2	1	4	22	4	19	2	2	3	3	.500	0	0-1	2	4.59
6 ML YEARS		181	51	2	65	460	1977	471	243	199	41	32	12	10	167	23	245	16	5	15	48	.238	0	20-28	9	3.89

Dmitri Young

Bats: Both **Throws:** Right **Pos:** 1B-10; PH-8   **Ht:** 6'2" **Wt:** 240 **Born:** 10/11/73 **Age:** 23

		BATTING																BASERUNNING				PERCENTAGES		
Year Team	Lg	G	AB	H	2B	3B	HR	(Hm	Rd)	TB	R	RBI	TBB	IBB	SO	HBP	SH	SF	SB	CS	SB%	GDP	Avg	OBP	SLG
1991 Johnson Cty	R+	37	129	33	10	0	2	—	—	49	22	22	21	1	28	2	0	2	2	1	.67	1	.256	.364	.380
1992 Springfield	A	135	493	153	36	6	14	—	—	243	74	72	51	3	94	5	0	4	14	13	.52	9	.310	.378	.493
1993 St. Pete	A+	69	270	85	13	3	5	—	—	119	31	43	24	3	28	2	0	5	3	4	.43	7	.315	.369	.441
Arkansas	AA	45	166	41	11	2	3	—	—	65	13	21	9	1	29	2	0	4	4	4	.50	5	.247	.294	.392
1994 Arkansas	AA	125	453	123	33	2	8	—	—	184	53	54	36	14	60	5	1	3	0	3	.00	6	.272	.330	.406
1995 Arkansas	AA	97	367	107	18	6	10	—	—	167	54	62	30	3	46	3	0	3	2	4	.33	11	.292	.347	.455
Louisville	AAA	2	7	2	0	0	0	—	—	2	3	0	1	0	1	0	0	0	0	0	.00	0	.286	.375	.286
1996 Louisville	AAA	122	459	153	31	8	15	—	—	245	90	64	34	8	67	1	0	3	16	5	.76	5	.333	.378	.534
1996 St. Louis	NL	16	29	7	0	0	0	(0	0)	7	3	2	4	0	5	1	0	0	0	1	.00	1	.241	.353	.241

Eric Young

Bats: Right **Throws:** Right **Pos:** 2B-139; PH-5   **Ht:** 5'9" **Wt:** 170 **Born:** 5/18/67 **Age:** 30

		BATTING																BASERUNNING				PERCENTAGES		
Year Team	Lg	G	AB	H	2B	3B	HR	(Hm	Rd)	TB	R	RBI	TBB	IBB	SO	HBP	SH	SF	SB	CS	SB%	GDP	Avg	OBP	SLG
1996 New Haven *	AA	3	15	1	0	0	0	—	—	1	0	0	3	0	3	0	0	0	0	0	.00	0	.067	.067	.067
Salem *	A+	3	10	3	3	0	0	—	—	6	2	0	3	0	1	0	0	0	2	0	1.00	0	.300	.462	.600
Colo. Sprng *	AAA	7	23	6	1	1	0	—	—	9	4	3	5	0	1	0	0	0	0	0	.00	—	.261	.393	.391
1992 Los Angeles	NL	49	132	34	1	0	1	(0	1)	38	9	11	8	0	9	0	4	0	6	1	.86	9	.258	.300	.288
1993 Colorado	NL	144	490	132	16	8	3	(3	0)	173	82	42	63	3	41	4	4	4	42	19	.69	9	.269	.355	.353
1994 Colorado	NL	90	228	62	13	1	7	(6	1)	98	37	30	38	1	17	2	5	2	18	7	.72	3	.272	.378	.430
1995 Colorado	NL	120	366	116	21	9	6	(5	1)	173	68	36	49	3	29	5	3	1	35	12	.74	4	.317	.404	.473
1996 Colorado	NL	141	568	184	23	4	8	(7	1)	239	113	74	47	1	31	21	2	5	53	19	.74	9	.324	.393	.421
5 ML YEARS		544	1784	528	74	22	25	(21	4)	721	309	193	205	8	127	32	18	12	154	58	.73	28	.296	.376	.404

Ernie Young

Bats: R **Throws:** R **Pos:** CF-133; RF-17; LF-8; PH-8   **Ht:** 6'1" **Wt:** 190 **Born:** 7/8/69 **Age:** 27

		BATTING																BASERUNNING				PERCENTAGES		
Year Team	Lg	G	AB	H	2B	3B	HR	(Hm	Rd)	TB	R	RBI	TBB	IBB	SO	HBP	SH	SF	SB	CS	SB%	GDP	Avg	OBP	SLG
1994 Oakland	AL	11	30	2	1	0	0	(0	0)	3	2	3	1	0	8	0	0	0	0	0	.00	1	.067	.097	.100
1995 Oakland	AL	26	50	10	3	0	2	(2	0)	19	9	5	8	0	12	0	0	0	0	0	.00	0	.200	.310	.380

Year Team	Lg	G	AB	H	2B	3B	HR	(Hm	Rd)	TB	R	RBI	TBB	IBB	SO	HBP	SH	SF	SB	CS	SB%	GDP	Avg	OBP	SLG
1996 Oakland	AL	141	462	112	19	4	19	(10	9)	196	72	64	52	1	118	7	3	4	7	5	.58	13	.242	.326	.424
3 ML YEARS		178	542	124	23	4	21	(12	9)	218	83	72	61	1	138	7	3	4	7	5	.58	15	.229	.313	.402

Kevin Young

Bats: R **Throws:** R **Pos:** 1B-27; PH-20; RF-15; 3B-7; DH-2; LF-2   **Ht:** 6'2" **Wt:** 219 **Born:** 6/16/69 **Age:** 28

Year Team	Lg	G	AB	H	2B	3B	HR	(Hm	Rd)	TB	R	RBI	TBB	IBB	SO	HBP	SH	SF	SB	CS	SB%	GDP	Avg	OBP	SLG
1996 Omaha *	AAA	50	186	57	11	1	13	—	—	109	29	46	12	5	41	4	0	2	3	0	1.00	2	.306	.358	.586
1992 Pittsburgh	NL	10	7	4	0	0	0	(0	0)	4	2	4	2	0	0	0	0	0	1	0	1.00	0	.571	.667	.571
1993 Pittsburgh	NL	141	449	106	24	3	6	(6	0)	154	38	47	36	3	82	9	5	9	2	2	.50	10	.236	.300	.343
1994 Pittsburgh	NL	59	122	25	7	2	1	(1	0)	39	15	11	8	2	34	1	2	1	0	2	.00	3	.205	.258	.320
1995 Pittsburgh	NL	56	181	42	9	0	6	(5	1)	69	13	22	8	0	53	2	1	3	1	3	.25	5	.232	.268	.381
1996 Kansas City	AL	55	132	32	6	0	8	(4	4)	62	20	23	11	0	32	0	0	0	3	3	.50	2	.242	.301	.470
5 ML YEARS		321	891	209	46	5	21	(16	5)	328	88	107	65	5	201	12	8	13	7	10	.41	20	.235	.292	.368

Greg Zaun

Bats: Both **Throws:** Right **Pos:** C-59; PH-1   **Ht:** 5'10" **Wt:** 170 **Born:** 4/14/71 **Age:** 26

Year Team	Lg	G	AB	H	2B	3B	HR	(Hm	Rd)	TB	R	RBI	TBB	IBB	SO	HBP	SH	SF	SB	CS	SB%	GDP	Avg	OBP	SLG
1990 Wausau	A	37	100	13	0	1	1	—	—	18	3	7	7	0	17	1	2	0	0	0	.00	2	.130	.194	.180
Bluefield	R+	61	184	57	5	2	2	—	—	72	29	21	23	1	15	1	0	1	5	5	.50	2	.310	.388	.391
1991 Kane County	A	113	409	112	17	5	4	—	—	151	67	51	50	1	41	2	3	4	4	4	.50	10	.274	.353	.369
1992 Frederick	A+	108	383	96	18	6	6	—	—	144	54	52	42	0	45	3	1	7	3	5	.38	10	.251	.324	.376
1993 Bowie	AA	79	258	79	10	0	3	—	—	98	25	38	27	4	26	1	0	1	4	7	.36	7	.306	.373	.380
Rochester	AAA	21	78	20	4	2	1	—	—	31	10	11	6	0	11	0	0	2	0	0	.00	1	.256	.302	.397
1994 Rochester	AAA	123	388	92	16	4	7	—	—	137	61	43	56	2	72	4	3	3	4	2	.67	5	.237	.337	.353
1995 Rochester	AAA	42	140	41	13	1	6	—	—	74	26	18	14	2	21	3	0	1	0	3	.00	0	.293	.367	.529
1996 Rochester	AAA	14	47	15	2	0	0	—	—	17	11	4	11	1	6	0	0	1	0	2	.00	0	.319	.441	.362
1995 Baltimore	AL	40	104	27	5	0	3	(1	2)	41	18	14	16	0	14	0	2	0	1	1	.50	2	.260	.358	.394
1996 Bal-Fla		60	139	34	9	1	2	(1	1)	51	20	15	14	3	20	2	1	2	1	0	1.00	5	.245	.318	.367
1996 Baltimore	AL	50	108	25	8	1	1	(1	0)	38	16	13	11	2	15	2	0	2	0	0	.00	3	.231	.309	.352
Florida	NL	10	31	9	1	0	1	(0	1)	13	4	2	3	1	5	0	1	0	1	0	1.00	2	.290	.353	.419
2 ML YEARS		100	243	61	14	1	5	(2	3)	92	38	29	30	3	34	2	3	2	2	1	.67	7	.251	.336	.379

Todd Zeile

Bats: Right **Throws:** Right **Pos:** 3B-135; 1B-28   **Ht:** 6'1" **Wt:** 200 **Born:** 9/9/65 **Age:** 31

Year Team	Lg	G	AB	H	2B	3B	HR	(Hm	Rd)	TB	R	RBI	TBB	IBB	SO	HBP	SH	SF	SB	CS	SB%	GDP	Avg	OBP	SLG
1989 St. Louis	NL	28	82	21	3	1	1	(0	1)	29	7	8	9	1	14	0	1	1	0	0	.00	1	.256	.326	.354
1990 St. Louis	NL	144	495	121	25	3	15	(8	7)	197	62	57	67	3	77	2	0	6	2	4	.33	11	.244	.333	.398
1991 St. Louis	NL	155	565	158	36	3	11	(7	4)	233	76	81	62	3	94	5	0	6	17	11	.61	15	.280	.353	.412
1992 St. Louis	NL	126	439	113	18	4	7	(4	3)	160	51	48	68	4	70	0	0	7	7	10	.41	11	.257	.352	.364
1993 St. Louis	NL	157	571	158	36	1	17	(8	9)	247	82	103	70	5	76	0	0	6	5	4	.56	15	.277	.352	.433
1994 St. Louis	NL	113	415	111	25	1	19	(9	10)	195	62	75	52	3	56	3	0	7	1	3	.25	13	.267	.348	.470
1995 StL-ChN	NL	113	426	105	22	0	14	(8	6)	169	50	52	34	1	76	4	4	5	1	0	1.00	13	.246	.305	.397
1996 Phi-Bal		163	617	162	32	0	25	(10	15)	269	78	99	82	4	104	1	0	4	1	1	.50	18	.263	.348	.436
1995 St. Louis	NL	34	127	37	6	0	5	(2	3)	58	16	22	18	1	23	1	0	2	1	0	1.00	2	.291	.378	.457
Chicago	NL	79	299	68	16	0	9	(6	3)	111	34	30	16	0	53	3	4	3	0	0	.00	11	.227	.271	.371
1996 Philadelphia	NL	134	500	134	24	0	20	(9	11)	218	61	80	67	4	88	1	0	4	1	1	.50	16	.268	.353	.436
Baltimore	AL	29	117	28	8	0	5	(1	4)	51	17	19	15	0	16	0	0	0	0	0	.00	2	.239	.326	.436
8 ML YEARS		999	3610	949	197	13	109	(54	55)	1499	468	523	444	24	567	15	5	42	34	33	.51	97	.263	.342	.415

Jon Zuber

Bats: Left **Throws:** Left **Pos:** 1B-22; PH-10   **Ht:** 6'0" **Wt:** 190 **Born:** 12/10/69 **Age:** 27

Year Team	Lg	G	AB	H	2B	3B	HR	(Hm	Rd)	TB	R	RBI	TBB	IBB	SO	HBP	SH	SF	SB	CS	SB%	GDP	Avg	OBP	SLG
1992 Batavia	A-	22	88	30	6	3	1	—	—	45	14	21	9	1	11	1	0	1	1	1	.50	1	.341	.404	.511
Spartanburg	A	54	206	59	13	1	3	—	—	83	24	36	33	1	31	1	0	1	3	1	.75	6	.286	.386	.403
1993 Clearwater	A+	129	494	152	37	5	5	—	—	214	70	69	49	5	47	0	3	4	6	6	.50	15	.308	.367	.433
1994 Reading	AA	138	498	146	29	5	9	—	—	212	81	70	71	4	71	1	1	5	2	4	.33	11	.293	.379	.426
1995 Scranton-WB	AAA	119	418	120	19	5	3	—	—	158	53	50	49	2	68	0	1	2	1	2	.33	12	.287	.360	.378
1996 Scranton-WB	AAA	118	412	128	22	5	4	—	—	172	62	59	58	3	50	1	2	4	4	2	.67	15	.311	.394	.417
1996 Philadelphia	NL	30	91	23	4	0	1	(1	0)	30	7	10	6	1	11	0	1	1	1	0	1.00	3	.253	.296	.330

1996 Team Statistics

We're always trying to make the *Handbook* more complete, so you'll be pleased to note we've greatly expanded the Team Statistics section this year. We've added a whole new page of breakdowns for each league showing won-lost records by month, division, in one-run games, and numerous other categories. We've also added a number of new stats to our traditional team stats pages—things like opponents' batting average, on-base and slugging, plus a number of new fielding stats including outfield assists, fielding and throwing errors, and pitcher/catcher pickoffs. Now you'll know more than ever about your favorite team.

1996 American League Final Standings

Overall

EAST				CENTRAL				WEST			
Team	W-L	Pct	GB	Team	W-L	Pct	GB	Team	W-L	Pct	GB
New York Yankees	92-70	.568	—	Cleveland Indians	99-62	.615	—	Texas Rangers	90-72	.556	—
Baltimore Orioles*	88-74	.543	4	Chicago White Sox	85-77	.525	14.5	Seattle Mariners	85-76	.528	4.5
Boston Red Sox	85-77	.525	7	Milwaukee Brewers	80-82	.494	19.5	Oakland Athletics	78-84	.481	12
Toronto Blue Jays	74-88	.457	18	Minnesota Twins	78-84	.481	21.5	California Angels	70-91	.435	19.5
Detroit Tigers	53-109	.327	39	Kansas City Royals	75-86	.466	24				

* represents playoff wild-card berth

East Division

Team	AT		VERSUS					CONDITIONS					RUNS		MONTHLY						ALL-STAR	
	Home	Road	East	Cent	West	LHS	RHS	Grass	Turf	Day	Night	XInn	1-R	5+R	Mar/Apr	May	June	July	Aug	Sep/Oct	Pre	Post
New York	49-31	43-39	32-20	37-24	23-26	21-24	71-46	82-60	10-10	38-22	54-48	4-6	25-16	25-22	13-10	16-11	18-11	16-10	13-17	16-11	52-33	40-37
Baltimore	43-38	45-36	29-23	34-26	25-25	30-25	58-49	76-67	12-7	28-26	60-48	10-8	25-18	29-24	14-12	14-10	14-14	11-16	19-11	16-11	46-39	42-35
Boston	47-34	38-43	33-19	23-37	29-21	26-19	59-58	76-67	9-10	22-29	63-48	8-12	20-19	25-25	7-19	14-12	13-14	13-13	22-9	16-10	36-49	49-28
Toronto	35-46	39-42	22-30	30-32	22-26	25-29	49-59	32-37	42-51	25-31	49-57	7-10	19-22	22-20	11-14	13-15	12-15	13-14	14-15	11-15	38-49	36-39
Detroit	27-54	26-55	14-38	19-42	20-29	14-22	39-87	45-99	8-10	21-38	32-71	4-9	12-21	16-47	9-18	4-23	10-17	12-14	14-15	4-22	27-61	26-48

Central Division

Team	AT		VERSUS					CONDITIONS					RUNS		MONTHLY						ALL-STAR	
	Home	Road	East	Cent	West	LHS	RHS	Grass	Turf	Day	Night	XInn	1-R	5+R	Mar/Apr	May	June	July	Aug	Sep/Oct	Pre	Post
Cleveland	51-29	48-33	40-20	32-20	27-22	28-23	71-39	85-57	14-5	30-21	69-41	6-9	28-20	33-15	16-8	19-9	14-14	16-11	15-13	19-7	52-35	47-27
Chicago	44-37	41-40	37-25	24-28	24-24	24-20	61-57	77-67	8-10	30-25	55-52	12-11	25-34	27-16	15-9	17-10	14-14	12-15	15-15	12-13	50-37	35-40
Milwaukee	38-43	42-39	27-33	31-21	22-28	19-23	61-59	70-73	10-9	30-31	50-51	11-6	24-18	25-26	12-12	11-16	17-11	12-16	14-16	14-11	43-43	37-39
Minnesota	39-43	39-41	30-31	21-31	27-22	20-18	58-66	30-37	48-47	27-24	51-60	9-4	22-18	25-25	13-12	10-16	15-13	13-14	16-14	11-15	41-45	37-39
Kansas City	37-43	38-43	27-34	22-30	26-22	21-36	54-50	66-76	9-10	15-29	60-57	10-6	14-26	20-25	9-18	15-12	10-17	14-13	14-15	13-11	38-50	37-36

West Division

Team	AT		VERSUS					CONDITIONS					RUNS		MONTHLY						ALL-STAR	
	Home	Road	East	Cent	West	LHS	RHS	Grass	Turf	Day	Night	XInn	1-R	5+R	Mar/Apr	May	June	July	Aug	Sep/Oct	Pre	Post
Texas	50-31	40-41	42-20	30-31	18-21	28-28	62-44	81-62	9-10	27-16	63-56	5-7	20-21	31-20	16-10	18-9	14-13	13-14	16-12	13-14	51-36	39-36
Seattle	43-38	42-38	31-30	31-30	23-16	23-17	62-59	33-35	52-41	24-23	61-53	7-4	21-22	31-21	15-10	12-14	14-12	16-12	12-17	15-11	46-39	39-37
Oakland	40-41	38-43	24-38	32-29	22-17	18-22	60-62	69-74	9-10	38-31	40-53	9-11	19-23	25-31	13-12	11-16	14-15	17-10	11-19	12-12	43-45	35-39
California	43-38	27-53	30-31	25-36	15-24	23-27	47-64	66-77	4-14	17-26	53-65	8-7	26-22	17-34	13-12	13-14	15-14	10-16	11-18	8-17	43-45	27-46

Team vs. Team Breakdown

	Bal	Bos	Cal	ChA	Cle	Det	KC	Mil	Min	NYA	Oak	Sea	Tex	Tor
Baltimore Orioles	—	7	6	4	5	11	9	9	7	3	9	7	3	8
Boston Red Sox	6	—	8	6	1	12	3	7	6	7	8	7	6	8
California Angels	6	4	—	6	4	6	4	7	4	7	6	5	4	7
Chicago White Sox	8	6	6	—	5	10	7	6	6	6	5	5	8	7
Cleveland Indians	7	11	9	8	—	12	7	7	10	3	6	8	4	7
Detroit Tigers	2	1	6	3	0	—	6	4	6	5	4	6	4	6
Kansas City Royals	3	9	8	6	6	6	—	4	6	4	5	7	6	5
Milwaukee Brewers	3	5	5	7	6	8	9	—	9	6	7	4	6	5
Minnesota Twins	5	6	8	7	3	6	7	4	—	5	6	6	7	8
New York Yankees	10	6	6	7	9	8	8	6	7	—	9	3	5	8
Oakland Athletics	4	5	7	7	6	8	7	5	7	3	—	8	7	4
Seattle Mariners	5	6	8	7	4	6	5	9	6	9	5	—	10	5
Texas Rangers	10	6	9	4	8	9	6	7	5	7	6	3	—	10
Toronto Blue Jays	5	5	5	5	7	8	7	7	5	5	8	7	2	—

(read wins across and losses down)

1996 National League Final Standings

Overall

EAST				CENTRAL				WEST			
Team	W-L	Pct	GB	Team	W-L	Pct	GB	Team	W-L	Pct	GB
Atlanta Braves	96-66	.593	—	St. Louis Cardinals	88-74	.543	—	San Diego Padres	91-71	.562	—
Montreal Expos	88-74	.543	8	Houston Astros	82-80	.506	6	Los Angeles Dodgers*	90-72	.556	1
Florida Marlins	80-82	.494	16	Cincinnati Reds	81-81	.500	7	Colorado Rockies	83-79	.512	8
New York Mets	71-91	.438	25	Chicago Cubs	76-86	.469	12	San Francisco Giants	68-94	.420	23
Philadelphia Phillies	67-95	.414	29	Pittsburgh Pirates	73-89	.451	15				

* represents playoff wild-card berth

East Division

	AT		VERSUS					CONDITIONS					RUNS		MONTHLY						ALL-STAR	
Team	Home	Road	East	Cent	West	LHS	RHS	Grass	Turf	Day	Night	XInn	1-R	5+R	Mar/Apr	May	June	July	Aug	Sep/Oct	Pre	Post
Atlanta	56-25	40-41	32-20	38-23	26-23	24-18	72-48	79-52	17-14	30-22	66-44	6-8	26-26	26-15	16-11	19-6	15-13	15-11	19-10	12-15	54-33	42-33
Montreal	50-31	38-43	24-28	39-22	25-24	17-17	71-57	24-33	64-41	26-22	62-52	7-5	33-23	22-18	17-9	14-14	16-10	11-15	14-14	16-12	49-38	39-36
Florida	52-29	28-53	25-27	33-27	22-28	20-12	60-70	68-63	12-19	16-32	64-50	9-8	26-23	22-22	11-16	16-11	12-14	10-17	16-13	15-11	40-47	40-35
New York	42-39	29-52	25-27	28-33	18-31	13-25	58-66	57-74	14-17	26-32	45-59	8-8	23-35	18-16	11-13	11-17	15-13	15-13	8-20	11-15	41-46	30-45
Philadelphia	35-46	32-49	24-28	21-40	22-27	15-16	52-79	21-35	46-60	24-23	43-72	4-4	25-22	12-25	13-11	13-15	6-21	11-16	11-19	13-13	37-49	30-46

Central Division

	AT		VERSUS					CONDITIONS					RUNS		MONTHLY						ALL-STAR	
Team	Home	Road	East	Cent	West	LHS	RHS	Grass	Turf	Day	Night	XInn	1-R	5+R	Mar/Apr	May	June	July	Aug	Sep/Oct	Pre	Post
St. Louis	48-33	40-41	29-32	37-15	22-27	16-19	72-55	70-60	18-14	27-27	61-47	8-6	30-25	28-18	12-15	12-14	17-10	15-11	15-15	17-9	46-41	42-33
Houston	48-33	34-47	33-28	24-28	25-24	19-13	63-67	20-35	62-45	29-27	53-53	9-10	28-23	19-23	13-14	14-14	15-12	15-12	17-11	8-17	47-42	35-38
Cincinnati	46-35	35-46	27-33	25-27	29-21	18-20	63-61	23-33	58-48	26-25	55-56	7-8	21-22	20-21	9-16	10-12	17-11	16-12	15-11	14-13	39-43	42-38
Chicago	43-38	33-48	31-30	19-33	26-23	15-15	61-71	66-64	10-22	43-52	33-34	8-11	21-34	19-24	13-14	9-17	16-11	14-12	15-13	9-19	41-46	35-40
Pittsburgh	36-44	37-45	25-36	25-27	23-26	17-19	56-70	28-29	45-60	23-29	50-60	7-9	13-27	19-28	12-14	9-18	15-12	12-15	8-20	17-10	39-48	34-41

West Division

	AT		VERSUS					CONDITIONS					RUNS		MONTHLY						ALL-STAR	
Team	Home	Road	East	Cent	West	LHS	RHS	Grass	Turf	Day	Night	XInn	1-R	5+R	Mar/Apr	May	June	July	Aug	Sep/Oct	Pre	Post
San Diego	45-36	46-35	39-23	28-33	24-15	22-21	69-50	73-58	18-13	35-19	56-52	13-11	32-23	28-20	17-10	17-10	9-19	15-12	18-10	15-10	48-41	43-30
Los Angeles	47-34	43-38	38-24	33-28	19-20	23-14	67-58	74-58	16-14	26-22	64-50	9-7	33-23	24-18	14-14	15-12	13-14	15-11	17-10	16-11	47-42	43-30
Colorado	55-26	28-53	28-33	36-26	19-20	18-19	65-60	72-59	11-20	35-27	48-52	7-3	23-16	21-21	11-14	14-11	15-14	14-14	16-14	13-12	42-44	41-35
San Francisco	38-44	30-50	28-33	24-38	16-23	14-22	54-72	55-77	13-17	35-42	33-52	6-10	17-29	20-29	14-12	12-14	10-17	10-17	12-15	10-19	38-48	30-46

Team vs. Team Breakdown

	Atl	ChN	Cin	Col	Fla	Hou	LA	Mon	NYN	Phi	Pit	SD	SF	StL
Atlanta Braves	—	7	7	5	6	6	5	10	7	9	9	9	7	9
Chicago Cubs	5	—	5	5	6	5	8	6	7	7	4	6	7	5
Cincinnati Reds	5	8	—	7	3	7	4	3	6	10	5	9	9	5
Colorado Rockies	7	7	6	—	5	8	6	3	7	6	7	8	5	8
Florida Marlins	7	6	9	8	—	7	6	5	7	6	5	3	5	6
Houston Astros	6	8	6	5	5	—	6	4	8	10	8	6	8	2
Los Angeles Dodgers	7	5	8	7	7	6	—	9	8	7	6	5	7	8
Montreal Expos	3	6	9	9	8	9	3	—	7	6	7	4	9	8
New York Mets	6	5	6	5	6	4	4	6	—	7	8	3	6	5
Philadelphia Phillies	4	6	2	6	7	2	6	7	6	—	7	4	6	4
Pittsburgh Pirates	3	9	8	5	7	5	6	5	5	5	—	4	8	3
San Diego Padres	4	6	3	5	9	6	8	8	10	8	9	—	11	4
San Francisco Giants	5	5	4	8	7	4	6	4	6	6	4	2	—	7
St. Louis Cardinals	4	8	8	4	6	11	4	4	7	8	10	8	6	—

(read wins across and losses down)

American League Batting

Tm	G	AB	H	2B	3B	HR	(Hm	Rd)	TB	R	RBI	TBB	IBB	SO	HBP	SH	SF	ShO	SB	CS	SB%	GDP	LOB	Avg	OBP	SLG
Sea	161	5668	1625	343	19	245	(121	124)	2741	993	954	670	57	1052	75	46	58	3	90	39	.70	122	1238	.287	.366	.484
Cle	161	5681	1665	335	23	218	(102	116)	2700	952	904	645	44	844	43	34	57	1	160	50	.76	163	1224	.293	.369	.475
Bal	163	5689	1557	299	29	257	(121	136)	2685	949	914	645	49	915	61	31	67	7	76	40	.66	132	1154	.274	.350	.472
Bos	162	5756	1631	308	31	209	(121	88)	2628	928	882	642	50	1020	67	33	47	9	91	44	.67	146	1251	.283	.359	.457
Tex	163	5702	1622	323	32	221	(112	109)	2672	928	890	660	51	1041	31	32	69	5	83	26	.76	126	1253	.284	.358	.469
ChA	162	5644	1586	284	33	195	(76	119)	2521	898	860	701	68	927	34	56	62	2	105	41	.72	138	1231	.281	.360	.447
Mil	162	5662	1578	304	40	178	(82	96)	2496	894	845	624	35	986	53	45	50	7	101	48	.68	113	1198	.279	.357	.441
Min	162	5673	1633	332	47	118	(61	57)	2413	877	812	576	42	958	65	20	63	5	143	53	.73	172	1194	.288	.357	.425
NYA	162	5628	1621	293	28	162	(76	86)	2456	871	830	632	56	909	41	41	72	5	96	46	.68	151	1258	.288	.360	.436
Oak	162	5630	1492	283	21	243	(113	130)	2546	861	823	640	36	1114	58	35	39	7	58	35	.62	132	1175	.265	.344	.452
Det	162	5530	1413	257	21	204	(100	104)	2324	783	741	546	26	1268	29	48	49	10	87	50	.64	132	1040	.256	.323	.420
Tor	162	5599	1451	302	35	177	(87	90)	2354	766	712	529	19	1105	92	38	37	9	116	38	.75	118	1169	.259	.331	.420
Cal	161	5686	1571	256	24	192	(104	88)	2451	762	727	527	40	974	29	45	33	6	53	39	.58	148	1209	.276	.339	.431
KC	161	5542	1477	286	38	123	(50	73)	2208	746	689	529	36	943	43	66	49	3	195	85	.70	99	1117	.267	.332	.398
AL	1133	79090	21922	4205	421	2742	(1326	1416)	35195	12208	11583	8592	609	14056	721	570	752	79	1454	634	.70	1892	16711	.277	.350	.445

American League Pitching

	HOW MUCH THEY PITCHED					WHAT THEY GAVE UP												THE RESULTS									
Tm	G	CG	Rel	IP	BFP	H	R	ER	HR	SH	SF	HB	TBB	IBB	SO	WP	Bk	W	L	Pct.	ShO	Sv-Op	Hld	OAvg	OOBP	OSLG	ERA
Cle	161	13	382	1452.1	6245	1530	769	700	173	39	46	39	484	44	1033	49	3	99	62	.615	9	46-59	58	.271	.331	.429	4.34
KC	161	17	322	1450	6251	1563	786	733	176	42	51	56	460	36	926	56	4	75	86	.466	8	35-52	38	.277	.335	.438	4.55
NYA	162	6	411	1440	6289	1469	787	744	143	44	45	49	610	56	1139	55	5	92	70	.568	9	52-69	62	.265	.341	.404	4.65
ChA	162	7	391	1461	6405	1529	794	733	174	41	42	36	616	68	1039	59	1	85	77	.525	4	43-75	50	.270	.343	.424	4.52
Tex	163	19	347	1449.1	6358	1569	799	749	168	33	55	43	582	51	976	38	9	90	72	.556	6	43-60	65	.278	.347	.430	4.65
Tor	162	19	303	1445.2	6271	1476	809	734	187	31	48	36	610	19	1033	61	3	74	88	.457	7	35-53	39	.266	.340	.427	4.57
Sea	161	4	403	1431.2	6351	1562	895	829	216	42	47	60	605	57	1000	37	3	85	76	.528	4	34-52	51	.279	.353	.459	5.21
Mil	162	6	385	1447.1	6437	1570	899	826	213	43	64	57	635	35	846	56	6	80	82	.494	4	42-65	58	.278	.354	.459	5.14
Min	162	13	387	1439.2	6355	1561	900	844	233	41	47	41	581	42	959	49	3	78	84	.481	5	31-52	39	.277	.346	.471	5.28
Oak	162	7	419	1456.1	6505	1638	900	841	205	52	55	52	644	36	884	60	6	78	84	.481	5	34-53	43	.287	.362	.463	5.20
Bal	163	13	378	1468.2	6460	1604	903	839	209	44	57	38	597	49	1047	38	5	88	74	.543	1	44-63	53	.280	.349	.449	5.14
Bos	162	17	409	1458	6633	1606	921	807	185	32	67	50	722	50	1165	51	6	85	77	.525	5	37-61	58	.279	.360	.436	4.98
Cal	161	12	383	1439	6461	1546	943	847	219	41	56	84	662	40	1052	80	8	70	91	.435	8	38-53	39	.275	.357	.449	5.30
Det	162	10	426	1432.2	6713	1699	1103	1015	241	45	72	80	784	26	957	82	4	53	109	.327	4	22-42	40	.296	.384	.491	6.38
AL	1133	163	5346	20271.2	89734	21922	12208	11241	2742	570	752	721	8592	609	14056	771	66	1132	1132	.500	79	536-809	693	.277	.350	.445	4.99

American League Fielding

Team	G	PO	Ast	OFAst	E	(Throw	Field)	TC	DP	GDP Opp	GDP	GDP%	PB	OSB	OCS	OSB%	CPkof	PPkof	AVG
Texas	163	4348	1647	25	87	(40	47)	6082	150	223	125	.561	10	62	56	.53	11	3	.986
New York	162	4320	1613	29	91	(43	48)	6024	146	216	117	.542	17	120	41	.75	1	14	.985
Baltimore	163	4406	1730	35	97	(44	53)	6233	173	231	147	.636	14	135	37	.78	0	3	.984
Minnesota	162	4319	1519	43	94	(48	46)	5932	142	189	115	.608	11	84	42	.67	0	2	.984
Oakland	162	4369	1778	43	103	(43	60)	6250	195	257	158	.615	11	117	41	.74	1	0	.984
Chicago	162	4383	1574	22	109	(41	68)	6066	145	201	120	.597	8	105	55	.66	1	6	.982
Kansas City	161	4350	1704	24	111	(44	67)	6165	184	251	154	.614	11	69	42	.62	0	6	.982
Toronto	162	4337	1606	33	110	(37	73)	6053	187	245	158	.645	16	74	41	.64	6	5	.982
Seattle	161	4295	1540	39	110	(52	58)	5945	155	218	132	.606	8	78	42	.65	2	5	.981
Cleveland	161	4357	1765	43	124	(53	71)	6246	156	224	130	.580	11	104	52	.67	2	3	.980
California	161	4317	1702	27	128	(42	86)	6147	156	227	133	.586	12	146	54	.73	1	7	.979
Milwaukee	162	4342	1693	36	134	(64	70)	6169	180	232	149	.642	9	96	40	.71	2	9	.978
Boston	162	4374	1638	37	135	(47	88)	6147	152	237	122	.515	23	147	37	.80	0	3	.978
Detroit	162	4298	1727	31	137	(56	81)	6162	157	246	132	.537	7	117	54	.68	1	5	.978
American League	1133	60815	23236	467	1570	(654	916)	85621	2278	3197	1892	.592	168	1454	634	.70	28	71	.982

Note: A"GDP Opp" is any situation with a runner on first and less than two out.

National League Batting

Tm	G	AB	H	2B	3B	HR	(Hm	Rd)	TB	R	RBI	TBB	IBB	SO	HBP	SH	SF	ShO	SB	CS	SB%	GDP	LOB	Avg	OBP	SLG
Col	162	5590	1607	297	37	221	(149	72)	2641	961	909	527	40	1108	82	81	52	4	201	66	.75	118	1108	.287	.355	.472
Cin	162	5455	1398	259	36	191	(89	102)	2302	778	733	604	47	1134	34	71	49	6	171	63	.73	115	1116	.256	.331	.422
Pit	162	5665	1509	319	33	138	(74	64)	2308	776	738	510	46	989	40	72	49	6	126	49	.72	105	1181	.266	.329	.407
Atl	162	5614	1514	264	28	197	(106	91)	2425	773	735	530	41	1032	27	69	50	8	83	43	.66	144	1154	.270	.333	.432
ChN	162	5531	1388	267	19	175	(97	78)	2218	772	725	523	48	1090	61	66	48	4	108	50	.68	125	1078	.251	.320	.401
SD	162	5655	1499	285	24	147	(75	72)	2273	771	718	601	62	1015	50	59	52	11	109	55	.66	144	1209	.265	.338	.402
StL	162	5502	1468	281	31	142	(70	72)	2237	759	711	495	59	1089	44	88	48	7	149	58	.72	121	1087	.267	.330	.407
Hou	162	5508	1445	297	29	129	(60	69)	2187	753	703	554	64	1057	84	68	55	10	180	63	.74	115	1172	.262	.336	.397
SF	162	5533	1400	245	21	153	(82	71)	2146	752	707	615	62	1189	48	77	43	12	113	53	.68	106	1198	.253	.331	.388
NYN	162	5618	1515	267	47	147	(64	83)	2317	746	697	445	54	1069	33	75	49	7	97	48	.67	114	1124	.270	.324	.412
Mon	162	5505	1441	297	27	148	(81	67)	2236	741	696	492	49	1077	58	79	36	8	108	34	.76	119	1119	.262	.327	.406
LA	162	5538	1396	215	33	150	(62	88)	2127	703	661	516	59	1190	22	74	35	12	124	40	.76	112	1113	.252	.316	.384
Fla	162	5498	1413	240	30	150	(73	77)	2163	688	650	553	51	1122	55	41	45	14	99	46	.68	138	1171	.257	.329	.393
Phi	162	5499	1405	249	39	132	(55	77)	2128	650	604	536	52	1092	45	54	37	8	117	41	.74	116	1207	.256	.325	.387
NL	1134	77711	20398	3782	434	2220	(1137	1083)	31708	10623	9987	7501	734	15253	683	974	648	117	1785	709	.72	1692	16037	.262	.330	.408

National League Pitching

Tm	G	CG	Rel	IP	BFP	H	R	ER	HR	SH	SF	HB	TBB	IBB	SO	WP	Bk	W	L	Pct.	ShO	Sv-Op	Hld	OAvg	OOBP	OSLG	ERA
Atl	162	14	408	1469	6132	1372	648	575	120	71	38	19	451	41	1245	49	5	96	66	.593	9	46-63	49	.247	.304	.370	3.52
LA	162	6	383	1466.1	6223	1378	652	564	125	77	47	39	534	59	1213	40	22	90	72	.556	9	50-72	43	.249	.317	.366	3.46
Mon	162	11	433	1441.1	6119	1353	668	605	152	67	45	56	482	49	1206	46	9	88	74	.543	7	43-60	49	.247	.313	.384	3.78
SD	162	5	411	1489	6292	1395	682	616	138	65	47	45	506	62	1194	59	10	91	71	.562	11	47-66	50	.248	.313	.375	3.72
Fla	162	8	417	1443	6183	1386	703	634	113	69	37	57	598	51	1050	49	5	80	82	.494	13	41-58	42	.256	.334	.376	3.95
StL	162	13	413	1452.1	6184	1380	706	641	173	64	49	35	539	59	1050	44	6	88	74	.543	11	43-66	68	.251	.319	.397	3.97
ChN	162	10	439	1456.1	6268	1447	771	705	184	61	42	55	546	48	1027	48	8	76	86	.469	10	34-51	60	.263	.330	.423	4.36
Cin	162	6	425	1443	6277	1447	773	692	167	80	58	42	591	47	1089	66	6	81	81	.500	8	52-73	56	.263	.336	.420	4.32
NYN	162	10	335	1440	6288	1517	779	675	159	78	48	44	532	54	999	60	12	71	91	.438	10	41-64	26	.272	.337	.411	4.22
Phi	162	12	387	1423.1	6138	1463	790	708	160	68	45	35	510	52	1044	71	7	67	95	.414	6	42-56	43	.267	.331	.422	4.48
Hou	162	13	371	1447	6364	1541	792	702	154	80	51	70	539	64	1163	65	12	82	80	.506	4	35-57	28	.274	.342	.420	4.37
Pit	162	5	422	1453.1	6338	1602	833	744	183	59	48	50	479	46	1044	62	8	73	89	.451	7	37-61	50	.281	.339	.443	4.61
SF	162	9	425	1442.1	6330	1520	862	755	194	79	48	67	570	62	997	58	10	68	94	.420	8	35-56	38	.273	.345	.441	4.71
Col	162	5	447	1422.2	6391	1597	964	884	198	56	45	69	624	40	932	66	11	83	79	.512	4	34-64	67	.285	.362	.464	5.59
NL	1134	127	5716	20289	87527	20398	10623	9500	2220	974	648	683	7501	734	15253	783	131	1134	1134	.500	117	580-867	652	.262	.330	.408	4.21

National League Fielding

Team	G	PO	Ast	OFAst	E	(Throw	Field)	TC	DP	GDP Opp	GDP	GDP%	PB	OSB	OCS	OSB%	CPkof	PPkof	AVG
Chicago	162	4369	1768	29	104	(45	59)	6241	147	206	114	.553	13	129	50	.72	1	5	.983
Florida	162	4329	1796	26	111	(40	71)	6236	187	253	156	.617	12	84	57	.60	1	5	.982
San Diego	162	4467	1768	15	118	(44	74)	6353	136	193	116	.601	14	136	54	.72	1	1	.981
Philadelphia	162	4270	1582	30	116	(55	61)	5968	145	212	117	.552	10	88	44	.67	1	7	.981
Cincinnati	162	4329	1694	29	121	(52	69)	6144	145	211	117	.555	7	146	50	.74	1	2	.980
Pittsburgh	162	4360	1868	31	128	(53	75)	6356	144	227	111	.489	10	185	57	.76	1	7	.980
Los Angeles	162	4399	1636	29	125	(39	86)	6160	143	209	123	.589	15	171	39	.81	1	2	.980
St. Louis	162	4357	1666	29	125	(49	76)	6148	139	210	116	.552	7	104	54	.66	0	8	.980
Montreal	162	4324	1713	26	126	(49	77)	6163	121	155	98	.632	10	156	48	.76	0	2	.980
Atlanta	162	4407	1808	28	130	(50	80)	6345	143	193	115	.596	11	116	44	.73	3	2	.980
San Francisco	162	4327	1637	31	136	(40	96)	6100	165	214	132	.617	13	108	69	.61	2	6	.978
Houston	162	4341	1692	44	138	(58	80)	6171	130	206	107	.519	14	115	55	.68	3	1	.978
Colorado	162	4268	1901	20	149	(72	77)	6318	167	239	139	.582	19	122	55	.69	1	16	.976
New York	162	4320	1717	42	159	(71	88)	6196	163	207	131	.633	10	125	33	.79	0	5	.974
National League	1134	60867	24246	409	1786	(717	1069)	86899	2075	2935	1692	.576	165	1785	709	.72	16	69	.979

Note: A "GDP Opp" is any situation with a runner on first and less than two out.

1996 Fielding Stats

Rabbit Maranville and Luis Aparicio probably never heard the term "range factor," but you can bet that Rey Ordonez and Edgar Renteria—and the people who evaluate them—have. Fielding statistics have evolved considerably over the past decade, and we at STATS always like to stay on the cutting edge. The original range factor was simply total successful chances (putouts + assists) per game played, but the range factor (Rng) you'll find here is a bit more precise: total successful chances per nine innings. You'll also find all the old standards, like assists, errors, double plays and games started by position. Another thing you won't find in other sources are our "special" catcher stats, including stolen- base data and one of our personal favorites, Catcher ERA (CERA).

The only important things you need to know before digging in are these: all the fielding stats are unofficial—an assist here or a putout there may change when the official stats arrive in December, but these are very close as they are. The regulars are sorted by range factor, except for the first basemen and the catchers in the first catcher section, who are sorted by fielding percentage. The catchers in the special catcher section are sorted by Catcher ERA. Remember to consider the pitching staff when looking at those CERAs, by the way. No matter what kind of game plan Brad Ausmus may have been able to dream up, he was going to be behind the eight-ball every game with that Tigers' staff. And finally, ties in range or percentage are, in reality, not ties at all, just numbers that don't show enough digits to be unique.

First Basemen - Regulars

Player	Tm	G	GS	Inn	PO	A	E	DP	Pct.	Rng
Olerud,John	Tor	101	92	823.0	782	55	2	107	.998	---
King,Jeff	Pit	92	76	683.1	746	45	2	61	.997	---
Joyner,Wally	SD	119	115	1044.0	1059	88	3	86	.997	---
Grace,Mark	ChN	141	139	1218.0	1259	107	4	119	.997	---
Martinez,Tino	NYA	151	149	1305.2	1238	84	5	119	.996	---
Clark,Will	Tex	117	116	994.2	954	70	4	89	.996	---
Colbrunn,Greg	Fla	134	131	1127.1	1168	102	6	130	.995	---
Palmeiro,Rafael	Bal	159	159	1418.2	1383	116	8	157	.995	---
Stahoviak,Scott	Min	114	103	902.2	800	90	5	78	.994	---
Offerman,Jose	KC	96	80	741.0	796	68	5	82	.994	---
Johnson,Mark	Pit	100	82	739.2	775	72	5	64	.994	---
Mabry,John	StL	146	139	1198.2	1172	75	8	107	.994	---
Morris,Hal	Cin	140	133	1173.2	1128	92	8	102	.993	---
Segui,David	Mon	114	113	988.2	943	89	7	79	.993	---
Snow,J.T.	Cal	154	149	1339.0	1274	105	10	136	.993	---
Clark,Tony	Det	86	86	760.0	766	53	6	82	.993	---
Thomas,Frank	ChA	139	139	1231.0	1097	84	9	111	.992	---
McGriff,Fred	Atl	158	158	1401.0	1415	121	12	118	.992	---
Jaha,John	Mil	85	82	718.0	675	59	6	84	.992	---
Galarraga,Andres	Col	159	158	1378.2	1528	115	14	151	.992	---
Fielder,Cecil	TOT	80	80	687.2	662	63	7	59	.990	---
Franco,Julio	Cle	97	96	832.2	851	74	9	90	.990	---
McGwire,Mark	Oak	109	107	896.1	913	59	10	117	.990	---
Karros,Eric	LA	154	154	1391.1	1314	118	15	131	.990	---
Sorrento,Paul	Sea	138	123	1099.1	955	80	11	112	.989	---
Bagwell,Jeff	Hou	162	162	1430.0	1336	136	16	115	.989	---
Carreon,Mark	TOT	107	102	863.0	836	56	10	88	.989	---
Vaughn,Mo	Bos	146	146	1309.0	1208	71	15	123	.988	---
Average	---	124	120	1060.1	1036	83	7	103	.993	---

First Basemen - The Rest

Player	Tm	G	GS	Inn	PO	A	E	DP	Pct.	Rng
Aldrete,Mike	Cal	1	0	1.0	0	0	0	0	.000	---
Aldrete,Mike	NYA	8	3	37.0	38	0	0	4	1.000	---
Alomar,Sandy	Cle	1	0	1.0	0	0	0	0	.000	---
Amaral,Rich	Sea	10	0	13.0	11	0	0	2	1.000	---
Amaro,Ruben	Phi	1	0	0.1	0	0	0	0	.000	---
Arias,Alex	Fla	1	0	1.1	1	0	0	0	1.000	---
Aude,Rich	Pit	4	4	28.0	28	3	1	3	.969	---
Baerga,Carlos	NYN	16	16	117.0	98	5	1	8	.990	---
Banks,Brian	Mil	1	1	9.0	14	1	0	0	1.000	---
Belk,Tim	Cin	6	4	38.0	28	0	0	2	1.000	---
Blowers,Mike	LA	6	1	15.2	20	2	0	0	1.000	---
Bogar,Tim	NYN	32	2	65.0	77	4	0	7	1.000	---
Bonilla,Bobby	Bal	9	3	36.0	27	1	1	4	.966	---
Borders,Pat	StL	1	0	1.1	1	0	1	0	.500	---
Brogna,Rico	NYN	52	49	422.2	439	32	2	47	.996	---
Brooks,Jerry	Fla	1	0	2.0	0	0	1	0	.000	---
Brosius,Scott	Oak	10	3	37.0	37	2	0	1	1.000	---
Brown,Brant	ChN	18	12	128.1	126	15	0	4	1.000	---
Busch,Mike	LA	1	0	2.0	2	0	0	0	1.000	---
Carreon,Mark	SF	73	70	587.2	533	37	8	65	.986	---
Carreon,Mark	Cle	34	32	275.1	303	19	2	23	.994	---
Carter,Joe	Tor	41	33	285.0	249	16	2	32	.993	---
Cianfrocco,Archi	SD	33	17	183.1	168	15	0	13	1.000	---
Cirillo,Jeff	Mil	2	0	3.0	5	0	0	0	1.000	---

First Basemen - The Rest

Player	Tm	G	GS	Inn	PO	A	E	DP	Pct.	Rng
Clark,Phil	Bos	1	0	1.0	2	0	0	0	1.000	---
Conine,Jeff	Fla	48	31	305.1	292	40	3	33	.991	---
Coomer,Ron	Min	57	36	318.1	243	39	2	27	.993	---
Cordero,Wil	Bos	1	1	9.1	7	0	0	2	1.000	---
Crespo,Felipe	Tor	2	0	6.0	3	1	0	0	1.000	---
Davis,Eric	Cin	1	1	6.0	7	0	0	0	1.000	---
Decker,Steve	SF	3	3	21.1	18	3	0	1	1.000	---
Delgado,Alex	Bos	1	0	2.0	1	1	0	0	1.000	---
Delgado,Carlos	Tor	27	25	226.2	221	13	4	22	.983	---
Espinoza,Alvaro	Cle	18	8	104.1	97	8	0	10	1.000	---
Espinoza,Alvaro	NYN	1	0	1.0	0	0	0	0	.000	---
Fielder,Cecil	Det	71	71	609.2	588	59	7	50	.989	---
Fielder,Cecil	NYA	9	9	78.0	74	4	0	9	1.000	---
Floyd,Cliff	Mon	2	1	15.0	16	0	1	1	.941	---
Franco,Matt	NYN	2	1	9.0	12	1	0	1	1.000	---
Gaetti,Gary	StL	14	9	86.1	85	6	1	6	.989	---
Garrison,Webster	Oak	1	0	2.0	1	1	0	0	1.000	---
Giambi,Jason	Oak	45	42	378.2	378	33	3	38	.993	---
Gomez,Leo	ChN	8	4	39.0	41	5	0	1	1.000	---
Gonzales,Rene	Tex	23	9	102.2	88	6	1	11	.989	---
Gonzalez,Luis	ChN	2	2	14.0	13	1	0	0	1.000	---
Greene,Willie	Cin	2	0	2.0	1	0	0	0	1.000	---
Greer,Rusty	Tex	1	0	0.0	0	0	0	0	.000	---
Gwynn,Chris	SD	1	0	0.2	0	1	0	0	1.000	---
Hale,Chip	Min	6	0	8.0	7	1	0	1	1.000	---
Hamelin,Bob	KC	33	28	243.0	233	19	4	26	.984	---
Hansen,Dave	LA	8	7	56.1	54	4	0	3	1.000	---
Harris,Lenny	Cin	16	14	124.0	122	11	1	10	.993	---
Haselman,Bill	Bos	2	1	11.2	13	0	0	2	1.000	---
Hocking,Denny	Min	1	0	1.0	1	0	0	0	1.000	---
Hoiles,Chris	Bal	1	0	1.0	0	0	0	0	.000	---
Hollins,Dave	Sea	1	0	1.0	0	0	0	0	.000	---
Houston,Tyler	Atl	10	0	22.0	15	1	0	1	1.000	---
Houston,Tyler	ChN	1	0	1.0	1	1	0	0	1.000	---
Howard,Dave	KC	2	0	4.0	4	0	0	0	1.000	---
Howell,Jack	Cal	2	1	10.0	11	0	1	1	.917	---
Hudler,Rex	Cal	7	5	42.0	44	0	1	3	.978	---
Hunter,Brian	Sea	41	26	219.1	219	7	2	19	.991	---
Huskey,Butch	NYN	75	69	575.0	570	42	10	55	.984	---
Hyers,Tim	Det	9	3	35.0	30	1	0	6	1.000	---
Jefferies,Gregg	Phi	53	53	446.1	411	38	1	38	.998	---
Jefferson,Reggie	Bos	16	14	124.0	117	16	1	8	.993	---
Johnson,Brian	SD	1	1	3.0	6	0	0	1	1.000	---
Jones,Chris	NYN	5	1	17.2	16	1	0	1	1.000	---
Jordan,Brian	StL	1	0	1.1	1	0	0	0	1.000	---
Jordan,Kevin	Phi	30	23	224.1	228	12	0	19	1.000	---
Jordan,Ricky	Sea	10	4	43.0	40	1	0	5	1.000	---
Kent,Jeff	Cle	20	12	120.0	112	9	1	13	.992	---
Klesko,Ryan	Atl	2	2	12.0	13	2	0	2	1.000	---
Kreuter,Chad	ChA	2	0	3.0	1	0	0	0	1.000	---
Leius,Scott	Cle	7	4	37.0	39	2	1	1	.976	---
Lesher,Brian	Oak	1	1	8.0	6	0	0	0	1.000	---
Leyritz,Jim	NYA	5	0	12.1	16	0	0	2	1.000	---
Livingstone,Scott	SD	22	15	135.2	138	10	1	15	.993	---
Lovullo,Torey	Oak	42	8	123.2	120	8	0	21	1.000	---
Magadan,Dave	ChN	10	5	54.0	59	4	0	4	1.000	---
Manto,Jeff	Bos	1	0	1.0	1	0	0	0	1.000	---
Marrero,Oreste	LA	1	0	1.0	1	0	0	0	1.000	---

First Basemen - The Rest

Player	Tm	G	GS	Inn	PO	A	E	DP	Pct.	Rng
Martinez,Dave	ChA	23	16	152.1	132	12	3	8	.980	---
Martinez,Edgar	Sea	4	4	33.0	28	1	1	3	.967	---
McCarty,Dave	SF	51	27	275.2	269	15	3	29	.990	---
McGee,Willie	StL	6	3	28.0	23	4	0	1	1.000	---
McIntosh,Tim	NYA	1	1	6.0	6	1	0	1	1.000	---
Merced,Orlando	Pit	1	0	2.1	1	1	0	1	1.000	---
Mitchell,Kevin	Cin	3	3	29.0	28	2	1	4	.968	---
Molitor,Paul	Min	17	17	145.2	138	13	1	13	.993	---
Mordecai,Mike	Atl	2	0	3.0	3	1	0	0	1.000	---
Morman,Russ	Fla	2	0	2.0	2	0	0	1	1.000	---
Murray,Eddie	Cle	1	1	9.0	10	1	0	0	1.000	---
Newfield,Marc	SD	2	1	10.0	9	1	1	0	.909	---
Nilsson,Dave	Mil	24	17	152.2	145	13	3	16	.981	---
O'Neill,Paul	NYA	1	0	1.0	0	0	0	0	.000	---
Oliver,Joe	Cin	3	1	12.0	9	1	0	0	1.000	---
Orsulak,Joe	Fla	2	0	5.0	3	1	0	1	1.000	---
Pagnozzi,Tom	StL	1	0	2.0	1	0	0	0	1.000	---
Paquette,Craig	KC	19	17	139.2	148	13	0	24	1.000	---
Parent,Mark	Det	1	0	2.0	1	0	0	0	1.000	---
Peltier,Dan	SF	13	10	102.0	87	6	0	11	1.000	---
Perez,Eddie	Atl	7	2	31.0	31	3	1	7	.971	---
Perez,Eduardo	Cin	8	6	58.1	56	7	0	6	1.000	---
Perry,Herbert	Cle	5	3	29.0	29	2	0	3	1.000	---
Petagine,Roberto	NYN	40	24	231.2	209	22	1	20	.996	---
Phillips,J.R.	SF	10	4	47.2	49	2	1	4	.981	---
Phillips,J.R.	Phi	11	8	67.2	70	3	0	7	1.000	---
Phillips,Tony	ChA	1	0	1.0	2	0	0	0	1.000	---
Pirkl,Greg	Sea	2	2	17.0	14	2	0	2	1.000	---
Pritchett,Chris	Cal	5	3	26.0	29	1	0	3	1.000	---
Randa,Joe	KC	7	2	27.0	21	3	0	2	1.000	---
Reboulet,Jeff	Min	13	6	64.0	57	8	0	7	1.000	---
Ripken,Billy	Bal	1	0	2.0	3	0	0	1	1.000	---
Robertson,Mike	ChA	2	1	10.2	12	1	0	2	1.000	---
Rodriguez,Henry	Mon	51	48	433.1	426	28	5	27	.989	---
Samuel,Juan	Tor	17	12	105.0	90	3	2	7	.979	---
Santiago,Benito	Phi	14	12	111.0	111	6	1	9	.992	---
Scarsone,Steve	SF	1	0	1.0	1	0	0	1	1.000	---
Schall,Gene	Phi	19	18	148.2	135	8	2	16	.986	---
Seitzer,Kevin	Mil	65	60	532.0	489	47	2	56	.996	---
Seitzer,Kevin	Cle	5	5	44.0	31	9	0	1	1.000	---
Servais,Scott	ChN	1	0	2.0	1	1	0	0	1.000	---
Sheaffer,Danny	StL	6	1	16.2	11	0	0	1	1.000	---
Silvestri,Dave	Mon	1	0	4.0	3	0	0	0	1.000	---
Simms,Mike	Hou	5	0	10.0	7	1	0	0	1.000	---
Spiers,Bill	Hou	4	0	7.0	9	1	0	2	1.000	---
Stairs,Matt	Oak	1	1	9.0	6	3	0	1	1.000	---
Steinbach,Terry	Oak	1	0	1.2	1	0	0	0	1.000	---
Stevens,Lee	Tex	18	15	146.0	152	14	1	21	.994	---
Stillwell,Kurt	Tex	1	0	4.0	3	0	0	0	1.000	---
Strange,Doug	Sea	3	0	6.0	4	0	0	1	1.000	---
Surhoff,B.J.	Bal	2	1	11.0	11	2	0	0	1.000	---
Sweeney,Mark	StL	15	6	62.1	67	2	2	7	.972	---
Tettleton,Mickey	Tex	23	23	182.0	161	11	4	14	.977	---
Thompson,Jason	SD	13	13	112.1	94	13	4	6	.964	---
Tomberlin,Andy	NYN	1	0	1.0	0	0	0	0	.000	---
Tucker,Michael	KC	9	7	55.0	52	3	0	6	1.000	---
Unroe,Tim	Mil	11	2	32.2	41	0	1	4	.976	---
Valle,Dave	Tex	5	0	6.0	5	0	0	1	1.000	---

First Basemen - The Rest

Player	Tm	G	GS	Inn	PO	A	E	DP	Pct.	Rng
Vander Wal,John	Col	10	4	44.0	38	2	1	2	.976	---
Ventura,Robin	ChA	14	6	63.0	56	8	1	8	.985	---
Vitiello,Joe	KC	9	6	55.0	40	5	0	4	1.000	---
Wallach,Tim	Cal	3	3	21.0	20	3	1	1	.958	---
Wilkins,Rick	SF	7	6	52.0	52	5	0	4	1.000	---
Williams,Eddie	Det	7	2	26.0	22	1	0	7	1.000	---
Williams,Matt	SF	13	12	106.0	90	12	1	10	.990	---
Wilson,Desi	SF	33	30	249.0	236	18	4	20	.984	---
Worthington,Craig	Tex	6	0	14.0	16	4	0	1	1.000	---
Young,Dmitri	StL	10	4	55.2	39	1	1	5	.976	---
Young,Kevin	KC	27	21	185.1	183	15	0	25	1.000	---
Zeile,Todd	Phi	28	28	244.0	223	15	4	30	.983	---
Zuber,Jon	Phi	22	20	181.0	146	11	2	10	.987	---

Second Basemen - Regulars

Player	Tm	G	GS	Inn	PO	A	E	DP	Pct.	Rng
Young,Eric	Col	139	136	1169.0	340	429	12	108	.985	5.92
Vina,Fernando	Mil	137	131	1165.2	331	413	16	115	.979	5.74
McLemore,Mark	Tex	147	145	1279.1	312	471	12	114	.985	5.51
Frye,Jeff	Bos	100	97	872.0	201	318	9	70	.983	5.36
Alomar,Roberto	Bal	142	140	1217.2	279	445	11	107	.985	5.35
Boone,Bret	Cin	141	138	1205.2	316	381	6	84	.991	5.20
Perez,Tomas	Tor	75	70	625.1	133	226	11	64	.970	5.17
Biggio,Craig	Hou	162	160	1409.1	361	442	10	75	.988	5.13
Cora,Joey	Sea	140	119	1071.2	299	311	13	88	.979	5.12
Baerga,Carlos	TOT	101	100	887.1	194	311	15	64	.971	5.12
Alicea,Luis	StL	125	104	954.0	242	289	24	70	.957	5.01
Vizcaino,Jose	TOT	138	136	1152.2	258	382	10	95	.985	5.00
Morandini,Mickey	Phi	137	133	1154.0	286	352	12	87	.982	4.98
Reed,Jody	SD	145	137	1245.0	274	412	9	87	.987	4.96
Lewis,Mark	Det	144	143	1240.2	265	412	9	94	.987	4.91
Lemke,Mark	Atl	133	132	1166.1	228	408	15	70	.977	4.91
Duncan,Mariano	NYA	104	98	774.0	182	239	11	58	.975	4.90
Lansing,Mike	Mon	159	158	1368.0	347	391	11	84	.985	4.86
Sandberg,Ryne	ChN	146	144	1234.0	228	421	6	81	.991	4.73
Knoblauch,Chuck	Min	151	150	1267.2	274	389	8	94	.988	4.71
DeShields,Delino	LA	154	149	1315.1	273	400	17	78	.975	4.60
Velarde,Randy	Cal	114	109	967.2	236	252	9	80	.982	4.54
Durham,Ray	ChA	150	145	1313.0	236	423	11	87	.984	4.52
Average	---	134	129	1132.2	265	370	11	84	.982	5.05

Second Basemen - The Rest

Player	Tm	G	GS	Inn	PO	A	E	DP	Pct.	Rng
Abbott,Kurt	Fla	20	15	140.1	35	39	0	6	1.000	4.75
Alexander,Manny	Bal	7	3	27.0	7	4	0	1	1.000	3.67
Alfonzo,Edgardo	NYN	66	56	518.0	122	174	8	42	.974	5.14
Amaral,Rich	Sea	15	10	89.0	16	21	0	2	1.000	3.74
Arias,Alex	Fla	1	0	2.2	0	2	0	0	1.000	6.75
Aurilia,Rich	SF	11	9	77.0	16	18	0	8	1.000	3.97
Baerga,Carlos	Cle	100	99	880.1	191	308	15	63	.971	5.10
Baerga,Carlos	NYN	1	1	7.0	3	3	0	1	1.000	7.71
Barberie,Bret	ChN	6	3	40.0	5	17	0	1	1.000	4.95
Bates,Jason	Col	37	20	210.2	58	79	3	16	.979	5.85
Batista,Tony	Oak	52	46	405.1	84	162	3	36	.988	5.46

Second Basemen - The Rest

Second Basemen - The Rest

Player	Tm	G	GS	Inn	PO	A	E	DP	Pct.	Rng
Bell,David	StL	20	16	133.2	22	54	1	9	.987	5.12
Belliard,Rafael	Atl	15	6	63.0	14	25	2	7	.951	5.57
Beltre,Esteban	Bos	8	5	43.0	16	10	1	4	.963	5.44
Benjamin,Mike	Phi	1	0	2.0	1	0	0	0	1.000	4.50
Bogar,Tim	NYN	8	1	33.1	4	11	0	4	1.000	4.05
Bournigal,Rafael	Oak	64	51	482.1	114	175	2	40	.993	5.39
Branson,Jeff	Cin	31	15	161.1	36	45	2	11	.976	4.52
Brito,Tilson	Tor	18	16	147.1	36	50	4	14	.956	5.25
Cairo,Miguel	Tor	9	8	67.2	22	18	0	5	1.000	5.32
Candaele,Casey	Cle	11	6	67.0	20	30	0	11	1.000	6.72
Canizaro,Jay	SF	35	26	237.0	60	79	4	16	.972	5.28
Castellano,Pedro	Col	3	3	18.0	4	10	0	2	1.000	7.00
Castillo,Luis	Fla	41	41	352.0	99	118	3	36	.986	5.55
Castro,Juan	LA	9	4	44.1	7	12	0	1	1.000	3.86
Cedeno,Domingo	Tor	62	58	516.1	109	169	9	47	.969	4.85
Cedeno,Domingo	ChA	2	1	9.0	0	0	0	0	.000	.00
Cianfrocco,Archi	SD	6	3	28.1	5	6	1	1	.917	3.49
Cirillo,Jeff	Mil	1	1	9.0	2	4	0	1	1.000	6.00
Cordero,Wil	Bos	37	36	332.1	75	109	10	18	.948	4.98
Crespo,Felipe	Tor	10	10	89.0	25	29	1	8	.982	5.46
Cruz,Fausto	Det	8	6	57.0	9	20	3	3	.906	4.58
Delgado,Alex	Bos	1	0	2.0	0	1	0	0	1.000	4.50
Doster,David	Phi	24	21	195.2	51	56	3	12	.973	4.92
Easley,Damion	Cal	9	4	47.2	12	11	1	2	.958	4.34
Easley,Damion	Det	8	6	64.0	14	24	1	4	.974	5.34
Eenhoorn,Robert	NYA	10	4	45.0	14	12	0	5	1.000	5.20
Eenhoorn,Robert	Cal	2	1	9.0	4	4	1	1	.889	8.00
Espinoza,Alvaro	Cle	5	2	20.1	5	11	1	5	.941	7.08
Espinoza,Alvaro	NYN	2	0	3.0	0	1	0	0	1.000	3.00
Fermin,Felix	ChN	6	2	25.0	2	5	1	1	.875	2.52
Fonville,Chad	LA	23	9	106.2	20	34	1	8	.982	4.56
Fox,Andy	NYA	72	37	375.2	77	104	8	21	.958	4.34
Frazier,Lou	Tex	1	0	2.0	0	1	0	0	.000	.00
Gallego,Mike	StL	43	41	359.2	85	118	3	31	.985	5.08
Garcia,Carlos	Pit	77	66	581.1	131	199	5	35	.985	5.11
Garciaparra,Nomar	Bos	1	0	2.0	2	1	0	0	1.000	13.50
Garrison,Webster	Oak	3	2	18.0	3	4	1	1	.875	3.50
Gates,Brent	Oak	64	63	547.2	140	183	9	48	.973	5.31
Giovanola,Ed	Atl	5	1	18.1	5	10	0	2	1.000	7.36
Gonzales,Rene	Tex	5	5	42.0	2	18	0	1	1.000	4.29
Graffanino,Tony	Atl	18	11	113.2	24	39	2	9	.969	4.99
Grebeck,Craig	Fla	29	21	203.1	68	65	2	24	.985	5.89
Gutierrez,Ricky	Hou	5	0	11.0	3	3	1	1	.857	4.91
Hajek,Dave	Hou	2	0	4.0	2	1	0	0	1.000	6.75
Hale,Chip	Min	14	2	39.0	8	13	0	2	1.000	4.85
Haney,Todd	ChN	23	12	137.1	29	59	2	12	.978	5.77
Hardtke,Jason	NYN	18	13	117.2	26	34	0	9	1.000	4.59
Harris,Lenny	Cin	8	5	42.2	11	15	1	4	.963	5.48
Hernandez,Jose	ChN	1	0	1.0	0	1	0	0	1.000	9.00
Hocking,Denny	Min	2	0	4.0	1	2	0	1	1.000	6.75
Holbert,Aaron	StL	1	1	5.0	0	1	0	0	1.000	1.80
Houston,Tyler	ChN	2	1	9.0	2	6	0	2	1.000	8.00
Howard,Dave	KC	3	2	24.1	9	9	0	3	1.000	6.66
Howard,Matt	NYA	30	10	117.0	17	26	1	5	.977	3.31
Howell,Jack	Cal	1	0	0.1	0	0	0	0	.000	.00
Hudler,Rex	Cal	53	45	398.1	96	115	4	35	.981	4.77
Huson,Jeff	Bal	12	6	57.0	20	16	1	6	.973	5.68
Jordan,Kevin	Phi	7	5	40.1	16	14	0	3	1.000	6.69

Player	Tm	G	GS	Inn	PO	A	E	DP	Pct.	Rng
Kelly,Pat	NYA	10	5	55.0	8	24	1	3	.970	5.24
Kent,Jeff	Cle	9	7	65.0	11	30	0	2	1.000	5.68
King,Jeff	Pit	71	63	554.2	145	181	7	40	.979	5.29
Leius,Scott	Cle	6	1	19.0	3	8	0	2	1.000	5.21
Leyritz,Jim	NYA	2	0	4.0	2	1	0	0	1.000	6.75
Liriano,Nelson	Pit	36	24	223.0	50	73	2	14	.984	4.96
Listach,Pat	Mil	12	11	98.2	29	26	1	8	.982	5.02
Lockhart,Keith	KC	84	61	589.1	111	207	8	54	.975	4.86
Lopez,Luis	SD	22	10	112.1	19	32	2	7	.962	4.09
Loretta,Mark	Mil	28	19	174.0	32	61	1	13	.989	4.81
Lovullo,Torey	Oak	2	0	3.0	4	1	0	1	1.000	15.00
Manto,Jeff	Bos	4	4	35.0	10	16	1	3	.963	6.69
Martin,Norberto	ChA	10	9	75.0	22	34	1	7	.982	6.72
Milliard,Ralph	Fla	24	18	163.2	42	65	5	14	.955	5.88
Mordecai,Mike	Atl	20	12	107.2	25	38	1	8	.984	5.27
Mueller,Bill	SF	8	8	72.0	17	20	2	7	.949	4.63
Munoz,Jose	ChA	7	5	50.0	12	12	2	2	.923	4.32
Naehring,Tim	Bos	1	0	0.1	0	0	0	0	.000	.00
Offerman,Jose	KC	38	31	254.0	64	81	1	29	.993	5.14
Owens,Eric	Cin	6	4	33.1	10	7	1	0	.944	4.59
Pena,Geronimo	Cle	1	1	9.0	2	3	0	1	1.000	5.00
Perez,Neifi	Col	4	3	25.0	6	8	1	3	.933	5.04
Phillips,Tony	ChA	2	2	14.0	4	5	0	2	1.000	5.79
Pozo,Arquimedez	Bos	10	8	68.0	18	22	3	3	.930	5.29
Raabe,Brian	Min	1	0	1.0	0	0	0	0	.000	.00
Randa,Joe	KC	15	6	66.2	15	26	1	4	.976	5.54
Reboulet,Jeff	Min	22	9	106.0	25	22	0	4	1.000	3.99
Relaford,Desi	Phi	4	3	25.1	8	11	0	4	1.000	6.75
Ripken,Billy	Bal	30	14	167.0	34	57	3	15	.968	4.90
Roberts,Bip	KC	63	57	488.2	101	188	4	41	.986	5.32
Santangelo,F.P.	Mon	5	1	17.0	5	7	0	2	1.000	6.35
Scarsone,Steve	SF	74	59	546.2	162	162	9	45	.973	5.33
Schofield,Dick	Cal	2	2	16.0	4	6	0	1	1.000	5.63
Sefcik,Kevin	Phi	1	0	6.0	1	1	0	0	1.000	3.00
Selby,Bill	Bos	14	12	103.1	22	28	1	5	.980	4.35
Sheets,Andy	Sea	18	10	77.0	18	29	2	9	.959	5.49
Shipley,Craig	SD	17	12	103.1	26	39	1	6	.985	5.66
Shumpert,Terry	ChN	4	0	10.0	2	2	0	0	1.000	3.60
Silvestri,Dave	Mon	1	0	1.0	0	0	0	0	.000	.00
Sojo,Luis	Sea	27	22	189.0	42	59	2	15	.981	4.81
Sojo,Luis	NYA	14	8	69.1	14	28	0	8	1.000	5.45
Spiers,Bill	Hou	7	2	22.2	7	4	0	2	1.000	4.37
Stankiewicz,Andy	Mon	19	3	55.0	12	19	1	2	.969	5.07
Stillwell,Kurt	Tex	21	13	126.0	24	29	2	4	.964	3.79
Strange,Doug	Sea	3	0	5.0	0	1	0	0	1.000	1.80
Stynes,Chris	KC	5	4	27.0	8	5	0	2	1.000	4.33
Thompson,Robby	SF	62	60	509.2	124	155	7	39	.976	4.93
Trammell,Alan	Det	11	7	112.1	15	23	2	6	.950	4.82
Veras,Quilvio	Fla	67	67	581.0	173	192	5	54	.986	5.65
Vizcaino,Jose	NYN	93	91	761.0	178	257	6	68	.986	5.14
Vizcaino,Jose	Cle	45	45	391.2	80	125	4	27	.981	4.71
Walker,Todd	Min	4	1	22.0	5	7	0	1	1.000	4.91
Wehner,John	Pit	12	7	70.1	19	18	1	3	.974	4.73
Womack,Tony	Pit	4	2	24.0	6	8	2	0	.875	5.25

Third Basemen - Regulars

Player	Tm	G	GS	Inn	PO	A	E	DP	Pct.	Rng
Arias,George	Cal	83	76	657.1	50	189	10	19	.960	3.27
Castilla,Vinny	Col	160	157	1374.0	96	389	20	43	.960	3.18
Andrews,Shane	Mon	123	107	939.0	64	256	15	13	.955	3.07
Kent,Jeff	TOT	95	94	788.2	77	190	21	18	.927	3.05
Fryman,Travis	Det	128	128	1116.1	97	275	8	24	.979	3.00
Brosius,Scott	Oak	109	108	946.1	83	231	10	25	.969	2.99
Caminiti,Ken	SD	145	142	1274.0	103	310	20	28	.954	2.92
Hayes,Charlie	TOT	143	135	1182.2	80	303	18	29	.955	2.91
Pendleton,Terry	TOT	149	146	1270.0	109	292	19	25	.955	2.84
Williams,Matt	SF	92	90	796.1	74	176	13	18	.951	2.83
Berry,Sean	Hou	110	110	871.1	67	194	22	13	.922	2.70
Hollins,Dave	TOT	144	142	1226.1	102	260	17	21	.955	2.66
Ventura,Robin	ChA	150	141	1274.1	133	238	10	35	.974	2.62
Naehring,Tim	Bos	116	113	989.0	81	206	11	17	.963	2.61
Gomez,Leo	ChN	124	98	854.1	69	174	7	16	.972	2.56
Wallach,Tim	TOT	91	85	747.1	65	146	10	8	.955	2.54
Zeile,Todd	TOT	135	135	1185.2	96	235	13	22	.962	2.51
Cirillo,Jeff	Mil	154	140	1243.1	105	239	18	18	.950	2.49
Surhoff,B.J.	Bal	106	104	926.1	80	174	14	22	.948	2.47
Thome,Jim	Cle	150	144	1277.1	86	261	17	24	.953	2.44
Gaetti,Gary	StL	133	130	1104.0	63	222	9	16	.969	2.32
Boggs,Wade	NYA	123	120	1026.2	60	202	7	24	.974	2.30
Sprague,Ed	Tor	148	148	1285.0	108	217	15	30	.956	2.28
Randa,Joe	KC	92	80	700.1	44	131	9	11	.951	2.25
Palmer,Dean	Tex	154	153	1321.1	105	218	16	17	.953	2.20
Blowers,Mike	LA	90	90	773.0	56	120	9	6	.951	2.05
Jones,Chipper	Atl	118	116	1037.0	48	184	13	9	.947	2.01
Average	**---**	**124**	**119**	**1043.2**	**81**	**223**	**13**	**20**	**.957**	**2.63**

Third Basemen - The Rest

Player	Tm	G	GS	Inn	PO	A	E	DP	Pct.	Rng
Abbott,Kurt	Fla	33	27	218.1	22	43	6	3	.915	2.68
Alexander,Manny	Bal	7	5	43.0	3	9	1	1	.923	2.51
Alfonzo,Edgardo	NYN	36	21	214.1	17	50	3	5	.957	2.81
Amaral,Rich	Sea	1	0	3.0	0	0	0	0	.000	.00
Arias,Alex	Fla	59	29	295.0	21	67	4	8	.957	2.68
Baerga,Carlos	NYN	6	3	33.0	2	4	3	0	.667	1.64
Barberie,Bret	ChN	2	2	17.0	1	2	0	0	1.000	1.59
Bates,Jason	Col	12	4	43.2	0	9	2	1	.818	1.85
Batista,Tony	Oak	18	5	68.0	9	18	2	3	.931	3.57
Batiste,Kim	SF	25	22	192.2	24	37	11	7	.847	2.85
Battle,Howard	Phi	1	0	2.0	0	0	0	0	.000	.00
Bell,David	StL	45	23	237.1	22	59	4	1	.953	3.07
Beltre,Esteban	Bos	13	10	99.2	11	13	0	1	1.000	2.17
Bogar,Tim	NYN	25	9	103.1	13	22	1	0	.972	3.05
Bonilla,Bobby	Bal	4	4	34.0	1	3	0	0	1.000	1.06
Booty,Josh	Fla	1	0	1.0	0	0	0	0	.000	.00
Branson,Jeff	Cin	64	42	407.1	31	93	9	12	.932	2.74
Busch,Mike	LA	23	18	158.2	16	25	3	1	.932	2.33
Candaele,Casey	Cle	3	0	6.0	1	3	0	1	1.000	6.00
Castellano,Pedro	Col	1	1	4.0	0	1	0	0	1.000	2.25
Castro,Juan	LA	23	0	54.2	5	3	1	1	.889	1.32
Cedeno,Andujar	SD	2	1	12.0	1	2	0	0	1.000	2.25
Cedeno,Andujar	Det	1	0	3.1	0	2	0	0	1.000	5.40
Cedeno,Andujar	Hou	1	0	1.0	0	1	0	0	1.000	9.00
Cedeno,Domingo	Tor	6	1	33.0	5	13	0	2	1.000	4.91

Third Basemen - The Rest

Player	Tm	G	GS	Inn	PO	A	E	DP	Pct.	Rng
Cianfrocco,Archi	SD	11	6	68.1	2	14	2	2	.889	2.11
Clark,Phil	Bos	1	0	1.0	0	1	0	0	1.000	9.00
Coomer,Ron	Min	9	3	39.0	2	3	0	0	1.000	1.15
Cora,Joey	Sea	1	0	1.0	0	0	0	0	.000	.00
Crespo,Felipe	Tor	6	3	33.2	6	8	0	2	1.000	3.74
Davis,Russ	Sea	51	49	427.1	31	67	7	5	.933	2.06
Decker,Steve	SF	2	1	7.0	2	2	0	0	1.000	5.14
Delgado,Alex	Bos	4	0	4.1	0	0	0	0	.000	.00
Doster,David	Phi	1	0	2.0	0	1	0	0	1.000	4.50
Duncan,Mariano	NYA	3	3	22.0	2	1	1	1	.750	1.23
Easley,Damion	Cal	3	1	13.0	0	4	0	0	1.000	2.77
Easley,Damion	Det	2	2	16.0	2	4	1	2	.857	3.38
Eenhoorn,Robert	NYA	2	0	5.0	2	1	0	0	1.000	5.40
Espinoza,Alvaro	Cle	20	7	73.0	7	11	1	1	.947	2.22
Espinoza,Alvaro	NYN	38	30	265.1	20	53	8	2	.901	2.48
Fonville,Chad	LA	2	1	10.0	2	2	0	0	1.000	3.60
Fox,Andy	NYA	31	9	136.1	9	38	1	3	.979	3.10
Franco,Matt	NYN	8	6	45.0	3	11	3	0	.824	2.80
Galarraga,Andres	Col	1	0	1.0	0	0	0	0	.000	.00
Gallego,Mike	StL	7	1	16.0	3	4	0	0	1.000	3.94
Garcia,Carlos	Pit	14	12	103.0	4	36	3	4	.930	3.50
Giambi,Jason	Oak	39	38	332.1	31	80	8	10	.933	3.01
Giovanola,Ed	Atl	6	1	29.0	1	6	0	1	1.000	2.17
Gonzales,Rene	Tex	15	4	63.0	7	16	0	3	1.000	3.29
Grebeck,Craig	Fla	1	0	1.0	0	0	0	0	.000	.00
Greene,Willie	Cin	74	58	536.2	45	145	15	13	.927	3.19
Gutierrez,Ricky	Hou	6	2	22.1	1	5	0	0	1.000	2.42
Hajek,Dave	Hou	3	1	17.0	1	6	0	0	1.000	3.71
Hale,Chip	Min	3	0	7.0	1	2	0	1	1.000	3.86
Haney,Todd	ChN	4	2	22.0	3	5	1	0	.889	3.27
Hansen,Dave	LA	19	10	85.0	6	19	1	1	.962	2.65
Harris,Lenny	Cin	24	19	174.0	21	37	4	2	.935	3.00
Hayes,Charlie	Pit	124	120	1044.2	66	273	18	25	.950	2.92
Hayes,Charlie	NYA	19	15	138.0	14	30	0	4	1.000	2.87
Hernandez,Jose	ChN	43	11	178.0	13	32	1	2	.978	2.28
Hiatt,Phil	Det	3	3	26.0	2	7	0	1	1.000	3.12
Hollins,Dave	Min	116	115	987.1	81	206	14	15	.953	2.62
Hollins,Dave	Sea	28	27	239.0	21	54	3	6	.962	2.82
Houston,Tyler	Atl	1	0	1.0	0	0	0	0	.000	.00
Houston,Tyler	ChN	9	5	38.2	6	9	1	0	.938	3.49
Howard,Matt	NYA	6	4	33.0	3	4	0	0	1.000	1.91
Howell,Jack	Cal	43	22	212.0	17	44	8	4	.884	2.59
Huff,Michael	Tor	3	3	23.0	1	2	0	1	1.000	1.17
Huskey,Butch	NYN	6	4	32.1	5	8	1	1	.929	3.62
Huson,Jeff	Bal	3	0	6.0	0	1	0	0	1.000	1.50
Johnson,Brian	SD	1	0	2.0	0	0	0	0	.000	.00
Jordan,Kevin	Phi	1	0	2.0	0	1	0	1	1.000	4.50
Kent,Jeff	NYN	89	89	746.2	75	183	21	17	.925	3.11
Kent,Jeff	Cle	6	5	42.0	2	7	0	1	1.000	1.93
King,Jeff	Pit	17	7	75.1	6	24	2	1	.938	3.58
Leius,Scott	Cle	8	4	41.0	3	6	0	0	1.000	1.98
Leyritz,Jim	NYA	13	10	70.0	3	10	4	0	.765	1.67
Liriano,Nelson	Pit	9	7	59.0	4	17	0	0	1.000	3.20
Livingstone,Scott	SD	16	12	109.2	5	24	1	2	.967	2.38
Lockhart,Keith	KC	55	44	371.0	27	75	5	5	.953	2.47
Lopez,Luis	SD	2	0	3.0	1	0	0	0	1.000	3.00
Loretta,Mark	Mil	23	9	99.0	9	23	0	4	1.000	2.91
Lovullo,Torey	Oak	11	7	72.2	9	12	1	2	.955	2.60

258

Third Basemen - The Rest

Player	Tm	G	GS	Inn	PO	A	E	DP	Pct.	Rng
Magadan,Dave	ChN	51	41	307.1	16	64	3	4	.964	2.34
Manto,Jeff	Sea	16	14	119.1	8	26	1	2	.971	2.56
Manto,Jeff	Bos	10	6	59.0	7	17	1	1	.960	3.66
Martin,Norberto	ChA	3	0	4.0	0	1	0	0	1.000	2.25
Martinez,Edgar	Sea	2	1	3.0	1	0	0	0	1.000	3.00
McIntosh,Tim	NYA	1	0	1.0	0	0	0	0	.000	.00
Miller,Orlando	Hou	30	11	148.1	14	24	2	1	.950	2.31
Mordecai,Mike	Atl	9	5	59.2	4	12	1	0	.941	2.41
Mueller,Bill	SF	45	40	366.0	34	79	4	10	.966	2.78
Munoz,Jose	ChA	1	0	1.0	0	0	0	0	.000	.00
Nevin,Phil	Det	24	23	203.0	17	49	4	6	.943	2.93
Norton,Greg	ChA	2	2	18.2	4	2	0	1	1.000	2.89
Osik,Keith	Pit	2	0	3.0	1	2	0	1	1.000	9.00
Owens,Eric	Cin	5	3	20.0	1	4	0	0	1.000	2.25
Paquette,Craig	KC	51	34	344.0	20	69	11	4	.890	2.33
Pena,Geronimo	Cle	3	1	11.0	0	0	0	0	.000	.00
Pendleton,Terry	Fla	108	106	927.2	82	214	12	20	.961	2.87
Pendleton,Terry	Atl	41	40	342.1	27	78	7	5	.938	2.76
Perez,Eduardo	Cin	3	3	20.0	3	4	0	0	1.000	3.15
Perez,Tomas	Tor	11	7	71.0	1	14	2	0	.882	1.90
Perry,Herbert	Cle	1	0	2.0	0	0	0	0	.000	.00
Pozo,Arquimedez	Bos	10	8	74.2	5	17	1	1	.957	2.65
Quinlan,Tom	Min	4	1	19.0	0	2	1	0	.667	0.95
Raabe,Brian	Min	6	1	20.0	2	4	1	1	.857	2.70
Reboulet,Jeff	Min	36	22	216.1	19	41	1	5	.984	2.50
Ripken,Billy	Bal	25	15	148.2	3	38	0	1	1.000	2.48
Ripken,Cal	Bal	6	6	49.0	5	16	0	1	1.000	3.86
Rodriguez,Tony	Bos	5	2	20.0	2	1	1	0	.750	1.35
Rolen,Scott	Phi	37	37	322.1	29	54	4	4	.954	2.32
Sabo,Chris	Cin	43	37	285.0	27	71	4	6	.961	3.09
Santangelo,F.P.	Mon	23	17	138.2	14	34	2	2	.960	3.12
Scarsone,Steve	SF	14	9	80.1	5	16	2	3	.913	2.35
Schofield,Dick	Cal	1	0	7.0	0	1	0	0	1.000	1.29
Schu,Rick	Mon	1	1	9.0	0	2	1	0	.667	2.00
Sefcik,Kevin	Phi	20	19	171.0	8	34	6	3	.875	2.21
Seitzer,Kevin	Mil	12	12	93.0	9	19	3	2	.903	2.71
Selby,Bill	Bos	14	10	95.0	6	15	3	0	.875	1.99
Sheaffer,Danny	StL	17	8	95.0	6	17	1	0	.958	2.18
Sheets,Andy	Sea	25	22	183.0	16	38	3	7	.947	2.66
Shipley,Craig	SD	4	1	19.0	1	5	0	0	1.000	2.84
Shumpert,Terry	ChN	10	3	39.0	8	4	1	0	.923	2.77
Silvestri,Dave	Mon	47	37	352.1	20	84	10	5	.912	2.66
Snopek,Chris	ChA	27	19	163.0	12	34	3	5	.939	2.54
Sojo,Luis	Sea	33	26	231.1	24	56	5	7	.941	3.11
Sojo,Luis	NYA	1	1	8.0	0	1	0	0	1.000	1.13
Spiers,Bill	Hou	76	38	387.0	22	93	5	8	.958	2.67
Spiezio,Scott	Oak	5	4	37.0	6	5	2	0	.846	2.68
Stankiewicz,Andy	Mon	1	0	2.0	0	1	1	0	.500	4.50
Stillwell,Kurt	Tex	6	0	11.0	0	1	0	1	1.000	0.82
Strange,Doug	Sea	39	22	224.2	11	38	2	3	.961	1.96
Stynes,Chris	KC	2	2	15.0	0	2	1	0	.667	1.20
Sveum,Dale	Pit	10	8	71.2	4	17	2	1	.913	2.64
Tatum,Jimmy	Bos	2	2	19.1	3	2	0	0	1.000	2.33
Tatum,Jimmy	SD	1	0	1.0	0	0	0	0	.000	.00
Trammell,Alan	Det	8	6	62.0	7	13	0	1	1.000	2.90
Unroe,Tim	Mil	3	1	12.0	0	10	0	0	1.000	7.50
Valentin,John	Bos	12	11	96.0	8	10	1	1	.947	1.69
Velarde,Randy	Cal	28	20	187.1	13	45	6	4	.906	2.79

Third Basemen - The Rest

Player	Tm	G	GS	Inn	PO	A	E	DP	Pct.	Rng
Voigt,Jack	Tex	1	0	3.0	0	1	0	0	1.000	3.00
Walker,Todd	Min	20	20	151.0	11	32	2	3	.956	2.56
Wallach,Tim	Cal	46	42	362.1	27	84	7	5	.941	2.76
Wallach,Tim	LA	45	43	385.0	38	63	3	3	.971	2.34
Wehner,John	Pit	24	8	96.2	8	24	0	3	1.000	2.98
Williams,Eddie	Det	3	0	6.0	0	1	0	0	1.000	1.50
Worthington,Craig	Tex	7	6	51.0	2	9	1	1	.917	1.94
Young,Kevin	KC	7	1	19.2	3	2	0	0	1.000	2.29
Zeile,Todd	Phi	106	106	924.0	72	179	10	13	.962	2.44
Zeile,Todd	Bal	29	29	261.2	24	56	3	9	.964	2.75

Shortstops - Regulars

Player	Tm	G	GS	Inn	PO	A	E	DP	Pct.	Rng
Sanchez,Rey	ChN	92	90	768.0	152	309	11	55	.977	5.40
Gonzalez,Alex	Tor	147	147	1316.0	280	465	21	123	.973	5.09
Bordick,Mike	Oak	155	153	1338.0	266	474	16	121	.979	4.98
Renteria,Edgar	Fla	106	103	922.1	162	344	11	76	.979	4.94
Valentin,Jose	Mil	151	145	1290.1	247	460	37	114	.950	4.93
Ordonez,Rey	NYN	150	145	1262.1	230	452	27	103	.962	4.86
Howard,Dave	KC	135	123	1109.0	196	403	11	109	.982	4.86
Elster,Kevin	Tex	157	155	1355.0	287	441	14	104	.981	4.84
Bell,Jay	Pit	151	143	1289.1	215	477	10	78	.986	4.83
Larkin,Barry	Cin	151	148	1242.1	231	426	17	80	.975	4.76
Dunston,Shawon	SF	78	77	634.0	116	218	15	51	.957	4.74
Weiss,Walt	Col	155	148	1275.0	220	449	30	89	.957	4.72
Gagne,Greg	LA	127	126	1126.2	184	404	21	86	.966	4.70
Stocker,Kevin	Phi	119	111	991.2	165	352	13	79	.975	4.69
DiSarcina,Gary	Cal	150	148	1290.0	212	460	20	94	.971	4.69
Valentin,John	Bos	118	117	1043.1	194	349	16	87	.971	4.68
Aurilia,Rich	SF	93	71	678.2	126	227	10	44	.972	4.68
Hernandez,Jose	ChN	87	71	670.0	134	214	19	50	.948	4.67
Clayton,Royce	StL	113	111	997.2	170	346	15	67	.972	4.65
Vizquel,Omar	Cle	150	149	1312.1	227	446	20	92	.971	4.62
Rodriguez,Alex	Sea	146	145	1267.2	239	403	15	92	.977	4.56
Gomez,Chris	TOT	136	126	1146.0	203	375	19	88	.968	4.54
Ripken,Cal	Bal	158	157	1379.2	229	466	14	109	.980	4.53
Jeter,Derek	NYA	157	156	1370.2	245	443	22	85	.969	4.52
Cedeno,Andujar	TOT	100	91	803.1	113	284	22	58	.947	4.45
Meares,Pat	Min	150	144	1249.1	257	344	22	85	.965	4.33
Grudzielanek,Mark	Mon	153	153	1328.2	181	454	27	78	.959	4.30
Guillen,Ozzie	ChA	146	129	1197.0	221	348	11	69	.981	4.28
Miller,Orlando	Hou	116	110	913.2	133	296	19	59	.958	4.23
Blauser,Jeff	Atl	79	78	654.1	84	207	23	41	.927	4.00
Average	---	130	125	1107.1	197	377	18	82	.969	4.67

Shortstops - The Rest

Player	Tm	G	GS	Inn	PO	A	E	DP	Pct.	Rng
Abbott,Kurt	Fla	44	41	360.0	67	123	6	34	.969	4.75
Alexander,Manny	Bal	21	6	89.0	14	33	3	6	.940	4.75
Alfonzo,Edgardo	NYN	15	8	85.0	7	22	0	5	1.000	3.07
Arias,Alex	Fla	20	18	158.1	26	60	3	15	.966	4.89
Barberie,Bret	ChN	1	0	3.0	0	0	0	0	.000	.00
Bates,Jason	Col	18	8	79.2	8	22	2	1	.938	3.39
Batista,Tony	Oak	4	3	27.0	4	11	0	1	1.000	5.00

Shortstops - The Rest

Player	Tm	G	GS	Inn	PO	A	E	DP	Pct.	Rng
Batiste,Kim	SF	7	4	42.0	11	4	0	4	1.000	3.21
Bell,David	StL	1	0	1.0	0	0	0	0	.000	.00
Belliard,Rafael	Atl	63	33	340.1	51	125	3	25	.983	4.65
Beltre,Esteban	Bos	6	2	20.0	4	3	0	0	1.000	3.15
Benjamin,Mike	Phi	31	30	252.1	37	87	6	14	.954	4.42
Blowers,Mike	LA	1	0	1.0	0	0	0	0	.000	.00
Bogar,Tim	NYN	19	6	62.1	10	23	0	6	1.000	4.76
Bournigal,Rafael	Oak	23	6	90.1	13	33	0	6	1.000	4.58
Branson,Jeff	Cin	38	14	198.2	30	63	3	17	.969	4.21
Brito,Tilson	Tor	5	5	40.2	6	10	0	3	1.000	3.54
Candaele,Casey	Cle	1	0	2.0	1	0	0	0	1.000	4.50
Canizaro,Jay	SF	7	4	35.1	4	12	2	3	.889	4.08
Castro,Juan	LA	30	26	224.2	40	69	2	21	.982	4.37
Cedeno,Andujar	SD	47	43	364.2	43	131	10	28	.946	4.29
Cedeno,Andujar	Det	51	47	429.2	67	147	12	27	.947	4.48
Cedeno,Andujar	Hou	2	1	9.0	3	6	0	3	1.000	9.00
Cedeno,Domingo	Tor	5	5	44.0	12	16	0	4	1.000	5.73
Cedeno,Domingo	ChA	2	2	18.2	6	4	1	2	.909	4.82
Cianfrocco,Archi	SD	10	6	56.1	13	16	0	2	1.000	4.63
Cruz,Fausto	Det	4	3	27.0	4	10	3	2	.824	4.67
Delgado,Wilson	SF	6	6	51.0	12	12	1	3	.960	4.24
Easley,Damion	Cal	13	5	69.0	9	24	2	10	.943	4.30
Easley,Damion	Det	8	8	56.0	6	19	1	6	.962	4.02
Eenhoorn,Robert	Cal	4	3	24.0	1	6	1	1	.875	2.63
Espinoza,Alvaro	Cle	16	8	96.0	16	29	1	2	.978	4.22
Espinoza,Alvaro	NYN	7	3	30.1	4	13	0	3	1.000	5.04
Fermin,Felix	ChN	2	1	8.0	3	2	0	0	1.000	5.63
Fonville,Chad	LA	20	10	114.0	11	33	3	5	.936	3.47
Fox,Andy	NYA	9	4	45.1	8	16	3	3	.889	4.76
Frye,Jeff	Bos	3	0	4.0	1	0	0	0	1.000	2.25
Fryman,Travis	Det	29	29	250.1	53	83	2	18	.986	4.89
Gallego,Mike	StL	1	1	11.0	3	4	0	1	1.000	5.73
Garcia,Carlos	Pit	19	16	133.2	25	49	3	14	.961	4.98
Garciaparra,Nomar	Bos	22	21	190.2	35	50	1	11	.988	4.01
Gil,Benji	Tex	5	2	20.0	5	7	1	0	.923	5.40
Giovanola,Ed	Atl	25	13	123.0	18	39	1	9	.983	4.17
Gomez,Chris	Det	47	38	344.0	77	114	6	34	.970	5.00
Gomez,Chris	SD	89	88	802.0	126	261	13	54	.968	4.34
Gomez,Leo	ChN	1	0	1.0	0	0	0	1	1.000	9.00
Gonzales,Rene	Tex	10	4	47.0	12	21	1	5	.971	6.32
Grebeck,Craig	Fla	2	0	2.1	0	1	0	0	1.000	3.86
Greene,Willie	Cin	1	0	2.0	0	2	0	0	1.000	9.00
Gutierrez,Ricky	Hou	74	47	483.1	82	140	11	32	.953	4.13
Haney,Todd	ChN	3	0	2.1	0	0	0	0	.000	.00
Hocking,Denny	Min	6	1	18.0	3	3	0	1	1.000	3.00
Hollins,Dave	Min	1	0	1.0	0	0	1	0	.000	.00
Jackson,Damian	Cle	5	2	21.0	3	13	0	4	1.000	6.86
Jones,Chipper	Atl	38	38	331.1	55	103	4	27	.975	4.29
Lansing,Mike	Mon	2	1	10.0	2	2	0	1	1.000	3.60
Liriano,Nelson	Pit	5	3	30.1	4	8	1	2	.923	3.56
Listach,Pat	Mil	7	6	46.0	5	10	1	1	.938	2.93
Lopez,Luis	SD	35	20	217.2	37	68	2	11	.981	4.34
Loretta,Mark	Mil	21	11	111.0	22	31	1	12	.981	4.30
Lovullo,Torey	Oak	1	0	1.0	0	0	0	0	.000	.00
Manto,Jeff	Bos	4	3	30.0	7	14	2	3	.913	6.30
Martin,Norberto	ChA	24	18	141.2	39	44	5	18	.943	5.27
Martinez,Pablo	Atl	1	0	9.0	0	2	0	1	1.000	2.00
Mordecai,Mike	Atl	6	0	11.0	1	1	0	0	1.000	1.64

Shortstops - The Rest

Player	Tm	G	GS	Inn	PO	A	E	DP	Pct.	Rng
Munoz,Jose	ChA	2	0	2.0	0	1	0	0	1.000	4.50
Norton,Greg	ChA	6	3	25.2	4	3	2	0	.778	2.45
Offerman,Jose	KC	37	32	269.0	54	85	10	30	.933	4.65
Paquette,Craig	KC	11	6	72.0	14	16	1	6	.968	3.75
Perez,Neifi	Col	14	6	68.0	15	20	1	8	.972	4.63
Perez,Tomas	Tor	5	5	45.0	17	10	2	4	.931	5.40
Reboulet,Jeff	Min	37	17	171.1	34	41	1	13	.987	3.94
Relaford,Desi	Phi	9	6	53.2	13	15	2	2	.933	4.70
Rodriguez,Tony	Bos	21	19	170.0	29	63	2	11	.979	4.87
Santangelo,F.P.	Mon	1	0	1.0	0	0	0	0	.000	.00
Scarsone,Steve	SF	1	0	0.1	0	0	0	0	.000	.00
Schofield,Dick	Cal	7	2	24.2	5	3	1	1	.889	2.92
Sefcik,Kevin	Phi	21	15	125.2	22	48	1	9	.986	5.01
Sheets,Andy	Sea	7	3	33.0	6	10	0	2	1.000	4.36
Shipley,Craig	SD	7	5	48.1	4	19	0	1	1.000	4.28
Shumpert,Terry	ChN	1	0	4.0	1	3	0	2	1.000	9.00
Silvestri,Dave	Mon	10	1	26.1	0	7	0	0	1.000	2.39
Smith,Ozzie	StL	52	50	442.2	90	162	8	36	.969	5.12
Snopek,Chris	ChA	12	10	76.0	13	31	2	5	.957	5.21
Sojo,Luis	Sea	19	13	131.0	30	44	1	10	.987	5.08
Sojo,Luis	NYA	4	2	24.0	2	8	0	2	1.000	3.75
Spiers,Bill	Hou	5	4	41.0	3	9	0	1	1.000	2.63
Stankiewicz,Andy	Mon	13	7	75.0	4	23	1	4	.964	3.24
Stillwell,Kurt	Tex	9	2	27.1	3	9	1	0	.923	3.95
Trammell,Alan	Det	43	37	325.2	52	108	4	15	.976	4.42
Velarde,Randy	Cal	7	3	31.1	6	9	1	2	.938	4.31
Vizcaino,Jose	Cle	4	2	21.0	3	10	0	4	1.000	5.57
Williams,Matt	SF	1	0	1.0	0	0	0	0	.000	.00

Left Fielders - Regulars

Player	Tm	G	GS	Inn	PO	A	E	DP	Pct.	Rng
Phillips,Tony	ChA	150	147	1309.0	344	13	7	3	.981	2.45
Cordova,Marty	Min	145	144	1278.1	327	9	3	0	.991	2.37
Greer,Rusty	Tex	136	135	1187.1	300	6	5	0	.984	2.32
Gilkey,Bernard	NYN	151	151	1290.2	310	18	6	2	.982	2.29
Anderson,Garret	Cal	140	140	1247.1	299	5	7	1	.977	2.19
Vaughn,Greg	TOT	137	135	1130.1	262	6	6	1	.978	2.14
Greenwell,Mike	Bos	75	74	614.0	137	9	4	2	.973	2.14
Belle,Albert	Cle	152	152	1343.0	308	11	10	0	.970	2.14
Newfield,Marc	TOT	79	72	623.2	143	3	1	1	.993	2.11
Bonds,Barry	SF	149	148	1272.2	282	10	6	2	.980	2.06
Gant,Ron	StL	116	116	991.2	216	4	5	2	.978	2.00
Henderson,Rickey	SD	114	98	932.1	197	3	3	0	.985	1.93
Burks,Ellis	Col	129	118	1031.1	216	4	5	1	.978	1.92
Gonzalez,Luis	ChN	139	131	1124.0	231	6	3	1	.988	1.90
Hollandsworth,T	LA	122	103	930.0	174	6	5	0	.973	1.74
Carter,Joe	Tor	115	109	935.2	167	7	7	1	.961	1.67
Conine,Jeff	Fla	128	123	1063.0	187	8	5	2	.975	1.65
Martin,Al	Pit	142	125	1126.1	180	5	7	0	.964	1.48
Klesko,Ryan	Atl	144	142	1211.1	190	6	5	1	.975	1.46
Rodriguez,Henry	Mon	89	88	702.0	101	5	6	0	.946	1.36
Average	---	127	122	1067.0	228	7	5	1	.978	1.99

Left Fielders - The Rest

Player	Tm	G	GS	Inn	PO	A	E	DP	Pct.	Rng
Abreu,Bob	Hou	6	3	30.0	6	0	0	0	1.000	1.80
Aldrete,Mike	Cal	4	1	16.0	2	0	0	0	1.000	1.13
Aldrete,Mike	NYA	6	5	34.1	5	0	0	0	1.000	1.31
Alexander,Manny	Bal	3	2	15.0	2	1	1	0	.750	1.80
Alou,Moises	Mon	33	27	216.1	51	2	2	0	.964	2.20
Amaral,Rich	Sea	63	48	415.1	105	3	0	0	1.000	2.34
Anthony,Eric	Cin	13	13	95.0	13	0	0	0	1.000	1.23
Anthony,Eric	Col	1	1	7.0	0	0	0	0	.000	.00
Ashley,Billy	LA	38	33	221.0	38	2	2	1	.952	1.63
Banks,Brian	Mil	3	0	6.0	1	0	0	0	1.000	1.50
Bartee,Kimera	Det	4	3	26.0	5	0	0	0	1.000	1.73
Battle,Allen	Oak	24	16	140.0	43	2	1	1	.978	2.89
Bautista,Danny	Det	12	9	78.1	19	0	0	0	1.000	2.18
Bautista,Danny	Atl	2	0	5.0	1	0	0	0	1.000	1.80
Beamon,Trey	Pit	5	4	34.0	8	0	1	0	.889	2.12
Becker,Rich	Min	15	12	108.1	32	1	0	0	1.000	2.74
Benard,Marvin	SF	5	0	7.1	1	0	0	0	1.000	1.23
Benitez,Yamil	Mon	3	0	8.0	1	0	0	0	1.000	1.13
Berroa,Geronimo	Oak	17	7	68.2	12	0	0	0	1.000	1.57
Bichette,Dante	Col	19	18	153.0	23	1	0	0	1.000	1.41
Bowers,Brent	Bal	21	10	99.0	22	2	0	0	1.000	2.18
Bradshaw,Terry	StL	4	1	21.0	3	0	0	0	1.000	1.29
Bragg,Darren	Sea	48	40	337.2	88	4	0	1	1.000	2.45
Bragg,Darren	Bos	7	0	9.1	2	0	0	0	1.000	1.93
Brosius,Scott	Oak	3	2	19.0	8	0	0	0	1.000	3.79
Brumfield,Jacob	Tor	18	11	111.1	33	1	0	0	1.000	2.75
Buford,Damon	Tex	14	5	59.2	18	0	0	0	1.000	2.72
Bullett,Scott	ChN	28	5	85.0	23	0	0	0	1.000	2.44
Burnitz,Jeromy	Cle	10	4	52.1	11	0	0	0	1.000	1.89
Cameron,Mike	ChA	2	0	3.2	1	0	0	0	1.000	2.45
Cangelosi,John	Hou	53	33	321.2	61	4	1	0	.985	1.82
Canseco,Jose	Bos	10	9	79.1	13	1	0	0	1.000	1.59
Carreon,Mark	SF	3	2	24.0	3	1	0	0	1.000	1.50
Castellano,Pedro	Col	1	0	2.0	0	0	0	0	.000	.00
Castro,Juan	LA	1	0	1.0	2	0	0	0	1.000	18.00
Cedeno,Roger	LA	20	9	100.2	21	0	1	0	.955	1.88
Cianfrocco,Archi	SD	1	1	9.0	0	0	0	0	.000	.00
Clark,Dave	Pit	34	24	203.2	47	1	0	0	1.000	2.12
Clark,Dave	LA	1	1	9.0	0	0	0	0	.000	.00
Coleman,Vince	Cin	20	17	150.2	28	2	1	0	.968	1.79
Cruz,Jacob	SF	6	5	46.0	8	1	0	0	1.000	1.76
Curtis,Chad	Det	48	27	257.2	61	3	2	0	.970	2.24
Daulton,Darren	Phi	5	5	38.0	6	0	0	0	1.000	1.42
Davis,Eric	Cin	14	12	104.2	22	1	0	0	1.000	1.98
Dawson,Andre	Fla	6	6	47.0	5	0	1	0	.833	0.96
Deer,Rob	SD	1	0	1.0	1	0	0	0	1.000	9.00
Delgado,Alex	Bos	5	1	15.0	4	1	0	0	1.000	3.00
Devereaux,Mike	Bal	35	27	233.1	41	1	1	1	.977	1.62
Diaz,Alex	Sea	19	12	117.0	36	0	0	0	1.000	2.77
Duncan,Mariano	NYA	2	1	9.0	2	0	0	0	1.000	2.00
Dunn,Todd	Mil	1	0	1.0	0	0	0	0	.000	.00
Dye,Jermaine	Atl	25	14	131.1	21	0	4	0	.840	1.44
Echevarria,Angel	Col	4	0	8.0	1	0	0	0	1.000	1.13
Eisenreich,Jim	Phi	43	34	320.1	72	0	1	0	.986	2.02
Erstad,Darin	Cal	11	11	96.2	17	2	1	0	.950	1.77
Everett,Carl	NYN	8	4	44.1	16	2	1	1	.947	3.65
Faneyte,Rikkert	Tex	2	1	8.2	6	0	0	0	1.000	6.23
Floyd,Cliff	Mon	69	36	373.1	70	2	3	0	.960	1.74

Left Fielders - The Rest

Player	Tm	G	GS	Inn	PO	A	E	DP	Pct.	Rng
Fonville,Chad	LA	19	8	86.0	14	1	1	0	.938	1.57
Frazier,Lou	Tex	12	9	84.2	22	3	1	0	.962	2.66
Frye,Jeff	Bos	2	2	15.0	2	0	0	0	1.000	1.20
Giambi,Jason	Oak	44	43	328.0	66	6	0	1	1.000	1.98
Gibralter,Steve	Cin	1	0	2.0	0	0	1	0	.000	.00
Giles,Brian S.	Cle	11	4	46.0	16	0	0	0	1.000	3.13
Glanville,Doug	ChN	19	11	110.1	25	1	1	0	.963	2.12
Gonzales,Rene	Tex	1	0	0.0	0	0	0	0	.000	.00
Goodwin,Curtis	Cin	9	1	32.0	8	0	0	0	1.000	2.25
Goodwin,Tom	KC	75	62	549.2	131	7	2	1	.986	2.26
Greene,Willie	Cin	9	6	55.2	10	0	1	0	.909	1.62
Guillen,Ozzie	ChA	2	0	3.0	2	0	0	0	1.000	6.00
Gwynn,Chris	SD	5	2	18.2	4	0	0	0	1.000	1.93
Hall,Mel	SF	3	0	6.0	0	0	0	0	.000	.00
Hammonds,Jeffrey	Bal	64	55	511.0	122	2	2	0	.984	2.18
Harris,Lenny	Cin	23	14	129.2	30	2	0	0	1.000	2.22
Hiatt,Phil	Det	1	0	1.0	1	0	0	0	1.000	9.00
Higginson,Bob	Det	63	54	474.2	94	4	3	1	.970	1.86
Hosey,Dwayne	Bos	7	5	43.1	10	0	0	0	1.000	2.08
Houston,Tyler	Atl	1	0	2.0	0	0	0	0	.000	.00
Howard,Thomas	Cin	51	27	273.0	50	2	0	1	1.000	1.71
Hubbard,Trent	Col	3	0	3.0	0	0	0	0	.000	.00
Hubbard,Trent	SF	8	6	58.1	14	0	0	0	1.000	2.16
Hudler,Rex	Cal	8	6	45.0	14	1	0	0	1.000	3.00
Huff,Michael	Tor	1	0	1.0	0	0	0	0	.000	.00
Hulse,David	Mil	24	3	61.1	18	0	0	0	1.000	2.64
Hunter,Brian	Sea	29	20	194.2	58	3	2	0	.968	2.82
Hyers,Tim	Det	1	1	8.0	3	0	0	0	1.000	3.38
Incaviglia,Pete	Phi	70	68	529.1	89	4	3	0	.969	1.58
Incaviglia,Pete	Bal	7	6	45.0	9	1	0	0	1.000	2.00
James,Dion	NYA	3	3	22.0	3	0	0	0	1.000	1.23
Jefferies,Gregg	Phi	51	50	436.0	110	1	0	0	1.000	2.29
Jefferson,Reggie	Bos	45	37	296.0	61	1	2	0	.969	1.89
Johnson,Mark	Pit	1	1	9.0	1	1	1	0	.667	2.00
Jones,Chris	NYN	17	6	77.0	14	0	2	0	.875	1.64
Kelly,Mike	Cin	6	5	39.0	6	1	1	1	.875	1.62
Kelly,Roberto	Min	6	6	48.0	11	0	1	0	.917	2.06
Kieschnick,Brooks	ChN	4	3	21.0	2	0	1	0	.667	0.86
Kingery,Mike	Pit	5	3	30.1	8	0	0	0	1.000	2.37
Kirby,Wayne	Cle	2	0	2.0	2	0	0	0	1.000	9.00
Kirby,Wayne	LA	8	2	42.1	9	1	2	0	.833	2.13
Koslofski,Kevin	Mil	6	0	10.0	1	0	0	0	1.000	0.90
Lawton,Matt	Min	1	0	2.0	0	0	0	0	.000	.00
Lennon,Patrick	KC	11	8	70.0	18	0	1	0	.947	2.31
Lesher,Brian	Oak	14	10	98.2	19	1	1	0	.952	1.82
Lewis,Darren	ChA	1	0	4.0	3	0	0	0	1.000	6.75
Leyritz,Jim	NYA	3	2	17.0	3	0	0	0	1.000	1.59
Listach,Pat	Mil	2	0	4.0	1	1	0	0	1.000	4.50
Lovullo,Torey	Oak	1	1	9.0	1	0	0	0	1.000	1.00
Mabry,John	StL	1	0	3.0	0	0	0	0	.000	.00
Magee,Wendell	Phi	6	5	50.0	6	0	1	0	.857	1.08
Malave,Jose	Bos	8	6	53.0	7	0	0	0	1.000	1.19
Manto,Jeff	Sea	1	0	1.0	0	0	0	0	.000	.00
Martinez,Dave	ChA	3	2	18.0	0	0	0	0	.000	.00
Martinez,Manny	Sea	2	1	12.0	1	1	0	0	1.000	1.50
Martinez,Manny	Phi	1	0	1.0	0	1	0	0	1.000	9.00
Mashore,Damon	Oak	35	9	120.2	33	0	1	0	.971	2.46
May,Derrick	Hou	70	65	524.0	123	4	4	0	.969	2.18

Left Fielders - The Rest

Player	Tm	G	GS	Inn	PO	A	E	DP	Pct.	Rng
McCarty,Dave	SF	5	1	16.0	0	1	0	0	1.000	0.56
McCracken,Q	Col	8	2	24.1	5	0	0	0	1.000	1.85
McGee,Willie	StL	35	18	190.2	37	1	2	0	.950	1.79
McMillon,Billy	Fla	15	10	91.1	17	0	0	0	1.000	1.68
Mejia,Miguel	StL	5	0	8.0	3	0	1	0	.750	3.38
Mieske,Matt	Mil	9	5	46.0	14	0	0	0	1.000	2.74
Mitchell,Keith	Cin	2	0	3.0	1	0	0	0	1.000	3.00
Mitchell,Kevin	Bos	1	1	8.0	1	0	0	0	1.000	1.13
Mitchell,Kevin	Cin	31	30	218.1	44	0	1	0	.978	1.81
Montgomery,Ray	Hou	5	2	18.1	5	0	0	0	1.000	2.45
Mouton,James	Hou	79	51	498.0	100	5	4	1	.963	1.90
Mouton,Lyle	ChA	22	13	122.1	26	0	2	0	.929	1.91
Munoz,Jose	ChA	1	0	1.0	0	0	0	0	.000	.00
Murray,Glenn	Phi	1	0	2.0	1	0	0	0	1.000	4.50
Myers,Rod	KC	4	1	15.0	3	0	0	0	1.000	1.80
Nevin,Phil	Det	9	7	55.2	16	1	1	0	.944	2.75
Newfield,Marc	SD	30	23	198.2	47	0	0	0	1.000	2.13
Newfield,Marc	Mil	49	49	425.0	96	3	1	1	.990	2.10
Newson,Warren	Tex	8	8	70.0	14	2	0	1	1.000	2.06
Nieves,Melvin	Det	21	21	182.1	47	2	4	0	.925	2.42
Nilsson,Dave	Mil	6	6	49.0	9	0	0	0	1.000	1.65
Norman,Les	KC	15	0	34.0	5	0	0	0	1.000	1.32
Nunnally,Jon	KC	7	4	36.2	5	0	1	0	.833	1.23
O'Leary,Troy	Bos	66	27	304.1	68	3	3	0	.959	2.10
Oliver,Joe	Cin	2	0	3.0	1	0	0	0	1.000	3.00
Orsulak,Joe	Fla	30	21	188.2	42	6	2	0	.960	2.29
Osik,Keith	Pit	2	1	12.0	1	0	0	0	1.000	0.75
Owens,Eric	Cin	52	37	337.0	65	3	1	1	.986	1.82
Palmeiro,Orlando	Cal	7	2	27.0	7	0	0	0	1.000	2.33
Paquette,Craig	KC	47	41	344.2	79	3	2	1	.976	2.14
Parker,Rick	LA	1	0	3.0	0	0	0	0	.000	.00
Peltier,Dan	SF	1	0	4.0	0	0	0	0	.000	.00
Pemberton,Rudy	Bos	1	0	2.0	1	0	0	0	1.000	4.50
Penn,Shannon	Det	1	0	1.0	0	0	0	0	.000	.00
Perez,Danny	Mil	2	0	3.0	1	0	0	0	1.000	3.00
Perez,Robert	Tor	59	39	360.2	90	3	2	0	.979	2.32
Plantier,Phil	Oak	67	59	534.1	136	8	4	2	.973	2.43
Polonia,Luis	Bal	32	26	245.2	53	1	1	0	.982	1.98
Polonia,Luis	Atl	7	2	39.0	4	1	1	0	.833	1.15
Pride,Curtis	Det	45	36	296.0	81	0	3	0	.964	2.46
Pulliam,Harvey	Col	3	2	19.0	4	0	0	0	1.000	1.89
Raines,Tim	NYA	51	47	408.0	78	3	1	0	.988	1.79
Reboulet,Jeff	Min	2	0	3.0	1	0	0	0	1.000	3.00
Rivera,Ruben	NYA	13	5	64.1	16	0	0	0	1.000	2.24
Roberson,Kevin	NYN	1	0	3.0	0	0	0	0	.000	.00
Roberts,Bip	KC	8	7	60.1	9	1	0	1	1.000	1.49
Samuel,Juan	Tor	8	3	37.0	5	0	0	0	1.000	1.22
Santangelo,F.P.	Mon	33	11	140.1	29	0	0	0	1.000	1.86
Selby,Bill	Bos	6	0	12.2	2	0	0	0	1.000	1.42
Sheaffer,Danny	StL	3	1	10.0	3	0	0	0	1.000	2.70
Sierra,Ruben	NYA	32	32	259.0	53	4	1	1	.983	1.98
Sierra,Ruben	Det	4	3	35.0	3	0	1	0	.750	0.77
Silvestri,Dave	Mon	1	0	1.0	0	0	0	0	.000	.00
Simms,Mike	Hou	9	8	55.0	14	0	0	0	1.000	2.29
Singleton,Duane	Det	3	1	16.0	3	0	0	0	1.000	1.69
Smith,Dwight	Atl	3	0	10.0	1	0	0	0	1.000	0.90
Smith,Mark	Bal	12	12	98.0	33	0	1	0	.971	3.03
Stairs,Matt	Oak	16	15	125.0	34	4	1	2	.974	2.74

Left Fielders - The Rest

Player	Tm	G	GS	Inn	PO	A	E	DP	Pct.	Rng
Stevens,Lee	Tex	5	5	34.0	5	0	0	0	1.000	1.32
Strange,Doug	Sea	10	6	46.0	10	0	0	0	1.000	1.96
Strawberry,Darryl	NYA	26	25	190.1	32	0	0	0	1.000	1.51
Stynes,Chris	KC	19	16	132.0	30	1	2	0	.939	2.11
Surhoff,B.J.	Bal	27	25	221.2	46	1	1	0	.979	1.91
Sweeney,Mark	StL	36	26	228.0	51	1	1	0	.981	2.05
Tavarez,Jesus	Fla	25	2	53.0	10	0	0	0	1.000	1.70
Thompson,Milt	LA	17	6	73.1	13	0	0	0	1.000	1.60
Thompson,Milt	Col	1	1	7.0	2	0	0	0	1.000	2.57
Timmons,Ozzie	ChN	25	12	116.0	31	1	0	0	1.000	2.48
Tinsley,Lee	Phi	18	0	46.2	6	0	0	0	1.000	1.16
Tinsley,Lee	Bos	4	0	6.0	1	0	0	0	1.000	1.50
Tomberlin,Andy	NYN	9	1	25.0	3	0	0	0	1.000	1.08
Trammell,Alan	Det	1	0	1.0	1	0	0	0	1.000	9.00
Tucker,Michael	KC	28	22	204.2	50	1	1	1	.981	2.24
Turner,Chris	Cal	1	1	7.0	1	0	0	0	1.000	1.29
Unroe,Tim	Mil	1	0	1.0	0	0	0	0	.000	.00
Vander Wal,John	Col	25	20	168.0	33	0	0	0	1.000	1.77
Vaughn,Greg	Mil	98	97	801.0	188	5	4	1	.980	2.17
Vaughn,Greg	SD	39	38	329.1	74	2	2	0	.974	2.08
Voigt,Jack	Tex	2	0	5.0	3	0	0	0	1.000	5.40
Walton,Jerome	Atl	23	4	70.1	22	0	0	0	1.000	2.82
Ward,Turner	Mil	15	2	40.0	13	0	0	0	1.000	2.93
Wehner,John	Pit	9	4	38.0	6	0	0	0	1.000	1.42
Whiten,Mark	Sea	36	34	308.0	87	4	2	0	.978	2.66
Williams,Gerald	NYA	70	42	436.0	89	0	2	0	.978	1.84
Williams,Keith	SF	1	0	8.0	1	0	0	0	1.000	1.13
Wilson,Nigel	Cle	1	1	9.0	0	0	0	0	.000	.00
Young,Ernie	Oak	8	0	13.0	4	0	0	0	1.000	2.77
Young,Kevin	KC	2	0	3.0	0	0	0	0	.000	.00

Center Fielders - Regulars

Player	Tm	G	GS	Inn	PO	A	E	DP	Pct.	Rng
Becker,Rich	Min	121	114	1012.1	335	18	2	9	.994	3.14
Griffey Jr,Ken	Sea	137	134	1173.0	374	10	4	1	.990	2.95
Young,Ernie	Oak	133	123	1061.2	339	8	1	4	.997	2.94
Nixon,Otis	Tor	125	125	1079.1	341	5	2	1	.994	2.89
Edmonds,Jim	Cal	111	105	921.2	280	6	1	2	.997	2.79
Damon,Johnny	KC	89	75	669.0	204	3	3	2	.986	2.78
Hamilton,Darryl	Tex	147	145	1266.1	388	2	0	0	1.000	2.77
Benard,Marvin	SF	102	97	848.0	254	6	3	0	.989	2.76
Otero,Ricky	Phi	100	98	834.1	247	8	4	2	.985	2.75
Lewis,Darren	ChA	137	95	933.0	284	0	3	0	.990	2.74
Johnson,Lance	NYN	157	156	1356.1	390	9	12	3	.971	2.65
Lankford,Ray	StL	144	142	1242.0	356	9	1	0	.997	2.64
Lofton,Kenny	Cle	153	153	1334.0	375	13	10	3	.975	2.62
Curtis,Chad	TOT	120	96	858.0	244	5	8	2	.969	2.61
Davis,Eric	Cin	115	102	893.2	251	3	3	0	.988	2.56
Goodwin,Tom	KC	81	68	613.1	173	0	3	0	.983	2.54
Anderson,Brady	Bal	143	143	1258.1	343	10	3	1	.992	2.52
Williams,Bernie	NYA	140	140	1232.0	334	10	5	3	.986	2.51
Hunter,Brian L.	Hou	127	117	1046.2	279	11	12	0	.960	2.49
Finley,Steve	SD	160	152	1416.2	384	7	7	2	.982	2.48
White,Rondell	Mon	86	83	734.1	185	5	2	0	.990	2.33
McRae,Brian	ChN	155	153	1358.2	343	2	5	1	.986	2.29
Grissom,Marquis	Atl	158	157	1380.0	338	10	1	1	.997	2.27

Center Fielders - Regulars

Player	Tm	G	GS	Inn	PO	A	E	DP	Pct.	Rng
White,Devon	Fla	139	137	1200.2	296	5	4	1	.987	2.26
Average	---	128	121	1071.2	305	6	4	1	.987	2.62

Center Fielders - The Rest

Player	Tm	G	GS	Inn	PO	A	E	DP	Pct.	Rng
Allensworth,J	Pit	61	55	501.2	139	4	3	0	.979	2.57
Alou,Moises	Mon	7	5	41.2	8	0	0	0	1.000	1.73
Amaral,Rich	Sea	26	21	191.2	60	0	0	0	1.000	2.82
Amaro,Ruben	Phi	7	2	28.2	7	0	0	0	1.000	2.20
Anderson,Garret	Cal	3	1	15.0	5	0	0	0	1.000	3.00
Anthony,Eric	Col	9	9	64.0	13	2	0	0	1.000	2.11
Bartee,Kimera	Det	95	62	593.2	211	1	2	0	.991	3.21
Battle,Allen	Oak	27	15	165.0	39	0	0	0	1.000	2.13
Bautista,Danny	Atl	2	0	5.0	1	0	0	0	1.000	1.80
Bell,Derek	Hou	2	1	13.2	1	0	0	0	1.000	0.66
Bonds,Barry	SF	6	3	36.0	5	0	0	0	1.000	1.25
Bradshaw,Terry	StL	3	1	10.0	1	0	0	0	1.000	0.90
Bragg,Darren	Sea	5	2	28.0	10	2	0	0	1.000	3.86
Bragg,Darren	Bos	47	46	369.2	101	4	0	2	1.000	2.56
Brosius,Scott	Oak	2	0	2.0	0	0	0	0	.000	.00
Brumfield,Jacob	Pit	22	17	152.1	34	1	2	1	.946	2.07
Brumfield,Jacob	Tor	39	30	282.2	74	3	2	0	.975	2.45
Buford,Damon	Tex	25	13	137.0	47	2	0	0	1.000	3.22
Bullett,Scott	ChN	11	6	60.2	14	1	0	0	1.000	2.23
Burks,Ellis	Col	32	31	250.0	64	2	0	1	1.000	2.38
Burnitz,Jeromy	Cle	5	1	27.1	8	0	0	0	1.000	2.63
Burnitz,Jeromy	Mil	8	7	64.0	16	0	0	0	1.000	2.25
Butler,Brett	LA	34	34	279.0	74	1	0	0	.987	2.42
Cameron,Mike	ChA	4	3	22.0	6	0	0	0	1.000	2.45
Cangelosi,John	Hou	29	26	198.2	52	1	2	0	.964	2.40
Carr,Chuck	Mil	27	25	200.1	75	4	0	1	1.000	3.55
Carreon,Mark	Cle	4	2	24.0	7	0	0	0	1.000	2.63
Cedeno,Roger	LA	50	33	324.0	90	1	1	0	.989	2.53
Cole,Alex	Bos	24	17	164.1	37	1	1	1	.974	2.08
Cummings,Midre	Pit	11	10	90.1	23	0	1	0	.958	2.29
Curtis,Chad	Det	80	76	626.0	182	3	7	1	.964	2.66
Curtis,Chad	LA	40	20	232.0	62	2	1	1	.985	2.48
Cuyler,Milt	Bos	30	24	199.0	66	0	0	0	1.000	2.98
Dascenzo,Doug	SD	1	1	7.0	0	0	0	0	.000	.00
Devereaux,Mike	Bal	30	19	196.1	65	4	0	2	1.000	3.16
Diaz,Alex	Sea	5	2	24.0	12	0	1	0	.923	4.50
Dunn,Todd	Mil	1	0	2.0	1	0	0	0	1.000	4.50
Dye,Jermaine	Atl	4	0	9.0	5	0	0	0	1.000	5.00
Dykstra,Lenny	Phi	39	34	303.2	103	3	0	1	1.000	3.14
Easley,Damion	Cal	2	0	3.0	1	0	0	0	1.000	3.00
Eisenreich,Jim	Phi	3	3	24.0	5	0	0	0	1.000	1.88
Erstad,Darin	Cal	36	35	309.1	102	0	2	0	.981	2.97
Everett,Carl	NYN	15	5	56.2	18	0	1	0	.947	2.86
Faneyte,Rikkert	Tex	4	1	13.0	5	0	0	0	1.000	3.46
Floyd,Cliff	Mon	16	7	78.1	20	0	1	0	.952	2.30
Fonville,Chad	LA	18	14	122.2	37	1	1	1	.974	2.79
Frazier,Lou	Tex	3	3	24.0	9	0	0	0	1.000	3.38
Frye,Jeff	Bos	1	1	6.0	2	0	0	0	1.000	3.00
Gibralter,Steve	Cin	1	0	3.0	0	0	0	0	.000	.00
Glanville,Doug	ChN	9	3	34.0	8	0	0	0	1.000	2.12
Goodwin,Curtis	Cin	28	23	212.0	40	0	2	0	.952	1.70

Center Fielders - The Rest

Player	Tm	G	GS	Inn	PO	A	E	DP	Pct.	Rng
Green,Shawn	Tor	2	0	2.0	1	0	0	0	1.000	4.50
Greenwell,Mike	Bos	1	0	1.0	0	0	0	0	.000	.00
Greer,Rusty	Tex	1	1	9.0	3	0	0	0	1.000	3.00
Guerrero,Vladimir	Mon	1	1	8.0	4	0	0	0	1.000	4.50
Hammonds,Jeffrey	Bal	1	0	1.0	0	0	0	0	.000	.00
Harris,Lenny	Cin	1	0	1.0	0	0	0	0	.000	.00
Henderson,Rickey	SD	10	9	65.1	11	0	1	0	.917	1.52
Hernandez,Jose	ChN	1	0	3.0	1	0	0	0	1.000	3.00
Herrera,Jose	Oak	19	14	112.0	31	0	1	0	.969	2.49
Higginson,Bob	Det	19	12	111.0	33	0	1	0	.971	2.68
Hollandsworth,T	LA	18	17	144.2	30	1	0	0	1.000	1.93
Hosey,Dwayne	Bos	20	14	139.2	50	2	1	1	.981	3.35
Howard,Dave	KC	1	0	3.0	0	0	0	0	.000	.00
Howard,Thomas	Cin	40	26	241.2	69	2	1	0	.986	2.64
Hubbard,Trent	Col	16	10	94.1	32	0	0	0	1.000	3.05
Hubbard,Trent	SF	1	1	8.0	5	1	0	0	1.000	6.75
Hudler,Rex	Cal	14	12	95.0	18	0	1	0	.947	1.71
Huff,Michael	Tor	4	2	22.0	11	0	0	0	1.000	4.50
Hulse,David	Mil	37	22	221.2	68	1	1	1	.986	2.80
Javier,Stan	SF	53	50	427.0	151	0	1	0	.993	3.18
Jones,Andruw	Atl	12	5	71.0	23	0	0	0	1.000	2.92
Jones,Chris	NYN	8	1	27.0	10	0	0	0	1.000	3.33
Jones,Dax	SF	29	11	123.1	41	1	0	0	1.000	3.06
Jones,Terry	Col	4	2	20.0	5	0	0	0	1.000	2.25
Jordan,Brian	StL	13	9	92.1	29	0	0	0	1.000	2.83
Kelly,Mike	Cin	10	9	78.2	25	0	0	0	1.000	2.86
Kelly,Roberto	Min	40	34	302.1	87	2	0	0	1.000	2.65
Kingery,Mike	Pit	64	47	441.2	109	2	2	0	.982	2.26
Kingsale,Gene	Bal	2	0	3.0	2	0	0	0	1.000	6.00
Kirby,Wayne	Cle	6	1	21.0	4	0	0	0	1.000	1.71
Kirby,Wayne	LA	47	44	356.0	84	1	1	0	.988	2.15
Koslofski,Kevin	Mil	14	10	96.0	34	0	1	0	.971	3.19
Lawton,Matt	Min	18	14	124.0	49	1	0	0	1.000	3.63
Listach,Pat	Mil	66	58	524.1	159	5	3	1	.982	2.82
Magee,Wendell	Phi	18	12	120.2	35	2	0	1	1.000	2.76
Martin,Al	Pit	26	23	180.0	36	0	1	0	.973	1.80
Martinez,Dave	ChA	73	64	504.0	166	1	1	1	.994	2.98
Martinez,Manny	Sea	4	2	15.0	2	1	0	0	1.000	1.80
Martinez,Manny	Phi	1	1	8.0	1	0	0	0	1.000	1.13
Mashore,Damon	Oak	7	7	54.2	15	0	0	0	1.000	2.47
McCracken,Q	Col	85	58	557.1	124	3	5	0	.962	2.05
McGee,Willie	StL	11	9	78.0	23	2	1	2	.962	2.88
Meares,Pat	Min	1	0	1.0	0	0	0	0	.000	.00
Mejia,Miguel	StL	11	1	30.0	9	0	0	0	1.000	2.70
Mieske,Matt	Mil	10	9	73.0	32	0	0	0	1.000	3.95
Mitchell,Keith	Cin	1	1	7.0	0	0	1	0	.000	.00
Montgomery,Ray	Hou	1	0	2.0	0	0	0	0	.000	.00
Moore,Kerwin	Oak	18	3	60.0	19	0	0	0	1.000	2.85
Mottola,Chad	Cin	1	1	6.0	0	0	0	0	.000	.00
Mouton,James	Hou	29	18	183.2	51	2	1	0	.981	2.60
Murray,Glenn	Phi	2	1	11.0	6	0	0	0	1.000	4.91
Myers,Rod	KC	15	14	122.2	30	0	0	0	1.000	2.20
Norman,Les	KC	3	1	18.0	7	0	0	0	1.000	3.50
O'Leary,Troy	Bos	17	11	88.0	16	1	0	0	1.000	1.74
Offerman,Jose	KC	1	1	8.0	6	0	0	0	1.000	6.75
Orsulak,Joe	Fla	14	14	101.2	22	0	1	0	.957	1.95
Palmeiro,Orlando	Cal	17	8	95.0	22	0	0	0	1.000	2.08
Parker,Rick	LA	3	0	8.0	1	0	0	0	1.000	1.13

Center Fielders - The Rest

Player	Tm	G	GS	Inn	PO	A	E	DP	Pct.	Rng
Perez,Danny	Mil	1	1	8.0	4	0	0	0	1.000	4.50
Phillips,Tony	ChA	2	0	2.0	0	0	0	0	.000	.00
Plantier,Phil	Oak	1	0	1.0	1	0	0	0	1.000	9.00
Rivera,Ruben	NYA	14	12	111.0	39	1	0	0	1.000	3.24
Roberts,Bip	KC	2	2	16.0	4	0	0	0	1.000	2.25
Samuel,Juan	Tor	5	2	28.0	2	0	0	0	1.000	0.64
Santangelo,F.P.	Mon	76	66	577.2	186	4	4	1	.979	2.96
Silvestri,Dave	Mon	1	0	1.0	0	0	0	0	.000	.00
Singleton,Duane	Det	15	12	102.0	26	3	0	1	1.000	2.56
Spiers,Bill	Hou	1	0	2.1	1	0	0	0	1.000	3.86
Stewart,Shannon	Tor	6	3	31.2	4	0	1	0	.800	1.14
Tarasco,Tony	Bal	1	1	10.0	6	0	0	0	1.000	5.40
Tavarez,Jesus	Fla	30	11	140.2	37	0	0	0	1.000	2.37
Thompson,Ryan	Cle	8	4	46.0	5	0	0	0	1.000	0.98
Tinsley,Lee	Phi	7	7	49.0	18	0	1	0	.947	3.31
Tinsley,Lee	Bos	79	49	490.1	131	8	1	1	.993	2.55
Vaughn,Greg	Mil	3	3	23.0	3	0	0	0	1.000	1.17
Walker,Larry	Col	54	52	437.0	116	3	1	0	.992	2.45
Walton,Jerome	Atl	1	0	4.0	2	0	0	0	1.000	4.50
Ward,Turner	Mil	3	2	20.0	11	0	0	0	1.000	4.95
Wehner,John	Pit	13	7	62.2	18	1	1	0	.950	2.73
Whiten,Mark	Phi	8	4	44.0	9	0	1	0	.900	1.84
Williams,Gerald	NYA	14	10	97.0	31	1	0	1	1.000	2.97
Williams,Gerald	Mil	25	25	215.0	72	3	1	1	.987	3.14
Womack,Tony	Pit	5	3	24.2	5	0	0	0	1.000	1.82

Right Fielders - Regulars

Player	Tm	G	GS	Inn	PO	A	E	DP	Pct.	Rng
Mieske,Matt	Mil	108	84	754.2	203	7	1	1	.995	2.50
Jordan,Brian	StL	128	122	1046.0	280	9	2	0	.993	2.49
Green,Shawn	Tor	127	114	991.1	253	10	2	3	.992	2.39
Tartabull,Danny	ChA	122	121	993.2	253	4	7	1	.973	2.33
Merced,Orlando	Pit	115	113	994.2	241	14	3	5	.988	2.31
Sosa,Sammy	ChN	124	124	1086.2	255	15	10	1	.964	2.24
Mondesi,Raul	LA	157	157	1407.1	338	11	12	3	.967	2.23
O'Neill,Paul	NYA	146	146	1241.2	294	7	0	3	1.000	2.18
Sanders,Reggie	Cin	80	79	692.1	160	7	2	1	.988	2.17
Salmon,Tim	Cal	153	152	1339.2	299	13	8	0	.975	2.10
Nieves,Melvin	Det	84	83	720.1	160	7	9	2	.949	2.09
Ochoa,Alex	NYN	76	72	633.2	135	8	5	3	.966	2.03
Ramirez,Manny	Cle	149	146	1303.1	272	19	9	4	.970	2.01
Bell,Derek	Hou	157	155	1371.1	283	16	7	4	.977	1.96
Alou,Moises	Mon	123	109	947.2	200	6	1	2	.995	1.96
Buhner,Jay	Sea	142	142	1230.1	251	10	3	1	.989	1.91
Bonilla,Bobby	Bal	108	107	915.1	184	8	5	1	.975	1.89
Bichette,Dante	Col	138	136	1167.0	232	4	9	1	.963	1.82
Hill,Glenallen	SF	98	97	826.0	159	6	7	3	.959	1.80
Gonzalez,Juan	Tex	102	102	855.1	164	6	2	0	.988	1.79
O'Leary,Troy	Bos	110	88	744.0	143	4	4	0	.974	1.78
Gwynn,Tony	SD	111	109	960.0	182	2	2	0	.989	1.73
Sheffield,Gary	Fla	161	160	1342.0	238	7	6	0	.976	1.64
Average	---	122	118	1024.1	225	8	5	1	.979	2.05

Right Fielders - The Rest

Player	Tm	G	GS	Inn	PO	A	E	DP	Pct.	Rng
Abreu,Bob	Hou	1	1	5.0	0	0	0	0	.000	.00
Aldrete,Mike	Cal	2	1	12.0	1	0	1	0	.500	0.75
Aldrete,Mike	NYA	4	1	12.0	2	0	0	0	1.000	1.50
Amaral,Rich	Sea	5	2	21.0	3	0	0	0	1.000	1.29
Amaro,Ruben	Phi	28	16	175.2	43	0	0	0	1.000	2.20
Anderson,Garret	Cal	6	5	45.2	12	0	0	0	1.000	2.36
Anthony,Eric	Cin	24	20	183.1	22	2	2	0	.923	1.18
Anthony,Eric	Col	10	6	54.1	7	0	0	0	1.000	1.16
Bartee,Kimera	Det	2	0	2.0	1	0	0	0	1.000	4.50
Bautista,Danny	Det	12	9	79.0	19	0	1	0	.950	2.16
Bautista,Danny	Atl	10	3	37.2	8	0	0	0	1.000	1.91
Beamon,Trey	Pit	11	7	69.1	16	0	0	0	1.000	2.08
Becker,Rich	Min	10	7	67.0	23	0	1	0	.958	3.09
Benard,Marvin	SF	38	21	202.2	54	1	2	0	.965	2.44
Benitez,Yamil	Mon	1	0	2.0	0	0	1	0	.000	.00
Berroa,Geronimo	Oak	54	50	398.0	79	6	2	1	.977	1.92
Bradshaw,Terry	StL	1	0	4.0	0	0	0	0	.000	.00
Bragg,Darren	Sea	16	9	105.0	19	0	1	0	.950	1.63
Bragg,Darren	Bos	29	11	127.2	33	1	2	0	.944	2.40
Brede,Brent	Min	7	5	40.0	12	1	0	0	1.000	2.93
Brooks,Jerry	Fla	2	0	7.0	2	0	0	0	1.000	2.57
Brumfield,Jacob	Tor	37	28	246.2	53	4	1	0	.983	2.08
Buford,Damon	Tex	44	16	185.1	28	1	0	0	1.000	1.41
Bullett,Scott	ChN	22	9	108.2	33	1	1	1	.971	2.82
Burnitz,Jeromy	Cle	15	11	92.0	25	0	0	0	1.000	2.45
Burnitz,Jeromy	Mil	14	13	110.0	22	1	1	0	.958	1.88
Cameron,Mike	ChA	5	0	6.0	0	0	0	0	.000	.00
Canseco,Jose	Bos	2	1	13.1	4	0	0	0	1.000	2.70
Carreon,Mark	SF	2	0	15.1	3	0	0	0	1.000	1.76
Carreon,Mark	Cle	1	0	4.0	0	0	0	0	.000	.00
Cedeno,Roger	LA	4	3	29.0	6	1	0	0	1.000	2.17
Cianfrocco,Archi	SD	7	4	39.0	7	0	0	0	1.000	1.62
Clark,Dave	Pit	28	21	198.1	34	2	1	1	.973	1.63
Cockrell,Alan	Col	1	0	1.0	0	0	0	0	.000	.00
Coomer,Ron	Min	23	17	143.0	29	0	2	0	.935	1.83
Cruz,Jacob	SF	17	15	128.2	33	0	1	0	.971	2.31
Cummings,Midre	Pit	10	10	87.0	26	0	0	0	1.000	2.69
Cuyler,Milt	Bos	22	10	111.0	38	0	3	0	.927	3.08
Damon,Johnny	KC	63	57	515.2	145	2	3	1	.980	2.57
Dascenzo,Doug	SD	9	0	15.1	3	0	0	0	1.000	1.76
Deer,Rob	SD	17	11	111.1	25	0	0	0	1.000	2.02
Delgado,Alex	Bos	2	0	3.0	1	0	0	0	1.000	3.00
Devereaux,Mike	Bal	62	22	255.1	64	2	2	0	.971	2.33
Diaz,Alex	Sea	5	2	23.0	7	1	0	0	1.000	3.13
Duncan,Mariano	NYA	1	0	5.0	1	0	0	0	1.000	1.80
Dunn,Todd	Mil	4	2	21.0	5	0	0	0	1.000	2.14
Dye,Jermaine	Atl	71	55	505.0	124	2	4	1	.969	2.25
Echevarria,Angel	Col	7	0	16.0	0	0	0	0	.000	.00
Eisenreich,Jim	Phi	50	43	371.0	90	3	3	1	.969	2.26
Erstad,Darin	Cal	1	1	8.0	2	0	0	0	1.000	2.25
Everett,Carl	NYN	37	27	231.2	61	2	5	0	.926	2.45
Floyd,Cliff	Mon	7	2	32.0	3	0	0	0	1.000	0.84
Fox,Andy	NYA	1	0	1.0	0	0	0	0	.000	.00
Frye,Jeff	Bos	2	2	16.0	6	0	0	0	1.000	3.38
Giambi,Jason	Oak	1	1	8.0	2	0	0	0	1.000	2.25
Giles,Brian S.	Cle	5	4	39.0	10	0	0	0	1.000	2.31
Glanville,Doug	ChN	8	0	14.0	2	0	0	0	1.000	1.29
Goodwin,Curtis	Cin	6	6	54.0	16	0	0	0	1.000	2.67

Right Fielders - The Rest

Player	Tm	G	GS	Inn	PO	A	E	DP	Pct.	Rng
Greene,Willie	Cin	1	0	2.0	0	0	0	0	.000	.00
Greenwell,Mike	Bos	1	0	1.0	0	0	0	0	.000	.00
Guerrero,Vladimir	Mon	7	5	45.1	7	0	0	0	1.000	1.39
Gwynn,Chris	SD	24	5	84.1	16	0	0	0	1.000	1.71
Hale,Chip	Min	3	0	3.0	0	0	0	0	.000	.00
Hall,Mel	SF	1	1	8.0	0	0	0	0	.000	.00
Hammonds,Jeffrey	Bal	11	9	77.0	23	1	1	0	.960	2.81
Harris,Lenny	Cin	18	7	77.1	14	0	0	0	1.000	1.63
Henderson,Rickey	SD	17	15	121.0	20	0	2	0	.909	1.49
Herrera,Jose	Oak	92	61	567.2	159	2	5	0	.970	2.55
Hiatt,Phil	Det	1	1	9.0	0	1	0	0	1.000	1.00
Higginson,Bob	Det	57	46	418.2	100	5	5	0	.955	2.26
Hocking,Denny	Min	33	30	265.1	62	4	1	0	.985	2.24
Hollandsworth,T	LA	9	2	30.0	12	0	0	0	1.000	3.60
Howard,Thomas	Cin	32	24	210.1	41	2	2	0	.956	1.84
Huff,Michael	Tor	4	3	21.0	1	0	0	0	1.000	0.43
Hulse,David	Mil	11	1	25.0	9	0	0	0	1.000	3.24
Hunter,Brian	Sea	2	1	5.1	3	0	1	0	.750	5.06
Huskey,Butch	NYN	40	40	292.0	64	2	4	2	.943	2.03
Huson,Jeff	Bal	1	0	1.0	0	0	0	0	.000	.00
Incaviglia,Pete	Phi	2	0	4.0	2	0	0	0	1.000	4.50
James,Dion	NYA	1	0	2.0	0	0	0	0	.000	.00
Javier,Stan	SF	18	18	151.0	29	2	2	0	.939	1.85
Jennings,Robin	ChN	11	11	79.1	19	2	0	0	1.000	2.38
Jones,Andruw	Atl	20	17	153.2	50	4	2	0	.964	3.16
Jones,Chipper	Atl	1	1	8.0	2	0	0	0	1.000	2.25
Jones,Chris	NYN	44	14	187.1	43	0	1	0	.977	2.07
Jones,Dax	SF	4	1	15.1	5	0	0	0	1.000	2.93
Justice,Dave	Atl	40	40	347.0	88	3	0	1	1.000	2.36
Kelly,Mike	Cin	1	1	9.0	3	0	0	0	1.000	3.00
Kelly,Roberto	Min	54	48	422.1	105	2	1	0	.991	2.28
Kieschnick,Brooks	ChN	5	1	13.0	3	0	0	0	1.000	2.08
Kingery,Mike	Pit	16	8	71.0	16	0	0	0	1.000	2.03
Kirby,Wayne	Cle	10	0	14.0	2	0	0	0	1.000	1.29
Koslofski,Kevin	Mil	2	0	3.0	0	0	0	0	.000	.00
Lawton,Matt	Min	60	51	464.0	147	3	3	0	.980	2.91
Lesher,Brian	Oak	14	9	83.2	21	1	0	0	1.000	2.37
Mabry,John	StL	13	4	57.1	12	0	0	0	1.000	1.88
Magee,Wendell	Phi	18	18	143.0	47	0	1	0	.979	2.96
Malave,Jose	Bos	30	19	180.0	36	1	1	0	.974	1.85
Martinez,Dave	ChA	73	22	296.0	69	3	2	0	.973	2.19
Martinez,Edgar	Sea	0	0	0.0	0	0	0	0	.000	.00
Martinez,Manny	Sea	3	2	19.0	9	0	0	0	1.000	4.26
Martinez,Manny	Phi	10	9	71.1	19	0	1	0	.950	2.40
Mashore,Damon	Oak	15	9	90.2	17	1	0	0	1.000	1.79
May,Derrick	Hou	3	1	11.2	2	1	0	0	1.000	2.31
McCarty,Dave	SF	15	6	69.1	22	1	0	1	1.000	2.99
McCracken,Q	Col	4	0	6.0	2	0	1	0	.667	3.00
McGee,Willie	StL	42	33	293.0	58	3	2	0	.968	1.87
McLemore,Mark	Tex	1	0	2.0	0	0	0	0	.000	.00
Mejia,Miguel	StL	6	0	12.0	2	0	0	0	1.000	1.50
Mitchell,Keith	Cin	2	2	18.0	6	0	0	0	1.000	3.00
Mitchell,Kevin	Bos	21	19	159.1	28	0	2	0	.933	1.58
Montgomery,Ray	Hou	2	0	5.0	1	0	0	0	1.000	1.80
Mottola,Chad	Cin	30	22	189.2	42	2	0	0	1.000	2.09
Mouton,James	Hou	5	4	31.1	6	0	0	0	1.000	1.72
Mouton,Lyle	ChA	28	19	165.1	39	1	0	0	1.000	2.18
Munoz,Pedro	Oak	14	13	109.1	15	0	0	0	1.000	1.23

Player	Tm	G	GS	Inn	PO	A	E	DP	Pct.	Rng
Murray,Glenn	Phi	24	22	187.0	45	1	0	0	1.000	2.21
Myers,Rod	KC	1	0	1.0	0	0	0	0	.000	.00
Newfield,Marc	SD	23	16	139.0	17	0	2	0	.895	1.10
Newson,Warren	Tex	58	44	397.2	108	3	1	1	.991	2.51
Nilsson,Dave	Mil	55	52	433.0	95	5	4	0	.962	2.08
Nixon,Trot	Bos	2	1	9.2	3	0	0	0	1.000	2.79
Norman,Les	KC	20	10	83.2	32	1	0	0	1.000	3.55
Nunnally,Jon	KC	24	20	188.1	56	0	1	0	.982	2.68
Obando,Sherman	Mon	47	36	315.2	74	2	3	0	.962	2.17
Oliver,Joe	Cin	1	1	7.0	1	0	0	0	1.000	1.29
Orsulak,Joe	Fla	19	2	65.0	16	0	1	0	.941	2.22
Palmeiro,Orlando	Cal	8	2	33.2	5	0	0	0	1.000	1.34
Pemberton,Rudy	Bos	12	11	93.0	8	0	0	0	1.000	0.77
Perez,Robert	Tor	25	9	109.0	24	0	0	0	1.000	1.98
Phillips,J.R.	Phi	15	14	110.0	42	1	2	1	.956	3.52
Plantier,Phil	Oak	1	1	7.0	0	0	0	0	.000	.00
Polonia,Luis	Bal	2	1	8.0	3	0	0	0	1.000	3.38
Pride,Curtis	Det	5	2	24.0	8	0	0	0	1.000	3.00
Reboulet,Jeff	Min	6	4	35.0	3	2	0	0	1.000	1.29
Rivera,Ruben	NYA	19	4	71.1	23	1	0	0	1.000	3.03
Roberson,Kevin	NYN	9	5	56.0	12	0	0	0	1.000	1.93
Roberts,Bip	KC	1	1	7.0	1	0	0	0	1.000	1.29
Rodriguez,Henry	Mon	2	0	3.2	1	0	0	0	1.000	2.45
Samuel,Juan	Tor	15	8	77.2	20	0	0	0	1.000	2.32
Santangelo,F.P.	Mon	18	10	94.0	16	0	0	0	1.000	1.53
Shipley,Craig	SD	3	2	19.0	4	1	0	0	1.000	2.37
Sierra,Ruben	NYA	1	1	8.0	3	1	0	0	1.000	4.50
Sierra,Ruben	Det	19	19	167.2	49	1	4	1	.926	2.68
Simms,Mike	Hou	3	1	17.0	3	0	0	0	1.000	1.59
Smith,Dwight	Atl	26	20	174.0	48	1	2	0	.961	2.53
Smith,Mark	Bal	8	6	57.0	17	0	0	0	1.000	2.68
Spehr,Tim	Mon	1	0	0.2	0	0	0	0	.000	.00
Spiers,Bill	Hou	1	0	5.2	2	0	0	0	1.000	3.18
Stairs,Matt	Oak	29	17	153.0	24	4	0	1	1.000	1.65
Strange,Doug	Sea	1	0	2.0	1	0	0	0	1.000	4.50
Strawberry,Darryl	NYA	8	6	56.0	13	1	0	0	1.000	2.25
Sweeney,Mark	StL	7	3	40.0	8	0	0	0	1.000	1.80
Tarasco,Tony	Bal	22	18	155.0	44	1	0	0	1.000	2.61
Tavarez,Jesus	Fla	12	0	29.0	10	0	0	0	1.000	3.10
Timmons,Ozzie	ChN	22	17	151.2	34	0	0	0	1.000	2.02
Tomberlin,Andy	NYN	8	4	39.1	5	1	0	0	1.000	1.37
Tucker,Michael	KC	73	63	571.1	133	4	1	0	.993	2.16
Valdes,Pedro	ChN	2	0	3.0	1	0	0	0	1.000	3.00
Vander Wal,John	Col	1	1	9.0	1	0	0	0	1.000	1.00
Vitiello,Joe	KC	1	0	1.0	0	0	0	0	.000	.00
Voigt,Jack	Tex	1	1	9.0	2	0	0	0	1.000	2.00
Walker,Larry	Col	33	19	169.1	36	1	0	0	1.000	1.97
Walton,Jerome	Atl	5	3	34.0	10	0	0	0	1.000	2.65
Ward,Turner	Mil	18	10	96.2	30	1	0	0	1.000	2.89
Wehner,John	Pit	8	3	32.1	8	0	0	0	1.000	2.23
Whiten,Mark	Phi	44	40	361.1	88	6	5	1	.949	2.34
Whiten,Mark	Atl	29	23	209.2	41	1	3	0	.933	1.80
Whiten,Mark	Sea	4	3	26.0	3	0	1	0	.750	1.04
Williams,Eddie	Det	2	2	12.0	3	0	0	0	1.000	2.25
Williams,Gerald	NYA	10	4	43.0	11	0	1	0	.917	2.30
Williams,Gerald	Mil	1	0	4.0	2	0	0	0	1.000	4.50
Williams,Keith	SF	3	3	26.0	7	0	0	0	1.000	2.42
Womack,Tony	Pit	1	0	0.2	0	0	0	0	.000	.00

Right Fielders - The Rest

Player	Tm	G	GS	Inn	PO	A	E	DP	Pct.	Rng
Young,Ernie	Oak	17	1	39.0	9	0	0	0	1.000	2.08
Young,Kevin	KC	15	10	82.0	14	1	1	0	.938	1.65

Catchers - Regulars

Player	Tm	G	GS	Inn	PO	A	E	DP	PB	Pct.
Girardi,Joe	NYA	120	110	973.2	803	45	3	8	10	.996
Wilson,Dan	Sea	135	130	1130.0	835	57	4	5	5	.996
O'Brien,Charlie	Tor	105	88	801.0	613	37	3	5	5	.995
Johnson,Charles	Fla	120	113	998.0	751	70	4	11	5	.995
Lopez,Javy	Atl	135	125	1112.2	993	81	6	9	11	.994
Manwaring,Kirt	TOT	86	72	618.0	438	45	3	7	3	.994
Karkovice,Ron	ChA	111	99	890.1	680	45	5	6	4	.993
Macfarlane,Mike	KC	99	92	819.1	511	35	4	2	5	.993
Fletcher,Darrin	Mon	112	104	857.0	722	30	6	5	6	.992
Piazza,Mike	LA	147	144	1255.2	1056	70	9	6	12	.992
Oliver,Joe	Cin	97	81	724.0	572	43	5	7	4	.992
Hundley,Todd	NYN	150	142	1265.1	911	72	8	7	10	.992
Hoiles,Chris	Bal	126	120	1036.0	777	41	7	3	7	.992
Steinbach,Terry	Oak	137	130	1140.2	732	45	7	7	6	.991
Wilkins,Rick	TOT	124	106	970.1	738	68	8	6	11	.990
Pagnozzi,Tom	StL	116	108	974.2	716	48	8	6	6	.990
Rodriguez,Ivan	Tex	147	141	1222.2	850	80	10	11	10	.989
Fabregas,Jorge	Cal	89	75	665.0	502	45	6	3	5	.989
Alomar,Sandy	Cle	124	111	992.0	724	48	9	6	7	.988
Ausmus,Brad	TOT	119	107	993.2	752	56	10	4	7	.988
Servais,Scott	ChN	128	125	1097.1	797	71	11	11	9	.987
Santiago,Benito	Phi	114	112	982.0	722	61	10	5	8	.987
Flaherty,John	TOT	118	107	963.2	714	40	10	4	5	.987
Stanley,Mike	Bos	105	98	846.2	654	19	10	2	18	.985
Matheny,Mike	Mil	104	97	826.2	476	40	8	5	3	.985
Myers,Greg	Min	90	81	714.0	488	26	8	5	6	.985
Reed,Jeff	Col	111	97	850.1	546	50	11	2	11	.982
Taubensee,Eddie	Cin	94	78	693.0	538	42	11	7	3	.981
Kendall,Jason	Pit	129	117	1060.1	797	70	18	10	8	.980
Average	---	116	107	947.1	703	51	7	6	7	.990

Catchers - The Rest

Player	Tm	G	GS	Inn	PO	A	E	DP	PB	Pct.
Ausmus,Brad	SD	46	38	372.0	300	22	6	0	5	.982
Ausmus,Brad	Det	73	69	621.2	452	34	4	4	2	.992
Ayrault,Joe	Atl	7	0	19.1	14	0	0	0	0	1.000
Bennett,Gary	Phi	5	5	40.0	35	5	0	0	0	1.000
Borders,Pat	StL	17	15	137.0	116	9	2	1	0	.984
Borders,Pat	Cal	19	14	139.2	111	14	2	1	1	.984
Borders,Pat	ChA	30	24	220.2	144	16	3	1	2	.982
Brito,Jorge	Col	8	5	45.2	36	7	0	1	1	1.000
Brown,Kevin L.	Tex	2	1	14.0	11	1	0	0	0	1.000
Casanova,Raul	Det	22	20	172.0	123	12	3	0	3	.978
Castillo,Alberto	NYN	6	4	33.2	23	0	0	0	0	1.000
Chavez,Raul	Mon	2	1	11.0	13	0	0	0	0	1.000
Cianfrocco,Archi	SD	1	0	1.0	0	0	0	0	0	.000
Decker,Steve	SF	30	26	234.0	183	12	0	4	5	1.000
Decker,Steve	Col	10	7	66.2	51	6	0	0	0	1.000
Delgado,Alex	Bos	14	1	21.0	16	0	2	1	0	.889
Devarez,Cesar	Bal	10	4	46.0	38	1	0	0	1	1.000
Diaz,Einar	Cle	4	0	4.0	4	0	0	0	0	1.000
Difelice,Mike	StL	4	2	18.0	15	1	0	0	0	1.000
Dorsett,Brian	ChN	15	9	90.2	79	5	0	1	1	1.000
Durant,Mike	Min	37	27	238.2	183	13	5	1	0	.975
Encarnacion,A	Pit	7	6	54.1	36	3	2	0	1	.951
Estalella,Bobby	Phi	4	4	35.0	24	1	0	0	0	1.000

Catchers - The Rest

Player	Tm	G	GS	Inn	PO	A	E	DP	PB	Pct.
Eusebio,Tony	Hou	48	38	333.0	255	24	1	1	1	.996
Fasano,Sal	KC	51	43	391.2	291	13	5	2	2	.984
Flaherty,John	Det	46	42	369.1	243	12	5	1	1	.981
Flaherty,John	SD	72	65	594.1	471	28	5	3	4	.990
Fordyce,Brook	Cin	4	3	26.0	18	0	0	0	0	1.000
Goff,Jerry	Hou	1	1	8.0	11	0	0	1	6	1.000
Greene,Charlie	NYN	1	0	2.0	1	0	0	0	0	1.000
Greene,Todd	Cal	26	18	178.0	119	19	0	1	1	1.000
Haselman,Bill	Bos	69	60	553.2	495	32	3	6	5	.994
Hatteberg,Scott	Bos	10	3	36.0	32	1	0	0	0	1.000
Hernandez,Carlos	LA	9	3	32.1	31	1	0	0	0	1.000
Houston,Tyler	ChN	27	22	198.1	130	9	2	0	2	.986
Hubbard,Mike	ChN	14	6	70.0	53	3	0	1	1	1.000
Jensen,Marcus	SF	7	6	52.0	37	5	2	1	1	.955
Johnson,Brian	SD	66	59	521.2	451	21	5	3	5	.990
Knorr,Randy	Hou	33	26	226.1	204	14	0	1	0	1.000
Kreuter,Chad	ChA	38	26	239.1	181	12	2	4	1	.990
Lampkin,Tom	SF	53	44	400.2	342	25	3	4	0	.992
Levis,Jesse	Mil	90	57	545.0	372	27	1	4	5	.998
Leyritz,Jim	NYA	55	50	440.0	363	19	2	3	7	.995
Lieberthal,Mike	Phi	43	41	366.1	285	19	3	4	0	.990
Machado,Robert	ChA	4	2	18.0	6	0	0	0	1	1.000
Manwaring,Kirt	SF	49	47	393.1	267	25	2	4	3	.993
Manwaring,Kirt	Hou	37	25	224.2	171	20	1	3	0	.995
Martinez,Sandy	Tor	75	68	587.2	413	33	3	9	8	.993
Marzano,John	Sea	39	29	270.2	194	10	3	1	3	.986
Mayne,Brent	NYN	21	16	139.0	85	3	0	2	0	1.000
McIntosh,Tim	NYA	1	0	2.0	0	0	0	0	0	.000
McKeel,Walt	Bos	1	0	0.2	0	0	0	0	0	.000
Mercedes,Henry	KC	4	0	10.0	2	0	0	0	0	1.000
Mirabelli,Doug	SF	8	5	47.0	29	2	0	0	0	1.000
Molina,Izzy	Oak	12	6	55.2	31	1	0	1	0	1.000
Mosquera,Julio	Tor	8	6	57.0	48	1	0	3	1	1.000
Natal,Bob	Fla	43	29	255.0	187	14	5	1	6	.976
Nevin,Phil	Det	4	2	20.0	12	1	0	0	1	1.000
Nilsson,Dave	Mil	2	0	3.0	2	1	0	0	0	1.000
Osik,Keith	Pit	41	39	336.2	235	23	6	2	1	.977
Owens,Jayhawk	Col	68	53	460.0	312	27	9	3	7	.974
Parent,Mark	Det	33	29	249.2	158	14	1	4	0	.994
Parent,Mark	Bal	18	11	93.1	73	2	1	1	2	.987
Pena,Tony	Cle	67	50	456.1	337	26	3	6	4	.992
Perez,Eddie	Atl	54	37	337.0	250	19	2	4	0	.993
Posada,Jorge	NYA	4	2	24.1	17	2	0	0	0	1.000
Prince,Tom	LA	35	15	178.1	161	11	1	2	3	.994
Sheaffer,Danny	StL	47	37	322.2	257	25	5	3	1	.983
Siddall,Joe	Fla	18	12	116.0	78	8	2	1	1	.977
Slaught,Don	Cal	59	53	452.1	338	27	3	1	5	.992
Slaught,Don	ChA	12	11	92.2	70	0	1	0	0	.986
Spehr,Tim	Mon	58	7	142.1	121	7	2	0	1	.985
Stinnett,Kelly	Mil	14	8	72.2	46	2	2	1	1	.960
Sweeney,Mike	KC	26	26	229.0	158	7	1	3	4	.994
Turner,Chris	Cal	3	1	4.0	2	2	0	0	0	1.000
Valle,Dave	Tex	35	21	212.2	145	13	1	2	0	.994
Walbeck,Matt	Min	61	54	487.0	326	18	2	2	5	.994
Webster,Lenny	Mon	63	50	430.2	390	25	1	3	3	.998
Wehner,John	Pit	1	0	2.0	1	0	0	0	0	1.000
Widger,Chris	Sea	7	2	31.0	18	1	2	0	0	.905
Wilkins,Rick	Hou	82	72	655.0	550	39	6	2	7	.990

Catchers - The Rest

Player	Tm	G	GS	Inn	PO	A	E	DP	PB	Pct.
Wilkins,Rick	SF	42	34	315.1	188	29	2	4	4	.991
Williams,George	Oak	43	26	260.0	154	12	3	1	5	.982
Zaun,Greg	Bal	49	28	293.1	215	9	3	3	4	.987
Zaun,Greg	Fla	10	8	74.0	60	6	0	0	0	1.000

Catchers - Regulars - Special

Player	Tm	G	GS	Inn	SBA	CS	PCS	CS%	ER	CERA
Piazza,Mike	LA	147	144	1255.2	189	34	8	.18	462	3.31
Johnson,Charles	Fla	120	113	998.0	84	40	2	.48	395	3.56
Lopez,Javy	Atl	135	125	1112.2	132	35	2	.27	450	3.64
Pagnozzi,Tom	StL	116	108	974.2	102	35	3	.34	418	3.86
Oliver,Joe	Cin	97	81	724.0	81	23	2	.28	333	4.14
Fletcher,Darrin	Mon	112	104	857.0	136	27	14	.20	396	4.16
Alomar,Sandy	Cle	124	111	992.0	111	35	10	.32	459	4.16
Santiago,Benito	Phi	114	112	982.0	92	28	2	.30	459	4.21
Servais,Scott	ChN	128	125	1097.1	139	40	0	.29	513	4.21
Hundley,Todd	NYN	150	142	1265.1	130	32	0	.25	600	4.27
O'Brien,Charlie	Tor	105	88	801.0	64	24	4	.38	392	4.40
Wilkins,Rick	TOT	124	106	970.1	128	40	4	.31	475	4.41
Taubensee,Eddie	Cin	94	78	693.0	113	26	0	.23	348	4.52
Karkovice,Ron	ChA	111	99	890.1	81	33	4	.41	452	4.57
Kendall,Jason	Pit	129	117	1060.1	177	41	10	.23	554	4.70
Manwaring,Kirt	TOT	86	72	618.0	83	37	4	.45	324	4.72
Rodriguez,Ivan	Tex	147	141	1222.2	94	48	4	.51	642	4.73
Macfarlane,Mike	KC	99	92	819.1	62	24	4	.39	437	4.80
Ausmus,Brad	TOT	119	107	993.2	121	40	6	.33	542	4.91
Fabregas,Jorge	Cal	89	75	665.0	83	22	2	.27	379	5.13
Girardi,Joe	NYA	120	110	973.2	120	30	8	.25	555	5.13
Flaherty,John	TOT	118	107	963.2	109	32	6	.29	557	5.20
Wilson,Dan	Sea	135	130	1130.0	100	39	10	.39	658	5.24
Reed,Jeff	Col	111	97	850.1	106	31	1	.29	497	5.26
Steinbach,Terry	Oak	137	130	1140.2	117	34	8	.29	671	5.29
Matheny,Mike	Mil	104	97	826.2	77	25	6	.32	490	5.33
Stanley,Mike	Bos	105	98	846.2	114	20	10	.18	502	5.34
Hoiles,Chris	Bal	126	120	1036.0	124	28	7	.23	616	5.35
Myers,Greg	Min	90	81	714.0	63	22	5	.35	426	5.37
Average	----	116	107	947.1	108	31	5	.29	482	4.58

Catchers - The Rest - Special

Player	Tm	G	GS	Inn	SBA	CS	PCS	CS%	ER	CERA
Ausmus,Brad	SD	46	38	372.0	47	15	0	.32	162	3.92
Ausmus,Brad	Det	73	69	621.2	74	25	6	.34	380	5.50
Ayrault,Joe	Atl	7	0	19.1	0	0	0	0	11	5.12
Bennett,Gary	Phi	5	5	40.0	5	3	0	.60	25	5.63
Borders,Pat	StL	17	15	137.0	12	6	1	.50	68	4.47
Borders,Pat	Cal	19	14	139.2	20	5	1	.25	87	5.61
Borders,Pat	ChA	30	24	220.2	30	9	3	.30	122	4.98
Brito,Jorge	Col	8	5	45.2	5	1	0	.20	29	5.72
Brown,Kevin L.	Tex	2	1	14.0	1	1	0	1.00	6	3.86
Casanova,Raul	Det	22	20	172.0	36	8	2	.22	131	6.85
Castillo,Alberto	NYN	6	4	33.2	4	0	0	0	8	2.14
Chavez,Raul	Mon	2	1	11.0	0	0	0	0	3	2.45
Cianfrocco,Archi	SD	1	0	1.0	0	0	0	0	0	0.00
Decker,Steve	SF	30	26	234.0	32	9	2	.28	116	4.46
Decker,Steve	Col	10	7	66.2	5	2	0	.40	40	5.40
Delgado,Alex	Bos	14	1	21.0	3	0	0	0	10	4.29
Devarez,Cesar	Bal	10	4	46.0	6	1	0	.17	21	4.11
Diaz,Einar	Cle	4	0	4.0	0	0	0	0	0	0.00
Difelice,Mike	StL	4	2	18.0	4	1	0	.25	12	6.00
Dorsett,Brian	ChN	15	9	90.2	5	3	0	.60	47	4.67
Durant,Mike	Min	37	27	238.2	17	6	1	.35	156	5.88
Encarnacion,A	Pit	7	6	54.1	7	1	0	.14	29	4.80
Estalella,Bobby	Phi	4	4	35.0	2	1	0	.50	14	3.60

Catchers - The Rest - Special

Player	Tm	G	GS	Inn	SBA	CS	PCS	CS%	ER	CERA
Eusebio,Tony	Hou	48	38	333.0	39	9	3	.23	158	4.27
Fasano,Sal	KC	51	43	391.2	29	10	1	.34	182	4.18
Flaherty,John	Det	46	42	369.1	31	9	0	.29	289	7.04
Flaherty,John	SD	72	65	594.1	78	23	6	.29	268	4.06
Fordyce,Brook	Cin	4	3	26.0	2	1	1	.50	11	3.81
Goff,Jerry	Hou	1	1	8.0	1	0	0	0	2	2.25
Greene,Charlie	NYN	1	0	2.0	0	0	0	0	0	0.00
Greene,Todd	Cal	26	18	178.0	24	8	2	.33	123	6.22
Haselman,Bill	Bos	69	60	553.2	60	16	1	.27	281	4.57
Hatteberg,Scott	Bos	10	3	36.0	7	1	0	.14	14	3.50
Hernandez,Carlos	LA	9	3	32.1	2	1	1	.50	10	2.78
Houston,Tyler	ChN	27	22	198.1	33	6	1	.18	110	4.99
Hubbard,Mike	ChN	14	6	70.0	2	1	0	.50	35	4.50
Jensen,Marcus	SF	7	6	52.0	6	3	0	.50	28	4.85
Johnson,Brian	SD	66	59	521.2	65	16	5	.25	186	3.21
Knorr,Randy	Hou	33	26	226.1	21	9	3	.43	117	4.65
Kreuter,Chad	ChA	38	26	239.1	33	11	1	.33	111	4.17
Lampkin,Tom	SF	53	44	400.2	33	17	3	.52	201	4.51
Levis,Jesse	Mil	90	57	545.0	51	14	2	.27	297	4.90
Leyritz,Jim	NYA	55	50	440.0	41	11	7	.27	182	3.72
Lieberthal,Mike	Phi	43	41	366.1	33	12	3	.36	210	5.16
Machado,Robert	ChA	4	2	18.0	3	1	1	.33	12	6.00
Manwaring,Kirt	SF	49	47	393.1	51	22	3	.43	214	4.90
Manwaring,Kirt	Hou	37	25	224.2	32	15	1	.47	110	4.41
Martinez,Sandy	Tor	75	68	587.2	49	17	0	.35	319	4.89
Marzano,John	Sea	39	29	270.2	19	3	1	.16	155	5.15
Mayne,Brent	NYN	21	16	139.0	24	1	0	.04	67	4.34
McIntosh,Tim	NYA	1	0	2.0	0	0	0	0	0	0.00
McKeel,Walt	Bos	1	0	0.2	0	0	0	0	0	0.00
Mercedes,Henry	KC	4	0	10.0	1	0	0	0	7	6.30
Mirabelli,Doug	SF	8	5	47.0	4	0	0	0	36	6.89
Molina,Izzy	Oak	12	6	55.2	9	0	0	0	41	6.63
Mosquera,Julio	Tor	8	6	57.0	2	0	0	0	23	3.63
Natal,Bob	Fla	43	29	255.0	36	10	2	.28	121	4.27
Nevin,Phil	Det	4	2	20.0	4	1	1	.25	15	6.75
Nilsson,Dave	Mil	2	0	3.0	0	0	0	0	3	9.00
Osik,Keith	Pit	41	39	336.2	58	15	3	.26	161	4.30
Owens,Jayhawk	Col	68	53	460.0	61	21	6	.34	318	6.22
Parent,Mark	Det	33	29	249.2	26	11	0	.42	200	7.21
Parent,Mark	Bal	18	11	93.1	6	2	0	.33	43	4.15
Pena,Tony	Cle	67	50	456.1	45	17	1	.38	241	4.75
Perez,Eddie	Atl	54	37	337.0	28	9	2	.32	114	3.04
Posada,Jorge	NYA	4	2	24.1	0	0	0	0	7	2.59
Prince,Tom	LA	35	15	178.1	19	4	0	.21	92	4.64
Sheaffer,Danny	StL	47	37	322.2	40	12	0	.30	143	3.99
Siddall,Joe	Fla	18	12	116.0	18	6	1	.33	72	5.59
Slaught,Don	Cal	59	53	452.1	72	18	5	.25	258	5.13
Slaught,Don	ChA	12	11	92.2	13	1	1	.08	36	3.50
Spehr,Tim	Mon	58	7	142.1	18	2	1	.11	51	3.22
Stinnett,Kelly	Mil	14	8	72.2	8	1	0	.13	36	4.46
Sweeney,Mike	KC	26	26	229.0	19	8	2	.42	107	4.21
Turner,Chris	Cal	3	1	4.0	1	1	0	1.00	0	0.00
Valle,Dave	Tex	35	21	212.2	23	7	0	.30	101	4.27
Walbeck,Matt	Min	61	54	487.0	46	14	1	.30	262	4.84
Webster,Lenny	Mon	63	50	430.2	50	19	8	.38	155	3.24
Wehner,John	Pit	1	0	2.0	0	0	0	0	0	0.00
Widger,Chris	Sea	7	2	31.0	1	0	0	0	16	4.65
Wilkins,Rick	Hou	82	72	655.0	77	22	2	.29	315	4.33

Catchers - The Rest - Special

Player	Tm	G	GS	Inn	SBA	CS	PCS	CS%	ER	CERA
Wilkins,Rick	SF	42	34	315.1	51	18	2	.35	160	4.57
Williams,George	Oak	43	26	260.0	32	7	1	.22	129	4.47
Zaun,Greg	Bal	49	28	293.1	36	6	0	.17	159	4.88
Zaun,Greg	Fla	10	8	74.0	3	1	0	.33	46	5.59

Pitchers Hitting & Fielding, and Hitters Pitching

In the introduction to this section in last year's *Major League Handbook*, we said that you'd find *everything* you'd ever want to know about this subject. Well. . . that wasn't quite the case. As part of our fine-tuning process, we found even *more* stuff you (and we) would want to know. We expanded our pitchers hitting data considerably to include on-base percentage, slugging percentage, doubles, triples, runs scored, walks, strikeouts, stolen bases and times caught stealing for the 1996 season. We increased our Career Hitting categories as well.

So what does all of this tell us? How about the rarity of a three-bagger for a hurler? A grand total of four pitchers legged out a triple in 1996: the Braves' Steve Avery, the Rockies' Roger Bailey, the Expos' Rheal Cormier and the Cubs' Kevin Foster. Stolen bases? A bit more common, but not much. Five pitchers registered a theft last season, including 40-year-old Danny Darwin. He must have gotten a great jump!

The pitchers fielding data remained the same—we simply separated it from the hitting, though Ben McDonald and Terry Mulholland may well wish we didn't include it at all. Greg Maddux even picked up an E-1. . . his only error in the past two seasons.

One final note for whichever team wins the Manny Alexander sweepstakes: Keep him away from the pitcher's mound! Enjoy.

Pitchers Hitting

Pitcher, Team	1996 Hitting														Career Hitting													
	Avg	OBP	SLG	AB	H	2B	3B	HR	R	RBI	BB	SO	SH	SB-CS	Avg	OBP	SLG	AB	H	2B	3B	HR	R	RBI	BB	SO	SH	SB-CS
Adams, Terry, ChN	.000	.143	.000	6	0	0	0	0	0	0	1	3	0	0-0	.000	.143	.000	6	0	0	0	0	0	0	1	3	0	0-0
Adamson, Joel, Fla	.000	.000	.000	0	0	0	0	0	0	0	0	0	0	0-0	.000	.000	.000	0	0	0	0	0	0	0	0	0	0	0-0
Alston, Garvin, Col	.000	.000	.000	0	0	0	0	0	0	0	0	0	0	0-0	.000	.000	.000	1	0	0	0	0	0	0	0	0	0	0-0
Alvarez, Tavo, Mon	.500	.500	.500	4	2	0	0	0	0	0	1	1	0	0-0	.125	.125	.125	16	2	0	0	0	1	0	5	3	0	0-0
Ashby, Andy, SD	.244	.239	.356	45	11	5	0	0	6	5	0	13	9	0-0	.168	.184	.208	202	34	8	0	0	13	10	4	81	40	1-0
Astacio, Pedro, LA	.088	.101	.088	68	6	0	0	0	1	3	1	28	8	0-1	.111	.119	.116	225	25	1	0	0	9	6	2	99	26	0-1
Aucoin, Derek, Mon	.000	.000	.000	0	0	0	0	0	0	0	0	0	0	0-0	.000	.000	.000	0	0	0	0	0	0	0	0	0	0	0-0
Avery, Steve, Atl	.239	.245	.500	46	11	4	1	2	5	11	1	12	1	0-0	.179	.200	.262	408	73	14	4	4	30	31	12	124	39	1-1
Ayala, Bobby, Sea	.000	.000	.000	0	0	0	0	0	0	0	0	0	0	0-0	.067	.067	.100	30	2	1	0	0	2	1	0	13	3	0-1
Bailey, Cory, StL	.000	.667	.000	1	0	0	0	0	2	0	2	0	1	0-0	.000	.667	.000	1	0	0	0	0	2	0	2	0	1	0-0
Bailey, Roger, Col	.263	.364	.526	19	5	0	1	1	4	5	3	4	3	0-0	.200	.282	.343	35	7	0	1	1	6	6	4	7	6	0-0
Barber, Brian, StL	.000	.000	.000	0	0	0	0	0	0	0	0	0	0	0-0	.125	.222	.125	8	1	0	0	0	0	0	1	2	0	0-0
Barton, Shawn, SF	.000	.000	.000	0	0	0	0	0	0	0	0	0	0	0-0	.000	.000	.000	0	0	0	0	0	0	0	0	1	0	0-0
Batchelor, Richard, StL	.000	.000	.000	1	0	0	0	0	0	0	0	1	0	0-0	.000	.000	.000	2	0	0	0	0	0	0	0	1	0	0-0
Batista, Miguel, Fla	.000	.000	.000	0	0	0	0	0	0	0	0	0	0	0-0	.000	.000	.000	0	0	0	0	0	0	0	0	0	0	0-0
Bautista, Jose, SF	.111	.111	.111	9	1	0	0	0	1	0	0	4	1	0-0	.100	.118	.100	50	5	0	0	0	2	1	1	17	4	0-0
Beck, Rod, SF	.333	.333	.333	3	1	0	0	0	0	1	0	2	0	0-0	.235	.235	.235	17	4	0	0	0	0	1	0	9	1	0-0
Beckett, Robbie, Col	.000	.000	.000	0	0	0	0	0	0	0	0	0	0	0-0	.000	.000	.000	0	0	0	0	0	0	0	0	0	0	0-0
Beech, Matt, Phi	.071	.071	.071	14	1	0	0	0	1	1	0	4	0	0-0	.071	.071	.071	14	1	0	0	0	1	1	0	4	0	0-0
Benes, Alan, StL	.148	.175	.197	61	9	3	0	0	4	5	2	25	7	0-0	.134	.159	.179	67	9	3	0	0	4	5	2	28	7	0-0
Benes, Andy, StL	.151	.158	.205	73	11	4	0	0	5	6	1	37	9	0-0	.130	.166	.183	447	58	12	0	4	25	30	17	205	57	0-0
Bergman, Sean, SD	.100	.100	.200	30	3	0	0	1	1	5	0	9	0	0-0	.100	.100	.200	30	3	0	0	1	1	5	0	9	0	0-0
Berumen, Andres, SD	.000	.000	.000	0	0	0	0	0	0	0	0	0	0	0-0	.000	.000	.000	1	0	0	0	0	0	0	0	1	0	0-0
Bielecki, Mike, Atl	.100	.250	.100	10	1	0	0	0	1	1	2	5	0	0-0	.079	.119	.079	280	22	0	0	0	11	13	13	143	35	1-0
Blair, Willie, SD	.000	.000	.000	3	0	0	0	0	0	0	0	1	0	0-0	.058	.090	.070	86	5	1	0	0	3	5	3	56	8	0-0
Blazier, Ron, Phi	1.000	1.000	1.000	1	1	0	0	0	0	0	0	0	0	0-0	1.000	1.000	1.000	1	1	0	0	0	0	0	0	0	0	0-0
Bochtler, Doug, SD	.000	.000	.000	0	0	0	0	0	0	0	0	0	0	0-0	.000	.000	.000	2	0	0	0	0	0	0	0	0	0	0-0
Boever, Joe, Pit	.000	.000	.000	1	0	0	0	0	0	0	0	1	0	0-0	.118	.118	.118	17	2	0	0	0	0	0	0	4	0	0-0
Bones, Ricky, Mil-NYA	.000	.000	.000	0	0	0	0	0	0	0	0	0	0	0-0	.077	.200	.077	13	1	0	0	0	1	1	2	5	4	0-0
Borbon, Pedro, Atl	1.000	1.000	1.000	1	1	0	0	0	0	0	0	0	0	0-0	.500	.500	.500	2	1	0	0	0	0	0	0	0	0	0-0
Borland, Toby, Phi	.000	.000	.000	4	0	0	0	0	0	0	0	2	0	0-0	.083	.077	.083	12	1	0	0	0	1	2	0	3	0	0-0
Borowski, Joe, Atl	.000	.000	.000	2	0	0	0	0	0	0	0	2	1	0-0	.000	.000	.000	2	0	0	0	0	0	0	0	2	1	0-0
Boskie, Shawn, Cal	.000	.000	.000	0	0	0	0	0	0	0	0	0	0	0-0	.184	.228	.270	141	26	5	2	1	9	8	8	42	9	0-0
Bottalico, Ricky, Phi	.333	.333	.667	3	1	1	0	0	0	0	0	2	0	0-0	.125	.125	.250	8	1	1	0	0	0	0	0	6	1	0-0
Bottenfield, Kent, ChN	.500	.500	.500	2	1	0	0	0	0	0	0	1	1	0-0	.246	.270	.246	61	15	0	0	0	3	3	1	19	5	1-0
Bourgeois, Steve, SF	.273	.385	.455	11	3	2	0	0	1	1	2	2	1	0-0	.273	.385	.455	11	3	2	0	0	1	1	2	2	1	0-0
Brantley, Jeff, Cin	.000	.000	.000	1	0	0	0	0	0	0	0	2	0	0-1	.118	.143	.132	68	8	1	0	0	5	5	2	23	10	0-0
Briscoe, John, Oak	.000	.000	.000	0	0	0	0	0	0	0	0	0	0	0-0	.000	.000	.000	0	0	0	0	0	0	0	0	0	0	0-0
Brocail, Doug, Hou	.000	.000	.000	0	0	0	0	0	0	0	0	4	0	0-0	.164	.164	.194	67	11	0	1	0	9	1	0	18	15	2-0
Brown, Kevin, Fla	.120	.185	.133	75	9	1	0	0	1	3	6	28	4	0-0	.118	.183	.132	76	9	1	0	0	1	3	6	28	4	0-0
Bruske, Jim, LA	.000	.000	.000	0	0	0	0	0	0	0	0	0	0	0-0	.000	.000	.000	0	0	0	0	0	0	0	0	0	0	0-0
Bullinger, Jim, ChN	.250	.368	.531	32	8	3	0	2	8	6	5	11	3	0-0	.180	.261	.320	122	22	8	0	3	12	17	13	42	17	1-0
Burba, Dave, Cin	.104	.143	.194	67	7	0	0	2	3	5	3	26	3	0-0	.120	.176	.179	117	14	1	0	2	6	8	8	52	13	0-0
Burke, John, Col	.500	.500	.500	2	1	0	0	0	0	1	0	0	0	0-0	.500	.500	.500	2	1	0	0	0	0	1	0	0	0	0-0
Burkett, John, Fla-Tex	.173	.173	.212	52	9	2	0	0	2	1	0	17	3	0-0	.088	.132	.100	419	37	5	0	0	16	14	20	178	47	0-0
Busby, Mike, StL	.500	.500	.500	2	1	0	0	0	0	0	0	0	0	0-0	.500	.500	.500	2	1	0	0	0	0	0	0	0	0	0-0
Byrd, Paul, NYN	.000	.000	.000	2	0	0	0	0	0	0	0	0	0	0-0	.333	.333	.333	3	1	0	0	0	0	0	0	0	0	0-0
Campbell, Mike, ChN	.364	.364	.545	11	4	2	0	0	2	1	0	5	1	0-0	.357	.357	.500	14	5	2	0	0	2	3	0	6	1	0-0
Candiotti, Tom, LA	.089	.106	.089	45	4	0	0	0	3	2	0	14	9	0-0	.117	.139	.132	266	31	4	0	0	11	10	6	61	42	0-0
Carlson, Dan, SF	.000	.000	.000	1	0	0	0	0	0	0	0	0	0	0-0	.000	.000	.000	1	0	0	0	0	0	0	0	0	0	0-0
Carrara, G., Tor-Cin	.000	.000	.000	7	0	0	0	0	1	0	0	1	0	0-0	.000	.000	.000	7	0	0	0	0	1	0	0	1	0	0-0
Carrasco, Hector, Cin	.200	.200	.200	5	1	0	0	0	0	0	0	4	0	0-0	.056	.056	.056	18	1	0	0	0	0	0	0	12	0	0-0
Casian, Larry, ChN	.000	.000	.000	0	0	0	0	0	0	0	0	0	0	0-0	.000	.000	.000	2	0	0	0	0	0	0	0	1	0	0-0
Castillo, Frank, ChN	.088	.119	.088	57	5	0	0	0	1	2	2	21	4	0-0	.108	.146	.108	268	29	0	0	0	6	8	12	87	30	0-1
Charlton, Norm, Sea	.000	.000	.000	0	0	0	0	0	0	0	0	0	0	0-0	.093	.152	.116	86	8	2	0	0	6	1	3	50	10	0-0
Christiansen, Jason, Pit	.000	.000	.000	4	0	0	0	0	0	0	0	4	1	0-0	.000	.000	.000	5	0	0	0	0	0	0	0	5	1	0-0
Clark, Mark, NYN	.043	.056	.058	69	3	1	0	0	3	2	1	26	10	0-0	.071	.079	.080	112	8	1	0	0	3	3	1	46	15	0-0
Clark, Terry, KC-Hou	.000	.000	.000	0	0	0	0	0	0	0	0	0	0	0-0	.500	.500	.500	2	1	0	0	0	0	1	0	0	0	0-0
Clemens, Roger, Bos	1.000	1.000	1.000	1	1	0	0	0	0	0	0	0	0	0-0	1.000	1.000	1.000	1	1	0	0	0	0	0	0	0	0	0-0
Clontz, Brad, Atl	.000	.500	.000	2	0	0	0	0	0	0	2	2	1	0-0	.000	.333	.000	4	0	0	0	0	0	1	2	2	1	0-0
Cooke, Steve, Pit	.000	.000	.000	1	0	0	0	0	0	0	0	0	0	0-0	.171	.176	.197	117	20	3	0	0	6	6	0	29	13	0-0
Cordova, Francisco, Pit	.125	.125	.125	16	2	0	0	0	1	2	0	7	2	0-0	.125	.125	.125	16	2	0	0	0	1	2	0	7	2	0-0
Cormier, Rheal, Mon	.186	.222	.233	43	8	0	1	0	2	4	2	12	11	0-0	.185	.202	.217	184	34	4	1	0	14	12	3	43	28	0-0
Crawford, Carlos, Phi	.000	.000	.000	1	0	0	0	0	0	0	0	1	0	0-0	.000	.000	.000	1	0	0	0	0	0	0	0	1	0	0-0
Creek, Doug, SF	.000	.000	.000	1	0	0	0	0	0	0	0	1	1	0-0	.000	.000	.000	1	0	0	0	0	0	0	0	1	1	0-0
Cummings, J., LA-Det	.000	.000	.000	0	0	0	0	0	0	0	0	0	0	0-0	.000	.000	.000	3	0	0	0	0	0	0	0	0	0	0-0
Daal, Omar, Mon	.000	.000	.000	11	0	0	0	0	0	0	0	5	0	0-0	.000	.083	.000	11	0	0	0	0	0	0	1	5	0	0-0
Darwin, Danny, Pit-Hou	.184	.184	.327	49	9	4	0	1	2	3	0	27	7	1-0	.136	.153	.215	242	33	9	2	2	13	19	5	130	15	2-0
DeLucia, Rich, StL	.250	.400	.250	4	1	0	0	0	1	0	1	0	0	0-0	.214	.313	.214	14	3	0	0	0	2	0	2	3	1	0-0
Dessens, Elmer, Pit	.400	.400	.400	5	2	0	0	0	1	2	0	0	0	0-0	.400	.400	.400	5	2	0	0	0	1	2	0	0	0	0-0
Dewey, Mark, SF	.000	.125	.000	7	0	0	0	0	0	1	1	3	0	0-0	.091	.286	.091	11	1	0	0	0	1	0	3	6	0	0-0
DiPoto, Jerry, NYN	.000	.000	.000	1	0	0	0	0	0	0	0	0	0	0-0	.000	.000	.000	6	0	0	0	0	0	0	0	4	1	0-0

272

	1996 Hitting														Career Hitting													
Pitcher, Team	Avg	OBP	SLG	AB	H	2B	3B	HR	R	RBI	BB	SO	SH	SB-CS	Avg	OBP	SLG	AB	H	2B	3B	HR	R	RBI	BB	SO	SH	SB-CS
Dishman, G., SD-Phi	.000	.000	.000	0	0	0	0	0	0	0	0	0	2	0-0	.200	.219	.200	30	6	0	0	0	4	4	0	13	4	0-0
Dougherty, Jim, Hou	.000	.000	.000	0	0	0	0	0	0	0	0	0	0	0-0	.125	.125	.125	8	1	0	0	0	1	0	0	2	1	0-0
Drabek, Doug, Hou	.179	.179	.196	56	10	1	0	0	5	3	0	12	7	0-0	.167	.193	.207	714	119	17	3	2	41	46	17	205	65	0-1
Dreifort, Darren, LA	.000	.000	.000	3	0	0	0	0	0	0	0	2	0	0-0	.250	.250	.250	4	1	0	0	0	0	1	0	2	1	0-0
Dyer, Mike, Mon	.000	.000	.000	7	0	0	0	0	0	0	0	4	0	0-0	.267	.267	.267	15	4	0	0	0	1	1	0	6	1	0-0
Eckersley, Dennis, StL	.000	.000	.000	1	0	0	0	0	0	0	0	0	0	0-0	.133	.173	.199	181	24	3	0	3	9	12	9	84	5	0-0
Eischen, Joey, LA-Det	.000	.000	.000	6	0	0	0	0	0	0	0	2	0	0-0	.000	.000	.000	7	0	0	0	0	0	0	0	3	0	0-0
Ericks, John, Pit	.000	.000	.000	5	0	0	0	0	0	0	0	1	0	0-0	.083	.083	.111	36	3	1	0	0	2	1	0	13	6	0-0
Estes, Shawn, SF	.158	.200	.158	19	3	0	0	0	3	1	1	8	6	0-0	.125	.160	.125	24	3	0	0	0	3	1	1	10	6	0-0
Farmer, Mike, Col	.400	.400	.400	10	4	0	0	0	1	0	0	0	0	0-0	.400	.400	.400	10	4	0	0	0	1	0	0	0	0	0-0
Fassero, Jeff, Mon	.094	.192	.094	64	6	0	0	0	5	4	8	32	14	1-0	.077	.147	.097	207	16	2	1	0	15	5	17	116	39	1-0
Fernandez, O., SF	.088	.088	.088	57	5	0	0	0	0	1	0	25	5	0-0	.088	.088	.088	57	5	0	0	0	0	1	0	25	5	0-0
Fernandez, Sid, Phi	.105	.217	.158	19	2	1	0	0	0	2	3	10	2	0-0	.182	.207	.223	538	98	15	2	1	28	34	16	208	67	1-0
Fetters, Mike, Mil	.000	.000	.000	0	0	0	0	0	0	0	0	0	0	0-0	.000	.000	.000	0	0	0	0	0	0	0	0	0	0	0-0
Florie, Bryce, SD-Mil	.000	.000	.000	3	0	0	0	0	0	0	0	1	0	0-0	.000	.000	.000	5	0	0	0	0	0	0	0	3	0	0-0
Fossas, Tony, StL	.000	.000	.000	1	0	0	0	0	0	0	0	0	0	0-0	.000	.000	.000	1	0	0	0	0	0	0	0	0	0	0-0
Foster, Kevin, ChN	.296	.406	.519	27	8	4	1	0	3	6	4	11	3	0-0	.216	.272	.319	116	25	5	2	1	12	15	8	39	11	2-0
Franco, John, NYN	.000	.000	.000	1	0	0	0	0	0	0	0	1	0	0-0	.097	.097	.097	31	3	0	0	0	2	1	0	12	3	0-0
Freeman, M., Col-ChA	.122	.163	.122	41	5	0	0	0	3	0	2	21	4	0-0	.114	.151	.164	140	16	1	0	2	11	7	4	83	19	0-0
Frey, Steve, Phi	.000	.000	.000	0	0	0	0	0	0	0	0	0	0	0-0	.000	.200	.000	4	0	0	0	0	0	0	1	3	0	0-0
Fyhrie, Mike, NYN	.000	.000	.000	0	0	0	0	0	0	0	0	0	0	0-0	.000	.000	.000	0	0	0	0	0	0	0	0	0	0	0-0
Gardner, Mark, SF	.162	.197	.176	68	11	1	0	0	6	4	2	26	8	0-0	.126	.151	.149	269	34	2	2	0	14	12	6	105	37	0-0
Glavine, Tom, Atl	.289	.333	.342	76	22	4	0	0	8	3	5	17	15	0-0	.199	.250	.229	632	126	12	2	1	50	44	42	166	86	1-0
Grace, Mike, Phi	.138	.219	.138	29	4	0	0	0	1	0	2	11	1	0-0	.129	.206	.129	31	4	0	0	0	1	0	2	13	3	0-0
Guthrie, Mark, LA	.000	.000	.000	3	0	0	0	0	0	0	0	0	0	0-0	.000	.000	.000	4	0	0	0	0	0	0	0	0	0	0-0
Habyan, John, Col	.000	.250	.000	3	0	0	0	0	0	0	1	1	0	0-0	.000	.286	.000	5	0	0	0	0	0	0	2	2	0	0-0
Hall, Darren, LA	.000	.000	.000	0	0	0	0	0	0	0	0	0	0	0-0	.000	.000	.000	0	0	0	0	0	0	0	0	0	0	0-0
Hamilton, Joey, SD	.162	.186	.235	68	11	2	0	1	7	4	2	32	11	0-0	.104	.133	.145	173	18	4	0	1	11	8	6	94	21	0-0
Hammond, Chris, Fla	.067	.125	.067	15	1	0	0	0	1	0	1	7	2	0-0	.205	.288	.297	229	47	7	1	4	30	14	27	92	19	0-0
Hampton, Mike, Hou	.238	.319	.262	42	10	1	0	0	9	3	4	11	7	0-0	.187	.267	.198	91	17	1	0	0	16	3	8	26	11	0-0
Hancock, Lee, Pit	.000	.000	.000	0	0	0	0	0	0	0	0	0	0	0-0	.000	.000	.000	0	0	0	0	0	0	0	0	0	0	0-0
Hancock, Ryan, Cal	1.000	1.000	1.000	1	1	0	0	0	1	0	0	0	0	0-0	1.000	1.000	1.000	1	1	0	0	0	1	0	0	0	0	0-0
Harnisch, Pete, NYN	.091	.121	.109	55	5	1	0	0	3	1	2	18	10	0-0	.119	.148	.157	319	38	12	0	0	25	15	10	86	37	0-2
Hartgraves, D., Hou-Atl	.000	.000	.000	1	0	0	0	0	0	0	0	0	1	0-0	.000	.000	.000	3	0	0	0	0	0	0	0	1	2	0-0
Hawblitzel, Ryan, Col	.000	.000	.000	1	0	0	0	0	0	0	0	0	0	0-0	.000	.000	.000	1	0	0	0	0	0	0	0	0	0	0-0
Heflin, Bronson, Phi	.000	.000	.000	0	0	0	0	0	0	0	0	0	0	0-0	.000	.000	.000	0	0	0	0	0	0	0	0	0	0	0-0
Helling, Rick, Tex-Fla	.111	.111	.111	9	1	0	0	0	1	0	0	3	0	0-0	.111	.111	.111	9	1	0	0	0	1	0	0	3	0	0-0
Henneman, Mike, Tex	.000	.000	.000	0	0	0	0	0	0	0	0	0	0	0-0	.000	.000	.000	1	0	0	0	0	0	0	0	1	0	0-0
Henry, Doug, NYN	.000	.000	.000	5	0	0	0	0	0	0	0	0	0	0-0	.143	.143	.143	7	1	0	0	0	1	0	0	1	1	0-0
Heredia, Felix, Fla	.000	.000	.000	0	0	0	0	0	0	0	0	0	0	0-0	.000	.000	.000	0	0	0	0	0	0	0	0	0	0	0-0
Hermanson, Dustin, SD	.000	.000	.000	0	0	0	0	0	0	0	0	0	0	0-0	.000	.000	.000	0	0	0	0	0	0	0	0	0	0	0-0
Hernandez, Livan, Fla	1.000	1.000	1.000	1	1	0	0	0	1	0	0	0	0	0-0	1.000	1.000	1.000	1	1	0	0	0	1	0	0	0	0	0-0
Hernandez, R., ChA	.000	.000	.000	0	0	0	0	0	0	0	0	0	0	0-0	.000	.000	.000	0	0	0	0	0	0	0	0	0	0	0-0
Hernandez, X., Cin-Hou	.000	.000	.000	2	0	0	0	0	0	0	0	1	1	0-0	.027	.077	.027	37	1	0	0	0	2	0	2	20	4	0-0
Hill, Ken, Tex	.000	.000	.000	0	0	0	0	0	0	0	0	0	0	0-0	.148	.209	.182	324	48	6	1	1	22	19	24	93	65	0-0
Hoffman, Trevor, SD	.000	.000	.000	8	0	0	0	0	0	0	0	4	1	0-0	.100	.100	.150	20	2	1	0	0	1	2	0	6	2	0-0
Holmes, Darren, Col	.000	.333	.000	2	0	0	0	0	0	0	1	1	0	0-0	.000	.200	.000	4	0	0	0	0	0	0	1	2	3	0-0
Holt, Chris, Hou	.000	.000	.000	1	0	0	0	0	0	0	0	0	0	0-0	.000	.000	.000	1	0	0	0	0	0	0	0	0	0	0-0
Holzemer, Mark, Cal	.000	.000	.000	0	0	0	0	0	0	0	0	0	0	0-0	.000	.000	.000	0	0	0	0	0	0	0	0	0	0	0-0
Honeycutt, Rick, StL	.000	.667	.000	1	0	0	0	0	0	1	2	1	0	0-0	.132	.210	.148	182	24	3	0	0	13	9	18	44	28	1-0
Hook, Chris, SF	.500	.500	.500	2	1	0	0	0	0	1	0	1	0	0-0	.200	.200	.200	5	1	0	0	0	0	1	0	3	0	0-0
Hope, John, Pit	.200	.200	.200	5	1	0	0	0	0	0	0	0	1	1-0	.143	.143	.143	21	3	0	0	0	0	0	0	8	1	1-0
Hudek, John, Hou	.000	.000	.000	0	0	0	0	0	0	0	0	0	0	0-0	1.000	1.000	1.000	1	1	0	0	0	0	2	0	0	0	0-0
Hunter, Rich, Phi	.167	.211	.222	18	3	1	0	0	2	0	1	5	4	0-0	.167	.211	.222	18	3	1	0	0	2	0	1	5	4	0-0
Hurst, Bill, Fla	.000	.000	.000	0	0	0	0	0	0	0	0	0	0	0-0	.000	.000	.000	0	0	0	0	0	0	0	0	0	0	0-0
Hutton, Mark, NYA-Fla	.316	.316	.474	19	6	0	0	1	2	1	0	6	1	0-0	.316	.316	.474	19	6	0	0	1	2	1	0	6	1	0-0
Isringhausen, J., NYN	.255	.291	.412	51	13	2	0	2	5	9	3	15	2	0-0	.218	.271	.333	78	17	3	0	2	7	9	5	25	6	0-0
Jackson, Danny, StL	.333	.333	.556	9	3	2	0	0	1	4	0	1	1	0-0	.127	.148	.167	408	52	12	2	0	27	28	9	211	53	0-1
Jackson, Mike, Sea	.000	.000	.000	0	0	0	0	0	0	0	0	0	0	0-0	.185	.214	.259	27	5	2	0	0	3	1	1	4	4	0-0
Jarvis, Kevin, Cin	.167	.167	.194	36	6	1	0	0	2	1	0	12	8	0-0	.164	.177	.197	61	10	2	0	0	4	2	0	21	11	0-0
Johns, Doug, Oak	.000	.000	.000	0	0	0	0	0	1	0	0	0	0	0-0	.000	.000	.000	0	0	0	0	0	1	0	0	0	0	0-0
Johnstone, John, Hou	.000	.000	.000	0	0	0	0	0	0	0	0	0	0	0-0	.000	.000	.000	0	0	0	0	0	0	0	0	0	1	0-0
Jones, Bobby, NYN	.117	.159	.150	60	7	2	0	0	6	2	3	20	9	0-0	.121	.140	.137	182	22	3	0	0	12	5	4	71	37	0-0
Jones, Doug, ChN-Mil	.000	.000	.000	0	0	0	0	0	0	0	0	0	0	0-0	.200	.200	.200	5	1	0	0	0	0	0	0	2	0	0-0
Jones, Todd, Hou	.000	.000	.000	1	0	0	0	0	0	0	0	0	0	0-0	.273	.273	.364	11	3	1	0	0	1	0	0	1	0	0-0
Jordan, Ricardo, Phi	.000	.000	.000	1	0	0	0	0	0	0	0	0	0	0-0	.000	.000	.000	1	0	0	0	0	0	0	0	0	0	0-0
Juden, Jeff, SF-Mon	.000	.000	.000	3	0	0	0	0	0	0	0	2	1	0-0	.057	.057	.143	35	2	0	0	1	1	5	0	24	6	0-0
Kile, Darryl, Hou	.137	.169	.192	73	10	4	0	0	3	5	3	34	7	0-0	.111	.162	.158	279	31	10	0	1	16	17	16	140	38	0-0
Knackert, Brent, Bos	.000	.000	.000	0	0	0	0	0	0	0	0	0	0	0-0	.000	.000	.000	0	0	0	0	0	0	0	0	0	0	0-0
Larkin, Andy, Fla	.000	.000	.000	2	0	0	0	0	0	0	0	1	0	0-0	.000	.000	.000	2	0	0	0	0	0	0	0	1	0	0-0
Leiper, Dave, Phi-Mon	.000	.000	.000	0	0	0	0	0	0	0	0	0	0	0-0	.250	.250	.250	4	1	0	0	0	0	1	0	2	0	0-0
Leiter, Al, Fla	.100	.149	.100	70	7	0	0	0	3	1	4	45	7	0-0	.100	.149	.100	70	7	0	0	0	3	1	4	45	7	0-0
Leiter, Mark, SF-Mon	.119	.157	.134	67	8	1	0	0	4	5	3	35	9	0-0	.109	.156	.117	128	14	1	0	0	6	10	7	68	18	0-0
Leskanic, Curt, Col	.333	.333	.667	3	1	1	0	0	0	1	0	2	1	0-0	.172	.200	.276	29	5	3	0	0	2	4	1	11	4	0-0

Pitcher, Team	1996 Hitting Avg	OBP	SLG	AB	H	2B	3B	HR	R	RBI	BB	SO	SH	SB-CS	Career Hitting Avg	OBP	SLG	AB	H	2B	3B	HR	R	RBI	BB	SO	SH	SB-CS
Lewis, Richie, Det	.000	.000	.000	1	0	0	0	0	0	0	0	0	0	0-0	.111	.273	.111	9	1	0	0	0	1	1	2	3	1	0-0
Lieber, Jon, Pit	.194	.256	.278	36	7	3	0	0	4	3	3	11	3	0-0	.125	.160	.167	96	12	4	0	0	7	3	4	39	5	0-0
Lilliquist, Derek, Cin	.000	.000	.000	0	0	0	0	0	0	0	0	0	0	0-0	.213	.220	.278	108	23	1	0	2	11	8	1	20	5	0-0
Lloyd, Graeme, Mil-NYA	.000	.000	.000	0	0	0	0	0	0	0	0	0	0	0-0	.000	.000	.000	0	0	0	0	0	0	0	0	0	0	0-0
Loaiza, Esteban, Pit	.118	.118	.118	17	2	0	0	0	1	1	0	2	5	0-0	.174	.183	.217	69	12	1	1	0	5	3	1	13	12	0-0
Loiselle, Rich, Pit	.250	.250	.375	8	2	1	0	0	0	2	0	3	0	0-0	.250	.250	.375	8	2	1	0	0	0	2	0	3	0	0-0
Lomon, Kevin, Atl	.000	.000	.000	0	0	0	0	0	0	0	0	0	0	0-0	.000	.000	.000	0	0	0	0	0	0	0	0	0	1	0-0
Ludwick, Eric, StL	.000	.000	.000	2	0	0	0	0	0	0	0	1	0	0-0	.000	.000	.000	2	0	0	0	0	0	0	0	1	0	0-0
Lyons, Curt, Cin	.000	.000	.000	5	0	0	0	0	0	0	0	2	1	0-0	.000	.000	.000	5	0	0	0	0	0	0	0	2	1	0-0
MacDonald, Bob, NYN	.000	.000	.000	0	0	0	0	0	0	0	0	0	0	0-0	.000	.000	.000	0	0	0	0	0	0	0	0	0	0	0-0
Maddux, Greg, Atl	.147	.183	.176	68	10	2	0	0	6	2	3	12	11	0-0	.179	.194	.208	784	140	17	0	2	61	37	14	212	81	3-1
Maduro, Calvin, Phi	.000	.000	.000	4	0	0	0	0	0	0	0	2	0	0-0	.000	.000	.000	4	0	0	0	0	0	0	0	2	0	0-0
Mantei, Matt, Fla	.000	.000	.000	1	0	0	0	0	0	0	0	1	0	0-0	.000	.000	.000	1	0	0	0	0	0	0	0	1	0	0-0
Manuel, Barry, Mon	.000	.125	.000	7	0	0	0	0	0	0	1	3	1	0-0	.000	.125	.000	7	0	0	0	0	0	0	1	3	1	0-0
Martinez, Pedro, Mon	.094	.171	.109	64	6	1	0	0	5	4	5	29	16	0-0	.096	.147	.113	177	17	1	1	0	8	11	8	83	28	0-0
Martinez, P.A., NYN-Cin	.000	.000	.000	0	0	0	0	0	0	0	0	0	0	0-0	.000	.100	.000	9	0	0	0	0	1	1	1	4	2	0-0
Martinez, Ramon, LA	.119	.148	.119	59	7	0	0	0	3	2	2	22	8	0-0	.149	.162	.175	510	76	10	0	1	24	31	7	170	58	0-2
Mathews, T.J., StL	.000	.000	.000	4	0	0	0	0	0	0	0	3	0	0-0	.000	.000	.000	6	0	0	0	0	0	0	0	4	0	0-0
Mathews, Terry, Fla-Bal	.000	.000	.000	4	0	0	0	0	0	0	0	2	0	0-0	.391	.391	.522	23	9	3	0	0	3	3	0	8	0	0-0
May, Darrell, Pit-Cal	.333	.333	.333	3	1	0	0	0	1	0	0	1	0	0-0	.333	.333	.333	3	1	0	0	0	1	0	0	1	0	0-0
McElroy, C., Cin-Cal	.000	.000	.000	2	0	0	0	0	0	0	0	0	0	0-0	.242	.242	.394	33	8	3	1	0	3	4	0	9	0	0-1
McMichael, Greg, Atl	.000	.000	.000	0	0	0	0	0	0	0	0	0	0	0-0	.000	.083	.000	11	0	0	0	0	0	0	1	6	0	0-0
Mercedes, Jose, Mil	.000	.000	.000	0	0	0	0	0	0	0	0	0	0	0-0	.000	.000	.000	0	0	0	0	0	0	0	0	0	0	0-0
Miceli, Dan, Pit	.000	.000	.000	13	0	0	0	0	0	0	0	4	0	0-0	.000	.000	.000	17	0	0	0	0	0	0	0	7	0	0-0
Miller, Kurt, Fla	.375	.375	.375	8	3	0	0	0	0	2	0	0	1	0-0	.286	.286	.286	14	4	0	0	0	1	2	0	2	2	0-0
Mimbs, Michael, Phi	.121	.121	.121	33	4	0	0	0	0	0	0	12	2	0-0	.132	.132	.147	68	9	1	0	0	2	2	0	24	10	0-0
Minor, Blas, NYN-Sea	.000	.000	.000	1	0	0	0	0	0	0	0	0	0	0-0	.154	.214	.231	13	2	1	0	0	1	0	0	7	1	0-0
Miranda, Angel, Mil	.000	.000	.000	0	0	0	0	0	0	0	0	0	0	0-0	.000	.000	.000	0	0	0	0	0	0	0	0	0	0	0-0
Mitchell, Larry, Phi	.000	.000	.000	2	0	0	0	0	0	0	0	1	0	0-0	.000	.000	.000	2	0	0	0	0	0	0	0	1	0	0-0
Mlicki, Dave, NYN	.100	.182	.100	10	1	0	0	0	0	0	1	3	0	0-0	.061	.207	.061	49	3	0	0	0	2	2	9	15	12	0-0
Montgomery, Jeff, KC	.000	.000	.000	0	0	0	0	0	0	0	0	0	0	0-0	.000	.000	.000	2	0	0	0	0	0	0	0	1	0	0-0
Moore, Marcus, Cin	.333	.333	.667	3	1	1	0	0	0	0	0	2	0	0-0	.200	.200	.400	5	1	1	0	0	0	0	0	4	0	0-0
Morel, Ramon, Pit	.000	.000	.000	4	0	0	0	0	0	0	0	2	1	0-0	.000	.000	.000	4	0	0	0	0	0	0	0	2	1	0-0
Morgan, Mike, StL-Cin	.050	.050	.050	40	2	0	0	0	1	0	0	17	11	0-0	.087	.111	.092	425	37	2	0	0	11	12	12	127	48	0-0
Morman, Alvin, Hou	.000	.000	.000	0	0	0	0	0	0	0	0	0	0	0-0	.000	.000	.000	0	0	0	0	0	0	0	0	0	0	0-0
Mulholland, T., Phi-Sea	.178	.178	.267	45	8	1	0	1	2	2	0	20	4	0-0	.091	.111	.120	450	41	5	1	2	17	11	9	200	34	1-1
Munoz, Bobby, Phi	.143	.143	.286	7	1	1	0	0	1	0	0	3	1	0-0	.174	.191	.261	46	8	1	0	1	4	6	1	16	3	0-0
Munoz, Mike, Col	.000	.000	.000	1	0	0	0	0	0	0	0	1	0	0-0	.250	.500	.500	4	1	1	0	0	1	1	2	3	0	0-0
Myers, Randy, Bal	.000	.000	.000	0	0	0	0	0	0	0	0	0	0	0-0	.186	.226	.237	59	11	3	0	0	5	7	3	32	5	0-0
Myers, Rodney, ChN	.000	.000	.000	5	0	0	0	0	0	0	0	4	0	0-0	.000	.000	.000	5	0	0	0	0	0	0	0	4	0	0-0
Navarro, Jaime, ChN	.130	.141	.143	77	10	1	0	0	1	3	0	26	8	0-0	.155	.167	.197	142	22	6	0	0	1	10	1	51	16	0-0
Neagle, Denny, Pit-Atl	.174	.194	.188	69	12	1	0	0	3	4	2	18	16	0-0	.138	.161	.186	210	29	4	0	2	10	19	6	63	30	0-1
Nen, Robb, Fla	.000	.000	.000	2	0	0	0	0	0	0	0	0	0	0-0	.000	.000	.000	9	0	0	0	0	0	0	0	1	0	0-0
Nied, Dave, Col	.000	.000	.000	1	0	0	0	0	0	0	0	1	0	0-0	.141	.187	.141	71	10	0	0	0	5	2	4	26	6	0-0
Nomo, Hideo, LA	.133	.156	.187	75	10	4	0	0	1	3	2	38	10	0-0	.113	.125	.142	141	16	4	0	0	3	7	2	71	15	0-0
Olivares, Omar, Det	.000	.000	.000	0	0	0	0	0	0	0	0	0	0	0-0	.229	.246	.323	201	46	7	0	4	19	21	5	58	13	0-0
Olson, Gregg, Det-Hou	.000	.000	.000	0	0	0	0	0	0	0	0	0	0	0-0	.000	.000	.000	2	0	0	0	0	0	0	0	2	0	0-0
Oquist, Mike, SD	.000	.000	.000	0	0	0	0	0	0	0	0	0	0	0-0	.000	.000	.000	0	0	0	0	0	0	0	0	0	0	0-0
Osborne, Donovan, StL	.220	.258	.339	59	13	4	0	1	6	10	3	24	10	0-1	.178	.217	.244	197	35	8	1	1	15	17	9	73	22	0-1
Osuna, Al, SD	.000	.000	.000	1	0	0	0	0	0	0	0	0	0	0-0	.000	.000	.000	3	0	0	0	0	1	1	0	1	1	0-0
Osuna, Antonio, LA	.000	.333	.000	1	0	0	0	0	0	1	1	0	0	0-0	.000	.200	.000	3	0	0	0	0	0	1	1	0	0	0-0
Pacheco, Alex, Mon	.000	.000	.000	0	0	0	0	0	0	0	0	0	0	0-0	.000	.000	.000	0	0	0	0	0	0	0	0	0	0	0-0
Painter, Lance, Col	.133	.133	.133	15	2	0	0	0	1	2	0	8	0	0-0	.164	.186	.236	55	9	2	1	0	6	5	2	27	7	0-0
Pall, Donn, Fla	.000	.333	.000	2	0	0	0	0	0	0	1	0	0	0-0	.000	.333	.000	2	0	0	0	0	0	0	1	0	0	0-0
Paniagua, Jose, Mon	.000	.154	.000	11	0	0	0	0	1	0	2	7	1	0-0	.000	.154	.000	11	0	0	0	0	1	0	2	7	1	0-0
Park, Chan Ho, LA	.053	.100	.053	19	1	0	0	0	0	2	1	9	3	0-0	.050	.095	.050	20	1	0	0	0	0	2	1	10	3	0-0
Parra, Jose, Min	.000	.000	.000	0	0	0	0	0	0	0	0	0	0	0-0	.000	.000	.000	0	0	0	0	0	0	0	0	0	2	0-0
Parrett, Jeff, StL-Phi	.000	.333	.000	2	0	0	0	0	1	0	1	1	0	0-0	.105	.171	.105	38	4	0	0	0	1	1	3	13	2	0-0
Parris, Steve, Pit	.167	.286	.167	6	1	0	0	0	1	0	1	1	2	0-0	.235	.257	.294	34	8	2	0	0	3	4	1	11	3	0-0
Patterson, Bob, ChN	.333	.333	.333	3	1	0	0	0	0	0	0	2	0	0-0	.127	.158	.145	55	7	1	0	0	3	4	2	24	6	0-0
Pena, Alejandro, Fla	.000	.000	.000	0	0	0	0	0	0	0	0	0	0	0-0	.110	.125	.144	181	20	3	0	1	9	7	3	73	9	0-0
Percival, Troy, Cal	.000	.000	.000	1	0	0	0	0	0	0	0	1	0	0-0	.000	.000	.000	1	0	0	0	0	0	0	0	1	0	0-0
Perez, Mike, ChN	.000	.000	.000	1	0	0	0	0	0	0	0	1	0	0-0	.000	.214	.000	11	0	0	0	0	1	0	3	7	3	0-0
Perez, Yorkis, Fla	.000	.000	.000	1	0	0	0	0	0	0	0	1	0	0-0	.000	.000	.000	5	0	0	0	0	0	0	0	4	0	0-0
Person, Robert, NYN	.143	.143	.190	21	3	1	0	0	1	0	0	12	5	0-0	.208	.208	.250	24	5	1	0	0	2	0	0	12	5	0-0
Peters, Chris, Pit	.211	.211	.263	19	4	1	0	0	2	1	0	8	1	0-0	.211	.211	.263	19	4	1	0	0	2	1	0	8	1	0-0
Petkovsek, Mark, StL	.188	.235	.188	16	3	0	0	0	1	0	0	3	0	0-0	.113	.200	.113	53	6	0	0	0	5	2	5	14	3	0-0
Plesac, Dan, Pit	.000	.000	.000	5	0	0	0	0	0	0	0	2	0	0-0	.071	.071	.071	14	1	0	0	0	0	0	0	9	0	0-0
Poole, Jim, Cle-SF	.000	.000	.000	2	0	0	0	0	0	0	0	1	0	0-0	.000	.000	.000	2	0	0	0	0	0	0	0	1	0	0-0
Portugal, Mark, Cin	.167	.184	.188	48	8	1	0	0	4	1	1	11	7	0-0	.193	.225	.252	393	76	15	1	2	27	32	16	75	49	0-0
Powell, Jay, Fla	.000	.000	.000	5	0	0	0	0	0	0	0	4	1	0-0	.000	.000	.000	5	0	0	0	0	0	0	0	4	1	0-0
Pugh, Tim, Cin-KC	.000	.000	.000	0	0	0	0	0	0	0	0	0	1	0-0	.202	.237	.239	109	22	4	0	0	6	4	4	38	14	0-0
Quirico, Rafael, Phi	.000	.000	.000	0	0	0	0	0	0	0	0	0	0	0-0	.000	.000	.000	0	0	0	0	0	0	0	0	0	0	0-0
Radinsky, Scott, LA	.000	.000	.000	1	0	0	0	0	0	0	0	0	0	0-0	.000	.000	.000	1	0	0	0	0	0	0	0	0	0	0-0

	1996 Hitting														Career Hitting													
Pitcher, Team	Avg	OBP	SLG	AB	H	2B	3B	HR	R	RBI	BB	SO	SH	SB-CS	Avg	OBP	SLG	AB	H	2B	3B	HR	R	RBI	BB	SO	SH	SB-CS
Rapp, Pat, Fla	.121	.121	.138	58	7	1	0	0	2	2	0	21	0	0-0	.128	.132	.149	188	24	4	0	0	7	11	1	72	16	0-0
Reed, Steve, Col	.333	.333	.333	3	1	0	0	0	0	0	0	1	0	0-0	.118	.118	.118	17	2	0	0	0	0	0	0	6	2	0-0
Rekar, Bryan, Col	.267	.313	.333	15	4	1	0	0	2	0	1	5	1	0-0	.122	.200	.146	41	5	1	0	0	3	0	4	20	5	0-1
Remlinger, Mike, Cin	.143	.250	.143	7	1	0	0	0	0	0	1	3	0	0-0	.032	.118	.032	31	1	0	0	0	2	1	3	11	7	0-0
Reyes, Al, Mil	.000	.000	.000	0	0	0	0	0	0	0	0	0	0	0-0	.000	.000	.000	0	0	0	0	0	0	0	0	0	0	0-0
Reynolds, Shane, Hou	.184	.215	.289	76	14	2	0	2	6	3	3	28	14	0-0	.157	.180	.213	178	28	4	0	2	11	6	5	73	33	0-0
Reynoso, Armando, Col	.173	.246	.192	52	9	1	0	0	4	2	5	25	7	0-0	.140	.192	.181	171	24	1	0	2	9	6	11	66	19	0-0
Rhodes, Arthur, Bal	.000	.000	.000	0	0	0	0	0	0	0	0	0	0	0-0	.000	.000	.000	0	0	0	0	0	0	0	0	0	0	0-0
Ritz, Kevin, Col	.231	.306	.308	65	15	2	0	1	7	5	7	28	11	0-0	.180	.243	.226	133	24	3	0	1	10	7	9	61	27	1-1
Rojas, Mel, Mon	.375	.375	.500	8	3	1	0	0	0	3	0	2	0	0-0	.121	.121	.138	58	7	1	0	0	1	3	0	32	6	0-0
Ruebel, Matt, Pit	.231	.286	.231	13	3	0	0	0	0	0	1	4	2	0-0	.231	.286	.231	13	3	0	0	0	0	0	1	4	2	0-0
Rueter, Kirk, Mon-SF	.125	.171	.125	32	4	0	0	0	2	3	2	5	2	0-0	.093	.147	.093	108	10	0	0	0	3	8	7	29	14	0-0
Ruffin, Bruce, Col	.000	.500	.000	1	0	0	0	0	0	0	1	1	0	0-0	.081	.148	.095	295	24	4	0	0	13	7	23	143	23	0-0
Ruffin, Johnny, Cin	.500	.500	.500	4	2	0	0	0	0	0	0	1	0	0-0	.176	.176	.176	17	3	0	0	0	1	0	0	5	0	1-0
Ryan, Ken, Phi	.143	.143	.143	7	1	0	0	0	0	0	0	4	1	0-0	.143	.143	.143	7	1	0	0	0	0	0	0	4	1	0-0
Salkeld, Roger, Cin	.031	.061	.031	32	1	0	0	0	1	0	1	21	4	0-0	.031	.061	.031	32	1	0	0	0	1	0	1	21	4	0-0
Sanders, Scott, SD	.194	.216	.278	36	7	3	0	0	2	1	1	11	4	0-0	.180	.216	.216	111	20	4	0	0	4	7	5	36	17	1-0
Schilling, Curt, Phi	.175	.188	.190	63	11	1	0	0	1	4	1	24	7	0-0	.158	.173	.176	273	43	5	0	0	10	14	5	90	34	0-0
Schmidt, Jason, Atl-Pit	.032	.091	.032	31	1	0	0	0	1	3	2	15	2	0-0	.056	.128	.056	36	2	0	0	0	1	3	3	17	3	0-0
Schourek, Pete, Cin	.263	.300	.263	19	5	0	0	0	1	2	1	5	5	0-0	.173	.199	.203	197	34	3	0	1	11	15	7	53	23	0-0
Schutz, Carl, Atl	.000	.000	.000	0	0	0	0	0	0	0	0	0	0	0-0	.000	.000	.000	0	0	0	0	0	0	0	0	0	0	0-0
Scott, Tim, Mon-SF	.000	.000	.000	5	0	0	0	0	0	0	0	4	0	0-0	.067	.067	.067	15	1	0	0	0	0	0	0	11	1	0-0
Service, Scott, Cin	.000	.000	.000	5	0	0	0	0	0	0	0	2	0	0-0	.067	.067	.067	15	1	0	0	0	0	1	0	8	0	0-0
Shaw, Jeff, Cin	.000	.167	.000	5	0	0	0	0	0	0	1	3	0	0-0	.091	.189	.091	33	3	0	0	0	4	0	4	15	1	0-0
Small, Mark, Hou	.000	.000	.000	1	0	0	0	0	0	0	0	1	0	0-0	.000	.000	.000	1	0	0	0	0	0	0	0	1	0	0-0
Smiley, John, Cin	.191	.236	.221	68	13	2	0	0	1	6	4	22	4	0-0	.149	.191	.190	464	69	13	0	2	21	33	25	173	43	0-0
Smith, Lee, Cal-Cin	.000	.000	.000	0	0	0	0	0	0	0	0	0	0	0-0	.047	.090	.094	64	3	0	0	1	2	2	3	42	4	0-0
Smith, Zane, Pit	.154	.154	.154	26	4	0	0	0	2	3	0	6	2	0-0	.158	.180	.187	551	87	12	2	0	27	32	13	108	72	1-0
Smoltz, John, Atl	.218	.253	.295	78	17	3	0	1	3	12	3	26	15	0-0	.153	.223	.202	535	82	12	1	4	44	35	47	212	72	2-1
Soderstrom, Steve, SF	.000	.000	.000	5	0	0	0	0	0	0	0	3	0	0-0	.000	.000	.000	5	0	0	0	0	0	0	0	3	0	0-0
Sparks, Steve, Mil	.000	.000	.000	0	0	0	0	0	0	0	0	0	0	0-0	.000	.000	.000	0	0	0	0	0	0	0	0	0	0	0-0
Spradlin, Jerry, Cin	.000	.000	.000	0	0	0	0	0	0	0	0	0	0	0-0	.000	.000	.000	2	0	0	0	0	0	0	0	1	0	0-0
Springer, Russ, Phi	.059	.059	.059	17	1	0	0	0	1	0	0	12	2	0-0	.056	.056	.056	18	1	0	0	0	1	0	0	13	3	0-0
Stanton, Mike, Bos-Tex	.000	.000	.000	0	0	0	0	0	0	0	0	0	0	0-0	.545	.583	.636	11	6	1	0	0	1	2	1	1	1	0-0
Stottlemyre, Todd, StL	.227	.301	.227	66	15	0	0	0	8	2	7	27	9	1-1	.224	.297	.224	67	15	0	0	0	8	2	7	28	9	1-1
Sturtze, Tanyon, ChN	.000	.000	.000	1	0	0	0	0	0	0	0	0	1	0-0	.000	.000	.000	1	0	0	0	0	0	0	0	0	1	0-0
Sullivan, Scott, Cin	.000	.000	.000	1	0	0	0	0	0	1	0	0	0	0-0	.000	.000	.000	2	0	0	0	0	0	1	0	1	0	0-0
Swartzbaugh, D., ChN	.000	.143	.000	6	0	0	0	0	0	0	1	3	0	0-0	.000	.143	.000	6	0	0	0	0	0	0	1	3	0	0-0
Swift, Bill, Col	.333	.333	.333	6	2	0	0	0	0	0	0	1	0	0-0	.215	.253	.268	205	44	8	0	1	25	13	11	48	25	1-0
Swindell, Greg, Hou-Cle	.333	.333	.500	6	2	1	0	0	0	0	0	1	0	0-0	.192	.204	.233	240	46	10	0	0	10	13	4	55	33	0-0
Tabaka, Jeff, Hou	.000	.000	.000	1	0	0	0	0	0	0	0	1	0	0-0	.333	.500	.667	3	1	1	0	0	1	0	1	1	1	0-0
Telemaco, A., ChN	.103	.133	.103	29	3	0	0	0	1	1	1	15	4	0-0	.103	.133	.103	29	3	0	0	0	1	1	1	15	4	0-0
Tewksbury, Bob, SD	.031	.074	.046	65	2	1	0	0	1	2	3	27	8	0-0	.131	.177	.150	374	49	7	0	0	20	18	21	146	41	0-0
Thobe, Tom, Atl	.000	.000	.000	1	0	0	0	0	0	0	0	0	0	0-0	.000	.000	.000	1	0	0	0	0	0	0	0	0	0	0-0
Thomas, Larry, ChA	.000	.000	.000	0	0	0	0	0	0	0	0	0	0	0-0	.000	.000	.000	0	0	0	0	0	0	0	0	0	0	0-0
Thompson, Mark, Col	.138	.153	.190	58	8	3	0	0	3	2	1	21	5	0-0	.173	.184	.213	75	13	3	0	0	5	2	1	32	7	0-0
Trachsel, Steve, ChN	.106	.119	.182	66	7	2	0	1	3	5	1	20	6	0-0	.177	.200	.226	164	29	5	0	1	10	11	4	48	20	0-1
Trlicek, Ricky, NYN	.000	.000	.000	0	0	0	0	0	0	0	0	0	0	0-0	.250	.250	.250	4	1	0	0	0	0	0	0	3	0	0-0
Urbani, Tom, StL-Det	.167	.167	.167	6	1	0	0	0	0	0	0	1	0	0-0	.246	.319	.308	65	16	1	0	1	6	4	7	18	7	0-0
Urbina, Ugueth, Mon	.103	.161	.103	29	3	0	0	0	3	1	2	17	3	0-0	.143	.189	.143	35	5	0	0	0	3	1	2	21	3	0-0
Valdes, Ismael, LA	.143	.155	.157	70	10	1	0	0	6	2	1	25	13	0-0	.119	.132	.127	134	16	1	0	0	8	3	2	52	20	1-0
Valdes, Marc, Fla	.000	.067	.000	14	0	0	0	0	0	0	1	2	0	0-0	.000	.059	.000	16	0	0	0	0	0	0	1	2	0	0-0
Valenzuela, F., SD	.143	.143	.175	63	9	2	0	0	4	2	0	15	3	0-0	.200	.206	.264	914	183	26	1	10	55	82	8	142	87	0-2
VanLandingham, SF	.131	.156	.148	61	8	1	0	0	3	2	2	31	6	0-0	.123	.135	.167	138	17	3	0	1	5	6	2	72	11	0-0
Veras, Dario, SD	.000	.000	.000	0	0	0	0	0	0	0	0	0	0	0-0	.000	.000	.000	0	0	0	0	0	0	0	0	0	0	0-0
Veres, Dave, Mon	.375	.375	.500	8	3	1	0	0	1	1	0	4	0	0-0	.267	.313	.333	15	4	1	0	0	1	1	1	9	2	0-0
Villone, Ron, SD-Mil	.000	.000	.000	0	0	0	0	0	0	0	0	0	0	0-0	.000	.000	.000	1	0	0	0	0	0	0	0	0	0	0-0
Wade, Terrell, Atl	.154	.214	.154	13	2	0	0	0	0	1	1	7	2	0-0	.154	.214	.154	13	2	0	0	0	0	1	1	7	2	0-0
Wagner, Billy, Hou	.000	.000	.000	5	0	0	0	0	0	0	0	2	0	0-0	.000	.000	.000	5	0	0	0	0	0	0	0	2	0	0-0
Wagner, Paul, Pit	.040	.111	.040	25	1	0	0	0	1	2	2	8	3	0-1	.168	.205	.181	149	25	2	0	0	9	9	7	44	15	0-1
Wainhouse, David, Pit	.000	.000	.000	1	0	0	0	0	0	0	0	0	0	0-0	.000	.000	.000	1	0	0	0	0	0	0	0	0	0	0-0
Walker, Pete, SD	.000	.000	.000	0	0	0	0	0	0	0	0	0	0	0-0	.000	.000	.000	0	0	0	0	0	0	0	0	0	0	0-0
Wall, Donne, Hou	.205	.239	.227	44	9	1	0	0	5	1	2	11	8	0-0	.184	.216	.204	49	9	1	0	0	5	1	2	13	11	0-0
Wallace, Derek, NYN	.000	.000	.000	0	0	0	0	0	0	0	0	0	0	0-0	.000	.000	.000	0	0	0	0	0	0	0	0	0	0	0-0
Watson, Allen, SF	.231	.286	.277	65	15	3	0	0	5	7	5	8	2	0-0	.255	.293	.339	165	42	12	1	0	13	19	9	21	13	0-0
Weathers, D., Fla-NYA	.158	.200	.316	19	3	0	0	1	1	2	0	13	0	0-0	.111	.146	.141	99	11	0	0	1	4	3	3	62	12	0-0
Wendell, Turk, ChN	.500	.667	.500	2	1	0	0	0	0	0	1	0	1	0-0	.111	.238	.111	18	2	0	0	0	0	0	3	8	1	0-0
West, David, Phi	.286	.444	.286	7	2	0	0	0	0	0	2	2	2	0-0	.182	.224	.273	55	10	2	0	1	3	5	3	22	9	0-0
Wetteland, John, NYA	.000	.000	.000	0	0	0	0	0	0	0	0	0	0	0-0	.146	.146	.244	41	6	1	0	1	3	7	0	19	9	0-0
Wickman, Bob, NYA-Mil	.000	.000	.000	0	0	0	0	0	0	0	0	0	0	0-0	.000	.000	.000	0	0	0	0	0	0	0	0	0	0	0-0
Wilkins, Marc, Pit	.222	.300	.222	9	2	0	0	0	1	1	1	6	0	0-0	.222	.300	.222	9	2	0	0	0	1	1	1	6	0	0-0
Williams, Mike, Phi	.157	.189	.157	51	8	0	0	0	4	1	2	11	6	1-0	.168	.192	.188	101	17	2	0	0	7	7	3	30	22	1-0
Wilson, Paul, NYN	.080	.115	.140	50	4	0	0	1	3	4	1	32	4	0-0	.080	.115	.140	50	4	0	0	1	3	4	1	32	4	0-0
Wohlers, Mark, Atl	.000	.000	.000	3	0	0	0	0	0	0	0	3	0	0-0	.100	.100	.100	10	1	0	0	0	1	0	0	9	1	0-0

	1996 Hitting														Career Hitting													
Pitcher, Team	Avg	OBP	SLG	AB	H	2B	3B	HR	R	RBI	BB	SO	SH	SB-CS	Avg	OBP	SLG	AB	H	2B	3B	HR	R	RBI	BB	SO	SH	SB-CS
Wojciechowski, S., Oak	.000	.000	.000	0	0	0	0	0	0	0	0	0	0	0-0	.000	.000	.000	0	0	0	0	0	0	0	0	0	0	0-0
Woodall, Brad, Atl	.200	.333	.200	5	1	0	0	0	0	0	1	2	0	0-0	.375	.444	.375	8	3	0	0	0	0	1	1	2	0	0-0
Worrell, Tim, SD	.150	.190	.150	20	3	0	0	0	1	2	1	10	6	0-0	.093	.125	.111	54	5	1	0	0	3	3	2	26	9	0-0
Worrell, Todd, LA	.000	.000	.000	0	0	0	0	0	0	0	0	0	0	0-0	.074	.107	.148	27	2	0	1	0	1	0	1	20	2	0-0
Wright, Jamey, Col	.077	.143	.154	26	2	2	0	0	3	0	2	13	5	0-0	.077	.143	.154	26	2	2	0	0	3	0	2	13	5	0-0
Young, Anthony, Hou	.000	.000	.000	2	0	0	0	0	0	0	0	2	0	0-0	.160	.177	.181	94	15	2	0	0	7	4	2	33	10	0-0

Pitchers Fielding and Holding Runners

1996 Fielding and Holding Runners

Pitcher, Team	G	Inn	PO	A	E	DP	Pct.	SBA	CS	PCS	PPO	CS%
Abbott, Jim, Cal	27	142.0	3	27	0	1	1.000	24	5	3	0	.33
Abbott, Kyle, Cal	3	4.0	0	1	0	0	1.000	0	0	0	0	.00
Acre, Mark, Oak	22	25.0	1	2	0	0	1.000	3	0	0	0	.00
Adams, Terry, ChN	69	101.0	8	11	0	1	1.000	8	2	0	0	.25
Adams, Willie, Oak	12	76.1	5	6	0	0	1.000	8	0	0	0	.00
Adamson, Joel, Fla	9	11.0	3	2	0	0	1.000	1	1	0	0	1.00
Aguilera, Rick, Min	19	111.1	13	5	2	0	.900	11	0	0	0	.00
Alberro, Jose, Tex	5	9.1	1	2	0	0	1.000	0	0	0	0	.00
Aldred, Scott, Det-Min	36	165.1	5	16	3	2	.875	21	6	1	0	.33
Alston, Garvin, Col	6	6.0	0	1	0	0	1.000	0	0	0	0	.00
Alvarez, Tavo, Mon	11	21.0	2	3	0	1	1.000	2	0	0	0	.00
Alvarez, Wilson, ChA	35	217.1	11	29	0	4	1.000	32	5	6	1	.34
Anderson, Brian, Cle	10	51.1	3	13	2	1	.889	12	3	3	0	.50
Andujar, Luis, ChA-Tor	8	37.1	1	2	0	0	1.000	2	1	0	0	.50
Appier, Kevin, KC	32	211.1	19	16	0	2	1.000	22	9	0	0	.41
Ashby, Andy, SD	24	150.2	10	29	2	3	.951	22	9	1	0	.45
Assenmacher, Paul, Cle	63	46.2	0	4	0	1	1.000	5	0	2	0	.40
Astacio, Pedro, LA	35	211.2	23	31	3	2	.947	20	5	1	0	.30
Aucoin, Derek, Mon	2	2.2	1	1	0	0	1.000	0	0	0	0	.00
Avery, Steve, Atl	24	131.0	8	26	2	0	.944	13	4	2	2	.46
Ayala, Bobby, Sea	50	67.1	5	9	0	1	1.000	8	2	1	0	.38
Bailey, Cory, StL	51	57.0	6	5	0	0	1.000	5	2	1	0	.60
Bailey, Roger, Col	24	83.2	11	26	1	2	.974	14	4	1	0	.36
Baldwin, James, ChA	28	169.0	12	16	3	1	.903	26	8	0	0	.31
Barber, Brian, StL	1	3.0	0	0	0	0	.000	2	0	0	0	.00
Barton, Shawn, SF	7	8.1	1	2	0	0	1.000	1	0	1	0	1.00
Batchelor, Richard, StL	11	15.0	0	1	0	0	1.000	0	0	0	0	.00
Batista, Miguel, Fla	9	11.1	0	1	0	0	1.000	1	0	0	0	.00
Bautista, Jose, SF	37	69.2	4	13	0	0	1.000	9	2	1	0	.33
Beck, Rod, SF	63	62.0	2	6	0	1	1.000	6	1	0	0	.17
Beckett, Robbie, Col	5	5.1	0	0	0	0	.000	0	0	0	0	.00
Beech, Matt, Phi	8	41.1	1	4	0	1	1.000	6	3	0	0	.50
Belcher, Tim, KC	35	238.2	18	32	2	4	.962	17	8	0	1	.47
Belinda, Stan, Bos	31	28.2	3	3	0	0	1.000	4	0	0	0	.00
Benes, Alan, StL	34	191.0	8	19	3	3	.900	21	13	0	1	.62
Benes, Andy, StL	36	230.1	8	24	2	1	.941	25	4	0	1	.16
Benitez, Armando, Bal	18	14.1	1	1	1	0	.667	2	0	0	0	.00
Bennett, Erik, Min	24	27.1	2	5	0	0	1.000	3	1	0	0	.33
Bere, Jason, ChA	5	16.2	1	3	1	0	.800	4	1	0	0	.25
Bergman, Sean, SD	41	113.1	11	19	0	0	1.000	19	2	0	0	.11
Bertotti, Mike, ChA	15	28.0	0	6	0	0	1.000	2	0	1	0	.50
Berumen, Andres, SD	3	3.1	0	0	0	0	.000	0	0	0	0	.00
Bevil, Brian, KC	3	11.0	2	1	0	0	1.000	1	1	0	0	1.00
Bielecki, Mike, Atl	40	75.1	3	14	0	0	1.000	10	1	0	0	.10
Blair, Willie, SD	60	88.0	6	6	2	0	.857	11	2	0	0	.18
Blazier, Ron, Phi	26	38.1	2	3	0	0	1.000	4	0	0	0	.00
Bluma, Jaime, KC	17	20.0	1	6	0	1	1.000	1	0	0	0	.00
Bochtler, Doug, SD	63	65.2	2	3	0	0	1.000	12	3	0	0	.25
Boehringer, Brian, NYA	15	46.1	2	4	0	0	1.000	4	0	0	1	.00
Boever, Joe, Pit	13	15.0	2	1	0	0	1.000	2	1	0	0	.50
Bohanon, Brian, Tor	20	22.0	2	2	0	0	1.000	2	0	0	0	.00
Bones, Ricky, Mil-NYA	36	152.0	11	15	1	4	.963	12	3	0	0	.25
Borbon, Pedro, Atl	43	36.0	4	5	1	1	.900	3	0	0	0	.00
Borland, Toby, Phi	69	90.2	4	7	0	1	1.000	8	2	0	0	.25
Borowski, Joe, Atl	22	26.0	0	12	0	1	1.000	3	1	0	0	.33
Bosio, Chris, Sea	18	60.2	3	10	0	1	1.000	5	2	0	0	.40
Boskie, Shawn, Cal	38	189.1	7	29	1	1	.973	19	2	0	3	.11
Bottalico, Ricky, Phi	61	67.2	1	5	0	1	1.000	3	1	0	0	.33
Bottenfield, Kent, ChN	48	61.2	6	12	0	2	1.000	10	1	0	1	.10
Bourgeois, Steve, SF	15	40.0	4	8	0	0	1.000	5	2	0	0	.40
Boze, Marshall, Mil	25	32.1	8	4	0	0	1.000	6	1	0	0	.17
Brandenburg, Tex-Bos	55	76.0	2	7	0	0	1.000	3	1	0	0	.33
Brantley, Jeff, Cin	66	71.0	7	4	0	0	1.000	5	1	0	0	.20
Brewer, Billy, NYA	4	5.2	0	1	0	0	1.000	0	0	0	0	.00
Briscoe, John, Oak	17	26.1	1	2	0	1	1.000	2	1	0	0	.50
Brocail, Doug, Hou	23	53.0	6	5	0	0	1.000	10	2	1	0	.30
Brow, Scott, Tor	18	38.2	3	4	0	0	1.000	5	2	0	0	.40
Brown, Kevin, Fla	32	233.0	29	54	1	4	.988	21	9	0	3	.43
Bruske, Jim, LA	11	12.2	0	2	0	0	1.000	0	0	0	0	.00
Bullinger, Jim, ChN	37	129.1	15	20	0	0	1.000	18	5	0	1	.28
Burba, Dave, Cin	34	195.0	15	14	2	2	.935	30	8	0	0	.27
Burke, John, Col	11	15.2	2	1	0	0	1.000	3	0	0	0	.00

1996 Fielding and Holding Runners

Pitcher, Team	G	Inn	PO	A	E	DP	Pct.	SBA	CS	PCS	PPO	CS%
Burkett, John, Fla-Tex	34	222.2	19	25	1	1	.978	23	8	0	1	.35
Burrows, Terry, Mil	8	12.2	2	1	0	0	1.000	0	0	0	0	.00
Busby, Mike, StL	1	4.0	0	1	1	0	.500	0	0	0	0	.00
Byrd, Paul, NYN	38	46.2	4	6	0	0	1.000	8	2	0	1	.25
Campbell, Mike, ChN	13	36.1	2	1	0	0	1.000	5	0	0	0	.00
Candiotti, Tom, LA	28	152.1	13	36	1	4	.980	21	3	0	0	.14
Carlson, Dan, SF	5	10.0	1	1	0	0	1.000	1	0	0	0	.00
Carmona, Rafael, Sea	52	90.1	2	14	1	0	.941	6	2	0	0	.33
Carpenter, Cris, Mil	8	8.1	0	0	0	0	.000	3	0	0	0	.00
Carrara, G., Tor-Cin	19	38.0	2	4	0	0	1.000	3	2	0	0	.67
Carrasco, Hector, Cin	56	74.1	3	12	2	1	.882	9	1	0	0	.11
Casian, Larry, ChN	35	24.0	2	5	1	1	.875	2	2	0	0	1.00
Castillo, Frank, ChN	33	182.1	18	23	3	2	.932	24	10	0	0	.42
Castillo, Tony, Tor-ChA	55	95.0	9	15	0	1	1.000	7	3	1	0	.57
Charlton, Norm, Sea	70	75.2	4	9	1	1	.929	5	0	0	0	.00
Chouinard, Bobby, Oak	13	59.0	3	13	0	2	1.000	3	1	1	0	.67
Christiansen, Jason, Pit	33	44.1	0	7	0	0	1.000	7	1	2	0	.43
Christopher, Mike, Det	13	30.0	1	3	0	0	1.000	1	0	0	0	.00
Clark, Mark, NYN	32	212.1	9	24	0	1	1.000	14	2	0	0	.14
Clark, Terry, KC-Hou	17	23.2	3	4	0	1	1.000	1	0	0	0	.00
Clemens, Roger, Bos	34	242.2	10	22	2	2	.941	43	10	3	1	.30
Clontz, Brad, Atl	81	80.2	1	18	1	1	.950	13	1	0	0	.08
Cone, David, NYA	11	72.0	7	4	1	1	.917	11	2	0	0	.18
Cook, Dennis, Tex	60	70.1	4	5	0	0	1.000	7	3	0	0	.43
Cooke, Steve, Pit	3	8.1	0	0	0	0	.000	0	0	0	0	.00
Coppinger, Rocky, Bal	23	125.0	6	8	0	1	1.000	24	2	1	0	.13
Corbin, Archie, Bal	18	27.1	0	1	0	0	1.000	1	0	0	0	.00
Cordova, Francisco, Pit	59	99.0	6	16	2	1	.917	12	0	0	0	.00
Cormier, Rheal, Mon	33	159.2	15	35	2	1	.962	22	2	9	0	.50
Corsi, Jim, Oak	57	73.2	6	17	0	2	1.000	3	2	1	0	1.00
Crabtree, Tim, Tor	53	67.1	4	10	1	1	.933	5	0	0	0	.00
Crawford, Carlos, Phi	1	3.2	0	0	1	0	.000	0	0	0	0	.00
Creek, Doug, SF	63	48.1	3	2	0	1	1.000	7	2	0	0	.29
Cummings, J., LA-Det	25	37.0	1	5	0	0	1.000	5	0	0	0	.00
D'Amico, Jeff, Mil	17	86.0	10	6	0	0	1.000	8	3	0	0	.38
Daal, Omar, Mon	64	87.1	4	16	1	0	.952	5	2	0	1	.40
Darwin, Danny, Pit-Hou	34	164.2	12	25	1	3	.974	15	3	0	0	.20
Darwin, Jeff, ChA	22	30.2	3	2	0	0	1.000	2	0	0	0	.00
Davis, Tim, Sea	40	42.2	3	5	1	1	.889	3	0	0	0	.00
Davison, Scott, Sea	5	9.0	3	0	0	0	1.000	1	1	0	0	1.00
DeLucia, Rich, SF	56	61.2	4	12	0	2	1.000	2	2	0	1	1.00
Dessens, Elmer, Pit	15	25.0	1	2	0	0	1.000	3	1	0	0	.33
Dewey, Mark, SF	78	83.1	8	17	0	2	1.000	9	4	0	0	.44
Dickson, Jason, Cal	7	43.1	3	5	1	0	.889	8	5	0	0	.63
DiPoto, Jerry, NYN	57	77.1	6	11	0	1	1.000	10	4	0	0	.40
Dishman, G., SD-Phi	7	9.1	1	0	0	0	1.000	1	1	0	0	1.00
Doherty, John, Bos	3	6.1	1	4	0	0	1.000	0	0	0	0	.00
Dougherty, Jim, Hou	12	13.0	1	3	0	0	1.000	1	0	0	0	.00
Drabek, Doug, Hou	30	175.1	17	23	3	0	.930	26	7	0	0	.27
Dreifort, Darren, LA	19	23.2	3	6	0	0	1.000	1	0	0	0	.00
Dyer, Mike, Mon	70	75.2	7	13	0	2	1.000	18	1	1	0	.11
Eckersley, Dennis, StL	63	60.0	3	6	1	0	.900	7	1	0	0	.14
Edenfield, Ken, Cal	2	4.1	1	0	0	0	1.000	0	0	0	0	.00
Eichhorn, Mark, Cal	24	30.1	2	6	0	0	1.000	5	1	0	0	.20
Eischen, Joey, LA-Det	52	68.1	0	11	0	2	1.000	9	0	2	0	.22
Eldred, Cal, Mil	15	84.2	4	10	0	0	1.000	8	1	0	0	.13
Ellis, Robert, Cal	3	5.0	0	0	0	0	.000	0	0	0	0	.00
Embree, Alan, Cle	24	31.0	1	2	0	0	1.000	7	2	0	0	.29
Ericks, John, Pit	28	46.2	1	2	0	0	1.000	11	1	0	0	.09
Erickson, Scott, Bal	34	222.1	30	43	2	6	.973	36	4	0	0	.11
Eshelman, Vaughn, Bos	39	87.2	5	16	3	0	.875	6	2	1	0	.50
Estes, Shawn, SF	11	70.0	2	11	0	0	1.000	3	3	0	0	1.00
Farmer, Mike, Col	7	28.0	1	3	0	0	1.000	4	0	1	0	.25
Farrell, John, Det	2	6.1	1	0	0	0	1.000	6	3	0	0	.50
Fassero, Jeff, Mon	33	231.2	12	41	1	2	.981	25	4	9	0	.52
Fernandez, Alex, ChA	35	258.0	27	43	2	7	.972	21	8	0	2	.38
Fernandez, O., SF	30	171.2	10	31	2	1	.953	12	2	3	3	.42
Fernandez, Sid, Phi	11	63.0	1	3	0	0	1.000	13	1	0	0	.08
Fetters, Mike, Mil	61	61.1	7	5	0	0	1.000	8	1	0	1	.13
Finley, Chuck, Cal	35	238.0	9	28	3	4	.925	32	6	2	1	.25
Flener, Huck, Tor	15	70.2	6	12	2	1	.900	2	0	0	0	.00
Fletcher, Paul, Oak	1	1.1	0	0	1	0	.000	0	0	0	0	.00

1996 Fielding and Holding Runners

Pitcher, Team	G	Inn	PO	A	E	DP	Pct.	SBA	CS	PCS	PPO	CS%
Florie, Bryce, SD-Mil	54	68.1	7	9	2	0	.889	10	1	0	0	.10
Fossas, Tony, StL	65	47.0	2	8	0	0	1.000	1	1	0	0	1.00
Foster, Kevin, ChN	17	87.0	6	16	1	0	.957	11	1	1	0	.18
Franco, John, NYN	51	54.0	1	8	0	0	1.000	2	1	0	1	.50
Freeman, M., Col-ChA	27	131.2	3	26	2	2	.935	21	2	0	0	.10
Frey, Steve, Phi	30	34.1	1	8	0	1	1.000	1	1	0	1	1.00
Frohwirth, Todd, Cal	4	5.2	0	0	0	0	.000	1	0	0	0	.00
Fyhrie, Mike, NYN	2	2.1	0	1	0	0	1.000	2	0	0	0	.00
Garces, Rich, Bos	37	44.0	1	8	1	2	.900	4	0	0	0	.00
Garcia, Ramon, Mil	37	75.2	6	10	0	2	1.000	6	1	0	0	.17
Gardner, Mark, SF	30	179.1	10	14	0	1	1.000	16	7	1	1	.50
Gibson, Paul, NYA	4	4.1	1	0	0	0	1.000	0	0	0	0	.00
Givens, Brian, Mil	4	14.0	1	0	1	0	.500	4	0	0	0	.00
Glavine, Tom, Atl	36	235.1	14	50	1	1	.985	14	7	0	0	.50
Gohr, Greg, Det-Cal	32	115.2	7	10	1	0	.944	16	4	0	0	.25
Gooden, Dwight, NYA	29	170.2	9	26	1	1	.972	29	5	0	4	.17
Gordon, Tom, Bos	34	215.2	14	30	3	3	.936	22	5	0	0	.23
Grace, Mike, Phi	12	80.0	6	17	0	0	1.000	4	0	0	1	.00
Granger, Jeff, KC	15	16.1	3	1	0	0	1.000	0	0	0	0	.00
Graves, Danny, Cle	15	29.2	2	2	0	0	1.000	4	0	0	0	.00
Grimsley, Jason, Cal	35	130.1	23	18	2	2	.953	19	3	0	0	.16
Groom, Buddy, Oak	72	77.1	2	6	1	0	.889	11	1	0	0	.09
Gross, Kevin, Tex	28	129.1	11	19	2	1	.938	12	5	1	0	.50
Grundt, Ken, Bos	1	0.1	0	0	0	0	.000	0	0	0	0	.00
Guardado, Eddie, Min	83	73.2	0	9	0	1	1.000	2	1	0	0	.50
Gubicza, Mark, KC	19	119.1	15	16	1	1	.969	6	3	0	0	.50
Guetterman, Lee, Sea	17	11.0	2	3	0	0	1.000	4	0	1	0	.25
Gunderson, Eric, Bos	28	17.1	0	0	0	0	.000	0	0	0	0	.00
Guthrie, Mark, LA	66	73.0	1	11	1	1	.923	9	0	1	0	.11
Guzman, Juan, Tor	27	187.2	9	22	3	2	.912	22	4	0	3	.18
Habyan, John, Col	19	24.0	1	2	0	0	1.000	7	2	0	0	.29
Hall, Darren, LA	9	12.0	0	0	0	0	.000	3	0	0	0	.00
Hamilton, Joey, SD	34	211.2	17	26	1	2	.977	22	5	1	0	.27
Hammond, Chris, Fla	38	81.0	6	13	2	1	.905	4	1	1	1	.50
Hampton, Mike, Hou	27	160.1	13	32	2	3	.957	15	3	3	1	.40
Hancock, Lee, Pit	13	18.1	3	7	1	2	.909	4	0	1	0	.25
Hancock, Ryan, Cal	11	27.2	2	3	0	1	1.000	3	1	0	0	.33
Haney, Chris, KC	35	228.0	9	27	0	1	1.000	14	6	3	0	.64
Hansell, Greg, Min	50	74.1	8	4	0	0	1.000	5	3	0	0	.60
Hanson, Erik, Tor	35	214.2	8	16	3	3	.889	20	11	1	0	.60
Harikkala, Tim, Sea	1	4.1	0	2	0	0	1.000	0	0	0	0	.00
Harnisch, Pete, NYN	30	194.2	10	16	3	1	.897	24	4	0	0	.17
Harris, Pep, Cal	11	32.1	1	6	0	1	1.000	1	0	0	0	.00
Harris, Reggie, Bos	4	4.1	0	0	0	0	.000	0	0	0	0	.00
Hartgraves, D., Hou-Atl	39	37.2	3	5	0	0	1.000	3	2	0	0	.67
Hawblitzel, Ryan, Col	8	15.0	2	2	0	0	1.000	1	1	0	0	1.00
Hawkins, LaTroy, Min	7	26.1	3	4	0	1	1.000	3	1	1	1	.67
Haynes, Jimmy, Bal	26	89.0	6	12	1	1	.947	9	3	0	1	.33
Heflin, Bronson, Phi	3	6.2	0	0	0	0	.000	0	0	0	0	.00
Helling, Rick, Tex-Fla	11	48.0	2	3	0	0	1.000	7	0	0	0	.00
Henneman, Mike, Tex	49	42.0	1	6	1	0	.875	0	0	0	0	.00
Henry, Doug, NYN	58	75.0	4	7	2	0	.846	10	1	0	0	.10
Hentgen, Pat, Tor	35	265.2	11	31	1	7	.977	16	7	2	0	.56
Heredia, Felix, Fla	21	16.2	0	0	0	0	.000	3	1	0	0	.33
Heredia, Gil, Tex	44	73.1	7	7	0	0	1.000	1	1	0	1	1.00
Hermanson, Dustin, SD	8	13.2	2	2	1	2	.800	1	0	0	0	.00
Hernandez, Livan, Fla	1	3.0	0	0	0	0	.000	0	0	0	0	.00
Hernandez, R., ChA	72	84.2	3	6	1	0	.900	9	2	0	0	.22
Hernandez, X., Cin-Hou	61	78.0	2	9	0	0	1.000	6	0	0	0	.00
Hershiser, Orel, Cle	33	206.0	20	47	2	3	.971	7	2	1	0	.43
Hill, Ken, Tex	35	250.2	22	37	1	5	.983	25	14	0	0	.56
Hitchcock, Sterling, Sea	35	196.2	6	23	3	2	.906	26	6	8	0	.54
Hoffman, Trevor, SD	70	88.0	8	6	0	0	1.000	6	1	1	0	.33
Holmes, Darren, Col	62	77.0	1	10	3	0	.786	9	4	1	1	.56
Holt, Chris, Hou	4	4.2	0	2	0	0	1.000	1	1	0	0	1.00
Holtz, Mike, Cal	30	29.1	2	4	0	0	1.000	3	1	0	0	.33
Holzemer, Mark, Cal	25	24.2	4	5	1	0	.900	2	1	0	0	.50
Honeycutt, Rick, StL	61	47.1	2	12	1	0	.933	1	0	0	0	.00
Hook, Chris, SF	10	13.1	3	3	0	0	1.000	1	0	0	0	.00
Hope, John, Pit	5	19.1	2	5	2	0	.778	3	0	0	0	.00
Howe, Steve, NYA	25	17.0	0	5	1	1	.833	3	1	0	0	.33
Hudek, John, Hou	15	16.0	1	5	0	0	1.000	1	0	0	0	.00
Hudson, Joe, Bos	36	45.0	1	9	2	1	.833	3	0	0	0	.00
Huisman, Rick, KC	22	29.1	0	5	0	0	1.000	4	0	0	0	.00
Hunter, Rich, Phi	14	69.1	5	13	1	0	.947	6	4	1	0	.83
Hurst, Bill, Fla	2	2.0	0	0	0	0	.000	1	0	0	0	.00
Hurtado, Edwin, Sea	16	47.2	3	9	0	1	1.000	11	1	0	1	.09
Hutton, Mark, NYA-Fla	25	86.2	6	4	2	0	.833	13	2	0	0	.15
Isringhausen, J., NYN	27	171.2	13	28	5	1	.891	22	3	0	2	.14
Jackson, Danny, StL	13	36.1	1	7	0	0	1.000	3	0	1	1	.33
Jackson, Mike, Sea	73	72.0	1	16	1	0	.944	6	2	0	0	.33
Jacome, Jason, KC	49	47.2	2	14	0	3	1.000	2	1	0	0	.50
James, Mike, Cal	68	81.0	5	12	0	2	1.000	4	2	1	0	.75
Janzen, Marty, Tor	15	73.2	5	6	2	1	.846	5	1	0	1	.20
Jarvis, Kevin, Cin	24	120.1	13	12	3	2	.893	18	5	0	0	.28
Johns, Doug, Oak	40	158.0	17	29	2	7	.958	16	3	1	0	.25
Johnson, Dane, Tor	10	9.0	2	1	0	0	1.000	0	0	0	0	.00
Johnson, Randy, Sea	14	61.1	1	8	1	0	.900	10	2	0	0	.20
Johnstone, John, Hou	9	13.0	1	1	0	0	1.000	0	0	0	0	.00
Jones, Bobby, NYN	31	195.2	11	31	1	3	.977	19	8	0	1	.42
Jones, Doug, ChN-Mil	51	64.0	1	6	0	1	1.000	2	1	0	0	.50
Jones, Stacy, ChA	2	2.0	0	0	0	0	.000	0	0	0	0	.00
Jones, Todd, Hou	51	57.1	4	6	0	0	1.000	7	1	0	0	.14
Jordan, Ricardo, Phi	26	25.0	0	3	0	0	1.000	1	0	0	0	.00
Juden, Jeff, SF-Mon	58	74.1	1	7	1	2	.889	14	2	0	0	.14
Kamieniecki, S., NYA	7	22.2	0	4	0	0	1.000	3	2	0	1	.67
Karchner, Matt, ChA	50	59.1	4	3	2	1	.778	4	1	0	0	.25
Karl, Scott, Mil	32	207.1	13	27	3	2	.930	15	5	3	2	.53
Keagle, Greg, Det	26	87.2	7	8	0	1	1.000	8	1	0	0	.13
Key, Jimmy, NYA	30	169.1	9	30	1	1	.975	8	4	2	1	.75
Keyser, Brian, ChA	28	59.2	6	16	1	3	.957	3	1	0	1	.33
Kiefer, Mark, Mil	7	10.0	0	0	0	0	.000	2	1	0	0	.50
Kile, Darryl, Hou	35	219.0	12	28	3	6	.930	24	7	0	0	.29
Klingenbeck, Scott, Min	10	28.2	6	3	0	0	1.000	4	2	0	0	.50
Klink, Joe, Sea	3	2.1	0	0	0	0	.000	0	0	0	0	.00
Knackert, Brent, Bos	8	10.0	0	4	0	1	1.000	0	0	0	0	.00
Krivda, Rick, Bal	22	81.2	1	10	0	0	1.000	10	3	1	0	.40
Lacy, Kerry, Bos	11	10.2	1	1	1	1	.667	0	0	0	0	.00
Langston, Mark, Cal	18	123.1	7	27	1	2	.971	20	2	4	3	.30
Larkin, Andy, Fla	1	5.0	1	0	0	0	1.000	1	0	0	0	.00
Leftwich, Phil, Cal	2	7.1	0	1	0	0	1.000	6	2	0	0	.33
Leiper, Dave, Phi-Mon	33	25.0	0	6	1	0	.857	2	1	0	0	.50
Leiter, Al, Fla	33	215.1	8	22	2	3	.938	16	8	1	0	.56
Leiter, Mark, SF-Mon	35	205.0	8	25	2	1	.943	31	6	2	2	.26
Leskanic, Curt, Col	70	73.2	4	7	1	0	.917	11	4	0	1	.36
Levine, Al, ChA	16	18.1	0	6	0	1	1.000	3	0	0	0	.00
Lewis, Richie, Det	72	90.1	4	6	0	1	1.000	17	5	0	0	.29
Lieber, Jon, Pit	51	142.0	17	25	0	0	1.000	27	8	0	0	.30
Lilliquist, Derek, Cin	5	3.2	1	2	0	0	1.000	0	0	0	0	.00
Lima, Jose, Det	39	72.2	11	17	0	1	1.000	4	1	0	0	.25
Linton, Doug, KC	21	104.0	9	10	2	1	.905	6	1	0	2	.17
Lira, Felipe, Det	32	194.2	18	33	0	4	1.000	21	4	0	2	.19
Lloyd, Graeme, Mil-NYA	65	56.2	2	7	0	1	1.000	6	0	1	0	.17
Loaiza, Esteban, Pit	10	52.2	6	12	1	0	.947	7	3	0	2	.43
Loiselle, Rich, Pit	5	20.2	2	5	0	0	1.000	2	1	0	0	.50
Lomon, Kevin, Atl	6	7.1	2	2	0	2	1.000	0	0	0	0	.00
Lopez, Albie, Cle	13	62.0	1	9	2	0	.833	6	3	0	0	.50
Ludwick, Eric, StL	6	10.0	1	1	1	0	.667	4	1	0	0	.25
Lyons, Curt, Cin	3	16.0	0	2	0	0	1.000	4	1	0	1	.25
MacDonald, Bob, NYN	20	19.0	1	2	0	0	1.000	1	0	0	0	.00
Maddux, Greg, Atl	34	245.0	35	69	1	6	.990	26	5	0	0	.19
Maddux, Mike, Bos	23	64.1	7	12	0	1	1.000	7	1	0	0	.14
Maduro, Calvin, Phi	4	15.1	0	1	0	0	1.000	2	1	0	1	.50
Magnante, Mike, KC	38	54.0	4	15	0	2	1.000	10	1	2	0	.30
Magrane, Joe, ChA	19	53.2	2	8	2	0	.833	5	2	0	0	.40
Mahomes, Pat, Min-Bos	31	57.1	4	8	0	0	1.000	5	1	0	1	.20
Mantei, Matt, Fla	14	18.1	3	4	0	0	1.000	5	1	1	0	.40
Manuel, Barry, Mon	53	86.0	1	11	0	1	1.000	20	1	0	0	.05
Martinez, Dennis, Cle	20	112.0	11	25	1	1	.973	8	3	0	0	.38
Martinez, Pedro, Mon	33	216.2	11	17	3	1	.903	32	3	0	0	.09
Martinez, P.A., NYN-Cin	9	10.0	0	1	0	0	1.000	3	0	0	0	.00
Martinez, Ramon, LA	28	168.2	6	28	2	1	.944	30	4	2	0	.20
Mathews, T.J., StL	67	83.2	0	6	2	0	.750	4	3	0	0	.75
Mathews, Terry, Fla-Bal	71	73.2	10	6	1	2	.941	6	3	1	0	.67
Maxcy, Brian, Det	2	3.1	1	1	0	0	1.000	1	0	0	0	.00
May, Darrell, Pit-Cal	10	11.1	0	2	0	0	1.000	2	0	0	0	.00
McCarthy, Greg, Sea	10	9.2	0	3	0	1	1.000	0	0	0	0	.00
McCaskill, Kirk, ChA	29	51.2	3	12	0	1	1.000	9	3	0	2	.33

1996 Fielding and Holding Runners

Pitcher, Team	G	Inn	PO	A	E	DP	Pct.	SBA	CS	PCS	PPO	CS%
McCurry, Jeff, Det	2	3.1	0	4	0	0	1.000	0	0	0	0	.00
McDonald, Ben, Mil	35	221.1	13	30	6	3	.878	25	6	1	1	.28
McDowell, Jack, Cle	30	192.0	20	26	1	0	.979	28	5	1	2	.21
McDowell, Roger, Bal	41	59.1	8	14	1	2	.957	7	2	0	1	.29
McElroy, C., Cin-Cal	52	49.0	3	12	1	1	.938	7	2	1	0	.43
McMichael, Greg, Atl	73	86.2	4	17	1	1	.955	10	3	0	0	.30
Meacham, Rusty, Sea	15	42.1	3	3	1	1	.857	1	1	0	0	1.00
Mecir, Jim, NYA	26	40.1	1	13	0	0	1.000	4	0	0	0	.00
Mendoza, Ramiro, NYA	12	53.0	2	11	0	0	1.000	7	0	0	0	.00
Menhart, Paul, Sea	11	42.0	5	7	1	2	.923	2	1	0	2	.50
Mercedes, Jose, Mil	11	16.2	0	2	0	0	1.000	2	1	0	0	.50
Mercker, Kent, Bal-Cle	24	69.2	8	4	1	0	.923	10	1	1	0	.20
Mesa, Jose, Cle	69	72.1	5	3	1	1	.889	8	3	0	0	.38
Miceli, Dan, Pit	44	85.2	6	3	3	0	.750	22	4	0	0	.18
Milacki, Bob, Sea	7	21.0	3	1	0	1	1.000	4	0	0	0	.00
Milchin, Mike, Min-Bal	39	32.2	3	5	0	0	1.000	1	1	0	0	1.00
Miller, Kurt, Fla	26	46.1	2	8	1	1	.909	4	1	1	0	.50
Miller, Travis, Min	7	26.1	0	2	0	0	1.000	7	1	2	0	.43
Miller, Trever, Det	5	16.2	1	4	0	0	1.000	1	1	0	0	1.00
Mills, Alan, Bal	49	54.2	4	7	0	2	1.000	6	2	0	0	.33
Mimbs, Michael, Phi	21	99.1	3	14	1	0	.944	7	4	1	0	.71
Minchey, Nate, Bos	2	6.0	0	1	0	0	1.000	2	0	0	0	.00
Minor, Blas, NYN-Sea	28	51.0	1	7	0	1	1.000	1	1	0	0	1.00
Miranda, Angel, Mil	46	109.1	3	14	2	0	.895	7	3	2	2	.71
Mitchell, Larry, Phi	7	12.0	1	0	1	0	.500	4	1	0	0	.25
Mlicki, Dave, NYN	50	90.0	3	6	2	2	.818	4	2	0	0	.50
Moehler, Brian, Det	2	10.1	0	1	1	0	.500	0	0	0	0	.00
Mohler, Mike, Oak	72	81.0	6	13	1	3	.950	5	1	2	0	.60
Monteleone, Rich, Cal	12	15.1	1	0	0	0	1.000	0	0	0	0	.00
Montgomery, Jeff, KC	48	63.1	6	13	0	1	1.000	5	1	0	0	.20
Montgomery, S., Oak	8	13.2	0	0	0	0	.000	2	0	0	0	.00
Moore, Marcus, Cin	23	26.1	0	1	0	0	1.000	6	1	0	0	.17
Morel, Ramon, Pit	29	42.0	4	3	0	0	1.000	3	2	0	0	.67
Morgan, Mike, StL-Cin	23	130.1	4	16	1	1	.952	25	6	2	1	.32
Morman, Alvin, Hou	53	42.0	2	8	1	0	.909	3	1	0	0	.33
Moyer, Jamie, Bos-Sea	34	160.2	6	25	3	2	.912	19	2	1	0	.16
Mulholland, T., Phi-Sea	33	202.2	6	26	6	2	.842	4	1	1	1	.50
Munoz, Bobby, Phi	6	25.1	0	3	0	0	1.000	8	1	1	0	.25
Munoz, Mike, Col	54	44.2	5	11	1	1	.941	1	0	0	0	.00
Mussina, Mike, Bal	36	243.1	14	34	0	3	1.000	14	8	0	0	.57
Myers, Jimmy, Bal	11	14.0	1	2	1	0	.750	1	1	0	0	1.00
Myers, Mike, Det	83	64.2	2	15	1	2	.944	9	1	1	0	.22
Myers, Randy, Bal	62	58.2	2	4	1	1	.857	3	0	0	0	.00
Myers, Rodney, ChN	45	67.1	9	4	1	0	.929	13	2	0	0	.15
Nagy, Charles, Cle	32	222.0	29	37	0	3	1.000	24	4	1	0	.21
Naulty, Dan, Min	49	57.0	7	5	0	1	1.000	6	1	0	0	.17
Navarro, Jaime, ChN	35	236.2	8	25	5	1	.868	36	12	0	1	.33
Neagle, Denny, Pit-Atl	33	221.1	5	30	1	4	.972	32	7	5	2	.38
Nelson, Jeff, NYA	73	74.1	4	15	1	1	.950	11	1	1	0	.18
Nen, Robb, Fla	75	83.0	3	9	0	1	1.000	4	2	0	0	.50
Nied, Dave, Col	6	5.1	0	0	0	0	.000	3	0	0	0	.00
Nitkowski, C.J., Det	11	45.2	2	5	0	0	1.000	10	2	3	0	.50
Nomo, Hideo, LA	33	228.1	12	20	1	0	.970	63	7	4	0	.17
Ogea, Chad, Cle	29	146.2	4	16	2	1	.909	17	9	0	1	.53
Olivares, Omar, Det	25	160.0	12	22	1	2	.971	9	3	0	0	.33
Oliver, Darren, Tex	30	173.2	4	23	1	3	.964	17	4	2	1	.35
Olson, Gregg, Det-Hou	52	52.1	6	3	0	0	1.000	10	4	0	0	.40
Oquist, Mike, SD	8	7.2	0	1	0	0	1.000	1	0	0	0	.00
Orosco, Jesse, Bal	66	55.2	2	8	0	0	1.000	6	0	0	0	.00
Osborne, Donovan, StL	30	198.2	6	23	1	0	.967	14	9	1	2	.71
Osuna, Al, SD	10	4.0	1	1	0	0	1.000	0	0	0	0	.00
Osuna, Antonio, LA	73	84.0	3	11	0	1	1.000	10	2	0	1	.20
Pacheco, Alex, Mon	5	5.2	0	0	0	0	.000	1	0	0	0	.00
Painter, Lance, Col	34	50.2	2	7	3	0	.750	6	0	1	0	.17
Pall, Donn, Fla	12	18.2	1	1	0	0	1.000	1	1	0	0	1.00
Paniagua, Jose, Mon	13	51.0	3	10	0	0	1.000	9	1	1	0	.22
Park, Chan Ho, LA	48	108.2	10	21	1	3	.969	9	4	1	0	.56
Parra, Jose, Min	27	70.0	7	7	0	2	1.000	6	3	0	0	.50
Parrett, Jeff, StL-Phi	51	66.1	3	9	0	1	1.000	2	0	0	0	.00
Parris, Steve, Pit	8	26.1	2	4	1	1	.857	3	0	0	0	.00
Patterson, Bob, ChN	79	54.2	1	3	0	0	1.000	4	1	0	0	.25
Patterson, Danny, Tex	7	8.2	0	2	0	0	1.000	1	1	0	0	1.00
Pavlas, Dave, NYA	16	23.0	2	3	0	0	1.000	0	0	0	0	.00
Pavlik, Roger, Tex	34	201.0	9	14	2	1	.920	14	7	0	1	.50

1996 Fielding and Holding Runners

Pitcher, Team	G	Inn	PO	A	E	DP	Pct.	SBA	CS	PCS	PPO	CS%
Pena, Alejandro, Fla	4	4.0	0	0	0	0	.000	0	0	0	0	.00
Pennington, B., Bos-Cal	22	20.1	0	2	0	0	1.000	2	0	0	0	.00
Percival, Troy, Cal	62	74.0	4	1	1	0	.833	15	1	0	0	.07
Perez, Mike, ChN	24	27.0	1	3	0	0	1.000	4	1	0	0	.25
Perez, Yorkis, Fla	64	47.2	2	9	2	0	.846	5	2	0	0	.40
Person, Robert, NYN	27	89.2	2	8	4	0	.714	8	1	0	0	.13
Peters, Chris, Pit	16	64.0	3	8	1	3	.917	9	0	0	1	.00
Petkovsek, Mark, StL	47	88.2	6	14	2	3	.909	8	1	0	1	.13
Pettitte, Andy, NYA	35	221.0	6	38	3	3	.936	21	4	7	4	.52
Pichardo, Hipolito, KC	57	68.0	7	13	1	2	.952	4	0	0	1	.00
Plesac, Dan, Pit	72	70.1	0	1	0	0	1.000	10	0	0	0	.00
Plunk, Eric, Cle	56	77.2	4	7	0	0	1.000	10	1	0	0	.10
Polley, Dale, NYA	32	21.2	0	4	1	0	.800	3	0	0	0	.00
Poole, Jim, Cle-SF	67	50.1	4	11	1	1	.938	6	0	2	0	.33
Portugal, Mark, Cin	27	156.0	11	16	2	1	.931	14	4	0	0	.29
Potts, Mike, Mil	24	45.1	3	2	0	0	1.000	9	2	0	0	.22
Powell, Jay, Fla	67	71.1	5	6	0	0	1.000	7	1	0	0	.14
Prieto, Ariel, Oak	21	125.2	10	17	0	0	1.000	17	6	0	0	.35
Pugh, Tim, Cin-KC	29	52.0	5	10	0	0	1.000	7	0	0	0	.00
Quantrill, Paul, Tor	38	134.1	4	23	0	1	1.000	10	5	1	1	.60
Quirico, Rafael, Phi	1	1.2	1	0	0	0	1.000	3	0	0	0	.00
Radinsky, Scott, LA	58	52.1	3	8	0	0	1.000	3	1	0	0	.33
Radke, Brad, Min	35	232.0	22	15	0	0	1.000	11	5	0	0	.45
Rapp, Pat, Fla	30	162.1	11	24	2	3	.946	20	10	0	0	.50
Reed, Steve, Col	70	75.0	3	8	0	1	1.000	6	2	1	0	.50
Rekar, Bryan, Col	14	58.1	2	9	1	1	.917	3	2	0	0	.67
Remlinger, Mike, Cin	19	27.1	3	5	0	0	1.000	5	0	1	0	.20
Reyes, Al, Mil	5	5.2	0	0	0	0	.000	1	0	0	0	.00
Reyes, Carlos, Oak	46	122.1	7	10	2	2	.895	13	5	0	0	.38
Reynolds, Shane, Hou	35	239.0	19	26	0	2	1.000	19	8	1	0	.47
Reynoso, Armando, Col	30	168.2	12	37	3	3	.942	11	2	0	8	.18
Rhodes, Arthur, Bal	28	53.0	1	2	0	0	1.000	5	1	1	1	.40
Risley, Bill, Tor	25	41.2	1	3	0	1	1.000	5	0	0	0	.00
Ritz, Kevin, Col	34	213.0	18	49	0	3	1.000	40	13	0	3	.33
Rivera, Mariano, NYA	60	107.2	4	13	0	0	1.000	4	1	0	1	.25
Roa, Joe, Cle	1	1.2	0	0	0	0	.000	0	0	0	0	.00
Robertson, Rich, Min	36	186.1	15	31	1	5	.979	23	6	2	0	.35
Robinson, Ken, KC	4	6.0	1	0	0	0	1.000	0	0	0	0	.00
Rodriguez, Frank, Min	38	206.2	24	30	2	4	.964	12	5	0	0	.42
Rodriguez, Nerio, Bal	8	16.2	1	0	0	0	1.000	2	0	0	0	.00
Rogers, Kenny, NYA	30	179.0	15	34	2	1	.961	10	1	5	1	.60
Rojas, Mel, Mon	74	81.0	4	13	1	0	.944	7	0	0	0	.00
Rosado, Jose, KC	16	106.2	3	15	1	1	.947	11	3	2	2	.45
Ruebel, Matt, Pit	26	58.2	7	9	1	0	.941	7	1	2	0	.43
Rueter, Kirk, Mon-SF	20	102.0	8	24	0	2	1.000	7	3	2	0	.71
Ruffcorn, Scott, ChA	3	6.1	1	0	0	0	1.000	4	1	0	0	.25
Ruffin, Bruce, Col	71	69.2	2	9	0	0	1.000	3	0	0	0	.00
Ruffin, Johnny, Cin	49	62.1	4	5	1	1	.900	13	2	0	0	.15
Russell, Jeff, Tex	55	56.0	1	8	0	0	1.000	6	2	0	0	.33
Ryan, Ken, Phi	62	89.0	8	11	0	3	1.000	13	4	0	0	.31
Sackinsky, Brian, Bal	3	4.2	0	0	0	0	.000	1	0	0	0	.00
Sager, A.J., Det	22	79.0	5	9	1	1	.933	8	5	0	0	.63
Salkeld, Roger, Cin	29	116.0	7	16	1	0	.958	15	3	0	0	.20
Sanders, Scott, SD	46	144.0	15	10	2	0	.926	11	3	0	0	.27
Sanderson, Scott, Cal	5	18.0	2	3	0	0	1.000	3	0	0	0	.00
Sauveur, Rich, ChA	3	3.0	0	1	0	1	1.000	1	1	0	0	1.00
Scanlan, Bob, Det-KC	17	22.1	1	4	4	0	.556	6	1	0	0	.17
Schilling, Curt, Phi	26	183.1	10	8	1	0	.947	9	6	0	0	.67
Schmidt, Jason, Atl-Pit	19	96.1	5	9	1	0	.933	10	1	0	0	.10
Schmidt, Jeff, Cal	9	8.0	0	0	0	0	.000	2	1	0	0	.50
Schourek, Pete, Cin	12	67.1	2	10	0	0	1.000	10	2	0	0	.20
Schutz, Carl, Atl	3	3.1	0	0	0	0	.000	2	1	0	0	.50
Scott, Tim, Mon-SF	65	66.0	5	7	0	1	1.000	12	3	0	0	.25
Sele, Aaron, Bos	29	157.1	8	18	1	1	.963	19	5	2	0	.37
Serafini, Dan, Min	1	4.1	0	0	0	0	.000	0	0	0	0	.00
Service, Scott, Cin	34	48.0	1	9	0	0	1.000	6	4	0	0	.67
Shaw, Jeff, Cin	77	104.2	13	14	1	3	.964	8	1	0	1	.13
Shepherd, Keith, Bal	13	20.2	1	2	0	0	1.000	3	0	0	0	.00
Shuey, Paul, Cle	42	53.2	3	5	0	1	1.000	7	3	1	0	.57
Silva, Jose, Tor	2	2.0	0	1	0	0	1.000	0	0	0	0	.00
Simas, Bill, ChA	64	72.2	9	5	1	1	.933	3	2	0	0	.67
Sirotka, Mike, ChA	15	26.1	0	3	1	0	.750	3	1	0	0	.33
Slocumb, H., Bos	75	83.1	8	12	0	4	1.000	15	1	0	0	.07
Small, Aaron, Oak	12	28.2	3	4	0	1	1.000	3	1	0	0	.33

1996 Fielding and Holding Runners

Pitcher, Team	G	Inn	PO	A	E	DP	Pct.	SBA	CS	PCS	PPO	CS%
Small, Mark, Hou	16	24.1	1	1	0	0	1.000	5	2	0	0	.40
Smiley, John, Cin	35	217.1	6	29	2	1	.946	25	9	0	0	.36
Smith, Lee, Cal-Cin	54	55.1	3	5	0	1	1.000	14	3	0	0	.21
Smith, Zane, Pit	16	83.1	1	13	1	1	.933	20	2	2	0	.20
Smoltz, John, Atl	35	253.2	27	26	1	2	.981	22	12	0	0	.55
Soderstrom, Steve, SF	3	13.2	0	1	0	0	1.000	3	1	0	0	.33
Sodowsky, Clint, Det	7	24.1	3	2	0	0	1.000	0	0	0	0	.00
Sparks, Steve, Mil	20	88.2	9	23	1	1	.970	6	2	0	3	.33
Spoljaric, Paul, Tor	28	38.0	1	5	0	3	1.000	2	0	0	0	.00
Spradlin, Jerry, Cin	1	0.1	0	0	0	0	.000	1	0	0	0	.00
Springer, Dennis, Cal	20	94.2	5	7	1	0	.923	20	7	0	0	.35
Springer, Russ, Phi	51	96.2	3	10	2	0	.867	10	1	1	0	.20
Stanton, Mike, Bos-Tex	81	78.2	2	7	0	0	1.000	10	2	3	1	.50
Stephenson, G., Bal	3	6.1	0	1	0	0	1.000	1	0	0	0	.00
Stevens, Dave, Min	49	58.0	7	6	0	0	1.000	6	1	1	0	.33
Stottlemyre, Todd, StL	34	223.1	8	38	2	2	.958	39	9	0	1	.23
Sturtze, Tanyon, ChN	6	11.0	0	2	0	1	1.000	0	0	0	0	.00
Sullivan, Scott, Cin	7	8.0	0	2	0	0	1.000	0	0	0	0	.00
Suppan, Jeff, Bos	8	22.2	0	2	0	0	1.000	6	0	1	0	.17
Suzuki, Makoto, Sea	1	1.1	0	0	0	0	.000	0	0	0	0	.00
Swartzbaugh, D., ChN	6	24.0	1	6	0	0	1.000	6	0	0	0	.00
Swift, Bill, Col	7	18.1	2	4	0	0	1.000	0	0	0	0	.00
Swindell, Greg, Hou-Cle	21	51.2	3	9	1	1	.923	11	1	4	0	.45
Tabaka, Jeff, Hou	18	20.1	1	0	0	0	1.000	3	1	0	0	.33
Tapani, Kevin, ChA	34	225.1	15	26	1	4	.976	18	6	2	0	.44
Tavarez, Julian, Cle	51	80.2	6	8	0	0	1.000	5	2	0	0	.40
Taylor, Billy, Oak	55	60.1	4	9	0	0	1.000	6	0	0	0	.00
Telemaco, A., ChN	25	97.1	9	9	1	0	.947	12	3	0	0	.25
Telgheder, Dave, Oak	16	79.1	3	14	0	1	1.000	4	0	0	0	.00
Tewksbury, Bob, SD	36	206.2	21	48	0	3	1.000	30	8	0	0	.27
Thobe, Tom, Atl	4	6.0	0	0	2	0	.000	0	0	0	0	.00
Thomas, Larry, ChA	57	30.2	2	4	0	1	1.000	5	1	0	0	.20
Thompson, Justin, Det	11	59.0	2	13	0	1	1.000	12	2	3	0	.42
Thompson, Mark, Col	34	169.2	14	21	5	2	.875	24	8	1	0	.38
Timlin, Mike, Tor	59	56.2	4	6	0	0	1.000	3	0	0	0	.00
Torres, Salomon, Sea	10	49.0	6	1	0	0	1.000	6	0	0	0	.00
Trachsel, Steve, ChN	31	205.0	16	29	1	0	.978	23	8	0	2	.35
Trlicek, Ricky, NYN	5	5.1	0	2	0	0	1.000	0	0	0	0	.00
Trombley, Mike, Min	43	68.2	6	6	0	0	1.000	8	2	0	0	.25
Urbani, Tom, StL-Det	19	35.1	0	4	0	0	1.000	6	2	0	0	.33
Urbina, Ugueth, Mon	33	114.0	6	10	1	2	.941	22	4	0	0	.18
Valdes, Ismael, LA	33	225.0	19	27	1	3	.979	27	4	0	1	.15
Valdes, Marc, Fla	11	48.2	6	3	0	0	1.000	7	0	0	0	.00
Valenzuela, F., SD	33	171.2	11	38	1	1	.980	25	2	6	1	.32
Valera, Julio, KC	31	61.1	5	7	1	1	.923	4	1	0	0	.25
Van Poppel, Oak-Det	37	99.1	3	10	1	1	.929	19	4	0	0	.21
VanEgmond, Tim, Mil	12	54.2	6	7	0	1	1.000	6	1	0	0	.17
VanLandingham,W., SF	32	181.2	14	15	2	0	.935	38	14	0	0	.37
VanRyn, Ben, Cal	1	1.0	0	1	0	0	1.000	0	0	0	0	.00
Veras, Dario, SD	23	29.0	0	6	0	0	1.000	4	0	0	0	.00
Veres, Dave, Mon	68	77.2	3	9	2	0	.857	11	2	0	0	.18
Veres, Randy, Det	25	30.1	0	0	0	0	.000	4	1	0	0	.25
Villone, Ron, SD-Mil	44	43.0	3	4	2	0	.778	6	0	2	0	.33
Viola, Frank, Tor	6	30.1	2	2	0	0	1.000	3	3	0	0	1.00
Vosberg, Ed, Tex	52	44.0	1	11	0	0	1.000	2	2	0	0	1.00
Wade, Terrell, Atl	44	69.2	2	9	1	1	.917	20	2	2	0	.20
Wagner, Billy, Hou	37	51.2	2	3	0	0	1.000	6	1	0	0	.17
Wagner, Matt, Sea	15	80.0	4	8	1	0	.923	2	1	0	0	.50
Wagner, Paul, Pit	16	81.2	10	14	0	1	1.000	21	6	0	1	.29
Wainhouse, David, Pit	17	23.2	3	7	1	1	.909	6	0	0	1	.00
Wakefield, Tim, Bos	32	211.1	13	18	2	4	.939	31	1	0	1	.03
Walker, Mike, Det	20	27.2	2	1	0	0	1.000	2	1	0	1	.50
Walker, Pete, SD	1	0.2	0	0	0	0	.000	0	0	0	0	.00
Wall, Donne, Hou	26	150.0	17	18	2	0	.946	17	7	1	0	.47
Wallace, Derek, NYN	19	24.2	3	2	0	0	1.000	4	1	0	0	.25
Ware, Jeff, Tor	13	32.2	3	5	0	1	1.000	1	0	0	0	.00
Wasdin, John, Oak	25	131.1	9	12	1	1	.955	17	3	0	0	.18
Watson, Allen, SF	29	185.2	6	21	1	2	.964	25	10	1	0	.44
Weathers, D., Fla-NYA	42	88.2	5	12	0	1	1.000	12	4	0	0	.33
Wells, Bob, Sea	36	130.2	8	12	2	1	.909	8	3	0	0	.38
Wells, David, Bal	34	224.1	15	39	1	4	.982	30	1	3	0	.13
Wendell, Turk, ChN	70	79.1	9	9	0	1	1.000	3	1	0	0	.33
Wengert, Don, Oak	36	161.1	19	8	0	0	1.000	13	3	1	0	.31
West, David, Phi	7	28.1	0	3	0	0	1.000	0	0	0	0	.00

1996 Fielding and Holding Runners

Pitcher, Team	G	Inn	PO	A	E	DP	Pct.	SBA	CS	PCS	PPO	CS%
Wetteland, John, NYA	62	63.2	0	7	0	1	1.000	10	2	0	0	.20
Whitehurst, Wally, NYA	2	8.0	1	1	0	0	1.000	1	0	0	0	.00
Whiteside, Matt, Tex	14	32.1	1	4	0	0	1.000	1	0	0	0	.00
Wickander, Kevin, Mil	21	25.1	1	4	0	0	1.000	1	0	1	0	1.00
Wickman, Bob, NYA-Mil	70	95.2	6	24	0	3	1.000	14	2	0	1	.14
Wilkins, Marc, Pit	47	75.0	2	10	0	3	1.000	17	4	1	0	.29
Williams, Brian, Det	40	121.0	6	17	2	3	.920	8	3	0	2	.38
Williams, Mike, Phi	32	167.0	19	32	1	4	.981	26	7	1	4	.31
Williams, Shad, Cal	13	28.1	1	0	0	0	1.000	6	1	0	0	.17
Williams, Woody, Tor	12	59.0	7	4	0	2	1.000	7	1	0	0	.14
Wilson, Paul, NYN	26	149.0	11	11	2	2	.917	28	4	0	0	.14
Witasick, Jay, Oak	12	13.0	0	0	0	0	.000	1	0	0	0	.00
Witt, Bobby, Tex	33	199.2	10	28	1	3	.974	21	9	1	0	.48
Wohlers, Mark, Atl	77	77.1	4	3	3	0	.700	13	1	0	0	.08
Wojciechowski, S., Oak	17	79.2	1	10	0	0	1.000	19	1	3	0	.21
Wolcott, Bob, Sea	30	149.1	10	19	0	3	1.000	1	1	0	1	1.00
Woodall, Brad, Atl	8	19.2	0	2	0	0	1.000	2	0	0	0	.00
Worrell, Tim, SD	50	121.0	8	9	2	0	.895	14	7	0	0	.50
Worrell, Todd, LA	72	65.1	3	6	1	0	.900	8	0	0	0	.00
Wright, Jamey, Col	16	91.1	9	20	2	1	.935	12	4	1	3	.42
Yan, Esteban, Bal	4	9.1	0	0	0	0	.000	0	0	0	0	.00
Young, Anthony, Hou	28	33.1	1	5	0	1	1.000	8	3	1	0	.50

Hitters Pitching

Player	1996 Pitching											Career Pitching										
	G	W	L	Sv	IP	H	R	ER	BB	SO	ERA	G	W	L	Sv	IP	H	R	ER	BB	SO	ERA
Aldrete, Mike	1	0	0	0	1.0	1	0	0	0	0	0.00	1	0	0	0	1.0	1	0	0	0	0	0.00
Alexander, Manny	1	0	0	0	0.2	1	5	5	4	0	67.50	1	0	0	0	0.2	1	5	5	4	0	67.50
Cangelosi, John	0	0	0	0	0.0	0	0	0	0	0	0.00	2	0	0	0	3.0	1	0	0	1	0	0.00
Canseco, Jose	0	0	0	0	0.0	0	0	0	0	0	0.00	1	0	0	0	1.0	2	3	3	3	0	27.00
Dascenzo, Doug	0	0	0	0	0.0	0	0	0	0	0	0.00	4	0	0	0	5.0	3	0	0	2	2	0.00
Davis, Chili	0	0	0	0	0.0	0	0	0	0	0	0.00	1	0	0	0	2.0	0	0	0	0	0	0.00
Espinoza, Alvaro	0	0	0	0	0.0	0	0	0	0	0	0.00	1	0	0	0	0.2	0	0	0	0	0	0.00
Gonzales, Rene	0	0	0	0	0.0	0	0	0	0	0	0.00	1	0	0	0	1.0	0	0	0	0	0	0.00
Howard, Dave	0	0	0	0	0.0	0	0	0	0	0	0.00	1	0	0	0	2.0	2	1	1	5	0	4.50
Martinez, Dave	0	0	0	0	0.0	0	0	0	0	0	0.00	2	0	0	0	1.1	2	2	2	4	0	13.50
O'Neill, Paul	0	0	0	0	0.0	0	0	0	0	0	0.00	1	0	0	0	2.0	2	3	3	4	2	13.50
Seitzer, Kevin	0	0	0	0	0.0	0	0	0	0	0	0.00	1	0	0	0	0.1	0	0	0	0	1	0.00
Tomberlin, Andy	0	0	0	0	0.0	0	0	0	0	0	0.00	1	0	0	0	2.0	1	0	1	1	1	0.00
Wallach, Tim	0	0	0	0	0.0	0	0	0	0	0	0.00	2	0	0	0	2.0	3	1	1	0	0	4.50

Park Data

In the charts that follow, the first block of columns shows how much the featured team totaled at home, how much opponents totaled against the featured team at its home and the grand totals of both. The second block of columns shows how much the featured team totaled in away games, how much opponents totaled in its away games and the grand totals of both. By combining both the featured team's and opponent totals, most team variance is negated and only the park variance is left.

Now for the Index. In a nutshell, the Index tells you whether the park favors the stat you happen to be looking at. For example, how much of an advantage did Rockies power hitters have hitting at Coors Field? In 1996, all batters hit 271 home runs in 5875 at-bats at Coors, a frequency of .0461 HR per AB; in Rockies road games, the frequency was .0279 HR per AB (148/5311). Dividing the Home frequency by the Road frequency gives us a figure of 1.66. This number is multiplied by 100 to make it more recognizable: 166. What does an Index of 166 mean? It means it was 66% easier for players to hit home runs at Coors than it was in other National League parks last season.

The greater the Index is over 100, the more favorable the park is for that statistic. The lower the Index is under 100, the less favorable the park is for that statistic. A park that was neutral in a category will have an Index of 100. *E-Infield* refers to infield *fielding* errors.

The indexes for the following categories are determined on a per at-bat basis: 2B, 3B, HR, BB, SO, LHB-HR and RHB-HR. The indexes for AB, R, H, E and E-Infield are determined using per-game ratios. All the other indexes are based on the raw figures shown in the chart.

For most parks you'll notice that we include 1996 data as well as three-year totals (1994-96). However, for parks where there have been changes over the last three years, we never combine data. For Busch Stadium in St. Louis, where they changed the dimensions and playing surface prior to last season, 1996 data is shown, but we only give 1994-95 data for comparison sake. We added a page which **ranks** the indices for runs, home runs and average from 1994 to 1996. "Alt" is the altitude of the city where the team plays.

Atlanta Braves—Atlanta-Fulton County Stadium

Alt: 1010 feet **Surface:** Grass

| | 1996 Season | | | | | | | 1994-1996 | | | | | | |
| | Home Games | | | Away Games | | | | Home Games | | | Away Games | | | |
	Braves	Opp	Total	Braves	Opp	Total	Index	Braves	Opp	Total	Braves	Opp	Total	Index
G	81	81	162	81	81	162	---	208	208	416	212	212	424	---
Avg	.281	.235	.258	.259	.259	.259	100	.267	.243	.255	.258	.247	.253	101
AB	2763	2820	5583	2851	2733	5584	100	6915	7199	14114	7374	7036	14410	100
R	434	300	734	339	348	687	107	986	826	1812	974	810	1784	104
H	777	664	1441	737	708	1445	100	1847	1746	3593	1900	1739	3639	101
2B	141	116	257	123	149	272	95	328	314	642	344	350	694	94
3B	18	13	31	10	16	26	119	34	32	66	39	31	70	96
HR	106	66	172	91	54	145	119	261	169	430	241	134	375	117
BB	275	204	479	255	247	502	95	684	619	1303	743	646	1389	96
SO	447	636	1083	585	609	1194	91	1180	1638	2818	1453	1559	3012	96
E	76	92	168	76	70	146	115	168	190	358	207	167	374	98
E-Infield	58	68	126	50	40	90	140	124	134	258	123	111	234	112
LHB-Avg	.297	.226	.267	.264	.268	.265	101	.286	.231	.263	.261	.261	.261	101
LHB-HR	68	13	81	38	19	57	138	172	40	212	124	35	159	130
RHB-Avg	.266	.241	.252	.254	.255	.254	99	.247	.249	.248	.255	.240	.247	101
RHB-HR	38	53	91	53	35	88	106	89	129	218	117	99	216	106

ATLANTA

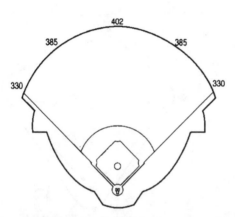

BALTIMORE

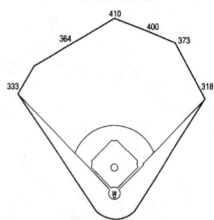

Baltimore Orioles—Oriole Park at Camden Yards

Alt: 148 feet **Surface:** Grass

| | 1996 Season | | | | | | | 1994-1996 | | | | | | |
| | Home Games | | | Away Games | | | | Home Games | | | Away Games | | | |
	Orioles	Opp	Total	Orioles	Opp	Total	Index	Orioles	Opp	Total	Orioles	Opp	Total	Index
G	82	82	164	81	81	162	---	209	209	418	210	210	420	---
Avg	.265	.276	.271	.282	.284	.283	96	.269	.264	.266	.269	.264	.267	100
AB	2770	2933	5703	2919	2791	5710	99	6957	7281	14238	7425	7015	14440	99
R	438	441	879	511	462	973	89	1089	1038	2127	1153	1002	2155	99
H	735	810	1545	822	794	1616	94	1870	1923	3793	2001	1851	3852	99
2B	128	135	263	171	149	320	82	322	355	677	391	371	762	90
3B	13	14	27	16	13	29	93	28	33	61	48	40	88	70
HR	121	108	229	136	101	237	97	286	262	548	283	227	510	109
BB	329	286	615	316	311	627	98	848	694	1542	809	777	1586	99
SO	468	544	1012	447	503	950	107	1190	1342	2532	1183	1301	2484	103
E	65	58	123	50	50	100	121	150	150	300	118	147	265	114
E-Infield	47	50	97	32	36	68	141	104	118	222	80	109	189	118
LHB-Avg	.290	.262	.278	.289	.300	.293	95	.291	.259	.277	.279	.261	.271	102
LHB-HR	75	34	109	78	33	111	97	153	83	236	155	62	217	110
RHB-Avg	.235	.285	.265	.273	.275	.274	97	.246	.267	.258	.260	.266	.263	98
RHB-HR	46	74	120	58	68	126	96	133	179	312	128	165	293	109

Boston Red Sox—Fenway Park

Alt: 15 feet **Surface:** Grass

| | 1996 Season | | | | | | | 1994-1996 | | | | | | |
| | Home Games | | | Away Games | | | | Home Games | | | Away Games | | | |
	Red Sox	Opp	Total	Red Sox	Opp	Total	Index	Red Sox	Opp	Total	Red Sox	Opp	Total	Index
G	81	81	162	81	81	162	---	217	217	434	204	204	408	---
Avg	.302	.282	.292	.265	.275	.270	108	.292	.278	.285	.261	.270	.265	107
AB	2865	2974	5839	2891	2788	5679	103	7501	7815	15316	7192	6939	14131	102
R	517	464	981	411	457	868	113	1224	1177	2401	1047	1063	2110	107
H	865	839	1704	766	767	1533	111	2193	2173	4366	1875	1875	3750	109
2B	180	160	340	128	132	260	127	488	406	894	328	357	685	120
3B	19	14	33	12	16	28	115	47	37	84	34	39	73	106
HR	121	93	214	88	92	180	116	259	223	482	245	209	454	98
BB	340	340	680	302	382	684	97	863	820	1683	743	828	1571	99
SO	494	598	1092	526	567	1093	97	1321	1470	2791	1345	1312	2657	97
E	91	57	148	68	67	135	110	231	189	420	164	164	328	120
E-Infield	59	39	98	52	47	99	99	157	137	294	120	120	240	115
LHB-Avg	.319	.286	.302	.264	.286	.275	110	.300	.278	.289	.268	.276	.272	106
LHB-HR	57	39	96	40	37	77	114	125	82	207	115	83	198	96
RHB-Avg	.288	.278	.283	.266	.266	.266	107	.285	.278	.281	.254	.265	.260	108
RHB-HR	64	54	118	48	55	103	117	134	141	275	130	126	256	99

BOSTON

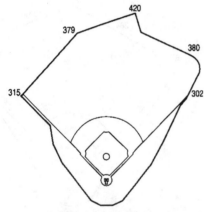

CALIFORNIA

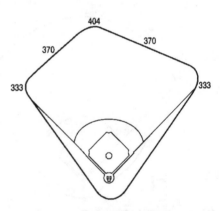

California Angels—Anaheim Stadium

Alt: 160 feet **Surface:** Grass

| | 1996 Season | | | | | | | 1994-1996 | | | | | | |
| | Home Games | | | Away Games | | | | Home Games | | | Away Games | | | |
	Angels	Opp	Total	Angels	Opp	Total	Index	Angels	Opp	Total	Angels	Opp	Total	Index
G	81	81	162	80	80	160	---	216	216	432	205	205	410	---
Avg	.277	.265	.271	.276	.286	.281	97	.272	.267	.269	.275	.283	.279	97
AB	2817	2897	5714	2869	2720	5589	101	7376	7681	15057	7272	6894	14166	101
R	387	451	838	375	492	867	95	1078	1162	2240	1028	1138	2166	98
H	780	768	1548	791	778	1569	97	2005	2051	4056	1998	1954	3952	97
2B	127	129	256	129	153	282	89	346	372	718	340	406	746	91
3B	8	3	11	16	15	31	35	28	16	44	37	40	77	54
HR	104	123	227	88	96	184	121	268	304	572	230	228	458	118
BB	256	307	563	271	355	626	88	779	787	1566	714	797	1511	98
SO	494	593	1087	480	459	939	113	1344	1449	2793	1234	1186	2420	109
E	71	76	147	78	59	137	106	191	175	366	164	162	326	107
E-Infield	47	46	93	60	43	103	89	127	119	246	116	114	230	102
LHB-Avg	.280	.264	.272	.293	.275	.285	96	.283	.278	.281	.280	.279	.280	100
LHB-HR	46	47	93	42	33	75	117	127	115	242	109	77	186	118
RHB-Avg	.275	.266	.270	.263	.292	.278	97	.262	.261	.262	.270	.286	.279	94
RHB-HR	58	76	134	46	63	109	124	141	189	330	121	151	272	117

Chicago Cubs—Wrigley Field

Alt: 658 feet **Surface:** Grass

| | 1996 Season | | | | | | | 1994-1996 | | | | | | |
| | Home Games | | | Away Games | | | | Home Games | | | Away Games | | | |
	Cubs	Opp	Total	Cubs	Opp	Total	Index	Cubs	Opp	Total	Cubs	Opp	Total	Index
G	81	81	162	81	81	162	---	212	212	424	207	207	414	---
Avg	.257	.253	.255	.246	.268	.256	99	.258	.261	.260	.258	.265	.261	99
AB	2729	2861	5590	2802	2701	5503	102	7136	7515	14651	7276	6984	14260	100
R	413	372	785	359	399	758	104	968	1009	1977	997	982	1979	98
H	700	724	1424	688	723	1411	101	1840	1965	3805	1878	1849	3727	100
2B	128	144	272	139	140	279	96	330	359	689	393	329	722	93
3B	11	16	27	8	18	26	102	38	40	78	46	43	89	85
HR	97	91	188	78	93	171	108	227	245	472	215	221	436	105
BB	273	258	531	250	288	538	97	682	729	1411	645	727	1372	100
SO	540	531	1071	550	496	1046	101	1359	1412	2771	1434	1258	2692	100
E	68	86	154	57	66	123	125	188	191	379	178	203	381	97
E-Infield	48	64	112	35	52	87	129	126	145	271	108	143	251	105
LHB-Avg	.296	.258	.276	.268	.275	.271	102	.283	.268	.275	.266	.268	.267	103
LHB-HR	25	29	54	29	38	67	82	72	82	154	66	85	151	101
RHB-Avg	.232	.250	.241	.231	.262	.246	98	.243	.257	.250	.253	.262	.257	97
RHB-HR	72	62	134	49	55	104	124	155	163	318	149	136	285	107

CHICAGO CUBS

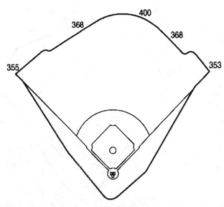

CHICAGO WHITE SOX

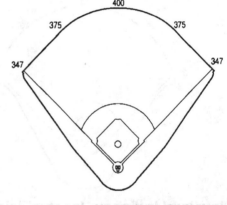

Chicago White Sox—Comiskey Park

Alt: 658 feet **Surface:** Grass

| | 1996 Season | | | | | | | 1994-1996 | | | | | | |
| | Home Games | | | Away Games | | | | Home Games | | | Away Games | | | |
	White Sox	Opp	Total	White Sox	Opp	Total	Index	White Sox	Opp	Total	White Sox	Opp	Total	Index
G	81	81	162	81	81	162	---	206	206	412	214	214	428	---
Avg	.277	.260	.268	.284	.280	.282	95	.283	.257	.270	.281	.276	.279	97
AB	2714	2839	5553	2930	2830	5760	96	6960	7190	14150	7686	7322	15008	98
R	398	370	768	500	424	924	83	1055	937	1992	1231	1113	2344	88
H	753	737	1490	833	792	1625	92	1973	1847	3820	2163	2020	4183	95
2B	122	119	241	162	173	335	75	310	314	624	401	372	773	86
3B	16	11	27	17	20	37	76	58	36	94	51	41	92	108
HR	76	90	166	119	84	203	85	197	206	403	265	247	512	83
BB	339	310	649	362	306	668	101	854	756	1610	920	854	1774	96
SO	407	507	914	520	532	1052	90	999	1300	2299	1263	1385	2648	92
E	56	52	108	75	56	131	82	147	150	297	194	190	384	80
E-Infield	40	32	72	47	34	81	89	111	108	219	140	120	260	88
LHB-Avg	.281	.251	.267	.288	.293	.290	92	.278	.253	.267	.286	.295	.290	92
LHB-HR	34	30	64	55	38	93	73	77	65	142	112	111	223	68
RHB-Avg	.273	.266	.269	.281	.269	.275	98	.290	.260	.273	.277	.262	.269	102
RHB-HR	42	60	102	64	46	110	94	120	141	261	153	136	289	95

Cincinnati Reds—Cinergy Field

Alt: 869 feet   **Surface:** Turf

| | 1996 Season | | | | | | | 1994-1996 | | | | | | |
| | Home Games | | | Away Games | | | | Home Games | | | Away Games | | | |
	Reds	Opp	Total	Reds	Opp	Total	Index	Reds	Opp	Total	Reds	Opp	Total	Index
G	81	81	162	81	81	162	---	213	213	426	208	208	416	---
Avg	.266	.249	.257	.248	.277	.262	98	.273	.253	.263	.266	.270	.268	98
AB	2632	2781	5413	2823	2723	5546	98	7028	7361	14389	7329	6997	14326	98
R	413	363	776	365	410	775	100	1077	934	2011	1057	952	2009	98
H	699	693	1392	699	754	1453	96	1916	1864	3780	1950	1890	3840	96
2B	153	125	278	106	155	261	109	402	356	758	345	351	696	108
3B	20	21	41	16	20	36	117	50	49	99	57	43	100	99
HR	89	86	175	102	81	183	98	224	209	433	252	206	458	94
BB	350	276	626	254	315	569	113	832	673	1505	679	681	1360	110
SO	540	545	1085	594	544	1138	98	1317	1426	2743	1501	1365	2866	95
E	68	63	131	72	84	156	84	151	194	345	173	200	373	90
E-Infield	54	39	93	48	60	108	86	107	122	229	115	148	263	85
LHB-Avg	.283	.253	.269	.255	.277	.264	102	.277	.260	.269	.263	.276	.268	100
LHB-HR	36	33	69	40	29	69	109	77	81	158	81	77	158	102
RHB-Avg	.251	.247	.249	.241	.277	.260	96	.269	.249	.259	.269	.267	.268	97
RHB-HR	53	53	106	62	52	114	91	147	128	275	171	129	300	90

CINCINNATI

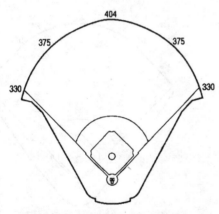

CLEVELAND

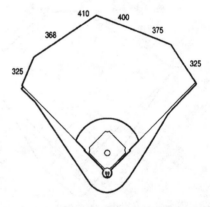

Cleveland Indians—Jacobs Field

Alt: 777 feet   **Surface:** Grass

| | 1996 Season | | | | | | | 1994-1996 | | | | | | |
| | Home Games | | | Away Games | | | | Home Games | | | Away Games | | | |
	Indians	Opp	Total	Indians	Opp	Total	Index	Indians	Opp	Total	Indians	Opp	Total	Index
G	80	80	160	81	81	162	---	203	203	406	215	215	430	---
Avg	.295	.273	.284	.291	.270	.281	101	.296	.261	.278	.287	.272	.280	99
AB	2746	2868	5614	2935	2768	5703	100	6996	7248	14244	7735	7315	15050	100
R	488	389	877	464	380	844	105	1223	909	2132	1248	1029	2277	99
H	810	782	1592	855	748	1603	101	2068	1895	3963	2223	1993	4216	100
2B	168	186	354	167	131	298	121	429	407	836	425	370	795	111
3B	15	9	24	8	16	24	102	39	23	62	27	42	69	95
HR	102	75	177	116	98	214	84	288	179	467	304	223	527	94
BB	350	259	609	321	225	546	113	807	628	1435	788	705	1493	102
SO	402	546	948	442	487	929	104	1019	1297	2316	1220	1328	2548	96
E	71	95	166	82	76	158	106	180	195	375	198	184	382	104
E-Infield	43	67	110	52	54	106	105	116	139	255	136	128	264	102
LHB-Avg	.304	.270	.286	.296	.284	.290	99	.307	.264	.285	.291	.283	.287	99
LHB-HR	44	26	70	48	44	92	78	133	71	204	126	103	229	93
RHB-Avg	.287	.275	.281	.288	.256	.273	103	.285	.259	.272	.285	.261	.273	99
RHB-HR	58	49	107	68	54	122	89	155	108	263	178	120	298	95

Colorado Rockies—Coors Field

Alt: 5282 feet **Surface:** Grass

| | 1996 Season | | | | | | | 1995-1996 | | | | | | |
| | Home Games | | | Away Games | | | | Home Games | | | Away Games | | | |
	Rockies	Opp	Total	Rockies	Opp	Total	Index	Rockies	Opp	Total	Rockies	Opp	Total	Index
G	81	81	162	81	81	162	---	153	153	306	153	153	306	---
Avg	.343	.304	.323	.228	.264	.246	132	.330	.309	.320	.237	.259	.248	129
AB	2909	2966	5875	2681	2630	5311	111	5424	5645	11069	5160	4993	10153	109
R	658	559	1217	303	405	708	172	1143	1049	2192	603	698	1301	168
H	997	903	1900	610	694	1304	146	1791	1746	3537	1222	1294	2516	141
2B	189	168	357	108	140	248	130	329	333	662	227	252	479	127
3B	26	25	51	11	23	34	136	57	53	110	23	31	54	187
HR	149	122	271	72	76	148	166	283	229	512	138	129	267	176
BB	298	314	612	229	310	539	103	555	566	1121	456	570	1026	100
SO	504	457	961	604	475	1079	81	926	915	1841	1125	908	2033	83
E	86	92	178	84	76	160	111	155	157	312	137	136	273	114
E-Infield	62	64	126	66	48	114	111	113	109	222	107	90	197	113
LHB-Avg	.319	.304	.310	.208	.287	.254	122	.320	.309	.314	.230	.282	.260	121
LHB-HR	33	40	73	14	29	43	156	66	76	142	37	50	87	150
RHB-Avg	.352	.305	.330	.235	.248	.241	137	.334	.309	.323	.240	.242	.241	134
RHB-HR	116	82	198	58	47	105	169	217	153	370	101	79	180	168

COLORADO

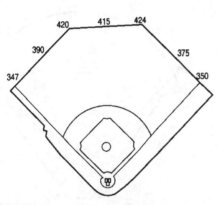

DETROIT

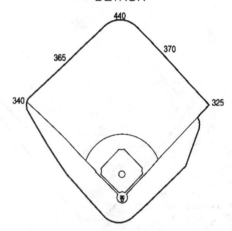

Detroit Tigers—Tiger Stadium

Alt: 633 feet **Surface:** Grass

| | 1996 Season | | | | | | | 1994-1996 | | | | | | |
| | Home Games | | | Away Games | | | | Home Games | | | Away Games | | | |
	Tigers	Opp	Total	Tigers	Opp	Total	Index	Tigers	Opp	Total	Tigers	Opp	Total	Index
G	81	81	162	81	81	162	---	211	211	422	210	210	420	---
Avg	.252	.287	.270	.259	.306	.282	96	.258	.285	.272	.253	.300	.276	98
AB	2691	2906	5597	2839	2825	5664	99	6995	7570	14565	7355	7294	14649	99
R	391	539	930	392	564	956	97	1095	1289	2384	994	1329	2323	102
H	678	835	1513	735	864	1599	95	1802	2160	3962	1863	2187	4050	97
2B	126	147	273	131	164	295	94	329	400	729	372	436	808	91
3B	10	15	25	11	25	36	70	44	43	87	31	54	85	103
HR	100	130	230	104	111	215	108	277	299	576	247	260	507	114
BB	256	405	661	290	379	669	100	849	874	1723	768	895	1663	104
SO	633	512	1145	635	445	1080	107	1569	1202	2771	1583	1044	2627	106
E	80	60	140	100	53	153	92	202	164	366	200	160	360	101
E-Infield	32	48	80	62	45	107	75	114	126	240	134	100	234	102
LHB-Avg	.271	.289	.282	.257	.321	.298	95	.263	.287	.277	.267	.311	.293	95
LHB-HR	42	53	95	39	51	90	106	110	130	240	87	116	203	117
RHB-Avg	.243	.286	.263	.260	.292	.273	96	.255	.284	.269	.247	.290	.266	101
RHB-HR	58	77	135	65	60	125	110	167	169	336	160	144	304	112

Florida Marlins—Pro Players Stadium

Alt: 7 feet   **Surface:** Grass

| | 1996 Season | | | | | | | 1994-1996 | | | | | | |
| | Home Games | | | Away Games | | | | Home Games | | | Away Games | | | |
	Marlins	Opp	Total	Marlins	Opp	Total	Index	Marlins	Opp	Total	Marlins	Opp	Total	Index
G	81	81	162	81	81	162	---	211	211	422	209	209	418	---
Avg	.264	.230	.247	.251	.281	.265	93	.270	.256	.263	.252	.272	.262	100
AB	2636	2677	5313	2862	2745	5607	95	7037	7260	14297	7273	6983	14256	99
R	369	277	646	319	426	745	87	945	939	1884	884	1013	1897	98
H	696	615	1311	717	771	1488	88	1898	1858	3756	1836	1896	3732	100
2B	108	105	213	132	147	279	81	296	326	622	338	363	701	88
3B	21	12	33	9	19	28	124	54	64	118	29	52	81	145
HR	73	44	117	77	69	146	85	187	174	361	201	198	399	90
BB	278	280	558	275	318	593	99	701	792	1493	718	796	1514	98
SO	537	543	1080	585	507	1092	104	1353	1398	2751	1431	1295	2726	101
E	63	71	134	68	70	138	97	210	160	370	178	161	339	108
E-Infield	41	47	88	50	42	92	96	134	114	248	120	111	231	106
LHB-Avg	.236	.254	.246	.235	.290	.267	92	.256	.267	.262	.246	.275	.263	100
LHB-HR	9	14	23	14	26	40	59	26	59	85	33	74	107	76
RHB-Avg	.276	.215	.247	.257	.275	.265	93	.276	.248	.263	.255	.269	.261	101
RHB-HR	64	30	94	63	43	106	95	161	115	276	168	124	292	96

FLORIDA

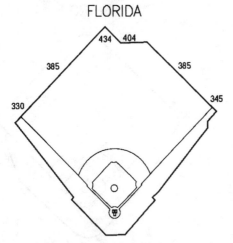

HOUSTON

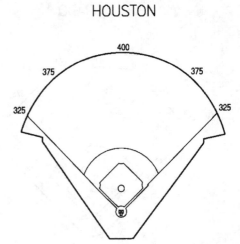

Houston Astros—The Astrodome

Alt: 96 feet   **Surface:** Turf

| | 1996 Season | | | | | | | 1994-1996 | | | | | | |
| | Home Games | | | Away Games | | | | Home Games | | | Away Games | | | |
	Astros	Opp	Total	Astros	Opp	Total	Index	Astros	Opp	Total	Astros	Opp	Total	Index
G	81	81	162	81	81	162	---	212	212	424	209	209	418	---
Avg	.268	.255	.261	.257	.294	.275	95	.270	.253	.261	.272	.285	.279	94
AB	2698	2869	5567	2810	2754	5564	100	7148	7441	14589	7412	7205	14617	98
R	364	347	711	389	445	834	85	992	884	1876	1110	1085	2195	84
H	722	732	1454	723	809	1532	95	1928	1886	3814	2019	2055	4074	92
2B	156	158	314	141	144	285	110	412	357	769	397	373	770	100
3B	11	13	24	18	16	34	71	31	42	73	45	49	94	78
HR	60	63	123	69	91	160	77	158	167	325	200	207	407	80
BB	277	254	531	277	285	562	94	740	655	1395	774	711	1485	94
SO	530	651	1181	527	512	1039	114	1398	1634	3032	1369	1324	2693	113
E	83	66	149	86	74	160	93	176	177	353	232	214	446	78
E-Infield	59	52	111	48	50	98	113	130	141	271	132	150	282	95
LHB-Avg	.246	.270	.263	.241	.294	.277	95	.279	.269	.273	.258	.290	.278	98
LHB-HR	8	27	35	10	29	39	86	28	70	98	54	73	127	76
RHB-Avg	.272	.246	.261	.261	.293	.275	95	.267	.243	.256	.277	.282	.279	92
RHB-HR	52	36	88	59	62	121	74	130	97	227	146	134	280	82

Kansas City Royals—Ewing M. Kauffman Stadium   Alt: 742 feet   Surface: Grass

| | 1996 Season | | | | | | | 1995-1996 | | | | | | |
| | Home Games | | | Away Games | | | Index | Home Games | | | Away Games | | | Index |
	Royals	Opp	Total	Royals	Opp	Total		Royals	Opp	Total	Royals	Opp	Total	
G	80	80	160	81	81	162	--	152	152	304	153	153	306	--
Avg	.266	.270	.268	.267	.284	.275	97	.267	.266	.266	.260	.280	.270	99
AB	2729	2854	5583	2813	2788	5601	101	5125	5351	10476	5320	5229	10549	100
R	372	369	741	374	417	791	95	657	715	1372	718	762	1480	93
H	726	771	1497	751	792	1543	98	1369	1421	2790	1383	1465	2848	99
2B	153	133	286	133	164	297	97	271	250	521	255	274	529	99
3B	24	26	50	14	16	30	167	44	41	85	29	30	59	145
HR	50	90	140	73	86	159	88	99	158	257	143	160	303	85
BB	252	216	468	277	244	521	90	476	475	951	528	488	1016	94
SO	433	425	858	510	501	1011	85	796	784	1580	996	905	1901	84
E	65	76	141	67	79	146	98	118	139	257	125	139	264	98
E-Infield	47	60	107	43	51	94	115	80	107	187	79	87	166	113
LHB-Avg	.263	.288	.274	.283	.274	.279	98	.274	.274	.274	.274	.283	.278	99
LHB-HR	15	34	49	28	38	66	77	39	67	106	57	65	122	90
RHB-Avg	.269	.257	.262	.246	.292	.272	97	.259	.259	.259	.241	.278	.262	99
RHB-HR	35	56	91	45	48	93	96	60	91	151	86	95	181	82

KANSAS CITY

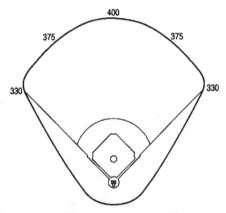

LOS ANGELES

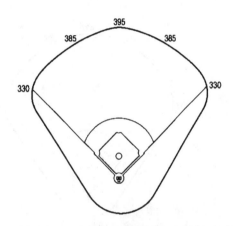

Los Angeles Dodgers—Dodger Stadium   Alt: 270 feet   Surface: Grass

| | 1996 Season | | | | | | | 1994-1996 | | | | | | |
| | Home Games | | | Away Games | | | Index | Home Games | | | Away Games | | | Index |
	Dodgers	Opp	Total	Dodgers	Opp	Total		Dodgers	Opp	Total	Dodgers	Opp	Total	
G	81	81	162	81	81	162	--	208	208	416	212	212	424	--
Avg	.244	.228	.236	.260	.271	.265	89	.252	.234	.242	.270	.270	.270	90
AB	2667	2759	5426	2871	2767	5638	96	6848	7116	13964	7536	7197	14733	97
R	314	283	597	389	369	758	79	825	768	1593	1044	1002	2046	79
H	650	628	1278	746	750	1496	85	1723	1662	3385	2031	1945	3976	87
2B	87	94	181	128	136	264	71	218	260	478	348	373	721	70
3B	11	5	16	22	14	36	46	30	18	48	63	52	115	44
HR	62	49	111	88	76	164	70	171	146	317	234	194	428	78
BB	234	256	490	282	278	560	91	646	609	1255	704	741	1445	92
SO	555	648	1203	635	565	1200	104	1354	1549	2903	1546	1456	3002	102
E	89	82	171	64	67	131	131	203	196	399	204	167	371	110
E-Infield	51	60	111	46	43	89	125	137	136	273	142	111	253	110
LHB-Avg	.231	.242	.237	.255	.263	.260	91	.247	.240	.243	.269	.268	.268	91
LHB-HR	5	20	25	13	32	45	55	21	74	95	39	89	128	77
RHB-Avg	.250	.217	.235	.262	.276	.269	87	.254	.228	.242	.270	.272	.271	89
RHB-HR	57	29	86	75	44	119	78	150	72	222	195	105	300	79

Milwaukee Brewers—County Stadium
Alt: 672 feet   **Surface:** Grass

| | 1996 Season | | | | | | | 1994-1996 | | | | | | |
| | Home Games | | | Away Games | | | Index | Home Games | | | Away Games | | | Index |
	Brewers	Opp	Total	Brewers	Opp	Total		Brewers	Opp	Total	Brewers	Opp	Total	
G	81	81	162	81	81	162	---	209	209	418	212	212	424	105
Avg	.281	.278	.280	.276	.279	.277	101	.278	.281	.280	.262	.271	.267	105
AB	2764	2871	5635	2898	2767	5665	99	7175	7483	14658	7465	7098	14563	102
R	451	460	911	443	439	882	103	1116	1197	2313	1065	1035	2100	112
H	778	798	1576	800	772	1572	100	1993	2105	4098	1959	1927	3886	107
2B	142	155	297	162	150	312	96	386	422	808	405	367	772	104
3B	22	17	39	18	19	37	106	54	47	101	49	47	96	105
HR	82	104	186	96	109	205	91	186	238	424	219	248	467	90
BB	336	325	661	288	310	598	111	805	851	1656	738	808	1546	106
SO	456	431	887	530	415	945	94	1145	1075	2220	1321	1047	2368	93
E	73	68	141	78	64	142	99	195	162	357	176	160	336	108
E-Infield	55	46	101	62	50	112	90	137	108	245	140	120	260	96
LHB-Avg	.280	.265	.272	.262	.302	.283	96	.281	.282	.282	.252	.276	.264	107
LHB-HR	19	44	63	32	58	90	69	62	95	157	80	117	197	78
RHB-Avg	.283	.288	.285	.285	.261	.274	104	.275	.281	.278	.270	.268	.269	103
RHB-HR	63	60	123	64	51	115	109	124	143	267	139	131	270	99

MILWAUKEE

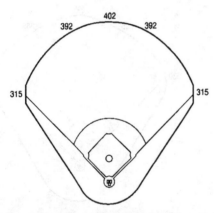

MINNESOTA

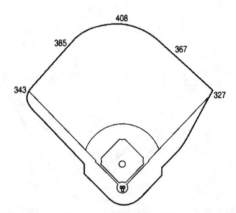

Minnesota Twins—Hubert H. Humphrey Metrodome
Alt: 834 feet   **Surface:** Turf

| | 1996 Season | | | | | | | 1994-1996 | | | | | | |
| | Home Games | | | Away Games | | | Index | Home Games | | | Away Games | | | Index |
	Twins	Opp	Total	Twins	Opp	Total		Twins	Opp	Total	Twins	Opp	Total	
G	82	82	164	80	80	160	---	213	213	426	206	206	412	---
Avg	.297	.275	.285	.279	.279	.279	102	.291	.278	.284	.273	.295	.284	100
AB	2838	2917	5755	2835	2728	5563	101	7309	7604	14913	7321	7102	14423	100
R	452	483	935	425	417	842	108	1139	1270	2409	1035	1207	2242	104
H	842	801	1643	791	760	1551	103	2127	2113	4240	1996	2095	4091	100
2B	184	180	364	148	160	308	114	447	466	913	394	451	845	104
3B	26	16	42	21	14	35	116	64	38	102	40	48	88	112
HR	61	121	182	57	112	169	104	168	329	497	173	267	440	109
BB	271	318	589	305	263	568	100	729	771	1500	677	731	1408	103
SO	478	511	989	480	448	928	103	1270	1269	2539	1239	1082	2321	106
E	62	78	140	46	71	117	117	157	170	327	163	185	348	91
E-Infield	48	56	104	32	45	77	132	107	126	233	111	129	240	94
LHB-Avg	.278	.269	.273	.251	.292	.271	101	.273	.272	.272	.250	.298	.276	99
LHB-HR	25	57	82	23	50	73	106	39	134	173	44	110	154	110
RHB-Avg	.309	.279	.294	.298	.269	.284	104	.300	.283	.292	.285	.293	.288	101
RHB-HR	36	64	100	34	62	96	102	129	195	324	129	157	286	109

Montreal Expos—Olympic Stadium

Alt: 187 feet   **Surface:** Turf

	1996 Season							1994-1996						
	Home Games			Away Games			Index	Home Games			Away Games			Index
	Expos	Opp	Total	Expos	Opp	Total		Expos	Opp	Total	Expos	Opp	Total	
G	81	81	162	81	81	162	---	205	205	410	215	215	430	---
Avg	.274	.237	.255	.250	.258	.254	100	.274	.249	.262	.257	.255	.256	102
AB	2708	2779	5487	2797	2689	5486	100	6861	7095	13956	7549	7206	14755	99
R	410	330	740	331	338	669	111	979	875	1854	968	885	1853	105
H	742	658	1400	699	695	1394	100	1880	1770	3650	1940	1839	3779	101
2B	167	116	283	130	128	258	110	434	330	764	374	326	700	115
3B	19	12	31	8	10	18	172	43	48	91	38	37	75	128
HR	81	76	157	67	76	143	110	166	178	344	208	202	410	89
BB	270	243	513	222	239	461	111	650	603	1253	621	583	1204	110
SO	497	605	1102	580	601	1181	93	1240	1454	2694	1407	1507	2914	98
E	66	74	140	83	83	166	84	199	189	388	192	233	425	96
E-Infield	46	46	92	57	53	110	84	133	113	246	134	159	293	88
LHB-Avg	.273	.267	.270	.244	.249	.247	109	.260	.260	.260	.251	.243	.247	105
LHB-HR	37	24	61	30	15	45	134	67	58	125	73	57	130	104
RHB-Avg	.275	.222	.248	.253	.263	.258	96	.281	.244	.262	.260	.262	.261	100
RHB-HR	44	52	96	37	61	98	99	99	120	219	135	145	280	82

MONTREAL

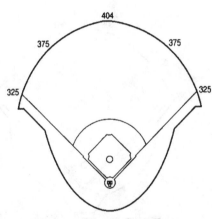

NEW YORK METS

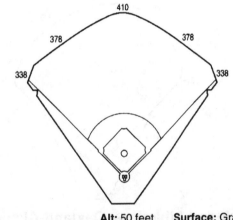

New York Mets—Shea Stadium

Alt: 50 feet   **Surface:** Grass

	1996 Season							1994-1996						
	Home Games			Away Games			Index	Home Games			Away Games			Index
	Mets	Opp	Total	Mets	Opp	Total		Mets	Opp	Total	Mets	Opp	Total	
G	81	81	162	81	81	162	---	206	206	412	213	213	426	---
Avg	.263	.261	.262	.276	.282	.279	94	.262	.264	.263	.265	.272	.269	98
AB	2748	2872	5620	2870	2714	5584	101	6949	7322	14271	7496	7154	14650	101
R	335	350	685	411	429	840	82	878	915	1793	1031	1008	2039	91
H	722	751	1473	793	766	1559	94	1819	1933	3752	1985	1949	3934	99
2B	113	111	224	154	129	283	79	274	337	611	375	368	743	84
3B	20	13	33	27	18	45	73	51	43	94	51	46	97	99
HR	64	72	136	83	87	170	79	180	200	380	209	209	418	93
BB	226	260	486	219	272	491	98	604	599	1203	623	666	1289	96
SO	508	536	1044	561	463	1024	101	1359	1314	2673	1511	1226	2737	100
E	94	79	173	102	87	189	92	227	212	439	202	205	407	112
E-Infield	58	57	115	64	67	131	88	157	138	295	140	149	289	106
LHB-Avg	.271	.268	.269	.300	.291	.296	91	.279	.271	.275	.273	.282	.277	99
LHB-HR	30	30	60	37	33	70	89	88	86	174	92	77	169	107
RHB-Avg	.258	.257	.257	.261	.276	.268	96	.249	.259	.254	.258	.265	.262	97
RHB-HR	34	42	76	46	54	100	73	92	114	206	117	132	249	84

New York Yankees—Yankee Stadium **Alt:** 60 feet **Surface:** Grass

| | 1996 Season | | | | | | | 1994-1996 | | | | | | |
| | Home Games | | | Away Games | | | | Home Games | | | Away Games | | | |
	Yankees	Opp	Total	Yankees	Opp	Total	Index	Yankees	Opp	Total	Yankees	Opp	Total	Index
G	80	80	160	82	82	164	---	210	210	420	210	210	420	---
Avg	.301	.263	.282	.276	.267	.272	104	.294	.260	.277	.275	.268	.272	102
AB	2709	2775	5484	2919	2766	5685	99	7074	7289	14363	7487	7108	14595	98
R	448	374	822	423	413	836	101	1150	957	2107	1140	1052	2192	96
H	815	731	1546	806	738	1544	103	2083	1895	3978	2058	1905	3963	100
2B	135	143	278	158	153	311	93	397	368	765	414	391	805	97
3B	13	5	18	15	17	32	58	34	31	65	44	43	87	76
HR	76	76	152	86	67	153	103	208	214	422	215	208	423	101
BB	315	301	616	317	309	626	102	868	708	1576	919	835	1754	91
SO	387	543	930	522	596	1118	86	1105	1337	2442	1315	1366	2681	93
E	33	77	110	68	85	153	74	123	162	285	159	213	372	77
E-Infield	27	45	72	54	49	103	72	91	100	191	117	137	254	75
LHB-Avg	.292	.267	.282	.265	.275	.269	105	.306	.267	.289	.278	.263	.272	107
LHB-HR	48	32	80	47	25	72	117	112	77	189	92	74	166	115
RHB-Avg	.311	.261	.282	.288	.261	.274	103	.282	.256	.267	.272	.271	.272	98
RHB-HR	28	44	72	39	42	81	91	96	137	233	123	134	257	92

NEW YORK YANKEES

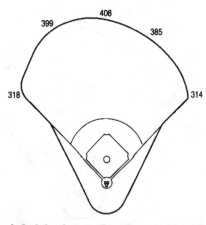

OAKLAND

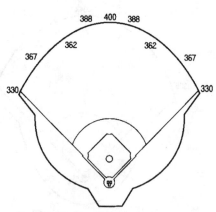

Oakland Athletics—Oakland-Alameda County Coliseum **Alt:** 42 feet **Surface:** Grass

| | 1996 Season | | | | | | | 1994-1995 | | | | | | |
| | Home Games | | | Away Games | | | | Home Games | | | Away Games | | | |
	Athletics	Opp	Total	Athletics	Opp	Total	Index	Athletics	Opp	Total	Athletics	Opp	Total	Index
G	75	75	150	87	87	174	---	128	128	256	130	130	260	---
Avg	.274	.281	.278	.258	.293	.275	101	.257	.247	.252	.266	.281	.273	92
AB	2531	2684	5215	3099	3016	6115	99	4235	4376	8611	4566	4331	8897	98
R	400	409	809	461	491	952	99	571	605	1176	708	745	1453	82
H	694	755	1449	798	883	1681	100	1090	1082	2172	1215	1217	2432	91
2B	134	148	282	149	166	315	105	174	175	349	232	233	465	78
3B	10	18	28	11	19	30	109	18	18	36	13	34	47	79
HR	103	89	192	140	116	256	88	131	129	260	151	152	303	89
BB	293	260	553	347	384	731	89	496	519	1015	486	547	1033	102
SO	492	424	916	622	460	1082	99	758	847	1605	839	775	1614	103
E	59	63	122	61	54	115	123	118	127	245	108	129	237	105
E-Infield	39	37	76	47	36	83	106	70	85	155	84	91	175	90
LHB-Avg	.282	.283	.283	.248	.286	.270	105	.227	.253	.244	.266	.292	.282	86
LHB-HR	16	39	55	37	50	87	74	28	61	89	47	75	122	75
RHB-Avg	.271	.280	.275	.262	.298	.278	99	.271	.241	.258	.266	.269	.267	97
RHB-HR	87	50	137	103	66	169	95	103	68	171	104	77	181	98

Philadelphia Phillies—Veterans Stadium

Alt: 5 feet   **Surface:** Turf

	1996 Season							1994-1996						
	Home Games			Away Games				Home Games			Away Games			
	Phillies	Opp	Total	Phillies	Opp	Total	Index	Phillies	Opp	Total	Phillies	Opp	Total	Index
G	81	81	162	81	81	162	---	213	213	426	208	208	416	---
Avg	.262	.258	.260	.249	.277	.263	99	.264	.254	.259	.255	.269	.262	99
AB	2742	2819	5561	2757	2660	5417	103	7190	7437	14627	7186	6855	14041	102
R	313	379	692	337	411	748	93	917	981	1898	869	964	1833	101
H	719	726	1445	686	737	1423	102	1899	1890	3789	1830	1842	3672	101
2B	132	159	291	117	145	262	108	388	399	787	332	323	655	115
3B	24	13	37	15	20	35	103	49	32	81	48	35	83	94
HR	55	82	137	77	78	155	86	151	200	351	155	192	347	97
BB	261	254	515	275	256	531	94	711	742	1453	718	683	1401	100
SO	527	561	1088	565	483	1048	101	1286	1479	2765	1401	1244	2645	100
E	59	68	127	80	66	146	87	166	197	363	189	180	369	96
E-Infield	39	50	89	54	38	92	97	128	133	261	131	102	233	109
LHB-Avg	.269	.250	.261	.267	.283	.273	95	.276	.255	.267	.263	.282	.271	99
LHB-HR	18	18	36	18	25	43	80	68	61	129	57	63	120	104
RHB-Avg	.256	.262	.259	.233	.274	.255	102	.251	.254	.252	.245	.261	.254	99
RHB-HR	37	64	101	59	53	112	89	83	139	222	98	129	227	93

PHILADELPHIA   PITTSBURGH

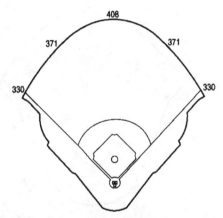

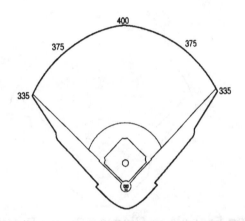

Pittsburgh Pirates—Three Rivers Stadium

Alt: 1137 feet   **Surface:** Turf

	1996 Season							1994-1996						
	Home Games			Away Games				Home Games			Away Games			
	Pirates	Opp	Total	Pirates	Opp	Total	Index	Pirates	Opp	Total	Pirates	Opp	Total	Index
G	80	80	160	82	82	164	---	213	213	426	207	207	414	---
Avg	.273	.279	.276	.261	.283	.272	101	.268	.280	.274	.256	.284	.270	102
AB	2730	2865	5595	2935	2835	5770	99	7196	7567	14763	7270	6994	14264	101
R	384	429	813	392	404	796	105	984	1116	2100	887	1033	1920	106
H	744	799	1543	765	803	1568	101	1927	2120	4047	1864	1983	3847	102
2B	162	162	324	157	136	293	114	414	427	841	348	364	712	114
3B	21	17	38	12	22	34	115	41	50	91	42	51	93	95
HR	74	81	155	64	102	166	96	188	209	397	155	221	376	102
BB	264	251	515	246	228	474	112	684	678	1362	631	648	1279	103
SO	482	550	1032	507	494	1001	106	1340	1370	2710	1346	1195	2541	103
E	79	72	151	72	86	158	98	213	212	425	193	170	363	114
E-Infield	53	50	103	52	62	114	93	137	130	267	139	130	269	96
LHB-Avg	.280	.294	.287	.268	.285	.275	104	.274	.286	.279	.259	.295	.275	102
LHB-HR	37	18	55	29	34	63	94	88	60	148	67	76	143	104
RHB-Avg	.267	.271	.269	.255	.282	.270	100	.264	.277	.271	.255	.277	.267	102
RHB-HR	37	63	100	35	68	103	98	100	149	249	88	145	233	101

San Diego Padres—San Diego/Jack Murphy Stadium **Alt:** 13 feet **Surface:** Grass

	1996 Season							1994-1995						
	Home Games			Away Games			Index	Home Games			Away Games			Index
	Padres	Opp	Total	Padres	Opp	Total		Padres	Opp	Total	Padres	Opp	Total	
G	78	78	156	84	84	168	---	129	129	258	132	132	264	---
Avg	.267	.247	.257	.264	.248	.256	100	.271	.243	.257	.274	.265	.270	95
AB	2610	2750	5360	3045	2879	5924	97	4274	4423	8697	4744	4437	9181	97
R	330	320	650	441	362	803	87	544	564	1108	603	639	1242	91
H	696	680	1376	803	715	1518	98	1160	1073	2233	1302	1177	2479	92
2B	122	115	237	163	135	298	88	196	181	377	235	202	437	91
3B	13	12	25	11	13	24	115	17	27	44	22	39	61	76
HR	67	71	138	80	67	147	104	106	129	235	102	112	214	116
BB	274	234	508	327	272	599	94	398	439	837	368	466	834	106
SO	461	594	1055	554	600	1154	101	773	983	1756	861	926	1787	104
E	79	49	128	58	90	148	93	118	120	238	134	117	251	97
E-Infield	53	33	86	46	60	106	87	90	72	162	96	91	187	89
LHB-Avg	.286	.246	.266	.294	.253	.275	97	.288	.235	.261	.307	.286	.297	88
LHB-HR	33	21	54	40	22	62	94	43	37	80	54	37	91	93
RHB-Avg	.252	.248	.250	.241	.245	.243	103	.258	.248	.253	.246	.251	.249	102
RHB-HR	34	50	84	40	45	85	111	63	92	155	48	75	123	133

SAN DIEGO

405
370   370
327   330

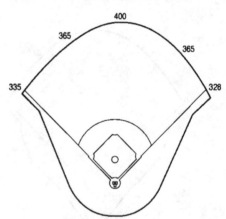

SAN FRANCISCO

400
365   365
335   328

San Francisco Giants—3Com Park **Alt:** 75 feet **Surface:** Grass

	1996 Season							1994-1996						
	Home Games			Away Games			Index	Home Games			Away Games			Index
	Giants	Opp	Total	Giants	Opp	Total		Giants	Opp	Total	Giants	Opp	Total	
G	82	82	164	80	80	160	---	214	214	428	207	207	414	---
Avg	.259	.266	.262	.247	.281	.264	100	.249	.261	.255	.254	.281	.268	95
AB	2748	2894	5642	2785	2672	5457	101	7149	7510	14659	7224	6906	14130	100
R	386	431	817	366	431	797	100	950	1053	2003	958	1085	2043	95
H	711	770	1481	689	750	1439	100	1782	1959	3741	1837	1943	3780	96
2B	120	151	271	125	139	264	99	306	368	674	327	369	696	93
3B	9	13	22	12	17	29	73	37	29	66	49	43	92	69
HR	82	98	180	71	96	167	104	214	250	464	214	239	453	99
BB	318	283	601	297	287	584	100	766	739	1505	685	708	1393	104
SO	589	549	1138	600	448	1048	105	1498	1372	2870	1470	1081	2551	108
E	81	99	180	77	62	139	126	205	217	422	162	196	358	114
E-Infield	57	63	120	57	50	107	109	143	155	298	114	146	260	111
LHB-Avg	.272	.280	.276	.271	.281	.275	100	.261	.263	.262	.270	.286	.278	94
LHB-HR	36	45	81	33	33	66	117	87	87	174	93	87	180	91
RHB-Avg	.251	.257	.254	.232	.281	.257	99	.243	.259	.251	.246	.279	.262	96
RHB-HR	46	53	99	38	63	101	95	127	163	290	121	152	273	104

Seattle Mariners—The Kingdome

Alt: 400 feet   **Surface:** Turf

| | 1996 Season | | | | | | | 1995-1996 | | | | | | |
| | Home Games | | | Away Games | | | | Home Games | | | Away Games | | | |
	Mariners	Opp	Total	Mariners	Opp	Total	Index	Mariners	Opp	Total	Mariners	Opp	Total	Index
G	81	81	162	80	80	160	---	154	154	308	152	152	304	---
Avg	.283	.273	.278	.290	.285	.288	97	.284	.266	.275	.279	.282	.281	98
AB	2780	2866	5646	2888	2730	5618	99	5235	5427	10662	5429	5182	10611	99
R	473	449	922	520	446	966	94	897	793	1690	892	810	1702	98
H	787	783	1570	838	779	1617	96	1487	1443	2930	1515	1462	2977	97
2B	182	159	341	161	150	311	109	336	312	648	283	276	559	115
3B	8	11	19	11	13	24	79	16	26	42	23	38	61	69
HR	121	116	237	124	100	224	105	222	189	411	205	176	381	107
BB	323	315	638	347	290	637	100	623	619	1242	596	577	1173	105
SO	525	546	1071	527	454	981	109	962	1152	2114	961	916	1877	112
E	67	60	127	57	56	113	111	127	101	228	113	115	228	99
E-Infield	51	52	103	43	40	83	123	95	85	180	91	89	180	99
LHB-Avg	.289	.300	.295	.289	.295	.292	101	.284	.288	.286	.278	.292	.285	100
LHB-HR	51	46	97	49	38	87	113	85	77	162	76	62	138	120
RHB-Avg	.280	.257	.268	.291	.279	.285	94	.284	.250	.267	.279	.275	.277	96
RHB-HR	70	70	140	75	62	137	101	137	112	249	129	114	243	100

SEATTLE

```
        405
   389
             380
331                    312
```

ST. LOUIS

```
        402
   372         375
330              330
```

St. Louis Cardinals—Busch Stadium

Alt: 535 feet   **Surface:** Grass

| | 1996 Season | | | | | | | 1994-1995 | | | | | | |
| | Home Games | | | Away Games | | | | Home Games | | | Away Games | | | |
	Cardinals	Opp	Total	Cardinals	Opp	Total	Index	Cardinals	Opp	Total	Cardinals	Opp	Total	Index
G	81	81	162	81	81	162	---	128	128	256	130	130	260	---
Avg	.278	.239	.258	.256	.263	.260	100	.260	.273	.267	.249	.282	.265	100
AB	2685	2774	5459	2817	2723	5540	99	4249	4497	8746	4432	4307	8739	102
R	391	326	717	368	380	748	96	559	631	1190	539	648	1187	102
H	746	664	1410	722	716	1438	98	1104	1228	2332	1104	1216	2320	102
2B	158	107	265	123	128	251	107	242	274	516	209	244	453	114
3B	18	7	25	13	16	29	87	30	25	55	21	32	53	104
HR	70	81	151	72	92	164	93	104	126	230	111	143	254	90
BB	250	264	514	245	275	520	100	426	396	822	444	404	848	97
SO	544	546	1090	545	504	1049	105	752	763	1515	854	711	1565	97
E	71	49	120	69	87	156	77	99	89	188	123	116	239	80
E-Infield	49	37	86	61	67	128	67	75	61	136	89	76	165	84
LHB-Avg	.290	.261	.275	.269	.281	.274	100	.277	.279	.278	.253	.268	.260	107
LHB-HR	18	35	53	27	34	61	89	48	42	90	46	46	92	98
RHB-Avg	.271	.226	.248	.248	.252	.250	99	.247	.270	.259	.246	.290	.269	96
RHB-HR	52	46	98	45	58	103	96	56	84	140	65	97	162	86

Texas Rangers—The Ballpark in Arlington
Alt: 551 feet   **Surface:** Grass

	1996 Season							1994-1996						
	Home Games			Away Games				Home Games			Away Games			
	Rangers	Opp	Total	Rangers	Opp	Total	Index	Rangers	Opp	Total	Rangers	Opp	Total	Index
G	81	81	162	82	82	164	---	216	216	432	205	205	410	---
Avg	.296	.280	.288	.273	.275	.274	105	.284	.279	.281	.269	.282	.276	102
AB	2768	2881	5649	2934	2764	5698	100	7337	7729	15066	7261	6990	14251	100
R	508	407	915	420	392	812	114	1221	1128	2349	1011	1088	2099	106
H	820	808	1628	802	761	1563	105	2084	2157	4241	1956	1973	3929	102
2B	149	141	290	174	136	310	94	371	361	732	397	354	751	92
3B	21	23	44	11	16	27	164	49	59	108	34	39	73	140
HR	112	86	198	109	82	191	105	256	226	482	227	251	478	95
BB	374	267	641	286	315	601	108	907	710	1617	716	780	1496	102
SO	491	506	997	550	470	1020	99	1311	1303	2614	1337	1194	2531	98
E	42	59	101	54	63	117	87	170	189	359	159	160	319	107
E-Infield	36	45	81	42	53	95	86	136	131	267	117	126	243	104
LHB-Avg	.307	.268	.288	.275	.282	.278	103	.283	.284	.284	.277	.285	.281	101
LHB-HR	42	38	80	31	27	58	140	99	104	203	67	98	165	118
RHB-Avg	.287	.290	.289	.272	.270	.271	107	.285	.275	.280	.263	.280	.272	103
RHB-HR	70	48	118	78	55	133	89	157	122	279	160	153	313	83

TEXAS

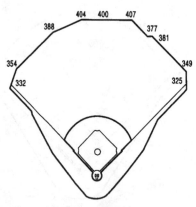

TORONTO

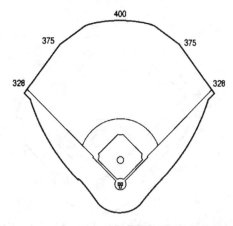

Toronto Blue Jays—SkyDome
Alt: 356 feet   **Surface:** Turf

	1996 Season							1994-1996						
	Home Games			Away Games				Home Games			Away Games			
	Blue Jays	Opp	Total	Blue Jays	Opp	Total	Index	Blue Jays	Opp	Total	Blue Jays	Opp	Total	Index
G	81	81	162	81	81	162	---	212	212	424	209	209	418	---
Avg	.255	.276	.266	.263	.256	.260	102	.260	.263	.262	.264	.270	.267	98
AB	2764	2882	5646	2835	2662	5497	103	7204	7506	14710	7393	6986	14379	101
R	364	433	797	402	376	778	102	979	1096	2075	995	1069	2064	99
H	706	794	1500	745	682	1427	105	1872	1977	3849	1952	1888	3840	99
2B	158	164	322	144	125	269	117	405	379	784	382	356	738	104
3B	16	14	30	19	6	25	117	46	39	85	46	35	81	103
HR	87	102	189	90	85	175	105	223	245	468	209	214	423	108
BB	254	324	578	275	286	561	100	708	887	1595	700	859	1559	100
SO	587	539	1126	518	494	1012	108	1410	1485	2895	1292	1274	2566	110
E	61	58	119	66	76	142	84	165	144	309	173	180	353	86
E-Infield	47	40	87	46	46	92	95	125	102	227	113	108	221	101
LHB-Avg	.268	.283	.276	.270	.249	.259	107	.267	.276	.272	.280	.274	.277	98
LHB-HR	31	49	80	29	33	62	133	66	120	186	78	85	163	116
RHB-Avg	.247	.270	.258	.258	.264	.260	99	.256	.252	.254	.254	.266	.260	98
RHB-HR	56	53	109	61	52	113	90	157	125	282	131	129	260	103

1994-96 Ballpark Index Rankings—Runs per Game

	AMERICAN LEAGUE										NATIONAL LEAGUE								
	Home Games				Away Games				Index		Home Games				Away Games				Index
	Gm	Team	Opp	Total	Gm	Team	Opp	Total			Gm	Team	Opp	Total	Gm	Team	Opp	Total	
Mil	209	1116	1197	2313	212	1065	1035	2100	112	Col*	153	1143	1049	2192	153	603	698	1301	168
Bos	217	1224	1177	2401	204	1047	1063	2110	107	Pit	213	984	1116	2100	207	887	1033	1920	106
Tex	216	1221	1128	2349	205	1011	1088	2099	106	Mon	205	979	875	1854	215	968	885	1853	105
Min	213	1139	1270	2409	206	1035	1207	2242	104	Atl	208	986	826	1812	212	974	810	1784	104
Det	211	1095	1289	2384	210	994	1329	2323	102	Phi	213	917	981	1898	208	869	964	1833	101
Bal	209	1089	1038	2127	210	1153	1002	2155	99	ChN	212	968	1009	1977	207	997	982	1979	98
Cle	203	1223	909	2132	215	1248	1029	2277	99	Cin	213	1077	934	2011	208	1057	952	2009	98
Oak**	75	400	409	809	87	461	491	952	99	Fla	211	945	939	1884	209	884	1013	1897	98
Tor	212	979	1096	2075	209	995	1069	2064	99	StL**	81	391	326	717	81	368	380	748	96
Cal	216	1078	1162	2240	205	1028	1138	2166	98	SF	214	950	1053	2003	207	958	1085	2043	95
Sea*	154	897	793	1690	152	892	810	1702	98	NYN	206	878	915	1793	213	1031	1008	2039	91
NYA	210	1150	957	2107	210	1140	1052	2192	96	SD**	78	330	320	650	84	441	362	803	87
KC*	152	657	715	1372	153	718	762	1480	93	Hou	212	992	884	1876	209	1110	1085	2195	84
ChA	206	1055	937	1992	214	1231	1113	2344	88	LA	208	825	768	1593	212	1044	1002	2046	79

*—Current dimensions began 1995; **—Current dimensions began 1996

1994-96 Ballpark Index Rankings—Home Runs per At Bat

	AMERICAN LEAGUE										NATIONAL LEAGUE								
	Home Games				Away Games				Index		Home Games				Away Games				Index
	Gm	Team	Opp	Total	Gm	Team	Opp	Total			Gm	Team	Opp	Total	Gm	Team	Opp	Total	
Cal	216	268	304	572	205	230	228	458	118	Col*	153	283	229	512	153	138	129	267	176
Det	211	277	299	576	210	247	260	507	114	Atl	208	261	169	430	212	241	134	375	117
Bal	209	286	262	548	210	283	227	510	109	ChN	212	227	245	472	207	215	221	436	105
Min	213	168	329	497	206	173	267	440	109	SD**	78	67	71	138	84	80	67	147	104
Tor	212	223	245	468	209	209	214	423	108	Pit	213	188	209	397	207	155	221	376	102
Sea*	154	222	189	411	152	205	176	381	107	SF	214	214	250	464	207	214	239	453	99
NYA	210	208	214	422	210	215	208	423	101	Phi	213	151	200	351	208	155	192	347	97
Bos	217	259	223	482	204	245	209	454	98	Cin	213	224	209	433	208	252	206	458	94
Tex	216	256	226	482	205	227	251	478	95	NYN	206	180	200	380	213	209	209	418	93
Cle	203	288	179	467	215	304	223	527	94	StL**	81	70	81	151	81	72	92	164	93
Mil	209	186	238	424	212	219	248	467	90	Fla	211	187	174	361	209	201	198	399	90
Oak**	75	103	89	192	87	140	116	256	88	Mon	205	166	178	344	215	208	202	410	89
KC*	152	99	158	257	153	143	160	303	85	Hou	212	158	167	325	209	200	207	407	80
ChA	206	197	206	403	214	265	247	512	83	LA	208	171	146	317	212	234	194	428	78

*—Current dimensions began 1995; **—Current dimensions began 1996

1994-96 Ballpark Index Rankings—Batting Average

	AMERICAN LEAGUE										NATIONAL LEAGUE								
	Home Games				Away Games				Index		Home Games				Away Games				Index
	Gm	Team	Opp	Avg	Gm	Team	Opp	Avg			Gm	Team	Opp	Avg	Gm	Team	Opp	Avg	
Bos	217	.292	.278	.285	204	.261	.270	.265	107	Col*	153	.330	.309	.320	153	.237	.259	.248	129
Mil	209	.278	.281	.280	212	.262	.271	.267	105	Mon	205	.274	.249	.262	215	.257	.255	.256	102
NYA	210	.294	.260	.277	210	.275	.268	.272	102	Pit	213	.268	.280	.274	207	.256	.284	.270	102
Tex	216	.284	.279	.281	205	.269	.282	.276	102	Atl	208	.267	.243	.255	212	.258	.247	.253	101
Oak**	75	.274	.281	.278	87	.258	.293	.275	101	StL**	81	.278	.239	.258	81	.256	.263	.260	100
Bal	209	.269	.264	.266	210	.269	.264	.267	100	SD**	78	.267	.247	.257	84	.264	.248	.256	100
Min	213	.291	.278	.284	206	.273	.295	.284	100	Fla	211	.270	.256	.263	209	.252	.272	.262	100
Cle	203	.296	.261	.278	215	.287	.272	.280	99	ChN	212	.258	.261	.260	207	.258	.265	.261	99
KC*	152	.267	.266	.266	153	.266	.280	.270	99	Phi	213	.264	.254	.259	208	.255	.269	.262	99
Det	211	.258	.285	.272	210	.253	.300	.276	98	Cin	213	.273	.253	.263	208	.266	.270	.268	98
Sea*	154	.284	.266	.275	152	.279	.282	.281	98	NYN	206	.262	.264	.263	213	.265	.272	.269	98
Tor	212	.260	.263	.262	209	.264	.270	.267	96	SF	214	.249	.261	.255	207	.254	.281	.268	95
Cal	216	.272	.267	.269	205	.283	.279	.279	97	Hou	212	.270	.253	.261	209	.272	.285	.279	94
ChA	206	.283	.257	.270	214	.281	.276	.279	97	LA	208	.252	.234	.242	212	.270	.270	.270	90

*—Current dimensions began 1995; **—Current dimensions began 1996

1996 Lefty-Righty Stats

Platoon splits are, quite simply, the most important statistical breakdowns in the game of baseball. They play a major role in just about every manager's lineup selection, and it's no exaggeration to say that the majority of in-game substitutions are devised to produce a favorable left-right match-up. For example, take a look at Tony La Russa's bullpen: it's built to attain one major goal—to give the Cardinals the platoon advantage when the game is on the line.

Although the platoon advantage is virtually universal—almost all hitters and pitchers perform better when they have the advantage—the *magnitude* of the effect differs from player to player, and there are exceptions to the rule. Certain left-handed hitters simply can't hit southpaw pitchers. Take Rich Becker. He was so bad against lefties that for years he tried to mask his weakness by switch-hitting. It didn't work: coming into 1996, he carried a .179 lifetime average against lefties. Finally, this year Becker gave up switch-hitting and went left-handed all the way. As a result, he had his best year yet, batting .291 overall. But you know what? His average against lefties actually *dropped* eight points, down to .171. Will he remain a regular? Maybe, but don't be surprised if he ends up as a platoon player.

Then you have your rare exception, like Angels' pitcher Jim Abbott. Although he throws left-handed, he's always had an unusual weakness for left-handed hitters. Early in the year, Roberto Alomar took advantage of this strange tendency. Getting set to hit against Abbott, the switch-hitting Alomar decided to try hitting from the *left* side. The result? A home run. On the following pages, one of the things you'll discover is that last year, lefties hit 38 points higher than righties did against Abbott. Who knows? Maybe Abbott is a natural *righthander*.

Batters vs. Left-Handed and Right-Handed Pitchers

Batter	vs	Avg	AB	H	2B	3B	HR	BI	BB	SO	OBP	SLG	Batter	vs	Avg	AB	H	2B	3B	HR	BI	BB	SO	OBP	SLG
Abbott,Kurt	L	.343	67	23	6	1	2	9	4	20	.380	.552	Baines,Harold	L	.333	105	35	4	0	4	27	9	12	.379	.486
Bats Right	R	.229	253	58	12	6	6	24	18	79	.288	.395	Bats Left	R	.305	390	119	25	0	18	68	64	50	.404	.508
Abreu,Bob	L	.000	0	0	0	0	0	0	0	0	.000	.000	Banks,Brian	L	1.000	2	2	1	0	1	2	1	0	1.000	3.000
Bats Left	R	.227	22	5	1	0	0	1	2	3	.292	.273	Bats Both	R	.400	5	2	1	0	0	0	0	2	.400	.600
Aldrete,Mike	L	.091	11	1	0	0	0	0	4	6	.333	.091	Barberie,Bret	L	.000	2	0	0	0	0	0	1	1	.333	.000
Bats Left	R	.227	97	22	6	0	6	20	10	13	.296	.474	Bats Both	R	.037	27	1	0	0	1	2	4	10	.161	.148
Alexander,M	L	.074	27	2	0	0	0	2	1	11	.107	.074	Barron,Tony	L	.000	0	0	0	0	0	0	0	0	.000	.000
Bats Right	R	.122	41	5	0	0	0	2	2	16	.163	.122	Bats Right	R	.000	1	0	0	0	0	0	0	1	.000	.000
Alfonzo,E	L	.258	89	23	3	2	1	13	9	12	.317	.371	Bartee,Kimera	L	.378	82	31	3	1	1	5	4	22	.407	.476
Bats Right	R	.262	279	73	12	0	3	27	16	44	.300	.337	Bats Right	R	.178	135	24	3	0	0	9	13	55	.250	.200
Alicea,Luis	L	.266	64	17	6	0	1	5	7	10	.351	.406	Bates,Jason	L	.238	42	10	3	0	0	4	7	7	.340	.310
Bats Both	R	.256	316	81	20	3	4	37	45	68	.350	.377	Bats Both	R	.195	118	23	5	1	1	5	16	27	.301	.280
Allensworth,J	L	.261	46	12	2	0	2	5	4	6	.320	.435	Batista,Tony	L	.277	65	18	2	1	2	9	7	11	.347	.431
Bats Right	R	.262	183	48	7	3	2	26	19	44	.341	.366	Bats Right	R	.306	173	53	8	1	4	16	12	38	.351	.434
Alomar,R	L	.313	192	60	14	2	9	37	32	26	.405	.547	Batiste,Kim	L	.200	35	7	4	0	1	2	2	8	.243	.400
Bats Both	R	.336	396	133	29	2	13	57	58	39	.414	.518	Bats Right	R	.211	95	20	2	0	2	9	3	25	.232	.295
Alomar,Sandy	L	.252	115	29	7	0	4	15	2	13	.267	.417	Battle,Allen	L	.146	48	7	0	0	0	1	9	11	.281	.146
Bats Right	R	.267	303	81	16	0	7	35	17	29	.311	.389	Bats Right	R	.220	82	18	3	0	1	4	8	15	.301	.293
Alou,Moises	L	.333	114	38	13	0	4	19	10	16	.384	.553	Battle,Howard	L	.000	1	0	0	0	0	0	0	1	.000	.000
Bats Right	R	.268	426	114	15	2	17	77	39	67	.328	.432	Bats Right	R	.000	4	0	0	0	0	0	0	1	.000	.000
Amaral,Rich	L	.293	147	43	8	2	1	16	23	19	.393	.395	Bautista,D	L	.282	39	11	1	0	1	5	7	6	.391	.385
Bats Right	R	.291	165	48	3	1	0	13	24	36	.391	.321	Bats Right	R	.178	45	8	1	0	1	4	4	14	.260	.267
Amaro,Ruben	L	.278	18	5	0	0	0	0	0	3	.278	.278	Beamon,Trey	L	.300	10	3	0	0	0	2	1	1	.364	.300
Bats Both	R	.323	99	32	10	0	2	15	9	15	.396	.485	Bats Left	R	.195	41	8	0	0	0	4	3	5	.250	.244
Anderson,B	L	.251	187	47	8	3	13	36	25	46	.355	.535	Becker,Rich	L	.171	105	18	5	0	0	9	6	37	.228	.219
Bats Left	R	.319	392	125	29	2	37	74	51	60	.416	.686	Bats Left	R	.321	420	135	26	4	12	62	62	81	.406	.488
Anderson,G	L	.292	212	62	14	0	3	21	2	43	.296	.401	Belk,Tim	L	.143	7	1	0	0	0	0	0	1	.143	.143
Bats Left	R	.281	395	111	19	2	9	51	25	41	.323	.408	Bats Right	R	.250	8	2	0	0	0	0	1	1	.333	.250
Andrews,Shane	L	.211	90	19	7	1	1	11	10	33	.287	.344	Bell,David	L	.250	64	16	4	0	0	4	5	9	.304	.313
Bats Right	R	.232	285	66	8	1	18	53	25	86	.297	.456	Bats Right	R	.185	81	15	2	0	1	5	5	13	.239	.247
Anthony,Eric	L	.136	22	3	1	0	0	0	3	9	.240	.182	Bell,Derek	L	.284	134	38	11	1	4	19	6	23	.312	.470
Bats Left	R	.258	163	42	7	0	12	22	29	47	.368	.521	Bats Right	R	.258	493	127	29	2	13	94	34	100	.311	.404
Arias,Alex	L	.273	55	15	4	1	0	4	3	7	.310	.382	Bell,Jay	L	.233	103	24	2	0	3	15	17	18	.339	.340
Bats Right	R	.278	169	47	7	1	3	22	14	21	.342	.385	Bats Right	R	.255	424	108	27	3	10	56	37	90	.318	.403
Arias,George	L	.293	82	24	0	0	3	12	2	13	.310	.402	Belle,Albert	L	.318	151	48	9	0	15	35	31	18	.439	.675
Bats Right	R	.212	170	36	8	1	3	16	14	37	.272	.324	Bats Right	R	.308	451	139	29	3	33	113	68	69	.400	.605
Ashley,Billy	L	.241	79	19	2	1	8	23	16	27	.371	.595	Belliard,R	L	.109	46	5	2	0	0	1	0	9	.109	.152
Bats Right	R	.097	31	3	0	0	1	2	5	17	.222	.194	Bats Right	R	.198	96	19	5	0	0	2	2	13	.212	.250
Aude,Rich	L	.214	14	3	0	0	0	1	0	8	.214	.214	Beltre,E	L	.154	13	2	0	0	0	1	0	2	.154	.154
Bats Right	R	.500	2	1	0	0	0	0	0	0	.500	.500	Bats Right	R	.286	49	14	0	0	0	5	4	12	.333	.327
Aurilia,Rich	L	.224	67	15	3	0	1	5	5	9	.278	.313	Benard,Marvin	L	.261	69	18	1	0	0	4	7	12	.338	.275
Bats Right	R	.243	251	61	4	1	2	21	20	43	.299	.291	Bats Left	R	.246	419	103	16	4	5	23	52	72	.333	.339
Ausmus,Brad	L	.144	90	13	3	0	2	10	6	15	.196	.244	Benitez,Yamil	L	.000	3	0	0	0	0	0	0	2	.000	.000
Bats Right	R	.246	285	70	13	0	3	25	33	57	.333	.323	Bats Right	R	.222	9	2	0	0	0	2	0	2	.222	.222
Ayrault,Joe	L	.333	3	1	0	0	0	0	0	1	.333	.333	Benjamin,Mike	L	.231	13	3	1	0	0	2	2	3	.333	.308
Bats Right	R	.000	2	0	0	0	0	0	0	0	.333	.000	Bats Right	R	.222	90	20	4	1	4	11	10	18	.314	.422
Baerga,Carlos	L	.220	123	27	7	0	0	12	12	11	.302	.276	Bennett,Gary	L	.000	2	0	0	0	0	0	0	1	.000	.000
Bats Both	R	.266	384	102	21	0	12	54	9	16	.290	.414	Bats Right	R	.286	14	4	0	0	0	1	2	5	.375	.286
Bagwell,Jeff	L	.364	110	40	13	0	3	21	33	25	.517	.564	Berroa,G	L	.341	135	46	10	0	8	29	15	24	.401	.593
Bats Right	R	.303	458	139	35	2	28	99	102	89	.434	.572	Bats Right	R	.275	451	124	22	1	28	77	32	98	.326	.514

Batters vs. Left-Handed and Right-Handed Pitchers

Batter	vs	Avg	AB	H	2B	3B	HR	BI	BB	SO	OBP	SLG
Berry,Sean	L	.264	106	28	11	0	3	21	7	16	.304	.453
Bats Right	R	.286	325	93	27	1	14	74	16	42	.335	.505
Bichette,D	L	.353	139	49	12	0	8	35	8	19	.377	.612
Bats Right	R	.302	494	149	27	3	23	106	37	86	.354	.508
Biggio,Craig	L	.328	125	41	7	1	5	20	18	14	.423	.520
Bats Right	R	.277	480	133	17	3	10	55	57	58	.376	.388
Blauser,Jeff	L	.209	67	14	1	0	3	12	14	20	.354	.358
Bats Right	R	.258	198	51	13	1	7	23	26	34	.357	.439
Blowers,Mike	L	.250	68	17	5	1	2	9	10	19	.350	.441
Bats Right	R	.269	249	67	14	1	4	29	27	58	.338	.382
Bogar,Tim	L	.190	42	8	3	0	0	3	3	10	.239	.262
Bats Right	R	.234	47	11	1	0	0	3	5	10	.327	.255
Boggs,Wade	L	.268	138	37	7	0	0	12	18	11	.350	.319
Bats Left	R	.328	363	119	22	2	2	29	49	21	.404	.416
Bonds,Barry	L	.307	150	46	5	1	12	39	24	27	.398	.593
Bats Left	R	.308	367	113	22	2	30	90	127	49	.483	.624
Bonilla,Bobby	L	.303	195	59	10	2	10	37	21	20	.362	.528
Bats Both	R	.280	400	112	17	3	18	79	54	65	.363	.473
Boone,Bret	L	.231	117	27	7	0	6	20	13	19	.303	.444
Bats Right	R	.233	403	94	14	3	6	49	18	81	.267	.328
Booty,Josh	L	.000	0	0	0	0	0	0	0	0	.000	.000
Bats Right	R	.500	2	1	0	0	0	0	0	0	.500	.500
Borders,Pat	L	.338	71	24	4	0	3	7	4	12	.373	.521
Bats Right	R	.248	149	37	3	0	2	11	5	31	.273	.309
Bordick,Mike	L	.226	137	31	4	1	1	13	12	15	.287	.292
Bats Right	R	.245	388	95	14	3	4	41	40	44	.314	.327
Bournigal,R	L	.210	62	13	4	0	0	4	2	4	.234	.274
Bats Right	R	.253	190	48	10	2	0	14	14	15	.307	.326
Bowers,Brent	L	.500	2	1	0	0	0	0	0	1	.500	.500
Bats Left	R	.297	37	11	2	0	0	3	0	6	.297	.351
Bradshaw,T	L	.667	3	2	0	0	0	1	1	0	.750	.667
Bats Left	R	.278	18	5	1	0	0	2	2	2	.350	.333
Bragg,Darren	L	.190	84	16	3	0	1	7	16	22	.330	.262
Bats Left	R	.279	333	93	23	2	9	40	53	52	.376	.441
Branson,Jeff	L	.200	55	11	3	0	2	9	7	12	.290	.364
Bats Left	R	.254	256	65	13	4	7	28	24	55	.317	.418
Brede,Brent	L	.000	1	0	0	0	0	0	0	0	.000	.000
Bats Left	R	.316	19	6	0	1	0	2	1	5	.350	.421
Brito,Jorge	L	.000	7	0	0	0	0	0	1	4	.125	.000
Bats Right	R	.143	7	1	0	0	0	0	0	4	.333	.143
Brito,Tilson	L	.385	26	10	3	0	0	3	2	4	.467	.500
Bats Right	R	.167	54	9	4	0	1	4	8	14	.286	.296
Brogna,Rico	L	.125	32	4	3	0	0	3	4	14	.216	.219
Bats Left	R	.282	156	44	7	1	7	27	15	36	.339	.474
Brooks,Jerry	L	.000	0	0	0	0	0	0	1	0	1.000	.000
Bats Right	R	.400	5	2	0	1	0	3	0	1	.500	.800
Brosius,Scott	L	.356	90	32	12	0	4	17	22	16	.482	.622
Bats Right	R	.290	338	98	13	0	18	54	37	69	.367	.488
Brown,Brant	L	.091	11	1	0	0	0	0	0	2	.091	.091
Bats Left	R	.345	58	20	1	0	5	9	2	15	.371	.621

Batter	vs	Avg	AB	H	2B	3B	HR	BI	BB	SO	OBP	SLG
Brown,K	L	.000	1	0	0	0	0	1	1	1	.333	.000
Bats Right	R	.000	3	0	0	0	0	0	1	1	.400	.000
Brumfield,J	L	.283	187	53	14	1	5	28	13	31	.335	.449
Bats Right	R	.229	201	46	14	1	9	32	16	44	.288	.443
Buford,Damon	L	.289	90	26	4	0	5	15	10	20	.356	.500
Bats Right	R	.273	55	15	5	0	1	5	5	14	.333	.418
Buhner,Jay	L	.304	125	38	9	0	11	32	23	33	.411	.640
Bats Right	R	.262	439	115	20	0	33	106	61	126	.357	.533
Bullett,Scott	L	.167	12	2	0	0	0	1	0	4	.167	.167
Bats Left	R	.216	153	33	5	0	3	15	10	50	.262	.307
Burks,Ellis	L	.427	143	61	15	3	8	26	15	20	.488	.741
Bats Right	R	.319	470	150	30	5	32	102	46	94	.383	.609
Burnitz,J	L	.269	26	7	1	0	1	6	4	11	.406	.423
Bats Left	R	.264	174	46	13	0	8	34	29	36	.372	.477
Busch,Mike	L	.267	30	8	4	0	1	8	1	9	.290	.500
Bats Right	R	.189	53	10	0	0	3	9	4	24	.246	.358
Butler,Brett	L	.313	32	10	0	1	0	4	1	8	.333	.375
Bats Left	R	.253	99	25	1	0	0	4	8	14	.306	.263
Cairo,Miguel	L	.167	18	3	2	0	0	0	2	5	.286	.278
Bats Right	R	.333	9	3	0	0	0	1	0	4	.333	.333
Cameron,Mike	L	.143	7	1	0	0	0	0	1	1	.250	.143
Bats Right	R	.000	4	0	0	0	0	0	0	2	.000	.000
Caminiti,Ken	L	.358	165	59	15	0	15	46	16	19	.412	.721
Bats Both	R	.312	381	119	22	2	25	84	62	80	.406	.577
Candaele,C	L	.211	19	4	1	0	0	0	1	5	.250	.263
Bats Both	R	.280	25	7	1	0	1	4	0	4	.280	.440
Cangelosi,J	L	.156	32	5	2	0	1	4	6	10	.289	.313
Bats Both	R	.278	230	64	9	4	0	12	38	31	.391	.352
Canizaro,Jay	L	.318	22	7	2	1	0	1	2	7	.375	.500
Bats Right	R	.173	98	17	2	0	2	7	7	31	.234	.255
Canseco,Jose	L	.326	95	31	7	1	6	23	19	19	.444	.611
Bats Right	R	.275	265	73	15	0	22	59	44	63	.384	.581
Carr,Chuck	L	.146	41	6	1	0	1	4	1	12	.167	.244
Bats Right	R	.354	65	23	5	1	0	7	5	9	.394	.462
Carreon,Mark	L	.287	108	31	10	1	2	13	8	11	.347	.454
Bats Right	R	.279	326	91	24	2	9	52	25	31	.336	.448
Carter,Joe	L	.247	166	41	10	3	6	24	12	18	.304	.452
Bats Right	R	.255	459	117	25	4	24	83	32	88	.307	.484
Casanova,Raul	L	.273	11	3	0	0	1	1	1	4	.333	.545
Bats Right	R	.176	74	13	1	0	3	8	5	14	.228	.311
Castellano,P	L	.091	11	1	0	0	0	1	1	4	.167	.091
Bats Right	R	.167	6	1	0	0	0	1	2	2	.444	.167
Castilla,V	L	.255	137	35	8	0	5	22	10	19	.315	.423
Bats Right	R	.317	492	156	26	0	35	91	25	69	.351	.583
Castillo,A	L	.200	5	1	0	0	0	0	0	2	.200	.200
Bats Right	R	.500	6	3	0	0	0	0	0	2	.500	.500
Castillo,Luis	L	.289	38	11	1	1	1	3	1	6	.308	.447
Bats Both	R	.254	126	32	1	0	0	5	13	40	.324	.262
Castro,Juan	L	.175	40	7	0	0	0	0	3	8	.233	.175
Bats Right	R	.207	92	19	5	3	0	5	7	19	.263	.326

Batters vs. Left-Handed and Right-Handed Pitchers

Batter	vs	Avg	AB	H	2B	3B	HR	BI	BB	SO	OBP	SLG	Batter	vs	Avg	AB	H	2B	3B	HR	BI	BB	SO	OBP	SLG
Cedeno,A	L	.219	96	21	1	0	5	13	6	18	.265	.385	Cuyler,Milt	L	.108	37	4	0	0	0	1	7	4	.261	.108
Bats Right	R	.209	239	50	5	3	5	25	9	52	.240	.318	Bats Both	R	.247	73	18	1	2	2	11	6	15	.321	.397
Cedeno,D	L	.250	84	21	3	1	0	4	1	17	.259	.310	Damon,Johnny	L	.226	133	30	4	1	1	15	13	19	.298	.293
Bats Both	R	.281	217	61	9	1	2	16	14	47	.326	.359	Bats Left	R	.286	384	110	18	4	5	35	18	45	.319	.393
Cedeno,Roger	L	.247	73	18	2	1	2	6	10	25	.337	.384	Dascenzo,Doug	L	.200	5	1	0	0	0	0	1	1	.333	.200
Bats Both	R	.246	138	34	9	0	0	12	,14	22	.320	.312	Bats Both	R	.000	4	0	0	0	0	0	0	1	.000	.000
Chavez,Raul	L	.000	3	0	0	0	0	0	1	1	.250	.000	Daulton,D	L	.000	0	0	0	0	0	0	0	0	.000	.000
Bats Right	R	.500	2	1	0	0	0	0	0	0	.500	.500	Bats Left	R	.167	12	2	0	0	0	0	7	5	.500	.167
Cianfrocco,A	L	.358	67	24	7	1	0	8	4	18	.411	.493	Davis,Chili	L	.290	176	51	7	0	9	33	25	38	.371	.483
Bats Right	R	.240	125	30	6	2	2	24	4	38	.262	.368	Bats Both	R	.294	354	104	17	0	19	62	61	61	.396	.503
Cirillo,Jeff	L	.311	161	50	15	1	6	12	19	23	.387	.528	Davis,Eric	L	.247	93	23	3	0	4	14	11	36	.340	.409
Bats Right	R	.331	405	134	31	4	9	71	39	46	.393	.494	Bats Right	R	.298	322	96	17	0	22	69	59	85	.409	.556
Clark,Dave	L	.207	29	6	1	0	1	4	6	14	.333	.345	Davis,Russ	L	.306	49	15	3	0	2	7	8	15	.414	.490
Bats Left	R	.279	197	55	11	2	7	32	28	39	.369	.462	Bats Right	R	.203	118	24	0	0	3	11	9	35	.266	.331
Clark,Phil	L	.000	2	0	0	0	0	0	0	1	.000	.000	Dawson,Andre	L	.294	17	5	1	0	0	2	0	3	.294	.353
Bats Right	R	.000	1	0	0	0	0	0	0	0	.000	.000	Bats Right	R	.268	41	11	1	0	2	12	2	10	.318	.439
Clark,Tony	L	.215	93	20	4	0	5	17	5	28	.253	.419	Decker,Steve	L	.250	60	15	1	0	1	10	5	7	.308	.317
Bats Both	R	.261	283	74	10	0	22	55	24	99	.314	.530	Bats Right	R	.241	87	21	2	0	1	10	13	22	.333	.299
Clark,Will	L	.246	134	33	7	0	4	18	11	21	.318	.388	Deer,Rob	L	.231	13	3	2	0	0	1	5	6	.444	.385
Bats Left	R	.301	302	91	18	1	9	54	53	46	.402	.457	Bats Left	R	.162	37	6	1	0	4	8	9	24	.326	.514
Clayton,Royce	L	.281	135	38	5	1	1	10	7	31	.315	.356	Delgado,Alex	L	.364	11	4	0	0	0	1	2	1	.462	.364
Bats Right	R	.275	356	98	15	3	5	25	26	58	.324	.376	Bats Right	R	.111	9	1	0	0	0	0	1	2	.200	.111
Cockrell,Alan	L	.200	5	1	1	0	0	0	0	3	.200	.400	Delgado,C	L	.152	92	14	4	1	2	10	8	39	.240	.283
Bats Right	R	.333	3	1	0	0	0	2	0	1	.250	.333	Bats Left	R	.298	396	118	24	1	23	82	50	100	.379	.538
Colbrunn,Greg	L	.327	113	37	6	0	6	17	5	14	.353	.540	Delgado,W	L	.000	2	0	0	0	0	0	0	1	.000	.000
Bats Right	R	.274	398	109	20	2	10	52	20	62	.328	.410	Bats Both	R	.400	20	8	0	0	0	2	1	4	.478	.400
Cole,Alex	L	.300	20	6	3	0	0	0	1	3	.333	.450	DeShields,D	L	.211	133	28	3	4	1	13	8	40	.257	.316
Bats Left	R	.192	52	10	2	1	0	7	7	8	.283	.269	Bats Left	R	.228	448	102	9	4	4	28	45	84	.296	.292
Coleman,Vince	L	.111	27	3	0	1	0	0	1	9	.143	.185	Devarez,Cesar	L	.000	3	0	0	0	0	0	0	1	.000	.000
Bats Both	R	.175	57	10	1	0	1	4	8	22	.277	.246	Bats Right	R	.133	15	2	0	1	0	0	1	2	.188	.267
Conine,Jeff	L	.393	122	48	5	0	9	31	13	17	.449	.656	Devereaux,M	L	.244	135	33	7	1	5	19	18	18	.333	.422
Bats Right	R	.267	475	127	27	2	17	64	49	104	.337	.440	Bats Right	R	.218	188	41	4	1	3	15	16	35	.283	.298
Coomer,Ron	L	.308	146	45	8	1	10	31	12	18	.356	.582	Diaz,Alex	L	.182	11	2	0	0	0	0	1	1	.308	.182
Bats Right	R	.276	87	24	4	0	2	10	5	6	.312	.391	Bats Both	R	.250	68	17	2	0	1	5	1	7	.268	.324
Cora,Joey	L	.218	55	12	2	0	0	4	3	8	.254	.255	Diaz,Einar	L	.000	0	0	0	0	0	0	0	0	.000	.000
Bats Both	R	.299	475	142	35	6	6	41	32	24	.349	.436	Bats Right	R	.000	1	0	0	0	0	0	0	0	.000	.000
Cordero,Wil	L	.237	59	14	6	0	0	10	4	14	.292	.339	Difelice,Mike	L	1.000	1	1	0	0	0	0	0	0	1.000	1.000
Bats Right	R	.309	139	43	8	0	3	27	7	17	.347	.432	Bats Right	R	.167	6	1	1	0	0	2	0	1	.167	.333
Cordova,Marty	L	.302	129	39	8	1	4	33	17	20	.395	.473	DiSarcina,G	L	.293	164	48	11	1	2	14	3	7	.304	.409
Bats Right	R	.311	440	137	38	0	12	78	36	76	.363	.480	Bats Right	R	.239	372	89	15	3	3	34	18	29	.278	.320
Crespo,Felipe	L	.188	16	3	1	0	0	2	3	5	.381	.250	Dorsett,Brian	L	.143	14	2	0	0	1	3	2	4	.235	.357
Bats Both	R	.182	33	6	3	0	0	2	9	8	.372	.273	Bats Right	R	.111	27	3	0	0	0	0	2	4	.172	.111
Cruz,Fausto	L	.286	7	2	0	0	0	0	0	2	.286	.286	Doster,David	L	.381	21	8	4	0	1	2	1	0	.409	.714
Bats Right	R	.226	31	7	2	0	0	0	1	9	.250	.290	Bats Right	R	.238	84	20	4	0	0	6	6	21	.289	.286
Cruz,Jacob	L	.273	11	3	0	0	1	5	2	5	.385	.545	Duncan,M	L	.317	123	39	11	1	2	19	4	26	.338	.472
Bats Left	R	.227	66	15	3	0	2	5	10	19	.346	.364	Bats Right	R	.350	277	97	23	2	6	37	5	51	.358	.513
Cummings,M	L	.182	22	4	1	0	0	2	0	4	.182	.227	Dunn,Todd	L	.333	3	1	0	0	0	0	0	0	.333	.333
Bats Left	R	.238	63	15	2	1	3	5	0	12	.234	.444	Bats Right	R	.286	7	2	1	0	0	1	0	3	.286	.429
Curtis,Chad	L	.301	143	43	7	0	3	15	18	25	.374	.413	Dunston,S	L	.255	55	14	2	1	0	3	2	10	.281	.327
Bats Right	R	.233	361	84	18	1	9	31	52	63	.328	.363	Bats Right	R	.310	232	72	10	1	5	22	11	30	.343	.427

Batters vs. Left-Handed and Right-Handed Pitchers

Batter	vs	Avg	AB	H	2B	3B	HR	BI	BB	SO	OBP	SLG	Batter	vs	Avg	AB	H	2B	3B	HR	BI	BB	SO	OBP	SLG
Durant,Mike	L	.245	49	12	2	0	0	2	7	9	.339	.286	Fonville,Chad	L	.169	59	10	2	0	0	3	3	13	.210	.203
Bats Right	R	.156	32	5	1	0	0	3	3	6	.222	.188	Bats Both	R	.218	142	31	2	1	0	10	14	18	.288	.246
Durham,Ray	L	.262	168	44	14	2	3	21	12	27	.308	.423	Fordyce,Brook	L	.000	2	0	0	0	0	0	2	0	.500	.000
Bats Both	R	.280	389	109	19	3	7	44	46	68	.367	.398	Bats Right	R	.400	5	2	1	0	0	1	1	1	.500	.600
Dye,Jermaine	L	.323	93	30	5	0	5	12	3	14	.340	.538	Fox,Andy	L	.172	29	5	0	0	1	3	2	3	.226	.276
Bats Right	R	.261	199	52	11	0	7	25	5	53	.287	.422	Bats Left	R	.200	160	32	4	0	2	10	18	25	.285	.263
Dykstra,Lenny	L	.421	38	16	1	1	2	5	11	6	.551	.658	Franco,Julio	L	.336	128	43	8	0	2	16	13	22	.397	.445
Bats Left	R	.198	96	19	5	2	1	8	15	19	.316	.323	Bats Right	R	.316	304	96	12	1	12	60	48	60	.411	.480
Easley,Damion	L	.333	48	16	1	0	3	10	4	9	.385	.542	Franco,Matt	L	.000	2	0	0	0	0	0	0	0	.000	.000
Bats Right	R	.219	64	14	1	0	1	7	6	16	.292	.281	Bats Left	R	.207	29	6	1	0	1	2	1	5	.250	.345
Echevarria,A	L	.273	11	3	0	0	0	4	2	2	.429	.273	Frazier,Lou	L	.176	17	3	1	0	0	1	5	3	.391	.235
Bats Right	R	.300	10	3	0	0	0	2	0	3	.250	.300	Bats Both	R	.303	33	10	1	1	0	4	3	7	.361	.394
Edmonds,Jim	L	.189	122	23	5	2	2	9	15	40	.293	.311	Frye,Jeff	L	.273	121	33	9	0	0	11	20	16	.375	.347
Bats Left	R	.350	309	108	23	1	25	57	31	61	.408	.673	Bats Right	R	.292	298	87	18	2	4	30	34	41	.371	.406
Eenhoorn,R	L	.100	10	1	0	0	0	1	1	1	.167	.100	Fryman,Travis	L	.248	125	31	7	0	3	15	18	33	.349	.376
Bats Right	R	.211	19	4	0	0	0	1	1	4	.238	.211	Bats Right	R	.273	491	134	25	3	19	85	39	85	.323	.452
Eisenreich,J	L	.375	40	15	1	0	0	7	2	5	.405	.400	Gaetti,Gary	L	.248	105	26	6	1	3	13	7	26	.289	.410
Bats Left	R	.359	298	107	23	3	3	34	29	27	.414	.487	Bats Right	R	.281	417	117	21	3	20	67	28	71	.336	.489
Elster,Kevin	L	.283	159	45	15	2	4	32	19	40	.350	.478	Gagne,Greg	L	.247	93	23	3	1	3	17	14	18	.346	.398
Bats Right	R	.239	356	85	17	0	20	67	33	98	.302	.455	Bats Right	R	.257	335	86	10	1	7	38	36	75	.330	.355
Encarnacion,A	L	.200	5	1	1	0	0	0	0	3	.200	.400	Galarraga,A	L	.326	141	46	9	1	12	42	12	29	.371	.660
Bats Right	R	.353	17	6	1	0	0	1	0	2	.353	.412	Bats Right	R	.297	485	144	30	2	35	108	28	128	.353	.584
Erstad,Darin	L	.308	65	20	1	1	1	9	4	10	.333	.400	Gallego,Mike	L	.222	36	8	0	0	0	1	5	8	.317	.222
Bats Left	R	.273	143	39	4	0	3	11	13	19	.333	.364	Bats Right	R	.206	107	22	2	0	0	3	7	23	.261	.224
Espinoza,A	L	.268	82	22	2	2	4	12	2	15	.291	.488	Gant,Ron	L	.202	94	19	2	0	5	10	18	18	.333	.383
Bats Right	R	.268	164	44	9	2	4	15	8	22	.309	.421	Bats Right	R	.258	325	84	12	2	25	72	55	80	.366	.538
Estalella,B	L	1.000	1	1	0	0	0	0	0	0	1.000	1.000	Garcia,Carlos	L	.292	72	21	4	0	1	7	5	7	.338	.389
Bats Right	R	.313	16	5	0	0	2	4	1	6	.353	.688	Bats Right	R	.283	318	90	14	4	5	37	18	51	.327	.399
Eusebio,Tony	L	.227	44	10	2	1	1	6	4	9	.292	.386	Garcia,Karim	L	.000	0	0	0	0	0	0	0	0	.000	.000
Bats Right	R	.287	108	31	5	1	0	13	14	11	.363	.352	Bats Left	R	.000	1	0	0	0	0	0	0	1	.000	.000
Everett,Carl	L	.250	36	9	3	0	0	5	4	9	.378	.333	Garciaparra,N	L	.161	31	5	0	1	1	5	2	5	.212	.323
Bats Both	R	.237	156	37	5	1	1	11	17	44	.312	.301	Bats Right	R	.286	56	16	2	2	3	11	2	9	.305	.554
Fabregas,J	L	.400	30	12	2	0	1	4	4	3	.457	.567	Garrison,W	L	.000	5	0	0	0	0	0	0	0	.000	.000
Bats Left	R	.272	224	61	4	0	1	22	13	24	.307	.304	Bats Right	R	.000	4	0	0	0	0	0	1	0	.200	.000
Faneyte,R	L	.200	5	1	0	0	0	1	0	0	.200	.200	Gates,Brent	L	.182	55	10	3	0	0	6	4	8	.250	.236
Bats Right	R	.000	0	0	0	0	0	0	0	0	.000	.000	Bats Both	R	.286	192	55	16	2	2	24	14	27	.335	.422
Fasano,Sal	L	.220	41	9	0	0	3	5	5	9	.319	.439	Giambi,Jason	L	.238	126	30	8	0	2	14	10	31	.307	.349
Bats Right	R	.196	102	20	2	0	3	14	9	16	.268	.304	Bats Left	R	.307	410	126	32	1	18	65	41	64	.370	.522
Fermin,Felix	L	.143	7	1	0	0	0	0	0	0	.143	.143	Gibralter,S	L	.000	0	0	0	0	0	0	0	0	.000	.000
Bats Right	R	.111	9	1	1	0	0	1	2	0	.273	.222	Bats Right	R	.000	0	0	0	0	0	0	0	2	.000	.000
Fielder,Cecil	L	.275	138	38	7	0	11	28	35	36	.423	.565	Gil,Benji	L	1.000	2	2	0	0	0	1	1	0	1.000	1.000
Bats Right	R	.245	453	111	13	0	28	89	52	103	.326	.459	Bats Right	R	.000	3	0	0	0	0	0	0	1	.000	.000
Finley,Steve	L	.267	180	48	9	4	4	19	13	25	.318	.428	Giles,B	L	.364	22	8	1	1	0	7	3	2	.440	.500
Bats Left	R	.309	475	147	36	5	26	76	43	63	.368	.571	Bats Left	R	.354	99	35	13	0	5	20	16	11	.432	.636
Flaherty,John	L	.312	93	29	7	0	1	17	9	12	.365	.419	Gilkey,B	L	.343	134	46	12	1	7	18	13	28	.399	.604
Bats Right	R	.276	323	89	17	0	12	47	8	49	.298	.440	Bats Right	R	.309	437	135	32	2	23	99	60	97	.392	.549
Fletcher,D	L	.295	61	18	4	0	1	12	3	9	.338	.410	Giovanola,Ed	L	.143	7	1	1	0	0	1	0	0	.143	.286
Bats Left	R	.261	333	87	18	0	11	45	24	33	.318	.414	Bats Left	R	.240	75	18	1	0	0	6	8	13	.318	.253
Floyd,Cliff	L	.235	34	8	3	0	0	4	2	9	.270	.324	Girardi,Joe	L	.257	136	35	9	0	0	9	5	18	.282	.324
Bats Left	R	.244	193	47	12	4	6	22	28	43	.351	.440	Bats Right	R	.311	286	89	13	3	2	36	25	37	.374	.399

Batters vs. Left-Handed and Right-Handed Pitchers

Batter	vs	Avg	AB	H	2B	3B	HR	BI	BB	SO	OBP	SLG	Batter	vs	Avg	AB	H	2B	3B	HR	BI	BB	SO	OBP	SLG
Glanville,D	L	.292	48	14	2	1	1	6	3	6	.327	.438	Gutierrez,R	L	.324	68	22	4	1	0	2	8	12	.403	.412
Bats Right	R	.171	35	6	3	0	0	4	0	5	.171	.257	Bats Right	R	.267	150	40	4	0	1	13	15	30	.339	.313
Goff,Jerry	L	.000	1	0	0	0	0	0	0	1	.000	.000	Gwynn,Chris	L	.200	5	1	0	0	0	1	2	1	.429	.200
Bats Left	R	.667	3	2	0	0	1	2	0	0	.667	1.667	Bats Left	R	.176	85	15	4	0	1	9	8	27	.247	.259
Gomez,Chris	L	.232	82	19	3	0	0	3	16	20	.357	.268	Gwynn,Tony	L	.353	136	48	6	1	1	20	9	2	.392	.434
Bats Right	R	.262	374	98	18	1	4	42	41	64	.344	.348	Bats Left	R	.352	315	111	21	1	2	30	30	15	.404	.444
Gomez,Leo	L	.283	113	32	8	0	3	18	19	30	.388	.434	Hajek,Dave	L	.000	0	0	0	0	0	0	1	0	1.000	.000
Bats Right	R	.217	249	54	11	0	14	38	34	64	.324	.430	Bats Right	R	.300	10	3	1	0	0	1	1	0	.364	.400
Gonzales,Rene	L	.220	50	11	3	0	1	1	7	5	.316	.340	Hale,Chip	L	.333	3	1	0	0	0	0	0	0	.333	.333
Bats Right	R	.214	42	9	1	0	1	4	3	6	.255	.310	Bats Left	R	.274	84	23	5	0	1	16	10	6	.347	.369
Gonzalez,Alex	L	.252	163	41	11	2	3	17	13	32	.309	.399	Hall,Mel	L	.333	3	1	0	0	0	1	0	1	.250	.333
Bats Right	R	.228	364	83	19	3	11	47	32	95	.296	.387	Bats Left	R	.091	22	2	0	0	0	4	1	3	.130	.091
Gonzalez,Juan	L	.376	141	53	12	0	20	47	15	20	.436	.887	Hamelin,Bob	L	.220	41	9	0	1	0	4	11	16	.382	.268
Bats Right	R	.293	400	117	21	2	27	97	30	62	.344	.558	Bats Left	R	.263	198	52	14	0	9	36	43	42	.393	.470
Gonzalez,Luis	L	.188	80	15	2	0	2	8	6	20	.244	.288	Hamilton,D	L	.264	182	48	3	3	1	17	17	23	.328	.330
Bats Left	R	.288	403	116	28	4	13	71	55	29	.374	.474	Bats Left	R	.306	445	136	26	1	5	34	37	43	.357	.402
Goodwin,C	L	.265	34	9	0	0	0	2	3	12	.324	.265	Hammonds,J	L	.247	81	20	5	1	2	7	8	15	.326	.407
Bats Left	R	.216	102	22	3	0	0	3	16	22	.322	.245	Bats Right	R	.216	167	36	5	0	7	20	15	38	.288	.371
Goodwin,Tom	L	.315	162	51	8	2	0	15	17	23	.380	.389	Haney,Todd	L	.105	19	2	0	0	0	0	1	3	.150	.105
Bats Left	R	.268	362	97	6	2	1	20	22	56	.313	.304	Bats Right	R	.143	63	9	1	0	0	3	6	12	.214	.159
Grace,Mark	L	.301	153	46	7	0	1	15	12	14	.352	.366	Hansen,Dave	L	.000	1	0	0	0	0	0	0	0	.000	.000
Bats Left	R	.343	394	135	32	1	8	60	50	27	.412	.490	Bats Left	R	.223	103	23	1	0	0	6	11	22	.296	.233
Graffanino,T	L	.182	11	2	0	0	0	0	2	3	.308	.182	Hardtke,Jason	L	.125	16	2	0	0	0	4	1	2	.176	.125
Bats Right	R	.171	35	6	1	1	0	2	2	10	.231	.257	Bats Both	R	.220	41	9	5	0	0	2	1	10	.256	.341
Grebeck,Craig	L	.333	15	5	0	0	1	2	0	1	.333	.533	Harris,Lenny	L	.311	45	14	3	0	1	7	4	6	.380	.444
Bats Right	R	.188	80	15	1	0	0	7	4	13	.230	.200	Bats Left	R	.280	257	72	14	2	4	25	17	25	.321	.397
Green,Shawn	L	.254	59	15	3	0	1	7	6	11	.343	.356	Haselman,Bill	L	.358	81	29	9	1	3	14	9	10	.422	.605
Bats Left	R	.284	363	103	29	3	10	38	27	64	.342	.463	Bats Right	R	.231	156	36	4	0	5	20	10	42	.281	.353
Greene,C	L	.000	0	0	0	0	0	0	0	0	.000	.000	Hatteberg,S	L	.000	0	0	0	0	0	0	0	0	.000	.000
Bats Right	R	.000	1	0	0	0	0	0	0	0	.000	.000	Bats Left	R	.182	11	2	1	0	0	0	3	2	.357	.273
Greene,Todd	L	.106	47	5	1	0	1	2	1	5	.125	.191	Hayes,Charlie	L	.277	112	31	4	0	4	16	9	15	.331	.420
Bats Right	R	.313	32	10	0	0	1	7	3	6	.389	.406	Bats Right	R	.246	414	102	20	2	8	59	28	75	.292	.362
Greene,Willie	L	.159	44	7	0	1	1	6	11	15	.321	.273	Henderson,R	L	.263	114	30	4	0	4	12	33	22	.433	.404
Bats Left	R	.259	243	63	5	4	18	57	25	73	.328	.535	Bats Right	R	.234	351	82	13	2	5	17	92	68	.403	.325
Greenwell,M	L	.346	81	28	5	1	0	9	2	7	.372	.432	Hernandez,C	L	.222	9	2	0	0	0	0	1	0	.300	.222
Bats Left	R	.276	214	59	15	0	7	35	16	20	.323	.444	Bats Left	R	.400	5	2	0	0	0	0	1	2	.500	.400
Greer,Rusty	L	.322	174	56	10	3	6	35	17	30	.381	.517	Hernandez,J	L	.173	81	14	3	0	1	5	4	25	.209	.247
Bats Left	R	.337	368	124	31	3	12	65	45	56	.405	.535	Bats Right	R	.264	250	66	11	1	9	36	20	72	.320	.424
Griffey Jr,K	L	.297	158	47	5	1	21	53	20	33	.382	.741	Herrera,Jose	L	.296	27	8	2	0	0	3	3	4	.387	.370
Bats Left	R	.305	387	118	21	1	28	87	58	71	.397	.581	Bats Left	R	.266	293	78	13	1	6	27	17	55	.311	.379
Grissom,M	L	.310	168	52	8	4	9	24	7	16	.333	.565	Hiatt,Phil	L	.182	11	2	0	0	0	0	1	7	.250	.182
Bats Right	R	.308	503	155	24	6	14	50	34	57	.354	.463	Bats Right	R	.200	10	2	0	1	0	1	1	4	.273	.400
Grudzielanek,M	L	.308	133	41	8	1	1	5	5	23	.331	.406	Higginson,Bob	L	.230	61	14	1	0	1	12	15	9	.358	.295
Bats Right	R	.305	524	160	26	3	5	44	21	60	.342	.395	Bats Left	R	.335	379	127	34	0	25	69	50	57	.413	.623
Guerrero,V	L	.200	15	3	0	0	0	0	0	1	.200	.200	Hill,G	L	.366	71	26	5	0	7	15	8	13	.425	.732
Bats Right	R	.167	12	2	0	0	1	1	0	2	.167	.417	Bats Right	R	.260	308	80	21	0	12	52	25	82	.326	.445
Guerrero,W	L	.000	1	0	0	0	0	0	0	1	.000	.000	Hocking,Denny	L	.167	30	5	2	0	0	2	2	4	.219	.233
Bats Right	R	.000	1	0	0	0	0	0	0	1	.000	.000	Bats Both	R	.206	97	20	4	0	1	8	6	20	.250	.278
Guillen,Ozzie	L	.239	117	28	5	0	1	5	1	6	.246	.308	Hoiles,Chris	L	.304	125	38	3	0	9	24	18	22	.386	.544
Bats Left	R	.270	382	103	19	8	3	40	9	21	.281	.385	Bats Right	R	.238	282	67	10	0	16	49	39	75	.343	.443

303

Batters vs. Left-Handed and Right-Handed Pitchers

Batter	vs	Avg	AB	H	2B	3B	HR	BI	BB	SO	OBP	SLG
Holbert,Aaron	L	.000	3	0	0	0	0	0	0	0	.000	.000
Bats Right	R	.000	0	0	0	0	0	0	0	0	.000	.000
Hollandsworth,T	L	.345	29	10	2	2	0	0	2	6	.387	.552
Bats Left	R	.287	449	129	24	2	12	59	39	87	.346	.430
Hollins,Dave	L	.326	135	44	9	0	5	24	24	29	.445	.504
Bats Both	R	.239	381	91	20	0	11	54	60	88	.353	.378
Hosey,Dwayne	L	.208	24	5	1	1	0	0	0	6	.208	.333
Bats Both	R	.222	54	12	1	1	1	3	7	11	.311	.333
Houston,Tyler	L	.200	5	1	0	0	0	0	1	2	.333	.200
Bats Left	R	.321	137	44	9	1	3	27	8	25	.359	.467
Howard,Dave	L	.205	146	30	4	2	3	18	15	27	.282	.322
Bats Both	R	.226	274	62	10	3	1	30	25	47	.295	.296
Howard,Matt	L	.115	26	3	0	0	1	2	1	5	.143	.231
Bats Right	R	.286	28	8	1	0	0	7	1	3	.310	.321
Howard,Thomas	L	.224	67	15	3	0	0	10	4	13	.278	.269
Bats Left	R	.283	293	83	16	10	6	32	13	38	.314	.468
Howell,Jack	L	.222	9	2	0	0	0	0	1	0	.300	.222
Bats Left	R	.274	117	32	4	1	8	21	9	30	.325	.530
Hubbard,Mike	L	.000	4	0	0	0	0	0	0	2	.000	.000
Bats Right	R	.118	34	4	0	0	1	4	0	13	.114	.206
Hubbard,Trent	L	.200	30	6	1	1	1	5	3	9	.273	.400
Bats Right	R	.220	59	13	4	1	1	9	8	18	.324	.373
Hudler,Rex	L	.345	139	48	11	2	9	21	6	27	.374	.647
Bats Right	R	.282	163	46	9	1	7	19	4	27	.304	.479
Huff,Michael	L	.136	22	3	0	1	0	0	1	3	.174	.227
Bats Right	R	.286	7	2	0	0	0	0	0	2	.286	.286
Hulse,David	L	.091	22	2	0	0	0	1	0	5	.091	.091
Bats Left	R	.253	95	24	3	0	0	5	8	11	.311	.284
Hundley,Todd	L	.196	153	30	9	0	6	21	21	57	.297	.373
Bats Both	R	.284	387	110	23	1	35	91	58	89	.379	.620
Hunter,Brian	L	.270	111	30	8	0	3	18	8	24	.317	.423
Bats Right	R	.264	87	23	2	0	4	10	7	19	.340	.425
Hunter,B	L	.260	131	34	9	1	0	7	2	18	.267	.344
Bats Right	R	.281	395	111	18	1	5	28	15	74	.307	.370
Huskey,Butch	L	.279	111	31	3	0	6	13	10	21	.336	.468
Bats Right	R	.277	303	84	13	2	9	47	17	56	.313	.422
Huson,Jeff	L	.400	5	2	0	0	0	0	1	1	.500	.400
Bats Left	R	.304	23	7	1	0	0	2	0	2	.292	.348
Hyers,Tim	L	.000	1	0	0	0	0	0	0	0	.000	.000
Bats Left	R	.080	25	2	1	0	0	0	4	5	.207	.120
Ibanez,Raul	L	.000	0	0	0	0	0	0	0	0	.000	.000
Bats Left	R	.000	5	0	0	0	0	0	0	1	.167	.000
Incaviglia,P	L	.351	74	26	4	0	8	19	9	12	.417	.730
Bats Right	R	.206	228	47	5	2	10	31	21	77	.285	.377
Jackson,D	L	.400	5	2	1	0	0	0	1	0	.400	.600
Bats Right	R	.200	5	1	1	0	0	1	1	3	.333	.400
Jaha,John	L	.371	124	46	9	0	7	27	29	27	.487	.613
Bats Right	R	.279	419	117	19	1	27	91	56	91	.369	.523
James,Dion	L	.000	0	0	0	0	0	0	0	0	.000	.000
Bats Left	R	.167	12	2	0	0	0	0	1	2	.231	.167
Javier,Stan	L	.282	78	22	7	0	1	5	8	13	.349	.410
Bats Both	R	.265	196	52	18	0	1	17	17	38	.330	.372
Jefferies,G	L	.287	87	25	5	0	1	12	6	4	.330	.379
Bats Both	R	.293	317	93	12	3	6	39	30	17	.352	.407
Jefferson,R	L	.320	50	16	3	0	1	9	5	15	.393	.440
Bats Left	R	.351	336	118	27	4	18	65	20	74	.387	.616
Jennings,R	L	.000	1	0	0	0	0	0	0	1	.000	.000
Bats Left	R	.228	57	13	5	0	0	4	3	8	.279	.316
Jensen,Marcus	L	.000	2	0	0	0	0	0	1	1	.333	.000
Bats Both	R	.235	17	4	1	0	0	4	7	6	.458	.294
Jeter,Derek	L	.340	162	55	5	1	2	12	16	25	.409	.420
Bats Right	R	.305	420	128	20	5	8	66	32	77	.355	.433
Johnson,Brian	L	.328	67	22	7	0	1	10	1	9	.333	.478
Bats Right	R	.250	176	44	6	1	7	25	3	27	.274	.415
Johnson,C	L	.207	87	18	5	0	1	6	9	16	.278	.299
Bats Right	R	.221	299	66	8	1	12	31	31	75	.296	.375
Johnson,Lance	L	.330	182	60	9	5	0	20	5	13	.346	.434
Bats Left	R	.334	500	167	22	16	9	49	28	27	.368	.496
Johnson,Mark	L	.233	30	7	1	0	2	4	3	8	.324	.467
Bats Left	R	.278	313	87	23	0	11	43	41	56	.365	.457
Jones,Andruw	L	.379	29	11	4	1	5	11	4	5	.455	1.103
Bats Right	R	.156	77	12	3	0	0	2	3	24	.188	.195
Jones,Chipper	L	.295	173	51	8	0	6	29	20	30	.366	.445
Bats Both	R	.315	425	134	24	5	24	81	67	58	.404	.565
Jones,Chris	L	.273	55	15	3	0	1	4	5	18	.344	.382
Bats Right	R	.223	94	21	4	0	3	14	7	24	.284	.362
Jones,Dax	L	.235	34	8	0	1	1	4	3	5	.297	.382
Bats Both	R	.083	24	2	0	1	0	3	5	7	.233	.167
Jones,Terry	L	.667	3	2	0	0	0	0	0	1	.667	.667
Bats Both	R	.143	7	1	0	0	0	1	0	2	.125	.143
Jordan,Brian	L	.343	108	37	11	0	3	17	9	25	.395	.528
Bats Right	R	.301	405	122	25	1	14	87	20	59	.337	.472
Jordan,Kevin	L	.130	23	3	0	0	1	1	0	7	.130	.261
Bats Right	R	.315	108	34	10	0	2	11	5	13	.345	.463
Jordan,Ricky	L	.240	25	6	0	0	1	4	1	6	.286	.360
Bats Right	R	.333	3	1	0	0	0	0	0	0	.333	.333
Joyner,Wally	L	.214	117	25	6	0	2	21	12	22	.290	.316
Bats Left	R	.301	316	95	23	1	6	44	57	49	.407	.437
Justice,Dave	L	.321	53	17	5	0	3	8	8	5	.413	.585
Bats Left	R	.322	87	28	4	0	3	17	13	17	.406	.471
Karkovice,Ron	L	.271	85	23	7	0	2	10	9	13	.347	.424
Bats Right	R	.204	270	55	15	0	8	28	15	80	.244	.348
Karros,Eric	L	.327	101	33	7	0	6	24	17	15	.417	.574
Bats Right	R	.247	507	125	22	1	28	87	36	106	.295	.460
Kelly,Mike	L	.176	17	3	1	0	1	2	3	4	.333	.412
Bats Right	R	.188	32	6	3	0	0	5	6	7	.333	.281
Kelly,Pat	L	.286	7	2	0	0	0	1	0	2	.286	.286
Bats Right	R	.071	14	1	0	0	0	1	2	7	.188	.071
Kelly,Roberto	L	.406	128	52	10	1	4	21	12	22	.462	.594
Bats Right	R	.268	194	52	7	3	2	26	11	31	.318	.366

Batters vs. Left-Handed and Right-Handed Pitchers

Batter	vs	Avg	AB	H	2B	3B	HR	BI	BB	SO	OBP	SLG
Kendall,Jason	L	.295	78	23	3	3	0	5	9	2	.371	.410
Bats Right	R	.301	336	101	20	2	3	37	26	28	.372	.399
Kent,Jeff	L	.325	123	40	10	1	0	14	16	14	.394	.423
Bats Right	R	.268	314	84	17	0	12	41	15	64	.302	.436
Kieschnick,B	L	.000	0	0	0	0	0	0	0	0	.000	.000
Bats Left	R	.345	29	10	2	0	1	6	3	8	.406	.517
King,Jeff	L	.285	137	39	10	3	7	21	24	15	.387	.555
Bats Right	R	.267	454	121	26	1	23	90	46	80	.333	.480
Kingery,Mike	L	.364	22	8	0	0	0	0	4	2	.481	.364
Bats Left	R	.236	254	60	12	2	3	27	19	27	.286	.335
Kingsale,Gene	L	.000	0	0	0	0	0	0	0	0	.000	.000
Bats Both	R	.000	0	0	0	0	0	0	0	0	.000	.000
Kirby,Wayne	L	.200	15	3	2	0	0	1	0	3	.200	.333
Bats Left	R	.275	189	52	9	1	1	11	19	16	.343	.349
Klesko,Ryan	L	.230	139	32	2	1	3	12	9	38	.285	.324
Bats Left	R	.301	389	117	19	3	31	81	59	91	.390	.604
Knoblauch,C	L	.388	147	57	10	3	4	19	24	19	.480	.578
Bats Right	R	.325	431	140	25	11	9	53	74	55	.438	.497
Knorr,Randy	L	.216	37	8	3	0	0	3	0	9	.216	.297
Bats Right	R	.180	50	9	2	0	1	4	5	9	.263	.280
Koslofski,K	L	.000	4	0	0	0	0	0	1	2	.200	.000
Bats Left	R	.237	38	9	3	2	0	6	3	10	.310	.421
Kreuter,Chad	L	.270	37	10	4	0	1	6	2	8	.308	.459
Bats Both	R	.195	77	15	4	0	2	12	11	21	.308	.325
Lampkin,Tom	L	.208	24	5	2	0	1	5	1	2	.269	.417
Bats Left	R	.235	153	36	6	0	5	24	19	20	.331	.373
Lankford,Ray	L	.246	122	30	8	3	0	22	7	30	.278	.361
Bats Left	R	.284	423	120	28	5	21	64	72	103	.389	.522
Lansing,Mike	L	.296	135	40	6	0	1	4	13	17	.358	.363
Bats Right	R	.283	506	143	34	2	10	49	31	68	.336	.417
Larkin,Barry	L	.298	121	36	8	1	9	24	30	11	.435	.603
Bats Right	R	.298	396	118	24	3	24	65	66	41	.402	.556
Lawton,Matt	L	.245	49	12	1	0	0	6	5	4	.339	.265
Bats Left	R	.261	203	53	6	1	6	36	23	24	.339	.389
Leius,Scott	L	.080	25	2	1	0	0	0	2	6	.148	.120
Bats Right	R	.222	18	4	3	0	1	3	0	2	.222	.556
Lemke,Mark	L	.219	128	28	4	0	3	7	21	11	.325	.320
Bats Both	R	.268	370	99	13	0	2	30	32	37	.323	.319
Lennon,P	L	.160	25	4	2	0	0	0	3	10	.250	.240
Bats Right	R	.600	5	3	1	0	0	1	4	0	.778	.800
Lesher,Brian	L	.216	37	8	0	0	3	8	2	10	.256	.459
Bats Right	R	.244	45	11	3	0	2	8	3	7	.300	.444
Levis,Jesse	L	.275	40	11	0	0	0	8	5	4	.356	.275
Bats Left	R	.228	193	44	6	1	1	13	33	11	.346	.285
Lewis,Darren	L	.188	112	21	3	0	1	14	13	12	.268	.241
Bats Right	R	.249	225	56	9	2	3	39	32	28	.346	.347
Lewis,Mark	L	.351	131	46	6	2	3	13	14	19	.408	.496
Bats Right	R	.244	414	101	24	1	8	42	28	90	.299	.365
Leyritz,Jim	L	.241	87	21	2	0	0	5	18	18	.383	.264
Bats Right	R	.275	178	49	8	0	7	35	12	50	.340	.438

Batter	vs	Avg	AB	H	2B	3B	HR	BI	BB	SO	OBP	SLG
Lieberthal,M	L	.241	29	7	3	0	1	4	1	4	.267	.448
Bats Right	R	.255	137	35	5	0	6	19	9	26	.303	.423
Liriano,N	L	.270	37	10	2	1	0	7	1	9	.289	.378
Bats Both	R	.267	180	48	12	1	3	23	13	13	.311	.394
Listach,Pat	L	.306	121	37	8	1	1	10	15	9	.387	.413
Bats Both	R	.199	196	39	8	1	0	23	21	42	.274	.250
Livingstone,S	L	.077	13	1	0	0	0	1	1	2	.143	.077
Bats Left	R	.314	159	50	4	1	2	19	8	20	.347	.390
Lockhart,K	L	.210	62	13	3	2	0	5	0	10	.222	.323
Bats Left	R	.283	371	105	30	1	7	50	30	30	.334	.426
Lofton,Kenny	L	.302	235	71	13	1	2	17	20	34	.357	.391
Bats Left	R	.326	427	139	22	3	12	50	41	48	.380	.475
Lopez,Javy	L	.301	113	34	5	0	4	17	8	17	.344	.451
Bats Right	R	.277	376	104	14	1	19	52	20	67	.315	.471
Lopez,Luis	L	.000	8	0	0	0	0	0	1	4	.000	.000
Bats Both	R	.191	131	25	3	0	2	11	8	31	.236	.260
Loretta,Mark	L	.230	74	17	0	0	0	5	10	7	.321	.230
Bats Right	R	.325	80	26	3	0	1	8	4	8	.357	.400
Lovullo,Torey	L	.192	26	5	2	0	0	3	1	5	.241	.269
Bats Both	R	.232	56	13	2	0	3	6	10	12	.358	.429
Lukachyk,Rob	L	.000	0	0	0	0	0	0	0	0	.000	.000
Bats Left	R	.000	2	0	0	0	0	0	0	1	.000	.000
Luke,Matt	L	.000	0	0	0	0	0	0	0	0	.000	.000
Bats Left	R	.000	0	0	0	0	0	0	0	0	.000	.000
Mabry,John	L	.351	97	34	7	1	3	19	4	20	.382	.536
Bats Left	R	.285	446	127	23	1	10	55	33	64	.333	.408
Macfarlane,M	L	.241	116	28	9	0	8	21	10	20	.297	.526
Bats Right	R	.289	263	76	15	2	11	33	21	37	.357	.487
Machado,R	L	.800	5	4	1	0	0	2	0	0	.800	1.000
Bats Right	R	.000	1	0	0	0	0	0	0	0	.000	.000
Magadan,Dave	L	.375	8	3	1	0	0	0	3	2	.545	.500
Bats Left	R	.248	161	40	9	0	3	17	26	21	.349	.360
Magee,Wendell	L	.200	10	2	0	0	0	1	2	2	.333	.200
Bats Left	R	.205	132	27	7	0	2	13	7	31	.245	.303
Malave,Jose	L	.255	55	14	2	0	3	13	0	12	.255	.455
Bats Right	R	.213	47	10	1	0	1	4	2	13	.260	.298
Manto,Jeff	L	.268	41	11	1	0	3	10	6	9	.375	.512
Bats Right	R	.148	61	9	5	1	0	0	11	15	.278	.262
Manwaring,K	L	.200	60	12	2	0	1	3	7	14	.294	.283
Bats Right	R	.240	167	40	7	0	0	15	12	26	.303	.281
Marrero,O	L	.000	0	0	0	0	0	0	0	0	.000	.000
Bats Left	R	.375	8	3	1	0	0	1	1	3	.444	.500
Martin,Al	L	.200	135	27	5	0	4	19	18	33	.290	.326
Bats Left	R	.327	495	162	35	1	14	53	36	83	.372	.487
Martin,N	L	.394	66	26	3	0	1	7	4	9	.423	.485
Bats Right	R	.311	74	23	4	0	0	7	2	8	.329	.365
Martinez,Dave	L	.311	74	23	4	3	1	10	11	12	.402	.486
Bats Left	R	.320	366	117	16	5	9	43	41	40	.391	.464
Martinez,E	L	.339	115	39	10	0	8	21	29	19	.473	.635
Bats Right	R	.323	384	124	42	2	18	82	94	65	.461	.583

Batters vs. Left-Handed and Right-Handed Pitchers

Batter	vs	Avg	AB	H	2B	3B	HR	BI	BB	SO	OBP	SLG	Batter	vs	Avg	AB	H	2B	3B	HR	BI	BB	SO	OBP	SLG
Martinez,M	L	.206	34	7	1	3	0	2	2	8	.250	.412	Milliard,R	L	.238	21	5	0	0	0	0	4	5	.360	.238
Bats Right	R	.263	19	5	1	0	0	1	2	8	.364	.316	Bats Right	R	.122	41	5	2	0	0	1	10	11	.288	.171
Martinez,Pablo	L	.000	1	0	0	0	0	0	0	0	.000	.000	Mirabelli,D	L	.000	5	0	0	0	0	0	1	0	.167	.000
Bats Both	R	1.000	1	1	0	0	0	0	0	0	1.000	1.000	Bats Right	R	.308	13	4	1	0	0	1	2	4	.400	.385
Martinez,S	L	.238	42	10	4	0	1	4	2	12	.273	.405	Mitchell,Keith	L	.182	11	2	0	0	0	1	0	3	.182	.182
Bats Left	R	.225	187	42	5	3	2	14	14	46	.291	.316	Bats Right	R	.500	4	2	1	0	1	2	1	0	.600	1.500
Martinez,Tino	L	.279	219	61	15	0	6	40	21	38	.336	.429	Mitchell,Kevin	L	.400	50	20	3	0	3	13	10	6	.500	.640
Bats Left	R	.301	376	113	13	0	19	77	47	47	.380	.487	Bats Right	R	.288	156	45	12	0	5	26	27	24	.395	.462
Marzano,John	L	.259	27	7	1	0	0	3	3	6	.375	.296	Molina,Izzy	L	.250	12	3	0	0	0	0	0	0	.250	.250
Bats Right	R	.241	79	19	5	0	0	3	4	9	.294	.304	Bats Right	R	.154	13	2	2	0	0	1	1	3	.214	.308
Mashore,Damon	L	.250	48	12	3	1	2	6	8	16	.351	.479	Molitor,Paul	L	.345	148	51	8	2	2	23	21	12	.426	.466
Bats Right	R	.281	57	16	4	0	1	6	8	15	.379	.404	Bats Right	R	.340	512	174	33	6	7	90	35	60	.379	.469
Matheny,Mike	L	.192	104	20	6	0	0	14	6	23	.241	.250	Mondesi,Raul	L	.274	113	31	5	1	4	20	7	25	.322	.442
Bats Right	R	.211	209	44	9	2	8	32	8	57	.243	.388	Bats Right	R	.301	521	157	35	6	20	68	25	97	.337	.507
May,Derrick	L	.154	13	2	0	0	0	1	1	2	.200	.154	Montgomery,R	L	.400	5	2	0	0	1	2	0	2	.400	1.000
Bats Left	R	.256	246	63	12	3	5	32	29	31	.337	.390	Bats Right	R	.111	9	1	1	0	0	2	1	3	.200	.222
Mayne,Brent	L	.300	10	3	1	0	0	1	0	3	.300	.400	Moore,Kerwin	L	.000	2	0	0	0	0	0	0	0	.000	.000
Bats Left	R	.258	89	23	5	0	1	5	12	19	.347	.348	Bats Both	R	.071	14	1	1	0	0	0	2	6	.188	.143
McCarty,Dave	L	.190	63	12	1	0	3	13	9	14	.293	.349	Morandini,M	L	.240	104	25	5	1	0	8	10	20	.322	.308
Bats Right	R	.232	112	26	2	0	3	11	9	29	.295	.330	Bats Left	R	.253	435	110	19	5	3	24	39	67	.321	.340
McCracken,Q	L	.279	68	19	4	0	0	6	6	13	.338	.338	Mordecai,Mike	L	.194	31	6	1	0	0	2	3	7	.257	.226
Bats Both	R	.293	215	63	9	6	3	34	26	49	.370	.433	Bats Right	R	.260	77	20	4	0	2	6	6	17	.313	.390
McGee,Willie	L	.295	88	26	5	1	3	13	2	21	.311	.477	Morman,Russ	L	.500	2	1	1	0	0	0	0	1	.500	1.000
Bats Both	R	.312	221	69	10	1	2	28	16	39	.363	.394	Bats Right	R	.000	4	0	0	0	0	0	1	1	.200	.000
McGriff,Fred	L	.325	200	65	11	1	11	41	15	34	.369	.555	Morris,Hal	L	.273	132	36	6	0	1	16	10	19	.322	.341
Bats Left	R	.281	417	117	26	0	17	66	53	82	.363	.465	Bats Left	R	.326	396	129	26	4	15	64	40	57	.390	.525
McGwire,Mark	L	.373	102	38	6	0	12	26	27	21	.511	.784	Mosquera,J	L	.222	9	2	0	0	0	1	0	1	.300	.222
Bats Right	R	.293	321	94	15	0	40	87	89	91	.453	.713	Bats Right	R	.231	13	3	2	0	0	1	0	2	.231	.385
McIntosh,Tim	L	.000	3	0	0	0	0	0	0	0	.000	.000	Mottola,Chad	L	.258	31	8	2	0	2	4	2	4	.303	.516
Bats Right	R	.000	0	0	0	0	0	0	0	0	.000	.000	Bats Right	R	.188	48	9	1	0	1	2	4	12	.250	.271
McKeel,Walt	L	.000	0	0	0	0	0	0	0	0	.000	.000	Mouton,James	L	.339	115	39	5	1	1	15	15	20	.415	.426
Bats Right	R	.000	0	0	0	0	0	0	0	0	.000	.000	Bats Right	R	.216	185	40	10	0	2	19	23	35	.299	.303
McLemore,Mark	L	.250	160	40	4	0	1	10	27	21	.354	.294	Mouton,Lyle	L	.296	125	37	6	0	3	23	10	29	.348	.416
Bats Both	R	.308	357	110	19	4	4	36	60	48	.405	.417	Bats Right	R	.292	89	26	2	1	4	16	12	21	.379	.472
McMillon,B	L	.000	3	0	0	0	0	0	0	1	.000	.000	Mueller,Bill	L	.321	28	9	2	0	0	3	2	6	.367	.393
Bats Left	R	.229	48	11	0	0	0	4	5	13	.302	.229	Bats Both	R	.331	172	57	13	1	0	16	22	20	.406	.419
McRae,Brian	L	.296	142	42	7	1	2	21	10	16	.346	.401	Mulligan,Sean	L	.000	1	0	0	0	0	0	0	0	.000	.000
Bats Both	R	.270	482	130	25	4	15	45	63	68	.364	.432	Bats Right	R	.000	0	0	0	0	0	0	0	0	.000	.000
Meares,Pat	L	.297	138	41	8	3	4	25	7	22	.333	.486	Munoz,Jose	L	.000	4	0	0	0	0	0	0	0	.000	.000
Bats Right	R	.256	379	97	18	4	4	42	10	68	.285	.356	Bats Both	R	.304	23	7	0	0	0	1	4	1	.407	.304
Mejia,Miguel	L	.000	6	0	0	0	0	0	0	4	.000	.000	Munoz,Pedro	L	.200	40	8	3	0	1	6	3	14	.256	.350
Bats Right	R	.118	17	2	0	0	0	0	0	6	.118	.118	Bats Right	R	.284	81	23	2	0	5	12	6	17	.333	.494
Merced,O	L	.263	114	30	9	1	2	16	14	24	.341	.412	Murray,Eddie	L	.269	156	42	3	0	6	21	23	19	.357	.404
Bats Left	R	.295	339	100	15	0	15	64	37	50	.362	.472	Bats Both	R	.256	410	105	18	1	16	58	38	68	.314	.422
Mercedes,H	L	.000	0	0	0	0	0	0	0	0	.000	.000	Murray,Glenn	L	.200	15	3	1	0	0	0	0	6	.200	.267
Bats Right	R	.250	4	1	0	0	0	0	0	1	.250	.250	Bats Right	R	.195	82	16	2	0	2	6	7	30	.258	.293
Mieske,Matt	L	.352	145	51	15	3	7	31	13	24	.400	.641	Myers,Greg	L	.290	31	9	1	0	0	4	2	7	.333	.323
Bats Right	R	.231	229	53	9	0	7	33	13	52	.274	.362	Bats Left	R	.285	298	85	21	3	6	43	17	45	.319	.436
Miller,O	L	.187	91	17	7	0	2	5	4	18	.229	.330	Myers,Rod	L	.353	17	6	3	0	0	1	2	3	.421	.529
Bats Right	R	.273	377	103	19	2	13	53	10	98	.306	.438	Bats Left	R	.261	46	12	4	0	1	10	5	13	.333	.413

Batters vs. Left-Handed and Right-Handed Pitchers

Batter	vs	Avg	AB	H	2B	3B	HR	BI	BB	SO	OBP	SLG	Batter	vs	Avg	AB	H	2B	3B	HR	BI	BB	SO	OBP	SLG
Naehring,Tim	L	.252	107	27	2	0	4	14	14	18	.336	.383	Owens,Eric	L	.236	106	25	4	0	0	3	12	11	.308	.274
Bats Right	R	.300	323	97	14	0	13	51	35	45	.373	.464	Bats Right	R	.162	99	16	2	0	0	6	11	27	.252	.182
Natal,Bob	L	.105	19	2	0	0	0	0	4	6	.261	.105	Owens,Jayhawk	L	.247	93	23	5	1	2	13	13	29	.336	.387
Bats Right	R	.141	71	10	1	1	0	2	11	25	.256	.183	Bats Right	R	.230	87	20	4	0	2	4	14	27	.340	.345
Nevin,Phil	L	.306	36	11	1	0	2	5	3	8	.375	.500	Pagnozzi,Tom	L	.303	76	23	5	0	3	11	5	13	.346	.487
Bats Right	R	.286	84	24	4	0	6	14	5	31	.322	.548	Bats Right	R	.263	331	87	18	0	10	44	19	65	.303	.408
Newfield,Marc	L	.292	89	26	8	0	1	11	5	22	.323	.416	Palmeiro,O	L	.261	23	6	1	0	0	0	2	6	.320	.304
Bats Right	R	.274	281	77	18	0	11	46	22	48	.334	.456	Bats Left	R	.297	64	19	5	1	0	6	6	7	.375	.406
Newson,Warren	L	.167	24	4	1	0	0	2	7	13	.355	.208	Palmeiro,R	L	.295	244	72	19	0	14	56	28	31	.367	.545
Bats Left	R	.265	211	56	13	1	10	29	30	69	.355	.479	Bats Left	R	.285	382	109	21	2	25	86	67	65	.389	.547
Nieves,Melvin	L	.218	101	22	3	2	4	18	6	30	.266	.406	Palmer,Dean	L	.303	152	46	7	1	12	31	17	40	.382	.599
Bats Both	R	.255	330	84	20	2	20	42	38	128	.339	.509	Bats Right	R	.272	430	117	19	1	26	76	42	105	.336	.502
Nilsson,Dave	L	.238	105	25	3	0	1	12	7	26	.293	.295	Paquette,C	L	.312	141	44	6	0	7	21	17	32	.381	.504
Bats Left	R	.359	348	125	30	2	16	72	50	42	.440	.595	Bats Right	R	.233	288	67	9	1	15	46	6	69	.251	.427
Nixon,Otis	L	.298	151	45	5	1	0	12	17	15	.369	.344	Parent,Mark	L	.167	42	7	1	0	2	3	2	9	.205	.333
Bats Both	R	.281	345	97	10	0	1	17	54	53	.380	.319	Bats Right	R	.253	95	24	6	0	7	20	3	28	.273	.537
Nixon,Trot	L	.500	2	1	1	0	0	0	0	0	.500	1.000	Parker,Rick	L	.500	4	2	1	0	0	0	0	1	.600	.750
Bats Left	R	.500	2	1	0	0	0	0	0	1	.500	.500	Bats Right	R	.200	10	2	0	0	0	1	0	1	.200	.200
Norman,Les	L	.133	30	4	0	0	0	0	6	9	.297	.133	Peltier,Dan	L	.250	4	1	0	0	0	0	1	2	.400	.250
Bats Right	R	.105	19	2	0	0	0	0	0	5	.105	.105	Bats Left	R	.255	55	14	2	0	0	9	6	7	.323	.291
Norton,Greg	L	.200	5	1	0	0	1	1	0	2	.200	.800	Pemberton,R	L	.462	26	12	4	0	1	9	2	4	.517	.731
Bats Both	R	.222	18	4	0	0	1	2	4	4	.364	.389	Bats Right	R	.600	15	9	4	0	0	1	0	0	.625	.867
Nunnally,Jon	L	.143	7	1	0	0	0	0	4	2	.455	.143	Pena,Geronimo	L	.000	4	0	0	0	0	0	0	2	.000	.000
Bats Left	R	.217	83	18	5	1	5	17	9	23	.290	.482	Bats Both	R	.200	5	1	0	0	1	2	1	2	.333	.800
O'Brien,C	L	.236	123	29	6	0	4	14	15	20	.345	.382	Pena,Tony	L	.226	62	14	1	0	1	8	3	2	.262	.290
Bats Right	R	.239	201	48	11	0	9	30	14	48	.322	.428	Bats Right	R	.179	112	20	3	0	0	19	12	23	.252	.205
O'Leary,Troy	L	.198	106	21	3	2	0	15	12	24	.286	.264	Pendleton,T	L	.179	112	20	0	0	1	13	9	13	.246	.205
Bats Left	R	.276	391	108	25	3	15	66	35	56	.338	.471	Bats Both	R	.252	456	115	26	1	10	62	32	98	.301	.379
O'Neill,Paul	L	.239	197	47	9	0	7	34	32	36	.348	.391	Penn,Shannon	L	.000	2	0	0	0	0	0	0	0	.000	.000
Bats Left	R	.338	349	118	26	1	12	57	70	40	.445	.521	Bats Left	R	.083	12	1	0	0	0	1	0	3	.083	.083
Obando,S	L	.188	69	13	4	0	2	9	8	18	.269	.333	Perez,Danny	L	.000	3	0	0	0	0	0	0	0	.000	.000
Bats Right	R	.284	109	31	5	0	6	13	14	30	.371	.495	Bats Right	R	.000	1	0	0	0	0	0	0	0	.000	.000
Ochoa,Alex	L	.330	91	30	7	3	2	12	6	7	.367	.538	Perez,Eddie	L	.220	50	11	1	0	1	4	4	9	.273	.300
Bats Right	R	.277	191	53	12	0	2	21	11	23	.320	.372	Bats Right	R	.274	106	29	8	1	3	13	4	10	.304	.453
Offerman,Jose	L	.249	193	48	9	2	4	13	20	33	.318	.378	Perez,Eduardo	L	.231	26	6	0	0	2	4	4	7	.333	.462
Bats Both	R	.332	368	122	24	6	1	34	54	65	.417	.438	Bats Right	R	.200	10	2	0	0	1	1	1	2	.273	.500
Olerud,John	L	.219	64	14	1	0	1	6	6	10	.301	.281	Perez,Neifi	L	.250	4	1	1	0	0	1	0	1	.250	.500
Bats Left	R	.284	334	95	24	0	17	55	54	27	.396	.509	Bats Both	R	.146	41	6	1	0	0	2	0	7	.146	.171
Oliver,Joe	L	.236	110	26	3	0	4	15	9	19	.301	.373	Perez,Robert	L	.329	143	47	10	0	2	17	6	12	.353	.441
Bats Right	R	.246	179	44	9	1	7	31	19	35	.317	.425	Bats Right	R	.322	59	19	0	0	0	4	2	5	.355	.322
Ordonez,Rey	L	.258	120	31	2	1	0	10	3	8	.276	.292	Perez,Tomas	L	.245	94	23	6	2	1	11	9	10	.311	.383
Bats Right	R	.257	382	98	10	3	1	20	19	45	.293	.306	Bats Both	R	.254	201	51	7	2	0	8	16	19	.311	.308
Orsulak,Joe	L	.273	22	6	1	0	0	3	1	4	.304	.318	Perry,Herbert	L	.200	5	1	1	0	0	0	1	0	.333	.400
Bats Left	R	.215	195	42	5	1	2	16	15	34	.270	.282	Bats Right	R	.000	7	0	0	0	0	0	0	2	.000	.000
Ortiz,Luis	L	.400	5	2	0	1	1	1	0	1	.400	1.400	Petagine,R	L	.231	13	3	0	0	1	3	1	4	.313	.462
Bats Right	R	.000	2	0	0	0	0	0	0	0	.000	.000	Bats Left	R	.233	86	20	3	0	3	14	8	23	.313	.372
Osik,Keith	L	.261	23	6	4	0	0	4	6	3	.414	.435	Phillips,J.R.	L	.000	9	0	0	0	0	0	0	8	.100	.000
Bats Right	R	.299	117	35	10	1	1	10	8	19	.349	.427	Bats Left	R	.179	95	17	5	0	7	15	11	43	.264	.453
Otero,Ricky	L	.227	75	17	2	0	0	3	6	8	.284	.253	Phillips,Tony	L	.302	149	45	8	1	3	17	41	33	.456	.430
Bats Both	R	.283	336	95	9	7	2	29	28	22	.340	.369	Bats Both	R	.269	432	116	21	2	9	46	84	99	.384	.389

Batters vs. Left-Handed and Right-Handed Pitchers

Batter	vs	Avg	AB	H	2B	3B	HR	BI	BB	SO	OBP	SLG	Batter	vs	Avg	AB	H	2B	3B	HR	BI	BB	SO	OBP	SLG
Piazza,Mike	L	.409	93	38	3	0	6	19	13	16	.477	.634	Robertson,M	L	.500	2	1	1	0	0	0	0	1	.500	1.000
Bats Right	R	.322	454	146	13	0	30	86	68	77	.410	.548	Bats Left	R	.000	5	0	0	0	0	0	0	0	.000	.000
Pirkl,Greg	L	.176	17	3	1	0	1	1	0	3	.176	.412	Rodriguez,A	L	.371	143	53	13	1	9	35	22	19	.449	.664
Bats Right	R	.167	6	1	0	0	0	0	0	1	.167	.167	Bats Right	R	.354	458	162	41	0	27	88	37	85	.403	.620
Plantier,Phil	L	.130	23	3	0	0	0	0	3	13	.231	.130	Rodriguez,H	L	.218	110	24	7	1	7	24	5	37	.263	.491
Bats Left	R	.221	208	46	8	1	7	31	25	43	.312	.370	Bats Left	R	.291	422	123	35	0	29	79	32	123	.341	.581
Polonia,Luis	L	.526	19	10	1	0	1	3	1	1	.550	.737	Rodriguez,I	L	.311	190	59	13	1	10	36	17	14	.364	.547
Bats Left	R	.241	187	45	3	1	1	13	10	22	.281	.283	Bats Right	R	.296	449	133	34	2	9	50	21	41	.332	.441
Posada,Jorge	L	.200	5	1	0	0	0	0	0	2	.200	.200	Rodriguez,T	L	.294	17	5	0	0	0	1	1	2	.368	.294
Bats Both	R	.000	9	0	0	0	0	0	1	4	.100	.000	Bats Right	R	.220	50	11	1	0	1	8	3	6	.264	.300
Pozo,A	L	.167	24	4	2	0	1	5	0	3	.167	.375	Rolen,Scott	L	.333	24	8	3	0	0	2	5	4	.448	.458
Bats Right	R	.176	34	6	1	1	0	6	2	7	.237	.265	Bats Right	R	.236	106	25	4	0	4	16	8	23	.291	.387
Pride,Curtis	L	.250	12	3	0	0	0	2	0	3	.250	.250	Sabo,Chris	L	.296	71	21	5	1	2	11	13	10	.405	.479
Bats Left	R	.302	255	77	17	5	10	29	31	60	.378	.525	Bats Right	R	.204	54	11	2	0	1	5	5	17	.283	.296
Prince,Tom	L	.333	15	5	2	0	0	2	3	3	.450	.467	Salmon,Tim	L	.268	164	44	8	1	10	27	41	38	.418	.512
Bats Right	R	.286	49	14	4	0	1	9	3	12	.333	.429	Bats Right	R	.293	417	122	19	3	20	71	52	87	.372	.496
Pritchett,C	L	.200	5	1	0	0	0	0	0	3	.200	.200	Samuel,Juan	L	.277	137	38	4	3	7	22	11	43	.338	.504
Bats Left	R	.125	8	1	0	0	0	1	0	0	.125	.125	Bats Left	R	.196	51	10	4	0	1	4	4	22	.268	.333
Pulliam,H	L	.222	9	2	0	0	0	0	2	2	.364	.222	Sanchez,Rey	L	.196	51	10	3	0	0	2	2	7	.241	.255
Bats Right	R	.000	6	0	0	0	0	0	0	4	.000	.000	Bats Right	R	.214	238	51	6	0	1	10	20	35	.279	.252
Quinlan,Tom	L	.000	5	0	0	0	0	0	0	3	.000	.000	Sandberg,Ryne	L	.239	117	28	8	0	12	27	17	22	.338	.615
Bats Right	R	.000	1	0	0	0	0	0	0	0	.000	.000	Bats Right	R	.245	437	107	20	4	13	65	37	94	.310	.398
Raabe,Brian	L	.143	7	1	0	0	0	1	0	1	.125	.143	Sanders,R	L	.258	62	16	5	0	2	2	14	17	.395	.435
Bats Right	R	.500	2	1	0	0	0	0	0	0	.500	.500	Bats Right	R	.249	225	56	12	1	12	31	30	69	.341	.471
Raines,Tim	L	.256	39	10	1	0	0	5	10	7	.412	.282	Santangelo,F	L	.307	75	23	4	0	1	13	13	10	.424	.400
Bats Both	R	.290	162	47	9	0	9	28	24	22	.376	.512	Bats Both	R	.270	318	86	16	5	6	43	36	51	.355	.409
Ramirez,Manny	L	.322	149	48	17	0	7	24	23	20	.411	.577	Santiago,B	L	.333	72	24	3	0	6	14	8	12	.400	.625
Bats Right	R	.304	401	122	28	3	26	88	62	84	.394	.584	Bats Right	R	.252	409	103	18	2	24	71	41	92	.320	.482
Randa,Joe	L	.340	147	50	15	0	1	22	12	20	.385	.463	Scarsone,S	L	.303	66	20	4	0	1	5	8	16	.378	.409
Bats Right	R	.274	190	52	9	1	5	25	14	27	.324	.411	Bats Right	R	.194	217	42	8	1	4	18	17	75	.257	.295
Reboulet,Jeff	L	.233	86	20	3	0	0	6	9	9	.305	.267	Schall,Gene	L	.273	11	3	2	0	0	2	1	1	.385	.455
Bats Right	R	.216	148	32	6	0	0	17	16	25	.293	.257	Bats Right	R	.273	55	15	3	1	2	8	11	14	.394	.473
Reed,Jeff	L	.233	30	7	0	0	2	4	2	6	.303	.433	Schofield,D	L	.250	4	1	0	0	0	0	1	0	.400	.250
Bats Left	R	.289	311	90	20	1	6	33	41	59	.371	.418	Bats Right	R	.250	12	3	0	0	0	0	0	1	.250	.250
Reed,Jody	L	.212	118	25	3	0	0	9	18	10	.319	.237	Schu,Rick	L	.000	1	0	0	0	0	0	0	0	.000	.000
Bats Right	R	.255	377	96	17	0	2	40	41	43	.327	.316	Bats Right	R	.000	3	0	0	0	0	0	0	0	.000	.000
Relaford,Desi	L	.000	4	0	0	0	0	0	0	2	.000	.000	Sefcik,Kevin	L	.176	17	3	0	1	0	1	2	1	.263	.294
Bats Both	R	.194	36	7	2	0	0	1	3	7	.256	.250	Bats Right	R	.303	99	30	5	2	0	8	7	15	.355	.394
Renteria,E	L	.244	90	22	6	1	2	9	8	20	.300	.400	Segui,David	L	.300	110	33	7	0	4	25	12	22	.369	.473
Bats Right	R	.326	341	111	12	2	3	22	25	48	.374	.399	Bats Both	R	.281	306	86	23	1	7	33	48	32	.377	.431
Ripken,Billy	L	.227	66	15	3	0	0	4	1	7	.250	.273	Seitzer,Kevin	L	.368	174	64	14	1	3	21	23	22	.439	.511
Bats Right	R	.232	69	16	5	0	2	8	8	11	.308	.391	Bats Right	R	.308	399	123	21	2	10	57	64	57	.407	.446
Ripken,Cal	L	.288	191	55	12	0	7	23	18	14	.351	.461	Selby,Bill	L	.100	10	1	1	0	0	0	1	4	.182	.200
Bats Right	R	.274	449	123	28	1	19	79	41	64	.337	.468	Bats Left	R	.294	85	25	3	0	3	6	8	7	.355	.435
Rivera,Ruben	L	.280	25	7	2	0	2	6	7	9	.424	.600	Servais,Scott	L	.228	101	23	4	0	3	20	10	17	.302	.356
Bats Right	R	.286	63	18	4	1	0	10	6	17	.361	.381	Bats Right	R	.276	344	95	16	0	8	43	20	58	.334	.392
Roberson,K	L	.200	5	1	1	0	0	2	0	1	.167	.400	Sheaffer,D	L	.217	60	13	2	2	1	11	4	6	.266	.367
Bats Both	R	.226	31	7	0	0	3	7	7	16	.375	.516	Bats Right	R	.232	138	32	7	1	1	9	5	19	.274	.319
Roberts,Bip	L	.277	112	31	5	1	0	8	4	13	.297	.339	Sheets,Andy	L	.209	43	9	3	0	0	5	9	19	.352	.279
Bats Both	R	.286	227	65	16	1	0	44	21	25	.346	.366	Bats Right	R	.179	67	12	5	0	0	4	1	22	.191	.254

Batters vs. Left-Handed and Right-Handed Pitchers

Batter	vs	Avg	AB	H	2B	3B	HR	BI	BB	SO	OBP	SLG
Sheffield,G	L	.313	99	31	5	0	9	26	26	7	.460	.636
Bats Right	R	.314	420	132	28	1	33	94	116	59	.466	.621
Shipley,Craig	L	.250	24	6	2	0	0	1	0	2	.240	.333
Bats Right	R	.338	68	23	3	0	1	6	2	13	.370	.426
Shumpert,T	L	.294	17	5	1	0	1	2	1	6	.316	.529
Bats Right	R	.143	14	2	0	0	1	4	1	5	.250	.357
Siddall,Joe	L	.000	1	0	0	0	0	0	0	0	.000	.000
Bats Left	R	.152	46	7	1	0	0	3	2	8	.188	.174
Sierra,Ruben	L	.316	158	50	13	0	2	26	16	19	.367	.437
Bats Both	R	.217	360	78	13	2	10	46	44	64	.300	.347
Silvestri,D	L	.172	29	5	1	0	0	4	6	4	.314	.207
Bats Right	R	.211	133	28	3	0	1	13	28	37	.346	.256
Simms,Mike	L	.143	28	4	0	0	1	2	2	5	.200	.250
Bats Right	R	.200	40	8	2	1	0	6	2	11	.256	.300
Singleton,D	L	.000	2	0	0	0	0	0	0	0	.000	.000
Bats Left	R	.167	54	9	1	0	0	3	4	15	.237	.185
Slaught,Don	L	.359	103	37	5	0	3	15	8	5	.411	.495
Bats Right	R	.279	140	39	5	0	3	21	7	17	.313	.379
Smith,Dwight	L	.000	7	0	0	0	0	0	1	3	.125	.000
Bats Left	R	.212	146	31	5	0	3	16	16	39	.293	.308
Smith,Mark	L	.214	42	9	1	0	3	4	0	8	.214	.452
Bats Right	R	.278	36	10	1	0	1	6	3	12	.381	.389
Smith,Ozzie	L	.240	25	6	0	1	0	3	4	3	.345	.320
Bats Both	R	.287	202	58	10	1	2	15	21	6	.360	.376
Snopek,Chris	L	.313	80	25	6	1	6	18	4	9	.349	.638
Bats Right	R	.083	24	2	0	0	0	0	2	7	.154	.083
Snow,J.T.	L	.199	186	37	3	1	3	17	11	38	.249	.274
Bats Both	R	.285	389	111	17	0	14	50	45	58	.363	.437
Sojo,Luis	L	.202	109	22	6	0	1	11	7	5	.250	.284
Bats Right	R	.230	178	41	4	1	0	10	4	12	.250	.264
Sorrento,Paul	L	.167	60	10	4	1	2	11	2	20	.242	.367
Bats Left	R	.307	411	126	28	0	21	82	55	83	.388	.528
Sosa,Sammy	L	.248	113	28	7	0	8	19	11	26	.312	.522
Bats Right	R	.281	385	108	14	2	32	81	23	108	.327	.577
Spehr,Tim	L	.000	13	0	0	0	0	0	0	4	.071	.000
Bats Right	R	.129	31	4	1	0	1	3	3	11	.206	.258
Spiers,Bill	L	.059	17	1	0	0	0	0	2	1	.200	.059
Bats Left	R	.269	201	54	10	1	6	26	18	33	.330	.418
Spiezio,Scott	L	.143	14	2	0	0	0	0	0	3	.143	.143
Bats Both	R	.467	15	7	2	0	2	8	4	1	.579	1.000
Sprague,Ed	L	.310	155	48	10	0	14	38	19	20	.385	.645
Bats Right	R	.225	436	98	25	2	22	63	41	126	.303	.443
Stahoviak,S	L	.276	29	8	1	0	1	3	7	12	.432	.414
Bats Left	R	.285	376	107	29	3	12	58	52	102	.371	.473
Stairs,Matt	L	.222	9	2	0	0	0	3	2	1	.417	.222
Bats Left	R	.281	128	36	5	1	10	20	17	22	.363	.570
Stankiewicz,A	L	.526	19	10	2	1	0	6	2	1	.591	.737
Bats Right	R	.207	58	12	3	0	0	3	4	11	.277	.259
Stanley,Mike	L	.302	106	32	5	0	10	26	23	20	.435	.632
Bats Right	R	.258	291	75	15	1	14	43	46	42	.363	.460
Steinbach,T	L	.292	120	35	3	1	9	15	14	25	.370	.558
Bats Right	R	.266	394	105	22	0	26	85	35	90	.333	.520
Stevens,Lee	L	.136	22	3	0	0	0	3	3	7	.240	.136
Bats Left	R	.268	56	15	2	3	3	9	3	15	.311	.571
Steverson,T	L	.000	0	0	0	0	0	0	0	0	.000	.000
Bats Right	R	.000	1	0	0	0	0	0	0	1	.000	.000
Stewart,S	L	.333	6	2	1	0	0	1	1	2	.429	.500
Bats Right	R	.091	11	1	0	0	0	1	0	2	.091	.091
Stillwell,K	L	.200	10	2	2	0	0	1	2	2	.333	.400
Bats Both	R	.284	67	19	2	0	1	3	8	9	.368	.358
Stinnett,K	L	.133	15	2	0	0	0	0	2	7	.278	.133
Bats Right	R	.000	11	0	0	0	0	0	0	4	.000	.000
Stocker,Kevin	L	.283	60	17	4	1	0	4	6	14	.353	.383
Bats Both	R	.249	334	83	18	5	5	37	37	75	.333	.377
Strange,Doug	L	.143	14	2	0	0	0	0	0	0	.143	.143
Bats Both	R	.243	169	41	7	1	3	23	14	31	.301	.349
Strawberry,D	L	.208	53	11	3	0	4	9	9	15	.323	.491
Bats Left	R	.282	149	42	10	0	7	27	22	40	.371	.490
Stynes,Chris	L	.310	58	18	2	0	0	5	2	3	.333	.345
Bats Right	R	.265	34	9	4	0	0	1	0	2	.265	.382
Surhoff,B.J.	L	.290	162	47	12	0	3	21	12	16	.348	.420
Bats Left	R	.293	375	110	15	6	18	61	35	63	.354	.509
Sveum,Dale	L	.000	3	0	0	0	0	0	0	3	.000	.000
Bats Both	R	.387	31	12	5	0	1	5	6	3	.486	.645
Sweeney,Mark	L	.375	16	6	1	0	0	3	0	3	.375	.438
Bats Left	R	.253	154	39	8	0	3	19	33	26	.388	.364
Sweeney,Mike	L	.245	49	12	2	0	1	7	7	10	.362	.347
Bats Right	R	.293	116	34	8	0	3	17	11	11	.356	.440
Tarasco,Tony	L	.417	12	5	0	0	0	3	0	1	.417	.417
Bats Left	R	.208	72	15	3	0	1	6	7	14	.278	.292
Tartabull,D	L	.271	133	36	7	1	4	27	29	33	.401	.429
Bats Right	R	.248	339	84	16	2	23	74	35	95	.314	.510
Tatum,Jimmy	L	.000	7	0	0	0	0	0	0	3	.000	.000
Bats Right	R	.250	4	1	0	0	0	0	0	0	.250	.250
Taubensee,E	L	.333	48	16	5	0	2	10	4	9	.377	.563
Bats Left	R	.283	279	79	15	0	10	38	22	55	.331	.444
Tavarez,Jesus	L	.235	34	8	1	0	0	1	3	2	.297	.265
Bats Both	R	.213	80	17	2	0	0	5	4	16	.250	.238
Tettleton,M	L	.245	155	38	14	0	6	21	33	41	.370	.452
Bats Both	R	.247	336	83	12	1	18	62	62	96	.365	.449
Thomas,Frank	L	.403	119	48	8	0	13	37	37	16	.544	.798
Bats Right	R	.333	408	136	18	0	27	97	72	54	.432	.576
Thome,Jim	L	.250	160	40	8	0	7	30	24	51	.355	.431
Bats Left	R	.339	345	117	20	5	31	86	99	90	.489	.696
Thompson,J	L	.000	3	0	0	0	0	0	0	2	.000	.000
Bats Left	R	.239	46	11	4	0	2	6	1	12	.250	.457
Thompson,Milt	L	.000	0	0	0	0	0	0	0	0	.000	.000
Bats Left	R	.106	66	7	2	0	0	3	7	13	.192	.136
Thompson,R	L	.259	54	14	6	0	2	5	4	20	.310	.481
Bats Right	R	.197	173	34	5	1	3	16	20	49	.298	.289

Batters vs. Left-Handed and Right-Handed Pitchers

Batter	vs	Avg	AB	H	2B	3B	HR	BI	BB	SO	OBP	SLG
Thompson,Ryan	L	.375	8	3	0	0	1	5	0	1	.375	.750
Bats Right	R	.286	14	4	0	0	0	0	1	5	.333	.286
Timmons,Ozzie	L	.211	76	16	4	0	3	8	11	13	.310	.382
Bats Right	R	.188	64	12	0	0	4	8	4	17	.246	.375
Tinsley,Lee	L	.175	63	11	1	0	0	4	3	20	.221	.190
Bats Both	R	.238	181	43	5	1	3	12	14	58	.296	.326
Tomberlin,A	L	.000	0	0	0	0	0	0	0	0	.000	.000
Bats Left	R	.258	66	17	4	0	3	10	9	27	.355	.455
Trammell,Alan	L	.327	49	16	1	0	0	2	0	3	.327	.347
Bats Right	R	.201	144	29	1	0	1	14	10	24	.248	.229
Tucker,M	L	.236	72	17	2	1	5	13	6	12	.313	.500
Bats Left	R	.266	267	71	16	3	7	40	34	57	.355	.427
Turner,Chris	L	.000	1	0	0	0	0	1	1	0	.333	.000
Bats Right	R	.500	2	1	0	0	0	0	0	0	.500	.500
Unroe,Tim	L	.333	3	1	0	0	0	0	1	0	.500	.333
Bats Right	R	.154	13	2	0	0	0	0	3	5	.313	.154
Valdes,Pedro	L	.000	1	0	0	0	0	0	0	1	.000	.000
Bats Left	R	.143	7	1	1	0	0	1	1	4	.250	.286
Valentin,John	L	.380	129	49	9	3	1	14	23	13	.481	.519
Bats Right	R	.269	398	107	20	0	12	45	40	46	.337	.410
Valentin,Jose	L	.248	121	30	3	2	2	18	14	40	.324	.355
Bats Both	R	.262	431	113	30	5	22	77	52	105	.340	.508
Valle,Dave	L	.500	22	11	1	1	2	10	2	2	.542	.909
Bats Right	R	.234	64	15	5	0	1	7	7	15	.310	.359
Vander Wal,J	L	.200	10	2	0	0	0	2	1	3	.273	.200
Bats Left	R	.255	141	36	6	2	5	29	18	35	.340	.433
Vaughn,Greg	L	.230	139	32	3	1	10	26	27	27	.357	.482
Bats Right	R	.271	377	102	16	0	31	91	55	103	.367	.560
Vaughn,Mo	L	.315	200	63	7	1	10	45	29	56	.414	.510
Bats Left	R	.331	435	144	22	0	34	98	66	98	.423	.616
Velarde,Randy	L	.283	152	43	11	1	3	18	28	30	.393	.428
Bats Right	R	.286	378	108	16	2	11	36	42	88	.363	.426
Ventura,Robin	L	.265	185	49	8	2	14	39	19	31	.332	.557
Bats Left	R	.297	401	119	23	0	20	66	59	50	.384	.504
Veras,Quilvio	L	.309	55	17	2	0	1	3	9	8	.415	.400
Bats Both	R	.237	198	47	6	1	3	11	42	34	.372	.323
Vina,Fernando	L	.218	110	24	3	0	0	8	8	11	.285	.245
Bats Left	R	.300	444	133	16	10	7	38	30	24	.356	.428
Vitiello,Joe	L	.257	109	28	7	0	4	21	20	34	.371	.431
Bats Right	R	.230	148	34	8	1	4	19	18	35	.320	.378
Vizcaino,Jose	L	.294	153	45	3	0	0	11	4	23	.316	.314
Bats Both	R	.298	389	116	14	8	1	34	31	59	.351	.383
Vizquel,Omar	L	.274	168	46	12	0	4	22	16	12	.342	.417
Bats Both	R	.307	374	115	24	1	5	42	40	30	.371	.417
Voigt,Jack	L	.000	5	0	0	0	0	0	0	1	.000	.000
Bats Right	R	.250	4	1	0	0	0	0	0	1	.250	.250
Walbeck,Matt	L	.284	74	21	4	0	1	10	2	7	.303	.378
Bats Both	R	.191	141	27	6	0	1	14	7	27	.227	.255
Walker,Larry	L	.280	75	21	5	2	5	15	3	14	.349	.600
Bats Left	R	.274	197	54	13	2	13	43	17	44	.339	.558

Batter	vs	Avg	AB	H	2B	3B	HR	BI	BB	SO	OBP	SLG
Walker,Todd	L	.188	16	3	0	0	0	0	0	3	.188	.188
Bats Left	R	.273	66	18	6	0	0	6	4	10	.301	.364
Wallach,Tim	L	.240	121	29	7	0	4	15	9	26	.292	.397
Bats Right	R	.229	231	53	3	1	8	27	21	53	.299	.355
Walton,Jerome	L	.440	25	11	4	0	0	2	3	3	.483	.600
Bats Right	R	.227	22	5	1	0	1	2	2	7	.280	.409
Ward,Turner	L	.071	14	1	1	0	0	2	3	4	.235	.143
Bats Both	R	.208	53	11	1	1	2	8	10	13	.328	.377
Webster,Lenny	L	.237	59	14	5	0	1	4	15	5	.400	.373
Bats Right	R	.226	115	26	5	0	1	13	10	16	.291	.296
Wehner,John	L	.282	85	24	4	1	2	12	6	12	.330	.424
Bats Right	R	.222	54	12	5	0	0	1	2	10	.250	.315
Weiss,Walt	L	.277	141	39	6	0	0	10	24	22	.381	.319
Bats Right	R	.285	376	107	14	2	8	38	56	56	.381	.396
White,Devon	L	.345	119	41	12	0	6	33	7	17	.389	.597
Bats Both	R	.254	433	110	25	6	11	51	31	82	.307	.416
White,Rondell	L	.379	95	36	8	3	0	13	3	11	.404	.526
Bats Right	R	.259	239	62	11	1	6	28	19	42	.315	.389
Whiten,Mark	L	.245	94	23	6	0	6	20	15	23	.366	.500
Bats Both	R	.267	318	85	14	1	16	51	55	104	.374	.469
Widger,Chris	L	.000	3	0	0	0	0	0	0	0	.000	.000
Bats Right	R	.250	8	2	0	0	0	0	0	5	.333	.250
Wilkins,Rick	L	.172	64	11	2	0	3	9	4	25	.225	.344
Bats Left	R	.256	347	89	16	2	11	50	63	96	.364	.409
Williams,B	L	.376	173	65	7	0	16	39	24	24	.447	.694
Bats Both	R	.272	378	103	19	7	13	63	58	48	.365	.463
Williams,E	L	.183	82	15	1	0	1	8	9	20	.264	.232
Bats Right	R	.211	133	28	4	0	5	18	9	30	.269	.353
Williams,George	L	.176	34	6	2	0	0	2	7	5	.317	.235
Bats Both	R	.143	98	14	3	0	3	8	21	27	.309	.265
Williams,Gerald	L	.290	124	36	9	1	4	14	9	18	.336	.476
Bats Right	R	.229	201	46	10	3	1	20	10	39	.276	.323
Williams,K	L	.250	8	2	0	0	0	0	0	3	.250	.250
Bats Right	R	.250	12	3	0	0	0	0	0	3	.250	.250
Williams,Matt	L	.233	90	21	3	0	7	21	14	22	.333	.500
Bats Right	R	.322	314	101	13	1	15	64	25	69	.377	.513
Wilson,Dan	L	.258	128	33	6	0	4	25	8	21	.297	.398
Bats Right	R	.295	363	107	18	0	14	58	24	67	.341	.460
Wilson,Desi	L	.500	6	3	0	0	0	1	1	2	.571	.500
Bats Left	R	.259	112	29	2	0	2	11	11	25	.325	.330
Wilson,Nigel	L	.000	0	0	0	0	0	0	0	0	.000	.000
Bats Left	R	.250	12	3	0	0	2	5	1	6	.308	.750
Womack,Tony	L	.000	0	0	0	0	0	0	0	0	.000	.000
Bats Left	R	.333	30	10	3	1	0	7	6	1	.459	.500
Worthington,C	L	.200	10	2	0	0	0	1	3	1	.385	.200
Bats Right	R	.111	9	1	0	0	1	3	3	2	.286	.444
Young,Dmitri	L	.200	10	2	0	0	0	1	0	2	.273	.200
Bats Both	R	.263	19	5	0	0	0	1	4	3	.391	.263
Young,Eric	L	.286	140	40	10	0	3	13	15	8	.375	.421
Bats Right	R	.336	428	144	13	4	5	61	32	23	.399	.421

Batters vs. Left-Handed and Right-Handed Pitchers

Batter	vs	Avg	AB	H	2B	3B	HR	BI	BB	SO	OBP	SLG
Young,Ernie	L	.276	127	35	5	1	6	16	15	32	.361	.472
Bats Right	R	.230	335	77	14	3	13	48	37	86	.312	.406
Young,Kevin	L	.322	87	28	6	0	7	20	10	14	.392	.632
Bats Right	R	.089	45	4	0	0	1	3	1	18	.109	.156
Zaun,Greg	L	.269	26	7	1	0	1	4	4	5	.367	.423
Bats Both	R	.239	113	27	8	1	1	11	10	15	.307	.354
Zeile,Todd	L	.280	118	33	7	0	6	20	20	11	.376	.492
Bats Right	R	.259	499	129	25	0	19	79	62	93	.341	.423
Zuber,Jon	L	.200	5	1	0	0	0	1	2	2	.429	.200
Bats Left	R	.256	86	22	4	0	1	9	4	9	.286	.337
AL	L	.277	--	--	--	--	--	--	--	--	.352	.439
	R	.277	--	--	--	--	--	--	--	--	.350	.447
NL	L	.264	--	--	--	--	--	--	--	--	.330	.411
	R	.262	--	--	--	--	--	--	--	--	.330	.407
MLB	L	.271	--	--	--	--	--	--	--	--	.343	.427
	R	.269	--	--	--	--	--	--	--	--	.340	.427

Pitchers vs. Left-Handed and Right-Handed Batters

Pitcher	vs	Avg	AB	H	2B	3B	HR	BI	BB	SO	OBP	SLG	Pitcher	vs	Avg	AB	H	2B	3B	HR	BI	BB	SO	OBP	SLG
Abbott,Jim	L	.336	119	40	10	1	10	32	13	11	.393	.689	Barton,Shawn	L	.400	10	4	0	0	0	2	0	0	.400	.400
Throws Left	R	.298	439	131	26	2	13	79	65	47	.388	.456	Throws Left	R	.455	33	15	1	0	2	9	1	3	.471	.667
Abbott,Kyle	L	.500	10	5	2	0	0	2	2	3	.583	.700	Batchelor,R	L	.238	21	5	2	0	0	2	1	6	.273	.333
Throws Left	R	.500	10	5	0	1	1	6	3	0	.615	1.000	Throws Right	R	.129	31	4	0	0	0	0	0	5	.129	.129
Acre,Mark	L	.353	51	18	2	2	1	10	7	10	.431	.529	Batista,M	L	.267	15	4	1	0	0	1	5	1	.450	.333
Throws Right	R	.328	61	20	6	0	3	11	2	8	.369	.574	Throws Right	R	.208	24	5	1	0	0	2	2	5	.269	.250
Adams,Terry	L	.234	145	34	4	1	3	12	14	21	.300	.338	Bautista,Jose	L	.287	115	33	6	1	6	21	11	14	.346	.513
Throws Right	R	.229	218	50	9	1	3	24	35	57	.336	.321	Throws Right	R	.220	150	33	6	0	4	19	4	14	.247	.340
Adams,Willie	L	.231	173	40	3	0	7	18	16	42	.293	.370	Beck,Rod	L	.219	105	23	6	1	4	16	3	23	.236	.410
Throws Right	R	.293	123	36	4	2	4	15	7	26	.356	.455	Throws Right	R	.254	130	33	6	0	5	16	7	25	.297	.415
Adamson,Joel	L	.231	13	3	0	0	0	1	2	1	.353	.231	Beckett,R	L	.429	7	3	0	0	1	4	3	1	.600	.857
Throws Left	R	.469	32	15	3	2	1	7	5	6	.541	.781	Throws Left	R	.214	14	3	0	0	2	6	6	5	.429	.643
Aguilera,Rick	L	.288	243	70	19	1	10	36	10	48	.319	.498	Beech,Matt	L	.250	28	7	1	0	1	2	1	6	.323	.393
Throws Right	R	.261	207	54	15	1	10	27	17	35	.319	.488	Throws Left	R	.318	132	42	8	1	7	28	10	27	.356	.553
Alberro,Jose	L	.222	18	4	2	0	1	4	6	1	.417	.500	Belcher,Tim	L	.288	510	147	22	4	12	56	41	54	.343	.418
Throws Right	R	.500	20	10	1	1	0	5	1	1	.500	.650	Throws Right	R	.273	421	115	22	4	16	52	27	59	.316	.458
Aldred,Scott	L	.325	151	49	15	1	7	30	14	23	.382	.576	Belinda,Stan	L	.276	58	16	4	0	1	10	10	10	.391	.397
Throws Left	R	.285	509	145	29	1	22	83	54	88	.356	.475	Throws Right	R	.268	56	15	3	0	2	11	10	8	.406	.429
Alston,Garvin	L	.400	10	4	2	0	0	2	1	1	.417	.600	Benes,Alan	L	.316	313	99	13	5	12	54	45	45	.402	.505
Throws Right	R	.357	14	5	0	1	1	5	2	4	.444	.714	Throws Right	R	.227	409	93	16	1	15	56	42	86	.303	.381
Alvarez,Tavo	L	.263	38	10	2	0	0	6	6	4	.364	.316	Benes,Andy	L	.269	368	99	19	1	11	45	43	43	.346	.416
Throws Right	R	.209	43	9	1	0	0	3	6	5	.320	.233	Throws Right	R	.230	504	116	19	2	17	53	34	117	.283	.377
Alvarez,W	L	.303	145	44	10	1	1	9	10	26	.350	.407	Benitez,A	L	.133	15	2	1	0	0	0	4	7	.316	.200
Throws Left	R	.248	693	172	49	1	20	86	87	155	.334	.408	Throws Right	R	.147	34	5	0	0	4	2	2	13	.189	.324
Anderson,B	L	.231	39	9	1	0	3	8	4	3	.302	.487	Bennett,Erik	L	.341	44	15	6	0	5	13	6	4	.420	.818
Throws Left	R	.312	157	49	12	2	6	20	10	18	.347	.529	Throws Right	R	.281	64	18	2	0	2	10	10	9	.390	.406
Andujar,Luis	L	.288	80	23	4	1	4	15	11	7	.370	.513	Bere,Jason	L	.341	44	15	2	1	1	10	10	13	.455	.500
Throws Right	R	.338	68	23	4	1	4	10	5	4	.377	.603	Throws Right	R	.379	29	11	3	0	2	8	8	6	.514	.690
Appier,Kevin	L	.260	427	111	23	2	11	41	55	114	.348	.400	Bergman,Sean	L	.289	180	52	7	3	5	24	22	37	.363	.444
Throws Right	R	.228	356	81	14	3	6	35	20	93	.269	.334	Throws Right	R	.263	255	67	11	1	9	35	11	48	.296	.420
Ashby,Andy	L	.278	252	70	12	1	6	20	21	34	.332	.405	Bertotti,Mike	L	.243	37	9	2	0	2	7	6	4	.341	.459
Throws Right	R	.244	315	77	10	0	11	33	13	51	.280	.381	Throws Left	R	.264	72	19	4	0	3	12	14	15	.384	.444
Assenmacher,P	L	.256	86	22	5	0	0	10	4	23	.293	.314	Berumen,A	L	.333	3	1	0	0	1	2	1	1	.500	1.333
Throws Left	R	.264	91	24	7	0	1	10	10	21	.352	.374	Throws Right	R	.200	10	2	1	0	0	0	1	3	.333	.300
Astacio,Pedro	L	.274	336	92	19	3	8	30	29	37	.330	.420	Bevil,Brian	L	.313	16	5	1	2	1	4	2	3	.368	.813
Throws Right	R	.252	457	115	15	2	10	42	38	93	.320	.359	Throws Right	R	.182	22	4	1	0	1	3	3	4	.280	.364
Aucoin,Derek	L	.000	5	0	0	0	0	0	1	1	.167	.000	Bielecki,Mike	L	.250	124	31	4	1	3	10	8	22	.293	.371
Throws Right	R	.600	5	3	0	0	0	1	0	0	.600	.600	Throws Right	R	.204	157	32	2	0	5	15	25	49	.310	.312
Avery,Steve	L	.256	90	23	4	0	0	11	6	18	.299	.300	Blair,Willie	L	.231	130	30	3	0	6	24	13	20	.293	.392
Throws Left	R	.291	423	123	22	2	10	48	34	68	.348	.423	Throws Right	R	.245	204	50	7	0	7	28	16	47	.323	.382
Ayala,Bobby	L	.304	135	41	7	1	7	27	10	33	.347	.526	Blazier,Ron	L	.241	54	13	4	0	2	7	4	7	.288	.426
Throws Right	R	.202	119	24	4	0	3	18	15	28	.301	.311	Throws Right	R	.346	104	36	5	1	4	17	6	18	.378	.529
Bailey,Cory	L	.224	76	17	3	0	1	5	16	13	.366	.303	Bluma,Jaime	L	.324	34	11	1	0	1	4	3	6	.378	.441
Throws Right	R	.284	141	40	6	0	0	14	14	25	.346	.326	Throws Right	R	.179	39	7	3	0	1	3	1	8	.233	.333
Bailey,Roger	L	.315	143	45	10	3	4	29	33	18	.439	.510	Bochtler,Doug	L	.189	111	21	2	2	1	10	23	24	.326	.270
Throws Right	R	.268	183	49	11	0	3	24	19	27	.335	.377	Throws Right	R	.200	120	24	4	0	5	18	16	44	.297	.358
Baldwin,James	L	.266	353	94	13	2	11	33	35	70	.332	.408	Boehringer,B	L	.256	86	22	8	0	4	15	13	14	.347	.488
Throws Right	R	.246	301	74	13	3	13	43	22	57	.305	.439	Throws Right	R	.264	91	24	8	1	2	14	8	23	.327	.440
Barber,Brian	L	.250	8	2	0	0	0	3	3	1	.429	.250	Boever,Joe	L	.385	26	10	0	0	1	6	3	1	.467	.500
Throws Right	R	.667	3	2	1	0	0	2	3	0	.833	1.000	Throws Right	R	.212	33	7	0	0	1	6	3	5	.278	.303

Pitchers vs. Left-Handed and Right-Handed Batters

Pitcher	vs	Avg	AB	H	2B	3B	HR	BI	BB	SO	OBP	SLG
Bohanon,Brian	L	.296	27	8	1	0	0	5	3	6	.406	.333
Throws Left	R	.306	62	19	5	0	4	21	16	11	.438	.581
Bones,Ricky	L	.330	330	109	21	0	20	47	33	24	.402	.576
Throws Right	R	.267	281	75	16	3	10	46	35	39	.350	.452
Borbon,Pedro	L	.150	40	6	0	2	0	3	2	16	.190	.250
Throws Left	R	.227	88	20	3	1	1	7	5	15	.277	.318
Borland,Toby	L	.284	134	38	4	0	3	17	11	25	.338	.381
Throws Right	R	.210	214	45	10	2	6	32	32	51	.320	.360
Borowski,Joe	L	.333	33	11	3	0	1	4	7	4	.450	.515
Throws Right	R	.319	69	22	4	0	3	13	6	11	.382	.507
Bosio,Chris	L	.297	118	35	7	2	3	23	17	15	.383	.466
Throws Right	R	.301	123	37	5	0	5	18	7	24	.343	.463
Boskie,Shawn	L	.251	390	98	16	1	20	49	43	77	.327	.451
Throws Right	R	.338	379	128	27	0	20	61	24	56	.392	.567
Bottalico,R	L	.217	92	20	4	1	3	12	12	27	.318	.380
Throws Right	R	.185	146	27	7	1	3	15	11	47	.241	.308
Bottenfield,K	L	.292	89	26	5	1	0	4	6	12	.337	.371
Throws Right	R	.232	142	33	7	1	3	17	13	21	.310	.359
Bourgeois,S	L	.310	71	22	5	0	2	10	10	6	.390	.465
Throws Right	R	.388	98	38	7	1	2	20	11	11	.465	.541
Boze,Marshall	L	.311	61	19	4	0	1	10	13	9	.432	.426
Throws Right	R	.406	69	28	3	0	4	21	12	10	.523	.623
Brandenburg,M	L	.286	126	36	10	2	3	21	15	28	.361	.468
Throws Right	R	.237	169	40	5	0	5	28	18	38	.314	.355
Brantley,Jeff	L	.248	121	30	3	0	2	5	19	33	.345	.322
Throws Right	R	.185	130	24	4	0	5	18	9	43	.232	.331
Brewer,Billy	L	.250	8	2	2	0	0	0	3	3	.455	.500
Throws Left	R	.313	16	5	3	0	0	4	5	5	.476	.500
Briscoe,John	L	.162	37	6	2	0	0	3	13	6	.373	.216
Throws Right	R	.235	51	12	2	0	2	8	11	8	.365	.392
Brocail,Doug	L	.354	79	28	7	0	4	12	10	9	.422	.595
Throws Right	R	.246	122	30	5	0	3	18	13	25	.326	.361
Brow,Scott	L	.288	80	23	4	0	4	15	12	12	.376	.488
Throws Right	R	.301	73	22	5	0	1	13	13	11	.407	.411
Brown,Kevin	L	.221	408	90	10	3	3	19	18	68	.260	.282
Throws Right	R	.220	441	97	12	3	5	31	15	91	.263	.295
Bruske,Jim	L	.300	20	6	0	0	1	3	1	5	.333	.450
Throws Right	R	.324	34	11	2	0	1	5	2	7	.378	.471
Bullinger,Jim	L	.270	222	60	13	2	6	35	27	38	.355	.428
Throws Right	R	.293	287	84	13	0	9	46	41	52	.386	.432
Burba,Dave	L	.255	314	80	21	2	8	32	47	49	.350	.411
Throws Right	R	.236	419	99	17	2	10	49	50	99	.314	.358
Burke,John	L	.370	27	10	2	0	0	5	3	6	.438	.444
Throws Right	R	.282	39	11	3	1	3	14	4	13	.349	.641
Burkett,John	L	.254	406	103	23	3	7	50	33	74	.311	.377
Throws Right	R	.282	447	126	25	1	12	57	25	81	.322	.423
Burrows,Terry	L	.333	15	5	0	1	1	3	2	1	.412	.667
Throws Left	R	.226	31	7	1	0	1	3	8	4	.400	.355
Busby,Mike	L	.462	13	6	1	1	2	6	2	2	.533	1.154
Throws Right	R	.333	9	3	1	0	2	6	2	2	.500	1.111

Pitcher	vs	Avg	AB	H	2B	3B	HR	BI	BB	SO	OBP	SLG
Byrd,Paul	L	.274	73	20	3	0	2	8	14	12	.391	.397
Throws Right	R	.259	108	28	6	1	5	21	7	19	.302	.472
Campbell,Mike	L	.220	50	11	6	1	1	4	4	5	.273	.440
Throws Right	R	.214	84	18	1	2	6	12	6	14	.267	.488
Candiotti,Tom	L	.268	272	73	9	0	10	37	22	32	.320	.412
Throws Right	R	.304	326	99	20	1	8	44	21	47	.349	.445
Carlson,Dan	L	.375	16	6	1	0	1	2	2	1	.444	.625
Throws Right	R	.269	26	7	1	0	1	3	0	3	.250	.423
Carmona,R	L	.335	158	53	9	0	7	22	29	30	.445	.525
Throws Right	R	.221	190	42	9	0	4	26	26	32	.313	.332
Carpenter,C	L	.308	13	4	1	0	1	3	0	0	.308	.615
Throws Right	R	.348	23	8	0	1	0	6	2	2	.385	.435
Carrara,G	L	.338	65	22	6	0	3	12	11	9	.434	.569
Throws Right	R	.337	95	32	6	1	8	20	14	14	.432	.674
Carrasco,H	L	.257	113	29	3	2	5	22	15	19	.341	.451
Throws Right	R	.184	158	29	3	1	1	13	30	40	.313	.234
Casian,Larry	L	.195	41	8	3	1	2	9	5	9	.292	.463
Throws Left	R	.176	34	6	1	0	0	2	6	6	.300	.206
Castillo,F	L	.265	291	77	14	1	8	29	27	65	.330	.402
Throws Right	R	.303	435	132	31	1	20	70	19	74	.338	.517
Castillo,Tony	L	.307	114	35	8	3	1	17	4	11	.339	.456
Throws Left	R	.241	249	60	8	1	9	35	20	46	.296	.390
Charlton,Norm	L	.187	75	14	2	1	0	7	10	16	.284	.240
Throws Left	R	.265	204	54	11	1	7	32	28	57	.353	.431
Chouinard,B	L	.241	116	28	7	0	1	13	20	17	.350	.328
Throws Right	R	.388	121	47	10	0	9	23	12	15	.449	.694
Christiansen,J	L	.264	53	14	3	1	3	11	6	16	.344	.528
Throws Left	R	.331	127	42	8	0	4	24	13	22	.387	.488
Christopher,M	L	.377	61	23	5	0	4	18	6	5	.414	.656
Throws Right	R	.329	73	24	6	3	8	19	5	14	.367	.822
Clark,Mark	L	.277	368	102	17	2	10	43	24	55	.324	.416
Throws Right	R	.254	452	115	24	2	10	36	24	87	.292	.383
Clark,Terry	L	.357	42	15	4	2	2	8	3	8	.400	.690
Throws Right	R	.403	72	29	6	0	2	14	6	9	.456	.569
Clemens,Roger	L	.236	513	121	23	5	10	59	74	146	.333	.359
Throws Right	R	.239	398	95	16	2	9	35	32	111	.296	.357
Clontz,Brad	L	.363	80	29	8	0	6	14	17	8	.465	.688
Throws Right	R	.217	226	49	6	1	5	39	16	41	.272	.319
Cone,David	L	.197	147	29	8	0	1	10	26	41	.318	.272
Throws Right	R	.198	106	21	4	0	2	11	8	30	.252	.292
Cook,Dennis	L	.206	107	22	7	2	1	22	11	37	.290	.336
Throws Left	R	.220	141	31	7	0	1	15	24	27	.345	.291
Cooke,Steve	L	.636	11	7	5	0	1	7	0	3	.636	1.364
Throws Left	R	.167	24	4	0	1	0	2	5	4	.300	.250
Coppinger,R	L	.323	220	71	12	1	14	40	38	33	.419	.577
Throws Right	R	.212	259	55	10	1	11	29	22	71	.276	.386
Corbin,Archie	L	.256	39	10	4	0	1	6	6	7	.370	.436
Throws Right	R	.200	60	12	1	0	1	7	16	13	.364	.267
Cordova,F	L	.362	149	54	13	1	4	27	10	13	.406	.544
Throws Right	R	.202	242	49	7	0	7	23	10	82	.237	.318

Pitchers vs. Left-Handed and Right-Handed Batters

Pitcher	vs	Avg	AB	H	2B	3B	HR	BI	BB	SO	OBP	SLG	Pitcher	vs	Avg	AB	H	2B	3B	HR	BI	BB	SO	OBP	SLG
Cormier,Rheal	L	.269	108	29	1	2	2	12	1	19	.288	.370	Eichhorn,Mark	L	.348	46	16	4	0	0	7	6	7	.423	.435
Throws Left	R	.270	504	136	24	3	14	54	40	81	.327	.413	Throws Right	R	.282	71	20	3	0	3	25	5	17	.338	.451
Corsi,Jim	L	.327	113	37	9	0	3	21	11	14	.398	.487	Eischen,Joey	L	.288	80	23	3	1	2	11	8	16	.374	.425
Throws Right	R	.227	150	34	5	0	3	15	23	29	.328	.320	Throws Left	R	.281	185	52	12	1	5	34	26	35	.369	.438
Crabtree,Tim	L	.227	119	27	7	0	1	13	11	29	.298	.311	Eldred,Cal	L	.305	164	50	11	0	5	19	24	21	.399	.463
Throws Right	R	.235	136	32	5	1	3	19	11	28	.298	.353	Throws Right	R	.209	153	32	8	1	3	20	14	29	.276	.333
Crawford,C	L	.250	4	1	0	0	0	0	1	2	.400	.250	Ellis,Robert	L	.000	7	0	0	0	0	0	1	3	.125	.000
Throws Right	R	.429	14	6	1	0	1	6	1	2	.500	.714	Throws Right	R	.000	8	0	0	0	0	0	3	2	.273	.000
Creek,Doug	L	.250	80	20	5	1	4	14	10	18	.341	.488	Embree,Alan	L	.186	43	8	2	0	0	3	7	14	.294	.233
Throws Left	R	.238	105	25	6	0	7	24	22	20	.375	.495	Throws Left	R	.301	73	22	5	1	10	26	14	19	.404	.808
Cummings,John	L	.294	51	15	3	0	0	15	6	11	.368	.353	Ericks,John	L	.273	77	21	6	0	2	7	12	19	.371	.429
Throws Left	R	.324	102	33	2	0	4	19	16	18	.418	.461	Throws Right	R	.304	115	35	5	0	9	27	7	27	.341	.583
D'Amico,Jeff	L	.292	185	54	11	1	12	28	17	37	.350	.557	Erickson,S	L	.322	475	153	29	5	10	65	32	46	.370	.467
Throws Right	R	.234	145	34	10	0	9	20	14	16	.298	.490	Throws Right	R	.268	406	109	26	1	11	52	34	54	.332	.419
Daal,Omar	L	.247	97	24	7	0	1	15	8	21	.302	.351	Eshelman,V	L	.226	84	19	1	0	3	15	8	21	.299	.345
Throws Left	R	.220	227	50	10	0	9	33	29	61	.310	.383	Throws Right	R	.337	276	93	17	1	10	49	50	38	.436	.514
Darwin,Danny	L	.330	276	91	18	1	9	34	9	31	.365	.500	Estes,Shawn	L	.258	31	8	0	0	0	3	6	3	.378	.258
Throws Right	R	.199	347	69	19	3	7	37	18	65	.245	.331	Throws Left	R	.241	228	55	9	3	3	19	33	57	.342	.346
Darwin,Jeff	L	.188	48	9	2	0	2	7	4	10	.250	.354	Farmer,Mike	L	.290	31	9	3	0	1	3	5	4	.389	.484
Throws Right	R	.266	64	17	2	0	3	8	5	5	.338	.438	Throws Left	R	.284	81	23	2	0	7	19	8	12	.348	.568
Davis,Tim	L	.295	61	18	4	0	0	8	10	8	.394	.361	Farrell,John	L	.381	21	8	4	0	0	4	4	0	.480	.571
Throws Left	R	.238	105	25	4	1	4	19	7	26	.296	.410	Throws Right	R	.500	6	3	0	0	2	2	1	0	.625	1.500
Davison,Scott	L	.333	15	5	1	0	2	4	2	3	.412	.800	Fassero,Jeff	L	.234	111	26	4	0	0	7	6	26	.271	.270
Throws Right	R	.273	22	6	0	0	4	5	1	6	.304	.818	Throws Left	R	.246	777	191	34	3	20	77	49	196	.292	.375
DeLucia,Rich	L	.314	86	27	8	0	4	19	17	13	.423	.547	Fernandez,A	L	.258	535	138	16	2	18	46	35	106	.306	.396
Throws Right	R	.229	153	35	4	2	4	19	14	42	.304	.359	Throws Right	R	.247	445	110	19	0	16	54	37	94	.308	.398
Dessens,Elmer	L	.311	45	14	3	0	1	4	3	3	.354	.444	Fernandez,O	L	.292	284	83	15	2	11	44	34	39	.375	.475
Throws Right	R	.441	59	26	6	0	1	14	1	10	.443	.593	Throws Right	R	.281	392	110	23	1	9	41	23	67	.327	.413
Dewey,Mark	L	.379	95	36	8	1	3	18	20	13	.483	.579	Fernandez,Sid	L	.313	32	10	0	0	1	5	2	9	.361	.406
Throws Right	R	.203	212	43	4	0	6	36	21	44	.286	.307	Throws Left	R	.199	201	40	12	1	4	16	24	68	.283	.328
Dickson,Jason	L	.333	93	31	9	0	2	8	13	13	.411	.495	Fetters,Mike	L	.279	136	38	5	0	3	19	12	24	.336	.382
Throws Right	R	.273	77	21	2	0	4	12	5	7	.325	.455	Throws Right	R	.267	101	27	4	0	1	10	14	29	.353	.337
DiPoto,Jerry	L	.310	129	40	8	0	2	20	19	18	.400	.419	Finley,Chuck	L	.234	124	29	6	0	5	17	13	33	.309	.403
Throws Right	R	.290	176	51	12	1	3	32	26	34	.382	.420	Throws Left	R	.268	792	212	40	1	22	81	81	182	.340	.404
Dishman,Glenn	L	.167	6	1	1	0	0	0	1	0	.286	.333	Flener,Huck	L	.210	62	13	4	0	1	8	4	8	.250	.323
Throws Left	R	.344	32	11	2	0	2	7	2	3	.371	.594	Throws Left	R	.263	209	55	14	1	8	27	29	36	.353	.455
Doherty,John	L	.294	17	5	1	0	0	3	2	2	.368	.353	Fletcher,Paul	L	.667	6	4	1	0	0	2	1	0	.714	.833
Throws Right	R	.250	12	3	0	0	1	6	2	1	.400	.500	Throws Right	R	.667	3	2	1	0	0	1	0	0	.667	1.000
Dougherty,Jim	L	.357	14	5	1	0	0	4	6	2	.571	.429	Florie,Bryce	L	.237	118	28	8	0	3	17	23	29	.361	.381
Throws Right	R	.250	36	9	1	0	2	7	5	4	.333	.444	Throws Right	R	.257	144	37	6	0	1	17	17	34	.353	.319
Drabek,Doug	L	.277	314	87	18	3	10	40	34	67	.349	.449	Fossas,Tony	L	.231	91	21	2	0	4	16	8	24	.290	.385
Throws Right	R	.314	385	121	17	3	11	50	26	70	.360	.460	Throws Left	R	.232	95	22	2	1	3	9	13	12	.324	.368
Dreifort,D	L	.302	43	13	2	0	1	8	3	8	.340	.419	Foster,Kevin	L	.269	167	45	9	1	6	20	18	30	.337	.443
Throws Right	R	.213	47	10	2	0	1	1	9	16	.339	.319	Throws Right	R	.306	173	53	10	2	10	39	17	23	.371	.561
Dyer,Mike	L	.229	105	24	3	0	1	10	18	22	.341	.286	Franco,John	L	.149	47	7	1	0	0	3	6	17	.245	.170
Throws Right	R	.306	180	55	7	0	6	35	16	29	.371	.444	Throws Left	R	.292	161	47	3	0	2	20	15	31	.352	.348
Eckersley,D	L	.290	100	29	7	0	4	10	1	22	.301	.480	Freeman,M	L	.308	221	68	14	3	7	37	24	23	.378	.493
Throws Right	R	.263	137	36	5	0	4	20	5	27	.299	.387	Throws Right	R	.287	303	87	9	2	14	53	34	49	.365	.469
Edenfield,Ken	L	.429	7	3	1	0	1	2	2	1	.556	1.000	Frey,Steve	L	.293	41	12	1	1	1	13	3	1	.326	.439
Throws Right	R	.438	16	7	0	0	1	4	0	3	.471	.625	Throws Left	R	.295	88	26	6	2	3	16	15	11	.398	.511

Pitchers vs. Left-Handed and Right-Handed Batters

Pitcher	vs	Avg	AB	H	2B	3B	HR	BI	BB	SO	OBP	SLG	Pitcher	vs	Avg	AB	H	2B	3B	HR	BI	BB	SO	OBP	SLG
Frohwirth,T	L	.462	13	6	1	0	1	6	1	0	.533	.769	Hall,Darren	L	.333	18	6	0	0	0	1	2	4	.400	.333
Throws Right	R	.286	14	4	2	0	0	4	3	1	.389	.429	Throws Right	R	.233	30	7	3	0	2	8	3	8	.303	.533
Fyhrie,Mike	L	.600	5	3	2	0	0	1	2	0	.714	1.000	Hamilton,Joey	L	.285	383	109	18	2	9	45	41	75	.357	.413
Throws Right	R	.167	6	1	0	0	0	1	1	0	.286	.167	Throws Right	R	.230	422	97	14	2	10	45	42	109	.306	.344
Garces,Rich	L	.313	64	20	6	1	0	11	19	14	.470	.438	Hammond,Chris	L	.307	88	27	6	0	3	21	5	11	.351	.477
Throws Right	R	.214	103	22	5	2	5	21	14	41	.295	.447	Throws Left	R	.318	242	77	15	3	11	46	22	39	.377	.541
Garcia,Ramon	L	.356	149	53	8	1	10	32	12	19	.401	.624	Hampton,Mike	L	.276	127	35	6	1	2	12	6	24	.313	.386
Throws Right	R	.215	144	31	7	1	7	27	9	21	.278	.424	Throws Left	R	.281	498	140	32	0	10	62	43	77	.339	.406
Gardner,Mark	L	.277	332	92	15	3	12	37	26	72	.333	.449	Hancock,Lee	L	.167	18	3	0	0	2	9	3	3	.286	.500
Throws Right	R	.289	374	108	17	0	16	59	31	73	.349	.463	Throws Left	R	.310	58	18	2	0	3	15	7	10	.403	.500
Gibson,Paul	L	.500	8	4	0	1	1	5	0	0	.500	1.125	Hancock,Ryan	L	.375	56	21	5	0	1	13	11	6	.485	.518
Throws Left	R	.182	11	2	0	0	0	0	0	3	.182	.182	Throws Right	R	.236	55	13	1	0	1	8	6	13	.323	.309
Givens,Brian	L	.467	15	7	2	0	0	2	1	3	.471	.600	Haney,Chris	L	.271	181	49	8	0	4	19	7	23	.307	.381
Throws Left	R	.431	58	25	6	0	3	17	6	7	.484	.690	Throws Left	R	.296	737	218	50	2	25	103	44	92	.335	.471
Glavine,Tom	L	.230	152	35	4	1	1	9	11	40	.280	.289	Hansell,Greg	L	.236	127	30	6	0	8	20	15	23	.326	.472
Throws Left	R	.253	740	187	43	1	13	68	74	141	.320	.366	Throws Right	R	.323	164	53	9	2	6	37	16	23	.379	.512
Gohr,Greg	L	.314	261	82	12	1	13	46	27	33	.375	.517	Hanson,Erik	L	.268	425	114	23	0	13	61	53	89	.350	.414
Throws Right	R	.348	233	81	9	0	18	41	17	42	.398	.618	Throws Right	R	.309	417	129	29	1	13	63	49	67	.380	.477
Gooden,Dwight	L	.254	382	97	23	1	10	46	50	80	.345	.398	Harikkala,Tim	L	.300	10	3	0	0	1	2	2	0	.417	.600
Throws Right	R	.266	271	72	16	2	9	41	38	46	.363	.439	Throws Right	R	.167	6	1	1	0	0	2	0	1	.286	.333
Gordon,Tom	L	.301	478	144	22	3	15	62	71	83	.391	.454	Harnisch,Pete	L	.275	353	97	15	4	11	44	34	44	.340	.433
Throws Right	R	.264	398	105	28	5	13	59	34	88	.319	.457	Throws Right	R	.247	396	98	17	0	19	51	27	70	.298	.434
Grace,Mike	L	.255	137	35	7	1	1	11	7	18	.292	.343	Harris,Pep	L	.275	69	19	7	1	2	9	12	8	.373	.493
Throws Right	R	.224	165	37	8	0	8	21	9	31	.269	.418	Throws Right	R	.226	53	12	3	0	2	6	5	12	.317	.396
Granger,Jeff	L	.150	20	3	1	0	1	3	6	4	.357	.350	Harris,Reggie	L	.667	6	4	2	0	0	2	4	1	.818	1.000
Throws Left	R	.383	47	18	3	3	2	10	4	7	.442	.702	Throws Right	R	.250	12	3	0	0	2	5	1	3	.308	.750
Graves,Danny	L	.268	56	15	3	1	2	9	5	10	.328	.464	Hartgraves,D	L	.238	42	10	1	0	3	10	4	7	.313	.476
Throws Right	R	.226	62	14	5	0	0	10	5	12	.279	.306	Throws Left	R	.247	97	24	5	1	1	10	19	23	.373	.351
Grimsley,J	L	.284	278	79	18	2	5	49	30	38	.353	.417	Hawblitzel,R	L	.241	29	7	2	0	0	3	1	4	.258	.310
Throws Right	R	.289	246	71	11	3	9	50	44	44	.418	.467	Throws Right	R	.333	33	11	2	1	2	9	5	3	.421	.636
Groom,Buddy	L	.268	123	33	3	0	2	16	10	25	.323	.341	Hawkins,L	L	.403	62	25	5	0	4	17	6	11	.449	.677
Throws Left	R	.291	179	52	8	0	6	31	24	32	.383	.436	Throws Right	R	.333	51	17	4	0	4	6	3	13	.370	.647
Gross,Kevin	L	.297	263	78	15	1	11	35	28	38	.362	.487	Haynes,Jimmy	L	.302	159	48	8	2	5	24	31	26	.414	.472
Throws Right	R	.290	252	73	23	1	8	37	22	40	.348	.484	Throws Right	R	.357	207	74	10	2	9	54	27	39	.429	.556
Grundt,Ken	L	1.000	1	1	1	0	0	0	0	0	1.000	2.000	Heflin,B	L	.438	16	7	2	0	0	6	2	1	.474	.563
Throws Left	R	.000	1	0	0	0	0	0	0	0	.000	.000	Throws Right	R	.286	14	4	0	0	1	2	1	3	.333	.500
Guardado,E	L	.198	111	22	2	1	2	13	7	28	.254	.288	Helling,Rick	L	.235	81	19	5	3	5	14	11	15	.323	.556
Throws Left	R	.250	156	39	10	1	10	28	26	46	.357	.519	Throws Right	R	.182	99	18	3	1	4	9	5	27	.221	.354
Gubicza,Mark	L	.306	265	81	10	2	9	34	22	21	.363	.460	Henneman,Mike	L	.295	78	23	3	0	3	13	10	14	.367	.449
Throws Right	R	.256	199	51	7	1	13	34	12	34	.307	.497	Throws Right	R	.222	81	18	3	0	3	12	7	20	.284	.370
Guetterman,L	L	.241	29	7	1	0	0	3	2	6	.290	.276	Henry,Doug	L	.237	139	33	3	1	3	14	25	32	.347	.338
Throws Left	R	.364	11	4	2	0	0	3	8	0	.632	.545	Throws Right	R	.304	161	49	8	1	4	28	11	26	.353	.441
Gunderson,E	L	.250	28	7	3	0	3	5	3	4	.313	.679	Hentgen,Pat	L	.249	507	126	25	0	14	53	46	82	.313	.381
Throws Left	R	.333	42	14	4	0	2	12	5	3	.420	.571	Throws Right	R	.233	481	112	24	2	6	45	48	95	.303	.328
Guthrie,Mark	L	.256	86	22	3	0	1	10	7	11	.309	.326	Heredia,Felix	L	.154	26	4	1	0	0	1	1	5	.185	.192
Throws Left	R	.232	185	43	7	0	2	18	15	45	.289	.303	Throws Left	R	.415	41	17	3	1	1	10	9	5	.510	.610
Guzman,Juan	L	.224	353	79	17	0	8	27	35	73	.297	.340	Heredia,Gil	L	.276	116	32	5	0	2	14	6	10	.311	.371
Throws Right	R	.233	339	79	16	0	12	32	18	92	.281	.386	Throws Right	R	.317	186	59	11	0	10	40	8	33	.345	.538
Habyan,John	L	.267	45	12	3	0	1	3	5	15	.340	.400	Hermanson,D	L	.273	22	6	1	0	1	6	2	6	.320	.455
Throws Right	R	.415	53	22	2	1	3	16	5	10	.500	.660	Throws Right	R	.387	31	12	4	0	2	10	2	5	.400	.710

Pitchers vs. Left-Handed and Right-Handed Batters

Pitcher	vs	Avg	AB	H	2B	3B	HR	BI	BB	SO	OBP	SLG	Pitcher	vs	Avg	AB	H	2B	3B	HR	BI	BB	SO	OBP	SLG
Hernandez,L	L	.250	4	1	0	0	0	0	2	2	.500	.250	Jacome,Jason	L	.276	76	21	4	0	1	9	8	17	.360	.368
Throws Right	R	.286	7	2	0	0	0	0	0	0	.286	.286	Throws Left	R	.374	123	46	8	1	4	22	14	15	.438	.553
Hernandez,R	L	.191	162	31	1	1	1	13	18	49	.271	.228	James,Mike	L	.237	131	31	3	2	3	16	22	31	.357	.359
Throws Right	R	.225	151	34	6	1	1	15	20	36	.314	.298	Throws Right	R	.195	159	31	5	0	4	20	20	34	.305	.302
Hernandez,X	L	.300	100	30	9	1	4	18	14	26	.383	.530	Janzen,Marty	L	.355	141	50	10	1	6	27	29	16	.460	.567
Throws Right	R	.236	199	47	9	0	9	29	14	55	.290	.417	Throws Right	R	.285	158	45	7	1	10	30	9	31	.327	.532
Hershiser,O	L	.314	459	144	31	2	7	50	36	47	.374	.436	Jarvis,Kevin	L	.314	220	69	11	3	11	34	20	21	.371	.541
Throws Right	R	.255	369	94	18	0	14	46	22	78	.301	.417	Throws Right	R	.299	278	83	14	1	6	42	23	42	.353	.421
Hill,Ken	L	.263	501	132	23	2	5	44	59	76	.343	.347	Johns,Doug	L	.283	138	39	10	1	4	14	15	13	.361	.457
Throws Right	R	.263	448	118	19	3	14	49	36	94	.320	.413	Throws Left	R	.301	492	148	33	4	17	81	54	58	.373	.488
Hitchcock,S	L	.229	166	38	11	0	3	17	13	31	.290	.349	Johnson,Dane	L	.167	18	3	0	0	0	0	2	4	.250	.167
Throws Left	R	.330	628	207	39	1	24	101	60	101	.389	.510	Throws Right	R	.154	13	2	0	0	0	2	3	3	.313	.154
Hoffman,T	L	.156	135	21	3	0	2	8	19	44	.260	.222	Johnson,Randy	L	.205	39	8	0	0	1	4	0	20	.225	.282
Throws Right	R	.165	176	29	7	1	4	19	12	67	.224	.284	Throws Left	R	.212	189	40	11	0	7	20	25	65	.307	.381
Holmes,Darren	L	.248	117	29	5	2	2	18	14	24	.331	.376	Johnstone,J	L	.316	19	6	0	0	1	4	4	2	.435	.474
Throws Right	R	.268	183	49	8	2	6	33	14	49	.320	.432	Throws Right	R	.324	34	11	1	0	1	6	1	3	.324	.441
Holt,Chris	L	.500	10	5	1	0	0	4	0	0	.500	.600	Jones,Bobby	L	.289	343	99	20	2	10	42	26	52	.336	.446
Throws Right	R	.000	9	0	0	0	0	0	3	0	.250	.000	Throws Right	R	.288	417	120	14	2	16	47	20	64	.324	.446
Holtz,Mike	L	.255	47	12	3	0	0	6	7	11	.364	.319	Jones,Doug	L	.270	111	30	7	1	5	20	9	32	.333	.486
Throws Left	R	.161	56	9	2	0	1	4	12	20	.324	.250	Throws Right	R	.290	145	42	8	1	2	23	11	28	.342	.400
Holzemer,Mark	L	.325	40	13	1	1	5	18	3	10	.364	.775	Jones,Stacy	L	.000	3	0	0	0	0	0	1	0	.250	.000
Throws Left	R	.328	67	22	5	0	2	13	5	10	.400	.493	Throws Right	R	.000	3	0	0	0	0	0	0	1	.000	.000
Honeycutt,R	L	.239	67	16	2	0	3	9	2	16	.257	.403	Jones,Todd	L	.316	95	30	3	0	3	17	15	23	.409	.442
Throws Left	R	.241	108	26	3	0	0	15	5	14	.270	.269	Throws Right	R	.242	128	31	6	0	2	19	17	21	.351	.336
Hook,Chris	L	.292	24	7	3	0	1	6	4	1	.400	.542	Jordan,R	L	.129	31	4	0	0	0	5	2	7	.176	.129
Throws Right	R	.321	28	9	0	0	2	4	10	3	.513	.536	Throws Left	R	.241	58	14	2	1	0	5	10	10	.353	.310
Hope,John	L	.185	27	5	1	0	2	5	5	5	.313	.444	Juden,Jeff	L	.198	106	21	3	0	4	9	18	24	.312	.340
Throws Right	R	.286	42	12	3	0	3	11	6	8	.392	.571	Throws Right	R	.240	167	40	8	2	4	24	16	37	.321	.383
Howe,Steve	L	.333	30	10	3	0	1	4	0	2	.333	.533	Kamieniecki,S	L	.326	43	14	3	0	4	11	12	5	.482	.674
Throws Left	R	.243	37	9	1	0	0	5	6	3	.364	.270	Throws Right	R	.393	56	22	5	0	2	15	7	10	.469	.589
Hudek,John	L	.316	19	6	1	1	0	2	2	7	.381	.474	Karchner,Matt	L	.276	98	27	3	1	4	18	19	16	.388	.449
Throws Right	R	.154	39	6	1	0	2	5	3	7	.214	.333	Throws Right	R	.262	130	34	6	0	6	25	22	30	.370	.446
Hudson,Joe	L	.337	86	29	4	0	2	15	13	8	.420	.453	Karl,Scott	L	.212	156	33	6	0	5	15	14	21	.305	.346
Throws Right	R	.301	93	28	6	0	2	23	19	11	.416	.430	Throws Left	R	.285	657	187	43	4	24	91	58	100	.343	.472
Huisman,Rick	L	.225	40	9	1	0	2	4	9	8	.367	.400	Keagle,Greg	L	.308	169	52	15	3	8	42	41	28	.452	.574
Throws Right	R	.235	68	16	4	0	2	9	9	15	.316	.382	Throws Right	R	.289	180	52	13	2	5	34	27	42	.382	.467
Hunter,Rich	L	.338	136	46	6	0	3	22	15	16	.403	.449	Key,Jimmy	L	.168	95	16	2	1	1	7	9	24	.248	.242
Throws Right	R	.271	140	38	5	1	7	22	18	16	.366	.471	Throws Left	R	.283	548	155	26	6	20	74	49	92	.340	.462
Hurst,Bill	L	.000	2	0	0	0	0	0	0	0	.000	.000	Keyser,Brian	L	.339	109	37	3	0	1	9	11	9	.393	.394
Throws Right	R	.429	7	3	1	0	0	1	1	1	.500	.571	Throws Right	R	.318	129	41	7	2	2	20	17	10	.395	.450
Hurtado,Edwin	L	.315	73	23	6	0	3	14	20	10	.453	.521	Kiefer,Mark	L	.300	20	6	0	0	1	5	1	3	.318	.450
Throws Right	R	.330	115	38	5	2	7	28	10	26	.375	.591	Throws Right	R	.429	21	9	3	0	0	5	4	2	.520	.571
Hutton,Mark	L	.257	152	39	3	1	5	17	28	24	.372	.388	Kile,Darryl	L	.316	405	128	24	4	9	48	50	89	.393	.462
Throws Right	R	.223	179	40	6	0	4	15	8	32	.267	.324	Throws Right	R	.240	438	105	16	2	7	51	47	130	.327	.333
Isringhausen,J	L	.315	276	87	9	1	3	39	30	39	.382	.388	Klingenbeck,S	L	.340	53	18	4	1	3	15	4	6	.390	.623
Throws Right	R	.262	393	103	12	2	10	45	43	75	.339	.379	Throws Right	R	.338	71	24	7	0	2	12	6	9	.390	.521
Jackson,Danny	L	.364	33	12	2	1	1	8	2	9	.400	.576	Klink,Joe	L	.500	4	2	0	0	1	1	1	1	.600	1.250
Throws Right	R	.204	103	21	3	0	2	10	14	18	.303	.291	Throws Left	R	.167	6	1	0	0	0	0	0	1	.167	.167
Jackson,Mike	L	.268	97	26	1	1	4	19	8	13	.336	.423	Knackert,B	L	.368	19	7	2	1	1	6	3	2	.435	.737
Throws Right	R	.201	174	35	8	0	7	32	16	57	.290	.368	Throws Right	R	.346	26	9	3	0	0	8	4	3	.433	.462

Pitchers vs. Left-Handed and Right-Handed Batters

Pitcher	vs	Avg	AB	H	2B	3B	HR	BI	BB	SO	OBP	SLG	Pitcher	vs	Avg	AB	H	2B	3B	HR	BI	BB	SO	OBP	SLG
Krivda,Rick	L	.288	52	15	4	0	0	3	16	6	.464	.365	Maddux,Mike	L	.287	122	35	6	0	7	19	13	19	.362	.508
Throws Left	R	.281	263	74	9	2	14	37	23	48	.337	.490	Throws Right	R	.301	136	41	8	1	5	18	14	13	.377	.485
Lacy,Kerry	L	.500	18	9	1	0	1	5	3	2	.571	.722	Maduro,Calvin	L	.207	29	6	1	0	0	0	2	8	.281	.241
Throws Right	R	.222	27	6	1	1	1	3	5	7	.364	.444	Throws Right	R	.259	27	7	2	0	1	4	1	3	.310	.444
Langston,Mark	L	.188	48	9	0	0	0	3	2	14	.235	.188	Magnante,Mike	L	.292	72	21	4	0	3	13	10	11	.407	.472
Throws Left	R	.254	421	107	19	3	18	58	43	69	.323	.442	Throws Left	R	.276	134	37	8	4	2	27	14	21	.336	.440
Larkin,Andy	L	1.000	1	1	0	0	0	0	1	0	1.000	1.000	Magrane,Joe	L	.368	38	14	2	0	0	8	6	6	.478	.421
Throws Right	R	.125	16	2	0	0	0	1	3	2	.300	.125	Throws Left	R	.308	182	56	13	1	10	33	19	15	.371	.555
Leftwich,Phil	L	.350	20	7	0	0	0	4	3	2	.435	.350	Mahomes,Pat	L	.321	112	36	14	0	7	22	17	15	.411	.634
Throws Right	R	.417	12	5	0	0	1	4	0	2	.417	.667	Throws Right	R	.295	122	36	7	1	6	26	16	21	.371	.516
Leiper,Dave	L	.341	44	15	2	0	4	10	3	8	.383	.659	Mantei,Matt	L	.190	21	4	1	0	1	3	8	12	.414	.381
Throws Left	R	.391	64	25	7	1	0	11	6	5	.443	.531	Throws Right	R	.200	45	9	2	0	1	6	13	13	.390	.311
Leiter,Al	L	.244	127	31	4	3	1	9	11	30	.307	.346	Manuel,Barry	L	.234	107	25	7	0	1	6	15	18	.333	.327
Throws Left	R	.194	629	122	32	1	13	53	108	170	.320	.310	Throws Right	R	.213	211	45	10	2	9	35	11	44	.269	.408
Leiter,Mark	L	.297	330	98	17	0	17	49	36	62	.370	.503	Martinez,D	L	.276	221	61	13	1	4	30	26	28	.351	.398
Throws Right	R	.257	471	121	28	3	20	67	33	102	.320	.456	Throws Right	R	.280	218	61	12	1	8	28	11	20	.317	.454
Leskanic,Curt	L	.233	129	30	7	2	7	26	15	35	.310	.481	Martinez,P.J.	L	.253	395	100	23	2	6	40	32	97	.310	.367
Throws Right	R	.327	159	52	8	1	5	28	23	41	.414	.484	Throws Right	R	.213	418	89	15	1	13	45	38	125	.278	.347
Levine,Al	L	.333	30	10	1	0	0	4	3	2	.412	.367	Martinez,P.A.	L	.350	20	7	2	0	2	7	1	5	.364	.750
Throws Right	R	.261	46	12	3	0	1	5	4	10	.314	.391	Throws Left	R	.286	21	6	1	0	0	5	7	4	.464	.333
Lewis,Richie	L	.198	131	26	5	1	1	13	28	25	.335	.275	Martinez,R	L	.247	267	66	11	0	6	24	55	61	.379	.356
Throws Right	R	.264	197	52	8	2	8	45	37	53	.379	.447	Throws Right	R	.243	358	87	9	2	6	34	31	73	.309	.330
Lieber,Jon	L	.282	259	73	10	4	5	33	15	33	.322	.409	Mathews,T.J.	L	.222	99	22	3	0	3	14	17	19	.336	.343
Throws Right	R	.277	300	83	10	1	14	34	13	61	.310	.457	Throws Right	R	.193	207	40	9	1	5	17	15	61	.254	.319
Lilliquist,D	L	.556	9	5	1	1	1	5	0	1	.556	1.222	Mathews,Terry	L	.349	106	37	7	0	6	19	12	17	.415	.585
Throws Left	R	.000	5	0	0	0	0	0	0	0	.000	.000	Throws Right	R	.232	181	42	4	1	4	33	22	45	.317	.331
Lima,Jose	L	.293	147	43	10	3	7	25	16	24	.361	.544	Maxcy,Brian	L	.400	10	4	0	0	1	2	0	0	.400	.700
Throws Right	R	.299	147	44	9	0	6	23	6	35	.342	.483	Throws Right	R	.571	7	4	0	0	1	3	2	1	.667	1.000
Linton,Doug	L	.286	213	61	17	1	5	19	17	46	.353	.446	May,Darrell	L	.308	13	4	0	0	0	2	1	1	.375	.308
Throws Right	R	.254	197	50	13	2	8	37	9	41	.294	.462	Throws Left	R	.368	38	14	1	0	6	17	5	5	.432	.868
Lira,Felipe	L	.281	409	115	18	3	18	57	39	61	.349	.472	McCarthy,Greg	L	.214	14	3	2	0	0	2	1	4	.421	.357
Throws Right	R	.256	348	89	14	0	12	42	27	52	.311	.399	Throws Left	R	.238	21	5	0	0	0	1	3	3	.320	.238
Lloyd,Graeme	L	.236	89	21	3	0	1	17	9	15	.300	.303	McCaskill,K	L	.337	92	31	7	1	1	19	13	14	.415	.467
Throws Left	R	.303	132	40	4	1	3	17	13	15	.367	.417	Throws Right	R	.350	117	41	11	2	5	22	18	14	.445	.607
Loaiza,E	L	.284	95	27	6	0	3	12	10	17	.358	.442	McCurry,Jeff	L	.500	8	4	2	0	1	4	1	0	.556	1.125
Throws Right	R	.328	116	38	6	1	8	17	9	15	.378	.603	Throws Right	R	.455	11	5	2	0	2	8	1	0	.500	1.182
Loiselle,Rich	L	.304	46	14	1	0	3	5	4	5	.360	.522	McDonald,Ben	L	.260	496	129	25	3	16	48	41	83	.317	.419
Throws Right	R	.222	36	8	3	0	0	0	4	4	.300	.306	Throws Right	R	.270	367	99	16	1	9	44	26	63	.322	.392
Lomon,Kevin	L	.250	8	2	0	0	0	3	1	0	.400	.250	McDowell,Jack	L	.283	424	120	21	5	12	53	41	74	.348	.441
Throws Right	R	.263	19	5	2	0	0	3	2	1	.333	.368	Throws Right	R	.280	336	94	21	2	10	44	26	67	.332	.443
Lopez,Albie	L	.301	136	41	7	0	7	18	13	26	.364	.507	McDowell,R	L	.304	92	28	4	1	1	15	10	7	.379	.402
Throws Right	R	.322	121	39	6	0	7	20	9	19	.374	.545	Throws Right	R	.291	141	41	3	0	6	25	13	13	.353	.440
Ludwick,Eric	L	.263	19	5	0	0	1	1	0	3	.263	.421	McElroy,Chuck	L	.231	65	15	2	0	1	12	5	18	.282	.308
Throws Right	R	.286	21	6	0	0	3	8	3	9	.385	.714	Throws Left	R	.254	118	30	8	0	3	18	18	27	.362	.398
Lyons,Curt	L	.429	28	12	4	0	1	4	5	3	.529	.679	McMichael,G	L	.290	176	51	8	1	3	23	5	44	.310	.398
Throws Right	R	.147	34	5	3	0	0	3	2	11	.194	.235	Throws Right	R	.212	156	33	11	1	1	18	22	34	.307	.314
MacDonald,Bob	L	.222	27	6	0	1	1	5	5	5	.344	.407	Meacham,Rusty	L	.383	81	31	5	0	4	16	8	10	.451	.593
Throws Left	R	.244	41	10	3	0	1	7	4	8	.304	.390	Throws Right	R	.280	93	26	1	1	5	13	5	15	.327	.473
Maddux,Greg	L	.225	423	95	14	5	4	26	13	93	.248	.310	Mecir,Jim	L	.247	77	19	1	0	5	21	12	15	.348	.455
Throws Right	R	.254	511	130	31	1	7	52	15	79	.277	.360	Throws Right	R	.303	76	23	7	1	1	17	11	23	.374	.461

Pitchers vs. Left-Handed and Right-Handed Batters

Pitcher	vs	Avg	AB	H	2B	3B	HR	BI	BB	SO	OBP	SLG	Pitcher	vs	Avg	AB	H	2B	3B	HR	BI	BB	SO	OBP	SLG
Mendoza,R	L	.369	122	45	17	0	4	26	4	13	.403	.607	Morgan,Mike	L	.276	203	56	16	1	4	21	26	24	.353	.424
Throws Right	R	.315	111	35	9	0	1	11	6	21	.353	.423	Throws Right	R	.297	303	90	11	3	12	48	21	50	.340	.472
Menhart,Paul	L	.313	96	30	5	2	4	19	17	8	.416	.531	Morman,Alvin	L	.239	71	17	2	0	1	8	9	21	.321	.310
Throws Right	R	.347	72	25	5	0	5	14	8	10	.427	.625	Throws Left	R	.277	94	26	6	0	7	27	15	10	.376	.564
Mercedes,Jose	L	.333	27	9	3	1	2	12	2	2	.367	.741	Moyer,Jamie	L	.309	152	47	5	0	7	24	11	19	.358	.480
Throws Right	R	.268	41	11	1	0	4	8	3	4	.318	.585	Throws Left	R	.265	490	130	20	2	16	54	35	60	.313	.412
Mercker,Kent	L	.286	56	16	2	0	1	5	8	5	.379	.375	Mulholland,T	L	.245	147	36	6	2	2	15	9	14	.289	.354
Throws Left	R	.300	223	67	10	4	12	46	30	24	.381	.543	Throws Left	R	.301	651	196	48	2	20	84	40	72	.342	.473
Mesa,Jose	L	.226	133	30	5	0	2	12	19	32	.325	.308	Munoz,Bobby	L	.377	53	20	3	0	2	8	6	6	.433	.547
Throws Right	R	.287	136	39	2	0	4	13	9	32	.338	.390	Throws Right	R	.373	59	22	5	2	3	17	1	2	.393	.678
Miceli,Dan	L	.295	132	39	11	2	5	24	17	20	.374	.523	Munoz,Mike	L	.200	60	12	2	0	2	3	6	17	.284	.333
Throws Right	R	.288	208	60	7	1	10	40	28	46	.371	.476	Throws Left	R	.352	122	43	11	2	2	25	10	28	.398	.525
Milacki,Bob	L	.347	49	17	3	0	1	11	8	7	.439	.469	Mussina,Mike	L	.251	495	124	31	1	8	46	44	118	.311	.366
Throws Right	R	.310	42	13	3	0	2	5	7	6	.408	.524	Throws Right	R	.302	464	140	32	0	23	80	25	86	.340	.519
Milchin,Mike	L	.327	52	17	5	0	3	10	4	15	.368	.596	Myers,Jimmy	L	.333	27	9	2	0	1	7	3	2	.400	.519
Throws Left	R	.342	79	27	6	0	3	12	13	14	.426	.532	Throws Right	R	.281	32	9	1	0	3	12	0	4	.265	.594
Miller,Kurt	L	.352	91	32	9	1	3	23	13	12	.433	.571	Myers,Mike	L	.229	118	27	7	0	1	10	11	42	.295	.314
Throws Right	R	.275	91	25	2	0	2	16	20	18	.412	.363	Throws Left	R	.309	139	43	9	0	5	29	23	27	.419	.482
Miller,Travis	L	.526	19	10	2	0	2	6	1	2	.550	.947	Myers,Randy	L	.208	48	10	0	0	3	10	11	16	.367	.396
Throws Left	R	.361	97	35	4	0	5	19	8	13	.410	.557	Throws Left	R	.281	178	50	8	1	4	20	18	58	.342	.404
Miller,Trever	L	.474	19	9	0	0	2	6	2	3	.500	.789	Myers,Rodney	L	.239	92	22	4	0	1	19	14	19	.345	.315
Throws Left	R	.352	54	19	1	0	1	9	7	5	.438	.426	Throws Right	R	.245	159	39	8	2	5	28	24	31	.342	.415
Mills,Alan	L	.229	70	16	5	0	2	10	10	11	.329	.386	Nagy,Charles	L	.260	434	113	22	2	10	42	36	81	.316	.389
Throws Right	R	.197	122	24	4	0	8	24	25	39	.331	.426	Throws Right	R	.249	417	104	22	1	11	39	25	86	.295	.386
Mimbs,Michael	L	.363	80	29	8	0	1	10	6	11	.402	.500	Naulty,Dan	L	.159	88	14	3	1	4	14	14	23	.275	.352
Throws Left	R	.277	314	87	17	0	12	45	35	45	.351	.446	Throws Right	R	.242	120	29	6	1	1	14	21	33	.355	.333
Minchey,Nate	L	.600	15	9	2	0	1	4	1	1	.625	.933	Navarro,Jaime	L	.270	374	101	22	5	10	38	34	71	.331	.436
Throws Right	R	.467	15	7	0	0	0	3	4	3	.550	.467	Throws Right	R	.269	532	143	26	2	15	64	38	87	.325	.410
Minor,Blas	L	.277	83	23	1	1	5	16	7	13	.330	.494	Neagle,Denny	L	.282	110	31	3	2	2	6	5	26	.313	.400
Throws Right	R	.241	112	27	3	0	5	15	10	21	.303	.402	Throws Left	R	.265	735	195	32	6	24	80	43	123	.307	.423
Miranda,Angel	L	.325	120	39	10	2	3	21	21	14	.427	.517	Nelson,Jeff	L	.283	127	36	9	2	5	20	11	25	.348	.504
Throws Left	R	.258	299	77	26	5	9	44	48	64	.355	.468	Throws Right	R	.245	159	39	5	0	1	14	25	66	.348	.296
Mitchell,L	L	.263	19	5	1	0	0	2	4	3	.391	.316	Nen,Robb	L	.243	140	34	8	0	0	15	11	32	.301	.300
Throws Right	R	.346	26	9	1	1	1	7	1	4	.357	.577	Throws Right	R	.209	158	33	8	0	2	11	10	60	.256	.297
Mlicki,Dave	L	.286	154	44	6	1	6	26	14	29	.351	.455	Nied,Dave	L	.444	9	4	0	0	0	3	5	2	.600	.444
Throws Right	R	.270	189	51	5	1	3	20	19	54	.346	.354	Throws Right	R	.091	11	1	0	0	1	3	3	2	.286	.364
Moehler,Brian	L	.190	21	4	2	1	0	3	6	0	.370	.381	Nitkowski,C	L	.350	40	14	2	0	1	7	6	8	.458	.475
Throws Right	R	.333	21	7	4	0	1	6	2	2	.391	.667	Throws Left	R	.327	147	48	6	3	6	33	32	28	.457	.531
Mohler,Mike	L	.263	99	26	5	2	4	21	14	29	.357	.475	Nomo,Hideo	L	.216	356	77	12	1	8	32	35	90	.285	.323
Throws Left	R	.264	201	53	10	3	5	29	27	35	.346	.418	Throws Right	R	.219	471	103	19	1	15	51	50	144	.294	.359
Monteleone,R	L	.318	22	7	2	0	1	3	0	1	.348	.545	Ogea,Chad	L	.265	306	81	14	1	11	40	25	52	.317	.425
Throws Right	R	.364	44	16	3	0	4	8	2	4	.391	.705	Throws Right	R	.268	261	70	20	1	11	37	17	49	.325	.479
Montgomery,J	L	.239	134	32	7	0	5	18	11	22	.304	.403	Olivares,Omar	L	.291	309	90	27	3	8	40	50	41	.386	.476
Throws Right	R	.267	101	27	4	1	9	18	8	23	.327	.594	Throws Right	R	.258	306	79	14	0	8	34	25	40	.329	.382
Montgomery,S	L	.182	22	4	1	0	1	2	7	4	.379	.364	Oliver,Darren	L	.226	106	24	5	2	2	11	9	25	.293	.368
Throws Right	R	.389	36	14	2	0	4	12	6	4	.476	.778	Throws Left	R	.288	576	166	27	2	18	69	67	87	.367	.436
Moore,Marcus	L	.290	31	9	0	0	0	6	12	8	.477	.290	Olson,Gregg	L	.260	104	27	4	0	3	21	12	22	.342	.385
Throws Right	R	.250	68	17	3	3	3	12	10	19	.354	.515	Throws Right	R	.277	101	28	3	0	4	27	23	15	.408	.426
Morel,Ramon	L	.343	70	24	0	1	2	10	5	4	.387	.457	Oquist,Mike	L	.273	11	3	0	0	0	0	4	2	.467	.273
Throws Right	R	.311	106	33	7	1	2	18	14	18	.393	.453	Throws Right	R	.200	15	3	1	0	0	0	0	2	.200	.267

Pitchers vs. Left-Handed and Right-Handed Batters

Pitcher	vs	Avg	AB	H	2B	3B	HR	BI	BB	SO	OBP	SLG	Pitcher	vs	Avg	AB	H	2B	3B	HR	BI	BB	SO	OBP	SLG
Orosco,Jesse	L	.216	74	16	1	1	2	10	12	19	.326	.338	Pichardo,H	L	.295	122	36	4	0	2	17	12	15	.360	.377
Throws Left	R	.202	129	26	3	0	3	13	16	33	.297	.295	Throws Right	R	.273	139	38	4	2	3	26	14	28	.342	.396
Osborne,D	L	.218	110	24	6	0	4	8	5	28	.252	.382	Plesac,Dan	L	.250	80	20	3	2	1	13	5	28	.291	.375
Throws Left	R	.260	643	167	31	2	18	68	52	106	.314	.398	Throws Left	R	.246	191	47	7	0	3	23	19	48	.311	.330
Osuna,Al	L	.308	13	4	2	1	0	4	0	2	.286	.615	Plunk,Eric	L	.237	135	32	4	0	3	13	17	40	.325	.333
Throws Left	R	.333	3	1	1	0	0	0	2	2	.667	.667	Throws Right	R	.170	141	24	2	0	3	13	17	45	.264	.248
Osuna,Antonio	L	.239	109	26	6	1	3	13	20	30	.351	.394	Polley,Dale	L	.150	40	6	1	0	1	4	3	12	.261	.250
Throws Right	R	.209	187	39	7	1	3	19	12	55	.260	.305	Throws Left	R	.362	47	17	4	0	4	8	8	2	.446	.702
Pacheco,Alex	L	.500	10	5	1	2	0	3	0	2	.500	1.000	Poole,Jim	L	.216	88	19	6	0	2	10	8	19	.286	.352
Throws Right	R	.200	15	3	0	0	2	3	1	5	.250	.600	Throws Left	R	.255	98	25	8	1	3	15	19	19	.376	.449
Painter,Lance	L	.250	52	13	1	0	1	7	9	15	.361	.327	Portugal,Mark	L	.239	234	56	9	2	7	20	18	43	.294	.385
Throws Left	R	.291	148	43	8	1	11	34	16	33	.365	.581	Throws Right	R	.254	355	90	18	4	13	51	24	50	.299	.437
Pall,Donn	L	.310	29	9	3	0	3	12	4	2	.382	.724	Potts,Mike	L	.283	53	15	0	0	3	13	8	11	.354	.453
Throws Right	R	.175	40	7	2	0	0	2	5	7	.267	.225	Throws Left	R	.333	129	43	4	1	4	15	22	10	.430	.473
Paniagua,Jose	L	.290	93	27	6	0	4	10	15	12	.385	.484	Powell,Jay	L	.252	111	28	3	3	3	18	17	23	.366	.414
Throws Right	R	.275	102	28	4	0	3	10	8	15	.345	.402	Throws Right	R	.257	167	43	8	1	2	25	19	29	.335	.353
Park,Chan Ho	L	.263	160	42	6	0	3	20	37	28	.401	.356	Prieto,Ariel	L	.257	280	72	11	3	6	28	40	50	.352	.382
Throws Right	R	.172	233	40	8	0	4	21	34	91	.287	.258	Throws Right	R	.296	196	58	14	1	3	29	14	25	.353	.423
Parra,Jose	L	.336	140	47	9	1	7	24	13	23	.395	.564	Pugh,Tim	L	.277	94	26	1	1	7	19	11	11	.349	.532
Throws Right	R	.281	146	41	7	1	8	26	14	27	.346	.507	Throws Right	R	.325	123	40	8	0	5	24	12	25	.396	.512
Parrett,Jeff	L	.256	86	22	6	2	0	9	16	20	.373	.372	Quantrill,P	L	.311	293	91	18	3	18	48	27	53	.362	.577
Throws Right	R	.253	166	42	10	0	2	22	15	44	.315	.349	Throws Right	R	.324	250	81	12	1	9	36	24	33	.386	.488
Parris,Steve	L	.367	49	18	2	1	0	7	2	8	.385	.449	Quirico,R	L	.000	0	0	0	0	0	0	0	0	.000	.000
Throws Right	R	.283	60	17	4	0	4	12	9	19	.386	.550	Throws Left	R	.444	9	4	2	0	1	7	5	1	.643	1.000
Patterson,Bob	L	.192	78	15	2	1	1	9	9	21	.267	.282	Radinsky,S	L	.242	66	16	3	0	0	7	2	18	.261	.288
Throws Left	R	.252	123	31	5	2	5	22	13	32	.326	.447	Throws Left	R	.275	131	36	8	2	2	24	15	30	.345	.412
Patterson,D	L	.400	15	6	0	0	0	3	0	1	.400	.400	Radke,Brad	L	.259	514	133	32	5	24	65	32	72	.304	.481
Throws Right	R	.200	20	4	0	0	0	2	3	4	.304	.200	Throws Right	R	.253	387	98	23	1	16	48	25	76	.298	.442
Pavlas,Dave	L	.333	42	14	9	0	0	7	4	5	.391	.548	Rapp,Pat	L	.310	290	90	11	1	5	35	47	29	.403	.407
Throws Right	R	.200	45	9	1	0	0	7	3	13	.265	.222	Throws Right	R	.293	321	94	21	2	7	48	44	57	.378	.436
Pavlik,Roger	L	.287	411	118	18	3	13	57	43	69	.354	.440	Reed,Steve	L	.284	102	29	6	0	5	16	9	17	.351	.490
Throws Right	R	.263	373	98	18	4	15	49	38	58	.336	.453	Throws Right	R	.213	174	37	7	0	6	26	10	34	.267	.356
Pena,A	L	.000	4	0	0	0	0	0	1	2	.200	.000	Rekar,Bryan	L	.400	100	40	10	4	3	24	16	10	.496	.670
Throws Right	R	.308	13	4	2	0	2	5	0	3	.308	.923	Throws Right	R	.309	152	47	6	2	8	33	10	15	.352	.533
Pennington,B	L	.091	22	2	0	0	1	5	9	4	.344	.227	Remlinger,M	L	.292	24	7	1	0	0	4	4	0	.433	.333
Throws Left	R	.188	48	9	2	0	1	8	22	16	.443	.292	Throws Left	R	.230	74	17	4	0	4	14	15	19	.363	.446
Percival,Troy	L	.128	133	17	3	0	2	9	18	51	.235	.195	Reyes,Al	L	.231	13	3	0	0	1	5	2	1	.333	.462
Throws Right	R	.172	122	21	2	0	6	15	13	49	.257	.336	Throws Right	R	.417	12	5	0	1	0	1	0	1	.417	.583
Perez,Mike	L	.326	46	15	4	0	0	7	4	5	.392	.413	Reyes,Carlos	L	.272	246	67	12	1	8	38	29	40	.345	.427
Throws Right	R	.219	64	14	3	0	2	11	9	17	.333	.359	Throws Right	R	.291	230	67	13	0	11	44	32	38	.375	.491
Perez,Yorkis	L	.295	88	26	4	1	1	16	10	23	.370	.398	Reynolds,S	L	.209	412	86	16	1	7	31	21	104	.247	.303
Throws Left	R	.255	98	25	3	0	1	19	21	24	.383	.316	Throws Right	R	.283	499	141	26	5	13	58	23	100	.321	.433
Person,Robert	L	.224	174	39	6	0	7	20	20	47	.306	.379	Reynoso,A	L	.313	281	88	20	3	9	41	19	31	.365	.502
Throws Right	R	.270	174	47	10	1	9	23	15	29	.326	.494	Throws Right	R	.276	388	107	19	1	18	49	30	57	.333	.469
Peters,Chris	L	.275	40	11	1	0	1	10	5	6	.340	.375	Rhodes,Arthur	L	.246	65	16	0	0	6	15	7	15	.315	.523
Throws Left	R	.289	211	61	14	4	8	31	20	22	.352	.507	Throws Left	R	.239	134	32	7	1	0	11	16	47	.320	.306
Petkovsek,M	L	.254	142	36	6	1	4	15	16	19	.327	.394	Risley,Bill	L	.186	59	11	4	2	1	8	14	7	.338	.373
Throws Right	R	.249	189	47	4	1	5	23	19	26	.333	.360	Throws Right	R	.244	90	22	4	1	6	18	11	22	.324	.511
Pettitte,Andy	L	.329	152	50	3	2	1	12	9	34	.368	.395	Ritz,Kevin	L	.294	337	99	21	3	10	50	50	45	.394	.463
Throws Left	R	.259	692	179	34	1	22	76	63	128	.321	.406	Throws Right	R	.274	500	137	18	5	14	66	55	60	.350	.414

Pitcher	vs	Avg	AB	H	2B	3B	HR	BI	BB	SO	OBP	SLG	Pitcher	vs	Avg	AB	H	2B	3B	HR	BI	BB	SO	OBP	SLG
Rivera,M	L	.215	214	46	4	0	1	15	20	52	.288	.248	Schmidt,Jeff	L	.333	9	3	0	0	0	2	3	1	.462	.333
Throws Right	R	.157	172	27	8	0	0	13	14	78	.219	.203	Throws Right	R	.417	24	10	0	0	2	9	5	1	.517	.667
Roa,Joe	L	.500	4	2	1	0	0	1	3	0	.714	.750	Schourek,Pete	L	.298	47	14	4	0	2	11	3	12	.340	.511
Throws Right	R	.500	4	2	1	0	0	2	0	0	.500	.750	Throws Left	R	.291	223	65	12	2	5	33	21	42	.355	.430
Robertson,R	L	.226	146	33	7	1	3	18	23	20	.347	.349	Schutz,Carl	L	.200	5	1	0	0	0	0	0	3	.200	.200
Throws Left	R	.285	576	164	25	4	19	79	93	94	.386	.441	Throws Left	R	.333	6	2	0	0	0	0	2	2	.500	.333
Robinson,Ken	L	.182	11	2	0	0	0	0	2	2	.308	.182	Scott,Tim	L	.235	98	23	3	1	3	18	15	17	.339	.378
Throws Right	R	.467	15	7	1	2	0	7	1	3	.471	.800	Throws Right	R	.280	150	42	10	2	5	25	15	30	.349	.473
Rodriguez,F	L	.274	441	121	27	4	12	56	50	48	.345	.435	Sele,Aaron	L	.322	339	109	25	1	9	57	40	67	.394	.481
Throws Right	R	.269	361	97	19	0	15	56	28	62	.327	.446	Throws Right	R	.281	295	83	12	0	5	41	27	70	.348	.373
Rodriguez,N	L	.259	27	7	2	0	0	2	4	5	.355	.333	Serafini,Dan	L	.000	3	0	0	0	0	1	1	0	.333	.000
Throws Right	R	.268	41	11	1	0	2	8	3	7	.326	.439	Throws Left	R	.438	16	7	2	0	1	4	1	1	.471	.750
Rogers,Kenny	L	.209	110	23	1	1	3	12	17	25	.326	.318	Service,Scott	L	.313	67	21	4	0	3	11	11	17	.418	.507
Throws Left	R	.271	576	156	29	0	13	67	66	67	.350	.389	Throws Right	R	.256	117	30	9	1	4	17	7	29	.323	.453
Rojas,Mel	L	.147	129	19	0	3	2	14	13	52	.224	.240	Shaw,Jeff	L	.194	160	31	7	0	2	13	19	22	.277	.275
Throws Right	R	.230	161	37	7	0	3	21	15	40	.298	.329	Throws Right	R	.292	233	68	14	1	6	36	10	47	.322	.438
Rosado,Jose	L	.316	76	24	3	0	2	4	7	17	.373	.434	Shepherd,K	L	.314	35	11	1	0	4	14	11	8	.478	.686
Throws Left	R	.233	330	77	19	3	5	30	19	47	.280	.355	Throws Right	R	.357	56	20	1	0	2	16	7	9	.422	.482
Ruebel,Matt	L	.156	45	7	2	0	2	6	6	3	.296	.333	Shuey,Paul	L	.237	93	22	3	0	1	8	15	20	.336	.301
Throws Left	R	.306	186	57	16	2	5	23	19	19	.374	.495	Throws Right	R	.225	102	23	4	0	5	15	11	24	.298	.412
Rueter,Kirk	L	.324	74	24	2	0	2	8	5	7	.367	.432	Silva,Jose	L	.400	5	2	0	0	1	3	0	0	.400	1.000
Throws Left	R	.264	322	85	18	0	10	31	22	39	.314	.413	Throws Right	R	.500	6	3	1	0	0	0	0	0	.500	.667
Ruffcorn,S	L	.385	13	5	0	0	0	1	3	1	.500	.385	Simas,Bill	L	.271	118	32	6	2	1	12	20	15	.383	.381
Throws Right	R	.357	14	5	0	2	1	6	3	2	.471	.714	Throws Right	R	.261	165	43	13	1	4	34	19	50	.339	.424
Ruffin,Bruce	L	.274	62	17	2	0	0	5	10	13	.370	.306	Sirotka,Mike	L	.219	32	7	1	1	0	2	1	4	.235	.313
Throws Left	R	.192	198	38	7	0	5	28	19	61	.260	.303	Throws Left	R	.355	76	27	8	2	3	25	11	7	.432	.632
Ruffin,Johnny	L	.297	91	27	5	3	2	18	15	22	.404	.484	Slocumb,H	L	.285	165	47	0	0	1	18	34	40	.405	.303
Throws Right	R	.289	152	44	2	0	8	22	22	47	.375	.461	Throws Right	R	.149	141	21	3	1	1	13	21	48	.269	.206
Russell,Jeff	L	.329	85	28	3	1	2	12	11	8	.400	.459	Small,Aaron	L	.279	61	17	2	0	2	8	8	9	.362	.410
Throws Right	R	.229	131	30	1	1	3	19	11	15	.301	.321	Throws Right	R	.339	59	20	5	0	1	15	14	8	.467	.475
Ryan,Ken	L	.241	133	32	8	0	0	16	29	22	.377	.301	Small,Mark	L	.206	34	7	1	1	0	4	6	6	.325	.294
Throws Right	R	.210	186	39	6	1	4	12	16	48	.276	.317	Throws Right	R	.356	73	26	8	1	1	20	7	10	.420	.534
Sackinsky,B	L	.417	12	5	0	0	0	1	2	1	.500	.417	Smiley,John	L	.276	127	35	14	3	4	16	11	33	.329	.528
Throws Right	R	.143	7	1	0	0	1	1	1	1	.250	.571	Throws Left	R	.253	681	172	33	5	16	72	43	138	.299	.386
Sager,A.J.	L	.296	152	45	4	0	4	10	24	23	.390	.401	Smith,Lee	L	.222	99	22	3	1	1	11	10	19	.297	.303
Throws Right	R	.291	158	46	9	1	6	31	5	29	.317	.475	Throws Right	R	.299	117	35	5	1	3	14	16	22	.381	.436
Salkeld,Roger	L	.249	189	47	10	0	7	25	14	26	.308	.413	Smith,Zane	L	.333	45	15	5	1	1	11	1	8	.340	.556
Throws Right	R	.271	247	67	17	1	11	38	40	56	.378	.482	Throws Left	R	.305	292	89	28	5	6	35	20	39	.355	.497
Sanders,Scott	L	.229	249	57	14	1	4	20	30	56	.309	.341	Smoltz,John	L	.221	394	87	16	2	5	28	36	112	.288	.310
Throws Right	R	.214	281	60	11	1	6	23	18	101	.262	.324	Throws Right	R	.212	528	112	29	0	14	61	19	164	.239	.347
Sanderson,S	L	.441	34	15	1	0	3	8	1	4	.472	.735	Soderstrom,S	L	.286	28	8	0	0	1	7	2	1	.323	.393
Throws Right	R	.429	56	24	5	0	2	11	3	3	.459	.625	Throws Right	R	.320	25	8	2	0	0	4	4	8	.438	.400
Sauveur,Rich	L	.000	2	0	0	0	0	0	2	0	.600	.000	Sodowsky,C	L	.365	52	19	1	0	3	10	9	4	.459	.558
Throws Left	R	.429	7	3	0	0	1	3	3	1	.600	.857	Throws Right	R	.375	56	21	4	0	2	18	11	5	.500	.554
Scanlan,Bob	L	.366	41	15	2	1	0	7	6	3	.447	.463	Sparks,Steve	L	.278	194	54	13	3	6	30	26	13	.364	.469
Throws Right	R	.286	49	14	1	0	2	7	6	3	.386	.429	Throws Right	R	.320	153	49	7	1	13	32	26	8	.426	.634
Schilling,C	L	.215	297	64	14	3	7	30	24	85	.273	.354	Spoljaric,P	L	.260	50	13	2	0	2	10	7	18	.373	.420
Throws Right	R	.228	372	85	21	1	9	33	26	97	.282	.363	Throws Left	R	.189	90	17	2	0	4	8	12	20	.282	.344
Schmidt,Jason	L	.336	152	51	9	2	4	28	29	25	.443	.500	Spradlin,J	L	.000	0	0	0	0	0	0	0	0	.000	.000
Throws Right	R	.253	225	57	6	0	6	30	24	49	.318	.360	Throws Right	R	.000	1	0	0	0	0	0	0	0	.000	.000

Pitchers vs. Left-Handed and Right-Handed Batters

Pitcher	vs	Avg	AB	H	2B	3B	HR	BI	BB	SO	OBP	SLG
Springer,D	L	.247	194	48	8	0	12	26	23	30	.330	.474
Throws Right	R	.254	169	43	4	0	12	21	20	34	.349	.491
Springer,Russ	L	.238	151	36	11	1	4	14	19	34	.324	.404
Throws Right	R	.293	239	70	13	1	8	45	19	60	.344	.456
Stanton,Mike	L	.263	114	30	5	1	1	19	7	28	.306	.351
Throws Left	R	.267	180	48	9	0	10	29	20	32	.337	.483
Stephenson,G	L	.400	10	4	1	0	1	4	1	2	.455	.800
Throws Right	R	.450	20	9	2	0	0	4	2	1	.522	.550
Stevens,Dave	L	.319	113	36	9	1	6	24	17	12	.398	.575
Throws Right	R	.206	107	22	5	0	6	14	8	17	.261	.421
Stottlemyre,T	L	.272	371	101	20	1	15	41	57	78	.367	.453
Throws Right	R	.198	455	90	16	1	15	51	36	116	.259	.336
Sturtze,T	L	.467	15	7	2	0	1	3	3	2	.556	.800
Throws Right	R	.290	31	9	0	0	2	8	2	5	.333	.484
Sullivan,S	L	.300	10	3	0	0	0	0	2	1	.462	.300
Throws Right	R	.222	18	4	0	0	0	0	3	2	.333	.222
Suppan,Jeff	L	.217	46	10	2	0	1	7	5	3	.288	.326
Throws Right	R	.452	42	19	2	2	2	11	8	10	.519	.738
Suzuki,Makoto	L	.333	3	1	0	0	0	0	1	1	.500	.333
Throws Right	R	.333	3	1	0	1	0	0	1	1	.500	1.000
Swartzbaugh,D	L	.356	45	16	3	0	1	7	7	6	.442	.489
Throws Right	R	.204	49	10	5	0	2	8	7	7	.304	.429
Swift,Bill	L	.303	33	10	2	1	1	4	4	3	.368	.515
Throws Right	R	.310	42	13	4	0	0	6	1	2	.326	.405
Swindell,Greg	L	.290	62	18	7	0	2	5	2	11	.318	.500
Throws Left	R	.316	152	48	15	1	11	38	17	25	.382	.645
Tabaka,Jeff	L	.412	34	14	3	0	1	8	7	4	.524	.588
Throws Left	R	.264	53	14	1	0	4	8	7	14	.371	.509
Tapani,Kevin	L	.274	441	121	28	4	21	68	41	81	.333	.499
Throws Right	R	.262	439	115	19	0	13	40	35	69	.319	.394
Tavarez,J	L	.371	151	56	13	4	4	27	14	17	.425	.589
Throws Right	R	.265	170	45	11	0	5	30	8	29	.293	.418
Taylor,Billy	L	.241	87	21	2	1	2	11	11	15	.333	.356
Throws Right	R	.225	138	31	6	0	3	16	14	52	.303	.333
Telemaco,A	L	.348	158	55	14	1	9	32	14	18	.400	.620
Throws Right	R	.233	227	53	8	0	11	28	17	46	.291	.414
Telgheder,D	L	.324	173	56	12	4	6	21	12	25	.367	.543
Throws Right	R	.254	142	36	8	1	6	13	14	18	.318	.451
Tewksbury,Bob	L	.266	320	85	15	3	4	44	23	42	.310	.369
Throws Right	R	.281	494	139	25	3	13	52	20	84	.310	.423
Thobe,Tom	L	.167	6	1	0	0	0	1	0	0	.143	.167
Throws Left	R	.235	17	4	0	0	1	1	0	1	.235	.412
Thomas,Larry	L	.286	63	18	3	0	1	11	6	12	.357	.381
Throws Left	R	.275	51	14	4	0	0	2	8	8	.393	.353
Thompson,J	L	.277	47	13	2	0	2	6	1	8	.320	.447
Throws Left	R	.265	185	49	10	0	5	25	30	36	.364	.400
Thompson,Mark	L	.291	299	87	16	2	12	41	35	40	.370	.478
Throws Right	R	.280	364	102	29	1	13	52	39	59	.364	.473
Timlin,Mike	L	.259	116	30	8	0	1	14	10	19	.313	.353
Throws Right	R	.191	89	17	1	1	3	10	8	33	.270	.326
Torres,S	L	.268	97	26	4	0	3	10	15	13	.366	.402
Throws Right	R	.212	85	18	6	0	2	14	8	23	.299	.353
Trachsel,S	L	.241	282	68	7	4	13	28	21	47	.293	.433
Throws Right	R	.232	487	113	28	1	17	45	41	85	.301	.398
Trlicek,Ricky	L	.333	6	2	0	0	0	2	1	1	.500	.333
Throws Right	R	.125	8	1	0	0	0	0	2	2	.300	.125
Trombley,Mike	L	.297	111	33	11	1	2	20	16	21	.395	.468
Throws Right	R	.189	148	28	6	1	0	18	9	36	.245	.243
Urbani,Tom	L	.311	45	14	1	1	2	10	8	10	.407	.511
Throws Left	R	.314	102	32	2	0	9	18	10	11	.383	.598
Urbina,Ugueth	L	.315	219	69	11	1	10	31	21	36	.373	.511
Throws Right	R	.153	216	33	9	0	8	18	23	72	.236	.306
Valdes,Ismael	L	.244	381	93	12	2	7	30	22	63	.286	.341
Throws Right	R	.256	493	126	27	2	13	54	32	110	.300	.398
Valdes,Marc	L	.366	82	30	6	0	4	12	15	3	.465	.585
Throws Right	R	.280	118	33	5	1	1	14	8	10	.320	.364
Valenzuela,F	L	.261	92	24	3	0	1	6	9	19	.327	.326
Throws Left	R	.270	567	153	35	1	16	65	58	76	.335	.420
Valera,Julio	L	.320	103	33	5	0	6	25	14	12	.398	.544
Throws Right	R	.298	141	42	11	0	1	18	13	19	.358	.397
Van Poppel,T	L	.377	212	80	21	2	16	62	42	25	.471	.722
Throws Right	R	.291	203	59	11	2	8	36	20	28	.358	.483
VanEgmond,T	L	.252	115	29	7	1	4	15	17	19	.343	.435
Throws Right	R	.299	97	29	7	2	2	10	6	14	.343	.474
VanLandingham	L	.289	301	87	13	2	9	43	23	23	.343	.435
Throws Right	R	.266	410	109	29	2	8	58	55	74	.359	.405
VanRyn,Ben	L	.500	2	1	0	0	0	0	0	0	.500	.500
Throws Left	R	.000	2	0	0	0	0	0	1	0	.333	.000
Veras,Dario	L	.182	44	8	2	0	2	9	7	12	.288	.364
Throws Right	R	.267	60	16	2	0	1	4	3	11	.313	.350
Veres,Dave	L	.309	123	38	8	1	3	14	19	23	.399	.463
Throws Right	R	.255	184	47	8	0	7	25	13	58	.322	.413
Veres,Randy	L	.323	62	20	3	1	3	16	12	15	.440	.548
Throws Right	R	.290	62	18	3	0	3	20	11	13	.390	.484
Villone,Ron	L	.208	53	11	0	0	1	10	11	10	.358	.264
Throws Left	R	.206	97	20	1	0	5	18	14	28	.322	.371
Viola,Frank	L	.207	29	6	0	0	1	2	1	7	.233	.310
Throws Left	R	.394	94	37	5	0	5	24	20	11	.496	.606
Vosberg,Ed	L	.254	67	17	1	0	2	14	9	10	.338	.358
Throws Left	R	.327	104	34	5	0	2	9	12	22	.397	.433
Wade,Terrell	L	.286	56	16	3	0	2	7	5	14	.349	.446
Throws Left	R	.210	195	41	14	1	7	17	42	65	.350	.400
Wagner,Billy	L	.087	23	2	1	0	0	1	5	8	.276	.130
Throws Left	R	.177	147	26	4	0	6	17	25	59	.301	.327
Wagner,Matt	L	.277	155	43	10	1	4	16	20	18	.361	.432
Throws Right	R	.293	164	48	9	0	11	40	18	23	.364	.549
Wagner,Paul	L	.257	140	36	6	0	1	17	22	37	.362	.321
Throws Right	R	.289	173	50	9	0	9	25	17	44	.358	.497
Wainhouse,D	L	.346	26	9	2	0	2	6	7	5	.485	.654
Throws Right	R	.210	62	13	2	0	1	9	3	11	.239	.290

Pitchers vs. Left-Handed and Right-Handed Batters

Pitcher	vs	Avg	AB	H	2B	3B	HR	BI	BB	SO	OBP	SLG
Wakefield,Tim	L	.289	454	131	30	0	14	63	55	64	.365	.447
Throws Right	R	.270	397	107	15	1	24	68	35	76	.340	.494
Walker,Mike	L	.389	54	21	2	2	5	16	9	8	.462	.778
Throws Right	R	.317	60	19	2	0	5	15	8	5	.406	.600
Walker,Pete	L	.000	1	0	0	0	0	0	3	1	.750	.000
Throws Right	R	.000	1	0	0	0	0	0	0	0	.000	.000
Wall,Donne	L	.254	244	62	17	3	6	26	16	39	.302	.422
Throws Right	R	.309	350	108	24	0	11	48	18	60	.348	.471
Wallace,Derek	L	.333	45	15	5	0	0	4	11	6	.464	.444
Throws Right	R	.255	55	14	0	0	2	9	3	9	.293	.364
Ware,Jeff	L	.230	61	14	3	0	3	11	16	7	.397	.426
Throws Right	R	.309	68	21	5	1	3	18	15	4	.440	.544
Wasdin,John	L	.312	269	84	22	2	14	53	36	32	.391	.565
Throws Right	R	.251	243	61	10	0	10	35	14	43	.296	.416
Watson,Allen	L	.198	101	20	3	1	3	13	9	19	.265	.337
Throws Left	R	.286	591	169	36	2	25	84	60	109	.352	.481
Weathers,Dave	L	.372	156	58	9	2	3	31	23	18	.454	.513
Throws Right	R	.253	198	50	10	0	5	27	19	35	.330	.379
Wells,Bob	L	.300	257	77	16	1	13	36	28	39	.372	.521
Throws Right	R	.248	258	64	18	2	12	39	18	55	.304	.473
Wells,David	L	.225	191	43	4	2	4	19	7	27	.254	.330
Throws Left	R	.302	675	204	40	3	28	99	44	103	.345	.495
Wendell,Turk	L	.221	113	25	3	0	2	9	19	26	.333	.301
Throws Right	R	.189	175	33	6	0	6	18	25	49	.299	.326
Wengert,Don	L	.306	346	106	18	2	18	55	35	33	.372	.526
Throws Right	R	.308	305	94	19	3	11	39	25	42	.364	.498
West,David	L	.200	15	3	0	1	0	1	1	2	.250	.333
Throws Left	R	.283	99	28	8	0	0	11	10	20	.349	.364
Wetteland,J	L	.285	144	41	9	1	7	24	13	32	.340	.507
Throws Right	R	.134	97	13	2	0	2	5	8	37	.200	.216
Whitehurst,W	L	.182	11	2	1	0	1	4	2	1	.308	.545
Throws Right	R	.391	23	9	2	0	0	2	0	0	.391	.478
Whiteside,M	L	.302	53	16	1	1	2	10	1	2	.309	.472
Throws Right	R	.333	81	27	1	1	6	18	10	13	.402	.593
Wickander,K	L	.250	36	9	1	0	0	9	7	9	.364	.278
Throws Left	R	.274	62	17	3	0	2	17	10	10	.370	.419
Wickman,Bob	L	.303	178	54	4	0	5	27	19	31	.383	.410
Throws Right	R	.265	196	52	12	0	5	45	25	44	.345	.403
Wilkins,Marc	L	.160	100	16	5	0	2	14	17	34	.283	.270
Throws Right	R	.324	182	59	9	1	4	23	19	28	.399	.451
Williams,B	L	.369	260	96	17	2	12	58	42	31	.457	.588
Throws Right	R	.226	217	49	8	1	9	46	43	41	.359	.396
Williams,Mike	L	.283	258	73	20	2	9	34	35	32	.370	.481
Throws Right	R	.295	390	115	18	2	16	63	32	71	.352	.474
Williams,Shad	L	.292	48	14	5	0	1	13	7	11	.386	.458
Throws Right	R	.373	75	28	6	0	6	23	14	15	.478	.693
Williams,W	L	.288	139	40	9	0	4	13	20	27	.379	.439
Throws Right	R	.264	91	24	1	0	4	12	1	16	.272	.407
Wilson,Paul	L	.294	265	78	16	4	6	44	33	42	.375	.453
Throws Right	R	.246	321	79	12	3	9	47	38	67	.339	.386

Pitcher	vs	Avg	AB	H	2B	3B	HR	BI	BB	SO	OBP	SLG
Witasick,Jay	L	.222	18	4	0	1	0	3	2	4	.286	.333
Throws Right	R	.258	31	8	0	0	5	7	3	8	.324	.742
Witt,Bobby	L	.294	436	128	24	5	14	56	51	80	.366	.468
Throws Right	R	.297	360	107	18	2	14	52	45	77	.374	.475
Wohlers,Mark	L	.197	137	27	5	1	3	12	13	56	.267	.314
Throws Right	R	.277	159	44	3	1	5	19	8	44	.316	.403
Wojciechowski	L	.234	47	11	2	0	2	4	5	5	.321	.404
Throws Left	R	.312	276	86	14	3	8	40	23	25	.364	.471
Wolcott,Bob	L	.351	308	108	27	3	15	48	36	31	.421	.604
Throws Right	R	.241	294	71	13	2	11	41	18	47	.295	.412
Woodall,Brad	L	.267	15	4	0	1	0	1	1	5	.313	.400
Throws Left	R	.348	69	24	9	1	4	16	3	15	.365	.681
Worrell,Tim	L	.257	206	53	12	3	0	16	21	34	.326	.345
Throws Right	R	.220	255	56	11	0	9	30	18	65	.286	.369
Worrell,Todd	L	.242	124	30	5	0	3	19	8	33	.286	.355
Throws Right	R	.286	140	40	5	0	2	15	7	33	.327	.364
Wright,Jamey	L	.315	165	52	18	3	3	24	20	27	.394	.515
Throws Right	R	.283	187	53	8	1	5	28	21	18	.369	.417
Yan,Esteban	L	.462	13	6	0	0	1	3	0	1	.462	.692
Throws Right	R	.269	26	7	1	0	2	3	3	6	.345	.538
Young,Anthony	L	.357	42	15	2	1	2	8	10	5	.472	.595
Throws Right	R	.241	87	21	4	0	2	10	12	14	.359	.356
AL	L	.281	--	--	--	--	--	--	--	--	.357	.445
	R	.274	--	--	--	--	--	--	--	--	.345	.445
NL	L	.270	--	--	--	--	--	--	--	--	.342	.412
	R	.258	--	--	--	--	--	--	--	--	.323	.405
MLB	L	.276	--	--	--	--	--	--	--	--	.350	.430
	R	.266	--	--	--	--	--	--	--	--	.334	.425

Leader Boards

For the first time in three years, baseball saw a full season's worth of *on-the-field* action. . . and it certainly seemed as though hitter's took out two years of pent-up frustration on the ball. If 1930 was the Year of the Hitter, 1996 will undoubtedly be remembered as the Year of the Slugger (at least until next season). Ah, say good-bye to truncated stats! For just the fourth time in big league history, *two* players reached the 50-homer mark in a single season. Mark McGwire's total of 52 was the highest since George Foster slugged his way to that plateau in 1977. For only the second time ever, three teammates walloped at least 40 homers, lead by Andres Galarraga's 47. The Big Cat also drove in 150 runs. . . you have to go all the way back to 1962 and the Dodgers' Tommy Davis to find a more productive campaign. Let's not give all the ink to the big boppers, however. Thanks to Paul Molitor—who also continued his steady climb up the all-time Leader Boards—and Lance Johnson, a player from each league posted at least 225 hits for the first time since that amazing 1930 campaign. Johnson's 21 triples may be the most eye-catching number in here when compared to the rest of his league.

Lest we get carried away with hitting, let's not forget that some moundsmen turned in stellar efforts in 1996. It's been 10 years since the National League has seen a pitcher post 24 wins, but one must wonder about the record Kevin Brown could have built with the luxury of John Smoltz's run support. If you want to point to the workhorse of 1996, move your finger in the direction of Pat Hentgen. Let's not get carried away, however. His total of 10 complete games is the lowest *ever* to lead the majors in a non-strike year (try as we might, we couldn't help but turn the discussion back to offense).

On your way through the career leaders, don't forget to stop and pay tribute to Eddie Murray's entrance into the 3,000-500 club. Any time a player can join the exclusive company of Aaron and Mays, there must be a piece of wall in Cooperstown reserved for his plaque. And if Molitor has as much left in *his* tank as he appeared to last season, a goal of cracking the top 10 in all-time hits is by no means out of the question. Maybe he'll stop at 3,142 (Robin Yount's total) just for old time's sake.

And don't forget the Bill James' Leader Boards. How else are you going to know that Erik Hanson led the league with 10 Cheap Wins? It's all about information. . . and you'll find hours of it here.

1996 American League Batting Leaders

Batting Average

Player, Team	AB	H	AVG
A Rodriguez, Sea	**601**	**215**	**.358**
F Thomas, ChA	527	184	.349
P Molitor, Min	660	225	.341
C Knoblauch, Min	578	197	.341
R Greer, Tex	542	180	.332
D Nilsson, Mil	453	150	.331
R Alomar, Bal	588	193	.328
E Martinez, Sea	499	163	.327
K Seitzer, Cle	573	187	.326
M Vaughn, Bos	635	207	.326

On-Base Percentage

Player, Team	PA*	OB	OBP
M McGwire, Oak	**548**	**256**	**.467**
E Martinez, Sea	634	294	.464
F Thomas, ChA	649	298	.459
J Thome, Cle	636	286	.450
C Knoblauch, Min	701	314	.448
M Vaughn, Bos	752	316	.420
K Seitzer, Cle	670	279	.416
A Rodriguez, Sea	671	278	.414
R Alomar, Bal	691	284	.411
P O'Neill, NYA	660	271	.411

* AB, BB, HBP, SF

Slugging Percentage

Player, Team	AB	TB	SLG
M McGwire, Oak	**423**	**309**	**.730**
J Gonzalez, Tex	541	348	.643
B Anderson, Bal	579	369	.637
A Rodriguez, Sea	601	379	.631
K Griffey Jr, Sea	545	342	.628
F Thomas, ChA	527	330	.626
A Belle, Cle	602	375	.623
J Thome, Cle	505	309	.612
E Martinez, Sea	499	297	.595
M Vaughn, Bos	635	370	.583

Games

C Ripken, Bal	**163**
R Palmeiro, Bal	162
P Molitor, Min	161
M Vaughn, Bos	161
C Fielder, NYA	160

Plate Appearances

M Vaughn, Bos	**752**
K Lofton, Cle	736
R Palmeiro, Bal	732
P Molitor, Min	729
T Phillips, ChA	719

At Bats

K Lofton, Cle	**662**
P Molitor, Min	660
C Ripken, Bal	640
I Rodriguez, Tex	639
M Vaughn, Bos	635

Hits

P Molitor, Min	**225**
A Rodriguez, Sea	215
K Lofton, Cle	210
M Vaughn, Bos	207
C Knoblauch, Min	197

Singles

P Molitor, Min	**167**
K Lofton, Cle	157
D Hamilton, Tex	145
D Jeter, NYA	142
K Seitzer, Cle	136

Doubles

A Rodriguez, Sea	**54**
E Martinez, Sea	52
I Rodriguez, Tex	47
J Cirillo, Mil	46
M Cordova, Min	46

Triples

C Knoblauch, Min	**14**
F Vina, Mil	10
4 players tied with	8

Home Runs

M McGwire, Oak	**52**
B Anderson, Bal	50
K Griffey Jr, Sea	49
A Belle, Cle	48
J Gonzalez, Tex	47

Total Bases

A Rodriguez, Sea	**379**
A Belle, Cle	375
M Vaughn, Bos	370
B Anderson, Bal	369
J Gonzalez, Tex	348

Runs Scored

A Rodriguez, Sea	**141**
C Knoblauch, Min	140
R Alomar, Bal	132
K Lofton, Cle	132
K Griffey Jr, Sea	125

Runs Batted In

A Belle, Cle	**148**
J Gonzalez, Tex	144
M Vaughn, Bos	143
R Palmeiro, Bal	142
K Griffey Jr, Sea	140

Ground Double Play

C Ripken, Bal	**28**
F Thomas, ChA	25
G Anderson, Cal	22
P Molitor, Min	21
P O'Neill, NYA	21

Sacrifice Hits

T Goodwin, KC	**21**
D Howard, KC	17
G DiSarcina, Cal	16
K Elster, Tex	16
D Lewis, ChA	15

Sacrifice Flies

B Bonilla, Bal	**17**
R Alomar, Bal	12
K Elster, Tex	11
4 players tied with	10

Stolen Bases

K Lofton, Cle	**75**
T Goodwin, KC	66
O Nixon, Tor	54
C Knoblauch, Min	45
O Vizquel, Cle	35

Caught Stealing

T Goodwin, KC	**22**
K Lofton, Cle	17
C Knoblauch, Min	14
O Nixon, Tor	13
5 players tied with	10

Walks

T Phillips, ChA	**125**
J Thome, Cle	123
E Martinez, Sea	123
M McGwire, Oak	116
F Thomas, ChA	109

Intentional Walks

F Thomas, ChA	**26**
M Vaughn, Bos	19
M McGwire, Oak	16
A Belle, Cle	15
K Griffey Jr, Sea	13

Hit by Pitch

B Anderson, Bal	**22**
C Knoblauch, Min	19
C O'Brien, Tor	17
M Vaughn, Bos	14
2 players tied with	13

Strikeouts

J Buhner, Sea	**159**
M Nieves, Det	158
M Vaughn, Bos	154
E Sprague, Tor	146
2 players tied with	145

1996 National League Batting Leaders

Batting Average

Player, Team	AB	H	AVG
T Gwynn, SD	**451**	**159**	**.353**
E Burks, Col	613	211	.344
M Piazza, LA	547	184	.336
L Johnson, NYN	682	227	.333
M Grace, ChN	547	181	.331
K Caminiti, SD	546	178	.326
E Young, Col	568	184	.324
B Gilkey, NYN	571	181	.317
J Bagwell, Hou	568	179	.315
G Sheffield, Fla	519	163	.314

On-Base Percentage

Player, Team	PA*	OB	OBP
G Sheffield, Fla	**677**	**315**	**.465**
B Bonds, SF	675	311	.461
J Bagwell, Hou	719	324	.451
M Piazza, LA	631	266	.422
R Henderson, SD	602	247	.410
B Larkin, Cin	627	257	.410
E Burks, Col	682	278	.408
K Caminiti, SD	638	260	.408
M Grace, ChN	616	244	.396
B Gilkey, NYN	656	258	.393

* AB, BB, HBP, SF

Slugging Percentage

Player, Team	AB	TB	SLG
E Burks, Col	**613**	**392**	**.639**
G Sheffield, Fla	519	324	.624
K Caminiti, SD	546	339	.621
B Bonds, SF	517	318	.615
A Galarraga, Col	626	376	.601
J Bagwell, Hou	568	324	.570
B Larkin, Cin	517	293	.567
S Sosa, ChN	498	281	.564
M Piazza, LA	547	308	.563
B Gilkey, NYN	571	321	.562

Games

C Biggio, Hou	**162**
J Bagwell, Hou	**162**
G Sheffield, Fla	161
S Finley, SD	161
2 players tied with	160

Plate Appearances

L Johnson, NYN	**724**
C Biggio, Hou	723
M Grissom, Atl	723
S Finley, SD	721
J Bagwell, Hou	719

At Bats

L Johnson, NYN	**682**
M Grissom, Atl	671
M Grudzielanek, Mon	657
S Finley, SD	655
M Lansing, Mon	641

Hits

L Johnson, NYN	**227**
E Burks, Col	211
M Grissom, Atl	207
M Grudzielanek, Mon	201
D Bichette, Col	198

Singles

L Johnson, NYN	**166**
M Grudzielanek, Mon	157
E Young, Col	149
M Grissom, Atl	142
2 players tied with	132

Doubles

J Bagwell, Hou	**48**
S Finley, SD	45
E Burks, Col	45
B Gilkey, NYN	44
H Rodriguez, Mon	42

Triples

L Johnson, NYN	**21**
T Howard, Cin	10
M Grissom, Atl	10
S Finley, SD	9
3 players tied with	8

Home Runs

A Galarraga, Col	**47**
G Sheffield, Fla	42
B Bonds, SF	42
T Hundley, NYN	41
4 players tied with	40

Total Bases

E Burks, Col	**392**
A Galarraga, Col	376
S Finley, SD	348
V Castilla, Col	345
K Caminiti, SD	339

Runs Scored

E Burks, Col	**142**
S Finley, SD	126
B Bonds, SF	122
A Galarraga, Col	119
G Sheffield, Fla	118

Runs Batted In

A Galarraga, Col	**150**
D Bichette, Col	141
K Caminiti, SD	130
B Bonds, SF	129
E Burks, Col	128

Ground Double Play

E Karros, LA	**27**
G Colbrunn, Fla	22
M Piazza, LA	21
J Mabry, StL	21
5 players tied with	20

Sacrifice Hits

D Neagle, Atl	**16**
P Martinez, Mon	**16**
T Glavine, Atl	15
J Smoltz, Atl	15
3 players tied with	14

Sacrifice Flies

D Bichette, Col	**10**
R Wilkins, SF	**10**
K Caminiti, SD	**10**
4 players tied with	9

Stolen Bases

E Young, Col	**53**
L Johnson, NYN	50
D DeShields, LA	48
B Bonds, SF	40
A Martin, Pit	38

Caught Stealing

E Young, Col	**19**
R Henderson, SD	15
R Clayton, StL	15
3 players tied with	12

Walks

B Bonds, SF	**151**
G Sheffield, Fla	142
J Bagwell, Hou	135
R Henderson, SD	125
B Larkin, Cin	96

Intentional Walks

B Bonds, SF	**30**
M Piazza, LA	21
J Bagwell, Hou	20
G Sheffield, Fla	19
K Caminiti, SD	16

Hit by Pitch

C Biggio, Hou	**27**
E Young, Col	21
A Galarraga, Col	17
J Kendall, Pit	15
2 players tied with	14

Strikeouts

H Rodriguez, Mon	**160**
A Galarraga, Col	157
T Hundley, NYN	146
S Sosa, ChN	134
R Lankford, StL	133

1996 American League Pitching Leaders

Earned Run Average

Pitcher, Team	IP	ER	ERA
J Guzman, Tor	**187.2**	**61**	**2.93**
P Hentgen, Tor	265.2	95	3.22
C Nagy, Cle	222.0	84	3.41
A Fernandez, ChA	258.0	99	3.45
K Appier, KC	211.1	85	3.62
K Hill, Tex	250.2	101	3.63
R Clemens, Bos	242.2	98	3.63
A Pettitte, NYA	221.0	95	3.87
B McDonald, Mil	221.1	96	3.90
T Belcher, KC	238.2	104	3.92

Won-Lost Percentage

Pitcher, Team	W	L	WL%
J Moyer, Sea	**13**	**3**	**.813**
C Nagy, Cle	17	5	.773
A Pettitte, NYA	21	8	.724
D Oliver, Tex	14	6	.700
P Hentgen, Tor	20	10	.667
R Pavlik, Tex	15	8	.652
J Baldwin, ChA	11	6	.647
M Mussina, Bal	19	11	.633
B Wells, Sea	12	7	.632
O Hershiser, Cle	15	9	.625

Opposition Average

Pitcher, Team	AB	H	AVG
J Guzman, Tor	**692**	**158**	**.228**
R Clemens, Bos	911	216	.237
P Hentgen, Tor	988	238	.241
K Appier, KC	783	192	.245
A Fernandez, ChA	980	248	.253
C Nagy, Cle	851	217	.255
B Radke, Min	901	231	.256
J Baldwin, ChA	654	168	.257
W Alvarez, ChA	838	216	.258
D Gooden, NYA	653	169	.259

Games

E Guardado, Min	83
M Myers, Det	83
M Stanton, Tex	81
H Slocumb, Bos	75
2 pitchers tied with	73

Games Started

M Mussina, Bal	36
11 pitchers tied with	35

Complete Games

P Hentgen, Tor	10
R Pavlik, Tex	7
K Hill, Tex	7
4 pitchers tied with	6

Games Finished

R Hernandez, ChA	61
H Slocumb, Bos	60
J Mesa, Cle	60
J Wetteland, NYA	58
M Timlin, Tor	56

Wins

A Pettitte, NYA	21
P Hentgen, Tor	20
M Mussina, Bal	19
C Nagy, Cle	17
3 pitchers tied with	16

Losses

J Abbott, Cal	18
E Hanson, Tor	17
R Robertson, Min	17
C Finley, Cal	16
B Radke, Min	16

Saves

J Wetteland, NYA	43
J Mesa, Cle	39
R Hernandez, ChA	38
T Percival, Cal	36
M Fetters, Mil	32

Shutouts

R Robertson, Min	3
P Hentgen, Tor	3
K Hill, Tex	3
R Clemens, Bos	2
F Lira, Det	2

Hits Allowed

C Haney, KC	267
M Mussina, Bal	264
S Erickson, Bal	262
T Belcher, KC	262
K Hill, Tex	250

Doubles Allowed

M Mussina, Bal	63
W Alvarez, ChA	59
C Haney, KC	58
S Erickson, Bal	55
B Radke, Min	55

Triples Allowed

T Belcher, KC	8
T Gordon, Bos	8
6 pitchers tied with	7

Home Runs Allowed

S Boskie, Cal	40
B Radke, Min	40
T Wakefield, Bos	38
A Fernandez, ChA	34
K Tapani, ChA	34

Batters Faced

P Hentgen, Tor	1100
A Fernandez, ChA	1071
K Hill, Tex	1061
M Mussina, Bal	1039
C Finley, Cal	1037

Innings Pitched

P Hentgen, Tor	265.2
A Fernandez, ChA	258.0
K Hill, Tex	250.2
M Mussina, Bal	243.1
R Clemens, Bos	242.2

Runs Allowed

T Wakefield, Bos	151
T Gordon, Bos	143
E Hanson, Tor	143
M Mussina, Bal	137
S Erickson, Bal	137

Strikeouts

R Clemens, Bos	257
C Finley, Cal	215
K Appier, KC	207
M Mussina, Bal	204
A Fernandez, ChA	200

Walks Allowed

R Robertson, Min	116
R Clemens, Bos	106
T Gordon, Bos	105
E Hanson, Tor	102
W Alvarez, ChA	97

Hit Batters

S Boskie, Cal	13
J Grimsley, Cal	13
O Hershiser, Cle	12
T Wakefield, Bos	12
3 pitchers tied with	11

Wild Pitches

C Finley, Cal	17
R Lewis, Det	14
E Hanson, Tor	13
K Tapani, ChA	13
J Abbott, Cal	13

Balks

K Hill, Tex	4
8 pitchers tied with	2

1996 National League Pitching Leaders

Earned Run Average

Pitcher, Team	IP	ER	ERA
K Brown, Fla	233.0	49	1.89
G Maddux, Atl	245.0	74	2.72
A Leiter, Fla	215.1	70	2.93
J Smoltz, Atl	253.2	83	2.94
T Glavine, Atl	235.1	78	2.98
S Trachsel, ChN	205.0	69	3.03
C Schilling, Phi	183.1	65	3.19
H Nomo, LA	228.1	81	3.19
J Fassero, Mon	231.2	85	3.30
I Valdes, LA	225.0	83	3.32

Won-Lost Percentage

Pitcher, Team	W	L	WL%
J Smoltz, Atl	24	8	.750
R Martinez, LA	15	6	.714
I Valdes, LA	15	7	.682
U Urbina, Mon	10	5	.667
A Benes, StL	18	10	.643
D Neagle, Atl	16	9	.640
M Gardner, SF	12	7	.632
J Hamilton, SD	15	9	.625
S Reynolds, Hou	16	10	.615
F Valenzuela, SD	13	8	.619

Opposition Average

Pitcher, Team	AB	H	AVG
A Leiter, Fla	756	153	.202
J Smoltz, Atl	922	199	.216
H Nomo, LA	827	180	.218
K Brown, Fla	849	187	.220
C Schilling, Phi	669	149	.223
T Stottlemyre, StL	826	191	.231
P Martinez, Mon	813	189	.232
S Trachsel, ChN	769	181	.235
G Maddux, Atl	934	225	.241
D Burba, Cin	733	179	.244

Games

B Clontz, Atl	81
B Patterson, ChN	79
M Dewey, SF	78
J Shaw, Cin	78
M Wohlers, Atl	77

Games Started

T Glavine, Atl	36
5 pitchers tied with	35

Complete Games

C Schilling, Phi	8
J Smoltz, Atl	6
4 pitchers tied with	5

Games Finished

T Worrell, LA	67
R Nen, Fla	66
M Rojas, Mon	64
M Wohlers, Atl	64
T Hoffman, SD	62

Wins

J Smoltz, Atl	24
A Benes, StL	18
K Brown, Fla	17
K Ritz, Col	17
4 pitchers tied with	16

Losses

P Rapp, Fla	16
F Castillo, ChN	16
4 pitchers tied with	14

Saves

J Brantley, Cin	44
T Worrell, LA	44
T Hoffman, SD	42
M Wohlers, Atl	39
M Rojas, Mon	36

Shutouts

K Brown, Fla	3
7 pitchers tied with	2

Hits Allowed

J Navarro, ChN	244
K Ritz, Col	236
D Kile, Hou	233
S Reynolds, Hou	227
D Neagle, Atl	226

Doubles Allowed

J Navarro, ChN	48
J Smiley, Cin	47
T Glavine, Atl	47
5 pitchers tied with	45

Triples Allowed

D Neagle, Atl	8
J Smiley, Cin	8
K Ritz, Col	8
P Wilson, NYN	7
J Navarro, ChN	7

Home Runs Allowed

M Leiter, Mon	37
P Harnisch, NYN	30
S Trachsel, ChN	30
T Stottlemyre, StL	30
4 pitchers tied with	28

Batters Faced

J Navarro, ChN	1007
J Smoltz, Atl	995
T Glavine, Atl	994
S Reynolds, Hou	981
G Maddux, Atl	978

Innings Pitched

J Smoltz, Atl	253.2
G Maddux, Atl	245.0
S Reynolds, Hou	239.0
J Navarro, ChN	236.2
T Glavine, Atl	235.1

Runs Allowed

K Ritz, Col	135
M Leiter, Mon	128
W VanLandingham, SF	123
A Benes, StL	120
2 pitchers tied with	116

Strikeouts

J Smoltz, Atl	276
H Nomo, LA	234
P Martinez, Mon	222
J Fassero, Mon	222
D Kile, Hou	219

Walks Allowed

A Leiter, Fla	119
K Ritz, Col	105
D Burba, Cin	97
D Kile, Hou	97
T Stottlemyre, StL	93

Hit Batters

D Kile, Hou	16
K Brown, Fla	16
M Leiter, Mon	16
M Thompson, Col	13
2 pitchers tied with	12

Wild Pitches

M Williams, Phi	16
J Isringhausen, NYN	14
J Hamilton, SD	14
3 pitchers tied with	13

Balks

I Valdes, LA	5
M Leiter, Mon	4
11 pitchers tied with	3

1996 American League Special Batting Leaders

Scoring Position

Player, Team	AB	H	AVG
S Brosius, Oak	**115**	**42**	**.365**
C Knoblauch, Min	110	40	.364
F Thomas, ChA	146	53	.363
M McGwire, Oak	103	37	.359
B Williams, NYA	146	52	.356
A Belle, Cle	154	54	.351
J Franco, Cle	120	42	.350
A Rodriguez, Sea	149	52	.349
B Higginson, Det	90	31	.344
T Martinez, NYA	180	61	.339

Leadoff On-Base%

Player, Team	PA	OB	OBP
B Higginson, Det	**152**	**76**	**.500**
C Knoblauch, Min	699	313	.448
R Alomar, Bal	227	92	.405
T Phillips, ChA	713	287	.403
B Anderson, Bal	483	194	.402
T Batista, Oak	157	63	.401
W Boggs, NYA	359	138	.384
D Jeter, NYA	195	74	.379
O Nixon, Tor	568	214	.377
T Raines, NYA	178	67	.376

Cleanup Slugging%

Player, Team	AB	TB	SLG
M McGwire, Oak	**419**	**304**	**.726**
J Gonzalez, Tex	536	347	.647
A Belle, Cle	586	369	.630
M Vaughn, Bos	126	79	.627
J Canseco, Bos	344	206	.599
R Palmeiro, Bal	409	243	.594
E Martinez, Sea	419	246	.587
T Salmon, Cal	224	131	.585
D Nilsson, Mil	184	104	.565
J Jaha, Mil	184	101	.549

Vs LHP

R Kelly, Min	**.406**
F Thomas, ChA	.403
C Knoblauch, Min	.388
J Valentin, Bos	.380
J Gonzalez, Tex	.376

Vs RHP

D Nilsson, Mil	**.359**
A Rodriguez, Sea	.354
P Molitor, Min	.340
J Thome, Cle	.339
P O'Neill, NYA	.338

Late & Close

D Nilsson, Mil	**.379**
P Meares, Min	.356
W Boggs, NYA	.354
J Girardi, NYA	.351
R Alomar, Bal	.349

Bases Loaded

B Higginson, Det	**.667**
W Cordero, Bos	.615
O Vizquel, Cle	.615
B Surhoff, Bal	.615
C Knoblauch, Min	.545

OBP vs LHP

F Thomas, ChA	**.544**
M McGwire, Oak	.511
J Jaha, Mil	.487
J Valentin, Bos	.481
C Knoblauch, Min	.480

OBP vs RHP

J Thome, Cle	**.489**
E Martinez, Sea	.461
M McGwire, Oak	.453
P O'Neill, NYA	.445
D Nilsson, Mil	.440

BA at Home

M Vaughn, Bos	**.380**
J Franco, Cle	.364
A Rodriguez, Sea	.364
P Molitor, Min	.359
R Greer, Tex	.358

BA on the Road

F Thomas, ChA	**.362**
K Seitzer, Cle	.356
A Rodriguez, Sea	.352
D Martinez, ChA	.350
J Cirillo, Mil	.350

SLG vs LHP

J Gonzalez, Tex	**.887**
F Thomas, ChA	.798
M McGwire, Oak	.784
K Griffey Jr, Sea	.741
B Williams, NYA	.694

SLG vs RHP

M McGwire, Oak	**.713**
J Thome, Cle	.696
B Anderson, Bal	.686
B Higginson, Det	.623
A Rodriguez, Sea	.620

SB Success %

R Durham, ChA	**88.2**
P Listach, Mil	83.3
J Damon, KC	83.3
J Frye, Bos	81.8
K Lofton, Cle	81.5

Times on Base

M Vaughn, Bos	**316**
C Knoblauch, Min	314
F Thomas, ChA	298
E Martinez, Sea	294
A Belle, Cle	293

AB per HR

M McGwire, Oak	**8.1**
K Griffey Jr, Sea	11.1
J Gonzalez, Tex	11.5
B Anderson, Bal	11.6
A Belle, Cle	12.5

Ground/Fly Ratio

O Nixon, Tor	**3.04**
T Goodwin, KC	2.37
D Jeter, NYA	2.11
P Molitor, Min	1.91
G DiSarcina, Cal	1.89

GDP/GDP Opp

J Valentin, Mil	**3.0**
T Goodwin, KC	3.1
D Nilsson, Mil	3.4
P Listach, Mil	3.6
J Damon, KC	3.7

% CS by Catchers

I Rodriguez, Tex	**51.1**
R Karkovice, ChA	40.7
D Wilson, Sea	39.0
B Ausmus, Det	33.8
M Matheny, Mil	32.5

Pitches Seen

T Phillips, ChA	**3051**
R Alomar, Bal	2953
C Knoblauch, Min	2953
M Vaughn, Bos	2872
J Thome, Cle	2837

Pitches per PA

J Thome, Cle	**4.46**
M Tettleton, Tex	4.33
E Martinez, Sea	4.27
T Phillips, ChA	4.24
R Alomar, Bal	4.22

% Pitches Taken

E Martinez, Sea	**67.3**
W Boggs, NYA	65.6
J Frye, Bos	64.9
M McLemore, Tex	64.8
M Tettleton, Tex	64.3

Steals of Third

K Lofton, Cle	**24**
O Nixon, Tor	12
T Goodwin, KC	11
P Listach, Mil	7
2 players tied with	6

1996 National League Special Batting Leaders

Scoring Position

Player, Team	AB	H	AVG
B Jordan, StL	147	62	.422
A Galarraga, Col	189	78	.413
B Gilkey, NYN	155	63	.406
K Caminiti, SD	155	60	.387
J Eisenreich, Phi	83	32	.386
T Gwynn, SD	84	32	.381
B Bonds, SF	115	43	.374
E Burks, Col	174	63	.362
L Gonzalez, ChN	114	40	.351
M Piazza, LA	140	49	.350

Leadoff On-Base%

Player, Team	PA	OB	OBP
R Henderson, SD	575	235	.409
J Cangelosi, Hou	227	91	.401
E Young, Col	615	241	.392
Q Veras, Fla	253	97	.383
L Dykstra, Phi	155	59	.381
O Smith, StL	161	61	.379
L Johnson, NYN	699	253	.362
B McRae, ChN	710	256	.361
M Grissom, Atl	718	251	.350
C Garcia, Pit	247	85	.344

Cleanup Slugging%

Player, Team	AB	TB	SLG
B Bonds, SF	136	91	.669
L Walker, Col	192	126	.656
A Galarraga, Col	257	164	.638
K Caminiti, SD	434	272	.627
G Sheffield, Fla	216	125	.579
S Sosa, ChN	447	258	.577
B Jordan, StL	288	151	.524
T Hundley, NYN	332	170	.512
M Williams, SF	325	163	.502
F McGriff, Atl	609	304	.499

Vs LHP

E Burks, Col	.427
J Conine, Fla	.393
J Bagwell, Hou	.364
K Caminiti, SD	.358
T Gwynn, SD	.353

Vs RHP

M Grace, ChN	.343
E Young, Col	.336
L Johnson, NYN	.334
A Martin, Pit	.327
H Morris, Cin	.326

Late & Close

T Gwynn, SD	.471
H Morris, Cin	.369
L Johnson, NYN	.368
J Bagwell, Hou	.360
C Jones, Atl	.352

Bases Loaded

L Gonzalez, ChN	.800
B Jordan, StL	.684
D Segui, Mon	.600
M Grace, ChN	.600
O Merced, Pit	.571

OBP vs LHP

J Bagwell, Hou	.517
E Burks, Col	.488
G Sheffield, Fla	.460
J Conine, Fla	.449
B Larkin, Cin	.435

OBP vs RHP

B Bonds, SF	.483
G Sheffield, Fla	.466
J Bagwell, Hou	.434
M Grace, ChN	.412
M Piazza, LA	.410

BA at Home

E Young, Col	.412
E Burks, Col	.390
D Bichette, Col	.366
A Galarraga, Col	.359
T Gwynn, SD	.351

BA on the Road

L Johnson, NYN	.369
M Piazza, LA	.353
J Mabry, StL	.331
M Grace, ChN	.319
K Caminiti, SD	.315

SLG vs LHP

E Burks, Col	.741
K Caminiti, SD	.721
A Galarraga, Col	.660
J Conine, Fla	.656
G Sheffield, Fla	.636

SLG vs RHP

B Bonds, SF	.624
G Sheffield, Fla	.621
T Hundley, NYN	.620
E Burks, Col	.609
R Klesko, Atl	.604

SB Success %

D Bell, Hou	90.6
L Walker, Col	90.0
B Bonds, SF	85.1
E Burks, Col	84.2
M Morandini, Phi	83.9

Times on Base

J Bagwell, Hou	324
G Sheffield, Fla	315
B Bonds, SF	311
E Burks, Col	278
C Biggio, Hou	276

AB per HR

B Bonds, SF	12.3
G Sheffield, Fla	12.4
S Sosa, ChN	12.4
T Hundley, NYN	13.2
A Galarraga, Col	13.3

Ground/Fly Ratio

R Ordonez, NYN	2.92
J Lopez, Atl	2.05
L Johnson, NYN	1.99
R Clayton, StL	1.97
D Bell, Hou	1.97

GDP/GDP Opp

R Aurilia, SF	1.7
T Hollandsworth, LA	2.2
S Andrews, Mon	2.9
A Ochoa, NYN	3.2
R Mondesi, LA	4.6

% CS by Catchers

C Johnson, Fla	47.6
K Manwaring, Hou	44.6
T Pagnozzi, StL	34.3
R Wilkins, SF	31.3
B Santiago, Phi	30.4

Pitches Seen

J Bagwell, Hou	2894
E Burks, Col	2735
G Sheffield, Fla	2699
R Henderson, SD	2696
2 players tied with	2678

Pitches per PA

R Henderson, SD	4.48
B Larkin, Cin	4.12
T Zeile, Phi	4.11
R Lankford, StL	4.08
T Hundley, NYN	4.06

% Pitches Taken

R Henderson, SD	69.4
T Zeile, Phi	65.1
W Weiss, Col	63.5
B Larkin, Cin	62.9
B Bonds, SF	62.6

Steals of Third

D Bell, Hou	11
B Larkin, Cin	10
B Hunter, Hou	10
L Johnson, NYN	10
3 players tied with	8

1996 American League Special Pitching Leaders

Baserunners Per 9 IP

Player, Team	IP	BR	BR/9
J Guzman, Tor	187.2	218	10.45
B Radke, Min	232.0	292	11.33
C Nagy, Cle	222.0	281	11.39
A Fernandez, ChA	258.0	327	11.41
P Hentgen, Tor	265.2	337	11.42
K Appier, KC	211.1	272	11.58
R Clemens, Bos	242.2	326	12.09
J Baldwin, ChA	169.0	229	12.20
D Wells, Bal	224.1	305	12.24
B McDonald, Mil	221.1	301	12.24

Run Support Per 9 IP

Player, Team	IP	R	R/9
T Gordon, Bos	215.2	176	7.34
M Mussina, Bal	243.1	185	6.84
B Witt, Tex	199.2	151	6.81
S Karl, Mil	207.1	156	6.77
D Oliver, Tex	173.2	128	6.63
S Aldred, Min	165.1	119	6.48
R Pavlik, Tex	201.0	143	6.40
A Pettitte, NYA	221.0	157	6.39
W Alvarez, ChA	217.1	153	6.34
S Erickson, Bal	222.1	151	6.11

Save Percentage

Player, Team	OP	SV	SV%
T Percival, Cal	39	36	.923
J Wetteland, NYA	47	43	.915
B Taylor, Oak	19	17	.895
J Mesa, Cle	44	39	.886
M Fetters, Mil	38	32	.842
M Henneman, Tex	37	31	.838
R Hernandez, ChA	46	38	.826
R Myers, Bal	38	31	.816
M Timlin, Tor	38	31	.816
H Slocumb, Bos	39	31	.795

Hits per 9 IP

J Guzman, Tor	7.58
R Clemens, Bos	8.01
P Hentgen, Tor	8.06
K Appier, KC	8.18
A Fernandez, ChA	8.65

Home Runs per 9 IP

P Hentgen, Tor	0.68
K Hill, Tex	0.68
R Clemens, Bos	0.70
K Appier, KC	0.72
K Rogers, NYA	0.80

Strikeouts per 9 IP

R Clemens, Bos	9.5
K Appier, KC	8.8
C Finley, Cal	8.1
J Guzman, Tor	7.9
M Mussina, Bal	7.5

GDP per 9 IP

S Erickson, Bal	1.5
E Hanson, Tor	1.2
T Belcher, KC	1.2
R Robertson, Min	1.1
C Nagy, Cle	1.1

Vs LHB

M Rivera, NYA	.215
J Guzman, Tor	.224
D Wells, Bal	.225
R Clemens, Bos	.236
D Springer, Cal	.247

Vs RHB

K Appier, KC	.228
P Hentgen, Tor	.233
J Guzman, Tor	.233
J Rosado, KC	.233
R Clemens, Bos	.239

OBP Leadoff Inning

A Fernandez, ChA	.274
J Guzman, Tor	.291
B Radke, Min	.293
T Belcher, KC	.293
C Ogea, Cle	.294

BA Allowed ScPos

R Lewis, Det	.184
J Guzman, Tor	.199
R Clemens, Bos	.199
C Nagy, Cle	.214
B McDonald, Mil	.224

SLG Allowed

P Hentgen, Tor	.355
R Clemens, Bos	.358
J Guzman, Tor	.363
K Appier, KC	.370
K Rogers, NYA	.378

OBP Allowed

J Guzman, Tor	.289
B Radke, Min	.302
C Nagy, Cle	.306
A Fernandez, ChA	.307
P Hentgen, Tor	.308

PkOf Throw/Runner

J Guzman, Tor	1.35
K Rogers, NYA	1.28
P Hentgen, Tor	1.07
K Appier, KC	0.98
S Boskie, Cal	0.94

SB% Allowed

J Key, NYA	25.0
C Haney, KC	35.7
E Hanson, Tor	40.0
K Rogers, NYA	40.0
M Mussina, Bal	42.9

Pitches per Batter

O Hershiser, Cle	3.36
S Erickson, Bal	3.50
C Haney, KC	3.51
B Radke, Min	3.63
F Rodriguez, Min	3.65

Grd/Fly Ratio Off

S Erickson, Bal	2.76
O Hershiser, Cle	2.26
C Nagy, Cle	2.01
A Pettitte, NYA	1.74
R Clemens, Bos	1.68

K/BB Ratio

J Guzman, Tor	3.11
M Mussina, Bal	2.96
A Fernandez, ChA	2.78
K Appier, KC	2.76
C Nagy, Cle	2.74

Wins in Relief

M Rivera, NYA	8
R Carmona, Sea	8
A Rhodes, Bal	8
B Wickman, Mil	7
M Karchner, ChA	7

Holds

M Rivera, NYA	27
M Stanton, Tex	22
J Russell, Tex	20
J Orosco, Bal	19
2 pitchers tied with	18

Blown Saves

J Montgomery, KC	10
H Slocumb, Bos	8
R Hernandez, ChA	8
M Karchner, ChA	8
3 pitchers tied with	7

% Inherited Scored

B Taylor, Oak	14.7
D Cook, Tex	19.8
N Charlton, Sea	20.5
L Thomas, ChA	21.2
J Orosco, Bal	21.7

1st Batter OBP

D Cook, Tex	.065
M Rivera, NYA	.089
T Percival, Cal	.107
M Myers, Det	.132
E Guardado, Min	.162

1996 National League Special Pitching Leaders

Baserunners Per 9 IP

Player, Team	IP	BR	BR/9
J Smoltz, Atl	**253.2**	**256**	**9.08**
K Brown, Fla	233.0	236	9.12
G Maddux, Atl	245.0	256	9.40
C Schilling, Phi	183.1	202	9.92
S Reynolds, Hou	239.0	279	10.51
H Nomo, LA	228.1	267	10.52
J Fassero, Mon	231.2	275	10.68
D Darwin, Hou	164.2	199	10.88
P Martinez, Mon	216.2	262	10.88
J Smiley, Cin	217.1	265	10.97

Run Support Per 9 IP

Player, Team	IP	R	R/9
K Ritz, Col	**213.0**	**171**	**7.23**
M Gardner, SF	179.1	136	6.83
R Martinez, LA	168.2	112	5.98
A Reynoso, Col	168.2	111	5.92
M Thompson, Col	169.2	108	5.73
J Smoltz, Atl	253.2	160	5.68
M Leiter, Mon	205.0	129	5.66
F Valenzuela, SD	171.2	108	5.66
A Benes, StL	191.0	115	5.42
M Clark, NYN	212.1	127	5.38

Save Percentage

Player, Team	OP	SV	SV%
M Rojas, Mon	**40**	**36**	**.900**
J Brantley, Cin	49	44	.898
R Bottalico, Phi	38	34	.895
M Wohlers, Atl	44	39	.886
D Eckersley, StL	34	30	.882
T Hoffman, SD	49	42	.857
T Wendell, ChN	21	18	.857
R Beck, SF	42	35	.833
R Nen, Fla	42	35	.833
T Worrell, LA	53	44	.830

Hits per 9 IP

A Leiter, Fla	**6.39**
J Smoltz, Atl	7.06
H Nomo, LA	7.09
K Brown, Fla	7.22
C Schilling, Phi	7.31

Home Runs per 9 IP

K Brown, Fla	**0.31**
G Maddux, Atl	0.40
T Glavine, Atl	0.54
A Leiter, Fla	0.59
R Martinez, LA	0.64

Strikeouts per 9 IP

J Smoltz, Atl	**9.8**
H Nomo, LA	9.2
P Martinez, Mon	9.2
D Kile, Hou	9.0
C Schilling, Phi	8.9

GDP per 9 IP

P Rapp, Fla	**1.3**
P Astacio, LA	1.2
M Thompson, Col	1.1
J Isringhausen, NYN	1.0
J Hamilton, SD	1.0

Vs LHB

S Reynolds, Hou	**.209**
C Schilling, Phi	.215
H Nomo, LA	.216
K Brown, Fla	.221
J Smoltz, Atl	.221

Vs RHB

A Leiter, Fla	**.194**
T Stottlemyre, StL	.198
D Darwin, Hou	.199
J Smoltz, Atl	.212
P Martinez, Mon	.213

OBP Leadoff Inning

G Maddux, Atl	**.216**
K Brown, Fla	.238
J Smoltz, Atl	.246
D Osborne, StL	.254
M Clark, NYN	.263

BA Allowed ScPos

S Trachsel, ChN	**.137**
K Brown, Fla	.188
D Burba, Cin	.193
A Leiter, Fla	.193
J Shaw, Cin	.202

SLG Allowed

K Brown, Fla	**.289**
A Leiter, Fla	.316
J Smoltz, Atl	.331
G Maddux, Atl	.337
R Martinez, LA	.341

OBP Allowed

J Smoltz, Atl	**.260**
K Brown, Fla	.262
G Maddux, Atl	.264
C Schilling, Phi	.278
S Reynolds, Hou	.288

PkOf Throw/Runner

A Reynoso, Col	**1.67**
M Leiter, Mon	1.46
O Fernandez, SF	1.26
I Valdes, LA	1.20
M Thompson, Col	1.19

SB% Allowed

D Osborne, StL	**28.6**
C Schilling, Phi	33.3
A Benes, StL	38.1
A Leiter, Fla	43.8
J Smoltz, Atl	45.5

Pitches per Batter

G Maddux, Atl	**3.10**
B Tewksbury, SD	3.26
D Darwin, Hou	3.38
P Astacio, LA	3.43
M Clark, NYN	3.47

Grd/Fly Ratio Off

K Brown, Fla	**3.42**
G Maddux, Atl	3.04
J Hamilton, SD	2.40
B Tewksbury, SD	1.99
K Ritz, Col	1.96

K/BB Ratio

G Maddux, Atl	**6.14**
J Smoltz, Atl	5.02
K Brown, Fla	4.82
S Reynolds, Hou	4.64
J Fassero, Mon	4.04

Wins in Relief

A Osuna, LA	**9**
T Hoffman, SD	**9**
J Shaw, Cin	8
M Petkovsek, StL	8
5 pitchers tied with	7

Holds

J Shaw, Cin	**22**
S Reed, Col	**22**
D Bochtler, SD	20
R Honeycutt, StL	19
G McMichael, Atl	18

Blown Saves

T Worrell, LA	**9**
J Franco, NYN	8
5 pitchers tied with	7

% Inherited Scored

M Wohlers, Atl	**16.7**
T Mathews, StL	**16.7**
T Hoffman, SD	17.1
L Casian, ChN	18.4
B Patterson, ChN	23.3

1st Batter OBP

R Bottalico, Phi	**.123**
H Carrasco, Cin	.130
D Bochtler, SD	.143
T Mathews, StL	.150
R Beck, SF	.150

1996 Active Career Batting Leaders

Batting Average

Player	AB	H	AVG
T Gwynn	7595	2560	.337
W Boggs	8100	2697	.333
F Thomas	3291	1077	.327
M Piazza	2002	653	.326
E Martinez	3276	1031	.315
K Lofton	2821	883	.313
M Grace	4903	1514	.309
H Morris	2922	902	.309
P Molitor	9795	3014	.308
R Greer	1236	380	.307
J Bagwell	3091	950	.307
C Knoblauch	3328	1019	.306
M Greenwell	4623	1400	.303
J Franco	6813	2061	.303
K Griffey Jr	3985	1204	.302
R Alomar	5048	1522	.302
W Clark	5548	1667	.300
J Cirillo	1020	305	.299
B Larkin	4946	1476	.298
R Palmeiro	5483	1636	.298
J Conine	2237	667	.298
C Baerga	3692	1100	.298
W McGee	6809	2028	.298
V Castilla	1644	488	.297
K Seitzer	5080	1504	.296

On-Base Percentage

Player	PA	OB	OBP
F Thomas	4140	1870	.452
W Boggs	9489	4000	.422
E Martinez	3899	1626	.417
R Henderson	10328	4198	.406
J Bagwell	3690	1498	.406
B Bonds	6710	2711	.404
J Thome	1988	803	.404
J Olerud	3684	1456	.395
T Salmon	2456	962	.392
C Knoblauch	3848	1505	.391
D Magadan	3884	1519	.391
T Gwynn	8334	3241	.389
M Piazza	2223	863	.388
M Vaughn	3143	1217	.387
R Greer	1422	549	.386
T Raines	9234	3558	.385
M Ramirez	1607	618	.385
F McGriff	6007	2302	.383
K Griffey Jr	4552	1733	.381
M Grace	5561	2117	.381
M McGwire	4973	1890	.380
G Sheffield	3745	1422	.380
K Lofton	3154	1196	.379
W Clark	6383	2420	.379
B Butler	9012	3402	.377

Slugging Percentage

Player	AB	TB	SLG
F Thomas	3291	1970	.599
A Belle	3441	1995	.580
M Piazza	2002	1119	.559
R Klesko	1133	631	.557
J Gonzalez	3130	1727	.552
M Ramirez	1377	757	.550
K Griffey Jr	3985	2187	.549
B Bonds	5537	3032	.548
M McGwire	4082	2221	.544
F McGriff	5129	2719	.530
J Thome	1647	873	.530
T Salmon	2085	1105	.530
K Mitchell	3948	2083	.528
M Vaughn	2692	1419	.527
J Bagwell	3091	1624	.525
J Canseco	5071	2640	.521
V Castilla	1644	849	.516
L Walker	3132	1597	.510
E Martinez	3276	1660	.507
D Strawberry	5045	2544	.504
J Edmonds	1339	675	.504
G Sheffield	3215	1612	.501
R Mondesi	1690	846	.501
D Justice	2858	1425	.499
M Williams	4139	2062	.498

Games

E Murray	2971
A Dawson	2627
O Smith	2573
P Molitor	2422
C Ripken	2381
R Henderson	2340
H Baines	2326
A Trammell	2293
T Wallach	2212
W Boggs	2123
C Davis	2115
G Gaetti	2113
T Raines	2112
B Butler	2108
R Sandberg	2029

Runs Scored

R Henderson	1829
P Molitor	1644
E Murray	1614
T Raines	1419
A Dawson	1373
W Boggs	1367
C Ripken	1366
B Butler	1307
R Sandberg	1264
O Smith	1257
A Trammell	1231
T Gwynn	1140
B Bonds	1121
H Baines	1113
C Davis	1099

Runs Batted In

E Murray	1899
A Dawson	1591
C Ripken	1369
H Baines	1356
J Carter	1280
C Davis	1195
G Gaetti	1155
P Molitor	1149
T Wallach	1125
J Canseco	1033
R Sierra	1024
A Trammell	1003
R Sandberg	997
B Bonds	993
B Bonilla	965

Stolen Bases

R Henderson	1186
T Raines	787
V Coleman	752
O Smith	580
B Butler	543
O Nixon	498
P Molitor	484
B Bonds	380
J Samuel	378
R Sandberg	337
W McGee	330
E Davis	329
K Lofton	327
M Grissom	323
A Dawson	314

Hits		Home Runs		Strikeouts		AB per HR	
E Murray	**3218**	**E Murray**	**501**	**A Dawson**	**1509**	**M McGwire**	**12.4**
P Molitor	3014	A Dawson	438	E Murray	1490	A Belle	14.2
A Dawson	2774	J Carter	357	C Davis	1484	J Gonzalez	14.6
W Boggs	2697	C Ripken	353	R Deer	1409	F Thomas	14.8
T Gwynn	2560	B Bonds	334	J Samuel	1401	R Klesko	14.9
C Ripken	2549	M McGwire	329	G Gaetti	1398	C Fielder	15.2
O Smith	2460	J Canseco	328	D Tartabull	1358	J Canseco	15.5
R Henderson	2450	H Baines	323	J Canseco	1349	M Piazza	15.6
H Baines	2425	F McGriff	317	A Galarraga	1328	F McGriff	16.2
A Trammell	2365	G Gaetti	315	T Wallach	1307	D Strawberry	16.4
T Raines	2352	D Strawberry	308	M Tettleton	1295	B Bonds	16.6
B Butler	2278	C Davis	298	T Phillips	1237	M Ramirez	16.6
R Sandberg	2268	C Fielder	289	D Strawberry	1237	J Buhner	16.7
C Davis	2089	R Sandberg	270	H Baines	1225	K Griffey Jr	16.7
T Wallach	2085	D Tartabull	262	2 players tied with	1221	M Williams	16.8

Doubles		Walks		K/BB Ratio		GDP/GDP Opp	
E Murray	**553**	**R Henderson**	**1675**	**W Boggs**	**0.49**	**E Williams**	**21.7**
P Molitor	544	E Murray	1318	T Gwynn	0.54	D Valle	26.4
W Boggs	518	W Boggs	1280	O Smith	0.55	J Lopez	26.9
A Dawson	503	T Raines	1168	E Young	0.62	T Pena	27.7
C Ripken	487	T Phillips	1099	M Grace	0.66	M Blowers	27.8
T Wallach	432	B Butler	1087	F Thomas	0.67	R Gonzales	28.5
H Baines	416	B Bonds	1082	R Henderson	0.71	J Franco	28.6
A Trammell	412	O Smith	1072	T Raines	0.72	P Meares	29.6
R Henderson	412	C Davis	1022	D Magadan	0.73	G Myers	30.0
T Gwynn	411	P Molitor	1004	J Reed	0.74	A Belle	30.2
O Smith	402	C Ripken	960	G Jefferies	0.74	B Mayne	30.3
T Raines	381	M Tettleton	946	L Dykstra	0.79	D Wilson	30.3
J Carter	380	H Baines	877	M Greenwell	0.79	T Steinbach	30.4
R Sandberg	377	A Trammell	850	B Butler	0.80	F Thomas	30.5
G Gaetti	376	F McGriff	812	B Bonds	0.80	D Clark	31.3

Triples		Intentional Walks		SB Success %		AB per RBI	
B Butler	**128**	**B Bonds**	**226**	**E Davis**	**85.9**	**F Thomas**	**4.5**
T Raines	109	E Murray	222	T Raines	85.2	A Belle	4.6
P Molitor	105	T Gwynn	177	B Larkin	84.4	M McGwire	4.7
L Johnson	99	W Boggs	169	S Javier	84.1	J Gonzalez	4.7
A Dawson	98	C Davis	164	M Grissom	82.6	M Ramirez	4.8
J Samuel	98	H Baines	162	K Lofton	82.2	M Piazza	4.9
W McGee	89	A Dawson	143	V Coleman	80.9	J Canseco	4.9
V Coleman	89	T Raines	142	R Henderson	80.9	M Vaughn	5.0
T Gwynn	82	W Clark	134	D Bell	80.0	C Fielder	5.0
R Sandberg	76	D Strawberry	127	L Dykstra	79.8	J Buhner	5.2
O Smith	69	K Griffey Jr	119	O Smith	79.7	R Klesko	5.2
D White	64	F McGriff	112	P Molitor	79.5	J Bagwell	5.2
S Finley	64	B Bonilla	110	R Alomar	79.2	D Strawberry	5.4
O Guillen	62	F Thomas	109	D White	79.2	D Tartabull	5.4
R Henderson	59	C Ripken	100	M Morandini	78.1	K Mitchell	5.4

1996 Active Career Pitching Leaders

Wins		Losses		Saves		Shutouts	
D Martinez	**240**	**D Martinez**	**182**	**L Smith**	**473**	**R Clemens**	**38**
D Eckersley	192	D Eckersley	165	D Eckersley	353	F Valenzuela	31
R Clemens	192	D Darwin	161	J Franco	323	D Martinez	29
F Viola	176	K Gross	157	R Myers	274	O Hershiser	25
M Langston	172	M Morgan	155	D Jones	242	D Gooden	24
F Valenzuela	171	F Viola	150	J Montgomery	242	D Drabek	21
D Gooden	168	M Langston	146	T Worrell	221	D Cone	21
O Hershiser	165	S Sanderson	143	R Aguilera	211	G Maddux	21
G Maddux	165	R Honeycutt	143	M Henneman	193	D Eckersley	20
J Key	164	F Valenzuela	141	J Russell	186	R Martinez	20
S Sanderson	163	T Candiotti	135	J Wetteland	180	M Langston	18
D Darwin	158	M Gubicza	135	G Olson	172	T Belcher	17
K Gross	140	D Jackson	122	R Beck	162	F Viola	16
T Glavine	139	B Witt	119	R McDowell	159	M Gubicza	16
D Drabek	137	O Hershiser	117	D Plesac	148	Z Smith	16

Games		Games Started		CG Freq		Innings Pitched	
L Smith	**997**	**D Martinez**	**548**	**D Eckersley**	**0.28**	**D Martinez**	**3860.0**
D Eckersley	964	F Viola	420	F Valenzuela	0.28	D Eckersley	3193.0
J Orosco	885	S Sanderson	407	R Clemens	0.26	F Valenzuela	2841.0
R Honeycutt	795	F Valenzuela	406	J McDowell	0.25	F Viola	2836.1
R McDowell	723	M Langston	398	G Maddux	0.23	R Clemens	2776.0
J Franco	712	R Clemens	382	C Schilling	0.22	M Langston	2772.0
P Assenmacher	685	K Gross	365	D Martinez	0.22	D Darwin	2711.1
D Darwin	652	O Hershiser	362	D Gooden	0.20	S Sanderson	2561.0
D Martinez	630	D Eckersley	361	M Langston	0.20	O Hershiser	2529.1
M Jackson	623	T Candiotti	346	K Brown	0.20	K Gross	2462.1
D Plesac	607	J Key	344	T Mulholland	0.19	G Maddux	2365.2
R Myers	605	D Drabek	335	D Cone	0.19	D Gooden	2340.1
J Russell	589	D Gooden	332	T Candiotti	0.19	T Candiotti	2317.2
J Jones	578	G Maddux	332	O Hershiser	0.19	J Key	2300.0
M Eichhorn	563	M Morgan	329	R Johnson	0.18	D Drabek	2257.0

Batters Faced		Home Runs Allowed		Walks Allowed		Strikeouts	
D Martinez	**16119**	**D Martinez**	**356**	**M Langston**	**1190**	**R Clemens**	**2590**
D Eckersley	13145	D Eckersley	332	B Witt	1121	M Langston	2335
F Valenzuela	11979	S Sanderson	297	D Martinez	1117	D Eckersley	2334
F Viola	11933	F Viola	294	F Valenzuela	1105	D Martinez	2070
M Langston	11682	M Langston	283	K Gross	966	F Valenzuela	2013
R Clemens	11384	D Darwin	272	F Viola	864	D Gooden	2001
D Darwin	11364	K Gross	226	R Clemens	856	F Viola	1844
S Sanderson	10709	J Key	225	C Finley	850	D Cone	1812
K Gross	10670	F Valenzuela	214	D Jackson	788	D Darwin	1769
O Hershiser	10525	G Swindell	201	M Gubicza	783	S Fernandez	1740
T Candiotti	9791	D Drabek	196	D Darwin	780	R Johnson	1709
D Gooden	9654	R Clemens	194	R Johnson	780	K Gross	1707
G Maddux	9637	M Morgan	192	O Hershiser	762	O Hershiser	1679
J Key	9490	C Finley	191	T Candiotti	750	G Maddux	1643
M Gubicza	9457	S Fernandez	190	D Cone	750	B Witt	1616

Earned Run Average

Player	IP	ER	ERA
J Franco	**876.0**	**250**	**2.57**
G Maddux	2365.2	753	2.86
L Smith	1268.1	420	2.98
J Orosco	1076.2	357	2.98
M Eichhorn	885.2	295	3.00
R Clemens	2776.0	943	3.06
A Pena	1057.1	365	3.11
O Hershiser	2529.1	888	3.16
D Cone	1994.0	701	3.16
J Fassero	850.0	302	3.20
R Myers	768.1	273	3.20
D Jones	785.1	280	3.21
D Gooden	2340.1	842	3.24
K Appier	1429.2	521	3.28
R McDowell	1050.0	385	3.30

Winning Percentage

Player	W	L	W%
M Mussina	**90**	**41**	**.687**
D Gooden	168	92	.646
R Clemens	192	111	.634
D Cone	136	80	.630
R Johnson	104	64	.619
G Maddux	165	104	.613
J Key	164	104	.612
P Hentgen	67	43	.609
J McDowell	119	77	.607
R Martinez	106	69	.606
J Guzman	67	44	.604
T Glavine	139	92	.602
K Appier	95	65	.594
O Hershiser	165	117	.585
K Rogers	82	59	.582

Opposition Batting

Player	AB	H	AVG
S Fernandez	**6774**	**1417**	**.209**
R Johnson	5503	1173	.213
M Jackson	2940	639	.217
J Orosco	3924	867	.221
D Cone	7336	1639	.223
R Clemens	10320	2359	.229
J Smoltz	6688	1545	.231
E Plunk	3454	799	.231
R Myers	2815	652	.232
L Smith	4699	1105	.235
K Appier	5330	1260	.236
R Martinez	5576	1319	.237
D Gooden	8731	2067	.237
C Schilling	3707	880	.237
G Maddux	8823	2102	.238

Hits Per 9 Innings

Player	IP	H	H/9
S Fernandez	**1861.2**	**1417**	**6.85**
R Johnson	1521.0	1173	6.94
M Jackson	810.0	639	7.10
J Orosco	1076.2	867	7.25
D Cone	1994.0	1639	7.40
R Myers	768.1	652	7.64
R Clemens	2776.0	2359	7.65
E Plunk	937.1	799	7.67
J Smoltz	1804.1	1545	7.71
L Smith	1268.1	1105	7.84
K Appier	1429.2	1260	7.93
R Martinez	1496.1	1319	7.93
D Gooden	2340.1	2067	7.95
G Maddux	2365.2	2102	8.00
C Schilling	988.1	880	8.01

Homeruns Per 9 Innings

Player	IP	HR	HR/9
R McDowell	**1050.0**	**50**	**0.43**
G Maddux	2365.2	119	0.45
J Franco	876.0	48	0.49
M Eichhorn	885.2	49	0.50
B Swift	1389.2	84	0.54
D Gooden	2340.1	142	0.55
D Jackson	2005.0	122	0.55
K Brown	1684.0	103	0.55
K Appier	1429.2	89	0.56
D Jones	785.1	49	0.56
Z Smith	1919.1	122	0.57
T Glavine	1956.1	127	0.58
O Hershiser	2529.1	168	0.60
J Fassero	850.0	57	0.60
L Smith	1268.1	87	0.62

Baserunners Per 9 Innings

Player	IP	BR	BR/9
G Maddux	**2365.2**	**2754**	**10.48**
S Fernandez	1861.2	2171	10.50
D Eckersley	3193.0	3774	10.64
M Mussina	1137.2	1351	10.69
R Clemens	2776.0	3301	10.70
C Schilling	988.1	1186	10.80
J Smoltz	1804.1	2201	10.98
D Gooden	2340.1	2856	10.98
J Smiley	1753.1	2145	11.01
D Cone	1994.0	2446	11.04
J Key	2300.0	2824	11.05
A Pena	1057.1	1303	11.09
D Drabek	2257.0	2790	11.13
K Appier	1429.2	1782	11.22
O Hershiser	2529.1	3156	11.23

Strikeouts per 9 Innings

Player	IP	K	K/9
R Johnson	**1521.0**	**1709**	**10.11**
R Myers	768.1	787	9.22
L Smith	1268.1	1236	8.77
E Plunk	937.1	878	8.43
S Fernandez	1861.2	1740	8.41
R Clemens	2776.0	2590	8.40
D Cone	1994.0	1812	8.18
J Orosco	1076.2	972	8.13
M Jackson	810.0	721	8.01
J Fassero	850.0	750	7.94
D Plesac	772.1	681	7.94
T Gordon	1365.1	1170	7.71
J Guzman	1010.2	865	7.70
D Gooden	2340.1	2001	7.70
B Witt	1900.1	1616	7.65

Walks per 9 Innings

Player	IP	BB	BB/9
B Tewksbury	**1490.0**	**241**	**1.46**
G Swindell	1800.0	391	1.96
D Eckersley	3193.0	722	2.04
D Jones	785.1	179	2.05
K Tapani	1461.0	349	2.15
M Mussina	1137.2	274	2.17
S Sanderson	2561.0	625	2.20
J Key	2300.0	563	2.20
G Maddux	2365.2	589	2.24
T Mulholland	1521.0	379	2.24
J Burkett	1408.1	360	2.30
J Smiley	1753.1	455	2.34
D Wells	1413.0	371	2.36
D Drabek	2257.0	606	2.42
R Aguilera	1033.1	284	2.47

Strikeout to Walk Ratio

Player	K	BB	K/BB
D Jones	**639**	**179**	**3.57**
D Eckersley	2334	722	3.23
G Swindell	1224	391	3.13
R Clemens	2590	856	3.03
R Aguilera	822	284	2.89
G Maddux	1643	589	2.79
M Mussina	760	274	2.77
C Schilling	800	291	2.75
B Tewksbury	660	241	2.74
J Fassero	750	274	2.74
D Gooden	2001	739	2.71
K Tapani	919	349	2.63
L Smith	1236	478	2.59
S Sanderson	1611	625	2.58
J Smiley	1164	455	2.56

1996 American League Bill James Leaders

Top Game Scores of the Year								
Pitcher	Date	Opp	IP	H	R	ER	BB	K	SC
R Clemens, Bos	9/18	Det	9.0	5	0	0	0	20	97
K Hill, Tex	5/3	Det	9.0	1	0	0	0	7	92

Top Game Scores of the Year								
Pitcher	Date	Opp	IP	H	R	ER	BB	K	SC
S Torres, Sea	9/15	Min	9.0	2	0	0	2	9	90

Offensive Win Pct

M McGwire, Oak	**.856**
E Martinez, Sea	.803
J Thome, Cle	.801
F Thomas, ChA	.799
A Rodriguez, Sea	.779
C Knoblauch, Min	.764
K Griffey Jr, Sea	.762
A Belle, Cle	.757
M Vaughn, Bos	.757
B Anderson, Bal	.748

Power/Speed Number

B Anderson, Bal	**29.6**
K Griffey Jr, Sea	24.1
K Lofton, Cle	23.6
B Williams, NYA	21.4
A Rodriguez, Sea	21.2
C Knoblauch, Min	20.2
J Valentin, Mil	19.9
R Alomar, Bal	19.2
A Belle, Cle	17.9
R Durham, ChA	15.0

Tough Losses

R Clemens, Bos	**6**
R Robertson, Min	**6**
J Guzman, Tor	5
F Lira, Det	5
T Gordon, Bos	4
K Tapani, ChA	4
J Rosado, KC	4
9 pitchers tied with	3

Runs Created

M Vaughn, Bos	**159**
A Rodriguez, Sea	157
A Belle, Cle	156
B Anderson, Bal	150
F Thomas, ChA	150
M McGwire, Oak	149
C Knoblauch, Min	147
J Thome, Cle	146
E Martinez, Sea	144
K Griffey Jr, Sea	142

Secondary Average

M McGwire, Oak	**.693**
J Thome, Cle	.545
E Martinez, Sea	.515
K Griffey Jr, Sea	.495
A Belle, Cle	.495
B Anderson, Bal	.494
F Thomas, ChA	.484
M Ramirez, Cle	.433
J Buhner, Sea	.433
R Palmeiro, Bal	.422

Slow Hooks

Angels	31
Orioles	28
Red Sox	28
Tigers	27
Blue Jays	27
Brewers	24
Royals	19
Athletics	19
Indians	17
White Sox	15
Rangers	15
Twins	14
Yankees	12
Mariners	9

Isolated Power (Power Pct)

M McGwire, Oak	**.418**
B Anderson, Bal	.340
J Gonzalez, Tex	.329
K Griffey Jr, Sea	.325
A Belle, Cle	.312
J Thome, Cle	.301
J Buhner, Sea	.285
F Thomas, ChA	.277
A Rodriguez, Sea	.273
M Ramirez, Cle	.273

Cheap Wins

B Witt, Tex	**7**
S Hitchcock, Sea	6
J McDowell, Cle	5
E Hanson, Tor	5
M Mussina, Bal	5
A Pettitte, NYA	5
9 pitchers tied with	4

Quick Hooks

Yankees	26
Mariners	26
White Sox	24
Brewers	24
Tigers	17
Orioles	15
Athletics	15
Indians	14
Royals	14
Rangers	14
Red Sox	12
Angels	12
Blue Jays	12
Twins	11

1996 National League Bill James Leaders

Top Game Scores of the Year

Pitcher	Date	Opp	IP	H	R	ER	BB	K	SC
C Schilling, Phi	8/21	LA	9.0	2	0	0	0	12	95
J Fassero, Mon	6/29	Phi	9.0	2	0	0	0	11	94
J Smiley, Cin	9/22	StL	9.0	1	0	0	0	8	93
J Smoltz, Atl	4/14	SD	8.0	1	0	0	1	13	92
H Nomo, LA	4/13	Fla	9.0	3	1	1	3	17	91
A Leiter, Fla	5/11	Col	9.0	0	0	0	2	6	91

Top Game Scores of the Year

Pitcher	Date	Opp	IP	H	R	ER	BB	K	SC
H Nomo, LA	9/17	Col	9.0	0	0	0	4	8	91
R Cormier, Mon	4/22	StL	9.0	3	0	0	0	9	90
M Gardner, SF	4/25	Atl	9.0	4	0	0	0	11	90
T Stottlemyre, StL	5/15	Fla	9.0	4	0	0	2	13	90
J Smoltz, Atl	5/29	ChN	9.0	4	0	0	2	13	90
J Smoltz, Atl	7/13	Fla	9.0	2	0	0	3	10	90

Offensive Win Pct

B Bonds, SF	.858
G Sheffield, Fla	.848
J Bagwell, Hou	.822
E Burks, Col	.817
K Caminiti, SD	.802
M Piazza, LA	.773
B Larkin, Cin	.760
C Jones, Atl	.748
A Galarraga, Col	.746
B Gilkey, NYN	.739

Power/Speed Number

B Bonds, SF	41.0
E Burks, Col	35.6
B Larkin, Cin	34.4
D Bichette, Col	31.0
R Lankford, StL	26.3
A Galarraga, Col	26.0
S Finley, SD	25.4
M Grissom, Atl	25.3
J Bagwell, Hou	25.0
S Sosa, ChN	24.8

Tough Losses

K Brown, Fla	9
G Maddux, Atl	7
C Schilling, Phi	7
H Nomo, LA	6
T Mulholland, Sea	5
T Stottlemyre, StL	5
A Watson, SF	5
J Isringhausen, NYN	5
7 pitchers tied with	4

Slow Hooks

Rockies	23
Mets	18
Cardinals	16
Giants	16
Braves	13
Astros	12
Cubs	11
Dodgers	10
Marlins	10
Phillies	9
Reds	8
Pirates	8
Padres	8
Expos	2

Runs Created

B Bonds, SF	163
G Sheffield, Fla	159
E Burks, Col	158
J Bagwell, Hou	156
K Caminiti, SD	138
A Galarraga, Col	136
C Jones, Atl	130
M Piazza, LA	125
B Larkin, Cin	124
B Gilkey, NYN	124

Secondary Average

B Bonds, SF	.663
G Sheffield, Fla	.597
J Bagwell, Hou	.518
B Larkin, Cin	.505
K Caminiti, SD	.449
E Burks, Col	.437
T Hundley, NYN	.433
R Henderson, SD	.419
R Lankford, StL	.407
C Jones, Atl	.388

Isolated Power (Power Pct)

G Sheffield, Fla	.310
B Bonds, SF	.308
A Galarraga, Col	.297
E Burks, Col	.295
K Caminiti, SD	.295
S Sosa, ChN	.291
T Hundley, NYN	.291
H Rodriguez, Mon	.286
B Larkin, Cin	.269
J Bagwell, Hou	.255

Cheap Wins

K Ritz, Col	5
A Reynoso, Col	5
P Rapp, Fla	5
T Mulholland, Sea	4
J Navarro, ChN	4
D Kile, Hou	4
A Benes, StL	4
11 pitchers tied with	3

Quick Hooks

Expos	32
Reds	29
Pirates	27
Braves	25
Padres	23
Cubs	17
Cardinals	17
Dodgers	16
Phillies	16
Astros	13
Rockies	13
Giants	12
Marlins	12
Mets	11

Player Profiles

As is our custom each year, we include in the *Major League Handbook* statistical profiles for a few of the game's premier players. Take a look at John Smoltz's numbers. Everyone remembers his magnificent run in the first few months of the season, but how many people noticed that his ERA actually went *down* in the second half? The Caminiti-for-MVP argument takes on a whole new dimension when you realize that he mashed 23 homers and drove in 61 runs during the Padres' stretch run in August and September. And behold the dominance of John Wetteland, who converted 43 of his 47 save opportunities—including all 15 in the month of June.

If you enjoy these profiles, you might want to check out the *STATS 1997 Player Profiles,* which has breakdowns like these for *every* player who appeared in the majors last season.

	Avg	G	AB	R	H	2B	3B	HR	RBI	BB	SO	HBP	GDP	SB	CS	OBP	SLG	IBB	SH	SF	#Pit	#P/PA	GB	FB	G/F
1996 Season	.326	146	546	109	178	37	2	40	130	78	99	4	14	11	5	.408	.621	16	0	10	2322	3.63	183	163	1.12
Last Five Years	.294	678	2527	389	743	160	6	110	436	283	420	8	62	45	22	.364	.493	60	3	26	10060	3.53	873	731	1.19

1996 Season

	Avg	AB	H	2B	3B	HR	RBI	BB	SO	OBP	SLG		Avg	AB	H	2B	3B	HR	RBI	BB	SO	OBP	SLG
vs. Left	.358	165	59	15	0	15	46	16	19	.412	.721	Scoring Posn	.387	155	60	12	1	15	100	40	31	.490	.768
vs. Right	.312	381	119	22	2	25	84	62	80	.406	.577	Close & Late	.253	95	24	4	0	9	25	14	21	.348	.579
Groundball	.349	146	51	13	1	8	31	15	27	.410	.616	None on/out	.287	122	35	9	0	12	12	10	17	.346	.656
Flyball	.299	87	26	7	1	4	24	8	18	.354	.540	Batting #3	.345	110	38	9	1	6	20	15	20	.422	.609
Home	.338	260	88	18	1	20	65	32	50	.407	.646	Batting #4	.323	434	140	28	1	34	110	63	79	.406	.627
Away	.315	286	90	19	1	20	65	46	49	.408	.598	Other	.000	2	0	0	0	0	0	0	0	.000	.000
Day	.310	174	54	12	0	10	41	28	36	.407	.552	April	.343	108	37	13	0	2	18	8	16	.393	.519
Night	.333	372	124	25	2	30	89	50	63	.408	.653	May	.229	35	8	1	0	3	6	4	1	.300	.514
Grass	.339	445	151	28	1	34	109	62	85	.417	.636	June	.257	113	29	2	0	6	19	11	19	.333	.434
Turf	.267	101	27	9	1	6	21	16	14	.364	.554	July	.357	98	35	10	0	6	26	21	20	.460	.643
First Pitch	.333	90	30	7	0	7	21	13	0	.410	.644	August	.344	96	33	4	1	14	38	17	20	.427	.844
Ahead in Count	.363	124	45	11	0	11	27	43	0	.524	.718	September/October	.375	96	36	7	1	9	23	17	23	.465	.750
Behind in Count	.253	225	57	12	0	11	41	0	79	.259	.453	Pre-All Star	.294	279	82	18	0	12	49	32	42	.371	.487
Two Strikes	.230	230	53	13	2	13	48	22	99	.300	.474	Post-All Star	.360	267	96	19	2	28	81	46	57	.443	.760

1996 By Position

Position	Avg	AB	H	2B	3B	HR	RBI	BB	SO	OBP	SLG	G	GS	Innings	PO	A	E	DP	Fld Pct	Rng Fctr	In Zone	Outs	Zone Rtg	MLB Zone
As 3b	.327	544	178	37	2	40	130	78	98	.409	.623	145	142	1274.0	103	310	20	28	.954	2.92	426	348	.817	.803

Last Five Years

	Avg	AB	H	2B	3B	HR	RBI	BB	SO	OBP	SLG		Avg	AB	H	2B	3B	HR	RBI	BB	SO	OBP	SLG
vs. Left	.301	857	258	64	2	42	177	80	103	.359	.527	Scoring Posn	.298	729	217	51	2	34	329	148	129	.405	.513
vs. Right	.290	1670	485	96	4	68	259	203	317	.366	.475	Close & Late	.260	396	103	24	0	15	53	63	83	.360	.434
Groundball	.298	781	233	47	2	29	127	66	115	.354	.475	None on/out	.276	633	175	37	1	26	26	32	95	.314	.461
Flyball	.275	437	120	37	2	18	84	55	94	.352	.492	Batting #4	.292	1211	354	73	1	63	234	160	221	.374	.510
Home	.303	1259	381	81	3	54	235	124	211	.363	.500	Batting #5	.282	713	201	47	2	22	99	59	105	.335	.446
Away	.285	1268	362	79	3	56	201	159	209	.364	.485	Other	.312	603	188	40	3	25	103	64	94	.375	.512
Day	.285	762	217	45	2	29	119	98	137	.368	.463	April	.281	327	92	27	1	9	57	29	59	.342	.453
Night	.298	1765	526	115	4	81	317	185	283	.362	.505	May	.290	365	106	28	1	19	68	30	47	.340	.529
Grass	.307	1302	400	74	2	74	249	158	227	.380	.538	June	.282	514	145	23	0	22	77	49	84	.347	.455
Turf	.280	1225	343	86	4	36	187	125	193	.346	.445	July	.297	478	142	31	1	15	81	65	75	.378	.460
First Pitch	.343	464	159	36	2	22	92	44	0	.395	.571	August	.296	433	128	28	2	22	78	53	77	.367	.522
Ahead in Count	.364	624	227	51	1	31	119	138	0	.478	.598	September/October	.317	410	130	23	1	23	75	57	78	.399	.546
Behind in Count	.216	966	209	49	0	34	135	0	352	.217	.373	Pre-All Star	.288	1384	398	92	3	54	231	132	218	.350	.475
Two Strikes	.214	1010	216	50	2	40	144	101	420	.285	.386	Post-All Star	.302	1143	345	68	3	56	205	151	202	.380	.514

Batter vs. Pitcher (career)

Hits Best Against	Avg	AB	H	2B	3B	HR	RBI	BB	SO	OBP	SLG	Hits Worst Against	Avg	AB	H	2B	3B	HR	RBI	BB	SO	OBP	SLG
Chuck McElroy	.727	11	8	1	0	1	3	0	1	.727	1.091	Mel Rojas	.000	9	0	0	0	0	0	3	2	.250	.000
W. VanLandingham	.538	13	7	2	0	1	7	1	3	.600	.923	Norm Charlton	.037	27	1	0	0	1	3	2	7	.103	.148
Jon Lieber	.533	15	8	1	1	1	5	1	2	.563	.933	Jaime Navarro	.091	11	1	0	0	0	0	1	4	.167	.091
Bob Patterson	.455	11	5	1	1	1	5	1	5	.500	1.000	Dave Nied	.100	10	1	0	0	0	0	1	1	.182	.100
Mark Portugal	.438	16	7	3	0	2	5	1	5	.471	1.000	Frank Viola	.118	17	2	0	0	0	0	1	4	.167	.118

	ERA	W	L	Sv	G	GS	IP	BB	SO	Avg	H	2B	3B	HR	RBI	OBP	SLG	CG	ShO	Sup	QS	#P/S	SB	CS	GB	FB	G/F
1996 Season	2.94	24	8	0	35	35	253.2	55	276	.216	199	45	2	19	89	.260	.331	6	2	5.68	25	109	10	12	285	218	1.31
Last Five Years	3.27	72	48	0	155	155	1071.1	355	1005	.227	899	180	18	89	387	.292	.349	21	7	4.93	95	106	45	32	1238	1058	1.17

1996 Season

	ERA	W	L	Sv	G	GS	IP	H	HR	BB	SO		Avg	AB	H	2B	3B	HR	RBI	BB	SO	OBP	SLG
Home	2.94	13	3	0	18	18	131.2	102	11	26	140	vs. Left	.221	394	87	16	2	5	28	36	112	.288	.310
Away	2.95	11	5	0	17	17	122.0	97	8	29	136	vs. Right	.212	528	112	29	0	14	61	19	164	.239	.347
Day	2.41	8	2	0	11	11	86.0	50	8	21	101	Inning 1-6	.203	728	148	30	2	14	63	44	226	.250	.308
Night	3.22	16	6	0	24	24	167.2	149	11	34	175	Inning 7+	.263	194	51	15	0	5	26	11	50	.300	.418
Grass	3.08	19	7	0	29	29	213.1	169	18	47	239	None on	.193	602	116	28	2	8	8	33	189	.237	.286
Turf	2.23	5	1	0	6	6	40.1	30	1	8	37	Runners on	.259	320	83	17	0	11	81	22	87	.303	.416
April	2.70	5	1	0	6	6	46.2	28	3	10	51	Scoring Posn	.264	174	46	9	0	5	65	18	53	.327	.402
May	1.73	6	0	0	6	6	41.2	26	3	11	46	Close & Late	.204	98	20	5	0	2	9	5	28	.240	.316
June	4.54	3	2	0	6	6	41.2	40	5	8	48	None on/out	.204	250	51	11	2	3	3	13	66	.246	.300
July	3.31	3	2	0	5	5	35.1	29	1	10	38	vs. 1st Batr (relief)	.000	0	0	0	0	0	0	0	0	.000	.000
August	2.49	3	2	0	6	6	43.1	39	3	6	45	First Inning Pitched	.228	127	29	4	0	4	16	12	41	.295	.354
September/October	3.00	4	1	0	6	6	45.0	37	4	10	48	First 75 Pitches	.204	604	123	27	2	12	51	38	182	.252	.315
Starter	2.94	24	8	0	35	35	253.2	199	11	55	276	Pitch 76-90	.205	117	24	8	0	1	8	3	36	.225	.299
Reliever	0.00	0	0	0	0	0	0.0	0	0	0	0	Pitch 91-105	.308	104	32	5	0	3	17	6	34	.342	.442
0-3 Days Rest (Start)	2.40	2	0	0	2	2	15.0	10	1	5	17	Pitch 106+	.206	97	20	5	0	3	13	8	24	.264	.351
4 Days Rest	2.97	18	6	0	27	27	191.0	154	15	40	204	First Pitch	.310	113	35	9	0	3	16	3	0	.331	.469
5+ Days Rest	3.02	4	2	0	6	6	47.2	35	3	10	55	Ahead in Count	.159	504	80	17	1	5	28	0	241	.160	.226
Pre-All Star	3.16	14	4	0	19	19	134.0	102	11	29	149	Behind in Count	.309	139	43	13	1	6	27	24	0	.404	.547
Post-All Star	2.71	10	4	0	16	16	119.2	97	8	26	127	Two Strikes	.142	506	72	18	1	5	26	28	276	.189	.211

Last Five Years

	ERA	W	L	Sv	G	GS	IP	H	HR	BB	SO		Avg	AB	H	2B	3B	HR	RBI	BB	SO	OBP	SLG
Home	3.56	30	25	0	76	76	517.2	442	55	179	480	vs. Left	.250	1981	495	93	12	37	190	216	397	.326	.365
Away	2.99	42	23	0	79	79	553.2	457	34	176	525	vs. Right	.204	1984	404	87	6	52	197	139	608	.257	.332
Day	2.85	25	16	0	50	50	353.2	272	31	113	357	Inning 1-6	.222	3255	723	142	14	71	313	293	862	.288	.340
Night	3.47	47	32	0	105	105	717.2	627	58	242	648	Inning 7+	.248	710	176	38	4	18	74	62	143	.308	.389
Grass	3.31	54	37	0	119	119	827.2	684	80	278	769	None on	.219	2417	530	119	10	44	44	184	619	.278	.331
Turf	3.14	18	11	0	36	36	243.2	215	9	77	236	Runners on	.238	1548	369	61	8	45	343	171	386	.313	.375
April	2.85	12	7	0	21	21	151.2	114	10	51	154	Scoring Posn	.223	857	191	35	5	23	283	129	243	.321	.356
May	3.25	13	10	0	29	29	196.1	163	13	78	177	Close & Late	.257	432	111	22	4	11	45	38	90	.316	.403
June	3.32	18	9	0	29	29	208.2	165	21	63	198	None on/out	.230	1035	238	48	7	20	20	86	237	.291	.348
July	3.24	9	8	0	26	26	177.2	159	11	62	170	vs. 1st Batr (relief)	.000	0	0	0	0	0	0	0	0	.000	.000
August	3.49	11	7	0	24	24	167.2	146	21	44	141	First Inning Pitched	.240	591	142	21	1	21	70	68	155	.319	.386
September/October	3.40	9	7	0	26	26	169.1	152	13	57	165	First 75 Pitches	.222	2676	593	114	10	60	245	246	703	.289	.339
Starter	3.27	72	48	0	155	155	1071.1	899	89	355	1005	Pitch 76-90	.234	513	120	26	2	12	53	35	129	.286	.363
Reliever	0.00	0	0	0	0	0	0.0	0	0	0	0	Pitch 91-105	.230	427	98	22	2	9	42	33	98	.284	.354
0-3 Days Rest (Start)	5.72	3	1	0	6	6	39.1	43	6	12	33	Pitch 106+	.252	349	88	18	4	8	47	41	75	.329	.395
4 Days Rest	3.06	49	31	0	106	106	740.2	618	59	238	686	First Pitch	.314	573	180	35	2	17	78	24	0	.345	.471
5+ Days Rest	3.46	20	16	0	43	43	291.1	238	24	105	286	Ahead in Count	.158	1955	308	58	10	21	120	0	865	.161	.230
Pre-All Star	3.13	45	30	0	87	87	611.2	488	49	212	583	Behind in Count	.312	735	229	54	6	30	109	170	0	.438	.524
Post-All Star	3.45	27	18	0	68	68	459.2	411	40	143	422	Two Strikes	.151	1997	302	57	7	23	108	161	1005	.218	.221

Pitcher vs. Batter (career)

Pitches Best Vs.	Avg	AB	H	2B	3B	HR	RBI	BB	SO	OBP	SLG	Pitches Worst Vs.	Avg	AB	H	2B	3B	HR	RBI	BB	SO	OBP	SLG
Dwight Smith	.000	19	0	0	0	0	0	0	2	.000	.000	Al Martin	.586	29	17	5	1	1	7	5	5	.647	.931
Phil Plantier	.000	14	0	0	0	0	0	0	5	.000	.000	Quivilo Veras	.500	10	5	3	2	0	1	2	3	.583	1.200
Kurt Stillwell	.000	13	0	0	0	1	0	0	3	.000	.000	Mike Aldrete	.500	8	4	1	1	0	1	3	0	.636	.875
Roberto Kelly	.000	13	0	0	0	0	0	1	2	.071	.000	Eric Davis	.438	32	14	2	0	5	8	5	5	.514	.969
Bret Boone	.071	14	1	0	0	0	0	0	8	.071	.071	Ellis Burks	.429	14	6	2	0	2	7	1	4	.467	1.000

John Wetteland — Yankees
Age 30 – Pitches Right (flyball pitcher)

	ERA	W	L	Sv	G	GS	IP	BB	SO	Avg	H	2B	3B	HR	RBI	OBP	SLG	GF	IR	IRS	Hld	SvOp	SB	CS	GB	FB	G/F
1996 Season	2.83	2	3	43	62	0	63.2	21	69	.224	54	11	1	9	29	.284	.390	58	14	6	0	47	8	2	55	76	0.72
Last Five Years	2.52	20	21	179	311	0	357.1	120	415	.202	262	44	10	29	139	.273	.319	273	137	36	0	214	48	8	301	410	0.73

1996 Season

	ERA	W	L	Sv	G	GS	IP	H	HR	BB	SO		Avg	AB	H	2B	3B	HR	RBI	BB	SO	OBP	SLG
Home	1.86	2	0	18	27	0	29.0	18	4	9	29	vs. Left	.285	144	41	9	1	7	24	13	32	.340	.507
Away	3.63	0	3	25	35	0	34.2	36	5	12	40	vs. Right	.134	97	13	2	0	2	5	8	37	.200	.216
Day	2.20	2	0	21	27	0	28.2	25	3	6	31	Inning 1-6	.000	0	0	0	0	0	0	0	0	.000	.000
Night	3.34	0	3	22	35	0	35.0	29	6	15	38	Inning 7+	.224	241	54	11	1	9	29	21	69	.284	.390
Grass	2.70	2	3	36	55	0	56.2	47	8	19	56	None on	.224	134	30	5	0	5	5	12	39	.288	.373
Turf	3.86	0	0	7	7	0	7.0	7	1	2	13	Runners on	.224	107	24	6	1	4	24	9	30	.280	.411
April	4.09	0	0	5	10	0	11.0	10	2	3	11	Scoring Posn	.179	67	12	3	0	2	19	6	22	.240	.313
May	2.16	0	1	5	9	0	8.1	5	1	5	12	Close & Late	.225	187	42	9	1	7	26	18	52	.290	.396
June	3.52	0	0	15	15	0	15.1	16	5	3	15	None on/out	.155	58	9	0	0	0	0	4	14	.210	.155
July	2.77	1	1	11	13	0	13.0	11	0	5	14	vs. 1st Batr (relief)	.190	58	11	1	0	1	6	3	13	.226	.259
August	5.40	0	1	2	5	0	5.0	6	1	1	3	First Inning Pitched	.228	228	52	10	1	9	29	18	66	.282	.399
September/October	0.00	1	0	5	10	0	11.0	6	0	4	14	First 15 Pitches	.232	164	38	6	1	8	19	15	42	.293	.427
Starter	0.00	0	0	0	0	0	0.0	0	0	0	0	Pitch 16-30	.211	76	16	5	0	1	10	6	26	.268	.316
Reliever	2.83	2	3	43	62	0	63.2	54	9	21	69	Pitch 31-45	.000	1	0	0	0	0	0	0	1	.000	.000
0 Days rest (Relief)	0.89	1	0	15	20	0	20.1	18	1	6	25	Pitch 46+	.000	0	0	0	0	0	0	0	0	.000	.000
1 or 2 Days rest	3.60	0	1	22	29	0	30.0	26	5	8	29	First Pitch	.333	30	10	4	0	2	6	2	0	.375	.667
3+ Days rest	4.05	1	2	6	13	0	13.1	10	3	7	15	Ahead in Count	.191	131	25	3	0	4	10	0	60	.191	.305
Pre-All Star	3.03	0	1	29	38	0	38.2	33	8	12	42	Behind in Count	.237	38	9	3	0	0	6	6	0	.333	.316
Post-All Star	2.52	2	2	14	24	0	25.0	21	1	9	27	Two Strikes	.167	138	23	1	1	5	11	13	69	.238	.312

Last Five Years

	ERA	W	L	Sv	G	GS	IP	H	HR	BB	SO		Avg	AB	H	2B	3B	HR	RBI	BB	SO	OBP	SLG
Home	3.04	13	11	86	159	0	177.2	133	16	55	189	vs. Left	.209	741	155	23	6	20	90	74	241	.283	.337
Away	2.00	7	10	93	152	0	179.2	129	13	65	226	vs. Right	.193	553	107	21	4	9	49	46	174	.259	.295
Day	2.92	7	7	57	105	0	120.1	98	13	34	146	Inning 1-6	.000	0	0	0	0	0	0	0	0	.000	.000
Night	2.32	13	14	122	206	0	237.0	164	16	86	269	Inning 7+	.202	1294	262	44	10	29	139	120	415	.273	.319
Grass	2.17	5	9	91	154	0	170.1	122	16	48	195	None on	.198	701	139	21	6	17	17	59	217	.262	.318
Turf	2.84	15	12	88	157	0	187.0	140	13	72	220	Runners on	.207	593	123	23	4	12	122	61	198	.285	.320
April	3.55	1	2	11	29	0	33.0	32	3	12	31	Scoring Posn	.209	387	81	14	2	7	106	44	130	.288	.310
May	3.39	4	5	27	57	0	71.2	53	9	28	83	Close & Late	.206	962	198	32	8	25	120	100	308	.283	.334
June	2.52	1	2	38	59	0	64.1	47	5	20	73	None on/out	.207	294	61	11	5	6	6	21	92	.260	.340
July	1.60	7	3	43	66	0	73.0	51	3	15	81	vs. 1st Batr (relief)	.210	286	60	12	3	6	22	21	85	.265	.336
August	3.88	4	7	27	50	0	58.0	54	7	29	66	First Inning Pitched	.211	1053	222	39	9	24	124	91	333	.276	.333
September/October	0.63	3	2	33	50	0	57.1	25	2	16	81	First 15 Pitches	.214	808	173	33	7	19	77	73	233	.283	.343
Starter	0.00	0	0	0	0	0	0.0	0	0	0	0	Pitch 16-30	.193	420	81	11	3	9	57	35	156	.258	.298
Reliever	2.52	20	21	179	311	0	357.1	262	29	120	415	Pitch 31-45	.129	62	8	0	0	1	4	11	25	.257	.177
0 Days rest (Relief)	1.90	3	5	64	89	0	99.1	78	5	31	110	Pitch 46+	.000	4	0	0	0	0	0	1	1	.200	.000
1 or 2 Days rest	2.77	14	11	83	151	0	175.2	123	14	65	208	First Pitch	.297	155	46	9	3	5	26	10	0	.343	.490
3+ Days rest	2.73	3	5	32	71	0	82.1	61	10	24	97	Ahead in Count	.148	721	107	14	3	12	53	0	353	.156	.226
Pre-All Star	2.79	9	10	91	169	0	197.0	152	18	64	223	Behind in Count	.322	174	56	10	1	6	36	45	0	.453	.494
Post-All Star	2.19	11	11	88	142	0	160.1	110	11	56	192	Two Strikes	.148	798	118	18	5	16	61	65	415	.217	.243

Pitcher vs. Batter (career)

Pitches Best Vs.	Avg	AB	H	2B	3B	HR	RBI	BB	SO	OBP	SLG	Pitches Worst Vs.	Avg	AB	H	2B	3B	HR	RBI	BB	SO	OBP	SLG
Jeff King	.059	17	1	0	0	0	1	1	7	.105	.059	Ozzie Smith	.556	9	5	0	0	0	2	2	1	.636	.556
Barry Larkin	.077	13	1	0	0	3	0	0	1	.071	.154	Kevin Mitchell	.444	9	4	0	0	0	1	3	2	.583	.444
Chris Sabo	.091	11	1	1	0	0	1	0	1	.091	.182	Benito Santiago	.438	16	7	1	0	0	1	1	4	.471	.500
Ryne Sandberg	.100	10	1	0	0	0	1	3	1	.308	.100	Craig Biggio	.417	12	5	0	0	2	6	3	4	.533	.917
Fred McGriff	.182	11	2	0	0	0	0	0	3	.182	.182	Kevin Elster	.333	9	3	0	0	1	4	2	4	.417	.667

Manager Tendencies

One of the things about baseball which appeals to many of us is the game's endless opportunities for analysis. . . and few things are analyzed more than managerial decisions. Major League skippers may not have batting averages and slugging percentages to point to at the end of the season, but when it comes time to judge their performance and production, that *doesn't* mean we can't take a look at their statistics.

Which manager posted the best stolen-base success rate?

Which skippers were constantly tinkering with their lineups?

Which managers wore out a path to the pitching mound?

It's questions like these that get our second-guessing juices going, and it's questions like these that inspired the following pages, which look at managerial tendencies in a number of situations. Once again, the skippers are compared based on offense, defense, lineups, and pitching use. We don't rank the managers; there is plenty of room for argument on whether certain moves are good or bad. We are simply providing fodder for the discussion.

Offensively, managers have control over bunting, stealing and the timing of hit-and-runs. The *Handbook* looks at the quantity, timing and success of these moves.

Defensively, the Handbook looks at the success of pitchouts, the frequency of intentional walks, and the pattern of defensive substitutions.

Most managers spend large amounts of their time devising lineups. The *Handbook* shows the number of lineups used, as well as the platoon percentage. The use of pinch hitters and pinch runners is also explored.

Finally, how does the manager use pitchers? For starters, the *Handbook* shows slow and quick hooks, along with the number of times a starter was allowed to throw more than 120 and 140 pitches. For relievers, we look at the number of relief appearances, mid-inning changes and how often a pitcher gets a save going more than one inning (a rare occurrence these days). The categories include:

Stolen Base Success Percentage: SB/Attempts

Pitchout Runners Moving: The number of times the opposition is running when a manager calls a pitchout.

Double Steals: The number of double steals attempted in 1996.

Out Percentage: The proportion of stolen bases on that count.

Sacrifice Bunt Attempts: A bunt is considered a sac attempt if no runner is on third, there are no outs, or the pitcher attempts a bunt.

Sacrifice Bunt Success %: A bunt that results in a sacrifice or a hit, divided by the number of attempts.

Favorite inning: The most common inning in which an event occurred.

Hit and Run Success: The hit and run results in baserunner advancement with no double play.

Intentional Walk Situation: Runners on base, first base open, and anyone but the pitcher up.

Defensive Substitutions: Straight defensive substitutions, with the team leading by four runs or less.

Number of Lineups: Based on batting order, 1-8 for National Leaguers, 1-9 for American Leaguers.

Percent LHB vs. RHSP and RHB vs. LHSP: A measure of platooning. A batter is considered to always have the platoon advantage if he is a switch hitter.

Percent PH platoon: Frequency the manager gets his pinch-hitter the platoon advantage. Switch hitters always have the advantage.

Score Diff: The most common score differential on which an intentional walk is called for.

Slow and Quick hooks: See the glossary for complete information. This measures how often a pitcher is left in longer than is standard practice, or pulled earlier than normal.

Mid-Inning Change: The number of times a manager changed pitchers in the middle of an inning.

1-Batter Appearance: The number of times a pitcher was brought in to face only one batter. Called the "Tony La Russa special" because of his penchant for trying to orchestrate specific match-ups for specific situations.

3 Pitchers (2 runs or less): The club gives up two runs or less in a game, but uses at least three pitchers.

Offense

	G	Att	SB%	Pitchout Rn Mvg	2nd SB-CS	3rd SB-CS	Home SB-CS	Double Steals	Out Percentage 0	Out Percentage 1	Out Percentage 2	Sac Bunt Att	Sac Bunt Suc. %	Sac Bunt Fav. Inning	Sqz	Hit&Run Att	Hit&Run Suc. %
AL Managers																	
Bell, Buddy, Det	162	137	63.5	5	74-43	13-5	0-2	4	10.9	46.7	42.3	63	85.7	3	1	87	36.8
Bevington, Terry, ChA	162	146	71.9	4	94-35	10-3	1-3	3	16.4	32.9	50.7	75	84.0	6	10	88	45.5
Boone, Bob, KC	161	280	69.6	11	161-67	25-14	9-4	8	17.5	30.0	52.5	93	81.7	6	9	172	37.2
Garner, Phil, Mil	162	149	67.8	7	87-38	14-7	1-3	5	18.1	35.6	46.3	72	72.2	7	6	73	35.6
Gaston, Cito, Tor	162	154	75.3	3	92-33	24-3	0-2	4	21.4	42.2	36.4	63	73.0	3	8	69	33.3
Hargrove, Mike, Cle	161	210	76.2	3	122-46	36-3	2-1	10	21.4	34.8	43.8	58	87.9	5	2	80	37.5
Howe, Art, Oak	162	93	62.4	1	55-30	3-3	0-2	1	16.1	40.9	43.0	49	77.6	7	0	61	42.6
Johnson, Davy, Bal	163	116	65.5	1	67-36	8-4	1-0	5	20.7	43.1	36.2	46	80.4	1	0	65	33.8
Kelly, Tom, Min	162	196	73.0	1	133-44	8-4	2-5	7	17.9	34.7	47.4	33	75.8	8	2	94	46.8
Kennedy, Kevin, Bos	162	135	67.4	1	83-37	6-5	2-2	1	16.3	33.3	50.4	39	94.9	2	1	75	32.0
Lachemann, Marcel, Cal	112	63	55.6	2	30-22	5-4	0-2	1	20.6	34.9	44.4	48	75.0	7	5	67	46.3
McNamara, John, Cal	50	29	62.1	1	17-11	1-0	0-0	0	17.2	37.9	44.8	18	50.0	9	1	26	53.8
Oates, Johnny, Tex	163	109	76.1	3	76-23	7-3	0-0	1	15.6	41.3	43.1	41	90.2	8	1	88	35.2
Piniella, Lou, Sea	161	129	69.8	5	71-33	19-6	0-0	4	25.6	37.2	37.2	65	78.5	8	1	65	33.8
Torre, Joe, NYA	162	142	67.6	4	83-38	9-6	4-2	8	19.0	37.3	43.7	53	81.1	7	9	70	45.7
NL Managers																	
Alou, Felipe, Mon	162	142	76.1	1	96-29	9-3	3-2	5	22.5	37.3	40.1	97	83.5	5	10	79	35.4
Baker, Dusty, SF	162	166	68.1	6	103-47	10-5	0-1	4	20.5	34.9	44.6	103	81.6	4	3	125	35.2
Baylor, Don, Col	162	267	75.3	8	173-46	25-16	3-4	6	21.0	41.2	37.8	115	79.1	3	6	126	38.9
Bochy, Bruce, SD	162	164	66.5	1	94-38	22-12	0-1	6	25.6	36.6	37.8	73	84.9	5	6	109	37.6
Boles, John, Fla	75	90	78.9	2	62-17	8-1	1-1	3	36.7	28.9	34.4	26	57.7	2	1	54	40.7
Collins, Terry, Hou	162	243	74.1	11	142-54	38-9	0-0	20	17.7	32.9	49.4	94	79.8	2	3	131	39.7
Cox, Bobby, Atl	162	126	65.9	2	73-38	9-4	1-1	3	15.1	40.5	44.4	90	82.2	2	5	66	37.9
Fregosi, Jim, Phi	162	158	74.1	5	99-38	17-2	1-1	5	17.1	33.5	49.4	77	74.0	7	8	80	27.5
Green, Dallas, NYN	131	125	71.2	6	71-31	17-4	1-1	7	22.4	42.4	35.2	69	89.9	3	6	83	39.8
Knight, Ray, Cin	162	234	73.1	10	133-53	36-6	2-3	8	20.9	34.6	44.4	96	78.1	7	9	113	38.1
La Russa, Tony, StL	162	207	72.0	11	126-47	23-7	0-4	8	24.2	34.8	41.1	117	87.2	8	1	141	39.0
Lachemann, Rene, Fla	86	55	50.9	1	24-23	4-3	0-1	1	30.9	45.5	23.6	42	61.9	8	1	32	40.6
Lasorda, Tom, LA	76	80	73.8	3	50-19	9-2	0-0	0	21.3	46.3	32.5	44	84.1	3	3	37	51.4
Leyland, Jim, Pit	162	175	72.0	5	106-38	17-9	3-1	8	16.0	40.0	44.0	101	75.2	3	11	116	39.7
Riggleman, Jim, ChN	162	158	68.4	4	90-43	17-2	1-4	4	19.6	34.2	46.2	79	86.1	8	3	102	46.1
Russell, Bill, LA	86	84	77.4	9	61-18	4-0	0-1	2	21.4	33.3	45.2	44	84.1	2	5	61	45.9
Valentine, Bobby, NYN	31	20	40.0	0	7-11	1-1	0-0	0	20.0	35.0	45.0	25	80.0	5	3	19	31.6

Defense

	G	Pitchout Total	Pitchout Runners Moving	Pitchout CS%	Non-PO CS%	IBB	IBB Pct. of Situations	IBB Favorite Score Diff.	Def. Subs Total	Def. Subs Favorite Inning	Pos. 1	Pos. 2	Pos. 3
AL Managers													
Bell, Buddy, Det	162	13	3	100.0	30.4	40	6.0	-2	17	9	cf-12	c-1	3b-1
Bevington, Terry, ChA	162	57	15	53.3	32.4	43	6.1	-1	52	8	rf-18	cf-16	ss-8
Boone, Bob, KC	161	38	6	83.3	35.2	21	3.2	0	28	9	lf-7	ss-6	2b-4
Garner, Phil, Mil	162	32	7	57.1	27.9	20	3.2	1	46	9	lf-13	cf-12	rf-7
Gaston, Cito, Tor	162	34	6		37.6	19	3.2	-1	11	8	1b-3	2b-3	3b-2
Hargrove, Mike, Cle	161	41	13	69.2	30.1	31	4.2	-1	25	9	3b-10	rf-6	2b-4
Howe, Art, Oak	162	37	12	8.3	27.4	49	7.2	0	40	9	lf-13	rf-11	cf-7
Johnson, Davy, Bal	163	13	3	66.7	20.7	27	4.3	0	38	9	rf-14	c-11	lf-7
Kelly, Tom, Min	162	12	2	50.0	33.1	21	3.4	-2	12	9	rf-5	3b-3	ss-3
Kennedy, Kevin, Bos	162	24	3	0.0	20.4	25	3.5	0	27	8	cf-13	lf-6	rf-5
Lachemann, Marcel, Cal	112	60	15	40.0	21.8	22	4.5	0	14	9	c-7	3b-2	cf-2
McNamara, John, Cal	50	22	6	100.0	27.1	12	6.9	-2	10	6	3b-5	c-2	cf-2
Oates, Johnny, Tex	163	8	1	0.0	47.9	32	5.8	0	21	8	rf-7	1b-4	lf-3
Piniella, Lou, Sea	161	40	7	42.9	34.5	40	6.3	-1	14	7	lf-7	cf-3	2b-2
Torre, Joe, NYA	162	19	3	166.7	22.8	27	4.1	-2	55	8	2b-21	lf-19	3b-6
NL Managers													
Alou, Felipe, Mon	162	25	11	36.4	22.8	25	3.8	0	30	9	c-10	lf-7	cf-6
Baker, Dusty, SF	162	96	16	56.3	37.3	45	7.0	-2	15	8	ss-5	3b-2	lf-2
Baylor, Don, Col	162	89	23	47.8	28.6	15	2.0	0	16	8	rf-5	c-3	lf-3
Bochy, Bruce, SD	162	65	18	61.1	25.0	42	6.6	-1	15	7	1b-3	ss-3	rf-3
Boles, John, Fla	75	11	2	0.0	27.3	10	3.9	-2	17	9	lf-6	3b-4	rf-3
Collins, Terry, Hou	162	35	8	25.0	32.7	42	5.8	0	38	9	3b-18	c-6	lf-5
Cox, Bobby, Atl	162	34	6	50.0	26.6	48	7.7	-2	27	9	lf-8	ss-6	rf-6
Fregosi, Jim, Phi	162	5	0	0.0	33.3	40	5.9	-2	6	8	lf-2	1b-1	ss-1
Green, Dallas, NYN	131	34	7	85.7	17.4	40	8.3	-2	21	8	1b-10	rf-7	c-1
Knight, Ray, Cin	162	36	12	25.0	25.5	50	6.9	-2	27	8	3b-7	lf-6	c-4
La Russa, Tony, StL	162	41	12	50.0	32.9	38	5.8	0	13	6	1b-5	2b-2	3b-2
Lachemann, Rene, Fla	86	4	0	0.0	52.8	20	7.1	0	2	5	2b-1	cf-1	None
Lasorda, Tom, LA	76	23	4	25.0	15.7	27	7.5	0	9	8	lf-4	3b-3	2b-1
Leyland, Jim, Pit	162	46	9	77.8	21.5	31	4.2	0	14	9	rf-8	2b-2	ss-2
Riggleman, Jim, ChN	162	65	13	30.8	27.7	38	5.5	-1	21	7	3b-17	c-1	ss-1
Russell, Bill, LA	86	26	6	66.7	18.0	25	6.3	0	12	7	3b-4	lf-4	cf-3
Valentine, Bobby, NYN	31	3	1	100.0	17.2	12	8.0	0	2	5	c-1	2b-1	3b-1

Lineups

		Starting Lineup			Substitutes					
	G	Lineups Used	%LHB Vs. RHSP	%RHB vs. LHSP	#PH	Percent PH Platoon	PH BA	PH HR	#PR	PR SB-CS
AL Managers										
Bell, Buddy, Det	162	128	36.6	96.9	123	75.6	0.120	3	29	2-2
Bevington, Terry, ChA	162	109	64.5	82.5	148	81.8	0.222	1	59	4-5
Boone, Bob, KC	161	152	71.6	78.8	172	84.9	0.284	2	53	2-3
Garner, Phil, Mil	162	114	47.6	90.1	115	76.5	0.264	3	48	5-2
Gaston, Cito, Tor	162	87	58.7	92.9	126	76.2	0.202	2	23	0-0
Hargrove, Mike, Cle	161	96	54.2	81.1	115	84.3	0.271	6	20	0-1
Howe, Art, Oak	162	124	34.5	91.4	121	67.8	0.259	4	74	3-0
Johnson, Davy, Bal	163	100	68.0	71.9	85	80.0	0.292	2	33	2-3
Kelly, Tom, Min	162	120	49.3	90.2	207	90.8	0.307	5	28	1-0
Kennedy, Kevin, Bos	162	124	49.3	72.6	151	74.2	0.238	2	54	3-3
Lachemann, Marcel, Cal	112	80	52.7	80.4	101	89.1	0.236	7	11	1-0
McNamara, John, Cal	50	39	55.9	76.9	45	86.7	0.289	0	11	0-0
Oates, Johnny, Tex	163	73	56.7	73.6	89	80.9	0.108	0	43	5-1
Piniella, Lou, Sea	161	99	45.6	89.7	190	86.3	0.226	5	28	5-0
Torre, Joe, NYA	162	131	62.3	73.0	92	72.8	0.231	1	62	1-1
NL Managers										
Alou, Felipe, Mon	162	113	43.5	85.2	240	54.6	0.244	4	31	1-0
Baker, Dusty, SF	162	129	43.2	81.5	250	66.0	0.204	6	17	0-0
Baylor, Don, Col	162	91	34.9	93.4	288	80.2	0.196	3	31	1-1
Bochy, Bruce, SD	162	114	46.5	77.2	289	70.9	0.227	4	29	2-3
Boles, John, Fla	75	50	36.2	97.2	132	48.5	0.260	3	13	0-0
Collins, Terry, Hou	162	111	21.3	97.4	257	67.7	0.192	6	30	0-1
Cox, Bobby, Atl	162	89	57.4	73.8	254	77.6	0.243	6	32	1-0
Fregosi, Jim, Phi	162	114	51.6	85.5	239	59.0	0.216	5	12	1-0
Green, Dallas, NYN	131	79	40.2	87.5	213	85.0	0.250	2	43	1-1
Knight, Ray, Cin	162	147	49.8	78.3	313	72.8	0.230	11	17	4-1
La Russa, Tony, StL	162	120	44.9	80.2	246	81.3	0.282	2	25	6-3
Lachemann, Rene, Fla	86	47	31.3	96.5	121	72.7	0.202	1	9	0-0
Lasorda, Tom, LA	76	44	38.1	84.4	149	83.9	0.210	1	12	0-1
Leyland, Jim, Pit	162	117	44.9	72.9	299	85.3	0.284	10	18	1-0
Riggleman, Jim, ChN	162	87	41.2	86.3	326	78.2	0.205	4	34	0-0
Russell, Bill, LA	86	37	35.2	86.7	154	76.0	0.232	6	33	0-0
Valentine, Bobby, NYN	31	28	47.4	88.9	88	87.5	0.250	1	7	0-0

Pitching

		Starters					Relievers					
	G	Slow Hooks	Quick Hooks	> 120 Pitches	> 140 Pitches	3 Days Rest	Relief App	Mid-Inning Change	Save > 1 IP	1st Batter Platoon Pct	1-Batter App	3 Pitchers (≤ 2 runs)
AL Managers												
Bell, Buddy, Det	162	27	17	26	0	1	426	250	8	63.6	34	9
Bevington, Terry, ChA	162	15	24	42	2	3	391	200	8	60.4	48	14
Boone, Bob, KC	161	19	14	26	0	6	322	170	12	61.5	29	16
Garner, Phil, Mil	162	24	24	13	0	1	385	224	12	55.2	26	25
Gaston, Cito, Tor	162	27	12	23	1	1	303	94	4	55.1	17	20
Hargrove, Mike, Cle	161	17	14	14	0	1	382	167	5	58.4	43	18
Howe, Art, Oak	162	19	15	7	0	1	419	229	13	64.1	35	18
Johnson, Davy, Bal	163	28	15	13	0	23	378	211	9	59.8	28	17
Kelly, Tom, Min	162	14	11	14	1	2	387	216	13	63.6	33	15
Kennedy, Kevin, Bos	162	28	12	45	7	1	409	215	7	59.4	41	10
Lachemann, Marcel, Cal	112	21	8	16	0	0	272	149	8	57.6	23	9
McNamara, John, Cal	50	10	4	11	0	1	113	68	4	57.5	15	7
Oates, Johnny, Tex	163	15	14	31	2	0	347	208	7	67.2	44	15
Piniella, Lou, Sea	161	9	26	15	0	6	403	245	14	61.7	23	25
Torre, Joe, NYA	162	12	26	22	1	4	411	190	10	57.9	36	25
NL Managers												
Alou, Felipe, Mon	162	2	32	13	0	1	433	178	18	61.9	31	24
Baker, Dusty, SF	162	16	12	15	0	3	425	193	8	63.5	35	18
Baylor, Don, Col	162	23	13	12	0	0	447	135	2	52.3	31	15
Bochy, Bruce, SD	162	8	23	10	0	7	411	153	12	60.6	21	32
Boles, John, Fla	75	5	9	4	0	0	200	74	5	59.0	10	15
Collins, Terry, Hou	162	12	13	9	0	9	371	145	10	60.0	27	14
Cox, Bobby, Atl	162	13	25	19	1	14	408	122	9	57.8	24	28
Fregosi, Jim, Phi	162	9	16	5	0	1	387	143	15	62.8	26	20
Green, Dallas, NYN	131	18	5	13	0	5	260	84	12	61.2	20	8
Knight, Ray, Cin	162	8	29	9	1	3	425	131	10	58.6	24	24
La Russa, Tony, StL	162	16	17	24	1	3	413	173	8	63.2	47	25
Lachemann, Rene, Fla	86	5	3	8	0	0	212	86	6	63.2	19	18
Lasorda, Tom, LA	76	3	10	5	0	1	178	63	4	59.0	11	19
Leyland, Jim, Pit	162	8	27	10	1	0	422	150	11	61.1	27	21
Riggleman, Jim, ChN	162	11	17	7	0	6	439	178	11	62.6	34	24
Russell, Bill, LA	86	7	6	12	0	0	205	69	1	58.5	10	12
Valentine, Bobby, NYN	31	0	6	0	0	0	75	23	1	59.5	3	5

Player Projections

Hello, and welcome to Braggin' Rites, STATS Inc's annual ritual of reviewing last year's batter projections, confessing our successes, acknowledging our even greater successes, and calling maximum possible attention to our greatest successes. Hi; I'm Bill James.

This *Handbook* each year projects the next season's performance for every major league player who seems to have a reasonable chance to get some at bats. We have done this for several years, at the instigation of John Dewan, using a series of formulas that I developed and filling in the gaps with guesswork and intuition. Sometimes we're right, sometimes we're wrong; we find it best not to make any claims to great accuracy, except in jest.

There is nothing profound about the projection system. Essentially, if a player hit .280 in 1995 and .300 in 1996, we're going to project him to hit .290 in 1997. If he actually hits .290, we'll be right, and if he hits .340, we'll be wrong. There's more to it than that, of course, but the rest is just details. We look at what the player has done every year of his career, we make a few park adjustments, and we make gentle adjustments for aging patterns. As a player ages, we expect him to increase his walks and increase his power (up to a point) but lose speed.

Our only really *surprising* successes come when

   a) we're lucky, or

   b) we correctly interpret a player's minor league statistics.

More on that in a moment. We have a "grading" system for last year's projections, based on similarity scores. A similarity score of 1000 would be a perfect projection—every number exactly right. That's never happened and never will, but for each difference between what we projected and what the player actually did, we make a deduction from 1000. If the similarity score is 980 or greater, that's an "A+". We had six "A+" projections last year, 6 out of 371 (there were a handful of players for whom we made predictions who retired, were hurt all season, went to Japan, or just didn't make a roster, but we're not going to count those.) An A+ projection is a nearly-perfect projection of a player's season, like this:

Ray Durham

	Avg.	G	AB	R	H	2B	3B	HR	RBI	BB	SO	SB	CS	SLG
Actual 1996	.275	156	557	79	153	33	5	10	65	58	95	30	4	.406
Projected 1996	.274	148	559	88	153	30	9	10	59	41	93	29	11	.413

Our projected on-base percentages aren't all that significant, because we don't project all the details like hit batsmen and sacrifice flies. Anyway, we were essentially right on every aspect of Durham's season except that he drew a few more walks than we had projected, and this scores as an A+ projection. We also had A+ projections for Tim Wallach, Mike Bordick, Bob Hamelin, Darrin Fletcher and Gary DiSarcina. I'll run DiSarcina:

Gary DiSarcina

	Avg.	G	AB	R	H	2B	3B	HR	RBI	BB	SO	SB	CS	SLG
Actual 1996	.256	150	536	62	137	26	4	5	48	21	36	2	1	.347
Projected 1996	.262	144	503	66	132	24	3	5	47	26	39	7	7	.352

DiSarcina had hit .238 in 1993, .260 in 1994, and .307 in 1995. When that happens, our computer guesses that he will land right in the middle, and it's amazing how often he does. Same thing with Bob Hamelin.

If the similarity between the projection and the actual season is 960-979, we would score that a straight "A", and if the similarity is 940-959, we would score that an A-minus. We had 57 straight A's, and 58 A minuses—thus, 121 of our 371 projections last year, just under a third, would have to be described as good. A typical "A" projection would be like Craig Biggio or Chris Hoiles:

Craig Biggio

	Avg.	G	AB	R	H	2B	3B	HR	RBI	BB	SO	SB	CS	SLG
Actual 1996	.288	162	605	113	174	24	4	15	75	75	72	25	7	.415
Projected 1996	.283	160	628	114	178	34	4	16	69	92	93	38	13	.427

Chris Hoiles

	Avg.	G	AB	R	H	2B	3B	HR	RBI	BB	SO	SB	CS	SLG
Actual 1996	.258	127	407	64	105	13	0	25	73	57	97	0	1	.474
Projected 1996	.268	137	447	69	120	19	0	24	71	82	102	1	1	.472

Those both score at 970, in the center of the "A" range. Albert Belle scores at 978:

Albert Belle

	Avg.	G	AB	R	H	2B	3B	HR	RBI	BB	SO	SB	CS	SLG
Actual 1996	.311	158	602	124	187	38	3	48	148	99	87	11	0	.623
Projected 1996	.308	159	603	115	186	42	3	46	131	85	95	15	8	.617

It's very unusual for us to do that well with a power hitter. We missed by only one hit, one at bat, one game. If one of his home runs had hit the top of the wall for a double, I think it would have been an A+ projection.

We were almost equally accurate on Manny Ramirez, projecting him at .309 based on 171/554 with 38 homers; he actually was at .309 on 170/550, with 33 homers. We had a straight-A projection on Doug Strange:

Doug Strange

	Avg.	G	AB	R	H	2B	3B	HR	RBI	BB	SO	SB	CS	SLG
Actual 1996	.235	88	183	19	43	7	1	3	23	14	31	1	0	.333
Projected 1996	.247	73	154	17	38	9	0	2	18	12	24	2	1	.344

We're pleased with those projections, but let's be honest: this is not rocket science. If you predict that Manny Ramirez will play every day and hit .300 with a bunch of homers and Doug Strange won't play very much and won't hit very much when he does, you'll probably be pretty close. Most of you could do this as well as we could.

Our projection for Darryl Strawberry was just dumb luck:

Darryl Strawberry

	Avg.	G	AB	R	H	2B	3B	HR	RBI	BB	SO	SB	CS	SLG
Actual 1996	.262	63	202	35	53	13	0	11	36	31	55	6	5	.490
Projected 1996	.246	87	211	35	52	9	1	10	38	36	50	1	2	.441

We didn't know how much Darryl Strawberry would play this year, and we certainly don't have any formula that can tell us that sort of thing. We just picked some numbers out of the air, and as it turned out we were pretty close. We take more pride in our projections for young players like John Mabry, Mark Lewis and Mark Newfield:

John Mabry

	Avg.	G	AB	R	H	2B	3B	HR	RBI	BB	SO	SB	CS	SLG
Actual 1996	.297	151	543	63	161	30	2	13	74	37	84	3	2	.431
Projected 1996	.276	150	550	65	152	31	1	14	67	30	67	4	7	.413

Mark Lewis

	Avg.	G	AB	R	H	2B	3B	HR	RBI	BB	SO	SB	CS	SLG
Actual 1996	.270	145	545	69	147	30	3	11	55	42	109	6	1	.396
Projected 1996	.267	131	487	71	130	26	1	10	56	37	77	5	4	.386

Mark Newfield

	Avg.	G	AB	R	H	2B	3B	HR	RBI	BB	SO	SB	CS	SLG
Actual 1996	.278	133	370	48	103	26	0	12	57	27	70	1	2	.446
Projected 1996	.273	117	319	38	87	19	0	11	42	20	42	1	1	.436

Mark Lewis had hit .205 in 1994 with Cleveland, and .339 with Cincinnati in 1995. Mark Newfield had only 244 major league at bats before last season, and had hit only .225 in those few at bats. We were able, factoring in their minor league records, to make accurate projections of what they would do if they got a chance to play. Other examples of that would be (moving on to the "A-" group), three Blue Jays: Carlos Delgado, Alex Gonzalez and Sandy Martinez:

Carlos Delgado

	Avg.	G	AB	R	H	2B	3B	HR	RBI	BB	SO	SB	CS	SLG
Actual 1996	.270	138	488	68	132	28	2	25	92	58	139	0	0	.490
Projected 1996	.286	121	427	67	122	21	1	25	78	62	97	3	2	.515

Alex Gonzalez

	Avg.	G	AB	R	H	2B	3B	HR	RBI	BB	SO	SB	CS	SLG
Actual 1996	.235	147	527	64	124	30	5	14	64	45	127	16	6	.391
Projected 1996	.267	138	501	74	134	27	5	14	58	46	115	20	8	.425

Sandy Martinez

	Avg.	G	AB	R	H	2B	3B	HR	RBI	BB	SO	SB	CS	SLG
Actual 1996	.227	76	229	17	52	9	3	3	18	16	58	0	0	.332
Projected 1996	.227	45	132	10	30	8	0	1	17	4	33	0	0	.311

Baseball men have long believed that you can't tell what a player will hit in the major leagues based on what he has hit in the minor leagues. The truth is that they can't tell what a player will hit in the majors based on what he has hit in the minors; we can. They can't tell because they don't know how to read minor league batting statistics. We can, because we do. A writer in the *Chicago Tribune* wrote after the season that "(Derek) Jeter is the hands-down favorite for AL Rookie of the Year because of his .314 average and 78 RBIs—not bad for a player considered to be a slick-fielding, no-hit shortstop." In all modesty, we knew exactly what Derek Jeter was going into the season:

Derek Jeter

	Avg.	G	AB	R	H	2B	3B	HR	RBI	BB	SO	SB	CS	SLG
Actual 1996	.314	157	582	104	183	25	6	10	78	48	102	14	7	.430
Projected 1996	.313	152	537	94	168	31	6	5	59	62	65	21	8	.421

This is not to deny that we make most of our "A" and "A-" projections on consistent major league players. Joe Carter was an "A-" last year, as were Frank Thomas, Cal Ripken and Wade Boggs:

Joe Carter

	Avg.	G	AB	R	H	2B	3B	HR	RBI	BB	SO	SB	CS	SLG
Actual 1996	.253	157	625	84	158	35	7	30	107	44	106	7	6	.475
Projected 1996	.247	156	607	81	150	30	2	27	104	46	107	10	3	.437

The guys who go out and ring up the same kind of numbers year-in and year-out, they're easy to project. The most common score for a projection is "B+", meaning a similarity score of 920 to 939. We had 62 of those; B+'s and "A's" of one stripe or another account for almost exactly 50% of our projections. A typical "B+" would be like Eric Anthony or Rich Becker:

Eric Anthony

	Avg.	G	AB	R	H	2B	3B	HR	RBI	BB	SO	SB	CS	SLG
Actual 1996	.243	79	185	32	45	8	0	12	22	32	56	0	2	.481
Projected 1996	.248	55	161	21	40	7	0	6	21	17	34	2	1	.404

We guessed Anthony's playing time about right and were close on his batting average, but he hit 12 homers when he had only expected six. We had all the production rates about right for Becker, but we shorted him almost a hundred at bats:

Rich Becker

	Avg.	G	AB	R	H	2B	3B	HR	RBI	BB	SO	SB	CS	SLG
Actual 1996	.291	148	525	92	153	31	4	12	71	68	118	19	5	.434
Projected 1996	.282	121	444	74	125	22	3	9	52	62	99	16	8	.405

Barry Bonds was a "B+", and Tony Clark:

Tony Clark

	Avg.	G	AB	R	H	2B	3B	HR	RBI	BB	SO	SB	CS	SLG
Actual 1996	.250	100	376	56	94	14	0	27	72	29	127	0	1	.503
Projected 1996	.266	98	316	41	84	15	1	16	56	37	92	1	1	.472

Clark was actually slightly less productive than we had expected him to be. He hit for more power, but his average was lower, and his strikeout and walk data was not as good as we had projected. Ron Coomer is a 29-year-old minor league veteran who was finally given a chance to play in the majors by Tom Kelly. Based almost entirely on his minor league statistics, we had pegged him as a player who should hit about .295:

Ron Coomer

	Avg.	G	AB	R	H	2B	3B	HR	RBI	BB	SO	SB	CS	SLG
Actual 1996	.296	95	233	34	69	12	1	12	41	17	24	3	0	.511
Projected 1996	.295	105	390	57	115	23	2	17	73	20	52	2	2	.495

That's a B+, because we gave him too much playing time. A B+ means that we missed on *something*, but not too badly. We had the playing time wrong, or we had his average off a little, or we missed by five or ten homers.

We had 42 straight B's, grading our own projections. . . here; I'll give you a full schedule:

A+	6	B+	62	C+	38	D+	5		
A	57	B	42	C	21	D	12	F	12
A–	58	B–	38	C–	14	D–	6		

A typical "Straight B" (similarity score 900-919) would be Jose Canseco, Will Clark or Tony Pena:

Jose Canseco

	Avg.	G	AB	R	H	2B	3B	HR	RBI	BB	SO	SB	CS	SLG
Actual 1996	.289	96	360	68	104	22	1	28	82	63	82	3	1	.589
Projected 1996	.267	122	464	75	124	22	1	27	85	56	120	10	6	.494

Will Clark

	Avg.	G	AB	R	H	2B	3B	HR	RBI	BB	SO	SB	CS	SLG
Actual 1996	.284	117	436	69	124	25	1	13	72	64	67	2	1	.436
Projected 1996	.301	143	525	93	158	31	3	19	95	80	69	2	2	.480

Tony Pena

	Avg.	G	AB	R	H	2B	3B	HR	RBI	BB	SO	SB	CS	SLG
Actual 1996	.195	67	174	14	34	4	0	1	27	15	25	0	1	.236
Projected 1996	.235	99	251	22	59	13	1	3	21	18	40	1	1	.331

Just like a "B+", only the errors are a little more serious. A "straight C" would mean a similarity score of 840-860. Straight C's would go to our projections for Jose Offerman, Reggie Sanders and Gary Sheffield:

Jose Offerman

	Avg.	G	AB	R	H	2B	3B	HR	RBI	BB	SO	SB	CS	SLG
Actual 1996	.303	151	561	85	170	33	8	5	47	74	98	24	10	.417
Projected 1996	.267	127	393	53	105	12	4	2	39	56	62	11	7	.359

Reggie Sanders

	Avg.	G	AB	R	H	2B	3B	HR	RBI	BB	SO	SB	CS	SLG
Actual 1996	.251	81	287	49	72	17	1	14	33	44	86	24	8	.463
Projected 1996	.274	154	562	97	154	29	6	25	94	67	146	33	14	.480

Gary Sheffield

	Avg.	G	AB	R	H	2B	3B	HR	RBI	BB	SO	SB	CS	SLG
Actual 1996	.314	161	519	118	163	33	1	42	120	142	66	16	9	.624
Projected 1996	.281	143	501	81	141	26	2	25	86	78	78	22	9	.491

We don't miss by that much too often, thank God. We graded 19% of our projections last year at "Straight C" or below. Of course, Sanders was hurt and projecting what Gary Sheffield will do next year is like chasing a humming bird with a whiffle bat, but I'm not here to alibi.

OK, let's deal with the bad ones. We had 23 projections last year which earned some sort of a D. The five who got "D+'s" for us were Carlos Baerga, Chad Fonville, Brett Butler, Todd Hollandsworth and F.P. Santangelo. Todd Hollandsworth was far better than we had projected he would be:

Todd Hollandsworth

	Avg.	G	AB	R	H	2B	3B	HR	RBI	BB	SO	SB	CS	SLG
Actual 1996	.291	149	478	64	139	26	4	12	59	41	93	21	6	.437
Projected 1996	.233	79	227	27	53	9	1	7	28	14	48	7	4	.374

And Baerga, of course, was far worse:

Carlos Baerga

	Avg.	G	AB	R	H	2B	3B	HR	RBI	BB	SO	SB	CS	SLG
Actual 1996	.254	126	507	59	129	28	0	12	66	21	27	1	1	.381
Projected 1996	.317	154	638	106	202	32	2	23	109	31	55	13	4	.481

In the "Straight D" class we have the probable National League MVP, Ken Caminiti, and his teammate Steve Finley:

Ken Caminiti

	Avg.	G	AB	R	H	2B	3B	HR	RBI	BB	SO	SB	CS	SLG,
Actual 1996	.326	146	546	109	178	37	2	40	130	78	99	11	5	.621
Projected 1996	.261	150	559	73	146	29	1	16	78	61	101	9	5	.403

Steve Finley

	Avg.	G	AB	R	H	2B	3B	HR	RBI	BB	SO	SB	CS	SLG
Actual 1996	.298	161	655	126	195	45	9	30	95	56	88	22	8	.531
Projected 1996	.272	147	580	84	158	21	6	9	47	46	71	27	10	.376

As to why I didn't assign these projections a score of "F", I can't really tell you, except to say that we did even worse in a few other cases. Our Mark McGwire projection is in the "Straight D" class, too; we had him pegged at .238 with 27 homers.

We made a "D" projection for Colorado catcher Jeff Reed; we had projected that he would bat only 83 times. The other eight "D" projections were all players that we had projected to get some playing time, but who didn't. Yamil Benitez, for example:

Yamil Benitez

	Avg.	G	AB	R	H	2B	3B	HR	RBI	BB	SO	SB	CS	SLG
Actual 1996	.167	11	12	0	2	0	0	0	2	0	4	0	0	.167
Projected 1996	.250	82	204	23	51	9	1	6	29	14	55	6	5	.392

The others in this class are Manny Alexander, Rich Aude, Dion James, David Justice, Scott Leius, Kelly Stinnett and Ryan Thompson. All of these are about like Benitez—guys that we projected to play some or quite a bit, who played very little or almost not at all.

I am afraid that I must take personal responsibility for all of these poor projections. We have an ongoing, year-to-year argument, as we make the projections, about how to assign playing time. We make the projections in early October, long before anyone knows what *team* many players will be on or who will be managing that team, let alone before anyone knows what role a player may be assigned coming out of spring training. I always argue, therefore, that if a player MIGHT play, we should assign him playing time in our projections. If a player MIGHT bat 500 times, we should assign him 500 at bats. Otherwise, I believe, we're not telling the reader what we DO know—how well these guys will play if they do play—out of deference to sheer speculation about who will play and who won't.

I am outranked and outvoted in this annual argument, but I win sometimes anyway, so we wind up assigning playing time to guys like Yamil Benitez and Kelly Stinnett, whose chance of playing was probably never all that good.

These types of errors dominate the nether regions of our projection success chart. The six "D-" projections include Vince Coleman, Carl Everett and Tony Tarasco— all guys that we thought might play, but who didn't. They also include Brady Anderson:

Brady Anderson

	Avg.	G	AB	R	H	2B	3B	HR	RBI	BB	SO	SB	CS	SLG
Actual 1996	.297	149	579	117	172	37	5	50	110	76	106	21	8	.637
Projected 1996	.244	151	599	95	146	26	5	14	59	87	109	31	9	.374

We got his playing time about right, got his triples right, his strikeouts and walks pretty close, and were OK on the speed categories. Unfortunately, we missed his slugging percentage by a cool 263 points. Todd Hundley was about the same; we had him projected for 14 homers, too. We also earned a "D-" on Reggie Jefferson. We come, finally, to the complete failures, the worst projections of the 1996 season. Nine of these 12 Failing grades, again, were for players whom we projected to play, but who didn't play much for one reason or another—Bret Barberie, David Bell, Darren Daulton, Benji Gil, Dwayne Hosey, Trent Hubbard, Pat Kelly, Herb Perry and Roberto Petagine. Speaking of Benji Gil, we didn't do a projection at all for Kevin Elster. Who knew? The projection for Herb Perry was the worst of the year, as measured by Similarity Scores:

Herb Perry

	Avg.	G	AB	R	H	2B	3B	HR	RBI	BB	SO	SB	CS	SLG
Actual 1996	.083	7	12	1	1	1	0	0	0	1	2	1	0	.167
Projected 1996	.299	119	412	65	123	27	1	10	62	39	55	5	4	.442

That scores at 656. What can we say; we thought he could hit. We still believe that he can, if he ever gets a chance to prove it. With the development of Brian Giles, we're not holding our breath.

These are our most common failures, but those going in the opposite direction are our most spectacular. It was an interesting year to be a guy named "Rodriguez". We had Henry Rodriguez pencilled in for four homers. All season.

Henry Rodriguez

	Avg.	G	AB	R	H	2B	3B	HR	RBI	BB	SO	SB	CS	SLG
Actual 1996	.276	145	532	81	147	42	1	36	103	37	160	2	0	.562
Projected 1996	.234	80	167	17	39	8	1	4	20	11	33	0	0	.365

I'd blame the lively ball if I hadn't spent so much time talking about all the things we got right. For Alex Rodriguez, we had an MLE (Major League Equivalency) for 1995, published in our *Minor League Handbook* last year, which showed that Alex should hit .338 in the majors with a slugging percentage of .580. Our experience has shown us time and time again that these MLEs DO predict what players will hit, but at the time, it just didn't seem possible that he could really be that good. When his MLE was combined with his dismal major league performance from 1994 and 1995, we produced what we thought at the time was a dangerously optimistic projection:

Alex Rodriguez

	Avg.	G	AB	R	H	2B	3B	HR	RBI	BB	SO	SB	CS	SLG
Actual 1996	.358	146	601	141	215	54	1	36	123	59	104	15	4	.631
Projected 1996	.271	137	521	60	141	23	4	18	69	33	143	11	7	.434

So we earned an "F" for that one, too.

And then, of course, there is the Colorado Rocky of the year. We always have one of these; we predict that next year we'll have one, too. We've caught up with Dante Bichette by now (we had an "A-" projection for him), and we're gradually catching up with Andres Galarraga and Vinny Castilla. But Ellis Burks caught us napping:

Ellis Burks

	Avg.	G	AB	R	H	2B	3B	HR	RBI	BB	SO	SB	CS	SLG
Actual 1996	.344	156	613	142	211	45	8	40	128	61	114	32	6	.639
Projected 1996	.260	120	361	56	94	23	3	14	53	46	83	6	4	.457

Hey, doesn't Duke Snider own a patent on those numbers? You sure you can use them without his permission, Ellis? Is Duke out of jail yet?

Well, we just started doing this for the fun of it. We didn't make any claims to accuracy to begin with, and we're not going to make them now. A few other publications have begun carrying their own projections of what players will do, and that being the case, I am sure there are people out there who claim they can do this better than we can. I encourage you to believe them. I am sure that there are people out there who knew that Alex Rodriguez would hit .358 with eight gazillion total bases. Speaking for myself, I enjoy being surprised once in awhile. Establishing the predictable establishes the parameters of our future surprises.   —*Bill James*

Pitcher Projections

Nostradamus and George Orwell had it easy. . . *they* never had to project the stats of a big league pitcher. Prognosticating about floods, earthquakes, Armageddon and "Big Brother" is nothing compared to the challenge of estimating what kind of numbers a pitcher will put up in his next season. The fickleness of a fastball or curve, the myriad injuries which can kill an arm for a season, the constant changing of roles and the delicate psyches of starters, relievers and their managers all make for one interesting equation. With that said, for the fourth-straight year we present the results of *our* equation (actually, it was developed by John Dewan and Mike Canter) . In the following section, you'll find 1997 projections for nearly 200 pitchers—the only requirements for a player making this list were 150 career games or 500 career innings.

So how reliable can they be? Maybe you should ask Ken Hill or Jamie Navarro, both of whom made our *1996* projections list:

Ken Hill

	ERA	W	L	G	IP	H	BB	SO	BR/9
Actual 1996	3.63	16	10	35	251	250	95	170	12.39
Projected 1996	3.87	15	10	34	214	204	90	117	12.34

Jamie Navarro

	ERA	W	L	G	IP	H	BB	SO	BR/9
Actual 1996	3.92	15	12	35	237	244	72	158	12.02
Projected 1996	3.91	13	13	33	228	237	64	150	11.88

Of course, we would never include numbers in our books which we wouldn't stand behind. . . or use ourselves. And believe us, we use these plenty. But this is by no means a "perfect" science, as Blue Jay fans would attest to after our 1996 predictions for their two aces:

Pat Hentgen

	ERA	W	L	G	IP	H	BB	SO	BR/9
Actual 1996	3.22	20	10	35	266	238	94	177	11.25
Projected 1996	4.73	12	14	34	232	235	104	180	13.25

Juan Guzman

	ERA	W	L	G	IP	H	BB	SO	BR/9
Actual 1996	2.93	11	8	27	188	158	53	165	10.12
Projected 1996	4.50	10	11	29	170	165	92	134	13.58

Who knew Guzman would find the strike zone again in '96? But that's half the fun. Nostradamus would love this stuff. . . we think you will too.

—*Tony Nistler*

Projections for 1997 Batters

Batter	Age	Avg	G	AB	R	H	2B	3B	HR	RBI	BB	SO	SB	CS	OBP	SLG
Abbott,Kurt, Fla	28	.249	129	422	53	105	21	5	12	46	28	118	4	2	.296	.408
Abreu,Bob, Hou	23	.273	121	362	53	99	17	7	8	52	44	91	11	9	.352	.425
Alexander,Manny, Bal	26	.228	52	171	23	39	7	1	2	15	9	29	9	5	.267	.316
Alfonzo,Edgardo, NYN	23	.274	131	435	51	119	22	3	8	54	31	50	5	4	.322	.393
Alicea,Luis, StL	31	.250	139	396	55	99	20	4	5	42	58	67	12	7	.346	.359
Allensworth,Jermaine, Pit	25	.267	136	464	72	124	26	5	5	41	37	80	21	13	.321	.377
Alomar,Roberto, Bal	29	.307	154	593	109	182	33	6	16	76	76	60	32	8	.386	.464
Alomar,Sandy, Cle	31	.268	118	384	53	103	20	1	12	49	21	43	4	2	.306	.419
Alou,Moises, Mon	30	.292	138	524	87	153	32	3	22	88	52	78	9	7	.356	.490
Amaral,Rich, Sea	35	.275	116	302	57	83	18	2	2	26	34	46	19	5	.348	.368
Anderson,Brady, Bal	33	.257	151	596	105	153	27	4	26	82	83	114	29	8	.348	.446
Anderson,Garret, Cal	25	.299	143	551	71	165	33	2	13	84	28	93	6	5	.333	.437
Andrews,Shane, Mon	25	.237	128	376	50	89	20	1	14	58	44	105	3	2	.317	.407
Anthony,Eric, Col	29	.249	93	253	33	63	11	1	10	31	33	66	3	2	.336	.419
Arias,Alex, Fla	29	.254	117	244	23	62	13	1	3	28	22	31	1	1	.316	.352
Arias,George, Cal	25	.272	151	537	76	146	25	3	22	87	43	108	2	1	.326	.453
Ashley,Billy, LA	26	.249	99	253	36	63	12	0	13	42	31	91	2	1	.331	.451
Aurilia,Rich, SF	25	.254	95	307	38	78	14	1	6	35	29	43	5	5	.318	.365
Ausmus,Brad, Det	28	.246	124	386	49	95	16	2	6	35	38	70	9	6	.314	.345
Baerga,Carlos, NYN	28	.291	142	584	90	170	30	2	20	93	26	40	8	3	.321	.452
Bagwell,Jeff, Hou	29	.303	154	561	114	170	37	3	31	113	114	113	18	7	.421	.545
Baines,Harold, ChA	38	.271	134	436	59	118	21	2	16	65	61	64	1	1	.360	.438
Bartee,Kimera, Det	24	.260	81	208	36	54	7	0	3	18	16	56	17	8	.313	.337
Bates,Jason, Col	26	.282	104	291	38	82	16	3	8	39	37	45	3	4	.363	.440
Batista,Tony, Oak	23	.274	121	435	60	119	24	2	14	59	28	86	8	6	.317	.434
Batiste,Kim, SF	29	.242	59	186	20	45	7	1	4	24	5	28	2	2	.262	.355
Battle,Allen, Oak	28	.280	81	250	46	70	17	2	2	27	33	42	9	4	.364	.388
Bautista,Danny, Atl	25	.235	56	102	11	24	4	0	2	12	5	21	2	1	.271	.333
Beamon,Trey, Pit	23	.294	74	126	17	37	6	1	1	14	10	17	4	2	.346	.381
Becker,Rich, Min	25	.277	152	556	87	154	28	3	10	66	67	126	17	8	.355	.392
Bell,David, StL	24	.244	73	201	19	49	7	1	4	22	11	27	1	2	.283	.348
Bell,Derek, Hou	28	.289	151	599	77	173	26	2	16	93	42	111	31	9	.335	.419
Bell,Jay, Pit	31	.253	153	576	79	146	31	4	12	61	61	116	5	5	.325	.384
Belle,Albert, Cle	30	.310	160	609	123	189	41	2	47	134	94	93	10	4	.403	.616
Benard,Marvin, SF	27	.273	109	370	59	101	17	2	4	31	36	56	15	9	.337	.362
Benjamin,Mike, Phi	31	.212	36	104	11	22	4	0	2	9	8	23	5	1	.268	.308
Berroa,Geronimo, Oak	32	.279	146	551	85	154	28	1	23	91	57	107	7	4	.347	.459
Berry,Sean, Hou	31	.282	134	422	49	119	24	1	16	71	33	64	11	6	.334	.457
Bichette,Dante, Col	33	.303	153	630	94	191	34	2	30	115	32	109	24	11	.337	.506
Biggio,Craig, Hou	31	.283	158	607	113	172	32	3	14	70	86	83	38	9	.372	.415
Blauser,Jeff, Atl	31	.248	126	460	68	114	21	2	11	47	58	96	7	4	.332	.374
Blowers,Mike, LA	32	.258	124	392	46	101	21	1	13	65	45	100	1	1	.334	.416
Boggs,Wade, NYA	39	.312	131	487	79	152	29	2	7	58	75	42	1	1	.404	.423
Bonds,Barry, SF	32	.285	155	536	117	153	33	3	35	107	130	76	36	11	.425	.554
Bonilla,Bobby, Bal	34	.270	151	570	85	154	31	3	23	89	69	104	2	3	.349	.456
Boone,Bret, Cin	28	.272	144	526	66	143	29	2	16	77	37	95	4	3	.320	.426
Borders,Pat, ChA	34	.238	102	302	24	72	15	1	5	25	14	55	1	1	.272	.344
Bordick,Mike, Oak	31	.246	147	499	47	123	17	2	5	46	45	55	8	4	.309	.319
Bournigal,Rafael, Oak	31	.246	64	171	15	42	8	0	0	15	9	11	1	1	.283	.292
Bragg,Darren, Bos	27	.287	119	411	70	118	27	2	10	51	55	77	16	6	.371	.436

Projections for 1997 Batters

Batter	Age	Avg	G	AB	R	H	2B	3B	HR	RBI	BB	SO	SB	CS	OBP	SLG
Branson,Jeff, Cin	30	.252	139	333	40	84	16	2	9	41	37	67	1	1	.327	.393
Brede,Brent, Min	25	.302	68	189	32	57	12	1	3	23	27	35	5	3	.389	.423
Brogna,Rico, NYN	27	.263	106	377	46	99	20	2	15	53	28	87	1	1	.314	.446
Brosius,Scott, Oak	30	.260	132	450	65	117	22	1	18	57	48	80	5	4	.331	.433
Brown,Brant, ChN	26	.274	61	106	13	29	6	1	2	11	6	19	2	2	.313	.406
Brumfield,Jacob, Tor	32	.268	123	355	61	95	23	2	8	34	33	63	17	9	.330	.411
Buford,Damon, Tex	27	.248	105	298	55	74	14	1	7	32	29	57	17	9	.315	.372
Buhner,Jay, Sea	32	.262	146	543	95	142	25	2	34	113	83	133	1	1	.359	.503
Bullett,Scott, ChN	28	.259	84	189	25	49	8	2	3	21	9	44	8	3	.293	.370
Burks,Ellis, Col	32	.292	141	554	103	162	31	4	29	97	65	123	19	6	.367	.520
Burnitz,Jeromy, Mil	28	.248	154	537	93	133	27	4	18	82	83	127	15	6	.348	.413
Butler,Brett, LA	40	.271	119	380	56	103	12	4	2	22	53	49	22	8	.360	.339
Cameron,Mike, ChA	24	.272	123	464	99	126	28	7	21	72	57	123	25	12	.351	.498
Caminiti,Ken, SD	34	.268	149	553	79	148	30	1	20	86	70	103	9	5	.350	.434
Cangelosi,John, Hou	34	.250	88	188	31	47	7	1	1	11	36	33	13	5	.371	.314
Canizaro,Jay, SF	23	.253	113	324	46	82	16	2	7	41	34	74	8	6	.324	.380
Canseco,Jose, Bos	32	.269	129	490	83	132	24	1	29	90	70	123	8	4	.361	.500
Carr,Chuck, Mil	28	.255	84	278	43	71	12	1	2	23	26	45	21	9	.319	.327
Carreon,Mark, Cle	33	.276	115	355	41	98	16	0	11	51	25	40	2	2	.324	.414
Carter,Joe, Tor	37	.248	152	601	77	149	30	2	26	103	44	102	9	3	.299	.434
Castilla,Vinny, Col	29	.294	160	603	86	177	37	3	32	104	35	93	6	5	.332	.524
Castillo,Luis, Fla	21	.280	140	435	69	122	11	5	1	27	44	91	39	13	.347	.336
Castro,Juan, LA	25	.235	70	187	21	44	8	1	1	17	10	27	2	2	.274	.305
Cedeno,Andujar, Hou	27	.236	116	382	40	90	19	2	9	45	27	87	4	3	.286	.366
Cedeno,Domingo, ChA	28	.241	99	290	39	70	10	3	3	24	19	60	4	3	.288	.328
Cedeno,Roger, LA	22	.257	73	202	28	52	7	1	1	18	21	34	9	4	.327	.317
Cianfrocco,Archi, SD	30	.254	87	232	26	59	12	1	6	33	11	55	1	1	.288	.392
Cirillo,Jeff, Mil	27	.294	155	555	93	163	37	3	16	78	64	75	7	5	.367	.458
Clark,Dave, LA	34	.266	114	199	29	53	8	1	7	31	25	42	2	1	.348	.422
Clark,Tony, Det	25	.268	155	568	81	152	24	1	33	103	62	168	1	1	.340	.488
Clark,Will, Tex	33	.294	138	504	87	148	29	3	17	91	80	71	2	1	.390	.464
Clayton,Royce, StL	27	.248	144	536	59	133	21	4	6	47	41	105	29	11	.302	.336
Colbrunn,Greg, Fla	27	.283	150	534	66	151	27	1	20	81	26	79	7	4	.316	.449
Conine,Jeff, Fla	31	.296	155	588	76	174	30	3	23	100	61	116	2	2	.362	.474
Coomer,Ron, Min	30	.303	99	327	48	99	19	1	14	62	19	37	3	2	.341	.495
Cora,Joey, Sea	32	.276	138	489	71	135	18	4	4	39	43	37	12	6	.335	.354
Cordero,Wil, Bos	25	.299	107	398	58	119	27	2	10	54	31	61	10	4	.350	.452
Cordova,Marty, Min	27	.299	152	569	92	170	36	3	23	96	56	109	18	8	.362	.494
Crespo,Felipe, Tor	24	.262	92	290	38	76	18	1	7	32	33	48	8	5	.337	.403
Cruz,Jacob, SF	24	.264	89	178	26	47	10	0	4	26	21	32	2	3	.342	.388
Cummings,Midre, Pit	25	.277	73	213	25	59	11	1	4	25	11	35	2	1	.313	.394
Curtis,Chad, LA	28	.261	155	570	91	149	26	3	15	60	68	91	28	16	.340	.396
Cuyler,Milt, Bos	28	.264	55	144	22	38	5	2	2	15	14	26	5	4	.329	.368
Damon,Johnny, KC	23	.291	150	549	79	160	23	9	11	61	44	55	24	7	.344	.426
Davis,Chili, Cal	37	.266	136	493	75	131	23	1	22	85	89	106	3	2	.378	.450
Davis,Eric, Cin	35	.233	107	335	57	78	14	1	14	52	56	108	15	6	.343	.406
Davis,Russ, Sea	27	.262	139	473	76	124	28	1	20	68	66	116	4	3	.353	.452
Decker,Steve, Col	31	.300	51	120	14	36	6	0	3	15	14	15	0	0	.373	.425
Delgado,Carlos, Tor	25	.275	144	509	72	140	25	1	28	88	64	132	1	1	.356	.493
DeShields,Delino, LA	28	.260	143	512	81	133	19	5	7	50	69	102	48	14	.348	.357

Projections for 1997 Batters

Batter	Age	Avg	G	AB	R	H	2B	3B	HR	RBI	BB	SO	SB	CS	OBP	SLG
Devereaux,Mike, Bal	34	.240	104	308	40	74	16	2	8	40	24	61	5	3	.295	.383
DiSarcina,Gary, Cal	29	.259	152	555	72	144	25	3	6	48	28	38	6	5	.295	.348
Doster,David, Phi	26	.245	55	184	21	45	12	0	4	21	12	25	3	2	.291	.375
Duncan,Mariano, NYA	34	.273	118	425	52	116	21	2	8	52	13	93	5	3	.295	.388
Dunn,Todd, Mil	26	.307	84	218	36	67	14	2	9	38	19	56	6	2	.363	.514
Dunston,Shawon, SF	34	.258	123	446	46	115	21	3	10	49	17	71	7	5	.285	.386
Durham,Ray, ChA	25	.275	154	574	87	158	31	8	11	67	51	97	29	9	.334	.415
Dye,Jermaine, Atl	23	.259	139	417	46	108	23	1	15	54	15	79	4	5	.285	.427
Dykstra,Lenny, Phi	34	.263	67	232	39	61	14	1	3	17	42	32	12	4	.376	.371
Easley,Damion, Det	27	.244	97	299	38	73	13	1	5	33	29	44	6	3	.311	.344
Echevarria,Angel, Col	26	.344	91	209	32	72	11	0	12	39	19	38	2	2	.399	.569
Edmonds,Jim, Cal	27	.292	137	497	87	145	28	3	23	80	50	116	3	3	.356	.499
Eisenreich,Jim, Phi	38	.289	129	381	44	110	19	2	5	46	39	43	8	2	.355	.388
Elster,Kevin, Tex	32	.236	144	499	64	118	26	1	15	74	51	120	2	1	.307	.383
Erstad,Darin, Cal	23	.286	153	584	96	167	25	4	10	59	59	90	12	10	.351	.394
Espinoza,Alvaro, NYN	35	.243	103	226	25	55	12	1	3	22	7	32	2	2	.266	.345
Estalella,Bobby, Phi	22	.228	57	162	19	37	5	0	7	24	19	46	1	1	.309	.389
Eusebio,Tony, Hou	30	.291	101	299	35	87	15	1	5	44	23	47	1	1	.342	.398
Everett,Carl, NYN	26	.276	94	286	48	79	14	2	9	40	26	62	9	7	.337	.434
Fabregas,Jorge, Cal	27	.259	106	316	29	82	12	0	3	35	22	36	1	1	.308	.326
Fasano,Sal, KC	25	.235	78	166	23	39	6	0	6	23	11	30	2	2	.282	.380
Fielder,Cecil, NYA	33	.243	151	564	80	137	20	1	32	100	79	144	1	0	.336	.452
Finley,Steve, SD	32	.276	150	604	103	167	25	6	17	65	54	77	28	11	.336	.422
Flaherty,John, SD	29	.243	132	403	39	98	21	0	10	46	18	59	2	2	.276	.370
Fletcher,Darrin, Mon	30	.261	135	414	43	108	22	1	12	59	36	35	0	0	.320	.406
Floyd,Cliff, Mon	24	.276	107	290	39	80	15	3	9	40	29	57	7	3	.342	.441
Fonville,Chad, LA	26	.249	90	233	34	58	4	1	1	15	18	30	12	5	.303	.288
Fox,Andy, NYA	26	.242	75	223	33	54	9	1	5	20	23	39	9	4	.313	.359
Franco,Julio, Cle	35	.273	128	487	68	133	22	2	11	79	66	90	7	4	.360	.394
Frye,Jeff, Bos	30	.276	118	431	65	119	28	2	3	43	53	56	12	4	.355	.371
Fryman,Travis, Det	28	.276	160	635	93	175	36	4	22	101	67	134	4	3	.345	.449
Gaetti,Gary, StL	38	.235	135	494	57	116	21	1	17	68	38	103	2	2	.289	.385
Gagne,Greg, LA	35	.243	136	470	51	114	22	3	8	55	43	90	6	7	.306	.353
Galarraga,Andres, Col	36	.282	152	588	93	166	32	2	32	111	34	159	13	5	.322	.507
Gallego,Mike, StL	36	.215	46	121	12	26	4	0	1	11	13	23	0	0	.291	.273
Gant,Ron, StL	32	.240	131	445	76	107	22	3	23	78	80	111	19	8	.356	.458
Garcia,Carlos, Pit	29	.274	120	464	61	127	22	3	8	49	26	72	15	9	.312	.386
Garciaparra,Nomar, Bos	23	.282	148	547	86	154	29	7	19	74	41	52	23	9	.332	.464
Gates,Brent, Oak	27	.274	111	416	50	114	24	2	5	48	37	57	3	2	.333	.377
Giambi,Jason, Oak	26	.285	144	561	89	160	43	0	19	91	70	89	1	1	.365	.463
Gibralter,Steve, Cin	24	.252	97	282	36	71	17	1	8	36	20	69	3	2	.301	.404
Gil,Benji, Tex	24	.236	56	144	16	34	5	1	3	16	10	43	2	2	.286	.347
Giles,Brian S., Cle	26	.302	155	549	93	166	26	5	21	84	69	62	6	4	.380	.483
Gilkey,Bernard, NYN	30	.277	151	566	86	157	34	4	18	83	63	101	18	11	.350	.447
Giovanola,Ed, Atl	28	.256	84	203	24	52	8	0	3	17	24	30	3	3	.335	.340
Girardi,Joe, NYA	32	.267	136	479	61	128	18	2	5	48	33	69	7	4	.314	.344
Glanville,Doug, ChN	26	.264	92	197	22	52	9	1	2	19	7	22	7	4	.289	.350
Gomez,Chris, SD	26	.245	144	481	55	118	23	1	8	55	55	94	5	3	.323	.347
Gomez,Leo, ChN	30	.234	124	351	47	82	18	0	14	50	52	77	2	2	.333	.405
Gonzalez,Alex, Tor	24	.248	153	557	75	138	30	5	15	66	58	142	18	8	.319	.400

Projections for 1997 Batters

Batter	Age	Avg	G	AB	R	H	2B	3B	HR	RBI	BB	SO	SB	CS	OBP	SLG
Gonzalez,Juan, Tex	27	.298	133	524	83	156	28	2	37	118	38	85	3	2	.345	.571
Gonzalez,Luis, ChN	29	.275	151	561	83	154	33	5	16	85	74	72	14	11	.359	.437
Goodwin,Curtis, Cin	24	.262	81	282	42	74	10	2	1	20	24	44	25	9	.320	.323
Goodwin,Tom, KC	28	.275	150	538	76	148	14	4	3	37	39	80	60	22	.324	.333
Grace,Mark, ChN	33	.301	149	571	84	172	34	2	11	71	65	52	4	3	.373	.426
Green,Shawn, Tor	24	.296	141	459	64	136	31	3	14	57	33	71	8	4	.343	.468
Greene,Todd, Cal	26	.278	112	367	52	102	17	0	20	56	19	64	3	3	.313	.488
Greene,Willie, Cin	25	.254	139	441	69	112	19	2	22	68	51	105	4	3	.331	.456
Greenwell,Mike, Bos	33	.286	113	416	58	119	24	2	11	59	36	34	6	3	.343	.433
Greer,Rusty, Tex	28	.291	147	516	78	150	32	3	16	78	72	88	3	1	.378	.457
Griffey Jr,Ken, Sea	27	.303	153	581	127	176	33	3	42	118	93	105	14	4	.399	.587
Grissom,Marquis, Atl	30	.278	159	663	107	184	30	5	16	61	53	77	38	13	.331	.410
Grudzielanek,Mark, Mon	27	.290	157	638	91	185	37	3	8	61	33	81	29	9	.325	.395
Guerrero,Vladimir, Mon	21	.320	127	435	71	139	31	5	14	64	36	48	12	9	.372	.510
Guerrero,Wilton, LA	22	.297	132	387	51	115	11	3	2	29	17	56	17	8	.327	.357
Guillen,Ozzie, ChA	33	.258	140	480	57	124	19	4	2	45	14	33	6	6	.279	.327
Gutierrez,Ricky, Hou	27	.264	100	284	37	75	10	2	1	26	29	52	6	4	.332	.324
Gwynn,Tony, SD	37	.336	135	524	71	176	29	4	7	67	47	23	9	4	.391	.447
Hamelin,Bob, KC	29	.237	105	312	47	74	17	1	15	49	55	70	3	3	.351	.442
Hamilton,Darryl, Tex	32	.279	131	501	70	140	22	3	5	45	51	50	12	4	.346	.365
Hammonds,Jeffrey, Bal	26	.281	112	402	65	113	21	3	12	53	34	64	8	4	.337	.438
Hansen,Dave, LA	28	.263	74	99	9	26	4	0	1	9	14	16	0	0	.354	.333
Harris,Lenny, Cin	32	.259	118	228	28	59	11	1	2	22	15	24	11	4	.305	.342
Haselman,Bill, Bos	31	.268	86	224	35	60	13	1	9	35	23	41	2	1	.336	.455
Hayes,Charlie, NYA	32	.260	127	435	46	113	22	1	10	57	37	72	4	2	.318	.384
Henderson,Rickey, SD	38	.251	114	378	72	95	18	2	8	33	89	72	28	11	.394	.373
Hernandez,Jose, ChN	27	.254	132	335	49	85	12	3	10	41	21	81	4	2	.298	.397
Herrera,Jose, Oak	24	.269	97	301	38	81	11	2	4	31	21	49	7	6	.317	.359
Hiatt,Phil, Det	28	.246	72	191	27	47	9	1	10	30	16	64	4	2	.304	.461
Higginson,Bob, Det	26	.280	152	579	98	162	34	4	29	85	80	110	12	7	.367	.503
Hill,Glenallen, SF	32	.261	130	467	65	122	22	2	19	70	40	101	20	7	.320	.439
Hoiles,Chris, Bal	32	.261	136	437	65	114	18	0	23	70	77	102	1	1	.372	.460
Hollandsworth,Todd, LA	24	.258	153	559	73	144	24	3	17	71	46	108	18	9	.314	.403
Hollins,Dave, Sea	31	.244	106	348	64	85	17	1	11	50	66	75	3	3	.365	.394
Hosey,Dwayne, Bos	30	.285	96	228	44	65	16	2	8	31	27	46	11	5	.361	.478
Houston,Tyler, ChN	26	.258	78	209	24	54	8	1	4	25	11	33	2	2	.295	.364
Howard,Dave, KC	30	.218	129	335	35	73	12	3	2	32	34	61	7	4	.290	.290
Howard,Thomas, Cin	32	.272	115	279	37	76	14	2	4	29	16	42	9	5	.312	.380
Hubbard,Trent, SF	31	.283	63	187	31	53	9	1	3	18	20	27	9	5	.353	.390
Hudler,Rex, Cal	36	.253	98	261	35	66	12	1	8	27	10	57	11	3	.280	.398
Hulse,David, Mil	29	.262	88	244	37	64	9	3	1	24	16	43	11	3	.308	.336
Hundley,Todd, NYN	28	.236	150	550	77	130	22	1	27	83	73	139	2	2	.326	.427
Hunter,Brian, Sea	29	.241	89	232	29	56	14	1	10	40	19	50	1	1	.299	.440
Hunter,Brian L., Hou	26	.301	129	491	78	148	23	4	6	42	30	71	35	12	.342	.401
Huskey,Butch, NYN	25	.245	129	441	54	108	17	1	17	64	36	88	7	5	.302	.404
Incaviglia,Pete, Bal	33	.231	120	320	39	74	18	1	15	47	27	99	1	1	.291	.434
Jaha,John, Mil	31	.277	146	549	92	152	28	1	27	97	73	120	4	2	.362	.479
Javier,Stan, SF	33	.253	128	467	70	118	16	2	6	43	52	80	30	7	.328	.334
Jefferies,Gregg, Phi	29	.300	124	490	68	147	27	2	12	63	46	28	18	9	.360	.437
Jefferson,Reggie, Bos	28	.304	115	342	54	104	21	2	14	55	28	71	0	0	.357	.500

Projections for 1997 Batters

Batter	Age	Avg	G	AB	R	H	2B	3B	HR	RBI	BB	SO	SB	CS	OBP	SLG
Jensen,Marcus, SF	24	.255	63	149	18	38	8	1	2	18	16	34	0	0	.327	.362
Jeter,Derek, NYA	23	.314	150	570	99	179	28	5	8	67	57	78	19	9	.376	.423
Johnson,Brian, SD	29	.262	101	294	29	77	18	1	7	43	14	47	0	0	.295	.401
Johnson,Charles, Fla	25	.238	128	407	46	97	19	1	16	52	50	89	2	2	.322	.408
Johnson,Lance, NYN	33	.296	152	629	93	186	20	12	5	56	34	37	44	11	.332	.390
Johnson,Mark, Pit	29	.252	139	436	66	110	21	1	18	63	64	104	8	5	.348	.429
Jones,Andruw, Atl	20	.288	142	545	85	157	31	2	31	89	30	135	20	7	.325	.523
Jones,Chipper, Atl	25	.293	159	597	109	175	30	6	24	101	89	97	11	5	.385	.484
Jones,Chris, NYN	31	.267	73	131	19	35	5	1	4	18	9	31	2	1	.314	.412
Jordan,Brian, StL	30	.287	147	520	77	149	27	4	18	83	31	90	22	9	.327	.458
Jordan,Kevin, Phi	27	.269	68	223	26	60	15	1	5	28	13	22	1	1	.309	.413
Joyner,Wally, SD	35	.272	133	478	63	130	28	1	11	71	70	68	3	2	.365	.404
Justice,Dave, Atl	31	.282	103	341	58	96	16	1	18	61	62	51	3	2	.392	.493
Karkovice,Ron, ChA	33	.215	114	325	42	70	14	0	11	40	37	93	2	2	.296	.360
Karros,Eric, LA	29	.263	158	608	81	160	30	2	28	104	56	110	5	2	.325	.457
Kelly,Mike, Cin	27	.222	54	180	25	40	7	1	6	21	17	54	5	2	.289	.372
Kelly,Pat, NYA	29	.254	90	256	33	65	14	1	4	30	18	55	6	3	.303	.363
Kelly,Roberto, Min	32	.288	83	229	30	66	11	1	5	27	14	37	8	4	.329	.410
Kendall,Jason, Pit	23	.304	141	454	71	138	26	3	6	58	42	26	7	4	.363	.414
Kent,Jeff, Cle	29	.273	140	516	67	141	28	2	18	69	32	98	4	4	.316	.440
Kieschnick,Brooks, ChN	25	.277	146	513	57	142	27	1	18	67	43	99	2	3	.333	.439
King,Jeff, Pit	32	.253	144	538	67	136	28	2	17	82	59	74	8	3	.327	.407
Kingery,Mike, Pit	36	.259	112	309	42	80	15	2	4	30	31	32	7	4	.326	.359
Kirby,Wayne, LA	33	.249	109	233	34	58	11	2	3	20	17	34	8	4	.300	.352
Klesko,Ryan, Atl	26	.277	150	548	85	152	23	3	35	95	71	118	6	4	.360	.522
Knoblauch,Chuck, Min	28	.301	155	607	116	183	34	6	10	66	85	87	52	16	.387	.427
Kreuter,Chad, ChA	32	.235	56	102	13	24	5	0	2	14	13	22	0	0	.322	.343
Lampkin,Tom, SF	33	.249	72	173	22	43	8	1	3	22	16	21	2	3	.312	.358
Lankford,Ray, StL	30	.265	152	562	101	149	33	6	21	81	82	137	27	11	.359	.457
Lansing,Mike, Mon	29	.266	156	590	74	157	34	2	9	60	43	69	25	9	.316	.376
Larkin,Barry, Cin	33	.283	149	548	102	155	28	4	16	67	83	63	41	8	.377	.436
Lawton,Matt, Min	25	.272	129	441	73	120	21	3	13	63	51	66	13	9	.348	.422
Lemke,Mark, Atl	31	.248	138	475	50	118	15	1	5	39	53	47	3	2	.324	.316
Levis,Jesse, Mil	29	.273	116	289	36	79	16	0	4	33	43	21	1	1	.367	.370
Lewis,Darren, ChA	29	.243	140	383	57	93	11	4	3	32	40	44	28	12	.314	.316
Lewis,Mark, Det	27	.267	153	558	75	149	29	2	12	62	50	103	4	3	.327	.391
Leyritz,Jim, NYA	33	.255	106	333	44	85	15	0	12	54	46	87	1	1	.346	.408
Lieberthal,Mike, Phi	25	.241	70	220	20	53	11	0	3	23	17	25	1	1	.295	.332
Liriano,Nelson, Pit	33	.259	123	297	34	77	18	3	4	39	32	40	2	1	.331	.380
Listach,Pat, Mil	29	.254	106	358	51	91	14	2	2	34	34	56	21	6	.319	.321
Livingstone,Scott, SD	31	.280	101	211	21	59	13	0	3	21	11	26	1	1	.315	.384
Lockhart,Keith, KC	32	.284	105	310	39	88	19	2	6	35	21	30	6	4	.329	.416
Lofton,Kenny, Cle	30	.313	151	626	124	196	29	9	11	67	63	74	77	21	.376	.441
Lopez,Javy, Atl	26	.279	138	477	55	133	22	2	21	67	26	84	2	2	.316	.465
Loretta,Mark, Mil	25	.277	82	260	33	72	11	2	2	33	21	25	4	3	.331	.358
Mabry,John, StL	26	.281	152	545	64	153	30	1	13	68	36	74	3	3	.325	.411
Macfarlane,Mike, KC	33	.240	129	425	58	102	24	1	16	58	42	85	2	1	.308	.414
Magadan,Dave, ChN	34	.273	90	220	28	60	13	1	2	25	42	33	1	1	.389	.368
Magee,Wendell, Phi	24	.256	51	160	18	41	8	1	4	18	13	27	3	3	.312	.394
Malave,Jose, Bos	26	.283	63	187	31	53	11	1	10	33	15	36	1	1	.337	.513

Projections for 1997 Batters

Batter	Age	Avg	G	AB	R	H	2B	3B	HR	RBI	BB	SO	SB	CS	OBP	SLG
Manto,Jeff, Bos	32	.259	82	174	25	45	11	0	8	27	23	37	1	1	.345	.460
Manwaring,Kirt, Hou	31	.227	113	339	23	77	12	1	3	30	26	58	1	1	.282	.295
Martin,Al, Pit	29	.289	153	567	93	164	29	6	18	65	59	112	32	14	.356	.457
Martin,Norberto, ChA	30	.268	96	254	38	68	11	2	2	25	12	32	8	4	.301	.350
Martinez,Dave, ChA	32	.281	146	469	67	132	20	5	8	50	50	53	12	7	.351	.397
Martinez,Edgar, Sea	34	.320	142	513	103	164	40	1	23	91	107	84	5	3	.437	.536
Martinez,Sandy, Tor	24	.235	90	272	21	64	14	1	4	30	13	62	0	0	.270	.338
Martinez,Tino, NYA	29	.274	158	580	83	159	32	1	28	105	69	89	1	1	.351	.478
Mashore,Damon, Oak	27	.249	66	181	24	45	9	1	3	19	17	44	5	2	.313	.359
Matheny,Mike, Mil	26	.228	104	268	26	61	15	1	4	33	17	57	2	1	.274	.336
May,Derrick, Hou	28	.276	120	341	43	94	18	1	8	47	30	39	4	2	.334	.405
Mayne,Brent, NYN	29	.250	75	108	10	27	5	0	1	10	11	16	0	0	.319	.324
McCarty,Dave, SF	27	.259	63	162	24	42	9	1	4	20	16	37	1	1	.326	.401
McCracken,Quinton, Col	27	.334	103	356	63	119	20	6	5	38	32	48	22	10	.389	.466
McGee,Willie, StL	38	.267	92	247	36	66	14	3	3	27	15	51	4	2	.309	.385
McGriff,Fred, Atl	33	.287	154	581	88	167	28	1	32	103	70	110	6	5	.364	.504
McGwire,Mark, Oak	33	.242	125	405	82	98	16	0	31	80	114	110	1	0	.408	.511
McLemore,Mark, Tex	32	.257	146	510	70	131	18	2	5	42	73	75	24	11	.350	.329
McMillon,Billy, Fla	25	.293	64	229	34	67	13	1	6	33	26	45	4	3	.365	.437
McRae,Brian, ChN	29	.269	158	635	102	171	32	7	12	59	69	96	34	12	.341	.398
Meares,Pat, Min	28	.262	154	561	71	147	26	4	9	63	25	104	12	7	.294	.371
Merced,Orlando, Pit	30	.283	138	505	74	143	27	3	13	76	61	77	7	3	.360	.426
Mieske,Matt, Mil	29	.250	137	368	52	92	23	3	13	59	32	74	3	5	.310	.435
Miller,Orlando, Hou	28	.247	136	449	49	111	25	4	11	56	21	111	4	5	.281	.394
Mitchell,Kevin, Cin	35	.297	73	219	27	65	15	0	8	39	37	35	0	0	.398	.475
Molitor,Paul, Min	40	.286	140	566	75	162	28	4	11	76	60	70	17	4	.355	.408
Mondesi,Raul, LA	26	.297	158	617	95	183	29	7	25	87	33	110	21	9	.332	.488
Morandini,Mickey, Phi	31	.266	140	508	60	135	23	5	5	40	48	75	17	7	.329	.360
Mordecai,Mike, Atl	29	.249	83	181	25	45	10	0	4	21	16	27	4	2	.310	.370
Morris,Hal, Cin	32	.303	139	509	69	154	29	2	13	77	46	71	5	3	.360	.444
Mouton,James, Hou	28	.262	122	324	48	85	20	2	4	32	33	59	26	9	.331	.373
Mouton,Lyle, ChA	28	.275	143	517	64	142	29	2	14	72	45	123	9	5	.333	.420
Mueller,Bill, SF	26	.288	139	524	76	151	24	4	3	50	57	61	4	4	.358	.366
Munoz,Pedro, Oak	28	.279	84	283	35	79	12	1	12	38	18	69	1	1	.322	.456
Murray,Eddie, Bal	41	.258	117	445	54	115	20	1	15	67	39	68	4	2	.318	.409
Myers,Greg, Min	31	.243	106	334	33	81	16	1	7	38	20	62	1	1	.285	.359
Naehring,Tim, Bos	30	.280	134	479	70	134	25	1	12	61	65	76	2	2	.366	.411
Nevin,Phil, Det	26	.266	138	443	67	118	20	1	18	70	52	101	3	2	.343	.438
Newfield,Marc, Mil	24	.287	139	516	74	148	36	1	19	81	39	80	1	1	.337	.471
Newson,Warren, Tex	32	.254	105	205	33	52	7	1	6	21	37	61	2	1	.368	.385
Nieves,Melvin, Det	25	.262	144	484	81	127	21	4	26	79	55	175	2	2	.338	.483
Nilsson,Dave, Mil	27	.295	142	529	79	156	33	3	18	91	55	77	2	2	.361	.471
Nixon,Otis, Tor	38	.257	135	544	72	140	11	1	1	30	65	85	47	16	.337	.287
Nunnally,Jon, KC	25	.256	119	371	68	95	20	5	19	61	55	98	8	7	.352	.491
O'Brien,Charlie, Tor	36	.210	97	276	26	58	15	0	7	30	30	58	0	0	.288	.341
O'Leary,Troy, Bos	27	.288	132	486	72	140	33	5	13	70	48	82	6	3	.352	.457
O'Neill,Paul, NYA	34	.285	142	516	83	147	29	1	20	89	89	80	2	3	.390	.461
Obando,Sherman, Mon	27	.278	90	263	32	73	17	2	8	33	21	46	1	0	.331	.449
Ochoa,Alex, NYN	25	.283	139	515	68	146	25	3	10	65	41	63	17	12	.336	.402
Offerman,Jose, KC	28	.271	148	550	77	149	20	6	4	49	82	94	13	9	.366	.351

Projections for 1997 Batters

Batter	Age	Avg	G	AB	R	H	2B	3B	HR	RBI	BB	SO	SB	CS	OBP	SLG
Olerud,John, Tor	28	.298	141	493	71	147	33	1	18	75	80	57	1	1	.396	.479
Oliver,Joe, Cin	31	.239	94	276	30	66	15	0	8	39	24	53	2	2	.300	.380
Ordonez,Rey, NYN	24	.236	153	517	54	122	18	4	2	45	23	52	7	8	.269	.298
Orsulak,Joe, Fla	35	.250	85	196	25	49	10	1	2	23	12	24	1	1	.293	.342
Ortiz,Luis, Tex	27	.291	54	179	22	52	9	1	4	23	10	17	1	1	.328	.419
Osik,Keith, Pit	28	.259	53	139	14	36	8	0	2	17	11	20	0	0	.313	.360
Otero,Ricky, Phi	25	.261	102	371	52	97	16	5	2	30	31	36	17	11	.318	.348
Owens,Eric, Cin	26	.258	61	128	19	33	5	1	2	11	12	19	8	3	.321	.359
Owens,Jayhawk, Col	28	.280	128	353	58	99	21	3	13	53	37	91	4	3	.349	.467
Pagnozzi,Tom, StL	34	.239	105	343	32	82	16	1	6	38	23	59	1	1	.287	.344
Palmeiro,Orlando, Cal	28	.294	73	119	17	35	5	1	0	12	13	11	3	2	.364	.353
Palmeiro,Rafael, Bal	32	.284	156	606	94	172	35	2	29	104	79	83	7	2	.366	.492
Palmer,Dean, Tex	28	.264	152	561	94	148	26	2	34	96	59	138	3	2	.334	.499
Paquette,Craig, KC	28	.238	129	420	55	100	21	2	17	61	21	106	5	3	.274	.419
Parent,Mark, Bal	35	.220	54	123	12	27	6	0	5	15	11	33	0	0	.284	.390
Pemberton,Rudy, Bos	27	.316	140	522	74	165	32	3	19	82	24	80	21	11	.346	.498
Pena,Tony, Cle	40	.238	53	130	12	31	5	0	2	13	9	20	0	0	.288	.323
Pendleton,Terry, Atl	36	.245	111	417	40	102	21	2	8	49	26	82	2	2	.289	.362
Perez,Eddie, Atl	29	.241	76	224	20	54	11	0	4	25	9	30	0	0	.270	.344
Perez,Neifi, Col	22	.305	144	528	67	161	36	9	11	59	20	48	10	8	.330	.470
Perez,Robert, Tor	28	.282	88	294	32	83	16	2	5	31	10	40	3	2	.306	.401
Perez,Tomas, Tor	23	.256	129	391	39	100	19	4	3	35	30	47	5	3	.309	.348
Perry,Herbert, Cle	27	.298	73	191	27	57	11	0	4	27	16	25	2	2	.353	.419
Petagine,Roberto, NYN	26	.275	118	182	26	50	11	0	6	29	26	48	1	1	.365	.434
Phillips,J.R., Phi	27	.226	81	230	29	52	15	1	10	33	20	73	2	2	.288	.430
Phillips,Tony, ChA	38	.264	143	541	104	143	21	2	12	51	120	138	13	8	.398	.377
Piazza,Mike, LA	28	.323	149	558	91	180	24	1	34	112	65	98	1	2	.393	.552
Plantier,Phil, Oak	28	.247	99	299	44	74	14	1	13	47	37	72	2	1	.330	.431
Polonia,Luis, Atl	32	.281	76	228	35	64	10	2	1	17	21	26	12	6	.341	.355
Pozo,Arquimedez, Bos	23	.286	96	248	33	71	13	2	7	34	17	23	3	2	.332	.440
Pride,Curtis, Det	28	.265	122	393	70	104	17	4	12	44	47	102	21	10	.343	.420
Raabe,Brian, Min	29	.291	83	199	31	58	11	1	3	21	18	7	4	2	.350	.402
Raines,Tim, NYA	37	.268	118	425	74	114	20	4	8	53	64	53	12	2	.364	.391
Ramirez,Manny, Cle	25	.307	155	550	98	169	39	1	36	116	86	115	8	6	.401	.578
Randa,Joe, KC	27	.264	129	405	46	107	22	2	7	46	29	49	6	4	.313	.380
Reboulet,Jeff, Min	33	.246	94	207	27	51	10	0	2	20	23	30	2	1	.322	.324
Reed,Jeff, Col	34	.260	108	331	31	86	13	1	4	28	47	62	1	1	.352	.341
Reed,Jody, SD	34	.256	129	449	54	115	26	1	3	45	59	42	4	4	.343	.339
Relaford,Desi, Phi	23	.220	72	218	23	48	8	1	3	16	17	41	9	4	.277	.307
Renteria,Edgar, Fla	21	.286	151	587	78	168	21	4	8	58	35	90	24	9	.326	.376
Ripken,Billy, Bal	32	.250	43	112	11	28	5	0	1	10	6	12	1	1	.288	.321
Ripken,Cal, Bal	36	.259	162	629	83	163	32	2	22	100	57	75	1	1	.321	.421
Rivera,Ruben, NYA	23	.253	121	304	52	77	17	3	11	43	35	87	13	9	.330	.438
Roberts,Bip, KC	33	.284	114	430	51	122	19	2	3	44	37	55	21	7	.340	.358
Rodriguez,Alex, Sea	21	.318	151	556	100	177	38	3	30	99	46	122	12	6	.370	.559
Rodriguez,Henry, Mon	29	.258	154	561	71	145	29	2	26	89	38	134	1	1	.306	.456
Rodriguez,Ivan, Tex	25	.301	154	602	89	181	34	2	19	86	35	59	4	3	.339	.458
Rolen,Scott, Phi	22	.285	143	540	70	154	36	1	17	74	57	89	8	8	.353	.450
Sabo,Chris, Cin	35	.244	47	123	16	30	10	0	3	17	9	22	1	0	.295	.398
Salmon,Tim, Cal	28	.300	159	594	113	178	34	2	37	112	102	139	5	4	.402	.551

Projections for 1997 Batters

Batter	Age	Avg	G	AB	R	H	2B	3B	HR	RBI	BB	SO	SB	CS	OBP	SLG
Samuel,Juan, Tor	36	.230	84	183	29	42	13	3	5	27	19	52	5	3	.302	.415
Sanchez,Rey, ChN	29	.255	101	337	37	86	14	2	2	24	18	38	5	3	.293	.326
Sandberg,Ryne, ChN	37	.253	154	538	77	136	25	3	18	81	54	118	10	8	.321	.411
Sanders,Reggie, Cin	29	.267	148	546	90	146	30	5	25	83	72	151	36	15	.353	.478
Santangelo,F.P., Mon	29	.246	132	341	41	84	19	1	3	33	42	47	5	4	.329	.334
Santiago,Benito, Phi	32	.251	124	415	50	104	19	2	14	56	37	80	2	1	.312	.407
Scarsone,Steve, SF	31	.251	89	219	28	55	12	1	6	23	20	59	2	2	.314	.397
Schall,Gene, Phi	27	.262	131	381	43	100	22	2	12	55	43	85	2	2	.337	.425
Sefcik,Kevin, Phi	26	.264	64	212	25	56	9	2	1	18	13	22	6	4	.307	.340
Segui,David, Mon	30	.270	135	467	67	126	22	1	11	59	54	56	3	4	.345	.392
Seitzer,Kevin, Cle	35	.287	139	523	65	150	27	2	7	65	70	69	3	1	.371	.386
Selby,Bill, Bos	27	.274	93	248	33	68	15	1	6	34	22	30	1	2	.333	.415
Servais,Scott, ChN	30	.238	128	408	44	97	22	0	12	56	33	73	1	1	.295	.380
Sheaffer,Danny, StL	35	.228	67	149	13	34	7	1	2	18	13	20	1	1	.290	.329
Sheets,Andy, Sea	25	.282	64	195	29	55	14	2	2	21	17	44	3	2	.340	.405
Sheffield,Gary, Fla	28	.284	154	560	109	159	30	2	33	108	130	86	25	12	.419	.521
Sierra,Ruben, Det	31	.260	120	446	60	116	25	3	16	78	40	68	6	4	.321	.437
Silvestri,Dave, Mon	29	.216	73	167	23	36	10	1	4	22	29	56	4	3	.332	.359
Slaught,Don, ChA	38	.274	89	263	26	72	14	1	4	32	29	32	0	0	.346	.380
Smith,Dwight, Atl	33	.250	101	140	17	35	7	1	3	19	12	33	2	2	.309	.379
Smith,Mark, Bal	27	.246	107	260	35	64	15	1	8	37	19	56	4	2	.297	.404
Snopek,Chris, ChA	26	.287	113	324	49	93	18	2	8	43	41	49	3	3	.367	.429
Snow,J.T., Cal	29	.262	142	523	68	137	21	1	19	79	54	91	2	3	.331	.415
Sojo,Luis, NYA	31	.253	82	249	29	63	11	1	3	24	13	19	3	1	.290	.341
Sorrento,Paul, Sea	31	.259	135	429	59	111	22	0	20	81	57	91	1	1	.346	.450
Sosa,Sammy, ChN	28	.272	143	570	85	155	21	4	33	101	47	134	30	11	.327	.496
Sprague,Ed, Tor	29	.238	161	584	76	139	30	1	21	79	56	132	0	0	.305	.401
Stahoviak,Scott, Min	27	.285	132	404	66	115	31	2	11	59	56	92	6	4	.372	.453
Stairs,Matt, Oak	29	.277	82	238	32	66	16	1	7	40	27	35	3	3	.351	.441
Stanley,Mike, Bos	34	.262	124	412	65	108	17	1	17	69	64	88	1	1	.361	.432
Steinbach,Terry, Oak	35	.253	137	487	55	123	22	1	16	70	38	95	2	2	.307	.400
Stewart,Shannon, Tor	23	.272	132	441	68	120	22	4	5	43	55	60	28	11	.353	.374
Stocker,Kevin, Phi	27	.250	135	444	51	111	20	3	4	43	54	79	5	3	.331	.336
Strange,Doug, Sea	33	.231	73	156	17	36	10	0	2	18	11	27	1	1	.281	.333
Strawberry,Darryl, NYA	35	.240	79	233	38	56	12	1	10	41	39	61	3	3	.349	.429
Stynes,Chris, KC	24	.287	83	244	33	70	13	2	4	28	12	15	6	4	.320	.406
Surhoff,B.J., Bal	32	.262	116	409	54	107	20	2	9	53	38	51	3	2	.324	.386
Sveum,Dale, Pit	33	.236	84	203	26	48	11	1	6	27	19	50	0	0	.302	.389
Sweeney,Mark, StL	27	.280	100	257	40	72	13	1	5	41	40	38	3	2	.377	.397
Sweeney,Mike, KC	23	.274	138	482	69	132	34	0	16	73	44	56	3	3	.335	.444
Tarasco,Tony, Bal	26	.273	87	205	31	56	8	1	7	24	22	34	10	3	.344	.424
Tartabull,Danny, ChA	34	.250	125	444	61	111	25	1	19	79	69	127	1	1	.351	.439
Taubensee,Eddie, Cin	28	.275	117	335	47	92	19	2	11	48	30	66	3	2	.334	.442
Tavarez,Jesus, Fla	26	.258	76	194	26	50	5	2	1	14	13	29	8	5	.304	.320
Tettleton,Mickey, Tex	36	.223	141	461	70	103	19	1	21	67	111	140	1	1	.374	.406
Thomas,Frank, ChA	29	.325	152	535	120	174	34	1	41	123	141	77	2	2	.466	.622
Thome,Jim, Cle	26	.298	155	557	115	166	30	3	34	99	115	146	4	4	.418	.546
Thompson,Robby, SF	35	.224	65	210	30	47	11	1	4	16	25	56	2	1	.306	.343
Timmons,Ozzie, ChN	26	.252	95	266	39	67	14	1	14	40	25	51	1	1	.316	.470
Tinsley,Lee, Bos	28	.254	98	248	42	63	12	3	4	29	27	64	11	6	.327	.375

Projections for 1997 Batters

Batter	Age	Avg	G	AB	R	H	2B	3B	HR	RBI	BB	SO	SB	CS	OBP	SLG
Tucker,Michael, KC	26	.271	137	462	63	125	20	5	14	60	51	91	10	6	.343	.426
Valentin,John, Bos	30	.288	144	552	95	159	36	2	19	80	78	69	12	7	.376	.464
Valentin,Jose, Mil	27	.243	148	543	85	132	28	4	17	77	67	138	20	8	.326	.403
Valle,Dave, Tex	36	.204	46	93	9	19	3	0	2	9	11	21	0	0	.288	.301
Vander Wal,John, Col	31	.248	94	117	14	29	6	1	4	18	16	29	1	1	.338	.419
Vaughn,Greg, SD	31	.234	140	513	83	120	24	1	26	88	74	131	11	5	.330	.437
Vaughn,Mo, Bos	29	.286	161	615	103	176	31	1	37	121	88	163	6	3	.376	.520
Velarde,Randy, Cal	34	.259	127	452	67	117	20	1	11	47	57	96	6	4	.342	.381
Ventura,Robin, ChA	29	.269	158	579	87	156	27	1	26	96	86	96	3	3	.364	.454
Veras,Quilvio, Fla	26	.265	112	392	68	104	16	4	4	32	64	53	35	16	.368	.357
Vina,Fernando, Mil	28	.261	142	556	89	145	17	8	6	48	44	39	14	7	.315	.353
Vitiello,Joe, KC	27	.275	93	291	35	80	17	1	10	45	31	58	1	1	.345	.443
Vizcaino,Jose, Cle	29	.275	151	574	69	158	19	5	3	51	42	86	10	8	.325	.341
Vizquel,Omar, Cle	30	.263	154	590	88	155	21	2	5	59	62	52	31	11	.333	.331
Walbeck,Matt, Min	27	.240	89	292	31	70	14	0	3	33	17	43	2	1	.282	.318
Walker,Larry, Col	30	.288	135	480	87	138	31	3	26	91	55	88	19	5	.361	.527
Walker,Todd, Min	24	.302	159	589	90	178	39	4	26	97	56	106	16	9	.363	.514
Wallach,Tim, LA	39	.226	93	314	33	71	16	1	8	38	29	71	0	0	.292	.360
Walton,Jerome, Atl	31	.265	72	113	17	30	5	0	2	11	11	20	5	4	.331	.363
Webster,Lenny, Mon	32	.253	74	174	19	44	11	0	3	18	19	23	0	0	.326	.368
Wehner,John, Pit	30	.268	83	213	29	57	12	1	3	22	17	28	7	4	.322	.376
Weiss,Walt, Col	33	.269	150	516	75	139	17	2	3	38	89	73	12	5	.377	.328
White,Devon, Fla	34	.256	144	543	74	139	27	4	13	63	34	111	19	6	.300	.392
White,Rondell, Mon	25	.294	158	581	90	171	34	6	16	76	48	93	25	9	.348	.456
Whiten,Mark, Sea	30	.249	135	453	72	113	18	3	17	65	64	117	15	7	.342	.415
Widger,Chris, Sea	26	.274	72	215	28	59	10	1	8	28	16	39	3	2	.325	.442
Wilkins,Rick, SF	30	.231	127	389	52	90	18	1	12	49	65	113	2	2	.341	.375
Williams,Bernie, NYA	28	.288	153	590	105	170	34	5	20	86	87	88	15	7	.380	.464
Williams,Eddie, Det	32	.273	57	165	22	45	7	0	7	28	14	26	0	0	.330	.442
Williams,George, Oak	28	.262	77	221	34	58	14	0	7	33	35	44	1	1	.363	.421
Williams,Gerald, Mil	30	.259	126	382	59	99	23	4	10	51	28	70	10	8	.310	.419
Williams,Matt, SF	31	.263	125	483	74	127	20	2	30	92	42	100	1	1	.322	.499
Wilson,Dan, Sea	28	.259	143	478	45	124	24	2	10	59	32	84	2	2	.306	.381
Wilson,Desi, SF	28	.276	59	199	25	55	10	1	2	23	12	39	5	4	.318	.367
Young,Dmitri, StL	23	.276	137	428	57	118	27	3	9	52	27	58	5	4	.319	.416
Young,Eric, Col	30	.301	145	582	103	175	24	7	9	66	69	39	53	20	.375	.412
Young,Ernie, Oak	27	.261	118	380	62	99	18	2	15	59	46	83	4	5	.340	.437
Young,Kevin, KC	28	.245	84	241	26	59	15	2	6	32	15	56	4	3	.289	.398
Zaun,Greg, Fla	26	.242	82	223	33	54	10	1	4	23	27	35	1	1	.324	.350
Zeile,Todd, Bal	31	.254	150	563	72	143	29	1	19	81	62	90	1	1	.328	.410
Zuber,Jon, Phi	27	.271	54	107	12	29	5	1	1	12	11	15	0	1	.339	.364

Projections for 1997 Pitchers

Pitcher	Age	ERA	W	L	Sv	G	GS	IP	H	HR	BB	SO	BR/9
Abbott,Jim, Cal	29	5.33	8	11	0	29	27	169	182	20	93	72	14.6
Aguilera,Rick, Min	35	4.65	1	2	27	56	0	60	65	10	15	49	12.0
Alvarez,Wilson, ChA	27	4.09	13	12	0	34	34	211	194	21	94	160	12.3
Appier,Kevin, KC	29	3.08	15	10	0	33	33	216	182	14	77	205	10.8
Ashby,Andy, SD	29	3.85	10	10	0	28	28	173	177	19	39	119	11.2
Assenmacher,Paul, Cle	36	2.80	5	2	0	60	0	45	41	2	14	43	11.0
Astacio,Pedro, LA	27	3.69	13	12	0	34	32	210	198	21	66	141	11.3
Avery,Steve, Atl	27	3.61	10	8	0	27	26	152	144	14	47	114	11.3
Ayala,Bobby, Sea	27	4.00	5	3	5	57	0	72	68	9	28	80	12.0
Bautista,Jose, SF	32	4.29	3	4	0	44	3	84	88	13	20	43	11.6
Beck,Rod, SF	28	3.57	2	4	36	65	0	63	57	9	16	46	10.4
Belcher,Tim, KC	35	4.62	11	15	0	34	34	226	254	27	64	114	12.7
Belinda,Stan, Bos	30	3.60	3	2	0	44	0	45	41	4	21	35	12.4
Benes,Andy, StL	29	3.77	12	13	0	36	34	222	208	23	74	180	11.4
Bere,Jason, ChA	26	6.29	3	6	0	13	13	63	56	7	68	52	17.7
Bielecki,Mike, Atl	37	4.38	3	4	2	35	7	78	75	12	33	59	12.5
Blair,Willie, SD	31	4.99	4	6	4	55	5	101	117	12	41	81	14.1
Boever,Joe, Pit	36	5.17	2	3	8	31	0	47	53	8	21	31	14.2
Bohanon,Brian, Tor	28	5.17	2	3	0	33	4	54	66	6	23	35	14.8
Bones,Ricky, NYA	28	5.17	7	9	0	36	18	148	162	20	66	59	13.9
Borland,Toby, Phi	28	4.19	4	5	0	65	0	88	91	5	44	71	13.8
Bosio,Chris, Sea	34	4.33	4	3	0	24	18	104	112	11	40	56	13.2
Boskie,Shawn, Cal	30	5.20	9	11	0	32	26	168	187	28	59	101	13.2
Brantley,Jeff, Cin	33	3.53	2	4	46	65	0	74	62	10	27	71	10.8
Brown,Kevin, Fla	32	3.07	15	10	0	31	31	220	220	14	31	150	10.3
Bullinger,Jim, ChN	31	4.69	7	10	0	34	22	142	145	12	75	93	13.9
Burba,Dave, Cin	30	4.10	11	12	0	33	33	189	169	18	94	154	12.5
Burkett,John, Tex	32	3.99	14	11	0	34	34	219	230	21	57	150	11.8
Candiotti,Tom, LA	39	4.11	10	11	0	30	29	173	180	18	49	112	11.9
Carrasco,Hector, Cin	27	3.29	5	4	0	61	0	82	69	4	46	62	12.6
Castillo,Frank, ChN	28	4.27	11	13	0	33	33	192	203	25	48	142	11.8
Castillo,Tony, ChA	34	3.76	5	4	2	57	0	91	88	9	29	53	11.6
Charlton,Norm, Sea	34	2.92	3	3	27	67	0	77	58	6	36	76	11.0
Clark,Mark, NYN	29	4.12	10	12	0	30	29	188	201	21	43	117	11.7
Clemens,Roger, Bos	34	3.83	15	10	0	31	31	214	190	20	94	217	11.9
Cone,David, NYA	34	3.49	16	10	0	32	32	227	181	20	107	197	11.4
Cook,Dennis, Tex	34	4.04	4	3	0	57	0	69	64	8	31	62	12.4
Cormier,Rheal, Mon	30	4.26	8	9	0	40	23	150	161	17	38	92	11.9
Corsi,Jim, Oak	35	3.41	4	3	0	52	0	66	56	4	33	38	12.1
Daal,Omar, Mon	25	4.23	3	4	0	53	4	66	64	7	31	54	13.0
Darwin,Danny, Hou	41	4.47	7	10	0	30	22	147	163	24	24	86	11.4
DeLucia,Rich, SF	32	4.38	4	5	0	58	0	72	68	11	33	69	12.6
Dewey,Mark, SF	32	3.63	4	4	0	62	0	67	64	5	29	46	12.5
DiPoto,Jerry, NYN	29	4.22	4	5	0	60	0	81	88	3	39	54	14.1
Drabek,Doug, Hou	34	4.11	11	12	0	32	32	186	190	17	64	145	12.3
Dyer,Mike, Mon	30	4.50	4	5	0	67	1	78	83	8	36	57	13.7
Eckersley,Dennis, StL	42	3.81	2	4	25	62	0	59	63	7	9	47	11.0
Eichhorn,Mark, Cal	36	3.00	2	1	0	24	0	30	29	1	8	17	11.1
Eldred,Cal, Mil	29	4.15	12	12	0	32	32	208	189	24	93	131	12.2
Erickson,Scott, Bal	29	4.66	12	14	0	35	34	222	259	21	66	110	13.2

365

Projections for 1997 Pitchers

Pitcher	Age	ERA	W	L	Sv	G	GS	IP	H	HR	BB	SO	BR/9
Fassero,Jeff, Mon	34	3.24	16	11	0	34	34	225	212	17	53	206	10.6
Fernandez,Alex, ChA	27	3.85	16	12	0	35	35	248	236	31	69	193	11.1
Fernandez,Sid, Phi	34	4.44	4	6	0	14	14	77	66	15	32	92	11.5
Fetters,Mike, Mil	32	4.17	2	3	36	56	0	54	56	3	29	44	14.2
Finley,Chuck, Cal	34	4.17	14	13	0	35	35	235	231	23	93	218	12.4
Fossas,Tony, StL	39	3.20	4	3	0	65	0	45	38	4	16	41	10.8
Franco,John, NYN	36	3.33	2	3	34	51	0	54	51	3	19	46	11.7
Freeman,Marvin, ChA	34	5.29	3	4	0	10	10	51	59	7	22	30	14.3
Frey,Steve, Phi	33	4.64	2	2	0	32	0	33	35	4	15	16	13.6
Gardner,Mark, SF	35	4.89	8	13	0	30	28	171	190	26	54	141	12.8
Glavine,Tom, Atl	31	3.66	15	12	0	35	35	231	224	13	84	163	12.0
Gooden,Dwight, NYA	32	4.53	10	11	0	29	29	171	163	18	88	126	13.2
Gordon,Tom, Bos	29	4.40	14	11	0	34	34	215	210	20	105	153	13.2
Groom,Buddy, Oak	31	5.38	3	5	0	62	2	72	87	9	35	52	15.3
Gross,Kevin, Tex	36	4.70	9	9	0	30	24	155	166	18	60	91	13.1
Guardado,Eddie, Min	26	5.10	4	5	8	74	2	83	93	12	38	70	14.2
Gubicza,Mark, KC	34	4.41	10	13	0	31	31	194	217	19	55	79	12.6
Guthrie,Mark, LA	31	4.13	4	5	0	67	0	72	75	7	26	59	12.6
Guzman,Juan, Tor	30	3.84	11	10	0	27	27	176	174	18	50	140	11.5
Habyan,John, Mon	33	3.98	3	2	0	35	0	43	45	3	18	39	13.2
Hamilton,Joey, SD	26	3.88	12	13	0	34	33	218	206	18	85	159	12.0
Hammond,Chris, Fla	31	4.18	4	5	0	35	15	114	124	12	36	79	12.6
Haney,Chris, KC	28	4.33	10	11	0	29	28	183	206	20	41	86	12.1
Hanson,Erik, Tor	32	4.77	11	15	0	34	34	213	225	20	101	157	13.8
Harnisch,Pete, NYN	30	3.95	9	11	0	27	27	171	160	23	54	111	11.3
Henneman,Mike, Tex	35	3.83	2	3	29	52	0	47	47	4	17	39	12.3
Henry,Doug, NYN	33	4.44	3	5	0	58	0	75	75	10	35	60	13.2
Hentgen,Pat, Tor	28	4.11	14	14	0	35	35	252	248	28	89	169	12.0
Heredia,Gil, Tex	31	3.93	5	4	2	44	7	94	107	8	16	66	11.8
Hernandez,Roberto, ChA	32	3.30	3	4	36	71	0	79	69	6	33	90	11.6
Hernandez,Xavier, Hou	31	3.98	5	5	3	63	0	86	83	10	34	82	12.2
Hershiser,Orel, Cle	38	4.14	14	10	0	32	32	200	207	23	56	127	11.8
Hill,Ken, Tex	31	3.93	15	12	0	35	34	236	233	17	90	144	12.3
Hitchcock,Sterling, Sea	26	4.69	12	11	0	33	33	194	207	24	72	135	12.9
Hoffman,Trevor, SD	29	2.96	3	4	39	67	0	79	61	9	27	90	10.0
Holmes,Darren, Col	31	4.14	5	4	0	67	0	76	75	7	36	74	13.1
Honeycutt,Rick, StL	43	2.94	4	3	5	60	0	49	42	5	9	27	9.4
Jackson,Danny, StL	35	4.06	2	2	0	16	10	62	65	5	21	41	12.5
Jackson,Mike, Sea	32	2.73	6	2	0	64	0	66	49	7	20	65	9.4
Johnson,Randy, Sea	33	3.03	18	7	0	32	32	223	170	18	91	307	10.5
Jones,Bobby, NYN	27	3.88	11	13	0	32	32	204	213	20	48	127	11.5
Jones,Doug, Mil	40	4.65	3	4	0	54	0	60	69	7	20	55	13.4
Jones,Todd, Hou	29	3.20	5	3	7	60	0	76	63	5	35	67	11.6
Kamieniecki,Scott, NYA	33	5.88	2	4	0	11	9	49	49	5	41	25	16.5
Key,Jimmy, NYA	36	4.43	11	11	0	32	32	185	198	18	63	120	12.7
Kile,Darryl, Hou	28	4.22	11	12	0	33	30	194	193	15	86	185	12.9
Langston,Mark, Cal	36	4.50	11	11	0	29	29	188	192	25	69	131	12.5
Leiper,Dave, Mon	35	3.82	2	2	0	41	0	33	33	3	13	17	12.5
Leiter,Al, Fla	31	4.08	12	13	0	33	33	212	190	15	117	187	13.0
Leiter,Mark, Mon	34	4.41	11	14	0	35	34	210	212	29	71	153	12.1

Projections for 1997 Pitchers

Pitcher	Age	ERA	W	L	Sv	G	GS	IP	H	HR	BB	SO	BR/9
Leskanic,Curt, Col	29	4.08	6	4	0	75	0	86	85	9	35	89	12.6
Lewis,Richie, Det	31	4.86	4	4	0	56	0	74	72	10	48	62	14.6
Lloyd,Graeme, NYA	30	3.96	4	3	0	56	0	50	51	5	16	28	12.1
MacDonald,Bob, NYN	32	4.50	1	2	0	26	0	30	31	4	14	25	13.5
Maddux,Greg, Atl	31	1.90	22	5	0	34	34	242	197	10	28	189	8.4
Maddux,Mike, Bos	35	4.16	4	3	0	32	6	80	85	9	22	52	12.0
Magnante,Mike, KC	32	4.75	2	3	0	36	0	53	60	6	21	29	13.8
Martinez,Dennis, Cle	42	3.91	10	7	0	24	24	145	143	14	48	71	11.9
Martinez,Pedro, Mon	25	3.07	16	10	0	33	33	217	179	19	70	209	10.3
Martinez,Ramon, LA	29	4.14	12	14	0	33	33	215	198	18	110	155	12.9
Mathews,Terry, Bal	32	4.05	5	4	0	69	0	80	82	9	27	60	12.3
McDonald,Ben, Mil	29	3.73	14	11	0	33	33	210	200	21	64	146	11.3
McDowell,Jack, Cle	31	4.24	14	10	0	31	31	210	217	20	73	153	12.4
McDowell,Roger, Bal	36	4.44	4	4	0	51	0	71	79	5	31	38	13.9
McElroy,Chuck, Cal	29	3.75	4	3	0	51	0	48	47	4	17	35	12.0
McMichael,Greg, Atl	30	3.07	6	4	2	74	0	88	81	5	29	79	11.3
Meacham,Rusty, Sea	29	4.94	2	2	5	28	3	51	60	7	15	31	13.2
Mercker,Kent, Cle	29	3.78	4	3	0	27	18	100	89	11	44	78	12.0
Mesa,Jose, Cle	31	3.75	3	3	41	69	0	72	73	6	24	65	12.1
Miceli,Dan, Pit	26	4.90	3	5	0	51	6	79	84	12	36	71	13.7
Mills,Alan, Bal	30	4.60	3	3	5	41	0	45	39	8	28	39	13.4
Minor,Blas, Sea	31	4.15	3	2	0	32	0	52	53	7	17	42	12.1
Montgomery,Jeff, KC	35	3.90	2	4	31	52	0	67	63	10	22	54	11.4
Morgan,Mike, Cin	37	4.43	7	9	0	23	23	136	144	14	49	70	12.8
Moyer,Jamie, Sea	34	4.26	10	7	0	29	21	150	156	19	43	78	11.9
Mulholland,Terry, Sea	34	4.66	12	11	0	33	31	191	216	26	46	82	12.3
Munoz,Mike, Col	31	4.89	3	3	0	60	0	46	49	5	25	39	14.5
Mussina,Mike, Bal	28	3.71	16	12	0	36	36	245	232	27	70	190	11.1
Myers,Randy, Bal	34	3.90	2	3	24	63	0	60	56	6	28	63	12.6
Nagy,Charles, Cle	30	4.02	15	10	0	32	32	215	223	22	59	164	11.8
Navarro,Jaime, ChN	29	4.29	12	15	0	34	34	233	251	23	71	152	12.4
Neagle,Denny, Atl	28	3.94	13	13	0	34	34	226	235	26	49	157	11.3
Nelson,Jeff, NYA	30	3.19	6	3	0	72	0	79	68	6	33	92	11.5
Nen,Robb, Fla	27	3.26	3	4	35	73	0	80	73	6	25	84	11.0
Olivares,Omar, Det	29	5.18	10	13	0	33	30	193	217	21	90	99	14.3
Olson,Gregg, Hou	30	4.79	2	3	2	43	0	47	46	4	32	32	14.9
Orosco,Jesse, Bal	40	2.73	5	2	0	68	0	56	37	5	29	58	10.6
Osborne,Donovan, StL	28	3.96	9	11	0	27	27	175	171	21	50	121	11.4
Parrett,Jeff, Phi	35	3.58	4	4	0	56	0	73	69	5	30	69	12.2
Patterson,Bob, ChN	38	3.38	5	4	8	76	0	56	49	6	18	49	10.8
Pavlik,Roger, Tex	29	4.54	12	12	0	34	34	206	208	25	83	146	12.7
Perez,Yorkis, Fla	29	3.86	4	4	0	69	0	49	43	4	26	48	12.7
Pichardo,Hipolito, KC	27	4.30	4	4	5	55	0	69	77	5	27	42	13.6
Plesac,Dan, Pit	35	3.73	4	4	8	70	0	70	68	6	22	69	11.6
Plunk,Eric, Cle	33	3.08	6	2	5	58	0	76	62	5	34	80	11.4
Poole,Jim, SF	31	3.63	4	3	0	60	0	52	46	5	22	43	11.8
Portugal,Mark, Cin	34	3.61	11	10	0	30	29	172	167	16	46	96	11.1
Quantrill,Paul, Tor	28	5.39	7	12	0	38	24	157	186	21	60	94	14.1
Radinsky,Scott, LA	29	4.41	3	4	0	56	0	49	54	4	19	33	13.4
Rapp,Pat, Fla	29	5.00	8	13	0	31	30	171	183	13	96	98	14.7

Projections for 1997 Pitchers

Pitcher	Age	ERA	W	L	Sv	G	GS	IP	H	HR	BB	SO	BR/9
Reed,Steve, Col	31	3.73	6	4	0	73	0	82	76	10	25	66	11.1
Reynolds,Shane, Hou	29	3.44	15	12	0	35	35	230	236	18	42	204	10.9
Reynoso,Armando, Col	31	4.84	9	9	0	28	27	147	168	19	43	72	12.9
Ritz,Kevin, Col	32	4.96	12	13	0	35	34	207	222	20	102	122	14.1
Rogers,Kenny, NYA	32	4.39	12	12	0	32	32	197	190	21	92	119	12.9
Rojas,Mel, Mon	30	3.19	3	4	34	71	0	79	70	6	27	80	11.1
Ruffin,Bruce, Col	33	3.97	2	3	26	61	0	59	56	5	29	58	13.0
Ruffin,Johnny, Cin	25	4.02	3	3	0	36	0	47	44	5	22	39	12.6
Russell,Jeff, Tex	35	4.50	3	3	4	51	0	50	55	5	17	29	13.0
Ryan,Ken, Phi	28	3.63	4	4	11	52	0	72	65	4	36	57	12.6
Schilling,Curt, Phi	30	3.49	12	12	0	31	31	214	197	23	58	211	10.7
Schourek,Pete, Cin	28	4.60	7	9	0	22	22	133	144	15	47	111	12.9
Scott,Tim, SF	30	3.57	4	4	0	67	0	68	64	5	26	51	11.9
Sele,Aaron, Bos	27	4.32	12	9	0	30	30	171	176	13	73	142	13.1
Shaw,Jeff, Cin	30	3.71	6	5	6	74	0	97	95	10	28	67	11.4
Slocumb,Heathcliff, Bos	31	3.60	3	3	30	73	0	80	77	2	40	74	13.2
Smiley,John, Cin	32	3.88	13	12	0	34	33	211	216	22	52	158	11.4
Smith,Lee, Cin	39	3.76	4	3	0	56	0	55	52	3	27	44	12.9
Smoltz,John, Atl	30	2.76	18	9	0	34	34	241	202	21	52	253	9.5
Stanton,Mike, Tex	30	4.10	5	4	4	72	0	68	69	7	28	47	12.8
Stevens,Dave, Min	27	5.29	3	4	0	54	0	63	68	11	29	38	13.9
Stottlemyre,Todd, StL	32	4.30	12	16	0	34	34	228	224	25	95	211	12.6
Swift,Bill, Col	35	4.33	2	2	0	12	9	52	57	5	16	30	12.6
Swindell,Greg, Cle	32	4.60	4	3	.0	26	14	92	106	13	22	53	12.5
Tapani,Kevin, ChA	33	4.78	12	14	0	35	34	222	247	27	75	150	13.1
Tewksbury,Bob, SD	36	4.40	10	12	0	32	30	186	220	17	39	98	12.5
Timlin,Mike, Tor	31	3.83	2	3	31	51	0	54	52	5	22	49	12.3
Trachsel,Steve, ChN	26	4.07	11	12	0	32	32	197	188	28	60	135	11.3
Trombley,Mike, Min	30	4.72	3	4	3	36	7	82	88	11	34	59	13.4
Valdes,Ismael, LA	23	3.17	15	11	0	34	32	224	204	19	54	171	10.4
Valenzuela,Fernando, SD	36	4.56	8	11	0	33	26	148	153	18	58	86	12.8
Van Poppel,Todd, Det	25	5.03	4	5	0	38	15	118	118	18	69	84	14.3
Veres,Dave, Mon	30	3.36	6	4	2	72	0	91	85	7	28	80	11.2
Vosberg,Ed, Tex	35	4.40	3	3	6	51	0	43	45	4	19	38	13.4
Wagner,Paul, Pit	29	4.89	5	9	0	23	19	116	125	11	56	94	14.0
Wakefield,Tim, Bos	30	4.71	13	12	0	31	31	214	217	29	91	136	13.0
Watson,Allen, SF	26	4.90	8	12	0	27	26	167	180	24	62	97	13.0
Wells,David, Bal	34	3.86	15	11	0	33	33	226	224	29	51	139	11.0
West,David, Phi	32	3.00	5	4	0	16	14	66	52	5	26	46	10.6
Wetteland,John, NYA	30	2.35	3	2	45	64	0	65	48	5	18	68	9.1
Whiteside,Matt, Tex	29	4.61	2	2	0	24	0	41	45	5	16	27	13.4
Wickman,Bob, Mil	28	4.02	5	5	0	70	0	94	94	8	40	69	12.8
Williams,Brian, Det	28	5.58	3	5	0	43	14	108	126	12	66	78	16.0
Witt,Bobby, Tex	33	5.14	10	13	0	33	32	198	220	21	95	159	14.3
Wohlers,Mark, Atl	27	3.20	3	4	39	76	0	76	67	4	31	95	11.6
Worrell,Todd, LA	37	3.22	2	4	42	70	0	67	62	5	18	67	10.7
Young,Anthony, Hou	31	4.26	2	2	0	31	0	38	38	4	16	20	12.8

These Guys Can Play Too And Might Get A Shot

Which players on the following list will get to play in '97? We can't tell you that any more than we can tell you how much it's going to snow next Christmas. But we *can* tell you this: *if* these guys get to play, their numbers probably will end up resembling the numbers we've listed below. These aren't projections, mind you; they're Major League Equivalencies. For an in-depth explanation of MLEs, you might want to consult the *STATS Minor League Handbook*, where we run MLEs for just about every player who played regularly in the high minors last year. Briefly, an MLE is a representation of what the player hit in the minors last year, expressed in major league terms. A projection is a little different—it answers the question, "What will this guy hit this year?" An MLE, on the other hand, answers the question, "What would this guy have hit last year if he'd been playing in the majors?" At any rate, look for a few of these players to break through in 1997.

Batter	Age	Avg	G	AB	R	H	2B	3B	HR	RBI	BB	SO	SB	CS	OBP	SLG
Abbott,Jeff	24	.317	113	435	63	138	25	0	13	59	31	51	10	4	.363	.464
Bonnici,James	25	.282	139	490	71	138	26	0	24	69	56	109	0	2	.355	.482
Boone,Aaron	24	.263	136	529	70	139	41	4	13	77	27	79	15	5	.299	.429
Bridges,Kary	25	.297	129	461	63	137	18	1	3	45	29	23	3	8	.339	.360
Brown,Kevin L.	24	.242	128	447	67	108	24	0	20	75	54	160	0	2	.323	.430
Brown,Ray	24	.302	115	351	55	106	24	3	11	42	37	64	1	0	.369	.481
Carey,Todd	25	.252	125	441	73	111	37	2	18	73	38	131	2	3	.311	.467
Catalanotto,Frank	23	.286	132	489	100	140	31	4	17	63	59	74	11	13	.363	.470
Evans,Tom	22	.261	120	383	72	100	25	0	15	53	80	124	2	0	.389	.444
Gibson,Derrick	22	.295	122	474	62	140	24	4	23	67	28	128	2	12	.335	.508
Helton,Todd	23	.359	114	404	60	145	32	3	11	66	56	50	1	5	.437	.535
Hidalgo,Richard	21	.272	130	497	58	135	31	1	11	69	21	62	8	7	.301	.404
Jennings,Robin	25	.271	86	325	48	88	14	4	16	51	29	55	1	0	.331	.486
Johnson,J.J.	23	.270	132	489	65	132	25	2	16	66	33	110	8	12	.316	.427
Johnson,Russ	24	.286	132	479	76	137	22	3	12	65	41	56	6	4	.342	.420
Konerko,Paul	21	.259	137	455	62	118	17	0	21	68	47	93	0	4	.329	.435
Ledee,Ricky	23	.288	135	483	90	139	29	3	26	86	48	123	5	5	.352	.522
Lee,Derrek	21	.255	134	483	77	123	32	1	30	81	43	180	8	6	.316	.511
McKeel,Walt	25	.300	128	463	80	139	21	0	14	73	47	55	1	3	.365	.436
Morales,Willie	24	.270	108	366	47	99	22	0	15	64	27	71	0	2	.321	.454
Orie,Kevin	24	.278	96	334	40	93	22	0	8	54	40	65	1	0	.356	.416
Patzke,Jeff	23	.278	124	414	57	115	29	3	3	54	56	115	4	4	.364	.384
Pirkl,Greg	26	.298	88	346	46	103	24	1	18	69	12	60	0	0	.321	.529
Posada,Jorge	25	.250	106	344	65	86	19	3	10	53	65	87	2	3	.369	.410
Powell,Dante	23	.253	137	498	78	126	23	1	18	66	53	102	30	13	.325	.412
Radmanovich,Ryan	25	.274	125	449	74	123	31	1	25	83	41	134	3	11	.335	.514
Ramirez,Alex	22	.312	131	500	70	156	27	8	12	76	12	78	14	10	.328	.470
Smith,Bubba	27	.270	134	497	71	134	25	0	25	82	35	129	0	0	.318	.471
Spencer,Shane	25	.238	135	467	66	111	20	0	26	82	53	108	2	3	.315	.448
Staton,T.J.	22	.290	112	376	62	109	23	2	12	49	42	106	12	6	.361	.457
Trammell,Bubba	25	.304	134	483	91	147	34	1	33	94	46	111	6	1	.365	.584
Valdes,Pedro	24	.282	103	390	55	110	21	0	13	54	28	59	1	0	.330	.436
Varitek,Jason	25	.262	134	503	63	132	38	0	13	67	58	106	5	5	.339	.416
Velazquez,Andy	21	.331	132	516	78	171	33	4	30	67	48	117	5	2	.388	.585
Wilson,Nigel	27	.285	128	473	80	135	22	4	27	87	45	121	3	4	.347	.520

The Favorite Toy

"The Favorite Toy," a Bill James invention, is one of *our* favorite toys as well. It's a mathematical formula created by Bill to project a player's chances to reach career offensive goals like 3,000 hits or 500 home runs. Rather than run the complex formula, we'll just say that The Favorite Toy uses a player's age and recent performances to estimate his chances of reaching the goal. So does Albert Belle have a chance to break Hank Aaron's career home run record? Is it better than 50/50 that Wade Boggs will make it to 3,000 hits? Here's what the formula says. (Age here is the player's age as of July 1, 1996).

— Don Zminda

Players with at least a 10% Chance for 3000 Hits

Player	Age	H	%Chance
Cal Ripken	35	2549	87
Tony Gwynn	36	2560	81
Wade Boggs	38	2697	58
Roberto Alomar	28	1522	37
Rafael Palmeiro	31	1636	26
Chuck Knoblauch	27	1019	25
Alex Rodriguez	20	259	19
Frank Thomas	28	1077	16
Marquis Grissom	29	1096	15
Carlos Baerga	27	1100	14
Barry Bonds	31	1595	14
Travis Fryman	27	1013	14
Craig Biggio	30	1279	14
Albert Belle	29	1014	13
Mark Grace	32	1514	13
Ken Griffey Jr	26	1204	13
Ruben Sierra	30	1675	13
Raul Mondesi	25	499	12
Harold Baines	37	2425	12
Mo Vaughn	28	794	12
Kenny Lofton	29	883	11
Brian McRae	28	966	11
Lance Johnson	32	1258	10
Bobby Bonilla	33	1643	10

Players with a 10% Chance for 500 Home Runs

Player	Age	HR	%Chance
Barry Bonds	31	334	89
Albert Belle	29	242	79
Mark McGwire	32	329	75
Ken Griffey Jr	26	238	73
Frank Thomas	28	222	61
Juan Gonzalez	26	214	56
Jose Canseco	31	328	47
Sammy Sosa	27	171	40

Player	Age	HR	%Chance
Cecil Fielder	32	289	40
Fred McGriff	32	317	38
Mo Vaughn	28	155	37
Rafael Palmeiro	31	233	32
Jay Buhner	31	213	30
Gary Sheffield	27	159	24
Matt Williams	30	247	21
Manny Ramirez	24	83	19
Jim Thome	25	93	19
Alex Rodriguez	20	41	19
Tim Salmon	27	120	15
Joe Carter	36	357	15
Jeff Bagwell	28	144	15
Dean Palmer	27	140	13
Greg Vaughn	30	179	11
Robin Ventura	28	144	11
Eric Karros	28	123	10

Players with a 10% chance for 600 Home Runs

Player	Age	HR	%Chance
Albert Belle	29	242	43
Ken Griffey Jr	26	238	39
Barry Bonds	31	334	37
Frank Thomas	28	222	31
Mark McGwire	32	329	29
Juan Gonzalez	26	214	29
Sammy Sosa	27	171	19
Mo Vaughn	28	155	17
Jose Canseco	31	328	11
Cecil Fielder	32	289	11
Jay Buhner	31	213	10

Players with a 5% chance for 700 Home Runs

Player	Age	HR	%Chance
Albert Belle	29	242	23
Ken Griffey Jr	26	238	20
Frank Thomas	28	222	14
Barry Bonds	31	334	13
Juan Gonzalez	26	214	13
Mark McGwire	32	329	8
Sammy Sosa	27	171	6
Mo Vaughn	28	155	5

Players with a 5% Chance for 756 Home Runs

Player	Age	HR	%Chance
Albert Belle	29	242	15
Ken Griffey Jr	26	238	12
Frank Thomas	28	222	8
Juan Gonzalez	26	214	6

Players with a 5% Chance for 800 Home Runs

Player	Age	HR	%Chance
Albert Belle	29	242	10
Ken Griffey Jr	26	238	7

Players with a 10% Chance for 2000 Runs Batted In

Player	Age	RBI	%Chance
Eddie Murray	40	1899	37
Albert Belle	29	751	26
Juan Gonzalez	26	659	23

Player	Age	RBI	%Chance
Frank Thomas	28	729	23
Ken Griffey Jr	26	725	20
Barry Bonds	31	993	17
Mo Vaughn	28	541	16
Rafael Palmeiro	31	848	11
Jeff Bagwell	28	589	10

Players with a 5% Chance for 2297 Runs Batted In

Player	Age	RBI	%Chance
Albert Belle	29	751	11
Juan Gonzalez	26	659	10
Frank Thomas	28	729	9
Ken Griffey Jr	26	725	7
Mo Vaughn	28	541	5

Glossary

% Inherited Scored

A Relief Pitching statistic indicating the percentage of runners on base at the time a relief pitcher enters a game that he allows to score.

% Pitches Taken

The number of pitches a batter does not swing at divided by the total number of pitches he sees.

1st Batter OBP

The On-Base Percentage allowed by a relief pitcher to the first batter he faces in a game.

Active Career Batting Leaders

Minimum of 1,000 At Bats required for Batting Average, On-Base Percentage, Slugging Percentage, At Bats Per HR, At Bats Per GDP, At Bats Per RBI, and K/BB Ratio. One hundred (100) Stolen Base Attempts required for Stolen Base Success %. Any player who appeared in 1996 is eligible for inclusion provided he meets the category's minimum requirements.

Active Career Pitching Leaders

Minimum of 750 Innings Pitched required for Earned Run Average, Opponent Batting Average, all of the "Per 9 Innings" categories, and Strikeout to Walk Ratio. Two hundred fifty (250) Games Started required for Complete Game Frequency. One hundred (100) decisions required for Win-Loss Percentage. Any player who appeared in 1996 is eligible for inclusion provided he meets the category's minimum requirements.

Bases Loaded

Batting Average with the Bases Loaded

BA ScPos Allowed

Batting Average Allowed with Runners in Scoring Position.

Batting Average

Hits divided by At-Bats.

Blown Save

Entering a game in a Save Situation (see Save Situation in Glossary) and allowing the tying or go-ahead run to score.

Catcher's ERA

The Earned Run Average of a club's pitchers with a particular catcher behind the plate. To figure this for a catcher, multiply the Earned Runs Allowed by the pitchers while he was catching times nine and divide that by his number of Innings Caught.

Cheap Wins/Tough Losses/Top Game Scores

First determine the starting pitcher's Game Score as follows: (1)Start with 50. (2)Add 1 point for each out recorded by the starting pitcher. (3)Add 2 points for each inning the pitcher completes after the fourth inning. (4)Add 1 point for each strikeout. (5)Subtract 2 points for each hit allowed. (6)Subtract 4 points for each earned run allowed. (7)Subtract 2 points for an unearned run. (8)Subtract 1 point for each walk.

If the starting pitcher scores over 50 and loses, it's a Tough Loss. If he wins with a game score under 50, it's a Cheap Win. The top Game Scores of 1996 are listed.

Cleanup Slugging%

The Slugging Percentage of a player when batting fourth in the batting order.

Complete Game Frequency

Complete Games divided by Games Started.

Earned Run Average

(Earned Runs times 9) divided by Innings Pitched.

Fielding Percentage

(Putouts plus Assists) divided by (Putouts plus Assists plus Errors).

Games Finished

The last pitcher of record for either team in any given game is credited with a Game Finished.

GDP

Ground into Double Play

GDP Opportunity

Any situation with a runner on first and less than two out.

Ground/Fly Ratio (Grd/Fly)

For batters, ground balls hit divided by fly balls hit. For pitchers, ground balls allowed divided by fly balls allowed. All batted balls except line drives and bunts are included.

Hold

A Hold is credited any time a relief pitcher enters a game in a Save Situation (see definition below), records at least one out, and leaves the game never having relinquished the lead. Note: a pitcher cannot finish the game and receive credit for a Hold, nor can he earn a hold and a save.

Isolated Power

Slugging Percentage minus Batting Average.

K/BB Ratio

Strikeouts divided by Walks.

Late & Close

A Late & Close situation meets the following requirements: (1)the game is in the seventh inning or later, and (2)the batting team is either leading by one run, tied, or has the potential tying run on base, at bat, or on deck. Note: this situation is very similar to the characteristics of a Save Situation.

Leadoff On Base%

The On-Base Percentage of a player when batting first in the batting order.

Offensive Winning Percentage

The Winning Percentage a team of nine Ken Caminitis (or anybody) would compile against average pitching and defense. The formula: (Runs Created per 27 outs) divided by the League average of runs scored per game. Square the result and divide it by (1+itself).

On Base Percentage

(Hits plus Walks plus Hit by Pitcher) divided by (At Bats plus Walks plus Hit by Pitcher plus Sacrifice Flies).

Opponent Batting Average

Hits Allowed divided by (Batters Faced minus Walks minus Hit Batsmen minus Sacrifice Hits minus Sacrifice Flies minus Catcher's Interference).

PA*

The divisor for On Base Percentage: At Bats plus Walks plus Hit By Pitcher plus Sacrifice Flies; or Plate Appearances minus Sacrifice Hits and Times Reached Base on Defensive Interference.

PCS (Pitchers' Caught Stealing)

The number of runners officially counted as Caught Stealing where the initiator of the fielding play was the pitcher, not the catcher. Note: such plays are often referred to as "pickoffs", but appear in official records as Caught Stealings. The most common "pitcher caught stealing scenario" is a 1-3-6 fielding play, where the runner is officially charged a Caught Stealing because he broke for second base. "Pickoff" (fielding play 1-3 being the most common) is not an official statistic.

Pitches per PA

For a hitter, the total number of pitches seen divided by total number of at-bats.

PkOf Throw/Runner

The number of pickoff throws made by a pitcher divided by the number of runners on first base.

Plate Appearances

At Bats plus Total Walks plus Hit By Pitcher plus Sacrifice Hits plus Sacrifice Flies plus Times Reached on Defensive Interference.

Power/Speed Number

A way to look at power and speed in one number. A player must score high in both areas to earn a high Power/Speed Number. The formula: (HR x SB x 2) divided by (HR + SB).

Quick Hooks and Slow Hooks

A Quick Hook is the removal of a pitcher who has pitched less than 6 innings and given up 3 runs or less. A Slow Hook occurs when a pitcher pitches more than 9 innings, or allows 7 or more runs, or whose combined innings pitched and runs allowed totals 13 or more.

Range Factor

The number of Successful Chances (Putouts plus Assists) times nine divided by the number of Defensive Innings Played. The average for a Regular Player at each position in 1996:

Second Base: 5.05	Left Field: 1.99
Third Base: 2.63	Center Field: 2.62
Shortstop: 4.67	Right Field: 2.05

Run Support Per 9 IP

The number of runs scored by a pitcher's team while he was still in the game times nine divided by his Innings Pitched.

Runs Created

A way to combine a batter's total offensive contributions into one number. The formula:

(H + BB + HBP - CS - GIDP) times (Total Bases + .26(TBB - IBB + HBP) + .52(SH + SF + SB)) divided by (AB + TBB + HBP + SH + SF).

Save Percentage

Saves (SV) divided by Save Opportunities (OP).

Save Situation

A Relief Pitcher is in a Save Situation when:

upon entering the game with his club leading, he has the opportunity to be the finishing pitcher (and is not the winning pitcher of record at the time), and meets any one of the three following conditions:

(1) he has a lead of no more than three runs and has the opportunity to pitch for at least one inning, or

(2) he enters the game, regardless of the count, with the potential tying run either on base, at bat, or on deck; or

(3) he pitches three or more innings regardless of the lead and the official scorer credits him with a save.

SB Success%

Stolen Bases divided by (Stolen Bases plus Caught Stealing).

Secondary Average

A way to look at a player's extra bases gained, independent of Batting Average. The formula: (Total Bases - Hits + TBB + SB) divided by At Bats.

Slugging Percentage

Total Bases divided by At Bats.

Total Bases

Hits plus Doubles plus (2 times Triples) plus (3 times Home runs).

Win-Loss Percentage or Winning Percentage

Wins divided by (Wins plus Losses).

About STATS, Inc.

STATS, Inc. is the nation's leading independent sports information and statistical analysis company, providing detailed sports services for a wide array of clients.

As one of the fastest-growing sports companies—in 1994, we ranked 144th on the "Inc. 500" list of fastest-growing privately held firms—STATS provides the most up-to-the-minute sports information to professional teams, print and broadcast media, software developers and interactive service providers around the country. Some of our major clients are ESPN, the Associated Press, *The Sporting News*, Electronic Arts, Motorola, SONY and Topps. Much of the information we provide is available to the public via STATS On-Line. With a computer and a modem, you can follow action in the four major professional sports, as well as NCAA football and basketball. . . as it happens!

STATS Publishing, a division of STATS, Inc., produces 11 annual books, including the *Major League Handbook*, *The Scouting Notebook*, the *Pro Football Handbook*, the *Pro Basketball Handbook* and the *Hockey Handbook*. These publications deliver STATS' expertise to fans, scouts, general managers and media around the country.

In addition, STATS offers the most innovative—and fun—fantasy sports games around, from *Bill James Fantasy Baseball* and *Bill James Classic Baseball* to *STATS Fantasy Football* and *STATS Fantasy Hoops*.

Information technology has grown by leaps and bounds in the last decade, and STATS will continue to be at the forefront as both a vendor and supplier of the most up-to-date, in-depth sports information available. For those of you on the information superhighway, you can always catch STATS at our site on America Online (Keyword: STATS).

For more information on our products, or on joining our reporter network, write us at:

STATS, Inc.
8131 Monticello Ave.
Skokie, IL 60076-3300

. . . or call us at 1-800-63-STATS (1-800-637-8287). Outside the U.S., dial 1-847-676-3383.

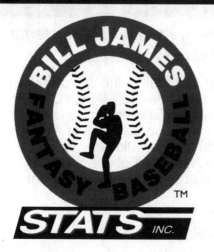 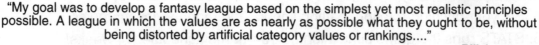

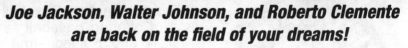 

STATS Fantasy Hoops

Soar into the 1996-97 season with STATS Fantasy Hoops! SFH puts YOU in charge. Don't just sit back and watch Grant Hill, Shawn Kemp, and Michael Jordan—get in the game and coach your team to the top!

How to Play SFH:
1. Sign up to coach a team.
2. You'll receive a full set of rules and a draft form with SFH point values for all eligible players - anyone who played in the NBA in 1995-96, plus all 1996 NBA draft picks.
3. Complete the draft form and return it to STATS.
4. You will take part in the draft with nine other owners, and we will send you league rosters.
5. You make unlimited weekly transactions including trades, free agent signings, activations, and benchings.
6. Six of the 10 teams in your league advance to postseason play, with two teams ultimately advancing to the Finals.

SFH point values are tested against actual NBA results, mirroring the real thing. Weekly reports will tell you everything you need to know to lead your team to the SFH Championship!

STATS Fantasy Football

STATS Fantasy Football puts YOU in charge! You draft, trade, cut, bench, activate players and even sign free agents each week. SFF pits you head-to-head against 11 other owners.

STATS' scoring system applies realistic values, tested against actual NFL results. Each week, you'll receive a superb in-depth report telling you all about both team and league performances.

How to Play SFF:
1. Sign up today!
2. STATS sends you a draft form listing all eligible NFL players.
3. Fill out the draft form and return it to STATS, and you will take part in the draft along with 11 other team owners.
4. Go head-to-head against the other owners in your league. You'll make week-by-week roster moves and transactions through STATS' Fantasy Football experts, via phone, fax, or on-line!

Order from  Today!

Use Order Form in This Book, or Call 1-800-63-STATS or 847-676-3383 or e-mail: info@stats.com

STATS On-Line

Now you can have a direct line to a world of sports information just like the pros use with STATS On-Line. If you love to keep up with your favorite teams and players, STATS On-Line is for you. From Charles Barkley's fast-breaking dunks to Mark McGwire's tape-measure blasts — if you want baseball, basketball, football and hockey stats, we put them at your fingertips!

STATS On-Line

- **Player Profiles and Team Profiles** — The #1 resource for scouting your favorite professional teams and players with information you simply can't find anywhere else! The most detailed info you've ever seen, including real-time stats.

- **NO monthly or annual fees**

- **Local access numbers** — avoid costly long-distance charges!

- **Unlimited access** — 24 hours a day, seven days a week

- **Downloadable files** — get year-to-date stats in an ASCII format for baseball, football, basketball, and hockey

- **In-progress box scores** — You'll have access to the most up-to-the-second scoring stats for every team and player. When you log into STATS On-Line, you'll get detailed updates, including player stats while the games are in progress!

- **Other exclusive features** — transactions and injury information, team and player profiles and updates, standings, leader and trailer boards, game-by-game logs, fantasy game features, and much more!

Sign-up fee of $30 (applied towards future use), 24-hour access with usage charges of $.75/min. Mon.-Fri., 8am-6pm CST; $.25/min. all other hours and weekends.

Order from  **Today!**

Use Order Form in This Book, or Call 1-800-63-STATS or 847-676-3383 or e-mail: info@stats.com

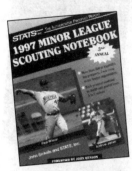

Bill James Presents:

STATS 1997 Batter Versus Pitcher Match-Ups!

- Complete stats for pitchers vs. batters (5+ career AB against them)
- Leader boards and stats for all 1996 major league players
- **Item #BP97, $14.95, Available Mid January, 1997!**

STATS Baseball Scoreboard 1997

- Lively analysis of all the hottest topics facing baseball today!
- Easy-to-understand charts answer the questions fans always ask
- Specific coverage for each major league team
- **Item #SB97, $18.95, Available March 1, 1996!**

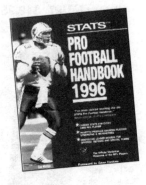

STATS Pro Basketball Handbook 1996-97

- Career stats for every player who logged minutes during 1995-96
- Team game logs with points, rebounds, assists and much more
- Leader boards from points per game to triple doubles
- **Item #BH97, $17.95, Available NOW!**

STATS Pro Football Handbook 1996

- A complete season-by-season register for every active 1995 player
- Numerous statistical breakdowns for hundreds of NFL players
- Leader boards in a number of innovative and traditional categories
- **Item #FH96, $17.95, Available NOW!**

    STATS Pro Football Handbook 1997 Available Early February 1997

Pro Football Revealed:
The 100-Yard War (1996 Edition)

- Profiles each team, complete with essays, charts and play diagrams
- Detailed statistical breakdowns on players, teams and coaches
- Essays about NFL trends and happenings by leading experts
- **Price: $16.95, Item #PF96 , Available NOW!**

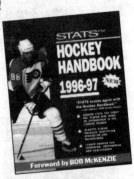

STATS Hockey Handbook 1996-97

- A complete season-by-season register for every active 1996 player
- Numerous statistical breakdowns for hundreds of NHL players
- Leader boards in numerous innovative and traditional categories
- **Item #HH97, $17.95, Available NOW!**

STATS, Inc. Order Form

Name_____

Address_____

City_____ State_____ Zip_____

Phone_____ Fax_____ Internet Address_____

Method of Payment (U.S. Funds Only):

❏ Check   ❏ Money Order   ❏ Visa   ❏ MasterCard

Credit Card Information:

Cardholder Name_____

Credit Card Number_____ Exp. Date_____

Signature_____

BOOKS (STATS publications now include free first class shipping)

Qty.	Product Name	Item Number	Price	Total
	STATS Major League Handbook 1997	HB97	$19.95	
	STATS Major League Handbook 1997 (Comb-bound)	HC97	$21.95	
	STATS Projections Update 1997	PJUP	$9.95	
	The Scouting Notebook: 1997	SN97	$18.95	
	The Scouting Notebook: 1997 (Comb-bound)	SC97	$20.95	
	STATS Minor League Scouting Notebook 1997	MN97	$18.95	
	STATS Minor League Handbook 1997	MH97	$19.95	
	STATS Minor League Handbook 1997 (Comb-bound)	MC97	$21.95	
	STATS Player Profiles 1997	PP97	$19.95	
	STATS Player Profiles 1997 (Comb-bound)	PC97	$21.95	
	STATS 1997 BVSP Match-Ups!	BP97	$14.95	
	STATS Baseball Scoreboard 1997	SB97	$18.95	
	Pro Football Revealed: The 100 Yard War (1996 Edition)	PF96	$16.95	
	STATS Pro Football Handbook 1996	FH96	$17.95	
	STATS Basketball Handbook 1996-97	BH97	$17.95	
	STATS Hockey Handbook 1996-97	HH97	$17.95	
	Prior Editions (Please circle appropriate year)			
	STATS Major League Handbook '90 '91 '92 '93 '94 '95 '96		$9.95	
	The Scouting Report/Notebook '94 '95 '96		$9.95	
	STATS Player Profiles '93 '94 '95 '96		$9.95	
	STATS Minor League Handbook '92 '93 '94 '95 '96		$9.95	
	STATS BVSP Match-Ups! '94 '95 '96		$3.95	
	STATS Baseball Scoreboard '92 '93 '94 '95 '96		$9.95	
	STATS Basketball Scoreboard/Handbook '93-'94 '94-'95 '95-'96		$9.95	
	Pro Football Revealed: The 100 Yard War '94 '95		$9.95	
	STATS Pro Football Handbook '95		$9.95	
	STATS Minor League Scouting Notebook '95 '96		$9.95	

MULTIMEDIA PRODUCTS (Prices include shipping & handling charges)

Qty.	Product Name	Item Number	Price	Total
	Bill James Encyclopedia CD-Rom	BJCD	$49.95	
	Macmillan's Baseball Encyclopedia CD-Rom	MACD	$44.95	
	Motorola SportsTrax for Baseball	BBTX	$199.00	
	STATS On-Line	STON	$30.00	

SEASON FINAL & YEAR-END REPORTS (Prices include shipping & handling charges)

Qty.	Product Name	Circle Format	Price	Total
	Season Final Report	Paper 3 1/2" disk 5" disk Mac	$12.95	
	Lefty/Righty Report	Paper 3 1/2" disk 5" disk Mac	$19.95	
	Stolen Base Report	Paper 3 1/2" disk 5" disk Mac	$34.95	
	Defensive Games by Position	Paper 3 1/2" disk 5" disk Mac	$9.95	
	Catcher Report	Paper 3 1/2" disk 5" disk Mac	$49.95	
	Relief Pitching Report	Paper 3 1/2" disk 5" disk Mac	$49.95	
	Zone Ratings/Outfield Arms Report	Paper 3 1/2" disk 5" disk Mac	$99.95	
	End of Season STATpak	Paper 3 1/2" disk 5" disk	$9.95	
	Team(s):			
	STATpak Subscription	Paper 3 1/2" disk 5" disk	$29.95	
	Team(s):			

FANTASY GAMES & STATSfax (STATSfax prices reflect the monthly charge for service)

Qty.	Product Name	Item Number	Price	Total
	Bill James Classic Baseball	BJCB	$129.00	
	How to Win the Classic Game	CGBK	$16.95	
	Classic Game STATSfax	CFX5	$20.00	
	STATS Fantasy Hoops	SFH	$85.00	
	STATS Fantasy Hoops STATSfax—5-Day	SFH5	$20.00	
	STATS Fantasy Hoops STATSfax—7-Day	SFH7	$25.00	
	STATS Fantasy Football	SFF	$69.00	
	STATS Fantasy Football STATSfax—3-Day	SFF3	$15.00	
	Bill James Fantasy Baseball	BJFB	$89.00	
	Fantasy Baseball STATSfax—5-Day	SFX5	$20.00	
	Fantasy Baseball STATSfax—7-Day	SFX7	$25.00	

1st Fantasy Team Name (ex. Colt 45's):_____ _____

What Fantasy Game is this team for?_____

2nd Fantasy Team Name (ex. Colt 45's):_____ _____

What Fantasy Game is this team for?_____

NOTE: $1.00/player is charged for all roster moves and transactions.

For Bill James Fantasy Baseball:

Would you like to play in a league drafted by Bill James?   ❏ Yes   ❏ No

For faster service, call:

1-800-63-STATS or 847-676-3383,

or fax this form to STATS:

847-676-0821

TOTALS		
	Price	Total
Product Total (excl. Fantasy Games)		
Canada—all orders—add:	$2.50/book	
Order 2 or more books—subtract:	$1.00/book	
(NOT to be combined with other specials)		
IL residents add 8.5% sales tax		
Subtotal		
Fantasy Games Total		
GRAND TOTAL		

All books now include free 1st class shipping!
Thanks for ordering from STATS, Inc.

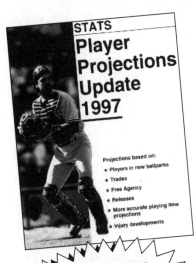